The University of Chicago School Mathematics Project

Algebra

Teacher's Edition

Authors

John W. McConnell
Susan Brown
Susan Eddins
Margaret Hackworth
Leroy Sachs
Ernest Woodward
James Flanders
Daniel Hirschhorn
Cathy Hynes
Lydia Polonsky
Zalman Usiskin

About the Cover

Graphed here is the path of a baseball that is lobbed from a height of 4 feet and attains a height of 12 feet after traveling a horizontal distance of 10 feet. The path is part of a parabola.

Scott, Foresman and Company

Editorial Offices: Glenview, Illinois Regional Offices: Sunnyvale, California • Atlanta, Georgia • Glenview, Illinois • Oakland, New Jersey • Dallas, Texas

Acknowledgments

Authors

John W. McConnell
Instructional Supervisor of Mathematics, Glenbrook South H.S., Glenview, IL

Susan Brown
Mathematics Teacher, York H.S., Elmhurst, IL

Susan Eddins
Mathematics Teacher, Illinois Mathematics and Science Academy, Aurora, IL

Margaret Hackworth
Mathematics Supervisor, Pinellas County Schools, Largo, FL

Leroy Sachs
Mathematics Teacher (retired), Clayton H.S., Clayton, MO

Ernest Woodward
Professor of Mathematics, Austin Peay State University, Clarksville, TN

James Flanders
UCSMP

Daniel Hirschhorn
UCSMP

Cathy Hynes
Mathematics Teacher, The University of Chicago Laboratory Schools

Lydia Polonsky
UCSMP

Zalman Usiskin
Professor of Education, The University of Chicago

Editorial Development and Design

Scott, Foresman staff, Publishers Services, Incorporated, Kristin Nelson Design, Jill Ruter Design

We wish to acknowledge the generous support of the **Amoco Foundation** and the **Carnegie Corporation of New York** in helping to make it possible for these materials to be developed and tested.

UCSMP Production and Evaluation

Series Editors: Zalman Usiskin, Sharon Senk (Michigan State University)
Technical Coordinator: Susan Chang
Director of Evaluations: Sandra Mathison (State University of New York, Albany)
Assistants to the Director: Penelope Flores, David Matheson, Catherine Sarther

A list of schools that participated in the research and development of this text may be found on page *iii*.

ISBN: 0-673-45264-6

56789—VHJ—969594939291

CONTENTS Teacher's Edition

The complete Contents for the Student Edition begins on page *vi*.

Note:
*The **Professional Sourcebook** is located at the back of the Teacher's Edition.*

UCSMP Helps You Update Your Curriculum and Better Prepare Your Students!

As reports from national commissions have shown, students currently are not learning enough mathematics, and the curriculum has not kept pace with changes in mathematics and its applications.

In response to these problems, UCSMP has developed a complete program for grades 7–12 that upgrades the school mathematics experience for the *average* student. The usual four-year high-school mathematics content—*and much more*—is spread out over six years. The result is that **students learn *more* mathematics** and **students are better prepared for the *variety* of mathematics** they will encounter in their future mathematics courses and in life.

In addition, UCSMP helps students view their study of mathematics as worthwhile, as full of interesting information, as related to almost every endeavor. With applications as a hallmark of all UCSMP materials, students no longer ask, "How does this topic apply to the world I know?"

For a more complete description of the series, see pages T19–T52 at the back of the Teacher's Edition.

In short, UCSMP. . .

- Prepares students to use mathematics effectively in today's world.
- Promotes independent thinking and learning.
- Helps all students improve their performance.
- Provides the practical support you need.

"Students have to read in order to use the material, plus so much of the material deals with real life, real world. There simply is no comparison with this kind of material and the other traditional math program."

**M. Gene Wagner, teacher,
Maple Dale School, Milwaukee, WI**

Years of field-testing and perfecting have brought impressive results!

Imagine using a text that has been developed as part of a coherent 7–12 curriculum design, one that has been tested on a large scale *before* publication, and most important, has bolstered students' mathematical abilities, which is reflected in test scores. Read on to find out how UCSMP has done that, and more.

For a detailed discussion of the development and testing of Algebra, *see pages T46–T50.*

UNIQUE DEVELOPMENT

This book was developed at the University of Chicago with funds provided by the Amoco Foundation and the Carnegie Corporation of New York.

PLANNING

Initial planning was done with input from professors, classroom teachers, school administrators, and district and state supervisors of mathematics, along with the recommendations by national commissions and international studies. In particular, the **UCSMP secondary curriculum is the first full mathematics curriculum to implement the recommendations of the NCTM Standards committees.**

AUTHORSHIP

Authors were chosen for expertise in the relevant areas of school mathematics and for classroom experience. *Algebra* and *Advanced Algebra* writing teams were selected from a nationwide competition.

FIELD-TESTING AND EVALUATION

Pilot testing began with teaching and revising based on **firsthand experience** by the initial team of authors. Then, evaluation was made from **local studies,** and the materials were revised again. Further evaluation and revisions were based on **national studies.** And finally, the **Scott, Foresman input** includes enhancements, such as color photography and nearly 600 blackline masters, to better meet the needs of teachers and students.

Applies and Extends Traditional Algebra Content

***Algebra* is designed to attract and keep students in mathematics —not to weed them out.** Students learn to describe the world around them with algebraic expressions, equations, graphs, and statistics. Applications, calculators, and computers provide a context for the abstract language of algebra.

Consistent organization leads to mastery.

*The following features are **built into every lesson,** providing a consistent path for learning:*

Lesson Introduction

gets students reading mathematics on a daily basis. Provided are key concepts, relevant vocabulary, and meaningful examples for students to read and discuss. Topics are placed in real-world settings so students know why they are studying them.

LESSON 9-2

Exponential Growth

Another important application of powers and exponents is population growth. The next example concerns rabbit populations, which can grow quickly. Rabbits are not native to Australia, and in 1859, 22 rabbits were imported from Europe as a new source of food. Australia's conditions were ideal for rabbits, and they flourished. Soon, there were so many rabbits that they damaged grazing land. By 1887, the government was offering a reward for a population control technique.

Example 1 Twenty-five rabbits are introduced to an area. Assume that the rabbit population doubles every six months. How many rabbits are there after 5 years?

Solution Since the population doubles twice each year, in 5 years it will double 10 times. The number of rabbits will be

$$25 \cdot \underbrace{2 \cdot 2 \cdot 2 \cdot 2 \cdot 2 \cdot 2 \cdot 2 \cdot 2 \cdot 2 \cdot 2}_{\text{10 factors}}.$$

To evaluate this expression on a calculator rewrite it as

$$25 \cdot 2^{10}.$$

Use the y^x key. After 5 years there will be 25,600 rabbits.

The rabbit population in Example 1 is said to grow exponentially. In **exponential growth,** the original amount is repeatedly *multiplied* by a nonzero number called the **growth factor.**

Growth model for powering:

When an amount is multiplied by g, the growth factor, in each of x time periods, then after the x periods, the original amount will be multiplied by g^x.

> ***“I firmly believe these materials are helping my students develop a higher level of reasoning and thinking, and [they] are learning more than the traditional Algebra I concepts.”***
>
> **Mary Babb, teacher,**
> **Liberty High School, Liberty, South Carolina**

Four Kinds of Questions

provide a variety of contexts, requiring students to really think about each problem.

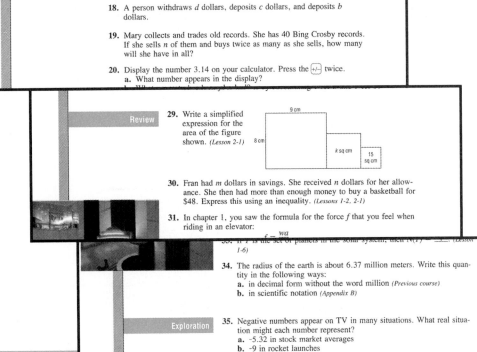

Questions

Covering the Reading

1. On the first play, a football team gained 7 yards. On the second play, the team lost 3 yards.
   a. Represent this situation on a number line.
   b. What was the net yardage for the two plays?
2. State the slide model for addition.
3. Add: a. -10 + -13 b. 9x + -11x c. -172 + 29

In 4 and 5, simplify.

4. 3 + -4 + x 5. -2 + y + -9

Applying the Mathematics

16. Describe a real situation that leads to -9 + 9 = 0.

In 17 and 18, write the addition expression suggested by each situation.

17. The temperature goes up x°, then falls 3°, then rises 5°.
18. A person withdraws d dollars, deposits c dollars, and deposits b dollars.
19. Mary collects and trades old records. She has 40 Bing Crosby records. If she sells n of them and buys twice as many as she sells, how many will she have in all?
20. Display the number 3.14 on your calculator. Press the +/- twice.
    a. What number appears in the display?

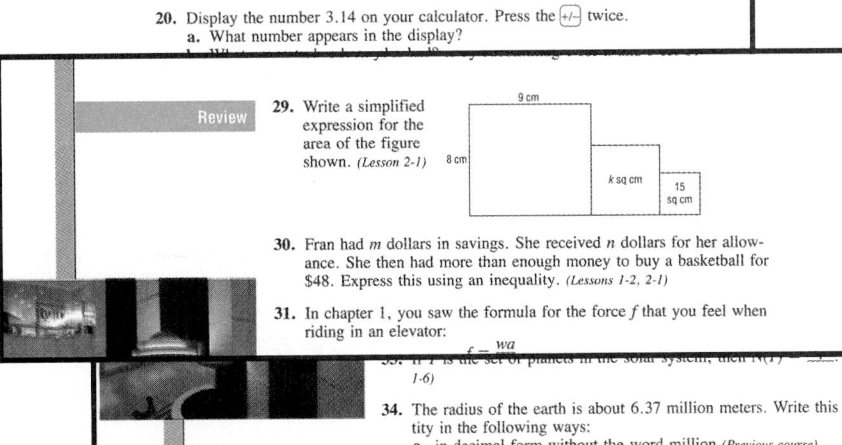

Review

29. Write a simplified expression for the area of the figure shown. *(Lesson 2-1)*

30. Fran had m dollars in savings. She received n dollars for her allowance. She then had more than enough money to buy a basketball for $48. Express this using an inequality. *(Lessons 1-2, 2-1)*
31. In chapter 1, you saw the formula for the force f that you feel when riding in an elevator:

1-6)

34. The radius of the earth is about 6.37 million meters. Write this quantity in the following ways:
    a. in decimal form without the word million *(Previous course)*
    b. in scientific notation *(Appendix B)*

Exploration

35. Negative numbers appear on TV in many situations. What real situation might each number represent?
    a. -5.32 in stock market averages
    b. -9 in rocket launches
    c. -3 in golf

LESSON 2-2 The Slide Model for Addition 67

1 COVERING THE READING

offers a variety of types of questions that allow students to try out what they've learned in the lesson introduction.

2 APPLYING THE MATHEMATICS

offers real-world and other applications of the lesson concepts.

3 REVIEW

keyed to past lessons, helps students maintain and improve performance on important skills and concepts, and previews ideas to prepare students for topics that will be studied later.

4 EXPLORATION

extends the lesson content, offering an interesting variety of applications, generalizations, and extensions, including open-ended experiments, research, and much more.

Prepares Students to Use Mathematics Effectively in Today's World

Real-world Applications

Students study each mathematical idea in depth through applications and practical problems, providing opportunities to develop skills and to understand the importance of mathematics in everyday life.

Lesson Integrating Statistics

LESSON **8-7**

Fitting a Line to Data

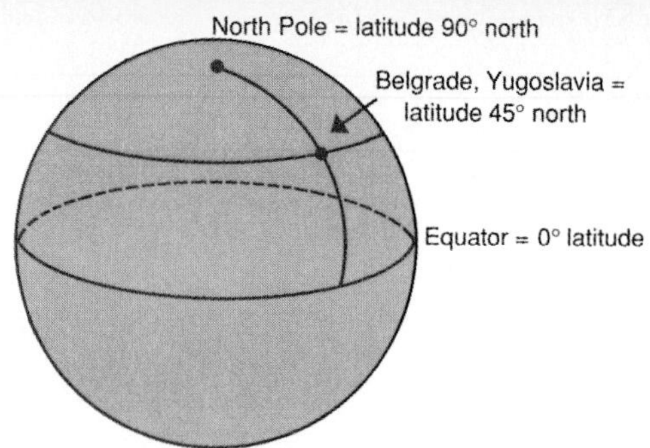

In many situations, there are more than two points. The points may not all lie on a line. Still an equation may be found that closely describes the coordinates. Finding that equation is the subject of this lesson.

The latitude of a place on the earth tells how far the place is from the equator. Latitudes in the Northern Hemisphere range from 0° at the equator to 90° at the North Pole.

In the table below are the latitude and mean high temperatures in April, for selected cities in the Northern Hemisphere. (The mean high temperature is the mean of all the high temperatures for the month.) Although in all of these cities temperature is measured in degrees Celsius, we have converted the temperatures to Fahrenheit for you.

Latitude and Temperature in Selected Cities

City	North Latitude	April Mean High Temperature (°F)
Lagos, Nigeria	6	89
San Juan, Puerto Rico	18	84

Probability Lesson

LESSON **4-8**

Multiplying Probabilities

Many TV watchers seldom change channels. So TV networks often put a new show after a popular one to boost the ratings of the new show. Suppose 25% of viewers watched show A and 80% of these stayed to watch show B. Then, since $.80 \cdot .25 = .20$, 20% of the viewers watched both shows.

If a viewer is called at random, then each of the percents can be interpreted as a probability.

25% = .25 = P(watched show A) = P(A)
80% = .80 = P(watched show B having already watched show A) = P(B given A)
20% = .20 = P(watched shows A and B) = P(A and B)

You have seen P(A) and P(A and B) before. P(B given A) is the probability that B occurs *given that A occurs*. P(B given A) is called a **conditional probability.** This situation illustrates the **Conditional Probability Formula.**

Conditional Probability Formula:
P(A and B) = P(A) · P(B given A).

You may see the Conditional Probability Formula with the intersection symbol.

Wider Scope

Algebra presents the history of major ideas and recent developments in mathematics and applications, which both teachers and students really like. In addition, it employs geometry, statistics, and probability to motivate, justify, extend, and enhance important concepts of algebra.

Lesson Integrating Geometry

LESSON **10-6**

Multiplying Monomials

In the last lesson, the Area Model for Multiplication was used to represent multiplying two polynomials. Recall that a polynomial with two terms is a binomial. You will multiply binomials often enough that we examine this as a special case.

The rectangle below has length $(a + b)$ and width $(c + d)$.

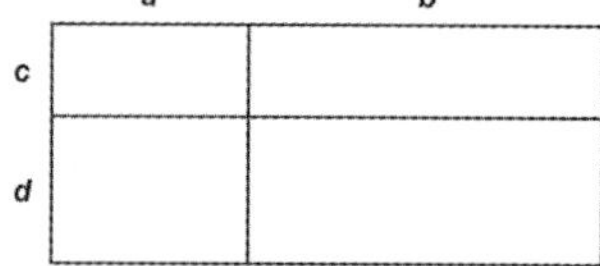

The area of the rectangle = length · width = $(a + b) \cdot (c + d)$. But the area of the rectangle also must equal the sum of the areas of the four small rectangles inside it.

	a	b
c	ac	bc
d	ad	bd

The sum of the areas of the four small rectangles = $ac + ad + bc + bd$. So,

$$(a + b) \cdot (c + d) = ac + ad + bc + bd.$$

Another way to show the pattern above is true is to chunk $(c + d)$ and distribute it over $(a + b)$ as follows:

$$(a + b) \cdot (c + d) = a(c + d) + b(c + d).$$

Example 3 Give the reciprocal of 1.25.

Solution The reciprocal of 1.25 is $\frac{1}{1.25}$. A calculator shows the quotient to be 0.8.

Check $1.25 \cdot 0.8 = 1$. So 1.25 and 0.8 are reciprocals because their product is 1.

If you know that the reciprocal of 1.25 is 0.8, you also know that the reciprocal of -1.25 is -0.8, since $-1.25 \cdot -0.8 = 1$.

Most scientific calculators have a reciprocal key [1/x]. To find the reciprocal of n, key in n [1/x]. The answer will be displayed as a decimal. You must apply a different process to write the reciprocal as a fraction. Use the fact that the reciprocal of a/b is b/a (unless a or b is zero).

Example 4 Give the reciprocal of $-\frac{3}{7}$.

Solution The reciprocal of $-\frac{3}{7}$ is $-\frac{7}{3}$.

Check $-\frac{3}{7} \cdot -\frac{7}{3} = \frac{21}{21} = 1$

Look back at the property of reciprocals. The term *nonzero* is emphasized because the property is not true for $a = 0$. Zero does not have a reciprocal because there is no number such that $0 \cdot x = 1$. In fact, you know that 0 times any real number is 0.

Multiplication Property of Zero:

For any real number a,

$$a \cdot 0 = 0 \cdot a = 0.$$

"I like the integration of material that connects concepts in exciting new ways."

Joyce Evans, teacher
Breck School, Minneapolis, MN

Technology

Students learn how to use calculators and computers—tools they'll need in the real world. The evidence shows that the appropriate use of technology enhances student mathematical understanding and improves problem-solving skills.

LESSON

12-2 Using an Automatic Grapher

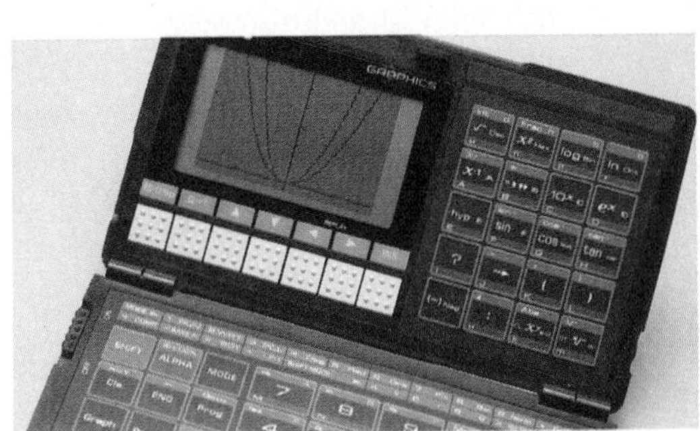

Graphs of equations are so helpful to have that there exist calculators that will automatically display part of a graph. Also, there are programs for every personal computer that will display graphs. Because computer screens are larger than calculator screens, they can more clearly show more of a graph, but graphing calculators are less expensive and more convenient.

Graphing calculators and computer graphing programs work in much the same way, and so we call them **automatic graphers** and do not distinguish them. Of course, no grapher is completely automatic. Each has particular keys to press that you must learn from a manual. Here we discuss what you need to know in order to use any of them.

The part of the coordinate grid that is shown is called a **window**. The screen at the right displays a window in which

$$-2 \le x \le 12$$
$$\text{and} \quad -3 \le y \le 7.$$

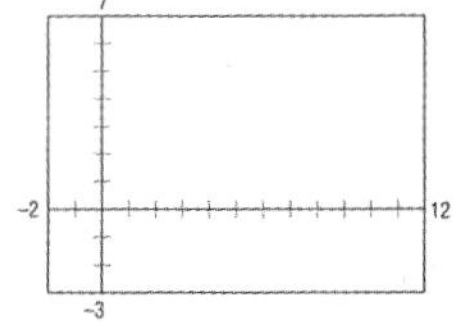

On calculators, the intervals for x and y may be left unmarked. Usually you need to pick the x-values at either end of the window. Some graphers automatically adjust and pick y-values so your graph will fit, but often you need to pick the y-values. If you don't do this, the grapher will usually pick a **default window** (perhaps $-10 \le x \le 10$, $-6 \le y \le 6$) and your graph may not appear on the screen.

On almost all graphers, the equation to be graphed must be a for-

A computer program can be used to evaluate formulas. In the next example, the programming statement INPUT is used. An **INPUT** statement makes the computer pause and wait for you to type in a value. The computer signals you by flashing its cursor (the symbol that shows you where you are on the screen). On some computers you may see a "?" printed on the screen as well.

Example 3 The circumference C of a circle can be estimated using the formula

$$C = \pi d$$

where d is the diameter of the circle and $\pi \approx 3.14159$.

a. Write a computer program to find C, given d.
b. Estimate the circumference of a circle with diameter 15.5 feet.

Solution

a.

```
10 PRINT "EVALUATE CIRCUMFERENCE FORMULA"
20 PRINT "GIVE DIAMETER"
30 INPUT DIAM
40 LET CIRC = 3.14159 * DIAM
50 PRINT "DIAMETER", "CIRCUMFERENCE"
60 PRINT DIAM, CIRC
70 END
```

Note: Using a comma in the PRINT statements makes the computer print in columns.

b. When the program is run, the lines EVALUATE CIRCUMFERENCE FORMULA and GIVE DIAMETER will automatically appear. Now type 15.5. When you press the RETURN or ENTER key you will see:

```
DIAMETER    CIRCUMFERENCE
15.5        48.694645
```

Questions

Develops Independent Thinking and Learning!

Reading

Great for Students:
Well-written explanations and examples enable students to successfully **apply** what they've read and also serve as a great reference tool, encouraging students to look for answers on their own. The reading also helps to **motivate** students by connecting mathematics to their world, which makes it more interesting to them.

Great for Teachers:
Because students can read and understand the text, you have the freedom to teach in a variety of ways. Instead of merely explaining every day what the text says, you can concentrate on developing further examples and explanations tailored to your students' needs.

Problem Solving

Every lesson contains a variety of problem-solving questions applying the mathematics. Students learn about the selection of problem-solving strategies to encourage efficient methods. In addition, requiring students to read helps develop thinkers who are more critical and aware.

LESSON 6-4

Repeated Addition and Subtraction

PARKING CHARGES	
1 HOUR	\$1.50
2 HOURS	2.30
3 HOURS	3.10
4 HOURS	3.90
5 HOURS	4.70
each additional hour	\$ .80

Equations of the form $ax + b = c$ often arise from situations of repeated addition or subtraction. For instance, consider the rates charged by a parking garage in a big city, as shown in the sign at the left. If a person left his car in the garage for a week, what would the parking charge be?

With 24 hours per day for 7 days, the person would be charged for 168 hours. Surely we don't want to add 80 cents each hour all these times.

A good strategy is to make a table to find the pattern. In this situation, we work back from the sign to figure out what 0 hours would cost. Then

Hours	Charges	Cost Pattern
0	.70 =	.70 + .80 · 0
1	.70 + .80 =	.70 + .80 · 1
2	.70 + .80 + .80 =	.70 + .80 · 2
3	.70 + .80 + .80 + .80 =	.70 + .80 · 3
4	.70 + .80 + .80 + .80 + .80 =	.70 + .80 · 4

Notice how the hours and cost pattern are related. The number on the far right is the number of hours. This signals an expression for the cost of parking t hours

276

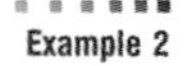

Example 2 A \$140,000 estate is to be split among three children and a grandchild. Each child gets the same amount and the grandchild gets one half as much. How much should each child receive?

Solution Let c represent each child's portion. Then $\frac{1}{2}c$ is the grandchild's portion.

$$c + c + c + \tfrac{1}{2}c = 140{,}000$$

Use the Multiplication Property of 1.

$$1c + 1c + 1c + \tfrac{1}{2}c = 140{,}000$$

Use the Distributive Property and change $\frac{1}{2}$ to .5.

$$3.5c = 140{,}000$$

Divide each side by 3.5.

$$c = 40{,}000$$

Example 2 A high school student wants to take a foreign language class in period 1, a music course in period 2, and an art course in period 3. The language classes available are French, Spanish, and German. The music classes available are chorus and band. The art classes available are drawing and painting. In how many ways can the student choose the three classes?

Solution Make a blank for each decision to be made.

_____ · _____ · _____
ways to choose language · ways to choose music · ways to choose art

There are 3 choices in foreign language, 2 choices in music, and 2 choices in art. Use the multiplication counting principle.

3 · 2 · 2
ways to choose language · ways to choose music · ways to choose art

There are 3 · 2 · 2 = 12 choices.

Check Organize the possibilities using a **tree diagram.**

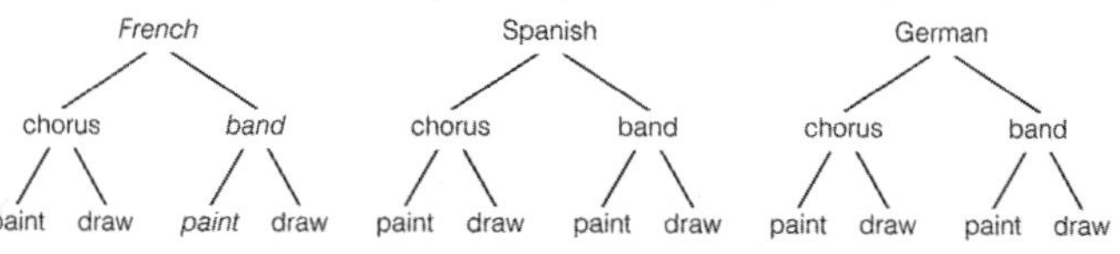

Each choice can be found by following a path along the diagram. One possible choice is shown in italics: *French—band—painting.* Counting shows there are 12 paths. Twelve different choices are pos-

es, and
think-
he
low-
neral-
5%.
would
ou pay
price.
sale
price

Chapter Review

The main objectives for the chapter are organized into sections corresponding to the four main types of understanding this book promotes: *Skills, Properties, Uses,* and *Representations.* Thus, the Chapter Review extends the multi-dimensional approach to understanding, offering a broader perspective that helps students put everything in place.

"This textbook teaches them how to think mathematics. It doesn't just give them the formula and tell them to do it, because that's not really helping them. How often in life do you get a formula— you usually get a problem."

Nancy Artinger, teacher, Lakeside Middle School, Irvine, CA

SKILLS deals with the procedures used to get answers.

Objective A. *Solve quadratic equations using the Quadratic Formula.* (*Lessons 12-4, 12-5*)

In 1–4, give the exact solutions to the equation.

1. $6y^2 + 7y - 20 = 0$

2. $x^2 + 7x + 12 = 0$

3. $4a^2 - 13a = 12$

4. $-q^2 - 6q + 12 = -4$

In 5 and 6, find a simpler equation that has the same solutions as the given equation. Then solve.

5. $10m^2 - 50m + 30 = 0$

6. $20y^2 + 14y - 24 = 0$

Objective B. *Factor quadratic trinomials.* (*Lessons 12-7, 12-9*)

In 15–20, factor.

15. $x^2 + 5x - 6$

16. $3y^2 + 2y - 8$

17. $10a^2 - 19a + 7$

18. $12m^3 + 117m^2 + 81m$

19. $x + 5x^2 - 6$

20. $-3 - 2k + 8k^2$

21. Given that -3 and 17 are solutions to $x^2 - 14x - 51 = 0$, write the factors of $x^2 - 14x - 51$.

PROPERTIES deal with the principles behind the mathematics.

Objective D. *Recognize properties of the parabola.* (*Lessons 12-1, 12-5*)

27. What shape is the graph of $y = -6x^2$?

28. *True or False* The parabola $y = -2x^2 + 3x + 1$ opens down.

29. What equation must you solve to find the x-intercepts of the parabola $y = ax^2 + bx + c$?

30. *True or false* The graph of $y = x^2 + 2x + 2$ intersects the x-axis twice.

CHAPTER 12 Chapter Review 633

USES deal with applications of mathematics in real situations.

Objective G. *Use the parabola and quadratic equations to solve real world problems.* (*Lesson 12-2, 12-3, 12-8*)

45. Consider again the quarterback in Lesson 12-2 who tosses a football to a receiver 40 yards downfield. The ball is at height h feet, x yards downfield where $h = -\frac{1}{40}(x - 20)^2 + 16$. If a defender is 6 yards in front of the receiver,
a. how far is he from the quarterback?
b. Would the defender have a chance to deflect the ball?

48. Refer to the graph below. It shows the height h in feet of a ball, t seconds after it is thrown from ground level at a speed of 64 feet per second.
a. Estimate from the graph at what height the ball will be after 1 second.
b. Estimate from the graph when the ball will reach a height of 35 feet.

REPRESENTATIONS deal with pictures, graphs, or objects that illustrate concepts.

Objective H. *Graph parabolas.* (*Lessons 12-1, 12-2*)

In 49–52, **a.** make a table of values; **b.** graph the equation.

49. $y = 3x^2$

50. $y = -\frac{1}{2}x^2$

51. $y = x^2 + 5x + 6$

52. $y = x^2 - 4$

53. *Multiple choice* Which equation has the

55. Describe the graphing window shown below.

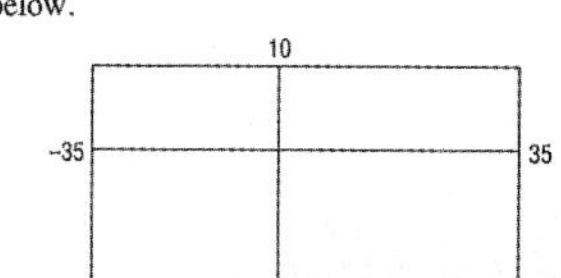

Skills include simple and complicated procedures for getting answers. The emphasis is on *how* to carry out algorithms.

Properties cover the mathematical justifications for procedures and other theory. To fully understand ideas, students must answer the common question, "But *why* does it work that way?"

Uses include real-world applications of the mathematics. To effectively apply what they learn, students must know *when* different models or techniques are relevant.

Representations provide concrete ways to conceptualize what it is that is being studied. Visual images, such as graphs and diagrams, are included here.

All these views have validity, and together they contribute to the deep understanding of mathematics that students need to have, in order to be independent thinkers and learners.

Helps Students Improve Their Performance

Strategies for increasing skill are combined in a unique fashion—and there is evidence that the result is a remarkable improvement in student achievement.

DAILY REVIEW reinforces skills learned in the chapter and combines and maintains skills from earlier chapters.

At least one **QUIZ** per chapter (in the Teacher's Resource File) offers further help to assess mastery.

The **SUMMARY** gives an overview of the entire chapter and helps students consider the material as a whole.

The **VOCABULARY** section provides a checklist of terms, symbols, and properties students must know. Students can refer to the lesson or to the Glossary for additional help.

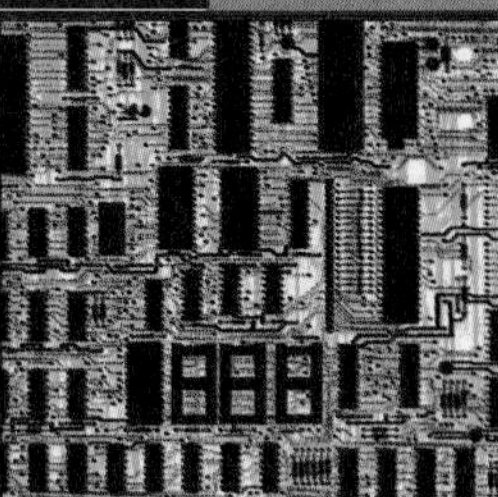

17. Calculators and computers are getting smaller and smaller. It has been estimated that the amount of information that can be stored on a silicon chip is doubling every 18 months. If today's chips have 5000 memory locations, how many might the same size chip have in 6 years?

In 18–21, simplify.

18. $(4y)^0$ when $y = \frac{1}{2}$

19. $7^0 \cdot 7^1 \cdot 7^2$

20. $(x + y)^0$ when $x = 3$ and $y = -8$

21. $(\frac{1}{2})^0 + (\frac{2}{3})^2$

Review

22. $2200 is deposited in a savings account.
a. What will be the total amount of money in the account after 6 years at an annual yield of 6%?
b. How much interest will have been earned in those 6 years? *(Lesson 9-1)*

23. Jeremy invests x dollars for 2 years at an annual yield of 7%. At the end of the 2 years he has $915.92 dollars in his account.
a. Write an equation describing this situation.
b. Find x. *(Lesson 9-1)*

24. A card is drawn randomly from a deck of 52 playing cards. Find **a.** P(a three); **b.** P(a king or an ace). *(Lessons 1-7, 3-5)*

25. Suppose a letter from the alphabet is chosen randomly. What is the probability that it is in the first half of the alphabet and is a vowel? *(Lesson 4-8)*

26. *Skill sequence* Solve. *(Lessons 7-4, 7-8)*
a. $y^2 = 144$ **b.** $(4y)^2 = 144$
c. $(4y - 20)^2 = 144$ **d.** $y^2 + 80 = 144$

In 27–30, simplify. *(Lessons 1-5, 6-9)*

CHAPTER 10

Summary

A term is a number, a product of numbers and variables, or a product of powers of numbers and variables. Polynomials are sums of terms and are classified by the number of terms. Polynomials arise from many situations. This chapter emphasizes situations where money is invested at the same rate but for different lengths of times. It also covers formulas for areas, acceleration, and counting the use of polynomials in some.

Like all algebraic expressions, polynomials can be added, subtracted, multiplied, and divided. All of these operations except division are studied in this chapter. Adding or subtracting polynomials is done by collecting like terms. Multiplying polynomials is done by multiplying each term of one polynomial by each term of the other, and then adding the products. Multiplication of polynomials can be represented by the area model.

Multiplication of binomials is a special case of multiplication of all polynomials and follows a pattern called FOIL.

$$(a + b)(c + d) = ac + ad + bc + bd$$

Certain special cases of this pattern are particularly important.

$$(a + b)(a + b) = a^2 + 2ab + b^2$$
$$(a - b)(a - b) = a^2 - 2ab + b^2$$
$$(a + b)(a - b) = a^2 - b^2$$

Reversing this process is called factoring. When the product of two or more factors is zero, then one of the factors must be zero. This Zero Product Property helps in solving certain equations.

Vocabulary

Below are the important new terms and phrases for this chapter. You should be able to give a general description and a specific example of each.

Lesson 10-1
polynomial
scale factor
polynomial in the variable x
constant term
degree of a polynomial
monomial, binomial, trinomial

Lesson 10-4
common monomial factoring

Lesson 10-5
Extended Distributive Property

Lesson 10-6
FOIL algorithm

Lesson 10-7
expanding a power of a polynomial
perfect square trinomial
Perfect Square Trinomial Patterns

Lesson 10-9
difference of squares
Difference of Two Squares Pattern

Lesson 10-10
Zero Product Property

Lesson 10-11
ruling out possibilities

“I’m interested in algebra this year. . . . It’s almost fun math, as opposed to dry arithmetic.”

Algebra **student, Van Buren High School, Albuquerque, New Mexico**

PROGRESS SELF-TEST provides the opportunity for feedback and correction—before students are tested formally. The Student Edition contains full solutions to questions on this test to enhance accurate self-evaluation.

CHAPTER REVIEW arranges questions according to the four dimensions of understanding—Skills, Properties, Uses, and Representations—to help students master those concepts that have not yet been mastered. Questions are keyed to objectives and lessons for easy reference.

CHAPTER TESTS in the Teacher’s Resource File give you a choice of formats. The regular chapter test comes in parallel Forms A and B and corresponds closely to the Chapter Review. An alternative format is a chapter test in Cumulative Form. You decide which format best suits your needs!

CHAPTER 2

Chapter Review

Questions on **SPUR** Objectives

SPUR stands for **S**kills, **P**roperties, **U**ses, and **R**epresentations. The Chapter Review questions are grouped according to the SPUR Objectives for this chapter.

SKILLS deal with the procedures used to get answers.

Objective A. *Add fractions.* (Lesson 2-3)

write as a single fraction.

$\frac{1}{3} + \frac{1}{4}$

d. $\frac{1}{2} + \frac{2}{3} + \frac{1}{3} + -\frac{3}{4}$

+ -.35

+ $(-4\frac{7}{10})$

$\frac{y}{3}$

6. $\frac{30}{a} + \frac{10}{a}$

+ $\frac{p}{q}$

8. $\frac{x}{5} + -\frac{3}{2}$

B. *Combine like terms.* (Lesson 2-2)

, simplify.

$4 + -2 + -6 + 1$

$+ -3x + 10x$

$+ 2b + -5 + 8a$

$+ 7x + 8 + 5 + 3x$

$1 + 2t + 2$

$n + 4m + -m$

$+ 6b + -5s$

$^2 + -7.5x + 8x^2$

Objective C. *Solve and check equations of the form* $a + x = b$. (Lessons 2-6, 2-7)

In 17–26, solve and check.

17. $2 + m = 12$

18. $x + -11 = 12$

19. $2.5 = t + 3.1$

20. $\frac{1}{3} + a + \frac{3}{4} = 5$

21. $21{,}625 + m = 29{,}112$

22. $(3 + n) + -11 = -5 + 4$

23. $-2 + y = -3$

24. Solve for p: $a + p = c$.

25. Solve for r: $15p + r = 20p$

26. Solve for t: $4s + 3s = t + 2s$

Objective D. *Solve inequalities of the form* $a + x < b$. (Lesson 2-7)

27. $x + 3 > 8$

28. $-28 > y + 22$

29. $-2 + (5 + x) > 4$

30. Solve for r: $d \le r + 45$

31. For the inequality $15 + x < 20$, Brian got the answer $x < 35$. Check whether Brian is correct.

ERTIES deal with the principles behind the mathematics.

E. *Identify properties of addition.* (Lessons 2-2, 2-3)

7, an instance of what property of addition is given?

$+ W) = 2(W + L)$

33. $x + 0 + 3 = x + 3$

34. $4+(28+-16)+-23=4+28+(-16+-23)$

35. $-(-31) = 31$

36. $\frac{2}{3} + \frac{5}{3} = \frac{7}{3}$

37. $8x + -13x = -5x$

CHAPTER 2

Progress Self-Test

Take this test as your would take a test in class. You will need graph paper. Then check your work with the solutions in the Selected Answers section in the back of the book.

1. What property of addition is illustrated by $(x + y) + -4 = x + (y + -4)$?

2. Write an equation to show how x and y are related to the given numbers in the rectangle below.

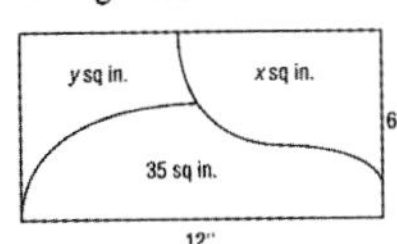

3. The temperature falls 10° then rises d°. Let t° be the change in temperature. Write an equation relating these numbers.

In 4–10, simplify.

4. $-11 + 85 + -47$

5. $x + 5 + x + -8 + -x$

6. $\frac{2}{n} + \frac{m}{n}$ **7.** $\frac{3}{4} + \frac{3}{5} + \left(-\frac{3}{10}\right)$

8. $-8\frac{1}{2} + \left(-3\frac{1}{3}\right)$ **9.** $-(-(-p))$

10. $3x + 4y + -5x$

11. *Multiple choice* Which of the following equals $\frac{a}{b} + \frac{c}{b}$?

(a) $\frac{a + c}{b + b}$ (b) $\frac{ab + bc}{b}$ (c) $\frac{a + c}{2b}$ (d) $\frac{a + c}{b}$

12. Marcia went on a diet. Below are the changes in her weight.

First week	Second week	Third week
lost 4 lb	gained $1\frac{1}{2}$ lb	lost 3 lb

a. Write an equation to find the change she must have the fourth week for a 10-lb overall loss.

b. Solve this equation.

13. What property is being illustrated? If $y + 11 = 3$, then $y + 15 = 7$.

In 14–17, solve.

14. $x + -4 = 12$

15. $-3.5 + a > 10.2$

16. $\frac{5}{2} + y = \frac{17}{4}$

17. $4 > 3 + (z + -10)$

18. Solve for b: $b + a = 100$.

19. Is -100 an element of the solution set of $15 \le x + 87$?

20. Graph the solutions of $-4 \ge 9 + x$.

21. Write, but do not solve, an inequality for this situation. Vern needs at least \$150 to buy a puppy. He has saved \$47.50. How much more money m does he need?

22. The perimeter of the triangle is 43. Find b when $a = 9$ and $c = 21$.

23. Carla’s age is C. What was her age 7 years ago?

24. Find the image of (5, -2) after a slide of 4 units to the left and 5 units up.

25. At the right, $\triangle A'B'C'$ is the image of $\triangle ABC$ under a slide. Under this slide, find B', the image of B.

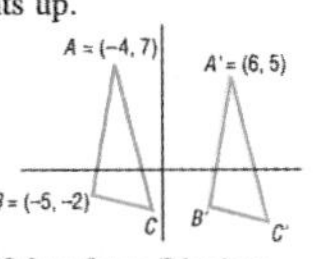

In 26 and 27, Wynken lives 30 km from Blynken. Blynken lives 12 km from Nod.

26. If x is the distance from Wynken to Nod, what inequalities must x satisfy?

27. What is the smallest possible value of x?

In 28–30, boys and girls fill a bus which seats 45 students. Let b be the number of boys on the bus and g be the number of girls.

28. Write an equation using b and g.

29. Find g in each ordered pair showing a possible combination (b, g) of boys and girls: (10, __?__), (20, __?__), (23, __?__), (44, __?__).

Provides the Practical Support You Need

Continual involvement of teachers and instructional supervisors —in planning, writing, rewriting, and evaluating—has made this program **convenient** and **adaptable** to your needs.

Before each chapter you'll find the following:

Daily Pacing Chart
shows you at a glance two alternate ways to pace the chapter.

Testing Options
list the chapter quizzes and tests for ease of planning.

Objectives are letter-coded and keyed to Progress Self-Test, Chapter Review, and Lesson Masters, showing a **direct correspondence between what is taught and what is tested.**

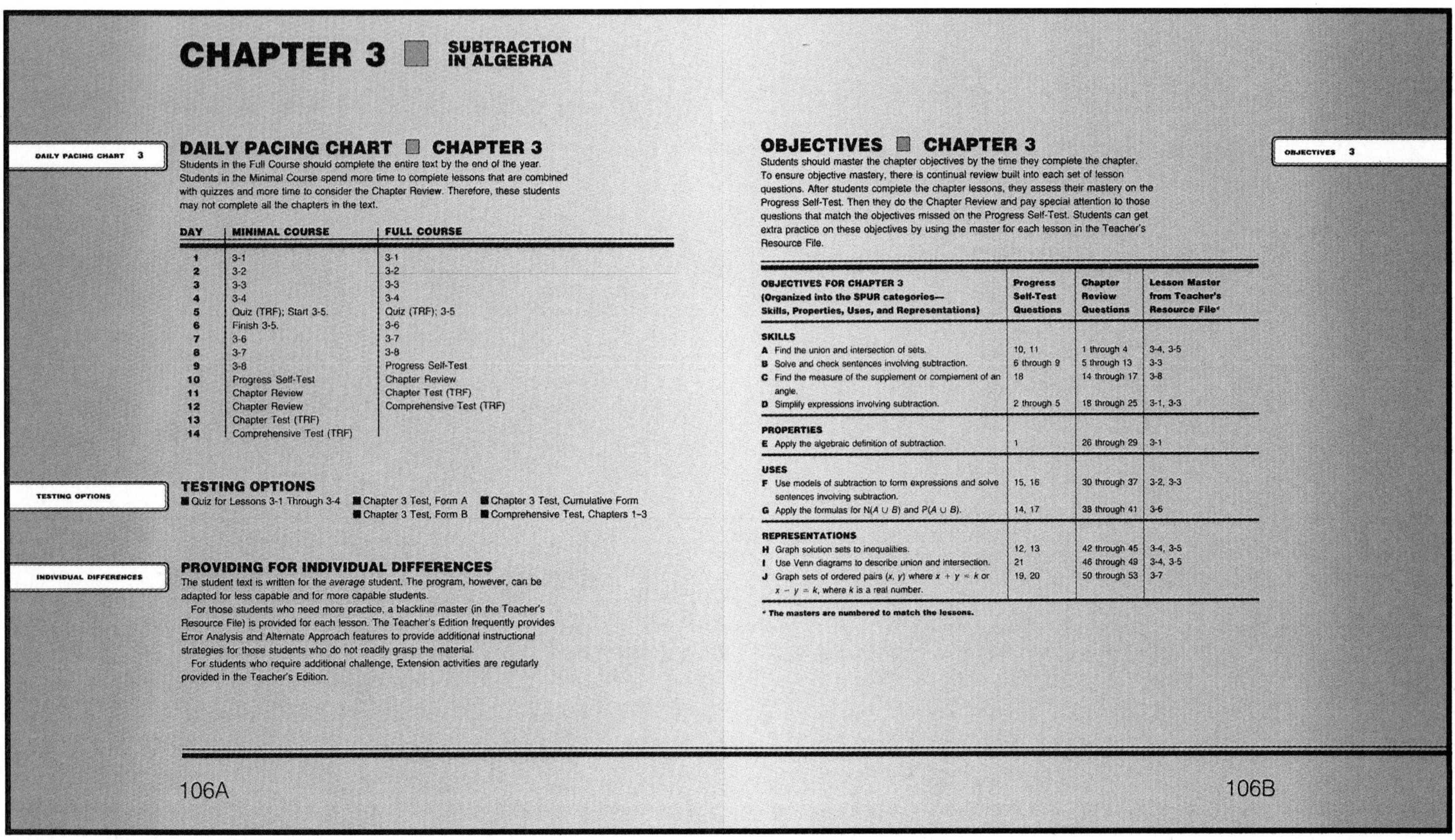

CHAPTER 3 SUBTRACTION IN ALGEBRA

DAILY PACING CHART 3

DAILY PACING CHART CHAPTER 3

Students in the Full Course should complete the entire text by the end of the year. Students in the Minimal Course spend more time to complete lessons that are combined with quizzes and more time to consider the Chapter Review. Therefore, these students may not complete all the chapters in the text.

DAY	MINIMAL COURSE	FULL COURSE
1	3-1	3-1
2	3-2	3-2
3	3-3	3-3
4	3-4	3-4
5	Quiz (TRF); Start 3-5.	Quiz (TRF); 3-5
6	Finish 3-5.	3-6
7	3-6	3-7
8	3-7	3-8
9	3-8	Progress Self-Test
10	Progress Self-Test	Chapter Review
11	Chapter Review	Chapter Test (TRF)
12	Chapter Review	Comprehensive Test (TRF)
13	Chapter Test (TRF)	
14	Comprehensive Test (TRF)	

TESTING OPTIONS

TESTING OPTIONS
- Quiz for Lessons 3-1 Through 3-4
- Chapter 3 Test, Form A
- Chapter 3 Test, Form B
- Chapter 3 Test, Cumulative Form
- Comprehensive Test, Chapters 1–3

INDIVIDUAL DIFFERENCES

PROVIDING FOR INDIVIDUAL DIFFERENCES

The student text is written for the *average* student. The program, however, can be adapted for less capable and for more capable students.

For those students who need more practice, a blackline master (in the Teacher's Resource File) is provided for each lesson. The Teacher's Edition frequently provides Error Analysis and Alternate Approach features to provide additional instructional strategies for those students who do not readily grasp the material.

For students who require additional challenge, Extension activities are regularly provided in the Teacher's Edition.

106A

OBJECTIVES 3

OBJECTIVES CHAPTER 3

Students should master the chapter objectives by the time they complete the chapter. To ensure objective mastery, there is continual review built into each set of lesson questions. After students complete the chapter lessons, they assess their mastery on the Progress Self-Test. Then they do the Chapter Review and pay special attention to those questions that match the objectives missed on the Progress Self-Test. Students can get extra practice on these objectives by using the master for each lesson in the Teacher's Resource File.

OBJECTIVES FOR CHAPTER 3 (Organized into the SPUR categories— Skills, Properties, Uses, and Representations)	Progress Self-Test Questions	Chapter Review Questions	Lesson Master from Teacher's Resource File*
SKILLS			
A Find the union and intersection of sets.	10, 11	1 through 4	3-4, 3-5
B Solve and check sentences involving subtraction.	6 through 9	5 through 13	3-3
C Find the measure of the supplement or complement of an angle.	18	14 through 17	3-8
D Simplify expressions involving subtraction.	2 through 5	18 through 25	3-1, 3-3
PROPERTIES			
E Apply the algebraic definition of subtraction.	1	26 through 29	3-1
USES			
F Use models of subtraction to form expressions and solve sentences involving subtraction.	15, 16	30 through 37	3-2, 3-3
G Apply the formulas for $N(A \cup B)$ and $P(A \cup B)$.	14, 17	38 through 41	3-6
REPRESENTATIONS			
H Graph solution sets to inequalities.	12, 13	42 through 45	3-4, 3-5
I Use Venn diagrams to describe union and intersection.	21	46 through 49	3-4, 3-5
J Graph sets of ordered pairs (x, y) where $x + y = k$ or $x - y = k$, where k is a real number.	19, 20	50 through 53	3-7

* The masters are numbered to match the lessons.

106B

> ❝I continue to marvel at the excitement I feel as each lesson goes on! The thinking required is so refreshing!!! Thank you for this opportunity to use such a good book!!!❞
>
> **Kathryn Shank, teacher, Irvine High School, Irvine, CA**

Overview

anticipates and addresses your needs for the upcoming chapter.

Perspectives,

a unique feature, provides the rationale for the inclusion of topics or approaches, provides mathematical background, and makes connections within UCSMP materials. This is interesting information you'll really use!

Professional Sourcebook for UCSMP

Also at your fingertips is a **wealth of information** that includes valuable background material on topics ranging from research to review. See pages T19–T52 at the back of the Teacher's Edition.

OVERVIEW 3

OVERVIEW ■ CHAPTER 3

In this chapter, subtraction is related to all of the following: addition, numbers of elements in sets, probabilities, applications from arithmetic, equations, and inequalities.

The first three lessons introduce the definition of subtraction, subtraction models, and solving $x - a = b$ and $x - a < b$. To solve these sentences, students are encouraged to change subtractions to additions, and then to proceed using the properties studied in Chapter 2.

Lessons 3-4 through 3-6 lead to the use of subtraction in solving both counting and probability problems in which sets overlap. The formulas for counts and probabilities employ the definitions of *union* and *intersection* of sets.

Lesson 3-7 deals with situations involving pairs of numbers whose sums are constant and the representation of these number pairs as lines. Lesson 3-8 applies the constant sum idea to important geometry situations. These two lessons offer an opportunity to consolidate the skills of this chapter. At the same time, these lessons present some significant uses of addition and subtraction which will be referred to later in the book.

PERSPECTIVES 3

PERSPECTIVES ■ CHAPTER 3

The Perspectives provide the rationale for the inclusion of topics or approaches, provide mathematical background, and make connections within UCSMP.

3-1
SUBTRACTION OF REAL NUMBERS

In the first grade, students learn their first "definition" of subtraction—referred to in Lesson 3-2 as the Take-away Model for Subtraction. Of course, "take-away" is not called a definition, but it serves that purpose. The problem with this early model is that it does not apply well to negative numbers.

In contrast, the algebraic definition of subtraction, $a - b = a + -b$, enables any subtraction to be converted to addition. This is particularly helpful because students already know how to add positive and negative numbers. Also, addition has the commutative and associative properties while subtraction does not. Converting to addition avoids errors in the order of operations when there are more than two numbers involved in the subtractions.

3-2
MODELS FOR SUBTRACTION

The two models for subtraction discussed in this lesson are review for students who have had *Transition Mathematics*.

The Take-away Model for Subtraction can be viewed as the counterpart to the Putting-together Model for Addition. The take-away model is the one most often encountered in school texts, and the situations are usually those in which the numbers are counts of discrete objects.

Students have also had a lot of experience with the Comparison Model for Subtraction. In general, we compare in the direction which gives a positive answer for the result. That is, we subtract the smaller number from the larger, and we use the context to decide whether the answer is positive or negative. The exception would be when a quantity changes over a period of time. There we subtract the earlier amount from the later one. The sign of the result shows whether the quantity increased or decreased over that period.

3-3
SOLVING $x - a = b$ AND $x - a < b$

This lesson tends to be easy for most students. It covers sentences of the forms $x - a = b$ and $x - a < b$ but purposely not those of the form $a - x = b$. Solution of this last sentence requires two major steps and is not treated until the next chapter.

This lesson is an opportunity for reviewing the checking process for inequalities.

3-4
INTERSECTION OF SETS

Several questions have been included in previous lessons in order to prepare students for this introduction of intersection. Students should not have trouble with this topic, but they may find the next lesson harder because they have to distinguish between intersection and union. Venn diagrams provide a visual representation.

The idea of intersection of sets is used in Lesson 3-6 in the formula to find the number of elements in the union. In Chapter 4, intersections are related to probabilities of events. In Chapter 11, intersections of sets are again found when discussing solutions to systems. Of course, intersections of sets of points are used throughout geometry. There are many applications throughout the text that use intersection.

3-5
UNION OF SETS

As with intersection, the union of sets is discussed through several related means: the definition, Venn diagrams, relative frequency, and graphing.

This lesson concentrates on identifying what elements would be in the union of sets. Example 1 shows that when considering the union of sets that overlap, the elements in both sets (namely, in the intersection) should *not* be listed twice when the union is enumerated. Specific formulas for the count of elements in a union of sets and for the probability of the union of sets are discussed in the next lesson.

3-6
ADDITION, SUBTRACTION, AND COUNTING

The simplest examples of addition are instances of the Putting-together Model where the addends do not overlap. In reality, however, overlap is a common occurrence. Our statistical examples show this quite frequently. In fact, many measurement problems involve overlap. It is important that the student encounter these situations and know how to handle them. The formula for the count of elements in the union of sets and the formula for the probability of the union of events are important formulas in mathematics.

The term *mutually exclusive* is introduced in the context of counting elements in the union. This term is used in connection with events and with probabilities of events. Here are three symbolic statements that two sets or events S and T are mutually exclusive:

$$N(S \cap T) = 0$$
$$P(S \cap T) = 0$$
$$S \cap T = \varnothing$$

Many books take as their Fundamental Counting Principle our Multiplication Counting Principle, which appears in Chapter 4. But our titles are very appropriate because addition situations tend to be more fundamental than multiplication ones.

3-7
ADDITION, SUBTRACTION, AND GRAPHING

Making a table is an important problem-solving strategy. Here, it is combined with the strategy of *drawing a graph*. Both ideas help students find patterns and make generalizations. By the end of the book, students will have seen a variety of tables and graphs which represent important linear and curvilinear patterns.

Using mathematics to describe the relationship between two variables is a fundamental component of scientific and statistical methods. This lesson is especially important if students have never graphed lines. The investigation of how the equation of a line relates to its graph is one of the major topics covered in this book.

Students should have graph paper for this assignment and many later lessons. One approach is to do the entire assignment on graph paper. Not only does this ensure a handy place to draw a graph, but it encourages neat work.

3-8
ADDITION, SUBTRACTION, AND GEOMETRY

Four important geometric concepts are covered in this lesson. Most students have studied them before. They should master them now. These concepts are the definitions of *supplementary angles* and *complementary angles*, the Triangle-Sum Property, and the convention for marking right angles. Prerequisites for understanding these concepts are some of the ideas in the Refresher material which precedes this chapter.

Supplementary angles, complementary angles, and the Triangle-Sum Property are rich sources of algebra questions because they are instances of the constant sum model:

$$a + b = \text{constant}.$$

As the development at the beginning of the lesson shows, solving for b gives

$$b = \text{constant} - a.$$

The definition in this book for *supplementary angles* does not explicitly state whether 0° and 180° could be the measures of supplementary angles. The graph in the lesson does not include the points (180, 0) and (0, 180). However, some books define angles with measure 180° and 0° and would therefore permit these two points.

106C

106D

Super Teaching Support
continued

1. **RESOURCES** save you time by coordinating all of the ancillaries to the lesson. In addition to Lesson Masters, ancillaries may include Computer Masters, Visual Masters, quizzes, and tests.

2. **OBJECTIVES** are letter-coded for easy reference.

3. **TEACHING NOTES** provide everything you need, including reading tips, suggestions for discussing the examples, calculator tips, mental math and estimation suggestions, dialogue to generate higher-order thinking, and more.

4. **ALTERNATE APPROACH** offers a different strategy for presenting the lesson, often using concrete materials or cooperative learning, for students needing additional help.

5. **ADDITIONAL EXAMPLES** provide parallel examples to those in the text for added flexibility.

6. **NOTES ON QUESTIONS** highlight important aspects of questions and provide helpful suggestions to enhance learning.

7. **ERROR ANALYSIS** pinpoints typical student errors and provides remediation strategies for correcting the errors.

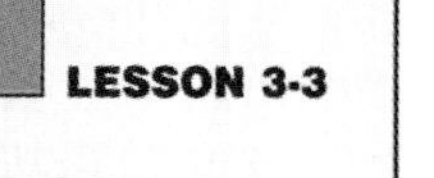

LESSON 3-3

1

RESOURCES
■ Lesson Master 3-3

2

OBJECTIVES

B Solve and check sentences involving subtraction.
D Simplify expressions involving subtraction.
F Use models of subtraction to form expressions and solve sentences involving subtraction.

3

TEACHING NOTES

Solving $x - a = b$ and $x - a < b$ is likely to be review for most students. Nevertheless, stress the sentence-solving techniques used in the lesson. This will benefit students who tend to confuse $x + a = b$ with $x - a = b$.

4

Alternate Approach
Instead of solving $x - a = b$ by changing the subtraction to addition, some people prefer to add a to each side right away.

Examples:
1. $x - 7 = -10$
$x - 7 + 7 = -10 + 7$
$x = -3$

2. $y - -20 < 5$
$y - -20 + -20 < 5 + -20$
$y < -15$

Students should be aware of both methods.

118

8. **MAKING CONNECTIONS** helps you connect present content and ideas to material covered in an earlier or later lesson, chapter, or text.

9. The **LESSON MASTER** is pictured where you need it for your convenience.

10. **MORE PRACTICE** lists the Lesson Master for additional practice of the lesson skills and concepts.

11. **EXTENSION** offers high-interest activities for all students, as well as enrichment activities for students needing additional challenge. These well-liked activities provide ideas for technology, estimation, mental math, carrers, and additional applications.

EVALUATION tells what you need to know about the quizzes and tests. It also provides **Alternative Assessment** suggestions to encourage different evaluation formats, such as oral presentation and cooperative learning.

5

ADDITIONAL EXAMPLES
1. Ross went shopping and spent \$43.50. When he got home he counted his money and had \$13.23. How much did he have when he started his shopping trip?
\$56.73

2. Solve and graph $-819 \le g - -406$.
$-1225 \le g$

-1225 g

3. Solve for x: $x - 12t = t$.
$x = 13t$

llow-Up helps you follow through

"It really gives you an opportunity to teach the whole child. If it's a science question, you can elaborate on that . . . If it's social studies, you can talk about that. And it takes the teacher out of this stiff role as the math teacher. It gives the teacher another dimension."

Eldora Muldrow, teacher, Crest Hills Middle School, Cincinnati, OH

6

NOTES ON QUESTIONS
Questions 3-5: By splitting these into parts **a** and **b**, we are emphasizing the rewriting step. If you use the alternate approach on page 118, part **a** is unnecessary.

7

Error Analysis for Question 8: Some students may erroneously solve $-6 > x - 4$ as $x > -2$. Then their graphs will be shaded on the wrong side of -2. Of course, they have switched the sides of the inequality without also reversing the sense. Stress the importance of checking. Choosing the value 4 for x will dramatically show that $x > -2$ is true but $-6 > x - 4$ is false.

8

Making Connections for Question 12: Students should first simplify the sentence to $1x - 3r = r$, then add $3r$ to both sides to get $1x = 4r$. To finish, they must realize that $1x = x$, a point that will be validated in Lesson 4-3 with the Multiplicative Identity Property of One.

Question 13: This shows the formula solved for p and s. You might ask students to solve for c.

Questions 14 and 15: These involve patterns. You might ask students to generalize. They could use the problem-solving strategies of *trying a simpler case* and *making a table*.

[$n - (n - 1 - (n - 2 - \ldots - 1)$*

$= \frac{n}{2}$ if n is even;

$= \frac{n+1}{2}$ if n is odd.

$1 - (2 - (3 - \ldots n)$*

$= \frac{-n}{2}$ if n is even;

$= \frac{n+1}{2}$ if n is odd.]

*We have omitted the many right-hand parentheses that should be used.

Question 17: When entering $120\frac{2}{5}$ into the calculator, the Equal Fractions Property can be used to make the work easier.
$120\frac{2}{5} = 120\frac{4}{10} = 120.4$.

ADDITIONAL ANSWERS
2a. Let M = Mercury's maximum temperature that day; then $M - (-23) = 797$
7a. Definition of subtraction
7b. Addition Property of Inequality
7c. Property of Opposites
7d. Additive Identity Property
8. $-2 > x$;

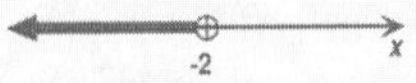

13a. Definition of subtraction
13b. Addition Property of Equality
13c. Associative Property of Addition
13d. Property of Opposites
13e. Additive Identity Property
18.

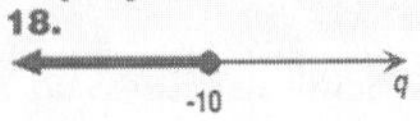

19.

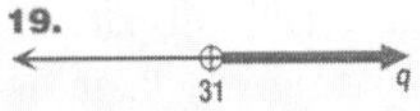

9

NAME ____________

LESSON **MASTER 3–3**
QUESTIONS ON SPUR OBJECTIVES

■SKILLS Objective B (See pages 150–152 for objectives.)
In 1–4, solve and check.

1. $p - 34 = -8$ $p = 26$; $26 - 34 = -8$
2. $4.5 = r - 3.8$ $r = 8.3$; $4.5 = 8.3 - 3.8$
3. $x - 11 > -5$ $x > 6$; $6 - 11 = -5$, and $7 - 11 > -5$
4. $\frac{5}{8} \geq y - \frac{3}{4}$ $y \leq \frac{11}{8}$; $\frac{5}{8} = \frac{11}{8} - \frac{3}{4}$, and $\frac{5}{8} > \frac{5}{4} - \frac{3}{4}$

In 5–10, solve for x.

5. $x - a = 19$ $x = 19 + a$
6. $k = x - 12$ $x = k + 12$
7. $x - p = 3p$ $x = 4p$
8. $-\frac{3}{4}d = x - \frac{d}{2}$ $x = -\frac{d}{4}$
9. $g < x - 32$ $x > g + 32$
10. $x - c > b$ $x > b + c$

■SKILLS Objective D
In 11–14, simplify.

11. $6h + h - 4h$ $3h$
12. $4 + (x - 8)$ $x - 4$
13. $3x + 5 - 2x$ $x + 5$
14. $-9x - x + 10x$ 0

■USES Objective F

15. The range of scores on an algebra test was R. The minimum score was 60. Write and solve an equation to find the maximum score h.
$h = R + 60$

16. To lose weight, Sonya had to reduce her daily caloric intake to less than 1800 calories. By eliminating desserts she removed 600 calories and is now losing weight. If her previous intake was c calories, write an inequality describing the situation.
$c - 600 < 1800; c < 2400$

17. Mr. Swenson has saved \$1500 for a down payment on an automobile. If the automobile costs T dollars, how much will he have to borrow?
$(T - 1500)$ dollars

Algebra © Scott, Foresman and Company   21

Making Connections for Question 24: Prior to this, students have not simplified fractions that have polynomial factors in the numerator or denominator. In this problem they need to use the cognitive skill of chunking—viewing small bits of information such as $(x + 3)$ as a single unit. Chunking is directly studied in Lesson 7-8.

Question 29b: Stress that $\frac{1}{2}x$ means "half of x."

Question 30: Students should not change the scientific notation to standard notation because a number like 235,000,000 cannot be entered directly into many calculators. Students may use scientific notation to enter the numbers, or they could use $1.27 \div 23.5$, and then adjust the decimal point.

FOLLOW-UP

10

MORE PRACTICE
For more questions on SPUR Objectives, use *Lesson Master 3-3*, shown on page 121.

11

EXTENSION
Computer Have students use the computer program in Lesson 2-6 (page 90) to solve equations of the form $x - a = b$. They will first have to change the form to $x + -a = b$.

Components Designed for Ease of Teaching

STUDENT EDITION,
full color

TEACHER'S EDITION,
annotated and with margin notes

TEACHER'S RESOURCE FILE
About 600 blackline masters
to cover your every classroom need!

Quiz and Test Masters

Quizzes (at least one per chapter)

Chapter Tests, Forms A and B (parallel forms)

Chapter Tests, Cumulative Form

Comprehensive Tests (four per text,
including Final Exam, primarily multiple choice)

Lesson Masters
(one or two per lesson)

Computer Masters

Answer Masters
(provide answers for questions in student text;
oversized type to enable display in class,
allowing students to grade their own work)

Teaching Aid Masters
(patterns for manipulatives;
masters for overhead transparencies;
forms, charts, and graphs from the PE;
coordinate grids; and more)

ADDITIONAL ANCILLARIES . . .

Solutions Manual

Computer Software

Visual Aids

"I've learned intense amounts this year."

Algebra **student, Crest Hills Middle School, Cincinnati, OH**

The University of Chicago School Mathematics Project

Algebra

Authors

John W. McConnell
Susan Brown
Susan Eddins
Margaret Hackworth
Leroy Sachs
Ernest Woodward
James Flanders
Daniel Hirschhorn
Cathy Hynes
Lydia Polonsky
Zalman Usiskin

About the Cover

Graphed here is the path of a baseball that is lobbed from a height of 4 feet and attains a height of 12 feet after traveling a horizontal distance of 10 feet. The path is part of a parabola.

Scott, Foresman and Company

Editorial Offices: Glenview, Illinois Regional Offices: Sunnyvale, California •
Atlanta, Georgia • Glenview, Illinois • Oakland, New Jersey • Dallas, Texas

Acknowledgments

Authors

John W. McConnell
Instructional Supervisor of Mathematics, Glenbrook South H.S., Glenview, IL

Susan Brown
Mathematics Teacher, York H.S., Elmhurst, IL

Susan Eddins
Mathematics Teacher, Illinois Mathematics and Science Academy, Aurora, IL

Margaret Hackworth
Mathematics Supervisor, Pinellas County Schools, Largo, FL

Leroy Sachs
Mathematics Teacher (retired), Clayton H.S., Clayton, MO

Ernest Woodward
Professor of Mathematics, Austin Peay State University, Clarksville, TN

James Flanders
UCSMP

Daniel Hirschhorn
UCSMP

Cathy Hynes
Mathematics Teacher, The University of Chicago Laboratory Schools

Lydia Polonsky
UCSMP

Zalman Usiskin
Professor of Education, The University of Chicago

Editorial Development and Design

Scott, Foresman staff, Publishers Services, Incorporated, Kristin Nelson Design, Jill Ruter Design

We wish to acknowledge the generous support of the **Amoco Foundation** and the **Carnegie Corporation of New York** in helping to make it possible for these materials to be developed and tested.

UCSMP Production and Evaluation

Series Editors: Zalman Usiskin, Sharon Senk (Michigan State University)
Technical Coordinator: Susan Chang
Director of Evaluations: Sandra Mathison (State University of New York, Albany)
Assistants to the Director: Penelope Flores, David Matheson, Catherine Sarther

A list of schools that participated in the research and development of this text may be found on page *iii*.

ISBN: 0-673-45263-8

5 6 7 8 9—VHJ—9 6 9 5 9 4 9 3 9 2 9 1

We cannot thank everyone who helped us on this book by name. We wish particularly to acknowledge Carol Siegel, who coordinated the use of these materials in schools, and Peter Bryant, Dan Caplinger, Janine Crawley, Kurt Hackemer, Michael Herzog, Maryann Kannappan, Mary Lappan, Teresa Manst, and Victoria Ritter of our technical staff.

The following teachers taught preliminary versions of this text, participated in the pilot and formative research, and contributed many ideas to help improve the text:

Ed Brennan
George Washington High School
Chicago Public Schools

Patricia Doliboa
Clearwater High School
Clearwater, Florida

Monica Hatfield
Morton East High School
Cicero, Illinois

Marie Hill
Glenbrook South High School
Glenview, Illinois

Martha Huberty
Aptakisic Junior High School
Prairie View, Illinois

Jacquie Jensen
O'Neill Junior High School
Downers Grove, Illinois

Rob Johan
O'Neill Junior High School
Downers Grove, Illinois

Joe Lee
Parkway West Junior High School
Chesterfield, Missouri

Edythe Olshan
Von Steuben Mathematics
and Science Academy
Chicago Public Schools

Janet Ramser
Northeast High School
Clarksville, Tennessee

Paula Rossino
Disney Magnet School
Chicago Public Schools

Candace Schultz
Wheaton-Warrenville Middle School
Wheaton, Illinois

Chris Senorski
Austin Academy
Chicago Public Schools

Barbara Simak
McClure Junior High School
Western Springs, Illinois

Mary Szczypta
Elk Grove High School
Elk Grove, Illinois

George Zerfass
Glenbrook South High School
Glenview, Illinois

The following schools used an earlier version of UCSMP *Algebra* in a nationwide study. Their comments, suggestions, and performance guided the changes made for this version.

Rancho San Joaquin High School
Lakeside Middle School
Irvine High School
Irvine, California

Mendocino High School
Mendocino, California

Lincoln Junior High School
Lesher Junior High School
Blevins Junior High School
Fort Collins, Colorado

Bacon Academy
Colchester, Connecticut

Rogers Park Junior High School
Danbury, Connecticut

Hyde Park Career Academy
Bogan High School
Chicago, Illiinois

Morton East High School
Cicero, Illinois

Springman Junior High School
Glenview, Illinois

Carl Sandburg Junior High School
Winston Park Junior High School
Palatine, Illinois

Fruitport High School
Fruitport, Michigan

Taylor Middle School
Roosevelt Middle School
Van Buren Middle School
Albuquerque, New Mexico

Crest Hills Middle School
Shroder Paideia
Walnut Hills High School
Cincinnati, Ohio

Easley Junior High School
Easley, South Carolina

R.C. Edwards Junior High School
Central, South Carolina

Liberty Middle School
Liberty High School
Liberty, South Carolina

Glen Hills Middle School
Glendale, Wisconsin

Robinson Middle School
Mapledale Middle School
Milwaukee, Wisconsin

We wish to acknowledge and thank the many other schools and students who have used earlier versions of these materials. We wish also to acknowledge the contribution of the text *Algebra Through Applications with Probability and Statistics,* by Zalman Usiskin (NCTM, 1979), developed with funds from the National Science Foundation, to some of the conceptualizations and problems used in this book.

UCSMP Algebra

The University of Chicago School Mathematics Project (UCSMP) is a long-term project designed to improve school mathematics in grades K-12. UCSMP began in 1983 with a 6-year grant from the Amoco Foundation. Additional funding has come from the Ford Motor Company, the Carnegie Corporation of New York, the National Science Foundation, the General Electric Foundation, GTE, and Citicorp.

The project is centered in the Departments of Education and Mathematics of the University of Chicago, and has the following components and directors:

Resources	Izaak Wirszup, Professor Emeritus of Mathematics
Primary Materials	Max Bell, Professor of Education
Elementary Teacher Development	Sheila Sconiers, Research Associate in Education
Secondary	Sharon L. Senk, Assistant Professor of Mathematics and Education, Syracuse University (on leave) Zalman Usiskin, Professor of Education
Evaluation	Larry Hedges, Professor of Education Susan Stodolsky, Professor of Education

From 1983-1987, the director of UCSMP was Paul Sally, Professor of Mathematics. Since 1987, the director has been Zalman Usiskin.

The text *Algebra* was developed by the Secondary Component (grades 7-12) of the project, and constitutes the second year in a six-year mathematics curriculum devised by that component. As texts in this curriculum complete their multi-stage testing cycle, they are being published by Scott, Foresman and Company. The schedule for first publication of the texts follows. Titles for the last two books are tentative.

Transition Mathematics	spring, 1989
Algebra	spring, 1989
Geometry	spring, 1990
Advanced Algebra	spring, 1989
Functions, Statistics, and Trigonometry, with Computers	spring, 1991
Precalculus and Discrete Mathematics	spring, 1991

A first draft of *Algebra* was written and piloted during the 1985-86 school year. After a major revision, a field trial edition was used in about ten schools in 1986-87. A second revision was given a comprehensive nationwide test during 1987-88. Results are available by writing UCSMP. The Scott, Foresman and Company edition is based on improvements suggested by the authors, editors, and some of the many teacher and student users of earlier editions.

Comments about these materials are welcomed. Address queries to Mathematics Product Manager, Scott, Foresman and Company, 1900 East Lake Avenue, Glenview, Illinois 60025, or to UCSMP, The University of Chicago, 5835 S. Kimbark, Chicago, IL 60637.

UCSMP *Algebra* is designed for a first-year course in algebra. It differs from other books for this course in six major ways. First, it has **wider scope** in content. It integrates geometry, statistics, and probability into the algebra. These topics are not isolated as separate units of study or enrichment. They are employed to motivate, justify, extend, and otherwise enhance important concepts of algebra.

Second, **reading and problem solving** are emphasized throughout. Students can and should be expected to read this book. The explanations were written for students and tested with them. The first set of questions in each lesson is called "Covering the Reading." The exercises guide students through the reading and check their coverage of critical words, rules, explanations, and examples. The second set of questions is called "Applying the Mathematics." These questions extend student understanding of the principles and applications of the lesson. To further widen student horizons, "Exploration" questions are provided in every lesson.

Third, there is a **reality orientation** towards both the selection of content and the approaches allowed the student in working out problems. Algebra is rich in applications and problem solving. Being able to do algebra is of little ultimate use to individuals unless they can apply that content. Real-life situations motivate algebraic ideas and provide the settings for practice of algebra skills. The variety of content of this book permits lessons on problem-solving strategies to be embedded in application settings.

Fourth, fitting the reality orientation, students are expected to use current **technology**. Calculators are assumed throughout this book because virtually all individuals who use mathematics today find it helpful to have them. Scientific calculators are recommended because they use an order of operations closer to that found in algebra and have numerous keys that are helpful in understanding concepts at this level. Computer exercises present important representations of the language and algorithms of algebra. To help the student develop a sense of when technology is appropriate, many lessons contain questions requiring mental computation.

Fifth, **four dimensions of understanding** are emphasized: skill in carrying out various algorithms; developing and using mathematical properties and relationships; applying mathematics in realistic situations; and representing or picturing mathematical concepts. We call this the SPUR approach: **S**kills, **P**roperties, **U**ses, **R**epresentations.

Sixth, the **instructional format** is designed to maximize the acquisition of both skills and concepts. The book is organized around lessons meant to take one day to cover. Ideas introduced in a lesson are reinforced through "Review" questions in the immediately succeeding lessons. This daily review feature allows students several nights to learn and practice important concepts and skills. The lessons themselves are sequenced into carefully constructed chapters. At the end of each chapter, a carefully focused Progress Self-Test and Chapter Review, keyed to objectives in all the dimensions of understanding, are then used to solidify performance of skills and concepts from the chapter so that they may be applied later with confidence. Finally, to increase retention, important ideas are again reviewed in "Review" questions of later chapters.

CONTENTS

Chapter 1 Basic Concepts 2

Chapter 2 Addition in Algebra 54

Chapter 3 Subtraction in Algebra 106

To the Student

With algebra, you can describe patterns of all kinds, work with formulas, discuss unknowns in problems, quickly graph ideas, and write computer programs. Algebra can be considered to be the language of mathematics. The first goal of UCSMP *Algebra* is to introduce you to this wonderful and rich language.

You will find algebra different from arithmetic. Sometimes algebra is harder, but often it's easier because there is less computation. Also, you will learn that graphs can describe many of the ideas in algebra, and these will help you.

For this book, you will need a ruler (to draw and measure along lines), with both centimeter and inch markings, and graph paper. It is best if the ruler is made of transparent plastic.

You will also need a scientific calculator in many places in this book, beginning in Chapter 1. Scientific calculators differ widely in the range of keys they have. If you are going to buy or borrow a calculator, it should have the following keys: $\boxed{x^y}$ or $\boxed{y^x}$ (powering), $\boxed{\sqrt{x}}$ (for square root), $\boxed{x!}$ (factorial), $\boxed{\pm}$ or $\boxed{+/-}$ (for negative numbers), $\boxed{\pi}$ (pi), and $\boxed{1/x}$ (reciprocals), and it should write very large or very small numbers in scientific notation. We recommend a *solar-powered* calculator so that you do not have to worry about batteries, though some calculators have batteries which can last for many years and work in dim light. A good calculator can last for many years.

There is another important goal of this book: to assist you to become able to learn mathematics on your own, so that you will be able to deal with the mathematics you see in newspapers, magazines, on television, on any job, and in school. The authors, who are all experienced teachers, offer the following advice.

1. You cannot learn much mathematics just by watching other people do it. You must participate. Some teachers have a slogan:

   Mathematics is not a spectator sport.

2. You are expected to read each lesson. Read slowly, and keep a pencil with you as you check the mathematics that is done in the book. Use the Glossary or a dictionary to find the meaning of a word you do not understand.

3. You are expected to do homework every day while studying from this book, so put aside time for it. Do not wait until the day before a test if you do not understand something. Try to resolve the difficulty right away and ask questions of your classmates or teacher. You are expected to learn many things by reading, but school is designed so that you do not have to learn everything by yourself.

4. If you cannot answer a question immediately, don't give up! Read the lesson again; read the question again. Look for examples. If you can, go away from the problem and come back to it a little later.

We hope you join the many thousands of students who have enjoyed this book. We wish you much success.

CHAPTER 1 ■ BASIC CONCEPTS

DAILY PACING CHART 1

DAILY PACING CHART ■ CHAPTER 1

Students in the Full Course should complete the entire text by the end of the year. Students in the Minimal Course spend more time to complete lessons that are combined with quizzes and more time to consider the Chapter Review. Therefore, these students may not complete all the chapters in the text.

For more information on pacing, see *General Teaching Suggestions: Pace* on page T35 of the Teacher's Edition.

DAY	MINIMAL COURSE	FULL COURSE
1	1-1	1-1
2	1-2	1-2
3	1-3	1-3
4	1-4	1-4
5	Quiz in Teacher's Resource File (TRF); Start 1-5.	Quiz in Teacher's Resource File (TRF); 1-5
6	Finish 1-5.	Appendix A (optional)
7	Appendix A (optional)	Appendix B (optional)
8	Appendix B (optional)	1-6
9	1-6	1-7
10	1-7	1-8
11	1-8	Progress Self-Test
12	Progress Self-Test	Chapter Review
13	Chapter Review	Chapter Test in Teacher's Resource File (TRF)
14	Chapter Review	
15	Chapter Test in Teacher's Resource File (TRF)	

TESTING OPTIONS

TESTING OPTIONS

- Quiz for Lessons 1-1 Through 1-4
- Chapter 1 Test, Form A
- Chapter 1 Test, Form B

INDIVIDUAL DIFFERENCES

PROVIDING FOR INDIVIDUAL DIFFERENCES

The student text is written for the *average* student. The program, however, can be adapted for less capable and for more capable students.

For those students who need more practice, a blackline master (in the Teacher's Resource File) is provided for each lesson. The Teacher's Edition frequently provides Error Analysis and Alternate Approach features to provide additional instructional strategies for those students who do not readily grasp the material.

For students who require additional challenge, Extension activities are regularly provided in the Teacher's Edition.

To the Student

With algebra, you can describe patterns of all kinds, work with formulas, discuss unknowns in problems, quickly graph ideas, and write computer programs. Algebra can be considered to be the language of mathematics. The first goal of UCSMP *Algebra* is to introduce you to this wonderful and rich language.

You will find algebra different from arithmetic. Sometimes algebra is harder, but often it's easier because there is less computation. Also, you will learn that graphs can describe many of the ideas in algebra, and these will help you.

For this book, you will need a ruler (to draw and measure along lines), with both centimeter and inch markings, and graph paper. It is best if the ruler is made of transparent plastic.

You will also need a scientific calculator in many places in this book, beginning in Chapter 1. Scientific calculators differ widely in the range of keys they have. If you are going to buy or borrow a calculator, it should have the following keys: $\boxed{x^y}$ or $\boxed{y^x}$ (powering), $\boxed{\sqrt{x}}$ (for square root), $\boxed{x!}$ (factorial), $\boxed{\pm}$ or $\boxed{+/-}$ (for negative numbers), $\boxed{\pi}$ (pi), and $\boxed{1/x}$ (reciprocals), and it should write very large or very small numbers in scientific notation. We recommend a *solar-powered* calculator so that you do not have to worry about batteries, though some calculators have batteries which can last for many years and work in dim light. A good calculator can last for many years.

There is another important goal of this book: to assist you to become able to learn mathematics on your own, so that you will be able to deal with the mathematics you see in newspapers, magazines, on television, on any job, and in school. The authors, who are all experienced teachers, offer the following advice.

1. You cannot learn much mathematics just by watching other people do it. You must participate. Some teachers have a slogan:

   Mathematics is not a spectator sport.

2. You are expected to read each lesson. Read slowly, and keep a pencil with you as you check the mathematics that is done in the book. Use the Glossary or a dictionary to find the meaning of a word you do not understand.

3. You are expected to do homework every day while studying from this book, so put aside time for it. Do not wait until the day before a test if you do not understand something. Try to resolve the difficulty right away and ask questions of your classmates or teacher. You are expected to learn many things by reading, but school is designed so that you do not have to learn everything by yourself.

4. If you cannot answer a question immediately, don't give up! Read the lesson again; read the question again. Look for examples. If you can, go away from the problem and come back to it a little later.

We hope you join the many thousands of students who have enjoyed this book. We wish you much success.

CHAPTER 1 ■ BASIC CONCEPTS

DAILY PACING CHART 1

DAILY PACING CHART ■ CHAPTER 1

Students in the Full Course should complete the entire text by the end of the year. Students in the Minimal Course spend more time to complete lessons that are combined with quizzes and more time to consider the Chapter Review. Therefore, these students may not complete all the chapters in the text.

For more information on pacing, see *General Teaching Suggestions: Pace* on page T35 of the Teacher's Edition.

DAY	MINIMAL COURSE	FULL COURSE
1	1-1	1-1
2	1-2	1-2
3	1-3	1-3
4	1-4	1-4
5	Quiz in Teacher's Resource File (TRF); Start 1-5.	Quiz in Teacher's Resource File (TRF); 1-5
6	Finish 1-5.	Appendix A (optional)
7	Appendix A (optional)	Appendix B (optional)
8	Appendix B (optional)	1-6
9	1-6	1-7
10	1-7	1-8
11	1-8	Progress Self-Test
12	Progress Self-Test	Chapter Review
13	Chapter Review	Chapter Test in Teacher's Resource File (TRF)
14	Chapter Review	
15	Chapter Test in Teacher's Resource File (TRF)	

TESTING OPTIONS

TESTING OPTIONS

■ Quiz for Lessons 1-1 Through 1-4

■ Chapter 1 Test, Form A

■ Chapter 1 Test, Form B

INDIVIDUAL DIFFERENCES

PROVIDING FOR INDIVIDUAL DIFFERENCES

The student text is written for the *average* student. The program, however, can be adapted for less capable and for more capable students.

For those students who need more practice, a blackline master (in the Teacher's Resource File) is provided for each lesson. The Teacher's Edition frequently provides Error Analysis and Alternate Approach features to provide additional instructional strategies for those students who do not readily grasp the material.

For students who require additional challenge, Extension activities are regularly provided in the Teacher's Edition.

OBJECTIVES ■ CHAPTER 1

Students should master the chapter objectives by the time they complete the chapter. To ensure objective mastery, there is continual review built into each set of lesson questions. After students complete the chapter lessons, they assess their mastery on the Progress Self-Test. Then they do the Chapter Review and pay special attention to those questions that match the objectives missed on the Progress Self-Test. Students can get extra practice on these objectives by using the master for each lesson in the Teacher's Resource File.

OBJECTIVES FOR CHAPTER 1 (Organized into the SPUR categories—Skills, Properties, Uses, and Representations)	**Progress Self-Test Questions**	**Chapter Review Questions**	**Lesson Master from Teacher's Resource File***
SKILLS			
A Operate with, and compare fractions.	4 and 5	1 through 8	1-1, 1-8
B Find solutions to open sentences using trial and error.	14 and 15	9 through 12	1-1
C Evaluate numerical and algebraic expressions.	1 through 3	13 through 20	1-4, 1-5
D Give the output for or write short computer programs and statements that evaluate expressions.	8	21 through 24	1-4
PROPERTIES			
E Read and interpret set language and notation.	12 and 25	25 through 31	1-6
F Find and interpret the probability of an event when outcomes are assumed to occur randomly.	21 through 23	32 through 35	1-7
USES			
G In real situations, choose a reasonable domain for a variable.	11	36 through 39	1-6
H Calculate the mean, median, and mode for a set of data.	6 and 7	40 through 43	1-2
I Evaluate formulas in real situations.	16 and 17	44 through 47	1-5
J Use relative frequency to determine information about surveys.	20	48 through 53	1-8
REPRESENTATIONS			
K Use graphs or symbols to describe intervals.	9 and 10, 24	54 through 59	1-1, 1-3
L Interpret dot frequency graphs.	18 and 19	60 and 61	1-2

*** The masters are numbered to match the lessons.**

OVERVIEW 1

OVERVIEW ■ CHAPTER 1

This chapter exhibits features which will be familiar to teachers and students who have used *Transition Mathematics,* the preceding text in this program.

The wider scope in content in this text compared to other algebra texts is evident in the use of statistics and probability. Neither the statistics nor the probability is separated from the algebra. Statistics is used to introduce graphing on the line in Lesson 1-2. The probability in Lesson 1-7 helps to review fractions. This work will be extended rapidly to algebraic fractions in Chapters 3 and 4.

Students are expected to read this text. If they never have had to read in a mathematics course before, they may be surprised, and you will need to state clear expectations in this regard. Notes provided with the individual lessons contain strategies to help you establish reading as a course requirement. Whether you use these ideas or develop your own, it is important to focus on reading carefully for comprehension. Although many students find reading uncomfortable at first, they almost always ease into it after the first few chapters and become quite accustomed to reading by the end of the year.

Notice the early use of computers and calculators. The representation of variables in computer programs, a major contemporary use of algebra, is first seen in Lesson 1-4. Scientific calculators are a necessity for some of the questions and examples starting in Lesson 1-5. Calculators are needed throughout this book and should be allowed on all tests, starting with this chapter.

The coverage of four dimensions of understanding—skills, properties, uses, and representations—begins in this chapter. As you can see from the Chapter Review (pages 50–53), this chapter is particularly rich in representations of algebra.

PERSPECTIVES 1

PERSPECTIVES ■ CHAPTER 1

The Perspectives provide the rationale for the inclusion of topics or approaches, provide mathematical background, and make connections within UCSMP.

1-1

NUMBERS IN ALGEBRA

This lesson introduces three of the basic tools of algebra: variables, sentences, and graphs. The chapter opener (pages 2–3) should be considered part of this lesson.

A very important goal of this lesson is to engender the expectation of reading. If your students have not had *Transition Mathematics,* they may be surprised at this expectation.

At this point, students are not expected to apply algebraic techniques to sentences like those in **Example 1.** They should use *trial and error.* Many later lessons are devoted to sentence-solving techniques. *Trial and error* (sometimes called "guess and check") is a technique that many people (including mathematicians) use in a variety of settings.

1-2

DESCRIBING DATA

This lesson covers the statistical topics of dot frequency diagrams and the measures of central tendency—mean, median, and mode.

Students are expected to know how to calculate the mean from previous courses. The dot frequency diagram is a good way to put data in order, which is the first step in finding the median. The diagram also makes it very easy to compare frequencies and pick out the mode(s).

Applications having to do with altitude, temperature, and money show the need for positive and negative numbers and provide models for the way they work. We assume that students have studied how to add and multiply integers. But they may be out of practice, so we touch lightly on these two skills in Review questions here and throughout this chapter and the next few chapters.

This lesson introduces the use of Review questions. A large part of the practice students will have on a topic is distributed throughout the Review sections in many lessons—some in the current chapter, some later in the book. Whenever students need help on Review questions, encourage them to use the lesson references at the end of each question to locate the appropriate material.

Note that except for the first lesson in a chapter, each Review section has questions from the previous lesson. This reflects an expectation that mastery should be attained by the end of the *chapter,* not necessarily by the end of each lesson. Reviews will also help students remember content from earlier chapters or courses. Thus, students should see reviews as an integral part of their daily assignments.

1-3

INTERVALS AND ESTIMATES

A commonly used statistic is the range. Range lends itself to descriptions using compound inequalities and graphs.

In an application, it may be difficult to tell whether an interval is closed (includes its endpoints) or open (excludes its endpoints). The interpretation may be a matter of opinion. The following language is useful: The interval "from a to b" includes the endpoints a and b and is denoted $a \le x \le b$; the interval "between a and b" does not include its endpoints and is denoted $a < x < b$. When an interval includes exactly one of its endpoints, it is sometimes called *half-open* and is more difficult to describe in English.

With intervals, the expression $a \pm b$ indicates the *interval with endpoints* $a - b$ and $a + b$. This is a different use from that found in the quadratic formula, where $a \pm b$ means only the *two numbers* $a - b$ and $a + b$.

The lesson shows that the midpoint of an interval is the average of the endpoints. This reinforces the geometric interpretation of average as the number in the middle.

1-4

ORDER OF OPERATIONS

Both the scientific calculator and the computer provide good motivation for a study of the order of operations. In this text, simple computer programs are employed to illustrate and motivate the order of operations.

Not all computer languages use the standard order of operations, but the most widely used ones, such as FORTRAN, COBOL, Pascal, and BASIC, do.

1-5

FORMULAS

Formulas are one of the mathematical tools most commonly used in everyday life. The examples and exercises show several realistic applications. Using calculators frees us from being limited to problems with "nice" but artificial numbers. Using computers enables large numbers of values to be calculated quickly. We expect that all students will have access to and use scientific calculators from this lesson on.

The formula in Example 1, like many useful formulas, produces only an estimate. This formula assumes the cars are traveling at a safe distance from one another. Actually, many cars do not travel at safe distances, so the number of cars on a road might be far greater than the formula indicates.

A conscious effort is made throughout this book to discuss, introduce, and review ideas from geometry. For example, the circumference of a circle and the area and perimeter of a rectangle are reviewed in this lesson.

The term *domain* is introduced in this lesson. This book does not use *range* in the sense of range of a function, as it might be confused with the statistical definition of *range* given in Lesson 1-3.

1-6

SETS

We have found that the vocabulary of sets enhances our explanation and development of major ideas, such as those in probability and systems. Also, set notation, particulary with intersection and union (to be discussed in Chapter 3), provides contrast to the operations of addition and multiplication. We do not develop an algebra of sets, but many of the properties of addition and multiplication which may seem trite to students usually have a less obvious counterpart in union and intersection.

We use the term *solution set* in this lesson, but we do not write solution sets in set-builder form $\{x: \ldots\}$ since there is no need for such formalism at this time.

We make special use of the notion of the number of elements in a set, denoted $N(S)$. The purpose is to provide an abbreviation for a common English phrase which will help lay the groundwork for function notation in this and later courses.

A distinction between discrete and continuous sets is made in this lesson. One way to describe the distinction is that while a discrete graph is made of individual dots, a continuous set can be graphed without lifting your pencil from the paper.

1-7

PROBABILITY

At first, students may be uncomfortable with the idea of measuring something intangible, which is the case with chance. The topic of probability continues in Chapters 3 and 4, where we consider compound events.

Here, we determine probabilities only in situations involving equally likely outcomes. We use the term *random* and give a rule for defining the probability of an event.

1-8

RELATIVE FREQUENCY AND THE EQUAL FRACTIONS PROPERTY

The term *relative frequency* is preferred by many people these days to the term *experimental probability.* Relative frequencies come from actual data, whereas probabilities are assumed, or they are deduced from assumptions. Although the probability of a *fair* coin coming up heads is 1/2, the relative frequency from an experiment in which a fair coin is tossed 100 times will not always be 1/2 but will center around 1/2. Often statisticians hypothesize a probability. Then they run an experiment to see if a relative frequency agrees with that probability.

CHAPTER 1

All lessons in this text are designed to be covered in one day. However, for the minimal course, a lesson should be covered over 2 days when it is combined with a quiz. (See the Daily Pacing Chart on page 2A.) Each lesson includes Review questions which will help students firm up content studied previously. At the end of the chapter, you should plan to spend 1 day to review the Progress Self-Test, 1 or 2 days for the Chapter Review, and 1 day for a test.

If your students have not used scientific calculators before, you should add Appendix A as a 1-day lesson after Lesson 1-5. If your students are not familiar with scientific notation, which will be used throughout this text, you should also introduce Appendix B as a 1-day lesson following Lesson 1-5.

Before beginning this chapter, make certain that the students have read the section entitled "To the Student" so that they know what materials they are expected to have.

CHAPTER 1

Basic Concepts

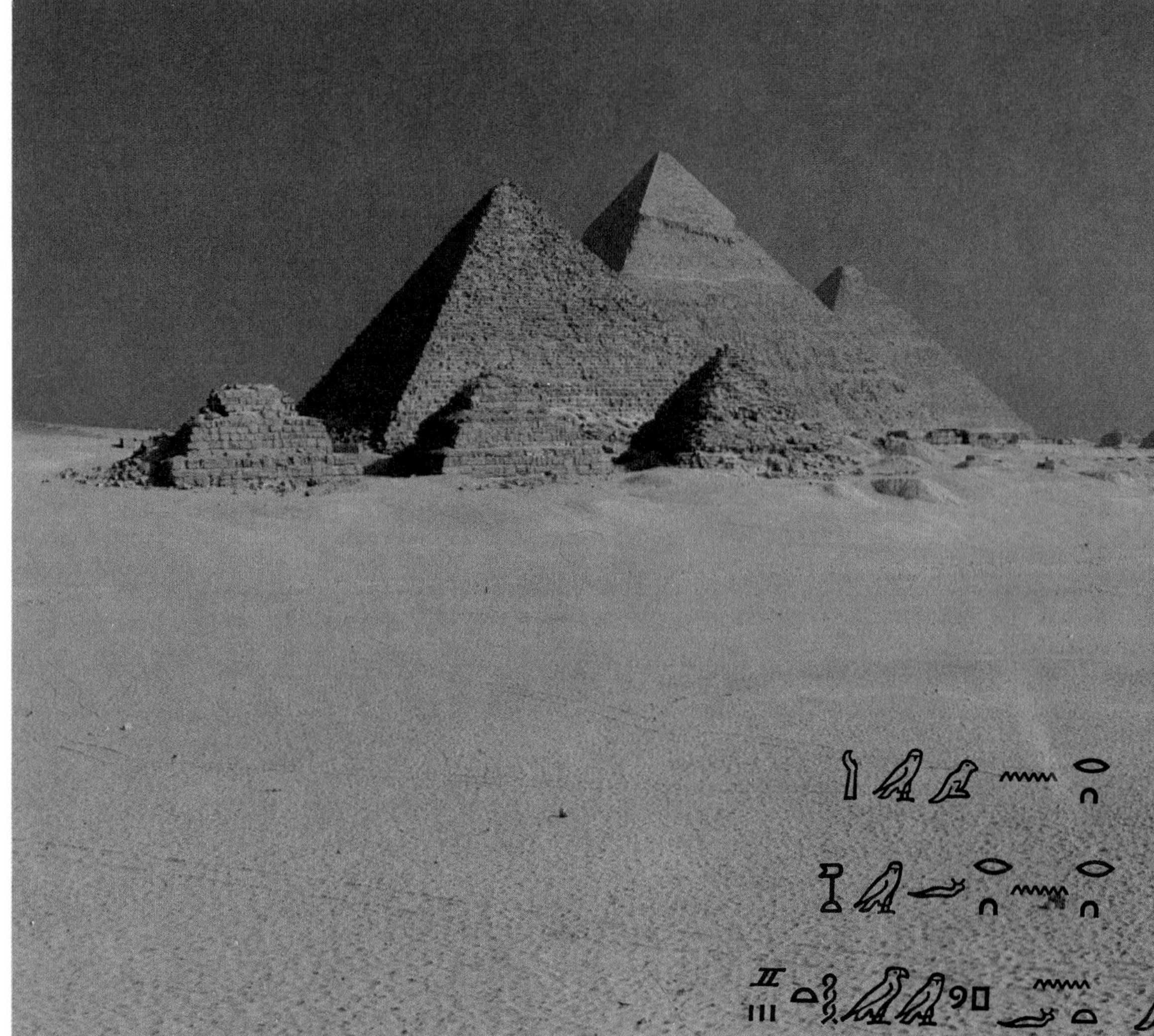

About 3500 years ago, and Egyptian wrote the hieroglyphics shown below. They tell how to find the area of a rectangle with length 10 units and width 2 units.

Today's description in English can be shorter.

The area of a rectangle equals its length times its width.

We can shorten the English statement by using symbols for equals and times.

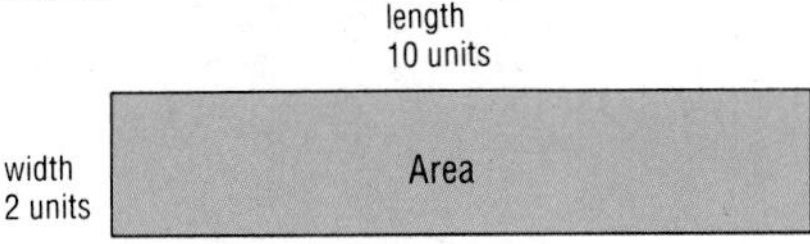

$$\begin{aligned}\text{Area of a rectangle} &= \text{length} \times \text{width}\\ &= 10 \text{ units} \times 2 \text{ units}\\ &= 20 \text{ square units}\end{aligned}$$

This statement can be abbreviated still more by using variables.

$$A = \ell w$$

By using variables, the area relationship is described in a very concise way. The formula $A = \ell w$ is much shorter than the hieroglyphics or the description in English. For many people, formulas are clearer and easier to use than words.

Variables are basic to the language of algebra. Formulas are one way in which algebra makes things easier to understand and use. In this chapter, you will study ideas fundamental to variables, to algebra, and to this book.

USING PAGES 2-3
Emphasize that these pages show different ways in which a sentence about area can be written. Point out that when using words, the sentence is long and perhaps confusing. When using variables and formulas, the sentence is concise and clear.

Students might be interested to know that the French mathematician François Viète is credited with the first systematic use, in 1591, of letters as variables in formulas. Before Viète, whole words were often used to stand for numbers.

LESSON 1-1

RESOURCES
■ Lesson Master 1-1
Visual for Teaching Aid 1: Number Lines
The Teaching Aids are available both as blackline masters and as overhead visuals.

OBJECTIVES

Letter codes refer to the SPUR Objectives on pages 50–53.

A Compare fractions.
B Find solutions to open sentences using trial and error.
K Use graphs or symbols to describe inequalities.

TEACHING NOTES

Reading To read well, a student must read carefully, watching for important terms and symbols. One way to begin is to have students read aloud, beginning with page 4. You may want to go around the class having students read one short paragraph each. This is a good way to get students involved from the beginning, and it lets you assess their reading skills.

When reading **Example 1,** students should see where each line of the work comes from—sometimes from the previous line, sometimes from looking back where the question was formulated.

For more information on reading skills, see *General Teaching Suggestions: Reading* on page T37 of the Teacher's Edition.

LESSON

1-1 Numbers in Algebra

There is an old *rule of thumb* for estimating your distance from a flash of lightning. First, determine the number of seconds between the flash and the sound of thunder. Divide this number by 5. The result is the approximate distance in miles. For example, if you count 10 seconds between the flash and the sound of thunder, you are $\frac{10}{5}$, or 2, miles from the lightning. In the language of algebra, if s is the number of seconds, then $\frac{s}{5}$ is your distance (in miles) from the lightning. The letter s is a variable. A **variable** is a letter or other symbol that can be replaced by any number (or other object) in some set.

In this situation the letter s was chosen because s is the first letter of "seconds." The full formula is:

$$n = \frac{s}{5}, \text{ where } n = \text{distance in miles; } s = \text{time in seconds.}$$

The sentence $n = \dfrac{s}{5}$ is called an **equation** because it uses the mathematical verb "=." Other verbs are shown below.

$\neq$	is not equal to	$\approx$	is approximately equal to
$<$	is less than	$>$	is greater than
$\leq$	is less than or equal to	$\geq$	is greater than or equal to

A sentence with one of the other verbs is called an **inequality**. For instance, the sentence $\frac{1}{2} < \frac{5}{8}$ is an inequality. A sentence with a variable is called an **open sentence**. $n = \frac{s}{5}$ is an open sentence. Open sentences are powerful mathematical statements because they allow you to symbolize many patterns and relationships in an efficient, organized way. A **solution** to a sentence is a replacement for the variable that makes the statement true.

Example 1 Which of the numbers 7, 8, or 9 is a solution to the open sentence

$$3 \cdot x + 15 = 4 \cdot x + 6?$$

Solution Try 7. Does $3 \cdot 7 + 15 = 4 \cdot 7 + 6$?
No, $36 \neq 34$.
Try 8. Does $3 \cdot 8 + 15 = 4 \cdot 8 + 6$?
No, $39 \neq 38$
Try 9. Does $3 \cdot 9 + 15 = 4 \cdot 9 + 6$?
Yes, $42 = 42$.

So 9 is a solution. The numbers 7 and 8 are not solutions.

In later chapters you will learn methods for finding solutions to equations. For now, you may have to solve equations by using trial and error.

When an open sentence has more than one solution, it may be easiest to describe the solutions with a graph or an inequality.

Example 2 Water will remain ice for all temperatures less than 0° Celsius.

a. Write an open sentence describing this situation.
b. Graph all the points which make the sentence true.

Solution

a. Let T represent the temperature of the water. Then water is ice if $T < 0°$. ($0° > T$ would also be a correct statement.)
b. Graph $T < 0°$. First mark $T = 0°$ with an open circle to indicate that 0° does not make $T < 0°$ true. Then draw a heavy arrow to the left to represent all points less than 0°.

Example 3 Carl's car gets at least 19.3 miles per gallon.

a. Write an algebraic sentence which describes this situation.
b. Graph the solutions to the sentence on a number line.

Solution

a. If m is the number of miles per gallon, m can be 19.3 or larger.

$$m \geq 19.3$$

One way to help retention is to summarize the lesson when finished. When the reading is completed, you could ask students for the important ideas and make a list on the board.

In **Examples 2 and 3,** point out that we label a number line with the variable in the sentence that is being graphed. This is equivalent to labeling axes when graphing ordered pairs.

When considering **Example 4,** point out that $a < b$ and $b > a$ are two ways of stating equivalent information, just as $2 = 1 + 1$ and $1 + 1 = 2$ are equivalent. Students will be asked in Question 11 to write the answer to **Example 3** in an equivalent form.

Inform your students that each of them will need to have a scientific calculator by Lesson 1-5.

ADDITIONAL EXAMPLES

1. Which of the numbers 7, 8, 9, or 10 is a solution to $2 \cdot x + 42 > 7 \cdot x$?
7, 8

2. Bob earns more than $25 each week.

a. Write an open sentence describing this situation.
$\mathbf{e > 25}$

b. Graph all the solutions.

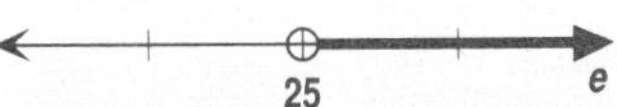

3. This elevator can carry at most 2750 lb.

a. Describe with an inequality.
$\mathbf{w \leq 2750}$

b. Graph all solutions.

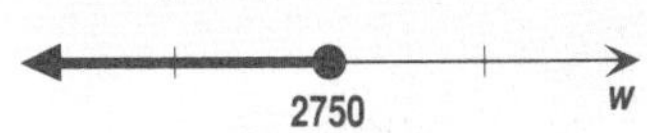

4. Write an inequality that compares $\frac{1}{6}$ and $\frac{2}{9}$.
$\frac{1}{6} < \frac{2}{9}$ or $\frac{2}{9} > \frac{1}{6}$

NOTES ON QUESTIONS
Question 1: This brings out the need for flexibility in writing numbers. The answer that the lightning formula gives is $\frac{8}{5}$ miles, but in this context $1\frac{3}{5}$ or 1.6 miles is easier to interpret. Ultimately, students need to learn which forms of an answer are clear or easy to use, and which are not. Hard and fast rules do not help, because taste is a factor in these decisions.

Still, you may want to establish the following conventions: If the problem is expressed with fractions or decimals, the answer should be in similar form; if the problem involves an application, decimal approximations are usually best; in purely mathematical contexts, an exact answer is usually preferred.

Error Analysis for Question 21: In this answer, some students may place the bar over all the digits to the right of the decimal point. Make sure they understand that the bar should appear only above the repeating digit(s).

b. Mark a dot on 19.3 and draw a heavy arrow to the right. (To find 19.3, you can separate the interval between 19 and 20 into ten equal parts.) The arrow indicates that numbers like 19.4, 19.35, 20, 50.2 and $70\frac{1}{2}$ all make the sentence $m \geq 19.3$ true. The closed circle means that 19.3 itself makes the sentence true.

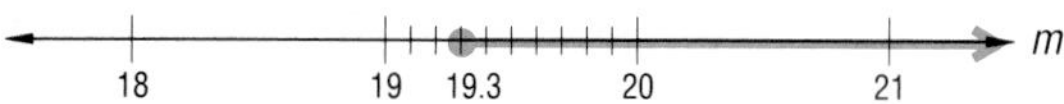

An inequality compares numbers. Often it is easier to compare numbers in decimal form than fraction form.

Example 4 Write an inequality that compares $\frac{1}{3}$ and $\frac{3}{8}$.

Solution A fraction indicates a division. Carry out that division to convert the fraction to a decimal.

$$\frac{1}{3} = 1 \div 3 = .\overline{3} \approx .333 \qquad \frac{3}{8} = 3 \div 8 = .375$$

In decimal form, $.\overline{3}$ is seen to be smaller than .375.

$$\text{So, } \frac{1}{3} < \frac{3}{8}.$$

A correct answer using the "is greater than" sign is $\frac{3}{8} > \frac{1}{3}$.

Questions

Covering the Reading

These questions check your understanding of the reading. If you cannot answer a question you should go back to the lesson to help you find the answer.

1. You clock the time between lightning and thunder as 8 seconds. How far away was the lightning? **1.6 miles**

2. What is a variable? **See margin.**

In 3–5, tell whether what is written is a sentence.

3. $5 \cdot x + 3 < 2$ **Yes** **4.** $8 - 2 \cdot y$ **No** **5.** $-5 \leq r$ **Yes**

6. What is the symbol for "is approximately equal to"? ≈

7. Which of the numbers 5, 9, 11 are solutions to $x \leq 9$? **5 and 9**

8. Which of the numbers 5, 6, or 7 is a solution of $2 \cdot y + 3 = 4 \cdot y - 9$? **6**

In 9 and 10, **a.** write an open sentence to describe the situation; **b.** graph all the points that make the sentence true.

9. Dan ran more than 3 miles. **a)** $m > 3$**; b) See margin.**

10. The temperature was below 10°F all day.
a) $T < 10$**; b) See margin.**

11. *Multiple choice* In Example 3, the inequality shown is $m \geq 19.3$. Which of the following means the same thing? **(b)**
(a) $m \approx 19.3$ (b) $19.3 \leq m$ (c) $19.3 < m$

In 12 and 13, write an inequality to compare the two numbers.

12. $\frac{5}{8}, \frac{4}{7}$ $\frac{4}{7} < \frac{5}{8}$ **or** $\frac{5}{8} > \frac{4}{7}$

13. $\frac{5}{6}, \frac{17}{20}$ $\frac{5}{6} < \frac{17}{20}$ **or** $\frac{17}{20} > \frac{5}{6}$

Applying the Mathematics

These questions extend your understanding of the content of the lesson. You should study the examples and explanations if you cannot get an answer. Check your answers with the Selected Answer section in the back of the book.

14. Before 1985, the average household in the United States contained more than 1.9 persons.
a. Write an inequality about the date using the variable d. $d < 1985$
b. Write an inequality about the average number of persons per household using the variable p. $p > 1.9$

In 15 and 16, write an inequality to describe each graph. Use the variable that is next to the graph.

15. (number line: 5, 10, 15, 20, 25; q) $q < 15$

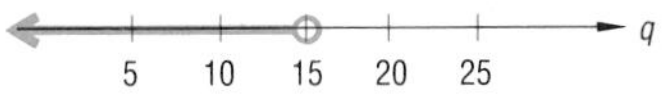

16. (number line: -3, -2, -1, 0, 1; t) $t \geq -2$

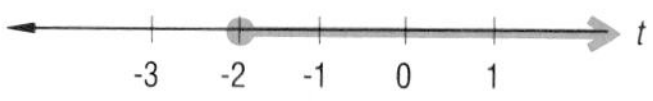

ADDITIONAL ANSWERS
2. a letter or other symbol that can be replaced by any number (or other object) in some set
9b.

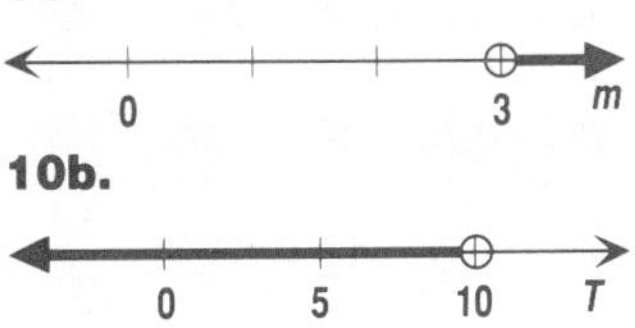

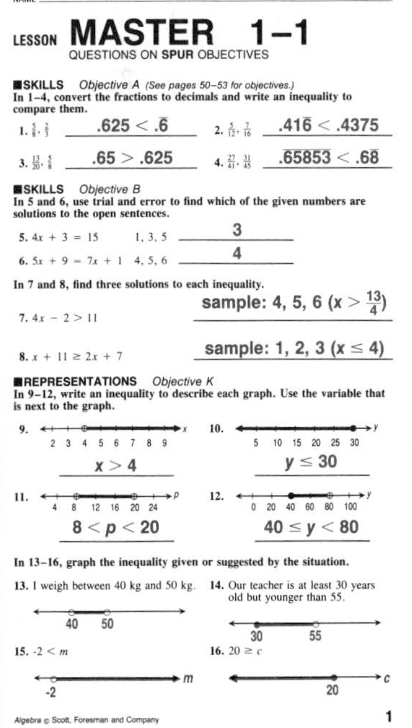
NAME ________

LESSON **MASTER 1–1**
QUESTIONS ON **SPUR** OBJECTIVES

■**SKILLS** *Objective A (See pages 50–53 for objectives.)*
In 1–4, convert the fractions to decimals and write an inequality to compare them.

1. $\frac{5}{8}, \frac{2}{3}$ $.625 < .\overline{6}$
2. $\frac{5}{12}, \frac{7}{16}$ $.41\overline{6} < .4375$
3. $\frac{13}{20}, \frac{5}{8}$ $.65 > .625$
4. $\frac{27}{41}, \frac{31}{45}$ $.\overline{65853} < .6\overline{8}$

■**SKILLS** *Objective B*
In 5 and 6, use trial and error to find which of the given numbers are solutions to the open sentences.

5. $4x + 3 = 15$ 1, 3, 5 3
6. $5x + 9 = 7x + 1$ 4, 5, 6 4

In 7 and 8, find three solutions to each inequality.

7. $4x - 2 > 11$ sample: 4, 5, 6 ($x > \frac{13}{4}$)
8. $x + 11 \geq 2x + 7$ sample: 1, 2, 3 ($x \leq 4$)

■**REPRESENTATIONS** *Objective K*
In 9–12, write an inequality to describe each graph. Use the variable that is next to the graph.

9. (2 3 4 5 6 7 8 9; x) $x > 4$
10. (5 10 15 20 25 30; y) $y \leq 30$
11. (4 8 12 16 20 24; p) $8 < p < 20$
12. (0 20 40 60 80 100; y) $40 \leq y < 80$

In 13–16, graph the inequality given or suggested by the situation.

13. I weigh between 40 kg and 50 kg. (40 50)
14. Our teacher is at least 30 years old but younger than 55. (30 55)
15. $-2 < m$ (-2; m)
16. $20 \geq c$ (20; c)

Algebra © Scott, Foresman and Company 1

NOTES ON QUESTIONS
Question 28: *Mental calculation* is a strand that runs throughout this book. These skills are important and should be emphasized.

Making Connections for Question 29: This question sets the stage for the Density Property, which is taught in Lesson 1-6.

FOLLOW-UP

MORE PRACTICE
For more questions on SPUR Objectives, use *Lesson Master 1-1,* shown on page 7.

EXTENSION
Have students generalize **Question 29** by asking the following: What is a general rule for finding a simple fraction (nonzero integer numerator, positive integer denominator) between any two given simple fractions? (sample: Add the numerators and denominators.)

EVALUATION
Alternative Assessment
You may wish to prepare an informal questionnaire which elicits students' feelings about their study of mathematics thus far. You might also ask them to describe in their own words what mathematics is. Use the questionnaire sometime early in the course. Then periodically through the course help students realize that they are expanding their conceptions of what mathematics is.

23a. sample: 4 (any number greater than 3)
23b. sample: 1 (any number less than 3)
26.

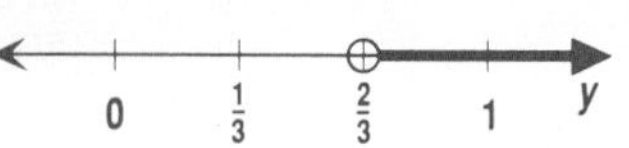

17. *Multiple choice* $z \geq 100$ is the same as c
(a) $z \leq 100$. (b) $100 \geq z$. (c) $100 \leq z$.

18. Which of the values 4, 8, or 16 solves $5 \cdot x < 40$? 4

In 19–21, use this information.
The mixed number $2\frac{1}{4} = 2 + \frac{1}{4}$.

Since $\frac{1}{4} = .25$ you can write

$$2\frac{1}{4} = 2 + .25$$
$$= 2.25$$

Write the mixed number as a decimal.

19. $3\frac{3}{8}$ 3.375 **20.** $1\frac{1}{9}$ $1.\overline{1}$ **21.** $112\frac{14}{15}$ $112.9\overline{3}$

22. Order from smallest to largest: $1\frac{1}{2}$, 1.52, $\frac{2.9}{2}$. $\frac{2.9}{2}$, $1\frac{1}{2}$, 1.52

23. Let $d = 3$. Find a value of n so that: a) See margin; b) See margin; c) 3
a. $\frac{n}{d} > 1$ **b.** $\frac{n}{d} < 1$ **c.** $\frac{n}{d} = 1$

24. Copy and complete so the statement describes the graph.

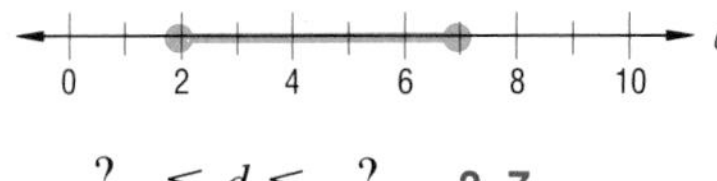

$\underline{\ ?\ } \leq d \leq \underline{\ ?\ }$ 2, 7

25. Which of the numbers -3, -2, 7, and -7 are included in the graph below? -3, -2 and 7

26. Graph $y > \frac{2}{3}$ on a number line. See margin.

27. Write in order from smallest to largest: $\frac{7}{10}$, $\frac{2}{3}$, $\frac{3}{4}$. $\frac{2}{3}$, $\frac{7}{10}$, $\frac{3}{4}$

Often it is quicker and more convenient to do problems in your head. Punching calculator keys for simple problems is time-consuming and may lead to careless mistakes. Do not use your calculator or work with paper and pencil on these problems. Just write an answer.

28. Compute in your head.
a. $10 \cdot 3.7$ 37 **b.** $1\frac{1}{2} \cdot 2$ 3 **c.** $4 \cdot \$2.25$ $9

Exploration

These questions ask you to explore mathematics topics related to the chapter. Often, these questions require that you use dictionaries and other books. Sometimes they will ask you to perform an experiment. Many exploration questions have more than one correct answer.

29. Find a fraction between $\frac{11}{20}$ and $\frac{14}{25}$. sample: $\frac{111}{200}$

LESSON

1-2

Describing Data

In Lesson 1-1, number lines were used to graph solutions to algebraic sentences. In this lesson, number lines are used to organize information and make sense out of data.

To illustrate a way to organize data on a number line, Mr. Tobias asked the students in his algebra class how many letters were in each of their last names. Here are the students' responses in the order in which they were given.

6, 6, 8, 4, 5, 6, 5, 4, 4, 5, 9, 7, 11, 6, 6, 5, 5, 9, 4, 8, 5

To picture this information, Mr. Tobias made a **dot frequency diagram**. First he drew a horizontal number line. For each student's response, he placed a dot above that number on the line.

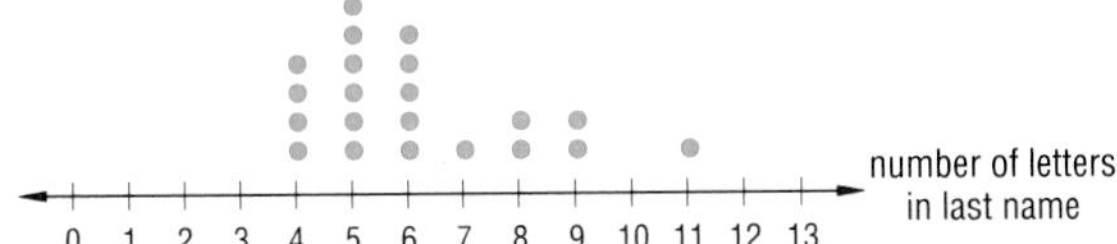

The number of dots above each number records how often that response occurred. From the drawing you can answer several questions about Mr. Tobias's class.

Example 1 Consider the dot frequency diagram above.

a. How many students' names have 6 letters?

b. How many students' names have more than 8 letters?

c. Would a response of 0 have made sense?

d. What is the mean (or average) number of letters per last name?

LESSON 1-2

RESOURCES

- Lesson Master 1-2
- Visual for Teaching Aid 2: Dot Frequency Diagrams for **Examples 1 and 3** and **Questions 1 and 7**

The Teaching Aids are available both as blackline masters and as overhead visuals.

OBJECTIVES

Letter codes refer to the SPUR Objectives on pages 50–53.

H Calculate the mean, median, and mode for a set of data.

L Interpret dot frequency graphs.

TEACHING NOTES

You and your students may want to replicate the activity that starts the lesson. It is a good way to introduce the statistics of mean, median, and mode, and it lets students introduce themselves to each other. Another set of data which your class can produce is the number of siblings (brothers and sisters) of each student.

Reading Again you may wish to help students with the reading. One strategy would be to read aloud through the definitions of *mean, median,* and *mode* on page 10. Have the students read the rest of the lesson silently; then ask them to describe how to find the mean, median, and mode.

Since the structure of this lesson is very straightforward, it is a good place to discuss taking notes.

Alternate Approach In **Example 1,** the dot frequency diagram can be used to set up a shortcut for finding the sum of the data. From it, you can see that 4 is used four times, 5 appears six times, 6 appears five times, and 8 and 9 are each used twice. So the sum can be found as follows:

$4 \cdot 4 + 5 \cdot 6 + 6 \cdot 5 + 7 + 2 \cdot 8 + 2 \cdot 9 + 11 = 128$

In **Example 3,** there are two middle values in the data, so the median is the average of the two. For data in which there are two *identical* middle values, the median has that same value.

The use of Review questions is introduced here. Make sure students understand how to use the lesson references, which are explained on page 13.

Solution

a. There are five dots above the number 6 on the dot frequency diagram, so five students have 6-letter last names.

b. There are three dots to the right of 8 on the number line. Three students have last names of more than 8 letters.

c. No. Every last name must have at least one letter.

d. Recall from your previous work that the mean is calculated as follows.

$$\text{mean} = \frac{\text{sum of the numbers}}{\text{number of numbers}} =$$

$$\frac{6+6+8+4+5+6+5+4+4+5+9+7+11+6+6+5+5+9+4+8+5}{21}$$

$$= \frac{128}{21}$$

$$\approx 6.1$$

The **mean** is a single number that represents a set of data. Numbers that represent sets of data are called **statistics**. Two other statistics used to describe data are the **median** and the **mode.** These statistics describe the middles or centers of the data. Statisticians call them measures of **central tendency.**

Statistics of Central Tendency:

The mean is the average of a set of numbers.

The median is the middle value of a set of numbers when the numbers are ranked in order.

The mode is the most frequently occurring number or category in a set of numbers or categories.

Example 2 Refer again to the responses in Mr. Tobias's class.

a. What is the mode for the set of data?

b. What is the median for the set of data?

Solution

a. The mode is the most frequently occurring value. The dot frequency diagram shows the most frequent response in Mr. Tobias's class was 5. The mode is therefore 5.

b. The median is the middle value of a set of numbers when the numbers are ranked in order. To calculate the median, first list the 21 values in order. You can use the dot frequency diagram to do this. Then cut the list into halves.

$$4, 4, 4, 4, 5, 5, 5, 5, 5, 5, \boxed{6}, 6, 6, 6, 6, 7, 8, 8, 9, 9, 11$$

There are 21 numbers, so the 11th number is the one in the middle. It is the number 6, so 6 is the median.

To find the median in Example 2, we counted until we found the middle value. If there are an even number of values, there is no single middle value. You must then find the *two* values in the middle. The mean of these is the median of the whole set of values.

Example 3 Sharma has test scores of 50, 60, 100, 70, 100, 60, 60, 100, 40, and 100.

a. If s represents a test score, for how many of Sharma's tests was $s \leq 60$?
b. What is her median score?
c. What is her mean score?
d. What is the mode?
e. Which statistic gives her the highest score?

Solution A dot frequency diagram helps to organize the data.

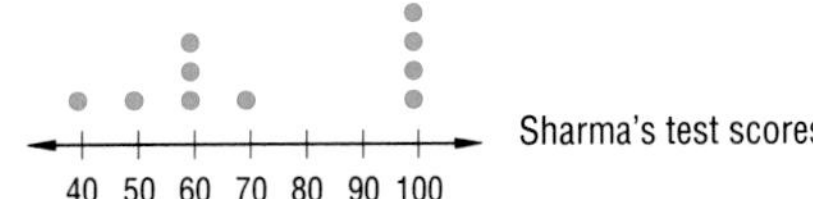

a. $s \leq 60$ means a score of 60 or lower. Sharma had one score of 40, one of 50, and three of 60. So Sharma had five tests for which $s \leq 60$.

b. List the scores in order from the diagram. There are an even number of scores, so locate the middle two.

40, 50, 60, 60, $\boxed{60, 70,}$ 100, 100, 100, 100

Find the mean of the middle scores. $\dfrac{60 + 70}{2} = 65$
Her median score is 65.

c. To find the mean, first add the scores. The sum is 740. There are 10 scores, so the mean is $\frac{740}{10} = 74$.

d. The mode is 100, the most common value.

e. The mode gives her the highest score. (The median gives her the lowest score.)

It is possible for a set of data to have more than one mode. For example, there are two modes for the set of scores 50, 70, 20, 70, 60, 40, and 20. Both 70 and 20 occur the same number of times. On the other hand, if no one piece of data occurs most often, the set of data has no mode. The set of scores 65, 90, 80, 60, 75, 77, and 56 has no mode.

ADDITIONAL EXAMPLES

A water polo team played 20 games last year. The dot frequency diagram below shows the number n of goals they scored for each game.

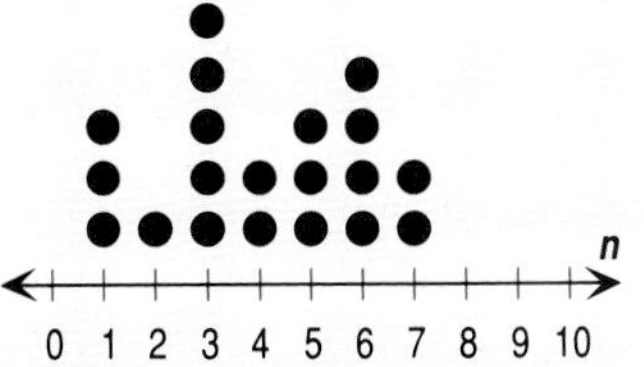

1. What is the mean?
4.05

2. What is the median?
4

3. What is the mode?
3

4. How many times did the team score fewer than 5 points?
11 times

5. Would a dot above 0 make sense?
yes, if they had scored no goals in a game

NOTES ON QUESTIONS

Error Analysis for Question 5b: Some students may erroneously obtain 57.5 as the median. This is the average of 75 and 40, the two middle scores as listed in the question. Emphasize that in order to find the median, you must first rank the scores in order—either from lowest to highest or from highest to lowest.

Error Analysis for Question 5c: If students give 2 as the mode, they are confusing the frequency of the mode with the mode itself. This error is more likely to occur when the mode is being determined from a dot frequency diagram, as in **Question 10.**

NOTES ON QUESTIONS
Questions 8 and 9: These may be difficult for students to answer because they involve matters of judgment. The mode is not usually the best description of central tendency, but it is useful in cases where "most popular" is important. For instance, when a hardware store stocks numbers that are used to put addresses on buildings, the mean is meaningless; the mode is most useful.

The median is preferred over the mean when a few extreme values would distort the mean. This type of distortion appears in **Question 10,** where the single high value makes the mean substantially higher than the median.

Questions 14-19: These questions review addition and multiplication of integers. The application in **Question 14** is intended to set the stage for **Questions 15 and 16.** In **Question 17,** cost can be thought of as a negative quantity, so -70 • 5 = -350. This is preparation for **Questions 18 and 19.**

Question 24: Students should do the *mental calculation* in **Question 24a** and realize that 1/3 of a number can be found by dividing by 3. Similarly, in **Question 24b,** 25% of 20 = 1/4 of 20 = 20/4 = 5.

ADDITIONAL ANSWERS
10a.

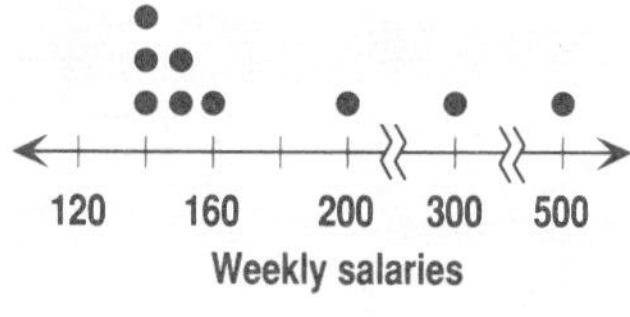

11b.

100 C

25a. The median strip is in the middle of the highway. The median is the middle value.
25b. *A la mode* means "fashionable." *Mode* means "most common or fashionable."

Questions

Covering the Reading

1. The dot frequency diagram below shows the number of students who received certain scores on an algebra test.

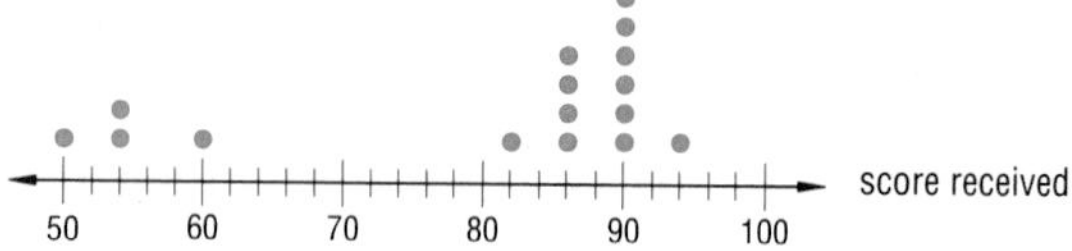

a. How many students received a score of 50? **1 student**
b. How many students received a score of more than 80? **12**
c. Find the mean or average score for the class. **79.875, or about 80**

2. The __?__ is the most frequently occurring number or category in a set of numbers or categories. **mode**

3. The middle value of a set of scores is 65. This is the __?__ for the set of scores. **median**

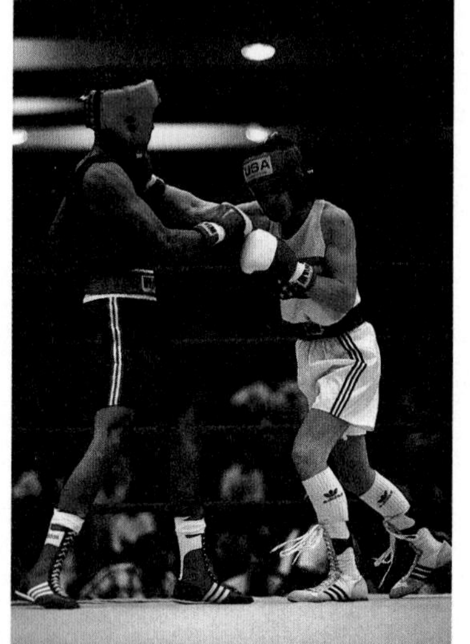

4. Seven members of a boxing team compete as flyweights. Their weights in pounds are: 112, 110, 111, 108, 107, 98, and 98. Find the median for these weights. **108 pounds**

5. For one quarter Sheila has scores of 68, 65, 80, 75, 40, 60, 62, and 80 in social studies. What is the **a.** mean; **b.** median; and **c.** mode of these scores? **d.** Which statistic gives her the highest measure of her scores? **a) 66.25; b) 66.5; c) 80; d) mode**

6. Give a set of data that has no mode.
sample: any set which has all different values

Applying the Mathematics

7. Shown below are the daily high temperature readings in degrees Fahrenheit for the first 27 days of January, 1979 in Sterling, Alaska.

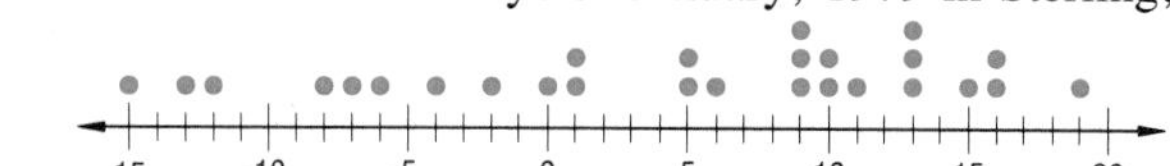

a. If the daily high temperature is T degrees, for how many days was $T < 0$? **8 days**
b. For how many days was $T > -10$? **24 days**
c. Give the mode or modes for this data. **9° and 13°**
d. Find the median. **6°**

8. In Question 4, does the median or mode give a better idea of the weights of the team members? **median**

9. Consider the mean, median and mode for the scores in Question 5. In your opinion, which statistic (the mean, median, or mode) is the *worst* description of how Sheila did that quarter? **mode**

10. The weekly salaries for workers in a small business are $160, $140, $140, $200, $150, $300, $150, $140 and $500.
a. Make a dot frequency diagram for this data. **See margin.**
b. Find the mean, median and mode. **≈ $209, $150, $140**

c. The company president wants to impress a prospective employee. Would the president be more likely to use the mean, median or mode to describe the workers' salaries? **mean**

d. The employees' union is negotiating for a raise. Would it be more likely to use the mean, median, or mode to describe the workers' salaries? **mode**

Review

Every lesson from here on contains review questions which give practice on ideas presented in earlier lessons. Lessons in parentheses after the questions indicate where the idea was first presented. If you cannot do a review question, look back at the indicated lesson. Some skills provide practice on ideas of previous courses.

11. The temperatures at which water is steam are all those greater than 100 °Celsius.
   a. Write an inequality describing this situation. **$C > 100$**
   b. Graph the inequality. *(Lesson 1-1)* **See margin.**

12. Write an inequality that has the same meaning as $-15 < y$. *(Lesson 1-1)*
$y > -15$

13. Put these numbers in order from least to greatest. *(Previous course)*

-10, 6.8, 5, -4, -15, 0, -2

-15, -10, -4, -2, 0, 5, 6.8

14. The Jets lost 11 yards on their first play and gained 7 on their second play. What was their net gain or loss? *(Previous course)*
4 yard loss

In 15 and 16, add. *(Previous course)*

15. -11 + 7 **-4**

16. -7 + -5 **-12**

17. For the first five days it was open, Harold's Electronics gave away pens to customers. The cost was $70.00 per day. What was the cost for all five days? *(Previous course)* **$350**

In 18 and 19, multiply. (Recall that a positive times a positive is positive; a negative times a negative is positive; and a positive times a negative is negative.) *(Previous course)*

18. $5 \cdot -70$ **-350**

19. $-10 \cdot -4$ **40**

20. Remember that x^2 means $x \cdot x$. Find **a.** 7^2 **49** **b.** 10^2 **100** **c.** 2^3 **8**
(Previous course)

In 21–23, multiply. *(Previous course)*

21. $\frac{2}{7} \cdot \frac{3}{5}$ **$\frac{6}{35}$**

22. $\frac{4}{9} \cdot \frac{3}{10}$ **$\frac{2}{15}$**

23. $\frac{2}{5} \cdot 10$ **4**

24. Compute in your head. *(Previous course)*
   a. $\frac{1}{3}$ of 9 **3**
   b. 25% of 20 **5**

Exploration

25. Mathematical terms are often borrowed from ordinary vocabulary. Explain the relationship between the following phrases and the statistical meaning of the underlined word. **a) See margin.; b) See margin.**
   a. median strip of a highway; **b.** pie a la mode

FOLLOW-UP

MORE PRACTICE

For more questions on SPUR Objectives, use *Lesson Master 1-2,* shown below.

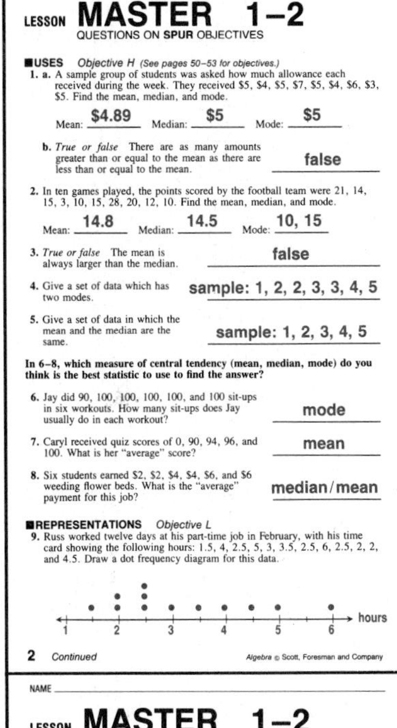

NAME ________________

LESSON **MASTER 1–2**
QUESTIONS ON **SPUR** OBJECTIVES

■**USES** *Objective H (See pages 50–53 for objectives.)*

1. a. A sample group of students was asked how much allowance each received during the week. They received $5, $4, $5, $7, $5, $4, $6, $3, $5. Find the mean, median, and mode.

Mean: **$4.89** Median: **$5** Mode: **$5**

b. *True or false* There are as many amounts greater than or equal to the mean as there are less than or equal to the mean. **false**

2. In ten games played, the points scored by the football team were 21, 14, 15, 3, 10, 15, 28, 20, 12, 10. Find the mean, median, and mode.

Mean: **14.8** Median: **14.5** Mode: **10, 15**

3. *True or false* The mean is always larger than the median. **false**

4. Give a set of data which has two modes. **sample: 1, 2, 2, 3, 3, 4, 5**

5. Give a set of data in which the mean and the median are the same. **sample: 1, 2, 3, 4, 5**

In 6–8, which measure of central tendency (mean, median, mode) do you think is the best statistic to use to find the answer?

6. Jay did 90, 100, 100, 100, 100, and 100 sit-ups in six workouts. How many sit-ups does Jay usually do in each workout? **mode**

7. Caryl received quiz scores of 0, 90, 94, 96, and 100. What is her "average" score? **mean**

8. Six students earned $2, $2, $4, $4, $6, and $6 weeding flower beds. What is the "average" payment for this job? **median/mean**

■**REPRESENTATIONS** *Objective L*

9. Russ worked twelve days at his part-time job in February, with his time card showing the following hours: 1.5, 4, 2.5, 5, 3, 3.5, 2.5, 6, 2.5, 2, 2, and 4.5. Draw a dot frequency diagram for this data.

2 *Continued* *Algebra* © Scott, Foresman and Company

NAME ________________

LESSON **MASTER 1–2**
(page 2)

10. Find the mean, median, and mode for the data given in the previous question.

Mean: **3.25** Median: **2.75** Mode: **2.5**

11. Parents of a group of students reported the years of schooling they had (excluding kindergarten). The dot frequency diagram shows their responses.

2 4 6 8 10 12 14 16 18 20 years

a. Find the mean, median, and mode.

Mean: **13.78** Median: **13** Mode: **12**

b. *True or false* Half of the parents had some schooling beyond high school. **true**

12. Below are the state sales tax rates charged on restaurant meals in the 50 states.

0 1 2 3 4 5 6 7 percent

a. How many states charge 4% or less? **33**

b. How many states use tax rates that involve a fraction of a percent? **6**

c. Find the mode for the data. **4**

d. Find the mean for the data. **3.44**

Algebra © Scott, Foresman and Company 3

LESSON 1-3

RESOURCES
■ Lesson Master 1-3

OBJECTIVE

The letter code refers to the SPUR Objectives on pages 50–53.

K Use graphs or symbols to describe intervals.

TEACHING NOTES

Reading Stress that students should notice the different symbols being used. They must notice how slight distinctions in symbols are used to differentiate among open, closed, and half-open intervals, both in their graphs and the inequalities that describe them.

Making Connections Point out that the interval meaning of ± is commonly found in everyday language ("I'll be there at 3:00, give or take 5 minutes"). The reference to the midpoint of the interval being the average of the endpoints gives a tool which will be useful in understanding the concept of *density* in Lesson 1-6.

Age can be considered either a discrete or a continuous variable. In the dot frequency diagram in **Example 1,** age is viewed in its everyday interpretation, as discrete. A person is n years old for a year; then on the next birthday the person becomes $n + 1$ years old. But a person does not jump in age, so age could also be viewed as continuous. A different

LESSON

1-3

Intervals and Estimates

An **interval** is the set of numbers between two numbers a and b, possibly including a and b. The numbers a and b are called the **endpoints** of the interval. Intervals occur often in real situations and are described in a variety of ways.

One way to describe an interval is with its middle point (midpoint) and a distance from that point. For instance, a pollster surveyed voters and reported: "Accurate to within 3%, I found that 58% of voters plan to vote for candidate A."

The graph below shows the percent of voters who could be expected to vote for candidate A.

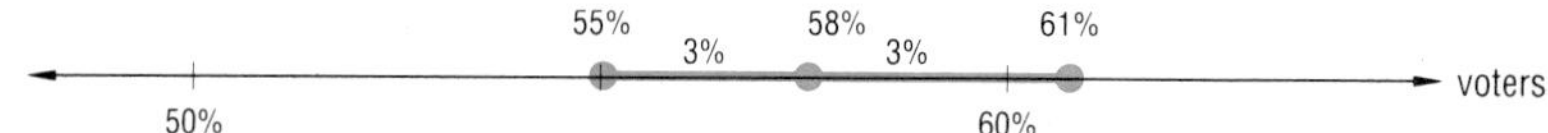

The percentage of voters who plan to vote for A can be 3% higher or lower than 58%. It can range from 55% to 61%. This interval can be described as

$$58\% \pm 3\%.$$

The symbol ± is read "plus or minus." Use the + sign to get the upper endpoint.

$$58\% + 3\% = 61\%$$

Use the − sign to get the lower endpoint.

$$58\% - 3\% = 55\%$$

Notice that the midpoint of the interval is the average of the endpoints. $58 = \dfrac{55 + 61}{2}$

14

A second way to describe an interval is by giving its endpoints as in the sentence: "You must be between 18 and 35 to enter the military." But the English language presents problems. The word *between* doesn't tell you whether 18 and 35 are included. An inequality is more precise. One way to interpret "between 18 and 35" is with the compound sentence $18 \le a \le 35$, where a represents a person's age. This interval is called a **closed interval** because it includes its endpoints.

Another interpretation of "between 18 and 35" does not include the endpoints. The interval $18 < a < 35$ is an **open interval.**

If an interval is described by words rather than symbols, you may have to decide from the situation if it is closed or open. In some situations, you may have a choice.

An interval can include one endpoint and not the other. Here is a graph of the positive numbers less than or equal to 10. $0 < x \le 10$

The endpoints are the numbers 0 and 10. 10 is included in the graph, but 0 is not.

The interval from the minimum to the maximum value of a set of data is useful for summarizing data on dot frequency diagrams.

Example 1 Shown below are the ages of U.S. presidents when they were first inaugurated. Describe the interval from the minimum to the maximum age using: **a.** an inequality; **b.** a graph; **c.** words.

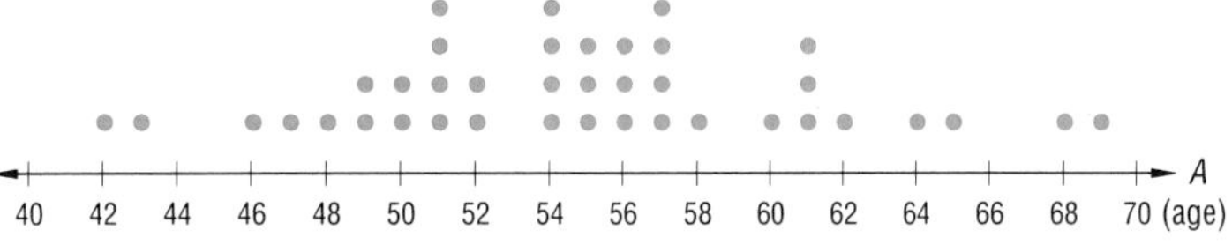

rationale—namely, convenience—causes us to draw the graph in **Example 1b** as continuous.

The term *range* is used in several ways here. The definition following **Example 1** gives its meaning as a statistic of spread. Note the distinction between this use of range as a *number* and the other use as an *interval* shown in **Example 3.**

Minimum and *maximum* are important terms that students will see throughout their mathematics studies. The use of the words seems natural here.

Making Connections
Do not get stalled on the subtraction of a negative number in **Example 3.** The physical model given in the example should be sufficient for justifying the answer. Subtraction will be treated in detail in Chapter 3.

ADDITIONAL EXAMPLES
1. With a Miller brand furnace thermostat, the furnace cycles on and off to keep the temperature within $1\frac{1}{2}$ degrees of the setting on the dial. Molly sets her thermostat at 70°. Describe the temperature in her home using **a.** the symbol $\pm$, **b.** an inequality of the form $a \le x \le b$, and **c.** a graph.
a. $70 \pm 1\frac{1}{2}$; **b.** $68\frac{1}{2} \le x \le 71\frac{1}{2}$
c.

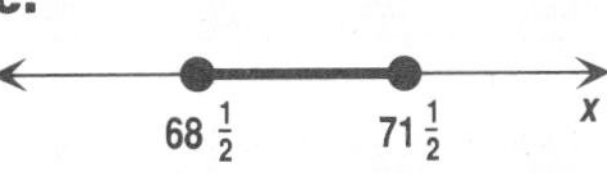

2. Ms. Cooper wanted to study the popularity of Cooper's Coffee Shop, so she recorded the number of customers every hour. The results are shown below.

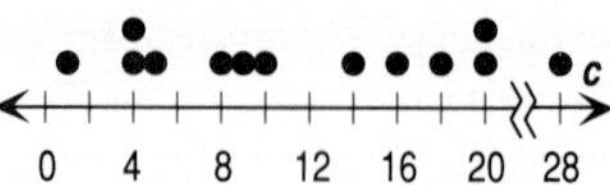

Describe the number of customers using **a.** an inequality, **b.** a graph, and **c.** words.
a. $1 \le c \le 28$
b.

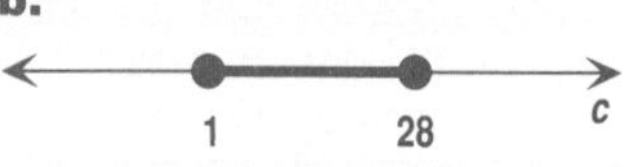

c. from 1 through 28

3. Find the range of the interval $17.3 < x < 40$.
22.7

4. A car's engine temperature started at -6° in the morning and went as high as 182°.

a. Graph the temperatures on a vertical number line.

b. Find the range of the interval.
188°

Solution

a. The maximum age is 69, the minimum is 42. The interval from minimum to maximum is $42 \le A \le 69$.

b.

(Technically, we might graph with dots from 42 to 69, but it is easier to draw a bar.)

c. Presidents' ages at inauguration range from 42 to 69.

Death Valley, California

The word *range* in solution c above indicates the interval. The **length of the interval** is also called its **range** and is found by subtracting the minimum value from the maximum value.

range = maximum value − minimum value

The range is a statistic which gives you an idea of the *spread* of data. In Example 1, the range is 69 years − 42 years = 27 years.

If an interval is open, use its endpoints as the maximum and minimum values.

Example 2 Find the range of the interval $3.5 < w < 18.07$.

Solution range = 18.07 − 3.5 = 14.57

Notice the two uses of range in the next example. When you are asked for the range in this book, you should give a number as an answer.

Example 3 Elevations in the state of California range from 86 meters below sea level (in Death Valley) to 4418 meters above sea level (on top of Mt. Whitney).

a. Graph the elevations in California on a vertical number line.
b. Calculate the range of the interval.

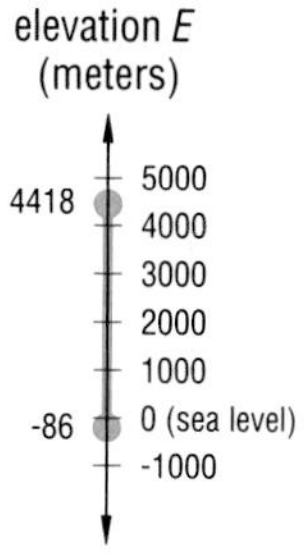

Solution

a. The question translates to graphing the inequality

$$-86 \le E \le 4418,$$

where E is an elevation in California. E can be any real number. The inequality is graphed at the left.

b. The maximum value is 4418 m. The minimum value is -86 m.

$$\begin{aligned} \text{range} &= \text{maximum} - \text{minimum} \\ &= 4418 - (-86) \\ &= 4418 + 86 \\ &= 4504 \end{aligned}$$

The range of elevation in California is 4504 meters.

Questions

Covering the Reading

1. What is an interval? **See margin.**

2. Graph the closed interval 29 ± 4. **See margin.**

3. A poll accurate within 5% showed that 47% of the voters plan to vote for Mamie.
  a. Describe this interval using the "±" symbol. **47% ± 5%**
  b. What are the endpoints of this interval? **42% and 52%**

4. **a.** Find the midpoint of the open interval from 100 to 180. **b.** Graph the interval. **a) 140; b) See margin.**

5. Use the following information. "Children ages five through twelve pay half price."
  a. Rewrite this using an inequality. **$5 \le a \le 12$**
  b. Is this a closed or open interval? **closed**
  c. What is the range of the interval? **7**

6. *Multiple choice* The graph 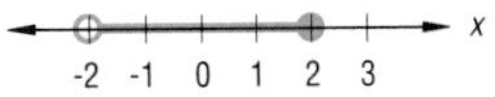 represents:

(a) $-2 \le x \le 2$ (b) $-2 < x < 2$ (c) $-2 \le x < 2$ (d) $-2 < x \le 2$
d

7. Suppose 15 students in a class were asked how much television they watched last week. The dot frequency diagram below shows their responses. Describe the interval from minimum to maximum time using **a.** an inequality, **b.** a graph, and **c.** words.
a) $5 \le n \le 35$; b) See margin; c) from 5 to 35 hours

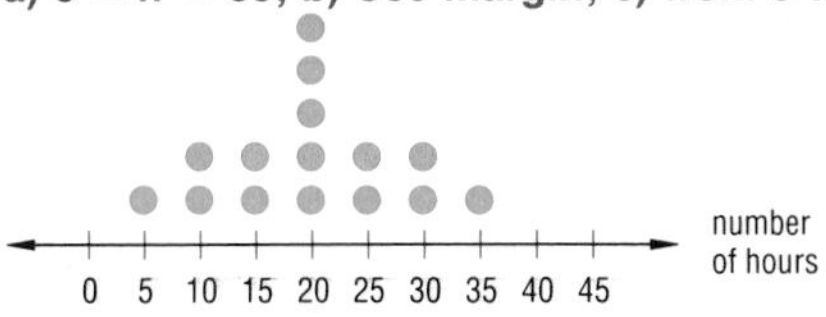

NOTES ON QUESTIONS

Question 8: This covers the idea that the midpoint of a segment is equidistant from the endpoints. The easiest method for finding m is to average the endpoints, something touched upon in the lesson. This idea is important in coordinate geometry, and also provides a helpful representation of the mean.

Questions 12 and 13: Since 1/2 and 1/8 convert to convenient decimals, the problems can be solved by finding $.5 \pm .125$. This may be easier than adding fractions.

Question 16: The selection of scale and unit markings for a graph to best fit the data is an important part of setting up frequency diagrams.

Making Connections for Question 19a: Many students are used to answering a question like this one by solving a proportion, such as

$$\frac{15}{100} = \frac{x}{24}.$$

In algebra, they need to break away from this method and learn to solve percent problems with multiplication ($.15 \times 24$). It is not just that the latter method is convenient and lends itself well to calculator use, but that it is essential in solving the exponential growth problems in Chapter 8.

ADDITIONAL ANSWERS

1. a set of numbers between two numbers *a* and *b*, possibly including *a* and *b*

2.

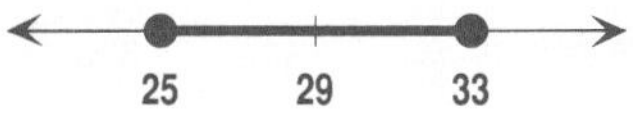

4b.

7b.

NOTES ON QUESTIONS
Question 19b: This problem can be done two ways. Students can either multiply their answer from **Question 19a** by 7, or multiply .15 by the number of hours in a week.

Question 19c: This problem can also be done two ways, but the methods will not yield equally good results. There are not exactly 52 weeks per year, so multiplying the answer to **Question 19b** by 52 is not as good as multiplying the answer to **Question 19a** by 365.

Questions 21-23: Here, students are introduced to the *Skill sequence* format, which will continue throughout the book. In *Skill sequences,* the questions progress so that answering one part gives a clue that helps in answering the next, or provides a contrast to answering the next.

Questions 24, 25, and 27: These require the use of references such as dictionaries and encyclopedias. Students of Transition Mathematics will be accustomed to such questions. Other students may be surprised. We wish to emphasize the many places one can find mathematical ideas.

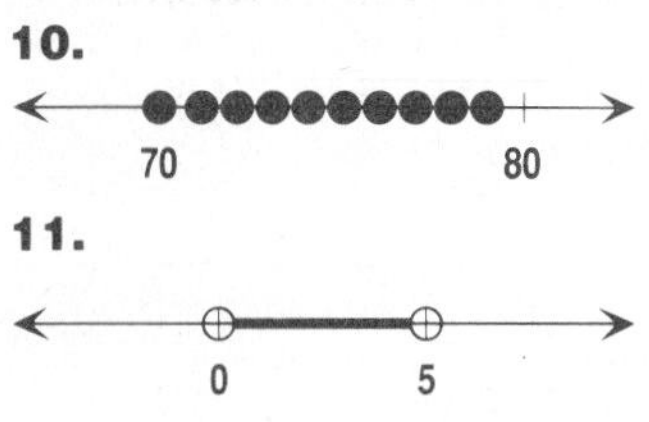

Applying the Mathematics

8. 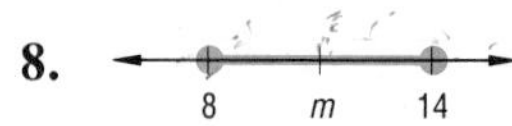

m is the coordinate of the midpoint of the interval graphed above.

a. What is the value of *m*? **11**

b. How much larger is 14 than *m*? **3**

c. How much smaller is 8 than *m*? **3**

d. Describe the interval using the "±" symbol. **11 ± 3**

9. Consider the interval graphed here.

20 — 20.5 *g*

a. Describe the interval using an inequality. **$20 \le g \le 20.5$**

b. What is the midpoint of this interval? **20.25**

In 10 and 11, graph the interval.

10. The best golfers had scores in the 70s. **See margin.**

11. Children under the age of 5 ride free. **See margin.**

In 12 and 13, consider the closed interval $\frac{1}{2} \pm \frac{1}{8}$.

12. What are the endpoints of the interval? **$\frac{3}{8}$ and $\frac{5}{8}$**

13. Describe this interval using an inequality. **$\frac{3}{8} \le x \le \frac{5}{8}$**

14. A machinist is making metal rods for lamps. The metal rods are to be 1.25″ in diameter with an allowable error of at most .005.″ (The number .005″ is called the *tolerance*.) Give an interval for the possible widths *w* of the rods. **$1.245 \le w \le 1.255$**

Review

15. A person makes more than \$1800 a month. Let *d* be the amount made.

a. What inequality describes this situation? *(Lesson 1-1)* **$d > 1800$**

b. Graph the inequality. *(Lesson 1-1)* **See margin.**

In 16 and 17, a survey was taken of the number of times the students in Ms. Lawson's class went swimming last month. Here are the data. Each number represents the number of swimming trips for a single student.

3	1	0	2	0
1	4	6	2	0
0	1	0	3	5

16. Which is the most appropriate number line for the data? *(Lesson 1-2)* **c**

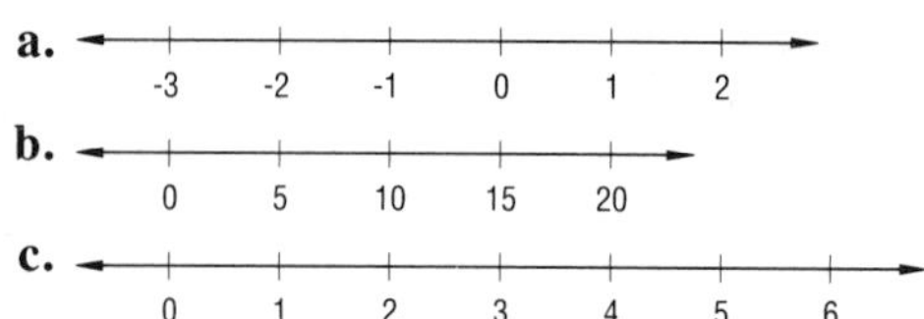

17. **a.** Construct a dot frequency diagram of the data using the appropriate number line from Question 16. **See margin.**
b. What is the mode of the data? **0**
c. What is the median of the data? *(Lesson 1-2)* **1**

18. Calculate 328 − x when x = 2.56. *(Previous course)* **325.44**

19. In 1983, the typical American teenager watched TV 15% of the time. *(Previous course)*
a. How many hours would this represent out of a 24-hour day? **3.6**
b. How many hours would this represent out of the hours in one week? **25.2**
c. How many days does this equal in a year?
54.75 or, in leap years, 54.9

20. A band performed at a party and earned $100, which the seven members want to share. How much will each person get, rounded to the nearest cent? *(Previous course)* **$14.29**

Skill sequences are questions intended to maintain and extend skills which you already have and will need in later chapters.

21. *Skill sequence* Find the sum. *(Previous course)*
a. $\frac{4}{5} + \frac{9}{5}$ **$\frac{13}{5}$** **b.** $\frac{4}{5} + \frac{9}{10}$ **$\frac{17}{10}$** **c.** $\frac{4}{5} + \frac{9}{11}$ **$\frac{89}{55}$**

22. Compute in your head. *(Previous course)*
a. 5 + -9 **-4** **b.** -5 + -9 **-14** **c.** -5 + 9 **4**

23. Compute in your head. *(Previous course)*
a. 7 · -8 **-56** **b.** -7 · 8 **-56** **c.** -7 · -8 **56**

Exploration

24. Each of the words below stands for an interval of time. How long is the interval? **See margin.**
a. decade **b.** century **c.** millenium
d. fortnight **e.** sennight **f.** lustrum

25. There is a third meaning of *range* suggested by Example 3. What is that meaning? **a mountain range**

26. Why did the nomad put a tent on his stove?
He wanted a home on the range.

27. Which presidents are represented by the endpoints of the interval in Example 1? **Theodore Roosevelt was the youngest. Ronald Reagan was the oldest.**

FOLLOW-UP

MORE PRACTICE
For more questions on SPUR Objectives, use *Lesson Master 1-3,* shown below.

EXTENSION
Industrial arts students may enjoy bringing in examples from their classes that are similar to **Question 14.**

15b.

17a.

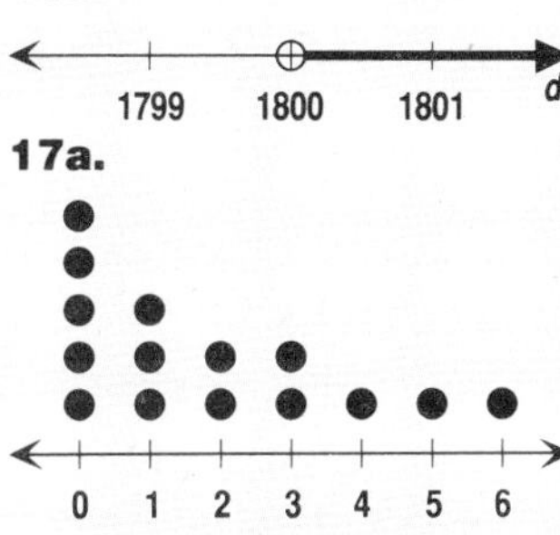

24a. 10 years; b. 100 years; c. 1000 years; d. 2 weeks; e. 1 week; f. 5 years.

NAME ______

LESSON **MASTER 1–3**
QUESTIONS ON **SPUR** OBJECTIVES

■**REPRESENTATIONS** *Objective K* *(See pages 50–53 for objectives.)*

1. An automobile manufacturer advertises that its car will get from 28 to 35 miles per gallon depending on the speed at which the car is driven.
a. Express this interval as an inequality using m for mileage.
$28 \le m \le 35$
b. Graph the inequality.

2. Graph the closed interval 16 ± 0.5.

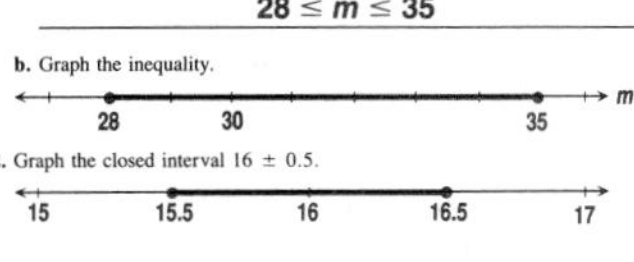

In 3–6, graph the inequality.

3. $2 \le x < 8$
4. $25 > y > 15$
5. {$n \le 5$ where n is a whole number}
6. {$p < 12$ where p is a whole number}
7. Graph the open interval from 20 to 50.

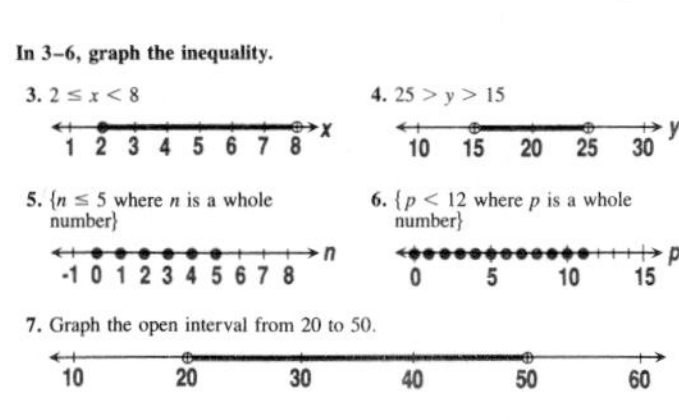

8. An interval has a range of 8 and midpoint 5. Graph the interval.

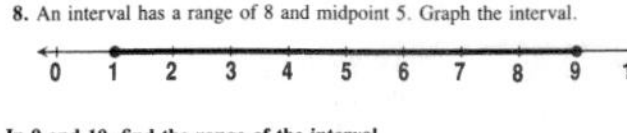

In 9 and 10, find the range of the interval.

9. 36 ± 8 **16** 10. 4 ± 1.2 **2.4**

11. The number of A's given by a group of algebra teachers varied from 2 to 9. Draw a graph showing this interval.

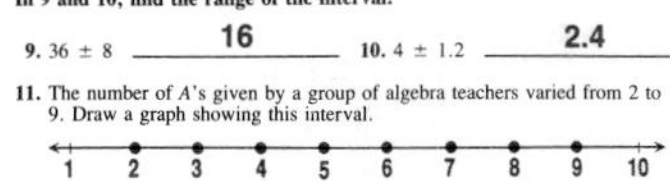

LESSON 1-4

RESOURCES
- Lesson Master 1-4
- Quiz on Lessons 1-1 Through 1-4
- Visual for Teaching Aid 3: Rules for Order of Operations
- Computer Master 1

The Teaching Aids are available both as blackline masters and as overhead visuals.

OBJECTIVES

Letter codes refer to the SPUR Objectives on pages 50–53.

C Evaluate numerical and algebraic expressions.
D Give the output for or write short computer programs and statements that evaluate expressions.

TEACHING NOTES

Emphasize that while the standard order of operations was originally a matter of choice, now it is part of the universal grammar of mathematics and is used throughout the world.

Alternate Approach
Students may find the following mnemonic helpful:

***P**lease **E**xcuse **M**y **D**ear **A**unt **S**ally*

P Parentheses
E Exponents (Powers)
M & D Multiplication and Division
A & S Addition and Subtraction

Make sure students understand that there is no priority

LESSON

1-4 Order of Operations

Finding the value of an expression is called **evaluating** the expression. **Numerical expressions** like $6 + 3^2 - 1$ combine numbers. If an expression includes one or more variables, like $4 + 3x$, it is called an **algebraic expression.** No matter which type of expression you are evaluating, if it involves several operations you must be careful to do them in the correct order.

Rules for Order of Operations

1. First do operations within parentheses or other grouping symbols.
2. Within grouping symbols or if there are no grouping symbols:
   a. Do all powers from left to right.
   b. Do all multiplications and divisions from left to right.
   c. Do all additions and subtractions from left to right.

To evaluate an algebraic expression you must have values to substitute for the variables. It is important to understand that $3x$ means $3 \cdot x$ and $5(A + B)$ means $5 \cdot (A + B)$.

Example 1 Evaluate $4 + 3x$ **a.** when $x = 9$ and **b.** when $x = -1$.

Solution

a. Let $x = 9$. Then $4 + 3x = 4 + 3 \cdot 9$ — Substitute 9 for x.
$= 4 + 27$ — Multiply first.
$= 31$ — Add.

b. Let $x = -1$. Then $4 + 3x = 4 + 3 \cdot -1$ — Substitute -1 for x.
$= 4 + -3$
$= 1$

The value of $4 + 3x$ depends upon what value is used for x.

Example 2 Evaluate $7n^3$ when $n = 2$.

Solution Substitute 2 for n. Do the power *before* the multiplication.

$$7 \cdot 2^3 = 7 \cdot 8$$
$$= 56$$

Suppose you did not follow the correct order and multiplied 7 and 2 first, then raised to the third power. Your answer would be 2744 instead of 56 and would be incorrect.

Most scientific calculators use the same order of operations as algebra. Though we do Examples 1 and 2 without calculators, because the numbers are easy, the following sequences will check them.

Example 1: 4 [+] 3 [×] 9 [=] 31

Example 2: 7 [×] 2 [x^y] 3 [=] 56

If you have never used a scientific calculator, see Appendix A.

Example 3 Evaluate $\frac{5(A + B)}{2}$ when $A = 3.4$ and $B = 7.2$.

Solution Substitute 3.4 for A and 7.2 for B.

Then $\frac{5(A + B)}{2} = \frac{5(3.4 + 7.2)}{2}$

$= \frac{5(10.6)}{2}$ Work inside the parentheses.

$= \frac{53}{2}$ Remove parentheses. 5(10.6) means $5 \cdot 10.6$.

$= 26.5$

Most computer languages follow the rules for order of operations. In **BASIC** (Beginner's All-Purpose Symbolic Instruction Code), the arithmetic symbols are + for addition, − for subtraction, * for multiplication, / for division, ^ for powering and ( ) for grouping. In computer symbols $5(A + B)$ is written 5 * (A + B). 2^3 is written 2 ^ 3.

Example 4 Use a computer to evaluate $3(4x - 5) + y$ when $x = 3.1$ and $y = 0.6$.

Solution Here is a computer program written in BASIC to evaluate the expression $3(4x - 5) + y$.

```
10 PRINT "ANSWER TO EXAMPLE 4"
20 LET X = 3.1
30 LET Y = 0.6
40 PRINT 3 * (4 * X - 5) + Y
50 END
```

Run the program. The computer should print

```
ANSWER TO EXAMPLE 4
22.8
```

between multiplication and division. You do them together in the order they appear as you move from left to right. The same holds true for addition and subtraction.

In **Example 2,** point out that the order of operations implies $7n^3$ means $7 \cdot n^3$. Because powers take precedence over multiplication, the exponent 3 applies to the n only. That is, make sure students do not interpret $7n^3$ as $(7n)^3$.

Reading Stress that when reading material that involves simplifying or evaluating expressions, students should analyze each step, seeing what was done, why it is allowed, and what the goal is.

Computer In **Example 1** we use the word *let* to prepare students for the LET commands in **Examples 4 and 5.** We also end programs with the END statement. Some implementations of BASIC forbid the LET statement and some do not require the END statement. You should test your computer's version before students run these programs.

If you expect students to have their own calculators, remind them that scientific calculators are needed for the next lesson. Advise them to bring the instructions to class.

ADDITIONAL EXAMPLES

1. Evaluate $5y + 6$ when $y = 3$ and when $y = .2$.
21; 7

2. Evaluate $2n^4$ when $n = 3$.
162

3. Evaluate $\frac{4(A - B)}{5}$ when $A = 6.3$ and $B = 4.7$.
1.28

4. After covering **Examples 4 and 5** in the student text, ask students to give the corresponding PRINT statements for evaluating the expressions in **Examples 1-3** in the student text.
1a. PRINT 4+3*9
1b. PRINT 4+3*(-1)
2. PRINT 7*2^3
3. PRINT 5*(3.4+7.2)/2
On some computers you may be able to type the symbol ? instead of the word PRINT.

Error Analysis In the PRINT statement given above for **Example 3,** some students may omit the symbol for multiplication and write: PRINT 5(3.4+7.2)/2. You may need to remind students that parentheses are strictly grouping symbols in BASIC and that the asterisk must always be used for multiplication.

A shortcut to writing the program in Example 4 is to do the substitutions in your head and type PRINT 3 * (4 * 3.1 − 5) + 0.6

When you press the return key, you should see 22.8

On a computer, when you evaluate expressions which are fractions, you must watch grouping carefully. You see that when you evaluate $\frac{10 + 4}{2 + 5}$ by hand, you get $\frac{14}{7} = 2$. If you type PRINT 10+4/2+5 you see 17 as the answer. The slash (/) is *not* a grouping symbol. The computer interprets 10 + 4 / 2 + 5 as 10 + (4/2) + 5. To get the correct interpretation, you must show your intended grouping with parentheses: (10 + 4)/(2 + 5).

Example 5 Use a computer to evaluate $\left(\frac{x + 10.7}{y + 4}\right)^7$ when $x = 3.1$ and $y = 0.6$.

Solution 1 To a computer the expression must be ((x + 10.7) / (y + 4))^7.
Substitute in your head and type PRINT ((3.1 + 10.7) / (0.6 + 4))^7

Press the return key and see 2187

Solution 2 Run the same program that is in Example 4 but change lines 10 and 40.

```
10 PRINT "ANSWER TO EXAMPLE 5"
20 LET X = 3.1
30 LET Y = 0.6
40 PRINT ((X + 10.7) / (Y + 4))^7
50 END
```

Questions

Covering the Reading

In 1–3, identify each expression as numerical or algebraic.

1. $\frac{8(7) + 2}{12}$ numerical **2.** $\frac{2x}{4 - 8}$ algebraic **3.** $a^2 + b^2$ algebraic

In 4–8, evaluate.

4. $10^2 \cdot 7^2$ 4900 **5.** $12 - 2 \cdot 4$ 4 **6.** $3(10 - 6)^3 + 15$ 207

7. $\frac{a + 2b}{5}$ when $a = 11.6$ and $b = 9.2$ **6**

8. .5 * H * (A + H) when H = 32 and A = .7 **523.2**

9. If you type PRINT 8+6/3−2 what will a computer print? **8**

10. What will the computer print on the screen when this program is run? **See margin.**

```
10 PRINT "ANSWER TO QUESTION 10"
20 LET A = 4.5
30 LET B = 2.6
40 PRINT 2 * (4 * A − 3) + B
50 END
```

11. Using the programs in the lesson as patterns, write a computer program or statement to evaluate $\left(\frac{m + 12.5}{n + 3}\right)^{10}$ when $m = 2.4$ and $n = 0.2$. **See margin.**

Applying the Mathematics

In 12–14, translate into BASIC.

12. $6xy$ **6 * X * Y**

13. $5x + 3y^{10}$ **5 * X + 3 * Y ^10**

14. $\frac{7x + y}{x + 7y}$ **(7 * X + Y)/(X + 7 * Y)**

15. The perimeter of the hexagon at the right is $4a + 2b$. Find the perimeter when $a = 10$ mm and $b = 35$ mm. **110 mm**

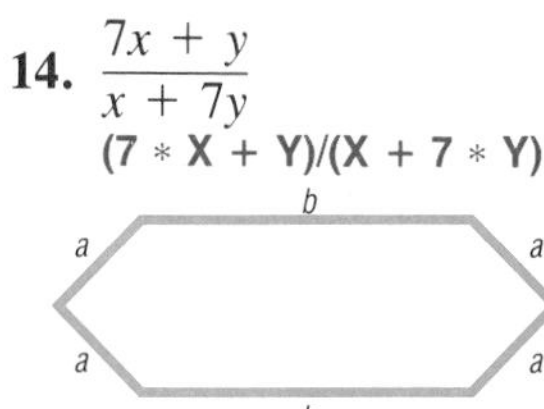

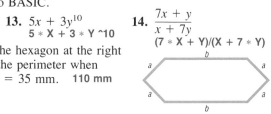

16. Begin with the innermost parentheses and work toward the outer parentheses. 6 − (5 − (4 − (3 − 2))). **4**

17. $\frac{1.4x - 2.3y}{4xy}$ = ___?___ ÷ ___?___. **(1.4x − 2.3y), 4xy**

18. Let d = number of days, t = number of trips, and m = number of meals.
   a. Write an expression representing the cost of a vacation at Hotel St. Jacques using d, t, and m. ***49d + 15t + 12m***
   b. Find the cost when $d = 3$, $t = 2$, and $m = 5$. **$237**

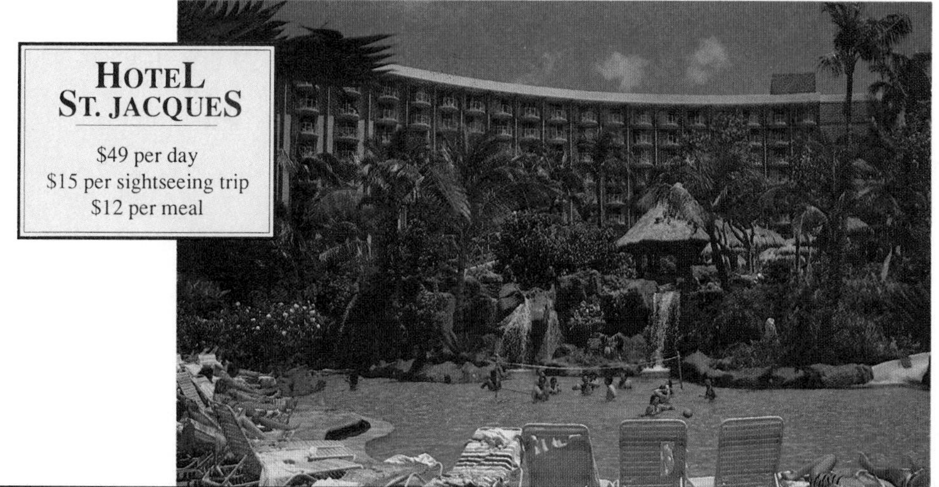

HOTEL
ST. JACQUES
$49 per day
$15 per sightseeing trip
$12 per meal

NOTES ON QUESTIONS

Question 22: This should be answered using *trial and error.*

Question 26: Students with correct answers will no doubt have noticed that the answer to 26c is the sum of the answers to 26a and 26b. We are setting up the Distributive Property.

Question 28: Here students are asked to translate numbers written as a combination of numerals and words into strictly numerical form. Numbers like these are often found in newspaper and magazine articles.

ADDITIONAL ANSWERS

10. ANSWER TO QUESTION 10
32.6

11.
```
10 PRINT "ANSWER TO QUESTION 11"
20 LET M=2.4
30 LET N=.2
40 PRINT ((M+12.5)/(N+3))^10
50 END
```

NAME ____________

LESSON **MASTER 1–4**
QUESTIONS ON **SPUR** OBJECTIVES

■SKILLS *Objective C (See pages 50–53 for objectives.)*
In 1–3, evaluate the numerical expressions.

1. 12 + 2 * 4 **20**

2. $16 - \frac{8}{2} + 6$ **18**

3. $\frac{3 + 7}{2} + 3$ **8**

4. *True or false* $3x^2 = (3x)^2$ **false**

5. Find the value of $3(m + n)$ when $m = 1.2$ and $n = 2.6$ **11.4**

6. Evaluate $\frac{r + s}{r - s}$ when $r = 5$ and $s = 3$. **4**

7. Evaluate $9b^2$ when $b = \frac{1}{3}$. **1**

8. Evaluate $\left(\frac{3n}{4}\right)^2$ when $n = 2$. $\frac{9}{4}$

■SKILLS *Objective D*

9. If the program below is run, and 1.6 is the input, what will be printed?

```
10 PRINT "EVALUATE AN EXPRESSION"
20 PRINT "ENTER A NUMBER"
30 INPUT X
40 PRINT 6 + 32/X − 10
50 END
```

EVALUATE AN EXPRESSION
ENTER A NUMBER, 16

10. The formula for changing Celsius temperature to Fahrenheit is:

$$F = \frac{9}{5}C + 32$$

   a. Write a computer program which will find F for an input of any C.

sample:
```
10 PRINT "FIND FAHRENHEIT FROM CELSIUS"
20 PRINT "ENTER A CELSIUS TEMPERATURE"
30 INPUT C
40 PRINT 9/5 * C + 32
50 END
```

   b. What is the Fahrenheit temperature when $C = 28$? **82.4**

 5

NOTES ON QUESTIONS
Computer for Question 30: Before assigning this question, test your computer's version of BASIC with regard to LET and END.

FOLLOW-UP

MORE PRACTICE
For more questions on SPUR Objectives, use *Lesson Master 1-4,* shown on page 23.

EXTENSION
Computer A nice class activity is to have students key in and run the programs in the examples or questions on a computer in the classroom.

Show students that by changing lines 20 and 30 in **Example 5,** they can vary the values for the variables to find other values for the expression. Indeed, you might tell students one would not want to run such a computer program unless values of the expression were desired for many values of *x* and *y*.

EVALUATION
A quiz covering Lessons 1-1 through 1-4 can be found on page 1 in the Teacher's Resource File.

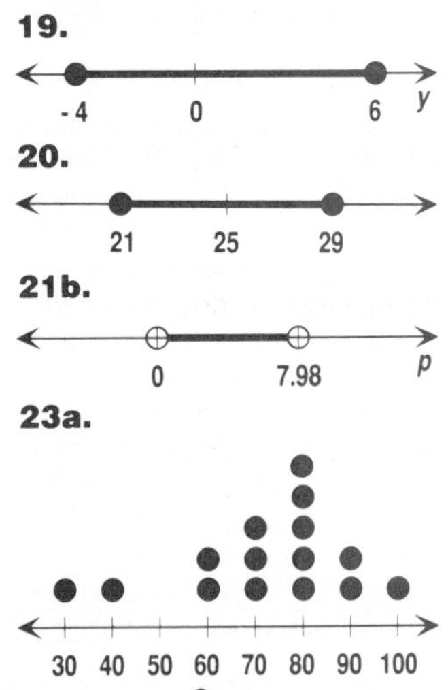

Review

19. Graph the interval $-4 \le y \le 6$. *(Lesson 1-3)* **See margin.**

20. Graph the closed interval 25 ± 4. *(Lesson 1-3)* **See margin.**

21. *P* is the sale price of a record whose list price is \$7.98. *(Lesson 1-3)*
a. Describe the possible values of *P* with an inequality.
b. Graph. **a) $0 < P < 7.98$ b) See margin.**

22. Which of the numbers -4, 2, 6 make the sentence $15 + n + -11 > 0$ true? *(Lesson 1-1)* **2 and 6**

23. Mrs. Marlowe gave her students a quiz. Their scores are shown below.

30	80	70	60	70
40	80	80	90	100
80	90	60	80	70

a. Construct a dot frequency diagram using the scores. **See margin.**
b. Find the mode of the scores. **80**
c. Find the median of the scores. **80**
d. Find the mean of the scores. **72**
e. Find the range of scores. **70**
f. On the basis of these statistics, are Mrs. Marlowe's students doing well? *(Lessons 1-2, 1-3)* **Answers will vary.**

24. *Skill sequence* Compute. *(Previous course)*
a. $\frac{2}{3} + \frac{4}{3}$ **2** **b.** $\frac{2}{3} + \frac{4}{9}$ $\frac{10}{9}$ **c.** $\frac{2}{3} + \frac{4}{13}$ $\frac{38}{39}$

25. *Skill sequence* If $x \cdot y = 85.7$, give
a. $-x \cdot y$ **-85.7** **b.** $x \cdot -y$ **-85.7** **c.** xy *(Previous course)* **85.7**

26. Compute in your head. *(Previous course)*
a. $.8 \cdot 5$ **4** **b.** $.8 \cdot .5$ **.4** **c.** $.8 \cdot 5.5$ **4.4**

27. *Multiple choice* Which of the following are sentences? *(Lesson 1-1)*
(a) Ten is more than the number. **(a) and (c)**
(b) Ten more than the number.
(c) Ten is less than the number.
(d) Ten less than the number.

28. Copy and complete with decimal answers. *(Previous course)*
a. 5.8 hundred = $5.8 \cdot 100$ = ___?___ **580**
b. 5.8 thousand = $5.8 \cdot$ ___?___ = ___?___ **1000; 5800**
c. 5.8 million = ___?___ $\cdot$ ___?___ = ___?___
5.8; 1,000,000; 5,800,000

29. Molly has one and three-eighths of a yard of ribbon and uses half of it to make a bow. Multiply $\frac{1}{2} \cdot 1\frac{3}{8}$ to find half of $1\frac{3}{8}$. *(Previous course)* $\frac{11}{16}$

Exploration

30. A computer can change the value of a variable. Find out what a computer will print when given the following instructions. **108**

```
10 LET X = 52
20 LET X = 4 + 2 * X
30 PRINT X
40 END
```

LESSON

1-5

Formulas

Almost everyone, at some time or another, has been in a lot of traffic. Perhaps you have been in a traffic jam on your way to an amusement park, or to a sports event, or to a concert. In big cities, adults may be in traffic jams every day on their way to work. Have you ever wondered how many cars are on the road?

An estimate to the answer can be calculated using the sentence below. Here N is the estimated number of cars on the road if they are traveling at safe distances from one another.

$$N = \frac{20Ld}{600 + s^2}$$

N = estimated number of cars
L = number of lanes of road
d = length of road (in feet)
s = average speed of the cars (in miles per hour)

This sentence is a *formula* for the number of cars *in terms of* the number of lanes of the road, the length of the road, and the average speed of the cars. A **formula** is a sentence in which one variable is given in terms of other variables and numbers. In this formula, N is given in terms of L, d, and s.

Example 1 How many cars are there on a 1-mile stretch of a 2-lane highway if the cars are going at an average speed of about 30 miles per hour?

Solution First determine the value of each variable. Here the only difficulty is that the length of the road is given in miles but is needed in feet. Recall that there are 5280 feet in a mile.

L = 2 lanes
d = 5280 feet
s = 30 miles per hour

Now replace the variables by their values.

$$N = \frac{20Ld}{600 + s^2}$$

$$N = \frac{20 \cdot 2 \cdot 5280}{600 + 30^2}$$

LESSON 1-5

RESOURCES
- Lesson Master 1-5
- Computer Master 1

OBJECTIVES

Letter codes refer to the SPUR Objectives on pages 50–53.

C Evaluate numerical and algebraic expressions.
D Give the output for or write short computer programs and statements that evaluate formulas.
I Evaluate formulas in real situations.

TEACHING NOTES

Reading The computer programs in this lesson are slightly more involved than those in the preceding lesson. Use them to emphasize that, in reading programs, students should relate each step to preceding steps, just as they do when reading worked-out examples.

Computer If possible, run the computer program in **Example 3** in class. The image of someone running the program over and over, each time entering a different value, helps to describe the idea that d can represent the diameter of any circle and πd will be its circumference. Use the program to calculate the distance around familiar circular objects. We will frequently use statements like PRINT A,B to print columns. You could expand the display to three columns by modifying the program. Replace lines 50 and 60 with the following:

```
50 LET RAD=DIAM/2
55 PRINT "DIAMETER",
   "RADIUS",
   "CIRCUMFERENCE"
60 PRINT DIAM, RAD,
   CIRC
```

Error Analysis In entering line 55 above, some students may place the comma(s) inside the quotation marks. The computer will then print the comma, but it will not space the entries in columns.

ADDITIONAL EXAMPLES

1. When you are traveling at r miles per hour in a car, it will come to a stop approximately d feet after you decide to hit the brakes where d is given by

$$d = r + \frac{r^2}{20}.$$

How many feet does it take to stop if you are going 45 miles per hour?
≈146 feet

2. Ames H.S. calculates students' grade-point averages on a scale in which an A is worth 4 points. If a student gets A's in a classes, B's in b classes, C's in c classes, D's in d classes and F's in f classes, the student's grade average (g) is found by

$$g = \frac{4a + 3b + 2c + d + f}{a + b + c + d + f}.$$

Find the average of a student who got two A's, one B, and three C's.
$2.8\bar{3}$

Evaluate using the order of operations. A calculator helps here.

$$N = \frac{211200}{1500}$$
$$N \approx 141$$

There are about 141 cars on the road.

The formula shows that the number of cars on a road depends quite a bit on the average speed of the cars. When cars go faster there should be a greater distance between them for safety.

Formulas do not necessarily work for all possible values of the variables. In the formula above, for example, it is meaningless to consider negative numbers for any of the variables and L should be a small whole number. All the values which *may* be meaningfully substituted for a variable make up the **domain** or **replacement set** of the variable. In Example 1, the domains for s and d are the positive real numbers, and the domain for L is the set of whole numbers excluding zero.

Example 2 In some bowling leagues, bowlers who average under 200 can get handicaps added to their score. The handicap H of a bowler, with average A, is often found by using the formula $H = .8(200 - A)$.

a. What is the handicap of a person whose average score is 145?
b. What would a bowler's final score be for a game in which his or her actual score was 145?
c. What happens when an average score greater than 200 is substituted into the formula?
d. What is the domain of A?

Solution

a. Substitute 145 in the formula for A and follow the order of operations.
$H = .8(200 - 145)$
$= .8(55)$
$= 44$
b. Add the handicap to the actual score. $145 + 44 = 189$
c. If $A > 200$, then $200 - A$ is negative. (This gives a negative handicap, which is ignored.)
d. $0 \le A \le 200$. Since the average must be less than or equal to 200 in order for this formula to work, the domain of A is the set of numbers satisfying $0 \le A \le 200$.

26

A computer program can be used to evaluate formulas. In the next example, the programming statement INPUT is used. An **INPUT** statement makes the computer pause and wait for you to type in a value. The computer signals you by flashing its cursor (the symbol that shows you where you are on the screen). On some computers you may see a "?" printed on the screen as well.

Example 3 The circumference C of a circle can be estimated using the formula

$$C = \pi d$$

where d is the diameter of the circle and $\pi \approx 3.14159$.

a. Write a computer program to find C, given d.

b. Estimate the circumference of a circle with diameter 15.5 feet.

Solution

a.

```
10 PRINT "EVALUATE CIRCUMFERENCE FORMULA"
20 PRINT "GIVE DIAMETER"
30 INPUT DIAM
40 LET CIRC = 3.14159 * DIAM
50 PRINT "DIAMETER", "CIRCUMFERENCE"
60 PRINT DIAM, CIRC
70 END
```

Note: Using a comma in the PRINT statements makes the computer print in columns.

b. When the program is run, the lines EVALUATE CIRCUMFERENCE FORMULA and GIVE DIAMETER will automatically appear. Now type 15.5. When you press the RETURN or ENTER key you will see:

```
DIAMETER CIRCUMFERENCE
15.5              48.694645
```

Questions

Covering the Reading

In 1–4, use the formula for the number of cars on a road.

1. In this formula, N is given in terms of _?_. *L, d* **and** *s*

2. About how many cars are on a 2-mile stretch of a 3-lane highway if the average speed of the cars is 50 mph? **204**

3. About how many cars are on a 1.5 mile part of a 4-lane highway if the average speed of the cars is 20 mph? **634**

4. In this formula, give the domain for: **a.** L, **b.** d, and **c.** s.
See margin.

NOTES ON QUESTIONS

Question 13: Students may not be familiar with the idea of acceleration. The unit *feet per second per second* will probably seem strange. The idea can be explained using **Question 13a;** an acceleration of 5 ft/sec/sec means that the elevator is speeding up 5 ft/sec every second. So if its speed averaged 5 feet a second during second 1, its speed will average 10 feet a second during second 2, and 15 feet a second during second 3.

ADDITIONAL ANSWERS

4a. the set of whole numbers excluding zero; b. the positive real numbers; c. the positive real numbers

NOTES ON QUESTIONS
Error Analysis for Question 14: Some students may not notice that they must convert 6 feet to inches. Take this opportunity to remind students of the importance of units in formulas.

Small Group Work for Questions 16 and 17: If you are in a region where crickets live, groups of your students might want to test the cricket-chirp formula.

Question 25: The fractions have been chosen so that the computations can be checked by converting to decimals. Reminds students of this check.

Question 27: Hideaki Tomoyori, a 55-year-old Japanese man, in 1988 memorized and recited (in front of a team of witnesses) the first 40,000 digits of pi. The recitation took him 17 hours and 20 minutes. So when your students complain about not being able to remember a few properties, remind them of Hideaki.

ADDITIONAL ANSWERS
8. You get the value zero. A bowler with average score 200 gets no handicap.
9. It makes the computer pause and wait for you to type in a value, which the computer then stores for the given variable.
15b. 40 in. is outside the domain of most adult heights, and the answer has no meaning. (No one has an ideal weight of 0.)
23. sample:

```
10 PRINT "ANSWER TO
   QUESTION 23"
20 LET X=5.7
30 LET Y=2.006
40 LET Z=51.46
50 PRINT X+Y+3*Z
60 END
```

28a. energy; mass of an object; speed of light;
b. the relationship between the mass of an object and the energy it contains

5. What is the formula for the handicap H of a bowler whose average score is A? **$H = .8(200 - A)$**

6. What is the handicap of a bowler whose average score is 120? **64**

7. *Multiple choice* A bowler with which average is not entitled to a handicap? **(d)**
(a) 95 (b) 145 (c) 195 (d) 205

8. Substitute 200 for A in the handicap formula. Explain what you get. **See margin.**

9. What does the INPUT statement make a computer do? **See margin.**

10. Using a _?_ in a PRINT statement makes a computer print in columns. **comma**

11. What is the circumference of a circle with diameter 7.3 in.? **≈ 22.9 in.**

Applying the Mathematics

12. a. Complete this program which computes area and perimeter of rectangles. Use these formulas: Area = LW, Perimeter = $2L + 2W$. **L*W, 2*L+2*W**

```
10 PRINT "AREA AND PERIMETER OF A RECTANGLE"
20 INPUT "LENGTH";L
30 INPUT "WIDTH";W
40 LET A = _?_
50 LET P = _?_
60 PRINT "AREA","PERIMETER"
70 PRINT A, P
80 END
```

b. What will the computer find for the area and perimeter when $L = 52.5$ and $W = 38$? **area = 1995 perimeter = 181**

13. The force you feel when riding an elevator is caused by the acceleration of the elevator acting against the pull of gravity.

$f = \frac{wa}{g}$, where
f = force in pounds
w = your weight in pounds
a = acceleration of elevator in feet per second per second
g = pull of gravity, usually taken to be 32 ft per second per second (32 ft/sec/sec)

a. What is the force when you weigh 120 lbs and the acceleration of the elevator is 5 ft/sec/sec? Use $g = 32$. **18.75 lb**
b. What happens to the force f as the acceleration of the elevator is increased? **It increases.**
c. On whom does the elevator exert a greater force, a heavy person or a light person? **a heavy person**

In 14 and 15, an adult's normal weight w (in pounds) can be estimated by the formula $w = \frac{11}{2}h - 220$ when his or her height h (in inches) is known.

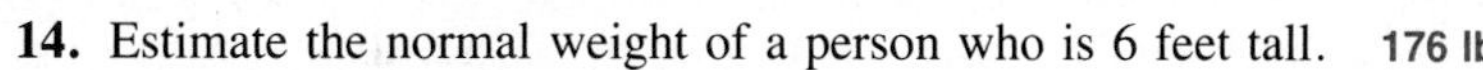

14. Estimate the normal weight of a person who is 6 feet tall. **176 lb**

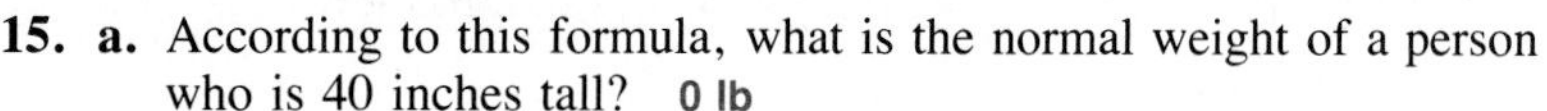

15. a. According to this formula, what is the normal weight of a person who is 40 inches tall? **0 lb**
    b. Explain your answer to part a by relating it to the domain of the variable h. **See margin.**

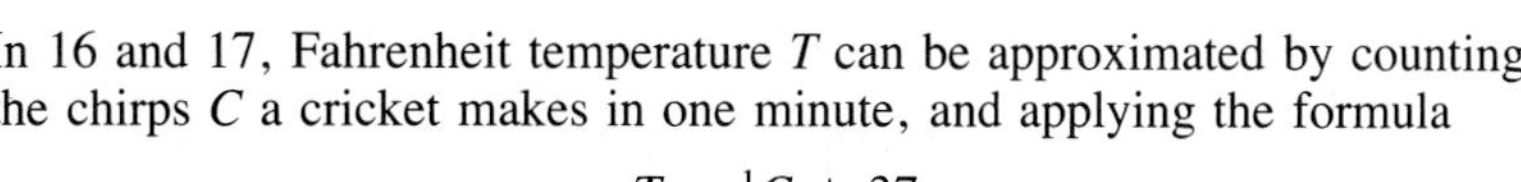

In 16 and 17, Fahrenheit temperature T can be approximated by counting the chirps C a cricket makes in one minute, and applying the formula

$$T = \frac{1}{4}C + 37.$$

16. A cricket chirps 200 times per minute. Estimate the temperature. **87 °F**
17. Estimate the temperature when a cricket chirps 180 times per minute. **82 °F**

Review

In 18–20, evaluate. *(Lesson 1-4)*

18. $(11 - 7)^3$ **64** 19. $5^2 \cdot 5^3$ **3125** 20. $57 - 3 \cdot 11$ **24**

21. What will the computer print on its screen when this program is run? *(Lesson 1-4)*

```
10 PRINT "ANSWER TO QUESTION 21"
20 LET M = 4.56
30 LET N = 3
40 PRINT 4 * M - 9/N
50 END
```

Answer to Question 21
15.24

22. Evaluate $28 - 3(x - 4)$ when $x = 9$. *(Lesson 1-4)* **13**

23. Write a computer program or statement that will print the value of $x + y + 3z$ when $x = 5.7$, $y = 2.006$, and $z = 51.46$. *(Lesson 1-4)* **See margin.**
24. Multiply 1234.5678 by 100,000 in your head. *(Previous course)* **123,456,780**
25. *Skill sequence* Find the sums. Write your result as a fraction or whole number. *(Previous course)*
    a. $\frac{3}{4} + \frac{1}{4}$ **1** b. $\frac{3}{8} + \frac{1}{4}$ **$\frac{5}{8}$** c. $\frac{3}{10} + \frac{1}{4}$ **$\frac{11}{20}$**

26. *Skill sequence*
    a. What is 16% of 24? **3.84**
    b. What is 16% of 2400? **384**
    c. Suppose 16% of the 24 million people aged 12–18 in the U.S. like jazz. How many people is this? *(Previous course)* **3,840,000**

27. The real number π has been calculated to more than 29.36 million decimal places. Write 29.36 million as a single number without a decimal point. *(Previous course)* **29,360,000**

Exploration

28. One of the world's most famous formulas was discovered by Albert Einstein in 1905. It is $E = mc^2$.
    a. What do E, m, and c stand for? **See margin.**
    b. What physical phenomenon does the formula describe? **See margin.**

FOLLOW-UP

MORE PRACTICE

For more questions on SPUR Objectives, use *Lesson Master 1-5,* shown below.

EXTENSION

The formula in **Questions 14 and 15** gives only one weight for a given height. However, most weight charts show an interval of normal weights for each height. Ask students to modify the formula using the ± symbol. For instance, a formula that gives weights within 5% of that given by the original formula is

$$w = \left(\frac{11}{2}h - 220\right) \pm .05\left(\frac{11}{2}h - 220\right).$$

Using inequality signs, the interval is

$$.95\left(\frac{11}{2}h - 220\right) \leq w \leq 1.05\left(\frac{11}{2}h - 220\right).$$

NAME ______

LESSON **MASTER 1–5**
QUESTIONS ON **SPUR** OBJECTIVES

■**SKILLS** *Objective D (See pages 50–53 for objectives.)*

1. When the program below is run, what will be printed if 3 is input?

```
10 PRINT "ENTER A NUMBER"
20 INPUT N
30 LET D = (N - 1) * (N + 1) + 2
40 PRINT N, D
50 END
```

ENTER A NUMBER; 3, 10

■**USES** *Objective I*

2. In a league with n teams, each team plays every other team twice (home and away). The total number of games played is $n(n - 1)$. How many games are played in an 8-team league? **56**

3. The distance, in feet, required to stop a car going s miles per hour is about
$$s + \frac{s^2}{20}.$$
How many feet will a car going 60 mph take to stop? **240**

4. The lateral area (where the label is placed) of a can of beans is $2\pi rh$, where r is the radius of the bottom, and h the height of the can. Find the lateral area if the radius is 5 cm and the height 14 cm. **140π cm²**

5. In some schools, the grade point average is given by:
$$\frac{4a + 3b + 2c + d}{a + b + c + d + f},$$
where a is the number of A's, b is the number of B's, c is the number of C's, d is the number of D's, and f is the number of F's. Carol had 2 A's, 2 B's and a D on her report card. Find her grade point average. **3**

6. Threshold weight is the maximum weight for a person in good health. For men aged 40–49, the threshold weight in pounds is given by
$$\left(\frac{h}{12.3}\right)^3 \quad h \text{ is height in inches}$$
What is the threshold weight for a 45-year-old man 67 in. tall? **≈162 lb**

LESSON 1-6

RESOURCES
- Lesson Master 1-6
- Visual for Teaching Aid 4: Density Property of Real Numbers

OBJECTIVES

Letter codes refer to the SPUR Objectives on pages 50–53.

E Read and interpret set language and notation.
G In real situations, choose a reasonable domain for a variable.

TEACHING NOTES

Reading This lesson is not straightforward to read because the subject matter is about discriminating among whole numbers, integers, and real numbers and between discrete and continuous sets. Emphasize that students, when reading contrasting terms, should ask themselves how the terms differ. For example, ask: Can you think of a whole number that is not an integer? (no) Can you think of an integer that is not a whole number? (yes, any negative integer)

We do not use the term *subset* in this book, but you may find it helpful. The set of whole numbers is a subset of the set of integers, which in turn is a subset of the set of real numbers. We do not mention the set of natural numbers, which is sometimes defined as {1, 2, 3, . . .} and sometimes as {0, 1, 2, 3, . . .}.

LESSON

1-6

Sets

A **set** is a collection of objects called **elements.** Usually the elements are put together for a purpose. Sets are found outside of mathematics, but with different names.

When a set is called	An element is often called
herd of dairy cattle	cow
team	player
committee	member
the U.S. Senate	senator
class	student
place setting	plate

A set often has different properties than its elements. For example, a team in baseball can win the World Series, but a player cannot. A cow moos, but a herd cannot. The Senate can pass legislation, but a senator cannot. A plate might have a radius, a place setting does not.

The standard symbols used for a set are braces {...}, and commas go between the elements. When Lulu, Mike, Nell, Oscar, Paula, and Quincy are the six members of a committee C, you could write

$$C = \{\text{Lulu, Mike, Nell, Oscar, Paula, Quincy}\}.$$

The order of naming elements makes no difference. {Oscar, Mike, Lulu, Nell, Paula, Quincy} is the same committee C. Two sets are **equal** if they have the same elements.

Some frequently used sets in mathematics are the set of whole numbers indicated by the letter W; the set of integers, indicated by I; and the set of real numbers, indicated by R.

W = The set of **whole numbers:** 0, 1, 2, 3, ... Other examples of whole numbers are 100; 1990; five; $\frac{16}{2}$; and 7,000,000.

I = The set of **integers** includes the whole numbers and their opposites. A list could begin 0, 1, -1, 2, -2, 3, -3, ... Other examples of integers are -17.00; $\frac{8}{2}$; 2001; and negative one thousand.

R = The set of **real numbers** consists of all numbers that can be represented as finite or infinite decimals. These include positive and negative numbers, whole numbers, zero, fractions, and decimals themselves. Examples of real numbers are 5; 100,000; -0.0042; $-3\frac{1}{3}$; 0; π; $.\overline{13}$; and $\sqrt{2}$.

Notice that all whole numbers are also integers, and all integers are also real numbers.

The set of real numbers possesses a property not held by the sets of whole numbers or integers. For instance, between 12.6 and 12.7 is the number 12.68. Even if you do not know the numbers, you can still find a number between them. One of the numbers between x and y is their mean, $\frac{x + y}{2}$. Because of the **Density Property**, the set of real numbers is an appropriate domain to use when a variable stands for a measure.

Density Property of Real Numbers:

Between any two real numbers are many other real numbers.

The three sets mentioned on pages 30–31 are often used as domains for variables. The domain of a variable in an open sentence is the set of numbers that might make sense as solutions. The **solution set** is the set of numbers from the domain that actually are solutions.

Example 1 Let x = number of people at a meeting.

a. Give a reasonable domain for x.

b. If there were more than 20 people, write this as an algebraic sentence using x.

c. Graph the solution set to part b.

Solution

a. Since x is a count of the number of people at the meeting, it does not make sense to have x be a fraction or negative. The domain for x is the set of whole numbers.

b. $x > 20$

c. You must show all the whole numbers greater than 20. The three dots next to the graph mean "and so on."

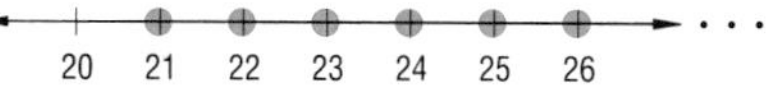

ADDITIONAL EXAMPLES

1. Carson's Used Cars sold from 24 to 30 cars each week last month. Let c = number of cars sold.

a. Give the domain of c.
whole numbers

b. Write an inequality to describe c.
$24 \le c \le 30$

c. Graph the solution set to the inequality in **1b.**

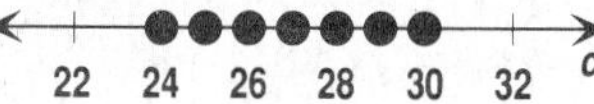

2. In the Beaufort scale, a force 11 wind is termed a storm. It includes winds of 64 to 75 miles per hour, which are strong enough to cause widespread damage. Let s = wind speed.

a. Give a reasonable domain for s.
nonnegative real numbers

b. Use an inequality to describe a force 11 wind.
$64 \le s \le 75$

c. Graph the solution to the inequality in **2b.**

(Your students might be interested to know that normal breathing approximates a force 2 wind on the Beaufort scale, described as a "light breeze.")

3. Let h represent the altitude of a group of mountain climbers.

a. Give a reasonable domain for h.
real numbers

b. The climbers used oxygen masks when they went above 14,000 feet. Write this as an inequality using h.
$h > 14{,}000$

c. Graph the solution to the inequality in **3b.**

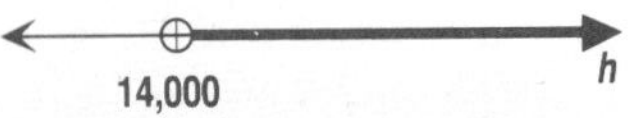

NOTES ON QUESTIONS
Making Connections for Questions 23 and 24:
In these questions, students explore the ideas of intersection and union of sets, which appear in Lessons 3-4 and 3-5.

Example 2 Let w = weight of a roast.

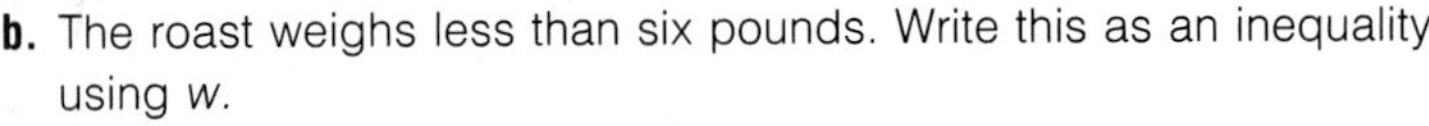

a Give a reasonable domain for w

b. The roast weighs less than six pounds. Write this as an inequality using w.

c. Graph the solution set to part b.

Solution

a. The roast can weigh a fraction of a pound, but not a negative number. The domain could be the set of positive real numbers.

b. $w < 6$, or $0 < w < 6$ (read "w is greater than 0 and less than 6.") Either is acceptable, since we know w is positive.

c.

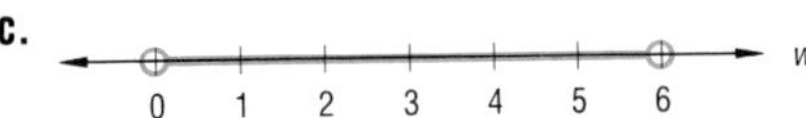

Example 3 Let t = temperature outside.

a. Give a reasonable domain for t.

b. It is colder than 6° outside. Write this as an inequality using t.

c. Graph the solution set to part b.

Solution

a. A temperature can be a fraction and it can be positive or negative. The domain is the set of real numbers.

b. $t < 6$

c.

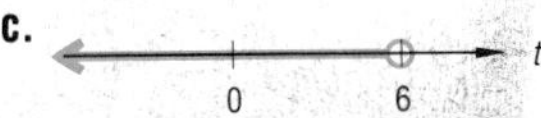

The situation determines whether you should use dots on its graph or whether you should indicate the numbers with a bar. Generally when a situation involves counting, the situation is called **discrete** and is graphed as dots. When a situation requires a measurement, like weight or time, it is called **continuous** and is graphed with a bar.

Sometimes, however, you may use a bar to describe discrete data. "From 34,000,000 to 40,000,000 people are expected to watch the next World Series game on TV" is a situation involving a discrete number of people. To graph the 6,000,001 dots (including endpoints) representing discrete people is time-consuming and the graph looks continuous anyway. Therefore the graph to describe this situation is a bar.

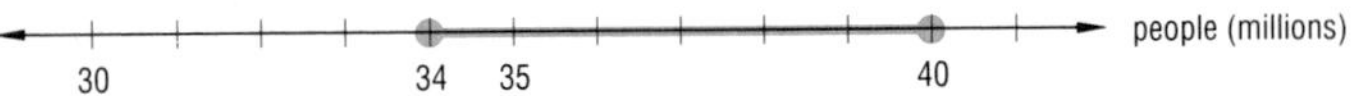

32

When a set S is discrete, you may want to know the number of elements in it. The symbol **N(*S*)** stands for the number of elements in S. N({3, 6, 12, 24}) = 4 because the set has 4 elements.

There is a set which has no elements in it. It is called the **empty set** or **null set.** The symbol { } can be used to refer to this set. The Danish letter ø is also used. The set ø might refer to

the set of points of intersection of two parallel lines,
the set of U.S. Presidents under 35 years of age,
the set of all the living dinosaurs,
the solution set of $x + 2 = x + 4$,

or many other things. N({ }) = N(ø) = 0

Questions

Covering the Reading

1. The objects in a set are called __?__. **elements**

In 2–5, a set and an element are given. **a.** State whether the set is discrete or continuous. **b.** Name another element in the set.

2. set: baseball team element: pitcher **a) discrete; b) sample: catcher**
3. set: family element: mother **a) discrete; b) sample: sister**
4. set: {2, 11, -6} element: -6 **a) discrete; b) 2 or 11**
5. set of real numbers element: 2 **a) continuous; b) See margin.**

6. Which of the following sets are equal? **A and C**
$A = \{0, 2, -5\}$ $B = \{2, -5\}$ $C = \{-5, 0, 2\}$

In 7–9, tell whether the number is an element of W, I, or R. (It is possible that a number belongs to more than one of these sets.)

7. -10 **I or R**
8. $\frac{6}{2}$ **W, I, or R**
9. 0.5 **R**

In 10–12, let S be the solution set for the sentence. **a.** Give the solution set. **b.** Find N(S).

10. $-5m = 25$ where the domain is R. **a) {-5}; b) 1**
11. $-3 < y < 3$ where the domain is W. **a) {0, 1, 2}; b) 3**
12. $-3 < y < 3$ where the domain is I. **a) {-1, -2, 0, 1, 2}; b) 5**

13. State the Density Property of Real Numbers. **See margin.**

Question 29: Problems similar to this have been asked before, but now the wording is more succinct because we have the term *domain.*

Alternate Approach for Question 30: Here are three ways to solve this problem.

Solution 1:
Find the mean of $\frac{3}{10}$ and $\frac{1}{3}$.

$\frac{1}{2}\left(\frac{3}{10} + \frac{1}{3}\right) = \frac{1}{2}\left(\frac{9}{30} + \frac{10}{30}\right)$
$= \frac{1}{2}\left(\frac{19}{30}\right) = \frac{19}{60}$

Then find the mean of $\frac{19}{60}$ and one of the given numbers.

Solution 2:
Write with the same denominator.
$\frac{3}{10} = \frac{9}{30}$ and $\frac{1}{3} = \frac{10}{30}$.

A number between them is $\frac{9.5}{30} = \frac{95}{300}$ or $\frac{19}{60}$.
Another is $\frac{9.6}{30} = \frac{96}{300}$ or $\frac{8}{25}$.

Solution 3:
Convert to decimals.
$\frac{3}{10} = .30$ and $\frac{1}{3} = .3\overline{3}$.
Some numbers between them are .31, .32, and .33.

Perhaps your students will come up with even more methods.

ADDITIONAL ANSWERS
5b. sample: any real number except 2
13. Between any two real numbers are many other real numbers.

NOTES ON QUESTIONS

Question 34: Students may be surprised that the range in this question is the same if the interval is closed as if it is open. This would not be the case if the set was discrete.

Question 36: Students will need an extensive dictionary for some parts of this question.

17c. the set of real numbers from 0 to 6194 (closed interval),

18c. the set of all real numbers from 12 to 15,

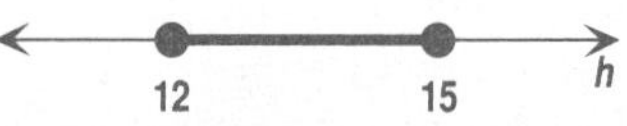

19b. sample: the set of all orange elephants

25.

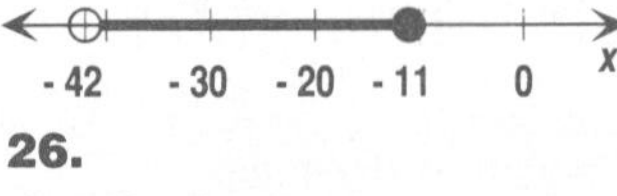

26.

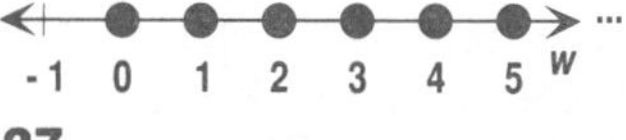

27.

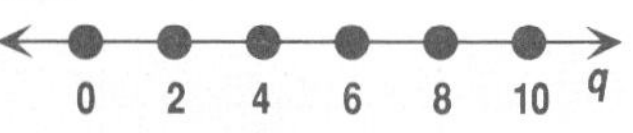

37. samples: society, citizen; chess set, rook; natural elements, hydrogen

In 14–16, write a real number that is between the two given numbers.

14. 3.4 and 3.5 sample: 3.45
15. a, b sample: $\frac{a+b}{2}$
16. -45 and -45.1 sample: -45.05

17. Let E = elevation of land in Alaska. b) $0 \le E \le 6194$
a. Give a reasonable domain for E. the set of real numbers
b. Elevations in Alaska range from sea level to 6194 meters (Mt. McKinley). Write this as an algebraic sentence involving E.
c. Write and graph the solution set to part b. See margin.

18. Let h = height of a dinosaur. b) $12 \le h \le 15$
a. Give a reasonable domain for h. the set of real numbers
b. Heights of adult *Tyrannosaurus rex* skeletons range from about 12 m to 15 m. Write this as an algebraic sentence involving h.
c. Write and graph the solution set to part b. See margin.

19. **a.** What does ø represent? the empty set (or null set)
b. Give a situation where ø might be used. See margin.

Applying the Mathematics

In 20–22, tell whether the set is discrete or continuous.

20. The police department will hire only people who are more than 63 inches tall. T is the set of acceptable heights. continuous

21. The Hubbard family has more than 5 children. C is the set of possible numbers of children. discrete

22. P is the set of prime numbers. discrete

In 23 and 24, use the following two sets.

$$C = \{-4, -2, 0, 2, 4\} \qquad D = \{2, 4, 6, 8\}$$

23. Which elements are in both sets C and D? {2, 4}

24. Which elements appear in set C or set D or both?
{-4, -2, 0, 2, 4, 6, 8}

In 25–27, graph the elements of the set on a number line.

25. solution set to $-42 < x \le -11$ where x is a real number
See margin.

26. {0, 1, 2, 3, 4, 5, ...} See margin.

27. the set of even whole numbers not greater than 10 See margin.

28. What is N(R) if $R = \{7, 8, 9, \dots, 18\}$? 12

29. Using {2, 5, 7, 9} as a domain, find the solution set of $4a + 1 > 20$. {5, 7, 9}

30. Give two real numbers that are between $\frac{3}{10}$ and $\frac{1}{3}$. sample: .31, .32

Review

31. Shoe size s and foot length F (in inches) for men are related by the formula $s = 3F - 24$. What is the shoe size of someone whose foot is $10\frac{1}{2}$ inches long? *(Lesson 1-5)* $7\frac{1}{2}$

32. *Multiple choice* Which expression summarizes the following directions? Begin with a number n. Find the product of n and 12.4. Subtract 11. Multiply the result by 6. *(Lesson 1-4)* (d)
(a) $n \cdot 12.4 - 11 \cdot 6$ (b) $n \cdot (12.4 - 11) \cdot 6$
(c) $(n \cdot 12.4) - (11 \cdot 6)$ (d) $(n \cdot 12.4 - 11) \cdot 6$

33. Insert parentheses around one of the subtractions so that the sentence is true. *(Lesson 1-4)*
$35 - 20 - 7 = 22$ $35 - (20 - 7) = 22$

34. Use this graph. *(Lesson 1-3)*

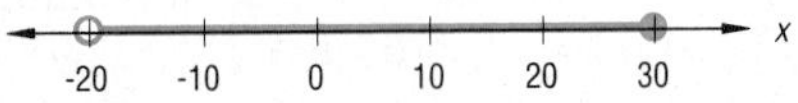

a. Copy and complete to describe the interval: __?__ $< x \le$ __?__. -20, 30
b. What is the range of the interval? 50

35. Evaluate in your head when $m = 3$. *(Lesson 1-4)*
a. $-2m$ -6 **b.** m^2 9
c. $2 + 2m$ 8 **d.** $m + -12$ -9

Exploration

36. Collections of animals frequently are given special names. Match the group name with the correct animal as in "school of fish."

Group name	Animal
cloud	ants
colony	bees
exaltation	crows
gaggle	fish
hive	foxes
leap	geese
mob	gnats
murder	kangaroos
pride	larks
nest	leopards
school	lions
skulk	nightingales
watch	oxen
yoke	vipers

DENNIS THE MENACE

"THIS WEEK WE'RE STUDYING REAL DEEP STUFF, LIKE: A BUNCH OF SHEEP IS A FLOCK... AND A FLOCK OF FLOWERS IS A BUNCH."

37. Name three sets outside of mathematics that are not mentioned in this lesson. For each, indicate what an element is usually called.
See margin.

FOLLOW-UP

MORE PRACTICE
For more questions on SPUR Objectives, use *Lesson Master 1-6,* shown below.

EXTENSION
Here is a famous puzzle that involves counting: A book is printed with 479 pages. How many *digits* are used to number the pages from 1 to 479? (1329) Explore this further: Let $d(n)$ be the number of digits needed to number the pages of an n-page book. The above question asks for $d(479)$. Is there any value of n for which $d(n) = 100$? (No, it takes an odd number of digits to number the first 9 pages and then an even number of digits for any of the next 90. Therefore, for $10 \le n \le 99$, $d(n)$ is an *odd* number from 11 to 189. For example, $d(54) = 99$ and $d(55) = 101$.)

NAME ____________

LESSON **MASTER 1–6**
QUESTIONS ON **SPUR** OBJECTIVES

■PROPERTIES *Objective E (See pages 50–53 for objectives.)*
In 1–3, use the set {3, 1.2, -4, 0, $\sqrt{3}$}.

1. Which elements are whole numbers? 3 and 0
2. Which elements are integers? 3, -4, and 0
3. Which elements are real numbers? 3, 1.2, -4, 0, and $\sqrt{3}$

In 4–6, let S be the solution set. Find N(S).

4. $4 < x \le 8$ where the domain is W, the set of whole numbers. 4
5. $n^2 = 4$ where the domain is I. 2
6. $x + 2 = 5$ where the domain is R. 1
7. If S = the set of states of the U.S. and R = the set of U.S. Senators, compare N(S) and N(R).
N(R) = 2N(S) or N(R) > N(S)
8. *True or false* The set of living dinosaurs = ø. true

■USES *Objective G*
In 9–12, a set is given. State whether the set is discrete or continuous and give a sample element of the set.

9. the set of tonight's TV programs discrete; M*A*S*H
10. the set of distances from school continuous; $\frac{1}{3}$ mile
11. the set of all integers discrete; 1
12. the set of fractions between 0 and 1 continuous; $\frac{1}{2}$

In 13–15, choose a domain for the variable from these:
real numbers whole numbers positive real numbers integers

13. n, the number of cars in a parking lot. whole numbers
14. t, the time it takes to walk to school. positive real numbers
15. m, the number of months the rainfall in Seattle was greater than 1 inch. whole numbers

 7

LESSON 1-7

RESOURCES
- ■ Lesson Master 1-7
- Visual for Teaching Aid 5: Possible Outcomes When 2 Dice Are Tossed
- Computer Master 2

OBJECTIVE

The letter code refers to the SPUR Objectives on pages 50–53.

F Find and interpret the probability of an event when outcomes are assumed to occur randomly.

TEACHING NOTES

Example 2 shows the important technique of listing all the outcomes and identifying the ones that are successes.

Emphasize that probability does not tell you what *will* occur, but rather, what *is likely* to occur.

Probabilities can be expressed as fractions, decimals, or percents. It is reasonable to accept answers in any one of these forms. Students should be guided by the type of information given in a problem.

In many cases, fractions are the most appropriate way of writing and computing with probabilities. In some probability problems, however, fractions in lowest terms are not best. For instance, when rolling two dice, is it more likely that the sum is 5 or 6? Comparing 1/9 and 5/36 is more difficult than comparing 4/36 and 5/36.

LESSON

1-7 Probability

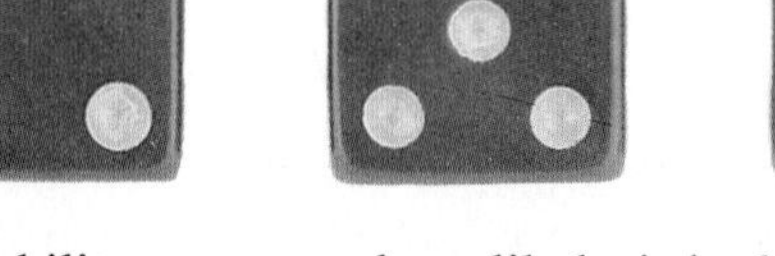

Probability measures how likely it is that something could happen. Suppose you toss an ordinary die once. There are six different faces which could show on the top of the die.

The result of tossing a die is called an **outcome.** There are six different outcomes: 1, 2, 3, 4, 5, 6. If each outcome is assumed to occur as often as any other outcome, the outcomes are called **equally likely** or **random.** Thus, the probability of tossing 4 is $\frac{1}{6}$, since 4 is one out of the six outcomes.

Example 1 Hurricanes happen often enough in Florida that public officials must have evacuation plans ready. These plans must take into account whether people are likely to be at home, work, or school. If a hurricane hits, what is the probability that it occurs on Sunday when there are the fewest people in schools and offices?

Solution Sunday is one out of the seven days of the week. If a hurricane occurs, the probability that it hits on Sunday is $\frac{1}{7}$.

Finding probabilities is often a matter of counting. Suppose you draw one card from an ordinary deck of 52 playing cards. What is the probability that it is a 5? In the situation "selecting a card from a deck" there are 52 equally-likely outcomes. Of these, "picking a 5" is not a single outcome, but a set of 4 different outcomes:

5♣ (5 of clubs)
5♦ (5 of diamonds)
5♥ (5 of hearts)
5♠ (5 of spades)

Since there are four ways to draw a 5 out of a possible 52 ways to choose a card from the deck, the probability of "picking a 5 from a deck of cards" is $\frac{4}{52}$. Here "choosing a 5" is called a *success*. "Not choosing a 5" is called a *failure*. To compute the **probability of a success**, you divide the number of outcomes that are successes by the total number of outcomes.

Definition:

Suppose a situation has T possible equally-likely outcomes of which S are successes. Then the probability of a success is $\frac{S}{T}$.

An **event** is a set of outcomes. Tossing a coin once has two possible outcomes, heads or tails. Many probabilities can be calculated simply by counting both the number of outcomes in the event and the number of all possible outcomes.

Example 2 A number is selected randomly from {1, 2, 3, 4, 5, 6, 7, 8, 9}. What is the probability that the number is prime?

Solution Remember that a prime number is a whole number greater than 1 that is divisible only by 1 and itself.

1 (2) (3) 4 (5) 6 (7) 8 9

The four ways to select a prime number are circled. The total number of outcomes is 9. Since the number is selected randomly, the probability that it is a prime is $\frac{4}{9}$.

When all outcomes of a situation like "tossing a die" have the same probability, the die is said to be *fair* or *unbiased*. In this lesson, dice, coins, and cards are assumed to be fair.

Example 3 When you roll a die, what is the probability that you will get

a. an even number?
b. a 7?
c. a number less than 7?

Solution The list of possible, equally-likely outcomes is 1, 2, 3, 4, 5, 6.

a. Three of the numbers, 2, 4, and 6 are even. The probability of tossing an even number is $\frac{3}{6}$, or $\frac{1}{2}$.
b. 7 is not a possible outcome. The number of successes is 0. The probability of tossing a 7 is $\frac{0}{6}$, or 0.
c. There are six successes: 1, 2, 3, 4, 5, 6. So the probability is $\frac{6}{6}$, or 1.

Notice in Example 3 that the event in part b is impossible and its probability is zero. This is the smallest number that a probability can be. The largest probability possible is 1. This happens in cases like part c that always happen. If P is a probability, then $0 \leq P \leq 1$.

The reading on page 36 assumes a knowledge of playing cards. In general, students are not as familiar with playing cards as are adults, so it may be necessary to discuss the size of a deck and the names of the cards. Some later questions in the chapter involve playing cards.

The dice array in **Example 4** may need to be explained. Understanding the set of all outcomes (called a *sample space*) makes solving dice problems much easier. You may want to make a table in class showing the probability of each of the sums that is possible on a single roll of two dice.

Sum	Probability
2	1/36
3	2/36
4	3/36
5	4/36
6	5/36
7	6/36
8	5/36
9	4/36
10	3/36
11	2/36
12	1/36

Making Connections
Students enjoy doing experiments in which they toss coins, roll dice, or draw cards. You can have them calculate the (theoretical) probabilities, then do experiments to calculate relative frequencies (to be discussed in Lesson 1-8). Each relative frequency can then be compared to the probability of that outcome. Explain that, in theory, if the trials for the outcome are indeed randomly generated, then the more times the experiment is carried out, the closer the relative frequency should be to the theoretical probability.

ADDITIONAL EXAMPLES

1. Sam replaces a burned-out light bulb. He has 8 replacement bulbs, but one of them is defective. If each bulb is equally likely to be chosen and Sam selects one, what is the probability that he picks one that works?
$\frac{7}{8}$

2. If a number is picked randomly from {11, 12, 13, 14, 15, 16, 17}, what is the probability that it is divisible by 3?
$\frac{2}{7}$

3. Suppose you have a 12-sided fair die, with the sides numbered from 1 to 12. When you roll the die once, what is the probability that you get

a. an even number?
$\frac{1}{2}$

b. a 7?
$\frac{1}{12}$

c. a number less than 7?
$\frac{1}{2}$

4. If two fair 6-sided dice are rolled once, what is the probability that the sum is greater than 10?
$\frac{1}{12}$

NOTES ON QUESTIONS
Encourage students to begin work on a probability question by listing all possible outcomes and identifying the successes.

Questions 9a and 9b: These bring out the idea of complementary events. Students should *discover* that they could find the answer to **Question 9b** by subtracting the answer to **Question 9a** from 1.

Questions 10-12: Here, students should use the diagram for **Example 4.**

Outcomes are not always equally likely. Consider the probability that you will find $1,000,000 on your way home today. There are two outcomes: finding the money and not finding it. This suggests that the probability of each is $\frac{1}{2}$. But "finding $1,000,000 today" and "not finding $1,000,000 today" are not equally-likely outcomes. The probability of finding the money is near zero; the probability of not finding it is near 1. You cannot use the probability formula $P = \frac{S}{T}$ in this situation.

Sometimes whether or not events are equally likely depends on how you look at them. For example, in many games you add numbers that you roll on two dice. There are eleven possible sums: 2, 3, 4, 5, 6, 7, 8, 9, 10, 11, and 12. However, these are not equally likely. A sum of 12 occurs less frequently than a sum of 7 or 8. However, you can overcome this problem by considering all 36 possible pairs of numbers rather than the 11 possible sums. The possible pairs are equally likely.

Example 4 Suppose two fair dice are thrown once. What is the probability that the sum of the dots is 7?

Solution Each die has 6 sides. The 36 possible outcomes are shown in the array below.
The 36 possible outcomes are equally likely, so the formula $P = \frac{S}{T}$ can be used. Here $T = 36$. The outcomes that give a sum of 7 are circled. There are six successes, so $S = 6$.

$$P = \frac{S}{T} = \frac{6}{36}$$
$$= \frac{1}{6}$$

38

Questions

Covering the Reading

1. For a situation with 400 outcomes occurring randomly, what is the probability of a single outcome? $\frac{1}{400}$

2. If a hurricane strikes, what is the probability that it hits on a weekday? $\frac{5}{7}$

3. If *T* outcomes are equally likely, and S are successes, what is the probability of a success? $\frac{S}{T}$

In 4 and 5, a single die is tossed once. Find each of the following:

4. the probability of tossing a 5 $\frac{1}{6}$

5. the probability that the die shows a number less than 3 $\frac{2}{6} = \frac{1}{3}$

6. Carlotta mails an entry to a magazine sweepstakes. She says: "The probability of winning is $\frac{1}{2}$, since either I will win or I won't." What is wrong with this argument? **See margin.**

In 7 and 8, a card is drawn from a deck of 52 playing cards. Find the probability of the event.

7. selecting the 7 of clubs $\frac{1}{52}$

8. selecting a queen $\frac{4}{52} = \frac{1}{13}$

9. A number is drawn randomly from the set {1, 2, 3, 4, 5}. What is probability that the number is
a. an even number? $\frac{2}{5}$
b. not an even number? $\frac{3}{5}$
c. a number less than 10? 1

10. A pair of dice is tossed once.
a. Show all the successful outcomes of getting a sum of 9. **See margin.**
b. Find the probability of getting a 9. $\frac{4}{36} = \frac{1}{9}$

Applying the Mathematics

In 11 and 12, a pair of dice is tossed once. For each event, **a.** list the set of successful outcomes; **b.** find the probability.

11. a sum greater than 9 **a) See margin; b)** $\frac{6}{36} = \frac{1}{6}$

12. a sum which is not greater than 3 **a) See margin; b)** $\frac{3}{36} = \frac{1}{12}$

13. You are holding a raffle. You want the chances of winning to be 1 in 10. If 80 people enter the raffle, how many prizes do you need? **8 prizes**

14. If a coin is flipped once, what is the probability that it lands on heads? $\frac{1}{2}$

Questions 14-16: These progress through the flipping of one, two, and three coins. You can extend the questions to more coins. Questions like these will arise frequently; students should learn how to list the outcomes in an ordered way (such as in alphabetical order).

Question 24: This can be solved by *estimation* and the following procedure: \$24.89 ≈ 25.00; 10% of \$25.00 is \$2.50; 5% of \$25.00 is half of that, or \$1.25; 15% is 10% + 5%, so the tip should be \$2.50 + \$1.25 = \$3.75.

Question 25: A common use of half-open intervals is illustrated here.

Making Connections for Question 29: This reviews a skill that we assume students have learned. Encourage students to solve this type of problem not with proportions, but by realizing that a percent is a ratio.

$$\frac{\text{240 students in music}}{\text{1600 students in school}} = .15 = 15\%.$$

Note that .15 and 15% stand for the ratio 15/100. This helps set up the idea of relative frequency in Lesson 1-8.

ADDITIONAL ANSWERS
6. Her entry is only one out of all the (no doubt more than 2) entries.
10a. (3, 6), (6, 3), (4, 5), (5, 4)
11a. (4, 6), (6, 4), (5, 5), (5, 6), (6, 5), (6, 6)
12a. (1, 1), (1, 2), (2, 1)

FOLLOW-UP

MORE PRACTICE
For more questions on SPUR Objectives, use *Lesson Master 1-7,* shown on page 41.

EXTENSION
Computer Students can investigate the random number function in BASIC and how to use it to simulate random events. The following program will simulate rolling a die 12 times. Note that the program uses a FOR/NEXT loop, a programming technique that is introduced in Chapter 6.

```
10 PRINT "ON ROLL#",
   "YOU ROLLED"
20 FOR ROLLN=1 TO 12
30 LET D=RND(1)*6
   (D will be chosen so
   0 ≤ D < 6.)
40 LET SCORE=INT
   (D+1)
   (Lets SCORE = the
   greatest integer less than
   D + 1)
50 PRINT ROLLN,SCORE
60 NEXT ROLLN
70 END
```

A word of caution: Different computers have slightly different formats for using a random number generator. For example, some may require the additional program line

```
25 RANDOMIZE TIMER
```

This will reseed (restart) the random number generator each time the program is run.

Have students run the computer program 5 times to randomly "roll" a die sixty times. Then have them count the times each number appeared. Are the results what they would expect?

15. A dime and a nickel are tossed once. The four possible outcomes are in the array below. The outcome HT means that the nickel came up heads and the dime came up tails. If the coins are fair, find:
a. the probability that both coins show heads. $\frac{1}{4}$
b. the probability that one coin shows a head and one shows a tail. $\frac{2}{4} = \frac{1}{2}$

		dime H	dime T
nickel	H	HH	HT
nickel	T	TH	TT

16. A dime, a nickel, and a penny are tossed once.
a. Write the eight possible outcomes. See margin.
b. If the coins are fair, find the probability that all three coins are heads. $\frac{1}{8}$
c. If the coins are fair, find the probability that only one coin shows heads. $\frac{3}{8}$

17. Tell why each of the following cannot represent a probability. See margin.
a. $\frac{50}{40}$ **b.** $\frac{7}{-14}$ **c.** 2

18. Bo T. Fell, one of the world's greatest algebra teachers, teaches only 3 of the 12 algebra classes at his school. If you were at his school and students were assigned randomly to classes, what is the probability you would not get Mr. Fell? $\frac{9}{12} = \frac{3}{4}$

19. If a letter is picked randomly from the alphabet, what is the probability it is between I and U (not including them)? $\frac{11}{26}$

Review

20. a. Write an inequality to describe this graph. *(Lesson 1-6)*
$y \geq -3$ or $y > -4$

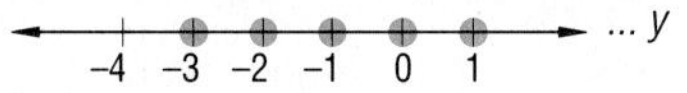

b. What is the domain? set of integers

21. The domain for g is {-3, 0, 5}. For each element of the domain, evaluate $10g^2$. *(Lesson 1-4, 1-6)* $10 \cdot (-3)^2 = 90$; $10 \cdot 0^2 = 0$; $10 \cdot 5^2 = 250$

22. a. Using I as a domain, graph $y > -1$ on one number line, and $y < 7$ on another. See margin.
b. What values appear on both graphs? *(Lessons 1-1, 1-6)*
{0, 1, 2, 3, 4, 5, 6}

23. Give a real number that is between x and y. *(Lesson 1-6)* sample: $\frac{x + y}{2}$

24. Often 15% of a restaurant bill is left for a tip. If a bill was $24.89, then what would be the tip? *(Previous course)* about $3.73

25. *Multiple choice* A theater has the following prices:

Infants (under 3)	-	free
Children (under 12)	-	\$2.50
Adults	-	\$5.00

Which graph shows the ages of people who will pay \$2.50? *(Lesson 1-3)*

(a)

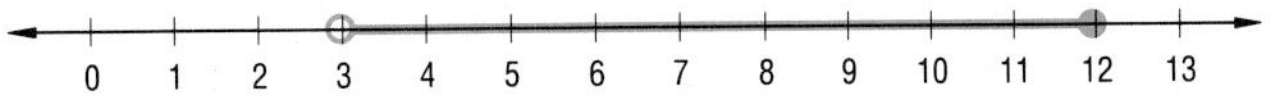

(b)

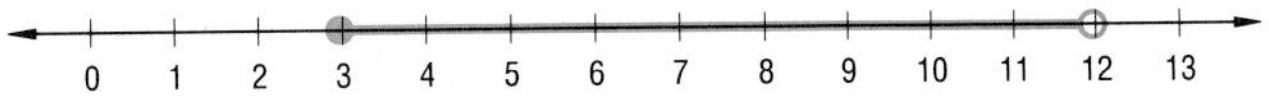

(c)

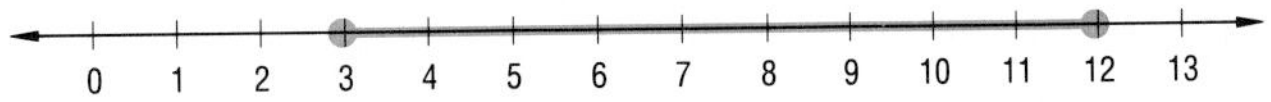

b

26. A certain pitcher has gotten a hit 20% of her times at bat. If the pitcher has batted 80 times, how many hits does she have? *(Previous course)* 16 hits

27. Compute in your head, given that $34 \cdot 651 = 22{,}134$. *(Previous course)*
a. $.01 \cdot 34 \cdot 651$ **b.** $.001 \cdot 34 \cdot 651$ **c.** $.0001 \cdot 34 \cdot 651$
a) 221.34; b) 22.134; c) 2.2134

28. Round 14.57052 to: **a.** the nearest tenth; **b.** the nearest hundredth; **c.** the nearest thousandth. *(Previous course)* a) 14.6; b) 14.57; c) 14.571

29. At Lowe High School, 240 students are in a musical group. If there are 1600 students in the school, what percent of the students are in a musical group? *(Previous course)* 15%

Exploration

30. When outcomes are not equally likely, the situation is called *biased*. Biased coins are sometimes called "weighted" or "two-headed." What are some names for **a.** a biased pair of dice; **b.** a biased deck of cards? a) sample: loaded; b) sample: stacked

16a. TTT, TTH, THT, THH, HTT, HTH, HHT, HHH
17a. You cannot have more successes than possible outcomes.
17b. You cannot have a negative number of outcomes.
17c. The largest probability possible is 1, when all possible outcomes are successes.
22a.

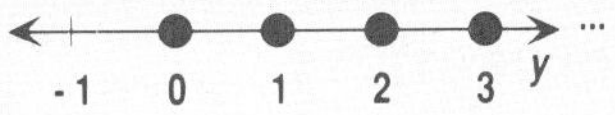

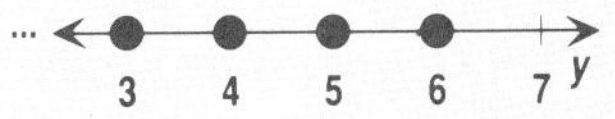

NAME ______

LESSON **MASTER 1–7**
QUESTIONS ON **SPUR** OBJECTIVES

■**PROPERTIES** *Objective F (See pages 50–53 for objectives.)*

1. A number is selected randomly from the set of integers between 1 and 50 inclusive. What is the probability that it is divisible by 7? $\frac{7}{50}$

2. Marie is in a class of 30 students. Five are to be picked at random for a committee. What is the probability that she will be picked? $\frac{1}{6}$

3. A hexagonal pencil (six faces) has printing on one face. When it is rolled, what is the probability that the printed face will not come up? $\frac{5}{6}$

4. In a "Pick Three" lottery you pick any three digits. If they come up in the same order as you picked them, you win. If you picked 587, what is the probability you will win? $\frac{1}{1000}$

5. Two fair dice are thrown. Find the probability of each of the following.
   a. Sum is 8. $\frac{5}{36}$
   b. Sum is not 2 or 12. $\frac{17}{18}$
   c. Sum is greater than 7. $\frac{5}{12}$

6. Jack is in a race with three other boys with about his speed. He says, "Either I will win or I won't. So the probability I will win is $\frac{1}{2}$." What is wrong with his argument?
Winning and losing are not equally likely.

7. A card is picked randomly from a standard deck of 52 playing cards. What is the probability that it is a heart? $\frac{1}{4}$

8. If an event has the probability of .75 of happening, what is the probability that it won't happen? .25

9. Which is more likely to happen: throwing a 2 with a die, or throwing a head with a fair coin? throwing a head

10. A letter is picked at random from the letters in the word *Mississippi*. What is the probability that it is an *s*? $\frac{4}{11}$

LESSON 1-8

RESOURCES
- Lesson Master 1-8
- Visual for Teaching Aid 6: Relative Frequency and Probability
- Computer Master 2

OBJECTIVES

Letter codes refer to the SPUR Objectives on pages 50–53.

A Operate with fractions.
J Use relative frequency to determine information about surveys.

TEACHING NOTES

Students may be puzzled by the instruction "estimate a probability." This means to use an experiment to determine a relative frequency and then use that value as an approximation for the probability. If students are still confused with relative frequency and probability after studying the examples, have them study the chart at the end of the lesson. It not only helps in making the distinction between relative frequency and probability, but points out important properties of each.

LESSON

1-8

Relative Frequency and the Equal Fractions Property

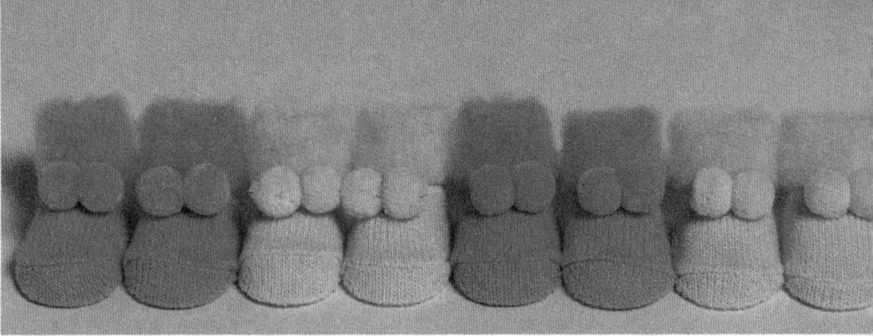

A **relative frequency** can be used to estimate how likely it is that a certain thing will happen. Consider the following question. How likely is it that a newborn baby will be a boy? One way to approach this problem is to use available data. In the U.S. in 1980, of about 3,612,258 children born, 1,852,616 were boys. The relative frequency of boys to births is found by dividing the number of boys by the total number of births.

$$\text{relative frequency} = \frac{\text{number of boys born}}{\text{total number of births}}$$

$$= \frac{1{,}852{,}616}{3{,}612{,}258} \approx 0.513 \approx 51.3\%$$

The definition of relative frequency is similar to the definition of probability.

Relative frequency of an event:

$$\frac{\text{number of times the event occurred}}{\text{total number of possible occurrences}}$$

Relative frequencies are sometimes given as decimals. A batter who has made 24 hits out of 90 times at bat is reported to have a "batting average" of $\frac{24}{90} \approx .267$. Survey results are typically reported in percent form. If a survey of 2000 adults shows that 1142 own a car, then the relative frequency of car owners is $\frac{1142}{2000} = .571 \approx 57\%$.

Relative frequencies and probabilities are not the same. A relative frequency always results from an actual experiment or data. A probability is always calculated from assumptions or is just assigned. In the example at the beginning of this lesson, the assumption might be that $\frac{1}{2}$, or 50%, of newborns are boys, but a more accurate probability would be 51.3%. However, we often use actual experiments to estimate the probability of an event.

Example 1 Suppose that 1025 people responded to the question "In which month do you feel the happiest?" with the following results:

January	19	June	138	November	24
February	12	July	153	December	182
March	33	August	47	No Choice	136
April	71	September	61		
May	96	October	53		

Estimate the probability that a randomly selected person would choose December as his or her happiest month.

Solution Calculate the relative frequency of those who said that December was their favorite month.

$$\text{relative frequency} = \frac{182}{1025} \approx 0.178$$

So, an estimate for the probability that a randomly selected person would select December is 0.178, or about 18%.

Suppose you asked eight friends the question, "Which do you prefer, chicken or hamburgers?" If two of your friends said "chicken," then the relative frequency of "chicken" answers is $\frac{2}{8} = .25 = 25\%$. Now suppose a marketing company asked the same question of 1200 people. If 300 of these people said "chicken," the relative frequency of "chicken" answers would be $\frac{300}{1200}$. Their relative frequency is the same as yours, since $\frac{2}{8} = \frac{300}{1200}$.

But people would certainly have more faith in 300 out of 1200 than in 2 out of 8. We might assign a probability of 0.25 to liking chicken more than hamburgers.

You know $\frac{2}{8}$ and $\frac{300}{1200}$ are equal, because they equal the same decimal, 0.25. But also, one fraction can be converted to the other.

$$\frac{2}{8} = \frac{2 \cdot 150}{8 \cdot 150} = \frac{300}{1200}$$

You have often rewritten fractions in this way. This is an instance of a general pattern we call the **Equal Fractions Property.**

Equal Fractions Property:

If $k \neq 0$ and $b \neq 0$, $\frac{a}{b} = \frac{ak}{bk}$.

The Equal Fractions Property can be used to simplify fractions. Very often, it helps to think of it "backwards," as $\frac{ak}{bk} = \frac{a}{b}$.

Reading The Equal Fractions Property is the first property in this book to use variables in describing properties of numbers. Students need to read the property carefully and know why the restrictions on k and b are made. They should also see that the property is used in two directions, either to change

$$\frac{a}{b} \text{ into } \frac{ak}{bk}$$

(as in the first portion of **Example 4**) or vice versa (as in **Examples 2 and 3** and the last portion of **Example 4**). You might point out that when a property is referenced, as in **Example 2,** students should pause and notice how the example applies the property.

ADDITIONAL EXAMPLES

1. A survey was taken of 60 people, asking what was their favorite animal as a pet. The results are shown below.

dog	23
cat	11
fish	5
bird	3
other	6
none	12

What is the relative frequency of a person's favorite pet being a cat?
$\frac{11}{60} \approx .183 \approx 18\%$

2. Simplify $\frac{10x}{15xy}$.
$\frac{2}{3y}$

3. A commercial reports that 3 out of 10 people use Sparkleclean detergent. Give some possible numbers for the persons surveyed and those using Sparkleclean.
sample: Out of 1000, 300 use Sparkleclean; out of 110, 33 use Sparkleclean.

Example 2 Simplify $\frac{34}{51}$.

Solution Look for common factors. $\frac{34}{51} = \frac{2 \cdot 17}{3 \cdot 17}$

Apply the Equal Fractions Property. $= \frac{2}{3}$

The Equal Fractions Property can also be used to rewrite fractions involving variables. For instance, $\frac{2mx}{3my} = \frac{2x}{3y}$ and $\frac{5x}{6w} = \frac{5xy}{6wy}$.

Note: Here and elsewhere, when a fraction is written, we assume its denominator is not zero.

Example 3 Simplify $\frac{2rt}{12rs}$.

Solution Look for common factors. $\frac{2rt}{12rs} = \frac{2 \cdot r \cdot t}{6 \cdot 2 \cdot r \cdot s}$

$= \frac{t}{6s}$

The Equal Fractions Property can be used to help interpret information you encounter in the media.

Example 4 A newspaper reports that its telephone survey of households showed 40% favored building a sports stadium. Give some possibilities of the number of households surveyed and the number favoring a sports stadium.

Solution You must find pairs of reasonable numbers. Each pair must form a ratio that is equal to 40%. 40% = .40 = $\frac{40}{100}$. So one possibility is that 40 favored the stadium out of 100 households surveyed.

The equal fractions property says that $\frac{40}{100} = \frac{40k}{100k}$ where $k \neq 0$.

One possibility is that $k = 6$.

Then $\frac{40}{100} = \frac{40 \cdot 6}{100 \cdot 6} = \frac{240}{600}$.

So another possibility is that 600 households were surveyed and 240 favored the sports stadium.

It is also possible that fewer than 100 households were surveyed.

$\frac{40}{100} = \frac{2 \cdot 20}{5 \cdot 20} = \frac{2}{5}$

Perhaps only 5 were surveyed, and 2 favored the stadium.

The table below summarizes some important similarities and differences between relative frequency and probability.

	Relative Frequency	Probability
1.	Between 0 and 1, inclusive	Between 0 and 1, inclusive.
2.	A relative frequency of 0 means that an event did not occur.	A probability of 0 indicates that an event is impossible.
3.	A relative frequency of 1 means that an event occurred every time.	A probability of 1 indicates that an event must happen.
4.	The more often an event occurred relative to the possible number of occurrences, the closer its relative frequency is to 1.	The more likely an event is, the closer its probability is to 1.

Questions

Covering the Reading

1. In 1970, of 3,791,258 children born in the U.S., 1,915,378 were boys. about .505
   a. What was the relative frequency of boys to births in 1970?
   b. Using this information, estimate the probability of a male birth in 1970. (Give your answer as a percent.) 50.5%
   c. How does this estimate compare to the estimate calculated with the data from 1980? It's smaller.
   d. Estimate the probability of a female birth in 1970. 49.5%

2. Relative frequencies are often used to __?__ probabilities that certain events will happen. estimate

In 3 and 4, use the data of Example 1. Give the relative frequency for a person responding:

3. October is his or her happiest month. (Write as a decimal and as a percent.) ≈.052 or 5.2%

4. Her or his happiest month begins in winter (January, February, or March). ≈.062 or 6.2%

5. State the Equal Fractions Property. If $k \neq 0$ and $b \neq 0$, then $\frac{a}{b} = \frac{ak}{bk}$.

6. In the fraction $\frac{x}{y}$, what value can y not have? 0

7. Simplify:
   a. $\frac{25}{85}$ $\frac{5}{17}$
   b. $\frac{42x}{420x}$ $\frac{1}{10}$
   c. $\frac{36}{9y}$ $\frac{4}{y}$

8. **a.** Simplify $\frac{2xy}{3ay}$. $\frac{2x}{3a}$ **b.** Rewrite $\frac{2x}{3a}$ with a denominator of $3ya$. $\frac{2yx}{3ya}$

NOTES ON QUESTIONS

Making Connections for Question 8b: This looks ahead to problems in which students will add algebraic fractions.

Questions 10 and 11: The distinction made here is an issue when using relative frequencies to approximate probabilities. For instance, prior to the *Challenger* explosion, no American had died in an actual space launch, but this did not mean that the probability of a fatality was zero.

Question 21: The goal of this question is not to have students cross-multiply but to have them realize that the numerator of $\frac{6y}{27}$ must be 18, making $y = 3$.

Question 22: This relates to the fact that in general,

$$\frac{a}{b} \neq \frac{a+x}{b+x}.$$

You could challenge your students to find examples in which the pattern in the problem works.

$\left(\frac{a}{b} = \frac{a+x}{b+x}\right.$ implies that $\left. a = b \text{ or } x = 0.\right)$

Making Connections for Question 23: Here, a Venn diagram is presented to illustrate sets. Venn diagrams will be used again in Chapters 3 and 4. It is important for students to realize that "girls who play softball" includes two categories: girls who play only softball and girls who play both softball and basketball.

NOTES ON QUESTIONS
Question 24: This introduces the P( ) notation to describe probability. Because it saves students from having to write out some words, they will probably like the notation. Of course, this is a foundation for function notation.

Question 26: Students are expected to answer this question by doing the computation

$$\frac{1}{5} \cdot \frac{9}{10} = \frac{9}{50}.$$

The solution can be checked by choosing a convenient number for the size of the student body, say 100. Then

$$\frac{1}{5} \cdot 100 = 20.$$

So, 20 students do not go to the dance. Since

$$\frac{9}{10} \cdot 20 = 18,$$

18 students have to work. The solution checks since

$$\frac{18}{100} = \frac{9}{50}.$$

Questions 30-32: We expect students to know and use the decimal forms of the common fractions $\frac{1}{2}$, $\frac{3}{4}$, and $\frac{4}{5}$.

Question 31: This can be done by division. $\frac{7}{2} > 3$ and $\frac{7}{3} < 3$ so $\frac{7}{2} > \frac{7}{3}$.

ADDITIONAL ANSWERS
14. sample: 2 out of 8, 3 out of 12, 100 out of 400
28. $7.2 \cdot 10^{15}$, $6.5 \cdot 10^{14}$, $9.4 \cdot 10^{13}$

9. In a survey of a neighborhood, 60% of those surveyed expressed a need for greater police protection.
  a. If 100 were surveyed, how many said they needed more police protection? **60 people**
  b. If 500 people were surveyed, how many said they needed more police protection? **300 people**
  c. If 5 people were surveyed, how many said they needed more police protection? **3 people**

10. If the probability of an event is 1, what do you know about that event? **It must happen.**

11. If the relative frequency of an event is 0, is the event impossible? **No, the event did not occur.**

Applying the Mathematics

Multiple choice In 12 and 13, find the relative frequency not equal to the other three.

12. (a) $\frac{9}{11}$ (b) $\frac{99}{121}$ (c) $\frac{90}{100}$ (d) $\frac{450}{550}$ **(c)**

13. (a) $\frac{100}{260}$ (b) $\frac{35}{91}$ (c) $\frac{38}{100}$ (d) $\frac{500}{1300}$ **(c)**

14. According to a survey in 1981, one out of four teenagers who worked earned more than \$200 a month. Use the Equal Fractions Property to write three possibilities for the total number of teenagers surveyed and the number who earned more than \$200. **See margin.**

15. Event X has a probability of $\frac{3}{4}$. Event Y has a probability of $\frac{1}{2}$. Event Z has a probability of $\frac{2}{3}$.
  a. If you could find actual relative frequencies of these events, which event would you expect to have the largest relative frequency? **X**
  b. Event Y has the smallest probability. Must it have the smallest relative frequency? **No, but it probably would.**

In 16 and 17, consider the following. A tire company tests 50 tires to see how long they last under typical road conditions. The results they obtained are shown at the right.

Mileage until worn out	Number of tires
10,000–14,999	1
15,000–19,999	3
20,000–24,999	6
25,000–29,999	15
30,000–34,999	14
35,000–39,999	7
40,000 or more	4

16. What is the relative frequency of a tire lasting less than 25,000 miles? (Write as a fraction.) $\frac{10}{50} = \frac{1}{5}$

17. What is the relative frequency of a tire lasting at least 10,000 miles? **1**

18. Since about 51% of people born in the U.S. are male, why aren't 51% of all living people in the U.S. male?
Possible answer: women tend to live longer than men.

19. *Multiple choice* An event occurred c times out of t possibilities. The relative frequency of the event was 30%. Which is true? **(a)**
  (a) $\frac{c}{t} = 0.3$ (b) $\frac{t}{c} = 0.3$
  (c) $ct = 0.3$ (d) $t - c = 0.3$

20. *Multiple choice* Of the people surveyed, $\frac{4}{9}$ thought the American League team would win the World Series. If 36n people were surveyed, how many thought the American League team would win?
(a) $\frac{4}{9}$n (b) 4n (c) 9n (d) 16n **(d)**

21. What is y if $\frac{6y}{27} = \frac{2}{3}$? (Hint: $\frac{2}{3}$ is how many twenty-sevenths?) **3**

22. *True or false* When $x = 1$, then $\frac{4 + x}{2 + x} = \frac{2}{1}$. **False**

23. In a certain school, out of 50 girls surveyed,
5 girls played both basketball and softball;
12 girls played basketball but not softball;
15 girls played softball but not basketball.
What percentage of girls surveyed played softball?
40%

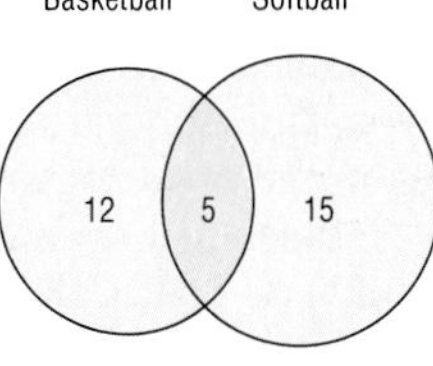

Review

24. Imagine tossing two fair dice once. Refer to Example 4 of Lesson 1-7 for a list of all possible outcomes. Find each of the following:
a. P(sum of 8), i.e., the probability of getting a sum of 8 **$\frac{5}{36}$**
b. P(sum not equal to 8) **$\frac{31}{36}$**
c. P(sum less than 13) *(Lesson 1-7)* **1**

25. A card is drawn randomly from a deck of 52 playing cards. Find each of the following:
a. P(7 of hearts) **$\frac{1}{52}$** b. P(a heart) **$\frac{13}{52} = \frac{1}{4}$** c. P(a king) *(Lesson 1-7)* **$\frac{4}{52} = \frac{1}{13}$**

26. One fifth of the students will not go to the dance. Of these, nine tenths have to work. What is the fraction of all the students who will not go to the dance because they have to work? *(Previous course)* **$\frac{9}{50}$**

27. *Skill sequence* What does each equal? *(Previous course)*
a. 3.95 from 12.8 **8.85**
b. 1.28 minus .395 **.885**
c. \$39.95 less \$1.52 **\$38.43**

28. Order from largest to smallest. *(Previous course, Appendix B)*
$6.5 \cdot 10^{14}$ $7.2 \cdot 10^{15}$ $9.4 \cdot 10^{13}$ **See margin.**

29. What is N(ø) + N({6, 7, 8,}) − N({2, 4})? *(Lesson 1-6)* **1**

In 30–32, determine in your head which is larger. *(Lesson 1-1)*

30. $2\frac{1}{2}$ or 2.45 **$2\frac{1}{2}$** 31. $\frac{7}{2}$ or $\frac{7}{3}$ **$\frac{7}{2}$** 32. $\frac{3}{4}$ or $\frac{4}{5}$ **$\frac{4}{5}$**

Exploration

Answers will vary.

33. In Example 4 of Lesson 1-7, two fair dice were thrown once. The probability of getting a sum of 7 was calculated to be $\frac{1}{6}$.
a. Try the corresponding experiment. Find a pair of dice and actually toss them 72 times. Record the results.
b. What relative frequency of getting a 7 do you get?
c. For any sums from 2 through 12, does any relative frequency you get match the corresponding probability?

FOLLOW-UP

MORE PRACTICE

For more questions on SPUR Objectives, use *Lesson Master 1-8,* shown below.

EXTENSION

To familiarize students with an almanac, you can ask them questions like:

1. What was the relative frequency that a new vehicle sold in a particular year was a passenger car? (In 1986, about 68.9%)

2. What is the relative frequency of English-speaking people on earth? (≈ 8.6%)

Small Group Work A list of such questions would make a good team activity. Students could write questions that are to be answered by other students.

NAME ______

LESSON **MASTER 1–8**
QUESTIONS ON **SPUR** OBJECTIVES

■**SKILLS** *Objective A (See pages 50–53 for objectives.)*
In 1–6, simplify using the Equal Fractions Property.

1. $\frac{42}{315}$ **$\frac{2}{15}$** 2. $\frac{4a}{9ab}$ **$\frac{4}{9b}$**
3. $\frac{4\pi r^2}{2\pi r}$ **$2r$** 4. $\frac{11abc}{44a}$ **$\frac{bc}{4}$**
5. $\frac{2(x + y)}{4(x + y)}$ **$\frac{1}{2}$** 6. $\frac{35rs^3}{21rs^2}$ **$\frac{5s}{3}$**

7. *True or false* By the Equal Fractions Property, $\frac{x + 3}{x + 6} = \frac{1}{2}$. **false**

8. What is x if $\frac{3x}{25} = \frac{24}{100}$? **2**

■**USES** *Objective J*

9. In a presidential preference poll, 52% preferred candidate A, 44% preferred candidate B, and 4% were undecided. Give two possibilities for the number of people polled, and how many were in each group.
samples: 100 people polled, 52 for A, 44 for B, 4 undecided; 200 people polled, 104 for A, 88 for B, 8 undecided.

10. In 1982 there were 26 physicians for every 100,000 people in India. If the population of India was 713 million, about how many physicians were there in India?
185,380

11. A 1982 Nielsen poll showed 50,150,000 American households out of 83,300,000 watched the final episode of M*A*S*H. What was the relative frequency of a household watching the program?
$\frac{50,150,000}{83,300,000} = \frac{59}{98}$, or about .6

12. An event occurs n times out of 100 possibilities. What is its relative frequency?
$\frac{n}{100}$

 9

SUMMARY

The Summary gives an overview of the entire chapter and provides an opportunity for students to consider the material as a whole. Thus, the Summary can be used to help students relate the concepts presented in the chapter.

VOCABULARY

Terms, symbols, and properties are listed by lesson to provide a checklist of things a student must know. Emphasize to students that they should read the vocabulary list carefully before starting the Progress Self-Test. If students do not understand the meaning of a term, they should refer back to the indicated lesson.

Definitions or descriptions of all terms in the vocabulary list may be found in the Glossary.

ADDITIONAL ANSWERS
8. ANSWER TO QUESTION
8
8.82
9.

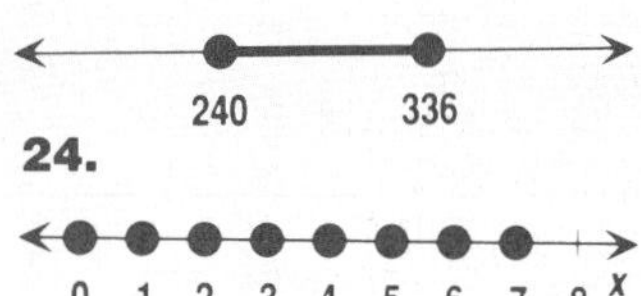

24.

0 1 2 3 4 5 6 7 8 x

Summary

Algebra is a language of numbers, operations, and variables. In this chapter, three important uses of variables are discussed. Variables describe number relationships, as in $k > 19.5$ or $-3 < g < 0$. Variables are a shorthand used in formulas like $A = \ell w$. And variables may represent unknowns, as in the open sentence $x + 5 = 8$.

Graphs help in understanding variables and numbers. Data can be pictured on a graph with a dot frequency diagram. Solutions to inequalities and intervals can be graphed on a number line.

Like any other language, algebra has its rules. Among these are the rules for order of operations: work in parentheses, then powers, then multiplications or divisions, then additions or subtractions. Scientific calculators and computers usually follow the same rules.

The language of sets helps with many ideas in this chapter. The domain of a variable is the set of values it may take. The solution set to a sentence is the set of values making that sentence true. An event is a set of outcomes.

Both relative frequencies and probabilities indicate the likelihood of an event. Relative frequencies are calculated from actual data. The relative frequency of an event E is the fraction of times E actually occurs out of the total number of possible occurrences. Probabilities are either taken from relative frequencies or calculated by assuming things about outcomes. If outcomes are assumed to occur randomly, the probability of an event E is the number of ways E can occur divided by the number of all possible outcomes.

Vocabulary

Below are the most important terms and phrases for this chapter. You should be able to give a general description and a specific example of each.

Lesson 1-1
variable
open sentence, solution
equation, inequality
$=, \neq, <, \leq, \approx, >, \geq$

Lesson 1-2
dot frequency diagram
statistics
mean, median, mode, central tendency

Lesson 1-3
interval, endpoints
open interval, closed interval
$\pm$, range, length of interval

Lesson 1-4
evaluating the expression
order of operations
numerical expression, algebraic expression
BASIC, PRINT, LET

Lesson 1-5
formula
domain, replacement set
INPUT

Lesson 1-6
set, element, {...}, equal sets
whole numbers, integers, real numbers
Density Property of Real Numbers
solution set, discrete, continuous
N(S)
empty set, null set, { }, ø

Lesson 1-7
outcome, equally likely or random
probability of a success
event

Lesson 1-8
relative frequency
Equal Fractions Property

Progress Self-Test

Take this test as you would take a test in class. Use a ruler and calculator. Then check your work with the solutions in the Selected Answers section in the back of the book.

In 1–3, evaluate each expression.

1. $2(a + 3b)$ when $a = 3$ and $b = 5$. **36**

2. $5 \cdot 6^n$ when $n = 4$. **6480**

3. $\dfrac{p + t^2}{p + t}$ when $p = 5$ and $t = 2$. $\frac{9}{7}$

4. Which is largest, $\frac{7}{12}$, $\frac{13}{22}$, or $\frac{3}{5}$? $\frac{3}{5}$

5. Simplify: $\dfrac{63abc}{28b}$. $\frac{9ac}{4}$ **6)** $\frac{50.7}{4} \approx 12.7$

6. The last four times Kevin ran the 100-meter dash his times were 13.1, 12.6, 12.7, and 12.3 seconds. Find the mean of his times.

7. Dennis earned \$6, \$4.50, \$10.00, \$5.00, \$5.00, and \$6 for six nights of babysitting. Find the median for these amounts. **\$5.50**

8. Here is a program to be run by a computer. What will be printed? **See margin.**

```
10 PRINT "ANSWER TO QUES. 8"
20 LET M = 6.3
30 LET N = 1.4
40 PRINT M * N
50 END
```

9. The Humbert family car goes from 240 to 336 miles on a tank of gas. Graph this interval on a horizontal number line. **See margin.**

10. A road has a 25 mph speed limit. A person is driving at S mph and is speeding. Express the possible values of S with an inequality. $S > 25$

In 11 and 12, W = the set of whole numbers, I = the set of integers, R = the set of real numbers, and P = the set of positive real numbers.

11. Which one of these sets is a reasonable domain for L, the length of an animal? **P; 12) I, R**

12. -5 is an element of which two of these sets?

13. A poll accurate to within 3% showed 67% of the registered voters planned to vote. What are the maximum and minimum percentages of voters planning to vote? **70%, 64%**

14. Which of the numbers 2, 5, and 8 makes the open sentence $4y + 7 = 2y + 23$ true? **8**

15. Give three values for x that make $3x < 24$ true. **sample: 0, 2, 4** **16) 85¢**

16. The formula $c = 20(n - 1) + 25$ gives the cost of first-class postage in 1988. In the formula, c is the cost in cents and n is the weight of the mail rounded up to the nearest ounce. What does it cost to mail a 3.2 ounce letter?

17. The area of a circle is given by the formula $A = \pi r^2$. To the nearest square meter, what is the area of a circle with radius 3 meters? (Use $\pi \approx 3.14159$.) $A = 3.14159(3)^2 \approx 28 \text{ m}^2$

In 18 and 19, a survey was done to determine the cost of granola bars. The prices (in cents per ounce) of 21 brands are shown on the dot frequency diagram below.

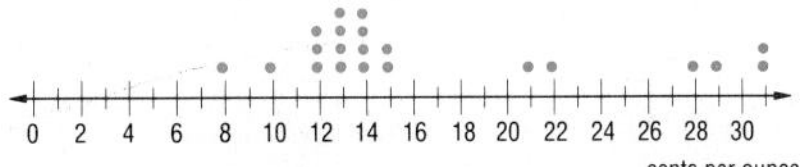

18. a. How many brands cost 12¢ per ounce? **3 brands**

b. How many brands cost 15¢ per ounce or more? **8 brands** **19)** $8 \le c \le 31$

19. Describe the range of costs using an inequality.

20. In 1981, a survey of 100,000 U.S. citizens showed 2284 born before 1901. What was the relative frequency of a 1981 U.S. citizen being born before 1901? $\frac{2284}{100{,}000}$ **or** $\approx .02$

21. There are 300 tickets in a raffle drawing for a 10-speed bike. If you buy 8 tickets, what is the probability you will win the bike? $\frac{8}{300}$ **or** $\frac{2}{75}$

22. A letter from the alphabet is chosen randomly. What is the probability it is a letter in the word CATS? $\frac{4}{26}$ **or** $\frac{2}{13}$

23. Alain is in the finals of a bowling tournament. He will face the winner of the match between Donna and Sarah. Alain has beaten Donna 6 games out of 9, while he has beaten Sarah 3 games out of 5. Which opponent is Alain more likely to beat? **Donna** **24) See margin.**

24. Let S be the solution set for $x < 8$ where the domain is W. Graph S on a number line.

25. If $G = \{-5, -4, -3, \ldots, 5\}$, what is N($G$)? **11**

PROGRESS SELF-TEST

For the development of mathematical competence, feedback and correction, along with the opportunity to practice, are necessary. The Progress Self-Test provides the opportunity for feedback and correction; the Chapter Review provides additional opportunities for practice.

We cannot overemphasize the importance of these end-of-chapter materials. It is at this point that the material "gels" for many students, allowing them to solidify skills and understanding. In general, student performance should be markedly improved after these pages.

USING THE PROGRESS SELF-TEST

Assign the Progress Self-Test as a one-night assignment. Worked-out *solutions* for all questions are in the Selected Answers section at the back of the student book. Encourage students to take the Progress Self-Test honestly, grade themselves, and then be prepared to discuss the test in class.

Advise students to pay special attention to those Chapter Review questions (pages 50–53) which correspond to questions missed on the Progress Self-Test. A chart provided in the Selected Answers section in the student text keys the Progress Self-Test questions to the lettered SPUR Objectives in the Chapter Review or to the Vocabulary. It also keys the questions to the corresponding lessons where the material is covered.

RESOURCES
- Chapter 1 Test, Form A
- Chapter 1 Test, Form B

CHAPTER REVIEW

The main objectives for the chapter are organized here into sections corresponding to the four main types of understanding this book promotes: Skills, Properties, Uses, and Representations.

Skills include simple and complicated procedures for getting answers; at higher levels they include the study of algorithms.

Properties cover the mathematical justifications for procedures and other theory; at higher levels they include proofs.

Uses include real-world applications of the mathematics; at higher levels they include modeling.

Representations include graphs and diagrams; at higher levels they include the invention of new objects or metaphors to discuss the mathematics.

Notice that the groupings are not in increasing order of difficulty—there may be hard skills and easy representations; some uses may be easier than anything else, and so on.

To the *lay person,* basic understanding of mathematics is generally found in Skills. The *mathematician* prefers to think of understanding in terms of Properties. The *engineer* often tests understanding by the ability to Use mathematics. The *psychologist* often views "true" understanding as being achieved through Representations or metaphors. The SPUR framework conveys the authors' belief that all

Chapter Review

Questions on SPUR Objectives

SPUR stands for **S**kills, **P**roperties, **U**ses, and **R**epresentations. The Chapter Review questions are grouped according to the SPUR Objectives for this chapter.

SKILLS deal with following a procedure to get an answer.

Objective A. *Operate with, and compare fractions. (Lessons 1-1, 1-8)* 1) $\frac{1}{6} > \frac{3}{20}$ or $\frac{3}{20} < \frac{1}{6}$

1. Write an inequality to compare $\frac{1}{6}$ and $\frac{3}{20}$.
2. Which is larger, $2\frac{3}{8}$ or $\frac{7}{3}$? $2\frac{3}{8}$
3. Which is larger, $\frac{3}{5}$ or $\frac{3}{4}$? $\frac{3}{4}$
4. Which is smaller, 1.7 or $1\frac{2}{3}$? $1\frac{2}{3}$

In 5–6, use the Equal Fractions Property to simplify fractions.

5. $\frac{11pq}{12mp}$ $\frac{11q}{12m}$
6. $\frac{49ab}{14b}$ $\frac{7a}{2}$

In 7 and 8, write as a single fraction.

7. $\frac{1}{5} + \frac{2}{3} - \frac{3}{4}$ $\frac{7}{60}$
8. $2\frac{1}{6} + 1\frac{1}{3}$ $3\frac{1}{2}$

Objective B. *Find solutions to open sentences using trial and error. (Lesson 1-1)*

9. Which of the numbers 3, 4, or 5 is a solution to $2x + 13 = 3x + 9$? 4
10. Using {1, 4, 7} as a domain, give the solution set of $7x - 13 < 2x$. {1}
11. Give three values for y that make $2y \geq 150$ true. sample: 75, 10^2, 387.2
12. Solve for z: $2 + z = 3$. $z = 1$

Objective C. *Evaluate numerical and algebraic expressions. (Lesson 1-4)*

13. Evaluate $-2p$ when $p = 3.5$. -7
14. Evaluate $4x^2$ when x = 1. 4
15. Evaluate $35 + 5 \cdot 2$. 45
16. *True or false* $2 - 3/5 + 6 = (2 - 3)/(5 + 6)$. False
17. Find the value of $4(p - q)$ when $p = 13.8$ and $q = 5.4$. 33.6 18) $\frac{7}{3}$
18. Evaluate $5(M - N)$ when $M = \frac{2}{3}$ and $N = \frac{1}{5}$.
19. Evaluate $2b^3$ when $b = 5$. 250
20. Evaluate $\left(\frac{n}{4}\right)^2$ when $n = 36$. 81

Objective D. *Give the output for or write short computer programs and statements that evaluate expressions. (Lessons 1-4, 1-5)*

In 21 and 22, what will the computer print if the statement is entered?

21. PRINT 8 * 3 − 28/2 10
22. PRINT -1 * (1.5 − 2.3) 0.8
23. If the program below is run, what will be printed after 2 is entered as input?

```
10 PRINT "ANSWER TO QUESTION 23"
20 PRINT "ENTER A NUMBER"
30 INPUT M
40 PRINT 3 + M/2 + M
50 END
```
See margin.

24. The area of a circle can be found by using the formula $A = \pi r^2$ where r is the radius of the circle and $\pi \approx 3.14159$.
    a. Write a computer program to find A given $r = 12.5$. (Hint: πr^2 is the same as $\pi \cdot r \cdot r$.) See margin.
    b. What is the area of a circle with radius 12.5 cm? $A = 3.14159(12.5)^2 = 490.9$ cm^2

PROPERTIES deal with the principles behind the mathematics.

Objective E. *Read and interpret set language and notation.* *(Lesson 1-6)*

25. Let B = the solution set to $-2 < n < 4$, where n is an integer.
    a. List the elements of B. -1, 0, 1, 2, 3
    b. What is N(B)? 5

26. Let $P = \{10, 20, 30, 40, 50\}$ and Q = the solution set to $x < 34$. Which elements are in both sets P and Q? 10, 20, 30

27. *True or false* $\frac{2}{1}$ is an element of the set of whole numbers. True 28) See margin.

28. a. What is ø called? b. What is N(ø)?

29. If S = the set of states in the USA, what is N(S)? 50

In 30 and 31, use these sets.
$A = \{-3, 0, 3, 6\}$ $B = \{6, 3, 0, -3\}$
$C = \{-3, 3, 6\}$ $D = \{-4, 0, 4, 8\}$

30. Which of the sets are equal? *A* and *B*

31. Find N(D) − N(C) + N(B). 5

Objective F. *Find and interpret the probability of an event when outcomes are assumed to occur randomly.* *(Lesson 1-7)*

32. A number is selected randomly from {2, 4, 6, 8, 10, 12}. What is the probability that the number is divisible by 5? $\frac{1}{6}$

33. A card is picked randomly from a standard deck of 52 playing cards. What is the probability that the card is a seven? $\frac{4}{52} = \frac{1}{13}$

34. Two fair dice are thrown once. What is the probability of a sum of 6? $\frac{5}{36}$

35. Event A has a probability of 0.3. Event B has a probability of $\frac{4}{9}$. Event C has a probability of 33%. Which event is
    a. most likely to happen? *B*
    b. least likely to happen? *A*

USES deal with applications of mathematics in real situations.

Objective G. *In real situations, choose a reasonable domain for a variable.* *(Lesson 1-6)*

In 36–39, choose a domain for the variable from these sets: See margin.

real numbers whole numbers
positive real numbers integers

Tell whether the domain is discrete or continuous.

36. d, the distance that a jogger runs

37. roast beef is being ordered for n people

38. P is the altitude of a point on the surface of the earth.

39. the weight w of a molecule

Objective H. *Calculate the mean, median, and mode for a set of data.* *(Lesson 1-2)*

In 40 and 41, use the following information. Nine kids were asked how much they paid for their jeans. They paid:
$22, $10.50, $14, $12, $12, $17, $38, $25 and $33.

40. Find the mean, median, and mode for these prices. $20.39, $17, $12

41. *True or false* The mode does not give an appropriate description of the amount the majority of kids paid. True

In 42 and 43, the ages of participants in an exercise class are 26, 49, 23, 52, 49, 23, 33, and 39.

42. Find the mean age of the participants. 36.75 years

43. *True or false* The median age is an integer. True

Objective I. *Evaluate formulas in real situations.* *(Lesson 1-5)*

44. The percent discount p on an item is given by the formula

$$p = 100\left(1 - \frac{n}{g}\right)$$

where g is the original price and n is the new price. Find the percent discount on a pair of jeans whose price is reduced from $20 to $15. 25%

these views have validity and that together they contribute to the deep understanding of mathematics we want students to have.

USING THE CHAPTER REVIEW

Whereas end-of-chapter material may be considered optional in some texts, in *Algebra* we have selected these objectives and questions with the expectation that they will be covered. Students should be able to answer these questions with about 85% accuracy after studying the chapter.

You may assign these questions over a single night to help students prepare for a test the next day, or you may assign the questions over a two-day period.

If you work the questions over two days, then we recommend assigning the *evens* for homework the first night so that students get feedback in class the next day, then assigning the *odds* the night before the test so students can use the answers provided in the book.

ADDITIONAL ANSWERS

23.
```
ANSWER TO
QUESTION 23
ENTER A NUMBER
?2
6
```

24a.
```
10 PRINT "EVALUATE
   AREA OF CIRCLE
   FORMULA"
20 PRINT "GIVE
   RADIUS"
30 INPUT R
40 LET A =
   3.14159*R*R
50 PRINT "RADIUS",
   "AREA"
60 PRINT R,A
```

28a. null set or empty set; **b.** 0

36. positive real numbers, continuous

37. whole numbers, discrete

38. real numbers, continuous

39. positive real numbers, continuous

EVALUATION
Two forms of a Chapter Test—Forms A and B—are provided in the Teacher's Resource Book. For more information on grading, see *General Teaching Suggestions: Grading* on page T44 of the Teacher's Edition.

ASSIGNMENT RECOMMENDATION
We strongly recommend that you assign Lesson 2-1, both reading and questions, for homework the evening of the test. It gives students work to do after they have completed the test and keeps the class moving. If you do not do this, you may cover one less *chapter* over the course of the year.

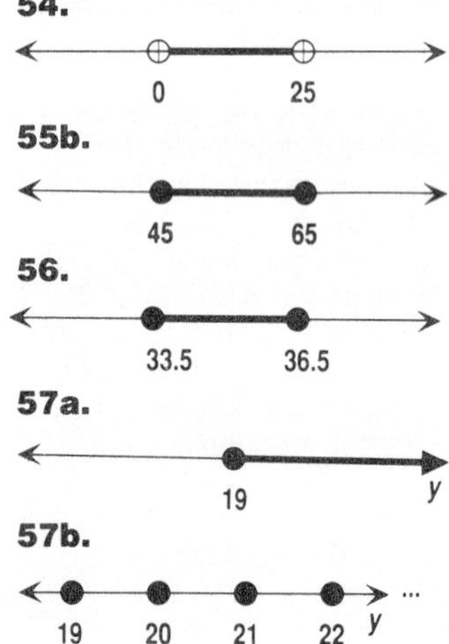

45. If a can of orange juice is h centimeters high and has a bottom radius of r centimeters, then the volume equals $\pi r^2 h$ cubic centimeters. What is the volume, to the nearest cubic centimeter, of a can 12 centimeters high with a radius of 6 centimeters? $\approx$ 1357 cm^3

In 46 and 47, use this information. The cost c of carpeting a room is given by $c = p\left(\frac{lw}{9}\right)$, where
p is the price of the carpeting per square yard and
l and w are the length and width of the room in feet.

46. Find the cost of carpeting a 12′ by 15′ room with carpeting that sells for \$19.95 per square yard. **\$399**

47. At \$5.99 per square yard, what is the cost of carpeting an 8′ by 30′ deck? **\$159.73**

Objective J. *Use relative frequency to determine information about surveys. (Lesson 1-8)*

48. One in four people refused to answer a market survey. Give three possibilities for the number of people surveyed and the number of people who refused to answer.
samples: 1000 and 250; 2500 and 625; 16 and 4

49. A survey found three fifths of amateur violinists to be women. If 400 violinists were surveyed, how many were women? **240**

50. At a shopping mall m people were asked about a certain product. w people liked the product. What is the relative frequency of people who liked the product? $\frac{w}{m}$

51. In 1980, France had a reported population of 54,652,000. There were 9,619,000 people over the age of 60. What is the relative frequency of people 60 or under? (Give your answer as a percent.) $\approx$ 82%

52. One in about 86 births in the U.S. results in twins.
a. What is the relative frequency of having twins? $\frac{1}{86}$
b. What is an estimate of the probability of having twins? $\frac{1}{86}$

53. *Multiple choice* An event occurred t times out of p possibilities. The relative frequency of the event was $\frac{1}{8}$. Which is true? **(a)**
(a) $\frac{t}{p} = \frac{1}{8}$ (b) $\frac{p}{t} = \frac{1}{8}$
(c) $\frac{t}{p+t} = \frac{1}{8}$ (d) $\frac{p}{p+t} = \frac{1}{8}$

REPRESENTATIONS deal with pictures, graphs, or objects that illustrate concepts.

Objective K. *Use graphs or symbols to describe intervals. (Lessons 1-1, 1-3)*

54. Kim bought stamps for less than \$25. On a number line, graph what she might have spent. See margin.

55. Consider the sign pictured.
a. Express the interval of legal speeds as an inequality using s to represent speed.
b. Graph all legal speeds.
See margin. 55a) $45 \le s \le 65$

SPEED LIMIT 65
45 MINIMUM

56. Graph the closed interval 35 ± 1.5. See margin.

57. Graph the solution set to $y \ge 19$, See margin.
a. if y is a real number;
b. if y is an integer.

In 58 and 59, choose from the three graphs below.

58. Which of these could be a graph of the solutions to $57 < n \le 62$? **(c)**

59. Which graph represents the statement "There are from 57 to 62 students with green eyes in the school"? **(b)**

(a) 56 57 58 59 60 61 62 63 n

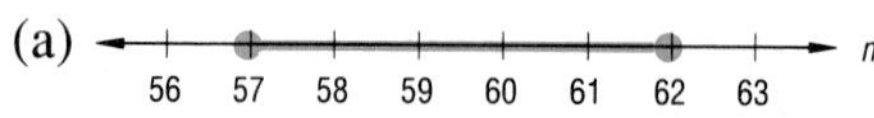

(b)

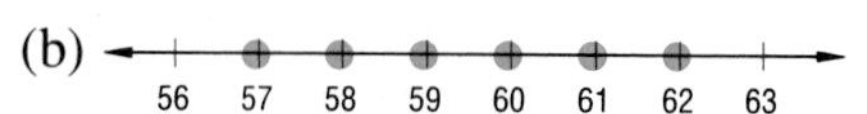

(c) 56 57 58 59 60 61 62 63 n

52

Objective L. *Interpret dot frequency graphs.* (Lesson 1-2)

60. A class of 16 students was asked how many hours of exercise they get a week. The dot frequency diagram below shows their responses.

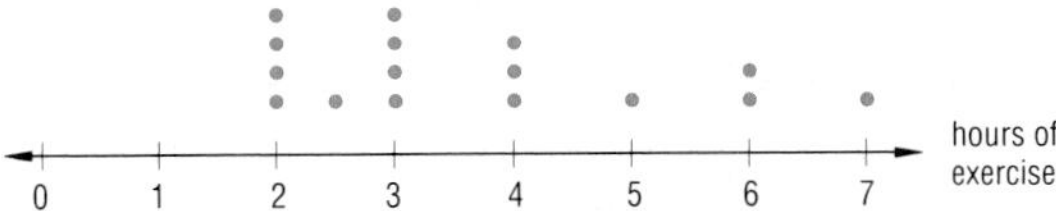

a. Describe the range of the hours with an inequality. **$2 \le h \le 7$**

b. What is the median number of hours exercised? **3 hours**

c. What is the mean number of hours exercised? **≈ 3.7 hours**

d. Give the modes of the responses. **2 and 3**

61. Below are the record high temperatures T in degrees Fahrenheit in the 50 states and the District of Columbia through 1986.

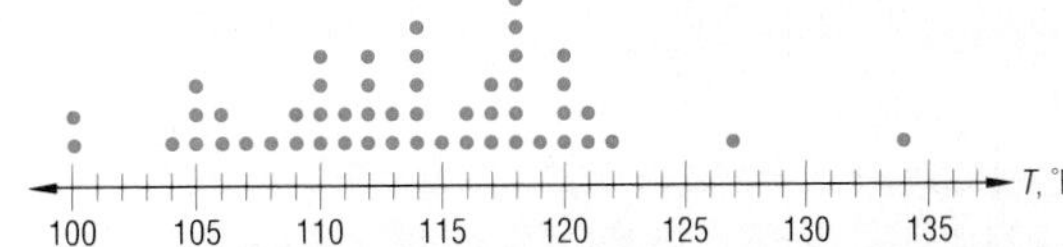

a. How many states had a record high of 105°? **3 states**

b. In how many states was $T \le 110°$? **16**

c. Give the mode for this data. **118°**

REFRESHER

Chapter 2, which discusses addition in algebra, assumes that you have mastered certain objectives in your previous mathematics courses. Use these questions to check your mastery.

A. Add any positive numbers or quantities.

1. 3.5 + 4.3 = **7.8**

2. 122.4 + 11 + .16 = **133.56**

3. 3.024 + 7.9999 = **11.0239**

4. $1\frac{1}{2} + 2\frac{1}{4} =$ **$3\frac{3}{4}$**

5. $\frac{2}{3} + 8\frac{1}{3} =$ **9**

6. $\frac{2}{5} + \frac{1}{6} + \frac{3}{7} =$ **$\frac{209}{210}$**

7. 6% + 12% = **18%**

8. 20% + 11.2% = **31.2%**

9. 11 cm + .03 cm = **11.03 cm**

10. .4 km + 1.9 km = **2.3 km**

11. 2′ 3″ + 9″ = **3′**

12. 6′ + 11″ + 4″ = **7′ 3″**

13. 30 oz + 8 lb = **9 lb 14 oz**

14. 4 lb 13 oz + 2 lb 12 oz = **7 lb 9 oz**

B. Add positive and negative integers.

15. 30 + -6 **24**

16. -11 + -4 **-15**

17. -1 + -1 + 3 **1**

18. -99 + 112 **13**

19. -2 + 4 + -6 **-4**

20. 8 + -8 + -8 + -8 **-16**

C. Graph ordered pairs on the coordinate plane.

21. (4, 3) **See margin.**

22. (5, -2)

23. (-2, 4)

24. (-3, -1)

25. (0, 4)

26. (0, -2)

27. (-3, 0)

28. (1, 0)

29. (0, 0)

D. Solve equations of the form $x + a = b$, where a and b are positive integers.

30. $x + 3 = 11$ **$x = 8$**

31. $9 + z = 40$ **$z = 31$**

32. $665 + w = 1072$ **$w = 407$**

33. $7 = m + 2$ **$m = 5$**

34. $2000 = n + 1461$ **$n = 539$**

35. $472 = 173 + s$ **$s = 299$**

RESOURCES

Visual for Teaching Aid 7: Coordinate Grid

REFRESHER

This optional material is intended to provide additional practice for students with weak backgrounds. The ideas covered will be used in Chapter 2. (Similar Refresher material is included before Chapters 3-5.)

If you assign these problems, they can be given whenever you feel it is appropriate. They can be given a few at a time or all at once. However, it is probably best not to spend a lot of time here.

ADDITIONAL ANSWERS 21-29.

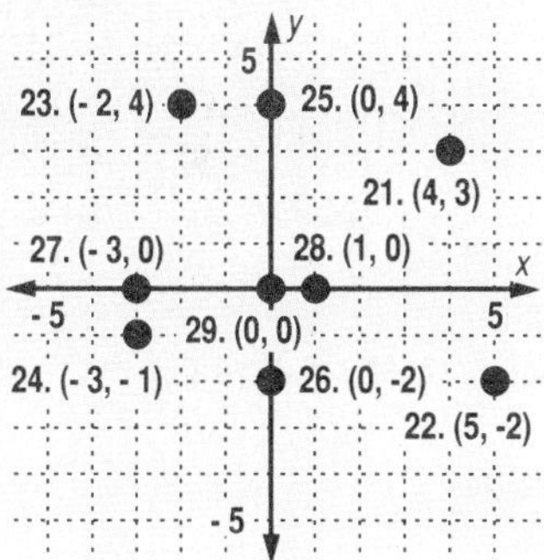

CHAPTER 2 ■ ADDITION IN ALGEBRA

DAILY PACING CHART 2

DAILY PACING CHART ■ CHAPTER 2

Students in the Full Course should complete the entire text by the end of the year. Students in the Minimal Course spend more time to complete lessons that are combined with quizzes and more time to consider the Chapter Review. Therefore, these students may not complete all the chapters in the text.

DAY	MINIMAL COURSE	FULL COURSE
1	2-1	2-1
2	2-2	2-2
3	2-3	2-3
4	2-4	2-4
5	Quiz (TRF); Start 2-5.	Quiz (TRF); 2-5
6	Finish 2-5.	2-6
7	2-6	2-7
8	2-7	2-8
9	2-8	Progress Self-Test
10	Progress Self-Test	Chapter Review
11	Chapter Review	Chapter Test (TRF)
12	Chapter Review	
13	Chapter Test (TRF)	

TESTING OPTIONS

TESTING OPTIONS

- Quiz for Lessons 2-1 Through 2-4
- Chapter 2 Test, Form A
- Chapter 2 Test, Form B
- Chapter 2 Test, Cumulative Form

INDIVIDUAL DIFFERENCES

PROVIDING FOR INDIVIDUAL DIFFERENCES

The student text is written for the *average* student. The program, however, can be adapted for less capable and for more capable students.

For those students who need more practice, a blackline master (in the Teacher's Resource File) is provided for each lesson. The Teacher's Edition frequently provides Error Analysis and Alternate Approach features to provide additional instructional strategies for those students who do not readily grasp the material.

For students who require additional challenge, Extension activities are regularly provided in the Teacher's Edition.

OBJECTIVES ■ CHAPTER 2

Students should master the chapter objectives by the time they complete the chapter. To ensure objective mastery, there is continual review built into each set of lesson questions. After students complete the chapter lessons, they assess their mastery on the Progress Self-Test. Then they do the Chapter Review and pay special attention to those questions that match the objectives missed on the Progress Self-Test. Students can get extra practice on these objectives by using the master for each lesson in the Teacher's Resource File.

OBJECTIVES FOR CHAPTER 2 (Organized into the SPUR categories— Skills, Properties, Uses, and Representations	**Progress Self-Test Questions**	**Chapter Review Questions**	**Lesson Master from Teacher's Resource File***
SKILLS			
A Add fractions.	6–8, 11	1 through 8	2-3
B Combine the terms.	4, 5, 10	9 through 16	2-2
C Solve and check equations of the form $a + x = b$.	14, 16, 18	17 through 26	2-6
D Solve inequalities of the form $a + x < b$.	15, 17, 19	27 through 31	2-7
PROPERTIES			
E Identify properties of addition.	1, 9	32 through 37	2-1, 2-2, 2-3
F Identify and apply properties used in solving equations and inequalities.	13	38 through 41	2-6, 2-7
G Use the Triangle Inequality to determine possible lengths of sides of triangles.	26, 27	42 through 45	2-8
USES			
H Use the models of addition to form and solve sentences involving addition.	2, 3, 12 21–23, 28	46 through 53	2-1, 2-2, 2-6, 2-7
I Apply the Triangle Inequality in real situations.	26, 27	54 through 55	2-8
REPRESENTATIONS			
J Graph solutions to inequalities on a number line.	20	56 through 59	2-7
K Plot points and interpret information on a coordinate graph.	29, 30	60 through 65	2-4
L Interpret two-dimensional slides on a coordinate graph.	24, 25	66 through 69	2-5

*** The masters are numbered to match the lessons.**

OVERVIEW ■ CHAPTER 2

Chapters 2 through 5 are organized around the four basic operations of arithmetic. Each chapter reviews models of an operation, then uses the models to establish properties and techniques of algebra. By the end of these chapters, students should be quite proficient at solving and applying one-step equations and inequalities.

This chapter introduces sentence-solving through a fresh look at addition. It stresses properties of addition, reviews addition of integers and fractions, introduces equations and inequalities, and discusses a variety of applications.

Lessons 2-1 and 2-2 use models to develop properties of addition and to picture integer addition. One of the models, the slide model, justifies the algebraic technique of combining like terms. Lesson 2-3 gives students a chance to practice fraction skills again, including the addition of simple algebraic fractions. Lessons 2-4 and 2-5 introduce the coordinate plane and the application of two-dimensional slides. Lessons 2-6 and 2-7 begin the systematic solution of algebra sentences with one-step addition equations and inequalities. Lesson 2-8 introduces an important application of simple inequalities in geometry.

Our approach assumes that, in previous courses, students have been introduced to addition, subtraction, multiplication, and division of signed numbers. Procedures for these operations are not explicitly stated, but the models throughout this chapter and the next three are used to illuminate the operations. Review questions in this chapter are intended to brush up students' skills with addition and multiplication. Subtraction and division of positive and negative numbers are deferred until Chapters 3 and 5, respectively.

PERSPECTIVES ■ CHAPTER 2

The Perspectives provide the rationale for the inclusion of topics or approaches, provide mathematical background, and make connections within UCSMP.

2-1

PUTTING-TOGETHER MODEL FOR ADDITION

In this lesson we introduce students to models for operations. You can think of a model for addition as an application postulate that connects addition to the real world. That is, it is an assumption about how the mathematics (in this case, addition) and the real world (in this lesson, putting together objects of a certain type) relate.

Models and properties of arithmetic operations share the trait that to represent them most efficiently, algebra is needed.

The Putting-together Model involves the most fundamental use of addition. Children first learn to add by combining two groups and counting the items in the result.

Most students do know when to add. So the contribution of models to students' correct choices among operations may become more helpful only in the later chapters. But models can also be used to verify properties. For example, in this lesson the Putting-together Model is used to verify the Commutative Property.

2-2

THE SLIDE MODEL FOR ADDITION

This lesson covers two topics. The first topic is integer addition. The number line provides a visual *representation*. The *uses* of addition (distance, temperature, money, and so on) help to give meaning to the process. The second topic of the lesson is *properties* of addition.

A slide or shift represents either an increase or a decrease from an initial state. In physical situations, a slide is usually achieved by adding or subtracting a positive number. However, a shift down or backwards may be achieved by adding a negative number. The slide model gives a method for visualizing the Additive Identity Property and the Property of Opposites. When we get to subtraction in Chapter 3, this will make the definition $a - b = a + -b$ quite natural.

The slide model also can be used to justify combining like terms. Measurement units can be considered scale factors. The statement $5.1 + 2.9 = 8$ can be developed on a line with an arbitrary unit. Scaling the line by a factor of q gives the corresponding statement $5.1q + 2.9q = 8q$. This idea is used in Lesson 2-3. We postpone the formal justification of adding like terms until the Distributive Property is presented in Chapter 6.

2-3

ADDITION OF FRACTIONS

Many algebra students still need practice in adding fractions. This lesson provides assistance in several ways. First, it uses the slide model to illustrate the idea. Second, it counters the common mistake of adding numerators and adding denominators. Third, two methods are shown for adding mixed numbers. Fourth, students are introduced to addition of signed fractions. Fifth, converting fractions to decimals is shown as a means of checking a problem, even if the decimal values are not exact.

Our later treatment of mixed numbers emphasizes commonly used fractions (for example, fourths, eighths, tenths). However, this lesson is intended to develop algebraic skills, so many of the fractions involve variables.

There exist a number of inexpensive calculators which can compute with fractions, but these calculators do not accept algebraic fractions. Some computer software, however, can perform operations with algebraic fractions.

2-4

THE COORDINATE PLANE

This lesson uses scattergrams to review graphing in the coordinate plane. It is another way in which data analysis is used to motivate an algebraic concept. Identifying patterns on coordinate graphs is fundamental to the development of the function concept.

The lesson focuses on graphs in the first quadrant. The next lesson will use all four quadrants.

Linking graphs to real situations as in the examples is a major step toward understanding why some of the graphs of later chapters are important to study.

2-5

TWO-DIMENSIONAL SLIDES

The words *slide* and *translation* are synonyms, but *slide* conveys a physical meaning and is usually used with younger students.

We study slides in the coordinate plane (that is, two-dimensional slides) for several reasons. First, they are an obvious application of the slide model for addition. Second, they give students the chance to practice the important graphing concepts that were introduced in the previous lesson and will be used throughout the book. Third, they give students practice in adding integers. Fourth, translations are important transformations both in geometry (where they relate congruent figures) and in algebra (where they relate graphs of functions and relations). Regarding the importance of slides in algebra, for example, the parabola $y = x^2 + 5$ is a translation image of the parabola $y = x^2$.

2-6

SOLVING $x + a = b$

This lesson provides the foundation for the solution of more complex equations. It also illustrates how real situations can be translated into algebraic sentences. Solving equations of this type will be practiced in the rest of the chapter. This practice should enable students to be proficient by the time the chapter test is given.

Because $x + a = b$ is a simple equation to solve, and because we expect students to have seen equations of this type before, we have increased their complexity by using more difficult numbers. The idea is to give students practice with decimals, fractions, and negative numbers while teaching them to solve, write, and use equations in a variety of settings.

2-7

SOLVING $x + a < b$

Checking inequalities is omitted from many books. But it is an accurate check, and it helps in understanding what it means to solve the inequality.

The next lesson covers a specific application of these inequalities, so you need not worry if students cannot solve them on the first day.

2-8

THE TRIANGLE INEQUALITY

The Triangle Inequality is the most important application of inequalities of the form $a + x > b$ that we know. It is a fundamental relationship in geometry and in advanced mathematics, but at the same time, it is the algebraic description of the popular adage "The shortest distance between two points is a straight line." Despite the obviousness of the adage, the problems do not strike students as trivial. Therefore, they view the solving of the inequality as a true help, and not merely as a hard way of doing something they could solve in their heads.

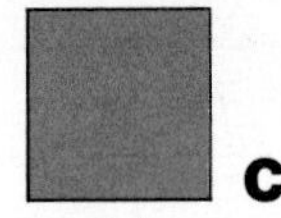

CHAPTER 2

RESOURCES

Visual for Teaching Aid 8: Prussian Army Table for Page 55

This chapter should take 8 or 9 days for the lessons and quiz, a day for the Progress Self-Test, 1 or 2 days for the Chapter Review, and 1 day for testing. The total is 11 to 13 days. Students who have studied from *Transition Mathematics* may be able to go more quickly, since they will be familiar with the models and many of the applications.

CHAPTER 2

Addition in Algebra

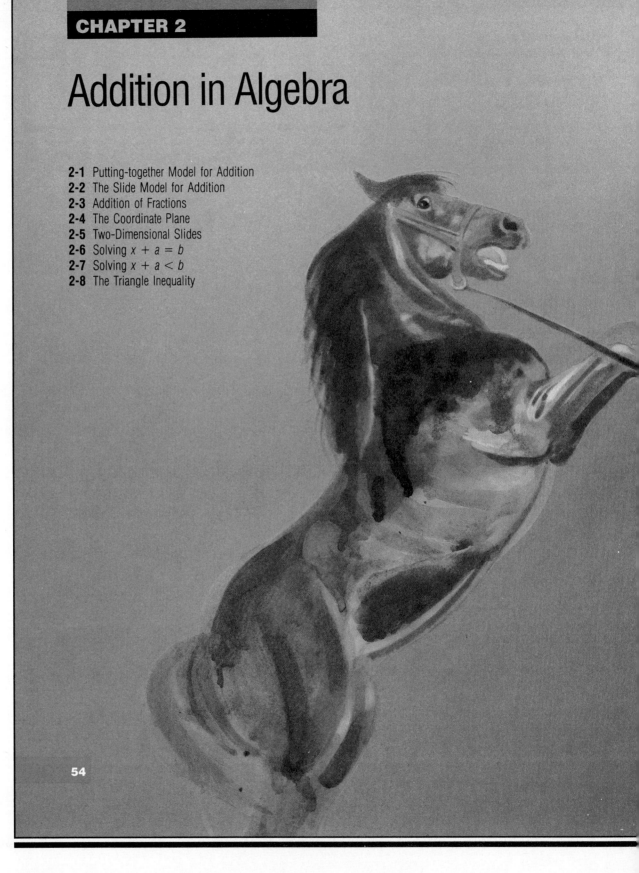

You often hear about automobile accidents. But life before automobile travel was not perfectly safe either. One hundred years ago, horses were a major means of transportation. However, travel on horseback could also be dangerous. Powerful kicks by the horse caused major injuries, even death. This was so serious a problem that the Prussian government kept records of how many men were killed by horse-kick in the Prussian army. A corps (pronounced core) was a major subdivision of the army that had about 10,000 men. Below are the data on eleven corps for 10 years.

Addition is used to total the numbers in each *row* across to find how many deaths there were each year. Addition is used to total the numbers in each *column* to find how many deaths there were in each corps for the 10-year period. The total of the columns is 79; this is also the total of the rows. In the decade 1880–1889, 79 men in the eleven listed corps were killed by horse-kick.

Number of Deaths by Horse-kick in the Prussian Army from 1880-1889 for 11 Corps

Year	I	II	III	IV	V	VI	VII	VIII	IX	X	XI	Total
1880	3	2	1	1	1				2	1	4	15
1881			2	1			1		1			5
1882	2					1		1	1	2	1	8
1883		1	2		1	2	1		1		3	11
1884		1					1			2		4
1885						1			2		1	4
1886	1			1	1	1			1		1	6
1887	1	2	1			3	2	1	1		1	12
1888	1	1			1	1					1	5
1889		1	1		1	1			1	2	2	9
Total	8	8	7	3	5	10	5	2	10	7	14	79

USING PAGES 54-55
The anecdote and table provide an amusing introduction to a familiar topic. *Teaching Aid 8* can be used to facilitate discussion. You may want to have students find the mode, median, mean, and range for both the 11 corps and the 10-year period. (per corps: modes 5, 7, 8, and 10; median 10; mean 7.2; range 12. per year: modes 4 and 5; median 7; mean 7.9; range 11.)

LESSON 2-1

RESOURCES

- Lesson Master 2-1
- Visual for Teaching Aid 9: Bar Graphs for Page 56

OBJECTIVES

E Identify the Commutative and Associative Properties of Addition.

H Use the Putting-together Model of addition to form and solve sentences involving addition.

TEACHING NOTES

Reading Encourage students to read the statements of properties with special care. Point out that if they are having difficulty understanding a property, they should substitute numbers for the variables. It also might help to reread the material leading up to the statement of the property. Usually this preceding material gives an example or a word statement of the property which will aid understanding.

The description of the Associative Property as the property that enables us to change the "order of additions" is different from the usual "change the grouping" description. We prefer the former because grouping is a more difficult concept for students. Use the language you prefer.

LESSON

2-1 Putting-together Model for Addition

Morgan Windows, Inc., manufactures custom-designed windows for houses. They have two plants, one in New York, and one in New Orleans. The company can keep track of its progress through charts and graphs. A **bar graph** with separate bars for the two plants presents a way to compare the two facilities. This is the graph shown at the left. You can see that the profits for the New York plant went down over the five-year period. The profits for the New Orleans plant increased until 1987 and then decreased in 1988.

Morgan Windows, Inc. 1984-1988 Profits

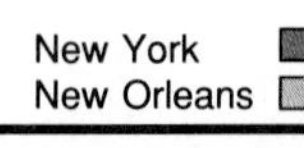

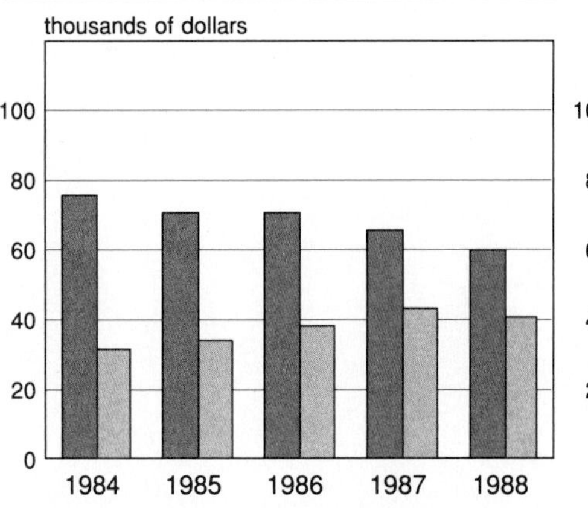

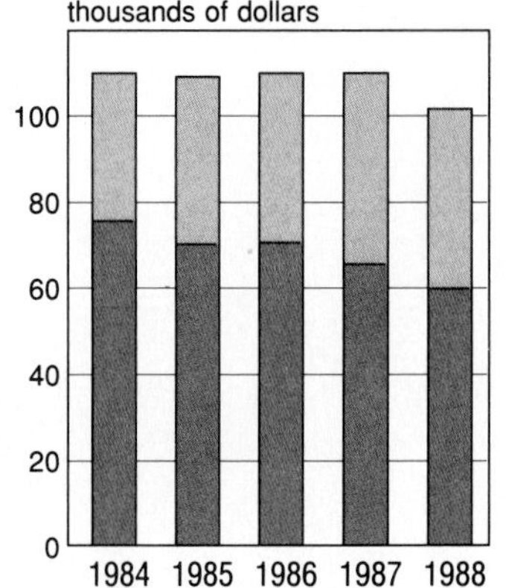

To determine whether overall profits were increasing or decreasing, the bar graph was rearranged into the **stacked bar graph** on the right. Each bar for New Orleans was placed on top of the bar representing New York for the same year. You can see that profits for the company were nearly constant until 1988.

To make this stacked bar graph, the two profits for each year shown in the left graph are added. For instance, in 1988, New York had a profit of \$60,000 and New Orleans had a profit of \$41,000. In total, they had a profit of \$101,000. So the bar for 1988 is drawn to the 101 mark.

A **model** for an operation is a general pattern that categorizes many of the uses of the operation. The stacked bar graph illustrates an important model for addition.

Putting-together Model for Addition:

A quantity x is put together with a quantity y *with the same units.* If there is no overlap, then the result is the quantity

$$x + y.$$

One important skill learned in algebra is called "simplifying expressions." Inform students that the term *simplify* has many meanings—to simplify a fraction may mean to write it in lowest terms while to simplify a radical may mean to write it with a smaller number under the radical sign. Here, *simplify* means "write an equal expression with fewer operation signs."

Example 1 Ms. Argonaut is given a daily allowance of $115.00 by her company for her travel expenses on a business trip. She spends $45.95 for her hotel room. She estimates that her automobile costs will be about $4.00 for gas and $7.50 for parking. Let E be the amount still available for other expenses. Write an equation to show how E is related to the other quantities.

Solution The different expenses do not overlap, so the putting-together model applies. The total allowance is $115.00. So,

$$49.95 + 4.00 + 7.50 + E = 115.00.$$

The next example involves sets and the putting-together model. Notice that the sets contain no common elements. If there were overlap, the putting-together model would have to be modified.

Example 2 Consider $A = \{1, 2, 3, \ldots, 10\}$ and $B = \{100, 101, 102, \ldots, 199\}$. If C is a set including all the elements from either A or B, find $N(C)$, the number of elements in set C.

Solution Since there is no overlap in A and B, $N(C) = N(A) + N(B)$. $N(A) = 10$ and $N(B) = 100$, so $N(C) = 10 + 100 = 110$.

When two or more quantities are put together, it does not make any difference which comes first. If the stacked bar graph on the previous page had the New York bars on top of the New Orleans bars, the total heights would be the same. For 1988,

$$\$41,000 + \$60,000 = \$60,000 + \$41,000.$$

In Example 2, $\quad N(A) + N(B) = N(B) + N(A).$

ADDITIONAL EXAMPLES

1. Paula baby-sat on three days last week: 2 hours on Monday, w hours on Wednesday, and $3\frac{1}{2}$ hours on Saturday. Altogether she baby-sat for 8 hours. Write an equation relating w and the other quantities.
$2 + w + 3\frac{1}{2} = 8$

2. Let $J = \{A, B, C, \ldots, H\}$ and $K = \{P, Q, X\}$. Let L be the set containing all the elements from either J or K. Find N(J), N(K), and N(L).
8; 3; 11

Example 2 gives instances of a general pattern named by Francois Servois in 1814. He used the French word "commutatif," which means "switchable." The English name is **commutative property.**

Commutative Property of Addition:

For any real numbers a and b,

$$a + b = b + a.$$

Sometimes you must change the order of numbers being added before you can carry out an addition.

Example 3 In making a square base for a coffee machine, there is to be $2\frac{1}{2}$ cm on each side of the circular warming tray. If the coffee pot is d cm in diameter, write a formula for the side of the base, b, in terms of d.

Solution First draw a picture.

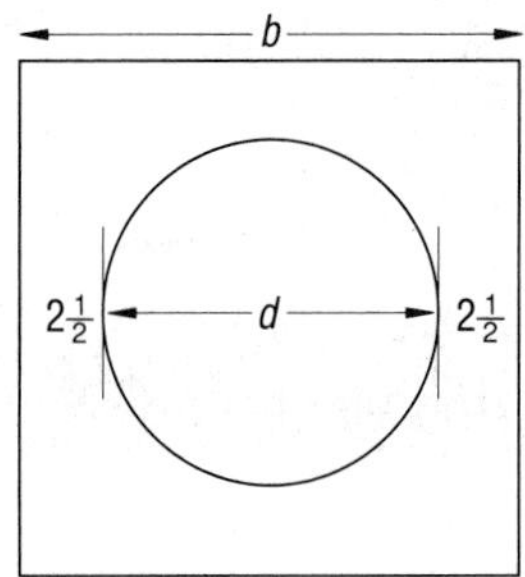

Putting together the distances gives

$$b = 2\tfrac{1}{2} + d + 2\tfrac{1}{2}.$$

The expression $2\frac{1}{2} + d + 2\frac{1}{2}$ can be simplified. There are three numbers to add. The order of operations says to do additions from left to right. So the above equation means

$$b = (2\tfrac{1}{2} + d) + 2\tfrac{1}{2}.$$

The commutative property allows you to switch the first two terms.

$$= (d + 2\tfrac{1}{2}) + 2\tfrac{1}{2}$$

But we would like to associate the middle term $2\frac{1}{2}$ with the other $2\frac{1}{2}$, not with d. The **associative property of addition** enables you to do this.

$$= d + (2\tfrac{1}{2} + 2\tfrac{1}{2})$$
$$= d + 5$$

Notice that $d + 5$ is simpler than $(2\frac{1}{2} + d) + 2\frac{1}{2}$. This is one reason for knowing the properties. The associative property was given its name by the Irish mathematician Sir William Rowan Hamilton.

Associative Property of Addition:

For any real numbers *a*, *b*, and *c*,

$$(a + b) + c = a + (b + c).$$

Both the commutative property and the associative property have to do with changing order. The commutative property says you can change the order of the *numbers* being added. The associative property says you can change the order of *additions* by *regrouping* the numbers. Together these properties enable you to add as many numbers as you please, in any order. This is why the totals of rows and columns in the Prussian horse-kick table on page 55 are the same.

Questions

Covering the Reading

1. What is a model for an operation? See margin.

2. State the putting-together model for addition. See margin.

In 3 and 4, refer to the graphs of the Morgan Windows, Inc., profits.

3. In which year did both the New York and New Orleans plants of Morgan Windows, Inc., show a decrease in profits? 1988

4. Approximately what were the combined profits of both plants in 1984? $110,000

5. Refer to Example 1. On another trip, Ms. Argonaut spent $52.50 for a hotel room, $23.75 for food, and $20 for a bus ticket. Write an equation to show how she accounts for these amounts and the amount still available for other expenses from her $115 daily allowance. See margin.

6. Let $E = \{3, 4, 5, 6, 7, 8\}$, $F = \{10, 11, 12, \ldots, 20\}$, and G = the set of numbers in either set E or set F. Find N(E), N(F), and N(G). N(E) = 6; N(F) = 11; N(G) = 17

7. Refer to Example 3. What size base would you need if the diameter of the pot was **a.** 12 cm? **b.** 10 cm? a. 17 cm; b. 15 cm

8. The commutative property for addition gets its name from a French word meaning __?__. switchable

9. Using the associative property involves __?__ the numbers. regrouping

10. Simplify $28 + k + 30$. $k + 58$

ADDITIONAL ANSWERS

1. A model for an operation is a general pattern that categorizes many of the uses of the operations.

2. A quantity *x* is put together with a quantity *y* with the same units. If there is no overlap, then the result is the quantity *x* + *y*.

5. Let *E* be the amount available for other expenses. Then 52.50 + 23.75 + 20 + *E* = 115.

NOTES ON QUESTIONS
Error Analysis for Question 17: Some students do not realize that 0, an element common to both *E* and *F* should only be counted once when finding N(*G*). Discuss an example where the elements of the sets are students in the class to dramatize that since an element cannot be in a set more than once, it cannot be counted more than once.

Question 18: Because *insufficient information is given* to answer this question, it causes some students problems. Students are so accustomed to having a single correct answer in mathematics that they think there must be an error in the book if a question has no answer. Emphasize that in the real world, *knowing when there is enough information to solve a problem* is one of the most basic problem-solving skills to learn. The need for such questions is evident since so many students find **Question 18** difficult. Note that the Putting-together Model is inappropriate because the sets overlap.

Question 20b: Students who know how to solve an equation can answer this question by doing so. Others can use *trial and error.* Both approaches are valid.

18. Cannot determine; there is an overlap; sample: Joe \$15, Dave \$10, Sarah \$20 or Joe \$10, Dave \$15, Sarah \$25

21. 49.95 + .05 + 59.28 + .72 = (49.95 + .05) + (59.28 + .72) = 50 + 60 = 110

30. When added, the sugar dissolves in the coffee, so their volumes overlap.

Questions 11–14 are *multiple choice*. Which addition property is illustrated?
(a) commutative only (b) both commutative and associative
(c) associative only (d) neither commutative nor associative

11. $2L + 2W = 2W + 2L$ **a**

12. $(2x + 3) + 4 = 2x + (3 + 4)$ **c**

13. The total for rows equals the total for columns in the Prussian horse-kick example. **b**

14. $[N(X) + N(Y)] + N(Z) = N(X) + [N(Z) + N(Y)]$ **b**

Applying the Mathematics

15. Rita got on a scale and weighed 50 kg. She took her cat in her arms and the scale went up x kg. It then read 54 kg. Write an addition equation relating x, 50, and 54. **50 + x = 54**

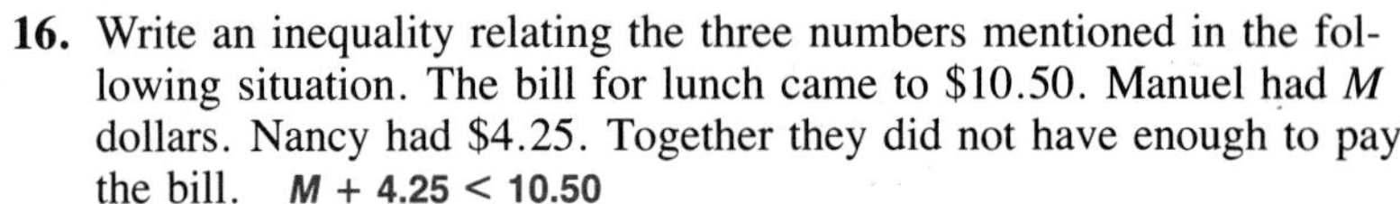

16. Write an inequality relating the three numbers mentioned in the following situation. The bill for lunch came to \$10.50. Manuel had M dollars. Nancy had \$4.25. Together they did not have enough to pay the bill. **$M + 4.25 < 10.50$**

17. Let $E = \{0, 2, 4, 6, 8\}$, and $F = \{0, 5, 10\}$. Suppose G is a set including all the elements in either E or F. Tell why $N(G) \neq N(E) + N(F)$. **There is overlap; zero is in both sets.**

18. Joe and his friend Dave together earned \$25 on a bike-a-thon. Joe and his sister Sarah together earned \$35 on the bike-a-thon. How much did the three of them earn altogether? **See margin.**

19. Write an expression for the perimeter of this triangle. **p + q + 26**

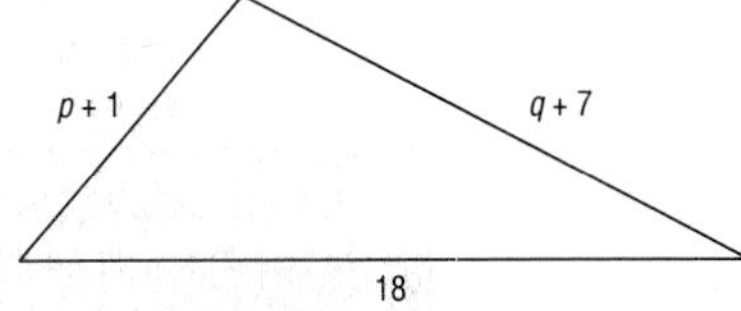

20. a. Write an equation to express the area of the largest rectangle in terms of the areas of the smaller rectangles. **54 = x + 18 + 24**

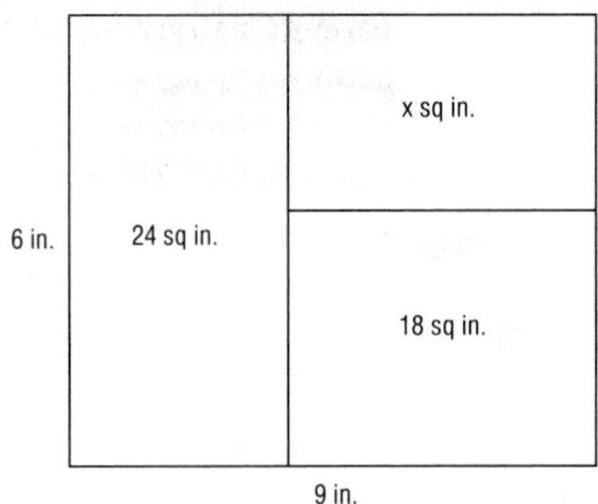

b. Find x. Use trial and error if necessary. **12**

21. Use the associative and commutative properties to add mentally:

$$49.95 + 59.28 + .05 + .72$$ **See margin.**

22. Find values of a, b, and c that show that $(a - b) - c = a - (b - c)$ is *not* always true. This indicates that, in general, subtraction is not associative.
sample: $(10 - 5) - 2 = 5 - 2 = 3$, but $10 - (5 - 2) = 10 - 3 = 7$

23. In each situation, tell whether "followed by" is a commutative operation.
 a. Putting on your socks, followed by putting on your shoes. **No**
 b. Putting cream in your coffee, followed by putting sugar in your coffee. **Yes**
 c. Writing on the blackboard, followed by erasing the blackboard. **No**
 d. Make up an example of your own. Tell whether it is commutative.
 sample: brushing your teeth followed by combing your hair; yes

Review

24. There are 12 National League (NL) baseball fields and 14 American League (AL) fields. Six NL fields are natural grass and eleven AL fields are artificial grass. What is the relative frequency of a major league ball park having natural grass? *(Lesson 1-8)* **$\frac{9}{26}$ or ≈ .346**

25. The Carter family has 35 classical CDs, 8 CDs of musicals, 10 folk CDs, and 15 rock-and-roll CDs. If Ben Carter picks a CD randomly, what is the probability the disk is classical? *(Lesson 1-7)*
$\frac{35}{68}$ or ≈ .515

26. Does $x + 14.7 = 20.3$ when $x = 5.6$? *(Lesson 1-4)* **Yes**

27. *Skill sequence* Simplify. *(Lesson 1-8)*
 a. $\frac{14}{21}$ **$\frac{2}{3}$** **b.** $\frac{14xy}{21xz}$ **$\frac{2y}{3z}$** **c.** $\frac{30ab}{45bn}$ **$\frac{2a}{3n}$**

28. *Multiple choice* During the championship basketball game, the Mustangs led by as many as 5 points and were down by as many as 3 points. If p is the point spread of the two teams, which graph best describes the game situation? *(Lesson 1-3)* **(c)**

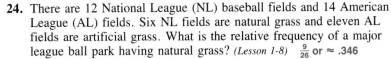

(a) 

(b) 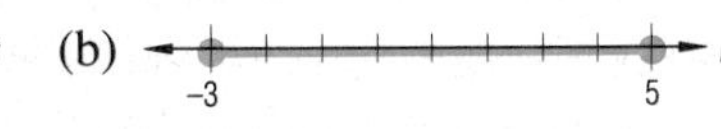

(c) 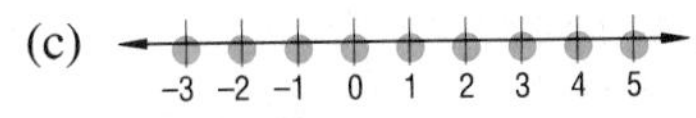

(d) 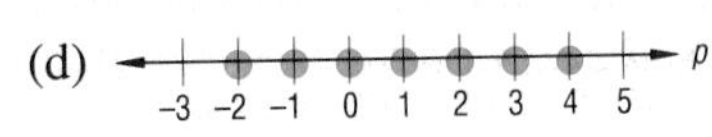

29. Rewrite as a simple fraction *(Previous course)*
 a. $8\frac{2}{3}$ **$\frac{26}{3}$** **b.** $-8\frac{2}{3}$ **$-\frac{26}{3}$** **c.** $5\frac{3}{10}$ **$\frac{53}{10}$**

Exploration

30. When $\frac{1}{3}$ cup of sugar is added to $\frac{2}{3}$ cup of coffee, the result does not fill a container that holds one cup. Why not? **See margin.**

31. The discussion about horse-kicks in the Prussian Army may be hard to believe, but it is true and uses real data.
 a. In what continent was Prussia? **Europe**
 b. What country or countries today cover the land which was once Prussia? **East Germany, West Germany, Poland, Soviet Union**

Question 31: Many students confuse Prussia (a former country roughly covering what is now Germany) with Russia. It is a natural confusion for those who have not studied much history and geography.

FOLLOW-UP

MORE PRACTICE

For more practice on SPUR Objectives, use *Lesson Master 2-1*, shown below.

EVALUATION

Alternative Assessment

For questions like **Question 18,** a good strategy is to have students orally explain the reasoning they used in arriving at an answer. This approach will enable you to assess thinking skills that are not readily apparent on written quizzes and tests.

NAME ______

LESSON **MASTER 2–1**
QUESTIONS ON **SPUR** OBJECTIVES

■PROPERTIES *Objective E (See pages 102–105 for objectives.)*
In 1–6, identify what property of addition is given.

1. $3 + -2 = -2 + 3$ **Commutative**
2. $(a + 4) + 6 = a + (4 + 6)$ **Associative**
3. $(x + 3) + 2 = 2 + (x + 3)$ **Commutative**
4. $4 + (6 + -2) = 4 + (-2 + 6)$ **Commutative**
5. $3 + (-2 + a) = (3 + -2) + a$ **Associative**
6. $m + (b + -3) + 3 = m + b + (-3 + 3)$ **Associative**

In 7–10, use the associative and commutative properties to add mentally.

7. $9 + -3 + 2 + -6$ **2**
8. $3.2 + -0.6 + -0.2 + 4.6$ **7**
9. $998 + 200 + 2 + 50$ **1250**
10. $\frac{3}{5} + \frac{-1}{3} + \frac{2}{5}$ **$\frac{2}{3}$**

■USES *Objective H*

11. For the first four months of the year (January–April), the profits of Patty's Pizza Co. were $540, $120, $460, and $180. Mentally find the total for this period. **$1300**

12. In a game show, Frank won $100 on the first question and n dollars on the second but lost q dollars on the third. He ended up with $300. Write a sentence relating these quantities. **$100 + n - q = 300$**

13. Before a summer storm, the temperature was 86°. It then fell d° and later rose 5°. The new temperature was less than 80°. Write a sentence for the final temperature and simplify. **$86 - d + 5 < 80, 11 < d$**

14. Write an expression for the perimeter of this triangle. **$(x - 1) + (x + 8) + 37$**

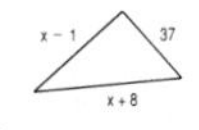

10 *Algebra* © Scott, Foresman and Company

LESSON 2-2

RESOURCES

- Lesson Master 2-2
- Visual for Teaching Aid 1: Number Lines

OBJECTIVES

B Combine like terms.
E Identify properties of addition (the Additive Identity Property, the Property of Opposites, and the Opposite of an Opposite [Op-op] Property.)
H Use the Slide Model of Addition to form and solve sentences involving addition.

TEACHING NOTES

This is a reasonable time to use slides to review addition of positive and negative numbers. Emphasize (as you will have to many times during the course of the year) that -*a* stands for a positive number when *a* is negative. This is the reason we call -*a* the "opposite of *a*" or "the additive inverse of *a*," and not "minus *a*" (However, many good mathematicians call it "minus *a*"!)

In **Example 2,** the result is given as y + -12 instead of $y - 12$ because the definition of subtraction has not yet been covered. If your students want to write $y - 12$, that is all right.

LESSON

2-2 The Slide Model for Addition

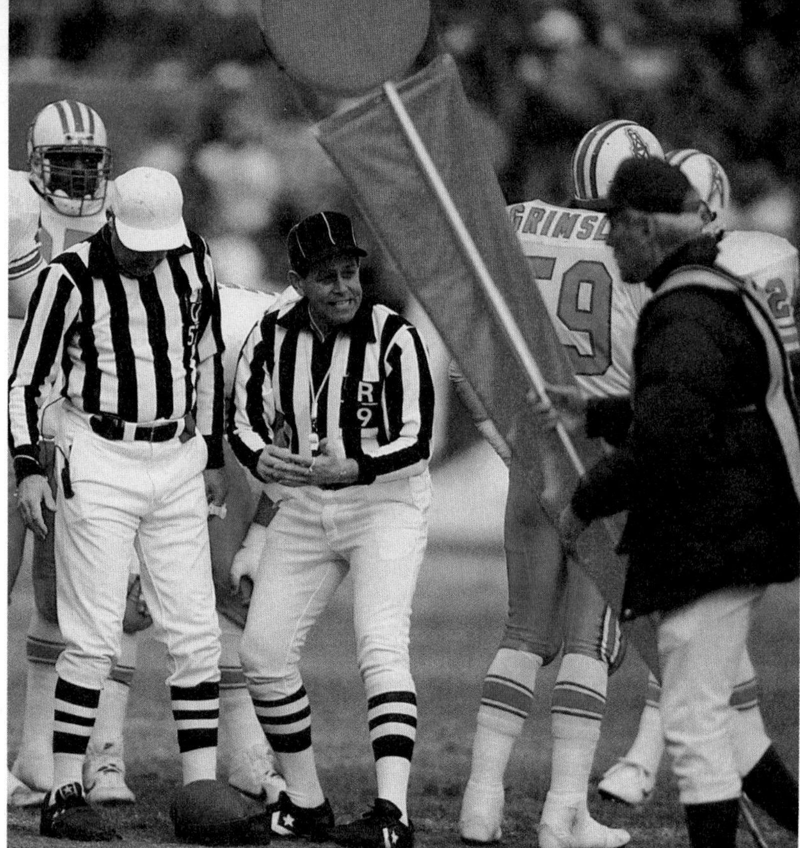

Many situations use both positive and negative numbers. You may add gains and losses in a football game, deposits and withdrawals in savings accounts, profits and losses in business endeavors, and so on. You can consider positive and negative numbers as being in opposite directions. Here is a situation that leads to the addition problem -4 + 6.

Example 1 A football team lost 4 yards on the first play and gained 6 yards on the second play. What is the net gain of these two plays?

Solution Think of -4 as a slide to the left. Think of 6 as a slide to the right. The net result is a slide to the right of 2 units. This means a net gain of 2 yards.

$$-4 + 6 = 2$$

Check The two plays can be represented on a number line where 0 is the "line of scrimmage."

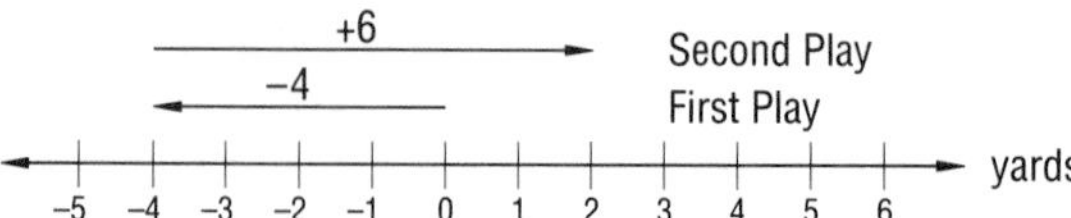

62

The lower arrow, from 0 to -4, indicates a loss of 4 yards. The upper arrow, from -4 to 2, represents a gain of 6 yards.

In the **slide model for addition,** positive numbers are shifts or slides in one direction. Negative numbers are slides in the opposite direction. The + sign means "followed by." The sum indicates the net result of the two slides.

Slide Model for Addition:

If a slide x is followed by a slide y, the result is the slide $x + y$.

The slide model gives a method for visualizing some properties of real numbers. Suppose you deposit \$480 in a bank. If you make no withdrawal or deposit, the amount you will have is \$480 + 0 or \$480. You can think of this as a slide of 480 followed by a slide of 0. A slide of zero does not change a position at all. Adding 0 to a number keeps the *identity* of that number. So 0 is called the **additive identity.**

Additive Identity Property:

For any real number a,

$$a + 0 = 0 + a = a.$$

What happens when you have one slide followed by another which is the same length, but in the opposite direction? The result is always 0.

$$7 + -7 = 0 \qquad 5 \cdot 10^{32} + -5 \cdot 10^{32} = 0$$

$$-11.2 + 11.2 = 0 \qquad -\frac{3}{5} + \frac{3}{5} = 0$$

Below is the graph of 7 + -7, which illustrates this result.

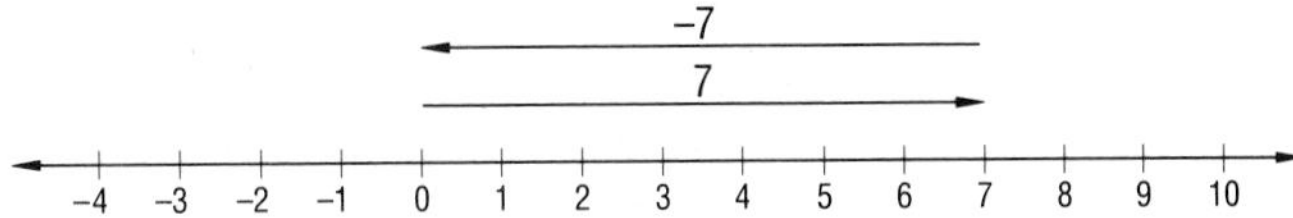

The numbers 7 and -7 are called **opposites** or **additive inverses** of each other. The opposite of any real number x is written **-*x*.**

ADDITIONAL EXAMPLES

1. During a drought, the level of Cottonwood Creek dropped 18 inches. After a storm, it rose 2 inches. Later, the level dropped 4 inches. Picture this on a number line and find the net change.

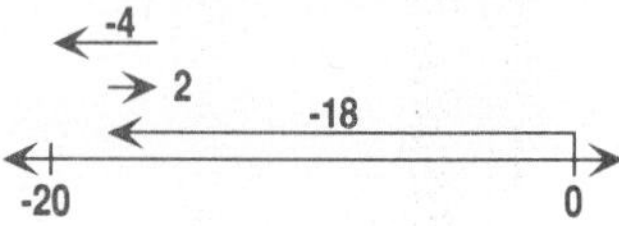

net change of -20 inches

2. Ms. Worth was driving at 40 miles per hour. She sped up 15 miles an hour and then slowed down 20 miles an hour. Write an addition problem to represent this, and find her resulting speed.
40 + 15 + -20; resulting speed 35 miles per hour

3. Simplify $(-6 + j) + (15 + k)$.
$\mathbf{j + k + 9}$

4. Simplify $-4n + -3n$ using a number line.

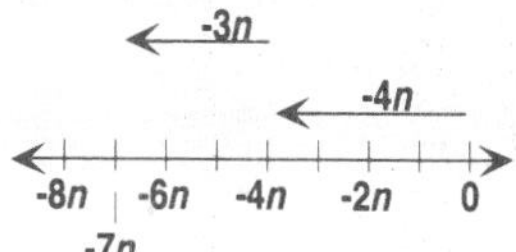

Property of Opposites:

For any real number a,
$$a + -a = 0.$$

If $a = -60$, then $-a$ is the opposite of -60, or $-a = 60$. So $-a$ is not always a negative number. *When a is negative, -a is positive.*

The numbers a and $-a$ are additive inverses, as are $-a$ and $-(-a)$. A number has only one additive inverse, so $-(-a) = a$. We call this the opposite-of-an-opposite property, or for short, the **Op-op Property.**

Op-op Property:

For any real number a,
$$-(-a) = a.$$

These properties apply to all numbers: positive, negative, or zero.

Example 2 Simplify $(-8 + y) + -4$.

Solution First change the order.

$(-8 + y) + -4 = (y + -8) + -4$ Commutative Property of Addition
$= y + (-8 + -4)$ Associative Property of Addition

Slides verify that $-8 + -4 = -12$.

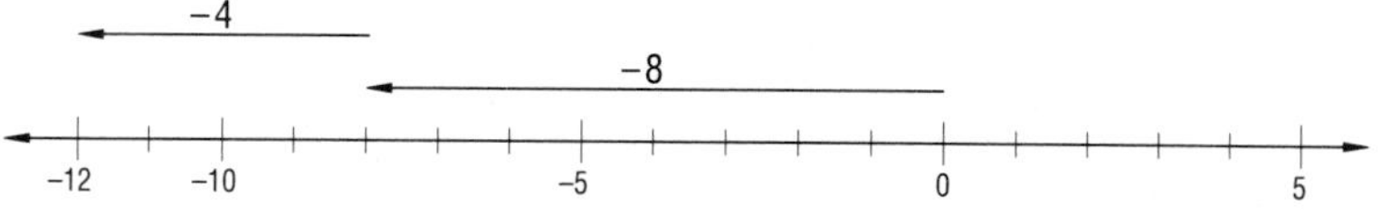

So $(-8 + y) + -4 = y + -12$.

Check For any particular value of y, $(-8 + y) + -4$ must give the same value as $y + -12$. We try $y = 7$ and follow order of operations.

Then $(-8 + y) + - 4 = (-8 + 7) + -4 = -1 + -4 = -5$
$y + -12 = 7 + -12 = -5.$

Since both expressions have a value of -5, they are equal.

You should find that with practice you can do some simplifying steps in your head. Often we write more steps than are needed so that you can follow closely. Ask your teacher how many steps you should write.

Number lines can show units. In Example 1, the units on the number line represent yards. The example shows that -4 yards + 6 yards = 2 yards. Sometimes the number line is in multiples of a number. The Morgan Windows, Inc., bar graphs in the last lesson were labeled in thousands. If the units or multiples are of the same number or quantity, their sum can be calculated.

Example 3 Simplify $7s + -2s$.

Solution Mark off a number line into segments of length s and then do the slide.

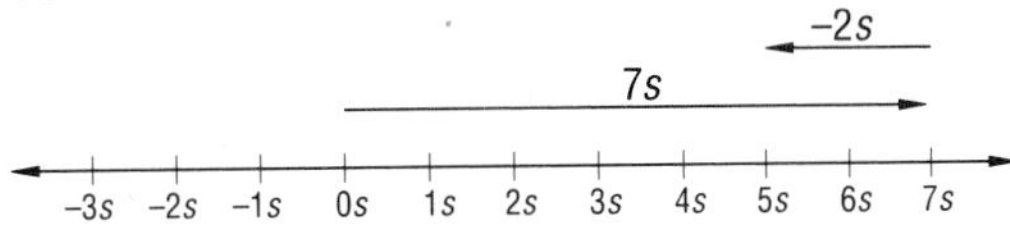

The slide ends at 5s. So $7s + -2s = 5s$.

The expressions $7s$ and $-2s$ are called **terms.** A term is either a single number or a product of numbers and variables. When the variables in the terms are the same, they are called **like terms** and the addition can be performed. This simplification is called **adding like terms**. Exponents of variables must match for terms to be like. The terms $5x^2$ and $9x^2$ are like terms. So, $5x^2 + 9x^2 = 14x^2$, just as 5 square inches + 9 square inches = 14 square inches. However, the expression $13t + -4a$ cannot be simplified because its terms are not like terms. Neither can $3 + 8x$ or $2x + x^5$ be simplified. Nor can 6 meters + 2 centimeters be simplified, unless you convert one unit to the other.

Adding Like Terms Property:

For any real numbers a, b, and x,

$$ax + bx = (a + b)x$$

Adding like terms is a special use of a more general property known as the Distributive Property. Your teacher may want you to call it by that name.

NOTES ON QUESTIONS

Questions 14, 15 and 28b: The checks are an important process because they point out what it means for expressions to be equal. They also give students a method of checking their answers to simplification problems and provide an opportunity to practice evaluating expressions. Students will develop a good sense of what a variable is, and will be more flexible in judging the correctness of their algebra manipulations. This checking technique is used extensively throughout the book.

Question 16: This question is intended to encourage students to write about mathematical ideas and to express themselves clearly. It is different from the more common question which sets forth a situation and asks students to give the equation.

Question 25: Note that the easiest way to add (17 + -35) + (36 + -18) is to change the order of operations as (17 + -18) + (-35 + 36).

NOTES ON QUESTIONS
Question 33: Sometimes asteroids are considered "minor planets." If they are included, then N(*T*) is unknown but quite large.

Question 35: When discussing this question, ask students for other examples of negative numbers on TV. (samples: In football, negative numbers mean yards lost. Temperatures below 0 are negative.)

ADDITIONAL ANSWERS
1a.

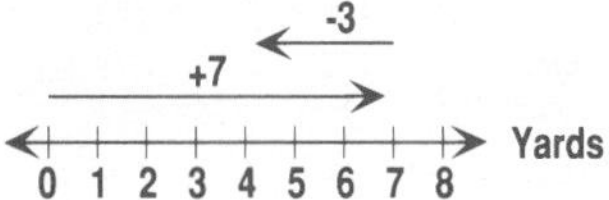

2. If a slide *x* is followed by a slide *y*, the result is the slide *x* + *y*.

6b. Adding 0 to a number does not change that number's value. The number keeps its "identity."

11. Property of Opposites

12. Additive Identity Property

13. Adding Like Terms Property

28b. Does 6 + 2 · 3 + 3 · 3 + 4 = 6 + 5 · 3 + 4? Does 6 + 6 + 9 + 4 = 6 + 15 + 4? Yes.

32a.

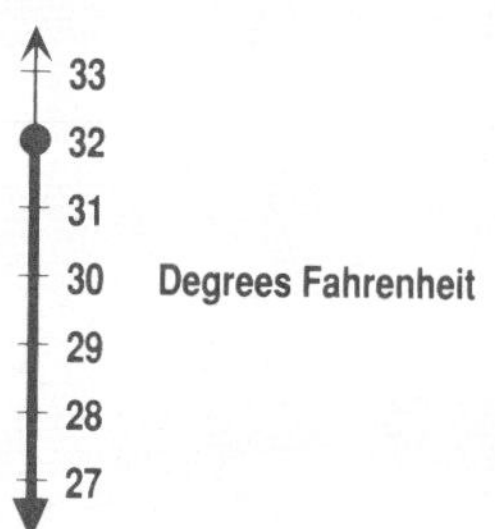

35a. sample: a fall in the Dow Jones Industrial Average

35b. sample: the number of seconds before a rocket is launched

Questions

Covering the Reading

1. On the first play, a football team gained 7 yards. On the second play, the team lost 3 yards.
a. Represent this situation on a number line. See margin.
b. What was the net yardage for the two plays? gain of 4 yards

2. State the slide model for addition. See margin.

3. Add: **a.** $-10 + -13$ **b.** $9x + -11x$ **c.** $-172 + 29$
3. a) -23 b) -2x c) -143

In 4 and 5, simplify.

4. $3 + -4 + x$ $x + -1$ **5.** $-2 + y + -9$ $y + -11$

6. a. $0 + -10 =$? . -10
b. Why is zero called the additive identity? See margin.

7. Another name for an additive inverse is ? . opposite

8. What is the additive inverse of $-x$? -(-x) or x

9. Give a value of n for which $-n$ is positive.
any negative value, such as -6

10. Simplify $-(-7)$. 7

In 11–13, an instance of what property is given? See margin.

11. $x + -x = 0$ **12.** $-y = 0 + -y$ **13.** $15x + 14x = 29x$

14. Check the answer in Example 3 by substituting 8 for s in $7s + -2s = 5s$.
Does 7 · 8 + -2 · 8 = 5 · 8? Does 56 + -16 = 40? Yes.

15. Check that $3 + 8x$ is not the same as $11x$ by substituting 4 for x.
$3 + 8 \cdot 4 \neq 44$

Applying the Mathematics

16. Describe a real situation that leads to $-9 + 9 = 0$.
sample: you spend $9 then earn $9

In 17 and 18, write the addition expression suggested by each situation.

17. The temperature goes up $x°$, then falls 3°, then rises 5°.
$x + -3 + 5$

18. A person withdraws d dollars, deposits c dollars, and deposits b dollars. $-d + c + b$

19. Mary collects and trades old records. She has 40 Bing Crosby records. If she sells n of them and buys twice as many as she sells, how many will she have in all? $40 - n + 2n$ or $40 + n$

20. Display the number 3.14 on your calculator. Press the [+/−] twice.
a. What number appears in the display? 3.14
b. What property has been checked? Op-op Property

21. If $p = -8$ and $q = -10$, then $-(p + q) =$? . 18

22. If Andy's age is A, write an expression for his age:
a. 3 years from now **b.** 4 years ago a. $A + 3$; b. $A + -4$

In 23–27, simplify.

23. $x + b + 0 + -x + -b + -c$ **-c**

24. $-(-(-4))$ **-4**

25. $(17 + -35) + (36 + -18)$ **0**

26. $-7t^2 + 22t^2$ **$15t^2$**

27. $11a + 3a - 4$ **$14a - 4$**

28. **a.** Simplify $a + 2b + 3b + 4$. **$a + 5b + 4$**
b. Check your answer by substituting 6 for a and 3 for b. **See margin.**

Review

29. Write a simplified expression for the area of the figure shown. *(Lesson 2-1)* **$(87 + k)$ sq cm**

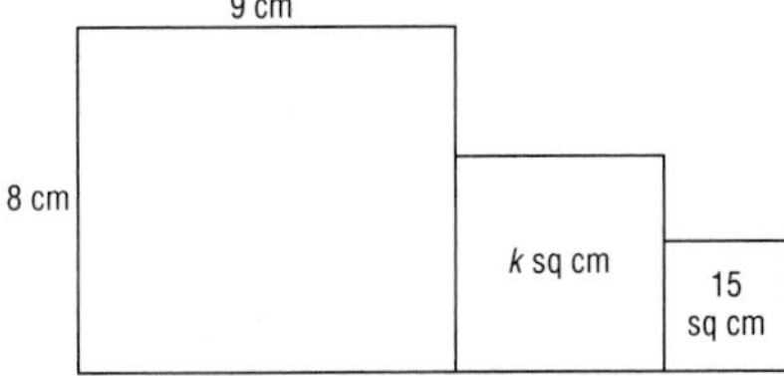

30. Fran had m dollars in savings. She received n dollars for her allowance. She then had more than enough money to buy a basketball for \$48. Express this using an inequality. *(Lessons 1-3, 2-1)* **$m + n > 48$**

31. In chapter 1, you saw the formula for the force f that you feel when riding in an elevator:

$$f = \frac{wa}{g}$$

where w = your weight, a = acceleration of the elevator, and $g \approx 32$ feet per second per second (gravity).

a. In the language BASIC, F = _?_. *(Lesson 1-4)* **F = W * A / G**

b. What force does a 90-pound person feel riding in an elevator accelerating at 4.5 feet per second per second? Round your answer to the nearest tenth of a pound. *(Lesson 1-5)* **12.6 pounds**

32. Freezing temperatures are those at or below 32 degrees Fahrenheit.

a. Graph all possibilities for freezing temperatures on a vertical number line. *(Lesson 1-1)* **See margin.**

b. Write an inequality representing all freezing temperatures in the Fahrenheit scale using x as the variable. *(Lesson 1-6)* **$x \le 32$**

33. If T is the set of planets in the solar system, then N(T) = _?_. *(Lesson 1-6)* **9**

34. The radius of the earth is about 6.37 million meters. Write this quantity in the following ways: **a) 6,370,000**

a. in decimal form without the word million *(Previous course)*

b. in scientific notation *(Appendix B)* **6.37×10^6**

Exploration

35. Negative numbers appear on TV in many situations. What real situation might each number represent?

a. -5.32 in stock market averages **See margin.**

b. -9 in rocket launches **See margin.**

c. -3 in golf **sample: three under par for a tournament**

FOLLOW-UP

MORE PRACTICE
For more practice on SPUR Objectives, use *Lesson Master 2-2,* shown below.

EXTENSION
Small Group Work Ask students to experiment to see if another operation on their calculator has the property described in **Question 20.** That is, pressing the key twice results in the return of the number originally entered. (the reciprocal key) Then ask students to find a pair of keys that can be pressed to return to the original value. (The pair they can understand now is x^2 and $\sqrt{x}$. Other pairs are e^x and ln, 10^x and log, sin and $\sin^{-1}$, cos and $\cos^{-1}$, tan and $\tan^{-1}$. These may require also pressing 2nd or INV keys.)

EVALUATION
Alternative Assessment
To evaluate students' understanding of properties, have them state each property in their own words. They can do this orally or in writing.

NAME ________

LESSON **MASTER 2–2**
QUESTIONS ON **SPUR** OBJECTIVES

■**SKILLS** *Objective B (See pages 102–105 for objectives.)*
In 1–8, simplify.

1. $-3 + t + -8$ — $t - 11$
2. $5x + -4x + 7x$ — $8x$
3. $6a + -7b + -3 + -2a$ — $4a - 7b - 3$
4. $0 + -5a$ — $-5a$
5. $-(-5) + y$ — $5 + y$
6. $7a + 6x + -7a$ — $6x$
7. $-12t^2 + 8t + -3t^2$ — $-15t^2 + 8t$
8. $2.3x + 5.1 + -4.6x$ — $5.1 - 2.3x$

■**PROPERTIES** *Objective E*
In 9–14, an instance of what property is given?

9. If $x = -3$, then $-x = 3$. — Op-op Property
10. $-ab + 0 = -ab$ — Additive Identity Property
11. $7y + -10y = -3y$ — Adding Like Terms Property
12. If $s = -6$, then $-(s) = 6$. — Op-op Property
13. $xy + -xy = 0$ — Property of Opposites
14. Jog 20 meters east, then 20 meters west, and you are back where you started. — Property of Opposites

■**USES** *Objective H*

15. A girl lost 10 lb, then gained 3 lb, then lost 4 lb. What is the total change in her weight? — -11 lb
16. A boy received gifts of g dollars and h dollars and spent x dollars, winding up with \$3.50. Write an equation representing this situation. — $g + h - x = 3.50$

 11

LESSON 2-3

RESOURCES

- Lesson Master 2-3
- Visual for Teaching Aid 7: Coordinate Grid
- Visual for Teaching Aid 10: Derivation of $\frac{a}{b} + \frac{c}{d} = \frac{ad + bc}{bd}$

OBJECTIVES

A Add fractions.
E Identify properties of addition.

TEACHING NOTES

You may be tempted to stay on this topic for more than one day. However, we recommend that you not stall here. There is a lot of review on addition of fractions in the rest of this chapter and in the Chapter Review. Most students should be able to add fractions when the chapter has been completed.

Reading The lesson shows a development of the formula

$$\frac{a}{b} + \frac{c}{d} = \frac{ad + bc}{bd}.$$

There are a lot of variables being used, and it is tempting to just look at the beginning and the end, skipping the middle of the derivation. This is not the way that mathematics should be read. Instead, the reader should follow each step, identifying what has been done and thinking about why the step is justified. After stepping through the process, they should look back and realize that the formula ties the beginning phrase with the final one, so the middle steps are omitted when applying the formula.

LESSON 2-3 Addition of Fractions

The slide model for addition can help you picture addition of fractions. For instance, the slide model confirms that $\frac{1}{4} + \frac{3}{4} = 1$.

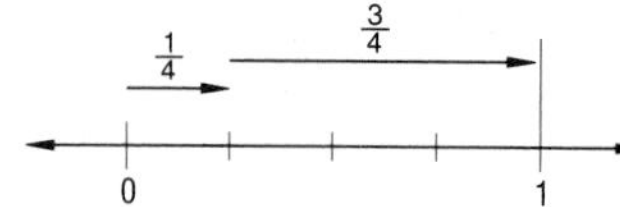

What does this tell you about adding fractions? It shows you that $\frac{1}{4} + \frac{3}{4} \neq \frac{1+3}{4+4} = \frac{4}{8}$. You do *not* add numerators and denominators. In fact, you add the numerators and keep the same denominator, called the **common denominator.**

Adding Fractions Property:

For all real numbers a, b, and c, with $c \neq 0$,

$$\frac{a}{c} + \frac{b}{c} = \frac{a + b}{c}.$$

Sometimes expressions involving fractions give a result which can be simplified.

Example 1 Simplify $\frac{-9 + 3b}{b} + \frac{9}{b}$.

Solution Since the denominators are the same, the Adding Fractions Property can be applied.

$$\frac{-9 + 3b}{b} + \frac{9}{b} = \frac{-9 + 3b + 9}{b}$$

$= \frac{3b}{b}$ Adding Like Terms Property, Additive Identity Property

$= 3$ Equal Fractions Property

The expression equals 3, regardless of the value of b.

Check We substitute 2 for b in the original expression and follow order of operations

$$\frac{-9 + 3 \cdot 2}{2} + \frac{9}{2} = \frac{-9 + 6}{2} + \frac{9}{2} = \frac{-3}{2} + \frac{9}{2} = \frac{6}{2} = 3.$$ It checks.

The Adding Fractions Property is quite similar to the Adding Like Terms Property. Instead of like terms, the denominators are the same. Both are special uses of a more general Distributive Property, which you will study in Chapter 6.

The rule for adding fractions is more complicated when the denominators are not the same. To picture adding $\frac{1}{2}$ and $\frac{1}{3}$, think of finding the coordinate of P.

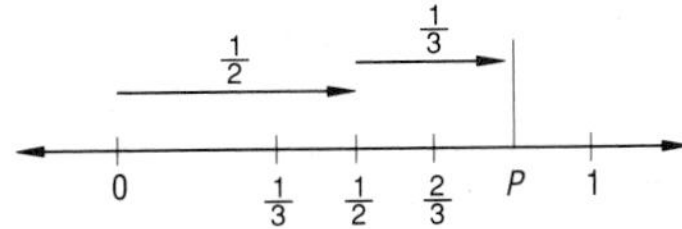

The difficulty lies in the fact that P does not lie on one of the tick marks. The interval between 0 and 1 must be divided into intervals which can measure both $\frac{1}{2}$ and $\frac{1}{3}$. Dividing it into sixths will work, since $\frac{1}{2}$ and $\frac{1}{3}$ can both be expressed as sixths. By the Equal Fractions Property, $\frac{1}{2} = \frac{3}{6}$ and $\frac{1}{3} = \frac{2}{6}$.

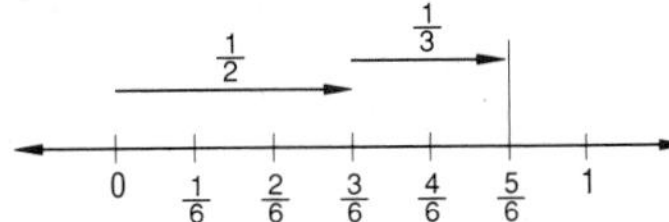

So $\frac{1}{2} + \frac{1}{3} = \frac{3}{6} + \frac{2}{6} = \frac{5}{6}$. Changing the interval on the number line to sixths illustrates the process of finding a common denominator.

The process of adding fractions with different denominators involves three steps. First, find a common denominator. Then use the Equal Fractions Property to rewrite the fractions with the common denominator. Last, add the numerators. Write this sum over the denominator. The next example involves mixed numbers, which have both whole number and fraction parts.

One complication when reading a book is that all the lines appear at once on the page. It might be helpful to show the class a copy of the derivation on an overhead projector, uncovering just one line at a time.

Some students prefer the preceding formula to the traditional method of employing least common denominators and they use it with good results. Of course, the formula does not always use the most efficient denominator, does not work well when more than two fractions are to be added, and often leads to answers that are not in lowest terms.

In **Example 4,** Solution 1, it may be helpful to look at the problem and identify the values of *a*, *b*, *c*, and *d* before showing how they are substituted into the formula.

Example 2 Find the perimeter of the triangle below.

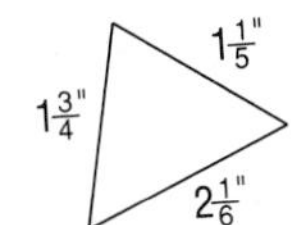

Solution 1 Change each mixed number to a fraction, then add.

$$1\tfrac{3}{4} + 2\tfrac{1}{6} + 1\tfrac{1}{5} = \tfrac{7}{4} + \tfrac{13}{6} + \tfrac{6}{5}$$

$$= \tfrac{105}{60} + \tfrac{130}{60} + \tfrac{72}{60}$$ A common denominator for $\frac{7}{4}$, $\frac{13}{6}$, and $\frac{6}{5}$ is 60.

$$= \tfrac{307}{60}$$

$$= 5\tfrac{7}{60} \text{ inches}$$

ADDITIONAL EXAMPLES

1. Simplify

$$\frac{5x + 2}{x} + \frac{3x + -2}{x}.$$

8

2. Find the perimeter of this rectangle.

$14\frac{1}{3}$

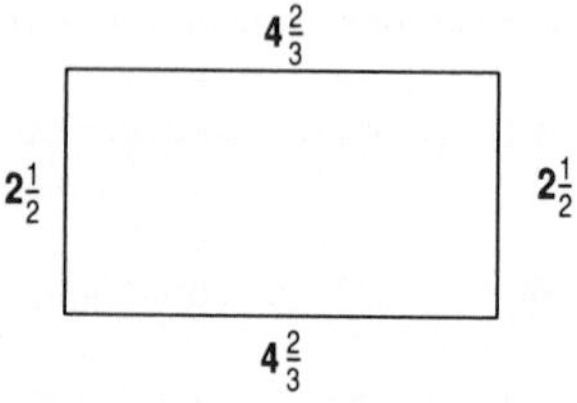

3. International Consolidated Stock dropped $1\frac{1}{8}$ dollars one day and rose $\frac{1}{2}$ dollar the next day. What was the net change?

The price dropped $\frac{5}{8}$ dollar.

4. Write as a single fraction.

$$\frac{5}{n} + \frac{11}{x}$$

$\frac{5x + 11n}{nx}$

Solution 2 The perimeter is $1\frac{3}{4} + 2\frac{1}{6} + 1\frac{1}{5}$.

Think of each mixed number as a sum. For example, $1\frac{3}{4} = 1 + \frac{3}{4}$.

$1\frac{3}{4} + 2\frac{1}{6} + 1\frac{1}{5} = 1 + \frac{3}{4} + 2 + \frac{1}{6} + 1 + \frac{1}{5}$

Group the whole numbers together and the fractions together.

$$\begin{aligned} &= 1 + 2 + 1 + \tfrac{3}{4} + \tfrac{1}{6} + \tfrac{1}{5} \\ &= 4 + \tfrac{45}{60} + \tfrac{10}{60} + \tfrac{12}{60} \\ &= 4 + \tfrac{67}{60} \\ &= 4 + 1\tfrac{7}{60} \\ &= 5\tfrac{7}{60} \text{ inches} \end{aligned}$$

A common denominator for $\frac{3}{4}$, $\frac{1}{6}$, and $\frac{1}{5}$ is 60.

Check Change the fractions to decimals. $1\frac{3}{4} = 1.75$, $2\frac{1}{6} \approx 2.17$, $1\frac{1}{5} = 1.2$, $5\frac{7}{60} \approx 5.12$. Is $1.75 + 2.17 + 1.2 \approx 5.12$? Yes.

The next example uses negative numbers in fraction form. Notice that $-\frac{9}{8}$ and $\frac{-9}{8}$ represent the same number.

Example 3 On Monday, McDonald's stock rose $\frac{3}{4}$ point; on Tuesday it fell $1\frac{1}{8}$. What was the net change?

Solution 1 A loss of $1\frac{1}{8}$ is a change of $-1\frac{1}{8}$. The answer can be found by computing $\frac{3}{4} + -1\frac{1}{8}$. You can use a common denominator of 8.

$$\frac{3}{4} + -1\frac{1}{8} = \frac{6}{8} + -1\frac{1}{8} = \frac{6}{8} + \frac{-9}{8} = \frac{6 + -9}{8} = -\frac{3}{8}.$$

The stock went down $\frac{3}{8}$ of a point.

Instead of rewriting the fractions with a common denominator, there is a formula that can be used when adding two fractions. You may find the formula helpful. It is developed by letting $\frac{a}{b}$ and $\frac{c}{d}$ stand for any two fractions. Then $b \neq 0$ and $d \neq 0$. A common denominator is bd. By the equal fractions property $\frac{a}{b} = \frac{ad}{bd}$ and $\frac{c}{d} = \frac{bc}{bd}$.

$$\begin{aligned} \frac{a}{b} + \frac{c}{d} &= \frac{ad}{bd} + \frac{bc}{bd} \\ &= \frac{ad + bc}{bd} \end{aligned}$$

This formula is used in the first solution of Example 2.

Example 4 Write $\frac{1}{4} + \frac{x}{3}$ as a single fraction.

Solution 1 Use the formula. $\frac{1}{4} + \frac{x}{3} = \frac{1 \cdot 3 + 4 \cdot x}{12}$

$$= \frac{3 + 4x}{12}$$

Solution 2 Use the common denominator 12.

$$\frac{1}{4} + \frac{x}{3} = \frac{1 \cdot 3}{4 \cdot 3} + \frac{4 \cdot x}{4 \cdot 3}$$
$$= \frac{3 + 4x}{12}$$

Check Substitute a number for x. We use $x = 2$. Then does

$$\frac{1}{4} + \frac{x}{3} = \frac{3 + 4x}{12}?$$

Does $\frac{1}{4} + \frac{2}{3} = \frac{3 + 4 \cdot 2}{12}$? Yes, both sides equal $\frac{11}{12}$.

Questions

Covering the Reading

1. To add two fractions by adding the numerators, what must be true of the denominators? **They must be equal.**

2. What common denominator can you use to help in adding $\frac{1}{3}$ and $\frac{7}{4}$? **12**

3. Use the slide model of addition to show $\frac{1}{4} + \frac{3}{8} = \frac{5}{8}$. **See margin.**

4. In Example 4, the final answer was $\frac{3 + 4x}{12}$. Show by substituting $x = 2$ that $\frac{7x}{12}$ is *not* the same as $\frac{3 + 4x}{12}$. $\frac{3 + 4 \cdot 2}{12} = \frac{11}{12}$, $\frac{7 \cdot 2}{12} = \frac{14}{12}$

5. Tell what your calculator gives for the following computations of $-\frac{5}{8}$ and $\frac{-5}{8}$: 5 [÷] 8 [=] [±] and 5 [±] [÷] 8 [=]. **-.625, -.625**

In 6–9, simplify.

6. $\frac{-3}{5} + \frac{1}{5}$ $-\frac{2}{5}$

7. $1\frac{1}{2} + 2\frac{2}{3} + \frac{1}{3}$ $4\frac{1}{2}$

8. $\frac{3}{4} + \frac{-2}{x}$ $\frac{3x + -8}{4x}$

9. $\frac{6y + 11}{2y} + \frac{-11}{2y}$ 3

Applying the Mathematics

10. *True or false* $\frac{a}{b} + \frac{c}{d} = \frac{a+c}{b+d}$. **False**

11. Write as a single fraction.
 a. $\frac{x}{5} + \frac{x}{3}$ $\frac{8x}{15}$
 b. $\frac{5}{x} + \frac{3}{x}$ $\frac{8}{x}$
 c. $\frac{f}{g} + \frac{3}{5}$ $\frac{5f + 3g}{5g}$
 d. $\frac{b}{c} + \frac{3}{x}$ $\frac{bx + 3c}{cx}$

NOTES ON QUESTIONS
Question 5: Calculator key sequences are used to show that $-\left(\frac{a}{b}\right) = \frac{-a}{b}$. You could have students verify that $\frac{a}{-b}$ is also equal to these. Watch for students who confuse the word *and* between the two key sequences with the *and* that means addition.

ADDITIONAL ANSWERS
3.

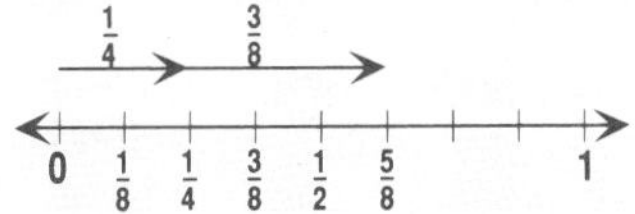

NOTES ON QUESTIONS
Making Connections for Question 16a: Finding the mean of two fractions may be unfamiliar to students. The formula for the mean of two numbers (given in Chapter 1), requires division by 2. Many students do not realize that division by 2 is equivalent to multiplying by 1/2, an easy procedure when working with fractions. This question therefore offers an opportunity to multiply algebraic fractions.

Question 16b: Students may not realize that variable expressions can represent real numbers, and may think that they are being asked for a numerical answer.

Making Connections for Question 28: Students are asked to name ordered pairs. For most students, this reviews ideas from earlier courses. Whether it is review or not, class discussion of this question will set the stage for Lesson 2-4, which discusses the coordinate plane.

FOLLOW-UP

MORE PRACTICE
For more practice on SPUR Objectives, use *Lesson Master 2-3,* shown on page 73.

20.

21. sample: the temperature ranged from -3 to 4 degrees

28. $A = (1, 4)$, $B = (5, 2)$, $C = (-2, 2)$, $D = (-5, 0)$, $E = (0, -2)$, $F = (-5, -3)$, $G = (3, -3)$, $H = (3, 0)$

12. a. Calculate $1\frac{3}{4} + 2\frac{1}{2} + -5\frac{7}{8}$. $-1\frac{5}{8}$

b. Check part a by changing the fractions to decimals and adding on a calculator.
1.75 + 2.5 + -5.875 = -1.625; $-1\frac{5}{8}$ = -1.625. It checks.

13. Add $\frac{k}{2} + \frac{2k}{3} + \frac{k}{4}$. $\frac{17k}{12}$

14. In a tug-of-war, team A pulled the rope $3\frac{1}{2}$ ft toward its side, then team B pulled it $1\frac{2}{3}$ ft toward its side. After another minute, team B pulled the rope $4\frac{5}{6}$ ft more in its direction. What is the status of the middle of the rope at this point? 3 ft toward team B's side

15. Simplify $(\frac{1}{3} + -\frac{1}{3}) + (f + \frac{1}{3})$. $f + \frac{1}{3}$ or $\frac{3f + 1}{3}$

Review

16. a. What is the mean of $\frac{x}{2}$ and $\frac{x}{3}$? $\frac{5x}{12}$ 16b) samples: $\frac{5x}{12}$, $\frac{2x}{5}$

b. Give a real number that is between $\frac{x}{2}$ and $\frac{x}{3}$. *(Lessons 1-2, 1-6)*

17. *Multiple choice* Which of the following *must* be a negative number? *(Lesson 2-2)*
(a) $-x$ (b) $-(-3)$ (c) $-(-(-\frac{1}{3}))$ (d) $-(-a)$ (c)

18. Write an expression to describe each situation. *(Lesson 2-2)*
a. Jamie's temperature went up 2°, then down y°, then down 2.4°.
b. Marie climbed u meters up the hill then d meters back down.
c. Stanley earned $7e$ dollars, then paid back $5e$ dollars to one friend while collecting c dollars from another.
a) $-y + -.4$; b) $u + -d$; c) $2e + c$

19. Complete the following: *(Previous course)*

Percent		Decimal		Fraction
40%	=	.40	=	$\frac{2}{5}$
60%	=	? .60	=	$\frac{3}{5}$
5%	=	.05	=	? $\frac{1}{20}$
? 10%	=	? .10	=	$\frac{1}{10}$

20. An acute angle has a measure between 0° and 90°. Graph the interval on a number line. *(Lesson 1-3)* See margin.

21. Give an example of a situation that could be represented by the graph at the left. *(Lesson 1-3)* See margin.

22. There are two children in the Windsor family. What is the probability that one is a boy and one is a girl? *(Lesson 1-7)* $\frac{2}{4}$ or $\frac{1}{2}$

23. Evaluate $4x^2 - 5y$, when $x = 3$ and $y = 5$. *(Lesson 1-4)* 11

24. Match each phrase with an equivalent expression. *(Previous course)*
a. three times a number ii
b. three more than a number i
c. the sum of three and a number i
d. the quotient of a number and 3 iv
e. a number to the third power iii

i. $n + 3$
ii. $3n$
iii. n^3
iv. $\frac{n}{3}$

72

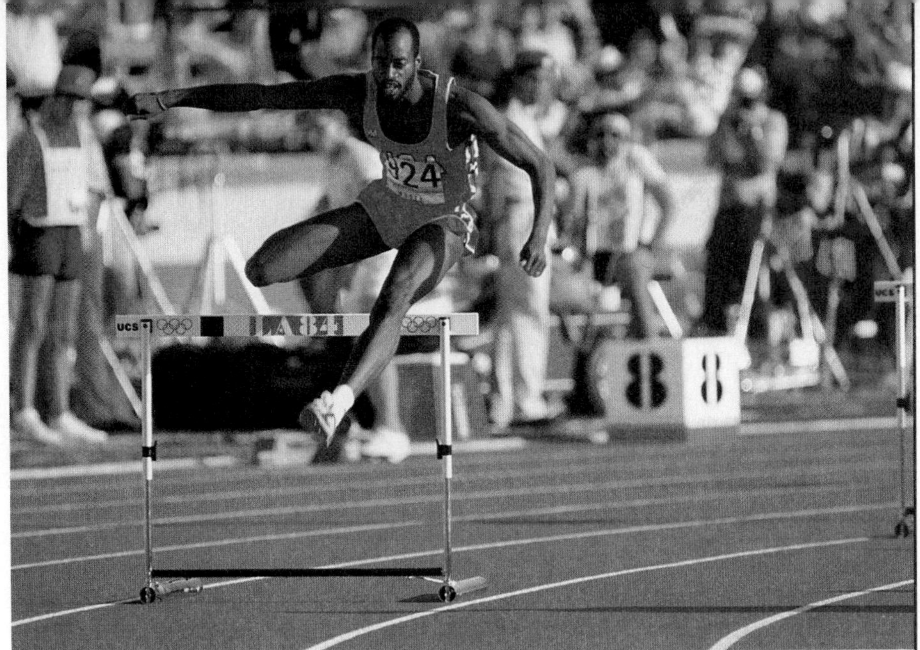

25. In the eleven-year period from 1977 through 1987, Edwin Moses won 122 consecutive victories, including an Olympic gold medal, in the 400-meter hurdles. What was his mean number of victories per year? *(Lesson 1-2)* **about 11.1**

26. *Multiple choice* Which is *not* equal to the others? *(Lesson 1-2)* **d**
(a) $1\frac{2}{5}$ (b) 1.4 (c) $\frac{14}{10}$ (d) $1.\overline{4}$

27. The pairs of lines in these drawings are called __?__. *(Previous course)* **perpendicular lines**

28. Give the coordinates of each ordered pair on this graph. *(Previous course)* **See margin.**

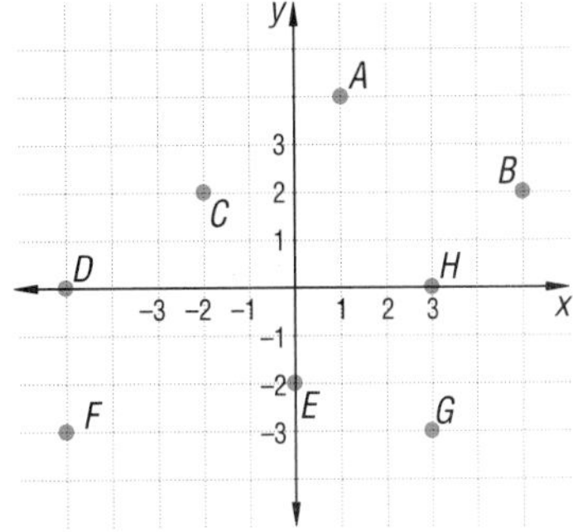

Exploration

29. **a.** Use your calculator to compute each sum.
i. $\frac{1}{2} + \frac{1}{4} + \frac{1}{8}$ **.875** **ii.** $\frac{1}{2} + \frac{1}{4} + \frac{1}{8} + \frac{1}{16}$ **.9375**
iii. $\frac{1}{2} + \frac{1}{4} + \frac{1}{8} + \frac{1}{16} + \frac{1}{32}$ **.96875**
b. If you could do an infinite addition problem, what do you think you would get as an answer to $\frac{1}{2} + \frac{1}{4} + \frac{1}{8} + \frac{1}{16} + \frac{1}{32} + \frac{1}{64} + \ldots$? **1**

EXTENSION
The exploration in **Question 29** brings up the idea of a finite sum of an infinite series. This topic frequently leads to a lively discussion. Some of your students may want to look up *Zeno's Paradoxes* and find out more about similar conditions that yield seemingly contradictory results.

One of the paradoxes involves Achilles and the tortoise in a race. Achilles ran 10 times as fast as the tortoise but the tortoise got a 100-cubit head start. After Achilles had run to the tortoise's starting point, the tortoise had run 10 cubits. When Achilles got to the tortoise's new point, it had moved 1 cubit. Can Achilles ever catch up? (Yes. This paradox confuses the fact that the finite distances covered by Achilles and the tortoise can be divided into infinitely many parts. Achilles must run $111\frac{1}{9}$ cubits to catch the tortoise, who in the same time will have run $11\frac{1}{9}$ cubits.)

NAME ____________

LESSON **MASTER 2–3**
QUESTIONS ON **SPUR** OBJECTIVES

SKILLS *Objective A* *(See pages 102–105 for objectives.)*
In 1–8, write as a single fraction.

1. $\frac{2}{3} + \frac{3}{4}$ **$\frac{17}{12}$**
2. $\frac{1}{3} + \frac{-1}{6} + \frac{3}{8}$ **$\frac{13}{24}$**
3. $-2\frac{3}{5} + -3\frac{8}{15}$ **$-\frac{92}{15}$**
4. $\frac{x}{5} + \frac{4}{5}$ **$\frac{x + 4}{5}$**
5. $\frac{p}{18} + \frac{5}{6}$ **$\frac{p + 15}{18}$**
6. $\frac{12}{c} + \frac{7}{c}$ **$\frac{19}{c}$**
7. $\frac{a}{m} + \frac{1}{n}$ **$\frac{an + m}{mn}$**
8. $\frac{x}{r} + \frac{y}{s}$ **$\frac{xs + ry}{rs}$**

9. Juan owned a stock whose value rose $\frac{5}{8}$ point on Monday, rose $\frac{1}{4}$ point on Tuesday, and fell $1\frac{1}{2}$ points on Wednesday. What was the overall change in his stock's value for these three days? **$-\frac{5}{8}$**

10. What is the perimeter of a rectangle with length $2\frac{1}{10}$ and width $1\frac{3}{5}$? **$7\frac{2}{5}$**

11. Represent the perimeter of a triangle with sides $1\frac{1}{8}$, $2\frac{4}{5}$, and x as a simplified algebraic expression. **$\frac{157}{40} + x$**

PROPERTIES *Objective E*
In 12–15, identify what property of addition is given.

12. $\frac{5}{12} + 0 = \frac{5}{12}$ **Add. Identity Prop.**
13. $3x + 5 + 2x = 5x + 5$ **Adding Like Terms Prop.**
14. $-(-x) = x$ **Op-op Prop.**
15. $\frac{x}{13} + \frac{-x}{13} = 0$ **Prop. of Opposites**

12 *Algebra* © Scott, Foresman and Company

LESSON 2-4

RESOURCES
- Lesson Master 2-4
- Quiz on Lessons 2-1 Through 2-4
- Visual for Teaching Aid 7: Coordinate Grid
- Visual for Teaching Aid 11: Graph and Chart for **Example 3**
- Visual for Teaching Aid 12: Graphs for Additional Examples 1 and 2
- Computer Master 3

OBJECTIVE

K Plot points and interpret information on a coordinate graph.

TEACHING NOTES

Reading When you read a novel, you read continuously along the page. But in reading this lesson, your eye should move back and forth from text to graph or chart. Students need to have this pointed out. You might have the lesson read aloud in class and mention places where the reader should look at a graph or chart.

LESSON

2-4 The Coordinate Plane

Coordinate graphs of the plane make it possible to picture relationships between pairs of numbers. They can display a lot of information and show trends in a small space. Here is an example of what you can do with such a graph.

DAILY BUGLE

TV Linked to Drop in Homework

Mrs. Hernandez, a teacher, read the headline in the newspaper at the left. To test whether the headline is true, Mrs. Hernandez asked her class to keep track of the time they spent at home studying and the time they spent watching TV. The next day, she had her students record their times on the board. The table below shows what her students reported.

Time Spent on TV and Homework (minutes)

Student	TV	Homework	Student	TV	Homework
Alex	60	30	Jim	120	75
Beth	0	60	Kerry	30	45
Carol	120	30	Lawanda	120	45
David	90	90	Meg	150	60
Evan	210	0	Nancy	180	15
Frank	150	30	Ophelia	60	120
Gary	0	90	Paula	90	75
Harper	90	60	Quincy	60	45
Irene	120	0			

To see if there is a connection between the time spent watching television and the time spent studying, Mrs. Hernandez graphed these data on a two-dimensional **coordinate graph.** She drew perpendicular number lines called **axes.** The point with coordinate 0 was the same on the axes. This point is called the **origin.**

Mrs. Hernandez then located a point for each student by starting at the origin and moving right the number of minutes spent watching TV. Then she moved up the number of minutes spent on homework. She drew a point on the graph and coded it with the student's initial.

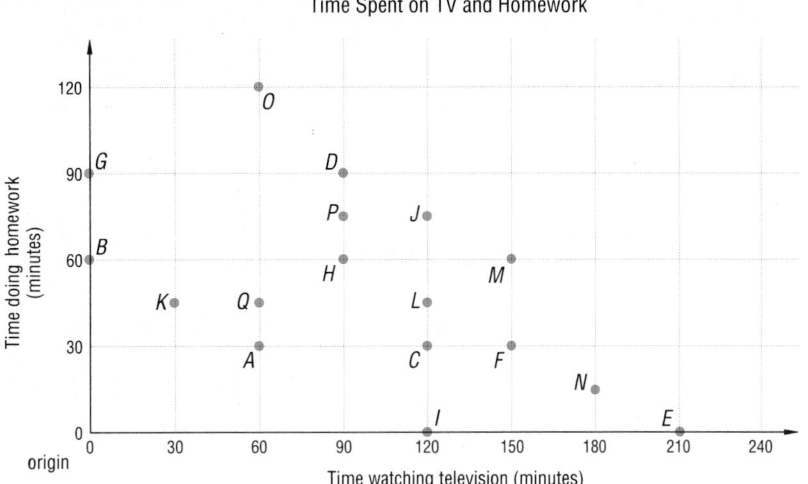

Paula's dot is at 90 right, 75 up since she spent 90 minutes watching TV and 75 minutes on homework. This point can be expressed as the ordered pair (90, 75) and is labeled as point P on the graph.

A two-dimensional coordinate graph is needed for these data since each response involves two numbers. This kind of graph is called a **scattergram.**

Example 1 Refer to the table and the scattergram on pages 74–75.

a. Responses of how many students are shown on the scattergram?
b. How many students reported doing homework for exactly 90 minutes?
c. How many students watched at least 120 minutes of television?
d. Who is represented by the ordered pair (60, 120)?

Solution

a. There are 17 student responses because there are 17 data points on the scattergram.
b. Two students (Gary, David) did exactly 90 minutes of homework because there are two data points on the horizontal line for 90.
c. The line for 120 minutes of TV is in the middle of the graph. Look for points on this line or to the right of it. There are 8 such points, so 8 students watched at least 120 minutes of TV.
d. The point at O, 60 right, 120 up, represents Ophelia.

From the pattern of dots, Mrs. Hernandez's class decided that the headline was generally true. As students watched more TV, they did less homework.

A scattergram can show trends that are not obvious from a table.

Even students who have had coordinate graphs in previous courses may still be unaccustomed to graphs in which the axes do not intersect at (0, 0) as in **Example 2.** In applications, the axes seldom intersect at (0, 0). Instead, the scales are picked so that the data can be conveniently displayed.

Making Connections
Three other comments can be made about **Example 2.** First, students may not realize the meaning of positive and negative net exports, that a negative value means the U.S. imported more than it exported. Second, in **Example 2b** the intention is that comparisons should be made simply by looking at the graph. Using subtraction to compare numbers will be covered in Lesson 3-2. Third, the solution of this example concludes by stating that the graph cannot be used to predict the future. You might add that economists do use graphs like these, but need much more information about what caused the trends before they make predictions.

ADDITIONAL EXAMPLES

1. The graph below shows the number of people in a classroom over a period of time.

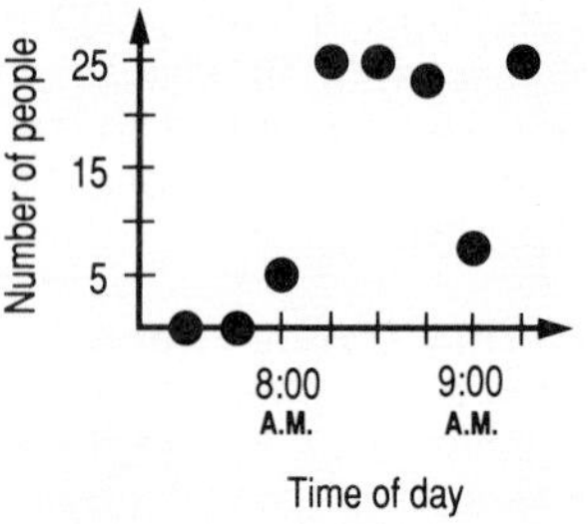

Invent a story that explains the graph.

sample: The teacher is in the room at 7:30. By 8:00 a few students have arrived. At 8:15 class has started. At 8:45 two students have left early. Nine o'clock is during a passing period, so only a few students are in the room. By 9:15 the next class has started.

2. A graph can be purposely made to be misleading by adjusting the scale. The two graphs below show the same data.

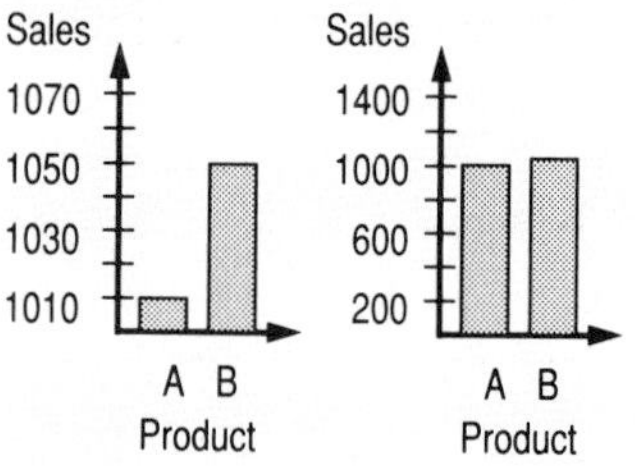

Which graph is misleading, and why?

The first graph, because it exaggerates the difference between the two companies' sales by not beginning the vertical axis at 0.

Example 2 United States "exports" are goods made in the U.S. and sold in another country. United States "imports" are goods made in another country and sold in the U.S. "Net exports" are calculated by subtracting imports from exports. They tell whether money is flowing in or out of a country.

a. Graph the information in this table.

b. In which year was the decline from the previous year greatest?

c. Is there an obvious trend from which to predict the future?

United States Net Exports of Goods and Services (billions of dollars)

Year	Amount
1975	23
1976	10
1977	-10
1978	-10
1979	-5
1980	10
1981	14
1982	0
1983	-37
1984	-99
1985	-103

Solution

a. The variable time is usually graphed on the horizontal axis. On the vertical axis, use a scale that allows numbers from -103 to 23. The table can be viewed as points named (1975, 23), (1976, 10), and so on.

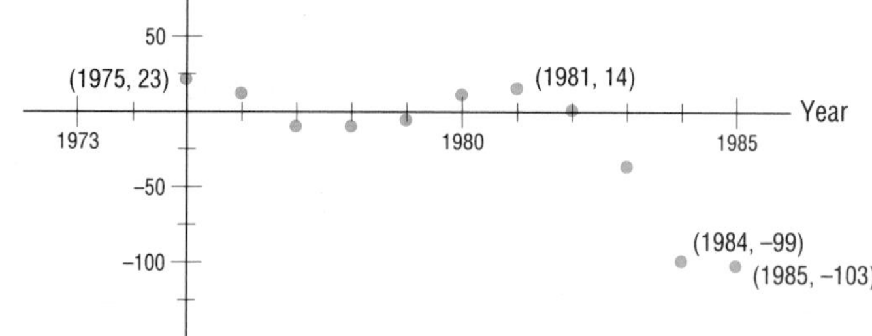

b. Read from left to right, when the dots go down, there is a decline. The biggest decline occurred in 1984.

c. From 1981 to 1985 there was a decline. That is one trend. But the years 1975 to 1981 show that trends can change from declines to increases. There is no obvious trend from which to predict the future.

Examples 1 and 2 use graphs to describe discrete situations. Example 3 displays a continuous situation with a graph.

Example 3 Here is a graph indicating the speed Harold Hooper traveled as he drove from home to work. Invent a story that explains the graph.

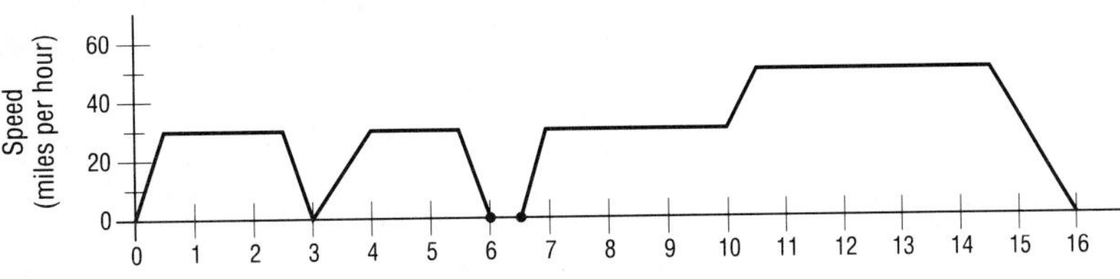

Solution Some key times are 3 minutes after he had left home, between 6 and $6\frac{1}{2}$ minutes after he left, and at 10 minutes after he left. He was going 0 miles per hour at the three-minute mark. He may have stopped for a stop sign. He was stopped for about $\frac{1}{2}$ minute beginning at the six-minute mark. This could have resulted from Harold's stopping at a stoplight. The change of speed at 10 minutes could be explained by a change of speed limit from 30 mph to 55 mph. (Of course, other stories are possible.)

Questions

Covering the Reading

1. The number lines used in a coordinate graph are called __?__ and share a point called the __?__. **axes, origin**

In 2–4, refer to Example 1.

2. Which ordered pair describes Alex's responses? **(60, 30)**

3. **a.** According to the graph, how many students did not watch any television? **2**
   b. How much time did each of these students spend on homework? **Beth, 60 minutes; Gary, 90 minutes**

4. What is the trend in this graph? **See margin.**

In 5–7, refer to Example 2.

5. Why are the numbers on the vertical axis given in billions of dollars? **to make the graph easier to use and to read**

6. When were the net exports the greatest? **1975**

7. How much less were the net exports in 1985 than in 1975? **$126 billion less**

Applying the Mathematics

8. Refer to the table and scattergram on pages 74 and 75.
   a. What is the median TV time? **90 minutes**
   b. What is the median homework time? **45 minutes**
   c. Which student's times are closest to the ordered pair of medians found in parts a and b? **Harper**

9. Refer to Example 3. What speed was the mode for Harold's trip to work? **30 mph**

NOTES ON QUESTIONS
Making Connections for Questions 10-12: These questions are examples of the type often found on college entrance exams. Also, **Questions 10 and 11** presage important work with lines in Chapters 7 and 8.

Questions 13-15: The graph related to these questions is a good example of the complexity found in real-world graphs. You may want to talk about the graph before assigning the questions so that students can move through the questions faster. Notice that the horizontal axis is not marked off in uniform lengths because the graph begins by including data at 10-year intervals and then includes data for the years 1974 and 1977. This was done to illustrate the rise in the price of coffee.

Error Analysis for Question 21: Students who use the formula from the previous lesson may give an answer of

$$\frac{17a}{5a^2},$$

not realizing that it can be reduced to

$$\frac{17}{5a}.$$

Students who use the LCD should get the correct answer in lowest terms.

ADDITIONAL ANSWERS
4. The students who watched more TV tended to spend less time doing homework.

NOTES ON QUESTIONS
Question 23: This is the first encounter with subscripts in this book. You might explain that subscripts are like people's last names. John Smith is a different person than John Jones, but without the last name, people might think they are the same person.

Question 25: The notation $m\angle PQR$ may be unfamiliar to your students, either because they are not used to naming angles or they may not realize that m means "the measure of the angle."

Question 31: Students are asked to survey some of their friends. Some people will undoubtedly contribute data to more than one student, so the answers will not be independent and are likely to be more similar than if everyone had used different friends.

FOLLOW-UP

MORE PRACTICE
For more questions on SPUR Objectives, use *Lesson Master 2-4,* shown on page 79.

EVALUATION
A quiz covering Lessons 2-1 through 2-4 is provided in the Teacher's Resource File on page 6.

16a.

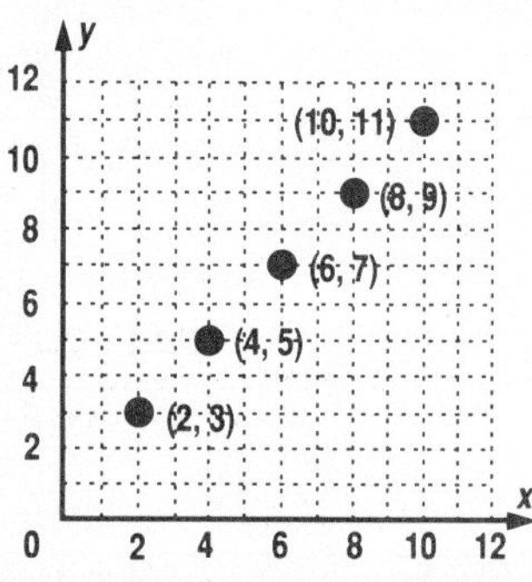

Questions 10 and 11 are *multiple choice*. Which of the following situations is represented by the graph? **10) a; 11) c**

(a) The distance traveled in h hours at 50 mph
(b) The distance traveled in h hours at 75 mph
(c) The distance you are from home if you started 150 miles from home and traveled at 50 mph

10.

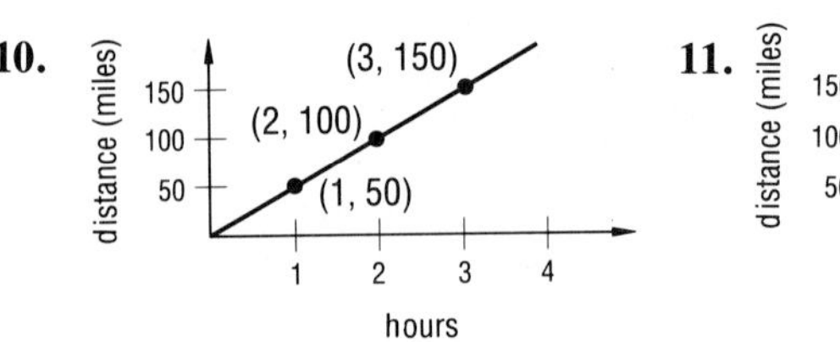

11.

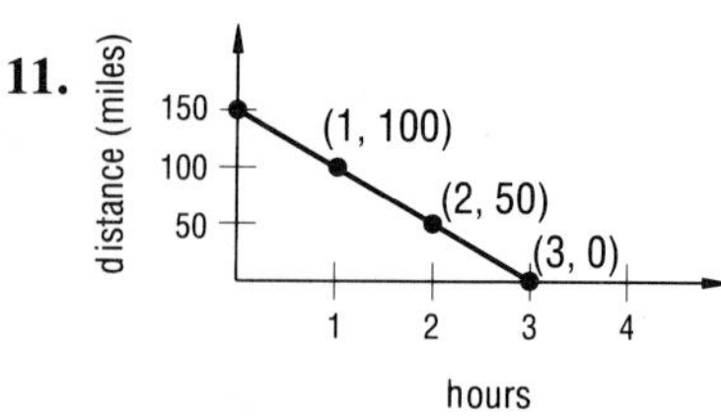

12. *Multiple choice* Which situation is represented by the graph at left?
(a) The cost d in dollars of h hamburgers at a cost of \$1 each.
(b) The cost d in dollars of h hamburgers at a cost of \$2 each.
(c) The change d that you could get back from a \$10 dollar bill, if you purchased h hamburgers at a cost of \$2 each.
(b)

hamburgers (h)
dollars (d)

In 13–15, use the graph below.

13. On the average, how many minutes did a worker have to work in 1940 to buy one dozen eggs? **31 minutes**

14. In general, would you say it took a greater or lower percentage of a person's time to buy the four items in 1970 than in 1930? **lower**

15. *Multiple choice* In dollars, the cost of the items in 1977 as compared with 1930 is **(c)**
(a) more (b) less (c) can't tell

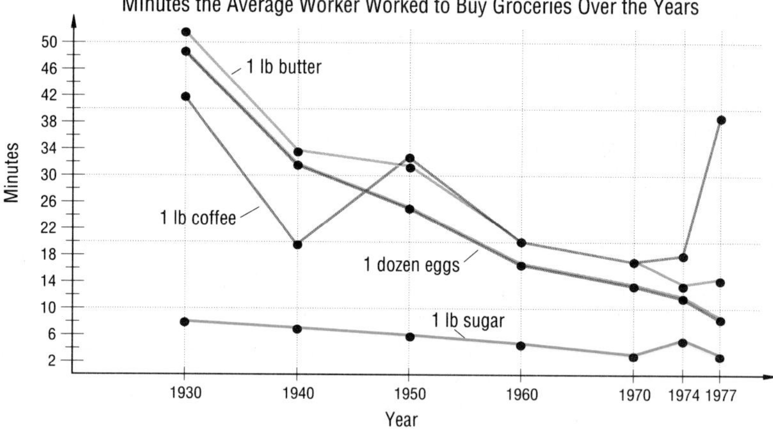

16. a. Make a coordinate graph showing the following set of points: {(2, 3), (4, 5), (6, 7), (8, 9), (10, 11)} **See margin.**

b. If the pattern continues, what is the missing coordinate in (100, __?__)? **101**

c. If the pattern continues, what is the missing coordinate in (m, __?__)? $m + 1$

Review

17. a. Add. -7 + 2 + -5 + 9 + 8 + -3 **4**
b. Add. $-7m + 2m + -5m + 9m + 8m + -3m$ *(Lesson 2-2)* **4m**

18. The value of IBM stock went down $2\frac{3}{8}$ points on July 30. On July 31 and August 1 it went up $\frac{3}{8}$ of a point each day. Find the net change in IBM stock over this three-day period. *(Lesson 2-3)* **down $1\frac{5}{8}$, or $-1\frac{5}{8}$**

19. Three distinct coins are tossed once. What is the probability that all three will land heads up? *(Lesson 1-7)* $\frac{1}{8}$

In 20–22, write as a single fraction. *(Lesson 2-3)*

20. $\frac{x}{3} + -\frac{2}{5}$ $\frac{5x + -6}{15}$ **21.** $\frac{2}{a} + \frac{7}{5a}$ $\frac{17}{5a}$ **22.** $\frac{3}{p} + -\frac{2}{q}$ $\frac{3q + -2p}{pq}$

23. Suppose $h_1 + h_2 = 0$ and $h_1 = 17.3$.
a. What is the value of h_2? **-17.3**
b. What property does this illustrate? *(Lesson 2-2)* **Property of Opposites**

24. Lucy lost two pounds, gained p pounds, then lost q pounds. Write an addition expression representing the change in Lucy's weight. *(Lesson 2-1)* **$-2 + p + -q$**

25. m∠PQR is 140°. Write an equation that relates 140, $x + 7$, and y. *(Lesson 2-1, Previous course)* **$x + 7 + y = 140$**

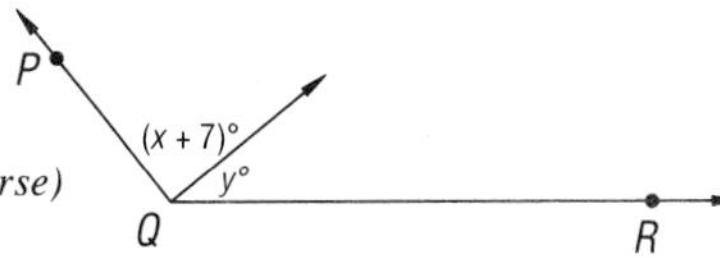

26. Write a set S with prime numbers as elements where N(S) = 5. *(Lesson 1-6)* **sample: {2, 3, 5, 7, 11}**

27. To estimate the number of bricks N needed in a wall, some bricklayers use the formula $N = 7LH$, where L and H are the length and height of the wall in feet. About how many bricks would a bricklayer need for a wall 8.5 feet high and 24.5 feet long? *(Lesson 1-5)* **1460**

28. To compute Jane's salary, use the formula $s = 4.50h + 6.75t$, where h is regular hours worked and t represents overtime. How much did she earn this week with 20 regular hours and 5 hours overtime? *(Lesson 1-5)* **$123.75**

29. Evaluate $-3x^3$ when $x = -1.4$. *(Lesson 1-4)* **8.232**

30. Evaluate in your head when $t = 4$. *(Lesson 1-4)*
a. $t + -9$ **b.** $-3t$ **c.** $-2t^2$ **a) -5; b) -12; c) -32**

Exploration

31. a. Do a survey of at least 10 of your friends. Ask them how much time they spent watching TV and how much they spent doing homework yesterday.
b. Plot your results on a scattergram.
c. Do your data agree with the newspaper headline in this lesson?
a., b., c.: Answers will vary. A sample is shown on page 75.

NAME ____________

LESSON MASTER 2–4
QUESTIONS ON **SPUR** OBJECTIVES

■REPRESENTATIONS *Objective K (See pages 102–105 for objectives.)*

1. Plot three vertices of a square (1, 3), (1, 6), and (4, 6). Find and plot the fourth vertex. Connect the vertices in order.

2. a. Toss four coins ten times. Plot the data as ordered pairs which show: (number of the toss, number of heads on the toss).

Sample:

b. Which number of heads occurred most often? **sample: 2**

Least often? **sample: 0 and 4**

3. a. The following ordered pairs show (year, net cash flow from U.S. Savings Bonds, in billions): (1975, 4), (1977, 4.7), 1979, -0.8), (1981, -4.3). Draw a graph for this data. Label the axes.

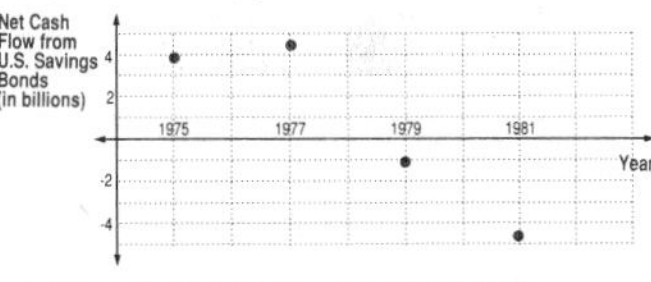

b. During which two-year period was the decrease greatest? **from 1977 to 1979**

c. What do the negative numbers mean in 1979 and 1981? **The net cash flow is to (not from) U.S. Savings Bonds.**

 Continued

NAME ____________

LESSON MASTER 2–4
(page 2)

4. a. A football team made the following gains and losses on their first four successive plays: 3, 4, -5, and 9. Plot the data (play number, yards made on that play).

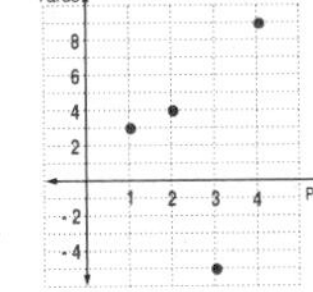

b. Did the team make a first down? That is, did they gain more than 10 yards? **yes**

5. This graph shows the number of kilowatts of electricity being used by a family during a day.

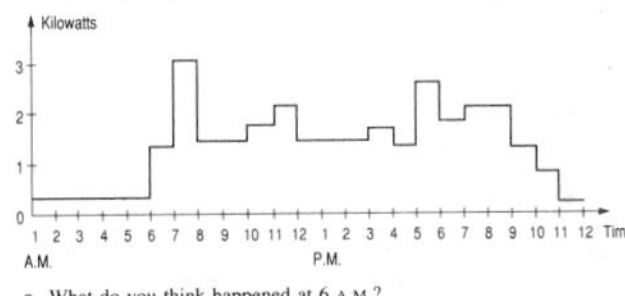

a. What do you think happened at 6 A.M.? **sample: Someone turned the lights on in the morning.**

b. How many kilowatts were being used between 7 and 8 A.M.? **3 kilowatts**

c. Why do you think it was so high? **sample: Someone used electrical appliances to cook.**

d. At what time do you think the last person went to bed for the night? **11P.M.**

LESSON 2-5

RESOURCES

- Lesson Master 2-5
- Visual for Teaching Aid 7: Coordinate Grid
- Visual for Teaching Aid 13: Graphs for **Example 2** and **Questions 8, 11, and 12**

OBJECTIVE

L Interpret two-dimensional slides on a coordinate graph.

TEACHING NOTES

Students will need graph paper for this lesson and for many other assignments throughout the year. Since review questions with graphs are scattered throughout the text, students should keep graph paper on hand.

Error Analysis Some students confuse the order of the coordinates. They should remember the correct order if you point out that it is alphabetic: horizontal (x), then vertical (y).

Some students who can graph ordered pairs cannot answer questions similar to **Example 1.** Oral questioning in class will demonstrate how quickly other students can find the coordinates of the image. This will make the task seem accessible for those who at first have trouble.

Emphasize that to go left or down, we add a negative number. In the next chapter, going left or down will be done by subtraction and will provide a nice example of how $a - b = a + -b$.

LESSON 2-5 Two-Dimensional Slides

You probably have played video games in which a character moves across the video screen. Programmers of games move the characters by first imagining them on a coordinate plane. In diagram 2 below, the *center* of the character's face is at the point (4,3).

1. how you see the screen

2. how the programmer sees the screen

One basic movement of a character is a **two-dimensional slide.** The movement from the original position or **preimage** to the final position or **image** is shown in diagram 3. The arrow shows the path the center takes. The programmer models this movement as a horizontal slide followed by a vertical slide, as shown in diagram 4.

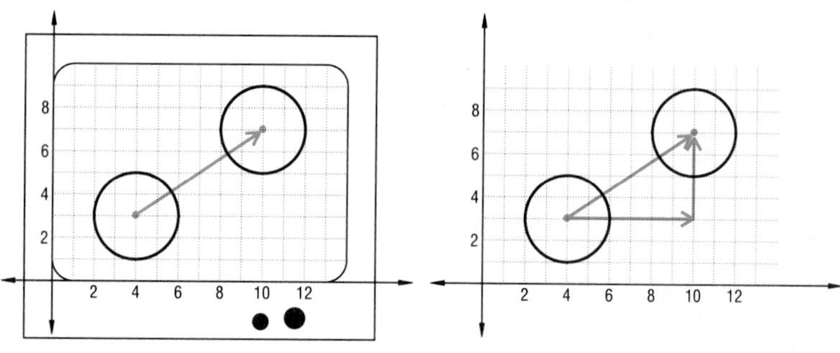

3. a slide of the figure

4. how the programmer sees the slide

In diagram 4, the slide is 6 units to the right and 4 units up. To slide a point 6 to the right, you must add 6 to the first coordinate of the point. To slide 4 units up, add 4 to the second coordinate. The center of the face was originally (4, 3). The new center is (4 + 6, 3 + 4), which is (10, 7).

To slide the entire preimage, a general pattern for sliding *any* point on the figure is needed. It is customary to call the general point (x, y). The first coordinate is called the **x-coordinate.** The horizontal axis is labeled x and called the **x-axis**. The second coordinate is called the **y-coordinate.** The vertical axis is labeled y and called the **y-axis**. If a preimage point is (x, y), then the image point after a slide 6 units to the right and 4 units up is $(x + 6, y + 4)$.

Using negative numbers, you can indicate a slide left or down.

Example 1 Find the image of the point $A = (12, 5)$ after a slide 10 units to the left and 8 units down.

Solution Add -10 to the first coordinate and -8 to the second coordinate. The image is (12 + -10, 5 + -8), or (2, -3). On the graph, the point A' (read "A prime") is the image of the point A.

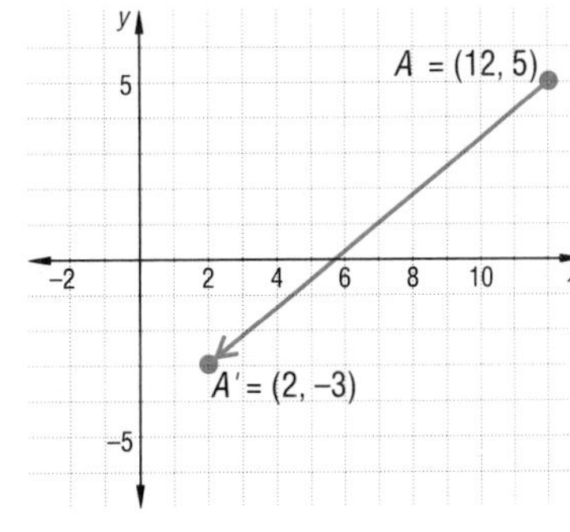

Check To check, graph the preimage (12, 5). Slide it 10 units to the left and 8 units down. It ends at the point (2, -3).

The more points the figure has, the easier it may be to see the slide.

Example 2 In $\triangle ABC$, let $A = (-2, 4)$, $B = (-1, 7)$, and $C = (2, 3)$. Slide the figure 1 unit to the right and 6 units down.

Solution Add 1 to each x-coordinate and -6 to each y-coordinate. Graph the image $\triangle A'B'C'$.

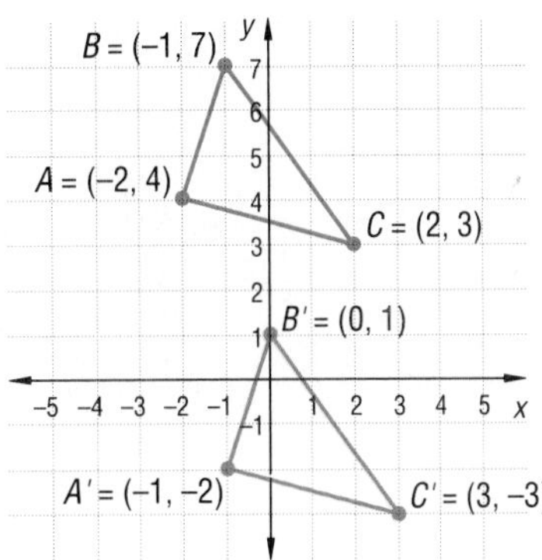

Check $\triangle ABC$ looks like it has been slid 1 unit to the right and 6 units down to get $\triangle A'B'C'$. (That is why this use of addition is called a two-dimensional slide.)

In **Example 2,** to slide the entire figure (which has infinitely many points), it is sufficient to find images of key points. The vertices of a triangle are obvious choices for key points. Use the opportunity to review the words *vertex* and *vertices.*

Alternate Approach
You can express a slide as an ordered pair and write preimage + slide = image. **Example 1** could be shown as (12, 5) + (-10, -8) = (2, -3). The general rule is vector addition:
$(a, b) + (c, d) = (a + c, b, + d)$.

ADDITIONAL EXAMPLES

1. Find the images of points $P = (7, 2)$ and $Q = (-8, 1)$ after a slide of 6 units to the right and 5 units down.
The image of *P* is (13, -3). The image of *Q* is (-2, -4).

2. In $\triangle RTX$, let $R = (-4, -1)$, $T = (3, 1)$, and $X = (0, -4)$. Graph the triangle and its image $\triangle R'T'X'$ after sliding left 3 units and up 7 units. Find the coordinates of R', T', and X'.

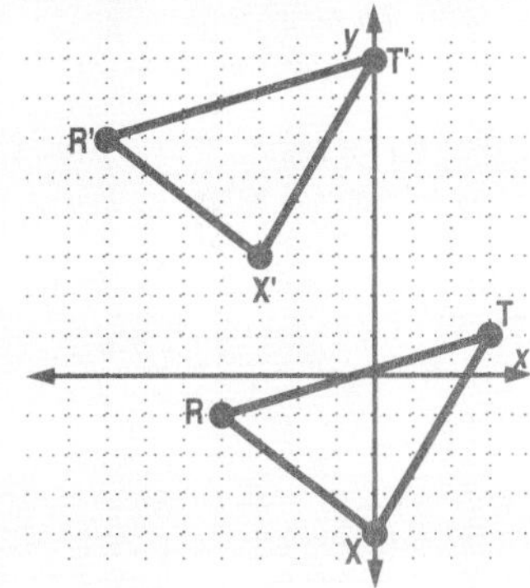

R' = (-7, 6), T' = (0, 8), and X' = (-3, 3).

3. Let (x, y) represent a point. Represent its image after a slide to the right of 4 units and 2 units down.
$(x + 4, y - 2)$

NOTES ON QUESTIONS
Question 12: Students may not realize that they can determine the slide that the figure undergoes by examining one convenient point, for instance the top of the head.

ADDITIONAL ANSWERS
5.

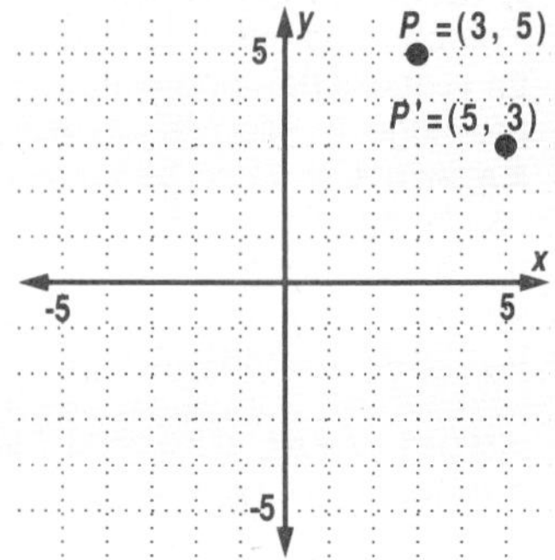

6.

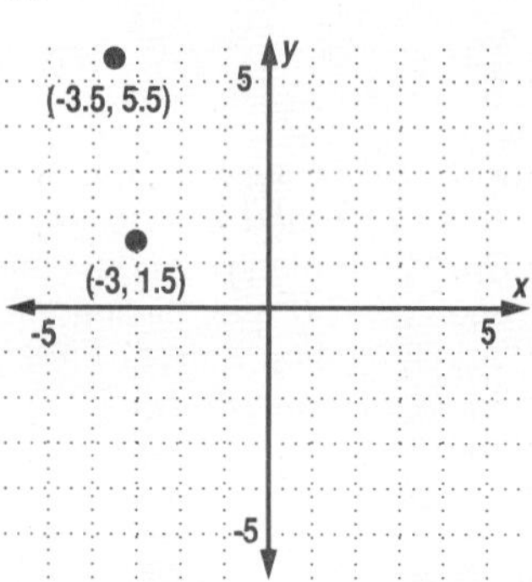

13.

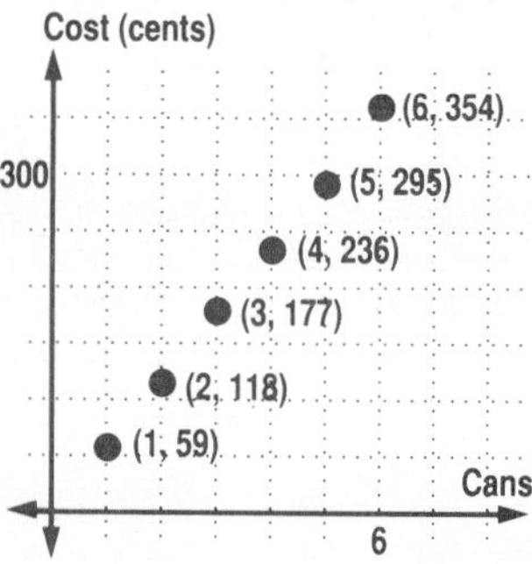

Example 3 A preimage point (x, y) is moved 7 units up. What is its image?

Solution (x, y) may be any point on the plane. But no matter what the values of x and y are, to move 7 units up, add 7 to the second coordinate. The image is $(x, y + 7)$. (There is no move left or right, so nothing is added to the first coordinate.)

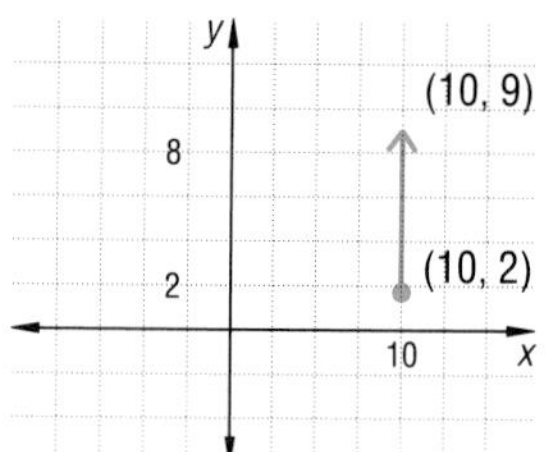

Check Substitute values for x and y and graph. Suppose $x = 10$ and $y = 2$. The preimage is then (10, 2). The image is (10, 2 + 7) or (10, 9). Is (10, 9) seven units above (10, 2)? The graph shows this, so it checks.

The x-axis and the y-axis divide the coordinate plane into four **quadrants.** The four quadrants are named I, II, III, and IV as shown below.

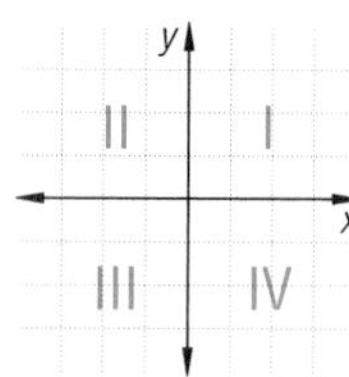

Questions

Covering the Reading

1. The first coordinate of a point is also called its _?_-coordinate. The second coordinate is also called its _?_-coordinate. **x; y**

2. When you slide a figure, the original figure is called the _?_ and the resulting figure is called its _?_. **preimage, image**

3. Write the image of (-2, -1) after a slide 1.5 units to the left and 6 units up. **(-3.5, 5)**

4. Find the image of (0, 0) after a slide 45 units up. **(0, 45)**

5. Draw a coordinate plane and graph the point $P = (3, 5)$ and its image after a slide of 2 units to the right and 2 units down. **See margin.**

6. A preimage is (-3, 1.5). Graph the preimage and its image after a slide 0.5 unit to the left and 4 units up. **See margin.**

7. Let point $P = (x, y)$.
   a. Write the image of P after a slide 3 units to the right and 7 units down. **(x + 3, y + -7)**
   b. Check your answer to part a by picking values for x and y and graphing.
   sample: x = 2, y = 0; (2 + 3, 0 + -7) = (5, -7)

Applying the Mathematics

8. a. Copy the triangle PQR with $P = (-5, -2)$, $Q = (-7, -5)$, and $R = (-3, -8)$.

b. On the same axes, graph the image of this figure by finding the image of each vertex after a slide of 3 units to the right and 4 units up.

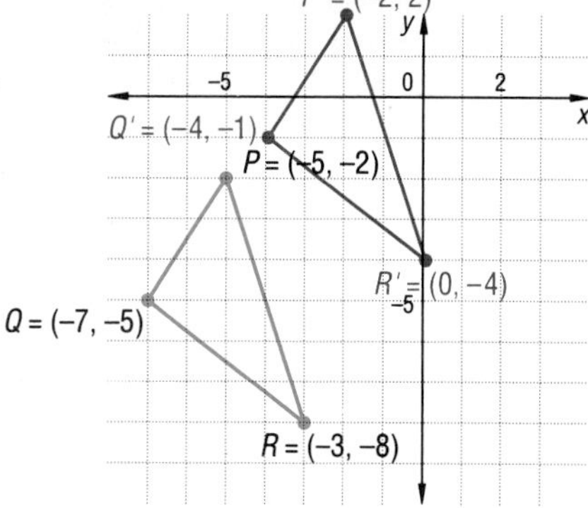

9. After a slide 3 units right and 9 units up, an image is (7, -1). What are the coordinates of its preimage? (Hint: You must work backwards.)
(4, -10)

10. A point is (7, 2) and its image is (15, -4). Describe the slide: _?_ units to the (left or right) and _?_ units (up or down).
8 right, 6 down

11. One route Tony can take to get to school is by going 2 blocks east, 4 blocks north, and another 2 blocks east. Name three other routes Tony can take to get from his house to school.
samples: 2N, 4E, 2N; 4E, 4N; 4N, 4E

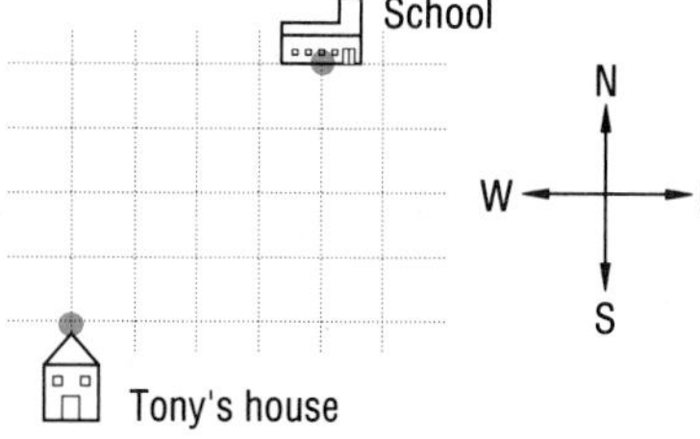

12. Examine the two-dimensional slide below.

a. Under this slide, the image of any point is _?_ units right and _?_ units above the preimage. **9; 8**

b. Under this slide, the image of (x, y) is (x + _?_, y + _?_). **9; 8**

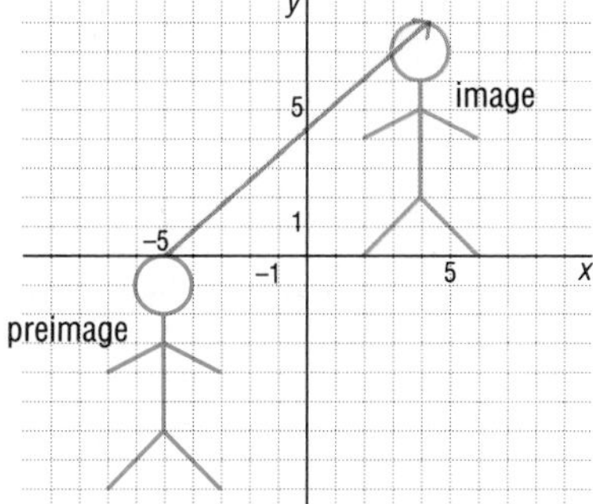

Review

13. A can of orange juice sells for \$.59 at the grocery store. On a coordinate graph, make *cost* the unit on one axis and *number of cans* the unit on the other axis. Plot a graph showing the cost of 1, 2, 3, 4, 5, and 6 cans. *(Lesson 2-4)* **See margin.**

In 14 and 15, simplify. *(Lesson 2-3)*

14. $\frac{3}{5} + (-2\frac{3}{10}) + 1\frac{1}{2}$ $\quad -\frac{1}{5}$

15. $\frac{2}{7} + \frac{x}{3}$ $\quad \frac{6 + 7x}{21}$

Question 24: Technically, BTU is the unit and the variable stands for the number of BTUs. However, this formula was found in a real-world source, where it is common to use BTU = 12,600 rather than number of BTUs = 12,600. It provides a nice noncomputer example where a variable is represented by a set of letters, not just by a single letter.

Question 27: DeSoto, Missouri, is a city about 50 miles south of St. Louis. Have students explain why they think the center of population is moving southwest. (The westward movement and, to some extent, the southerly movement are consistent with the historical development of the United States. Originally, the population was centered in the northeastern part of the country. The center moved west and south as territories were added and people moved into them. The southern component of the movement has increased recently with the movement of industry into the once largely rural Sunbelt.)

NAME

LESSON **MASTER 2–5**
QUESTIONS ON **SPUR** OBJECTIVES

■REPRESENTATIONS *Objective L (See pages 102–105 for objectives.)*
In 1–4, find the image of the point after the given slide.

1. (-3, -1); 15 units left and 20 units up. **(-18, 19)**
2. (-6, 14); 4 units left and 9 units down. **(-10, 5)**
3. (7.3, -4.9); 3.5 units right and 4.6 units up. **(10.8, -0.3)**
4. (x, y); 63 units right and 26 units down. **(x + 63, y − 26)**

In 5–7, the image of a point after the indicated slide is given. Find the preimage. (Hint: Work backwards.)

5. (4, -2); 6 units left and 4 units up. **(10, -6)**
6. (-5, -8); 4 units right and 3 units down. **(-9, -5)**
7. (x + 6, y + 9); 3 units right and 6 units up. **(x + 3, y + 3)**

In 8 and 9, find *a* and *b*.

8. (3 + a, 2 + b) = (-7, 10) $\quad a =$ **-10** $\quad b =$ **8**
9. (a + -4, b + -6) = (1, 0) $\quad a =$ **5** $\quad b =$ **6**

10. Graph the image of the triangle after a slide of 3 units right and 4 units down.

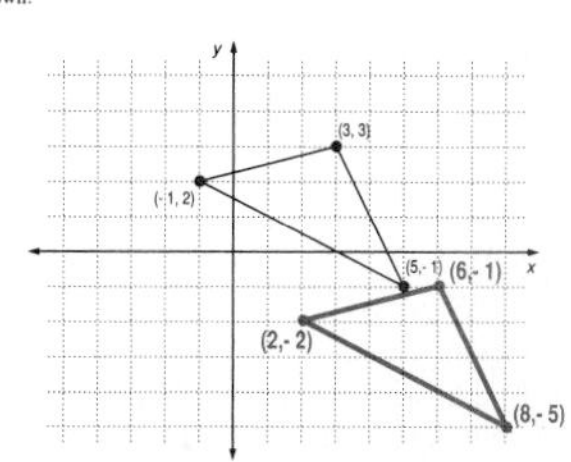

FOLLOW-UP

MORE PRACTICE
For more practice on SPUR Objectives, use *Lesson Master 2-5,* shown on page 83.

EXTENSION
Have students consider the following questions, which are related to **Question 27:**

1. The center of population of the U.S. moves 58 feet west and 29 feet south each day. Will it continue to move at that rate until the year 2020? (Probably not. Because the time interval is so long, it would be difficult to predict whether population trends will continue. Most likely, they will not.)

2. Find the geographical center of the United States by consulting a reference book. An almanac is often an excellent source for information of this nature. (Including Alaska and Hawaii the geographical center is in Butte County, South Dakota, west of Castle Rock.)

25.

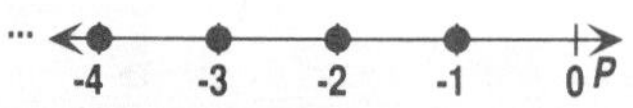

27a. 847,380 ft (160.5 miles) west, 423,690 ft (80.2 miles) south

27b. near Crane, Missouri, about 15 miles southwest of Springfield

16. John wants $\frac{1}{2}$ of a pizza. Sue wants $\frac{1}{3}$ of the same pizza, and Anne wants $\frac{1}{6}$ of the same pizza. Will one pizza be large enough for the three of them? *(Lesson 2-3)* **Yes**

17. The Ceramco Co. showed a loss of \$5 million in 1983 and a profit of \$3.2 million in 1984. What was the net change over the two years? *(Lesson 2-2)* **-\$1.8 million**

In 18–21, simplify. *(Lessons 2-2, 2-3)*

18. $-x + 14 + x$ **14**

19. $\frac{1}{2} + \frac{1}{3} + \frac{1}{2}$ **$1\frac{1}{3}$**

20. $-2.5y + 3.5y$ **y**

21. 40% of 100 **40**

22. *Skill sequence* If $2y + 1 = 8$, evaluate. *(Lesson 1-4)* **a) 24; b) 18; c) 33**
a. $3(2y + 1)$ **b.** $(2y + 1) + 10$ **c.** $2y + 26$

23. a. Which property tells you segments $\overline{AB}$ and $\overline{CD}$ below have the same length? **Commutative Property of Addition**
b. Express that length in terms of x and y. *(Lesson 2-1)* **x + y**

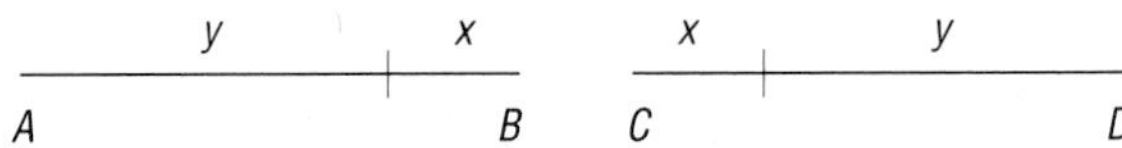

24. An air conditioning unit with a high energy efficient ratio (EER) gives more cooling with less electricity. To find the EER of a unit, divide the BTU (British Thermal Unit) number by the number of watts. The higher the EER, the more efficient the air conditioner.

$$\text{EER} = \frac{\text{BTU}}{\text{watts}}$$

a. Find the EER to the nearest tenth for an air conditioner having BTU = 12,600 and watts = 1315. **9.6**
b. Find the EER to the nearest tenth for an air conditioner having BTU = 5000 and watts = 850. **5.9**
c. Which air conditioner, in part a or part b, is more efficient? *(Lesson 1-5)* **a**

25. $P = \{$all integers less than 0$\}$. Graph P. *(Lesson 1-6)* **See margin.**

26. Refer to the information about the Prussian Army on page 55 of this chapter. Here are the data for a twelfth corps.

1880	'81	'82	'83	'84	'85	'86	'87	'88	'89	Total
d	0	4	0	1	0	*d*	2	1	0	14

What is the value of d? *(Lessons 2-1, 2-2)* **3**

Exploration

27. In 1980, the U.S. center of population was 1/4 mile west of De Soto, Missouri. According to American Demographics, the center of population moves 58 feet west and 29 feet south each day. **See margin.**
a. At this rate, how far will it have moved by the year 2020?
b. Where will it be? (You will need to consult a map.) **See margin.**

LESSON

2-6

Solving $x + a = b$

You have been solving some simple equations by trial and error. For more complex equations, guessing at solutions is not easy and is too slow. It is important, therefore, to have a more systematic way of solving equations. Here is the idea behind a property that is particularly helpful in solving equations.

Suppose Tina's age is T years and Robert's age is R years. If Tina and Robert are the same age, then

$$T = R.$$

Eight years from now, Tina's age will be $T + 8$ years and Robert's age will be $R + 8$ years. They will still be the same age, so

$$T + 8 = R + 8.$$

Similarly, Tina's age three years ago was $T + -3$ and Robert's age was $R + -3$. Thus,

$$T + -3 = R + -3$$

since they would have been the same age then as well.

The general property used is the **Addition Property of Equality.**

Addition Property of Equality:

For all real numbers a, b, and c:
if $a = b$,
then $a + c = b + c$.

In solving an equation, this property indicates that you can add any number c to both sides of the equation without changing its solutions. In the equation $a = b$, a and b may represent algebraic expressions.

Example 1 Solve: $x + -126 = 283$.

Solution 1 Beginners put in all the steps.

$(x + -126) + 126 = 283 + 126$	Addition Property of Equality (126 is added to both sides.)
$x + (-126 + 126) = 409$	Associative Property of Addition (The additions can be done in any order.)
$x + 0 = 409$	Property of Opposites (-126 and 126 are opposites.)
$x = 409$	Additive Identity Property (Replace $x + 0$ with x.)

LESSON 2-6

RESOURCES
■ Lesson Master 2-6

OBJECTIVES

C Solve and check sentences of the form $x + a = b$.
F Identify and apply properties used in solving equations.
H Use the models of addition to form and solve sentences involving addition.

TEACHING NOTES

To illustrate the Addition Property of Equality, this lesson begins with an example about persons' ages. In this context, the Addition Property of Equality means: If two people have the same age, then any number of years from now (in either direction—past or future) their ages are also the same.

Alternate Approach To illustrate the Addition Property of Equality, you can use the balance scale idea (see **Question 20**) in which a and b are weights that balance on each side. Obviously, if the same weight is added to each side, the scale will still balance. And if the weights are removed (adding a negative), the scale will still balance.

Making Connections
Examples 1 and 2 include two solutions. The first, "for beginners," puts in all the steps. The second, "for experts," shows only the addition step. This beginner-expert approach is used again in Chapter 6 when students learn to solve more complicated equations.

Allow students to solve *easy* equations in their head. Mental solving of equations has the advantage that students must keep track of what the answer means. That is, they check the solution at the same time they are finding it.

Notice that the Addition Property of Equality is stated in its right-hand form, where c is added on the right side in each member of the equation. However, in **Example 3,** this property is used in its left-hand form; namely, if $a = b$, then $c + a = c + b$. We will continue to use the form that is more convenient for the equation in question.

Check Substitute 409 for x in the original equation. Does $409 + {}^-126 = 283$? Yes. So 409 is the solution.

Solution 2 Experts do some work mentally and may write fewer steps.

$x + {}^-126 = 283$
$x = 283 + 126$ Addition Property of Equality
$x = 409$

Check Experts still check. This is done like the check in Solution 1.

All the steps were shown in Solution 1 to Example 1 to illustrate the properties that justify this process. Like the expert, you do not always need to include all steps in solving an equation. Directions in the problem and your teacher's instructions will guide you in choosing what steps to include.

The key to solving equations is knowing what should be done to both sides. In Example 1, 126 is added to both sides because it is the opposite of -126. So the left side simplifies to just x. For this type of equation there is only one step to remember.

To solve an equation of the form

$$x + a = b$$

add $-a$ to both sides and simplify.

In an equation, the variable can be on either side. And, since addition is commutative, the variable may be first or second on that side. In each of the four equations below, -47 can be added to both sides to find the same solution, 51.

$$x + 47 = 98$$
$$47 + x = 98$$
$$98 = x + 47$$
$$98 = 47 + x$$

To solve more complicated addition equations, you can use the commutative and associative properties to simplify one side to the form $x + a$.

Example 2 Solve $-10 = -3.2 + (x + 8.2)$

Solution 1 For beginners

$-10 = (-3.2 + x) + 8.2$	Associative Property of Addition
$-10 = (x + -3.2) + 8.2$	Commutative Property of Addition
$-10 = x + (-3.2 + 8.2)$	Associative Property of Addition
$-10 = x + 5$	
$-10 + -5 = (x + 5) + -5$	Addition Property of Equality
$-10 + -5 = x + (5 + -5)$	Associative Property of Addition
$-15 = x + 0$	Property of Opposites
$-15 = x$	Additive Identity Property

Check Substitute -15 for x on the right side of the original equation.

$$-10 = -3.2 + (-15 + 8.2)$$
$$-10 = -3.2 + -6.8$$
$$-10 = -10$$

Since -15 makes the equation true, -15 is the solution.

Solution 2 For experts

$-10 = -3.2 + (x + 8.2)$	Commutative and Associative Properties of Addition
$-10 = x + 5$	
$-10 + -5 = x$	Addition Property of Equality
$-15 = x$	

Check The check is identical to that in Solution 1.

Many equations with addition can be solved mentally. In working with complicated numbers or in rearranging formulas, however, the Addition Property of Equality can be particularly useful.

Example 3 The perimeter p of a triangle with sides of lengths a, b, and c is given by the formula $p = a + b + c$. Solve this equation for c.

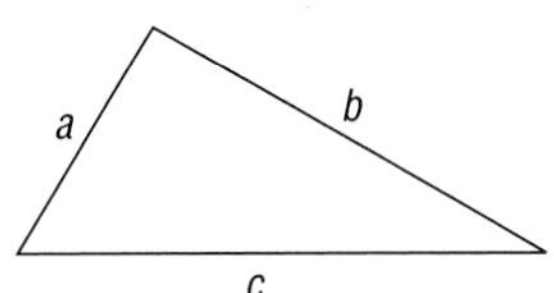

Solution To solve for c means to rewrite the equation so that c is alone on one side.

$$p = a + b + c$$

Add $-a$ to each side.

$$-a + p = -a + a + b + c$$
$$-a + p = 0 + b + c$$
$$-a + p = b + c$$

Add $-b$ to each side.

$$-b + -a + p = -b + b + c$$

Simplify again.

$$-b + -a + p = 0 + c$$
$$-b + -a + p = c$$

ADDITIONAL EXAMPLES

1. Solve: $240 = y + 650$.
-410

2. Solve:
$(150 + k) + -28 = 46$.
-76

3. Solve
$k = -2a + b + n$ for b.
$2a + k + -n = b$ or $b = 2a + k + -n$.

4. Solve for n.
$-4x = n + 15x$
$-19x = n$ or $n = -19x$.

NOTES ON QUESTIONS
Questions 11, 12, and 19: Solving literal equations illustrates the need for using the properties of equality to solve equations. Be sure that students understand the instruction "solve for" in this type of problem. It means to find a formula that expresses the given variable in terms of the others.

Questions 24-29: These questions are about a rating like those found in consumer magazines. Students may be surprised to see negative numbers here, but 0 is an appropriate middle value on many judgment scales. Although these questions take up quite a bit of room, they are not difficult to do.

Most people prefer to put the variable for which they are solving on the left side of the equation. Thus, $c = -b + -a + p$

Check When $a = 10$, $b = 15$, and $c = 20$, then $p = 45$. Substitute these values in the answer. Does $20 = -15 + -10 + 45$? Yes.

Example 4 Solve for y. $3x + y = 11x$

Solution Add $-3x$ to both sides. $-3x + 3x + y = -3x + 11x$
Combine terms. $y = 8x$

Check Substitute $8x$ for y. Does $3x + 8x = 11x$? Yes.

When you solve equations, we *strongly recommend* that you arrange your work so that the equal signs of each line are directly below each other (as the examples show). This helps to avoid confusion.

Questions

Covering the Reading

In 1–4, suppose your age is A and a friend's age is B. What does each sentence mean? See margin.

1. $A = B$

2. $A + 4 = B + 4$

3. $A + -6 = B + -6$

4. If $A = B$, then $A + C = B + C$.

5. State the Addition Property of Equality. See margin.

In 6 and 7, consider these steps in solving the equation $-173 + a = 209$.

a. $-173 + a = 209$
b. $173 + -173 + a = 173 + 209$
c. $0 + a = 382$
d. $a = 382$

6. What property was used to get from step a to step b?
Addition Property of Equality

7. What property was used to get from step c to step d?
Additive Identity Property

In 8 and 9, **a.** What number should be added to each side when solving the equation? **b.** Find the solution. **c.** Check your answer. See margin.

8. $m + 42 = 87$

9. $-12 + y = -241$

10. Solve: $8 = -5 + (x + 2)$ $x = 11$

11. Let p be the perimeter of a triangle. Let a, b, and c represent the lengths of the sides of the triangle.
a. What is a formula for p in terms of a, b, and c? $a + b + c = p$
b. Solve the formula for b. $b = p + -a + -c$
c. Find b if $a = 21$, $c = 47$, and $p = 101$. $b = 33$

12. Consider the equation $g + 9h = 85h$.
  a. Solve for g. **$g = 76h$**
  b. Check your work by letting $h = 2$ and solving the resulting equation. **Does 76 (2) + 9 (2) = 85 (2)? Does 152 + 18 = 170? Yes.**

Applying the Mathematics

13. *Multiple choice* Which equation does not have the same solution as the others? **(b)**
  (a) $15 + x = -3$ (b) $-3 + x = 15$
  (c) $x + 15 = -3$ (d) $-3 = x + 15$

14. Hank has \$5.27. A solar calculator costs \$14. Let n be how much more he needs.
  a. What addition equation could be solved to find out how much more money he needs? **$5.27 + n = 14$**
  b. Solve this equation. **$n = 8.73$**

In 15 and 16, **a.** simplify the left side. **b.** Solve and check.

15. $C + 48 + -5 = 120$ **a) C+ 43 = 120; b) See margin.**

16. $x + 3 + 5 + -x + 8 + x = 29$ **a) x + 16 = 29; b) See margin.**

In 17 and 18, **a.** find the solution. **b.** Check your answer.

17. $3\frac{1}{4} + x = 10\frac{1}{2}$ **18.** $15.2 = f + 2.15$ **See margin.**

19. Solve for d: $a + d = c$. **$d = c + -a$**

20.a.

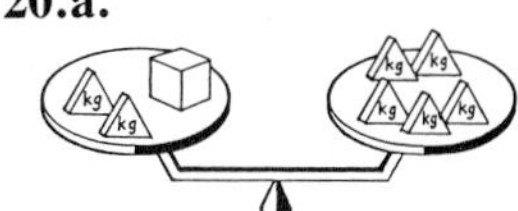

20.b.

20. Pictured at left top is a balance scale. On the left side of the top scale is 1 box and 2 one-kilogram weights. They balance with 5 kilograms on the right side. If b is the weight of the box, the situation is described by the equation $b + 2 = 5$.
  a. How much does the box weigh? **3 kg**
  b. Describe the situation for the bottom scale using an equation. **$b + 4 = 7$**

In 21 and 22, write an equation, solve and check.

21. The temperature was 25°F yesterday and now it is -12°F. Let c be the change in temperature. By how much has the temperature changed? **25 + c = -12, c = -37; fallen 37°, 25 + -37 = -12**

22. On June 1, Carlos's savings account showed a balance of \$4347.59. During the next month he deposited a total of \$752.85 and withdrew \$550.00. On July 1, he asked the bank to tell him how much was in the account. The teller said \$4574.14 including interest. How much interest had been earned during June? **4347.59 + 752.85 − 550 + I = 4574.14, I = \$23.70, 4347.59 + 752.85 − 550 + 23.70 = 4574.14**

Review

23. Triangle $D'E'F'$ is a slide image of triangle DEF. $D = (0, 0)$, $E = (1, 4)$, $F = (3, 6)$ and $F' = (5, 2)$.
  a. Describe the slide choosing the appropriate directions: ___?___ units (left or right) and ___?___ units (up or down). **2 right, 4 down**
  b. What are the coordinates of D' and E'? *(Lesson 2-5)* **$D' = (2,-4)$; $E' = (3,0)$**

ADDITIONAL ANSWERS

1. My friend and I are the same age.

2. In 4 years, we will be the same age.

3. Six years ago we were the same age.

4. We will always be the same age.

5. For all real numbers a, b, and c: if a = b, then a + c = b + c.

8a. -42; b. m = 45; c. Does 45 + 42 = 87? Yes.

9a. 12; b. y = -229; c. Does -12 + -229 = -241? Yes.

15b. c = 77. Does 77 + 43 = 120? Yes.

16b. x = 13. Does 13 + 16 = 29? Yes.

17a. $7\frac{1}{4}$; b. Does $3\frac{1}{4} + 7\frac{1}{4} = 10\frac{1}{2}$? Yes.

18a. 13.05 b. Does 15.2 = 13.05 + 2.15? Yes.

NAME ____________

LESSON **MASTER 2–6**
QUESTIONS ON **SPUR** OBJECTIVES

■SKILLS *Objective C (See pages 102–105 for objectives.)*
In 1–4, solve the equations in your head.

1. $x + 5 = 11$ **x = 6**
2. $2 + h + 3 = 60$ **h = 55**
3. $15 = p + 6$ **p = 9**
4. $20 = 5 + x + -4$ **x = 19**

In 5–9, solve and check the equations.

5. $x + -9 = 11$ **x = 20** **20 + -9 = 11**
6. $-8 + c + 7 = -12$ **c = -11** **-8 + -11 + 7 = -12**
7. $-12.4 + s = -14$ **s = -1.6** **-12.4 + -1.6 = -14**
8. $p + -5.7 = -2.3$ **p = 3.4** **3.4 + -5.7 = -2.3**
9. $2 = \frac{1}{3} + \frac{t}{6} + \frac{1}{3}$ **t = 8** **$2 = \frac{1}{3} + \frac{8}{6} + \frac{1}{3}$**

In 10–13, solve for x.

10. $x + a = c$ **x = c + -a**
11. $x + -p = r$ **x = r + p**
12. $k + x = m$ **x = m + -k**
13. $w = x + -v$ **x = w + v**

■PROPERTIES *Objective F*
Multiple choice **In 14 and 15, circle the equation that does not have the same solution as the others.**

14. (a) $4 + x = -8$ (b) $x + 4 = -8$ (c) $-8 + x = 4$ (circled) (d) $-8 = 4 + x$
15. (a) $y + 6 = -3$ (b) $6 + y = -3$ (c) $-3 = 6 + y$ (d) $6 = y + -3$ (circled)

■USES *Objective H*
16. The temperature is -10°C. By how much must it increase to become 4°C? **14°C**

In 17 and 18, a. write an equation to describe the situation. b. Solve.

17. Peggy opened a savings account with \$40. She made a deposit of x dollars, and withdrew \$20. Her balance now is \$90.
  a. **90 = 40 + x − 20** b. **x = 70**

18. A triangle has sides of 13, 8, and y. The perimeter is 28.
  a. **13 + 8 + y = 28** b. **y = 7**

16

NOTES ON QUESTIONS

Question 30: The estimates made here could be done by rounding to the place of the *leading digit*. However, this is not the only way to estimate in doing these problems. Ask students how they made their estimates.

Computer for Question 31: In some versions of BASIC, one or more spaces between expressions or values within a PRINT statement have the same effect as using a semicolon. However, at the end of a PRINT statement, a semicolon should be used if you want the next PRINT statement to begin on the same line.

FOLLOW-UP

MORE PRACTICE

For more questions on SPUR Objectives, use *Lesson Master 2-6*, shown on page 89.

31a.

```
SOLVE AN EQUATION
X + A = B
GIVE A AND B
THE SOLUTION TO X + 3 = 2
IS X = -1
```

31b.

```
10 PRINT "SOLVE AN
   EQUATION
   X + A + B = C"
20 PRINT "GIVE A, B,
   and C"
30 INPUT A, B, C
40 PRINT "THE SOLUTION
   TO X+";A;"+";B;"=";C
50 PRINT "IS X="; C+
   (-A)+(-B)
60 END
```

31c.

```
SOLVE AN EQUATION
X + A + B = C
GIVE A, B, AND C
5, 7, 2
THE SOLUTION TO
X + 5 + 7 = 2
IS -10
```

Cost and Ratings for Popular Strawberry Ice Creams

Brand	Cost per Serving	Rating
Berry N'ice	57	3
Perfect Parfait	55	5
Delicious	52	5
Merry Berry	49	-1
Sundae Special	46	3
Gourmet	43	2
Fabulous Flavors	26	1
Bon Appetit	22	2
Betty's Best	19	3
Select	18	-1
Mmm Good	18	1
Creamy Creations	17	-2
Mix-In Magic	17	-2
I. Scream	16	3
Ambrosia	16	-1
Tasty Treat	12	-2
Nuts and Berries	12	-2
Sweet Swirl	12	-3

In 24–29, a consumer research organization evaluated the flavor and texture of popular strawberry ice creams. The rating scale had a maximum possible score of 6 (flavor and texture very good) and a minimum possible of -6 (very bad). See the chart at the left for data. A scattergram is shown below. *(Lesson 2-4)*

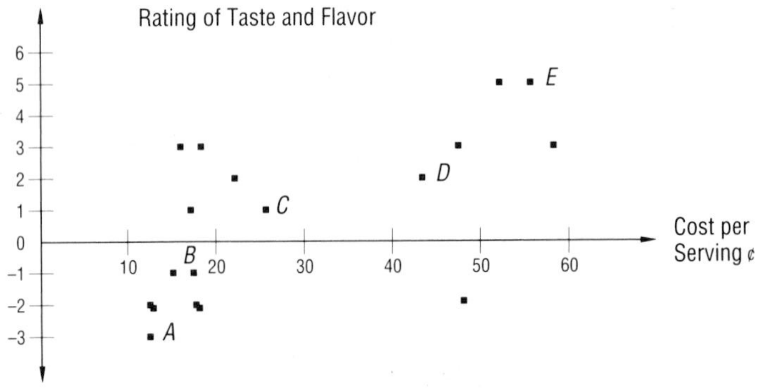

24. Which point (A, B, C, D, or E) represents Gourmet? **D**

25. Which point represents Select? **B**

26. What is the range for cost ? **45¢**

27. Which ice cream seems to be a poor value; that is, it costs a lot but has a low rating? **Merry Berry**

28. Is there a tendency for ice cream which costs more to taste better? **Yes**

29. Find the median cost for the 18 brands. **18.5¢**

30. Estimate the answers in your head. *(Previous course)*
a. 496 − 308 **b.** 983 ÷ 102 **c.** 29^2
Sample: a) 200; b) 10; c) 900

Exploration

31. Here is a computer program.

```
10 PRINT "SOLVE AN EQUATION X + A = B"
20 PRINT "GIVE A AND B"
30 INPUT A, B
```

The semicolons in lines 40 and 50 below instruct the computer to print the following character on the same line as the previous one with one space between them.

```
40 PRINT "THE SOLUTION TO X + ";A;" = ";B
50 PRINT "IS X = ";B+(-A)
60 END
```

a. What will the computer print after this program is run with the input 3, 2? **See margin.**
b. Change this computer program so that it will solve $x + 5 + 7 = 2$. Use the command INPUT A,B,C. **See margin.**
c. Run this program. **See margin.**

LESSON

2-7

Solving $x + a < b$

Suppose your age is x and an *older* friend's age is y. Then

$$x < y.$$

Five years from now you will still be younger.

$$x + 5 < y + 5$$

In general, j years from now you will be younger than your friend.

$$x + j < y + j$$

In the same way, k years ago you were younger.

$$x + -k < y + -k$$

These examples illustrate the **Addition Property of Inequality.**

Addition Property of Inequality:

For all real numbers a, b, and c,
if $a < b$,
then $a + c < b + c$.

The Addition Property of Inequality allows you to add the same number to both sides of an inequality. So you can solve an inequality in the same way that you solved an equation.

To solve an inequality of the form

$$x + a < b,$$

add $-a$ to both sides and simplify.

LESSON 2-7

RESOURCES

■ Lesson Master 2-7

OBJECTIVES

D Solve and check sentences of the form $x + a < b$.
F Identify and apply properties used in solving equations and inequalities.
H Use the models of addition to form and solve sentences involving addition.
J Graph solutions to inequalities on a number line.

TEACHING NOTES

Emphasize that the steps used in solving $x + a < b$ correspond to those used in solving $x + a = b$. However, inequalities differ from equations in significant ways. There are often infinitely many solutions, and they cannot be listed. So the answer has to be given either as an equivalent inequality or it has to be graphed.

Error Analysis Many students have difficulty solving inequalities even though the goal of isolating the variable is the same as for an equation. Also, the idea of graphing inequalities is new to students. The following approach should help most students. Begin with **Example 1** and ask for a "number for x that works." Then ask for another. If students are giving positive solutions, ask if there are any negative ones. If students are giving integers, ask for ones that are not. Finally, ask: How can we describe all the numbers that work? ($x < 11$.)

Students need to be cautioned about switching the sides of an inequality. The paragraph following **Example 3** provides an opportunity to remind them to change the sense of the inequality when reversing the sides. Notice, however, that in **Example 3** the solution is expressed with the variable as the right member. This is acceptable, though you may prefer that students always put the variable on the left-hand side.

Example 1 Solve: $x + 31 < 42$

Solution Add -31 to each side. $x + 31 + -31 < 42 + -31$
Now simplify. $x + 0 < 11$
$x < 11$

Note that it's just like solving an equation.

Check The answer $x < 11$ means that any number less than 11 will work in the original sentence $x + 31 < 42$. Since this inequality has infinitely many solutions, you cannot check the answer by substituting a single number. You must do two things.

Step 1: Check the number 11 by substituting it in the original inequality. It should make both sides equal. Does $11 + 31 = 42$? Yes.

Step 2: Pick some number that works in the answer $x < 11$. This number should also work in the original inequality. We pick the number 7.
Is $7 + 31 < 42$? Yes, $38 < 42$.

Since both steps worked, $x < 11$ is the solution to $x + 31 < 42$.

Inequalities often have many solutions. Because all the solutions in Example 1 cannot be listed, we either write them in the form of a simpler inequality, $x < 11$, or we graph them.

Here is a graph of $x < 11$.

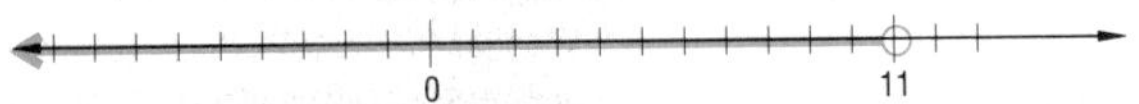

Inequalities with the $>$ sign are solved just like those with the $<$ sign. Here is why. Suppose your age is a, and a friend's age is b. If you are older than your friend now, you will be older c years from now. So, if $a > b$, then $a + c > b + c$. The same idea works for $\leq$ and $\geq$.

Thus, sentences with $=$, $<$, $>$, $\leq$, or $\geq$ that involve addition can all be solved in the same way.

> You can add the same number to both sides of an equation or inequality without affecting the solutions.

Example 2 You can vote in government elections in the U.S. if you are 18 years old or over. Joan will be able to vote in an election three years from now. How old is she now?

Solution Let J be Joan's age. Three years from now her age is $J + 3$. Since she will be able to vote, she will be at least 18.

$$J + 3 \geq 18$$

Add -3 to each side. $\quad J \geq 15$

Joan is at least 15 years old.

Check

Step 1. Try 15. If Joan is now 15. Will she be able to vote in 3 years? Yes.

Step 2. Try a number that works in $J \geq 15$. We use 28. If Joan is 28, will she be able to vote in 3 years? Yes.

Notice in Example 2 that $J = 15$ would not be the correct answer because it does not also tell you that she may be older than 15. $J \geq 15$ is the best way to describe her possible age. $J \geq 15$ is also read "Joan is *at least* 15." In the next example, some steps are omitted to simplify the work.

Example 3 Graph all solutions to $-87 \geq x + 6$.

Solution Use the Addition Property of Inequality. Add -6 to both sides.

$$-87 + -6 \geq x + 6 + -6$$
$$-93 \geq x$$

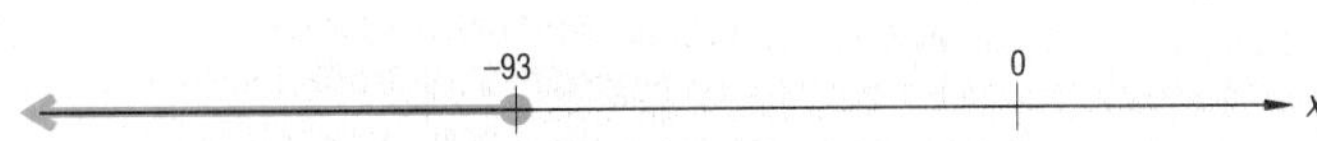

Check

Step 1: Does $-87 = -93 + 6$? Yes.

Step 2: Try a number that is a solution to $-93 \geq x$, such as -100. Does -100 work in the original sentence? Yes, because $-87 \geq -100 + 6$.

The expression $-93 \geq x$ can be read several ways. One way is $x \leq -93$. Another way is "x is *at most* -93."

ADDITIONAL EXAMPLES

1. Solve: $-16 > n + -4$.
$-12 > n$ or $n < -12$.

2. In order to ride the Thrillorama at the amusement park, a child must be at least 36 inches tall. Janet was n inches tall last year and has grown 2 inches since then. This year she can ride the Thrillorama.

a. Write an inequality relating 36, 2, and n.
$n + 2 \geq 36$

b. How tall was Janet last year?
$n \geq 34$, so Janet was at least 34 inches tall.

3. Graph all solutions to $18 + a \geq 7$.

NOTES ON QUESTIONS
Questions 6 and 11: These two questions serve to remind students to change the sense of an inequality when interchanging its sides.

Questions 23 and 24: Questions like these provide opportunities to teach or review some geometry. Here, the angles with measures x and y, or a and b, are complementary.

Question 26: Here, the mean and the median are very close: 64.8 and 64, respectively. This situation occurs when the distribution of data is symmetric about the mean. You may want to ask students how to change the data so that the mean is no longer close to the median. For example, you could change the hottest temperature (74°) to 100°. This will increase the mean by roughly 2°.

ADDITIONAL ANSWERS
13b.

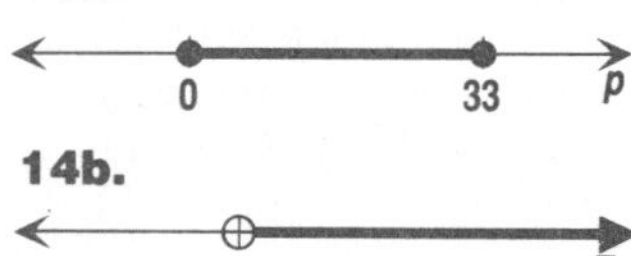

14b.

6 T

15. $x \geq 1\frac{3}{4}$. **Step 1: Does** $\frac{1}{2} + 1\frac{3}{4} + \frac{3}{4} = 3$? **Yes. Step 2: Try 3. Is** $\frac{1}{2} + 3 + \frac{3}{4} \geq 3$? **Yes,** $4\frac{1}{4} \geq 3$.

27b.

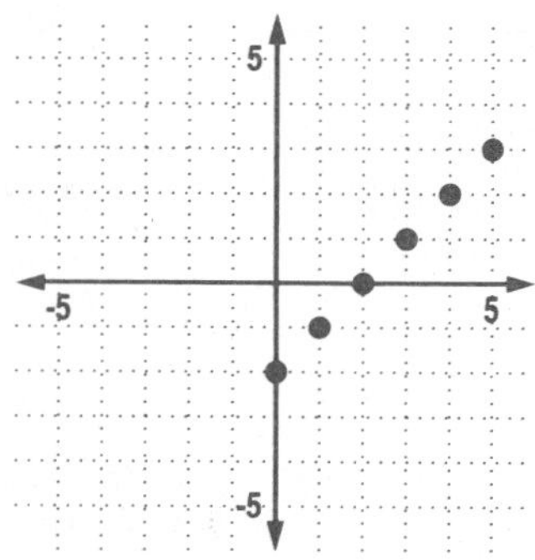

Questions

Covering the Reading

In 1–3, suppose your age is x and an older friend's age is y.

1. What inequality relates x and y? **$x < y$**

2. What inequality relates the ages fifty years from now? **$x + 50 < y + 50$**

3. What inequality relates the ages six years ago? **$x + -6 < y + -6$**

In 4 and 5, solve.

4. $-7 + x \leq 2$ **$x \leq 9$**

5. $y + 4.6 \geq 4.79$ **$y \geq 0.19$**

6. For the inequality $12 < x + 8$, Miko got the answer $x < 4$.
- **a.** Substitute 4 in the original inequality. Does it make the two sides equal? **Yes**
- **b.** Choose some number that works in $x < 4$. Does it make the original inequality true? **No, $x > 4$.**
- **c.** Is Miko's answer correct? **No**

7. *Multiple choice* Which inequality represents the situation, Frank is at least 50 years old? **(d)**
(a) $E < 50$ (b) $E > 50$ (c) $E \leq 50$ (d) $E \geq 50$

8. *Multiple choice* Which inequality represents the situation, Rosa is at most 29 years old? **(c)**
(a) $R < 29$ (b) $R > 29$ (c) $R \leq 29$ (d) $R \geq 29$

9. Liz will be able to vote in an election 2 years from now.
- **a.** Write an inequality whose solutions tell Liz's possible ages.
- **b.** Solve. **$z \geq 16$ 9a) $z + 2 \geq 18$**

10. Given are steps in the solution of the inequality $t + 18 < -3$. Name the property that supports each step.

Step 1:	$t + 18 + -18 < -3 + -18$	**Addition Property of Inequality**
Step 2:	$t + 0 < -21$	**Property of Opposites**
Step 3:	$t < -21$	**Additive Identity Property**

Applying the Mathematics

11. *True or false* The graph of $x + 3 < 17$ is the same as the graph of $14 > x$. **True**

12. Solving $46 + x < -39$ you get $x < -85$. Use this information to solve $46 + x > -39$ in your head. **$x > -85$**

In 13 and 14, **a.** answer the question. **b.** Graph the solutions.

13. Your class is planning a picnic for the first graders. There is \$162 to spend for refreshments and prizes. The food costs \$129. You do not have to spend all the money. How much can be spent for prizes? **a) $129 + p \leq 162$; $p \leq 33$; b) See margin.**

14. The temperature is now 31 °C. The high temperature record for this date is 37 °C. How much does the temperature have to change to break the record? **a) $31 + T > 37$; $T > 6$; b) See margin.**

15. Solve and check: $\frac{1}{2} + (x + \frac{3}{4}) \geq 3$. **See margin.**

16. Solve for n: $18m + n \geq 19m$. **$n \geq m$**

Review

In 17–19, solve in your head. *(Lesson 2-6)*

17. $3 + x = 3$ **0** **18.** $10 = y + 4$ **6** **19.** $-3 = z + 2\frac{1}{2}$ **$-5\frac{1}{2}$**

In 20 and 21, solve using the Addition Property of Equality. *(Lesson 2-6)*

20. $a + -11.2 = 24$ **35.2** **21.** $9 + B = -11.6$ **-20.6**

22. Solve $-11 = (2 + y) + -7$. *(Lesson 2-6)* **-6**

In 23 and 24, use the rectangle at the right. $x + y = 90°$, and $a + b = 90°$.

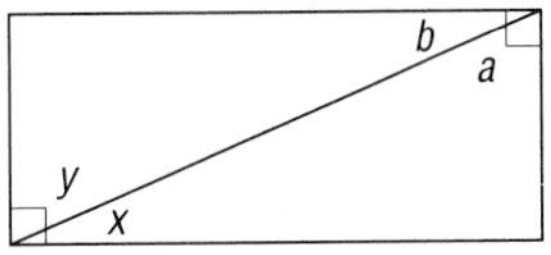

23. If $x = 30°$, find y. *(Lesson 2-6)* **60°**

24. Solve the equation $a + b = x + y$ for b. *(Lesson 2-6)* **$b = x + y + -a$; $b = 90 + -a$**

25. Find the image of the point $P = (3, 6)$ after a slide of 4 units to the right and 6 units up. *(Lesson 2-5)* **(7, 12)**

26. Here is a list of the average monthly temperatures (in °F) in Los Angeles for one year.

57	58	59	62	65	68
73	74	73	68	63	58

a. Find the mean of the monthly temperatures. **$64.8\overline{3}°$**
b. Find the median. *(Lesson 1-2)* **64°**

27. Copy and complete the ordered pairs below.
(0, _?_), (1, _?_), (2, _?_), (3, _?_), (4, _?_), (5, _?_)
a. Complete so that the second coordinate of each ordered pair is 2 less than the first coordinate. **(0,-2), (1,-1), (2,0), (3,1), (4,2), (5,3)**
b. Graph these points on a coordinate plane. *(Lesson 2-5)* **See margin.**

28. Simplify $\frac{-3}{4} + \frac{x^2}{5}$. *(Lesson 2-3)* **$\frac{-15 + 4x^2}{20}$**

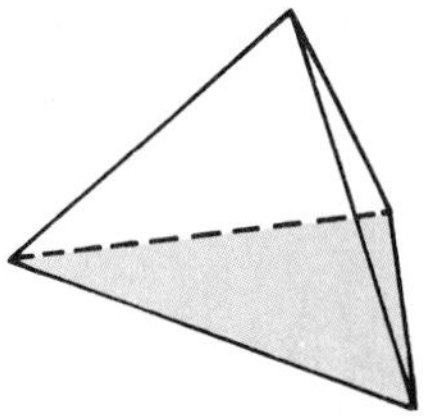

29. Darrell has a pair of 4-sided dice like the one at left. The sides are numbered 1 to 4 and all outcomes are equally likely. If the two dice are rolled once, what is the probability of rolling a sum of 6 on the two dice? (The face that is counted is the one that is down.) *(Lesson 1-7)* **$\frac{3}{16}$**

Exploration

30. Give five inequalities whose solutions can be described by $x < 24$.
samples: $x + 5 < 29$, $x - 8 < 16$, $23 > x - 1$, $x + 1.5 < 25.5$, $x - 3\frac{1}{2} < 20\frac{1}{2}$

Question 29: The figure is a tetrahedron. Such continual review of geometry will benefit students (and their teachers) in later courses.

Question 30: This question is important because it reverses the idea of solving an inequality. Given a solution, can you determine what inequality might have led to it? For some students, doing this problem finally clarifies the process of solving inequalities.

FOLLOW-UP

MORE PRACTICE
For more practice on SPUR Objectives, use *Lesson Master 2-7,* shown below.

EXTENSION
Computer Students can adapt the computer program from **Question 31** in Lesson 2-6 to solve $x + a < b$. This will further emphasize the similarity in the solution processes. (In lines 10, 40, and 50, change = to <.)

NAME ____________

LESSON **MASTER 2–7**
QUESTIONS ON **SPUR** OBJECTIVES

■SKILLS *Objective D (See pages 102–105 for objectives.)*
In 1–4, solve.

1. $-13 < d + 5$ **$d > -18$** 2. $11 + w \leq 20$ **$w \leq 9$**

3. $d + -9.3 \leq -13.7$ **$d \leq -4.4$** 4. $\frac{2}{5} + a > \frac{3}{4}$ **$a > \frac{7}{20}$**

5. Solve for x: $3a + x < -5a$ **$x < -8a$**

6. Solve for y: $y + -8b \geq -12b$ **$y \geq -4b$**

In 7–10, solve in your head.

7. $x + 4 \leq 7$ **$x \leq 3$** 8. $-3 + y < 6$ **$y < 9$**

9. $2.5 + p > 5.5$ **$p > 3$** 10. $r + \frac{1}{2} \geq \frac{3}{4}$ **$r \geq \frac{1}{4}$**

■PROPERTIES *Objective F*

11. If $s + 13 < -5$, then $s + 13 + -13 < -5 + -13$. This is an instance of what property? **The Addition Property of Inequality**

12. Mike adds -8 to both sides of $x + 8 \geq 11$. What sentence results? **$x \geq 3$**

13. *Multiple choice* Circle the inequality that has the same solutions as $-4 < x < 10$.
(a) $10 < x < -4$ (b) $10 \geq x > -4$ **(c) $10 > x > -4$** (d) $-4 \leq x \leq 10$

■USES *Objective H*

14. Edna saved \$11 and received \$5 as a gift. If jeans cost at least \$25, how much more does she need? **at least \$9**

15. The temperature was 10°C. It increased by $n°$. Now it is more than T°C.
a. Give a sentence relating 10, T, and n. **$10 + n > T$**
b. Solve for n. **$n > T - 10$**

■REPRESENTATIONS *Objective J*
In 16 and 17, solve and graph the solution set.

16. $y + -1.2 < 5.6$ **$y < 6.8$** 17. $\frac{1}{2} + a \leq \frac{-3}{2}$ **$a \leq -2$**

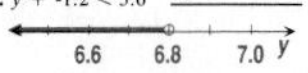

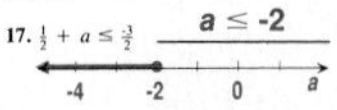

LESSON 2-8

RESOURCES
■ Lesson Master 2-8

OBJECTIVES

G Use the Triangle Inequality to determine possible lengths of third sides of triangles.
I Apply the Triangle Inequality in real situations.

TEACHING NOTES

Three different situations are discussed here: when three points are collinear, when three points determine a triangle, and when either case could be true.

A demonstration of the Triangle Inequality can be used to illustrate Solution 2 in **Example 1.** Take a regular one-foot ruler and a yardstick. Hold them together at one end and ask how far apart the other ends could be. The sum and difference of the lengths give the maximum and minimum values. The values in between are found by the Triangle Inequality.

Alternate Approach
Discuss **Example 2.** Rather than solving the problem algebraically, you can use a diagram. Consider the extreme cases, where the distance between Larry's house and school is the greatest and the least. In both cases, the three points are collinear. Make a drawing of each situation.

LESSON

2-8

The Triangle Inequality

In geometry, capital letters usually name points. The distance from point A to point B is written AB. This is not multiplication because points cannot be multiplied. The line segment connecting A and B is written $\overline{AB}$.

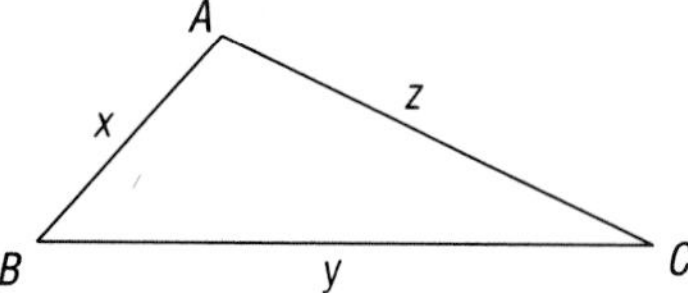

Suppose A, B, and C are 3 points. If A, B, and C lie on the same straight line, and B is between A and C, then $AC = AB + BC$. That is, at right, $AC = x + y$. You put together the smaller lengths to get the larger length.

However, A, B, and C might be the 3 vertices of a triangle.

To determine the possible values for AC, you can apply an important relationship called the **triangle inequality.**

Triangle Inequality: The sum of the lengths of two sides of any triangle is greater than the length of the third side.

In $\triangle ABC$ drawn above, this relationship means three inequalities are true.

$$x + y > z \qquad x + z > y \qquad y + z > x$$

Example 1 Suppose two sides of a triangle have lengths 15 and 22. What are the possible lengths of the third side?

Solution 1 Let $x = 15$ and $y = 22$. Substitute into the Triangle Inequality to find the possible values of z.

$$15 + 22 > z \text{ and } 15 + z > 22 \text{ and } 22 + z > 15$$

Solve each inequality.

$$37 > z \text{ and } \quad z > 7 \text{ and } \quad z > -7$$

The first two inequalities show that when two sides of a triangle are 15 and 22, the third side must be shorter than 37 but longer than 7. This can be written as $7 < z < 37$. This expression can be read several ways. One way is "x is greater than 7 *and* x is less than 37." Another is "x is *between* 7 and 37." (The third inequality shows that it must also be longer than -7. But that is obvious since length is always positive.)

96

Solution 2 Draw pictures. Let $AB = 15$ and $BC = 22$. Think of a hinge connected at point B. $\overline{AB}$ is fixed. $\overline{BC}$ moves.

Hinge wide open. AC is almost 37.

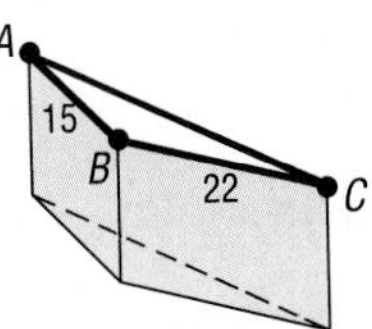

Hinge partially open. AC can be any number between 7 and 37.

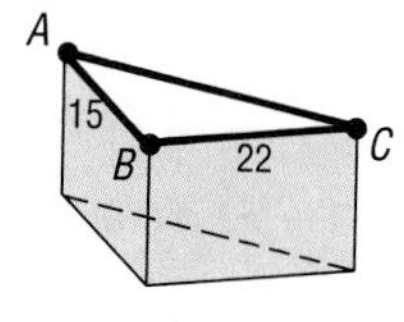

Hinge almost closed. AC is near 7.

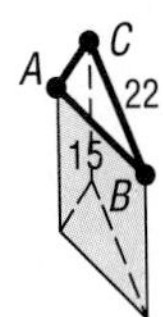

The hinge can open so that A, B, and C are on the same line and are no longer vertices of a triangle. Then $AC = 37$.

15 22
A B C

When the hinge is fully closed, A, B, and C are on the same line and are not vertices of a triangle. Then $AC = 7$.

7 15
C A B

So AC must have a value less than when the hinge is completely open (37) and greater than when the hinge is closed (7). Hence $7 < AC < 37$.

If you know nothing about A, B, and C, then either $AB + BC = AC$ (they are on the same line) or $AB + BC > AC$ (they are vertices of a triangle). So $AB + BC \geq AC$ is always true.

Example 2 Amy lives one mile from school and 0.4 mile from Larry. How far does Larry live from school?

School
Larry's house
1.0 miles
0.4 miles
Amy's house

Solution Let d be the distance from school to Larry's house. Then, by the Triangle Inequality,

$$1.0 + 0.4 \geq d \text{ and } 0.4 + d \geq 1.0 \text{ and } 1.0 + d \geq 0.4.$$

There are equal signs in the inequalities since the houses and the school could be on the same road. Solve each inequality.

$$1.4 \geq d \quad \text{and} \quad d \geq 0.6 \quad \text{and} \quad d \geq -0.6$$

$1.4 \geq d$ means Larry can live no more than 1.4 miles from school, $d \geq 0.6$ means the distance Larry lives from school must be at least 0.6 mile. Since distance is always positive, $d \geq -0.6$ yields no new information. So Larry lives from 0.6 to 1.4 miles from school. The solution is given by the interval

$$0.6 \leq d \leq 1.4.$$

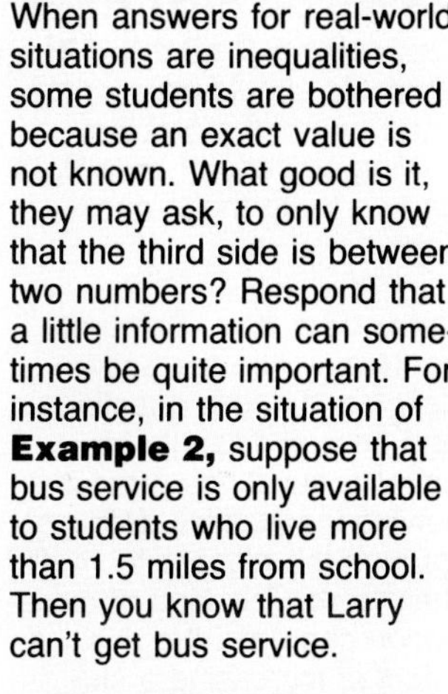
When answers for real-world situations are inequalities, some students are bothered because an exact value is not known. What good is it, they may ask, to only know that the third side is between two numbers? Respond that a little information can sometimes be quite important. For instance, in the situation of **Example 2,** suppose that bus service is only available to students who live more than 1.5 miles from school. Then you know that Larry can't get bus service.

ADDITIONAL EXAMPLES

1. If two sides of a triangle have lengths 3 and 19, write an interval to describe the possible lengths of the third side.
$16 < x < 22$

2. Pinehurst is 18 miles from Quincy and 27 miles from Randall. How far is Quincy from Randall?
at least 9 miles and at most 45 miles.

NOTES ON QUESTIONS
Questions 2 and 8–12: Students should be encouraged to use the problem-solving strategy of *drawing a picture* to do these questions.

Question 8b: Some students may see the pattern developed in this question and answer Triangle Inequality questions without solving inequalities. Still, go through the algebra to verify their work. This kind of explanation can have the positive effect of increasing a student's faith in algebraic processes, even if it doesn't convince the student that algebra was the way to do it in the first place.

Question 10: You might discuss that airplane *fares* are not always consistent with the Triangle Inequality. That is, it sometimes costs less (not more) to fly from *A* to *B* to *C* than to fly from *A* to *C* directly.

Question 24: This question has surprisingly few answers. It's a case where the Triangle Inequality determines more than seems possible at first.

ADDITIONAL ANSWERS

3. The sum of the lengths of two sides of any triangle is greater than the length of the third side.

5a. $4 + 5 > x$, $x + 4 > 5$, $x + 5 > 4$

5b. $x < 9$, $x > 1$, $x > -1$

6a. $32 + 20 \geq PQ$, $32 + PQ \geq 20$, $20 + PQ \geq 32$

10c.

20. \$38,250 for Von, \$25,500 for Winnie, \$12,750 for Xenia, and \$8500 for Yuri

Questions

Covering the Reading

1. In the drawing below, A is on $\overline{BC}$. How long is BC? **10 + d**

10 d
B A C

2. If M is between P and Q on a line, $PM = 5$, and $PQ = 7$, what is MQ? **2**

3. State the Triangle Inequality. **See margin.**

4. Refer to the triangle at the right. Copy and complete.

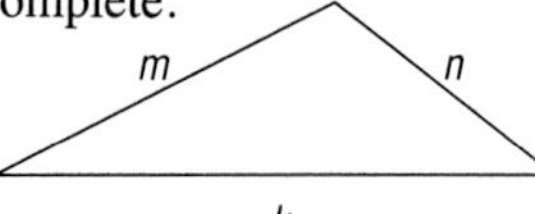

a. $k + n >$ _?_ **m**
b. $n + m >$ _?_ **k**
c. _?_ + _?_ $> n$ **m, k or k, m**

5. Refer to the triangle at the right.

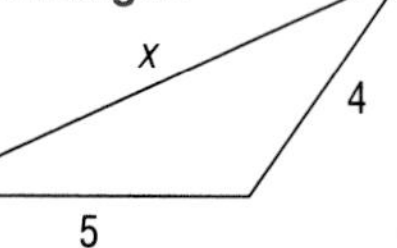

a. Name three inequalities that involve x. **See margin.**
b. Solve each inequality for x. **See margin.**
c. x must be less than _?_. **9**
d. x must be greater than _?_. **1**
e. _?_ $< x <$ _?_. **1, 9**

32 cm P
20 cm Q

6. Two metal plates are joined by a hinge as in the drawing at the left.
a. Name the three inequalities PQ must satisfy. **See margin.**
b. PQ can be no shorter than _?_ cm. **12**
c. PQ can be no longer than _?_ cm. **52**

7. Suppose Larry lives 1.3 km from school and 0.8 km from Amy. The distance Amy lives from school must be greater than or equal to _?_ but less than or equal to _?_. **0.5 km, 2.1 km**

Applying the Mathematics

8. a. If two sides of a triangle have lengths $100x^2$ and $75x^2$, the third side can have any length between _?_ and _?_. **$25x^2$, $175x^2$**
b. If two sides of a triangle have lengths a and b, with $a > b$, then the third side c can have any length between _?_ and _?_. **$a + b$, $a - b$ (with $a > b$)**

9. Why is there no triangle with sides of lengths 1 cm, 2 cm, and 4 cm? **because $1 + 2 < 4$**

10. By air, it is 1061 miles from Miami to St. Louis and 1724 miles from St. Louis to Seattle. Use only this information to answer the questions.
a. What is the shortest possible air distance from Miami to Seattle? **10a) 663 miles**
b. What is the longest possible air distance? **2785 miles**
c. Graph the possible distances on a number line. **See margin.**

11. Sirius, the brightest star in the nighttime sky, is 8.7 light-years from Earth. Procyon, a bright star near Sirius, is 11.3 light-years from Earth. Let m be the distance between Sirius and Procyon. What values can m have? **$2.6 < m < 20$ light-years**

12. Betty can walk to school in 25 minutes. She can walk to her boyfriend's house in 10 minutes. Let t be the length of time for her boyfriend to walk to school. If they walk at the same rate, what are the possible values of t? **$15 \leq t \leq 35$ minutes**

Review

In 13–15, solve. *(Lesson 2-6)*

13. $\frac{4}{3} = x + \frac{1}{6}$ $\frac{7}{6}$ or $1\frac{1}{6}$

14. $-423 = -234 + y$ -189

15. $z + (2 + -z) + 6 = z$ 8

16. Ben had S dollars in his savings account. He made deposits of \$28.75 and \$36.57. His balance was then \$137.48.

a. Relate these four quantities in an addition equation.

b. Solve for S. *(Lesson 2-6)* $S = \$72.16$ a) $S + 28.75 + 36.57 = 137.48$

In 17 and 18, simplify each expression. *(Lesson 2-3)*

17. $-(-p^3 + p^3)$ 0

18. $b + c + d + (-c)$ $b + d$

19. *Skill sequence* If $4x - 7y = 3$, evaluate. *(Lesson 1-4)*

a. $5(4x - 7y)$ 15

b. $(4x - 7y)^2$ 9

c. $6(4x - 7y) - (4x - 7y)$ 15

20. An estate was divided among four heirs in the following manner:

Von	45%
Winnie	30%
Xenia	15%
Yuri	10%

If the estate was worth \$85,000 how much did each heir receive? *(Previous course)* See margin.

21. Which is larger, 45% of 85,000 or 85% of 45,000? *(Previous course)* They are equal.

22. What is $\frac{1}{2}\%$ of 400? *(Previous course)* 2

23. A squirrel slid down 50 cm and then climbed up an unknown amount c, then slid down 20 cm, winding up 210 cm above its starting position. Find c. *(Lesson 2-6)* $-50 + c + -20 = 210; c = 280$

Exploration

24. The perimeter of a triangle is 15 cm. The sides all have different integer lengths. How many different combinations of sides are possible? (Hint: The answer may be fewer than you think. Use trial and error and the Triangle Inequality.) three; they are 2, 6, 7; 3, 5, 7; and 4, 5, 6.

FOLLOW-UP

MORE PRACTICE

For more questions on SPUR Objectives, use *Lesson Master 2-8,* shown below.

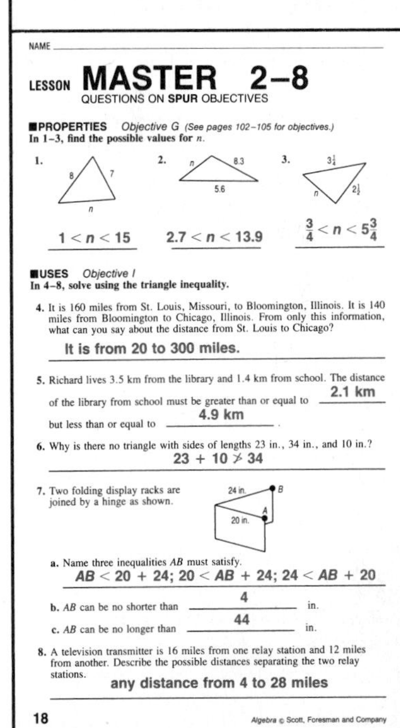

NAME ____________

LESSON **MASTER 2–8**
QUESTIONS ON **SPUR** OBJECTIVES

■**PROPERTIES** *Objective G (See pages 102–105 for objectives.)*
In 1–3, find the possible values for n.

1. $1 < n < 15$
2. $2.7 < n < 13.9$
3. $\frac{3}{4} < n < 5\frac{3}{4}$

■**USES** *Objective I*
In 4–8, solve using the triangle inequality.

4. It is 160 miles from St. Louis, Missouri, to Bloomington, Illinois. It is 140 miles from Bloomington to Chicago, Illinois. From only this information, what can you say about the distance from St. Louis to Chicago? It is from 20 to 300 miles.

5. Richard lives 3.5 km from the library and 1.4 km from school. The distance of the library from school must be greater than or equal to 2.1 km but less than or equal to 4.9 km.

6. Why is there no triangle with sides of lengths 23 in., 34 in., and 10 in.? $23 + 10 \not> 34$

7. Two folding display racks are joined by a hinge as shown.

a. Name three inequalities AB must satisfy. $AB < 20 + 24$; $20 < AB + 24$; $24 < AB + 20$

b. AB can be no shorter than 4 in.

c. AB can be no longer than 44 in.

8. A television transmitter is 16 miles from one relay station and 12 miles from another. Describe the possible distances separating the two relay stations. any distance from 4 to 28 miles

18

SUMMARY

The Summary gives an overview of the entire chapter and provides an opportunity for students to consider the material as a whole. Thus, the Summary can be used to help students relate the concepts presented in the chapter.

VOCABULARY

Terms, symbols, and properties are listed by lesson to provide a checklist of things a student must know. Emphasize to students that they should read the vocabulary list carefully before starting the Progress Self-Test. If students do not understand the meaning of a term, they should refer back to the indicated lesson.

Definitions or descriptions of all terms in the vocabulary list may be found in the Glossary.

ADDITIONAL ANSWERS

20. $-13 \geq x$;

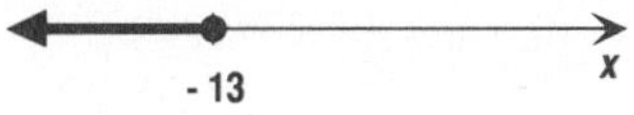

24. $(5 + -4, -2 + 5) = p' = (1, 3)$

26. $x \leq 30 + 12$, $x + 12 \geq 30$, and $x + 30 \geq 12$ gives $18 \leq x \leq 42$

Summary

In algebra as in arithmetic, addition is a basic operation. This chapter discusses sets, properties, uses, equations, inequalities, and graphs related to addition.

The most frequent applications of addition occur in situations which are represented by a putting-together or a slide. Putting-together occurs when quantities that do not overlap are combined. A slide occurs when you start with a quantity and go higher or lower by a given amount. Slides help picture addition of integers, addition of fractions, and combining like terms.

The properties of addition can be verified through their uses. For example, putting-together quantities in a different order yields the same sum, so addition is commutative. Other properties are mentioned below, in the Vocabulary.

Graphing provides a picture that can help clarify solutions to a problem or trends in data. If the relationship between two quantities is being considered, a coordinate graph in a plane is needed to show both values. A two-dimensional slide can be represented as a combination of a horizontal and vertical slide on a coordinate graph.

The simplest sentences to solve are of the form $x + a = b$ or $x + a < b$. The first step in solving each is to add $-a$ to both sides. Then simplify. One simple application of inequalities is in finding possible lengths of third sides in a triangle.

Vocabulary

Below are the most important terms and phrases for this chapter. You should be able to give a general description and specific examples of each.

Lesson 2-1
bar graph, stacked bar graph
Putting-together Model for Addition
Commutative Property of Addition
Associative Property of Addition

Lesson 2-2
Slide Model for Addition
additive identity
Additive Identity Property
opposite, additive inverse
Property of Opposites
Op-op Property
terms, like terms
Adding Like Terms Property

Lesson 2-3
common denominator
Adding Fractions Property

Lesson 2-4
coordinate graph
axes
origin
scattergram

Lesson 2-5
two-dimensional slide
preimage
image
x-coordinate, *y*-coordinate
x-axis, *y*-axis
quadrant

Lesson 2-6
Addition Property of Equality

Lesson 2-7
Addition Property of Inequality

Lesson 2-8
Triangle Inequality

Progress Self-Test

Take this test as your would take a test in class. You will need graph paper. Then check your work with the solutions in the Selected Answers section in the back of the book.

1. What property of addition is illustrated by $(x + y) + -4 = x + (y + -4)$? **Associative**
2. Write an equation to show how x and y are related to the given numbers in the rectangle below. **$x + y + 35 = 12 \cdot 6$**

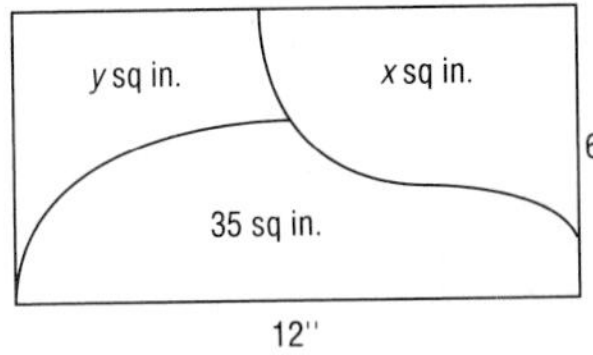

3. The temperature falls 10° then rises d°. Let t° be the change in temperature. Write an equation relating these numbers. **$t = -10 + d$**

In 4–10, simplify.

4. $-11 + 85 + -47$ **27**
5. $x + 5 + x + -8 + -x$ **$x + -3$**
6. $\frac{2}{n} + \frac{m}{n}$ **$\frac{2 + m}{n}$**
7. $\frac{3}{4} + \frac{3}{5} + \left(-\frac{3}{10}\right)$ **$1\frac{1}{20}$**
8. $-8\frac{1}{2} + \left(-3\frac{1}{3}\right)$ **$-11\frac{5}{6}$**
9. $-(-(-p))$ **$-p$**
10. $3x + 4y + -5x$ **$-2x + 4y$**
11. *Multiple choice* Which of the following equals $\frac{a}{b} + \frac{c}{b}$? **(d)**
    (a) $\frac{a + c}{b + b}$ (b) $\frac{ab + bc}{b}$ (c) $\frac{a + c}{2b}$ (d) $\frac{a + c}{b}$
12. Marcia went on a diet. Below are the changes in her weight.

First week	Second week	Third week
lost 4 lb	gained $1\frac{1}{2}$ lb	lost 3 lb

   a. Write an equation to find the change she must have the fourth week for a 10-lb overall loss. **$-4 + 1\frac{1}{2} + -3 + L = -10$**
   b. Solve this equation. **$-4\frac{1}{2}$; $4\frac{1}{2}$ lb loss**
13. What property is being illustrated?
    If $y + 11 = 3$, then $y + 15 = 7$.
    Addition Property of Equality

In 14–17, solve.

14. $x + -4 = 12$ **$x = 16$**
15. $-3.5 + a > 10.2$ **$a > 13.7$**
16. $\frac{5}{2} + y = \frac{17}{4}$ **$y = \frac{7}{4}$**
17. $4 > 3 + (z + -10)$ **$11 > z$**
18. Solve for b: $b + a = 100$. **$b = 100 + -a$**
19. Is -100 an element of the solution set of $15 \le x + 87$? **No**
20. Graph the solutions of $-4 \ge 9 + x$. **See margin.**
21. Write, but do not solve, an inequality for this situation. Vern needs at least \$150 to buy a puppy. He has saved \$47.50. How much more money m does he need? **$m + 47.50 \ge 150$**
22. The perimeter of the triangle is 43. Find b when $a = 9$ and $c = 21$. **$b = 13$**

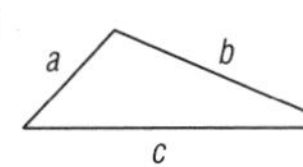

23. Carla's age is C. What was her age 7 years ago? **$C + -7$**
24. Find the image of (5, -2) after a slide of 4 units to the left and 5 units up. **(1, 3)**
25. At the right, $\triangle A'B'C'$ is the image of $\triangle ABC$ under a slide. Under this slide, find B', the image of B.
    $B' = (5, -4)$

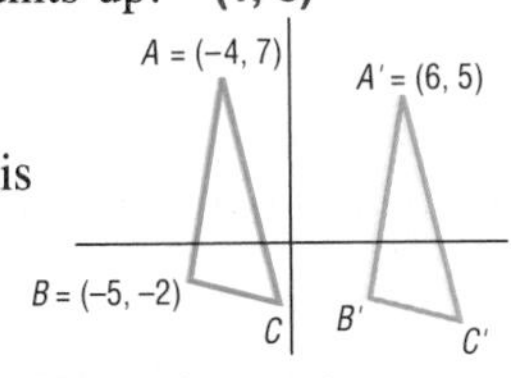

In 26 and 27, Wynken lives 30 km from Blynken. Blynken lives 12 km from Nod.

26. If x is the distance from Wynken to Nod, what inequalities must x satisfy? **See margin.**
27. What is the smallest possible value of x?
    18 km

In 28–30, boys and girls fill a bus which seats 45 students. Let b be the number of boys on the bus and g be the number of girls.

28. Write an equation using b and g. **$b + g = 45$**
29. Find g in each ordered pair showing a possible combination (b, g) of boys and girls: (10, __?__), (20, __?__), (23, __?__), (44, __?__).
    (10, 35), (20, 25), (23, 22), (44, 1)
30. On a coordinate graph, plot points with b on the horizontal axis and g on the vertical axis.
    See margin.

PROGRESS SELF-TEST

We cannot overemphasize the importance of these end-of-chapter materials. It is at this point that the material "gels" for many students, allowing them to solidify skills and understanding. In general, student performance should be markedly improved after these pages.

USING THE PROGRESS SELF-TEST

Assign the Progress Self-Test as a one-night assignment. Worked-out *solutions* for all these questions are in the Selected Answers section in the back of the student book. Encourage students to take the Progress Self-Test honestly, grade themselves, and then be prepared to discuss the test in class.

Advise students to pay special attention to those Chapter Review questions (pages 102–105) which correspond to questions missed on the Progress Self-Test. A chart provided in the Selected Answers section in the student text keys the Progress Self-Test questions to the lettered SPUR Objectives in the Chapter Review or to the Vocabulary. It also keys the questions to the corresponding lessons where the material is covered.

30.

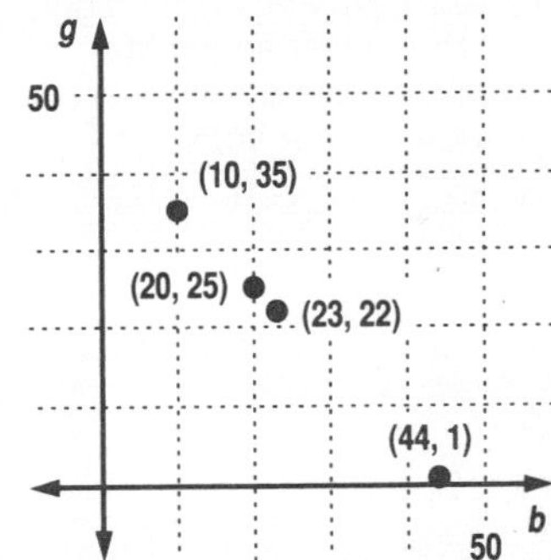

RESOURCES
- Chapter 2 Test, Form A
- Chapter 2 Test, Form B
- Chapter 2 Test, Cumulative Form

CHAPTER REVIEW

The main objectives for the chapter are organized here into sections corresponding to the four main types of understanding this book promotes: Skills, Properties, Uses, and Representations.

USING THE CHAPTER REVIEW
Whereas end-of-chapter material may be considered optional in some texts, in *Algebra* we have selected these objectives and questions with the expectation that they will be covered. Students should be able to answer these questions with about 85% accuracy after studying the chapter.

You may assign these questions over a single night to help students prepare for a test the next day, or you may assign the questions over a two-day period.

If you work the questions over two days, then we recommend assigning the *evens* for homework the first night so that students get feedback in class the next day, then assigning the *odds* the night before the test so the students can use the answers provided in the book.

Chapter Review

Questions on SPUR Objectives

SPUR stands for **S**kills, **P**roperties, **U**ses, and **R**epresentations. The Chapter Review questions are grouped according to the SPUR Objectives for this chapter.

SKILLS deal with the procedures used to get answers.

Objective A. *Add fractions.* *(Lesson 2-3)*

In 1–8, write as a single fraction.

1. $\frac{1}{2} + \frac{1}{3} + \frac{1}{4}$ **$\frac{13}{12}$**

2. Add. $\frac{1}{2} + \frac{2}{3} + \frac{1}{3} + \frac{-3}{4}$ **$\frac{3}{4}$**

3. $\frac{-7}{10} + -.35$ **$-\frac{21}{20}$**

4. $-1\frac{3}{8} + (-4\frac{7}{10})$ **$-\frac{243}{40}$**

5. $\frac{x}{3} + \frac{y}{3}$ **$\frac{x+y}{3}$**

6. $\frac{30}{a} + \frac{10}{a}$ **$\frac{40}{a}$**

7. $\frac{m}{n} + \frac{p}{q}$ **$\frac{mq+np}{nq}$**

8. $\frac{x}{5} + -\frac{3}{2}$ **$\frac{2x+-15}{10}$**

Objective B. *Combine like terms.* *(Lesson 2-2)*

In 9–16, simplify.

9. $8 + 4 + -2 + -6 + 1$ **5**

10. $8x + -3x + 10x$ **15x**

11. $4a + 2b + -5 + 8a$ **12a + 2b + -5**

12. $2x + 7x + 8 + 5 + 3x$ **12x + 13**

13. $t + 1 + 2t + 2$ **3t + 3**

14. $-3m + 4m + -m$ **0**

15. $5s + 6b + -5s$ **6b**

16. $13x^2 + -7.5x + 8x^2$ **$21x^2 + -7.5x$**

Objective C. *Solve and check equations of the form $a + x = b$.* *(Lesson 2-6)*

In 17–26, solve and check.

17. $2 + m = 12$ **m = 10**

18. $x + -11 = 12$ **x = 23**

19. $2.5 = t + 3.1$ **t = -0.6**

20. $\frac{1}{3} + a + \frac{3}{4} = 5$ **$a = 3\frac{11}{12}$**

21. $21{,}625 + m = 29{,}112$ **m = 7487**

22. $(3 + n) + -11 = -5 + 4$ **n = 7**

23. $-2 + y = -3$ **y = -1**

24. Solve for p: $a + p = c$. **p = c + -a**

25. Solve for r: $15p + r = 20p$ **r = 5p**

26. Solve for t: $4s + 3s = t + 2s$ **5s = t**

Objective D. *Solve inequalities of the form $a + x < b$.* *(Lesson 2-7)*

27. $x + 3 > 8$ **x > 5**

28. $-28 > y + 22$ **y < -50**

29. $-2 + (5 + x) > 4$ **x > 1**

30. Solve for r: $d \leq r + 45$ **$r \geq d + -45$**

31. For the inequality $15 + x < 20$, Brian got the answer $x < 35$. Check whether Brian is correct. **15 + 35 = 50; not correct**

PROPERTIES deal with the principles behind the mathematics.

Objective E. *Identify properties of addition.* *(Lessons 2-1, 2-2, 2-3)*

In 32–37, an instance of what property of addition is given? **See margin.**

32. $2(L + W) = 2(W + L)$

33. $x + 0 + 3 = x + 3$

34. $4+(28+-16)+-23=4+28+(-16+-23)$

35. $-(-31) = 31$

36. $\frac{2}{3} + \frac{5}{3} = \frac{7}{3}$

37. $8x + -13x = -5x$

Objective F. *Identify and apply properties used in solving equations and inequalities.* (*Lessons 2-6, 2-7*) 38) Addition Property of Inequality

In 38 and 39, an instance of what property is given? 39) Addition Property of Equality

38. If $t + 18 < -3$, then $t + 18 + -18 < -3 + -18$.

39. You can add 64 to both sides of an equation without affecting the solutions.

40. Hillary adds -14 to both sides of $x + -7 = 14$. What sentence results? $x + -21 = 0$

41. *Multiple choice* Which inequality has the same solution set as $3 < x \le 15$? (c)
(a) $15 < x \le 3$ (b) $15 > x \ge 3$
(c) $15 \ge x > 3$ (d) $3 \le x < 15$

42) $7 + 8 > 13$, $8 + 13 > 7$, $13 + 7 > 8$;
43) $a + b > c$, $b + c > a$, $c + a > b$

Objective G. *Use the Triangle Inequality to determine possible lengths of sides of triangles.* (*Lesson 2-8*)

In 42 and 43, use the Triangle Inequality to write the three inequalities which must be satisfied by lengths of sides in the triangle.

42.

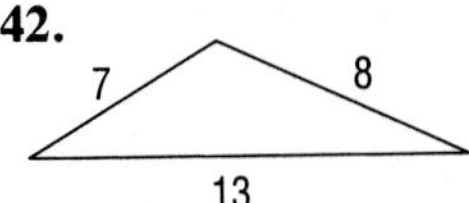

43.

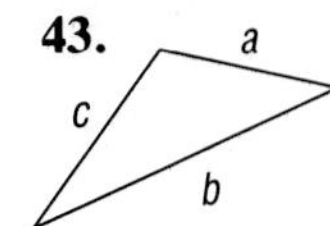

In 44 and 45, find the possible values for y.

44.

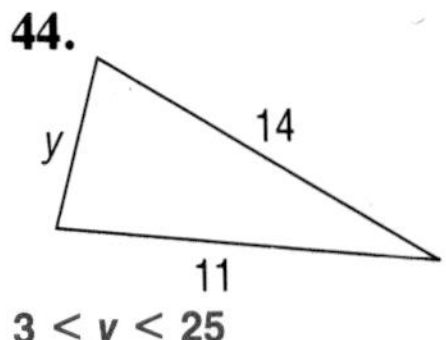

$3 < y < 25$

45.

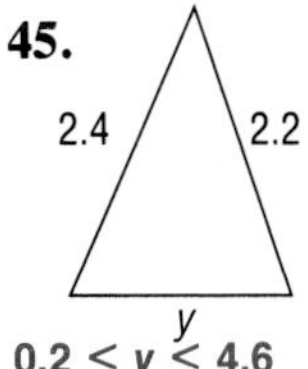

$0.2 < y < 4.6$

USES deal with applications of mathematics in real situations.

Objective H. *Use the models of addition to form and solve sentences involving addition.* (*Lessons 2-1, 2-2, 2-6, 2-7*)

46. Two children wish to buy a $50 present for their parents. If one child has saved $5, how much does the other child need to have saved?

a. Do this problem in your head. $45

b. Imagine that you couldn't do the problem mentally. Write an equation that might help answer the question.
$5 + x = 50$

47. If the temperature is -11°C, by how much must it increase to become 13°C? 24°

48. The two largest milk-producing states are Wisconsin and California. One year, Wisconsin produced 2.246 billion pounds of milk. Together these states produced 3.652 billion pounds of milk. How much milk was produced in California that year?

49. Mark has $5.40 and would like to buy a pair of jeans for $26. He earns d dollars babysitting and $7.50 for mowing the lawn, but still does not have enough money. What sentence relates $5.40, $26, $7.50, and d?

48) 1.406 billion lb
49) $5.40 + d + 7.50 < 26$

50. Eli needs $5 more for a concert ticket. How much must he earn to go to the concert and have at least $4 to spend on bus fare and food? at least $9

51. The temperature was T_1 degrees. It changed by C degrees. Now it is more than T_2 degrees. Give a sentence relating T_1, C, and T_2. $T_1 + C > T_2$

52. Represent the perimeter of the quadrilateral below as a simplified algebraic expression.

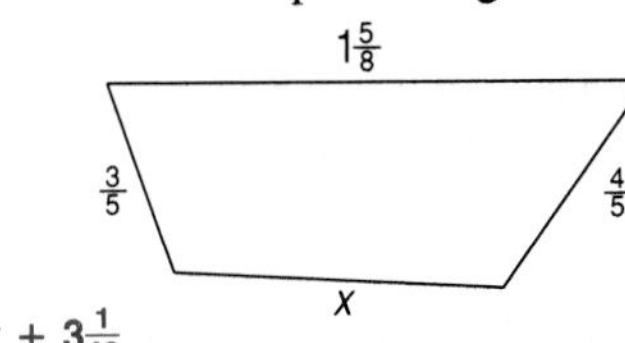

$x + 3\frac{1}{40}$

53. Bessie's stock rose $1\frac{1}{4}$ points Monday, rose $\frac{1}{8}$ point Tuesday, and fell $\frac{3}{4}$ point Wednesday. What was the overall change in her stock for these three days? $+\frac{5}{8}$

ADDITIONAL ANSWERS

32. Commutative Property of Addition

33. Additive Identity Property

34. Associative Property of Addition

35. Op-op Property

36. Adding Fractions Property

37. Adding Like Terms Property

EVALUATION
Three tests are provided for this chapter in the Teacher's Resource File. Chapter 2 Test, Forms A and B, cover just Chapter 2. The third test is Chapter 2, Cumulative Form. Two thirds of this test covers Chapter 2; one third covers Chapter 1. For information on grading, see *General Teaching Suggestions; Grading* on page T44 in the Teacher's Edition.

ASSIGNMENT RECOMMENDATION
On the day your students take the chapter test, we suggest you make an assignment in the first section of the next chapter.

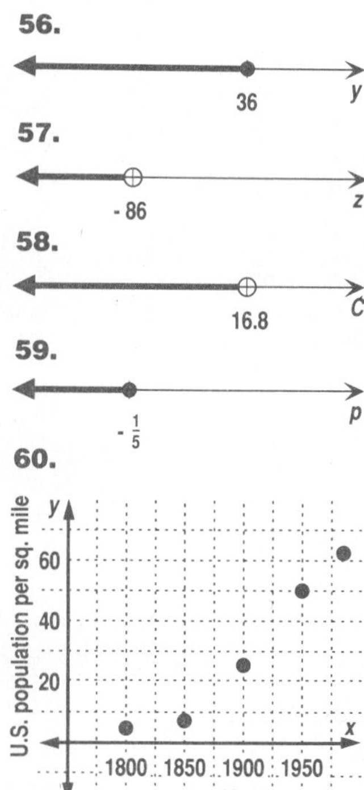

Objective I. *Apply the Triangle Inequality relationship in real situations. (Lesson 2-8)*

54. It is 346 miles from El Paso to Phoenix and 887 miles from Dallas to Phoenix. From only this information, what can you say about the distance from Dallas to El Paso? **more than 541 miles and less than 1233 miles**

55. Malinda lives 20 minutes by train from Roger and 30 minutes by train from Charles. By train, how long would it take to get from Roger's place to Charles's place? (Assume all trains go at the same rate.) **more than 10 and less than 50 minutes**

REPRESENTATIONS deal with pictures, graphs, or objects that illustrate concepts.

Objective J. *Graph solutions to inequalities on a number line. (Lesson 2-7)*

In 56–59, graph all solutions to the inequality.

56. $12 + y \leq 48$ **56–59) See margin.**

57. $-66 > z + 20$

58. $1.5 + C - 6.2 < 12.1$

59. $\frac{1}{5} + \frac{2}{10} \geq \frac{3}{5} + p$

60) See margin.

Objective K. *Plot points and interpret information on a coordinate graph. (Lesson 2-4)*

60. Draw a graph to illustrate these data (year, the U.S. population per square mile). Label the axes. (1800, 6.1), (1850, 7.9), (1900, 25.6), (1950, 50.7), (1980, 62.6)

In 61 and 62, the graph below shows the height of a boy's head from the ground as he rides in a ferris wheel. *(Lesson 2-4)*

61. Where is the boy (top, bottom, halfway up) after 40 seconds on the ride? **halfway up**

62. After everyone is on, how many times does the ferris wheel go around before it begins to let people off? **4 times**

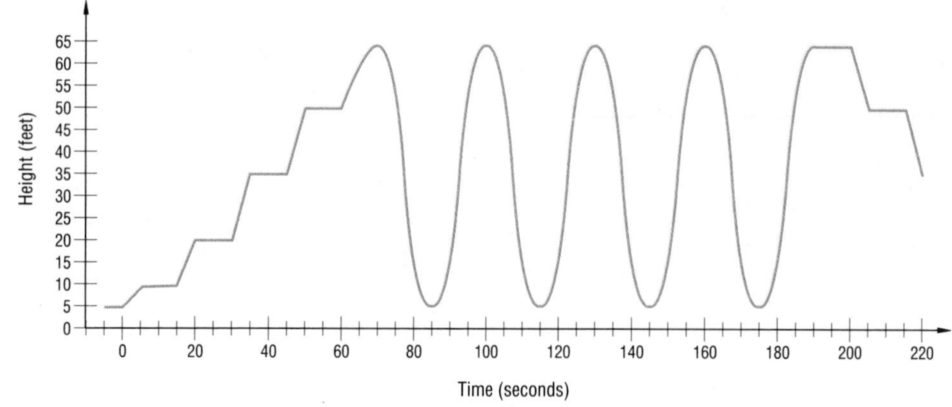

104

In 63–65, use the graph below.

63. Which state had more people in 1930, Texas or Ohio? **Ohio**

64. In which decade was there a time when the populations in Ohio and Texas were the same? **around 1965**

65. In which ten-year interval did Ohio show the greatest increase in population? **1950–1960**

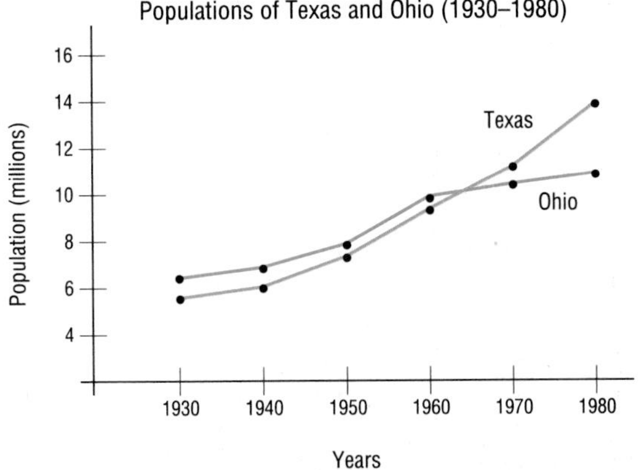

Objective L. *Interpret two-dimensional slides on a coordinate graph.* (Lesson 2-5) **67) (x + 4, y + -10)**

66. Find the image of (2, -4) after a slide of 40 units to the left and 60 units up. **(-38, 56)**

67. Find the image of (x, y) after a slide of 4 units to the right and 10 units down.

68. Find a and b when $(4 + a, 9 + b) = (3, 17)$.

69. After a slide, the image of C is $C' = (6,4)$. Graph the image of $\triangle ABC$ below by finding the image of each vertex.

68) a = -1, b = 8

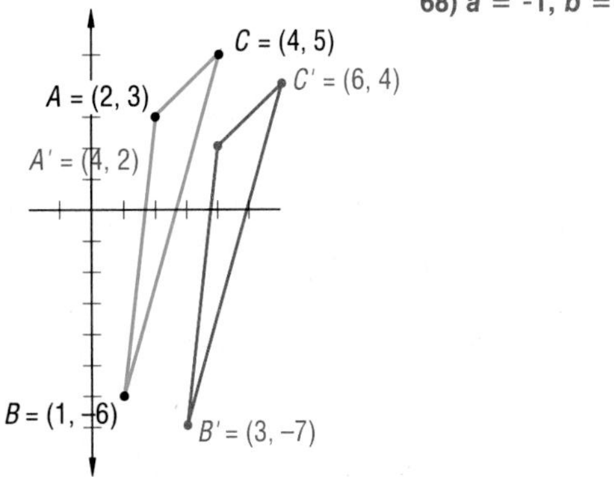

REFRESHER

Chapter 3, which discusses subtraction in algebra, assumes that you have mastered certain objectives in your previous mathematics studies. Use these optional questions to check your mastery.

A. Subtract positive and negative integers.

1. 40 − 200 **-160** **2.** 76 − 79 **-3**
3. -2 − 6 **-8** **4.** -12 − -11 **-1**
5. 111 − -88 **199** **6.** -2 − -3 **1**

B. Measure angles.

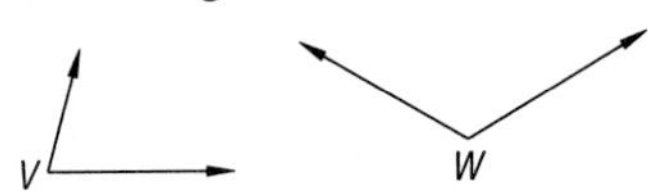

7. *Multiple choice*
The measure of angle V is **b**
(a) between 0° and 45°
(b) between 45° and 90°
(c) greater than 90°

8. *Multiple choice*
The measure of angle W is **c**
a. between 0° and 45°
b. between 45° and 90°
c. greater than 90°

9. Measure $\angle V$ to the nearest degree. **75°**

10. Measure $\angle W$ to the nearest degree. **120°**

11. Draw an angle whose measure is 110°. **See margin.**

C. Solve simple equations of the form $x - a = b$ when a and b are positive integers.

12. $x - 40 = 11$ **x = 51**

13. $878 = y - 31$ **909 = y**

14. $w - 64 = 49$ **w = 113**

15. $100 = z - 402$ **502 = z**

RESOURCES
Visual for Teaching Aid 14: Protractors

REFRESHER
This optional material provides practice with ideas that will be used in Lessons 3-2, 3-3, and 3-8. If your students have had little experience with these ideas, you can assign these problems, either all at once or scattered throughout the early sections of Chapter 3. Students must use protractors in Problems 9–11. In class, you can use a clear plastic protractor to demonstrate how to draw and measure angles.

ADDITIONAL ANSWERS
11.

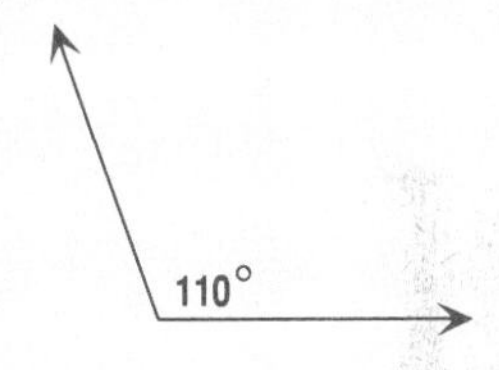

CHAPTER 3 ■ SUBTRACTION IN ALGEBRA

DAILY PACING CHART 3

DAILY PACING CHART ■ CHAPTER 3

Students in the Full Course should complete the entire text by the end of the year. Students in the Minimal Course spend more time to complete lessons that are combined with quizzes and more time to consider the Chapter Review. Therefore, these students may not complete all the chapters in the text.

DAY	MINIMAL COURSE	FULL COURSE
1	3-1	3-1
2	3-2	3-2
3	3-3	3-3
4	3-4	3-4
5	Quiz (TRF); Start 3-5.	Quiz (TRF); 3-5
6	Finish 3-5.	3-6
7	3-6	3-7
8	3-7	3-8
9	3-8	Progress Self-Test
10	Progress Self-Test	Chapter Review
11	Chapter Review	Chapter Test (TRF)
12	Chapter Review	Comprehensive Test (TRF)
13	Chapter Test (TRF)	
14	Comprehensive Test (TRF)	

TESTING OPTIONS

TESTING OPTIONS

- Quiz for Lessons 3-1 Through 3-4
- Chapter 3 Test, Form A
- Chapter 3 Test, Form B
- Chapter 3 Test, Cumulative Form
- Comprehensive Test, Chapters 1–3

INDIVIDUAL DIFFERENCES

PROVIDING FOR INDIVIDUAL DIFFERENCES

The student text is written for the *average* student. The program, however, can be adapted for less capable and for more capable students.

For those students who need more practice, a blackline master (in the Teacher's Resource File) is provided for each lesson. The Teacher's Edition frequently provides Error Analysis and Alternate Approach features to provide additional instructional strategies for those students who do not readily grasp the material.

For students who require additional challenge, Extension activities are regularly provided in the Teacher's Edition.

OBJECTIVES ■ CHAPTER 3

Students should master the chapter objectives by the time they complete the chapter. To ensure objective mastery, there is continual review built into each set of lesson questions. After students complete the chapter lessons, they assess their mastery on the Progress Self-Test. Then they do the Chapter Review and pay special attention to those questions that match the objectives missed on the Progress Self-Test. Students can get extra practice on these objectives by using the master for each lesson in the Teacher's Resource File.

OBJECTIVES FOR CHAPTER 3 (Organized into the SPUR categories— Skills, Properties, Uses, and Representations)	**Progress Self-Test Questions**	**Chapter Review Questions**	**Lesson Master from Teacher's Resource File***
SKILLS			
A Find the union and intersection of sets.	10, 11	1 through 4	3-4, 3-5
B Solve and check sentences involving subtraction.	6 through 9	5 through 13	3-3
C Find the measure of the supplement or complement of an angle.	18	14 through 17	3-8
D Simplify expressions involving subtraction.	2 through 5	18 through 25	3-1, 3-3
PROPERTIES			
E Apply the algebraic definition of subtraction.	1	26 through 29	3-1
USES			
F Use models of subtraction to form expressions and solve sentences involving subtraction.	15, 16	30 through 37	3-2, 3-3
G Apply the formulas for $N(A \cup B)$ and $P(A \cup B)$.	14, 17	38 through 41	3-6
REPRESENTATIONS			
H Graph solution sets to inequalities.	12, 13	42 through 45	3-4, 3-5
I Use Venn diagrams to describe union and intersection.	21	46 through 49	3-4, 3-5
J Graph sets of ordered pairs (x, y) where $x + y = k$ or $x - y = k$, where k is a real number.	19, 20	50 through 53	3-7

*** The masters are numbered to match the lessons.**

OVERVIEW ■ CHAPTER 3

In this chapter, subtraction is related to all of the following: addition, numbers of elements in sets, probabilities, applications from arithmetic, equations, and inequalities.

The first three lessons introduce the definition of subtraction, subtraction models, and solving $x - a = b$ and $x - a < b$. To solve these sentences, students are encouraged to change subtractions to additions, and then to proceed using the properties studied in Chapter 2.

Lessons 3-4 through 3-6 lead to the use of subtraction in solving both counting and probability problems in which sets overlap. The formulas for counts and probabilities employ the definitions of *union* and *intersection* of sets.

Lesson 3-7 deals with situations involving pairs of numbers whose sums are constant and the representation of these number pairs as lines. Lesson 3-8 applies the constant sum idea to important geometry situations. These two lessons offer an opportunity to consolidate the skills of this chapter. At the same time, these lessons present some significant uses of addition and subtraction which will be referred to later in the book.

PERSPECTIVES ■ CHAPTER 3

The Perspectives provide the rationale for the inclusion of topics or approaches, provide mathematical background, and make connections within UCSMP.

3-1

SUBTRACTION OF REAL NUMBERS

In the first grade, students learn their first "definition" of subtraction—referred to in Lesson 3-2 as the Take-away Model for Subtraction. Of course, "take-away" is not called a definition, but it serves that purpose. The problem with this early model is that it does not apply well to negative numbers.

In contrast, the algebraic definition of subtraction, $a - b = a + -b$, enables any subtraction to be converted to addition. This is particularly helpful because students already know how to add positive and negative numbers. Also, addition has the commutative and associative properties while subtraction does not. Converting to addition avoids errors in the order of operations when there are more than two numbers involved in the subtractions.

3-2

MODELS FOR SUBTRACTION

The two models for subtraction discussed in this lesson are review for students who have had *Transition Mathematics.*

The Take-away Model for Subtraction can be viewed as the counterpart to the Putting-together Model for Addition. The take-away model is the one most often encountered in school texts, and the situations are usually those in which the numbers are counts of discrete objects.

Students have also had a lot of experience with the Comparison Model for Subtraction. In general, we compare in the direction which gives a positive answer for the result. That is, we subtract the smaller number from the larger, and we use the context to decide whether the answer is positive or negative. The exception would be when a quantity changes over a period of time. There we subtract the earlier amount from the later one. The sign of the result shows whether the quantity increased or decreased over that period.

3-3

SOLVING $x - a = b$ AND $x - a < b$

This lesson tends to be easy for most students. It covers sentences of the forms $x - a = b$ and $x - a < b$ but purposely not those of the form $a - x = b$. Solution of this last sentence requires two major steps and is not treated until the next chapter.

This lesson is an opportunity for reviewing the checking process for inequalities.

3-4

INTERSECTION OF SETS

Several questions have been included in previous lessons in order to prepare students for this introduction of intersection. Students should not have trouble with this topic, but they may find the next lesson harder because they have to distinguish between intersection and union. Venn diagrams provide a visual representation.

The idea of intersection of sets is used in Lesson 3-6 in the formula to find the number of elements in the union. In Chapter 4, intersections are related to probabilities of events. In Chapter 11, intersections of sets are again found when discussing solutions to systems. Of course, intersections of sets of points are used throughout geometry. There are many applications throughout the text that use intersection.

3-5

UNION OF SETS

As with intersection, the union of sets is discussed through several related means: the definition, Venn diagrams, relative frequency, and graphing.

This lesson concentrates on identifying what elements would be in the union of sets. Example 1 shows that when considering the union of sets that overlap, the elements in both sets (namely, in the intersection) should *not* be listed twice when the union is enumerated. Specific formulas for the count of elements in a union of sets and for the probability of the union of sets are discussed in the next lesson.

3-6

ADDITION, SUBTRACTION, AND COUNTING

The simplest examples of addition are instances of the Putting-together Model where the addends do not overlap. In reality, however, overlap is a common occurrence. Our statistical examples show this quite frequently. In fact, many measurement problems involve overlap. It is important that the student encounter these situations and know how to handle them. The formula for the count of elements in the union of sets and the formula for the probability of the union of events are important formulas in mathematics.

The term *mutually exclusive* is introduced in the context of counting elements in the union. This term is used in connection with events and with probabilities of events. Here are three symbolic statements that two sets or events S and T are mutually exclusive:

$$N(S \cap T) = 0$$
$$P(S \cap T) = 0$$
$$S \cap T = \emptyset$$

Many books take as their Fundamental Counting Principle our Multiplication Counting Principle, which appears in Chapter 4. But our titles are very appropriate because addition situations tend to be more fundamental than multiplication ones.

3-7

ADDITION, SUBTRACTION, AND GRAPHING

Making a table is an important problem-solving strategy. Here, it is combined with the strategy of *drawing a graph.* Both ideas help students find patterns and make generalizations. By the end of the book, students will have seen a variety of tables and graphs which represent important linear and curvilinear patterns.

Using mathematics to describe the relationship between two variables is a fundamental component of scientific and statistical methods. This lesson is especially important if students have never graphed lines. The investigation of how the equation of a line relates to its graph is one of the major topics covered in this book.

Students should have graph paper for this assignment and many later lessons. One approach is to do the entire assignment on graph paper. Not only does this ensure a handy place to draw a graph, but it encourages neat work.

3-8

ADDITION, SUBTRACTION, AND GEOMETRY

Four important geometric concepts are covered in this lesson. Most students have studied them before. They should master them now. These concepts are the definitions of *supplementary angles* and *complementary angles,* the Triangle-Sum Property, and the convention for marking right angles. Prerequisites for understanding these concepts are some of the ideas in the Refresher material which precedes this chapter.

Supplementary angles, complementary angles, and the Triangle-Sum Property are rich sources of algebra questions because they are instances of the constant sum model:

$$a + b = \text{constant}.$$

As the development at the beginning of the lesson shows, solving for b gives

$$b = \text{constant} - a.$$

The definition in this book for *supplementary angles* does not explicitly state whether 0° and 180° could be the measures of supplementary angles. The graph in the lesson does not include the points (180, 0) and (0, 180). However, some books define angles with measure 180° and 0° and would therefore permit these two points.

CHAPTER 3

RESOURCES

Visual for Teaching Aid 15: Roman-Numeral Puzzle

This chapter should take 8 or 9 days for the lessons and quiz; 1 day for the Progress Self-Test; 1 or 2 days for the Chapter Review; and 1 day for testing. The total is 11 to 13 days. Allow an additional day for the Comprehensive Test.

CHAPTER 3

Subtraction in Algebra

Here is a puzzle originally done with matchsticks. Given are six incorrect equations involving adding or subtracting whole numbers written as Roman numerals. Can you correct each by repositioning just one match?

Subtraction has uses more important than puzzles. Any quantities related by addition (3, 4, and 7, for example) are also related by subtraction. In this chapter you will review what you know about subtraction and apply that knowledge to solving equations and inequalities, to counting problems, to graphing, and to geometry.

106

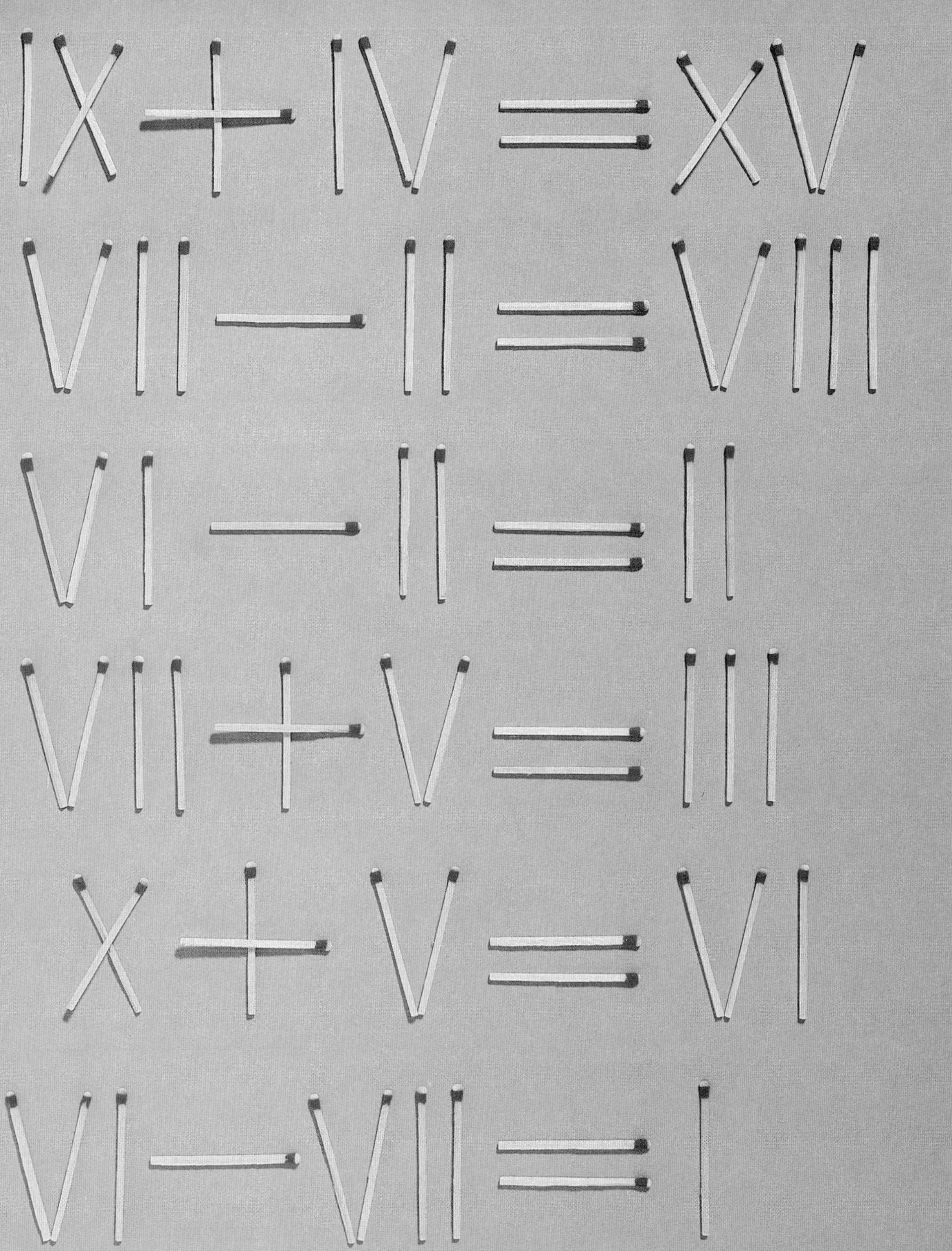

USING PAGES 106–107
The Roman-numeral puzzle in the chapter opener should stimulate student interest. *Teaching Aid 15* can be used as a discussion aid or as a worksheet.

LESSON 3-1

RESOURCES
■ Lesson Master 3-1

OBJECTIVES

D Simplify expressions involving subtraction.
E Apply the algebraic definition of *subtraction.*

TEACHING NOTES

Emphasize that there are two ways to approach subtraction problems. One approach is to think of a use of subtraction, as in **Example 1.** No formal definition is needed. The other is to use the algebraic definition of subtraction, as in **Example 2.** The formal definition is more efficient on problems such as **Example 3.**

In **Example 4,** students should not leave the answer as $y + \text{-}10$. The preferred simplified form is $y - 10$ since it uses fewer symbols. However, you might allow $\text{-}10 + y$ since the form $\text{-}2x + y$ is sometimes useful.

Error Analysis In problems like **Example 5,** a common mistake is to simplify $5x - x$ to 5. If students do this, use a number line to show combining terms.

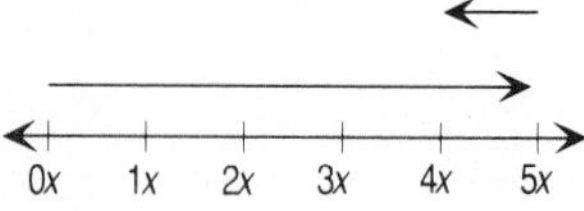

LESSON

3-1 Subtraction of Real Numbers

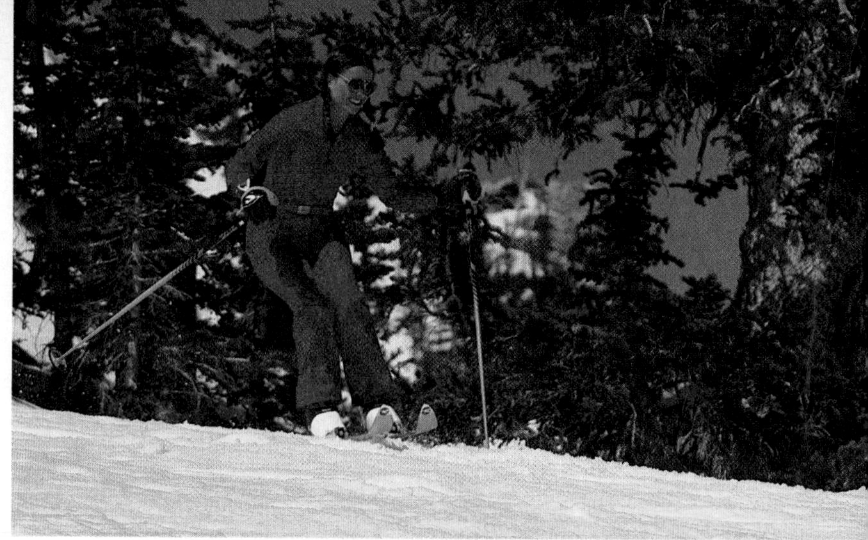

You learned how to subtract with questions like this one.

Question: If you have 7 pennies and take 2 away, how many pennies are left?

Answer: $7 - 2 = 5$

The same question can be answered by adding: $7 + \text{-}2 = 5$. So $7 - 2 = 7 + \text{-}2$. Here is another question that can be answered either by adding or by subtracting.

Example 1 A temperature is -5°C. It falls 3°. What is the new temperature?

Solution 1 Begin with -5. Subtract 3.
$\text{-}5 - 3 = \text{-}8$ The new temperature is -8 °C.

Solution 2 Begin with -5. Add -3.
$\text{-}5 + \text{-}3 = \text{-}8$ The new temperature is -8 °C.

These instances show that subtracting a number is the same as adding its opposite. The general pattern is the **algebraic definition of subtraction.**

Algebraic Definition of Subtraction:

For all real numbers a and b,
$$a - b = a + \text{-}b.$$

Changing a subtraction problem into an addition problem is especially helpful when the numbers are not integers.

Example 2 Evaluate $x - y$ when $x = 7.31$ and $y = -5.62$.

Solution Substitution gives $x - y = 7.31 - -5.62$.
The opposite of -5.62 is 5.62, so by the algebraic definition of subtraction

$$= 7.31 + 5.62$$
$$= 12.93.$$

Check Use a calculator.

7.31 [−] 5.62 [+/−] [=]
You should see 12.93 displayed.

Caution: Subtraction is *not* associative. A computation like $3 - 9 - 1$ will not give the same answer if you do $3 - 9$ first as when you do $9 - 1$ first. You must follow the order of operations and work from left to right. (Do $3 - 9$ first.) However, you can gain flexibility by changing the subtractions to adding the opposites. $3 + -9 + -1$. Now either addition can be done first, and the answer is -7.

Example 3 During the week of June 10, 1985, the price of IBM stock changed as follows:

Monday	Tuesday	Wednesday	Thursday	Friday
up $\frac{1}{4}$	down $1\frac{5}{8}$	down $5\frac{1}{4}$	down $2\frac{1}{8}$	up $2\frac{1}{2}$

Find the net change in the price of IBM stock for the week.

Solution The net change is figured by combining all of the daily changes for the week. Up means add. Down means subtract.

$$\text{net change} = \tfrac{1}{4} - 1\tfrac{5}{8} - 5\tfrac{1}{4} - 2\tfrac{1}{8} + 2\tfrac{1}{2}$$

By changing each subtraction to adding the opposite, the numbers may be added in any order.

$$= \tfrac{1}{4} + -1\tfrac{5}{8} + -5\tfrac{1}{4} + -2\tfrac{1}{8} + 2\tfrac{1}{2}$$

Now use the commutative and associative properties of addition. Group the positives and the negatives.

$$= (\tfrac{1}{4} + 2\tfrac{1}{2}) + (-1\tfrac{5}{8} + -5\tfrac{1}{4} + -2\tfrac{1}{8})$$
$$= 2\tfrac{3}{4} + -9$$
$$= -6\tfrac{1}{4}$$

The net change is down $6\frac{1}{4}$.

Check Convert to decimals and use a calculator.
Net change = $0.25 - 1.625 - 5.25 - 2.125 + 2.5 = -6.25$

Another explanation emphasizes units: 5 inches − 1 inch = 4 inches. Still another explanation is with order of operations: the multiplication in $5x$ is done before the subtraction. With the last explanation, substitute a number for x.

ADDITIONAL EXAMPLES

1. Prospectors in Death Valley enter their mine on the valley floor (elevation -86 ft) and go down the shaft 30 feet. What is their elevation?
-116 ft

2. Evaluate $x - y$ when $x = -16.8$ and $y = 21.4$.
-38.2

3. A hospital patient's temperature is 101.2° at 8 P.M. Over the next two days, it undergoes the following changes.

	8 A.M.	8 P.M.
Day 1	up .3°	down 1.1°
Day 2	down .4°	up .8°

What is the patient's temperature at 8 P.M. of Day 2?
100.8°

4. Simplify $-a - (-b)$.
$\boldsymbol{b - a}$ **or** $\boldsymbol{-a + b}$

5. Simplify $4j - 7j + 5x + j$.
$\boldsymbol{5x - 2j}$ **or** $\boldsymbol{-2j + 5x}$

NOTES ON QUESTIONS
Question 1: This question parallels **Example 1.** Carefully review this question to insure that students have a concrete basis for the algebraic definition of *subtraction.*

Questions 20c and 22: These establish a handy pattern: $(a - b) = -(b - a)$.

Question 21: This reinforces the general problem-solving strategy of *eliminating possibilities.* Point out that the mathematical term *domain of x* could have been used in place of *choices for x.*

You could keep the whole number parts separate from the fraction parts in Example 3. But be careful. Whereas $1\frac{5}{8}$ means $1 + \frac{5}{8}$, so $-1\frac{5}{8}$ means $-1 - \frac{5}{8}$ or $-1 + -\frac{5}{8}$.

Example 4 Simplify $-10 - (-y)$.

Solution By the algebraic definition of subtraction,

$$\begin{aligned} -10 - (-y) &= -10 + y \\ &= y + -10 \\ &= y - 10 \end{aligned}$$

Check Let $y = 25$. Then $-10 - (-y) = -10 - (-25) = -10 + 25 = 15$. Also, $y - 10 = 25 - 10 = 15$.

Example 5 Simplify $5x + 3y - 2 - x$.

Solution Think of x as $1x$. Use the algebraic definition of subtraction.

$5x + 3y - 2 - 1x = 5x + 3y + -2 + -1x$

Combine like terms. $= 4x + 3y + -2$

Apply the algebraic definition of subtraction. $= 4x + 3y - 2$

Questions

Covering the Reading

1. The temperature is 12 °F. It falls 15°. **a) 12 + -15; b) 12 − 15**
   a. Write an addition expression to find the new temperature.
   b. Write a subtraction expression to find the new temperature.

2. State the algebraic definition of subtraction. **See margin.**

In 3–5, apply the algebraic definition of subtraction to rewrite the subtraction as an addition.

3. $-2 - 7$ **-2 + -7** **4.** $28 - -63$ **28 + 63** **5.** $x - (-d)$ **x + d**

6. During one week, the price of World Wide Widget stock changed as follows. Find the net change. **down $\frac{3}{8}$**

Monday	Tuesday	Wednesday	Thursday	Friday
down $2\frac{1}{4}$	up $\frac{1}{2}$	down $\frac{1}{8}$	down $\frac{1}{2}$	up 2

In 7 and 8, **a.** rewrite each subtraction as an addition; **b.** evaluate the expression.

7. $\frac{3}{5} - -\frac{7}{10}$ **a) $\frac{3}{5} + \frac{7}{10}$; b) $\frac{13}{10}$** **8.** $-3 - 4 - -7 - -11$
a) -3 + -4 + 7 + 11; b) 11

9. a. *True or false* $(3 - 9) - 1 = 3 - (9 - 1)$ **False**
   b. What property is or is not verified in part a? **Associative Property of Subtraction**

In 10 and 11, calculate.

10. $20 - 4 - 3$ **13**

11. $-7 - 30 - 20$ **-57**

12. Write the key sequence to do $-73 - -91$ on your calculator:
    a. using the [−] key; b. using the [+] key. **See margin.**

In 13 and 14, simplify.

13. $10p - 2q + 4 + 8q$ **$10p + 6q + 4$**

14. $-2a - 3a + 4b - b$ **$-5a + 3b$**

Applying the Mathematics

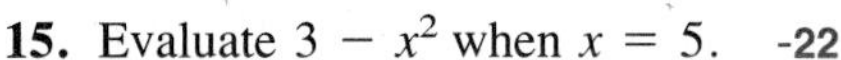

15. Evaluate $3 - x^2$ when $x = 5$. **-22**

16. Evaluate $-x - y$ when $x = -12$ and $y = 2$. **10**

17. Evaluate $a - y - b$ when $a = -1$, $b = 2$, and $y = -3$. **0**

18. What problem does this key sequence answer? 8.37 [+/−] [−] 7.01 [=]
    Evaluate $-8.37 - 7.01$.

19. Mr. Whittaker's doctor advised him to lose weight. The changes in Mr. Whittaker's weight were:

First Week	Second Week	Third Week	Fourth Week
lost 4 lb	lost 3 lb	lost 3 lb	gained 5 lb

    a. Write an expression for the net change using addition.
    b. Write an expression for the net change using subtraction.
    c. What was the net change for the four weeks ? **-5 lb**
    a) $-4 + -3 + -3 + 5$; b) $-4 - 3 - 3 + 5$

20. Let t be Toni's weight. Let f be Fred's weight. Suppose $t - f = 35$.
    a. Find a value for t and a value for f such that $t - f = 35$. **See margin.**
    b. Who is heavier, Toni or Fred? **Toni**
    c. Use values for t and f from part a. Find the value of $f - t$. **-35**

21. Find all possible values for x using the clues. **-1, 1**

    Choices for x: -7, -4, -3, -1, 1, 3, 4, 7
    Clue 1: $x > 0 - 2$
    Clue 2: $x < 4 - -1$
    Clue 3: $x \neq 2 - -1$
    Clue 4: $-x \neq -4$

22. Evaluate $a - b$ and $b - a$ when
    a. $a = 5$ and $b = -1$ **6, -6**
    b. $a = 1$ and $b = 3$ **-2, 2**
    c. $a = -2$ and $b = 0$ **-2, 2**
    d. $a = -3$ and $b = -6$ **3, -3**
    e. From part a to part d, does subtraction seem to be commutative? **No**

23. a. Simplify $-x - 2x - 3x - 4x - 5x$. **$-15x$**
    b. Simplify $y - y - 2y - 3y - 4y - 5y$. **$-14y$**
    c. Simplify $6x - (5x - (4x - (3x - 32)))$. Begin with the innermost parentheses and work toward the outer parentheses. **$2x + 32$**
    d. Simplify $x - (3x - 6x)$. **$4x$**

ADDITIONAL ANSWERS

2. For all real numbers *a* and *b*, $a - b = a + -b$.

12a.
73 [+/−] [−] 91 [+/−] [=]

12b.
73 [+/−] [+] 91 [=]

20a. sample: $t = 150$, $f = 115$

NAME ____________

LESSON **MASTER 3–1**
QUESTIONS ON **SPUR** OBJECTIVES

■SKILLS *Objective D* *(See pages 150–152 for objectives.)*
In 1–7, simplify.

1. $11x - 3x + 7x$ **15x**
2. $-1.8r - .4r + 2.3r$ **0.1r**
3. $3d - \frac{d}{4} - \frac{-5d}{2}$ **$\frac{21d}{4}$**
4. $x^2 - -2x - 3x^2$ **$-2x^2 + 2x$**
5. $4t - (-6t + 4)$ **$10t - 4$**
6. $-63 - 44 + 17 - -40 - 6$ **-56**
7. $-6z^2 - -4z^3 + 8z^3 - 9z^2$ **$-15z^2 + 12z^3$**

■PROPERTIES *Objective E*
In 8–10, rewrite each subtraction as addition.

8. $4 - 6 - -10$ **$4 + -6 + 10$**
9. $2a - 3b + c$ **$2a + -3b + c$**
10. $-3 - h + 4h - -6$ **$-3 + -h + 4h + 6$**
11. Write a key sequence to compute $-47 - -86$ using the [+] and [+/−] keys on your calculator.
    47 [+/−] [+] 86 [=]
12. Evaluate $-f - g$ when $f = -10$ and $g = 12$. **-2**
13. Evaluate $-(2u - 3v)$ when $u = 4$ and $v = 7$. **13**
14. Evaluate $6 - (-x - y)$ when $x = 2$ and $y = -5$. **3**

FOLLOW-UP

MORE PRACTICE
For more questions on SPUR Objectives, use *Lesson Master 3-1,* shown on page 111.

EXTENSION
Have students apply the definition of subtraction to rewrite each equation below as addition and then solve, writing the answers as Roman numerals.

1. XXXIV − -LXXXIII − XLVII =
[XXXIV + LXXXIII + -XLVII = LXX
(34 + 83 + -47 = 70)]

2. MDXLVI − DLXXXVII =
[MDXLVI + -DLXXXVII = CMLIX (1546 + -587 = 959)]

3. CCCLXVII − CDXXXII − MCCV =
[CCCLXVII + -CDXXXII + -MCCV = MCCLXX
(367 + -432 + -1205 = -1270)]

24. $7 \le x$;

Review

24. Find and graph the solution set: $3 \le x + -4$. *(Lesson 2-7)* **See margin.**

25. *Skill sequence* Solve. *(Lesson 2-6)*
a. $-3 = x + (-7)$ **x = 4**
b. $2.7 + y = 3.4$ **y = 0.7**
c. $z + (-1\frac{1}{4}) = -\frac{3}{4}$ **$z = \frac{1}{2}$**

26. *Multiple choice* Tell which graph best fits each description. *(Lesson 2-4)*
a. The number of people in a restaurant from 6 A.M. to 6 P.M. **26a) Graph II**
b. The number of people in a school from 6 A.M. to 6 P.M. **Graph I**
c. The number of people in a hospital from 6 A.M.to 6 P.M. **Graph III**

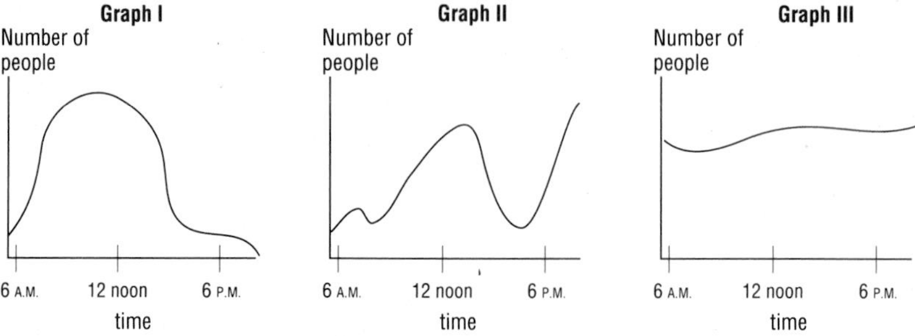

27. Evaluate in your head when $b = 20$. *(Lesson 1-4)*
a. $-3 + b$ **17** **b.** $\frac{1}{2}b$ **10** **c.** $2b^2$ **800**

28. Event A has a probability of 66%, event B has a probability of $\frac{3}{5}$, and event C has a probability of 0.7. Which event is most likely to happen? *(Lesson 1-7)* **Event C with a probability of 0.7**

29. Solve for y: $2x + y + 5x = 28x + 3$. *(Lesson 2-6)* **y = 21x + 3**

Exploration

30. The puzzles in the chapter opener are written with Roman numerals. Match each Roman numeral at left with its decimal form at right. *(Previous course)*

a. L **50** 1
b. M **1000** 5
c. C **100** 10
d. D **500** 50
e. V **5** 100
f. X **10** 500
g. I **1** 1000

31. Roman numerals were the most common way of writing numbers in Western Europe from about 100 B.C. to A.D. 1700. Even in this century, they have often been used to name years and on timepieces. Match each year with its corresponding Roman numeral.

a. the year Christopher Columbus first sailed for the New World
b. the year the character "Mickey Mouse" first appeared in a cartoon
c. the year the first gasoline-powered automobile appeared
d. the year Joan of Arc was killed

i. MDCCCLXXXV
ii. MCDXXXI
iii. MCDXCII
iv. MCMXXVIII

a) 1492 (iii); b) 1928 (iv); c) 1885 (i); d) 1431 (ii)

LESSON

3-2

Models for Subtraction

Pine Island had an area of 27.8 square miles. During a hurricane, 1.6 square miles of beach were washed away. The area of the island left was 27.8 − 1.6, or 26.2 square miles. This illustrates an important model for subtraction.

Take-Away Model for Subtraction:

If a quantity y is taken away from an original quantity x, the quantity left is $x - y$.

The take-away model leads to algebraic expressions involving subtraction.

Example 1 In baseball, the batter hits into a playing field. The foul lines form a 90° angle. Suppose on a hard-hit ground ball each of the four infielders can cover an angle of about 13°. The pitcher can cover about 6°. How much of the infield is left for the hitter to hit through?

shortstop
2nd baseman
1st baseman
3rd baseman
pitcher
13°
6°
13°
13°
13°
foul
foul
batter

Solution The infielders and the pitcher can cover 13° + 13° + 13° + 13° + 6° = 58° of the hitting region. Subtract 58° from the 90° region: 90° − 58° = 32°. A hit can occur in about 32° of the field.

LESSON 3-2

RESOURCES

■ Lesson Master 3-2

OBJECTIVES

D Simplify expressions involving subtraction.
F Use models of subtraction to form expressions and solve sentences involving subtraction.

TEACHING NOTES

As this lesson is discussed, you may want to use discrete sets to review the models for subtraction.

Take-away Model

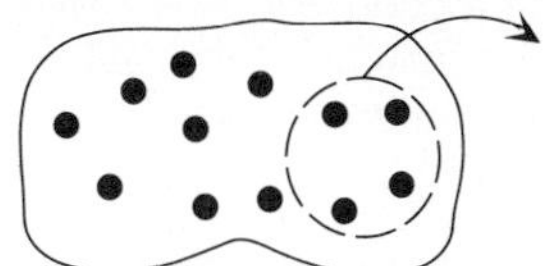

How many are left?

Comparison Model

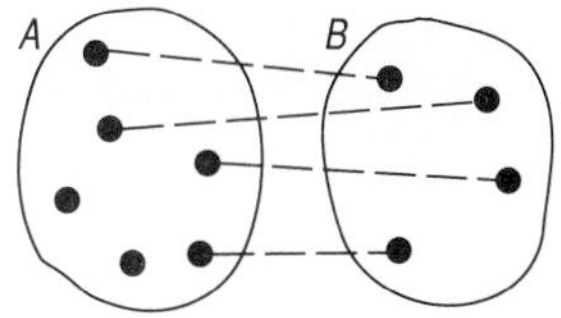

How many more or less?

In **Example 4,** the answer $x^2 - y^2$ is not wrong, but it would give a negative number. Emphasize that the order should be the larger number minus the smaller number.

ADDITIONAL EXAMPLES

1. Sal's Sandwich Shop began the day with $17\frac{1}{2}$ pounds of pastrami. Two people each bought a pound of pastrami, five people each bought $\frac{1}{2}$ pound, and one person bought $2\frac{1}{2}$ pounds. How much pastrami is left?
$10\frac{1}{2}$ lb

2. Yesterday, the high temperature was 22°F and the low temperature was -12°F. What was the range of temperatures?
34°F

3. Yesterday, it was 97°. Today, it is even hotter, and the temperature is T degrees. How much warmer is it today than yesterday?
$T - 97$ degrees

4. A cube with side e is inside a cube with side f. What is the volume of the space between the two cubes?
$f^3 - e^3$

If each infielder could cover 15°, with the pitcher covering 6°, then by the same procedure, there would be 24° of the infield for a ball to get through. In general, if all infielders can cover d degrees and the pitcher can cover P degrees, then there are $90 - 4d - P$ degrees remaining for a hard-hit ground ball to get through.

A second model for subtraction is used when two quantities are compared.

Comparison Model for Subtraction:

The quantity $x - y$ tells how much quantity x differs from the quantity y.

You saw one application of the comparison model for subtraction in Lesson 1-3 when you computed the range of a set of numbers. Recall that the interval from the minimum to the maximum is called the range. It is found by subtracting the minimum value from the maximum value. The range tells you how much the maximum differs from the minimum.

Example 2 The greatest recorded difference in temperature during a single day was in Browning, Montana, in January, 1916. During one 24-hour period, the low temperature was -56°F and the high temperature was 44°F. What was the range of the temperature?

Solution Compare the numbers by subtracting.

$$\begin{aligned} \text{range} &= \text{maximum} - \text{minimum} \\ &= 44 - (-56) \\ &= 44 + 56 \\ &= 100 \end{aligned}$$

The range of the temperatures was 100°.

Examples 3 and 4 use the comparison model with variables to describe relationships.

Example 3 Andrea is A years old. Her younger brother, Tim, is 12 years old. How much older is Andrea than Tim?

Solution To compare the ages, use the comparison model. Subtract the numbers. Therefore Andrea is $A - 12$ years older than her brother.

Check If Andrea is 15, she is 3 years older than her brother. If $A = 15$, then $A - 12 = 3$, which checks.

114

Example 4 The Transamerica Building in San Francisco has the shape of a pyramid. Each floor is approximately square. Let x be the side of one floor and let y be the side of a lower floor. Write an expression to compare the areas of the two floors.

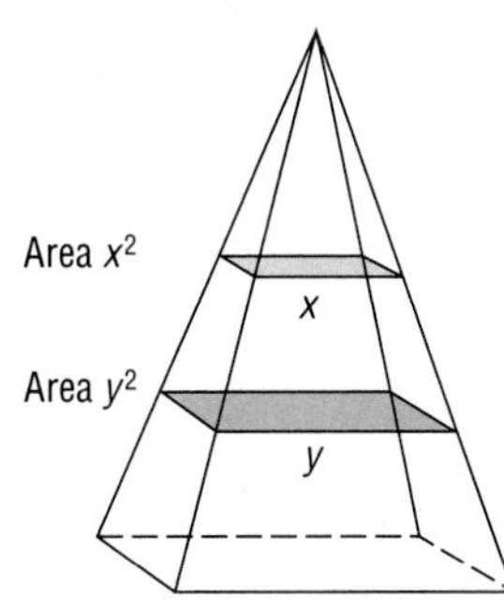

Solution The two floors have areas x^2 and y^2. Since floor y has the larger area, the difference in area is $y^2 - x^2$.

In Example 4, be careful to use order of operations. Take powers before subtracting. If $y = 50$ meters and $x = 30$ meters, the difference in areas is $50^2 - 30^2$ square meters, which is $2500 - 900$, or 1600 square meters.

ADDITIONAL ANSWERS

1. If a quantity y is taken away from an original quantity x, the quantity left is $x - y$.

3. The quantity $x - y$ tells how much quantity x differs from the quantity y.

Questions

Covering the Reading

1. State the take-away model for subtraction. **See margin.**

2. In the baseball example, if each infielder could cover 14° and the pitcher 7°, how much of the infield is there for ground balls to get through? **27°**

3. State the comparison model for subtraction. **See margin.**

4. A most unusual recorded temperature change occurred in Spearfish, South Dakota on January 22, 1943. Over a period of two minutes the temperature rose from -4° F to 45° F. What was the range of temperature? **49°**

In 5–6, use Example 3.

5. Andrea's older cousin Sam is 18. How much older is Sam than Andrea? **$18 - A$**

6. Suppose Andrea is 17 years old. How much older is she than her brother Tim? **5 years**

7. Suppose one side of a floor in the Transamerica Building has length 40 meters. Let b meters be the length of a side of a higher floor. Write an expression for the difference in the areas of the two floors. **$1600 - b^2$**

Applying the Mathematics

8. The Arnold Company buys a piece of property which has an area of 14,000 square feet. On it the company builds a store with area S square feet and a parking lot with area 2580 square feet. Write an expression for the area left for the lawn. **$(14{,}000 - S - 2580)$ square feet**

NOTES ON QUESTIONS
Questions 11 and 12: Students should subtract the earlier value from the later value. In **Question 12,** the direction of the change (positive or negative) is important when finding the median and the mean.

Questions 15 and 17: These diagrams give pictorial representations for the Take-away Model for Subtraction.

Question 16: What matters is the amount of difference, not whether the estimate was over or under. In a later lesson, we use this type of situation to help introduce absolute value.

Question 23: Remind students to think of moving to the right on a number line (or up, on a vertical number line) as adding a positive number and moving to the left (or down) either as adding a negative or as subtracting a positive.

Making Connections for Question 24: This reviews the use of variables to describe general patterns. If your students have had *Transition Mathematics,* this type of question will be familiar. There is a question on patterns in the next lesson, so be sure your students understand this one.

3 P.M. 6 P.M. 9 P.M.

In 9 and 10, Bernie's age is B, John's age is $B - 3$, and Robin's age is $B - 7$.

9. **a.** Who is older, Robin or Bernie? **b.** How much older?
a) Bernie; b) 7 yrs

10. **a.** Who is older, John or Robin? **b.** How much older?
a) John; b) 4 years

11. These thermometers at the left show a hospital patient's temperature at three times.
a. What was the change from 3 P.M. to 6 P.M.? **0.5°**
b. What was the change from 3 P.M. to 9 P.M.? **-1.5°**

12. Some students studied a chapter for which they took a pretest and a posttest.
a. Complete the table below. The change may be negative.

Student	Pretest	Posttest	Change
Chui, L.	57	65	8
Fields, S.	43	41	? **-2**
Ivan, J.	63	? **68**	5
Washington, C.	? **54**	51	-3

b. What is the median change? **1.5**
c. What is the mean of the changes? **2**

13. In New York City, the sun's rays make a $72\frac{1}{2}°$ angle with the ground at noon on the first day of summer (about June 21). On the first day of winter (about December 21), the angle is $25\frac{1}{2}°$. By how much do the angles differ? **47°**

14. Neanderthal man lived in Europe, North Africa, and Central Asia from about 200,000 B.C. to about 30,000 B.C. How long was this?
170,000 yrs

15. A carpenter has a board that is x feet long. He cuts a 3-foot piece from it. Write an expression for the length of the remaining piece. **(x − 3) feet**

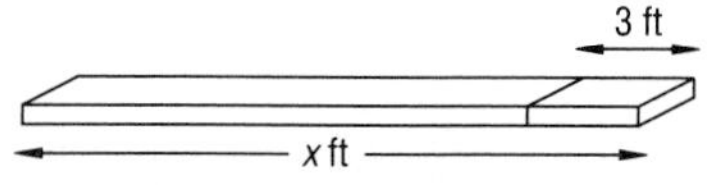

16. At a carnival, John estimates that there are 325 marbles in a barrel. Maria's estimate is 500. The actual count is 422. Who has a closer estimate? **Maria**

17. What is the difference in area between the two rectangles at the right? **4x**

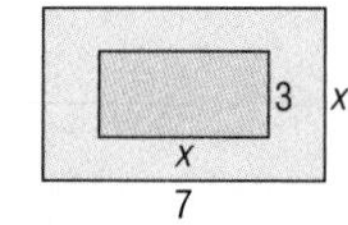

Review

In 18-22, simplify. *(Lesson 3-1)*

18. 42,531 − 36,195 − (-14,259) **20,595**

19. -8.7 − 16.03 **-24.73**

20. $-p - (-q)$ **q − p or -p + q**

21. $-7ab + 2a - 5b - 6ab - 4a + b$ **-13ab − 2a − 4b**

22. $y + (6 - (2.7y + 0.4y))$ **-2.1y + 6 or 6 − 2.1y**

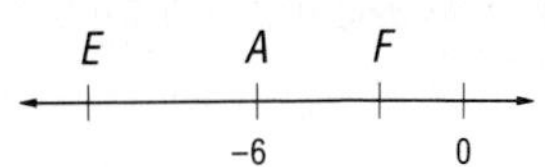

23. E is 4 units to the left of A. F is n units to the right of A.
   a. What is the coordinate of E? **-10**
   b. Write an expression for the coordinate of F. *(Lesson 2-2)* **$-6 + n$**

24. Four instances of a pattern are given below. Describe the general pattern using two variables. *(Previous course)* **$a^2 - b^2 = (a + b)(a - b)$**

$$9^2 - 4^2 = (9 + 4)(9 - 4)$$
$$31^2 - 29^2 = (31 + 29)(31 - 29)$$
$$7^2 - 8^2 = (7 + 8)(7 - 8)$$
$$3.5^2 - 2.5^2 = (3.5 + 2.5)(3.5 - 2.5)$$

25. A formula in a computer program is J = 3 * I + 1. Find the value of J when I = 12. *(Lesson 1-4)* **37**

26. In Tinytown, the only gas station is 1 mile from the elementary school and 0.4 mile from the high school. Explain why it is impossible for the two schools to be 2 miles apart. *(Lesson 2-8)* **See margin.**

27. The image of (x, y) is $(7, -1)$. It results from a slide four units to the right and two units down. Find x and y. *(Lesson 2-5)* **$x = 3$, $y = 1$**

In 28 and 29, use this information: At Central High, all graduates must take either earth science or biology. There were G graduates last year. E of them took only earth science. B of them took only biology. A of them took both. Suppose a science reporter picks at random a graduate to interview. *(Lesson 1-7)*

28. What is the probability that the student took both biology and earth science? **A/G**

29. What is the probability the student took earth science but not biology? **E/G**

30. *Skill sequence* Solve. *(Lesson 2-7)*
   a. $x - 8 > 5$ **$x > 13$**
   b. $16 + x > 1 - 0$ **$x > -15$**
   c. $-28.3 > x + 17.5$ **$-45.8 > x$**

31. The area of a right triangle is $\frac{1}{2}$ the product of its legs. Find the areas in your head. *(Lesson 1-4)*
a) $\frac{1}{2}b^2$; b) $6h^2$; c) $\frac{1}{16}$

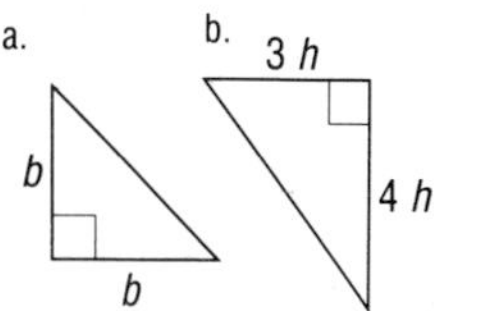

Exploration

32. The number of years between historical events can be calculated by subtracting the years in which the events occurred. You will be within a year of being correct. (December 31, 1985 and January 1, 1986 are one day apart, not one year apart.)
   a. How many years apart are the Declaration of Independence and the end of the Civil War? **89 years**
   b. How many years are between the death of Archimedes in 222 B.C. and the death of Julius Caesar in A.D. 43. (Be careful! There was no year 0.) **264 years**
   c. Nicholas and Nicole have birth years one year apart. What is the smallest and largest possible difference in their birth days?
   Smallest difference is 1 day; largest difference is 2 years less 1 day.

FOLLOW-UP

MORE PRACTICE

For more questions on SPUR Objectives, use *Lesson Master 3-2*, shown below.

EXTENSION

1. Trajan was emperor of Rome until CXVII A.D. He ruled for XIX years. In what year did his reign begin? (Write your answer in Roman numerals.) [XCVIII A.D. (98 A.D.)]

2. The Roman poet Virgil wrote the *Aeneid* between XXX B.C. and XIX B.C. If it took him this entire time to write this work, how many years of his life were spent writing the *Aeneid?* (Write your answer in Roman numerals.) [XI years (11 years)]

26. Distance is at least (1 − 0.4) miles and at most (1 + 0.4) miles.

NAME ______

LESSON **MASTER 3–2**
QUESTIONS ON **SPUR** OBJECTIVES

USES *Objective F (See pages 150–152 for objectives.)*

1. The label on a can of paint says it will cover 550 square feet. Tim has used part of the can to paint a wall of W square feet. How much more area can be covered by what is left in the can?
$(550 - W)$ square feet

2. A dealer sells a TV set for S dollars. This price includes overhead expenses E and a profit P. How much did the TV cost the dealer?
$(S - (E + P))$ dollars or $(S - E - P)$ dollars

3. After cutting 115 square meters of a lawn, Carlos has less than 28 square meters to cut. If the lawn area is M square meters, write an inequality to describe the possible values of M.
$M - 115 < 28$

4. Last year Mrs. Chen's arithmetic class mean was 7 points below passing on a basic skills test. This year it was 8 points above passing. By how much did it improve this year?
15 points

5. In the first football game, the fullback's average gain per carry was -2.3 yards. In the second game it was 3.2 yards. By how much did it increase?
5.5 yards

6. The highest temperature ever recorded in Fairbanks, Alaska, is 84°F. The lowest temperature is -40°F. What is the difference between these two temperatures?
124°F

7. The closing price for ABC stock was d dollars. If the change for the day was $-3\frac{1}{8}$, what was the opening price?
$\left(d + 3\frac{1}{8}\right)$ dollars

8. In a presidential poll, n% favored candidate A, m% favored candidate B, and the rest had no opinion. What percent had no opinion?
$(100 - (n + m))$% or $(100 - n - m)$%

20

LESSON 3-3

RESOURCES
■ Lesson Master 3-3

OBJECTIVES

B Solve and check sentences involving subtraction.
D Simplify expressions involving subtraction.
F Use models of subtraction to form expressions and solve sentences involving subtraction.

TEACHING NOTES

Solving $x - a = b$ and $x - a < b$ is likely to be review for most students. Nevertheless, stress the sentence-solving techniques used in the lesson. This will benefit students who tend to confuse $x + a = b$ with $x - a = b$.

Alternate Approach
Instead of solving $x - a = b$ by changing the subtraction to addition, some people prefer to add a to each side right away.

Examples:

1. $x - 7 = -10$
$x - 7 + 7 = -10 + 7$
$x = -3$

2. $y - -20 < 5$
$y - -20 + -20 < 5 + -20$
$y < -15$

Students should be aware of both methods.

LESSON 3-3

Solving $x - a = b$ and $x - a < b$

The range of temperatures recorded on the planets of our solar system is 682°C. The minimum temperature of -220°C was recorded on Pluto. The maximum was recorded on Venus. To find the maximum recorded temperature you can use a subtraction equation.

Let T = the maximum temperature recorded. Substitute into the formula for range.

$$\text{range} = \text{maximum} - \text{minimum}$$
$$682 = T - (-220)$$

Notice that you can change the subtraction to addition.

$$682 = T + 220$$

Solve as you would an addition equation. Add -220 to each side.

$$682 + -220 = T + 220 + -220$$
$$462 = T$$

The maximum recorded temperature is 462°C.

The subtraction equation above was changed to one involving addition. You can do this with *any* sentence involving subtraction. Then you can use all you know about solving addition sentences.

Example 1 Hometown Bank and Trust requires a minimum balance of $1500 for free checking. If Mr. Archer can withdraw $3276 and still have free checking, how much is in his account?

Solution Let M be the amount of money in Mr. Archer's account. Then the amount left after the withdrawal is $M - 3276$. This quantity must be greater than or equal to $1500.

$$M - 3276 \geq 1500$$

Change subtraction to addition. $M + -3276 \geq 1500$

Add 3276 to both sides of the inequality. $M + -3276 + 3276 \geq 1500 + 3276$

$$M \geq 4776$$

The answer, $M \geq 4776$, means that Mr. Archer has to have at least \$4776 in his account in order to keep free checking after a withdrawal of \$3276.

Check As with any inequality, check the answer with two steps.
Step 1: Check 4776 by substituting in the original inequality.
Does $4776 - 3276 = 1500$? Yes.
Step 2: Check some number that works in $M \geq 4776$. We choose 5000.
Is $5000 - 3276 \geq 1500$?
Yes, since $1724 \geq 1500$.

In Example 2, each line of the solution includes the reason for that step.

Example 2 Solve $-1 > x - 4.2$ and graph its solutions.

Solution

$-1 > x + -4.2$	algebraic definition of subtraction
$-1 + 4.2 > x + -4.2 + 4.2$	Addition Property of Inequality
$-1 + 4.2 > x + 0$	Property of Opposites
$3.2 > x$	Additive Identity Property

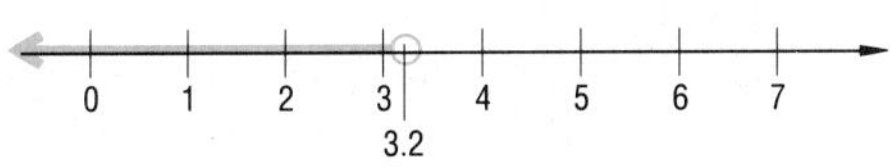

Check Step 1: Check 3.2. This should make the sides equal.
Does $-1 = 3.2 - 4.2$? Yes.
Step 2: Check a value smaller than 3.2, like 0.
Is $-1 > 0 - 4.2$?
Is $-1 > -4.2$? Yes, it checks.

To summarize: in order to solve sentences of the form

$$x - a = b \quad \text{or} \quad x - a < b,$$

rewrite as $x + -a = b$ or $x + -a < b$,
and solve as you would any addition sentences.

ADDITIONAL EXAMPLES

1. Ross went shopping and spent \$43.50. When he got home he counted his money and had \$13.23. How much did he have when he started his shopping trip?
\$56.73

2. Solve and graph $-819 \leq g - -406$.
$\mathbf{-1225 \leq g}$

3. Solve for x: $x - 12t = t$.
$\mathbf{x = 13t}$

NOTES ON QUESTIONS
Questions 3-5: By splitting these into parts **a** and **b,** we are emphasizing the rewriting step. If you use the alternate approach on page 118, part **a** is unnecessary.

Error Analysis for Question 8: Some students may erroneously solve $-6 > x - 4$ as $x > -2$. Then their graphs will be shaded on the wrong side of -2. Of course, they have switched the sides of the inequality without also reversing the sense. Stress the importance of checking. Choosing the value 4 for x will dramatically show that $x > -2$ is true but $-6 > x - 4$ is false.

Making Connections for Question 12: Students should first simplify the sentence to $1x - 3r = r$, then add $3r$ to both sides to get $1x = 4r$. To finish, they must realize that $1x = x$, a point that will be validated in Lesson 4-3 with the Multiplicative Identity Property of One.

Question 13: This shows the formula solved for p and s. You might ask students to solve for c.

Questions 14 and 15: These involve patterns. You might ask students to generalize. They could use the problem-solving strategies of *trying a simpler case* and *making a table.*

[$n - (n - 1 - (n - 2 - \ldots - 1)$*
$= \frac{n}{2}$ if n is even;
$= \frac{n+1}{2}$ if n is odd.
$1 - (2 - (3 - \ldots n)$*
$= \frac{-n}{2}$ if n is even;
$= \frac{n+1}{2}$ if n is odd.]

*We have omitted the many right-hand parentheses that should be used.

Questions

Covering the Reading

1. To solve $x - a = b$, first rewrite the sentence as $x +$ __?__ $= b$, and then solve like any addition sentence. **$-a$**

2. The range of temperatures recorded on Mercury one day was 797°F. The minimum temperature recorded that day was -23°F. Using the definition of range,
   a. write an equation to find Mercury's maximum recorded temperature that day; **See margin.**
   b. solve to find the maximum. **$M = 774°$**

In 3–5, **a.** rewrite as an addition sentence and **b.** solve.

3. $s - 1240 = 20{,}300$ **a) $s + -1240 = 20{,}300$; b) $s = 21{,}540$**

4. $5.3 = w - -4.1$ **a) $5.3 = w + 4.1$; b) $w = 1.2$**

5. $x - -60 < 140$ **a) $x + 60 < 140$; b) $x < 80$**

6. Refer to Example 1. How much would be in Mr. Archer's account if he can withdraw $4582 and still have free checking? **$6082 or more**

7. The steps in the solution of the inequality $K - 25 < 755$ are given. State the reason for each step. **See margin.**

Step 1:	$K + -25 < 755$	**a.** __?__
Step 2:	$K + -25 + 25 < 755 + 25$	**b.** __?__
Step 3:	$K + 0 < 755 + 25$	**c.** __?__
Step 4:	$K < 780$	**d.** __?__

8. Graph all solutions to $-6 > x - 4$. **See margin.**

Applying the Mathematics

9. Write, but do not solve, an inequality for the following problem: Houston Investment provides free travelers' checks to customers having at least $1000 in a savings account. Marilyn Pulowski wants to withdraw $2768.00 for a trip. How much should be in her account so that she can make the withdrawal and still qualify for free travelers' checks? **$A - 2768 \geq 1000$**

10. The range of temperatures that have been used in laboratory experiments is about $8.2 \cdot 10^6$ kelvins. The minimum recorded lab temperature is $5 \cdot 10^{-8}$ kelvins. Write a subtraction equation which you could use to solve for the maximum recorded temperature M. You do not have to solve this sentence. **$8.2 \cdot 10^6 = M - 5 \cdot 10^{-8}$**

In 11 and 12, solve for x.

11. $x - 35 \leq y$ **$x \leq y + 35$**

12. $8x - 3r - 7x = r$ **$x = 4r$**

13. The formula $p = s - c$ relates profit, selling price, and cost. Here the formula is solved for s. Give a reason for each step. **See margin.**

Step 1:	$p = s + -c$	**a.**	?
Step 2:	$p + c = (s + -c) + c$	**b.**	?
Step 3:	$p + c = s + (-c + c)$	**c.**	?
Step 4:	$p + c = s + 0$	**d.**	?
Step 5:	$p + c = s$	**e.**	?

Review

In 14–15, simplify. *(Lessons 1-4, 3-1)*

14. $5 - (4 - (3 - (2 - 1)))$ **3**

15. $1 - (2 - (3 - (4 - 5)))$ **3**

16. $m - (2m - 4m)$ **3m**

17. Subtract and check with a calculator. *(Lesson 3-1)*

$120\frac{2}{5} - 19\frac{9}{10}$ **$100\frac{1}{2}$**

In 18 and 19, solve for q and graph the solution set. Do *not* use a calculator.

18. $q + 21 \le 11$ *(Lesson 2-7)* **$q \le -10$; see margin.**

19. $3 + q - 12 > 4 - -18$ *(Lessons 2-7, 3-3)* **$q > 31$; see margin.**

20. Solve for a: $a + -2b = 10$. *(Lesson 2-6)* **$a = 2b + 10$**

21. Four instances of a pattern are given below. Describe the general pattern using one variable. *(Previous course)* **$2a + a = 3a$**

$2 \cdot 5 + 5 = 3 \cdot 5$
$2 \cdot 7 + 7 = 3 \cdot 7$
$2 \cdot 81 + 81 = 3 \cdot 81$
$2 \cdot 90 + 90 = 3 \cdot 90$

22. The Goldens celebrated their 50th (golden) wedding anniversary in year y. In what year were they married? *(Lesson 3-2)* **$y - 50$**

23. The Valases will celebrate their nth wedding anniversary in 2000. In what year were they married? *(Lesson 3-2)* **$2000 - n$**

Question 17: When entering $120\frac{2}{5}$ into the calculator, the Equal Fractions Property can be used to make the work easier. $120\frac{2}{5} = 120\frac{4}{10} = 120.4$.

ADDITIONAL ANSWERS

2a. Let M = Mercury's maximum temperature that day; then $M - (-23) = 797$

7a. Definition of subtraction

7b. Addition Property of Inequality

7c. Property of Opposites

7d. Additive Identity Property

8. $-2 > x$;

13a. Definition of subtraction

13b. Addition Property of Equality

13c. Associative Property of Addition

13d. Property of Opposites

13e. Additive Identity Property

18.

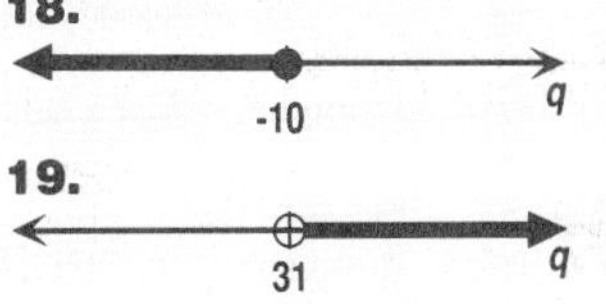

19.

NAME ______

LESSON **MASTER 3–3**
QUESTIONS ON **SPUR** OBJECTIVES

■**SKILLS** *Objective B (See pages 150–152 for objectives.)*
In 1–4, solve and check.

1. $p - 34 = -8$ **$p = 26$**; **$26 - 34 = -8$**

2. $4.5 = r - 3.8$ **$r = 8.3$**; **$4.5 = 8.3 - 3.8$**

3. $x - 11 > -5$ **$x > 6$**; **$6 - 11 = -5$, and $7 - 11 > -5$**

4. $\frac{5}{8} \ge y - \frac{3}{4}$ **$y \le \frac{11}{8}$**; **$\frac{5}{8} = \frac{11}{8} - \frac{3}{4}$, and $\frac{5}{8} > \frac{5}{4} - \frac{3}{4}$**

In 5–10, solve for x.

5. $x - a = 19$ **$x = 19 + a$**

6. $k = x - 12$ **$x = k + 12$**

7. $x - p = 3p$ **$x = 4p$**

8. $-\frac{3}{4}d = x - \frac{d}{2}$ **$x = -\frac{d}{4}$**

9. $g < x - 32$ **$x > g + 32$**

10. $x - c > b$ **$x > b + c$**

■**SKILLS** *Objective D*
In 11–14, simplify.

11. $6h + h - 4h$ **$3h$**

12. $4 + (x - 8)$ **$x - 4$**

13. $3x + 5 - 2x$ **$x + 5$**

14. $-9x - x + 10x$ **0**

■**USES** *Objective F*

15. The range of scores on an algebra test was R. The minimum score was 60. Write and solve an equation to find the maximum score h.
$h = R + 60$

16. To lose weight, Sonya had to reduce her daily caloric intake to less than 1800 calories. By eliminating desserts she removed 600 calories and is now losing weight. If her previous intake was c calories, write an inequality describing the situation.
$c - 600 < 1800$; $c < 2400$

17. Mr. Swenson has saved $1500 for a down payment on an automobile. If the automobile costs T dollars, how much will he have to borrow?
(T − 1500) dollars

 21

Making Connections for Question 24: Prior to this, students have not simplified fractions that have polynomial factors in the numerator or denominator. In this problem they need to use the cognitive skill of chunking—viewing small bits of information such as $(x + 3)$ as a single unit. Chunking is directly studied in Lesson 7-8.

Question 29b: Stress that $\frac{1}{2}x$ means "half of x."

Question 30: Students should not change the scientific notation to standard notation because a number like 235,000,000 cannot be entered directly into many calculators. Students may use scientific notation to enter the numbers, or they could use 1.27 ÷ 23.5, and then adjust the decimal point.

FOLLOW-UP

MORE PRACTICE
For more questions on SPUR Objectives, use *Lesson Master 3-3*, shown on page 121.

EXTENSION
Computer Have students use the computer program in Lesson 2-6 (page 90) to solve equations of the form $x - a = b$. They will first have to change the form to $x + -a = b$.

24. Simplify $\frac{50(x + 3)}{2(x + 3)}$ where $x \neq -3$. *(Lesson 1-8)* **25**

25. Elaine White and Cynthia Wong invested a total of $10,000 to purchase an office supplies business. Ms. White put up $5500 of the investment. What is the difference in investments between White and Wong? *(Lesson 2-6)*
$5500 − 4500 = $1000

In 26 and 27, use the number line.

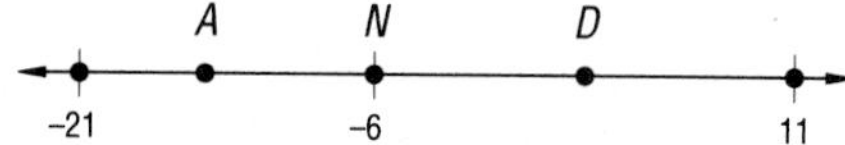

26. Find the coordinate of D if D is 9 units from N. *(Lesson 2-2)* **3**

27. Find the coordinate of A if A is 8 units from N. *(Lesson 2-2)* **-14**

28. Jan's Sports sells camping equipment and clothing. In 1985, 71% of sales were of clothing. What percent of the sales were of equipment? *(Previous course)* **29%**

29. Estimate the value of x. Do *not* use a calculator.
a. $999{,}999 - x = 800{,}000$ **200,000**
b. $\frac{1}{2}x = 4.98$ **10**
c. $x + 10^{-20} = 5$ **5**

30. The population of the United States is about $2.35 \cdot 10^8$ and the population of Los Angeles Metropolitan area is about 1.27×10^7. If a person living in the United States is selected randomly, what is the probability that the person lives in the Los Angeles area? *(Lesson 1-8)*
≈5.4%

Exploration

31. During gym class, the students formed a circle and counted off. (The first student counted "1," the second student counted "2," etc.)
a. Student number 7 was directly across the circle from student number 28. How many students are in this class? **42 students**
b. Suppose student number 7 was directly across from student number n. Then how many students are in this class? **$(n - 7) \cdot 2$ students**

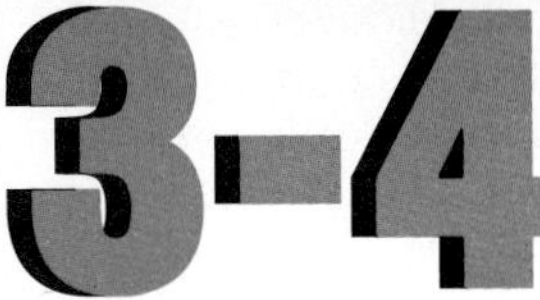

Intersection of Sets

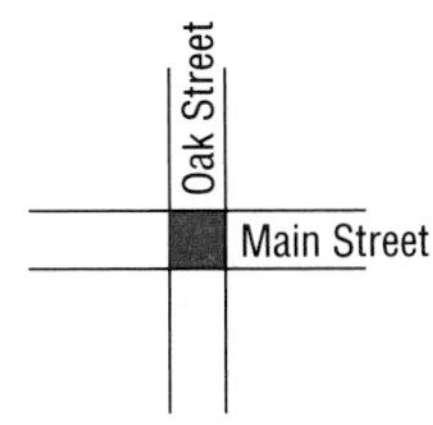

A police report of an accident stated that "the pedestrian was in the intersection of Main and Oak Streets when he was struck by the car." The intersection of the streets is colored in the map at the left. It is the area where the two streets overlap. Since the pedestrian was in the intersection, he was both in Main Street and in Oak Street.

The term intersection has a similar meaning when used with sets. The **intersection** of two sets is the set of elements in both.

Example 1 Let $A = \{1, 3, 5, 7, 9\}$ and $B = \{1, 4, 7, 10\}$. Give the intersection of A and B.

Solution The elements that are in both A and B are 1 and 7. The intersection is $\{1, 7\}$.

The symbol for intersection is $\cap$. So in Example 1,

$$A \cap B = \{1, 3, 5, 7, 9\} \cap \{1, 4, 7, 10\} = \{1, 7\}.$$

This notation lets us write the following definition.

Definition:

The intersection of sets A and B, written $A \cap B$, is the set of elements that are in both A *and* B.

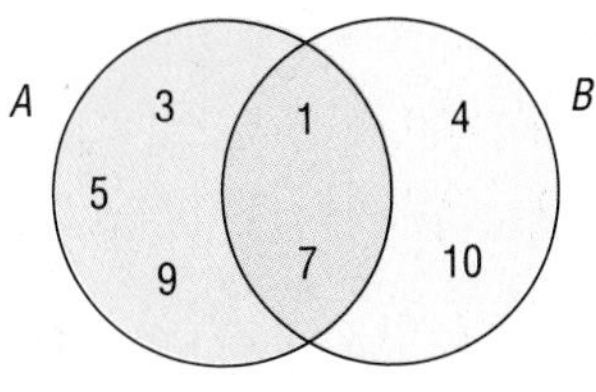

The sets A, B, and $A \cap B$ can be illustrated by the diagram at left, called a **Venn diagram.** The elements in A are in the circle labeled A. The elements in B are in the circle labeled B. The circles overlap because both contain 1 and 7. The overlap represents $A \cap B$.

If sets are infinite, the elements in their intersection cannot be all listed. But they may be described algebraically or graphed.

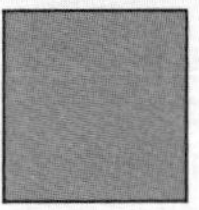

LESSON 3-4

RESOURCES
- Lesson Master 3-4
- Quiz on Lessons 3-1 Through 3-4
- Visual for Teaching Aid 16: Venn Diagrams (for use when discussing set relationships and solving problems)
- Computer Master 4

OBJECTIVES

A Find the union and intersection of sets.
H Graph solution sets to inequalities.
I Use Venn diagrams to describe union and intersection.

TEACHING NOTES

Associate for students the symbol $\cap$, the word *and*, and the term *intersection*. This may help to avoid trouble in the next lesson distinguishing $\cap$ from $\cup$.

Alternate Approach Example 2 presents the intersection of solution sets of inequalities on the number line. Although we show three number lines for the problem, you may want students to work on one line. In that case the two graphs for the given inequalities should appear alongside (one above, the other below) the number line with only the "answer" on the number line. Transparencies using different colors are especially effective for this type of problem.

Reading In **Example 3,** we have abbreviated the event description P (tossing an even number and *tossing a number* greater than two), to the shorter statement P (even number *and* greater than two). If students have difficulty with this abbreviation, you might need to restate the last paragraph of the solution.

Example 2 Kim is cooking dinner in a rush and wants to bake a casserole and muffins at the same time. The casserole recipe calls for an oven temperature from 325° to 375°, depending on how long it is cooked. The muffins can bake at any temperature from 350° to 450°.

a. Describe each of the two intervals with an inequality.

b. Describe the intersection of the two intervals (the temperature settings that are right for both the casserole and muffins) algebraically.

c. Graph the intersection.

Solution

a. Let t be an appropriate oven temperature. Then for the casserole, $325 \le t \le 375$ and for the muffins, $350 \le t \le 450$.

b. The temperature settings all right for both are from 350° to 375°, described by the interval $350 \le t \le 375$.

c. First graph the solution to each sentence separately. Be careful to line up the scales on the two number lines.

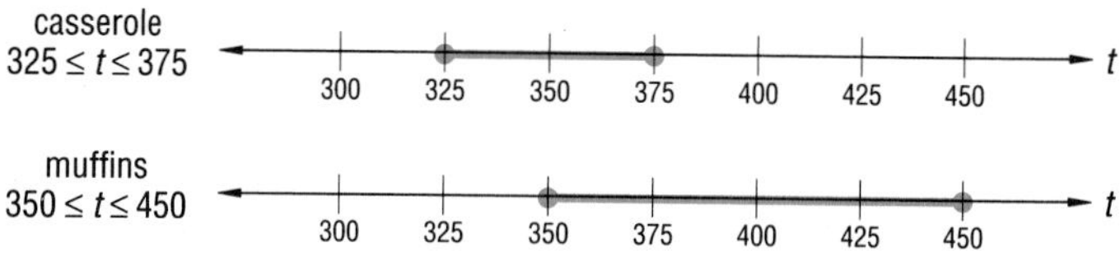

The intersection is that part of the number line where the two graphs overlap.

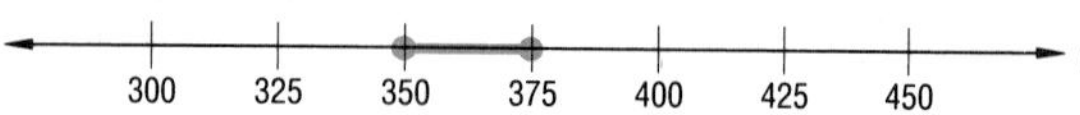

Many probability problems deal with the intersection of two events. To save space, when E is an event, we often write **P(E)** for "the probability of E."

Example 3 Consider tossing an unbiased die. What is the probability of tossing an even number greater than two?

Solution Tossing an even number greater than two is the intersection of two events:
A = tossing an even number; B = tossing a number greater than two.
First list the outcomes of each event.

A = tossing an even number = {2, 4, 6}.
B = tossing a number greater than two = {3, 4, 5, 6}.

The question asks for P (even *and* greater than two). $A \cap B = \{4, 6\}$. There are two faces of the die with a number that is both even and greater than two. Since there are six outcomes in all, the probability is $\frac{2}{6}$ or $\frac{1}{3}$. That is, $P(A \cap B) = \frac{1}{3}$.

124

Intersections arise whenever there are two or more conditions to be satisfied. When you applied the Triangle Inequality in the last chapter, you found the intersection of three conditions. Example 4 is a type of question you have seen before in Lesson 2-8, but the solution is worded in the language of the intersection of sets.

Example 4 Two sides of a triangle have lengths 30 and 40. What are the possible lengths for the third side?

30 40 x

Solution Draw a picture, calling the third length x. Using the Triangle Inequality,

$30 + 40 > x$ *and* $30 + x > 40$ *and* $40 + x > 30$.

So the intersection of the solution sets to these inequalities is desired. Solving them,

$x < 70$ *and* $x > 10$ *and* $x > -10$.

The intersection is the set of numbers between 10 and 70. That set is described as $10 < x < 70$.

Questions

Covering the Reading

1. Define: intersection of two sets. See margin.
2. If $A = \{2, 4, 6, 8, 10\}$ and $B = \{3, 6, 9, 12, 15\}$, give the intersection of A and B. $A \cap B = \{6\}$
3. Find $\{3, 6, 9, 12, 15, 18\} \cap \{2, 4, 6, 8, 10, 12\}$. $\{6, 12\}$
4. One food requires an oven temperature between 275° and 325°. A second food requires a temperature over 300°.
   a. Algebraically describe the temperatures t at which both foods can bake. $300 < t \leq 325$
   b. Graph the temperatures t at which both foods can bake. See margin.
5. Oxygen is a liquid or solid below -183 °C. Nitrogen is liquid or solid below -196 °C. A scientist needs both oxygen and nitrogen in liquid or solid form. Graph the possible temperatures for obtaining both. See margin.

In 6 and 7, imagine tossing a fair die with six possible outcomes {1, 2, 3, 4, 5, 6}.

6. Find the probability of tossing an even prime number. $\frac{1}{6}$
7. Find the probability of tossing an odd prime number. $\frac{1}{3}$

ADDITIONAL EXAMPLES

1. Let P = {cat, dog, canary, fish} and C = {car, can, cat, canary}. Give $P \cap C$.
{cat, canary}

2. In women's clothing, petite sizes are intended for those less than 5 feet 4 inches tall. To be a flight attendant for Mid-Central Airways you must be at least 58 inches and at most 74 inches tall. Graph the heights (in inches) of Mid-Central female flight attendants who might wear petite sizes and describe it with an inequality.

$58 \leq x < 64$

3. Graph the set of all real numbers n such that $n > -2$ and $n > 5$.

4. When tossing a pair of dice, what is the probability that the sum is even and less than 6? (See *Teaching Aid 5* or the picture on p. 38.)
$\frac{1}{9}$

ADDITIONAL ANSWERS

1. $A \cap B$ is the set of elements that are in both A and B.

4b.

5.

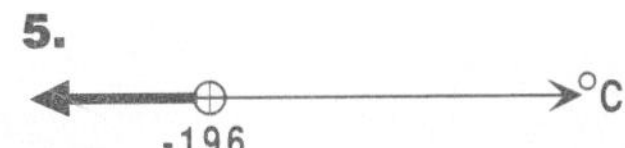

NOTES ON QUESTIONS
Question 17b: Here, parentheses are used as grouping symbols with set notation. As in numerical problems, students should simplify inside parentheses first.

Making Connections for Questions 19 and 20: These set the stage for the work in Lesson 3-6, which covers intersection used in problems involving union.

8.

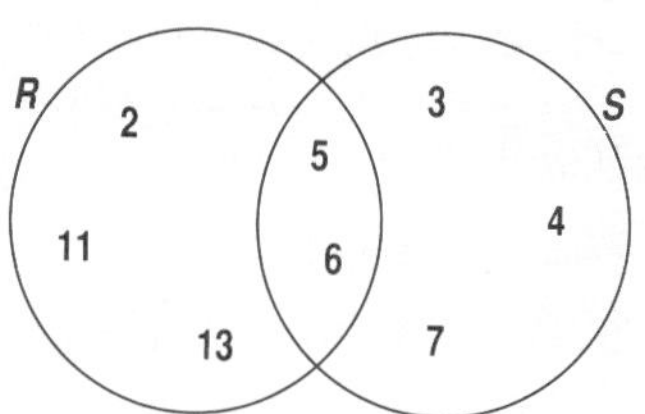

10a. $6 + L > 10$, $10 + L > 6$, $10 + 6 > L$

11a.

11b.

20a.

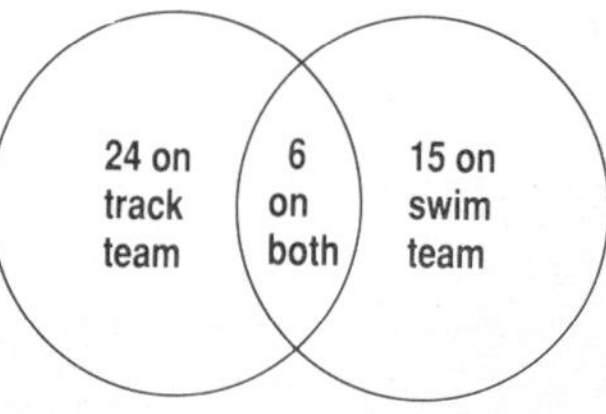

8. Draw a Venn diagram to illustrate R, S, and $R \cap S$ if $R = \{2, 5, 6, 11, 13\}$ and $S = \{3, 4, 5, 6, 7\}$. **See margin.**

9. Intersections arise whenever there are __?__ conditions to be satisfied. **two or more**

10. Two sides of a triangle have lengths 6 and 10.
 a. According to the Triangle Inequality, which three inequalities must be satisfied by the length L of the third side? **See margin.**
 b. Solve the inequalities. $L > 4$, $L > -4$, and $16 > L$
 c. Algebraically describe the possible values of L. $4 < L < 16$

11. Graph the set of all real numbers y, so that
 a. $y \geq -1$ and $y \leq 2$ **See margin.**
 b. $-1 < y < 2$ **See margin.**

Applying the Mathematics

12. Find $\{1, 3, 7, 10\} \cap \{2, 4, 8, 9\}$. { } or ϕ

In 13 and 14, suppose a letter from the alphabet is chosen at random.

13. Find P (the letter is in the word "antic" and in the word "antique").

14. Find P (the letter is a consonant and in the first half of the alphabet).
13) $\frac{4}{26}$ or $\frac{2}{13}$; **14)** $\frac{10}{26}$ or $\frac{5}{13}$

In 15 and 16, write answers as fractions. If one element x is chosen at random from $\{1, 2, 3, \ldots, 30\}$, find the probability for each of the following:

15. $x > 3$ and $x > 15$ $\frac{15}{30}$ or $\frac{1}{2}$ **16.** $x < 8$ and $x > 21$ 0

17. $A = \{1, 3, 5, 7, 9, 11\}$; $B = \{1, 4, 7, 10, 13, 16\}$; $C = \{1, 5, 10, 15, 20, 25\}$
 a. Find $A \cap B$. {1, 7} **b.** Find $(A \cap B) \cap C$. {1}

18. Remember that N(P) means "the number of elements in set P." If $P = \{20, 22, 28, 29, 35\}$ and $Q = \{25, 26, 27, 28, 29, 30\}$, find
 a. N(P) 5 **b.** N(Q) 6 **c.** N($P \cap Q$) 2

19. T girls are on the track team. S girls are on the swim team. B are on both. How many are on at least one of the teams? $T + S - B$

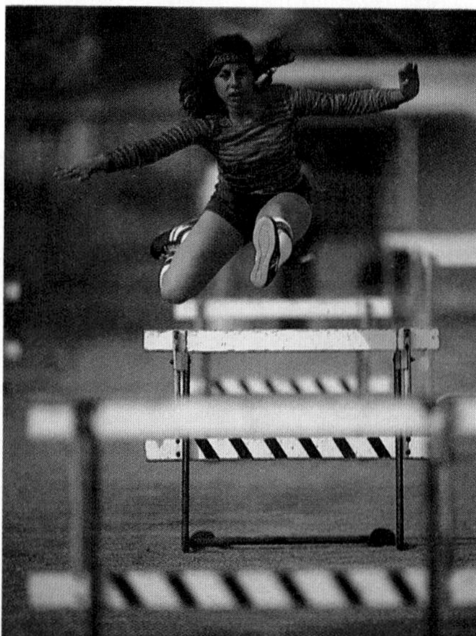

20. Thirty boys are on the school's track team. Twenty-one boys are on the swim team. Six are on both. **a) See margin.**
   a. Copy and complete the Venn diagram of this situation.
   b. How many are on at least one of the teams? **45**

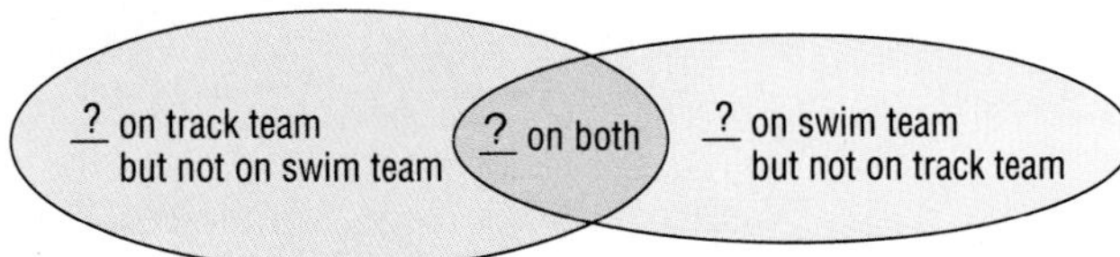

Review

In 21–23, solve. *(Lesson 3-3)*

21. $t - 153 = -12$ **$t = 141$**

22. $4.2 \geq z - 18.3 + 5$ **$17.5 \geq z$**

23. $-3b + 4b - 1 = 3$ **$b = 4$**

24. *Multiple choice* Suppose $j < n$. Then $j - n$ **(b)**
   (a) is always positive
   (b) is always negative
   (c) can be either positive or negative. *(Lesson 3-3)*

25. Simplify: $-10 - p + p - -6$. *(Lesson 3-1)* **-4**

26. You purchase P granola bars. Here are four expressions.
   i. $P + 3$ **ii.** $P - 3$
   iii. $0.5\,(P - 1)$ **iv.** $P - 1$

   Match each expression with the description of how many bars you have after
   a. you eat 3 bars, **ii**
   b. then you buy 6 more, **i**
   c. then you give 5 to your brother but take 1 back, **iv**
   d. then your dog eats half your bars. *(Lessons 2-2, 3-2)* **iii**

27. *Skill sequence* Evaluate. *(Lessons 2-3, 3-1)*
   a. $4 - 7$ **-3**
   b. $\frac{4}{5} - \frac{7}{5}$ **$\frac{-3}{5}$**
   c. $\frac{4}{x} - \frac{7}{x}$ **$\frac{-3}{x}$**

28. Evaluate in your head when $x = -3$ and $y = 4$. *(Lessons 2-2, 3-1)*
   a. $x + 2y$ **5**
   b. $x - 2y$ **-11**
   c. $2y - x$ **11**

Exploration

29. A, B, and C are sets of integers between 1 and 10. What might be the elements of these sets if $N(A) = 4$, $N(B) = 6$, and $N(A \cap B) = 3$?
   sample: $A = \{1, 2, 3, 4\}$; $B = \{2, 3, 4, 5, 6, 7\}$; $A \cap B = \{2, 3, 4\}$

Question 26: Each of the parts **a-d** assumes the previous parts have been completed.

Question 28c: This problem is not easily done by simply taking the opposite of the answer to **28b.**

FOLLOW-UP

MORE PRACTICE
For more questions on SPUR Objectives, use *Lesson Master 3-4,* shown below.

EVALUATION
A quiz covering Lessons 3-1 through 3-4 is provided in the Teacher's Resource File on page 13.

NAME ______

LESSON **MASTER 3–4**
QUESTIONS ON **SPUR** OBJECTIVES

■**SKILLS** *Objective A (See pages 150–152 for objectives.)*
In 1–6, find the intersection of the sets.

1. $A = \{4, 9, 13, 17\}$, $B = \{1, 9, 15, 17\}$ **{9, 17}**
2. $C = \{1, 3, 5\}$, $D = \{3, 5, 7, 9, 11\}$ **{3, 5}**
3. $F = \{12, 14\}$, $G = \{14, 16\}$, $H = \{14, 15\}$ **{14}**
4. $J = \{20, 30, 40\}$, $K = \{10, 20, 30, 40\}$ **{20, 30, 40}**
5. $L = \{101, 102, 103\}$, $M = \{104, 105, 106\}$ **ø**
6. $P = \emptyset$, $Q = \{2, 4, 6\}$ **ø**

■**REPRESENTATIONS** *Objective H*
In 7–11, graph the solutions. The domain is the real numbers.

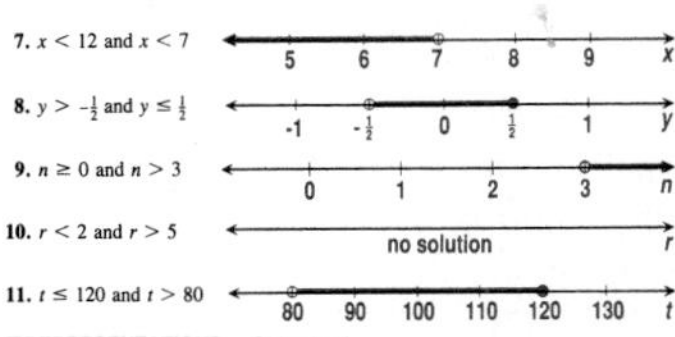

■**REPRESENTATIONS** *Objective I*
In 12 and 13, draw a Venn diagram showing the two sets.

12. $A = \{-3, -1, 0, 5\}$
    $B = \{-8, -1, 0, 7\}$

13. $C = \{1, 2, 3, 4\}$
    $D = \{0, 1, 2, 3, 4, 5\}$

14. Refer to the Venn diagram. What can you say about $X \cap Y$? **$X \cap Y = \emptyset$**

15. Shade in $Z \cap W$.

22 *Algebra* © Scott, Foresman and Company

LESSON 3-5

RESOURCES
- Lesson Master 3-5
- Visual for Teaching Aid 16: Venn Diagrams (for use when discussing set relationships and solving problems)
- Computer Master 4

OBJECTIVES

A Find the union and intersection of sets.
H Graph solution sets to inequalities.
I Use Venn diagrams to describe union and intersection.

TEACHING NOTES

Emphasize the relationship of the term *union,* the connective *or,* and the symbol ∪. Make sure students realize that *or* is used in the inclusive sense of "one *or* the other *or* both."

Error Analysis Now that both intersection and union have been introduced, students must learn not to confuse the two. You might use the analogy of the *intersection* of two streets. Points in the intersection are on one street *and* the other. Points in the *union* are on one street *or* the other. You might also use a mnemonic based on alphabetical order:

intersection ↔ **a**nd
union ↔ **o**r

Both **i** and **a** come before **u** and **o.**

The symbols are usually not confusing, since the union symbol looks like the letter *U*.

LESSON

3-5 Union of Sets

With one game to go in the season the Blues lead the Reds by one game. The Blues are playing the Purples; the Reds are playing the Greens. From the standings at the right, you can see that the Blues will win the league title if
(a) the Blues beat the Purples *or*
(b) the Greens beat the Reds.

Teams	Wins	Losses
Blues	6	1
Reds	5	2
.	.	.
.	.	.
.	.	.
Greens	2	5
Purples	2	5

The key word in this situation is "or." Unlike the intersection of events, in which two conditions must all be satisfied, here *either* condition *or both* will cause the Blues to win. This is the idea behind the **union** of two sets. The symbol for union looks like the letter U.

Definition:

The union of sets A and B, written $A \cup B$, is the set of elements in either A *or* B (or in both).

Contrast the definition of union with that of intersection. The key word for intersection is "and"; the key word for union is "or." Notice that the union of two sets is not just the result of "putting them together." Elements are not repeated if they are in both sets.

Example 1 **a.** Give the union of {1,3,5,7,9,11} and {1,4,7,10,13,16}.
b. Make a Venn diagram of the two sets and shade the union.

Solution

a. The union is the set of elements in one set or the other (or both). {1,3,5,7,9,11} ∪ {1,4,7,10,13,16} = {1,3,5,7,9,11,4,10,13,16} Notice that the elements 1 and 7 are in both sets, but they are only written once.

b.

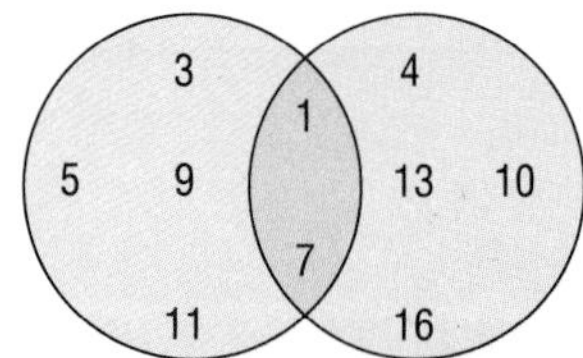

As in the case of intersections, unions can often be represented on the number line.

Example 2 Graph the set of all numbers s such that $s > -2$ or $s \leq -10$.

Solution Include all points that satisfy either or both conditions.

Example 3 George remembered that yesterday's temperature was either below 40°F or below freezing. What might have been the temperature?

Solution Let T be the temperature in °F. Either $T < 40$ or $T < 32$. Draw graphs for each inequality. (You may do this in your head.)

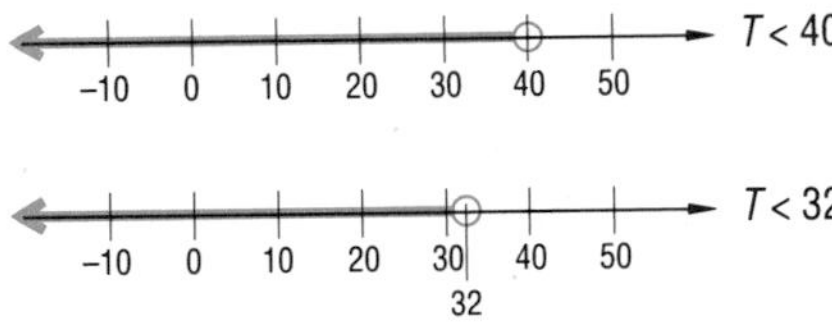

Include all points that are on either graph.

$T < 40$ or $T < 32$

−10 0 10 20 30 40 50

$T < 40$ or $T < 32$ is equivalent to $T < 40$ alone. The temperature might have had any value less than 40 °F.

Example 4 shows how the idea of union can be applied to a relative frequency problem.

Example 4 To determine how many late buses were needed, some of the students in Hillcrest High were surveyed. They were asked, "Do you sometimes stay after school for an activity or sport?" and "How do you get home—bus, car, or walk?" The data are summarized in the table at the right.

		Travel home		
		bus	car	walk
Stay after	yes	20	40	30
	no	85	65	70

a. What is the relative frequency of students walking home?
b. What is the relative frequency of students staying after?
c. What is the relative frequency of students walking home or staying after?

ADDITIONAL EXAMPLES

1. Give the union of {P, N, X, K} and {K, Q, N}.
{P, N, X, K, Q}

2. Graph all numbers y such that $y > 5$ or $y > -6$.

3. The label of a paint can says "For best results do not use if the temperature is above 90° or below 50°." Graph the temperatures in which you should not paint.

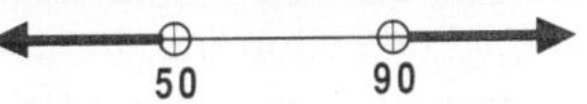

4. If a card is picked from a deck, what is the probability that it is a jack or a heart?
$\frac{4}{13}$

NOTES ON QUESTIONS
Making Connections for Question 12: This offers preparation for the next lesson. Students will have to do some figuring and drawing to think this through.

Question 13: Students should realize that this question involves three steps: solving the inequalities, graphing the inequalities, and finding the union.

Question 19: Students should use chunking, treating $\frac{7}{5}x$ as a unit and solving for it. Discuss this and point out that solving for x is not the efficient way to do this problem. This type of question encourages students to read carefully and to think about what is being asked.

ADDITIONAL ANSWERS

2. $A \cup B$ is the set of elements in either A or B (or both).

3. {2, 3, 4, 6, 8, 9, 10, 12, 15}

6.

10.

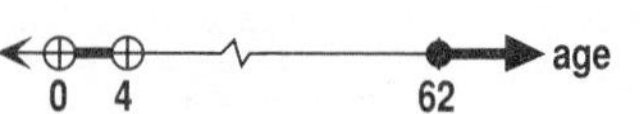

11.

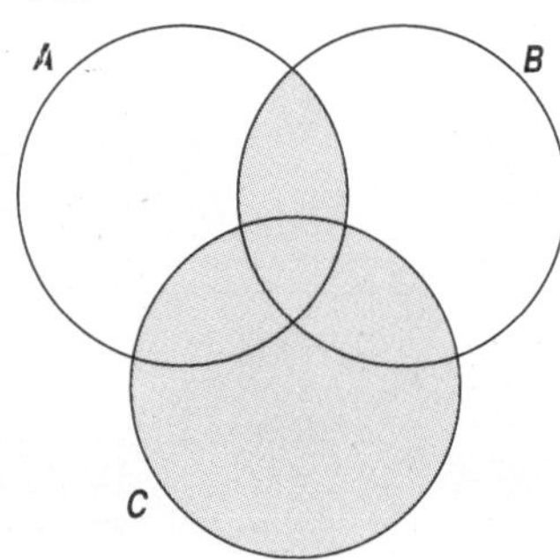

12. 21;

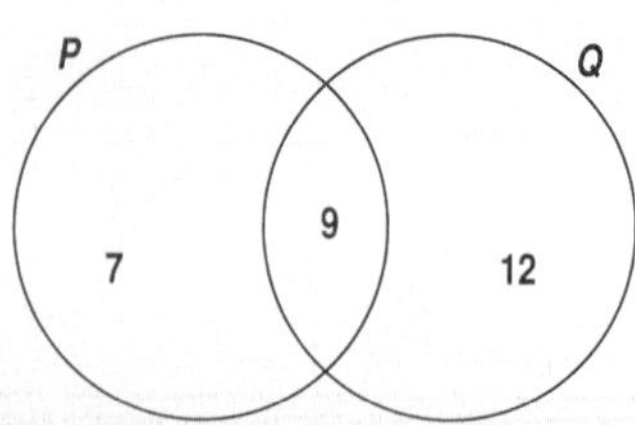

Solution There are a total of 310 students in the survey.

a. 100 walk home; relative frequency $= \frac{100}{310} \approx 32\%$

b. 90 stay after; relative frequency $= \frac{90}{310} \approx 29\%$

c. There are $20 + 40 + 30 + 70 = 160$ who walk or stay after.
Relative frequency $= \frac{160}{310} \approx 52\%$.

Notice that the answers to parts a and b do not add up to the answer in part c. Some students do both.

Questions

Covering the Reading

1. How can the Greens wind up the season ahead of the Purples? **The Greens beat the Reds and the Blues beat the Purples.**
2. Define: union of two sets. **See margin.**
3. Give the union of {2,4,6,8,10} with {3,6,9,12,15}. **See margin.**
4. Find $\{1,3,7,10\} \cup \{2,4,8,9\}$. **{1, 2, 3, 4, 7, 8, 9, 10}**
5. Match each sentence below with its graph at the left.
   a. $y < -8$ or $y > 2$ **I**
   b. $y < -8$ or $y < 2$ **III**
   c. $y > -8$ and $y < 2$ **II**

I: −8, 2, y
II: −8, 2, y
III: −8, 2, y

6. Graph the set of all numbers z such that $z < -2$ or $z \leq 4$. **See margin.**
7. Refer to Example 4.
   a. What is the relative frequency of students taking the bus and staying after? **≈ 6%**
   b. What is the relative frequency of students taking the bus or staying after? **≈ 56%**

Applying the Mathematics

In 8 and 9, let E = the odd numbers from 1 to 10. Let F = all multiples of 3 between 1 and 10.

8. Find **a.** $E \cap F$; **b.** $E \cup F$; **c.** $N(E \cup F)$. **a. {3, 9}; b. {1, 3, 5, 6, 7, 9}; c. 6**
9. Now let G = the prime numbers between 1 and 10. Find **a.** $(E \cap F) \cap G$; **b.** $(E \cup F) \cup G$. **a) {3}; b) {1, 2, 3, 5, 6, 7, 9}**
10. Graph the ages that have free admission under the following rule: You will get in free if you are younger than 4 or a senior citizen (62 or older). **See margin.**
11. Copy the Venn diagram at the left and shade in $(A \cap B) \cup C$. **See margin.**

A B C

130

12. $N(P) = 16$. $N(P \cap Q) = 9$. $N(P \cup Q) = 28$. Find $N(Q)$. (Hint: Make a Venn diagram.) **See margin.**

13. Graph the numbers that are solutions to $k + 7 > 6$ or $k + 12 > -17$. **See margin.**

14. A group of students who played baseball were asked "How do you bat—right-handed, left-handed, or both?" and "Do you belong to an organized league—yes or no?" Here are the results.

		Batter's stance		
		right	left	both
Belong to league	yes	10	2	5
	no	15	20	0

What is the relative frequency of students who
a. belong to an organized league? **≈ 33%**
b. belong to an organized league or bat left-handed? **≈ 71%**

15. Graph the union of the solution set to $-10 < y < 1$ and the solution set to $0 < y < 16$. **See margin.**

16. Members of the Jordan family have the following ages: Mr. Jordan, 44; Mrs. Jordan, 43; Michael, 20; Barbara, 16; Louis, 13. If a person from the family is selected at random, what is the probability that
a. it is a teenager or a female? $\frac{3}{5}$
b. it is a teenager and a female? $\frac{1}{5}$

Review

17. Solve in your head. *(Lessons 2-6, 3-3)*
a. $2 = x - 5.4$ **$x = 7.4$**
b. $1\frac{1}{2} + y = 4$ **$y = 2\frac{1}{2}$**
c. $z + 1.5 = 0$ **$z = -1.5$**

18. Solve for v: $a^2 + v = 10$. *(Lesson 2-7)* **$v = 10 + -(a^2)$**

19. If $\frac{7}{5}x + 3 = -2$, find $\frac{7}{5}x$. *(Lesson 2-6)* **$\frac{7}{5}x = -5$**

20. Solve for q: $-2r < q + 8r$. *(Lesson 2-7)* **$-10r < q$**

21. *Skill sequence* *(Lesson 2-3)*
a. $\frac{1}{2} - \frac{2}{3}$ **$\frac{-1}{6}$**
b. $\frac{x}{2} - \frac{2x}{3}$ **$\frac{-x}{6}$**
c. $\frac{x}{2a} + \frac{2x}{3a}$ **$\frac{7x}{6a}$**

22. Write in simplest terms: $\frac{15ab}{12bc} + \frac{3a}{4c}$. *(Lesson 2-3)* **$\frac{2a}{c}$**

23. Two sides of a triangle both have length 12. What are the possible lengths of the third side? *(Lessons 2-8, 3-3)*
$0 < s < 24$ where s is length of third side

24. A baseball player made 30 hits out of the last 100 times at bat. Estimate the probability that the player will get a hit the next time at bat. *(Lesson 1-8)* **$\frac{30}{100}$ or 30%**

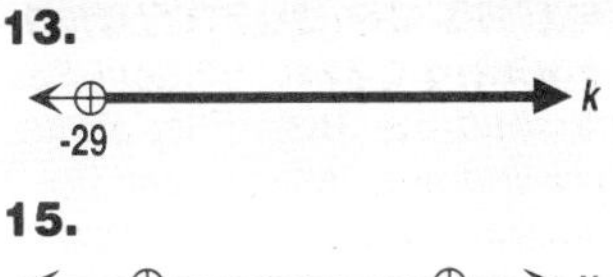

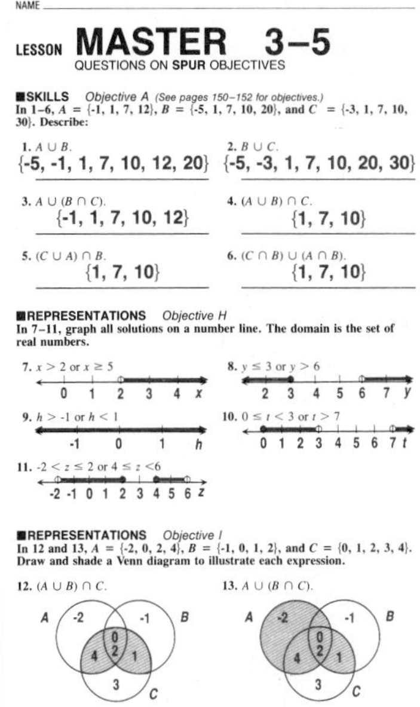

NAME ______

LESSON **MASTER 3–5**
QUESTIONS ON **SPUR** OBJECTIVES

SKILLS *Objective A (See pages 150–152 for objectives.)*
In 1–6, $A = \{-1, 1, 7, 12\}$, $B = \{-5, 1, 7, 10, 20\}$, and $C = \{-3, 1, 7, 10, 30\}$. Describe:

1. $A \cup B$. **{-5, -1, 1, 7, 10, 12, 20}**
2. $B \cup C$. **{-5, -3, 1, 7, 10, 20, 30}**
3. $A \cup (B \cap C)$. **{-1, 1, 7, 10, 12}**
4. $(A \cup B) \cap C$. **{1, 7, 10}**
5. $(C \cup A) \cap B$. **{1, 7, 10}**
6. $(C \cap B) \cup (A \cap B)$. **{1, 7, 10}**

REPRESENTATIONS *Objective H*
In 7–11, graph all solutions on a number line. The domain is the set of real numbers.

7. $x > 2$ or $x \ge 5$
8. $y \le 3$ or $y > 6$
9. $h > -1$ or $h < 1$
10. $0 \le t < 3$ or $t > 7$
11. $-2 < z \le 2$ or $4 \le z < 6$

REPRESENTATIONS *Objective I*
In 12 and 13, $A = \{-2, 0, 2, 4\}$, $B = \{-1, 0, 1, 2\}$, and $C = \{0, 1, 2, 3, 4\}$. Draw and shade a Venn diagram to illustrate each expression.

12. $(A \cup B) \cap C$.
13. $A \cup (B \cap C)$.

NOTES ON QUESTIONS
Question 27: Students can find the answer by substituting a small number (for example, 3) for y and checking which answer agrees with the value of the given expression. It is not necessary for students to use properties of exponents to answer a multiple-choice question of this type.

FOLLOW-UP

MORE PRACTICE
For more questions on SPUR Objectives, use *Lesson Master 3-5,* shown on page 131.

EXTENSION
Ask students whether $\cap$ and $\cup$ have the properties of commutativity and associativity. Students will have to formulate the properties [for $\cap$ these could be expressed $A \cap B = B \cap A$ and $A \cap (B \cap C) = (A \cap B) \cap C$] and test the patterns to see if they seem to hold. (They do.)

28a. red, narrow; red, medium; blue, narrow; blue, medium; green, narrow; green, medium; yellow, narrow; yellow, medium

29a. sample: $A = \{1, 2, 3, \ldots, 11\}$ $B = \{2, 3, 4, \ldots, 12\}$ $A \cap B = \{2, 3, 4, \ldots, 11\}$ $A \cup B = \{1, 2, 3, \ldots, 12\}$

29b. No, all elements in $A \cap B$ are also in $A \cup B$. $A \cap B$ cannot have more elements than $A \cup B$.

25. *Multiple choice* Which of the following real world situations is represented by the graph below? *(Lesson 2-4)* a

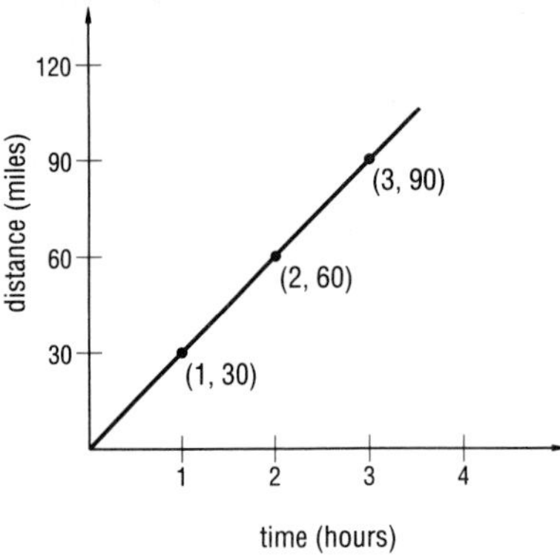

(a) The distance traveled in h hours at 30 mph
(b) The distance traveled in h hours at 50 mph
(c) The distance you are from home if you started 90 miles from home and traveled home at 30 mph

26. The volume of a cone is $V = \frac{1}{3}\pi r^2 h$ where r is the radius and h the height. Find the volume of a cone with a radius 3 cm and height 15 cm. Round your answer to the nearest cubic centimeter. *(Lesson 1-5)* ≈141 cubic centimeters

27. *Multiple choice* $2y^2 \cdot y^3 =$? *(Lesson 1-4)* (a)
(a) $2y^5$ (b) $2y^6$ (c) $(2y)^5$ (d) $4y^6$

28. Camisha is buying a spiral notebook. She has a choice of four colors (red, blue, green, orange) and 2 line widths (narrow, medium).
a. List all the possible types of notebooks. See margin.
b. If Camisha picks a type at random, what is the probability that she chooses one that is blue and has narrow lines? *(Lesson 1-7)* $\frac{1}{8}$

Exploration

29. a. Give an example of two sets A and B with $N(A \cap B) = 10$ and $N(A \cup B) = 12$. See margin.
b. Is it possible to have sets A and B with $N(A \cap B)$ larger than $N(A \cup B)$? Explain why or why not. See margin.
c. Is it possible to have $N(A \cap B) = N(A \cup B)$? Explain why or why not. Yes, if sets A and B are identical.

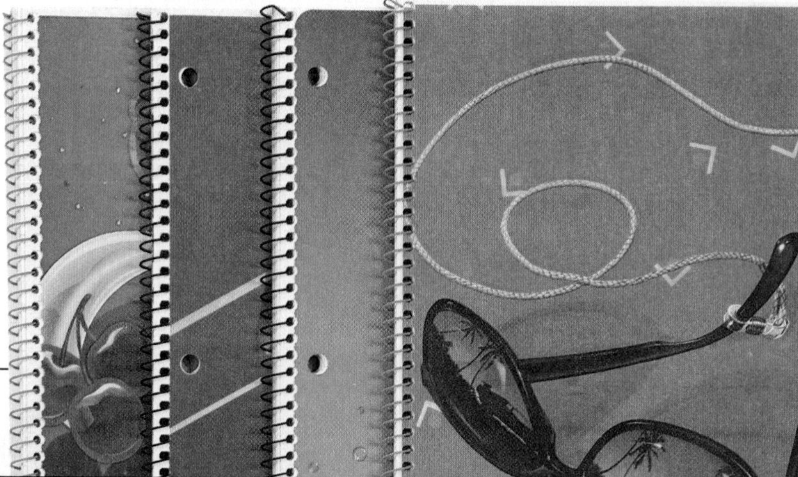

LESSON

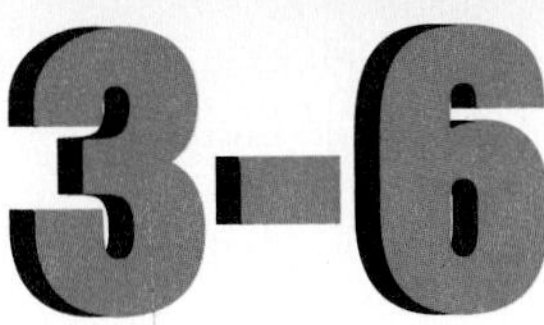

Addition, Subtraction, and Counting

Mr. Drummond's 4th period science class has 23 students. Ms. Whitefeather's 4th period math class has 25 students. If D and W are the sets of students in these classes,

$$N(D) = 23 \text{ and } N(W) = 25.$$

Because the classes meet at the same time, they have no students in common. They are called **mutually exclusive.** It is easy to calculate the number of students in one or the other of the classes.

$$\begin{aligned} N(D \cup W) &= N(D) + N(W) \\ &= 23 + 25 \\ &= 48 \end{aligned}$$

The Venn diagram for mutually exclusive sets, like D and W, is two circles that do not overlap.

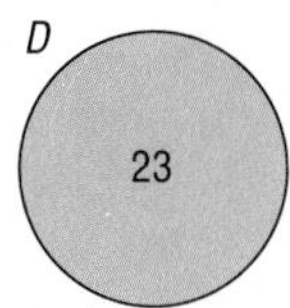

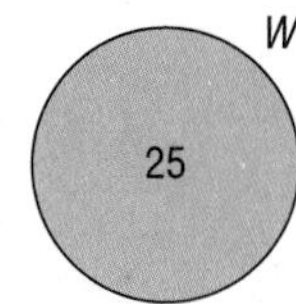

Now consider sets with overlap. Let L be the set of students in Ms. Lee's 5th period science class. Set L has 30 students, 6 of whom are in Ms. Whitefeather's class. Here is a Venn diagram for W and L.

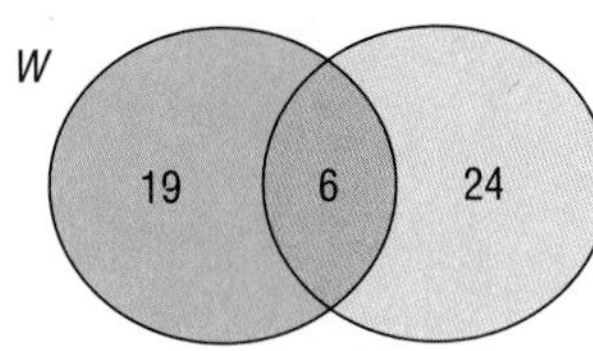

$N(W) = 25$ and $N(L) = 30$, but the total number of students either in Ms. Whitefeather's math class or in Ms. Lee's science class is not 55. If we added the numbers, we would be counting 6 students twice. The six students are in the intersection of the classes; they are the elements of $W \cap L$. The total of 49 students can be found by adding $N(W)$ and $N(L)$, then subtracting $N(W \cap L)$.

$$\begin{aligned} N(W \cup L) &= N(W) + N(L) - N(W \cap L) \\ 49 &= 25 \quad + 30 \quad - 6 \end{aligned}$$

This example illustrates the Fundamental Counting Principle.

Fundamental Counting Principle:

Let A and B be finite sets.
Then $N(A \cup B) = N(A) + N(B) - N(A \cap B)$.

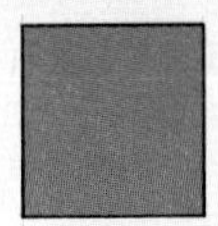

LESSON 3-6

RESOURCES

- Lesson Master 3-6
- Visual for Teaching Aid 16: Venn Diagrams (for use when discussing set relationships and solving problems)

OBJECTIVE

G Apply the formulas for $N(A \cup B)$ and $P(A \cup B)$.

TEACHING NOTES

To reinforce the example in the first paragraph of this lesson, talk about your class and other teachers' classes, choosing some groups that are mutually exclusive and some that are not.

Many of the questions in this lesson can be answered with the aid of a Venn diagram, the formula for $N(A \cup B)$, or the formula for $P(A \cup B)$. A student can become confused trying to decide which method is the correct one, not realizing that all may be correct.

In **Example 2** the number of members of each group is not known, and the formula for probability can be used. Alternatively, a Venn diagram can illustrate the overlap of probabilities.

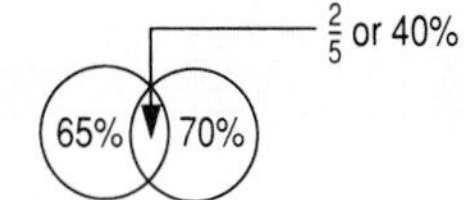

ADDITIONAL EXAMPLES

1. When tossing two dice, what is the probability that you get a 4 on the first or second die? (Explain that this can be described as rolling at least one 4.)
$\frac{11}{36}$

2. Of the 9 members of an interschool softball team, 4 are female. There are 4 teachers on the team, only one of whom is female. If a player comes up to bat, what is the probability the player is

a. female and a teacher?
$\frac{1}{9}$

b. female or a teacher?
$\frac{7}{9}$

3. In a recent year, of the total U.S. population, 8.5% lived alone, 3.3% were males living alone, and 48.1% of the population was male. What is the probability that a resident of the U.S. was a male or lived alone?
53.3%

Example 1 A clothing company makes a line of blouses and skirts to be worn as mix-and-match outfits. Of all possible outfits, the company recommends 76 of them as stylish. The orange blouse is used in 5 outfits and the blue skirt in 9 outfits. The orange blouse and blue skirt are used together in 3 outfits. How many outfits include the orange blouse or the blue skirt?

Solution Let G = the set of outfits with the orange blouse.
Let L = the set of outfits with the blue skirt.
Then N (outfits with the orange blouse or blue skirt) =

$$\begin{aligned} N(G \cup L) &= N(G) + N(L) - N(G \cap L) \\ &= 5 + 9 - 3 \\ &= 11 \end{aligned}$$

If two sets A and B are mutually exclusive, the situation is simpler. $N(A \cap B) = 0$ and there is nothing to subtract. That is why $N(D \cup W) = N(D) + N(W)$ on page 133.

The Fundamental Counting Principle leads to a property of probabilities. Here is a Venn diagram of the same three classes considered on page 133. There are 72 students in all.

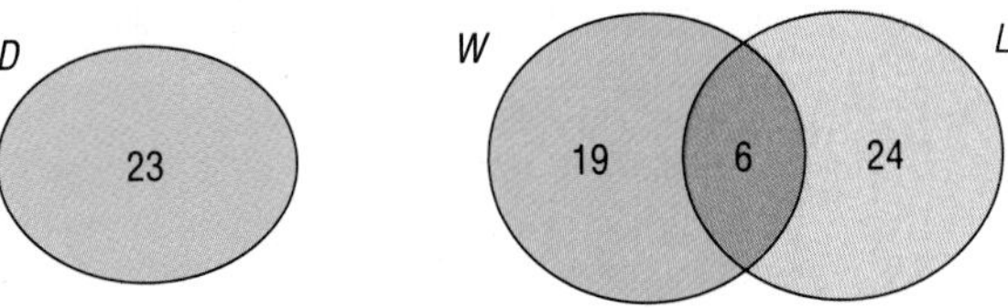

Let a student be chosen randomly from these classes. It's easy to calculate these probabilities.

P(student is in Mr. Drummond's class) $= P(D) = \frac{23}{72}$

P(student is in Ms. Whitefeather's class) $= P(W) = \frac{25}{72}$

P(student is in Ms. Lee's class) $= P(L) = \frac{30}{72}$

Probabilities of unions and intersections are also easy to find. For instance,

$$P(W \cup L) = \frac{49}{72}$$
$$P(W \cap L) = \frac{6}{72}.$$

All these probabilities are the same as the numbers in the sets divided by 72. So it is not surprising that

P(student is in W or L) = P(in W) + P(in L) − P(in both W and L).
That is, $P(W \cup L) = P(W) + P(L) - P(W \cap L)$.
To verify: $\frac{49}{72} = \frac{25}{72} + \frac{30}{72} - \frac{6}{72}$

134

The general principle is a formula for the probability of a union of events.

Probability of a Union of Events:

$$P(A \cup B) = P(A) + P(B) - P(A \cap B)$$

Written with the words "and" and "or" this formula says that

$$P(A \text{ or } B) = P(A) + P(B) - P(A \text{ and } B).$$

Example 2 At Cardioid Hospital, 65% of the patients have high blood pressure, 70% have clogged arteries, and 2 out of 5 have both conditions. If a patient has either condition, he or she has high risk of a heart attack. What is the probability that a Cardioid Hospital patient has either one of the conditions?

Solution Let H = high blood pressure. Let C = clogged arteries. We want $P(H \cup C)$. The following information is given.

$$P(H) = .65$$
$$P(C) = .70$$
$$P(H \cap C) = \tfrac{2}{5}$$

Use the Probability of a Union of Events.

$$\begin{aligned} P(H \cup C) &= P(H) + P(C) - P(H \cap C) \\ &= .65 + .70 - \tfrac{2}{5} \\ &= .65 + .70 - .40 \\ &= .95 \end{aligned}$$

As a percent, the probability is 95%.

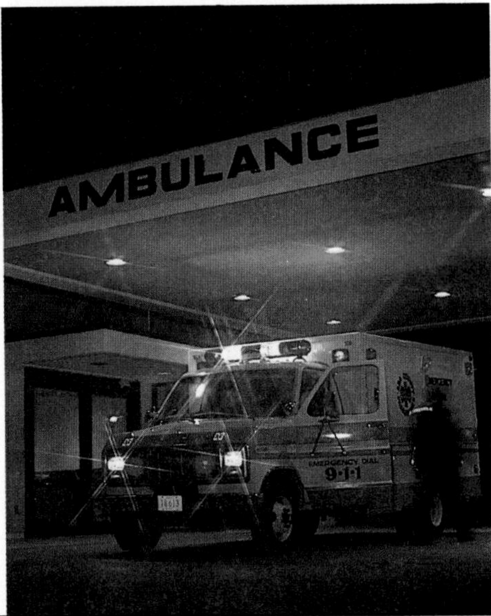

NOTES ON QUESTIONS

Question 5: For practice in solving application problems using *or* and *and*, this question is written using the words *or* and *and* instead of $\cap$ and $\cup$.

Question 10c: This can be answered by multiplying 500 students by the appropriate percent, or by multiplying the result from **Question 10b** by 5.

Questions 17b and c: Students should be encouraged to solve these problems by chunking rather than by simplifying the given equation. From part **a,** $x = 9$. Seeing the similarities between the first and second equations, you know $3 + y = 9$, so $y = 6$. Looking at the second and third equations, $z + 4 = 6$, so $z = 2$.

NOTES ON QUESTIONS

Question 18: This can be solved by simplifying first or by adding 4, 3, and then 2 to each side.

Error Analysis for Question 21: Some students may get 1.6 as the answer. These students have not followed the correct order of operations; they have calculated $3x$ first and have then squared the result. Have these students explain the difference in meaning between $3x^2$ and $(3x)^2$. Periodically, we have exercises of this type so students will be reminded of the correct order of operations.

Question 22: When reading the question, students should stop and ask themselves where the expressions $\frac{p}{3}$ and $\frac{2p}{5}$ come from.

ADDITIONAL ANSWERS

8. When $A \cap B = \varnothing$ or when A and B are mutually exclusive.

13b.

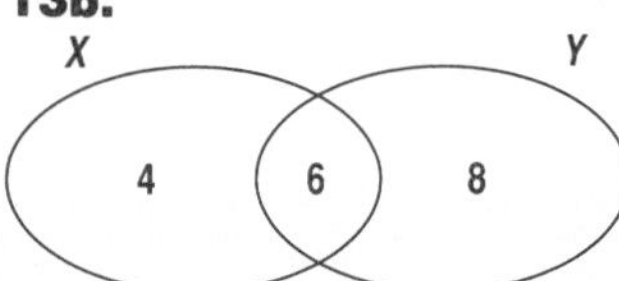

14a.

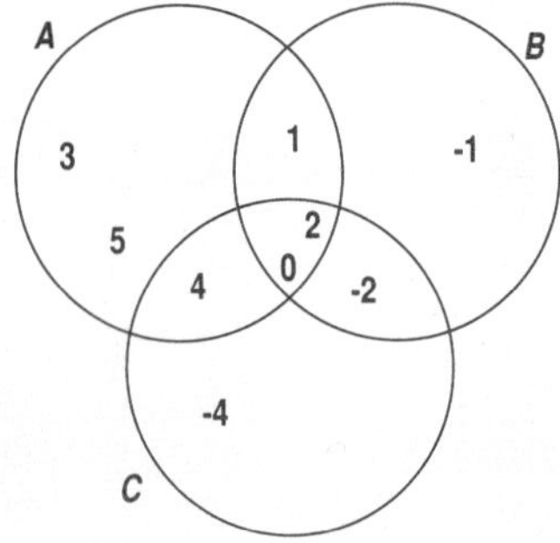

25a. sample: R(E) = .44, R(L) = .16, R(E ∪ L) = .49, R(E ∩ L) = .11

25b. Yes; R(E ∪ L) = R(E) + R(L) − R(E ∩ L)

Questions

Covering the Reading

In 1–4, refer to the science and math classes discussed in this lesson.

1. Give the numerical value.

a. $N(D)$ 23 **b.** $N(W)$ 25 **c.** $N(L)$ 30
d. $N(D \cap W)$ 0 **e.** $N(W \cap L)$ 6 **f.** $N(D \cap L)$ 0
g. $N(D \cup W)$ 48 **h.** $N(W \cup L)$ 49 **i.** $N(D \cup L)$ 53

2. Complete the formula: $N(W \cup L) = N(W) + N(L) -$ _?_. $N(W \cap L)$

3. Let a student be randomly selected from these classes. Calculate:

a. $P(W)$ $\frac{25}{72}$ **b.** $P(L)$ $\frac{30}{72}$ or $\frac{5}{12}$ **c.** $P(W \cup L)$ $\frac{49}{72}$

4. Complete the formula: $P(W \cup L) = P(W) + P(L) -$ _?_. $P(W \cap L)$

5. Find N(*A* or *B*) if N(*A* and *B*) = 6, N(*A*) = 20 and N(*B*) = 11. 25

6. Refer to Example 1. A fuchsia blouse is used in 2 outfits. No outfits use both a fuchsia and an orange blouse.

a. How many outfits include an orange or a fuchsia blouse? 7 outfits

b. What is the probability of choosing at random an outfit including an orange or a fuchsia blouse? $\frac{7}{76}$

7. When are sets mutually exclusive? when they have no overlap

8. When is $P(A \cup B) = P(A) + P(B)$? See margin.

9. Refer to Example 2. At Cardioid Hospital, if $P(H) = .59$, $P(C) = .62$, and $P(H \cap C) = .34$, what is $P(H \cup C)$? .87

Applying the Mathematics

10. At Central High School, 15% of the students received an A in English, 20% received an A in Math, and 6% received an A in both subjects.

a. Find the percent of students who got an A in English or an A in Math. 29%

b. Find N(A in English or A in Math) if there are 100 students at Central. 29

c. Find N(A in English or A in Math) if there are 500 students at Central. 145

11. If $N(A \cup B) = 30$, $N(A) = 24$ and $N(B) = 12$, calculate $N(A \cap B)$. 6

12. A class has s students. On a test 10 students received A's and 4 students received B's. A student is selected at random. What is the probability the student got an A or a B? $\frac{14}{s}$

13. $N(X) = 10$; $N(Y) = 14$; $N(X \cup Y) = 18$

a. Find $N(X \cap Y)$. 6

b. Copy the diagram and fill in the correct numbers in each region. See margin.

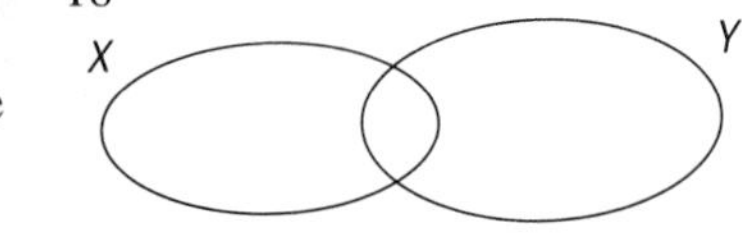

14. If $A = \{0, 1, 2, 3, 4, 5\}$, $B = \{-2, -1, 0, 1, 2\}$, and $C = \{-4, -2, 0, 2, 4\}$

a. draw a Venn diagram showing A, B, and C; See margin.

b. find $N(A \cup B \cup C)$. 9

15. $P(A) = \frac{1}{2}$, $P(B) = \frac{1}{3}$, and $P(A \cap B) = \frac{1}{4}$. Find $P(A \cup B)$. $\frac{7}{12}$

16. A company produces 41 different frozen dinners. 14 dinners have beef, 21 have chicken, 5 have broccoli, and 3 have both beef and broccoli. If a dinner is picked at random, what is the probability that
a. it has beef or broccoli? $\frac{16}{41}$
b. it has beef or chicken? (No dinner has both.) $\frac{35}{41}$

Review

17. *Skill sequence* Solve. *(Lesson 2-6)*
a. $-2 + x = 7$ **x = 9** **b.** $-2 + (3 + y) = 7$ **y = 6**
c. $-2 + (3 + (z + 4)) = 7$ **z = 2**

18. Solve $((m - 2) - 3) - 4 = -5$. *(Lesson 3-3)* **m = 4**

19. If you celebrated your 12th birthday in year y:
a. In what year were you born? **y − 12**
b. In what year will you celebrate your 50th birthday? *(Lesson 3-2)* **y + 38**

20. Alicia is d years older than her brother Jim. **a.** Five years from now, how many years older than Jim will she be? **b.** Write an equation relating their ages A and J. *(Lesson 3-2)* **a) d years; b) A = J + d**

21. Evaluate $\frac{3x^2}{2y}$ when $x = 1.1$ and $y = 3.4$. Round to nearest tenth. *(Lesson 1-4)* **≈.5**

22. You eat a third of a pizza. A friend eats a fifth of a pizza twice the size. Let p stand for the size of the smaller pizza. Simplify $\frac{p}{3} - \frac{2p}{5}$ to determine who has eaten more pizza, and by how much. *(Lesson 3-1)* $-\frac{p}{15}$ **your friend**

23. Christopher played golf on several different courses last summer. A positive result means above par, a negative result means below par. If his results were 5, -3, 8, -4, -2, 0, -1, -2, 3, find his average compared to par. *(Lesson 1-2)* $\frac{4}{9}$; **slightly above par**

24. Match each % with its equivalent fraction. *(Previous course)*

a. 60%	i	**i.**	$\frac{3}{5}$
b. 62.5%	iii	**ii.**	$\frac{2}{3}$
c. $66.\overline{6}$%	ii	**iii.**	$\frac{5}{8}$

Exploration

25. Do relative frequencies follow formulas like those for counting and probability in this lesson? Try this experiment. Toss two dice 50 times. Let E = tossing an even number. Let L = tossing a number larger than 9. Let $R(X)$ be the relative frequency of an event X.
a. Find $R(E)$, $R(L)$, $R(E \cup L)$, and $R(E \cap L)$. **See margin.**
b. Do these numbers add to or subtract from each other in some way? If so, how? If not, are they close? **See margin.**

26. Find out how many sides a die would have if it were in the shape of **a.** a tetrahedron; **b.** an icosahedron. **a) 4 sides; b) 20 sides**

Question 26: Ask if any students have unusual dice like those mentioned here. Encourage them to bring such dice to class. (These kinds of dice can be bought from various educational supply houses and are sold in some specialty card and game shops.)

FOLLOW-UP

MORE PRACTICE
For more questions on SPUR Objectives, use *Lesson Master 3-6,* shown below.

EVALUATION
Alternative Assessment
Have **small groups** of students formulate their own problems for situations that involve overlap. Then have them pose their problems for the class and explain how the Fundamental Principle of Counting can be used to solve the problems.

NAME ____________

LESSON **MASTER 3–6**
QUESTIONS ON **SPUR** OBJECTIVES

■USES *Objective G (See pages 150–152 for objectives.)*
In 1 and 2, find N(A ∪ B) if A and B are mutually exclusive.

1. $N(A) = 4$, $N(B) = 9$ **13**
2. $N(A) = 72$, $N(B) = 36$ **108**

In 3 and 4, find N(A ∪ B).

3. $N(A) = 32$, $N(B) = 24$, $N(A \cap B) = 8$ **48**
4. $N(A) = 153$, $N(B) = 147$, $N(A \cap B) = 94$ **206**

5. On the Sluggers baseball squad, a total of 8 players can play infield (includes pitchers and catchers), 7 can play outfield and 3 can play either infield or outfield. How many players are on the squad? **12 players**

6. There are 28 students in the Drama Club and 32 students in the Chorus. If there are 50 students altogether, how many are in both? **10 students**

7. In a poll of fast food preferences, 100 liked hamburgers, 75 liked pizza, 50 like chicken, 10 liked hamburgers and pizza only, 10 liked hamburgers and chicken only, 5 liked pizza and chicken only, and 10 liked all three. How many people were polled? Draw a Venn diagram to illustrate the situation. **180 people**

C H P 25 10 70 10 5 10 50

In 8 and 9, find P(A ∪ B).

8. $P(A) = \frac{1}{2}$, $P(B) = \frac{1}{3}$, $P(A \cap B) = 0$ $\frac{5}{6}$
9. $9(A) = \frac{1}{4}$, $P(B) = \frac{4}{9}$, $P(A \cap B) = \frac{5}{36}$ $\frac{5}{9}$

10. What is the probability of rolling either an even number or a prime number with a single die? $\frac{5}{6}$

11. In a group of 100 car owners, 47 change their own oil, 61 wash their own car, and 38 do both. If someone were chosen at random from this group, what is the probability they either change their oil or wash their own car? $\frac{7}{10}$

LESSON 3-7

RESOURCES
- Lesson Master 3-7
- Visual for Teaching Aid 17: Diagram and Hints for **Question 28**
- Visual for Teaching Aid 7: Coordinate Grid
- Computer Master 5

OBJECTIVE

J Graph sets of ordered pairs (x, y) where $x + y = k$ or $x - y = k$, where k is a real number.

TEACHING NOTES

Emphasize that each point on a graph satisfies the equation that is being graphed. For each graph, pick a few points and substitute the coordinates in the equation to reinforce this idea.

In the chart at the beginning of the lesson, students may expect there to be twelve, not thirteen, ordered pairs. They may need to reflect on why there are 13 integer values from 0 through 12.

In **Example 1,** be sure students realize that they can choose any number as a value of x.

Reading The paragraph following **Example 1** discusses the equation $y - x = -2$. Ask your students if, when they read the lesson, they stopped and figured out from where this equation came. Also, in this paragraph the word *constant* is used. Discuss what a constant is, as opposed to a variable. (A constant is a value that does not change in the course of a problem.)

LESSON

3-7

Addition, Subtraction, and Graphing

Suppose Tim wants to buy a dozen muffins. He likes raisin muffins and bran muffins. The ways he can purchase a dozen muffins of the two kinds can be expressed as thirteen ordered pairs, listed in the table at the left.

R Raisin	B Bran	(R, B) Ordered Pairs
0	12	(0, 12)
1	11	(1, 11)
2	10	(2, 10)
3	9	(3, 9)
.	.	.
.	.	.
.	.	.
10	2	(10, 2)
11	1	(11, 1)
12	0	(12, 0)

Using variables makes the pattern easier to write. If Tim buys R raisin muffins and B bran muffins, then Tim's choices can be represented by ordered pairs (R, B) where $R + B = 12$. We could solve for B and write $B = 12 - R$.

Here is a graph of Tim's possible choices for a dozen muffins.

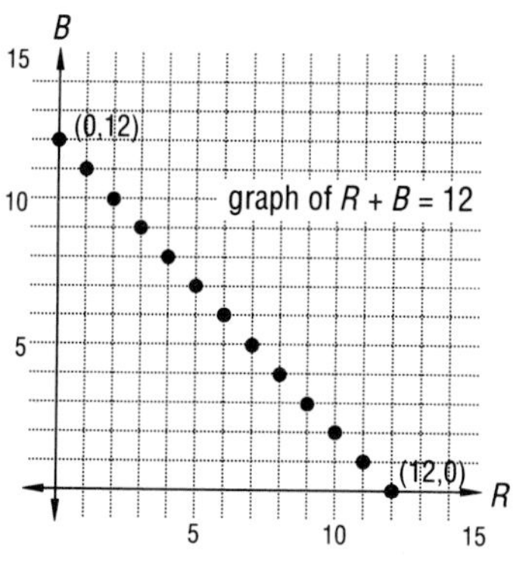

The points are all on the same line. There are 13 points on the graph because there are 13 combinations of muffins Tim can buy. He cannot have a fraction of a muffin and he certainly can't have a negative number of muffins. This graph is discrete and the set of points is finite.

However, suppose you wanted to graph *all the pairs* of numbers whose sum is 12. You would have pairs with negative numbers and fractions, like (15, -3) and (4.5, 7.5). In fact, there are an infinite number of pairs whose sum is 12. But they all still lie in a straight line when they are graphed. This graph is continuous and is the entire line. Its algebraic representation is $x + y = 12$, where x and y can be any real numbers.

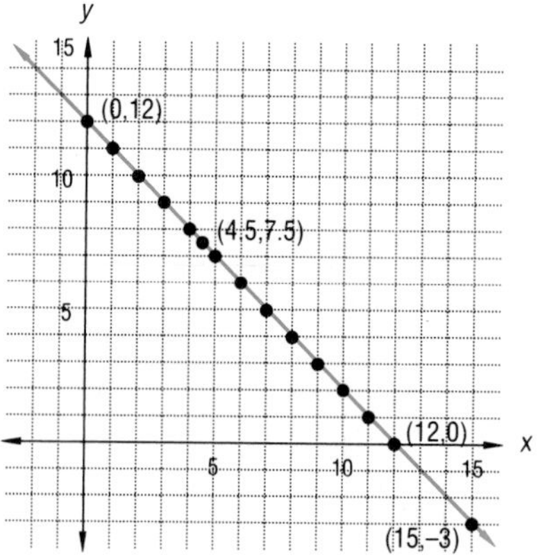

The graph of any constant sum situation will look much like this one.

138

To graph all pairs of numbers that satisfy a condition, first make a chart showing some sample pairs. Then plot the points on a graph. If the graph is continuous, draw a line through the points.

Example 1 Make a graph of all ordered pairs of real numbers (x, y) for which $y = x - 2$.

x	y	(x, y)
-3	-5	(-3, -5)
-2	-4	(-2, -4)
-1	-3	(-1, -3)
0	-2	(0, -2)
1	-1	(1, -1)
2	0	(2, 0)
3	1	(3, 1)

Solution Choose some numbers for x, say the integers from -3 to 3. For each value of x, find the corresponding value of y and fill in the chart.

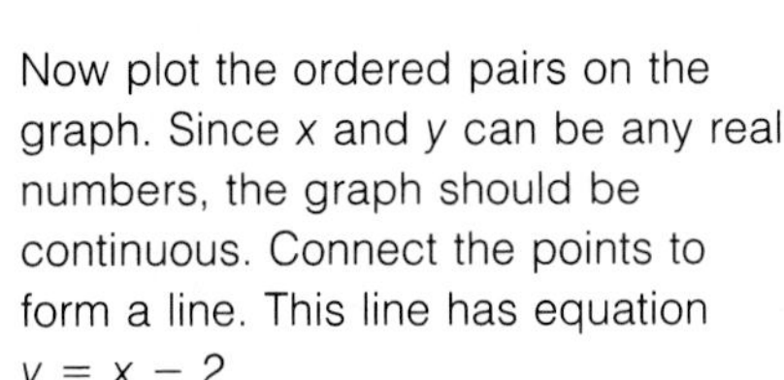

Now plot the ordered pairs on the graph. Since x and y can be any real numbers, the graph should be continuous. Connect the points to form a line. This line has equation $y = x - 2$.

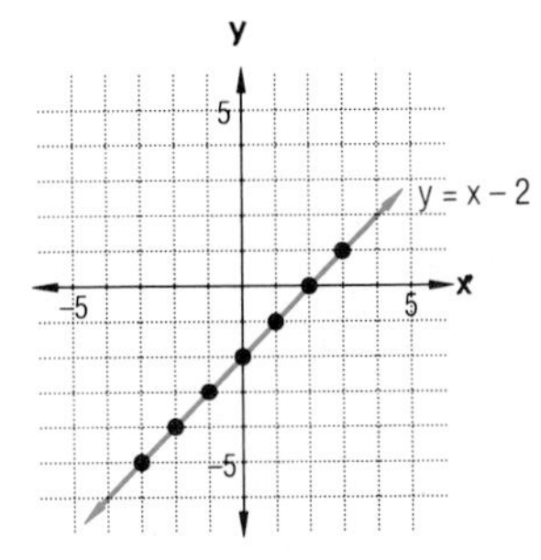

Notice that in Example 1, $y - x = -2$. So the difference of y and x is constant. The graph of any constant difference situation is a line.

Questions

Covering the Reading

In 1–3, consider the muffin example in this lesson.

1. If Tim buys 10 raisin muffins, how many bran muffins did he buy? 2

2. The table of values in the muffin problem is missing some ordered pairs. Copy and complete.
a. (_?_, 4) 8 **b.** (6, _?_) 6

3. When a graph is made of all pairs of real numbers whose sum is 12, a _?_ is formed. line

See margin.

4. a. Extend the chart from Example 1 by copying the chart at the right and filling in the empty columns.
b. Are these points on the line in Example 1? Yes

x	y	(x, y)
4		
5		
6		

ADDITIONAL EXAMPLES

1. Carlos is 7 years older than his sister Alice. Neither one is yet old enough to drive.

a. Assuming the minimum driving age is 16, make a table of values for (C, A).

C	7	8	9	10	11	12	13	14	15
A	0	1	2	3	4	5	6	7	8

b. Graph.

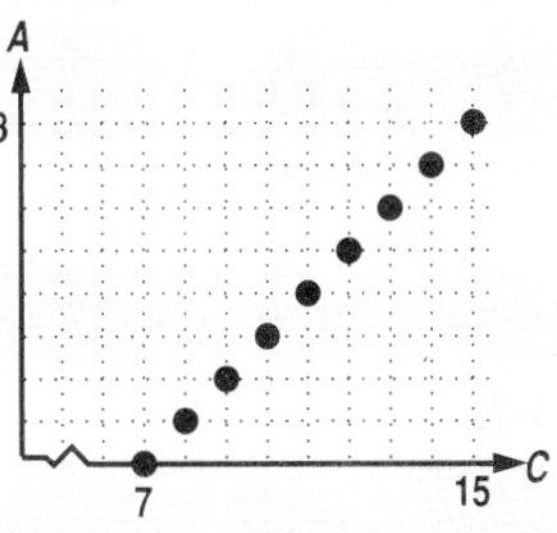

(Note: The age of 0 indicates Alice is less than 1 year old.)

2a. Make a table of ordered pairs for which $x - y = -1$.

b. Graph all ordered pairs satisfying $x - y = -1$.

a. sample

x	y
5	6
2	3
0	1

b.

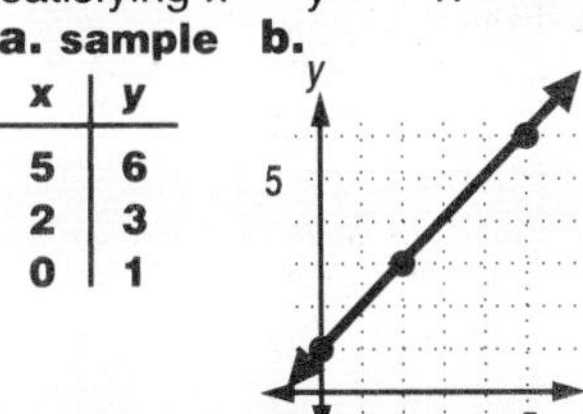

NOTES ON QUESTIONS
Making Connections for Questions 6 and 7b: These are intended to start forming some ideas that will be used in Chapter 11 with systems of equations. Note that in **7b** there are many ordered pairs that satisfy either condition taken alone, but only one ordered pair that satisfies both. Mention the connection with intersections of sets.

ADDITIONAL ANSWERS

4a.

x	y	x, y
4	2	(4, 2)
5	3	(5, 3)
6	4	(6, 4)

NOTES ON QUESTIONS
Question 16: Discuss two ways to answer this question, one using the formula and the other using a Venn diagram.

Making Connections for Question 17: The next lesson has a similar problem, so be sure that students understand each step in this one.

Question 28: *Teaching Aid 17* provides some guidelines for answering this question.

5a.

x	y	x, y
1	6	(1, 6)
2	7	(2, 7)
3	8	(3, 8)
4	9	(4, 9)
5	10	(5, 10)
6	11	(6, 11)

5b.

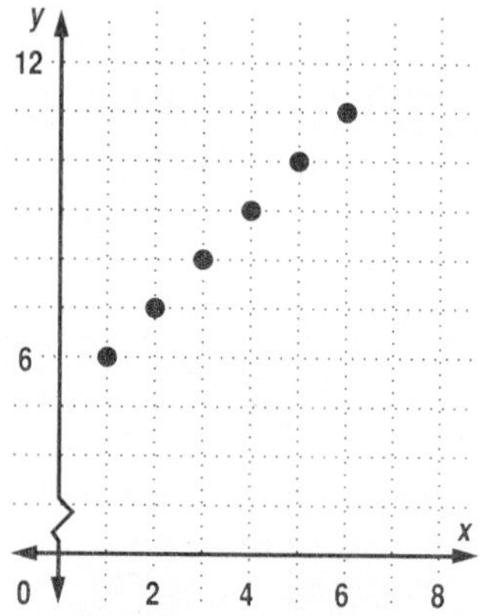

8a.

x	y	x, y
-2	2	(-2, 2)
-1	1	(-1, 1)
0	0	(0, 0)
1	-1	(1, -1)
2	-2	(2, -2)

8b.

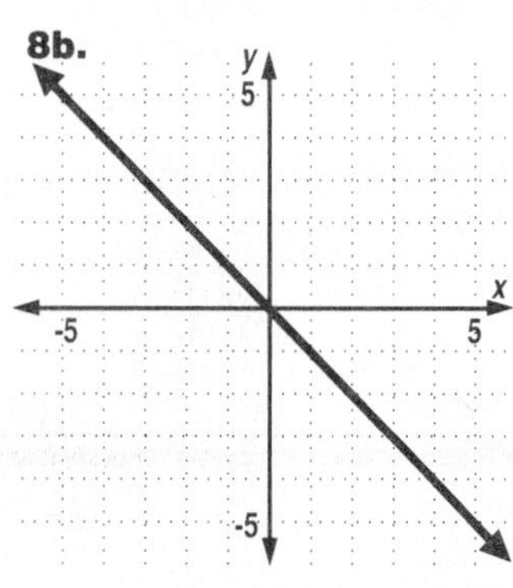

5. Xandra and Yvonne each have earned medals in track and field events. Yvonne has 5 more medals than Xandra.
   a. Copy and fill in the chart to show some possible numbers of medals for the girls. **See margin.**
   b. Graph the ordered pairs from the chart. **See margin.**

x Xandra	y Yvonne	(x, y) Ordered Pairs
1	6	
2		
3		(3, 8)
4		
5	10	
6		

Applying the Mathematics

6. In the muffin example, suppose Tim has twice as many bran muffins as raisin muffins. How many bran muffins does he have? **8**

(1, 7), (2, 6), (3, 5), (4, 4), (5, 3), (6, 2), (7, 1)

7. Sally and Alvin each have tropical fish. Together they have eight fish.
   a. Find all possible number pairs of Sal's fish and Al's fish.
   b. If Sal has two more fish than Al, how many fish does Al have? **3**

8. a. Copy and fill in the chart at the right to show ordered pairs where the y-coordinate is the opposite of the x-coordinate. **See margin.**
   b. On a coordinate plane, graph all ordered pairs of real numbers for which $y = -x$. **See margin.**

x	y	(x, y)
-2	2	(-2, 2)
-1		
0		
1		
2		

In 9 and 10, make a list of the four ordered pairs graphed. Then choose the equation that describes the points. **See margin.**

9.

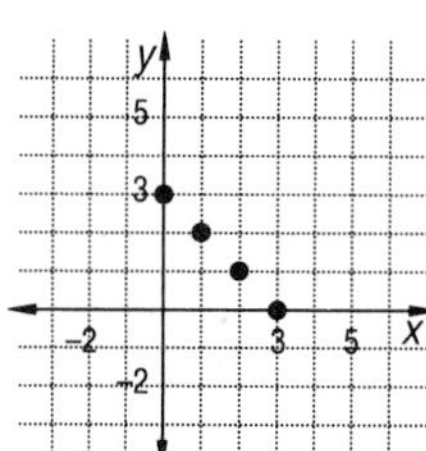

a. $y = 3x$
b. $y = x + 3$
c. $y = 3 - x$

10.

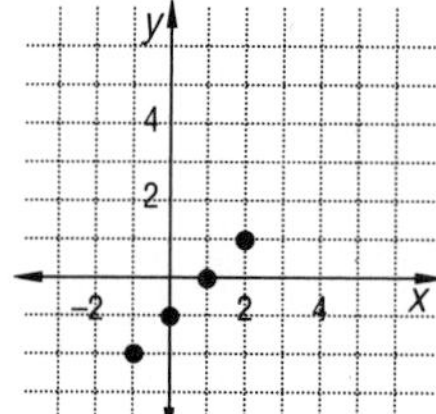

a. $y = 1x$
b. $y = x + 1$
c. $y = x - 1$

11. Write an equation that describes the points in Question 5. **$y = x + 5$**

12. Calvin is giving away 10 records to Jorge and Maria.
   a. Make a chart showing the possible ways to divide the records.
   b. Graph the possibilities with the number of Jorge's records on the horizontal axis and the number of Maria's records on the vertical axis. **See margin.**
   c. *True or false* This graph is a line. **False**

Review

13. Solve $10.4 = y - 12.2$. *(Lesson 3-3)* **22.6**

14. Solve $x - k = 50$ for x. *(Lesson 3-3)* **$x = 50 + k$**

15. Last weekend, 2250 students went to the football game Friday night. On Saturday night, 276 attended the dance. If 200 students were at both events, find N(attended game or attended dance). *(Lesson 3-6)* **2326**

16. If $N(A) = 15$, $N(A \cap B) = 7$ and $N(A \cup B) = 20$, find $N(B)$. *(Lesson 3-6)* **12**

17. In the fall election, 80% of the students voted for Millie for president, 60% voted for Moe for vice-president, and 45% voted for both.

a. What percent voted for Millie or Moe? **95%**

b. If 453 students voted, how many voted for Millie or Moe? *(Lesson 3-6)* **430**

18. Copy the diagram at the left for each question.

a. Shade $A \cup B$. **See margin.**

b. Shade $(A \cup B) \cap C$. **See margin.**

c. Shade $A \cap B \cap C$. *(Lessons 3-4, 3-5)* **See margin.**

19. A = {instruments in a symphony orchestra} and B = {instruments in a marching band}. Name an instrument in A but not in $A \cap B$. *(Lesson 3-4)* **sample: violin, piano, kettle drum**

20. The 1984 population of Illinois was about $1.14 \cdot 10^7$. The population of Chicago was about $7.10 \cdot 10^6$. A person living in Illinois is randomly selected. Approximate the probability that he or she lives in Chicago. *(Lesson 1-7)* **≈.62 or 62%**

21. *Multiple choice* The measure of this angle is closest to **(a)**

(a) 45° (b) 90°

(c) 135° (c) 180° *(Previous course)*

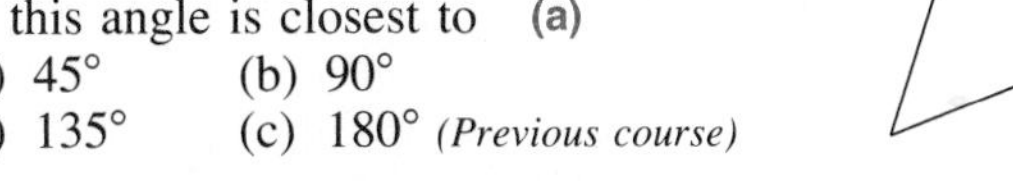

22. At 3:00, what is the measure of the angle between the hands of a clock? *(Previous course)* **90°**

23. A factory packs 5-pound packages of mixed peanuts and cashews. If c pounds of cashews are in a package, the price p of the package is found by the formula

$$p = 2.39c + 1.69(5 - c)$$

If a package contains 1.5 pounds of cashews, find its price. *(Lesson 1-5)* **$9.50**

24. Graph: **a.** $y \le 11$; **b.** $y \le 11$ or $y \ge 15$; **c.** $y \le 11$ and $y \le 7$. *(Lessons 3-4, 3-5)* **See margin.**

9. (0, 3), (1, 2), (2, 1), (3, 0); c

10. (-1, -2), (0, -1), (1, 0), (2, 1); c

12a.

Jorge	Maria
1	9
2	8
3	7
4	6
5	5
6	4
7	3
8	2
9	1

12b.

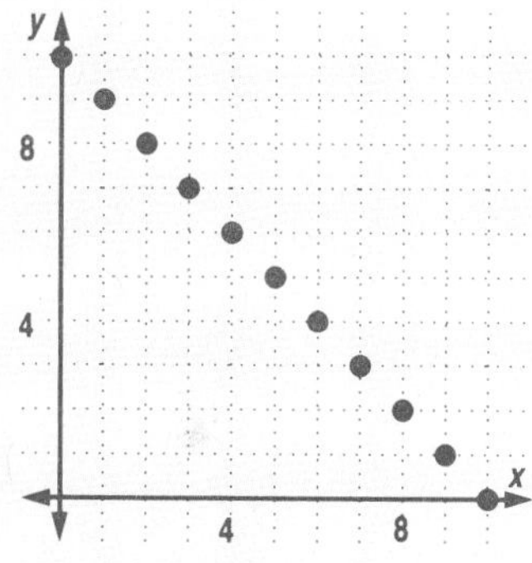

18., 24. See margin, page 142.

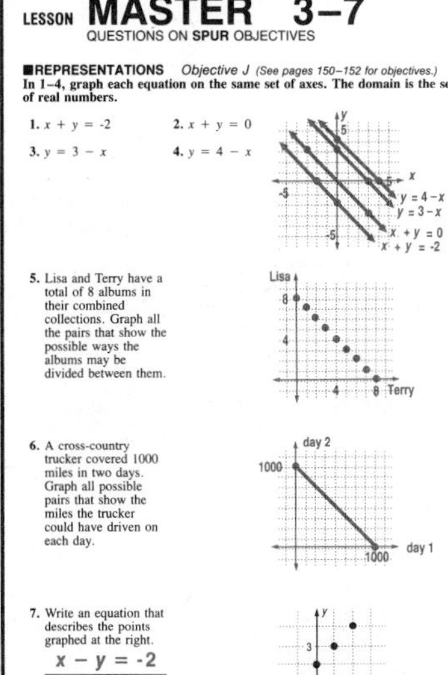

NAME ______

LESSON **MASTER 3–7**
QUESTIONS ON **SPUR** OBJECTIVES

■**REPRESENTATIONS** *Objective J* *(See pages 150–152 for objectives.)*
In 1–4, graph each equation on the same set of axes. The domain is the set of real numbers.

1. $x + y = -2$ **2.** $x + y = 0$

3. $y = 3 - x$ **4.** $y = 4 - x$

5. Lisa and Terry have a total of 8 albums in their combined collections. Graph all the pairs that show the possible ways the albums may be divided between them.

6. A cross-country trucker covered 1000 miles in two days. Graph all possible pairs that show the miles the trucker could have driven on each day.

7. Write an equation that describes the points graphed at the right. **x − y = -2**

 25

FOLLOW-UP

MORE PRACTICE
For more questions on SPUR Objectives, use *Lesson Master 3-7*, shown on page 141.

18a.

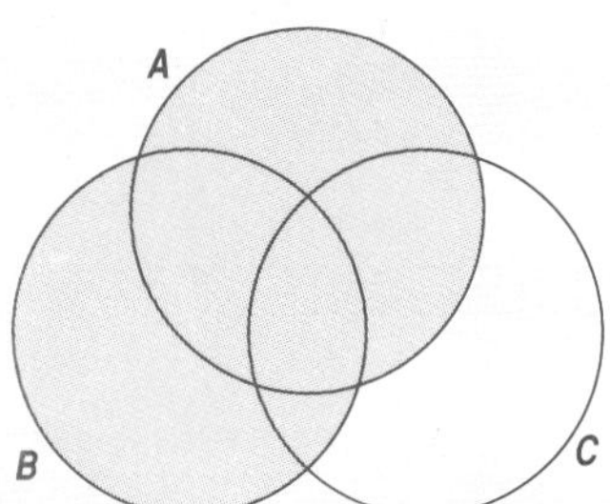

18b.

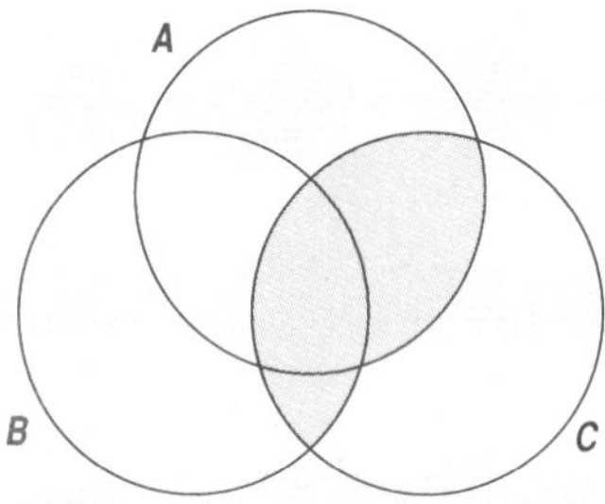

18c.

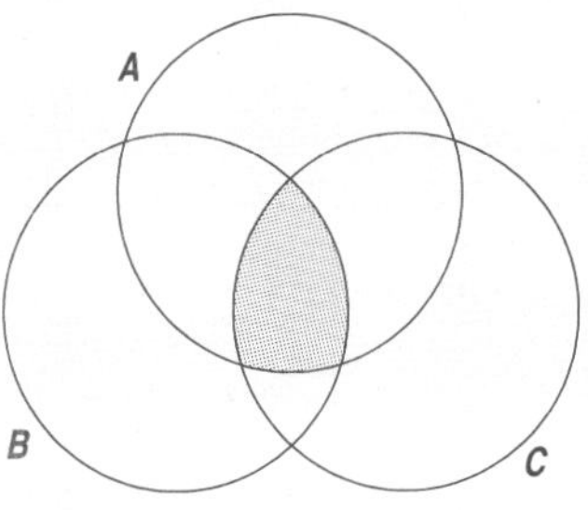

24a.

24b.
24c.

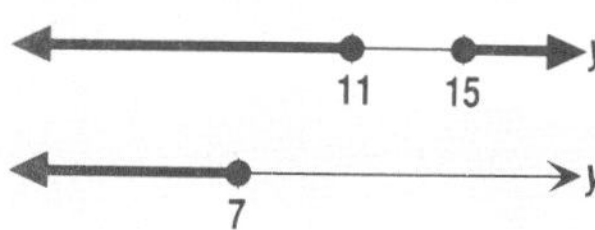

27a. 2735 − 1986 = 749. Add 749 to obtain Babylonian year. 1066 + 749 = 1815 Babylonian year. 5746 − 1986 = 3760. Add 3760 to obtain Jewish year. 1066 + 3760 = 4826 Jewish year.

28. The sum for any year is usually 100.

25. *Skill sequence* Evaluate in your head when $x = 10$. *(Lesson 1-4)*
a. x^3 **1000** **b.** $2x^3$ **2000** **c.** $(\frac{1}{2}x)^3$ **125**

26. *Multiple choice* Which fraction is not equivalent to the others? *(Lesson 2-3)* **(d)**
(a) $\frac{-3}{2}$ (b) $\frac{3}{-2}$ (c) $-\left(\frac{-3}{-2}\right)$ (d) $-\left(\frac{-3}{2}\right)$

Exploration

27. a. The year 1986 roughly corresponds to the year 2735 in the Babylonian calendar and the year 5746 in the Jewish calendar. The Norman conquest of England occurred in 1066. What year is 1066 in the Babylonian and the Jewish calendars? **See margin.**

b. If you graph ordered pairs (J, G), where J is the year in the Jewish calendar and G the year in the Gregorian calendar (the official one in the United States), the graph is a line. Does the line slant up or down as you go to the right? **up**

c. Look in an almanac or other reference book. What other calendars are there? **sample: Islamic, Chinese, Julian**

28. This graph is roughly symmetric, that is, the graph of the Democrats and that of the Republicans are nearly reflection images of each other. What causes this? **See margin.**

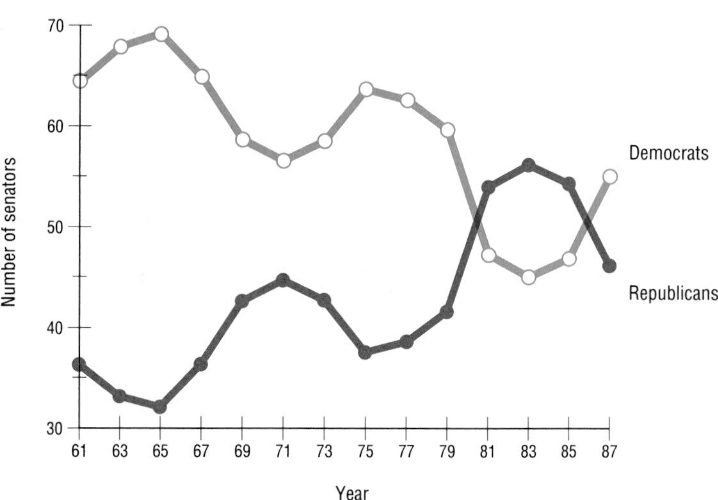

142

Addition, Subtraction, and Geometry

Constant sums occur in many places in geometry.

In each picture at the right, the pendulum makes two angles with the crossbar of the clock. As the pendulum swings, the angle measures x and y vary. But since the crossbar of the clock is a straight line, the sum of the measures of the angles is always 180°.

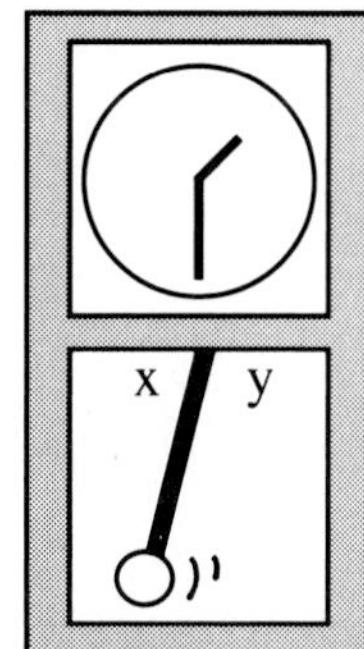

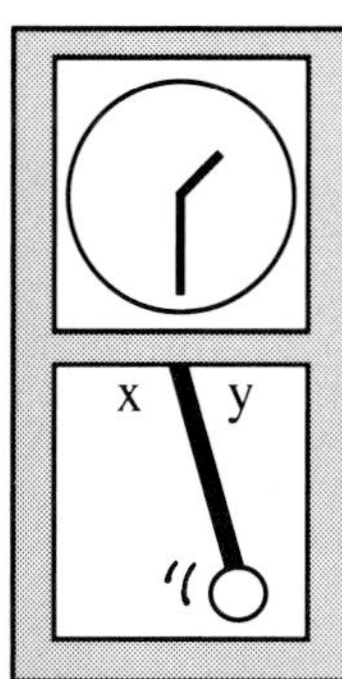

$$x + y = 180$$

Solving for y,

$$-x + x + y = 180 + -x$$
$$0 + y = 180 + -x$$
$$y = 180 - x$$

So if x is known, y can be found by subtracting x from 180°.

Example 1 In the angles shown above, find y if x is 128°.

Solution 1 $y = 180 - x$ (from preceding explanation)
$= 180 - 128$
$= 52$

Solution 2

$x + y = 180$

Substitute 128 for x. $128 + y = 180$

$y = 52$

(0, 180)
(128, 52)
(180, 0)

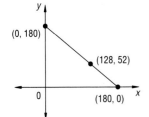

Two angles whose sum is 180° occur often in geometry, so they are given a name. These angles are called **supplementary** (no matter what the position of the angles). The angles are **supplements.**

If the pairs of possible measures of supplementary angles are graphed, they lie on the part of the line $x + y = 180$ that is in the first quadrant. At left is a graph of these pairs. The point (128, 52) from Example 1 is identified.

LESSON 3-8

RESOURCES

- Lesson Master 3-8
- Visual for Teaching Aid 14: Protractors
- Visual for Teaching Aid 18: Diagrams for **Question 33**

OBJECTIVE

C Find the measure of the supplement or complement of an angle.

TEACHING NOTES

A protractor with two scales, one beginning at each side, can be used to show measures of linear pairs (adjacent supplementary angles). With the protractor in position, the measure of one angle can be read from one scale and its linear pair from the other scale. A clear plastic protractor can be used directly on the overhead projector.

To illustrate the Triangle-Sum Property, make a triangle out of paper and label the measures of the angles $a°$, $b°$, and $c°$. Then tear the triangle into three parts and reassemble to form a straight angle.

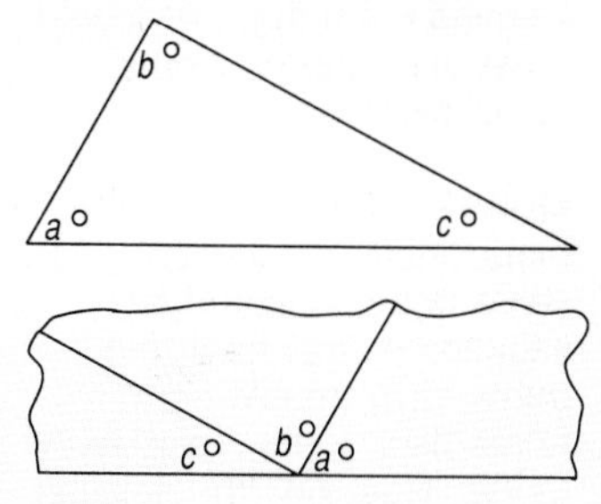

Vary this activity and make pairs of supplements and complements.

Additional Example 1 provides some algebra problems which follow the constant sum model: $a + b =$ constant. Students who have no trouble with specific numerical values in constant sum situations often struggle with representing a general value. It seems strange to them that a problem involving a sum can result in a subtraction expression. Relating back to the Take-away Model of Subtraction may help make the idea clear.

ADDITIONAL EXAMPLES

1. Suppose $x + y = 32k^2$.

a. If $x = 5$, what is y?
$32k^2 - 5$

b. If $y = 12z$, what is x?
$32k^2 - 12z$

c. If $x = 14k^2$, what is y?
$32k^2 - 14k^2 = 18k^2$

2. In a triangle, two angles have the same measure x and the measure of the third angle is 70°. Find x.
55°

3. If the measures of complementary angles are x and y, write an equation relating x and y.
$x + y = 90$

4. Find the measure of a supplement of a right angle.
90°

NOTES ON QUESTIONS

Questions 6-8: Many students will be able to do these problems as arithmetic exercises without having to write and solve an equation. Remind them that they could have done the problems using algebra.

Question 12: Writing an expression to represent one value in a constant sum situation is important. If students have trouble here, relate back to the Take-away Model. Checking the solution helps: $m\angle B = 90 - W$. So $m\angle A + m\angle B = W + (90 - W) = 90$.

You may already know that in a triangle, regardless of its shape, the sum of the measures of the three angles is 180.

Triangle-Sum Property:

In any triangle with angle measures a, b, and c, $a + b + c = 180$.

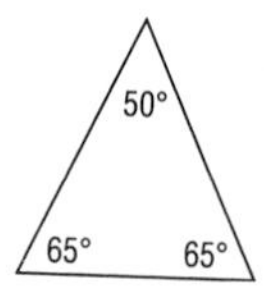

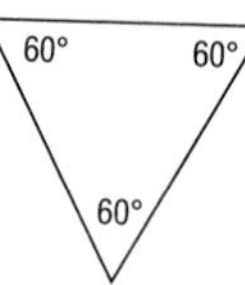

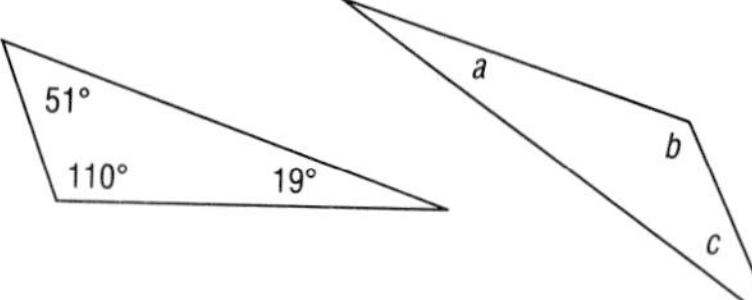

So, if you know the measures of two angles of a triangle, you can find the measure of the third angle.

Example 2 In the triangle at the right, find n.

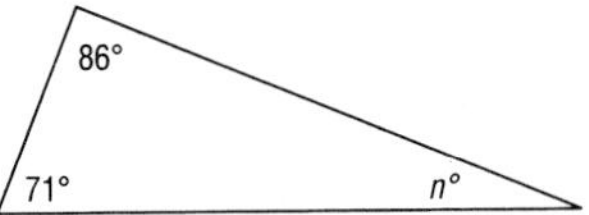

Solution 1 In any triangle with angle measures a, b, and c,
$a + b + c = 180$.

Substitute for a, b, and c.	$71 + 86 + n = 180$
Simplify.	$157 + n = 180$
Solve.	$n = 23$

So the third angle is 23°.

Solution 2 Add the given measures. Then subtract from 180.

$180 - (71 + 86) = 180 - 157 = 23$

In a right triangle, one of the angles measures 90°. In drawings, a 90° angle is often marked with the symbol ⌐.

Example 3 Write an expression for p in the triangle at the right.

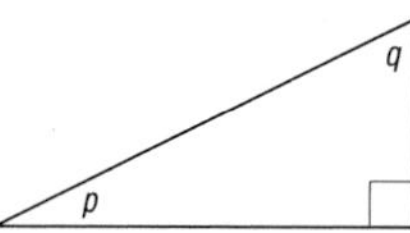

Solution

	$a + b + c = 180$
Substitute for a, b, and c.	$p + q + 90 = 180$
Solve for p and simplify.	$p = 180 - 90 - q$
	$p = 90 - q$

In Example 3, angles p and q are called **complements.** Two angles are **complementary** if the sum of their measures is 90°.

Questions

Covering the Reading

In 1–3, use the drawing at the right.

1. If $x = 42°$, what is y? **138°**

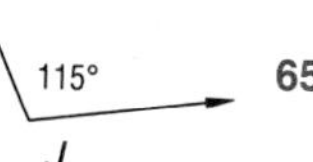

2. Find x if y is 137.5°. **42.5°**

3. Represent y in terms of x. **$y = 180 - x$**

4. If $m\angle F = 58°$ and $m\angle G = 132°$, are $\angle F$ and $\angle G$ supplementary? **No**

5. Find the measure of a supplement of $\angle J$. **65°**

115°
J

In 6–8, find the value of the variable.

6. **7.** **8.**

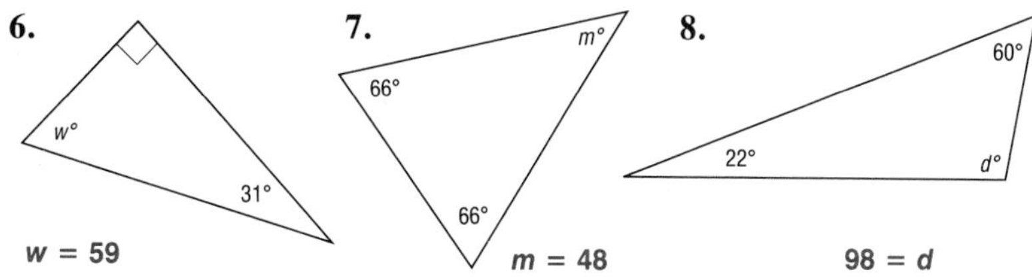

$w = 59$ **$m = 48$** **$98 = d$**

9. *True or false* 65° and 25° are measures of complementary angles. **True**

10. If $m\angle Q$ is 29°, what is the measure of a complement? **61°**

11. a. Give the measures of five pairs of complementary angles, then write the measures as ordered pairs. **See margin.**

b. Graph your pairs on the coordinate plane. **See margin.**

c. Show the possible measures of all pairs of complementary angles on your graph. **See margin.**

Applying the Mathematics

12. Angles A and B are complementary. If $m\angle A = W$, write an expression to represent the measure of $\angle B$. **$90 - W$**

13. $\angle C$ is the supplement of $\angle A$. $\angle T$ is the complement of $\angle C$. $m\angle A = 155°$. Find the measures of $\angle C$ and $\angle T$. **$m\angle C = 25°$, $m\angle T = 65°$**

14. This triangle has two angles the same size. The third angle is 102°. Find e. **39°**

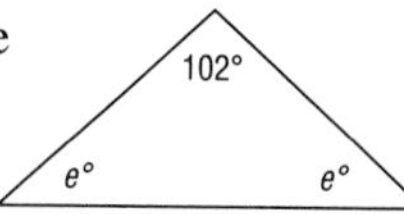

In 15 and 16, use this fact. The sum of the angles of a quadrilateral is always 360°.

15. Find p. **50°**

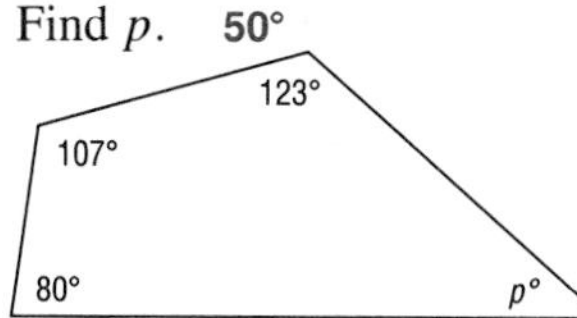

16. Find q. **73°**

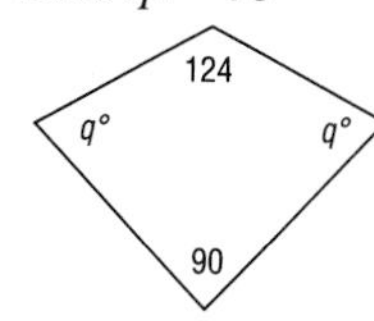

NOTES ON QUESTIONS:

Questions 14 and 16: Although we have not yet solved two-step equations like $2e + 102 = 180$, students should be able to do these problems by subtracting from 180 or 360, then dividing the result by 2.

Questions 15 and 16: These deal with the sum of the measures of the angles in a quadrilateral. You might want to verify the quadrilateral sum for your students. This can be done by drawing a diagonal to decompose a quadrilateral into two triangles.

Question 18: Make sure that students do use graph paper and make the graph for this question. Stating that the domain is R says that the graph is a continuous line rather than a set of discrete points. Often this will be assumed rather than stated.

Computer for Question 27: In this computer program, a single INPUT statement is used to enter values for the two variables A and B.

Questions 31 and 32: Point out that these questions are essentially identical. Half of a number is the same as that number divided by 2; a third of a number is the same as dividing the number by 3; 3/4 of a number can be found by multiplying it by 3, then dividing by 4.

ADDITIONAL ANSWERS

11a. sample: (10, 80), (30, 60), (45, 45), (70, 20), (85, 5)

11b, c.

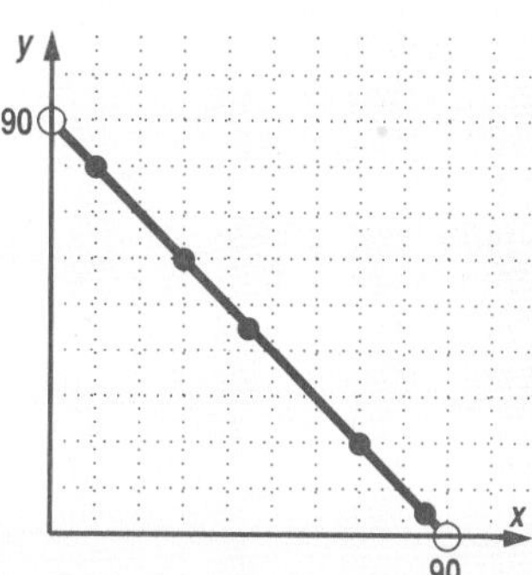

NOTES ON QUESTIONS
Question 33: While each of the four corners at an intersection could count as a different location for the theater, we don't count the additional distance one would have to travel to cross the street. *Teaching Aid 18* provides several repetitions of the diagram for this question.

18a.

x	y	x, y
-2	-5	(-2, -5)
-1	-4	(-1, -4)
0	-3	(0, -3)
1	-2	(1, -2)
2	-1	(2, -1)

18b.

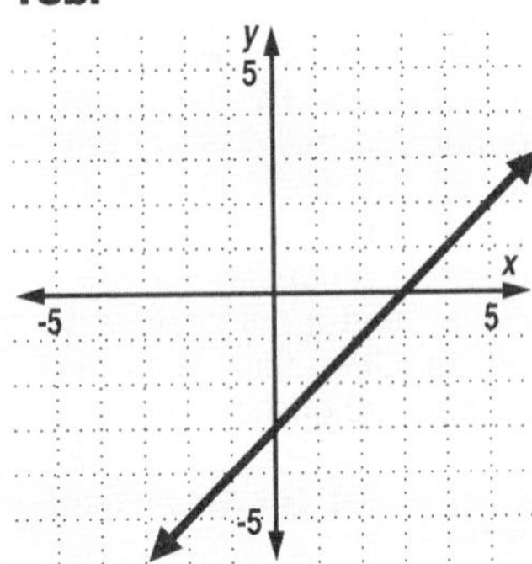

26a.

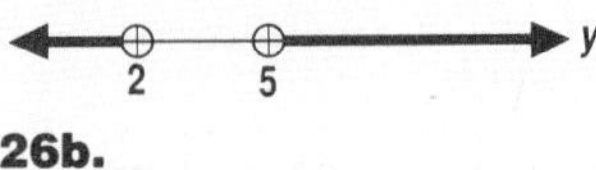

26b.

2 5 y

27. **EVALUATE A * B**
GIVE A AND B
?13.94, 6.06
84.4764

33.

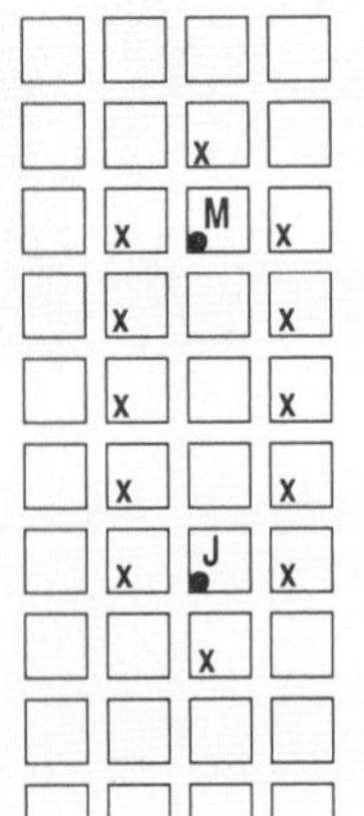

17. Write an expression to represent m∠C in terms of m∠A and m∠B. **m∠C = 180 − (m∠A + m∠B)**

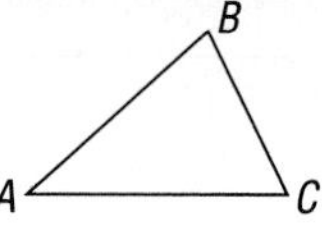

Review

18. Assume for points (x, y) that $x - y = 3$. *(Lessons 1-5, 3-7)*
  a. Make a table of some points (x, y). **See margin.**
  b. Graph $x - y = 3$. The domain for both variables is the set of real numbers. **See margin.**

In 19–21, solve.

19. Solve: $z - 43 < 65$. *(Lesson 3-3)* **$z < 108$**

20. Solve: $3.1 = w - 7.48$. *(Lesson 3-3)* **$w = 10.58$**

21. Solve: $3 + x + {}^-8 = 5$. *(Lesson 2-6)* **$x = 10$**

22. The total cost of a hamburger and a milk shake is \$1.96. If h is the cost of the hamburger, what is the cost of the milk shake? *(Lesson 3-2)* **$1.96 - h$**

23. In a town, 24% of the residents voted for a tax increase. 86% reduced their water consumption. 17% voted for the increase and reduced their water consumption. Of 3526 residents, how many voted for the increase or reduced their water consumption? *(Lesson 3-6)* **3279**

24. The only even prime number is 2. There are 25 even numbers and 15 prime numbers less than or equal to 50. If an integer is chosen at random from the interval $1 \le x \le 50$, what is the probability it is even or a prime? *(Lesson 3-6)* **$\frac{39}{50} = .78$**

25. The variable y stands for the same number in both figures below. The perimeter of the triangle is 73. What is the area of the square? *(Lesson 2-6)* **961**

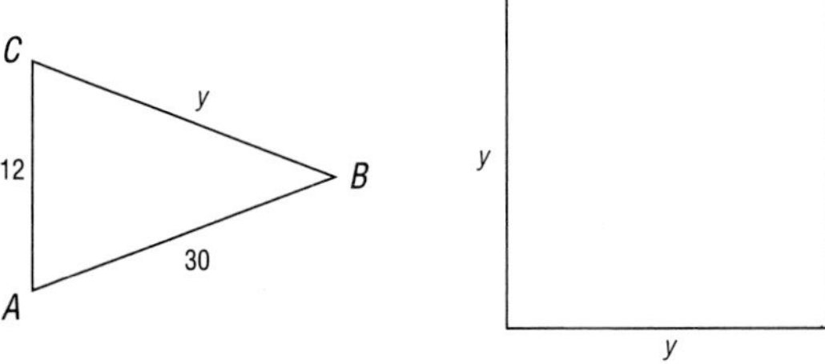

26. Graph: **a.** $y < 2$ or $y > 5$; **b.** $y < 2$ and $y > 5$. *(Lessons 3-4,3-5)* **See margin.**

27. When this program is run on the computer, what will be printed if 13.94, 6.06 is the input? *(Lesson 1-4)* **See margin.**

```
10 PRINT "EVALUATE A * B"
20 PRINT "GIVE A AND B"
30 INPUT A,B
40 PRINT A * B
50 END
```

28. Here is a list of National Football League scoring leaders over a 10-year period.

Year	Leader	Points
1986	Kevin Butler, Chicago	120
1985	Kevin Butler, Chicago	144
1984	Ray Wersching, San Francisco	131
1983	Mark Mosely, Washington	161
1982	Wendell Tyler, Los Angeles	78
1981	Ed Murray, Detroit	121
1980	Ed Murray, Detroit	116
1979	Mark Mosely, Washington	114
1978	Frank Corrall, Los Angeles	118
1977	Walter Payton, Chicago	96

a. What is the median of points for the leaders? **119**
b. What is the mean of points? **119.9**
c. What is the range of points? *(Lesson 1-2)* **83**

29. *Multiple choice* Which of the following is *not* equal to $w + -k$? *(Lesson 3-1)* **(b)**
(a) $w - k$ (b) $k - w$ (c) $-k + w$

30. Simplify. *(Lessons 2-2, 3-1)* **30. a) $4b$; b) $10p^5$; c) $n + .1m$**
a. $2b + -3b + 5b$ **b.** $15p^5 - 10p^5 + 5p^5$ **c.** $.2n + .3m + .8n - .2m$

In 31 and 32, simplify. *(Lessons 2-3, 3-1)*

31. $\frac{1}{2}x - \frac{1}{3}x - \frac{3}{4}x$ $-\frac{7}{12}x$ 32. $\frac{y}{2} - \frac{y}{3} - \frac{3y}{4}$ $-\frac{7y}{12}$

Exploration

33. Below is a map of Centerville. John lives at the corner marked J. His girl friend Mary lives by the corner marked M. John and Mary each walk directly to the theater along streets and meet there. The sum of the distances they walk is 6 blocks. Copy the diagram. On your copy show all possible locations of the theater. **See margin.**

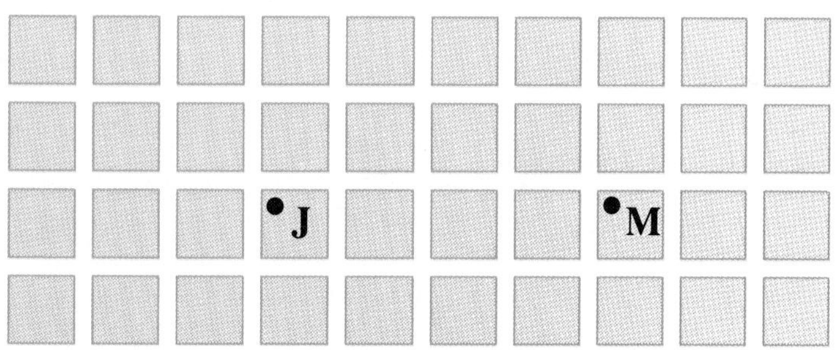

FOLLOW-UP

MORE PRACTICE

For more questions on SPUR Objectives, use *Lesson Master 3-8,* shown below.

EXTENSION

1. Have students determine the sum of the measures of the angles of a pentagon. (540°)

2. Have students find a formula for the sum of the measures of an *n*-gon. [$s = (n - 2)180°$]

EVALUATION
Alternative Assessment

You may want students to write a brief essay (one or two paragraphs) on "The Most Important Things I Learned in this Chapter About Subtraction."

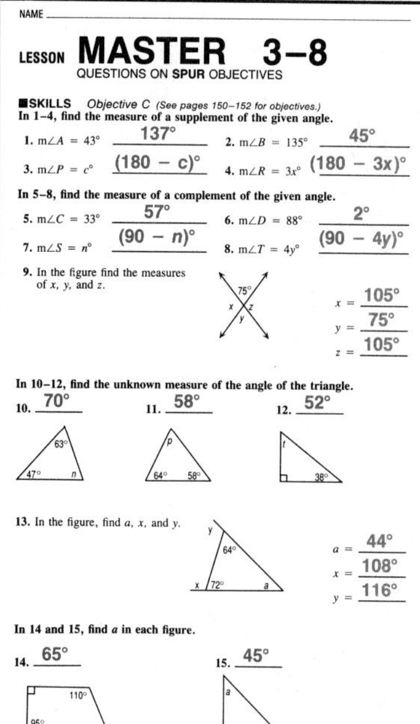

NAME ____

LESSON **MASTER 3–8**
QUESTIONS ON **SPUR** OBJECTIVES

SKILLS *Objective C (See pages 150–152 for objectives.)*
In 1–4, find the measure of a supplement of the given angle.

1. $m\angle A = 43°$ **137°** 2. $m\angle B = 135°$ **45°**
3. $m\angle P = c°$ **(180 − c)°** 4. $m\angle R = 3x°$ **(180 − 3x)°**

In 5–8, find the measure of a complement of the given angle.

5. $m\angle C = 33°$ **57°** 6. $m\angle D = 88°$ **2°**
7. $m\angle S = n°$ **(90 − n)°** 8. $m\angle T = 4y°$ **(90 − 4y)°**

9. In the figure find the measures of x, y, and z.

$x =$ **105°**
$y =$ **75°**
$z =$ **105°**

In 10–12, find the unknown measure of the angle of the triangle.

10. **70°** 11. **58°** 12. **52°**

13. In the figure, find a, x, and y.

$a =$ **44°**
$x =$ **108°**
$y =$ **116°**

In 14 and 15, find *a* in each figure.

14. **65°** 15. **45°**

26

SUMMARY

The Summary gives an overview of the entire chapter and provides an opportunity for students to consider the material as a whole. Thus, the Summary can be used to help students relate the concepts presented in the chapter.

VOCABULARY

Terms, symbols, and properties are listed by lesson to provide a checklist of things a student must know. Emphasize to students that they should read the vocabulary list carefully before starting the Progress Self-Test. If students do not understand the meaning of a term, they should refer back to the indicated lesson.

Definitions or descriptions of all terms in the vocabulary list may be found in the Glossary.

ADDITIONAL ANSWERS

12.

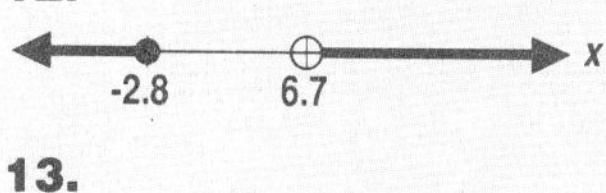

13.

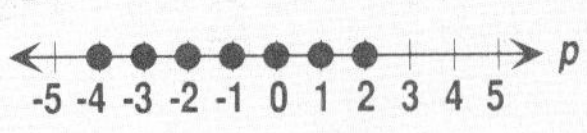

19.

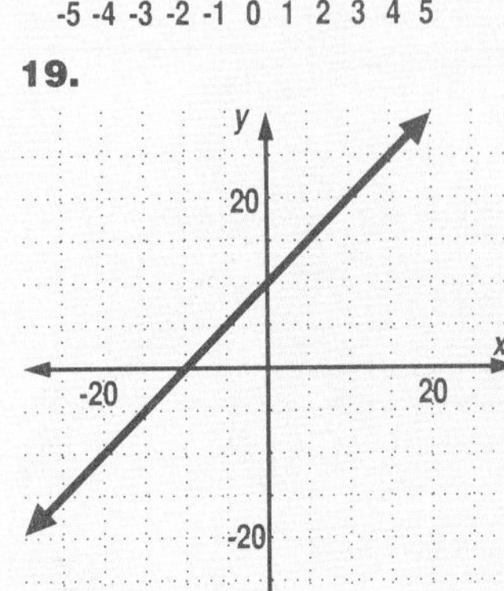

Summary

You can think of this chapter as having three parts. The first part concerns the algebraic definition and uses of subtraction, and solving subtraction sentences. The second part deals with the relationships of addition and subtraction to the union and intersection of sets and to counting and probability. The third part applies these ideas to the graphing of lines and to properties of geometric figures.

The algebraic definition of subtraction is in terms of addition: $a - b = a + -b$. This definition enables subtraction sentences of the form $x - a = b$ or $x - a < b$ to be solved by converting them to addition. Such sentences arise from the uses of subtraction. The two major models for subtraction are take-away and comparison.

Given two sets A and B, their union $A \cup B$ consists of those elements in A *or* in B (or in both). Their intersection $A \cap B$ consists of those elements in A *and* in B. The number of elements in $A \cup B$ is denoted by $N(A \cup B)$.

$$N(A \cup B) = N(A) + N(B) - N(A \cap B)$$

If A and B are events, then $A \cup B$ consists of the event where either A or B occurs, and

$$P(A \cup B) = P(A) + P(B) - P(A \cap B)$$

In both these formulas, subtraction compensates for counting elements in the intersection twice.

When an equation has two variables, its solutions may be graphed on a coordinate plane. In this chapter, ordered pairs (x, y) satisfying $x + y = a$ and $x - y = a$ were graphed. In each case, the graph is a line. Constant sums like these occur in geometry. Two angles whose measures add to 180° are supplementary; two angles whose measures add to 90° are complementary. The three angles of a triangle give the constant sum 180°.

Vocabulary

Below are the most important terms and phrases for this chapter. You should be able to give a general description and a specific example of each.

Lesson 3-1
algebraic definition of subtraction

Lesson 3-2
take-away model for subtraction
comparison model for subtraction

Lesson 3-4
intersection of sets, $\cap$
"and"
Venn diagram

Lesson 3-5
union of sets, $\cup$
"or"

Lesson 3-6
mutually exclusive
Fundamental Counting Principle
Probability of a Union of Events

Lesson 3-8
supplementary angles, supplements
complementary angles, complements
⌐ symbol for 90° angle
Triangle Sum Property

Progress Self-Test

Take this test as you would take a test in class. You will need graph paper. Then check your work with the solutions in the Selected Answers section in the back of the book.

1. According to the algebraic definition of subtraction, adding -7 is the same as doing what else? **subtracting 7**

In 2–5, simplify.

2. $n - 16 - 2n - (-12)$ **$-n - 4$**
3. $-8x - (2x - x)$ **$-9x$**
4. $\frac{3}{4} - \frac{7}{8}$ **$-\frac{1}{8}$**
5. $\frac{m}{2a} - \frac{3m}{4a}$ **$-\frac{m}{4a}$**

In 6 and 7, solve.

6. $y - 13 = -7$ **$y = 6$** 7. $m - 2 < 6$ **$m < 8$**

8. Solve for b: $b - a = 100$. **$b = 100 + a$**
9. Solve for m: $m - 7n = -22n$. **$m = -15n$**

In 10 and 11, $A = \{-3, -1, 1, 3, 5, 7\}$ and $B = \{-6, -3, 0, 3, 6, 9\}$.

10. Find $A \cap B$. **$\{-3, 3\}$** 11. $A \cup B$. **$\{-6, -3, -1, 0, 1, 3, 5, 6, 7, 9\}$**

In 12 and 13, graph on a number line.

12. $x > 6.7$ or $x \leq -2.8$. **12–13) See margin.**
13. $p > -5$ and $p \leq 2$, where p is an integer
14. Park's Pet Shop mailing list has 480 customers, each of whom has cats or dogs. Of these, 321 customers have dogs and 215 have cats. How many customers have both cats and dogs? **$(321 + 215) - 480 = 56$**
15. If the 1990 population of Vermont is V and the 1990 population of New Hampshire is H, how many more people are in Vermont than in New Hampshire in 1990? **$V - H$**
16. A store had B boxes of paper clips at the beginning of the week, sold S of them, used 3 boxes itself, and received a shipment of N new boxes. How many boxes were there after all this? **$B - S - 3 + N$**

17. Last summer 30 students in the school spent some time in England. Of these, 15 visited France; 11 visited Germany; and 20 visited either France or Germany. If one of these students is chosen at random to be interviewed by the school newspaper, what is the probability that student visited all three countries? **$\frac{6}{30}$**
18. *Multiple choice* In which pair are angles X and Y complementary? **(c)**
    (a) $m\angle X = 67°$, $m\angle Y = 113°$
    (b) $m\angle X = 38°$, $m\angle Y = 38°$
    (c) $m\angle X = 5°$, $m\angle Y = 85°$
    (d) none of (a)–(c)
19. Today it is 10 degrees cooler than yesterday. If x = today's temperature and y = yesterday's temperature, graph all ordered pairs (x, y) that fit this description. **See margin.**
20. On a coordinate plane, graph all ordered pairs of numbers whose sum is 7. **See margin.**
21. Which Venn diagram represents $(X \cap Y) \cup Z$? **(c)**

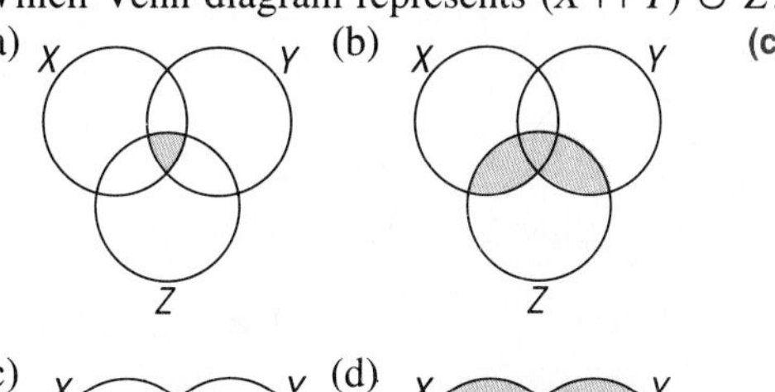

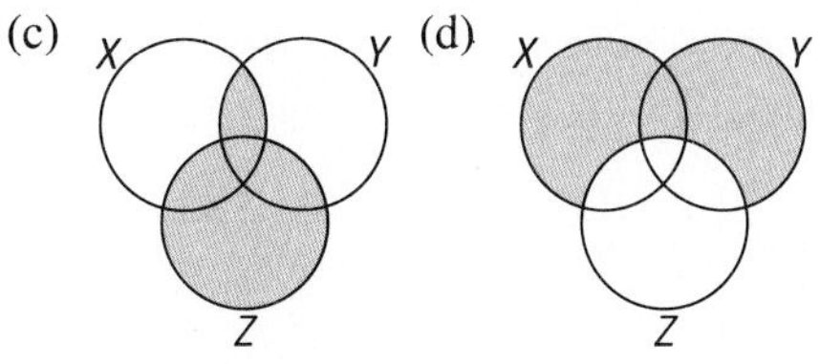

PROGRESS SELF-TEST

We cannot overemphasize the importance of these end-of-chapter materials. It is at this point that the material "gels" for many students, allowing them to solidify skills and understanding. In general, student performance should be markedly improved after these pages.

USING THE PROGRESS SELF-TEST

Assign the Progress Self-Test as a one-night assignment. Worked-out *solutions* for all questions are in the Selected Answers section at the back of the student book. Encourage students to take the Progress Self-Test honestly, grade themselves, and then be prepared to discuss the test in class.

Advise students to pay special attention to those Chapter Review questions (pages 150–152) which correspond to questions missed on the Progress Self-Test. A chart provided in the Selected Answers section in the student text keys the Progress Self-Test questions to the lettered SPUR Objectives in the Chapter Review or to the Vocabulary. It also keys the questions to the corresponding lessons where the material is covered.

20.

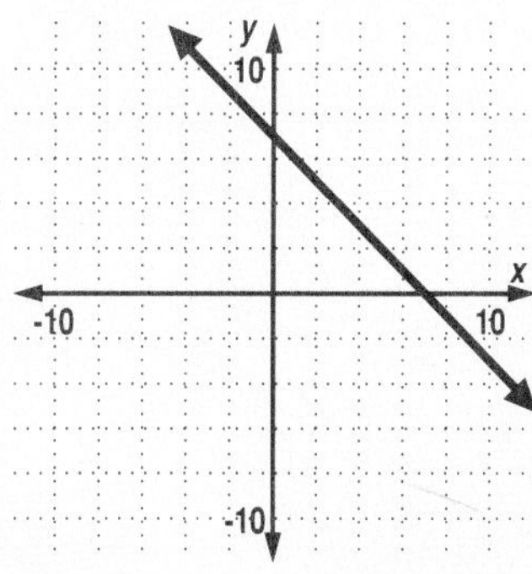

RESOURCES
- Chapter 3 Test, Form A
- Chapter 3 Test, Form B
- Chapter 3 Test, Cumulative Form
- Comprehensive Test, Chapters 1-3

CHAPTER REVIEW

The main objectives for the chapter are organized here into sections corresponding to the four main types of understanding this book promotes: Skills, Properties, Uses, and Representations. You may assign these questions over a single night to help students prepare for a test the next day, or you may assign the questions over a two-day period.

If you work the questions over two days, then we recommend assigning the *evens* for homework the first night so that students get feedback in class the next day, then assigning the *odds* the night before the test so the students can use the answers provided in the book.

Chapter Review

Questions on SPUR Objectives

SPUR stands for **S**kills, **P**roperties, **U**ses, and **R**epresentations. The Chapter Review questions are grouped according to the SPUR Objectives for this chapter.

SKILLS deal with the procedures used to get answers.

Objective A. *Find the union and intersections of sets.* *(Lessons 3-4, 3-5)*

In 1–2, $A = \{11, 15, 19, 23, 25\}$, $B = \{10, 15, 20, 25, 30\}$.

1. Find $A \cap B$. **{15, 25}**

2. Find $A \cup B$. **{10, 11, 15, 19, 20, 23, 25, 30}**

In 3–4, $C = \{2, 8, 9\}$, $D = \{4, 8, 12\}$, $E = \{6, 8, 9\}$.

3. Find $(C \cup D) \cap E$. **{8, 9}**

4. Find $C \cup (D \cap E)$. **{2, 8, 9}**

Objective B: *Solve and check sentences involving subtraction.* *(Lesson 3-3)*

5. Solve and check: $x - 47 = -2$. **$x = 45$**

6. Solve: $2.5 = t - 3.34$. **$t = 5.84$**

7. Solve: $\frac{3}{2} + y - \frac{1}{4} = \frac{3}{4}$. **$y = -\frac{1}{2}$**

8. Solve for x: $x - z = 4$. **$x = 4 + z$**

9. Solve: $z - 12 < 11$. **$z < 23$**

10. Solve: $-3 < m + 2$. **$-5 < m$**

11. For the inequality $x - 30 \geq 40$, Brian got the answer $x \geq 10$. Check whether Brian is correct. **Does 10 − 30 = 40? No. He is wrong.**

12. Solve for r: $r - 45 \geq d$. **$r \geq d + 45$**

13. Solve for y: $-8z = y - 7z$ **$-z = y$**

Objective C: *Find the measure of the supplement or complement of an angle.* *(Lesson 3-8)*

14. If $m\angle Q = 17°$, find the measure of the supplement of $\angle Q$. **163°**

15. $\angle A$ and $\angle B$ are complementary. If $m\angle B = 62.5°$, find $m\angle A$. **27.5°**

16. $m\angle L = a°$. What is the measure of the supplement of $\angle L$? **$180 - a$**

17. $\angle R$ and $\angle S$ are complements. $m\angle R = x°$ and $m\angle S = z°$. Write an equation relating x and z. **$x + z = 90$**

Objective D: *Simplify expressions involving subtraction.* *(Lessons 3-1, 3-3)*

In 18–25, simplify.

18. $3x - 4x + 5x$ **$4x$**

19. $-\frac{2}{3} - \frac{4}{5}$ **$-1\frac{7}{15}$**

20. $\frac{3a}{2} - \frac{9a}{2}$ **$-3a$**

21. $-\frac{28}{3} - \frac{48}{3}$ **$-25\frac{1}{3}$**

22. $c - \frac{c}{3} - 2c - 2$ **$-\frac{4c}{3} + -2$**

23. $y - (2y - y)$ **0**

24. $-41 - 233 + 30 - -52 - 6 - 5$ **-203**

25. $z^3 - 7 + 8 - 4z^3$ **$1 + -3z^3$**

PROPERTIES deal with the principles behind the mathematics.

Objective E: *Apply the algebraic definition of subtraction.* *(Lesson 3-1)*

In 26 and 27, rewrite each subtraction as addition.

26. $x - y + z$ **$x + -y + z$**

27. $-8 - v = 42$ **$-8 + -v = 42$**

28. *True or false* The sum of $m - k$ and $k - m$ is zero. **True**

29. *Multiple choice* Which does *not* equal the others? **(d)**

(a) $a - b$ (b) $a + -b$
(c) $-b + a$ (d) $b + -a$

USES deal with applications of mathematics in real situations.

Objective F: *Use models of subtraction to form expressions and solve sentences involving subtraction.* (Lessons 3-2, 3-3)

30. Last week Carla earned E dollars, saved S dollars, and spent P dollars. Relate E, S, and P in a subtraction sentence. $E - P = S$

31. An elevator won't run if it holds more than L kilograms. A person weighing 80 kg gets on a crowded elevator and an "overload" light goes on. How much did the other passengers weigh? See margin.

32. The total floor area of a three-story house is advertised as 3500 sq ft. If the first floor's area is F sq ft and the third floor's area is 1000 sq ft, what is the area of the second floor? $S = 2500 - F$ 33) $S - 40 < 3$; $S < 43$

33. After spending \$40, Mort has less than \$3 left. If he started with S dollars, write an inequality to describe the possible values of S.

34. Donna is 5 years older than Eileen. If Donna's age is D, how old is Eileen? $D - 5$

35. A plane 30,000 feet above sea level is radioing a submarine 1500 feet below sea level. What is the difference in their altitudes? 31,500 feet

36. General Computer Co. had a profit of \$4 million last year and a loss of \$0.3 million this year. By how much do these amounts differ? 4.3 million

37. There were 5000 people at the game. Herb guessed there were H people. Herb's guess was too low. How far off was the guess? $5000 - H$

Objective G: *Apply the formulas for $N(A \cup B)$ and $P(A \cup B)$.* (Lesson 3-6)

38. Of Mrs. Schubert's 20 piano students, 13 can play either a Beethoven sonata or a Chopin mazurka, 6 can play only the Beethoven, and 5 can play only the Chopin. How many can play both? See margin.

39. Of the 25 students in Mr. Young's algebra class, 16 studied some on Saturday, 15 studied some on Sunday, and 9 studied both Saturday and Sunday. What is the probability that a student in this class studied on either of the days? $\frac{22}{25}$

40. $P(A) = \frac{1}{4}$, $P(B) = \frac{1}{13}$, $P(A \cap B) = \frac{1}{52}$. What is $P(A \cup B)$? $\frac{4}{13}$

41. Fifty-six people signed the Declaration of Independence. Forty people signed the U.S. Constitution. Five people signed both documents. How many people signed the Constitution or the Declaration of Independence? 91

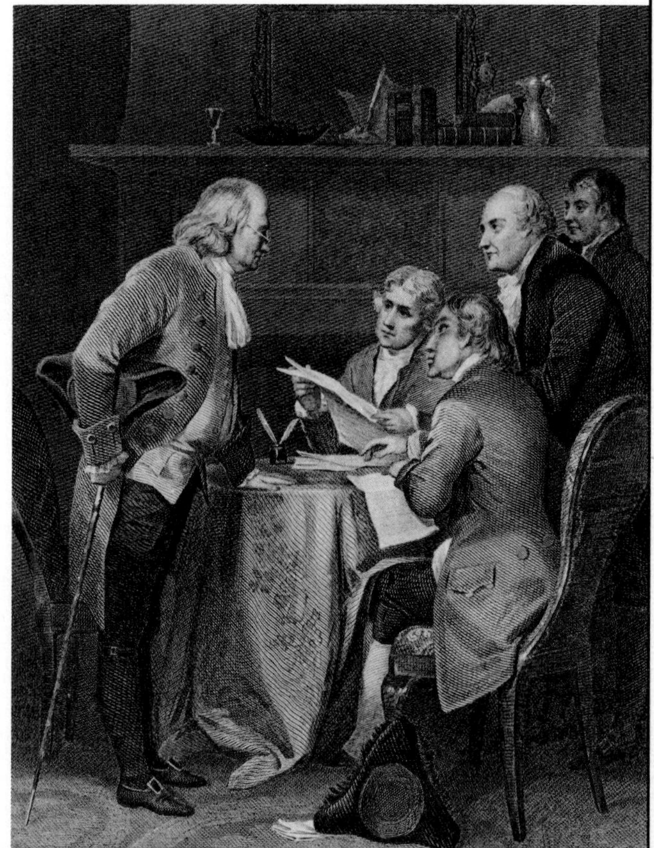

Drawing up the Declaration of Independence are (from left to right) Benjamin Franklin, Thomas Jefferson, Robert R. Livingston, John Adams, and Roger Sherman

ADDITIONAL ANSWERS

31. $p + 80 > L$ where p = weight of other passengers; $p > L - 80$

38. $6 + 5 + x = 13$; $x = 2$; Two students can play both.

42.

43.

44.

45.

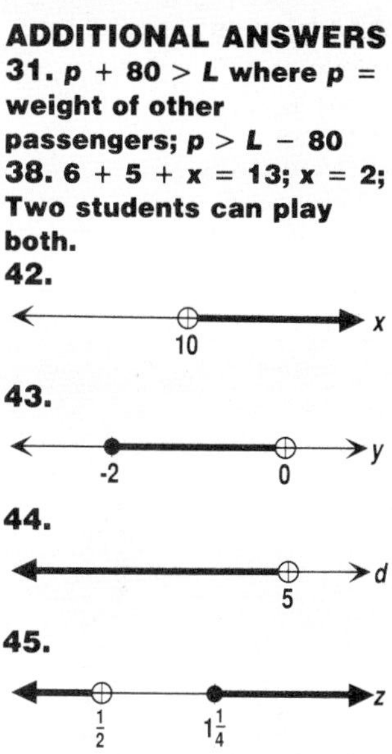

42.–45. See margin, page 151.

48.

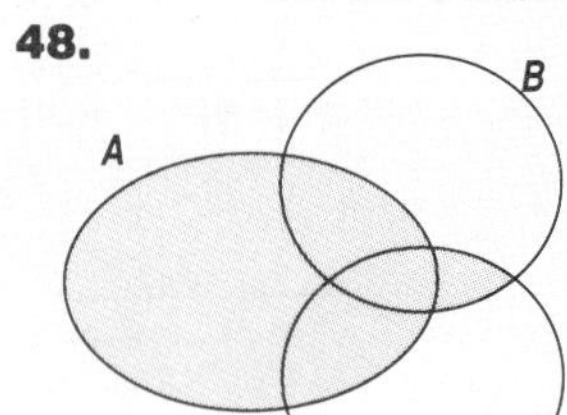

49.

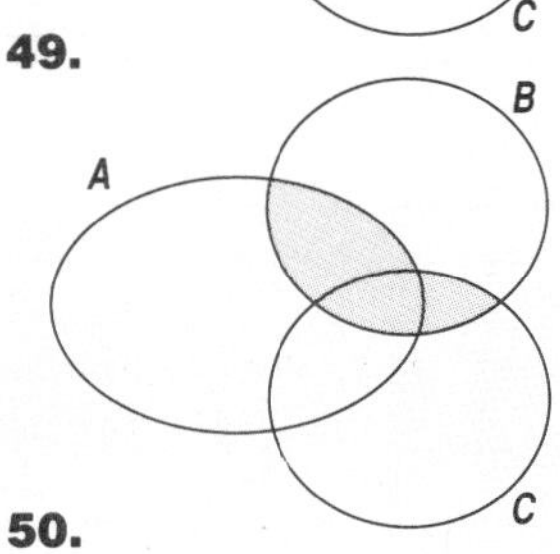

50.

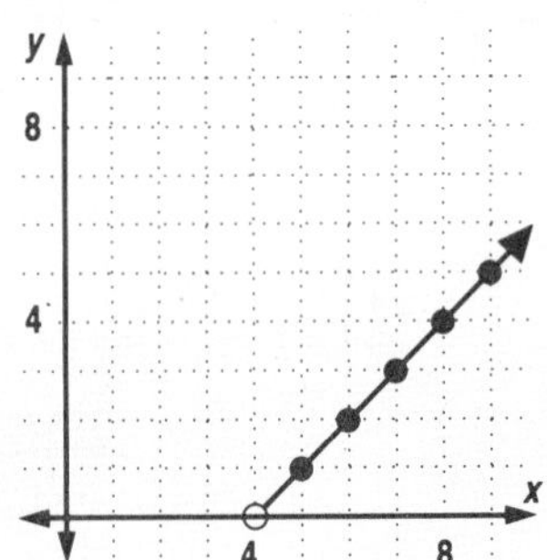

51.

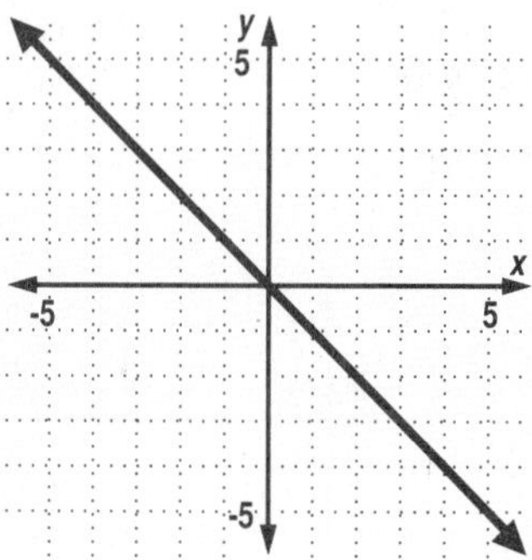

52.

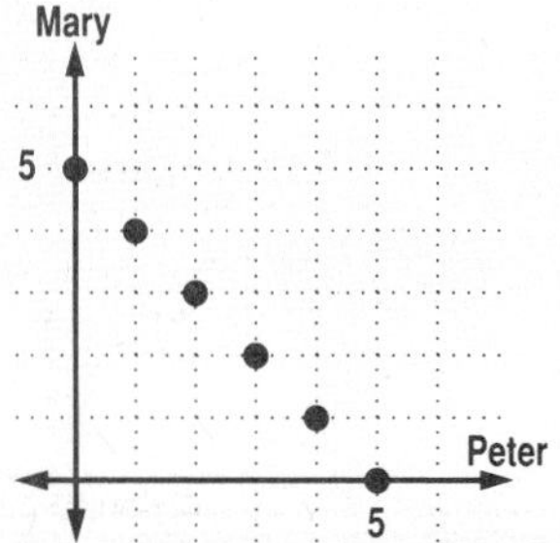

REPRESENTATIONS deal with pictures, graphs, or objects that illustrate concepts.

Objective H: *Graph solution sets to inequalities.* *(Lessons 3-4, 3-5)*

In 42–45, graph on a number line. The domain for all variables is the real numbers.

42. $x > 10$ and $x \geq -\frac{1}{2}$ **42–45) See margin.**

43. $-2 \leq y \leq 3$ and $y < 0$

44. $d \leq -15$ or $d < 5$

45. $z < \frac{1}{2}$ or $z \geq 1\frac{1}{4}$

Objective I: *Use Venn diagrams to describe union and intersection.* *(Lessons 3-4, 3-5)*

In 46 and 47, $A = \{-11, -1, 0, 2, 10\}$ and $B = \{-20, -10, 0, 10, 20\}$.

46. Write the set that is represented by the colored area in the Venn diagram. **{0, 10}**

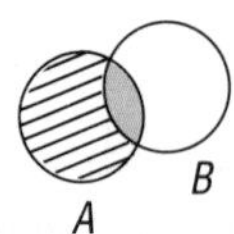

47. Write the set that is represented by the striped area. **{-11, -1, 2}**

In 48 and 49, use the figure below.

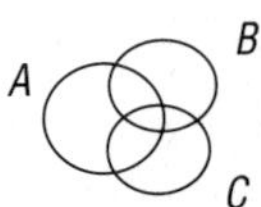

48. Copy the figure. Shade $A \cup (B \cap C)$.

49. Copy the figure. Shade $(A \cap B) \cup (C \cap B)$. **See margin.**

Objective J: *Graph sets of ordered pairs (x, y) where x + y = k or x − y = k, where k is a real number.* *(Lesson 3-7)*

50. Xavier is four years older than his sister Yvonne. Graph all possible ordered pairs that represent their ages. Let x represent Xavier's age and y represent Yvonne's age. **See margin.**

51. The sum of two numbers is 0. Graph all possible pairs of numbers. **See margin.**

52. Mary and Peter have a total of 5 pets. Graph all possible ways the pets may be divided between them. **See margin.**

53. Graph all ordered pairs (x, y) with $x - y = 30$. **See margin.**

53.

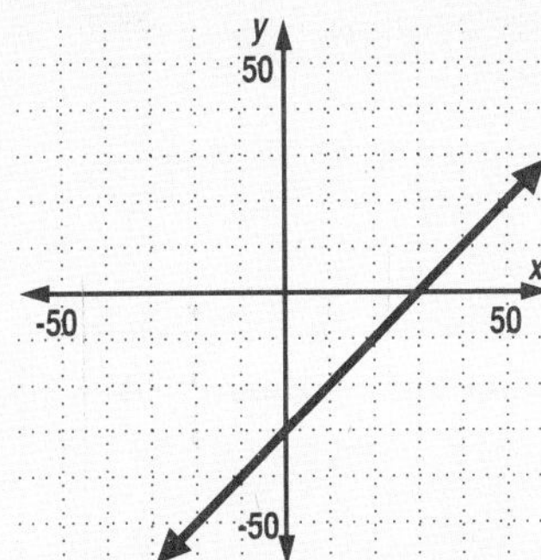

REFRESHER

Chapter 4, which discusses multiplication in algebra, assumes that you have mastered certain objectives in your previous mathematics courses. Use these optional questions to check your mastery.

A. Multiply any positive numbers or quantities.

1. $4.7 \cdot 3.21$ **15.087**

2. $0.04 \cdot 312$ **12.48**

3. $666 \cdot 0.00001$ **0.00666**

4. $.17 \cdot .02$ **0.0034**

5. $\frac{2}{3} \cdot 30$ **20**

6. $\frac{5}{2} \cdot 11$ $27\frac{1}{2}$

7. $\frac{2}{9} \cdot \frac{3}{4}$ $\frac{1}{6}$

8. $\frac{1}{4} \cdot \frac{1}{3} \cdot \frac{1}{2}$ $\frac{1}{24}$

9. $1\frac{1}{4} \cdot 2\frac{1}{8}$ $2\frac{21}{32}$

10. $5 \cdot 6\frac{2}{3}$ $33\frac{1}{3}$

11. $17 \cdot \$2.31$ **$39.27**

12. $\frac{3}{4} \cdot \$125$ **$93.75**

13. $\frac{1}{2} \cdot 10\frac{1}{2}$ inches $5\frac{1}{4}$ **inches**

14. $30\% \cdot 120$ **0.3 · 120 = 36**

15. $3\% \cdot \$6000$ **0.03 · $6000 = $180**

16. $5.25\% \cdot 1500$ **0.0525 · 1500 = 78.75**

B. Multiply positive and negative integers.

17. $3 \cdot -2$ **-6**

18. $11 \cdot -11$ **-121**

19. $-6 \cdot 4$ **-24**

20. $-5 \cdot -5$ **25**

21. $0 \cdot -1$ **0**

22. $-14 \cdot 130$ **-1820**

23. $-60 \cdot -59$ **3540**

24. $-3 \cdot -2 \cdot -1 \cdot -1$ **6**

C. Solve equations of the form $ax = b$, when a and b are positive integers.

25. $3x = 12$ $x = 4$

26. $5y = 110$ $y = 22$

27. $10z = 5$ $z = \frac{1}{2}$

28. $1 = 9w$ $\frac{1}{9} = w$

29. $6 = 50a$ $\frac{3}{25} = a$

30. $b \cdot 21 = 14$ $b = \frac{2}{3}$

31. $8c = 4$ $c = \frac{1}{2}$

32. $7 = 2d$ $3\frac{1}{2} = d$

D. Determine the area of a rectangle below left given its dimensions.

33. length 15″, width 12″ **180 in.^{2}**

34. length 4.5 cm, width 3.2 cm **14.4 cm^2**

35. length 2 m, width 4 m **8 m^2**

36. length 100′, width 82′ **8200 ft^2**

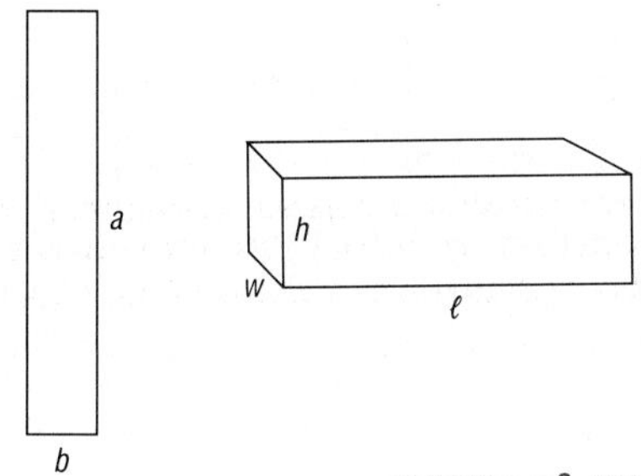

37) 96 cm^3; 38) 162 in.^{3}

E. Determine the volume of a rectangular solid above right given its dimensions.

37. length 8 cm, width 4 cm, height 3 cm

38. length 12 in., width 9 in., height $1\frac{1}{2}$ in.

39. length $\frac{1}{2}$ ft, width $\frac{1}{2}$ ft, height $\frac{1}{2}$ ft $\frac{1}{8}$ **ft^3**

40. length 60 m, width 50 m, height 10 m **30,000 m^3**

EVALUATION

Three tests are provided for this chapter in the Teacher's Resource File. Chapter 3 Test, Forms A and B, cover just Chapter 3. The third test is Chapter 3 Test, Cumulative Form. About 50% of this test covers Chapter 3, 25% covers Chapter 2, and 25% covers Chapter 1. A Comprehensive Test covering Chapters 1–3 is also included with this chapter. For more information on grading, see *General Teaching Suggestions: Grading* on page T44 in the Teacher's Edition.

ASSIGNMENT RECOMMENDATION

On the day your students take the chapter test, we suggest you make an assignment in the first section of the next chapter.

REFRESHER

The major topic of Chapter 4 is multiplication. If your students have a particularly weak background in multiplication, you may wish to assign this optional Refresher material to prepare them better for the chapter. Parts D and E on this page involve ideas that will be reviewed in Lesson 4-1. Parts A, B, and C can be assigned while covering Lessons 4-1 through 4-3, so students will be ready to work with more difficult equations in Lesson 4-4.

CHAPTER 4  MULTIPLICATION IN ALGEBRA

DAILY PACING CHART 4

DAILY PACING CHART ■ CHAPTER 4

Students in the Full Course should complete the entire text by the end of the year. Students in the Minimal Course spend more time to complete lessons that are combined with quizzes and more time to consider the Chapter Review. Therefore, these students may not complete all the chapters in the text.

DAY	MINIMAL COURSE	FULL COURSE
1	4-1	4-1
2	4-2	4-2
3	4-3	4-3
4	Quiz (TRF); Start 4-4.	Quiz (TRF); 4-4
5	Finish 4-4.	4-5
6	4-5	4-6
7	4-6	Quiz (TRF); 4-7
8	Quiz (TRF); Start 4-7.	4-8
9	Finish 4-7.	4-9
10	4-8	Progress Self-Test
11	4-9	Chapter Review
12	Progress Self-Test	Chapter Test (TRF)
13	Chapter Review	
14	Chapter Review	
15	Chapter Test (TRF)	

TESTING OPTIONS

TESTING OPTIONS

- Quiz for Lessons 4-1 Through 4-3
- Quiz for Lessons 4-4 Through 4-6
- Chapter 4 Test, Form A
- Chapter 4 Test, Form B
- Chapter 4 Test, Cumulative Form

INDIVIDUAL DIFFERENCES

PROVIDING FOR INDIVIDUAL DIFFERENCES

The student text is written for the *average* student. The program, however, can be adapted for less capable and for more capable students.

For those students who need more practice, a blackline master (in the Teacher's Resource File) is provided for each lesson. The Teacher's Edition frequently provides Error Analysis and Alternate Approach features to provide additional instructional strategies for those students who do not readily grasp the material.

For students who require additional challenge, Extension activities are regularly provided in the Teacher's Edition.

OBJECTIVES ■ CHAPTER 4

Students should master the chapter objectives by the time they complete the chapter. To ensure objective mastery, there is continual review built into each set of lesson questions. After students complete the chapter lessons, they assess their mastery on the Progress Self-Test. Then they do the Chapter Review and pay special attention to those questions that match the objectives missed on the Progress Self-Test. Students can get extra practice on these objectives by using the master for each lesson in the Teacher's Resource File.

OBJECTIVES FOR CHAPTER 4 (Organized into the SPUR categories—Skills, Properties, Uses, and Representations)	**Progress Self-Test Questions**	**Chapter Review Questions**	**Lesson Master from Teacher's Resource File***
SKILLS			
A Multiply fractions.	3	1 through 4	4-2
B Solve and check equations of the form $ax = b$.	6, 7	5 through 10	4-4, 4-5
C Solve and check equations of the form $a - x = b$.	10	11 through 14	4-5
D Solve and check inequalities of the form $ax < b$.	8, 9	15 through 20	4-6
E Evaluate expressions containing a factorial symbol.	1	21 through 26	4-9
PROPERTIES			
F Identify and apply properties of multiplication. Commutative Property, Associative Property, Property of Reciprocals, Multiplication Property of Zero, Multiplication Property of Equality, Multiplication Property of Inequality, Multiplicative Identity Property of 1, Multiplication Property of -1.	2, 4, 11, 12	27 through 38	4-1, 4-3, 4-4, 4-6
USES			
G Apply the area and rate factor models for multiplication.	13, 17, 18	39 through 45	4-1, 4-2
H Apply the Multiplication Counting Principle.	4	46 through 49	4-7
I Apply the Conditional Probability Formula.	19, 21	50 through 53	4-8
J Apply the Permutation Theorem.	5	54 through 56	4-9
K Solve sentences of the form $ax = b$ and $ax < b$ to answer questions from real situations.	20	57 through 60	4-1, 4-2, 4-4, 4-6
REPRESENTATIONS			
L Use area, arrays, and volume to picture multiplication.	5	61 through 70	4-1

*** The masters are numbered to match the lessons.**

OVERVIEW ■ CHAPTER 4

The chapter begins with applications of multiplication, proceeds to the solution of equations and inequalities involving multiplication, and concludes with further applications.

The Area Model for Multiplication, reviewed in Lesson 4-1, appears both in a continuous form (area of rectangles) and a discrete form (elements of an array). The geometric concept of area of a rectangle appears in several later chapters to justify algebraic properties such as multiplication of binomials. The area model helps to justify the Commutative and Associative Properties of Multiplication.

The Rate Factor Model for Multiplication is used in Lesson 4-2 to provide readiness for Lesson 4-4, in which students solve equations of the form $ax = b$. Students are also given extensive practice in the Rate Factor Model, which will be used later as the basis for the study of both exponential growth and division, and as an interpretation of slope of lines.

Lesson 4-2 focuses on units in rates to give an algebraic representation of arithmetic operations on fractions. Rate factors (with units) help to develop the multiplication properties in Lesson 4-3 and to justify the solution of equations in Lesson 4-4.

By the time the student reaches Lessons 4-4 to 4-6, the solving of equations and inequalities, there are a wealth of applications which can be treated.

In Lesson 4-7 the discrete version of the Area Model (array) is generalized to obtain the Multiplication Counting Principle. This serves as a basis for the probability and counting problems of Lessons 4-8 and 4-9.

PERSPECTIVES ■ CHAPTER 4

The Perspectives provide the rationale for the inclusion of topics or approaches, provide mathematical background, and make connections within UCSMP.

4-1

AREAS, ARRAYS, AND VOLUMES

This lesson discusses two versions of the Area Model for Multiplication. The continuous version is based on the area of a rectangle ($A = \ell w$). This gives a rationale for the Commutative Property of Multiplication. It is extended to the volume formula ($V = \ell wh$) to justify the Associative Property of Multiplication. The area model is continuous in the sense that any measure could be used for lengths. This is contrasted with the discrete version, the application to arrays. For arrays, the measures used must be whole numbers.

Although formal development of rules of exponents is in Chapter 9, students will encounter the square ($x \cdot x = x^2$) and cube ($x^2 \cdot x = x^3$) cases in this chapter.

4-2

MULTIPLYING FRACTIONS AND RATES

This lesson sets the stage for many later lessons. In the next chapter, there is a Rate Model for Division. When we cover equations of lines, slope is viewed as a rate. Also, some work with positive and negative numbers will be explained using this model.

In this lesson, the word *factor* is used as a noun to denote one of the components of a multiplication expression. *Factor* will be used later as a verb to indicate that a student should write an addition expression as a product, as in "factor $6x + 10$."

There is a fundamental difference between the rate factor and area models. In the rate factor model, each factor plays a different role, and one thinks of multiplying by a rate, rather than multiplying two numbers together. That is, "multiplication by x" becomes a phrase that is used, instead of "multiplication of x and y."

In science, the arithmetic of units as given here is called "dimensional analysis." This topic is not included in many algebra books, but recent research has shown that it does help students analyze and solve application problems. It is useful because students do not have to figure out from the setting whether to multiply or divide, but can arrange the factors so that the units cancel properly. It also allows you to write sentences like 7 feet = 84 inches, which would be incorrect without the units.

4-3

SPECIAL NUMBERS IN MULTIPLICATION

The four properties in this lesson are essential to the use of multiplication in expressions involving variables. Students have probably seen these properties already.

The reciprocal key on the calculator is introduced in this lesson. This will give you an opportunity to discuss when a calculator should be used and when it shouldn't. In general, if a number or its reciprocal is an integer or if the reciprocal is to be expressed as a fraction, the calculator isn't appropriate. When the number is in decimal form, the calculator is appropriate.

4-4

SOLVING $ax = b$

The Rate Model for Multiplication motivates the Multiplication Property of Equality, which is basic to solving $ax = b$. At this time, we solve these equations by multiplying by $1/a$. (Sentences like $\frac{3}{5}x = 9$ are most readily solved by multiplying by the reciprocal.) Later, in Chapter 6, students get a choice between multiplying by $1/a$ or dividing by a.

4-5

SPECIAL NUMBERS IN EQUATIONS

This lesson introduces students to some situations which have no solution and other situations which are identities and thus true for all real numbers. Students will continue to see some of these special situations occasionally. In Chapter 11, after discussing systems of equations involving parallel lines, an entire lesson is devoted to situations which either always or never happen.

The solving of $-x = b$ leads to the solving of $a - x = b$, our first two-step equation. Equations of the form $a - bx = c$ are studied in Chapter 6. You may wish to introduce some of them here, but we recommend that testing and teaching for mastery be delayed until Chapter 6.

4-6

SOLVING $ax < b$

In previous lessons students have worked with the Addition Property of Equality, the Addition Property of Inequality, and the Multiplication Property of Equality. Since neither of these properties distinguishes between positive and negative numbers, students may be surprised that the Multiplication Property of Inequality makes such a distinction. In particular, the second part of the Multiplication Property of Inequality is difficult for some students.

The special case of multiplying both sides of an inequality by -1 can be deduced directly from the Addition Property of Inequality, as below. (The Associative and Identity Properties of Addition are needed also, but not specifically mentioned here.)

Given $a < b$

Add $-a$ to each side.

$$-a + a < -a + b$$
$$0 < -a + b$$

Add $-b$ to each side.

$$0 + -b < -a + b + -b$$
$$-b < -a$$
$$-a > -b$$

4-7

THE MULTIPLICATION COUNTING PRINCIPLE

The Multiplication Counting Principle is often not taught until 11th or 12th grade, in connection with permutations and combinations. Because of its importance in mathematics and its applications, and since it is not a difficult topic, its discussion need not be delayed that long.

Although the Multiplication Counting Principle is quite easy to apply, it is not at all obvious to students. The pictures of arrays and the tree diagrams given in this lesson help to connect the idea of multiplication with the counting situations that are discussed.

In this lesson, the Multiplication Counting Principle is applied to those situations in which the number of ways available for a particular choice is unrelated to the number of ways available for a previous choice. In the next two lessons, a special case of the Multiplication Counting Principle is considered. In this special case, the number of ways available for a particular choice is one less than the number of ways available for the preceding choice.

The Multiplication Counting Principle is sometimes given the name "Fundamental Counting Principle." The name reflects its role as a powerful tool in counting problems.

4-8

MULTIPLYING PROBABILITIES

The concept of conditional probability is important in its own right. However, the reasons for placing this lesson at this point are (1) the Multiplication Counting Principle is reinforced and (2) multiplication of fractions is reviewed.

Conditional probability is discussed without using all the formal notation for it. The development is based on the conditional probability formula $P(A \cap B) = P(A) \cdot P(B|A)$. Instead of the vertical line $|$, we use the word *given*. Thus conditional probability appears as $P(A \cap B) = P(A) \cdot P(B \text{ given } A)$.

This conceptualization follows the reasoning commonly used to compute probabilities of compound events, and it works in all situations, whether or not events are independent. Two events A and B are independent if $P(B \text{ given } A) = P(B)$, that is, if the occurrence of A does not affect the probability of B. Thus, in independent events A and B, $P(A \cap B) = P(A) \cdot P(B)$.

4-9

THE FACTORIAL SYMBOL

The Permutation Theorem is a special case of the Multiplication Counting Principle, one that is limited in two senses. First, there is only one kind of situation or data being considered. Contrast this with Example 2 in Lesson 4-7, which had three situations: language class, music class, and art class. Second, once an element has been used, it cannot be used again. Contrast this with Example 3 in Lesson 4-7: if you answered "A" to multiple choice Question 1, you could still answer "A" to Question 2. The difference is that in factorial situations there is no *replacement*.

CHAPTER 4

This chapter should be covered in 12 to 15 days: 9 to 11 days for the lessons and quizzes; 1 day for the Progress Self-Test; 1 or 2 days for the Chapter Review; and 1 day for testing.

CHAPTER 4

Multiplication in Algebra

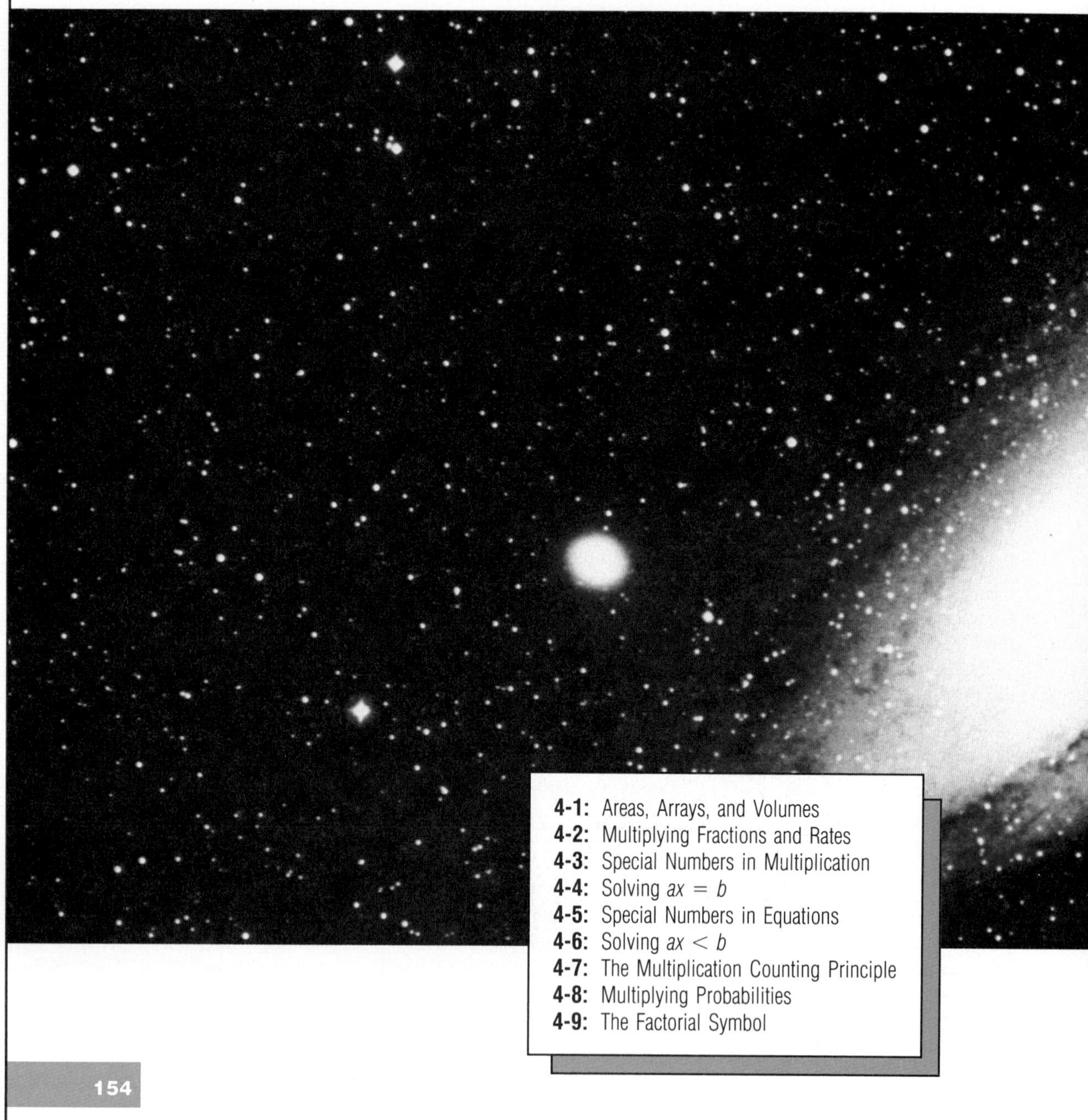

Our galaxy looks somewhat like the Andromeda Galaxy pictured here. Is there life on some other planet in our galaxy?

A formula for computing the number of planets N currently supporting intelligent life involves the product of seven numbers.

$$N = T \cdot P \cdot E \cdot L \cdot I \cdot C \cdot A$$

Of course you need to know what the letters in the formula represent. Here are their meanings and an estimated value for each. No one knows these values exactly.

T = *Total* number of stars in our galaxy.
P = fraction of stars with a *Planetary* system.
E = fraction of planetary systems with a planet that has an *Ecology* able to sustain life.
L = fraction of planets able to sustain life on which *Life* actually develops.
I = fraction of planets with life on which that life is *Intelligent*.
C = fraction of planets with intelligent life on which that life could *Communicate* outwardly.
A = fraction of planets with communicating life which is *Alive* now.

In *Space,* a novel by James Michener, these variables are given the values $T = 400{,}000{,}000{,}000$, $P = \frac{1}{4}$, $E = \frac{1}{2}$, $L = \frac{9}{10}$, $I = \frac{1}{10}$, $C = \frac{1}{3}$, and $A = \frac{1}{100{,}000{,}000}$. This yields a value of 15 for N. But people disagree on the values. Changing the values can change the value of N by a great deal. For instance if $P = \frac{1}{10}$ with the other values above, then $N = 6$ instead of 15. In this chapter, we discuss many other situations involving multiplication.

USING PAGES 154-155
The formula on page 155 is taken from James Michener's novel *Space*, a fictionalized account that is based on a forty-year period of American space exploration. The only operation expressed in the formula is multiplication.

Students might enjoy the following activity, which also uses only multiplication: By assigning values to the letters in the alphabet, say $A = 1$, $B = 2$, $C = 3$, etc, ask your students to determine the product of the letters in their name. For example, if your name is David, you would get a product of 3168. $(4 \cdot 1 \cdot 22 \cdot 9 \cdot 4 = 3168)$ See whose name gives the highest product.

LESSON 4-1

RESOURCES
- Lesson Master 4-1
- Visual for Teaching Aid 19: Diagrams from **Questions 6, 19, and 20**
- Visual for Teaching Aid 20: Diagrams for Additional Examples 1 and 3
- Computer Master 6

OBJECTIVES

F Identify and apply the Commutative and Associative Properties of Multiplication.
G Apply the Area Model for Multiplication.
K Solve sentences of the form $ax = b$ and $ax < b$ to answer questions from real situations.
L Use area, arrays, and volume to picture multiplication.

TEACHING NOTES

Alternate Approach
Some problems involving decomposition of regions into rectangles can be done by subtraction as well as by addition. Here is a different way to do **Example 1.**

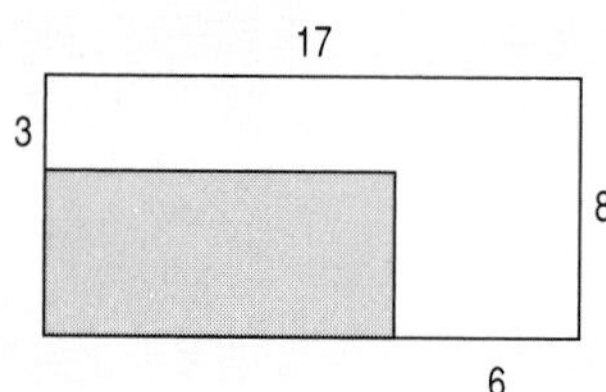

Area = 17 • 8 − 11 • 5
= 136 − 55 = 81

4-1 Areas, Arrays, and Volumes

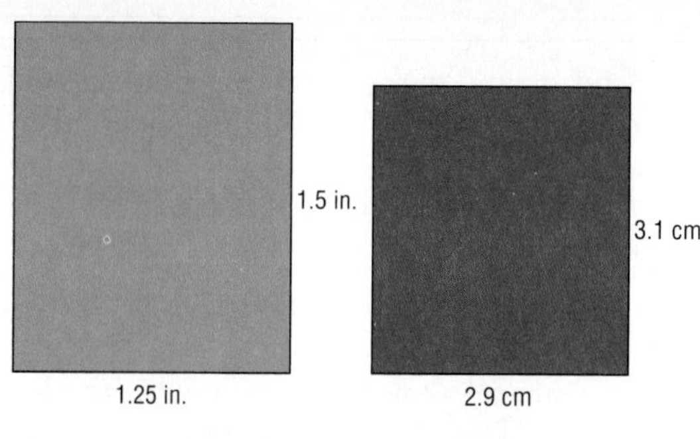

The operation of multiplication can be pictured using area. The area of any rectangle is the product of its two dimensions. The rectangles above are actual size.

Area = 1.25 in. · 1.5 in.	Area = 2.9 cm · 3.1 cm	Area = 6 cm · 0.5 cm
= 1.875 square in.	= 8.99 square cm	= 3 square cm
= 1.875 in.^{2}	= 8.99 cm^2	= 3 cm^2

The area is in square units because both the numbers and units are multiplied.

These examples are instances of a general pattern, the **area model for multiplication.** This model applies only to positive real numbers since the dimensions of a rectangle are lengths.

Area Model for Multiplication:

The area of a rectangle with length ℓ and width w is ℓw.

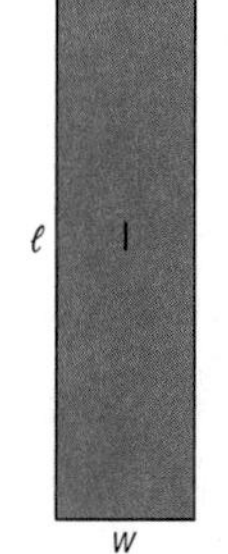

Area = ℓw

Rectangle I at the left has been rotated to give rectangle II. The two rectangles have the same dimensions. They must have the same area. So the area formula could be written $A = wl$ as well as $A = lw$.

In this way, the area model pictures the **Commutative Property of Multiplication,** which holds for all real numbers.

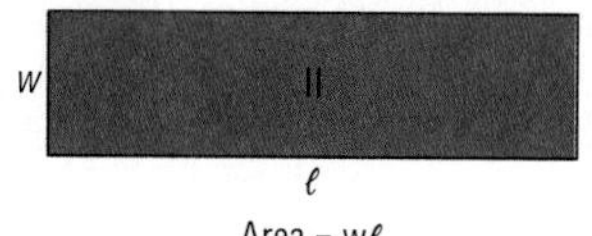

Area = $w\ell$

Commutative Property of Multiplication:

For any real numbers a and b,
$ab = ba$.

By combining the area model with models for addition and subtraction, areas of some regions which are not rectangles can be determined.

Example 1 A driveway to a house has the shape at the right. All angles are right angles. Find the area of the driveway.

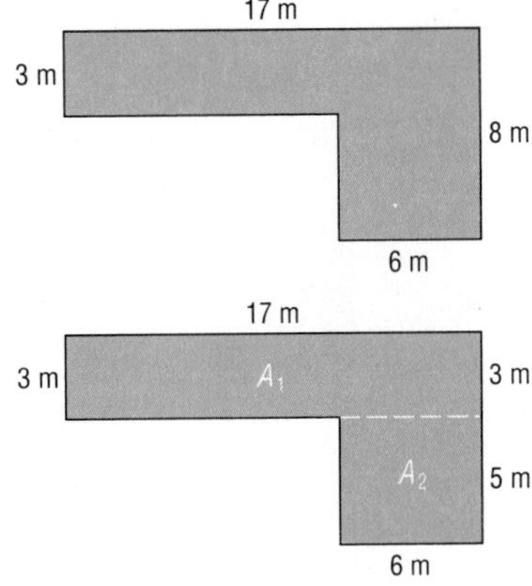

Solution There is no simple formula for an irregular shape like this. But the shape can be split into two rectangles. One way to split the figure is shown at right. This splits the right side into lengths of 3 m and 5 m.

Call the smaller areas A_1 and A_2. The top rectangle has dimensions 3 m and 17 m, so $A_1 = 51\text{ m}^2$. Also, $A_2 = 5\text{ m} \cdot 6\text{ m}$ or 30 m^2. Putting the areas together,

$$\begin{aligned}\text{Area of driveway} &= A_1 + A_2 \\ &= 51\text{ m}^2 + 30\text{ m}^2 \\ &= 81\text{ m}^2\end{aligned}$$

The stars below form a **rectangular array** with 5 rows and 9 columns. It is called a 5-by-9 array. The numbers 5 and 9 are the **dimensions** of the array. The area model of multiplication applies to rectangular arrays. The total number of stars is 45, the product of the dimensions. The graph is discrete.

Area Model (discrete version):

The number of elements in a rectangular array with x rows and y columns is xy.

Here is another illustration of the Commutative Property of Multiplication. Imagine the stars in the array following **Example 1** are boxes. If you think of them as stacks of boxes, there would be 9 stacks with 6 boxes in each. If you turn the array 90°, then you would say that there are 6 stacks with 9 boxes in each. Either way, there are 54 boxes.

ADDITIONAL EXAMPLES

1. Find the area. (There are at least 3 ways to do this problem. Ask students for suggestions.)

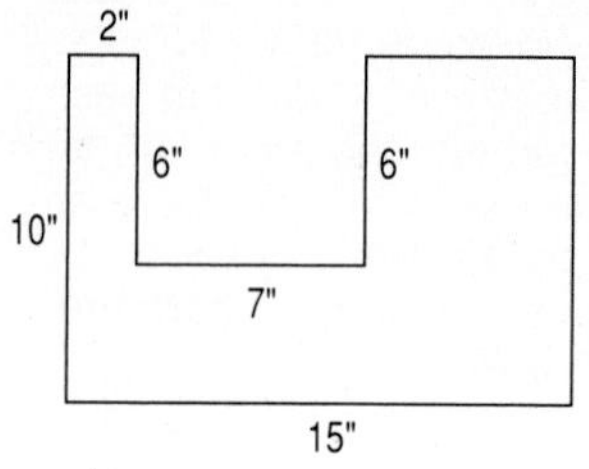

108 sq in.

2. The Stuart Soup Company packs soup cans in cartons that measure 40 cm wide, 48 cm long, and 20 cm tall. How many cans will fit in one carton if each can has a diameter of 8 cm and is 10 cm in height?
60

3. What is the area of this figure? (You can also ask for the perimeter. It is $16x + 2y + 8$.)

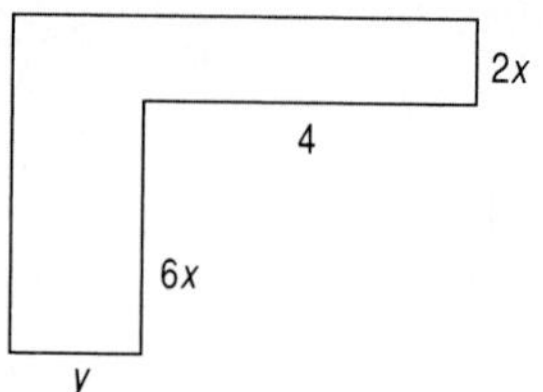

$(8x + 8xy)$ sq. units

The area model can be extended to three-dimensional figures. The **volume** of a **rectangular solid** or **box** is the product of its three dimensions.

$$\text{Volume} = \text{length} \cdot \text{width} \cdot \text{height}$$
$$V = lwh$$

Example 2 Find the volume of the rectangular solid at the left.

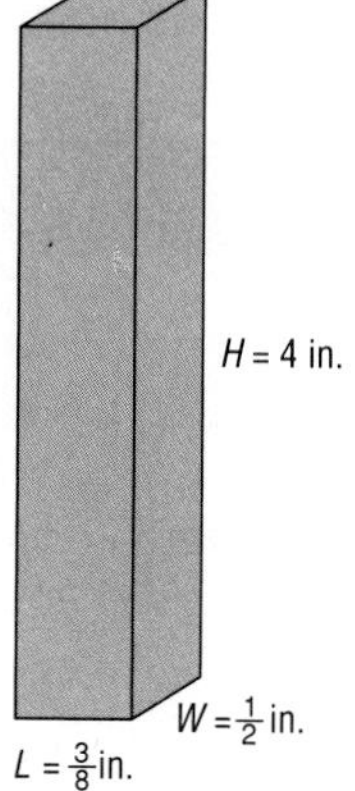

Solution $V = \ell wh$
$= \frac{3}{8} \text{ in.} \cdot \frac{1}{2} \text{ in.} \cdot 4 \text{ in.}$

Recall that the product of fractions is the product of the numerators divided by the product of the denominators. So

$$V = \frac{3}{16} \text{ in.}^2 \cdot 4 \text{ in.}$$
$$= \frac{12}{16} \text{ in.}^3$$
$$= \frac{3}{4} \text{ in.}^3.$$

(Volume is measured in cubic units; in.^{3} means cubic inches.)

Check Rewrite the dimensions as decimals.

$$\frac{3}{8} \cdot \frac{1}{2} \cdot 4 = .375 \cdot 0.5 \cdot 4$$
$$= .1875 \cdot 4$$
$$= .75$$

Since $\frac{3}{4} = .75$, the answer checks.

In Example 2, you may have noticed that you did not have to follow order of operations and multiply from left to right. You could first multiply $\frac{1}{2}$ in. by 4 in. This gives 2 in.^{2}, which is easy to multiply by $\frac{3}{8}$ in. This illustrates that

$$(l \cdot w) \cdot h = l \cdot (w \cdot h).$$
Doing left multiplication first = Doing right multiplication first

The general property, true for all numbers, is called the **Associative Property of Multiplication.**

Associative Property of Multiplication:

For any real numbers a, b, and c,
$(ab)c = a(bc)$.

Since lw is the area of the base, you may see the volume formula expressed as B, the area of the base, times the height.

$$V = Bh$$

Example 3 What is the volume of a box in which the height is $4x$ and the area of the base is $5x^2$?

Solution

Volume = Area of base · height

$V = (5x^2)4x$

$= 4(5x^2)x$ Commutative Property of Multiplication

$= (4 \cdot 5)(x^2 \cdot x)$ Associative Property

$= 20x^3$ $x^2 \cdot x = x^3$

The volume of the box is $20x^3$.

Check Let $x = 2$. Use the volume formula, $V = Bh$. If $x = 2$, the height is 8 and the area of the base is 20, so the volume is 160. Now evaluate the answer $20x^3$.

$$20x^3 = 20 \cdot 2^3 = 20 \cdot 8 = 160, \text{ which checks.}$$

When units are not given, as in Example 3, you can assume they are the same—all inches, all centimeters, or all something else. Otherwise, you should be careful to make sure units are the same before multiplying.

Questions

Covering the Reading

1. State the area model for multiplication. **See margin.**

2. $lw = wl$ is an instance of what property of multiplication? **See margin.**

3. If the length and width of a rectangle are measured in inches, the area is measured in what unit? **square inches**

In 4 and 5, find the area of a rectangle with the given dimensions.

4. length 7.2 cm and width 4.3 cm **30.96 cm²**

5. length 8 in. and width y in. **$8y$ in.²**

6. In the figure at the right, all angles are right angles. Find its area. **188 square units**

22
6
13
8

7. Compute the number of dots in a rectangular array containing 48 rows and 83 columns. **3984**

In 8–10, find the volume of the rectangular solid in which:

8. the dimensions are $\frac{1}{4}$ ft by $\frac{2}{3}$ ft by $\frac{1}{8}$ ft. **$\frac{1}{48}$ cubic ft**

9. the length is 3, width is $7x$, height is y. **$21xy$ cubic units**

10. the area of the base is $9p^2$ and the height is $12p$. **$108p^3$ cubic units**

NOTES ON QUESTIONS

Question 6: There are several ways to get the answer. Elicit these from your students and then ask which one they prefer.

Questions 6, 9, and 10: Units are specified in the answers. In **Question 6,** the answer 188 is correct. We have listed the answer as 188 square units to emphasize the difference between linear measure and area measure. Encourage your students to specify the generic "units" when measures are not specified.

ADDITIONAL ANSWERS

1. The area of a rectangle with length *L* and width *W* is *LW*.

2. Commutative Property of Multiplication

NOTES ON QUESTIONS
Question 16: Encourage students to draw a diagram in answering this question.

Making Connections for Questions 17 and 18: Here, the Area Model is used to give a representation of multiplication of fractions. Although discussion will take time, it will prepare students for reading the next lesson on multiplication of fractions. You may want to give some additional examples which are similar to **Questions 17 and 18.** Point out that when multiplying with fractions between 0 and 1, the product will be smaller than the factors, for example, $\frac{1}{2} \cdot \frac{1}{2} = \frac{1}{4}$. Some students think that the result of a multiplication must be a number larger than the factors.

Question 21: Here, compliment students for creative thinking if they give dimensions that are not integers.

Question 29: This situation can also be described using a ± sign.

Making Connections for Question 30: This question gives practice in multiplying signed numbers, a topic justified in the next lesson.

18.

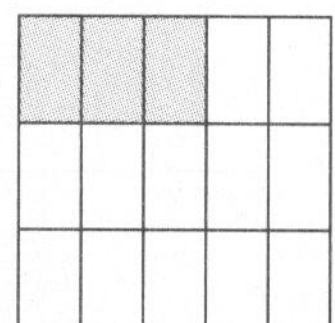

21. samples: 3 by 4 by 7, 2 by 6 by 7, 14 by 2 by 3, 28 by 1 by 3, $\frac{1}{2}$ by $\frac{1}{2}$ by 336

28a. If Carl runs *d* miles, then *d* > 3.

28b.

29a. If *p* pounds of meat are eaten, then 17 ≤ *p* ≤ 23.

29b.

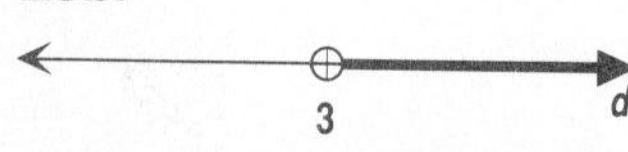

Applying the Mathematics

11. How many square tiles, each one foot on a side, are needed to cover an area $9a$ feet by $5b$ feet? **45ab**

12. The O'Leary's garden is a rectangle 45 ft by 60 ft.
 a. What is the area of their garden? **2700 sq ft**
 b. If they put a fence around the garden, how long will the fence be? **210 ft**

13.

Write an expression for the area of the rectangle at the left. ***kn***
Write an expression for its perimeter. **2*k* + 2*n***

14. How many cubic inches are in a box 5 inches wide, 1 foot long, and 3 inches high? **180 in.^{3}**

15. What is the volume of a rectangular solid in which the length is $6x$ cm, the width is $2x$ cm, and the height is x cm? **$12x^3$cm^3**

16. What is the volume of a rectangular solid in which the width and height have the same measurement z and the length is twice that measurement? **$2z^3$ cubic units**

In 17 and 18, use the following information. Area can be used to picture multiplication with fractions. The sides of the square below are 1 unit long. To picture $\frac{3}{4} \cdot \frac{2}{3}$, one side is divided into fourths, an adjacent side into thirds. Each of the small rectangles is $\frac{1}{12}$ the area of the square.

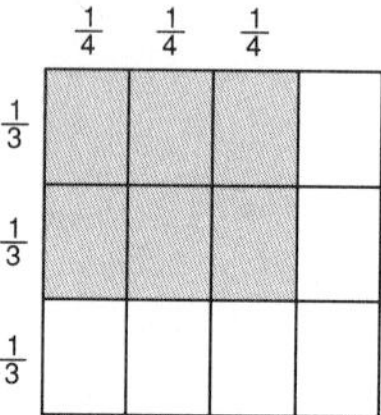

At the left, the rectangle with dimensions $\frac{3}{4}$ and $\frac{2}{3}$ is colored. The area of the colored part is $\frac{6}{12}$ of the total area since 6 small rectangles are colored. Since $A = lw$, $A = \frac{3}{4} \cdot \frac{2}{3}$ = colored area = $\frac{6}{12}$. The fraction $\frac{6}{12}$ can be reduced to $\frac{1}{2}$.

17. a. What multiplication problem is pictured? **$\frac{1}{2}$ in. · $\frac{3}{4}$ in.**
 b. What fraction of the square is colored? **$\frac{3}{8}$**
 c. The picture shows $\frac{1}{2} \cdot \frac{3}{4}$ = ? **$\frac{3}{8}$**

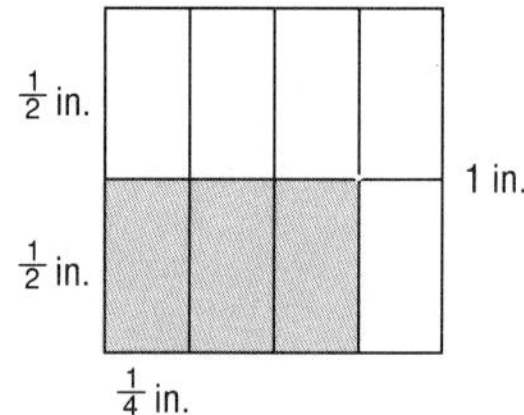

18. Draw a one-inch square. Divide one side into fifths and an adjoining side into thirds. Color the drawing to represent $\frac{1}{3} \cdot \frac{3}{5}$. **See margin.**

19. Find the area of the figure below. All angles are right angles. The unit is meters. **576 m^2**

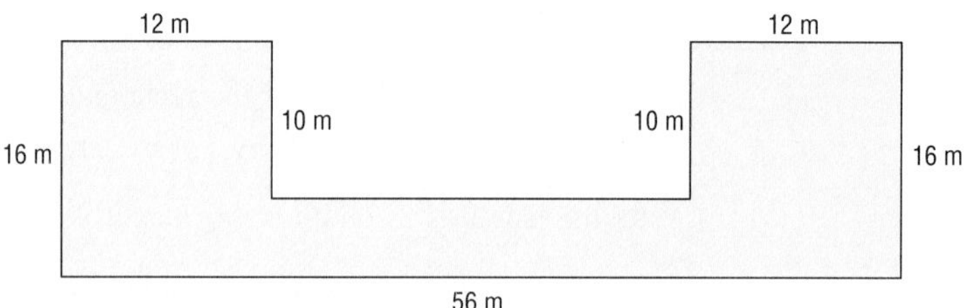

160

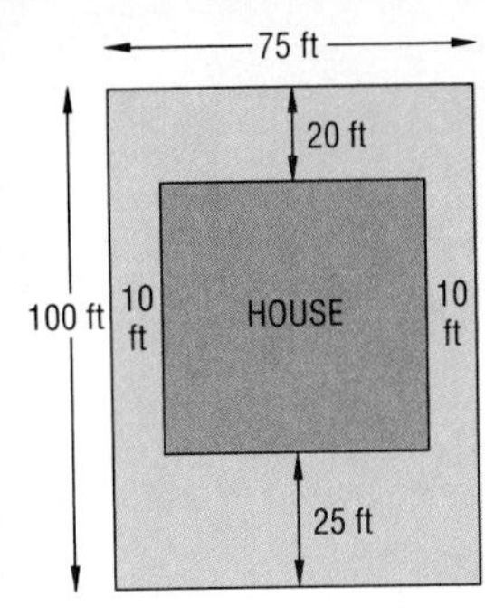

20. A single-story house is to be built on a lot 75 feet wide by 100 feet deep. The shorter side of the lot faces the street. The house must be set back from the street 25 feet. It must be 20 feet from the back lot line, and 10 feet from each side lot line. What is the maximum square footage (area) the house can have? **3025 sq ft**

21. The volume of the rectangular solid at the right is 84. Give four different sets of dimensions the box might have. **See margin.**

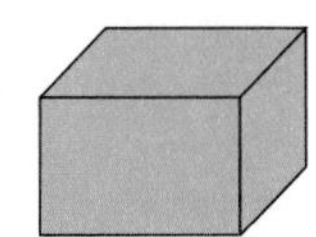

In 22 and 23, use the associative and commutative properties to do the multiplication in your head.

22. $25 \cdot x \cdot 4 \cdot 34$ **3400x** **23.** $(2 \cdot 3x)(8x \cdot 5)$ **240x²**

Review

24. Which property tells you that $(x + -3) + 3 = x + (-3 + 3)$? *(Lesson 2-1)* **Associative Property of Addition**

In 25–27, evaluate each expression when $a = 7$, $b = 5$, $x = 4.7$, and $y = 2.3$.

25. $3(x + y) - 2(a - b)$ *(Lesson 1-4)* **17**

26. $\dfrac{5(4b - 2a)}{b^2}$ *(Lesson 1-4)* **$\frac{6}{5}$ or 1.2**

27. ab^2 *(Lesson 1-4)* **175**

28. Carl runs more than three miles every morning.
 a. Write an inequality to describe this situation. **See margin.**
 b. Graph on a number line. *(Lesson 1-1)* **See margin.**

29. A caterer estimates that 20 lb of meat will be eaten. She is within 3 lb of the actual amount used. **See margin.**
 a. Write an inequality showing the actual amount possibly eaten.
 b. Graph on a number line. *(Lessons 1-1, 3-9)* **See margin.**

30. Compute in your head. *(Previous course)*
 a. $-2 \cdot -\frac{1}{2}$ **1** **b.** $3 \cdot -5 \cdot -0.1$ **1.5** **c.** $-2 \cdot 8.5$ **-17**

Exploration

31. You can make a box by cutting out square corners from a rectangular piece of paper. **a) See student's work.**
 a. Begin with a piece of $8\frac{1}{2}''$ by $11''$ notebook paper. Cut a $1''$ square from each corner. Fold to make a box and use tape to hold it.
 b. What is the volume of the box you have made? **58.5 in.³**
 c. Estimate the size of the square you should cut out from each corner to make the box with largest volume. (Use trial and error.) **≈1.6 in.**

FOLLOW-UP

MORE PRACTICE
For more practice on SPUR Objectives, use *Lesson Master 4-1,* shown below.

EXTENSION
You can illustrate how to compute with monomials by using the area and volume models. For instance, the diagram below illustrates that $2x \cdot 4x = 8x^2$. The figure shows the area is made up of eight squares, each one having an area of x^2.

	x	x	x	x	
x	x^2	x^2	x^2	x^2	2x
x	x^2	x^2	x^2	x^2	
		4x			

NAME ____________

LESSON **MASTER 4–1**
QUESTIONS ON **SPUR** OBJECTIVES

■PROPERTIES *Objective F (See pages 204–207 for objectives.)*
In 1–4, identify what property of multiplication is given.

1. $a(bc) = (bc)a$ **Commutative** 2. $2 \cdot 3h = 6h$ **Associative**
3. $k(x + y) = (x + y)k$ **Commutative** 4. $4(25 \cdot 3) = (4 \cdot 25)3$ **Associative**

In 5–8, simplify.

5. $3x \cdot 4y$ **12xy** 6. $am \cdot an$ **a^2mn**
7. $2ab \cdot 3bc \cdot 4ac$ **$24a^2b^2c^2$** 8. $\frac{1}{2}a \cdot \frac{2}{3}b$ **$\frac{1}{3}ab$**

■USES *Objective G*
9. Find the area of a walk 3 ft wide around a rectangular pool 27 ft by 32 ft. **390 square feet**
10. Find the area of the shaded part. **78 square units**
11. How many trees are in the orchard around the barn? **31 trees**

■USES *Objective K*
12. A calculator comes in a box 2 cm × 8 cm × 10 cm. How many calculators can be shipped in a box 30 cm × 48 cm × 60 cm? **540 calculators**
13. A standard room is 10 ft high. What does the area of the floor have to be for the volume to be 7200 cubic feet? **720 square feet**

■REPRESENTATIONS *Objective L*
In 14 and 15, the squares have length 1. What multiplication of fractions does each drawing represent, and what is the area of the shaded part?

14. 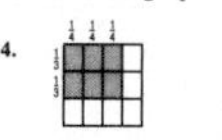 $\frac{2}{3} \cdot \frac{3}{4}$; $\frac{1}{2}$

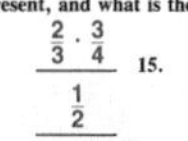

15. 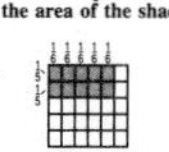 $\frac{2}{5} \cdot \frac{5}{6}$; $\frac{1}{3}$

 27

LESSON 4-2

RESOURCES

- Lesson Master 4-2
- Visual for Teaching Aid 21: Model for Multiplying Fractions

OBJECTIVES

A Multiply fractions.
G Apply the Rate Factor Model for Multiplication.
K Solve sentences of the form $ax = b$ and $ax < b$ to answer questions from real situations.

TEACHING NOTES

Discuss the multiplication problems that correspond to the other three quadrants of the array of stars on page 162. *Teaching Aid 21* may be used. Generalize to the rule for multiplying fractions.

Questions like that in **Example 3** can be solved as proportions, but that is not the intention here. Not only is the rate method efficient, but it works easily in problems involving more than two factors, as demonstrated in **Example 4.** Require students to use this model, where it is appropriate, in completing the exercises.

LESSON

Multiplying Fractions and Rates

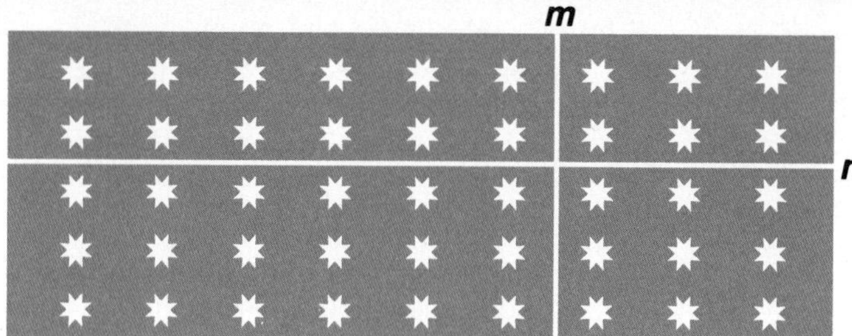

In the array above, $\frac{6}{9}$ of the stars are to the left of line m. Also, $\frac{2}{5}$ of the stars are above the horizontal line n. What fraction of the stars are both to the left of m and above n?

There are $6 \cdot 2$ or 12 stars both left and above. There are $9 \cdot 5$ or 45 stars in all. So $\frac{12}{45}$ of the stars are to the left and above. Another way of answering this question is by multiplying $\frac{6}{9} \cdot \frac{2}{5}$ in the familiar way.

$$\frac{6}{9} \cdot \frac{2}{5} = \frac{6 \cdot 2}{9 \cdot 5} = \frac{12}{45}$$

The general pattern is very easy to describe with variables.

Rule for Multiplication of Fractions:

For all real numbers a, b, c, and d, with b and d not zero,

$$\frac{a}{b} \cdot \frac{c}{d} = \frac{ac}{bd}.$$

Example 1 Multiply $\frac{3}{4}$ by $\frac{14x}{15}$.

Solution 1 $\frac{3}{4} \cdot \frac{14x}{15} = \frac{3 \cdot 14x}{4 \cdot 15} = \frac{42x}{60}$

Since 6 is a common factor of the numerator and denominator, the answer can be simplified using the Equal Fractions Property.

$$= \frac{6 \cdot 7x}{6 \cdot 10}$$

$$= \frac{7x}{10}$$

Solution 2 Take out the common factors 2 and 3 before multiplying.

$$\frac{\overset{1}{\cancel{3}}}{\underset{2}{\cancel{4}}} \cdot \frac{\overset{7}{\cancel{14}}x}{\underset{5}{\cancel{15}}} = \frac{7x}{10}$$

162

Example 2 Simplify $\frac{2}{5y} \cdot 10y$.

Solution

$$\frac{2}{5y} \cdot \frac{10y}{1} = \frac{2}{\cancel{5y}_{1\cdot 1}} \cdot \frac{\cancel{10y}^{2\cdot 1}}{1}$$

$$= 4$$

Fraction forms often appear in situations involving rates. Rate units can be expressed using a slash "/" or horizontal bar "—." The slash or bar is read "per."

rate	with a slash	with a bar
99 cents per pound	99 cents/lb	$99 \frac{\text{cents}}{\text{lb}}$
80 kilometers per hour	80 km/hr	$80 \frac{\text{km}}{\text{hr}}$
W words per minute	*W* words/min	$W \frac{\text{words}}{\text{min}}$

Rates can be multiplied by other quantities. The units are treated as if they were factors in a multiplication.

Example 3 An airplane flies 380 miles each hour. How far will it have flown in 12 hours?

Solution Write the rate of travel as

$$380 \frac{\text{miles}}{\text{hour}}.$$

Multiply by the number of hours. The "hours" unit on the left cancels the "hour" in the denominator.

$$12 \cancel{\text{hours}} \cdot 380 \frac{\text{miles}}{\cancel{\text{hour}}} = 4560 \text{ miles}$$

Two or more rates may be multiplied. The units are treated like numbers in fractions.

Example 4 Each week a student must study 4 grammar lessons. There are 3 pages per lesson. The student spends 20 minutes per page. How many minutes does she spend studying grammar each week?

Solution Think rates: 3 pages per lesson, 20 minutes per page.

$$4 \cancel{\text{lessons}} \cdot 3 \frac{\cancel{\text{pages}}}{\cancel{\text{lessons}}} \cdot 20 \frac{\text{min}}{\cancel{\text{page}}} = 240 \text{ minutes}$$

In **Example 5** you should discuss the relationship of 12 pages/minute to 1/12 minute/page. Point out that the choice of which of these reciprocal rates to use was made by seeing which units would cancel. Discuss the meaning of reciprocals of common rates such as miles per hour, revolutions per minute, dollars per hour (wages), or dollars per gallon of gasoline.

Notice the use of the word *cancel* in **Example 5.** This is the term commonly used with rates in science, so we use it here. However, with numbers we use the Equal Fractions Property, as in Lesson 1-8, and avoid the word *cancel*, which causes confusion for some students.

ADDITIONAL EXAMPLES

1. Multiply $\frac{8}{x} \cdot \frac{3x}{10}$.

$\mathbf{\frac{12}{5}}$

2. Multiply $16n$ by $5a$.

80*an*

3. It takes Rob 20 minutes to walk one mile. At this rate, how long does it take him to walk 7 miles?

140 minutes or 2 hours and 20 minutes

4. In 1962, Wilt Chamberlain set an NBA season scoring record, averaging 50.4 points per game. On the average, how many points did he score per minute? (There are 48 minutes in a basketball game.)

1.05 $\frac{\text{points}}{\text{minute}}$

5. A football field is 120 yards long from goal post to goal post. How many football fields make a mile? (There are 5280 feet in 1 mile.)

$14.\overline{6} \approx 14.7$ football fields

The general idea behind these situations is a second model for multiplication, the **rate factor model.**

Rate Factor Model for Multiplication:

When a rate is multiplied by another quantity, the unit of the product is the product of units. Units are multiplied as though they were fractions. The product has meaning when the units have meaning.

The rate factor model can be applied to both positive and negative rates. Suppose a farmer's topsoil is eroding at a rate of 0.5 inch per year. The rate of change is

$$-0.5\ \frac{\text{inch}}{\text{year}}.$$

If erosion continues at this rate for 20 years, multiplying gives the total loss.

$$20\ \cancel{\text{years}} \cdot -0.5\ \frac{\text{inch}}{\cancel{\text{year}}} = -10 \text{ inches}$$

The final answer is negative, which means that 10 inches of topsoil will be *lost* over the twenty years.

This instance confirms the rules for multiplication of positive and negative numbers.

If two numbers have the same + or − sign, their product is positive. If two numbers have different signs, their product is negative.

Sometimes a given rate does not fit into the rate factor model, but its reciprocal does. For example, if a computer printer prints 12 pages in 1 minute, then it takes $\frac{1}{12}$ minute to print 1 page. The two rates $\frac{1}{12}\ \frac{\text{min}}{\text{page}}$ and $12\ \frac{\text{pages}}{\text{min}}$ are *reciprocal rates*, each describing the same situation from a different point of view. Reciprocals do not usually equal each other, but reciprocal *rates* are equal quantities.

164

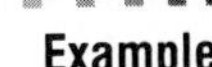

Example 5 A computer prints at the rate of 12 pages/min. How long will it take to print 2400 documents with 3 pages per document?

Solution There are two rates: 12 pages/min and 3 pages/document. Write the product.

$$2400\ \cancel{\text{doc}} \cdot 3\ \frac{\text{pages}}{\cancel{\text{doc}}} \cdot 12\ \frac{\text{pages}}{\text{min}}$$

The document units cancel but pages and min do not cancel. So use the reciprocal rate to rewrite $12\ \frac{\text{pages}}{\text{min}}$ as $\frac{1}{12}\ \frac{\text{min}}{\text{page}}$.

$$2400\ \cancel{\text{doc}} \cdot 3\ \frac{\cancel{\text{pages}}}{\cancel{\text{doc}}} \cdot \frac{1}{12}\ \frac{\text{min}}{\cancel{\text{pages}}} = 600 \text{ minutes}$$

It will take 600 minutes to print the documents.

Questions

Covering the Reading

1. What fraction of the dots are above the horizontal line ℓ and to the right of the vertical line m? **$\frac{10}{33}$**

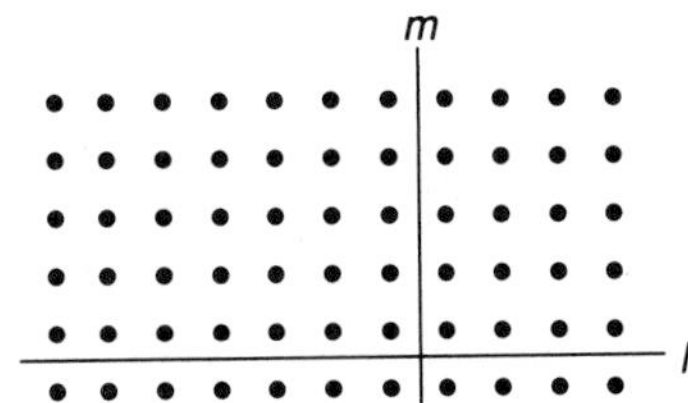

2. Multiply. **a.** $\frac{5}{x} \cdot \frac{3}{2}$ **b.** $\frac{a}{b} \cdot \frac{m}{n}$ **a) $\frac{15}{2x}$; b) $\frac{am}{bn}$**

In 3–5, compute.

3. $\frac{3m}{n} \cdot \frac{7m}{9}$ **$\frac{7m^2}{3n}$**

4. $\frac{3}{8} \cdot 32z$ **12z**

5. $81 \cdot \frac{2k}{27}$ **6k**

6. *Multiple choice* Which is not equal to the others? **(c)**

(a) $\frac{20}{11} \cdot r$ (b) $\frac{20r}{11}$ (c) $\frac{20}{11r}$ (d) $\frac{r}{11} \cdot 20$

In 7 and 8, **a.** copy the sentence and underline the rate; **b.** use a slash to write the rate unit; **c.** use a fraction bar to write the rate unit.

7. A typist types 70 words per minute. **See margin.**

8. Roast beef costs $2.99 a pound. **See margin.**

9. Joanne runs 5.85 miles each hour. At the same rate, how far will she run in 3 hours? **17.55 miles**

10. Each week Myron must study k grammar lessons. There are 4 pages per lesson. He spends 30 minutes per page. How many minutes does he spend studying grammar each week? **120k**

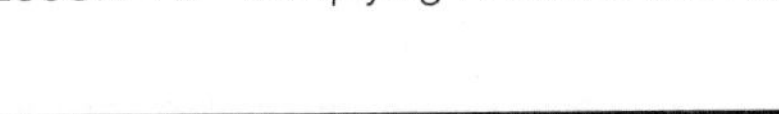

ADDITIONAL ANSWERS

7a. A typist types 70 words per minute.

7b. 70 words/minute

7c. 70 $\frac{\text{words}}{\text{minute}}$

8a. Roast beef costs $2.99 per pound.

8b. 2.99 dollars/pound

8c. 2.99 $\frac{\text{dollars}}{\text{pound}}$

NOTES ON QUESTIONS
Questions 14 and 15: To decide what form of a rate to use in these questions, students need to look at the units specified for the answer. For example, in **Question 14,** they want shrimp/dollar. Therefore 6 dollars/pound must be rewritten as $\frac{1}{6}$ lb/dollar.

Question 21: The birth rate of 15.5 babies per 1000 population is typical of the way that demographic statistics are expressed. One way of setting up this problem is to treat the USA population as 226,000 thousand people.

Making Connections for Question 24: Here, we begin examining situations that fit the pattern $y = mx + b$. In these settings, there is a beginning quantity (corresponding to the y-intercept) that changes at a constant rate (the slope). We include this kind of problem often as a lead-up to Chapter 8.

Question 27: Point out that the answer from the multiplication matches the answer found by counting the smaller rectangles.

Question 29: You may wish to use a physical model of a cylinder to explain the surface area of a cylinder.

14b. sample: Shrimp costs 6 dollars per pound. If there are 30 shrimp per pound, how many shrimp can you get for a dollar?

15b. A printer is printing 15-page documents at the rate of 1/2 page per minute. How many minutes will it take to print each document?

11. **a.** A farmer's topsoil is eroding at a rate of 0.3 inches per year. What is the total change after 5 years ? -1.5 inches
b. $5 \cdot -0.3 =$ ______

12. *Multiple choice* What is the reciprocal rate of $40 \frac{\text{miles}}{\text{gallon}}$? (b)
(a) $40 \frac{\text{gallons}}{\text{mile}}$ (b) $\frac{1}{40} \frac{\text{gallon}}{\text{mile}}$ (c) $\frac{1}{40} \frac{\text{mile}}{\text{gallon}}$

13. Which choice of Question 12 is a quantity equal to $40 \frac{\text{miles}}{\text{gallon}}$? (b)

In 14 and 15, **a.** use the reciprocal of the rates to do the multiplication; **b.** invent a situation for which the multiplication would be appropriate.

14. $6 \frac{\text{dollars}}{\text{lb}} \cdot 30 \frac{\text{shrimp}}{\text{lb}} = \_\_\_\_\_\_ \frac{\text{shrimp}}{\text{dollar}}$ a) 5; b) See margin.

15. $15 \frac{\text{pages}}{\text{doc}} \cdot \frac{1}{2} \frac{\text{page}}{\text{min}} = \_\_\_\_\_\_ \frac{\text{min}}{\text{doc}}$ a) 30; b) See margin.

16. Suppose a laser printer prints 5 pages per minute. How long will it take to print 2400 documents with 3 pages per document?
1440 min or 24 hr

Applying the Mathematics

17. Multiply $\frac{8b}{7c} \cdot \frac{21a}{2x} \cdot 5c$. $\frac{60ab}{x}$

18. While Phyllis exercises, her heart rate is 150 beats per minute. If she exercises for m minutes at this rate, how many times will her heart beat? $150m$ beats

19. There are 16 bottles per case. There are 8 ounces of liquid per bottle.
a. How many ounces are in 12 cases? 1536 oz
b. How many ounces are in c cases? $128c$ oz

20. **a.** Find the rent for two years on an apartment which rents for $595 per month. $14,280
b. Find the rent for y years on this apartment. $7140y$ dollars

21. In 1983, the U.S. birth rate was 15.5 babies per 1000 population. The population was 226,000,000. Use this multiplication,

$$15.5 \frac{\text{babies}}{1000 \text{ people}} \cdot 226{,}000{,}000 \text{ people},$$

to determine how many babies were born in 1983. 3,503,000 babies

22. Marty can wash k dishes per minute. His sister Sue is twice as fast.
a. How many dishes does Sue wash per minute? $2k \frac{\text{dishes}}{\text{minute}}$
b. How many minutes does Sue spend per dish? $\frac{1}{2k} \frac{\text{minutes}}{\text{dish}}$

23. As a magician at a birthday party, Kelly charges D dollars per party. If he performed at s parties, how much did he earn altogether?
Ds dollars

24. Pat adds K dollars to her bank account each week.
a. How much has she added after 20 weeks? $20K$ dollars
b. If she started with $150 in her account, write an expression for the amount she has after 20 weeks. $150 + 20K$ dollars

25. A sky diver "free falls" at about 120 mi/hr which is 176 ft/sec. How many seconds does it take the diver to "free fall" 2000 ft?
≈11.4 sec

Review

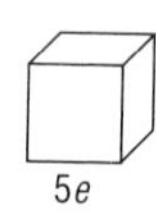

26. Write an expression for the volume of a cube having edges of length $5e$. *(Lesson 4-1)*
$125e^3$ cubic units

$\frac{1}{4}$"　$\frac{1}{6}$"　1"

27. What is the area of the colored portion of the figure at the left? Write your answer as a reduced fraction. *(Lesson 4-1)* **$\frac{1}{2}$ in.^{2}**

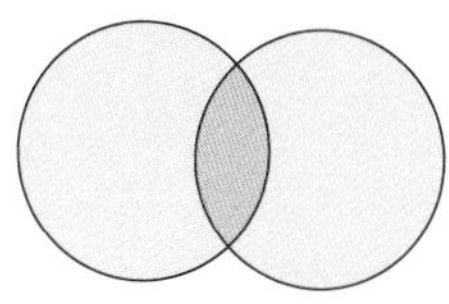

28. Thirty-seven people attended the Spanish Club picnic. Twenty-one people ate hamburgers and twenty-eight ate hot dogs. If everyone ate either hamburgers or hot dogs, how many people ate both? *(Lesson 3-6)* **12**

29. What is the output from line 60 of the program below if 5, 12 is input in line 30? *(Lesson 1-4)* **5　12　534.072**

```
10 PRINT "TOTAL SURFACE AREA OF A CYLINDER"
20 PRINT "GIVE RADIUS AND HEIGHT"
30 INPUT R, H
40 LET A = 2 * 3.1416 * R * R + 2 * 3.1416 * R * H
50 PRINT "RADIUS", "HEIGHT", "AREA"
60 PRINT R, H, A
70 END
```

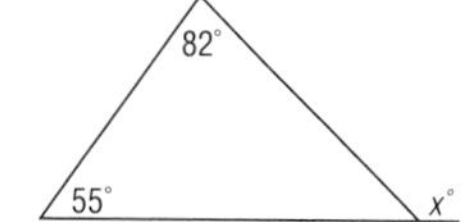

30. Use the triangle at the right. Find x. *(Lessons 2-6, 3-8)* **137°**

31. *Skill sequence*　*True or false* *(Lesson 1-6)*
   a. $4x = 18$ if $x = 4.5$ **True**
   b. $-9y = 42$ if $y = -\frac{14}{3}$ **True**
   c. $\frac{4}{5}z = -96$ if $z = 120$ **False**

32. Compute in your head using the associative and commutative properties of multiplication. *(Lesson 4-1)*
   a. $2 \cdot 7 \cdot 4 \cdot 5$ **280** **b.** $\frac{1}{2} \cdot \frac{3}{4} \cdot \frac{2}{3}$ **$\frac{1}{4}$** **c.** $2.5 \cdot 6 \cdot 2$ **30**

Exploration

33. The abbreviation mph stands for the rate unit "miles per hour." For what rate does each of these abbreviations stand?
   a. mpg **b.** rpm **c.** psi
   a) miles per gallon; b) revolutions per minute; c) pounds per square inch

FOLLOW-UP

MORE PRACTICE

For more practice on SPUR Objectives, use *Lesson Master 4-2,* shown below.

NAME ______

LESSON **MASTER 4–2**
QUESTIONS ON **SPUR** OBJECTIVES

■**SKILLS** *Objective A (See pages 204–207 for objectives.)*
In 1–8, multiply.

1. $\frac{5}{8x} \cdot \frac{2x}{3}$ **$\frac{5}{12}$**
2. $\frac{4ab}{9} \cdot \frac{3}{5a}$ **$\frac{4b}{15}$**
3. $\frac{ax}{3} \cdot \frac{2}{ay}$ **$\frac{2x}{3y}$**
4. $3\frac{1}{3} \cdot 1\frac{1}{5}$ **4**
5. $\frac{7m}{12} \cdot \frac{3n}{4m} \cdot \frac{1}{7n}$ **$\frac{1}{16}$**
6. $42g \cdot \frac{3}{7}$ **18g**
7. $\frac{24}{11k} \cdot \frac{22r}{9} \cdot \frac{3k}{8}$ **2r**
8. $\frac{8p}{15} \cdot 45$ **24p**

■**USES** *Objective G*

9. In 1984 in the U.S., there were 22.8 motor vehicle deaths per 100,000 population. How many motor vehicle deaths would you then expect in a U.S. city of 3.5 million people? **798 deaths**

10. A baseball player's batting average (hits/times at bat) is .300. At that rate, how many times at bat would the player need to get 120 hits? **400 hits**

11. There are 85 calories in one cooked egg, and 3 eggs in an omelet. How many calories are in 2 omelettes? **510 calories**

12. In 1982, there were 77.2 lb of beef per person consumed in the United States. The average family consisted of 3.1 people. Farmers received 57 cents per lb for beef. On the average, how many cents did the farmers receive from each family's purchase of beef? **13,641.24¢**

■**USES** *Objective K*

13. Susan has 75 stamps in her collection and adds 7 stamps to her collection every month. In how many months will she have 110 stamps? Write an equation to represent this problem and solve the problem.
$75 + 7m = 110$
5 months

28　

LESSON 4-3

RESOURCES
- Lesson Master 4-3
- Quiz on Lessons 4-1 Through 4-3

OBJECTIVE

F Identify and apply the following properties of multiplication:
Multiplicative Identity Property of 1;
Multiplication Property of -1;
Property of Reciprocals;
Multiplication Property of Zero.

TEACHING NOTES

Students may have trouble recognizing the use of the Multiplicative Identity Property of 1 in **Example 1.** Explain that 2.54 cm/inch is equal to 1; thus multiplying by this rate factor does not change the value of an expression, only its form. Another example of rate factor identities is currency conversions.

Discuss the parallel structures of addition and multiplication, along with their special numbers, 0 and 1. This chart may be helpful.

	Addition	Multiplication
Identity Element	0	1
Identity Property	$a + 0 = a$	$a \cdot 1 = a$
Inverse Property	$a + -a = 0$	$a \cdot 1/a = 1$
Related Operation	$a - b = a + -b$	$a \div b = a \cdot 1/b$*

* To be covered in Lesson 5-1

LESSON

4-3 Special Numbers in Multiplication

The numbers 1, 0, and -1 have special roles in multiplication. The number 1 is the **multiplicative identity.**

Multiplicative Identity Property of 1:

For any real number a,
$$a \cdot 1 = 1 \cdot a = a.$$

This simple property is used in ways that are not always obvious. For instance, 2.54 cm = 1 inch. Since the quantities are equal, dividing one by the other gives reciprocal rates

$$\frac{2.54 \text{ cm}}{1 \text{ inch}} \text{ and } \frac{1 \text{ inch}}{2.54 \text{ cm}}$$

each equal to the number one.

Multiplying by such a rate does not change a quantity. It only converts the quantity to different units.

Example 1 Elise needs to buy 7 inches of ribbon. It is sold in the store by the centimeter. How many centimeters does she need?

Solution Multiply 7 inches by the rate factor $2.54 \frac{\text{cm}}{\text{inch}}$.

$$7 \cancel{\text{inches}} \cdot 2.54 \frac{\text{cm}}{\cancel{\text{inch}}} = 17.78 \text{ cm}$$

In Example 1, because 7 inches is multiplied by 1, the actual length of ribbon Elise needs is not being changed. Some other useful rates equal to 1 are $\frac{5280 \text{ ft}}{1 \text{ mi}}$, $\frac{16 \text{ ounces}}{1 \text{ pound}}$, and $\frac{1 \text{ min}}{60 \text{ sec}}$.

Just as multiplication by 1 has special uses, multiplying a number by -1 yields an important result. Think about the farmer in Lesson 4-2 whose topsoil is eroding by 0.5 inch per year. So one year ago there was 0.5 inch *more* soil than there is now. Going back is a negative direction in time. The time is -1 year. Here is the multiplication.

$$-1\ \cancel{\text{year}} \cdot -0.5\frac{\text{inch}}{\cancel{\text{year}}} = 0.5\ \text{inch}$$

a year ago — rate — 0.5 inch more soil

This situation illustrates that multiplication by -1 changes a number to its opposite.

Multiplication Property of -1:

For any real number a,
$$a \cdot -1 = -1 \cdot a = -a.$$

Example 2 Simplify $-x \cdot -y$.

Solution Since $-x = -1x$ and $-y = -1y$

then $-x \cdot -y$
$= -1x \cdot -1y$
$= (-1 \cdot -1)\ xy$
$= 1xy$
$= xy$

When x and y are positive, $-x$ and $-y$ are negative. The result of Example 2 shows that the product of two negative numbers is positive. $-4 \cdot -3 = 4 \cdot 3 = 12$.

Remember that 8 and -8 are opposites (additive inverses) because their sum is the additive identity, 0. Similarly, the numbers 8 and $\frac{1}{8}$ are **reciprocals** or **multiplicative inverses** because their product is the multiplicative identity, 1.

Property of Reciprocals:

For any *nonzero* real number a,
$$a \cdot \frac{1}{a} = \frac{1}{a} \cdot a = 1.$$

The reciprocal of n can always be written $\frac{1}{n}$ or $1/n$. The bar or slash indicates division. You can calculate the reciprocal of a number by dividing 1 by the number.

Making Connections Example 5 previews the Zero Product Property which is used to solve quadratics in Chapter 10. This property should be explained very simply at this time.

ADDITIONAL EXAMPLES

1. Mr. Moy is a Canadian traveling in the U.S. His car has a 75-liter gas tank. How many gallons will the tank hold? (Use 1 gallon = 3.785 liters.)
≈ 19.8 gallons

2. Simplify $-2x \cdot -xy$.
$2x^2y$

3. Give the reciprocal of 0.3125.
3.2

4. Give the reciprocal of $5\frac{1}{4}$.
$\frac{4}{21}$

5. Evaluate
$(n - 3)(n + 7)(n - 18)$
for $n = -3$ and $n = -7$.
504; 0

NOTES ON QUESTIONS
Error Analysis for Question 17e: Students may confuse reciprocals and opposites, thinking that the reciprocal of a number must have the opposite sign. Point out that the reciprocal and original number have a product of *positive* one, and thus must have the same sign.

Question 19: This type of problem solving is helpful when traveling in a foreign country. Conversion between metric and customary units is necessary for someone in the U.S. who travels in almost any other country.

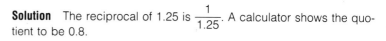

Example 3 Give the reciprocal of 1.25.

Solution The reciprocal of 1.25 is $\frac{1}{1.25}$. A calculator shows the quotient to be 0.8.

Check $1.25 \cdot 0.8 = 1$. So 1.25 and 0.8 are reciprocals because their product is 1.

If you know that the reciprocal of 1.25 is 0.8, you also know that the reciprocal of -1.25 is -0.8, since $-1.25 \cdot -0.8 = 1$.

Most scientific calculators have a reciprocal key [1/x]. To find the reciprocal of n, key in n [1/x]. The answer will be displayed as a decimal. You must apply a different process to write the reciprocal as a fraction. Use the fact that the reciprocal of a/b is b/a (unless a or b is zero).

Example 4 Give the reciprocal of $-\frac{3}{7}$.

Solution The reciprocal of $-\frac{3}{7}$ is $-\frac{7}{3}$.

Check $-\frac{3}{7} \cdot -\frac{7}{3} = \frac{21}{21} = 1$

Look back at the property of reciprocals. The term *nonzero* is emphasized because the property is not true for $a = 0$. Zero does not have a reciprocal because there is no number such that $0 \cdot x = 1$. In fact, you know that 0 times any real number is 0.

Multiplication Property of Zero:

For any real number a,
$$a \cdot 0 = 0 \cdot a = 0.$$

Example 5 Evaluate $(w + 4.7)(2.6 - w)(w + 7.1)$ when $w = -4.7$.

Solution Substituting gives

$$(-4.7 + 4.7)(2.6 - -4.7)(-4.7 + 7.1).$$

Since -4.7 and 4.7 are opposites, their sum is 0.

$$= (0)(2.6 - -4.7)(4.7 + 7.1)$$
$$= 0$$

The product is 0. There is no need to do the computation in the second or third parentheses.

Questions

Covering the Reading

1. a. What number is the multiplicative identity? **1**
b. What number is the additive identity? **0**

2. State the property of reciprocals. **See margin.**

3. Reciprocals are also called __?__. **multiplicative inverses**

4. Zero has the same role in __?__ that 1 has in __?__.
addition, multiplication

5. Copy and complete the following:
a. -18 and 18 are __?__ because their sum is __?__.
b. 18 and $\frac{1}{18}$ are __?__ because their product is __?__.
a) opposites or additive inverses, zero; b) reciprocals, one

6. To what real number does the property of reciprocals *not* apply? **zero**

In 7–11, give the reciprocal and check your answer. **See margin.**

7. 10 **8.** 1/9 **9.** $4\frac{3}{5}$ **10.** 2.5 **11.** $-\frac{6}{7}$

12. Evaluate $(x + 1)(x + 2)(x + 3)(x + 4)$ when $x = -3$. **0**

13. Refer to Example 1.
a. Suppose Elise needs 10 more inches of ribbon. How many more centimeters must she buy? **10 in. · 2.54 $\frac{\text{cm}}{\text{in.}}$ = 25.4 cm**
b. Suppose Elise needed x inches of ribbon. How many centimeters is this? **x in. · 2.54 $\frac{\text{cm}}{\text{in.}}$ = 2.54x cm**

14. a. Simplify: $z \cdot -w$. **-zw or -wz**
b. If z and w are positive numbers, then part **a** indicates that the product of a __?__ number and a __?__ number is __?__.
positive; negative; negative.

Applying the Mathematics

15. Simplify: $a \cdot -b \cdot c \cdot -d \cdot e$. ***abcde***

16. *Multiple choice* Which does *not* equal the multiplicative identity?
(a) c/c when $c \neq 0$ (b) $0.8 \cdot 5/4$ (c) $4.1 - 4.1$ (d) $.9 + .1$
(c)

17. Which pairs of numbers are reciprocals? **a and d**
a. 200 and 0.005 **b.** 7 and .7 **c.** $\frac{1}{4}$ and 0.25
d. 1.5 and $\frac{2}{3}$ **e.** $\frac{3}{5}$ and $-\frac{3}{5}$

18. How many feet are in x miles if 5280 ft = 1 mile? **5280x**

19. Don bought a 34-inch belt. His waist measures 75 cm. Is the belt long enough for him to wear? **Yes**

ADDITIONAL ANSWERS

2. For any nonzero real number a,
$a \cdot \frac{1}{a} = \frac{1}{a} \cdot a = 1$

7. $\frac{1}{10}$, $10 \cdot \frac{1}{10} = 1$

8. 9; $\frac{1}{9} \cdot 9 = 1$

9. $\frac{5}{23}$; $\frac{23}{5} \cdot \frac{5}{23} = 1$

10. $\frac{2}{5}$; $\frac{5}{2} \cdot \frac{2}{5} = 1$

11. $-\frac{7}{6}$; $-\frac{6}{7} \cdot -\frac{7}{6} = 1$

NAME ____________

LESSON **MASTER 4–3**
QUESTIONS ON **SPUR** OBJECTIVES

■PROPERTIES *Objective F* *(See pages 204–207 for objectives.)*
In 1–8, simplify and name the multiplication property used.

1. $4 \cdot \frac{a}{a}$ **4**; **Multiplicative Identity Prop.**
2. $6x \cdot \frac{1}{6x}$ **1**; **Property of Reciprocals**
3. $-1 \cdot -2y$ **2y**; **Multiplication Property of -1**
4. $8(2n - 2n)$ **0**; **Multiplication Property of 0**
5. $(-6)(ab)$ **-6ab**; **Associative Property of Mult.**
6. $\frac{4k}{4k}(2c - 1)$ **2c − 1**; **Multiplicative Identity Prop.**
7. $(x + y) \cdot \frac{1}{(x + y)}$ **1**; **Property of Reciprocals**
8. $(2t + 1)(3t - 1)(0)$ **0**; **Multiplication Property of 0**

In 9–12, write the reciprocal.

9. -1.5 **$-\frac{2}{3}$** **10.** $\frac{8}{3}$ **$\frac{3}{8}$**
11. $\frac{5}{2x}$ **$\frac{2x}{5}$** **12.** $\frac{6}{y - 1}$ **$\frac{y - 1}{6}$**

In 13–18, for what value of the variable is the reciprocal undefined?

13. $\frac{2x}{15}$ **$x = 0$** **14.** $\frac{n}{-5}$ **$n = 0$**
15. $\frac{a - 5}{7}$ **$a = 5$** **16.** $\frac{c + 4}{9b}$ **$c = -4$**
17. y **$y = 0$** **18.** $\frac{0}{x}$ **all of them**

NOTES ON QUESTIONS
Question 20: You may wish to have students name the property illustrated by this question. (Multiplication Property of Zero)

Question 23: Here, students should use associativity and commutativity to position reciprocals next to each other.

FOLLOW-UP

MORE PRACTICE
For more practice on SPUR Objectives, use *Lesson Master 4-3,* shown on page 171.

EXTENSION
Ask students to find in a newspaper, the exchange rates between the dollar and the yen, between the dollar and the British pound, and between the dollar and the deutsche mark. Keep track of these rates over a period of time. Determine whether it is getting less or more expensive for a traveler from the United States to visit these countries. What about travelers from other countries who wish to visit the U.S.?

EVALUATION
A quiz covering Lessons 4-1 through 4-3 is provided in the Teacher's Resource File on page 22.

Alternative Assessment
Again you might evaluate student understanding of properties by having them state the properties in their own words.

32.

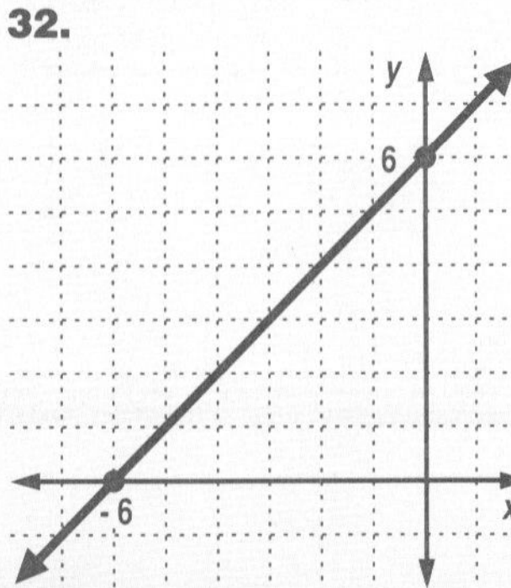

20. To attract people to a grocery store, the manager decides to sell milk at her cost and make 0¢ profit for each bottle sold. How much profit is made when b bottles of milk are sold? **0¢**

21. Find the particular values of a and b such that $x = ax + b$ is true for all values of x. **$a = 1, b = 0$**

22. Suppose $D = (w + 2)(w - 3)(w + 6)$. For what three values of w will D have a value of 0? **$w = -2, 3, -6$**

In 23 and 24, simplify.

23. $\frac{4}{3} \cdot 3a \cdot \frac{3}{4} \cdot \frac{1}{3a} \cdot 10x$ **10x**

24. Compute in your head.
a. $3 \cdot \frac{5}{3}$ **5** **b.** $\frac{9}{x} \cdot x$ **9** **c.** $a \cdot \frac{b}{a}$ **b**

Review

25. *Skill sequence* Multiply. *(Lesson 4-2)*
a. $\frac{4}{3} \cdot 24p$ **32p** **b.** $\frac{-5}{y} \cdot 25y$ **-125** **c.** $\frac{x}{3} \cdot 3x$ **x^2**

26. *Multiple choice* Which is not equal to the others? *(Lesson 4-2)* **(d)**
(a) $\frac{7}{4} \cdot 6x$ (b) $\frac{42}{4}x$ (c) $\frac{42x}{4}$ (d) $\frac{7}{24x}$

27. Write the rate "33 math problems per night" using a slash. *(Lesson 4-2)*
33 math problems/night

28. Suppose a seven-month-old baby weighing w kg has been gaining 0.01 kg per day. At this rate,
a. How much will the baby gain in 60 days? **0.6 kg**
b. How much will the baby weigh in 60 days? *(Lesson 4-2)* **(w + 0.6) kg**

stage 8'
15'
40'
80'

29. An auditorium has dimensions 40′ by 80′. It contains a stage that is 8′ by 15′.
a. What is the area of the remaining floor space? **3080 ft²**
b. If each audience member needs 6 square feet of floor space, how many people will the auditorium hold? *(Lesson 4-1)* **513 people**

30. Solve for y: $3x + y = 2$. *(Lesson 2-6)* **$y = -3x + 2$**

31. John spent T total hours on homework. One hour was spent on science and $\frac{1}{2}$ hour on math. How much time did John spend on other subjects? *(Lesson 3-2)* **$T - \frac{3}{2}$ hours**

32. Let x and y be any real numbers. Graph all solutions to $x = y - 6$. *(Lesson 3-7)* **See margin.**

Exploration

33. The expression *numero uno* is Spanish for "number one." Translate 1 into three other languages.
samples: unus: Latin; un: French; ein: German

172

LESSON

4-4 Solving $ax = b$

Sara earns \$400/week as a zoo attendant. This is equal to a salary rate of \$20,800/year.

Original salary: \$400/week = \$20,800/year

To reward Sara for excellent work the zoo decides to multiply her salary by 1.2. (This is a 20% raise.)

After raise: $1.2 \cdot \$400\text{/week} = 1.2 \cdot \$20{,}800\text{/year}$
\$480/week = \$24,960/year

Multiplied by 1.2, her salary is \$480/week or \$24,960/year. These rates are still equal. This situation is an instance of **Multiplication Property of Equality.**

Multiplication Property of Equality:

For all real numbers a, b, and c: if $a = b$,
then $ca = cb$.

The most important use of this property is in solving equations.

Example 1 An auditorium can seat 40 people in each row. For a talk, the audience should sit as close to the stage as possible. How many rows are needed if 600 people are expected to attend the talk?

Solution It helps to draw a picture.

r rows { 40 seats/row

The total number of seats is $40r$. The equation to solve is $40r = 600$. The solution for this equation is on page 174.

LESSON 4-4

RESOURCES
- Lesson Master 4-4

OBJECTIVES

B Solve and check equations of the form $ax = b$.
F Identify and apply the Multiplication Property of Equality and the Multiplicative Identity Property of 1.
K Solve sentences of the form $ax = b$ to answer questions from real situations.

TEACHING NOTES

Making Connections
The introductory example points out that multiplying Sara's salary by 1.2 is the same as giving her a 20% raise. This is explained in detail in Chapter 5. For now, explain that after Sara gets a 20% raise, her salary will be 120% of her old salary. The decimal form of 120% is 1.20, or 1.2.

Any real-world situation that leads to $ax = b$ can be solved as the simple division b/a. For instance, **Examples 1 and 5** can each be solved directly by division. Do not discourage such quick solutions, but point out that here we are looking at their representation as multiplication equations.

Examples 2-4 have been chosen to involve difficult numbers so that students must use algebraic techniques. If students are given mostly simple problems (for example, solve $3x = 39$), many are able to pass algebra tests without fully understanding the procedures they need to use to solve a more difficult equation.

The distance equation $d = rt$ is an example of a formula derived from a rate. Another example of such a formula is given in **Question 17.** These offer a view of literal equations which link to applications.

ADDITIONAL EXAMPLES

1. When Brad writes essays, he fits about 250 words on a page. He must write a 1500-word essay. About how long will it be? Write an equation and solve it.
250x = 1500; 6 pages

2. Solve $-128 = -20x$.
6.4

3. Solve $-\frac{3}{8}k = 24$.
-64

4. Solve $1.95 = .13x$.
15

5. A race car driver completes a lap around a 6.75-mile course in 4.5 minutes. Write an equation and find his speed in miles per minute. Convert this rate to miles per hour.
$6.75 = 4.5x$; $1.5\frac{\text{mi}}{\text{min}} = 90\frac{\text{mi}}{\text{hr}}$

To solve, multiply both sides by $\frac{1}{40}$, the reciprocal of 40.

$40r = 600$	
$\frac{1}{40} \cdot 40r = \frac{1}{40} \cdot 600$	Multiplication Property of Equality
$(\frac{1}{40} \cdot 40)r = \frac{600}{40}$	Associative Property of Multiplication
$1 \cdot r = \frac{600}{40}$	Property of Reciprocals
$r = 15$	Multiplication Property of 1

So 15 rows are needed.

Check Will 15 rows hold 600 seats? Yes. $15 \cdot 40 = 600$.

To solve $ax = b$ for x (when a is not zero) multiply both sides of the equation by the reciprocal of a.

In the term ax, a is called the **coefficient** of x. So to solve $ax = b$, multiply both sides by the reciprocal of the coefficient of x.

Example 2 Solve $-6x = 117$.

Solution The reciprocal of -6 is $-\frac{1}{6}$.
Multiply both sides of the equation by $-\frac{1}{6}$.

$$-6x = 117$$
$$-\frac{1}{6} \cdot -6x = -\frac{1}{6} \cdot 117$$
$$x = -\frac{117}{6}$$
$$x = -19.5$$

Check $-6x = -6 \cdot -19.5 = 117$

Example 3 Solve $\frac{4}{5}y = 56$.

Solution The reciprocal of $\frac{4}{5}$ is $\frac{5}{4}$.
Multiply both sides of the equation by $\frac{5}{4}$.

$$\frac{4}{5}y = 56$$
$$\frac{5}{4} \cdot \frac{4}{5}y = \frac{5}{4} \cdot 56$$
$$y = \frac{5}{\cancel{4}_1} \cdot \cancel{56}^{14}$$
$$y = 70$$

Check $\frac{4}{5} \cdot y = \frac{4}{5} \cdot 70 = 56$

Example 4 Solve $3.4w = -85$.

Solution The reciprocal of 3.4 can be written as $\frac{1}{3.4}$. Multiply both sides of the equation by $\frac{1}{3.4}$.

$$3.4w = -85$$
$$\frac{1}{3.4} \cdot 3.4w = \frac{1}{3.4} \cdot -85$$
$$w = -\frac{85}{3.4}$$
$$w = -25$$

Check $3.4w = 3.4 \cdot -25 = -85$

A rate like $\frac{\text{miles}}{\text{hr}}$ is calculated as follows: divide miles representing distance by hours representing time. This gives the formula:

$$\frac{\text{distance}}{\text{time}} = \text{rate}.$$

In short, $$\frac{d}{t} = r.$$

Solving this equation for d gives a related formula.

Multiply both sides by t. $$t \cdot \frac{d}{t} = r \cdot t$$

$$d = rt$$

That is, $$\text{distance} = \text{rate} \cdot \text{time}.$$

Example 5 How long would it take to drive from Detroit to Indianapolis, a distance of 290 miles, if you travel at 55 mph?

Solution Let t be the length of time, in hours.

$$d = r \cdot t$$
$$290 \text{ miles} = 55 \frac{\text{miles}}{\text{hour}} \cdot t \text{ hours}$$
$$290 = 55t$$

Multiply both sides of the equation by $\frac{1}{55}$.

$$\frac{1}{55} \cdot 290 = \frac{1}{55} \cdot 55t$$
$$5.27 \approx t$$

It will take about 5.27 hours.

Check If you travel at 55 mph for 5.27 hours, will you travel about 290 miles? Yes, because

$$55 \frac{\text{mi}}{\cancel{\text{hr}}} \cdot 5.27 \cancel{\text{hr}} \approx 290 \text{ mi}$$

NOTES ON QUESTIONS

Question 12: The answer may be given as $-\frac{4}{3}m$ or $\frac{-4m}{3}$. It is important to consider both answers so that students realize their equality.

Question 13: This involves a law used with levers:
force = weight • distance from fulcrum.

Question 15: This question uses $C = \pi d$. The answer given is based on computation with the pi key on the calculator. Students who approximate pi with 3.14 will be about .01 off the answer given.

Question 17: This gives an example from science of a formula derived from a rate: weight/volume = density. The corresponding multiplication equation is weight = density • volume. (Note: In everyday contexts, the term *weight* is used. In scientific contexts, the term *mass* is used.)

NOTES ON QUESTIONS

Questions 20 and 21: These are simple enough that there are several methods students might use. However, we suggest that you stress solution by rate factor multiplication, so that students are prepared to use this method in more complicated problems.

Question 21: Here, an estimate can be found as follows:

0.27 hr $\approx \frac{1}{4}$ hr = 15 minutes.

Error Analysis for Question 23: This question uses $A = \pi r^2$. Your students may confuse area with circumference. It is helpful to draw pictures illustrating these two measurements.

Question 27c: This involves a percent greater than 100%. Students should learn that % means multiply by $\frac{1}{100}$ or .01.

ADDITIONAL ANSWERS

1b. Multiplication Property of Equality

9. d = distance, r = rate, t = time

26.

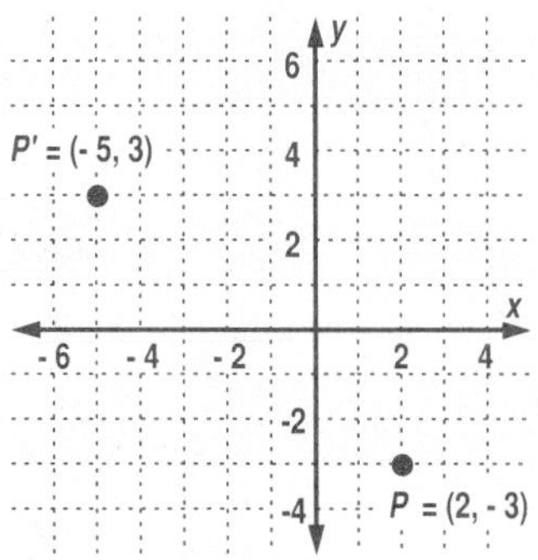

28a. $A = \frac{1}{2}bh$, A = area, b = base, h = height

28b. $P = 2\ell + 2w$, P = perimeter, ℓ = length, w = width

28c. $C = 2\pi r$, C = circumference, r = radius

28d. $I = prt$, I = interest, p = principal, r = rate, t = time

28e. $F = ma$, F = force, m = mass, a = acceleration

Questions

Covering the Reading

1. a. If $a = b$, then $6a$ = __?__. 6b

b. What property is used to answer part a? See margin.

2. If 920 people were expected at the talk of Example 1, how many rows of seats would be needed? 23 rows

In 3–5, **a.** What is the coefficient of the unknown? **b.** By what number should you multiply both sides to solve the equation? **c.** Solve.

3. $-32x = 416$ a) -32 b) $-\frac{1}{32}$ c) -13

4. $-210 = 4.2y$ a) 4.2 b) $\frac{1}{4.2}$ c) -50

5. $\frac{3}{32}A = \frac{3}{4}$ a) $\frac{3}{32}$ b) $\frac{32}{3}$ c) 8

6. To solve $ax = b$ for x, multiply both sides of the equation by __?__. $\frac{1}{a}$

7. Solve $-240x = 12$. -.05

8. Solve $\frac{1}{5} = \frac{1}{80}y$. 16

9. In the formula $d = rt$, what do d, r, and t represent? See margin.

10. Refer to Example 5. If you travel from Detroit to Indianapolis at 65 mph, how long will it take to get there? ≈4.5 hours

11. Julie thinks $\frac{1}{4}$ is the solution to the equation $\frac{1}{3} \cdot m = \frac{4}{3}$. Is she correct? No

Applying the Mathematics

12. Solve for k: $-3k = 4m$. $\frac{-4m}{3}$

13. Jose and Maria want to use the seesaw at the left. Jose weighs 40 kg and sits 150 cm from the turning point. Maria weighs 30 kg. Where should she sit to balance Jose? (Note: To balance, weight times distance on one side must equal weight times distance on the other.) 200 cm from the turning point

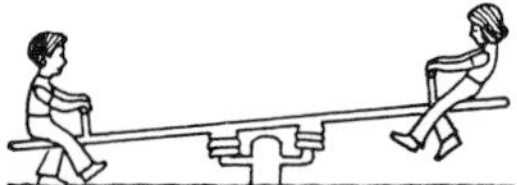

14. On a day in the U.S., a mean of about 10,205 people each give a pint of blood. About how many days will it take to get one million pints of blood? about 98 days

15. The circumference of a circle is 39 cm. Find its diameter to the nearest hundredth. (Remember: $C = \pi d$.) 12.41 cm

16. The volume of a box needs to be 500 cubic centimeters. The base of the box has dimensions 12.5 cm and 5 cm. How high must the box be? 8 cm

17. Density D of a material is defined as the rate M/V, where M is the weight of material and V is the volume.

a. What equation results when both sides of $D = M/V$ are multiplied by V? $DV = M$

b. If the density of water is 62.4 pounds per cubic foot, find the weight of 10.4 cubic feet of water. 648.96 pounds

Review

18. *Multiple choice* Which results are equal to the multiplicative identity? *(Lesson 4-3)* **(a, d)**

(a) $\frac{2y}{2y}$ (b) $.4 \cdot \frac{2}{5}$ (c) $-6.4 + 6.4$ (d) $.8 + .2$

19. *Multiple choice* Which pair of numbers are reciprocals? *(Lesson 4-3)* **(a)**

(a) $2y$ and $\frac{1}{2y}$ (b) 0.4 and $\frac{2}{5}$ (c) -6.4 and 6.4 (d) 0.8 and 0.2

20. About how many quarts are in x liters, if 1 liter $\approx$ 1.06 quarts? *(Lesson 4-3)* **1.06x**

21. In this lesson, the answer to Example 5 is 5.27 hr. How many minutes is 0.27 hr? *(Lesson 4-2)* **16.2 minutes**

22. If Irma dribbles a basketball 2 times per second, and moves 4.5 ft per second, how many dribbles will she make moving 60 ft down court? *(Lesson 4-2)* **≈27 dribbles**

10 cm
3 cm
r = 8 cm

23. The formula for the area of a circle is $A = \pi r^2$, where π is about 3.14 and r is the radius. Find the area of the colored region if the radius of the circle is 8 cm and the rectangle is 3 cm by 10 cm *(Lesson 3-2, 4-1)* **≈171 cm²**

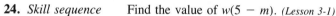

24. *Skill sequence* Find the value of $w(5 - m)$. *(Lesson 3-1)*

a. $w = 20, m = -7$ **240**
b. $w = 20, m = 7$ **-40**
c. $w = -20, m = 7$ **40**

25. Solve for a. *(Lessons 2-6, 2-7)*

a. $a + 43 = 36$ **$a = -7$**
b. $a - 31 \leq 17$ **$a \leq 48$**
c. $a + c > 166$ **$a > 166 - c$**

26. Graph the point (2, -3) and its image after a slide of 7 units to the left and 6 units up. *(Lesson 2-5)* **See margin.**

27. Write as a percent: **a.** 0.24 **b.** 0.3 **c.** 1.4 *(Previous course)*
a) 24%; b) 30%; c) 140%

Exploration

28. A number of well-known equations are of the same form as $d = rt$. Some of them are listed below. For each equation, find out what the variables represent. **See margin.**

a. $A = \frac{1}{2}bh$ **b.** $P = 2\ell + 2w$ **c.** $C = 2\pi r$
d. $I = prt$ **e.** $F = ma$

FOLLOW-UP

MORE PRACTICE

For more practice on SPUR Objectives, use *Lesson Master 4-4,* shown below.

EXTENSION

Computer Have students adapt the computer program in Lesson 2-6 (on page 90) to solve A∗X = B.
sample:

```
10 PRINT "SOLVE AN EQUATION A * X = B, WHERE A <> 0."
20 PRINT "GIVE A AND B."
30 INPUT A,B
40 PRINT "SOLUTION TO";A;"*X = ";B
50 PRINT "IS X = ";B/A
60 END
```

NAME ____________

LESSON MASTER 4–4
QUESTIONS ON **SPUR** OBJECTIVES

■**SKILLS** *Objective B (See pages 204–207 for objectives.)*
In 1–8, solve and check.

1. $17n = 51$ **$n = 3$; $17 \cdot 3 = 51$**
2. $-13k = 65$ **$k = -5$; $(-13)(-5) = 65$**
3. $-5s = -1.25$ **$s = .25$; $(-5)(.25) = -1.25$**
4. $-8.978 = 1.34t$ **$t = -6.7$; $-8.978 = 1.34(-6.7)$**
5. $\frac{3}{4}x = 27$ **$x = 36$; $\frac{3}{4}(36) = 27$**
6. $-7c = 4\frac{1}{5}$ **$c = -\frac{3}{5}$; $-7\left(-\frac{3}{5}\right) = 4\frac{1}{5}$**
7. $-\frac{6}{25} = -\frac{4}{5}p$ **$p = \frac{3}{10}$; $-\frac{6}{25} = -\frac{4}{5}\left(\frac{3}{10}\right)$**
8. $6y - 8y = 2$ **$y = -1$; $6(-1) - 8(-1) = 2$**

In 9–12, solve for x.

9. $3x = a$ **$x = \frac{a}{3}$** 10. $-bx = h$ **$x = -\frac{h}{b}$**
11. $\frac{x}{n} = 12$ **$x = 12n$** 12. $\frac{a}{b}x = c$ **$x = \frac{bc}{a}$**

■**PROPERTIES** *Objective F*
13. What property tells you that $6x = 18.6$ is equivalent to $x = 3.1$?
Multiplication Property of Equality

14. To solve $\frac{a}{b}x = \frac{c}{d}$ for x, multiply both sides by **$\frac{b}{a}$**.

■**USES** *Objective K*
15. A plane flies from St. Louis to Chicago, a distance of 297 miles, in 45 minutes. Use the formula $d = rt$ to find its average speed. **396 mph**

16. Use the formula $I = prt$ to determine the annual rate of interest r a bank pays if \$120 earns \$6 in one year. **5%**

30

LESSON 4-5

RESOURCES

■ Lesson Master 4-5

OBJECTIVES

B Solve and check equations of the form $ax = b$.

C Solve and check equations of the form $a - x = b$.

TEACHING NOTES

Continue to stress checking solutions to equations. One benefit is that the solutions of the special situations that appear in **Examples 1-3** should make intuitive sense.

Error Analysis In **Example 5,** make sure that students realize that there are two distinct steps to be carried out and that they should not stop when $-c$ has been isolated. First, isolate $-c$; then transform $-c = -1.23$ into an equation with just c on the left.

Alternate Approach Instead of writing an equation to solve the question in **Example 5,** a number line could have been used. Think of the correct length of the rod as the origin.

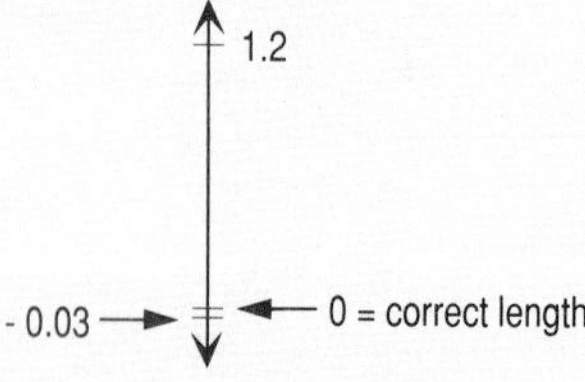

Therefore, the amount cut off is 1.2 − -0.03, or 1.23.

LESSON

4-5 Special Numbers in Equations

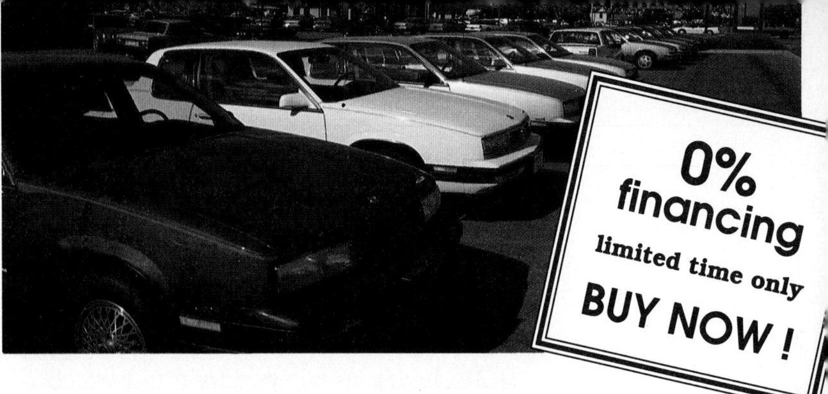

When a and b are real numbers, the equation $a + x = b$ has exactly one solution. This may lead you to think that all simple equations have exactly one solution. That is not so, even with some equations of the form $ax = b$.

Example 1 Solve $0x = 4$.

Solution By the Multiplication Property of 0, for any value of x, $0x = 0$. So $0x$ cannot equal 4. There is no solution.
Write: There is no solution.

Example 2 Solve $0y = 0$.

Solution This is the Multiplication Property of 0. It is always true.
Write: All real numbers are solutions.

Notice that in Examples 1 and 2, you cannot multiply both sides by the reciprocal of 0. Why?—because 0 has no reciprocal! That signals you to be careful when 0 is the coefficient of the unknown. Zero is the only number that causes such problems.

In the next example, the coefficient of t has a reciprocal. The result is that there is exactly one solution.

Example 3 Solve $13t = 0$.

Solution 1 This equation can be solved by multiplying both sides by $\frac{1}{13}$.

$$\frac{1}{13} \cdot 13t = \frac{1}{13} \cdot 0$$
$$t = 0$$

Solution 2 Do it in your head. The only number that 13 can be multiplied by to get 0 is 0 itself. So $t = 0$.
Write: The solution is 0.

To avoid writing sentences as explanations of solutions, solution sets can be written. For Examples 1, 2, and 3, the solutions are as follows.

Equation	Sentence	Solution set
$0x = 4$	There is no solution.	{ } or ø
$0y = 0$	All real numbers are solutions.	R
$13t = 0$	The solution is 0.	{0}

Notice that {0} and { } are different. The set { } or ø has no elements and indicates that no number works in $0x = 4$. The set {0} contains the element 0, and indicates that 0 works in $13t = 0$.

The Multiplication Property of -1, $-1 \cdot a = -a$, is useful in solving equations where the opposite of the unknown has been found.

Example 4 Solve $-x = 3.824$.

Solution 1 Use the Multiplication Property of -1.

$$-1 \cdot x = 3.824$$

Multiply both sides by -1 (which happens to be the reciprocal of -1).

$$-1 \cdot -1 \cdot x = -1 \cdot 3.824$$
$$x = -3.824$$

Solution 2 Translate the equation into words and find the solution in your head. The opposite of what number is 3.824? Answer: -3.824

Equations like the one above arise when a variable has been subtracted. The next example leads to a situation of the form $a - x = b$.

Example 5 A rod was 1.2 cm too long. It was shortened and found to be 0.03 cm too short. How much was cut off?

Solution Let the amount cut off be c. "Too short" means -0.03. From the Take-away Model for Subtraction, the answer is the solution to

$$1.2 - c = -0.03.$$

Use the definition of subtraction. Change to addition.

$$1.2 + -c = -0.03$$

Apply the Addition Property of Equality. Add -1.2 to both sides.

$$-1.2 + 1.2 + -c = -1.2 + -0.03$$
$$-c = -1.23$$

Apply the Multiplication Property of Equality. Multiply both sides by -1.

$$c = 1.23$$

The amount cut off was 1.23 cm.

ADDITIONAL EXAMPLES
In Examples 1-5, solve.

1. $3.6 = 0x$.
There is no solution.

2. $0 = 0a$.
All real numbers are solutions.

3. $0 = 7.2y$.
0

4. $-x = -\frac{7}{8}$.
$\mathbf{\frac{7}{8}}$

5. $83 - x = 91$.
-8

NOTES ON QUESTIONS

Question 5: Some students may not distinguish between { } and {ϕ}. Explain that {ϕ} cannot be the empty set because it has an element in it.

Error Analysis for Question 20: Students often solve equations like this mentally but get the wrong answer because they multiply by the coefficient rather than by its reciprocal. To solve $12r = -4$, you do not multiply by 12, but by 1/12. (Similarly, to solve $x + 7 = 20$, you do not add 7, but -7.) Stress the need to check answers to help combat this mistake. Also reinforce the idea that in solving an equation you do not carry out the operation that is written in the equation.

ADDITIONAL ANSWERS

2a. The solution is 0; b. {0}

3a. There is no solution;

b. { } or ϕ

4a. All real numbers are solutions; b. R

22a. Yes; b. $\frac{5}{12}$ m

24.

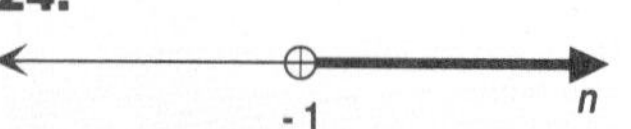

25c. When the number of factors is even, the value is 1. When the number of factors is odd, the value is -1.

26. ≈ 2.9 crates; so 3 crates are needed

Questions

Covering the Reading

1. Why can't both sides of $3 = 0x$ be multiplied by the reciprocal of 0?
0 has no reciprocal.

In 2–4, describe the solutions **a.** with a sentence; **b.** with the solution set.

2. $7y = 0$ **3.** $0 \cdot w = 14$ **4.** $0 = a \cdot 0$ **See margin.**

5. *Multiple choice* Which set is the same as ø? **(d)**
(a) {ø} (b) {0} (c) 0 (d) { }

6. Write the Multiplication Property of -1, beginning with "For any real number c, ..." **For any real number c, $c \cdot -1 = -1 \cdot c = -c$.**

In 7–12, solve.

7. $-1 \cdot x = 40$ **$x = -40$** **8.** $-y = -3$ **$y = 3$** **9.** $-z = 0$ **$z = 0$**

10. $16 - w = 102$ **$w = -86$** **11.** $1.74 - v = -2$ **$v = 3.74$** **12.** $-6 - x = 8$ **$x = -14$**

13. A TV program is found to be 1 minute 14 seconds too long for its time slot. It is shortened and a second version is 15 seconds too short. By how much was it shortened? **x = 89 seconds**

Applying the Mathematics

14. If $90 - x = 11$, what is x? **$x = 79$**

15. a. Solve for y: $m - y = 25$. **$y = m - 25$**
b. Check your answer to part a by letting $m = 27$ and $y = 2$.
$y = m - 25$; $2 = 27 - 25$

16. Solve for z: $300z - 299z - z = 0$.
$0z = 0$; All real numbers are solutions.

17. Refer to the formula on page 155. Some people believe that, other than the Earth, the value of $L = 0$. What effect does this have on the value of N? **$N = 0$**

Review

In 18–20, solve. *(Lesson 4-4)*

18. $\frac{7}{9}q = 140$ **$q = 180$** **19.** $-4p = 12$ **$p = -3$** **20.** $12r = -4$ **$r = -\frac{1}{3}$**

21. The circumference C of a circle can be found from the formula $C = 2\pi r$, where r is the radius of the circle. If $C = 60\pi$, what is r? *(Lesson 4-4)* **$r = 30$**

22. The volume of a box is half a cubic meter. The length of the box is 1.5 meters and the width is 0.8 meter. **a.** Is this possible? **b.** If so, find the height of the box. If not, explain why not. *(Lessons 4-1, 4-4)*
See margin.

23. Simplify: $-1 \cdot 4 \cdot -8 + 2 \cdot -5 \cdot 9 - -3 \cdot 6 \cdot -10$. *(Lessons 2-2, 3-1, 4-3)*
-238

24. Graph all solutions to $n > -1$. *(Lesson 1-1)* **See margin.**

25. a. Evaluate $-1 \cdot -1 \cdot -1 \cdot -1 \cdot -1 \cdot -1 \cdot -1 \cdot -1$. **1**
b. Evaluate $-1 \cdot -1 \cdot \ldots \cdot -1$, where there are 25 factors. **-1**
c. Give a general rule for answering questions like part b. *(Previous course)* **See margin.**

26. A crate contains 12 cases. Each case has 24 boxes. Each box has 60 packages of batteries. Each package has 2 batteries. How many crates will it take to ship 100,000 batteries? *(Lessons 4-2, 4-4)* **See margin.**

In 27–29, which is larger? *(Previous course)*

27. $3 + -4$ or $4 + -3$? **4 + -3**

28. $1 \cdot -8$ or $2 \cdot -8$? **1 · -8**

29. $-432 \cdot -175$ or $-346 \cdot 811$? **-432 · -175**

Exploration

30. Consider the following pattern.

row 1	$x = 10$
row 2	$\frac{1}{2}x = 10$
row 3	$\frac{1}{3}x = 10$
⋮	⋮
row 100	

a. What will be written in row n? **$\frac{1}{n}x = 10$**
b. What is the solution to the equation in row n? **$x = 10n$**
c. What will be written in row 100? **$\frac{1}{100}x = 10$**
d. What is the solution to the equation in row 100? **$x = 1000$**
e. To what equation are the equations getting closer and closer?
$0x = 10$. The solutions become larger and larger, approaching infinity.

FOLLOW-UP

MORE PRACTICE
For more practice on SPUR Objectives, use *Lesson Master 4-5*, shown below.

EVALUATION
Alternative Assessment
To evaluate student understanding of equation-solving procedures, ask them to write equations for which you give the solution procedure. For example, **1.** Write an equation that can be solved by adding -12 to both sides. (sample: $x + 12 = 14$) **2.** Write an equation that can be solved by multiplying both sides by $\frac{1}{7}$. (sample: $7y = 3$)

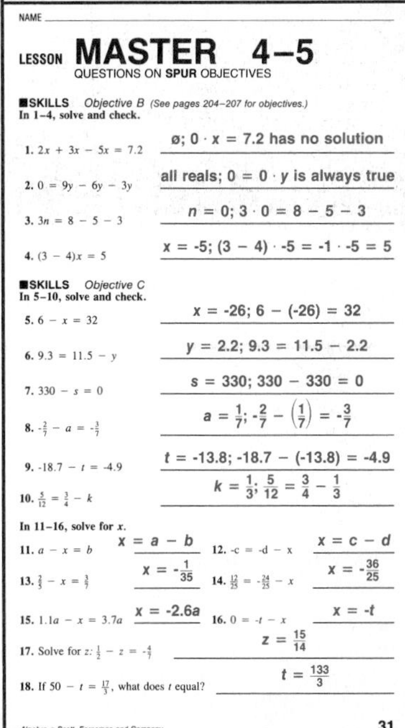

NAME ______

LESSON **MASTER 4–5**
QUESTIONS ON **SPUR** OBJECTIVES

■SKILLS *Objective B* *(See pages 204–207 for objectives.)*
In 1–4, solve and check.

1. $2x + 3x - 5x = 7.2$ **ø; $0 \cdot x = 7.2$ has no solution**
2. $0 = 9y - 6y - 3y$ **all reals; $0 = 0 \cdot y$ is always true**
3. $3n = 8 - 5 - 3$ **$n = 0$; $3 \cdot 0 = 8 - 5 - 3$**
4. $(3 - 4)x = 5$ **$x = -5$; $(3 - 4) \cdot -5 = -1 \cdot -5 = 5$**

■SKILLS *Objective C*
In 5–10, solve and check.

5. $6 - x = 32$ **$x = -26$; $6 - (-26) = 32$**
6. $9.3 = 11.5 - y$ **$y = 2.2$; $9.3 = 11.5 - 2.2$**
7. $330 - s = 0$ **$s = 330$; $330 - 330 = 0$**
8. $-\frac{2}{7} - a = -\frac{3}{7}$ **$a = \frac{1}{7}$; $-\frac{2}{7} - \left(\frac{1}{7}\right) = -\frac{3}{7}$**
9. $-18.7 - t = -4.9$ **$t = -13.8$; $-18.7 - (-13.8) = -4.9$**
10. $\frac{5}{12} = \frac{3}{4} - k$ **$k = \frac{1}{3}$; $\frac{5}{12} = \frac{3}{4} - \frac{1}{3}$**

In 11–16, solve for x.

11. $a - x = b$ **$x = a - b$** **12.** $-c = -d - x$ **$x = c - d$**
13. $\frac{2}{5} - x = \frac{3}{7}$ **$x = -\frac{1}{35}$** **14.** $\frac{12}{25} = -\frac{24}{25} - x$ **$x = -\frac{36}{25}$**
15. $1.1a - x = 3.7a$ **$x = -2.6a$** **16.** $0 = -t - x$ **$x = -t$**
17. Solve for z: $\frac{1}{2} - z = -\frac{4}{7}$ **$z = \frac{15}{14}$**
18. If $50 - t = \frac{17}{3}$, what does t equal? **$t = \frac{133}{3}$**

 31

LESSON 4-6

RESOURCES
- Lesson Master 4-6
- Quiz on Lessons 4-4 Through 4-6
- Visual for Teaching Aid 22: Diagram for Alternate Approach

OBJECTIVES

D Solve and check inequalities of the form $ax < b$.
F Identify and apply the Multiplication Property of Inequality.
K Solve sentences of the form $ax < b$ to answer questions from real situations.

TEACHING NOTES

Emphasize the two-step check, as in the examples:

1. Check to see whether the boundary point is correct.

2. Check whether the sense of the inequality is correct.

This check is very important in helping students grasp the essential elements of the problem.

Error Analysis Some students will at first look for any negative in the problem. They will change $5x < -25$ to $x > -5$, for example. Continually ask what both sides were being multiplied by. If students do not know, ask what they would multiply by if given $5x = -25$. Stress that the number both sides are multiplied by is the same for the equality and the related inequality.

LESSON

4-6 Solving $ax < b$

Here are some numbers in increasing order.

-10 -6 5 30 30.32 870

Because the numbers are in order, you could put the inequality sign $<$ between any two of them. Now multiply these numbers by some fixed *positive* number, say 11. Here are the products.

-110 -66 55 330 333.52 9570

The order is the same. You could still put an $<$ sign between any of the numbers. This illustrates that if $x < y$, then $11x < 11y$. In general, multiplication by a positive number keeps order.

Multiplication Property of Inequality (part 1):

If $x < y$ and a is positive, then $ax < ay$.

Each of the signs $>$, $\leq$, or $\geq$ between numbers or expressions also indicates order. The Multiplication Property of Inequality works with any of those signs. Many inequalities can be solved using this property.

Example 1 Solve $4x \leq 20$.

Solution Multiply both sides by $\frac{1}{4}$. Since $\frac{1}{4}$ is positive, the inequality sign remains the same.

$$\frac{1}{4} \cdot 4x \leq \frac{1}{4} \cdot 20$$
$$x \leq 5$$

Check As with other inequalities you have solved, there are two steps to the check.

Step 1: Substitute 5 in the original inequality. It should make the two sides equal. It does. $4 \cdot 5 = 20$.

Step 2: Check some number that works in $x \leq 5$. We pick 3. Is $4 \cdot 3 \leq 20$? Yes, $12 \leq 20$.

Since both steps worked, the solution $x \leq 5$ is correct.

Example 2 The length of a rectangle is 50 cm. Its area is greater than 175 cm^2. Find the width of the rectangle.

length = 50 cm

width = w cm

Solution It helps to draw a picture. $A = \ell w$, and $\ell = 50$, so the area of the rectangle is $50w$. The situation is described by the inequality $50w > 175$.

To solve, multiply both sides by $\frac{1}{50}$, the reciprocal of 50.

$$\frac{1}{50} \cdot 50w > \frac{1}{50} \cdot 175$$

It's just like solving equations. Simplifying yields

$$w > 3.5.$$

The width is more than 3.5 cm.

Check Step 1: Does $50 \cdot 3.5 = 175$? Yes.
Step 2: Pick some value that works in $w > 3.5$ cm, such as 10. Is $50 \cdot 10 > 175$? Yes.

Multiplying both sides of an inequality by a *positive* number is straightforward. Multiplying by a *negative* number requires one more step. Here are the numbers from the beginning of this lesson.

-10 -6 5 30 30.32 870

Multiplying these numbers by -3,

30 18 -15 -90 -90.96 -2610

The first row of numbers is in *increasing* order. The second row is in *decreasing* order. The order has been reversed. Multiplication by a negative number changes order. So, if you multiply both sides of an inequality by a negative number, you must **change the direction of the inequality.**

Multiplication Property of Inequality (part 2):

If $x < y$ and a is negative then $ax > ay$.

Example 3 Solve $-7x \geq 126$.

Solution Multiply both sides by $-\frac{1}{7}$, the reciprocal of -7. Since $-\frac{1}{7}$ is a negative number, remember to *change the inequality sign* from $\geq$ to $\leq$.

$$-\tfrac{1}{7} \cdot -7x \leq -\tfrac{1}{7} \cdot 126$$

Now simplify.

$$x \leq -\tfrac{126}{7}$$
$$x \leq -18$$

Check Step 1: Does $-7 \cdot -18 = 126$? Yes.
Step 2: Try a number that works in $x \leq -18$. We use -20. Is $-7 \cdot -20 \geq 126$? Yes, $140 \geq 126$.

Changing from $<$ to $>$, or from $\leq$ to $\geq$, or vice-versa, is called **changing the sense** of the inequality. Note this is the same as changing the direction of the inequality. The only time you have to change the sense is when you are multiplying both sides by a negative number. Otherwise, solving $ax < b$ is just like solving $ax = b$.

Some students will give a single number as the solution to an inequality. Remind them that we are looking for all numbers that work in the original sentence.

Alternate Approach
Mappings from one number line to another show the change of the sense of an inequality under multiplication by a negative. Following are three graphs. The first shows addition of -2. The second shows multiplication by 2. The third shows multiplication by -1. In the last example the lines connecting a number to its product cross over. This indicates a change in the sense of the inequality.

Addition of -2

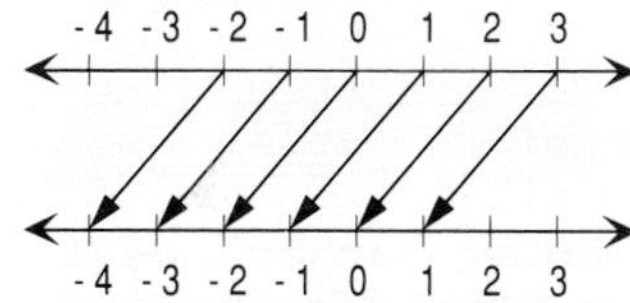

Multiplication by 2

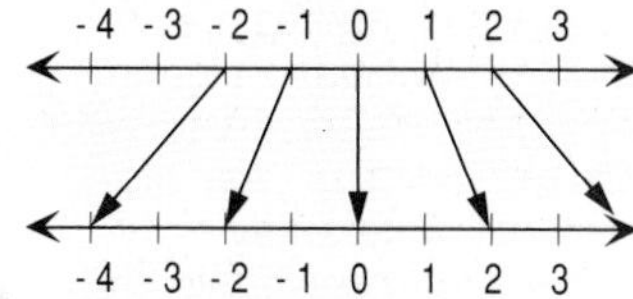

Multiplication by -1

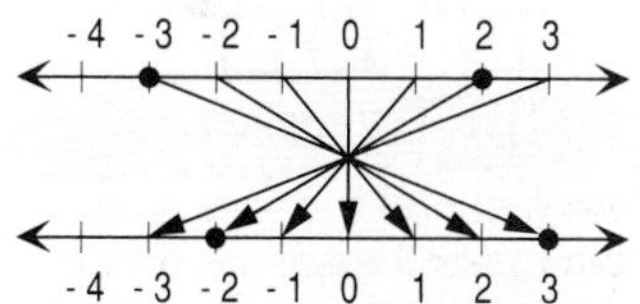

In the last example, notice that $-3 < 2$. But under multiplication by -1, the -3 is mapped to 3 and the 2 to -2. Clearly, $3 > -2$.

ADDITIONAL EXAMPLES

1. Solve $\frac{2}{3}x > 30$.
$\mathbf{x > 45}$

2. Meg is hiking at a rate of 2.5 miles per hour. She knows that it is at least 13.5 miles to Bear Lake. How long will it take Meg to hike there? Write a sentence and solve it.
$2.5t \geq 13.5$; at least 5.4 hours

3. Solve $-4m < 50$.
$m > -\frac{25}{2}$

NOTES ON QUESTIONS

Question 20: This illustrates an inequality in which the answer needs to be rounded. The solution of the inequality is $x < 90\frac{10}{11}$, but it makes more sense to say that there could be at most 90 guests, rather than at most $90\frac{10}{11}$ guests. (In fact, there are almost always costs one is unprepared for, and if these numbers were correct, it probably would be best to have no more than 75 or 80 guests.)

Question 31: Ask students to imagine they have folded the pattern and have them draw the resulting box. Many students have poor intuition for problems of this type.

Making Connections for Question 37: Division of fractions is reviewed here. This is a precursor for Chapter 5 which addresses the topic of division in algebra.

Question 38: Ask students to write a key sequence to solve this problem in general. [For $a < x^2 < b$, one solution is a [+] b [=] [÷] 2 [=] [√]. That is, find the mean of a and b and then take the square root.]

ADDITIONAL ANSWERS

4. If $x < y$ and a is positive, then $ax < ay$. If $x < y$ and a is negative, then $ax > ay$.

36.

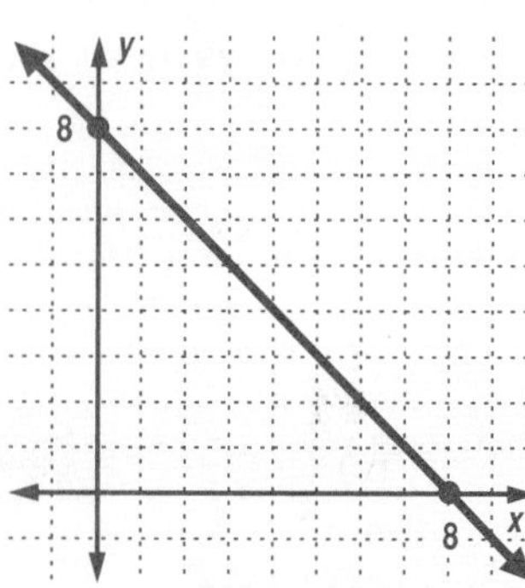

You can see why the two-step check of an inequality is important. The first step checks the number in the solution. The second step checks the sense of the inequality.

Questions

Covering the Reading

In 1–3, consider the inequality $20 < 30$. What inequality results if:

1. you multiply both sides of this inequality by 6? $120 < 180$
2. you multiply both sides of this inequality by $\frac{2}{3}$? $\frac{40}{3} < 20$
3. you multiply both sides of this inequality by -4? $-80 > -120$
4. Give both parts of the multiplication property of inequality. See margin.

In 5 and 6, change the sense of each inequality.

5. $<$ $>$
6. $\geq$ $\leq$

7. Tell whether or not these numbers are solutions to $-9x < -18$.

a. 2	b. -2	c. 3	d. -3	e. -1	f. 0
No	No	Yes	No	No	No

In 8–13, solve and check each sentence.

8. $5x \geq 10$ $x \geq 2$
9. $-3y < 300$ $y > -100$
10. $-4A < -124$ $A > 31$
11. $13 > 2z$ $\frac{13}{2} > z$
12. $\frac{2}{3}P \leq \frac{1}{4}$ $P \leq \frac{3}{8}$
13. $0.09 > -9c$ $-0.01 < c$

14. The length of a rectangle is 20 cm. Its area is less than 154 cm^2. Find the width of the rectangle. less than 7.7 cm

Applying the Mathematics

In 15–17, multiply both sides by -1 to solve the sentence.

15. $-m < 8$ $m > -8$
16. $-2 \leq -n$ $2 \geq n$
17. $-t < 0$ $t > 0$

18. The area of the foundation of a rectangular building is not to exceed 20,000 square feet. The width of the foundation is to be 125 feet. How long can the foundation be? less than or equal to 160 ft

19. An auditorium has at least 1500 seats. There are 50 seats in each row. There must be at least how many rows? 30 rows

20. Parents of the bride have budgeted $2500 for the dinner after the wedding. Each person's dinner will cost $27.50. At most how many people can attend the dinner? at most 90 people

21. Three fourths of a number is less than two hundred four. What are the possible values of the number? $n < 272$

22. You are to travel more than 100 km in 3 hours. Write an inequality to describe your rate. $r > \frac{100 \text{ km}}{3 \text{ hr}}$ or $r > 33\frac{1}{3} \frac{\text{km}}{\text{hr}}$

23. Use the clues to find x. **$x = 4$**
Clue 1: x is an integer.
Clue 2: $2x < 10$.
Clue 3: $-3x < -9$.

Review

In 24–29, solve. *(Lessons 2-2, 4-4, 4-5)*

24. $8 = -2a$ **$-4 = a$**

25. $\frac{1}{2}b = 5$ **$b = 10$**

26. $-200 - c = -144$ **$c = -56$**

27. $3d + 3d = 42$ **$d = 7$**

28. $8 + g = 0$ **$g = -8$**

29. $30\pi = \pi d$ **$30 = d$**

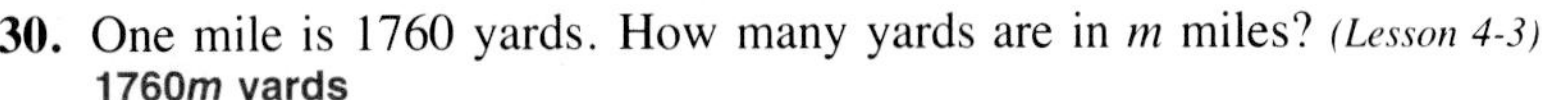

30. One mile is 1760 yards. How many yards are in m miles? *(Lesson 4-3)* **1760m yards**

31. A box is made by folding the pattern at the left along the dotted lines and taping the edges. What is the volume of the box? *(Lesson 4-1)* **57 cubic units**

32. *Skill sequence* Subtract. *(Lesson 3-1)*
a. $143 - 256$ **-113** **b.** $143 - -256$ **399** **c.** $-143 - 256$ **-399** **d.** $1.43 - 2.56$ **-1.13**

33. A number n is randomly selected from {10, 11, 12, 13, 14, 15} *(Lessons 1-7, 3-6)*
a. Find P($n > 12$). $\frac{1}{2}$ **b.** P(n is odd) $\frac{1}{2}$
c. P($n > 12$ and n is odd) $\frac{1}{3}$ **d.** P($n > 12$ or n is odd) $\frac{2}{3}$

34. **a.** Find a nonzero value of x for which $\frac{6 + x}{2 + x}$ does not equal 3.
b. Find a nonzero value of x for which $\frac{6 \cdot x}{2 \cdot x}$ does not equal 3.
(Lessons 1-4, 1-8)
a) any values other than 0 and -2; b) No such nonzero values exist.

35. You can see that the formula $A = \frac{1}{2}bh$ for the area of a triangle is true for a right triangle because a right triangle is half of a rectangle with sides b and h. Write a formula for the area of a triangle that is half of a square with sides of length s. *(Lesson 1-5)* **$A = \frac{1}{2}s^2$**

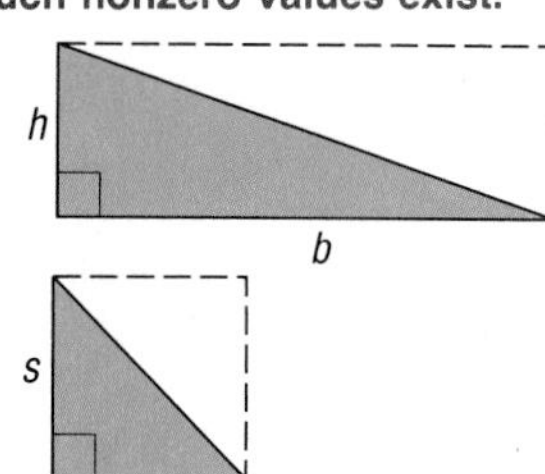

36. Graph all solutions to $x + y = 8$. Start with letting x and y be whole numbers. *(Lesson 3-7)* **See margin.**

37. *Skill sequence* Divide. *(Previous course)*
a. $\frac{2}{5} \div \frac{1}{3}$ $1\frac{1}{5}$ **b.** $2 \div \frac{1}{3}$ 6 **c.** $2.5 \div \frac{1}{3}$ 7.5 **d.** $\frac{1}{2} \div 3$ $\frac{1}{6}$

Exploration

38. Using your calculator, find a number $x < 0$ such that $.05 < x^2 < .06$.
Sample: -0.23; any values between -0.224 and -0.244 are possible answers.

FOLLOW-UP

MORE PRACTICE

For more practice on SPUR Objectives, use *Lesson Master 4-6*, shown below.

EXTENSION

Remind students that the two parts of the Multiplication Property of Inequality cover the result of multiplying both sides of $ax < b$ by a positive and by a negative. Then ask: What happens when you multiply both sides by zero? (Both sides are equal and the original inequality is lost.)

EVALUATION

A quiz covering Lessons 4-4 through 4-6 can be found on page 23 in the Teacher's Resource File.

NAME ____________

LESSON **MASTER 4–6**
QUESTIONS ON **SPUR** OBJECTIVES

■SKILLS *Objective D* *(See pages 204–207 for objectives.)*
In 1–8, solve and check.

1. $6c \le 42$ — $c \le 7; 6 \cdot 7 = 42, 6 \cdot 6 \le 42$
2. $-68 > 17d$ — $d < -4; -68 = 17(-4), -68 > 17(-5)$
3. $-9k > 108$ — $k < -12; -9(-12) = 108, -9(-13) > 108$
4. $5.5x \le 45.1$ — $x \le 8.2; 5.5(8.2) = 45.1, 5.5(8.1) \le 45.1$
5. $-.36 < .144n$ — $n > -2.5; -.36 = .114(-2.5), -.36 < .114(-2.4)$
6. $-.7y \ge -6.3$ — $y \le 9; -.7(9) = -6.3, -.7(8) \ge -6.3$
7. $\frac{2}{5}a \ge 8$ — $a \ge 20; \frac{2}{5}(20) = 8, \frac{2}{5}(21) \ge 8$
8. $-\frac{5}{12} < -\frac{3}{8}b$ — $b < \frac{10}{9}; -\frac{5}{12} = \left(-\frac{3}{8}\right)\left(\frac{10}{9}\right), -\frac{5}{12} < -\frac{3}{8}(1)$

■PROPERTIES *Objective F*

9. If $-x < a$, then x __>__ $-a$.

10. What inequality results if both sides of $-3z \ge -2$ are multiplied by $-\frac{1}{3}$? — $z \le \frac{2}{3}$

■USES *Objective K*

11. At least how much must the radius of a circle be in order for the circumference to be at least 88? — $\frac{44}{\pi}$ or ≈ 14

12. The class has collected \$75.50 for a pizza party. A large pizza costs \$9.95.
   a. Write an inequality to find how many pizzas the class can buy. — $9.95x \le 75.50$
   b. Solve the inequality. — $x \approx 7.6$; 7 pizzas

13. In 4 minutes, a drain can empty at most 40 gallons from a tank.
   a. Write an inequality that tells the rate at which the drain empties water from the tank. — $r \le \frac{40 \text{ gallons}}{4 \text{ minutes}}$
   b. Solve the inequality. — $r \le 10$ gallons/minute

32

LESSON 4-7

RESOURCES
- Lesson Master 4-7
- Computer Master 7

OBJECTIVE

H Apply the Multiplication Counting Principle.

TEACHING NOTES

Try to make this material as concrete as possible. For instance, in **Example 1,** use a diagram of the stadium to trace some of the paths that are described in the solution.

Alternate Approach It is important that students realize many problems can be described by more than one of the methods in this lesson. You can show how to solve **Example 1** with a tree diagram and also with the Multiplication Counting Principle. You may also wish to write the possible schedules in **Example 2** as ordered triples and to describe some of the possible quiz papers in **Example 3.**

The y^x key on a calculator can help with some calculations in this lesson. Your students may need instruction on using this key.

LESSON

4-7 Multiplication Counting Principle

In mathematics, a procedure is said to be *elegant* if it is clever and simple at the same time. For instance, area and multiplication are helpful in solving many types of counting problems. The area model of multiplication allows you to organize the items being counted into rectangular arrays, and then multiply to get totals. Here is an example of such a situation.

Example 1 A stadium has 9 gates. Gates *A*, *B*, *C*, and *D* are on the north side. Gates *E*, *F*, *G*, *H* and *I* are on the south side. In how many ways can you enter the stadium through a north gate and leave through a south gate?

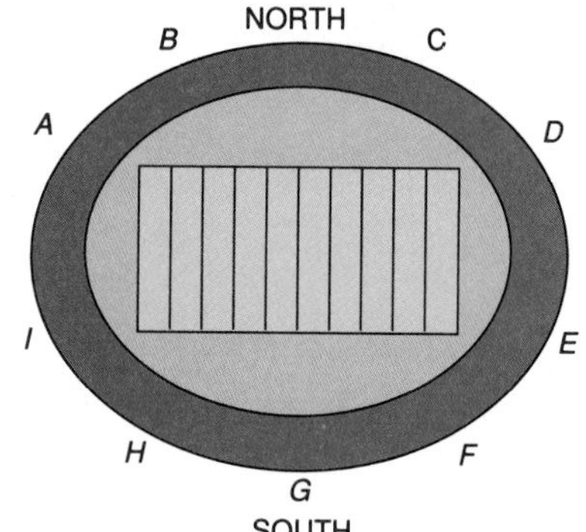

Solution Create a rectangular array where each entry in the array is an ordered pair. The first letter represents a gate you enter. The second letter stands for a gate you exit. The ordered pair (*C*, *H*) means you enter at gate *C* and leave through gate *H*.

		South Gate				
		E	*F*	*G*	*H*	*I*
	A	(*A*,*E*)	(*A*,*F*)	(*A*,*G*)	(*A*,*H*)	(*A*,*I*)
North	B	(*B*,*E*)	(*B*,*F*)	(*B*,*G*)	(*B*,*H*)	(*B*,*I*)
Gate	C	(*C*,*E*)	(*C*,*F*)	(*C*,*G*)	(*C*,*H*)	(*C*,*I*)
	D	(*D*,*E*)	(*D*,*F*)	(*D*,*G*)	(*D*,*H*)	(*D*,*I*)

Since the array has 4 rows and 5 columns, there are $4 \cdot 5 = 20$ pairs in the table. There are 20 ways of entering through a north gate and leaving through a south gate.

This elegant use of multiplication occurs often enough that it is given a special name, the **Multiplication Counting Principle.**

Multiplication Counting Principle:

If one choice can be made in m ways and a second choice can be made in n ways, then there are mn ways of making the first choice followed by the second choice.

The Multiplication Counting Principle can be extended to situations where more than two choices must be made.

Example 2 A high school student wants to take a foreign language class in period 1, a music course in period 2, and an art course in period 3. The language classes available are French, Spanish, and German. The music classes available are chorus and band. The art classes available are drawing and painting. In how many ways can the student choose the three classes?

Solution Make a blank for each decision to be made.

ways to choose language	·	ways to choose music	·	ways to choose art

There are 3 choices in foreign language, 2 choices in music, and 2 choices in art. Use the multiplication counting principle.

3	·	2	·	2
ways to choose language		ways to choose music		ways to choose art

There are $3 \cdot 2 \cdot 2 = 12$ choices.

Check Organize the possibilities using a **tree diagram.**

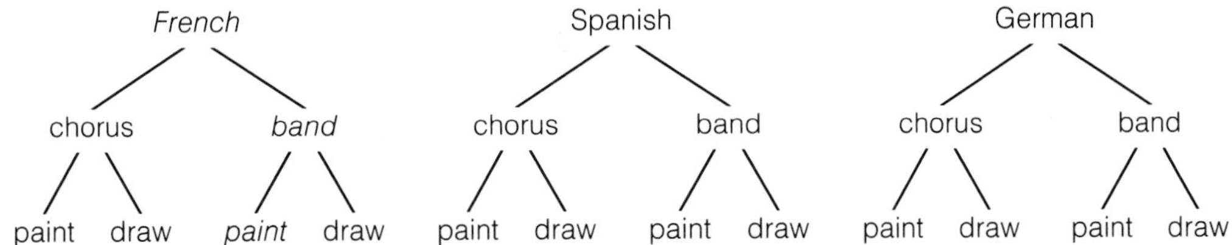

Each choice can be found by following a path along the diagram. One possible choice is shown in italics: *French—band—paint.* Counting shows there are 12 paths. Twelve different choices are possible.

ADDITIONAL EXAMPLES

1. A math contest event involves a student-teacher pair. The Centralville varsity team has five members (Alice, Bert, Carl, Denise, and Ellen) and two sponsors (Mr. Price and Ms. Quill).

a. How many pairs can compete?
10

b. List them.
(A, P), (A, Q), (B, P), (B, Q), (C, P), (C, Q), (D, P), (D, Q), (E, P), (E, Q)

2. A restaurant offers a special breakfast with eggs, meat, and juice. The eggs can be cooked in one of three different ways (scrambled, fried, poached); there are two choices for the meat (bacon, sausage) and three choices for the juice (orange, grape, tomato). How many different breakfasts can be ordered?
18

3. While Kari was at summer camp it was sunny for 7 days and then rained for 3 days. Each day Kari could do one special activity. On sunny days she had a choice of five different outside activities and on rainy days she had a choice of two different inside activities. How many ways could she choose her special activities in camp?
$\mathbf{5^7 \cdot 2^3 = 625{,}000}$

NOTES ON QUESTIONS
Question 9: The answer to part **a** is quite large. Therefore, the answer to part **b** is very small. Students may be more surprised at the size of the answer if they express the answer to part **b** as a decimal.

Question 17: Students may need help setting up a chart. Then they must generalize.

Question 36: This can be illustrated using the Area Model for Multiplication. Start with a square. Partition one side to show the school separated into French students and others. Partition an adjacent side to separate the French students into Ms. Walker's students and others.

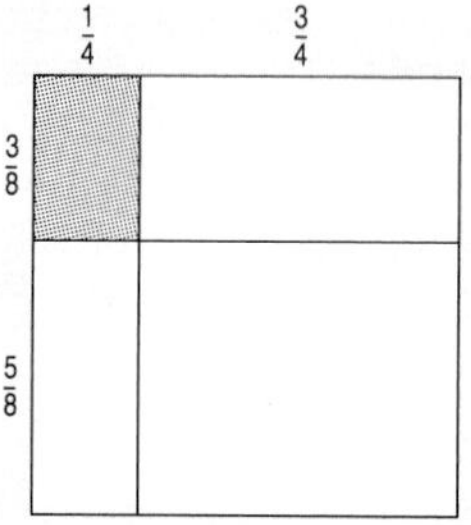

Ms. Walker has 3/8 • 1/4 = 3/32 of the students.

ADDITIONAL ANSWERS
2. If one choice can be made in *m* ways and a second choice be made in *n* ways, then there are *mn* ways of making the two choices in order.

5.

North Gate \ South Gate	I	F	E
A	(A, I)	(A, F)	(A, E)
B	(B, I)	(B, F)	(B, E)
C	(C, I)	(C, F)	(C, E)

Example 3 Mr. Graff gave his algebra class a quiz with five questions. Since Angie had not done her homework, she had to guess the answers. The quiz had two multiple-choice questions with choices A, B, C, and D, and three true-false questions. What is the probability that Angie gets all the questions correct?

Solution There are 4 ways to answer the multiple-choice question and 2 ways to answer each true-false question. Use the Multiplication Counting Principle.

4	•	4	•	2	•	2	•	2
ways to answer #1		ways to answer #2		ways to answer #3		ways to answer #4		ways to answer #5

There are $4 \cdot 4 \cdot 2 \cdot 2 \cdot 2 = 128$ different ways of answering the five questions, so there are 128 outcomes. Since only one of those outcomes is "all correct answers," with random guessing, Angie only has 1 chance out of 128 of getting all the questions correct.

P(all answers correct) $= \frac{1}{128}$

Example 4 Mr. Graff has already written the chapter test. It has three multiple-choice questions each with m possible answers, two multiple-choice questions each with n possible answers and five true-false questions. How many ways are there to answer the questions?

Solution Make a blank for each of the 10 questions. Fill it with the number of possible answers for that question.

Question #	1	2	3	4	5	6	7	8	9	10
Choices	m	m	m	n	n	2	2	2	2	2

Apply the Multiplication Counting Principle and multiply these to get $m \cdot m \cdot m \cdot n \cdot n \cdot 2 \cdot 2 \cdot 2 \cdot 2 \cdot 2$ sets of answers. Using exponents, this can be expressed as $m^3n^22^5$, or $32m^3n^2$.

Questions

Covering the Reading

1. In mathematics, a procedure is said to be elegant if __?__. **it is simple and clever at the same time**
2. State the Multiplication Counting Principle. **See margin.**
3. Can the Multiplication Counting Principle be applied in problems involving more than 2 choices? **Yes**

188

In 4 and 5, refer to Example 1.

4. In how many ways can a person enter through a north gate and leave through gate G? 4

5. Suppose the stadium closed gates D, G, and H. Using an array, list the ways a person could enter the stadium through a north gate and leave through a south gate. **See margin.**

6. Suppose the school in Example 2 offered Russian as a fourth language choice. How many choices could a student make? 16

7. Using exponents, simplify $5 \cdot m \cdot m \cdot n \cdot n \cdot n \cdot n$. $5m^2n^4$

8. Suppose Mr. Graff's quiz had two questions with x choices, and three true-false questions. Give the number of ways to answer the items on the test with an expression: a) $x \cdot x \cdot 2 \cdot 2 \cdot 2$; b) $2^3x^2 = 8x^2$
   a. not using exponents **b.** using exponents.

9. All the questions on a quiz can be answered with true or false. There are 20 questions. If a student guesses randomly,
   a. how many ways are there of answering the test? $2^{20} = 1{,}048{,}576$
   b. what are the chances of getting all the answers correct? 1/1,048,576

10. In Example 4, if all the multiple choice questions had q possible answers, how many different ways are there for answering the test? $q^5 \cdot 2^5 = 32q^5$

Applying the Mathematics

11. Satoshi, Izumi, Mitsuo, and Takeshi are candidates for Winter Carnival King. Reiko, Akiko, and Kimiko are the nominees for Winter Carnival Queen. Name all the possible "Royal Couples." **See margin.**

12. Radio station call letters must start with W or K, like WNEW or KYRZ.
   a. How many choices are there for the first letter? 2
   b. How many choices are there for the second letter? 26
   c. How many different 4-letter station names are possible? **See margin.**

13. Telephone area codes consist of 3 digits. The first digit must be chosen from 2 through 9. The second digit must be 0 or 1. The third digit cannot be 0. How many area codes are possible? 144

14. Suppose in Example 1 that a person could enter through any gate and leave through any gate. In how many ways can this be done? 81

15. Suppose in Example 1 that a person could enter through any gate and leave through any *other* gate. In how many ways can this be done? 72

16. At the Fulton College cafeteria, the main dish last Thursday was chicken. The vegetables served were carrots and beans. There were three dessert choices: an apple, pudding, and cake.
   a. Organize the possible meals consisting of a main dish, vegetable, and a dessert using a tree diagram. **See margin.**
   b. How many different such meals are possible? 6

17. A quiz has Q true-false questions. How many sets of answers are possible? (Hint: Make a list. Express the answer when $Q = 1$, $Q = 2$, $Q = 3$, and $Q = 4$. Then find the general pattern.) 2, 4, 8, 16; 2^Q

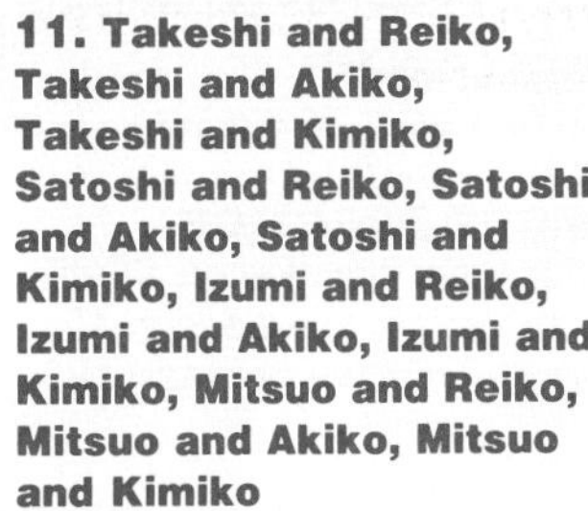

11. Takeshi and Reiko, Takeshi and Akiko, Takeshi and Kimiko, Satoshi and Reiko, Satoshi and Akiko, Satoshi and Kimiko, Izumi and Reiko, Izumi and Akiko, Izumi and Kimiko, Mitsuo and Reiko, Mitsuo and Akiko, Mitsuo and Kimiko

12c. $2 \cdot 26 \cdot 26 \cdot 26 = 35{,}152$

16a.

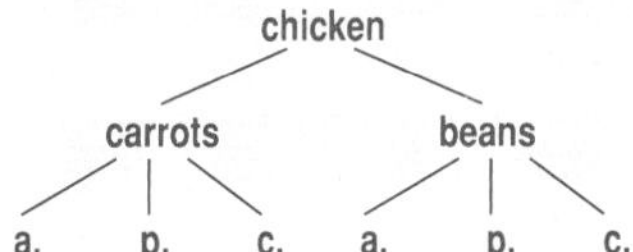

a: apple; p: pudding; c: cake

29. Commutative Property of Multiplication
30. Commutative Property of Addition
31. Property of Opposites
32. Additive Identity Property

38a. National Aeronautics and Space Administration
38b. United Nations Children's Emergency Fund
38c. Central Intelligence Agency

NAME ____________

LESSON **MASTER 4–7**
QUESTIONS ON **SPUR** OBJECTIVES

■USES *Objective H (See pages 204–207 for objectives.)*

1. Combination locks have 36 numbers used in three-number combinations. How many different combinations are there? (Assume that the same number cannot be used twice in a row.) **44,100 combinations**

2. A car can be ordered in six different colors, with a choice of two engines and three transmissions. How many different cars can be ordered? **36 cars**

3. On a special sale, pizza can be ordered with two toppings. Suppose there are eight different toppings available.
   a. How many pizzas can be ordered with two different toppings? **28 pizzas**
   b. Suppose you can also order "doubles" (pizzas with a double order of the same topping). How many different pizzas can be ordered? **36 pizzas**

4. A certain state uses three letters followed by three digits for its license plates. The letters I, O, and Q are not used, because they might be read as one or zero. How many licence plates are possible? **12,167,000 license plates**

5. How many different batting lineups can a 9-member baseball team have if the pitcher must bat last? **40,320 batting lineups**

6. Suppose a flag is to be made with three stripes of equal areas. Each of the colors red, white, and blue must be used, but can be chosen in any order. If the stripes can be either all vertical or all horizontal, how many different flags can be made? **12 flags**

7. The digits 0, 1, and 8 read the same right side up or upside down.
   a. How many different two-digit numbers read the same either way? (A number may not begin with zero.) **6 numbers**
   b. How many different three-digit numbers can be read the same either way? (A number may not begin with zero.) **18 numbers**

 33

FOLLOW-UP

MORE PRACTICE
For more practice on SPUR Objectives, use *Lesson Master 4-7,* shown on page 189.

EXTENSION
1. Have students solve this problem: A pizza parlor wants to be able to advertise that more than 100 combinations of pizza toppings are available. How many toppings must they have available? [With n toppings, 2^n combinations are possible. (The idea is the same as in **Question 17.**) Only 7 different choices of toppings will make 128 choices possible.]

2. You may want to perform a simulation of **Question 9.** Tell your students that you are going to test their ability to read minds. Tell them you are thinking of three true-false questions which they must answer T or F. Determine the answer key by tossing a coin or by using a random number generator on a calculator. (Let an odd digit stand for false and an even digit stand for true.) About 1/8 of your students will have perfect papers. Does that mean they are good mind readers? Repeat this for 5 and 10 questions. About 1/32 of the students will get all correct on a 5-question random true-false test and about 1/1000 on a 10-question test.

29-32., 38a-c. See margin, page 189.

38d. International Business Machines

38e. Intercontinental ballistic missile

38f. American Federation of Labor—Congress of Industrial Organization

38g. National Football League

38h. North Atlantic Treaty Organization

38i. United Nations Educational, Scientific and Cultural Organization

Review

In 18–23, solve. *(Lessons 4-4, 4-5, 4-6)*

18. $6j = 11$ $j = \frac{11}{6}$ **19.** $-20k = \frac{2}{5}$ $k = -\frac{1}{50}$ **20.** $-\ell = 3 - 5$ $\ell = 2$

21. $4m < \frac{1}{10}$ $m < \frac{1}{40}$ **22.** $-90 \geq -6n$ $15 \leq n$ **23.** $d + 2d < 39$ $d < 13$

24. If apples cost 49¢ a pound and 5 apples weigh 3 pounds, about how much should 1 apple cost? *(Lesson 4-2)* **29.4¢ each**

25. A farmer harvests 40 bales of hay per acre. How many acres would produce a harvest of 236 bales? *(Lessons 4-2, 4-4)* **5.9**

26. All angles in this figure are right angles. Write an expression for the area of the figure. *(Lesson 4-1)* **48 + 2x**

27. The length of a rectangle is 5 units longer than twice its width. If the width is w units long, write an expression for its area. *(Lesson 4-1)* $(2w + 5)w$

28. David weighs D pounds. His brother, Carl, weighs 17 pounds more.
a. Write an expression for Carl's weight. $D + 17$
b. Write an expression for their total weight. *(Lesson 2-2)* $2D + 17$

In 29–32, name the property illustrated. *(Lessons 2-2, 2-3)* **See margin.**

29. $a(3 + b) = (3 + b)a$ **30.** $a(3 + b) = a(b + 3)$

31. $a + (3 + -3) = a + 0$ **32.** $(a + 3) + 0 = a + 3$

33. Evaluate $\frac{4\pi r^3}{3}$ on your calculator when $r = 2.1$. Round your answer to the nearest tenth. *(Lesson 1-4)* ≈ 38.8

34. Evaluate $6(3x - y)$ when $x = -\frac{7}{3}$ and $y = -\frac{32}{5}$. Write your answer as a fraction. *(Lessons 1-4, 2-3)* $-\frac{18}{5}$

35. Evaluate when $d = \frac{1}{2}$. *(Lesson 1-4)*
a. d^2 $\frac{1}{4}$ **b.** $3d + 4$ $\frac{11}{2}$ **c.** $-8d^3$ -1

36. At Harwood High, $\frac{3}{8}$ of the students take French and $\frac{1}{4}$ of the French students are in Ms. Walker's French class. What fraction of Harwood High Students are in Ms. Walker's French class? *(Previous course)* $\frac{3}{32}$

37. If the probability of rain tomorrow is 30%, what is the probability of no rain tomorrow? *(Lesson 1-7)* **70%**

Exploration

In 38 and 39, use the fact that an *acronym* is a name made from first letters of words or parts of words. **See margin.**

38. Here are some famous acronyms. Tell what the letters stand for.
a. NASA **b.** UNICEF **c.** CIA
d. IBM **e.** ICBM **f.** AFL-CIO
g. NFL **h.** NATO **i.** UNESCO

39. *True or false* Over a half million 4-letter acronyms are possible in English. (Hint: Use the Multiplication Counting Principle.) **False**

LESSON

4-8

Multiplying Probabilities

Many TV watchers seldom change channels. So TV networks often put a new show after a popular one to boost the ratings of the new show. Suppose 25% of viewers watched show A and 80% of these stayed to watch show B. Then, since $.80 \cdot .25 = .20$, 20% of the viewers watched both shows.

If a viewer is called at random, then each of the percents can be interpreted as a probability.

$$\begin{aligned} 25\% = .25 &= \text{P(watched show A)} &&= \text{P}(A) \\ 80\% = .80 &= \text{P(watched show B having already watched show A)} &&= \text{P}(B \text{ given } A) \\ 20\% = .20 &= \text{P(watched shows A and B)} &&= \text{P}(A \text{ and } B) \end{aligned}$$

You have seen P(A) and P(A and B) before. P(B given A) is the probability that B occurs *given that A occurs*. P(B given A) is called a **conditional probability.** This situation illustrates the **Conditional Probability Formula.**

Conditional Probability Formula:

$$\text{P}(A \text{ and } B) = \text{P}(A) \cdot \text{P}(B \text{ given } A).$$

You may see the Conditional Probability Formula with the intersection symbol.

$$\text{P}(\text{A} \cap \text{B}) = \text{P(A)} \cdot \text{P(B given A)}.$$

Here is an example that makes use of this formula.

Example 1 A department store knows that $\frac{4}{5}$ of its customers are female. The probability that a U.S. female wears contact lenses is about $\frac{3}{50}$. If a customer is chosen at random, what is the probability that the customer is a female and wearing contact lenses?

LESSON 4-8

RESOURCES
- Lesson Master 4-8
- Computer Master 8

OBJECTIVE

I Apply the Conditional Probability Formula.

TEACHING NOTES

Reading To aid in student understanding, suggest that they focus on the meaning of the Conditional Probability Formula rather than the words and symbols. The probability that A and B both happen is the probability that A occurs times the probability that B also happens. Questions in this lesson usually give students information that is ordered, to help them determine which event should be considered A and which one B.

Explain that to find P(A *and* B), you first find the fraction of the time that A happens, namely, P(A). Second, you find the fraction of those times that B happens also, namely, P(B *given* A).

In **Example 1,** 4/5 of the customers are females, and 3/50 of those 4/5 also wear contact lenses. So P(female and wearing contacts) = 4/5 • 3/50. This can also be shown with the diagram below where a square represents all the customers.

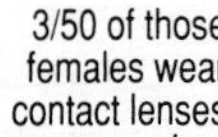

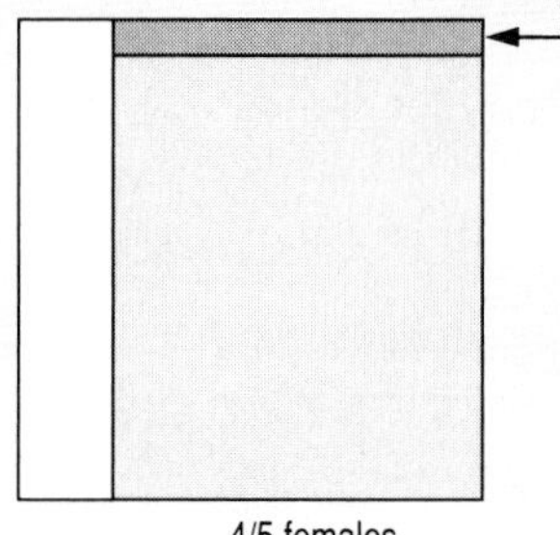

Solution You are asked to find $P(A \cap B)$, where A = customer is a female and B = customer is wearing contacts. You are given $P(A) = \frac{4}{5}$.

P(B given A) means the probability that a person wears contacts given that the person is a female. Here

$$\begin{aligned} P(B \text{ given } A) &= \frac{3}{50} \\ P(A \text{ and } B) &= P(A) \cdot P(B \text{ given } A) \\ &= \frac{4}{5} \cdot \frac{3}{50} \\ &= \frac{12}{250} \\ &= 0.048 \end{aligned}$$

Since 0.048 = 4.8%, there is about a 5% chance that a randomly chosen customer is a female who wears contact lenses.

The situation of Example 1 can be pictured in a tree diagram.

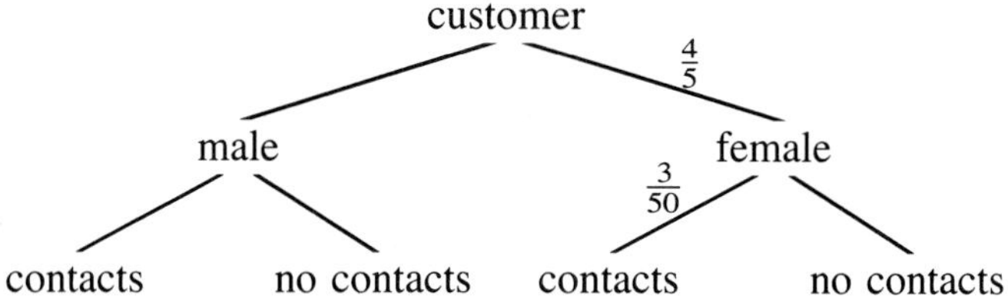

The tree diagram helps to see what other probabilities could be calculated. For instance, $\frac{47}{50}$ of females do not wear contacts. Can you find the probability that the customer is a female who doesn't wear contact lenses?

Example 2 Suppose that two cards are drawn from a well-shuffled deck. The first card is *not* put back before the second is drawn. What is the probability that both cards are hearts?

Solution
Let A = drawing a heart as the first card.
Let B = drawing a heart as the second card.
The problem is to compute P(A and B).
There are 13 hearts in the deck of 52, so $P(A) = \frac{13}{52}$.
After the first heart has been drawn there are 12 hearts left in a deck of 51. So $P(B \text{ given } A) = \frac{12}{51}$.

$$\begin{aligned} P(A \text{ and } B) &= P(A) \cdot P(B \text{ given } A) \\ &= \frac{13}{52} \cdot \frac{12}{51} \\ &= \frac{1}{4} \cdot \frac{4}{17} \\ &= \frac{1}{17} \end{aligned}$$

192

In the following example, the occurrence of the first event does not affect the probability of the second event. However, the formula for multiplying probabilities still works.

Example 3 Ken plays a game at a carnival in which he draws a marble from each of two jars. He wins a prize if both marbles are green.

Look at the jars at the left. Find the probability that both marbles Ken draws are green.

Solution Looking at the jar, P(1st is green) = $\frac{1}{10}$. Notice that the second color drawn does not depend on what color the first marble is. So P(2nd is green given 1st is green) = $\frac{3}{7}$.

$$\begin{aligned}\text{P(1st is green and 2nd is green)} &= \text{P(1st is green)} \cdot \text{P(2nd is also green)}\\ &= \frac{1}{10} \cdot \frac{3}{7}\\ &= \frac{3}{70} \approx .04\end{aligned}$$

Probability situations like these can lead to equations of the form $ax = b$, where both a and b are fractions.

Example 4 In a survey, $\frac{2}{15}$ of the people surveyed were men who liked Brand X Toothpaste. If $\frac{3}{5}$ of the people surveyed were men, what fraction of men like Brand X?

Solution
Let A = person surveyed is a man.
Let B = person liked Brand X.
Then we know that P(A and B) = $\frac{2}{15}$ and P(A) = $\frac{3}{5}$.
We want P(B given A), the probability that a man liked Brand X. Call this t.

$$\text{Now P(A and B)} = \text{P(A)} \cdot \text{P(B given A)}$$
$$\frac{2}{15} = \frac{3}{5} \cdot t$$

Solve the equations as usual. Multiply both sides by $\frac{5}{3}$.

$$\frac{5}{3} \cdot \frac{2}{15} = \frac{5}{3} \cdot \frac{3}{5} \cdot t$$
$$\frac{2}{9} = t$$

Thus the probability that a man likes Brand X is $\frac{2}{9}$.

ADDITIONAL EXAMPLES

1. Radio station WWWW estimates that it has $\frac{1}{8}$ of the local listening audience. Of all those local listeners, $\frac{1}{50}$ buy WWWW T-shirts. What is the probability that a person listens to WWWW and has a WWWW T-shirt?
$\frac{1}{8} \cdot \frac{1}{50} = \frac{1}{400}$
You might replace the fractions with percents and recompute the answer.

2. At the store, a shelf contains 80 cartons of eggs. Six of the cartons have broken eggs. If Bob picks up two cartons, what is the probability that both cartons have broken eggs?
$\frac{6}{80} \cdot \frac{5}{79} = \frac{3}{632}$

3. In **Example 3,** if Kevin picks a marble from each jar, what is the probability that neither one is green?
$\frac{9}{10} \cdot \frac{4}{7} = \frac{18}{35}$

4. During last year's baseball season, Will got a hit in $\frac{2}{15}$ of the team's games. Will played in $\frac{3}{5}$ of the games. In what fraction of the games that Will played did he get a hit?
$\frac{3}{5} \cdot x = \frac{2}{15}$, so $x = \frac{2}{9}$

NOTES ON QUESTIONS

Question 10: The Rate Factor Model for Multiplication can help explain this question:

$$\frac{2}{3}\frac{\text{males}}{\text{people surveyed}} \cdot (x)\frac{\text{males watching TV}}{\text{males}} = \frac{3}{10}\frac{\text{males watching TV}}{\text{people surveyed}}.$$

Reading for Question 11: Students may need help with the subtleties distinguishing choice (b) from choice (c). Choice (b) involves

$$\frac{\text{opera likers}}{\text{people over 20}},$$

while choice (c) uses

$$\frac{\text{people over 20}}{\text{opera likers}}.$$

Question 14: You may explain this question by using specific values for r and t. For example, if $r = 7$ and $t = 12$, then P(both red) $= \frac{7}{12} \cdot \frac{6}{11} = \frac{42}{132}$.

Check Draw a tree diagram with the given information and the solution found.

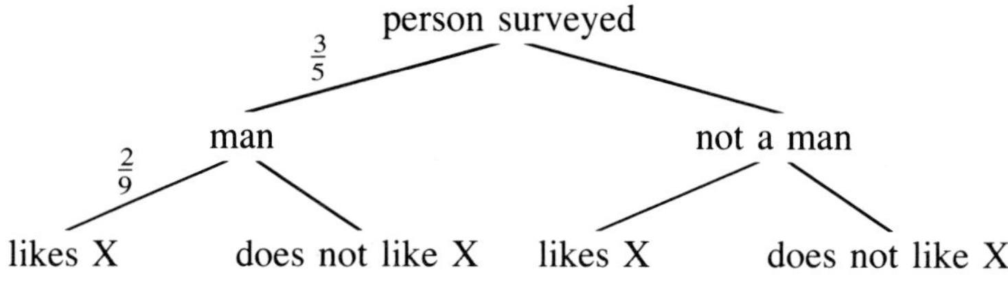

From the diagram, $\frac{3}{5} \cdot \frac{2}{9} = \frac{2}{15}$, the given probability that a person surveyed is a man who likes Brand X.

Questions

Covering the Reading

1. **a.** Give the Conditional Probability Formula for P(A and B). P(A) · P(B given A)
   b. If P(A) $= \frac{1}{10}$ and P(B given A) $= \frac{2}{3}$, what is P(A and B)? $\frac{2}{30}$ or $\frac{1}{15}$

2. **a.** If 28% of TV viewers watched Channel 5 from 7:00 to 7:30 and 75% of these stayed to watch the Channel 5 program at 7:30, what percent of viewers watched both? 21%
   b. Part **a** can be done using the Conditional Probability Formula. Describe the events A and B, B given A, and A. See margin.

In 3 and 4, refer to Example 1.

3. **a.** What is the probability that a customer in the store is female?
   b. What is the probability that a customer in the store is female and wears contact lenses? ≈5%

4. **a.** What is the probability that a female in the U.S. does not wear contacts? $\frac{47}{50}$
   b. Use the tree diagram to calculate the probability that a customer in the store is female and does not wear contacts. ≈75%

5. Refer to Example 1. At Horst's Shoes, 5 out of 7 customers are females. If a customer is chosen at random, find the probability that the person is a female and is wearing contact lenses. Write your answer as a percent. $\frac{3}{70} \approx .043$ or 4.3%

6. Here is a tree diagram for Example 2. Copy and compute the probabilities. a) $\frac{13}{52}$ or $\frac{1}{4}$; b) $\frac{12}{51}$ or $\frac{4}{17}$; c) $\frac{39}{52}$ or $\frac{3}{4}$; d) $\frac{39}{51}$ or $\frac{13}{17}$

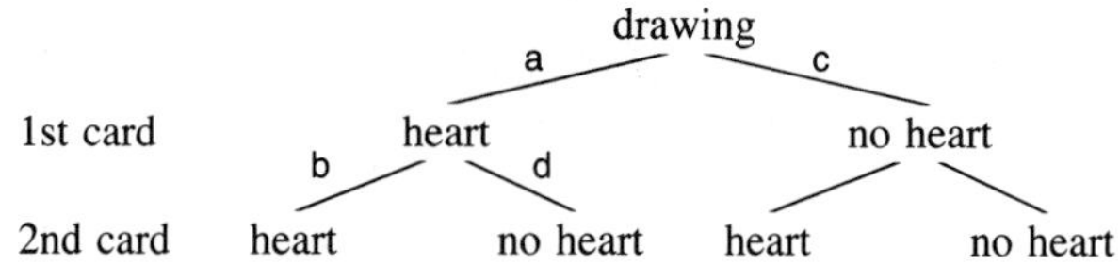

7. In the situation of Example 2, what is the probability that neither card drawn is a heart? $\frac{19}{34}$

8. Suppose that two cards are drawn from a deck. The first card is not put back before the second is drawn. What is the probability that both cards are kings? **$\frac{1}{221} \approx 0.005$**

9. Ken draws a marble from each of two jars. The probability that the first marble is red is $\frac{8}{15}$. The probability that the second one is red is $\frac{1}{3}$. Find the probability that both marbles are red. **≈18%**

10. Two thirds of the people surveyed were male. Three tenths of those surveyed were males who had watched television the previous night. What fraction of males watched television last night? **$\frac{9}{20}$**

Applying the Mathematics

11. *Multiple choice* Suppose X = is over 20 years old and Y = likes opera. Which describes P(Y given X)? **(b)**
(a) the probability that a person is over 20 and likes opera
(b) the probability that a person who is over 20 also likes opera
(c) the probability that a person who likes opera is over 20

12. In a certain town it was determined that 90% of the blocks have fire hydrants. Of those blocks with fire hydrants, 72% have more than one. What percent of blocks in the town have more than one fire hydrant? **≈65%**

13. There are two traffic lights on the way to the store. One is red 60% of the time. The other light is red 50% of the time no matter what color the first light is. What is the probability of being stopped by a red light at both traffic signals? **30%**

14. There are r red balls out of a total of t balls in a jar. A ball is drawn and kept out of the jar. Then a second ball is drawn. Write an expression for each of the following:
a. P(first ball is red and second ball is red) **$\frac{r}{t} \cdot \frac{r-1}{t-1}$**
b. P(first ball is *not* red and second ball is red) **$\frac{t-r}{t} \cdot \frac{r}{t-1}$**

15. There are 20 books in a pile: 3 history books, 7 biographies, and 10 novels. You close your eyes and choose a book at random without putting it back into the pile. Your friend then closes his eyes and chooses a book at random. Find each of the following:
a. P(you choose a novel) **$\frac{1}{2}$**
b. P(your friend then chooses a biography) **$\frac{7}{19}$**
c. P(you choose a novel and your friend chooses a biography) **$\frac{7}{38}$**

In 16 and 17, find P(A and B).

16. P(A) = $\frac{x}{z}$, P(B given A) = $\frac{y}{x}$ **$\frac{y}{z}$** 17. P(A) = $\frac{m}{3n}$, P(B given A) = $\frac{5m}{3n}$ **$\frac{5m^2}{9n^2}$**

18. Before an oil company decides to drill a well, geologists test the site to determine if there is a good chance of striking oil. In 1986, the Oliff Oil Company geologists found that 23% of the sites were favorable. Wells were drilled on those sites and 8% of the drilled wells struck oil.
a. Estimate the probability that a site will seem favorable and produce oil. **1.8% or ≈ 2%**
b. Next year the Oliff Oil Company plans to test 50 sites. How many sites can be expected to produce oil? **50 · 2% = 1 site**

ADDITIONAL ANSWERS
2b. P($A \cap B$) = P(A) · P(B given A) = .28 · .75 = .21

NAME ____________

LESSON **MASTER 4–8**
QUESTIONS ON **SPUR** OBJECTIVES

USES *Objective I* *(See pages 204–207 for objectives.)*
In 1–4, find P(A and B).

1. P(A) = $\frac{3}{5}$, P(B given A) = $\frac{5}{8}$ **$\frac{3}{8}$**
2. P(B) = .45, P(A given B) = .30 **.135**
3. P(B) = .6n, P(A given B) = .4n **$.24n^2$**
4. P(A) = $\frac{p}{3}$, P(B given A) = $\frac{1}{p}$ **$\frac{1}{3}$**

In 5 and 6, find P(B given A).

5. P(A and B) = $\frac{5}{8}$, P(A) = $\frac{3}{4}$ **$\frac{5}{6}$**
6. P(A and B) = $\frac{p}{3}$, P(A) = $\frac{2p}{5}$ **$\frac{5}{6}$**

In 7 and 8, find P(A).

7. P(A and B) = $\frac{1}{12}$, P(B given A) = $\frac{2}{3}$ **$\frac{1}{8}$**
8. P(A and B) = .32r, P(B given A) = .56r **$\frac{4}{7}$; or about .57**

9. If two light bulbs in a display are connected in series and one goes out, the other will also go out. The probability that a light bulb will last a month is .95. What is the probability that the display will last a month? **.9025**

10. In basketball, a one-and-one free throw means that if you make the first one, you get to shoot again. Suppose a player usually makes 75% of his free throws. What is the probability that he will make both shots of a one-and-one free throw? **$\frac{9}{16}$, .5625 or 56.25%**

11. At a carnival booth, you get a prize if you hit a target and knock it off the shelf. The probability that you will hit the target is $\frac{1}{4}$. The probability that it will fall off the shelf if you hit it is $\frac{1}{2}$. What is the probability that you will win a prize? **$\frac{1}{8}$**

12. Two letters are picked at random from the letters in the word *mathematics*, without replacement. What is the probability that they are both vowels? **$\frac{6}{55}$**

NOTES ON QUESTIONS
Question 19a:
Let A = first child is a girl. Let B = second child is a girl. From the given, P(A) = .5. Also, since births do not affect one another, P(B given A) = .5. So P(A and B) = P(A) • P(B given A) = .5 • .5. We have used 1/2 in this question to emphasize the fractions. Using conditional probability helps dispel faulty reasoning such as "I have had 5 daughters. That means my next child is almost certainly going to be a son."

Recall that the relative frequency of male births is 51.3% (Lesson 1-8). You may wish to have students do the problem with the relative frequency of female births (48.7%) instead of the fraction 1/2.

Question 30b: This can be answered by rounding each number to the nearest half, so the answer is approximately 1/2 + 1/2 + 1 = 2. (National Assessments show students are poor at estimating sums of fractions.)

Question 32: To give this answer as a decimal, there are two orders in which the calculations can be carried out. One way is 1750 − 1714 = 36 people who didn't show up; 36/1750 ≈ 2%. Another method is 1714/1750 ≈ 98%; 100% − 98% = 2%.

Small Group Work for Question 33: Instead of having one person draw a card 100 times, you might divide the class into groups. Have each group do some of the drawings, then combine the results.

FOLLOW-UP

MORE PRACTICE
For more practice on SPUR Objectives, use *Lesson Master 4-8,* shown on page 195.

28a. $32 \div \frac{1}{8} = 256$
28b. 8, 16, 32, 64, 128

19. If the probability of a newborn being a girl is $\frac{1}{2}$, find the probability of the birth of
a. two girls in a row. $\frac{1}{4}$ **b.** three girls in a row. $\frac{1}{8}$

Review

20. How many different outfits can be made from 3 shirts, 4 pairs of slacks and 2 pairs of shoes, all of which go together? *(Lesson 4-7)* **24 outfits**

21. A certain state makes car license plates with 3 letters and then 3 numbers. For example, WEZ 123 is a car license number in this state. So is WEW 002. How many license plates are possible? *(Lesson 4-7)* **17,576,000**

22. *Skill sequence* Solve. *(Lessons 3-3, 4-4, 4-5, 4-6)*
a. $x - \frac{3}{8} = -\frac{1}{4}$ $x = \frac{1}{8}$ **b.** $\frac{3}{8} - y = -\frac{1}{4}$ $y = \frac{5}{8}$
c. $\frac{3}{8}z = -\frac{1}{4}$ $z = -\frac{2}{3}$ **d.** $\frac{3}{8}z < -\frac{1}{4}$ $z < -\frac{2}{3}$

23. A rectangular array of d dots has c columns and r rows. How are c, r, and d related? *(Lesson 4-1)* $cr = d$

24. *Multiple choice* $3x^2 \cdot x^4 =$ **(b)**
(a) $3x^8$ (b) $3x^6$ (c) $9x^8$ (d) $24x$ *(Lesson 1-4)*

In 25–27, multiply. *(Lessons 1-8, 4-2)* 25) $\frac{6}{5}$; 26) $\frac{15a^2b}{2}$; 27) $\frac{1}{a}$

25. $\frac{3 \cdot 2 \cdot 1}{5 \cdot 4 \cdot 3 \cdot 2 \cdot 1} \cdot 4 \cdot 3 \cdot 2 \cdot 1$ **26.** $\frac{5ab}{8m} \cdot 12am$ **27.** $\frac{6x^2}{4a} \cdot \frac{2}{3x^2}$

28. Five instances in a general pattern are given below. **a.** Give the next instance. **b.** Calculate the values of each instance. *(Previous course)*

$32 \div 4$ $32 \div 2$ $32 \div 1$ $32 \div \frac{1}{2}$ $32 \div \frac{1}{4}$
See margin.

29. Solve for x: $mx = -12$. *(Lesson 4-4)* $x = -\frac{12}{m}$

30. In your head, estimate each result to the nearest whole number. *(Previous course)*
a. $8.93 \cdot 2.06$ 18 **b.** $\frac{1}{2} + \frac{5}{8} + \frac{3}{4}$ 2 **c.** $75.36 \div 2.0000965$ 38

31. Find the image of the point (-7, 2) after a slide of:
a. 8 units to the right and 5 units down (1, -3)
b. r units up $(-7, r + 2)$
c. m units to the right and n units down *(Lesson 2-5)* $(-7 + m, 2 - n)$

32. A restaurant found that out of 1750 people who made reservations last month, 1714 actually showed up. What is the relative frequency of people who did not show up? *(Lesson 1-8)* ≈2%

Exploration

33. Repeat the experiment of Example 2, one hundred times.
a. How often do you pick two hearts? **Answers will vary; about 6 times**
b. How often do you pick two cards of the same suit? **about 24 times**
c. Is the probability calculated in Example 2 verified in your experiment? **Yes, if both cards were hearts about $\frac{6}{100}$ of the time.**

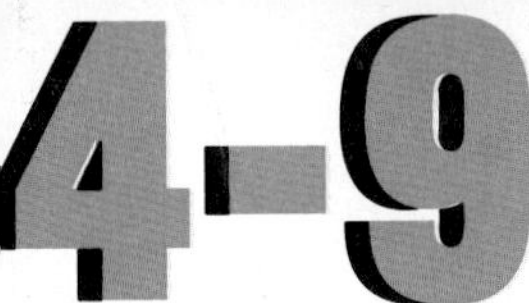

LESSON 4-9

The Factorial Symbol

A special case of the Multiplication Counting Principle occurs when a list of things is to be ranked or ordered.

Some students were asked to rank these famous basketball stars in order of preference: Magic Johnson, Michael Jordan, Larry Bird, Dominique Wilkins. How many possible rankings can there be in the poll?

To answer this question, you might try to list all the possible outcomes. Here are just three of the possible rankings.

Larry Bird	Dominique Wilkins	Michael Jordan
Magic Johnson	Michael Jordan	Magic Johnson
Dominique Wilkins	Larry Bird	Dominique Wilkins
Michael Jordan	Magic Johnson	Larry Bird

It seems like it would take a long time to list all rankings. But the number of rankings can be found using the Multiplication Counting Principle. There are 4 people who could finish first. After choosing one for first place there are only 3 people left who could finish second. Then, after 1st and 2nd place have been chosen, there are only 2 people left who could finish third, and the remaining person will finish last.

4	·	3	·	2	·	1
ways to choose 1st place		ways to choose 2nd place		ways to choose 3rd place		ways to choose 4th place

The answer is $4 \cdot 3 \cdot 2 \cdot 1 = 24$.

A shortcut way to write $4 \cdot 3 \cdot 2 \cdot 1$ is 4! This is read "four factorial."

Definition:

The symbol ***n!*** (read ***n* factorial**) means the product of the integers from *n* down to 1.

LESSON 4-9

RESOURCES
- Lesson Master 4-9
- Computer Master 8

OBJECTIVES

E Evaluate expressions containing a factorial symbol.
J Apply the Permutation Theorem.

TEACHING NOTES

At this point, let students treat the word *theorem* as synonymous with *property*. Explain that we may call a property a theorem when it follows logically from other properties.

Make sure that all students know how to find a factorial on their brand of calculator.

The evaluation in **Example 3** is motivated by the need to simplify expressions such as 99!/95!. You cannot enter either of the two factorials on most calculators, but the reduced form, 99 • 98 • 97 • 96, *is* computable.

ADDITIONAL EXAMPLES

1. Evaluate 7!
5040

2. In how many different orders can the four members of a relay track team run?
24

3. Evaluate $\frac{9!}{6!3!}$.
84

Example 1 Evaluate 5!

Solution $5! = 5 \cdot 4 \cdot 3 \cdot 2 \cdot 1$
$= 120$

An arrangement of letters, names, or objects is called a **permutation.** We have found that there are 4! permutations of 4 names. In general:

Permutation Theorem:

There are $n!$ possible permutations of n objects when each object is used exactly once.

Factorials are used when you are making arrangements of all the items in a set.

Scientific calculators usually have a factorial key [n!]. To evaluate $n!$, key in n [x!]. On some calculators you may have to use a second function key, [inv] or [2nd]. Then key in n [inv] [x!].

Example 2 A baseball manager is setting a batting order for his 9 starting players. How many batting orders are possible?

Solution The batting order is an arrangement of the starting players. Each player is used only once so the permutation theorem applies.

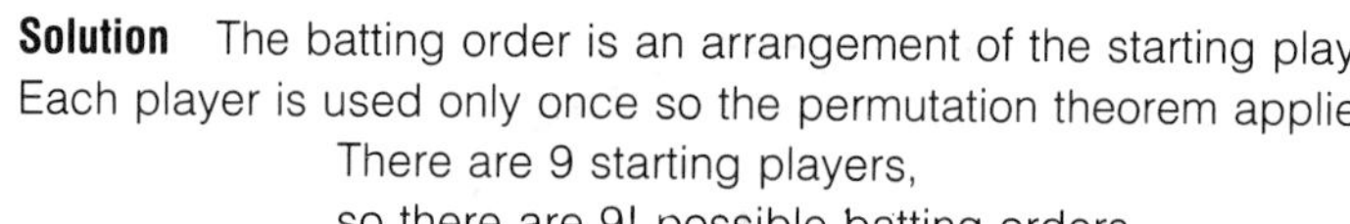

There are 9 starting players,
so there are 9! possible batting orders.

Using the calculator, key in 9 [x!]

$$9! = 362{,}880$$

Sometimes you can do a problem more quickly with pencil and paper than with a calculator. When working with fractions, see whether you can simplify first. Large numbers can often be managed using this method.

Example 3 Evaluate $\frac{12!}{10!}$.

Solution 1 Express the factorials as multiplications and simplify.

$$\begin{aligned}\frac{12!}{10!} &= \frac{12 \cdot 11 \cdot 10 \cdot 9 \cdot 8 \cdot 7 \cdot 6 \cdot 5 \cdot 4 \cdot 3 \cdot 2 \cdot 1}{10 \cdot 9 \cdot 8 \cdot 7 \cdot 6 \cdot 5 \cdot 4 \cdot 3 \cdot 2 \cdot 1} \\ &= 12 \cdot 11 \\ &= 132\end{aligned}$$

Solution 2 Only write out as many of the factors of the factorials as necessary.

$$\begin{aligned}\frac{12!}{10!} &= \frac{12 \cdot 11 \cdot 10!}{10!} \\ &= 12 \cdot 11 \\ &= 132\end{aligned}$$

Check Use a calculator to evaluate the factorials. Key in 12 [x!] [÷] 10 [x!] [=].

$$\begin{aligned}\frac{12!}{10!} &= \frac{4.79 \cdot 10^8}{3{,}628{,}800} \\ &= 132\end{aligned}$$

12! is so large that the calculator must express it in scientific notation.

Questions

Covering the Reading

1. Make a list of all possible rankings in a poll with Michael Jordan, Magic Johnson, and Larry Bird. **See margin.**
2. If you take a poll ranking 4 basketball stars, how many outcomes can there be in the poll? **24**
3. A short way to write $4 \cdot 3 \cdot 2 \cdot 1$ is __?__. **4!**
4. The symbol n! means __?__. **See margin.**
5. Evaluate n! when n equals:
   a. 1 **1** **b.** 2 **2** **c.** 3 **6** **d.** 4 **24**
   e. 5 **120** **f.** 6 **720** **g.** 7 **5040** **h.** 8 **40,320**

In 6 and 7, evaluate with a calculator.

6. 15! **1.3077×10^{12}**
7. 30! **2.6525×10^{32}**

ADDITIONAL ANSWERS
1. Bird, Jordan, Johnson; Bird, Johnson, Jordan; Jordan, Johnson, Bird; Jordan, Bird, Johnson; Johnson, Bird, Jordan; Johnson, Jordan, Bird
4. *n* factorial (the product of the integers from *n* down to 1)

NOTES ON QUESTIONS
Question 12: The most efficient way to answer this question is to realize 10! = 10 • 9! and use the answer to **Example 2.**

Question 14: When you discuss this question, expand the factorials to show the common factors in the numerator and denominator. Remind students that the common factors can be removed because of the Equal Fractions Property $\frac{ak}{bk} = \frac{a}{b}$.

Question 15: This question is intended to help differentiate between situations that involve factorials and those that use the Multiplication Counting Principle. It is important that students see this difference.

Question 19: Call attention to the denominators of these answers. In parts **a** and **c** we are considering the entire class, but in **b** we are only looking at students with the flu.

Making Connections for Question 33: Have students rewrite this question as 8*c* • 8*c*, then multiply. We will formalize properties of exponents in Chapter 9.

Alternate Approach for Question 36: You can also ask for the largest *n* for which *n*! is displayed as a number in standard form (as opposed to a display in scientific notation).

19.

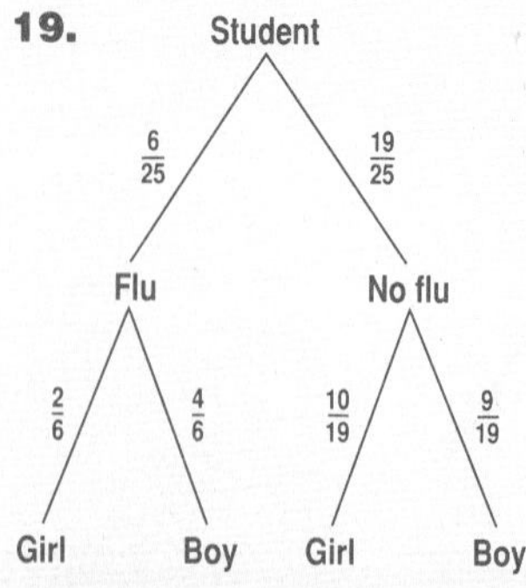

35. Answers will vary. On some calculators, the largest value of *n* is 69.

In 8 and 9, evaluate.

8. $\frac{6!}{3!}$ 120

9. $\frac{100!}{99!}$ 100

10. An arrangement of objects is called a __?__. permutation

11. The number of permutations of *n* objects is __?__. *n*!

12. In softball, there are 10 people who can bat. In how many ways can the manager of a softball team arrange the batting order? 10! = 3,628,800

Applying the Mathematics

In 13 and 14, evaluate.

13. (3!)! 720

14. $\frac{7!}{4!\,3!}$ 35

15. Suppose 8 horses are in a race.
a. In how many ways can first and second place be awarded? 8 · 7 = 56
b. In how many different orders can all eight horses finish? 8! = 40,320

16. Twenty pictures are placed in a line on a wall. In how many ways can they be arranged? Write your answer in scientific notation. $20! = 2.4329 \cdot 10^{18}$

17. a. Evaluate $\frac{n!}{(n-1)!}$ when $n = 10$. 10
b. Generalize part a. $\frac{n!}{(n-1)!} = n$

Review

18. Michelle has three outfits she can wear to school tomorrow. One is blue, one is green, and the third is purple. Let *A* = she wears the blue outfit in tomorrow's math class. Let *B* = she wears the blue outfit in tomorrow's English class. Estimate: *(Lesson 4-8)*
a. P(*A*) $\frac{1}{3}$ **b.** P(*B*) $\frac{1}{3}$ **c.** P(*B* given *A*) 1 **d.** P($A \cap B$) $\frac{1}{3}$

19. Six students in a class of 25 have the flu. Two of these six are girls. Thirteen of the 25 students in the class are boys. Draw a tree diagram.
a. What is the probability that a randomly chosen student is a girl? $\frac{12}{25}$
b. What is the probability that a randomly chosen student with the flu is a girl? $\frac{2}{6}$ or $\frac{1}{3}$ 19) See margin for tree diagram.
c. What is the probability that a randomly chosen student is a girl with the flu? *(Lesson 4-8)* $\frac{6}{25} \cdot \frac{2}{6} = \frac{2}{25}$

20. On three questions of a five question multiple-choice test there are four choices. On two questions there are five choices. If Mary guesses on all the questions, what are her chances of getting them all correct? *(Lesson 4-7)* **$\frac{1}{1600}$**

In 21–26, solve. *(Lessons 4-4, 4-5, 4-6)*

21. $10x = 723$ **72.3**

22. $7a \geq -2$ **$a \geq \frac{-2}{7}$**

23. $\frac{3}{8}y < \frac{5}{4}$ **$y < \frac{10}{3}$**

24. $1.6 = 2.5x$ **$.64 = x$ or $\frac{16}{25} = x$**

25. $(2 - 3)t \leq 8$ **$t \geq -8$**

26. $8v - 8v = 0$ **$0v = 0$; v = any number**

27. Simplify: $\frac{7}{5} \cdot 5x + 0 \cdot x + -7x$. *(Lesson 4-3)* **0**

28. Write the reciprocal of $\frac{50n^3}{233m^5}$. *(Lesson 4-3)* **$\frac{233m^5}{50n^3}$**

29. There are about 16,000 grains of sand per cubic inch and 1728 cubic inches per cubic foot. About how many grains of sand are in a 25 cubic foot sandbox? *(Lesson 4-2)* **≈691,200,000 grains**

30. A rectangular solid is twice as long as it is wide. It is three units higher than it is wide. If w is the width, write an expression for its volume. *(Lesson 4-1)* **$2w^2(w + 3)$**

In 31–33, simplify. *(Lesson 4-1)*

31. $3.3(2a)$ **$6.6a$**

32. $(6b)(3b)$ **$18b^2$**

33. $(8c)^2$ **$64c^2$**

Exploration

In 34–36, use a calculator.

34. What is the smallest value of n for which $n!$ is divisible by 100? **10**

35. What is the largest value of n for which the calculator can calculate or estimate $n!$? **See margin.**

36. Key in 2.5 [x!]. Explain what happens. **An error message is displayed.**

FOLLOW-UP

MORE PRACTICE

For more practice on SPUR Objectives, use *Lesson Master 4-9*, shown below.

EXTENSION

1. Have students consider the following questions: In **Example 2,** if the manager wants the shortstop to bat last, how many batting orders are possible? ($8! \cdot 1 = 40{,}320$) If he wants the left fielder to bat fourth and the shortstop to bat last, how many batting orders are possible? ($7! = 5040$)

2. Computer Students can enter and run the following program:

```
10 PRINT "EVALUATE 1! TO N!"
20 PRINT "WHAT IS N?"
30 INPUT N
40 LET X = 1
50 FOR I = 1 TO N
60 LET X = X * I
70 PRINT I "!=" X
80 NEXT I
90 END
```

NAME ______

LESSON **MASTER 4–9**
QUESTIONS FOR **SPUR** OBJECTIVES

■SKILLS *Objective E (See pages 204–207 for objectives.)*
In 1–6, write as a decimal.

1. $6!$ **720**
2. $3! \cdot 2!$ **12**
3. $2! + 5!$ **122**
4. $7 \cdot 6 \cdot 5!$ **5040**
5. $\frac{5!}{3!2!}$ **10**
6. $\frac{15!}{13!}$ **210**

In 7 and 8, simplify.

7. $\frac{(n + 1)!}{n!}$ **$n + 1$**
8. $n \cdot (n - 1)!$ **$n!$**

In 9–12, use a calculator to estimate.

9. $16!$ **$\approx 2.1 \times 10^{13}$**
10. $8!7!$ **$\approx 2.03 \times 10^8$**
11. $\frac{10!}{6!4!}$ **210**
12. $\frac{9! + 4!}{6!}$ **504**

■USES *Objective J*

13. a. Eight gymnasts compete in an event. In how many ways can first and second place be awarded? **56**
b. In how many different orders can all eight gymnasts finish? **40,320**

14. a. Twelve members of a college basketball squad line up for the national anthem. How many different ways could this be done? **4.79×10^8**
b. The members select a captain and co-captain from their 12. How many ways can this be done? **132**

15. In how many ways can 6 different books be arranged on a shelf? **720**

16. a. How many ways can the letters in the word CATS be arranged? **24**
b. Write the arrangements that are English words. **CATS, ACTS, SCAT, CAST**

17. Four boys and four girls are to be seated in a row on a stage, alternating boy, girl, boy, girl, etc. How many different seating arrangements are there? **576 seating arrangements**

SUMMARY

The Summary gives an overview of the entire chapter and provides an opportunity for students to consider the material as a whole. Thus, the Summary can be used to help students relate the concepts presented in the chapter.

VOCABULARY

Terms, symbols, and properties are listed by lesson to provide a checklist of things a student must know. Emphasize to students that they should read the vocabulary list carefully before starting the Progress Self-Test. If students do not understand the meaning of a term, they should refer back to the indicated lesson.

Definitions or descriptions of all terms in the vocabulary list may be found in the Glossary.

Summary

Multiplication has many uses. The product xy of two numbers x and y may stand for:

Area Model the area of a rectangle with length x and width y

Area Model (discrete version) the number of elements in a rectangular array with x rows and y columns

Rate Factor Model the result of multiplying a rate x by a secondary quantity y

Multiplication Counting Principle the number of ways of making a first choice followed by a second choice if the first choice can be made in x ways and the second choice can be made in y ways

Conditional Probability Formula $P(A \cap B)$ if $P(A) = x$ and $P(B \text{ given } A) = y$)

The product of three numbers xyz is the volume of a box with dimensions, x, y, and z. The product of the integers from 1 to n, written $n!$, is the number of ways of arranging n objects.

The numbers 0, 1, and -1 are special in multiplication. Multiplying any number by zero gives the same result ... 0. For this reason, equations of the form $0x = b$ are either true for all real numbers or for none. Multiplying any number by 1 yields that number. A conversion factor is the number 1 written using different units, so multiplying by it does not change the value of a quantity. Multiplying any number by -1 changes it to its opposite.

These many applications mean that equations of the form $ax = b$ and inequalities of the form $ax < b$ are quite common. When $a \neq 0$, such sentences can be solved by multiplying both sides by the number $\frac{1}{a}$, the reciprocal of a. The only caution is to remember to change the sense of the inequality if a is negative.

Vocabulary

Below are the most important terms and phrases for this chapter. You should be able to give a general description and a specific example of each.

Lesson 4-1
Area Model for Multiplication
Commutative Property of Multiplication
Associative Property of Multiplication
rectangular array, dimensions
rectangular solid, box
volume

Lesson 4-2
Rule for Multiplication of Fractions
Rate Factor Model for Multiplication
reciprocal rates

Lesson 4-3
Multiplicative Identity Property of 1
Multiplication Property of -1
reciprocal, multiplicative inverse, [1/x]
Property of Reciprocals
Multiplication Property of Zero

Lesson 4-4
Multiplication Property of Equality

Lesson 4-6
Multiplication Property of Inequality
changing sense of an inequality, changing direction of an inequality

Lesson 4-7
Multiplication Counting Principle
tree diagram

Lesson 4-8
P(A and B)
P(B given A), conditional probability
Conditional Probability Formula

Lesson 4-9
n factorial, $n!$
permutation
Permutation Theorem

Progress Self-Test

Take this test as you would take a test in class. You will need graph paper. Then check your work with the solutions in the Selected Answers section in the back of the book.

1. Evaluate $\frac{5!}{3!2!}$. **10**
2. Evaluate $7(v + 2.9)(2v + 3.1)(2.4 - v)$ when $v = 2.4$. **0**
3. Simplify $1\frac{2}{3} \cdot \frac{x}{5}$. $\frac{x}{3}$
4. a. Give an instance of the Associative Property of Multiplication. **See margin.**
   b. Give an instance of the Property of Reciprocals. **See margin.**
5. Use a square to show that $\frac{1}{2} \times \frac{3}{5} = \frac{3}{10}$. **See margin.**

In 6–10, solve.

6. $30x = 10$ $x = \frac{1}{3}$
7. $\frac{1}{4}k = -24$ $k = -96$
8. $15 \leq 3m$ $5 \leq m$
9. $-y \leq -2$ $y \geq 2$
10. $1.46 = 2.7 - t$ $1.24 = t$
11. What is the reciprocal of $3m$? $\frac{1}{3m}$ 12) $n \cdot 1 = n$
12. Write using symbols: The product of a number and the multiplicative identity is that number.
13. Find the area of the figure below. (All angles are right angles.) **See margin.**

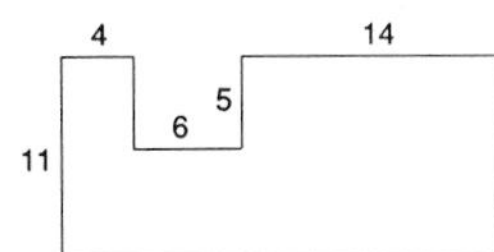

14. A sports stadium has 4 north gates and 5 south gates. In how many ways can a person enter through a north gate and leave through a south gate? $4 \cdot 5 = 20$
15. Dianne, Juan, Myisha, Sari, and Ted ran for class representative. No two of them received the same number of votes. If they are ranked from most votes to least votes, how many possible rankings are there? $5! = 120$
16. What is the price of s shirts that sell for \$15.50 a shirt? **\$15.50s**

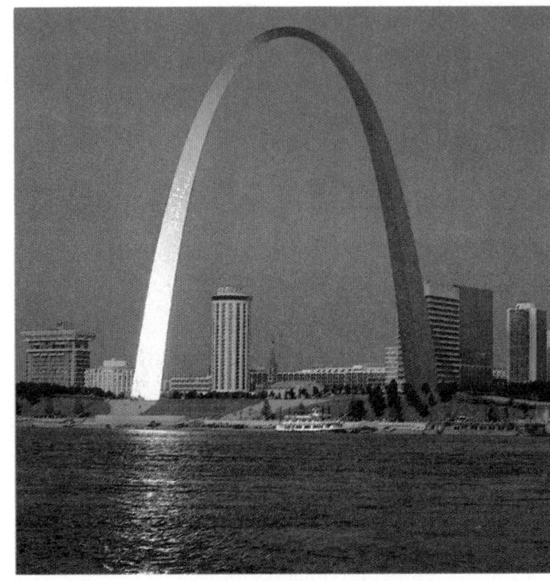

17. How much driving time is there from Chicago to St. Louis, a distance of 300 miles, if you travel at an average of 55 mph? **about $5\frac{1}{2}$ hours**
18. There are 2.54 cm/in. How many centimeters are there in 8 inches? **20.32 cm**
19. A drawer contains 4 black socks and 3 red socks. If one sock is picked at random from the drawer and not put back, and then another is picked, what is the probability that both are red? $\frac{1}{7}$
20. A box holds 1000 cm^3. Its length is 16 cm and its depth is 5 cm.
    a. Write an equation to find the width w of the box. $16 \text{ cm} \cdot w \cdot 5 \text{ cm} = 1000 \text{ cm}^3$
    b. Solve for w. $w = 12.5$ cm
21. Fourteen of the first forty U.S. Presidents served before the Civil War. Of the Presidents who served before that war, half were born in Virginia. Only one of the Presidents who served after that war was born in Virginia. What is the probability that a randomly chosen U.S. President served before the Civil War and was born in Virginia? $\frac{7}{40}$

PROGRESS SELF-TEST

We cannot overemphasize the importance of these end-of-chapter materials. It is at this point that the material "gels" for many students, allowing them to solidify skills and understanding. In general, student performance should be markedly improved after these pages.

USING THE PROGRESS SELF-TEST

Assign the Progress Self-Test as a one-night assignment. Worked-out *solutions* for all questions are in the Selected Answers section in the back of the student book. Encourage students to take the Progress Self-Test honestly, grade themselves, and then be prepared to discuss the test in class.

Advise students to pay special attention to those Chapter Review questions (pages 204–207) which correspond to questions missed on the Progress Self-Test. A chart provided in the Selected Answers section in the student text keys the Progress Self-Test questions to the lettered SPUR Objectives in the Chapter Review or to the Vocabulary. It also keys the questions to the corresponding lessons where the material is covered.

ADDITIONAL ANSWERS

4a. sample: $(2 \cdot 5) \cdot 8 = 2 \cdot (5 \cdot 8)$

4b. sample: $6 \cdot \frac{1}{6} = \frac{1}{6} \cdot 6 = 1$

5.

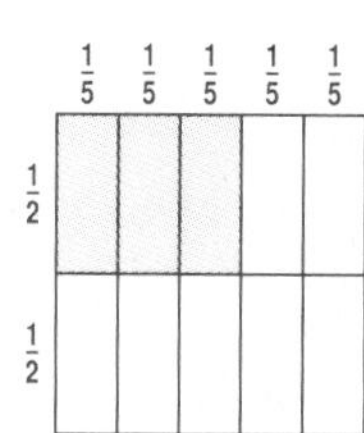

13. $11 \cdot (14 + 6 + 4) - (5 \cdot 6) = (11 \cdot 24) - 30 = 264 - 30 = 234$

RESOURCES
- Chapter 4 Test, Form A
- Chapter 4 Test, Form B
- Chapter 4 Test, Cumulative Form

CHAPTER REVIEW

The main objectives for the chapter are organized here into sections corresponding to the four main types of understanding this book promotes: Skills, Properties, Uses, and Representations.

USING THE CHAPTER REVIEW

Whereas end-of-chapter material may be considered optional in some texts, in *Algebra* we have selected these objectives and questions with the expectation that they will be covered. Students should be able to answer these questions with about 85% accuracy after studying the chapter.

You may assign these questions over a single night to help students prepare for a test the next day, or you may assign the questions over a two-day period.

If you work the questions over two days, then we recommend assigning the *evens* for homework the first night so that students get feedback in class the next day, then assigning the *odds* the night before the test so the students can use the answers provided in the book.

ADDITIONAL ANSWERS

33a. $(-6.2 + 3.8) \cdot (4.3 - -6.2) \cdot (0) = 0$

34. **Multiplication Property of Equality**

Chapter Review

Questions on **SPUR** Objectives

SPUR stands for **S**kills, **P**roperties, **U**ses, and **R**epresentations. The Chapter Review questions are grouped according to the SPUR Objectives for this chapter.

SKILLS deal with the procedures used to get answers.

Objective A. *Multiply fractions. (Lesson 4-2)*

1. $\frac{9x}{10} \cdot \frac{3}{4x}$ $\frac{27}{40}$

2. $1\frac{5}{8} \cdot 2\frac{2}{3}$ $\frac{13}{3}$

3. $\frac{a}{b} \cdot \frac{c}{d} \cdot \frac{b}{a}$ $\frac{c}{d}$

4. $\frac{ax}{3} \cdot \frac{6}{a}$ 2x

Objective B. *Solve and check equations of the form $ax = b$. (Lessons 4-4, 4-5)*

In 5–10, solve and check.

5. $2.4m = 360$ $m = 150$

6. $-\frac{1}{2}k = -10$ $k = 20$

7. $-10f = 23$ $f = -2.3$

8. $-2 = 0.4h$ $\frac{1}{.04} \cdot -2 = \frac{1}{.04} \cdot 0.4h$; $-5 = h$

9. $\frac{4}{25}A = \frac{6}{5}$ $A = \frac{15}{2}$

10. $\frac{2}{9} = 4c - 2c - 2c$ $\frac{2}{9} = 0c$; no solution

Objective C. *Solve and check equations of the form $a - x = b$. (Lesson 4-5)*

In 11–14, solve and check.

11. $31 - x = 43$ $x = -12$

12. $7.6 = -5.2 - y$ $-12.8 = y$

13. $\frac{1}{5} - z = \frac{2}{5}$ $z = -\frac{1}{5}$

14. $0 - x = 1$ $x = -1$

Objective D. *Solve and check inequalities of the form $ax < b$. (Lesson 4-6)*

In 15–20, solve and check.

15. $8m \le 16$ $m \le 2$

16. $-250 < 5y$ $-50 < y$

17. $6u > -12$ $u > -2$

18. $-x \ge -1$ $x \le 1$

19. $\frac{1}{2}g \le 5$ $g \le 10$

20. $3.6h < 720$ $h < 200$

Objective E. *Evaluate expressions containing a factorial symbol. (Lesson 4-9)*

In 21–23, write as a decimal.

21. $4! + 3!$ 30

22. $\frac{6!}{4!2!}$ 15

23. $\frac{16!}{14!}$ 240

In 24–26, use a calculator to estimate.

24. $15!$ $\approx 1.3077 \cdot 10^{12}$

25. $\frac{20!}{15!\,5!}$ 15,504

26. $(4!)!$ $24! = 6.2 \cdot 10^{23}$

PROPERTIES deal with the principles behind the mathematics.

Objective F. *Identify and apply properties of multiplication. (Lessons 4-1, 4-3, 4-4, 4-6)*

Commutative Property
Associative Property
Property of Reciprocals
Multiplication Property of Zero
Multiplication Property of Equality
Multiplication Property of Inequality
Multiplicative Identity Property of 1
Multiplication Property of -1.

27. **a.** Simplify in your head: $4 \cdot x \cdot 25 \cdot 22$. **2200x**

b. What properties aid in the simplification? **Associative and Commutative Properties of Multiplication**

28. $3 \cdot a = a \cdot 3$ is an instance of what property? **Commutative Property of Multiplication**

29. Write in symbols: The product of a number and its reciprocal is the multiplicative identity. $n \cdot \frac{1}{n} = 1$

In 30–32, write the reciprocal of the given number.

30. -2 $-\frac{1}{2}$ **31.** 0.6 $\frac{1}{0.6}$ **or** $\frac{5}{3}$ **32.** $\frac{3}{4x}$ $\frac{4x}{3}$

33b) Multiplication Property of Zero

33. **a.** Evaluate $(k + 3.8)(4.3 - k)(k + 6.2)$ when $k = -6.2$. **See margin.**

b. What property aids in this evaluation?

34. Of what property is this an instance? If $m = n$, then $12m = 12n$. **See margin.**

35. Multiplication by -1 changes a number to its __?__. **opposite**

36. If $-12x < 4$, what inequality results from multiplying both sides by $-\frac{1}{12}$? $x > -\frac{1}{3}$

In 37 and 38, give an example of an equation of the form $ax = b$ that has:

37. no solution. **sample: $0x = 5$**

38. all real numbers as solutions. **sample: $0n = 0$**

USES deal with applications of mathematics in real situations.

Objective G. *Apply the area and rate factor models for multiplication. (Lessons 4-1, 4-2)*

39. Consider the sketch of the $9' \times 12'$ area rug at the right. What is the area of the colored part? **48 ft²**

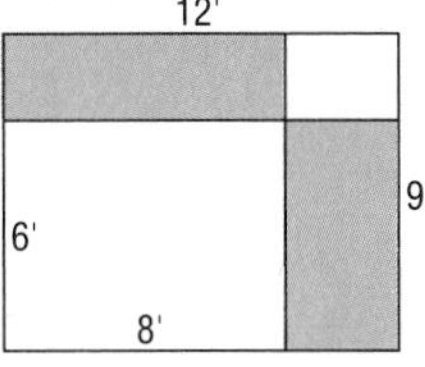

40. What is the volume of a box that is 12 cm long, 15 cm high, and 8 cm wide? **1440 cm³**

41. Find the rent for k months on an apartment that rents for \$350 per month. **\$350k**

42. At 30 miles per gallon of gas and \$1.00 per gallon of gas, what is the gas cost per mile? **$3\frac{1}{3}$¢/mile**

43. There are 43,560 sq ft/acre. How many square feet are there in 24 acres? **1,045,440 sq. ft.**

44. A hairdresser charges 15 dollars per cut. How much will he earn in 5 hours if he does 3 cuts per hour? **\$225**

45. On average, B books fit on 1 foot of shelf space. A bookcase has 24 feet of shelf. How many books can fit on C bookcases?
C bookcases $\cdot\, 24 \frac{\text{ft}}{\text{bookcase}} \cdot B \frac{\text{books}}{\text{ft}} = 24 \cdot B \cdot C$ books

Objective H. *Apply the Multiplication Counting Principle. (Lesson 4-7)*

ΑΒΓΔΕΖΗΘΙΚΛΜ
ΝΞΟΠΡΣΤΥΦΧΨΩ

46. The Greek alphabet has 24 letters. How many 3-letter monograms are possible? (3-letter Greek monograms often are used to name fraternities and sororities.) **13,824**

47. All 10 questions on a quiz are multiple choice, each with 5 possible choices. How many different sets of answers are possible on the test? **9,765,625**

48. A sports stadium has n north gates and s south gates. In how many ways can a person enter through a north gate and leave through a south gate? $n \cdot s$ **49)** $\frac{1}{3} \cdot \frac{2}{8} = \frac{1}{12}$

49. Claire has 3 skirts. One is red and two are black. She has 8 blouses: 2 are white, 2 are yellow, 3 are floral, and 1 is plaid. In a rush one morning she pulls out a skirt and a blouse at random. What is the probability that she takes a red skirt and a white blouse?

63.

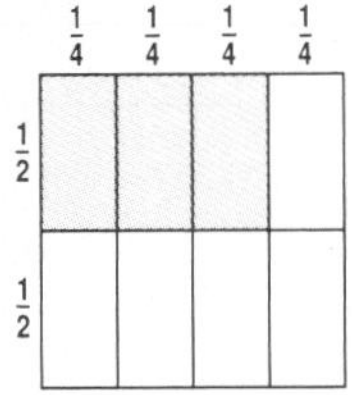

64.

X X
X X
X X
$3 \cdot 2 = 6$

X X X
X X X
$2 \cdot 3 = 6$

Objective I. *Apply the Conditional Probability Formula.* (Lesson 4-8)

50. Bill is a streak hitter in baseball. He gets hits 25% of the time he is at bat. But when he gets a hit his first time up, the probability he will get a hit the next time up is 32%. What is the probability Bill will get hits twice in a row at the beginning of a game? **$.25 \cdot .32 = .08$ or 8%**

51. Ten of the 30 students in a class are boys. Three students were absent yesterday; two of those were boys. A student from the class is to be randomly selected to get a special test on this chapter. **See below.**

a. What is the probability that if a boy is selected, the boy was absent yesterday?

b. What is the probability that a boy who was absent yesterday will be selected?

52. The estimated probability of being able to roll your tongue is $\frac{1}{8}$. The estimated probability of having attached earlobes is $\frac{1}{16}$. What is the probability of a person being able to roll his or her tongue and having attached earlobes? **$\frac{1}{128}$**

53. Two cards are drawn from a standard deck. What is the probability of drawing:
a. two clubs? **b.** two kings?

a) $\frac{13}{52} \cdot \frac{12}{51} = \frac{3}{51}$; b) $\frac{4}{52} \cdot \frac{3}{51} = \frac{1}{221}$

51a) $\frac{2}{10}$ or $\frac{1}{5}$; b) $\frac{10}{30} \cdot \frac{2}{10} = \frac{2}{30}$ or $\frac{1}{15}$

Objective J. *Apply the Permutation Theorem.* (Lesson 4-9)

54. The number of permutations of n objects is __?__. **$n!$** **55a) $9! = 362{,}880$; b) 3.6288×10^5**

55. Nine students are lining up outside a classroom. **a.** In how many ways can they arrange themselves? **b.** Write the answer in scientific notation.

56. Jesse, Simon, Arlene, and Ed ran for class president. No two received the same number of votes. How many possible orders, by votes received, are there? **$4! = 24$**

Objective K. *Solve sentences of the form $ax = b$ and $ax < b$ to answer questions from real situations.* (Lessons 4-1, 4-2, 4-3, 4-4, 4-6) **8.22 hr or ≈ 8 hr 15 min**

57. How long does it take to drive from Chicago to Minneapolis, a distance of 411 miles, if a person can average 50 mph?

58. The volume of a rectangular storage area needs to be 10,000 cubic feet. The floor has dimensions 40 feet and 80 feet. What should the height be? **3.125 ft**

59. Daniel budgeted $550 for accommodations. His hotel costs $45 a day. At most how many days can he stay at the hotel?

60. At least how many 16 oz bottles are needed to hold 300 oz of mineral water?
$b \geq 18.75$; At least 19 bottles are needed.
59) $d \leq 12.\overline{2}$; at most 12 days

REPRESENTATIONS deal with pictures, graphs, or objects that illustrate concepts.

Objective L. *Use area, arrays, and volume to picture multiplication.* (Lesson 4-1)

61. What property of multiplication is illustrated below, where $A_1 = A_2$?

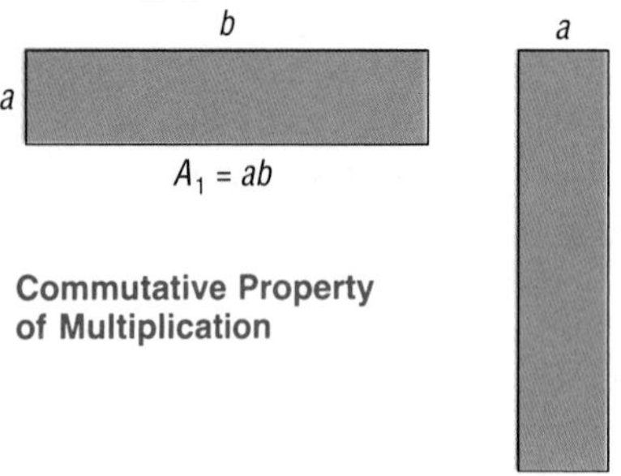

Commutative Property of Multiplication

62. The large square at the right has length 1. What multiplication of fractions does the drawing represent?
$\frac{1}{2} \times \frac{2}{3} = \frac{1}{3}$

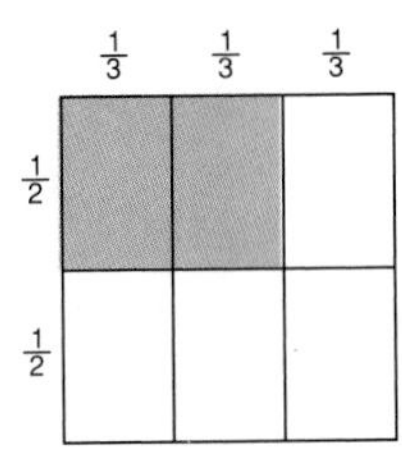

63. Use a square to show that $\frac{1}{2} \times \frac{3}{4} = \frac{3}{8}$.

64. Use two arrays to show that $2 \times 3 = 3 \times 2$.
See margin.

65. If a dot is picked at random, what is the probability that it is to the right of line l and below line m?

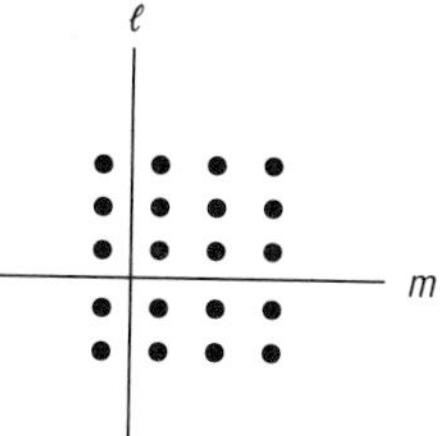

$\frac{3}{4} \cdot \frac{2}{5} = \frac{6}{20}$ or $\frac{3}{10}$

66. How many dots are in the array below? **36**

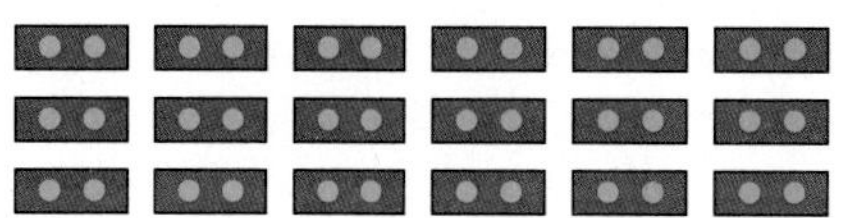

67. How many square tiles, each one foot on a side, are needed to cover an area $4q$ feet by 5 feet? **20q tiles**

68. How many cubes, one centimeter on each edge, can be placed in a box with base p cm^2 and height 3 cm? **3p cubes**

69. What is the volume of a box with dimensions $3k$, $2k$, and $4k$? **$24k^3$**

70. What is the volume of a box with dimensions 0.3 meter, 0.45 meter, and x meters? **.135x meters^3**

REFRESHER

Chapter 5, which discusses division in algebra, assumes that you have mastered certain objectives in your previous mathematics work. Use these optional questions to check your mastery.

A. Divide.

1. 40 ÷ 100 **0.40**
2. 100 ÷ 40 **2.5**
3. 7.2 ÷ 3 **2.4**
4. 80 ÷ .05 **1600**
5. .06 ÷ .3 **.2**
6. 6.8 ÷ 34 **.2**
7. 1 ÷ 625 **.0016**
8. 11.27 ÷ 2.35 **≈4.8**
9. $\frac{12}{7} \div \frac{2}{7}$ **6**
10. $\frac{3}{5} \div \frac{3}{4}$ **$\frac{4}{5}$**
11. $\frac{2}{9} \div \frac{1}{3}$ **$\frac{2}{3}$**
12. $\frac{3}{2} \div \frac{4}{5}$ **$1\frac{7}{8}$**
13. 6 ft ÷ 2 **3 ft**
14. $10m$ ÷ 4 **2.5m**
15. 100 kg ÷ 7 **$14\frac{2}{7}$ kg**
16. 6 lb ÷ 25 **.24 lb**

B. Convert any simple fraction to a decimal or percent.

In 17–20, give the decimal and percent equivalent.

17. $\frac{1}{2}$ **.5; 50%**
18. $\frac{3}{4}$ **.75; 75%**
19. $\frac{1}{40}$ **.025; 2.5%**
20. $\frac{73}{100}$ **.73; 73%**

In 21–24, round to the nearest hundredth.

21. $\frac{1}{7}$ **.14**
22. $\frac{20}{3}$ **6.67**
23. $\frac{110}{17}$ **6.47**
24. $\frac{3467}{1103}$ **3.14**

In 25–28, give to the nearest percent.

25. $\frac{11}{5}$ **220%**
26. $\frac{27}{101}$ **27%**
27. $\frac{8}{9}$ **89%**
28. $\frac{11}{60}$ **18%**

C. Convert percents to decimals and fractions.

29. 30% **.3; $\frac{3}{10}$**
30. 1% **.01; $\frac{1}{100}$**
31. 300% **3.0; $\frac{3}{1}$**
32. 2.46% **.0246; $\frac{123}{5000}$**
33. .03% **.0003; $\frac{3}{10,000}$**
34. $\frac{1}{4}$% **.0025; $\frac{1}{400}$**

D. Give a percent of a number or quantity.

35. 32% of \$750 **\$240**
36. 94% of 72 questions **68 questions**
37. 7.3% of 40,296 voters **2942 voters**
38. 100% of 12,000 square miles **12,000 sq mi**
39. 0% of 60 students **0 students**

E. Divide.

40. -8 ÷ -4 **2**
41. -40 ÷ 5 **-8**
42. 60 ÷ -120 **-.5**
43. 2 ÷ -80 **-.025**
44. $\frac{-3}{-6}$ **$\frac{1}{2}$**
45. $\frac{400}{-4}$ **-100**

F. Identify the divisor, dividend, and quotient in a division situation.

46. 21 ÷ 3 = 7 **3; 21; 7**
47. 0.2 = 20 ÷ 100 **100; 20; 0.2**
48. $\frac{56}{7} = 8$ **7; 56; 8**

EVALUATION
Three tests are provided for this chapter in the Teacher's Resource File. Chapter 4 Test, Forms A and B, cover just Chapter 4. The third test is Chapter 4 Test, Cumulative Form. About 50% of this test covers Chapter 4, 25% covers Chapter 3, and 25% covers earlier chapters. For information on grading, see *General Teaching Suggestions: Grading* on page T44 in the Teacher's Edition.

ASSIGNMENT RECOMMENDATION
On the day your students take the chapter test, we suggest you make an assignment in the first section of the next chapter.

REFRESHER
The major topic of Chapter 5 is division. If your students have a particularly weak background in division, you may wish to assign this optional Refresher material to better prepare them for the chapter. Parts A, E, and F involve ideas that will be reviewed in Lesson 5-1. Parts B, C, and D review ideas that will be covered throughout the rest of the chapter.

CHAPTER 5 ■ DIVISION IN ALGEBRA

DAILY PACING CHART 5

DAILY PACING CHART ■ CHAPTER 5

Students in the Full Course should complete the entire text by the end of the year. Students in the Minimal Course spend more time to complete lessons that are combined with quizzes and more time to consider the Chapter Review. Therefore, these students may not complete all the chapters in the text.

DAY	MINIMAL COURSE	FULL COURSE
1	5-1	5-1
2	5-2	5-2
3	5-3	5-3
4	5-4	5-4
5	Quiz (TRF); Start 5-5.	Quiz (TRF); 5-5
6	Finish 5-5.	5-6
7	5-6	5-7
8	5-7	5-8
9	5-8	Progress Self-Test
10	Progress Self-Test	Chapter Review
11	Chapter Review	Chapter Test (TRF)
12	Chapter Review	
13	Chapter Test (TRF)	

TESTING OPTIONS

TESTING OPTIONS

- Quiz for Lessons 5-1 Through 5-4
- Chapter 5 Test, Form A
- Chapter 5 Test, Form B
- Chapter 5 Test, Cumulative Form

INDIVIDUAL DIFFERENCES

PROVIDING FOR INDIVIDUAL DIFFERENCES

The student text is written for the *average* student. The program, however, can be adapted for less capable and for more capable students.

For those students who need more practice, a blackline master (in the Teacher's Resource File) is provided for each lesson. The Teacher's Edition frequently provides Error Analysis and Alternate Approach features to provide additional instructional strategies for those students who do not readily grasp the material.

For students who require additional challenge, Extension activities are regularly provided in the Teacher's Edition.

OBJECTIVES ■ CHAPTER 5

Students should master the chapter objectives by the time they complete the chapter. To ensure objective mastery, there is continual review built into each set of lesson questions. After students complete the chapter lessons, they assess their mastery on the Progress Self-Test. Then they do the Chapter Review and pay special attention to those questions that match the objectives missed on the Progress Self-Test. Students can get extra practice on these objectives by using the master for each lesson in the Teacher's Resource File.

OBJECTIVES FOR CHAPTER 5 (Organized into the SPUR categories—Skills, Properties, Uses, and Representations)	**Progress Self-Test Questions**	**Chapter Review Questions**	**Lesson Master from Teacher's Resource File***
SKILLS			
A Divide real numbers and simplify division expressions.	1 through 4, 10	1 through 10	5-1
B Solve percent problems using equations or in your head.	7 through 9	11 through 18	5-4
C Solve proportions.	5, 6	19 through 24	5-7
PROPERTIES			
D Identify restrictions on a variable in a division situation.	12	25 through 28	5-2
E Use the language of proportions and the Means-Extremes Property.	11, 13	29 through 32	5-7, 5-8
USES			
F Use the Rate Model for Division.	16	33 through 42	5-2
G Use a ratio to compare two quantities.	14, 15	43 through 47	5-3
H Solve percent and size change problems from real situations.	17	48 through 53	5-4, 5-6
I Solve problems involving proportions in real situations.	19, 20	54 through 57	5-7
REPRESENTATIONS			
J Find probabilities involving geometric regions.	18, 25	58 through 61	5-5
K Find missing lengths in similar figures.	23, 24	62 through 67	5-8
L Use the IF-THEN command in computer programs.	21	68 through 69	5-2
M Apply the Size Change Model for Multiplication on the coordinate plane.	22	70 through 73	5-6

*** The masters are numbered to match the lessons.**

OVERVIEW ■ CHAPTER 5

The chapter uses properties, applications, and geometric representations as well as skill development to cover a broad range of mathematics centered on the algebra of division. It concludes the study of the four fundamental operations of arithmetic. In the next chapter, students will encounter combinations of the operations in expressions and equations.

This chapter starts by relating division to multiplication. This conceptualization of division from the standpoint of properties is followed by two models for division, the Rate Model and the Ratio Model. The models are used extensively in applications later in the book and lead to the important topic of proportions. The Means-Extremes Property is used to solve proportions, which are then applied to the geometry of similar figures.

Division is applied in three additional areas: percent, probability, and size change. The first of these focuses on translating percent problems into equations which the student already knows how to solve. Lesson 5-5 applies division to compute probabilities involving geometry. The Size-Change Model stated in Lesson 5-6 can be used in many ways: on the coordinate plane, in percent problems, and in numerical conversions.

PERSPECTIVES ■ CHAPTER 5

The Perspectives provide the rationale for the inclusion of topics or approaches, provide mathematical background, and make connections within UCSMP.

5-1

THE DEFINITION OF DIVISION

The structure of Chapters 4 and 5 on multiplication and division parallels that of Chapters 2 and 3 on addition and subtraction. In Chapter 3 we defined subtraction as adding the opposite. Here we define division as multiplication by the reciprocal.

One model of division not specifically discussed in this book is the Splitting-Up Model illustrated by the introductory example. This idea is used when an item or set of items is divided into equal parts. Although many uses of division involve this model, these uses can also be interpreted as one of the two models given in this chapter as follows: (1) splitting 10 apples among 2 students could be solved using the Rate Model for Division:

$$\frac{10 \text{ apples}}{2 \text{ students}} = 5\frac{\text{apples}}{\text{student}}.$$

(2) Splitting 10 apples into groups of 2 could be solved using the Size Change Model of Multiplication:

$$\frac{10 \text{ apples}}{2} = 5 \text{ apples}.$$

Equations with fractions are usually easier to solve with paper-and-pencil multiplication than with calculator division. When students solve equations in this lesson and throughout the chapter, you may want to emphasize an example like the following: If you multiply both sides of the equation $\frac{2}{3}x = 20$ by the reciprocal $\frac{3}{2}$, you will get the exact solution $x = 30$. Students who approximate $\frac{2}{3}$ and divide both sides of the equation by .67 will get the cumbersome approximation $x \approx 29.85$.

5-2

RATES

The Rate Model for Division summarizes an exceedingly important application of this operation. From the early splitting-up problems of grade school through calculus and beyond, rate is a fundamental idea. Examples 1–3 exhibit a variety of arithmetic situations to which this idea applies.

Students have already worked with rate in problems involving rate factor multiplication. Here the emphasis is on finding the rate. The rate model is applied repeatedly in this book. For example, the concept of slope in Chapter 8 is approached as a rate of change.

5-3

RATIOS

As the lesson states, both subtraction and division are used to compare two quantities. However, students may not distinguish between these two methods. They may be surprised to realize that if numbers have a constant difference, they will not have a constant ratio. For instance, suppose Mrs. Alma is 30 and her son is 2. Now her age is 15 times his. This ratio will change, though. In 2 years her age will be 8 times his age. However, the difference in their ages will remain the same. Similarly, if numbers have a constant ratio, the differences will vary.

In a sense, a ratio can be viewed as a rate. For instance, in Example 3, instead of thinking of the unit as $\frac{\text{skunks}}{\text{skunks}}$, think of $\frac{\text{rabid skunks}}{\text{normal skunks}}$. This interpretation fits if we were to predict the number of rabid skunks in a forest with 2000 skunks.

5-4

SOLVING PERCENT PROBLEMS USING EQUATIONS

In arithmetic, students may have learned about the three different computations involving percent which are illustrated in Example 1. They had to learn three different ways of finding the correct answers. This lesson shows the strength of algebra. It gives the student one way to set up the problem. After the equation is set up, the student can apply the laws of algebra to find the solution.

The numbers used in real percent problems are often quite large, as Examples 2 and 3 demonstrate. Use of the calculator is most appropriate in percent problems. But the percent key is often programmed in special ways. That is why we do not use it in this chapter.

We include work with percents greater than 100% because this will be important in working with exponential growth in Chapter 9. Students need to be comfortable with the idea and be able to convert the percent form to a decimal.

5-5

PROBABILITY WITHOUT COUNTING

In this book, probabilities have been ratios of the numbers of elements in sets. The problems in this lesson show that you don't have to count to find probabilities if you have some other way of finding the ratios.

The geometric representation of probability gives students a model which facilitates the understanding of the probability of an event. Geometric probabilities may be ratios of lengths, angle measures, areas, or volumes. Many geometric applications are very familiar, such as Example 3, which deals with the probability of a specific outcome on a spinner. The problems give a good introduction to or review of geometry formulas.

Geometric interpretations of probability are quite important in statistics. The normal curve used in standardized tests exhibits this idea. Areas of sections under the curve are related to probabilities that students will achieve certain scores.

5-6

SIZE CHANGES

The Size Change Model for Multiplication is in this chapter because the comparisons made between image and preimage use ratio division.

In this lesson, we consider the multiplication, namely, the size change. In Lessons 5-7 and 5-8, we consider the results of size changes in discussing proportions and similar figures.

You can think of a multiplication being a size change when the factor has no unit. This occurs in "times as many" and "part of" situations, and in all percent applications. All of these illustrate one-dimensional size changes; there is a quantity (perhaps $50), a size change factor (say 20%) and a product quantity with the same unit as the original ($10).

The coordinate diagrams in this lesson are two-dimensional. Seeing a size change in two-dimensions is easier and gives twice the practice with the multiplications. You might want students to consider situations in three-dimensions that involve a size change (Example: a balloon). You can also decrease the dimensions and look at one-dimensional size changes of segments on a number line. The effect of multiplying by a negative value of k may be easier to see there than on a plane.

The idea of similar figures is introduced in this lesson. The equality of angle measures in similar figures could be discussed, but the focus here is on the change in lengths. The proportionality of sides can be illustrated using the size change factor. Further work with similarity will be done in Lesson 5-8.

5-7

PROPORTIONS

Proportions arise from equal rates and from equal ratios. They are often used in applications to describe realistic situations as Examples 1 and 2 indicate.

The Means-Extremes Property is the standard method of solving a proportion, and it is unique to this type of equation.

The Means-Extremes Property is a theorem, a statement which can be deduced from other properties. The steps in the deduction are given in the paragraph preceding the statement of the property. To emphasize this, you could call this property the Means-Extremes Theorem.

5-8

SIMILAR FIGURES

Similar figures were treated briefly in Lesson 5-6 by using multiplication by a size change factor. The current lesson uses proportions to find lengths of sides of similar figures. The proportions come from ratios of lengths of corresponding sides.

In this book, similar figures are almost always represented with corresponding sides parallel, as in the pictures in this lesson. Using colored chalk or pens to indicate corresponding sides can help students see the pairing, a task that increases in difficulty with the number of sides in the polygons. The emphasis in algebra is on writing and solving proportions, not on recognizing when two figures are similar. Notice that in the problem with the flagpole, we assume students accept that the triangles are similar. More on the topic is saved until geometry.

CHAPTER 5

This chapter should take 8 or 9 days for the lessons and quiz; 1 day for the Progress Self-Test; 1 or 2 days for the Chapter Review; and 1 day for testing. The total is 11 to 13 days.

CHAPTER 5

Division in Algebra

Can the big 6-by-7 rectangle be split into little regions of the T-shape at the left below? A person could start solving this problem by using trial and error.

Below is a start that leads to a situation which does not work. But maybe the start was wrong.

There's another way to examine the problem. The rectangle's area is 42 square units. The T-shaped region has area 4 units. If the rectangle can be split up, there will be $\frac{42}{4}$, or 10.5 T-shaped regions. Since the number of regions must be an integer, no way will work.

Division starts with questions of splitting up things. In this chapter, you will study this and other uses of division.

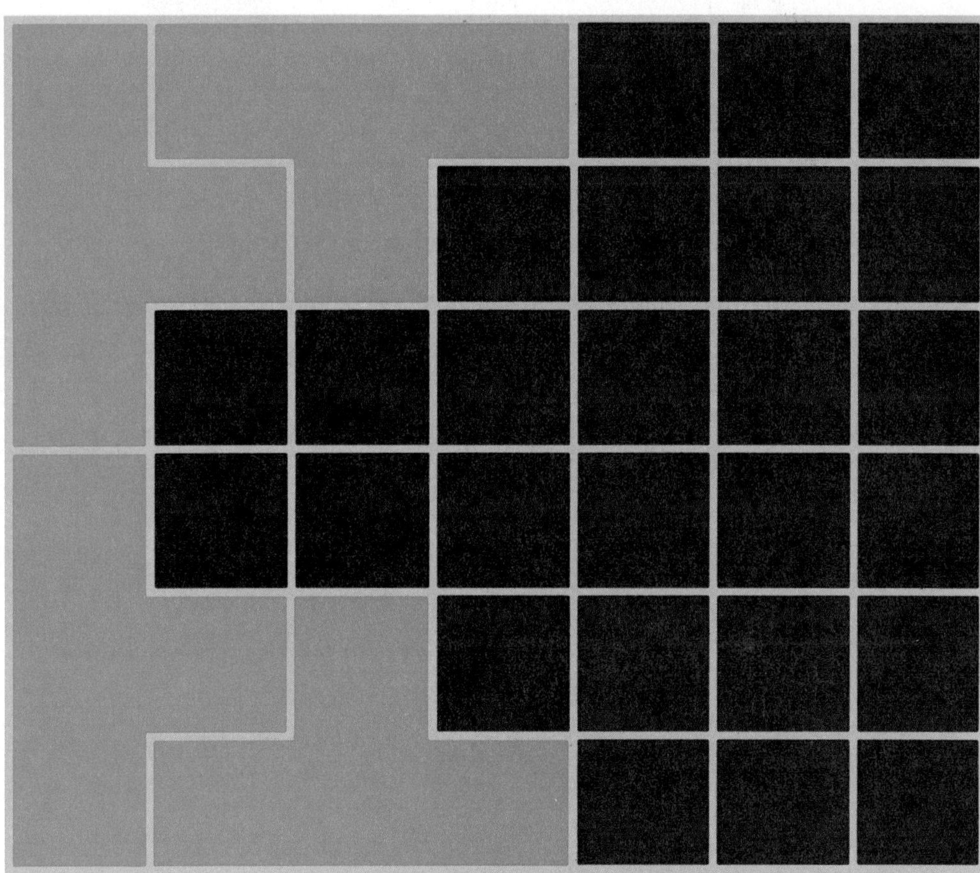

USING PAGES 208-209
From the example given, students should not jump to the conclusion that a rectangle whose area is divisible by 4 can always be split up into the T-shaped regions. You might consider the two rectangles below.

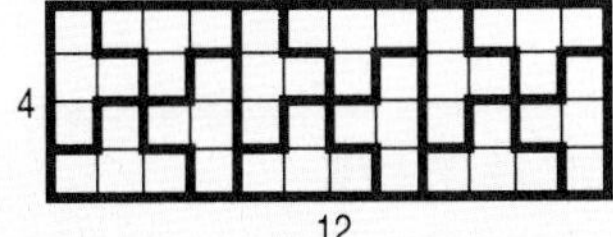

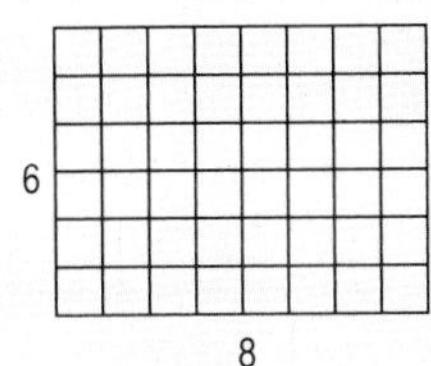

The area of each is 48, and $\frac{48}{4} = 12$. The first rectangle can be split into 12 T-shaped regions as shown. The second cannot be split up in this manner.

LESSON 5-1

RESOURCES

- Lesson Master 5-1
- Visual for Teaching Aid 23: Diagram for **Question 33**

OBJECTIVE

A Divide real numbers and simplify division expressions.

TEACHING NOTES

The first three examples in the lesson deal with expressions. The expressions replicate problems students have seen in earlier work with arithmetic, but each example has an algebraic twist. **Example 1** uses variables, **Example 2** uses a negative number, and **Example 3** uses the number π, which looks like a variable to many students.

Example 4 contrasts the multiplication approach with the division approach by using both operations to solve the same equation. We will now use either method.

When you work with **Examples 2 and 3,** we recommend that you avoid using the Equal Fractions Property, the technique of multiplying numerator and denominator by the LCD (except as a check). The emphasis in this lesson is on the definition of division. Complex fractions should be expressed as division problems as in the examples.

LESSON

5-1 The Definition of Division

Abe divided a quart of orange juice equally among his five children. How many ounces of orange juice did each child receive?

This question can be answered either by multiplication or division. Either way you must change 1 quart to 32 ounces. You can view this problem as 32 ounces divided among 5 children,

$$32 \div 5 = 6.4$$

or each child gets $\frac{1}{5}$ of the orange juice,

$$32 \cdot \frac{1}{5} = 6.4$$

Each way the answer is 6.4 ounces. Dividing by 5 is the same as multiplying by $\frac{1}{5}$.

In general, dividing by b is the same as multiplying by its reciprocal, $\frac{1}{b}$.

Algebraic Definition of Division:

For any real numbers a and b, $b \neq 0$,

$$a \div b = a \cdot \frac{1}{b}.$$

Recall that $a \div b$ can also be written as a/b or $\frac{a}{b}$. So $a \div b = \frac{a}{b} = a/b = a \cdot \frac{1}{b}$.

The definition of division allows any division situation to be converted to multiplication. For instance, consider $\frac{a}{b} \div \frac{c}{d}$. According to the definition of division, dividing by $\frac{c}{d}$ is the same as multiplying by $\frac{d}{c}$. So,

$$\frac{a}{b} \div \frac{c}{d} = \frac{a}{b} \cdot \frac{d}{c}.$$

For example $\frac{5}{2} \div \frac{9}{7} = \frac{5}{2} \cdot \frac{7}{9} = \frac{35}{18}$. Variables are dealt with in the same way.

210

Example 1 Simplify $\frac{x}{5} \div \frac{3}{4}$.

Solution $\frac{x}{5} \div \frac{3}{4} = \frac{x}{5} \cdot \frac{4}{3} = \frac{4x}{15}$

Check Let $x = 2$. Does $\frac{2}{5} \div \frac{3}{4} = \frac{4 \cdot 2}{15}$? To determine this, change each fraction to a decimal. Does $0.4 \div 0.75 = \frac{8}{15}$? Yes, each side is equal to $0.\overline{53}$.

Dividing fractions with negative numbers can be dealt with in the same way. In Example 2, the fraction is converted to the equivalent division problem.

Example 2 Simplify $\frac{\frac{1}{6}}{-\frac{2}{3}}$.

Solution $\frac{\frac{1}{6}}{-\frac{2}{3}}$ means $\frac{1}{6} \div -\frac{2}{3}$

Use the definition of division to convert the division to a multiplication. The reciprocal of $-\frac{2}{3}$ is $-\frac{3}{2}$. Thus

$$\frac{1}{6} \div -\frac{2}{3} = \frac{1}{\cancel{6}_2} \cdot -\frac{\cancel{3}^1}{2}$$

$$= -\frac{1}{4}$$

In Example 2, a positive number is divided by a negative number. This is converted into multiplication of a positive by a negative. So the quotient is negative. Generally, the signs of answers to division problems follow the same rules as in multiplication.

> If two numbers have the same + or − sign, their quotient is positive. If two numbers have different signs, their quotient is negative.

Remember that π is a number and can be multiplied and divided like any other number. Example 3 on page 212 uses π in a division problem.

ADDITIONAL EXAMPLES

In 1-3, simplify.

1. $\frac{2n}{5} \div \frac{10n}{7}$ **$\frac{7}{25}$**
2. $\frac{\frac{x}{6}}{\frac{5}{x}}$ **$\frac{x^2}{30}$**
3. $\frac{\frac{4xy}{11}}{22x}$ **$\frac{2y}{121}$**
4. Solve $2.3w = 18.4$. **8**

NOTES ON QUESTIONS
Questions 2-8: In these questions students must apply the algebraic definition of division.

Error Analysis for Questions 5b and 5c: Some students think that these questions are the same. To illustrate that they are quite different, imagine that a cafeteria uses 50 apples for dessert. Compare the number of people served if each gets $\frac{1}{2}$ of an apple as opposed to the number served if a helping is 2 apples.

Questions 9 and 10: These are examples of complex fractions which might look intimidating. This in itself increases the difficulty of the questions. Rewriting the division using the sign ÷ results in an expression which will be familiar to students. Explain that the ability to write a fraction as a division (and vice versa) gives students a second way to think about division, and thus is quite beneficial.

Question 15: Students may need a hint that the first step is to convert the mixed numbers to fractions.

Question 17: This should be interpreted as $\frac{1}{2} \div 3$, and then converted to the multiplication $\frac{1}{2} \cdot \frac{1}{3}$. Draw a picture to verify that 1/6 is the correct answer.

ADDITIONAL ANSWERS
2. For real numbers a and b, $b \neq 0$, $a \div b = a \cdot \frac{1}{b}$.

21. A positive number divided by a positive number is positive; a negative number divided by a negative number is positive; a negative number divided by a positive number is negative; a positive number divided by a negative number is negative.

Example 3 Simplify $\dfrac{7\pi}{\frac{\pi}{21}}$

Solution Use the definition of division to rewrite as a multiplication.

$$7\pi \div \frac{\pi}{21} = 7\pi \cdot \frac{21}{\pi}$$

Follow the properties of multiplication.

$$= \frac{7\not\pi}{1} \cdot \frac{21}{\not\pi}$$

$$= 147$$

The definition of division leads to another method for solving equations of the form $ax = b$. In the next example, one method of solution uses multiplication. However, multiplying by $-\frac{1}{31}$ is the same as dividing by -31. So a second method uses division.

Example 4 Solve $-31m = 527$.

Solution 1 Multiply both sides by $-\frac{1}{31}$.

$$-\frac{1}{31} \cdot -31m = -\frac{1}{31} \cdot 527$$
$$m = -\frac{527}{31}$$
$$m = -17$$

Solution 2 Divide both sides by -31.

$$-31m = 527$$
$$\frac{-31m}{-31} = \frac{527}{-31}$$
$$m = -17$$

Both methods of Example 4 are acceptable. You may prefer one or the other.

Questions

Covering the Reading

1. Suppose Abe had divided a quart of orange juice equally among his five children *and himself*. Show two ways to determine how many ounces of orange juice each person received.
   $32 \div 6 = 5.\overline{3}$, $32 \cdot \frac{1}{6} = 5.\overline{3}$ ounces
2. State the algebraic definition of division. See margin.

212

In 3–5, fill in the blanks.

3. a. $\frac{m}{n} = m \div$ ___?___. n

b. $\frac{m}{n} = m \cdot$ ___?___ $\frac{1}{n}$

4. a. $\frac{\frac{a}{b}}{\frac{c}{d}} = \frac{a}{b} \div$ ___?___. $\frac{c}{d}$ **b.** $\frac{a}{b} \div \frac{c}{d} = \frac{a}{b} \cdot$ ___?___. $\frac{d}{c}$

5. a. $50 \div \frac{1}{2} = 50 \cdot$ ___?___. 2

b. $\frac{50}{\frac{1}{2}} = 50 \cdot$ ___?___. 2

c. $\frac{50}{2} = 50 \cdot$ ___?___. $\frac{1}{2}$

d. If 50 boxes of flyers are split so each campaign worker gets $\frac{1}{2}$ of a box, how many campaign workers are needed to distribute all the flyers? **100**

6. Consider $\frac{3}{4} \div \frac{3}{16}$. **a.** Rewrite as a multiplication. **b.** Evaluate. **a) $\frac{3}{4} \cdot \frac{16}{3}$; b) 4**

In 7 and 8, simplify.

7. $\frac{5}{4} \div \frac{n}{10}$ $\frac{25}{2n}$ **8.** $\frac{12\pi}{5} \div \frac{\pi}{4}$ $\frac{48}{5}$

In 9 and 10, **a.** rewrite with the ÷ sign; **b.** rewrite as a multiplication; **c.** simplify.

9. $\frac{\frac{6}{25}}{\frac{10}{7}}$ $\frac{6}{25} \div \frac{10}{7}; \frac{6}{25} \cdot \frac{7}{10} = \frac{21}{125}$ **10.** $\frac{x}{-\frac{1}{2}}$ $x \div -\frac{1}{2}; x \cdot -2 = -2x$

11. When solving $-3j = -48$,
a. by what would you multiply both sides? $-\frac{1}{3}$
b. by what would you divide both sides? -3

In 12–14, solve.

12. $143 = -13x$ **-11** **13.** $-1.5q = -75$ **50** **14.** $2.5k = -0.7$ **-0.28**

Applying the Mathematics

15. Simplify: $1\frac{2}{3} \div 3\frac{1}{3}$. $\frac{1}{2}$

16. Ruth divided a gallon of milk equally among x people. How many ounces did each person receive? $\frac{128}{x}$

17. Half of a pizza was divided equally among 3 people. How much of the original pizza did each person receive? $\frac{1}{6}$

18. Le Parfum Company produces perfume in 200-ounce batches and bottles it in quarter-ounce bottles. Suppose you want to know how many bottles are needed per batch.
a. Write a division problem that will tell you. $200 \div \frac{1}{4} = B$
b. Find the answer. **800**

23.

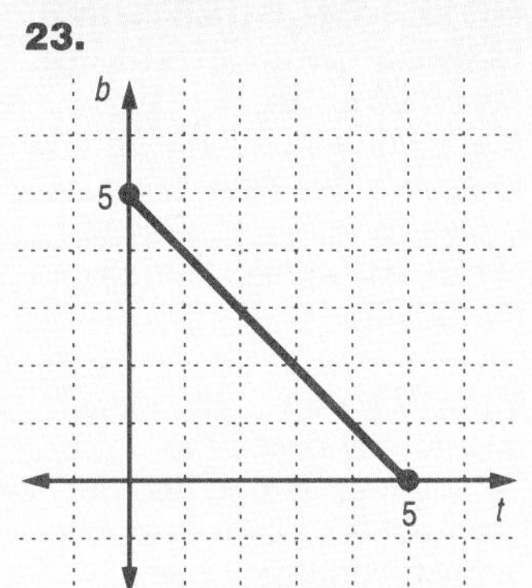

t = amount of turkey
b = amount of beef
$t + b = 5$
$t \geq 0$
$b \geq 0$

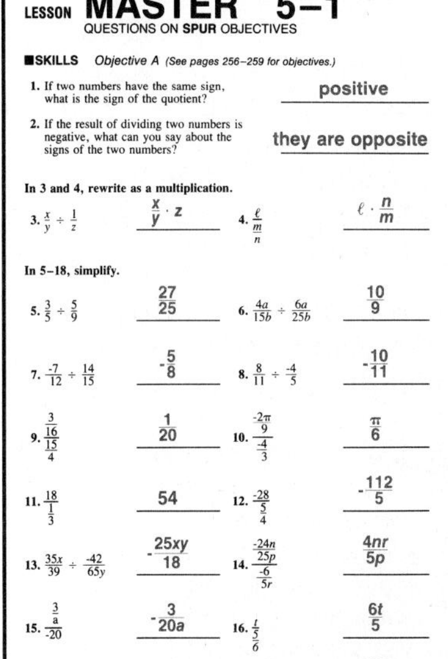

NAME ____________

LESSON **MASTER 5–1**
QUESTIONS ON **SPUR** OBJECTIVES

■SKILLS *Objective A (See pages 256–259 for objectives.)*

1. If two numbers have the same sign, what is the sign of the quotient? **positive**

2. If the result of dividing two numbers is negative, what can you say about the signs of the two numbers? **they are opposite**

In 3 and 4, rewrite as a multiplication.

3. $\frac{x}{y} \div \frac{1}{z}$ $\frac{x}{y} \cdot z$ **4.** $\frac{\ell}{\frac{m}{n}}$ $\ell \cdot \frac{n}{m}$

In 5–18, simplify.

5. $\frac{3}{5} \div \frac{5}{9}$ $\frac{27}{25}$ **6.** $\frac{4a}{15b} \div \frac{6a}{25b}$ $\frac{10}{9}$

7. $\frac{-7}{12} \div \frac{14}{15}$ $-\frac{5}{8}$ **8.** $\frac{8}{11} \div \frac{-4}{5}$ $-\frac{10}{11}$

9. $\frac{\frac{3}{16}}{\frac{15}{4}}$ $\frac{1}{20}$ **10.** $\frac{\frac{-2\pi}{9}}{\frac{-4}{3}}$ $\frac{\pi}{6}$

11. $\frac{18}{\frac{1}{3}}$ 54 **12.** $\frac{-28}{\frac{5}{4}}$ $-\frac{112}{5}$

13. $\frac{35x}{39} \div \frac{-42}{65y}$ $-\frac{25xy}{18}$ **14.** $\frac{\frac{-24n}{25p}}{\frac{-6}{5r}}$ $\frac{4nr}{5p}$

15. $\frac{\frac{3}{a}}{-20}$ $-\frac{3}{20a}$ **16.** $\frac{t}{\frac{5}{6}}$ $\frac{6t}{5}$

17. $\frac{\frac{-15w}{38x}}{\frac{45z}{57y}}$ $-\frac{wy}{2xz}$ **18.** $\frac{\frac{-9f}{56g}}{\frac{-15h}{49k}}$ $\frac{21fk}{40gh}$

36

NOTES ON QUESTIONS
Making Connections for Question 29: Be sure that students understand how to do this question, because problems involving areas of circles will appear throughout the chapter.

Question 31: Students should first divide the 24 squares by 6 to find out how many squares should be in each congruent piece.

FOLLOW-UP

MORE PRACTICE
For more practice on SPUR Objectives, use *Lesson Master 5-1,* shown on page 213.

EXTENSION
Computer If you have students who are familiar with the INT function in BASIC, you can ask them to write a program that accepts the dividend and divisor of a division problem as input and prints the quotient (under integer division) with remainder. For instance, when the problem is $\frac{25}{7}$, the computer should print "25/7 = 3 WITH REMAINDER 4". Here is a program that accomplishes that.

```
10 PRINT "THIS
   PROGRAM WILL DO
   THE DIVISION A/B."
20 INPUT "ENTER THE
   VALUE OF A.";A
30 INPUT "ENTER THE
   VALUE OF B.";B
40 PRINT
50 PRINT A; "/";B; "=";
   INT(A/B); "WITH
   REMAINDER";
   A-INT(A/B)*B
```

At least one calculator on the market also does this integer division.

21, 23. See margin, pages 212-213.

19. a. Write as a decimal: $\frac{-7}{2}$, $\frac{7}{-2}$, and $-\frac{7}{2}$. **-3.5, -3.5, and -3.5**

b. Write as a decimal: $\frac{-3}{11}$, $\frac{3}{-11}$, and $-\frac{3}{11}$. **$-.\overline{27}$, $-.\overline{27}$, and $-.\overline{27}$**

c. Generalize the pattern of parts a and b using variables. **$\frac{-x}{y} = \frac{x}{-y} = -\frac{x}{y}$**

20. Simplify $\frac{xy}{21} \div \frac{x}{4y}$. **$\frac{4y^2}{21}$**

21. In 1577, Guillaume Gosselin published a book titled *De Arte Magna*. It contained some of the first work on positive and negative numbers. It was written in Latin. Here are some rules Gosselin wrote.

1. P in P diviso quotus est P.
2. M in M diviso quotus est P.
3. M in P diviso quotus est M.
4. P in M diviso quotus est M.

Translate these rules into English. **See margin.**

Review

22. Suppose $x = -.0046928146$ and $y = -.0046928146$. What is $\frac{x}{y}$? *(Previous course)* **1**

23. Your uncle is having a party and he asked you to buy 5 pounds of meat. You can buy sliced turkey or roast beef. Graph all the possible ways you could buy the two different meats so they total 5 pounds. Let t = amount of turkey and b = amount of beef. *(Lesson 3-7)* **See margin.**

24. Simplify: **a.** $7 + \frac{3}{7}$ **b.** $7 \cdot \frac{3}{7}$ **c.** $x \cdot \frac{y}{x}$ *(Lesson 2-3, 4-2)*
a) $7\frac{3}{7}$; b) 3; c) y

25. You bought 5 new shirts today. How many different ways can you choose the order in which to wear them? *(Lesson 4-9)* **120**

26. After paying $213.00 tax, Cliff still had more than $4700 in his account. How much did he have before the tax? *(Lesson 3-3)*
more than $4913

27. The perimeter of quadrilateral *URSA* at the left is 25.
a. Find x. **3** **b.** Find UR. *(Lesson 2-6)* **10**

28. *Skill sequence* Solve and check. *(Lessons 2-6, 4-4)*
a. $\frac{3}{5} + r = 8$ **$7\frac{2}{5}$** **b.** $\frac{3}{5}r = 8$ **$\frac{40}{3}$**
c. $\frac{48}{6} = 0 \cdot r + r + .6$ **7.4** **d.** $\frac{3rt}{5t} = 2^3$ **$r = \frac{40}{3}$**

29. A circle has a radius of 1.2 m. Find its area to the nearest tenth of a square meter. (Hint: $A = \pi r^2$.) *(Lesson 1-5)* **4.5 m^2**

30. Evaluate in your head. *(Previous course, Lessons 4-2, 4-3)*
a. $(2)^3$ **8** **b.** $(-1)^3$ **-1** **c.** $(\frac{2}{3})^3$ **$\frac{8}{27}$**

Exploration

31. Congruent figures are figures with the same size and shape. Split this region into 6 congruent pieces.

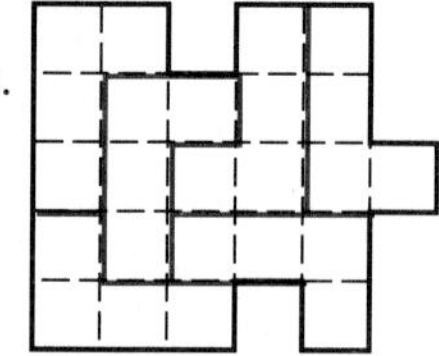

214

LESSON

5-2

Rates

In Lesson 4-2, you multiplied with rates. For example, if you travel at 45 miles per hour, then in 5 hours, you will travel 225 miles because

$$5 \text{ hours} \cdot 45 \frac{\text{miles}}{\text{hour}} = 225 \text{ miles.}$$

If you are not given a rate, you may be able to calculate it using division.

Example 1 Joe took a trip of 400 miles. The trip took him 8 hours. What was his average rate?

Solution 1 Divide the distance in miles by the time in hours.

$$\frac{400 \text{ miles}}{8 \text{ hours}}$$

Separate the numerical parts from the measurement units.

$$\frac{400 \text{ miles}}{8 \text{ hours}} = \frac{400}{8}\,\frac{\text{miles}}{\text{hours}}$$
$$= 50 \text{ miles per hour}$$

He was traveling at a rate or speed of 50 miles per hour.

Solution 2 You could also divide the time by the distance.

$$\frac{8 \text{ hours}}{400 \text{ miles}} = \frac{8}{400}\,\frac{\text{hours}}{\text{miles}}$$
$$= \frac{1}{50} \text{ hour per mile}$$

This means that, on the average, it took him $\frac{1}{50}$ of an hour to travel each mile.

LESSON 5-2

RESOURCES
- Lesson Master 5-2
- Computer Master 9

OBJECTIVES

D Identify restrictions on a variable in a division situation.
F Use the Rate Model for Division.
L Use the IF-THEN command in computer programs.

TEACHING NOTES

In **Example 1,** Jane's rate could have been found by using the formula $d = rt$ and solving the resulting equation. But the emphasis here is on the Rate Model. Because rates are meaningless without units, insist that the students show them!

Reading For many students, *rate* means "speed" and **Example 1** is an example of this. **Examples 2 and 3,** however, are not. Explain that the word *per* can be used whenever there is a rate. It isn't the speed measured by miles per hour that makes that a rate, it is the word *per* (or an equivalent, such as *for each*).

The explanation following **Example 3** uses the Rate Model to show that "you cannot divide by zero."

Computer Do not skip the computer program which closes the lesson, even if you don't have a computer available. "If-then" reasoning is at the heart of mathematics. The mechanical representation of this reasoning in a computer language gives students good experience with conditional statements. This program can also be adapted to show what happens when attempting to divide by zero. Replace lines 50 and 60 with the single line

50 PRINT 7/(K–5)

Then run the program using 5 for your input. Show the class the error message. Also have students try to divide by zero on their calculators.

Make sure that students know that $x \neq y$ in algebra becomes X<>Y in BASIC. Most computer languages do not handle the $\neq$ symbol.

The first solution gives Joe's rate in *miles per hour*. You are familiar with the meaning of this rate from speed limit signs or watching the speedometer in a car. The second solution gives the rate in *hours per mile*, or how long it takes to travel one mile. Notice that $\frac{1}{50}$ of an hour is $\frac{1}{50} \cdot 60$ min or 1.2 minutes. In other words, it takes a little over a minute to go one mile. Either rate is correct. The one you use depends on the situation in which you use it.

This situation is an instance of the **Rate Model for Division.**

Rate Model for Division:

If a and b are quantities with different units, then $\frac{a}{b}$ is the amount of quantity a per quantity b.

Example 2 In 1986, total medical costs in the United States were about \$458,200,000,000. That year the population was about 240,500,000. What did a person spend for medical costs on the average?

Solution This situation should prompt you to find dollars per person. To get this rate, divide the total spent by the number of people.

$$\frac{458{,}200{,}000{,}000 \text{ dollars}}{240{,}500{,}000 \text{ people}} = \frac{458{,}200{,}\cancel{000}{,}\cancel{000} \text{ dollars}}{240{,}5\cancel{00}{,}\cancel{000} \text{ people}}$$
$$\approx 1905 \text{ dollars/person}$$

Rates can be negative quantities.

Example 3 The temperature goes down 12 degrees in 5 hours. What is the rate of temperature change?

Solution The rate here is degrees per hour. To find it, divide the number of degrees by the number of hours.

$$\frac{\text{drop of 12 degrees}}{\text{5 hours}} = \text{drop of 2.4 degrees per hour}$$

This can be written as

$$\frac{\text{-12 degrees}}{\text{5 hours}} = \text{-2.4 degrees per hour.}$$

The temperature drops at a rate of 2.4 degrees per hour.

Consider the rate $\frac{10 \text{ meters}}{0 \text{ seconds}}$. It means you are traveling 10 meters in 0 seconds. To be true, you would have to be in two places at the same time. Since that is impossible, this model illustrates that it is meaningless to think of $\frac{10}{0}$. *Division by zero is impossible*. The denominator of a fraction cannot be zero. When variables appear in divisions, you sometimes must take precautions so that you don't attempt to divide by zero.

Example 4 What value can k *not* have in $\frac{7}{k - 5}$?

Solution The denominator can't be 0, so $k - 5$ cannot be 0. Thus k cannot be 5.

Check If $k = 5$, then $\frac{7}{k - 5} = \frac{7}{5 - 5} = \frac{7}{0}$.

If a computer is instructed to divide by zero, it won't do it! The program will stop running and an error message will appear on the screen. To avoid this, you can have the computer decide in advance if an expression will involve division by zero. An **IF-THEN** command has the computer make a decision. When the sentence between the words IF and THEN is true, the computer executes the statement following the THEN. When the sentence is false, the statement following the THEN is completely ignored by the computer.

In Example 4 you saw that if k is 5, the expression $\frac{7}{k - 5}$ has no meaning. The following program evaluates $\frac{7}{k - 5}$ for different values of k, as long as $k \neq 5$. Otherwise, it prints a message about division by zero.

```
10 PRINT "EVALUATE 7/(K – 5)"
20 PRINT "ENTER VALUE OF K"
30 INPUT K
40 PRINT "VALUE OF 7/(K – 5)"
50 IF K = 5 THEN PRINT "DIVISION BY ZERO IS IMPOSSIBLE"
55 REM      THE COMPUTER SYMBOL FOR "NOT EQUAL" IS < >.
60 IF K <> 5 THEN PRINT 7/(K - 5)
70 END
```

ADDITIONAL EXAMPLES

1. Carlos worked $7\frac{1}{2}$ hours last week and earned \$38.55. What was his salary?
5.14 dollars/hour or \$5.14/hr

2. In the 1984 Olympics, Carlos Lopez of Portugal set an Olympic record for the 26.2-mile marathon. He ran the race in about 2.16 hours. What was his average speed?
≈ 12.1 miles per hour

3. From 1984 to 1989, the enrollment at Middlewood School dropped by 148 students. How fast was the enrollment changing?
$\frac{\textbf{-148 students}}{\textbf{5 years}} = \textbf{-29.6}\frac{\textbf{students}}{\textbf{year}}$

4. What value can n not have in $\frac{n + 3}{10 - n}$? **10**

NOTES ON QUESTIONS
Questions 8 and 9: Students should be able to see what value of the variable makes the denominator 0. Point out that if the answer were not obvious, it could be found by setting the denominator equal to zero and solving the resulting equation.

Computer for Question 11: This question presents an opportunity to remind students that the fraction bar in $\frac{K}{K-5}$ acts as a grouping symbol. Because BASIC does not use that symbol, the parentheses must be used to group.

Question 12: This is an example of reciprocal rates. Consumer decisions are often based on "pennies (cost) per ounce." Would "ounces per penny" do just as well in making a decision? How would you judge the better buy using "ounces per penny"? (The better buy gives more ounces per penny.)

Computer for Question 18: For this computer activity, students can pattern their program after the one given in the lesson. Since hours should be positive, they only have to test HOURS>0 rather than HOURS<>0.

Questions

Covering the Reading

1. Suppose Joe took a trip of 300 miles and it took him 8 hours.
  a. What was his average speed in miles per hour? **37.5 mph**
  b. On the average, how long did it take him to travel a mile? **$\frac{2}{75}$ or ≈ .027 hour**

2. State the rate model for division. **See margin.**

3. a. To calculate degrees per hour, you should divide _?_ by _?_. **degrees, hours**
  b. The temperature drops 11 degrees in 5 hours. What is the rate of temperature change? **-2.2 degrees per hour**

4. Give a rate suggested by each situation.
  a. A family drove 24 miles in $\frac{2}{3}$ hours. **36 mph**
  b. A family drove m miles in $\frac{2}{3}$ hours. **1.5*m* mph**
  c. A family drove 24 miles in h hours. **24/*h* mph**
  d. A family drove m miles in h hours. ***m*/*h* mph**

In 5–7, calculate a rate suggested by each situation.

5. In 9 days Julian earned $495. **$55 per day**

6. c cans of natural lemonade cost $2.10. **2.10/c dollars per can**

7. You travel 270 miles and use 7.8 gallons of gasoline. **See margin.**

In 8 and 9, what value can the variable *not* have in each expression?

8. $\frac{18}{k-4}$ **4**

9. $\frac{x-6}{x+1}$ **-1**

In 10 and 11, refer to the computer program in this lesson.

10. Tell what the computer will print if the value entered for K is:
  a. 19 **0.5** **b.** 0 **-1.4** **c.** 5. **IMPOSSIBLE**

11. Why are parentheses needed around $K - 5$?
  so that the program will divide by the result of *K*-5

Applying the Mathematics

12. In one store a 20-ounce can of pineapple costs 89¢ and a 6-ounce can of the same kind of pineapple costs 39¢.
  a. Calculate the unit cost of the 20-ounce can. **4.5 cents**
  b. Calculate the unit cost of the 6-ounce can. **6.5 cents**
  c. Based on the unit cost, which is the better buy? **20-ounce can**

A street in Bangladesh

13. For each place, find the number of people per square mile. (This is called the *population density*.) **a) 1544.1 people per sq mi**

a. Bangladesh: population 85,122,000; area 55,126 sq mi

b. Greenland: population 50,000; area 840,000 sq mi **.06 person per sq mi**

14. A fast runner can run a half mile in 2 minutes. What is the average rate, then, in miles per *hour*? **15 mph**

15. *Multiple choice* In m minutes, a copy machine made c copies. At this rate, how many copies per *hour* can be made? **(b)**

(a) $\frac{60m}{c}$ (b) $\frac{60c}{m}$ (c) $\frac{c}{60m}$ (d) $\frac{m}{60c}$

16. In $\frac{5n + 1}{2n}$, what value can n not have? **0**

17. What happens on your calculator when you divide by 0? **An error message (E) appears.**

18. Write a computer program to calculate rate of speed in miles per hour. It should ask for the number of miles and number of hours. If the user enters zero hours, it should print IMPOSSIBLE. **See margin.**

Review

19. $\frac{x}{3} \div 5$ is the same as what multiplication problem? *(Lesson 5-1)* $\frac{x}{3} \cdot \frac{1}{5}$

In 20–24, simplify. *(Lesson 5-1)*

20. $\frac{5}{\frac{2}{3}}$ **15/2 or 7.5**

21. $\frac{-3}{4} \div \frac{-3}{2}$ $\frac{1}{2}$

22. $\frac{x}{2y} \div \frac{11y}{3}$ $\frac{3x}{22y^2}$

23. $6 \div \frac{1}{2}$ **12**

24. $\frac{x}{2} \div \frac{x}{4}$ **2**

ADDITIONAL ANSWERS

2. If a and b are quantities with different units, then $\frac{a}{b}$ is the amount of quantity a per quantity b.

7. ≈34.6 miles per gallon

18.

```
10 PRINT
   "CALCULATE
   RATE OF
   SPEED"
20 PRINT "ENTER
   NUMBER OF
   MILES M."
30 INPUT M
40 PRINT "ENTER
   NUMBER OF
   HOURS H."
50 INPUT H
60 IF H=0
   THEN PRINT
   "IMPOSSIBLE"
70 IF H>0
   THEN PRINT
   "RATE OF
   SPEED IS";M/H;
   "MILES/HOUR"
```

NAME ____________

LESSON **MASTER 5–2**
QUESTIONS ON **SPUR** OBJECTIVES

■PROPERTIES *Objective D (See pages 256–259 for objectives.)*

In 1–6, what value(s) can the variable not have?

1. $\frac{2}{x}$ **x can't be 0**
2. $\frac{a}{a-4}$ **a can't be 4**
3. $\frac{b-3}{b+5}$ **b can't be -5**
4. $\frac{n+9}{n-11}$ **n can't be 11**
5. $\frac{1.5k}{k-1.5}$ **k can't be 1.5**
6. $\frac{c-6.1}{8.3+c}$ **c can't be -8.3**

■USES *Objective F*

7. Andre Dawson of the Chicago Cubs earned \$1,850,000 in 1988. If he played in all 162 games, how much was his salary per game? **\$11,419.75**

8. There are 30 slices in a certain loaf of bread and 2400 calories per loaf. How many calories are in each slice? **80 calories/slice**

9. Bobby ran $\frac{3}{10}$ of a mile in $1\frac{1}{2}$ minutes. How many minutes per mile is this? **5 minutes/mile**

10. In a recent year, there were 46,000 deaths from motor vehicle accidents in the U.S. If the population was approximately 226.5 million, what was the death rate per 100,000 population due to motor vehicle accidents? **$\frac{\text{20.3 deaths}}{\text{100,000 people}}$**

■REPRESENTATIONS *Objective L*

11. For the program, what will be printed if the input is

a. 6? **IMPOSSIBLE** b. -4? **.2**

```
10 PRINT "EVALUATE AN EXPRESSION."
20 PRINT "ENTER A VALUE OF A."
30 INPUT A
40 IF A = 6 THEN PRINT "IMPOSSIBLE"
50 IF A <> 6 THEN PRINT (A+2)/(A-6)
60 END
```

12. Write a program to evaluate $(n + 4)/(n + 9)$ for any value of n that is entered. If the input makes the expression meaningless, the computer should print "IMPOSSIBLE."

SAMPLE:

```
10 PRINT "ENTER A VALUE OF N."
20 INPUT N
30 IF N = -9 THEN PRINT "IMPOSSIBLE"
40 IF N <> -9 THEN PRINT (N + 4)/(N + 9)
50 END
```

 37

NOTES ON QUESTIONS
Question 28: This question involves the geometric concepts of length, area, and perimeter which students need to review periodically.

Small Group Work for Questions 34 and 35: You may wish to have students work in small groups while researching these questions.

FOLLOW-UP

MORE PRACTICE
For more practice on SPUR Objectives, use *Lesson Master 5-2,* shown on page 219.

EXTENSION
An almanac is a good source of sports statistics, many of which lend themselves to rate questions. It is interesting to compare rates. Ask students to find the rates (in kilometers per hour) of the Olympic record-holders in the following events. Then tell which record-holder was faster. (The answers given are as of 1988.)

1. the men's 100-meter run and the men's 10,000-meter run (36.4 km/hr; 21.7 km/hr; The 100-meter runner was faster.)

2. the men's 100-meter run and the men's 100-meter freestyle swimming (36.4 km/hr; 7.4 km/hr; The runner was faster.)

3. the women's 1500-meter run and the women's 1500-meter speedskating (23.1 km/hr; 43.8 km/hr; The speedskater was faster.)

34. sample: In 1985, the debt per capita was $7514.51.

In 25 and 26, solve. *(Lessons 4-4, 5-1)*

25. $.45x = -135$ **-300**

26. $\frac{5}{8}m = \frac{10}{3}$ $\frac{16}{3}$

27. Solve $-19 = 1.9tn$ for n. *(Lesson 5-1)* $-\frac{10}{t}$

28. If the area of square S is 9 and the perimeter of square T is 20, find the area of square R. *(Previous course)* **64**

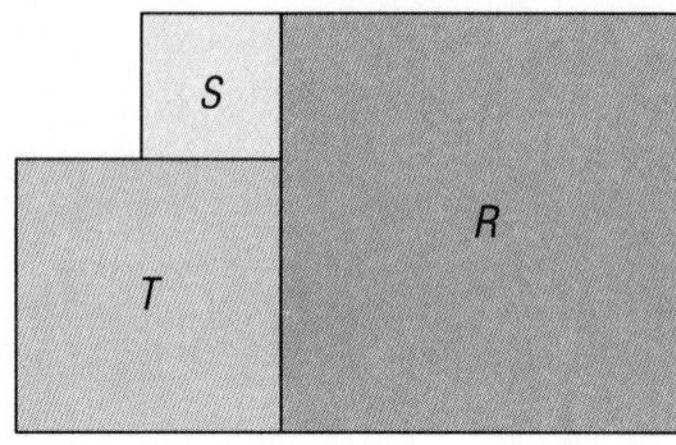

29. In the summer of 1987, an American dollar was worth about .62 English pound and one dollar would buy about 6.1 French francs. About how many francs could be bought for 75 pounds? *(Lesson 4-3)* **≈ 738 francs**

30. There are 3 teachers of freshman English, 4 of freshman math, and 2 of freshman science. Lionel wants Mr. Novel for English, Mrs. Euclid for math, and Mr. Bunson for science. If students are randomly assigned to classes, what is the probability Lionel will get all his favorite teachers? *(Lesson 4-8)* $\frac{1}{24}$

In 31–33, solve and check. *(Lessons 2-3, 3-3)*

31. $8 = x - 5$ **13**

32. $-7 = y - 2.5$ **-4.5**

33. $13 - 15 + z = 2\frac{1}{2} + \frac{-3}{4}$ $\frac{15}{4}$

Exploration

34. Use an almanac or some other source to find the national debt. Find the U.S. population. Then calculate the average debt per capita (the phrase "per capita" means "per person"). **See margin.**

35. See Question 13. What is the population density of the community or city where you live? **Answers will vary.**

LESSON

5-3 Ratios

Being overweight increases the probability that a person will suffer from heart disease. The chart below left shows a way to test whether an adult has an increased risk. Dividing the waist measure by the hip measure results in a **ratio** which can be used to compare them.

1. Measure waist and hips. Call these w and h.
2. For women, risk of heart disease increases if $\frac{w}{h} > 0.8$.
3. For men, risk of heart disease increases if $\frac{w}{h} > 1.0$.

Example 1 Ms. Mott's waist measure is 26″. Her hip measure is 35″. According to the chart at left, does she run an increased risk of heart disease?

Solution $\frac{\text{waist measure}}{\text{hip measure}} = \frac{26''}{35''} \approx 0.74$

Since $0.74 < 0.8$, her risk (according to this test) is not high.

The direction of the comparison is important. If Ms. Mott compared her hip measure to her waist measure, the result would be $\frac{35''}{26''} \approx 1.35$, which is greater than 0.8. She would be using the wrong number and would misinterpret the test.

Subtraction provides one way to compare quantities. Division is another way.

Ratio Model for Division:

Let a and b be quantities with the same units. Then the ratio $\frac{a}{b}$ compares a to b.

The ratio $\frac{b}{a}$ compares b to a.

Notice the difference between a rate and a ratio. In a rate, the units for a and b are different. When forming a ratio, be sure that the quantities are measured in the same units.

LESSON 5-3

RESOURCES

- Lesson Master 5-3
- Computer Master 10

OBJECTIVE

G Use a ratio to compare two quantities.

TEACHING NOTES

For clarity, we distinguish rates from ratios, but we do not stress the difference. Notice that only **Question 8** in this lesson addresses this issue. (See also the last paragraph of the Perspective for this lesson.)

Alternate Approach **Example 2** was done by comparing minutes to minutes. Instead, both measurements could have been in hours.

$\frac{\text{Ms. Harper's time}}{\text{Mr. Garcia's time}} =$

$\frac{\frac{1}{6}\text{hr}}{\frac{3}{4}\text{hr}} = \frac{1}{6} \div \frac{3}{4} =$

$\frac{1}{6} \cdot \frac{4}{3} = \frac{2}{9}.$

The percent of discount is a common application that students need to understand. Have students make or collect lists of original and sale prices of items in stores or newspaper advertisements. Then have them calculate the percent of discount for each.

ADDITIONAL EXAMPLES

1. Bob's height is 5 feet 10 inches. His daughter is 40 inches tall. What is the ratio of their heights?
$\frac{7}{4}$

2. For many years the Empire State Building (1250 feet tall) was the world's tallest building. That record is currently held by the Sears Tower (1454 feet tall) in Chicago. The height of the Empire State Building is what percent of the height of the Sears Tower?
≈86%

3. When the first U.S. census was taken in 1790, the area of the country was 891,364 square miles. In the last census it was 3,618,770 square miles. How many times as large is the United States now than it was in 1790?
≈4.1

4. A pair of tennis shoes was originally being sold for $40. Now they are on sale for $8 less. What is the percent of discount on the tennis shoes?
20%

Example 2 It takes Mr. Garcia $\frac{3}{4}$ hour to go to work and it takes Ms. Harper 10 minutes to go to work. Find a ratio comparing Ms. Harper's time to Mr. Garcia's time.

Solution The units of measure for 10 minutes and $\frac{3}{4}$ hour are not the same. We change hours to minutes. Since Ms. Harper is first in the word description of the ratios, her time must be in the numerator. The ratio of Ms. Harper's time to Mr. Garcia's time is

$$\frac{\text{Ms. Harper's time}}{\text{Mr. Garcia's time}} = \frac{10 \text{ minutes}}{\frac{3}{4} \text{ hour}} = \frac{10 \text{ minutes}}{\frac{3}{4} \cdot 60 \text{ minutes}} = \frac{10 \text{ minutes}}{45 \text{ minutes}} = \frac{2}{9}$$

This means that, on the average, Ms. Harper travels 2 minutes for every 9 minutes that Mr. Garcia travels. You could also say that it takes Ms. Harper $\frac{2}{9}$ of the time it takes Mr. Garcia to go to work.

Often ratios are written as percentages. In Example 2, $\frac{2}{9} = .\overline{22} \approx 22\%$, and you could say that it takes Ms. Harper about 22% of the time it takes Mr. Garcia. A percentage can always be interpreted as a ratio, in this case about $\frac{22}{100}$.

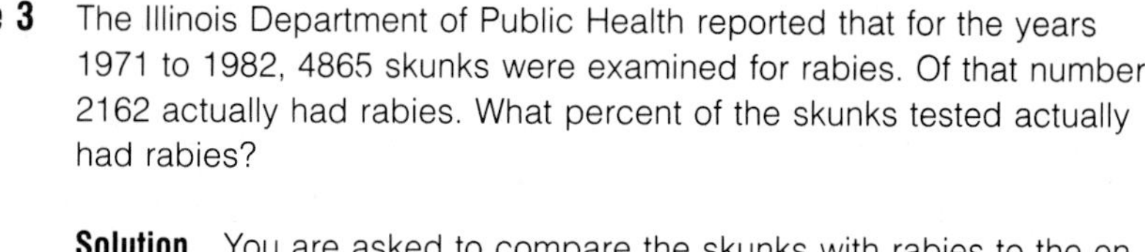

Example 3 The Illinois Department of Public Health reported that for the years 1971 to 1982, 4865 skunks were examined for rabies. Of that number, 2162 actually had rabies. What percent of the skunks tested actually had rabies?

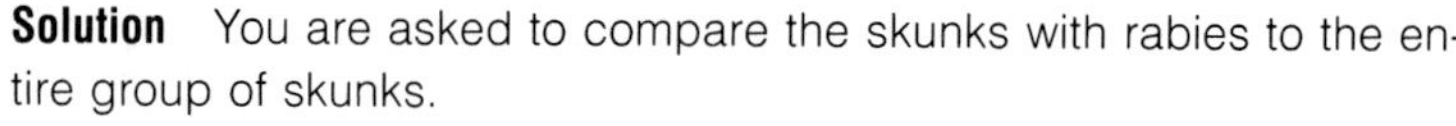

Solution You are asked to compare the skunks with rabies to the entire group of skunks.

$$\frac{2162 \text{ skunks}}{4865 \text{ skunks}} = \frac{2162}{4865} \approx .444 \approx 44.4\%$$

Thus about 44% of the tested skunks actually had rabies.

If asked to compare quantities without being given any order, you can make the comparison either way.

Example 4 Life expectancy has increased from an estimated 18 years in 3000 B.C. to 73.8 years in 1980. Using a ratio, compare these life expectancies.

Solution 1 $\frac{\text{1980 expectancy}}{\text{3000 B.C. expectancy}} \approx \frac{73.8 \text{ years}}{18 \text{ years}} = 4.1$

This means that the life expectancy in 1980 was about 4 times what it was in 3000 B.C.

222

Solution 2 $\frac{\text{3000 B.C. expectancy}}{\text{1980 expectancy}} \approx \frac{\text{18 years}}{\text{73.8 years}} \approx .244$

Since $.244 \approx .25$, the answer indicates that life expectancy in 3000 B.C. was about $\frac{1}{4}$ of what it was in 1980.

In a problem involving discount, the *percent of discount* is the ratio of the discount to the selling price.

Example 5 The selling price of an item originally costing $30 is reduced $6. What is the percent of discount?

Solution
$$\frac{\text{amount of discount}}{\text{original price}} = \frac{\text{6 dollars}}{\text{30 dollars}} = \frac{1}{5} = .2 = 20\%$$

Questions

Covering the Reading

In 1 and 2, refer to the method for testing heart disease risk.

1. Does a woman run an increased risk of heart disease if her waist and hip measurements are 32″ and 37″, respectively? **Yes**

2. Does a man run an increased risk of heart disease if his waist is 34″ and his hips are 36″? **No**

3. Let x and y be two quantities with the same units. Write two ratios comparing x and y. **x/y, y/x**

4. Suppose it takes Ms. Lopez 25 minutes to complete a particular job and it takes Mr. Sampson half an hour to complete the same job. Write a ratio which:
a. compares Ms. Lopez's time to Mr. Sampson's time; **5/6**
b. compares Mr. Sampson's time to Ms. Lopez's time. **6/5**

5. The Illinois Department of Health reported that for the years 1971 to 1982, of 230 horses tested for rabies only 16 actually had the disease. What percentage of horses tested had rabies? **≈7%**

6. An item costing $40 is reduced by $5. What is the percent of discount? **12.5%**

7. What is the difference between a rate and a ratio? **See margin.**

ADDITIONAL ANSWERS
7. A ratio is the quotient of quantities with the same units; a rate is the quotient of quantities with different units.

NOTES ON QUESTIONS
Question 11: The most common answer given to this ratio problem is $\frac{w}{h} > 1$. However, this inequality can be transformed into $w > h$ by multiplying both sides by h (since $h > 0$). It is an opportunity to apply the Multiplication Property of Inequality, for $w > h$ gives a more meaningful description of a person's measurements.

Questions 17 and 18: These problems concern ratios of geometric quantities. These exercises give the students some experience in working with ratios in similar figures. They should figure out the ratio from the formulas given in the question.

Questions 25a-25c: Here, geometry is applied to help students move from units to variables. In **Question 25b,** m might be interpreted to be a variable or to be an abbreviation. Either way, the answer can be written $\frac{1}{3}m^2$. If m stands for meter, then m² stands for square meters. "Multiplication of units" yields valid results for the derived unit.

Question 26c: Here, chunking can be used. In **26a** we find that $b = 8$, so in **26b,** $5 + d = 8$ and $d = 3$.

Making Connections for Question 29: One purpose of this question is to familiarize students with subscripts before they see the slope formula in Lesson 8-2. Notice that the values of the variables are given in the same order as they would be read from two ordered pairs. A similar problem appears in Lesson 5-7.

12. Answer must be between 0.8 and 1.0. sample: $\frac{27}{30} = 0.9$.

8. *Multiple choice* Which is not a ratio? **(b)**
(a) $\frac{14 \text{ seconds}}{23 \text{ seconds}}$ (b) $\frac{150 \text{ miles}}{3 \text{ hours}}$ (c) $\frac{27 \text{ cookies}}{13 \text{ cookies}}$

9. *Multiple choice* A girl born today in the United States has a life expectancy of about 79 years. A boy has a life expectancy of about 72 years. Compare a girl's life expectancy to a boy's. **(b)**
(a) 1.09 (b) 1.1 (c) .91 (d) 9

Applying the Mathematics

10. The ratio of x to y is the __?__ of the ratio of y to x. **reciprocal**

11. If w is a man's waist measure and h is his hip measure, write a formula describing when a man's risk of heart disease increases. $\frac{w}{h} > 1$

12. Give an example of waist and hip measurements which would not run a risk of heart disease for a man, but would for a woman. **See margin.**

13. According to a teacher group, the average teacher salary for 1987–88 was \$28,031. In 1870 it was \$189. The 1980 salary is about how many times the 1870 salary? **≈148**

14. An item in a store sells for \$15.00. The store's profit on that item is \$6.00.
a. Write a ratio of profit to selling price. $\frac{6}{15} = \frac{2}{5}$
b. What is the percent of profit? **40%**

15. A store charges 64¢ tax on a \$16.00 purchase.
a. Write a ratio of tax to purchase price. $\frac{.64}{16} = \frac{1}{25}$
b. What is the percent of tax? **4%**

16. Banner High School has won 36 of its last 40 football games.
a. Write a ratio of games won to games played. $\frac{36}{40} = \frac{9}{10}$
b. What percent of these 40 games has it won? **90%**
c. Winning percentages are often written as a three-place decimal. Write the answer from part a as a three-place decimal. **.900**

In 17 and 18, refer to the circles. Lengths of their radii are given.

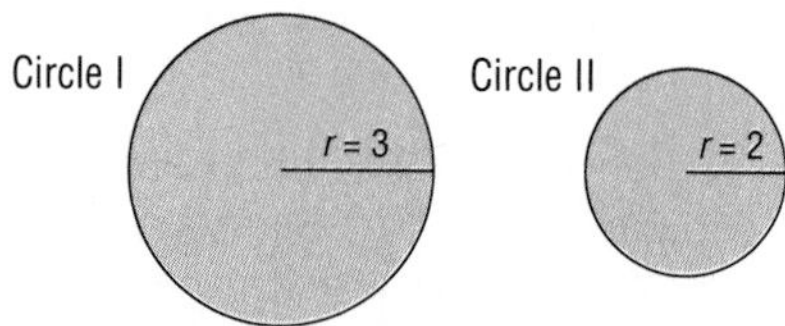

17. The diameter of a circle is twice its radius. Find the ratio of the diameter of Circle I to the diameter of Circle II. $\frac{6}{4} = \frac{3}{2}$

18. In a circle, Area $= \pi r^2$.
a. Give the ratio of the area of Circle I to the area of Circle II, in lowest terms. $\frac{9}{4}$
b. Write this ratio as a decimal. **2.25**

19. Frieda owns x sweaters while her brother-in-law Fred owns y sweaters. How many times as many sweaters does Fred own as Frieda? $\frac{y}{x}$

224

Review

20. It took Patrick 6 hours and 30 minutes to travel 314 miles. What was his average rate for the trip? *(Lesson 5-2)* **≈48 mph**

21. Simplify: $-\frac{8}{3} \div \frac{7}{2}$. *(Lesson 5-1)* $-\frac{16}{21}$

22. *Multiple choice* Which of the following is *not* equal to $-\frac{a}{b}$? *(Lesson 5-1)* **(c)**
(a) $\frac{a}{-b}$ (b) $\frac{-a}{b}$ (c) $\frac{-a}{-b}$ (d) $-\frac{-a}{-b}$

23. To use a mainframe computer, a school pays \$500 per hour. What is this in minutes per dollar? *(Lesson 5-2)* **.12**

24. In Seattle, Washington, it rained or snowed an average of 150 days per year over a 30-year period. What was the relative frequency of precipitation? *(Lesson 1-8)* **≈.41**

25. Remember the area of a rectangle is $\ell \cdot w$. Find the area of the rectangle. *(Lesson 4-1)* **a) 13.5 ft²; b) 1/3 m²; c) 6x²**

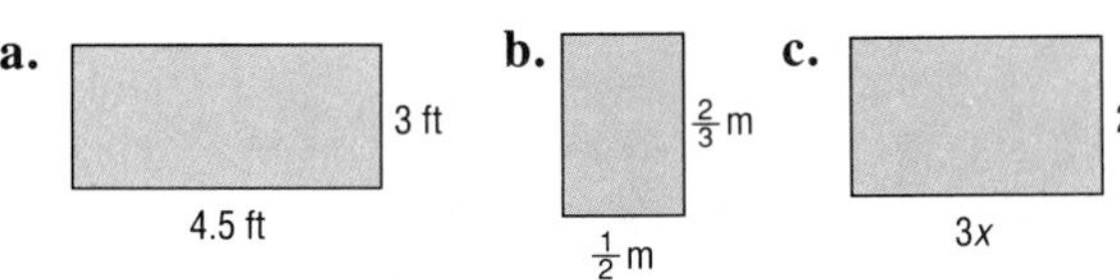

26. *Skill sequence* Solve. *(Lessons 3-3,4-5)*
a. $b - 12 = -4$ **b = 8**
b. $12 - c = -4$ **c = 16**
c. $(5 + d) - 12 = -4$ **d = 3**

27. In 1986, salaries for state governors were as high as \$100,000 (New York) and as low as \$35,000 (Arkansas and Maine).
a. What is the range of salaries? **\$65,000**
b. What is the mean of the two extreme salaries? *(Lesson 1-2)* **\$67,500**

28. In a slide, the preimage (3, 4) has image (6, 1). Under the same slide
a. what is the image of (0, 8)? **(3, 5)**
b. what is the preimage of (-2, -7)? *(Lesson 2-5)* **(-5, -4)**

29. Evaluate $\frac{y_2 - y_1}{x_2 - x_1}$ when $x_1 = 6$, $y_1 = 1$, $x_2 = 8$ and $y_2 = 23$. *(Lesson 1-5)* **11**

Exploration

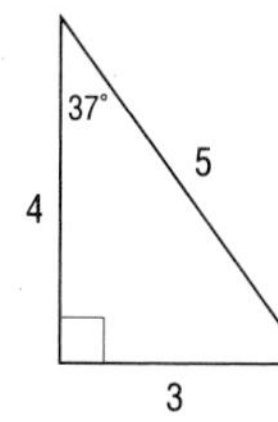

30. Consider this right triangle with an angle of about 37°. The three sides can form six different ratios.
a. Write the values of all six of these ratios.
b. Some of these ratios have special names. One of these is called the sine. For the triangle to the left, it is written sin 37°. Compute sin 37° on your calculator using the key sequence **a)** $\frac{3}{4}, \frac{3}{5}, \frac{4}{5}, \frac{4}{3}, \frac{5}{3}, \frac{5}{4}$; **b) .601815;** $\frac{3}{5}$

37 [sin]

and determine which of the six ratios in part a is the sine.
c. Compute cos 37° on your calculator and determine which of the six ratios in part a is the cosine. **.7986355;** $\frac{4}{5}$
d. Compute tan 37° on your calculator and determine which of the six ratios in part a is the tangent. **.7535541;** $\frac{3}{4}$

FOLLOW-UP

MORE PRACTICE
For more practice on SPUR Objectives, use *Lesson Master 5-3,* shown below.

EXTENSION
It is possible to have ratios of more than two numbers. However, these are usually not written in fraction form. Instead, the numbers are separated by colons. These ratios can be simplified like ordinary ratios. For example, the ratio 9:12:15 can be reduced to 3:4:5. Have students consider the following problems:

1. Find three integers that are in the ratio 1:5:6 and whose sum is 36. ($x + 5x + 6x = 36$, so $x = 3$; the numbers are 3, 15, 18)

2. Find four integers that are in the ratio 1:2:3:7 and whose sum is 52. ($x + 2x + 3x + 7x = 52$, so $x = 4$; the numbers are 4, 8, 12, 28)

NAME __________

LESSON **MASTER 5–3**
QUESTIONS ON **SPUR** OBJECTIVES

■USES *Objective G (See pages 256–259 for objectives.)*

1. In a recent year, there were 11,068 births and 9,928 deaths in Alaska. Write the ratio of births to deaths. **$\frac{11068}{9928} \approx 1.115$**

2. Jack gets an allowance of \$7.50 a week and spends \$3.50 a week for lunches. What percent of his allowance is spent for lunch? **$\frac{3.50}{7.50} = 46.\overline{6}\%$**

3. In the 1980 presidential election there were 35.5 million votes cast for the Democratic candidate and 43.9 million votes for the Republican. What was the ratio of Republican to Democratic votes? **$\frac{43.9}{35.5} \approx 1.24$**

4. *Multiple choice* The rectangle that is considered to be most pleasing to the eye has a length to width ratio of about 1.618. Which rectangle has dimensions which are closest to this ratio?
(a) 6 cm by 9 cm (b) 8.5 in. by 11 in.
(c) 3 in. by 5 in. (d) 4 ft by 8 ft **c**

5. A pair of jeans which usually sells for \$24 is on sale for \$6 less. What is the percent of discount? **25%**

6. What is the percent of discount of a \$119.95 suit which is selling for \$99? **≈17%**

7. What is the sales tax rate if you pay 60¢ on a \$12.00 item? **5%**

8. What is the sales tax rate for a tax of t dollars on an item costing c dollars? **$\left(100\frac{t}{c}\right)\%$**

9. A school swim team won 6 out of 8 swimming meets. What is the team's winning percentage? **75%**

10. Mr. Gaston bought a stock for d dollars, and sold it for $d + p$ dollars. What was the ratio of his profit to his purchase price? **$\frac{p}{d}$**

38 *Algebra* © Scott, Foresman and Company

LESSON 5-4

RESOURCES
- Lesson Master 5-4
- Quiz for Lessons 5-1 Through 5-4
- Visual for Teaching Aid 24: 10 × 10 grids

OBJECTIVES

B Solve percent problems using equations or in your head.
H Solve percent and size change problems from real situations.

TEACHING NOTES

Alternate Approach All the examples in this lesson are solved with equations of the form $a \cdot b = c$. However, when finding a percent as in **Example 1c,** it may be easier to use the Ratio Model from the previous lesson and simply divide.

Stress that the symbol % means "multiplied by .01." Thus to change from a percent to a decimal, move the decimal point two places to the left as you would when multiplying by .01. To change from a decimal to percent, reverse the process. Suggest to students that they can verify such changes by remembering common equivalences (for example, 10% = .1 and 1% = .01).

Percent-to-decimal conversions can also be checked by relating unfamiliar situations to familiar ones. For instance, in **Example 1a,** to check the change of 112% to decimal form, add the decimal equivalents of 100% and 12%. The first answer is 1 and the second answer is

LESSON

5-4 Solving Percent Problems Using Equations

The word **percent** (often written as the two words per cent) comes from the Latin words *per centum,* meaning "per 100." So 7% literally means 7 per 100, or the ratio $\frac{7}{100}$, or 0.07. The symbol % for percent is only about 100 years old.

In many situations, a percent of an original quantity is a known quantity.

50% of 120,000 is 60,000.
$5\frac{1}{4}$% of \$3000 is \$157.50.

Often, however, you only know two of the three numbers. One method for solving such percent problems is to translate the words into an equation of the form $ab = c$.

Example 1
a. 112% of 650 is what number?
b. 7% of what number is 31.5?
c. What percent of 3.5 is.84?

Solution

a. 112% of 650 is what number?

$$a \cdot b = c$$
$$1.12 \cdot 650 = c$$ Change 112% to 1.12.
$$728 = c$$

The answer is 728.

b. 7% of what number is 31.5?

$$a \cdot b = c$$
$$.07 \cdot b = 31.5$$ 7% is .07.
$$\frac{.07b}{.07} = \frac{31.5}{.07}$$ Divide both sides by .07.
$$b = 450$$

The answer is 450.

Check 7% of 450 = .07 · 450 = 31.5

c. What % of 3.5 is .84?

$$a \cdot b = c$$
$$a \cdot 3.5 = .84$$
$$\frac{a \cdot 3.5}{3.5} = \frac{.84}{3.5}$$ Divide both sides by 3.5.
$$a = .24$$
$$= 24\%$$

Check 24% · 3.5 = .24 · 3.5 = .84

Example 2 It was reported in 1987 that 55% of the 51.5 million married couples in the U.S.A. had two incomes. Approximately how many couples had two incomes?

Solution Let c be the number of couples with two incomes.

$$.55 \cdot 51.5 = c$$
$$28.325 = c$$

Approximately 28.3 million couples had two incomes.

Example 3 In 1983, only 43,200 or 2.4% of America's enlisted military personnel were college graduates. How many enlisted personnel were there in all?

Solution Let x be the number of enlisted personnel then,

$$2.4\% \cdot x = 43{,}200$$
$$.024 \cdot x = 43{,}200$$
$$x = \frac{43{,}200}{.024}$$
$$x \approx 1{,}800{,}000$$

There were approximately 1,800,000 enlisted personnel.

.12. In **Example 3** change 2.4% by referring to the decimal form of 2%, then putting the extra digit at the end.

Making Connections
Example 4 is very similar to **Example 5** of the previous lesson, but notice the extra step. The amount of discount must be calculated before the percent of discount can be found.

ADDITIONAL EXAMPLES

1. a. 64% of 175 is what number?
112

b. 125% of what number is 230?
184

c. 473 out of 671 is what percent?
≈70.5

2. It is estimated that in 1990 about 8% of farmers will use a personal computer. If there are 3 million farmers, how many of them will use a computer?
240,000

3. Tickets to a concert cost $15.50 if purchased in advance, and $18 if purchased at the ticket window. What is the percent of discount for tickets purchased in advance?
$\frac{2.50}{18.00} \approx$ **14%**

4. Here is a newspaper quote in which the arithmetic is incorrect: The 400-page report says that "the average citizen had a better than 18 percent chance of falling victim to a serious crime, with an average of 5,480 offenses per 100,000 Americans." Where is the error?
It appears that the reciprocal $\frac{100{,}000}{5480}$ was used instead of the correct ratio $\frac{5480}{100{,}000}$. The correct percent can be estimated as follows:
$\frac{5480}{100{,}000} \div \frac{1000}{1000} \approx$ **5.5%.**

NOTES ON QUESTIONS
Reading for Question 8: Some students may answer by saying 29%, not seeing the difference between finding the number of couples and the percent of couples. Have them reread the question. Then ask whether the word *many* indicates they should find a number or a percent.

Question 14: Here, there are two ways to solve the problem. The first way is to multiply .14 • 1850 to find the drop in enrollment, and then to subtract from 1850. The second method is to realize that if enrollment is down 14%, then it will be 86% of its present size. So calculate .86 • 1850. The second method is more efficient and relates to the way we will do exponential decrease problems. Students should see this method here.

Question 16: This can be done mentally by realizing that 45 minutes is 3/4 of an hour and knowing that 3/4 = 75%. Students should know the percent forms of 1/2, thirds, fourths, fifths, and tenths. Also, some students will find it convenient to remember the percent forms of sixths and eighths.

Question 19: Here, the retail price of the bike is 166% of the wholesale price, so the wholesale price was marked up 66%.

Problems related to business often involve percents.

Example 4 A camera is on sale for \$60. Its original cost was \$80. What is the percent of discount?

Solution The discount is \$20. So we ask:

$$\underbrace{\text{What \%}}_{a} \text{ of } \underbrace{\$80}_{b} \text{ is } \underbrace{\$20?}_{c}$$

$$a \cdot b = c$$

$$a \cdot 80 = 20$$
$$a = \frac{20}{80}$$
$$a = .25$$

The percent of discount is 25%.

Check 75% of $80 = .75 \cdot 80 = 60$

Percent problems are so common that almost all calculators have a [%] key. If you press 5 [%] you will see .05, which equals 5%. This key is not needed for percent problems like those in this chapter.

Questions

Covering the Reading

1. In 1987, how many married couples were there in the U.S.? **51.5 million**
2. In 1983, what percent of America's enlisted military personnel were college graduates? **2.4%**
3. One method of solving percent problems is to use an equation of the form _?_. $ab = c$

In 4–6, use an equation to solve.

4. 123% of 780 is what number? **959.4**
5. 40% of what number is 440? **1100**
6. What % of 4.7 is .94? **20%**
7. A camera is on sale for \$49. Its original cost was \$59. What is the percent of discount? **≈17%**
8. Refer to Example 2. How many married couples in 1987 did not have two incomes? **≈23.2 million**

228

9. About 70,000 or 12.4% of America's navy personnel are officers.
   a. Write an equation that you can use to determine how many navy personnel there are in all. **$.124x = 70{,}000$**
   b. Solve the equation. **$x = 564{,}516$**

Applying the Mathematics

10. If 2.4% of America's enlisted military personnel are college graduates, what percent are *not* college graduates? **97.6%**

11. Convert .325823224 to the nearest whole percent. **33%**

In 12 and 13, use this information. In 1985, 57.7 million people in the U.S. attended at least one game of baseball, football, basketball, or ice hockey.

12. Suppose 36% of all spectators attended a baseball game. How many people attended a baseball game? (Round to the nearest tenth of a million.) **20.8 million**

13. Suppose 18.8 million spectators attended a football game. What % of the people went to a football game? (Round your answer to the nearest whole number percent.) **33%**

14. Clearwater High School expects a 14% decrease in enrollment next year. There are 1850 students enrolled this year. How many students will the school lose? **259**

15. On a mathematics test there were 8 As, 12 Bs, 10 Cs, 2 Ds and 0 Fs. What percent of the students earned As? **25%**

16. It takes Angela 60 minutes to do her homework. What percent of her homework time is 45 minutes? **75%**

17. Mr. and Mrs. Thompson insured their house for $74,800, which is 85% of its value. What is the value of their house? **$88,000**

18. A TV originally cost $320. It is on sale for $208. What is the percent of discount? **35%**

19. A bicycle costs $256 wholesale. If Better Bikes sells it for $425, write this price compared to the wholesale cost as a percent. **≈166%**

Making Connections for Question 26: Since examples and questions in the next lesson deal with areas of circles, the formula is reviewed here.

Making Connections for Question 33: This question employs the ideas of percent increase and decrease that students will use in Chapter 9. To increase by 30%, multiply by 130% or 1.30. To decrease by 30%, multiply by 70% or .70. If you begin with x, the result is $x \cdot 1.3 \cdot .70 = .91x$, or 91% of the beginning amount.

NAME ____________

LESSON MASTER 5–4
QUESTIONS ON **SPUR** OBJECTIVES

SKILLS *Objective B* *(See pages 256–259 for objectives.)*

1. What is 60% of 25? **15**
2. 16 is what percent of 40? **40%**
3. 38 is what percent of 20? **190%**
4. 65% of what number is 195? **300**
5. What is 140% of 72? **100.8**
6. 4.5% of what number is .09? **2**
7. 4.62 is what percent of 1.76? **262.5%**
8. What is 0.5% of 40? **.2**

USES *Objective H*

9. A dealer wants to raise the price of a car by 6.5%. How much should the dealer add to the price of a $7800 car? **$507**

10. The population of Omaha, Nebraska went from 346,929 in 1970 to 313,939 in 1980. The 1980 population was what percent of the 1970 population? **90.5%**

11. The United States has about 134 million metric tons of copper deposits. This represents about 18.5% of the world deposits. How many million metric tons of copper deposits does the world have? **724.3 million metric tons**

12. Sara withdrew $50 from her savings account of $168. About what percent did she withdraw? **30%**

13. In the first 50 years of the all-star baseball games, 53 games were played between the National and American Leagues. The National League won 34 of them. What percent did the American League win? **35.8%**

 39

FOLLOW-UP

MORE PRACTICE
For more practice on SPUR Objectives, use *Lesson Master 5-4,* shown on page 229.

EXTENSION
Students can research the history of the symbol % and write a paragraph or two about it. (sample: The word *percent* comes from the Latin *per centum*, which means "for a hundred." By the fifteenth century, *per centum* was abbreviated to *per cento.* Then further abbreviating took place, resulting in the present day symbol. Some earlier forms that were used follow: per c̊, p c̊, per $\frac{o}{o}$, $\frac{o}{o}$)

EVALUATION
A quiz covering Lessons 5-1 through 5-4 is provided in the Teacher's Resource File on page 30.

Alternative Assessment
To evaluate students' understanding of the percent concept, have them use 10 × 10 grids and shade them to give pictorial representations of percents like 50%, 5%, 0.5%, 15%, and 10.5%. *Teaching Aid 24* can be used for this purpose.

ADDITIONAL ANSWERS
32.

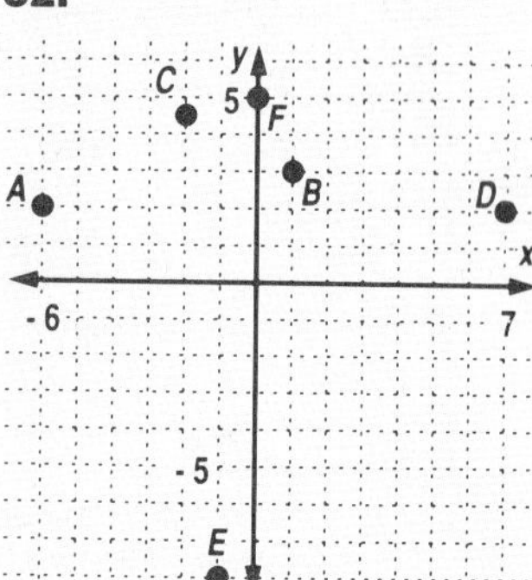

33a. .91 times the number chosen

Review

20. $1.72 = \underline{\ ?\ }\%$ *(Previous course)* **172%**

21. In 1987, the Los Angeles Lakers defeated the Boston Celtics in the NBA Championship series 4 games to 2. What percent of the series games were won by the Lakers? *(Lesson 5-3)* **$66\frac{2}{3}\%$**

22. Stanley took $1\frac{1}{4}$ hours to do his homework; Jenile took 35 minutes.
a. What is the ratio of Jenile's homework time to Stanley's? **$\frac{35}{75}$ or $\frac{7}{15}$**
b. What is the ratio of Stanley's homework time to Jenile's? *(Lesson 5-3)* **$\frac{75}{35}$ or $\frac{15}{7}$**

23. Ben charges $2.25 per hour to babysit. How much will he earn if he starts a job at 7:00 p.m. and leaves at 10:45 p.m.? Round to the nearest 50 cents. *(Lesson 4-2)* **$8.50**

In 24 and 25, simplify. *(Lesson 5-1)*

24. $\frac{5}{6} \div \frac{1}{3}$ **$\frac{5}{2}$**

25. $-\frac{4x}{y} \div \frac{2x}{3y}$ **-6**

26. What is the area of a circle with radius r? *(Previous course)* **Area = πr^2**

27. $\frac{2}{3}$ of a number is 87. Find the number. *(Lesson 4-4)* **130.5**

28. Use the pentagon at the right. Find x if
a. its perimeter is 56 cm. *(Lesson 2-2)* **x = 37**
b. its perimeter is at least 56 cm. *(Lesson 2-7)* **x ≥ 37**

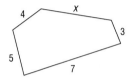

29. Solve for y: $-4x + 3y = 10x$. *(Lesson 2-6)* **$y = \frac{14x}{3}$**

In 30 and 31, solve. *(Lessons 4-4, 4-6)*

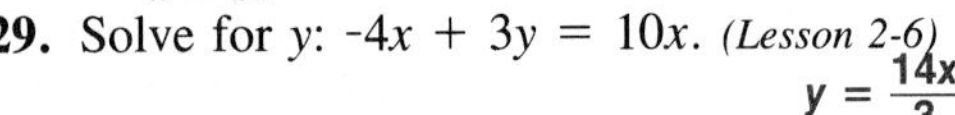

30. $\frac{2}{3}a = 6$ **9**

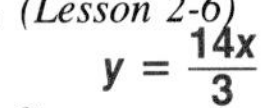

31. $5c > 2$ **$c > \frac{2}{5}$**

32. On a coordinate plane, graph the following points. Use the letters to label each point. $A = (-6, 2)$ $B = (1, 3)$ $C = (-2, 4\frac{1}{2})$ $D = (7, 2)$ $E = (-1, -8)$ $F = (0, 5)$ *(Lesson 2-4)* **See margin.**

Exploration

33. Take a number and increase it by 30%. Decrease this result by 30%. You shouldn't end up with the number you started with.
a. What number should you end up with? **See margin.**
b. Explain why this happened.
After the 1st change, the number x becomes 1.3x; after the 2nd change, it becomes .7(1.3x) = .91x.

LESSON 5-5

Probability Without Counting

In Chapter 1, we defined the probability of an event as the ratio of the number of successes to the total number of equally-likely possibilities. Since probabilities are ratios, they are often found by dividing. Division can help find probabilities even when it is not possible to find an answer by counting.

Example 1 The picture at the left represents a square dart board with dimensions as shown. Assume a person throws a dart which sticks to the board at a random place. What is the probability that it is a "bull's eye"? (The bull's eye circle is the smaller circle.)

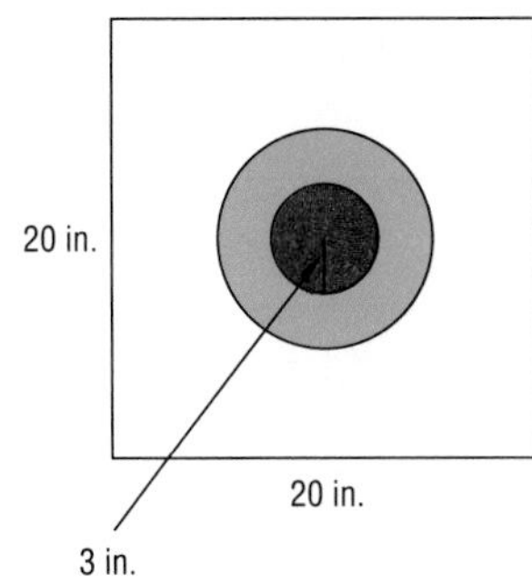

Solution Recall that the area of a circle with radius r is πr^2. Compare the area of the bull's eye circle to the area of the whole board.

$$\frac{\text{area of bull's eye circle}}{\text{area of whole board}} = \frac{(\pi \cdot 3^2)\text{ sq in.}}{(20 \cdot 20)\text{ sq in.}} = \frac{9\pi}{400} \approx 0.071 \text{ or about } 7\%$$

In Example 1, the probability is the ratio of two areas. In Example 2, the probability is the ratio of two lengths.

Example 2 A, B, C, D, and E are exits on an interstate highway. If accidents occur at random between points A and E, what is the probability that an accident occurs between B and C?

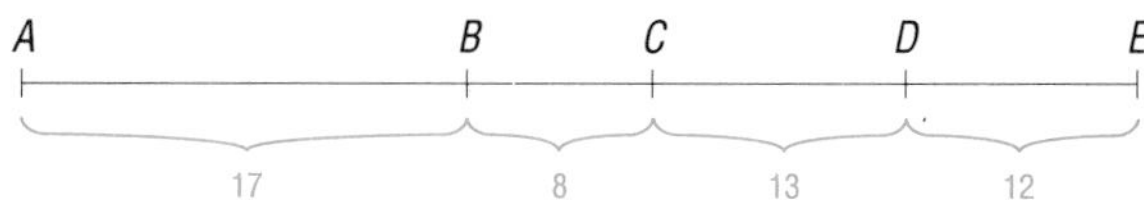

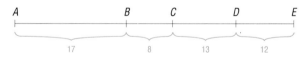

Solution Using the Putting-together Model of Addition, the length of $\overline{AE}$ is 50 miles.

$$\text{probability the accident is in } \overline{BC} = \frac{\text{length of } \overline{BC}}{\text{length of } \overline{AE}} = \frac{8 \text{ miles}}{50 \text{ miles}} = .16 \text{ or } 16\%$$

LESSON 5-5

RESOURCES

- Lesson Master 5-5
- Visual for Teaching Aid 25: Diagrams for **Examples 1, 2, and 3**
- Visual for Teaching Aid 26: Diagrams for Additional Examples

OBJECTIVE

J Find probabilities involving geometric regions.

TEACHING NOTES

You may want to run a simulation of **Example 3.** Use an ordinary bobby pin for the arrow and hold it in place with a pencil point. Students enjoy seeing this demonstrated on the overhead projector. Spin many times, counting the number of times one of the letters comes up. The relative frequency should be compared to the probability predicted by the geometric ratio.

Ask students to estimate when the relative frequency would convince them that the spinner was biased. With a spinner like the one in **Example 3,** P(B) = 1/4. Ask: If you spin the pointer 100 times, which would be reasonable for a fair spinner: 10 B's, 24 B's, 30 B's, 55 B's? (24 B's) This kind of question is formalized in statistics courses. It is proper to ask it informally now to emphasize the difference between a relative frequency and a probability.

Reading Example 4 uses the term *inscribed.* Ask students what the word means, to see if they have picked up the definition from the context. You might ask them to draw examples of other inscribed figures.

ADDITIONAL EXAMPLES

1. A round dart board has a large "bull's eye" of radius 5". The board has a radius of 7". If a dart lands randomly on any point of the board, what is the probability that it lands on the "bull's eye"?

$\frac{25\pi}{49\pi} = \frac{25}{49} \approx$ **51%**

2. The Roadrunner runs down a mile-long stretch of highway. He will stop once at random. If the Roadrunner stops on the 100-foot section patrolled by the Coyote, the Coyote will begin to chase him. What is the probability that this will happen?
≈1.9%, about 1 in 50

3. A spinner is equally likely to land at any position on a dial with four regions. See diagram. What is the probability that it lands on region B? Region C or D?
$\frac{1}{9}, \frac{29}{36}$

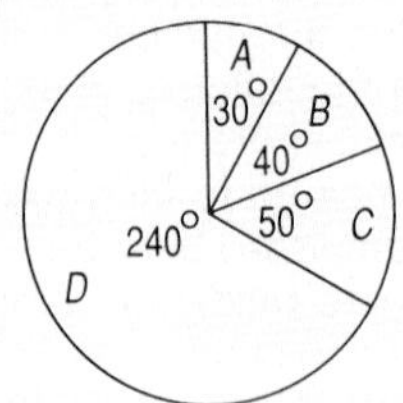

4. In this square, everything outside the triangle has been shaded. If a point is chosen at random, what is the probability that it will lie in the shaded portion? (Remember that area of a triangle = $\frac{1}{2}$ • base • height.)
$\frac{7}{9}$

9"
2.5" 4" 2.5"

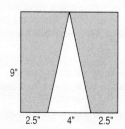

Here is an example which involves angle measure.

Example 3 At the left is a picture of a spinner like that used in many games. Suppose the spinner is equally likely to point in any direction. The spinner is spun once. What is the probability that it lands in region *A*?

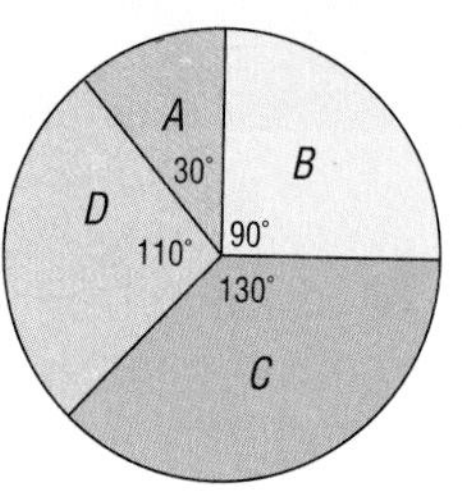

Solution The sum of the measures of all angles around the center of the circle is 360°. Probability (spinner lands in *A*) $= \frac{30°}{360°} = \frac{1}{12}$.
(Notice that in this example it is convenient to write the probability as a fraction.)

All of these examples have illustrated the following **Probability Formula for Geometric Regions.**

Probability Formula for Geometric Regions

If all points occur randomly in a region, then the probability P of an event is given by

$$P = \frac{\text{measure (area, length, etc.) of region for event}}{\text{measure of entire region}}$$

Example 4 A circle is inscribed in a square as shown here. If a point is selected at random from inside the square, what is the probability that it lies in the colored region (outside the circle)?

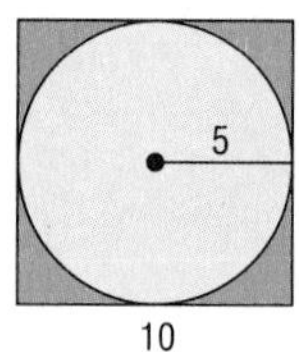

Solution Probability of a point in shaded region =

$$\frac{\text{area of shaded region}}{\text{area of square}}$$

Using subtraction,
the area of the shaded region = area of square − area of circle

$$= 10^2 - \pi 5^2$$
$$= 100 - 25\pi$$

Thus the probability is $\frac{100 - 25\pi}{100}$

$$\approx \frac{100 - 25(3.14)}{100}$$
$$\approx \frac{21.5}{100}$$
$$\approx 21.5\%$$

Questions

Covering the Reading

1. Consider the dart board at the right. A person throws a dart. What is the probability that it is a bull's eye?
a. Write your answer as a decimal. **≈.08**
b. Write your answer as a percent. **≈8%**

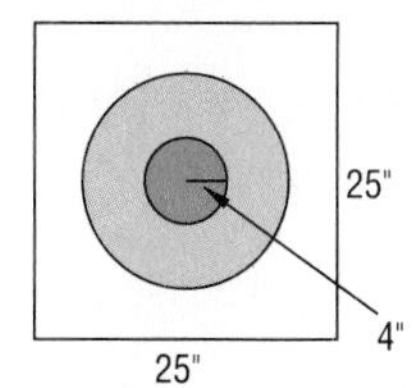

In 2 and 3, refer to Example 2. What is the probability an accident occurs

2. between exits B and E? **.66** **3.** between exits C and E? **.5**

In 4 and 5, refer to Example 3.

4. What is the probability that the spinner will land in region B? $\frac{1}{4}$

5. What is the probability that the spinner will land in region C? $\frac{13}{36}$

6. In general, how can you calculate the probability of an event involving a geometric region? **See margin.**

7. Refer to Example 4.
a. What is the area of the square? **100**
b. What is the area of the shaded region? **$100 - 25\pi \approx 21.5$**
c. What is the probability that a randomly selected point in the square lies inside the circle? **$\frac{\pi}{4} \approx 78.5\%$**
d. If p is the probability that the point lies in the colored region and q is the probability that it lies in the circle, what is $p + q$? Why? **100%; $p + q$ is the probability of the point lying somewhere in the entire region.**

Applying the Mathematics

8. An electric clock with a second hand is stopped by a power failure. What is the probability that the second hand stopped between
a. 12 and 3? $\frac{1}{4}$
b. 1 and 5? $\frac{1}{3}$
c. 11 and 1? $\frac{1}{6}$

9. Suppose the larger circle of the dart board of Example 1 has a radius of 6 in.
a. What is the probability that the dart lands inside the larger circle? **≈.28**
b. What is the probability that the dart lands inside the larger circle but outside the bull's eye? **≈.21**

NOTES ON QUESTIONS

Question 7d: Students may be puzzled that P(inside circle) + P(outside circle) = 1, leaving 0 probability that the point is on the circle itself. This is because the arc of the circle has no area. (The area of a circle is the size of the region enclosed by it.) In a similar fashion, in **Example 2,** the probability of choosing a specific single point on the segment is zero, since a point has no length.

Question 8: This question can be solved by thinking of the circle as being divided into twelfths or by realizing that for each hour the arc is 30°. The first method is more intuitive.

Question 9b: It may help students to make a drawing and shade in the region described. They may have trouble seeing that they must find the area of two circles and subtract the smaller area from the larger one in order to find the area of the "ring." One image that may help is to think of making a doughnut by cutting out a circle of dough and removing the doughnut hole.

ADDITIONAL ANSWERS

6. The measure of the region of an event divided by the measure of the entire region.

NOTES ON QUESTIONS
Small Group Work for Question 24: This activity works well with small groups of students.

FOLLOW-UP

MORE PRACTICE
For more practice on SPUR Objectives, use *Lesson Master 5-5,* shown on page 235.

23.

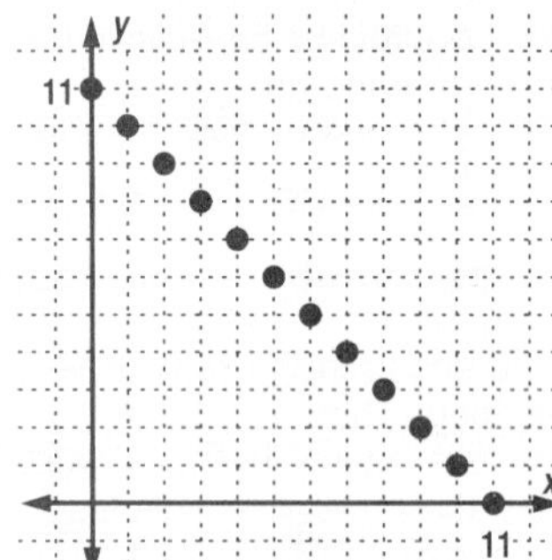

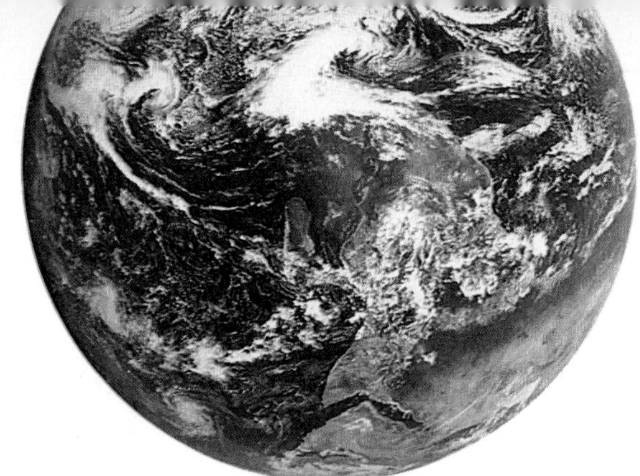

10. The land area of the earth is about 57,510,000 square miles and the water surface area is about 139,440,000 square miles. Give the probability that a meteor hitting the surface of the earth will:
a. fall on land; **≈.29** **b.** fall on water. **≈.71**

11. In a rectangular yard of dimensions q ft by p ft, there is a garden of dimensions b ft by a ft. If a newspaper is thrown randomly into the yard, what is the probability that a point on it lands in the garden? $\frac{ab}{pq}$

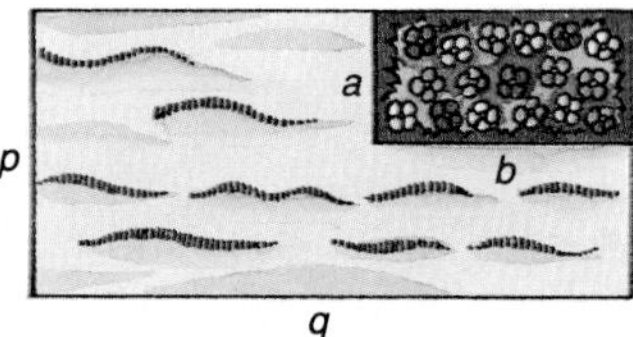

Review

12. Answer in your head. *(Lesson 5-4)*
a. What is 25% of 60? **15** **b.** 50% of what number is 13? **26**
c. 8 is what percent of 24? **$33\frac{1}{3}$%**

13. According to the census, in 1980 about 167 million people lived in urban areas in the U.S. while 59.5 million lived in rural areas. What percent of the U.S. population lives in a rural area? *(Lesson 5-4)* **≈26.3%**

14. A world record in the 100-meter dash was set by American Calvin Smith in 1983, at 9.93 seconds. The world record in the 200-meter dash, set by Italian Pietro Mennea in 1979, is 19.72 seconds.
a. Find the average number of meters per second in each record run.
b. By this measure, which runner is faster? Can you account for this? *(Lesson 5-2)* **Mennea; Mennea covered more meters per second.**
14a) 10.07 for the 100 m; 10.14 for the 200 m

In 15–17, perform the operation and simplify. *(Lessons 4-2, 5-1)*

15. $1\frac{5}{9} \div 2\frac{1}{7}$ $\frac{98}{135}$ **16.** $\frac{2x}{s} \div \frac{x}{10}$ $\frac{20}{s}$ **17.** $bd \cdot \frac{a}{b}$ **ad**

18. In the U.S. army, a *squad* is usually 10 enlisted men. A *platoon* is 4 squads. A *company* is 4 platoons. A *battalion* is 4 companies. A *brigade* is 3 battalions. A *division* is 3 brigades. A *corps* is 2 divisions. A *field army* is 2 corps. How many enlisted men are there in a field army? *(Lesson 4-2)* **23,040**

19. The volume of a box is to be more than 1700 cm^3. The base has dimensions 8 cm by 15 cm. What are the possible heights of the box? *(Lesson 4-6)* **more than $\frac{85}{6}$ (≈14.2) cm**

20. If $12(n - 7) = 48$, **a.** find the value of $n - 7$ **4** and **b.** find the value of n. *(Lesson 4-4)* **11**

21. *Skill sequence* Evaluate. *(Lesson 4-9)*

a. $10!$ **3,628,800** **b.** $\frac{12!}{10!}$ **132** **c.** $\frac{8!}{3!\,5!}$ **56**

22. *Skill sequence* Solve. *(Lessons 2-6, 2-7, 4-4, 4-6)*

a. $x + .7 = 1$ **0.3** **b.** $x - .7 = 1$ **1.7**

c. $.7x = 1$ **≈1.43** **d.** $-.7x > -1$ **$x < 1.43$**

23. Let x and y be whole numbers. Graph all solutions to $x + y = 11$. *(Lesson 3-7)* **See margin.**

Exploration

24. In 1760, the French mathematician Buffon discovered the following amazing property. Draw a set of parallel lines as close to exactly ℓ units apart as you can, where ℓ is the length of a needle. Drop the needle onto the lines and count how often it touches a line and how often it doesn't.

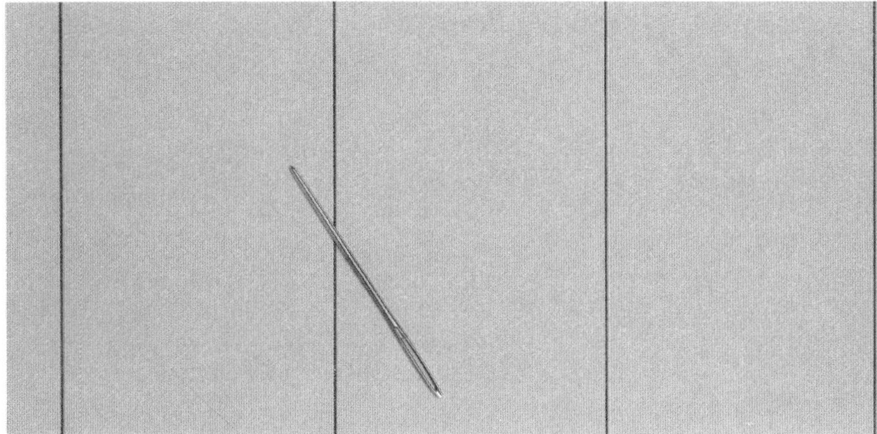

The probability the needle touches a line is $\frac{2}{\pi}$. That is,

$$\frac{\text{number of times needle touches line}}{\text{number of times needle is dropped}} = \frac{2}{\pi}.$$

Try Buffon's experiment, drawing the lines and dropping the needle at least 100 times. How close do you get to $\frac{2}{\pi}$? **Answers will vary.**

EXTENSION

Computer The program below will simulate spinning the spinner in **Example 3** twenty-five times. Students can run this program to determine relative frequencies and compare them with the probabilities. This program introduces a string variable (Z$).

```
10  PRINT "ON SPIN",
    "THE SPINNER
    LANDED ON"
20  FOR X=1 TO 25
30  LET Y =
    INT(RND(1)*360)
40  IF Y ≤ 30 THEN LET
    Z$ = "A"
50  IF Y > 30 AND
    Y ≤ 120 THEN
    LET Z$ = "B"
60  IF Y > 120 AND
    Y ≤ 250 THEN
    LET Z$ = "C"
70  IF Y > 250 THEN
    LET Z$ = "D"
80  PRINT X,Z$
90  NEXT X
100 END
```

The random number function on your computer may have different requirements.

NAME ____________

LESSON **MASTER 5–5**
QUESTIONS ON **SPUR** OBJECTIVES

■REPRESENTATIONS *Objective J (See pages 256–259 for objectives.)*

1. Two squares are drawn inside the rectangle. If a point is selected at random, what is the probability that it lies in the shaded region? **.85**

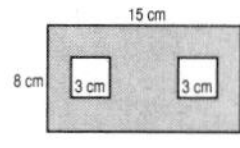

2. A 20-minute audio tape has four songs with times in minutes and seconds as follows: A, 4:30; B, 4:00; C, 5:30; D, 6:00. If the tape is started at any random position, what is the probability that it will be playing song A or C? **.5**

3. The total area of the United States is 3,623,420 square miles. This includes 79,537 square miles of water. What is the probability that a satellite which falls at a random location in the U.S. will land in water? **.022**

4. In the spinner, any position is equally likely. What is the probability that the spinner lands in region A or C? $\frac{60 + k}{360}$

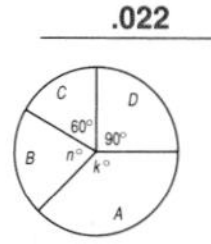

5. A dart lands randomly on the crossword puzzle board. What is the probability that it will land in an unshaded square? **.78**

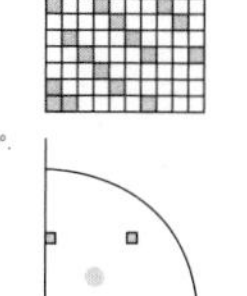

6. The baseball foul lines form an angle of 90°. Suppose that a batter hits a ball with no control over its direction. What is the probability that the ball will go outside the foul lines? $\frac{3}{4}$

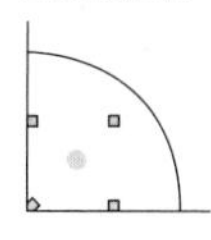

LESSON 5-6

RESOURCES
- Lesson Master 5-6
- Visual for Teaching Aid 27: Graphs from **Examples 1 and 2**
- Visual for Teaching Aid 7: Coordinate Grid

OBJECTIVES

H Solve percent and size change problems from real situations.
M Apply the Size Change Model for Multiplication on the coordinate plane.

TEACHING NOTES

You may wish to extend the opening discussion as follows: Suppose a copy machine can be adjusted to make size changes for values of k from 50% to 200%. How would you make an enlargement that is 4 times as big as the original? (enlarge by 200% twice) 3 times as big? (perhaps 150%, then 200%) $\frac{1}{8}$ of the original? (50% three times)

Alternate Approach
When considering size changes in the coordinate plane, as in **Example 1,** you may want to first show the image of (x, y) as k(x, y), then as (kx, ky). This idea is employed with vectors in the operation called *scalar multiplication.*

LESSON

5-6 Size Changes

Some photocopy machines can reduce a picture to 75% or 64% of its original size. They can also enlarge it to 120% of its original size. In these examples the numbers 75%, 64%, and 120% are called **size change factors**. Notice below that lengths and widths (not the area) of the top figure are multiplied by each size change factor.

Original figure

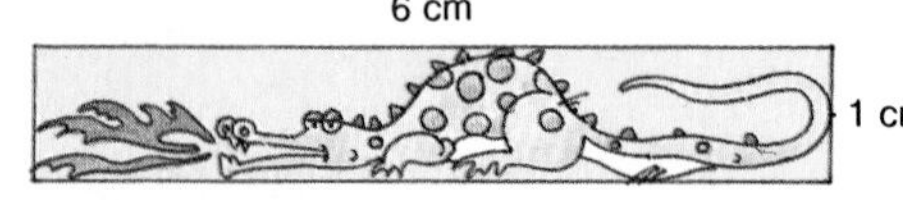

A. Size change factor of 75%:

$.75 \cdot 6 = 4.5$
$.75 \cdot 1 = .75$

B. Size change factor of 64%:

$.64 \cdot 6 = 3.84$
$.64 \cdot 1 = .64$

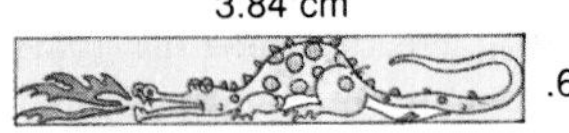

C. Size change factor of 120%:

$1.20 \cdot 6 = 7.2$
$1.20 \cdot 1 = 1.20$

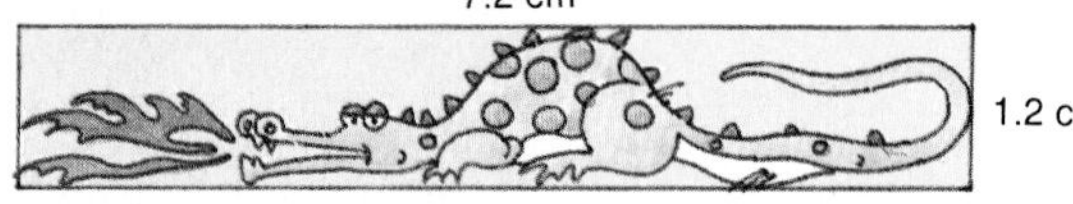

These and similar situations lead to a **Size Change Model for Multiplication.**

Size Change Model for Multiplication:

If a quantity x is multiplied by a size change factor k, $k \neq 0$, then the resulting quantity is kx.

When the size change factor k is greater than 1 or less than -1, the size change is an **expansion**. Since 120% = 1.2, the size change pictured in C above illustrates an expansion. If k is between -1 and 1, the size change is a **contraction**. Since 75% = 0.75 and 64% = 0.64, the size changes pictured in A and B above are contractions.

Expansions and contractions also occur with figures in a coordinate plane. In geometric situations, the size change factor is called the **magnitude of the size change.**

Example 1 A quadrilateral in a coordinate plane has vertices (3, 0), (0, 3), (6, 6), and (6, 3). What is its image under a size change of magnitude $\frac{1}{3}$?

Solution Multiply the coordinates of each vertex by $\frac{1}{3}$ and draw the new quadrilateral.

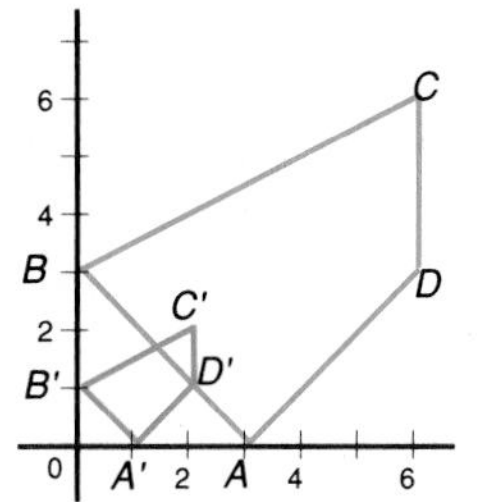

Preimage point	Image point
$A = (3, 0)$	$A' = (\frac{1}{3} \cdot 3, \frac{1}{3} \cdot 0) = (1, 0)$
$B = (0, 3)$	$B' = (\frac{1}{3} \cdot 0, \frac{1}{3} \cdot 3) = (0, 1)$
$C = (6, 6)$	$C' = (\frac{1}{3} \cdot 6, \frac{1}{3} \cdot 6) = (2, 2)$
$D = (6, 3)$	$D' = (\frac{1}{3} \cdot 6, \frac{1}{3} \cdot 3) = (2, 1)$

In this example, notice that under a size change of magnitude $\frac{1}{3}$, the image of (x, y) is $(\frac{1}{3}x, \frac{1}{3}y)$. In general, on the coordinate plane,

> Multiplying coordinates of all points of a figure by k, $k \neq 0$, performs a size change of magnitude k.

In Example 1, the magnitude k is $\frac{1}{3}$. Since $-1 < \frac{1}{3} < 1$, the size change is a contraction. The image is smaller than the preimage. Negative size change factors are possible. In Example 2, the coordinates of the points are multiplied by -2. Notice that multiplying by a negative number changes the size and rotates the figure 180° about the point (0, 0). It turns the figure upside down.

Example 2 A figure in a coordinate plane has vertices (-2, 0), (-1, -4), (-2, -2), and (-4, -2). What is its image under a size change of magnitude -2?

Solution Multiply the coordinates of each vertex by -2 and draw the new quadrilateral.

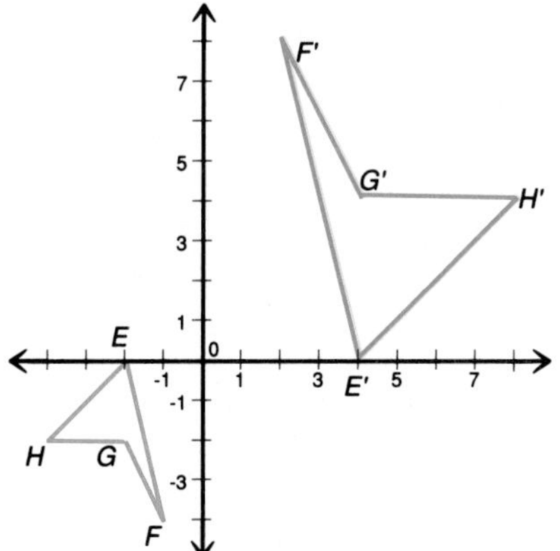

Preimage points
$E = (-2, 0)$
$F = (-1, -4)$
$G = (-2, -2)$
$H = (-4, -2)$

Image points
$E' = (4, 0)$
$F' = (2, 8)$
$G' = (4, 4)$
$H' = (8, 4)$

Explain that in **Example 2,** the preimage is rotated 180° about the origin in forming the image. This is the result of multiplying by a negative value of k. The size change can be broken down into two steps to illustrate this point. First multiply by 2, then by -1. Are the operations commutative? Students may be surprised that it works even if the preimage figure contained points with negative coordinates. (See Additional Example 2.)

ADDITIONAL EXAMPLES

1. Graph the triangle with vertices A = (0, 8), B = (8, 10) and C = (2, 4) and draw its image under a size change of magnitude $\frac{3}{4}$.
The vertices of the image are A′ = (0, 6), B′ = (6, 7.5), and C′ = (1.5, 3).

2. Graph the rectangle with vertices (2, -1), (3, -1), (3, 4), and (2, 4). Draw its image under a size change of magnitude -4.
The vertices of the image are (-8, 4), (-12, 4), (-12, -16), and (-8, -16).

3. From 1967 to 1986, the cost of consumer goods, as measured by the consumer price index, increased on the average by a factor of 331%. If an item cost $10 in 1986, about how much would it have cost in 1967?
$3.02

The size change in Example 2 is an expansion since $-2 < -1$. In an expansion the image is larger than the preimage. Because the magnitude is negative, the figure has been rotated 180°. Turn the page upside down to see that it looks like the original, only it is larger.

Examples 1 and 2 show that size changes do not change shape. Each angle and its image have the same measure. Also, the corresponding sides of the preimage and image are parallel. (However, the corresponding sides need not be parallel.) When two figures have the same shape, they are called **similar figures**. In a size change, the preimage and image are always similar figures.

Example 3 After a size change of magnitude 75%, a figure is 10 cm long. What was its original length?

Solution 75% · original length = 10 cm
Let L be the original length. Change 75% to 0.75. The equation becomes

$$0.75L = 10$$
$$\frac{0.75L}{0.75} = \frac{10}{0.75} \quad \text{Divide both sides by 0.75.}$$
$$L = 13.\overline{3}$$

The original length was $13\frac{1}{3}$ cm.

Check 75% of 13.3 is just about 10. So the solution checks.

The idea of size change can involve quantities other than lengths.

Example 4 A window washer receives time-and-a-half for overtime. If he gets $14.10 for an overtime hour, what is his normal hourly wage?

Solution Time-and-a-half means the overtime wage is $1\frac{1}{2}$ times the normal wage. Let W be the normal hourly wage.

$$1\tfrac{1}{2} \cdot W = \$14.10$$

That is, $1.5W = 14.10$

Divide both sides by 1.5. $W = \frac{14.10}{1.5}$

$$W = 9.40$$

The normal hourly wage is $9.40.

Check Half of $9.40 is $4.70, and that added to $9.40 gives $14.10.

Questions

Covering the Reading

1. In the photocopy machine example at the beginning of this lesson, the magnitude of the size change factor in A is .75. What is the magnitude of the size change factor in B? **0.64**

2. A(n) _?_ results from a size change of magnitude k where $-1 < k < 1$. **contraction**

3. A(n) _?_ results from a size change of magnitude k where $k > 1$ or $k < -1$. **expansion**

4. In a size change a preimage figure and its image are always _?_. **similar figures**

5. A picture with dimensions 10 inches by 15 inches is reduced on a photocopy machine with a factor of 64%. What are the dimensions of the reduced picture? **6.4 in. by 9.6 in.**

6. The image at the right is to be enlarged on a photocopy machine by a factor of 120%. How tall will the image be in the new diagram? **6.6 cm**

5.5 cm

7. State the size change model for multiplication. **See margin.**

8. What is the image of (3, -9) under a size change of magnitude -7? **(-21, 63)**

9. What is the image of (x, y) under a size change of magnitude 8? **(8x, 8y)**

10. **a.** Graph the quadrilateral $ABCD$ in Example 1. **a–c) See margin.**
    b. Graph its image under a size change of magnitude 2.
    c. Graph its image under a size change of magnitude -2.

11. $J'K'L'M'N'$ is the image of pentagon $JKLMN$ under a size change of magnitude $\frac{3}{2}$.
    a. Find the coordinates of J', K', L', M' and N'.
    b. Graph pentagon $J'K'L'M'N'$.

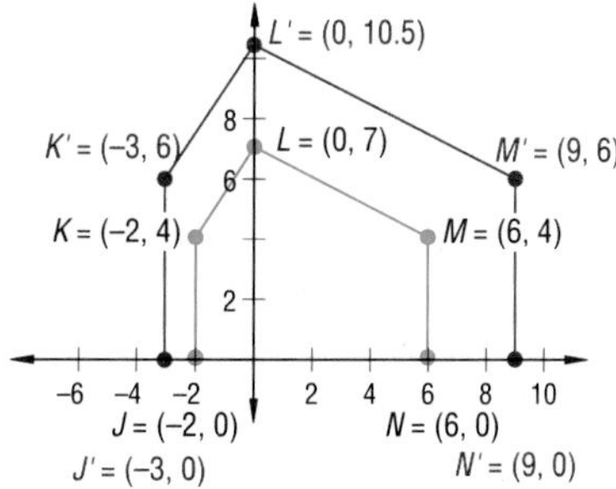

12. After a size change of 120%, a figure is 18 cm long.
    a. Write an equation using L for the original length. **1.2L = 18**
    b. What was its original length? **L = 15**

13. A worker receives time-and-a-half for overtime. If the worker gets \$11.70 for an overtime hour, what is the worker's normal hourly wage? **\$7.80/hr**

NOTES ON QUESTIONS
Question 10: This is an instance of the effect of multiplying by a negative size change factor rather than a positive one.

ADDITIONAL ANSWERS
7. If a quantity *x* is multiplied by a size change factor *k*, then the resulting quantity is *kx*, and *k* is called the magnitude of the size change.

10.

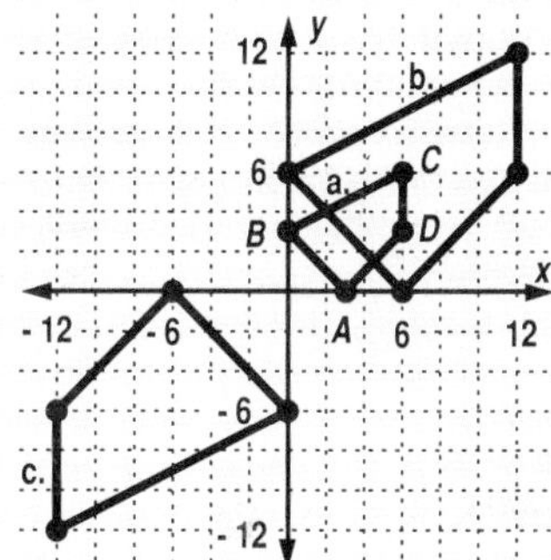

NOTES ON QUESTIONS
Question 31: Here, students could estimate 35% of 24 as 1/3 of 24.

Question 33: Students can solve this most efficiently by realizing that here $-x$ and $-y$ are both positive. However, the question can also be answered by testing a special case.

Question 36: The first paragraph of the lesson mentions that under a size change the area does not change in the same way as the length and width. Lead students toward the idea that if the size change factor is k, the area changes by a factor of k^2.

Applying the Mathematics

14. Lorenzo is one year old and weighs 21 lb. This is $3\frac{1}{2}$ times his birth weight. What did he weigh at birth? **6 lb**

15. A human hair is 0.1 mm thick. Under a microscope it appears 15 mm thick. How many times is it magnified?
150

16. Under a size change of magnitude 6, the image P' of a point P is (9, -42). What are the coordinates of P?
$(\frac{3}{2}, -7)$

17. **a.** Describe the graph of the image of the quadrilateral at the right under a size change of magnitude 1. **17a) Same as given**
b. What property of multiplication does this size change represent?
Multiplicative Identity Property of 1

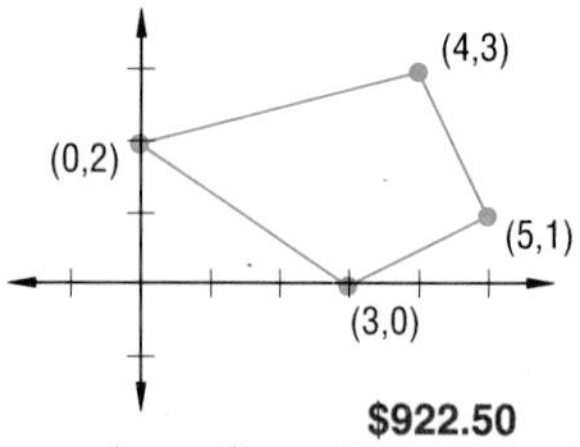

18. Refer to the poster below.
a. What would it cost for a party of five people to fly to Hawaii? **$922.50**
b. What would it cost for a party of p people? (Assume $p \geq 3$.) **$553.50 + 123(p - 2)$**

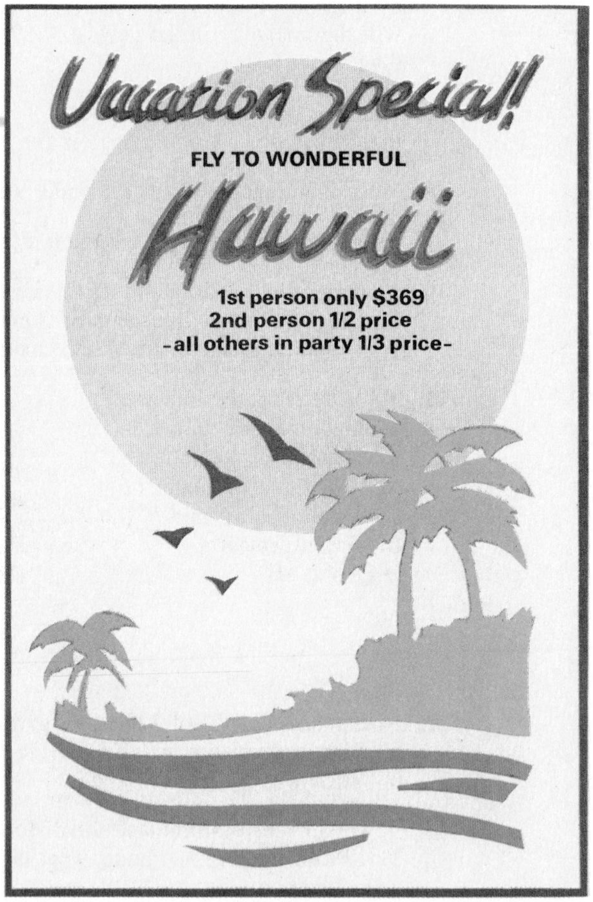

240

Review

19. A football field has measurements given at the right. If a balloon floats down to a random spot on the field, what is the probability it will land in the darker area of play? *(Lesson 5-5)* **≈14%**

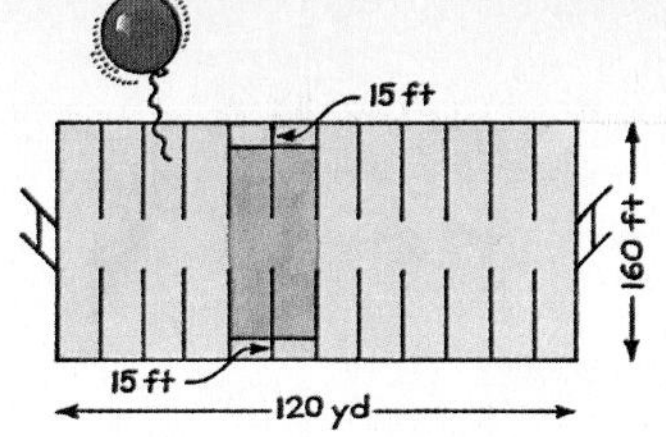

20. In 1985, 93.5 million of the 110 million workers in the U.S. commuted by car. What percent is this? *(Lesson 5-5)* **85%**

21. A scarf normally sells for \$23.95. It is on sale for 30% off.
    a. What percent of the price does the customer pay? **70%**
    b. Write an equation to find the sale price. **c = .7(23.95)**
    c. How much does the scarf cost on sale? *(Lesson 5-5)* **\$16.77**

In 22–24, solve. *(Lessons 4-4, 4-6)*

22. $-6.5x = -117$ **x = 18**

23. $-117 \geq -6.5x$ **18 ≤ x**

24. $19 = \frac{x}{4}$ (Hint: rewrite $\frac{x}{4}$ as a multiplication.) **76**

25. Solve for y: $xy = 53$. $y = \frac{53}{x}$

In 26–28, **a.** write an equation, and **b.** solve.

26. Five-eighths of what number is 80? *(Lesson 4-4)*
    a) $\frac{5}{8}x = 80$; b) x = 128

27. Five-eighths more than what number is 80? *(Lesson 2-6)*
    a) $\frac{5}{8} + x = 80$; b) $x = 79\frac{3}{8}$

28. Fifty-eight more than what number is 80? *(Lesson 2-6)*
    a) 58 + x = 80; b) x = 22

In 29–31, estimate without a calculator. *(Previous course)*

29. $\frac{1}{4}$ of 398 **≈100**

30. 987,925 ÷ 991 **≈1000**

31. 35% of 24 **≈8**

32. Find the value of $-9a(b - 2)$ when $a = 0$ and $b = -20$. *(Lesson 4-3)* **0**

33. Suppose $x < 0$ and $y < 0$.
    a. Is $-x \cdot -y$ positive or negative? **positive**
    b. Is $-x + -y$ positive or negative? *(Lessons 2-2, 4-3)* **positive**

a	e	i
o	u	h
k	l	m
n	p	w

Hawaiian alphabet

34. A manufacturer of copy machines advertises that its new machine will produce 3 times as many copies per minute as brand A's machine. Brand A's machine produces c copies per minute. In 4 minutes, how many copies will the new machine produce? *(Lesson 4-2)* **12c**

35. How many different two-letter "words" are possible using the 12 letters of the Hawaiian alphabet? *(Lesson 4-7)* **144**

36. Draw a rectangle. Now draw a new rectangle whose sides are $\frac{1}{4}$ the length of sides of the first rectangle. How many of the small rectangles can fit in the large rectangle? **16**

FOLLOW-UP

MORE PRACTICE
For more practice on SPUR Objectives, use *Lesson Master 5-6,* shown below.

EXTENSION
Have students consider this size change: The parallelogram below has vertices (2, 2), (1, 4), (-2, -2), and (-1, -4).

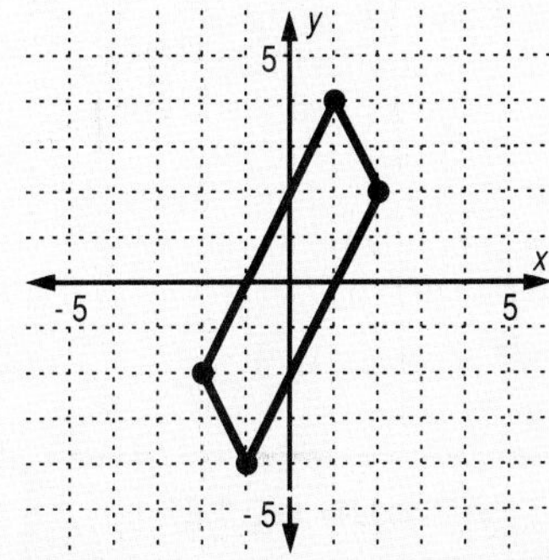

Draw the image of this figure under a size change of magnitude -1. What special relationship do the image and preimage have? (They are identical.)

NAME ____________

LESSON **MASTER 5–6**
QUESTIONS ON **SPUR** OBJECTIVES

■**USES** *Objective H (See pages 256–259 for objectives.)*

1. Helene received a Christmas bonus of 1.5 times her weekly salary. If her weekly salary was W dollars, how much was her bonus? **1.5*W* dollars**

2. After a period of growth, a crystal was 1.2 times its original length. If its new length was 6.4 mm long, what was the original length of the crystal? **about 5.3 mm**

3. A blade of grass appears to be 2" thick under a 250-power microscope. What is its actual thickness? **.008 in.**

■**REPRESENTATIONS** *Objective M*

In 4 and 5, give the image of point *P* under a size change of magnitude 3.

4. $P(2, 4)$ **(6, 12)**

5. $P(-5, -8)$ **(-15, -24)**

In 6 and 7, give the image of point *P* under a size change of magnitude $-\frac{1}{2}$.

6. $P(-4, 1)$ $\left(2, -\frac{1}{2}\right)$

7. $P(x, -y)$ $\left(-\frac{x}{2}, \frac{y}{2}\right)$

8. Graph the image of the triangle ABC under a size change of magnitude 2.

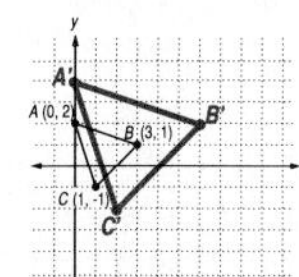

9. Graph the image of the triangle PQR under a size change of $-\frac{2}{3}$.

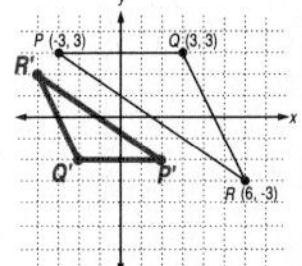

LESSON 5-7

RESOURCES
■ Lesson Master 5-7

OBJECTIVES

C Solve proportions.
E Use the language of proportions and the Means-Extremes Property.
I Solve problems involving proportions in real situations.

TEACHING NOTES

Alternate Approach
Some problems which can be solved by the Means-Extremes Property can be solved more efficiently by other methods. For instance,

Three apples cost 60¢; how much does a dozen apples cost?

This can be solved by using $\frac{60}{3} = \frac{x}{12}$, but it is easier to get the cost of a single apple and then multiply it by 12.

Another method for solving proportions deals with the idea of scale factor. For the above problem, a dozen apples is 4 times as many as 3 apples, so the cost must be 4 times as much.

Point out that there are many correct ways to set up a proportion. This is an advantage but also a difficulty. Equal rates can be used just as well as equal ratios. For each correct equation, another can be found by inverting each side. In general, we have found that students prefer setting up rates on each side to ratios. That is, in **Example 2,** they tend to prefer Solution 1 to Solution 2.

LESSON

5-7 Proportions

A **proportion** is a statement that two fractions are equal. In general, any equation of the form

$$\frac{a}{b} = \frac{c}{d}$$

is called a proportion. The numbers b and c are the **means** of the proportion. The numbers a and d are the **extremes** of the proportion. For example, $\frac{30}{x} = \frac{6}{7}$ is a proportion. Its means are 6 and x. Its extremes are 30 and 7. The equation $\frac{x}{2} + \frac{5}{4} = \frac{1}{2}$ is not a proportion because the left side of the equation is not a single fraction.

Suppose two fractions are equal. We show a specific case and the general idea.

$$\frac{9}{12} = \frac{30}{40} \qquad\qquad \frac{a}{b} = \frac{c}{d}$$

Multiply both sides by the product of the denominators. $12 \cdot 40 = 480$, and $b \cdot d = bd$.

$$480 \cdot \frac{9}{12} = 480 \cdot \frac{30}{40} \qquad\qquad bd \cdot \frac{a}{b} = bd \cdot \frac{c}{d}$$

Simplifying leads to another equation using the same numbers as in the original fraction.

$$40 \cdot 9 = 12 \cdot 30 \qquad\qquad da = bc$$

The **Means-Extremes Property** enables you to shorten your work by skipping the middle step.

Means-Extremes Property:

For all real numbers a, b, c, and d (b and d nonzero),

if $\frac{a}{b} = \frac{c}{d}$, then $ad = bc$.

Many questions can be answered by writing a proportion from two equal ratios or two equal rates.

Example 1 A motorist traveled 283.5 miles on 9 gallons of gas. With the same driving conditions, how far could the car go on a full tank of 14 gallons of gas?

Solution Let x be the number of miles traveled on 14 gallons. Since conditions are the same, $\frac{\text{mi}}{\text{gal}}$ using 9 gallons $= \frac{\text{mi}}{\text{gal}}$ using 14 gallons.

$$\frac{283.5 \text{ miles}}{9 \text{ gallons}} = \frac{x \text{ miles}}{14 \text{ gallons}}$$
$$\frac{283.5}{9} = \frac{x}{14}$$

Use the Means-Extremes property.

$$283.5 \cdot 14 = 9x$$
$$441 = x$$

The car could travel 441 miles on 14 gallons.

The above example was set up by equating *rates*. Proportions can also be set up using equal *ratios*. In Example 2 below, Solution 1 uses rates. Solution 2 uses ratios.

Example 2 In the map below, 1 inch represents 880 miles. On the map the distance between New York and Miami is $1\frac{1}{4}$ inches. How far apart are the cities?

Solution 1 Let x be the actual distance between the cities. Set up a proportion using equal rates in inches per mile.

$$\frac{1 \text{ inch}}{880 \text{ miles}} = \frac{1\frac{1}{4} \text{ inches}}{x \text{ miles}}$$
$$1 \cdot x = 880 \cdot 1\frac{1}{4}$$
$$x = 1100$$

The cities are 1100 miles apart.

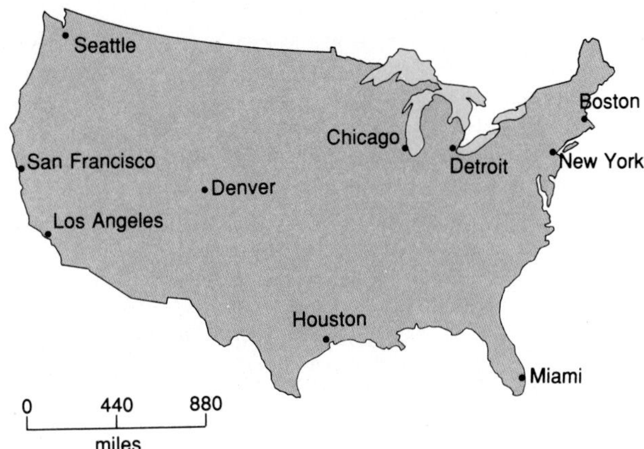

Scale: 1 inch = 880 miles

ADDITIONAL EXAMPLES

1. During the last three years, a town's population grew by 2406 people. If it continues to increase by the same amount, by how much will the population change in the next 10 years?

$\frac{2406}{3} = \frac{x}{10}$, **8020 people**

2. A drawing of a steam locomotive is made to the scale .125 inch = 1 foot. The drawing is 6.75 inches long. How long is the real locomotive?

$\frac{.125}{1} = \frac{6.75}{x}$, **54 feet**

NOTES ON QUESTIONS
Reading for Questions 2-5: Here, students are asked to recognize proportions. This requires paying careful attention to the symbolic patterns when reading. Have students discuss why the equation in **Question 3** is a proportion, and why the equation in **Question 2** and the expressions in **Questions 4 and 5** are not proportions. Stress that a proportion is the only type of problem that is solved by the Means-Extremes Property.

Question 9: Note that proportions with the same solutions have the same numbers positioned diagonally. This is true in general.

Computer for Question 20: Some students might enjoy using the computer program in this question to check their work in other problems.

Solution 2 Set up a proportion using equal ratios. One ratio compares inches, the other miles.

$$\frac{1 \text{ inch}}{1\frac{1}{4} \text{ inches}} = \frac{880 \text{ miles}}{x \text{ miles}}$$
$$1 \cdot x = 880 \cdot 1\tfrac{1}{4}$$
$$x = 1100$$

The cities are 1100 miles apart.

Often several correct proportions can be used to solve a problem. There are two other proportions which could have been used to find the distance from New York to Miami.

$$\frac{880 \text{ miles}}{1 \text{ inch}} = \frac{x \text{ miles}}{1\frac{1}{4} \text{ inches}} \text{ or } \frac{1\frac{1}{4} \text{ inches}}{1 \text{ inch}} = \frac{x \text{ miles}}{880 \text{ miles}}$$

Each gives the same final answer.

Questions

Covering the Reading

1. *True* or *false* A proportion results when two fractions are equal.
True

In 2–5, tell whether the expression or sentence is a proportion.

2. $2 + \frac{x}{3} = \frac{1}{5}$ No

3. $\frac{a}{d} = \frac{b}{x}$ Yes

4. $\frac{a}{b} \cdot \frac{c}{d}$ No

5. $\frac{2}{3} + \frac{4}{5}$ No

6. According to the Means-Extremes Property, if $\frac{x}{y} = \frac{z}{w}$, then __?__.
$xw = yz$

7. A motorist keeps records of his car's gas mileage. The last time he filled the tank, he had gone 216 miles on 13.8 gallons of gas. At this rate, how far can the car go on a full tank of 21 gallons?
≈328.7 miles

8. On the map in Example 2, the distance between Seattle and San Francisco is $\frac{3}{4}$ in.
   a. Write two proportions that can be used to find the distance between the two cities. $\frac{880 \text{ mi}}{1 \text{ in.}} = \frac{d \text{ mi}}{3/4 \text{ in.}}$, $\frac{3/4 \text{ in.}}{1 \text{ in.}} = \frac{d \text{ mi}}{880 \text{ mi}}$
   b. What is the distance?
   660 miles

9. For parts a–c, write the equation that results from using the Means-Extremes Property.
   a. $\frac{3}{5} = \frac{n}{7}$ $21 = 5n$
   b. $\frac{3}{7} = \frac{n}{5}$ $15 = 7n$
   c. $\frac{7}{5} = \frac{n}{3}$ $21 = 5n$
   d. Which of the proportions in part a, b, or c has a different solution than the others? b

10. If $\frac{3}{4x} = \frac{5}{11}$ then $3 \cdot 11 =$ __?__. $20x$

244

A picture is worth a thousand words.

In 11 and 12, **a.** write the equation that you get from using the Means-Extremes Property; **b.** solve. Write your answer as a fraction.

11. $\frac{x}{7} = \frac{3}{11}$ $11x = 21; x = \frac{21}{11}$ **12.** $\frac{5}{9} = \frac{3m}{2}$ $10 = 27m; \frac{10}{27} = m$

Applying the Mathematics

13. If a picture is worth a thousand words, what is the worth of 325 words? $\frac{13}{40}$ or .325 of a picture

14. A basketball team scores 17 points in the first 6 minutes of play. At this rate, how many points will the team score in a 32-minute game? about 91

15. About 0.75 inch of rain fell in 3 hours. At this rate, how many inches of rain will fall in 9 hours? 2.25 inches

In 16 and 17, solve using the Means-Extremes Property. Write your answer as a fraction.

16. $\frac{2}{a} = \frac{-14}{15}$ $-\frac{30}{14} = -\frac{15}{7}$ **17.** $\frac{2}{b} = 7$ $b = \frac{2}{7}$

The Means-Extremes Property can be used to determine whether fractions are equal. The fractions $\frac{a}{b}$ and $\frac{c}{d}$ will be equal only if $ad = bc$. In 18 and 19, tell whether the given fractions are equal.

18. $\frac{1}{3}, \frac{33}{100}$ not equal **19.** $\frac{4.5}{-5}, \frac{-153}{170}$ equal

20. a. If $A \neq 0$ and $B \neq 0$, solve $\frac{A}{B} = \frac{C}{x}$ for x. $x = \frac{BC}{A}$

b. Complete line 40 so the program solves $\frac{A}{B} = \frac{C}{X}$, when the values for A, B, and C are entered. B * C/A

```
10 PRINT "SOLVE PROPORTION A/B = C/X"
20 PRINT "ENTER A, B AND C"
30 INPUT A, B, C
40 LET X = ?
50 PRINT "X IS "; X
60 END
```


NAME ______

LESSON MASTER 5–7

QUESTIONS ON **SPUR** OBJECTIVES

■SKILLS *Objective C (See pages 256–259 for objectives.)*

In 1–8, solve.

1. $\frac{x}{40} = \frac{7}{8}$ $x = 35$
2. $\frac{-3}{5} = \frac{9}{y}$ $y = -15$
3. $\frac{7}{n} = 2.8$ $n = 2.5$
4. $\frac{3p}{-16} = \frac{21}{4}$ $p = -28$
5. $\frac{4k}{5} = -18$ $k = -\frac{45}{2}$
6. $\frac{1.8}{t} = \frac{4.2}{0.5}$ $t = .214$
7. $\frac{a}{\frac{1}{2}} = \frac{4}{\frac{1}{3}}$ $a = 6$
8. $\frac{-3.5}{0.4t} = \frac{-0.5}{6.6}$ $t = 115.5$

■PROPERTIES *Objective E*

9. If $\frac{p}{r} = \frac{2q}{3s}$, then by the Means-Extremes Property $3ps = 2qr$.
10. If $\frac{3x}{5} = \frac{-2y}{7}$, then $\frac{7}{-2y} = \frac{5}{3x}$.

■USES *Objective I*

11. Mr. Swenson can plow 3.5 acres in 1.5 hours. At that rate, how long would it take him to plow 10.5 acres? 4.5 hours
12. A certain recipe to serve 4 people calls for 280 grams of flour. How many grams of flour are needed if 7 people are to be served the same size portion? 490 grams
13. Anne earns $48 for each 100 envelopes she addresses. At that rate, how many envelopes will she have to address to earn $200? 417 envelopes
14. Ben used 8 gallons of gas to go 230 miles. Under the same driving conditions, how many gallons will he need to go 310 miles? 10.8 gallons
15. Jon used 2.5 gallons of paint to cover 900 square feet. How many gallons will he need to cover 1300 square feet? $3.6\overline{1}$ gallons

NOTES ON QUESTIONS
Making Connections for Question 22: This question looks ahead to the next lesson, in which proportional sides of similar figures are studied.

FOLLOW-UP

MORE PRACTICE
For more practice on SPUR Objectives, use *Lesson Master 5-7*, shown on page 245.

EVALUATION
Alternative Assessment
Use problems like those in **Questions 13-15.** Have students solve these problems at the chalkboard. Then each student should explain his or her solution to the class.

ADDITIONAL ANSWERS
22a.

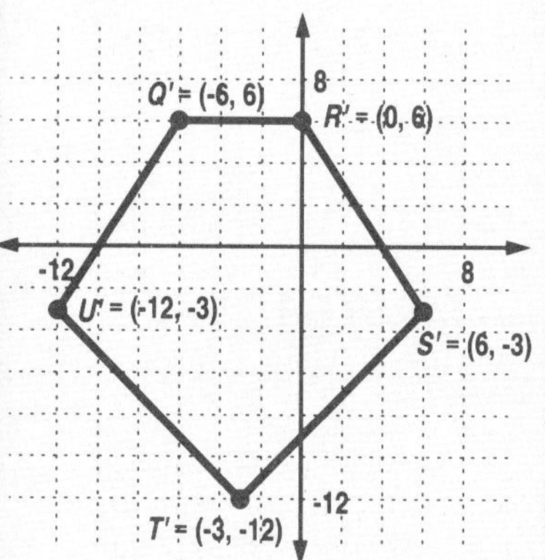

30. samples: Leaves are to an oak tree as needles are to a pine tree. Numbers are to arithmetic as variables are to algebra.

Review

21. **a.** Find the image of (-3, 6) under a size change of magnitude $-\frac{5}{3}$. (5, -10)
b. Is the size change an expansion or a contraction? *(Lesson 5-6)* expansion

22. **a.** Copy the figure at the right. Draw the image of figure *QRSTU* under a size change of magnitude 3. Call the image $Q'R'S'T'U'$. See margin.
b. What is the length of $\overline{QR}$? 2
c. What is the length of $\overline{Q'R'}$? *(Lesson 5-6)* 6

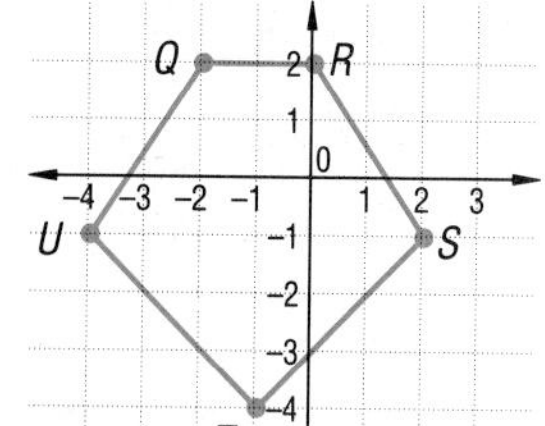

23. What is the probability of a randomly picked point being in the colored region at right? *(Lesson (5-5)* $\frac{4x - 3y}{4x}$

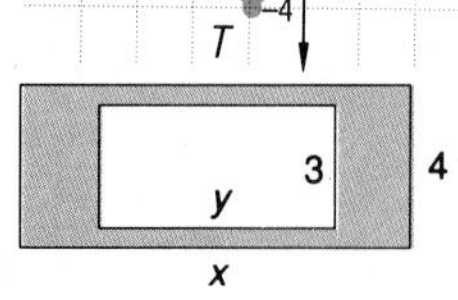

24. *Karat* is a measure of fineness used for gold and other precious materials. Pure gold is 24-karats. Gold of 18-karat fineness is 18 parts pure gold and 6 parts other metals giving 24 parts altogether.
a. A bracelet is 18-karat gold. What percent gold is this? (Hint: Write a ratio.) 75%
b. A necklace is 10-karat gold. What percent gold is this? *(Lesson 5-3)* ≈42%

25b. ≈60%

25. In the 1988 congressional election, Senator Lloyd Bentsen of Texas got 3,120,348 votes out of 5,232,113 cast. Express his part of the votes as **a.** a ratio; **b.** a percent. *(Lesson 5-3)* a. $\frac{3,120,348}{5,232,113}$

26. What value(s) can m *not* have in the expression $\frac{m - 7}{m + 5}$? *(Lesson 5-2)* -5

27. Evaluate $\frac{y_2 - y_1}{x_2 - x_1}$ when $x_1 = 4$, $y_1 = 2$, $x_2 = 3$, and $y_2 = 5$. *(Lesson 1-5)* -3

28. Solve. *(Lessons 2-6, 4-4, 4-5)*
a. $p + 8 = 23$ 15
b. $8p = 23$ $\frac{23}{8}$
c. $8 - p = 23$ -15
d. $\frac{1}{8}p = 23$ 184

Exploration

29. The statement, "driver is to car as pilot is to airplane" is called an *analogy*. This analogy corresponds to the proportion $\frac{a}{b} = \frac{c}{d}$, where a = driver, b = car, c = pilot and d = airplane. Here is a list of analogies. Solve for the missing word.
a. Soup is to bowl as water is to __?__. glass
b. Inch is to centimeter as __?__ is to kilogram. pound
c. __?__ is to earth as earth is to sun. moon
d. Cow is to __?__ as hen is to chick. calf
e. Hoop is to __?__ as net is to soccer. basketball
f. Washington is to first as Reagan is to __?__. fortieth
g. __?__ is to Maryland as Sacramento is to California. Annapolis
h. Motorist is to car as __?__ is to bicycle. sample: bicyclist

30. Make up two analogies similar to those in Question 29. See margin.

246

LESSON 5-8

Similar Figures

In Lesson 5-6, you learned that with expansions and contractions, the image and the preimage are similar. At the left $\triangle PQR$ is the image of $\triangle ABC$ under a contraction of magnitude $\frac{1}{2}$. So the triangles are similar. In this lesson you will learn more about what happens when two figures are similar.

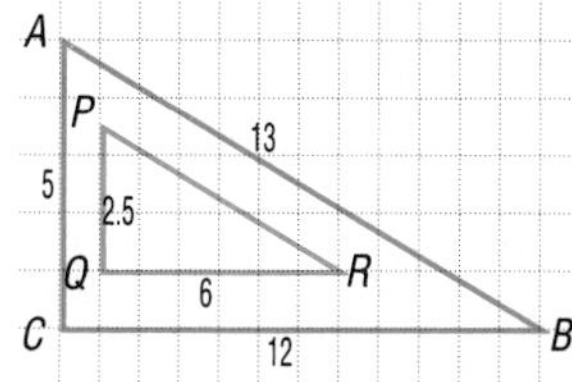

A segment and its image are corresponding sides. Notice what happens when we write ratios to compare the lengths of two of the three pairs of corresponding sides. PQ is the length of $\overline{PQ}$.

$$\frac{PQ}{AC} = \frac{2.5}{5} = \frac{1}{2} \qquad \frac{QR}{CB} = \frac{6}{12} = \frac{1}{2}$$

The ratios are equal: $\frac{PQ}{AC} = \frac{QR}{CB}$. This suggests the following generalization.

> In similar figures, ratios of lengths of corresponding sides are equal.

A ratio of corresponding sides for two similar figures is called a **ratio of similitude**. This ratio is the same as the magnitude of a size change between the figures. It can represent an expansion or a contraction. In the figure at the left, the ratio of similitude is $\frac{1}{2}$ or 2. This ratio equals the magnitude of the contraction.

Example 1 In the figure at the top left, find PR.

Solution $\overline{PR}$ and $\overline{AB}$ are corresponding sides. $\overline{PR}$ is smaller.

Since the triangles are similar,	$\frac{PR}{AB} = \frac{QR}{CB}$.
Substitute for AB, QR, and CB.	$\frac{PR}{13} = \frac{6}{12}$
Apply the Means-Extremes Property.	$12 \cdot PR = 78$
Divide both sides by 12.	$PR = 6.5$

Check $\frac{PR}{AB} = \frac{6.5}{13} = 0.5$, which is $\frac{1}{2}$.

LESSON 5-8

RESOURCES

- Lesson Master 5-8
- Visual for Teaching Aid 28: Diagrams for **Questions 6, 11, and 12**
- Visual for Teaching Aid 7: Coordinate Grid

OBJECTIVES

E Use the language of proportions and the Means-Extremes Property.

K Find missing lengths in similar figures.

TEACHING NOTES

Error Analysis Students may have difficulty thinking of a symbol like AB as a number. They may not see that $\frac{PQ}{AC} = \frac{QR}{CB}$ relates four numbers. Further, they may see $12 \cdot PR$ as $12 \cdot P \cdot R$. Therefore, this notation should be given special attention throughout the lesson. For example, point out that PQ means "the distance from point P to point Q," and therefore, PQ stands for a number.

To help students see the origin of the proportion in **Example 1,** you might redraw the figure with the two triangles side-by-side, marking the known lengths of the sides with their measures. The ratio of similitude can be either 1/2 or 2 because no order is implied. However, in size changes there is a sense of "first length" and "second length," so having only one scale factor seems natural.

Point out that Check 1 of **Example 2** is a "rough check." Advise students to always *check their answers for reasonableness*; usually a rough check is the best way to do this.

Students need a ruler and graph paper to do questions in this assignment.

ADDITIONAL EXAMPLES

1.

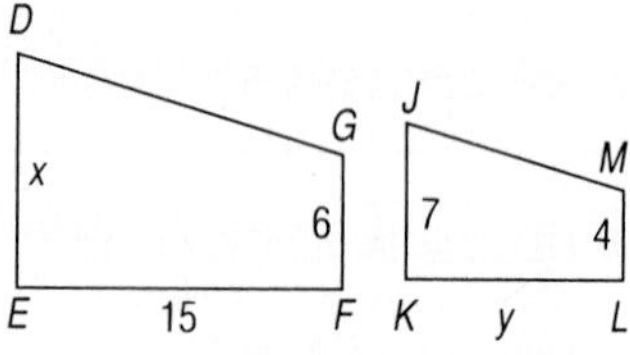

The quadrilaterals are similar. Find x and y.
10.5, 10

2.

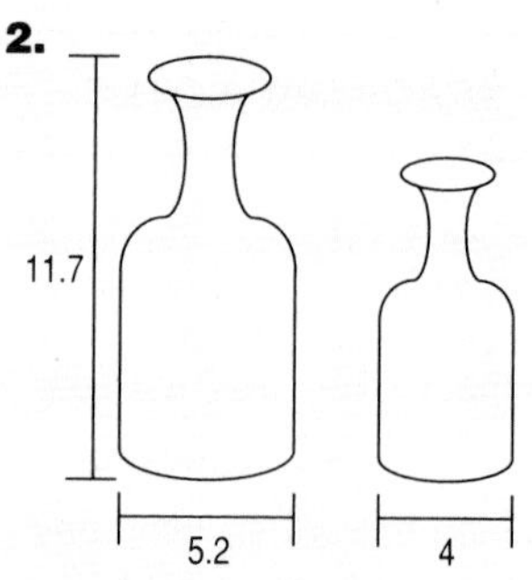

The small vase is similar to the large vase. Find the height of the small vase.
9 units

Example 2 The two quadrilaterals below are similar. The figures have been drawn with corresponding sides parallel. (This means that the lines containing the corresponding sides never intersect or that the corresponding sides lie on the same line.) Find CD.

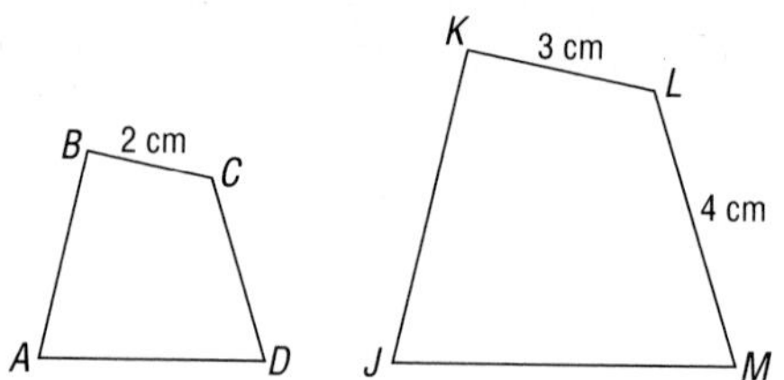

Solution You want to find the length of $\overline{CD}$, so find the side corresponding to it. That is $\overline{LM}$. Now find corresponding sides whose lengths you know. These are $\overline{BC}$ and $\overline{KL}$. Since the figures are similar, the ratios of lengths of these corresponding sides are equal.

$$\frac{CD}{LM} = \frac{BC}{KL}$$

Substitute. $$\frac{CD}{4} = \frac{2}{3}$$

Use the Means-Extremes Property. $$3 \cdot CD = 2 \cdot 4$$

$$CD = \frac{8}{3} \text{ cm}$$

Check 1 CD, at $\frac{8}{3}$ cm, is bigger than BC. This is fine, because LM is bigger than KL.

Check 2 Find the ratios of similitude first using BC and KL, then using CD and LM.

$$\frac{BC}{KL} = \frac{2}{3} \qquad \frac{CD}{LM} = \frac{\frac{8}{3}}{4} = \frac{8}{3} \div 4 = \frac{8}{3} \cdot \frac{1}{4} = \frac{8}{12} = \frac{2}{3}$$

They are equal.

248

Using similar figures, you can find the height of an inaccessible object.

Harold Hanking wanted to find the height h of the flagpole in front of Hatcher Heights High. Here is how he did it. He held a yardstick parallel to the flagpole and measured the length of its shadow. Then he measured the length of the shadow of the flagpole. He drew the following picture.

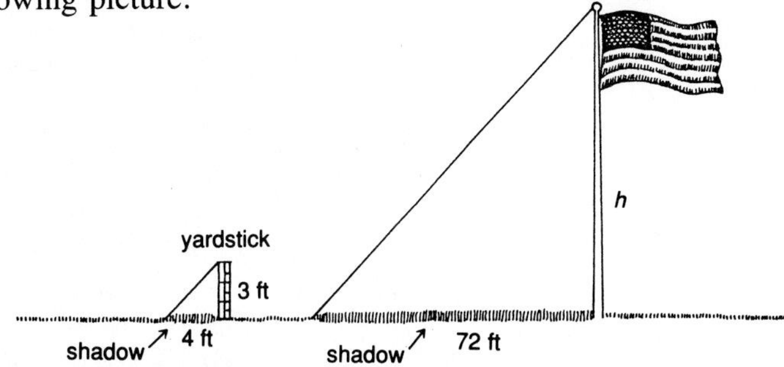

He recognized that the two triangles were similar. Then using ratios of corresponding sides he wrote:

$$\frac{3}{h} = \frac{4}{72}$$
$$4h = 72 \cdot 3$$
$$4h = 216$$
$$h = 54$$

The flagpole is 54 feet tall.

Questions

Covering the Reading

1. In similar figures, _?_ of lengths of corresponding _?_ are equal. **ratios; sides**
2. Refer to the triangles at the beginning of the lesson. *True or false* $\frac{CB}{QR} = \frac{AC}{PQ}$. **True**
3. The two triangles below are similar. Corresponding sides are parallel. Which side of $\triangle BIG$ corresponds to: **a.** $\overline{AT}$; **b.** $\overline{CT}$? **a) $\overline{BG}$; b) $\overline{IG}$**

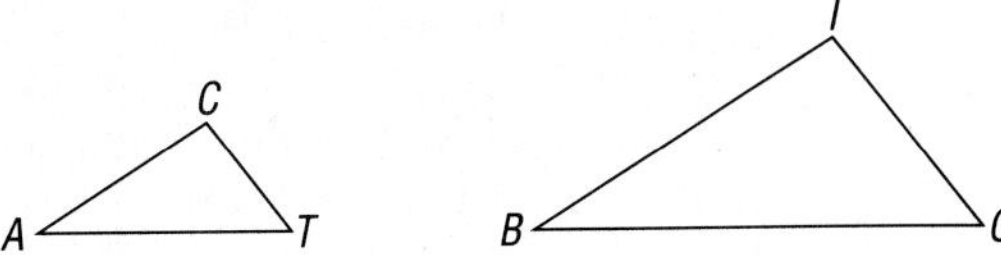

4. How can you calculate a ratio of similitude for two similar figures? **See margin.**

ADDITIONAL ANSWERS
4. Calculate the ratio of any two corresponding sides.

NOTES ON QUESTIONS
Question 9: If students have a hard time seeing where the shadows fall, demonstrate by using a flashlight to stand for the sun and books to represent the tree and Jim.

Question 10: Students should realize that the complex fraction is eliminated after the Means-Extremes Property is used.

Question 11: Students must measure the width of the house and the height to the peak of the roof to get the information they need to solve the problems.

Question 12: Students need to realize that in their drawing the segments should be parallel to (slant the same way as) the segments in the original drawing.

ADDITIONAL ANSWERS
6a.

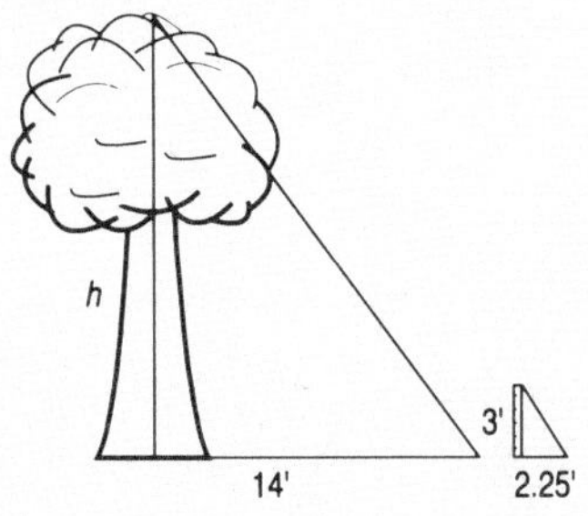

5. Refer to these similar quadrilaterals. Corresponding sides are parallel.

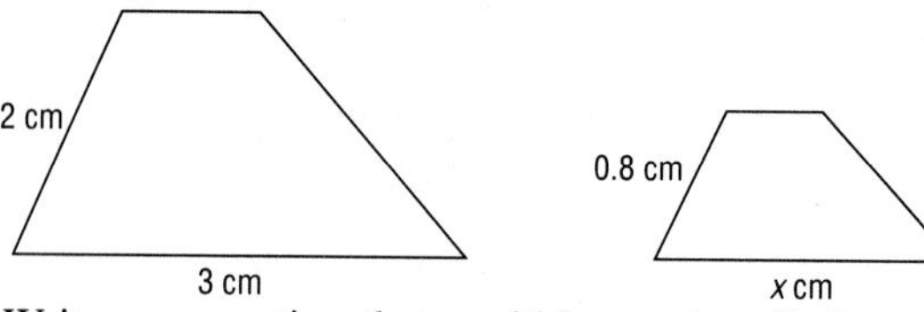

a. Write a proportion that could be used to find x. **sample:** $\frac{x}{3} = \frac{0.8}{2}$
b. Solve the proportion you wrote in part a. $x = 1.2$
c. What are two possible ratios of similitude? **.4 or 2.5**

6. A tree casts a shadow that is 14 ft long. A yardstick casts a shadow that is 2.25 ft long.

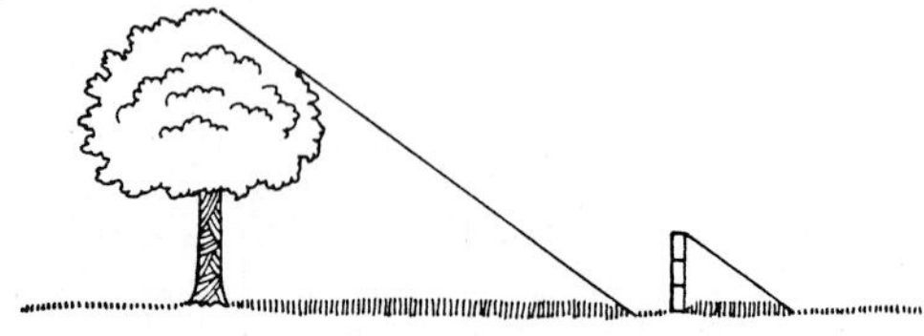

a. Copy this diagram and put in the given lengths. **See margin.**
b. Write a proportion that describes this situation. $\frac{h}{3} = \frac{14}{2.25}$
c. How tall is the tree? **≈18.67 ft**

Applying the Mathematics

7. Write four equal ratios for these similar figures. Corresponding sides are parallel. **sample:** $\frac{p}{t} = \frac{a}{s} = \frac{r}{e} = \frac{k}{w}$

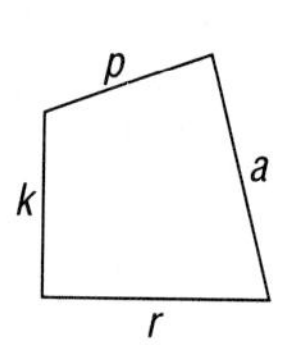

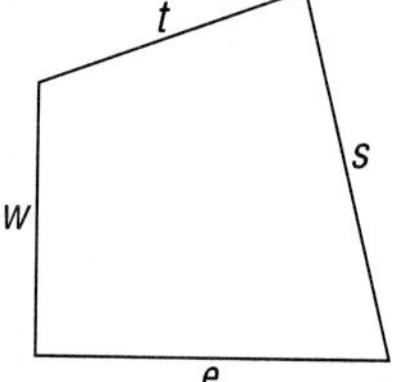

8. The quadrilaterals below are similar. Corresponding sides are shown in the same color. Write a proportion and solve for x. $\frac{2x}{20} = \frac{6}{15}$; $x = 4$

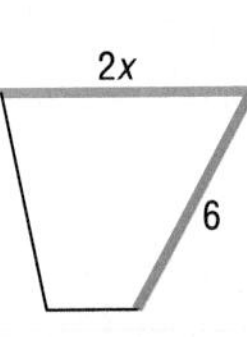

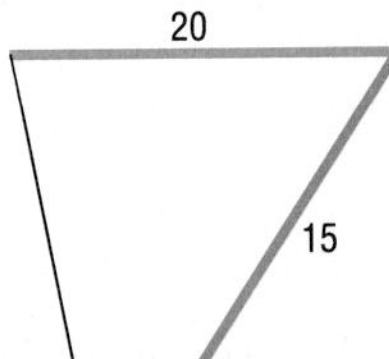

9. On a sunny day Jim, who is 6 feet tall, casts a shadow that is 10 feet long. A nearby tree, which is t feet tall, casts a shadow that is 25 feet long. **See margin.**
a. Draw a diagram of this situation. Write in the lengths.
b. Write a proportion that describes this situation. $\frac{t}{6} = \frac{25}{10}$
c. How tall is the tree? **15 ft**

250

10. Triangles ABC and DEF are similar. Corresponding sides are parallel.

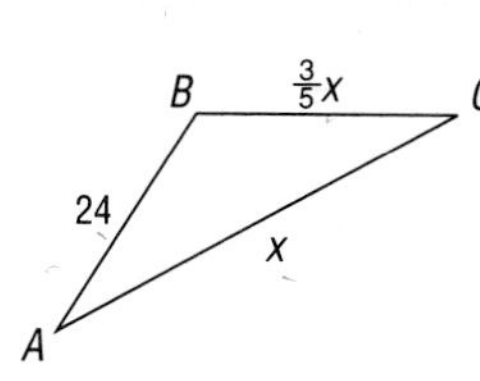

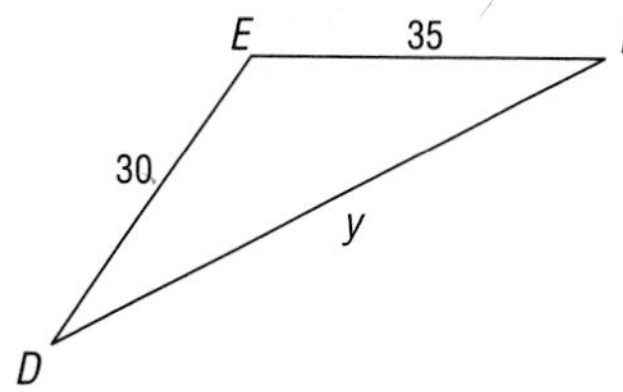

a. *Multiple choice* Which proportion should you use to find x? **III**

I. $\frac{24}{30} = \frac{x}{y}$ II. $\frac{\frac{3}{5}x}{y} = \frac{x}{35}$ III. $\frac{24}{30} = \frac{\frac{3}{5}x}{35}$

b. Solve the equation you chose for x. **$x = 46\frac{2}{3}$**

c. Use your solution to part **b** to find y. **$y = 58\frac{1}{3}$**

d. Based on your answers to parts b and c, what is the ratio of the *perimeter* of ABC to the *perimeter* of DEF? **$\frac{4}{5}$**

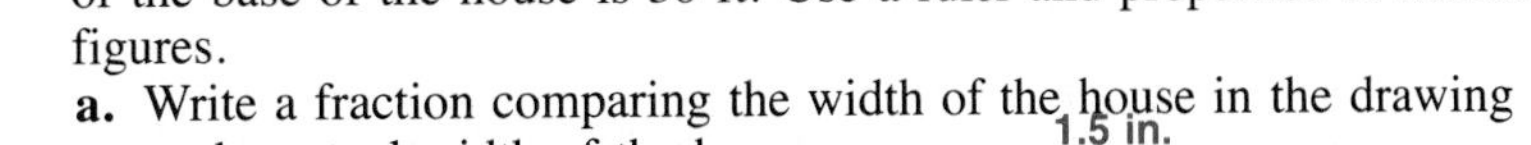

11. Use the scale drawing of a house shown at the left. The actual width of the base of the house is 30 ft. Use a ruler and properties of similar figures.

a. Write a fraction comparing the width of the house in the drawing to the actual width of the house. **$\frac{1.5 \text{ in.}}{30 \text{ ft}}$**

b. Write a proportion you could use to find the actual height to the peak of the roof. **$\frac{1.5}{30} = \frac{1}{x}$**

c. Solve your answer to part b. **20 ft**

12. Pentagon $ABCDE$ is given. $\overline{PT}$ is given and corresponds to $\overline{AE}$. Copy the second drawing and draw the complete similar pentagon $PQRST$. **$\frac{PT}{AE} = \frac{2}{4} = \frac{1}{2}$; see margin.**

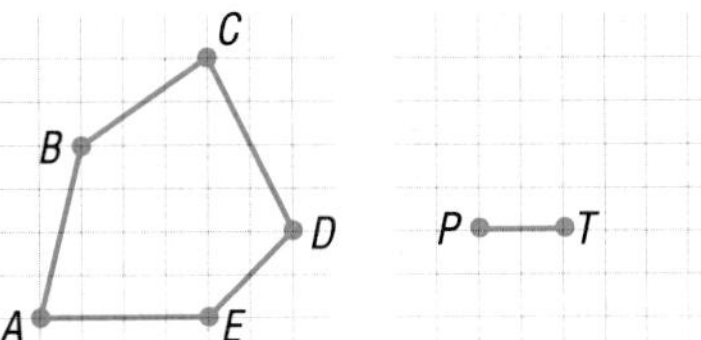

Review

In 13–16, solve. *(Lessons 2-3, 5-7)*

13. $\frac{1}{2} + A = \frac{3}{4}$ **$A = \frac{1}{4}$**

14. $\frac{3}{B} = \frac{9}{12}$ **$B = 4$**

15. $\frac{2}{3} = \frac{5}{C}$ **$C = \frac{15}{2}$**

16. $\frac{48}{2x} = \frac{9}{5}$ **$x = \frac{40}{3}$**

17. This year there are 1250 students in Harwood Junior High School. Five years ago there were only 800 students. Calculate the rate of growth of the school population during this period. *(Lesson 5-2)*

$\left(\text{Hint: rate of growth} = \frac{\text{change in population}}{\text{change in time}}\right)$ **90 students per year**

18. Refer to the sketches in Question 12. What is a ratio of similitude of the two pentagons? *(Lesson 5-6)* **$\frac{1}{2}$ or 2**

9a.

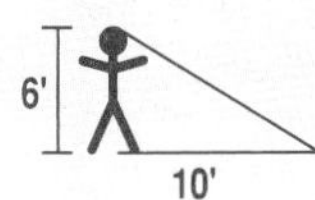

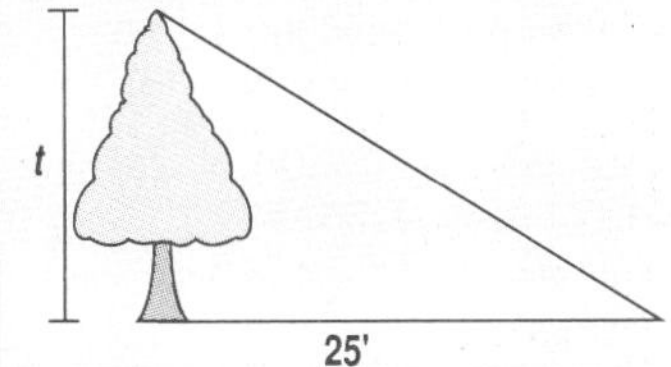

12.

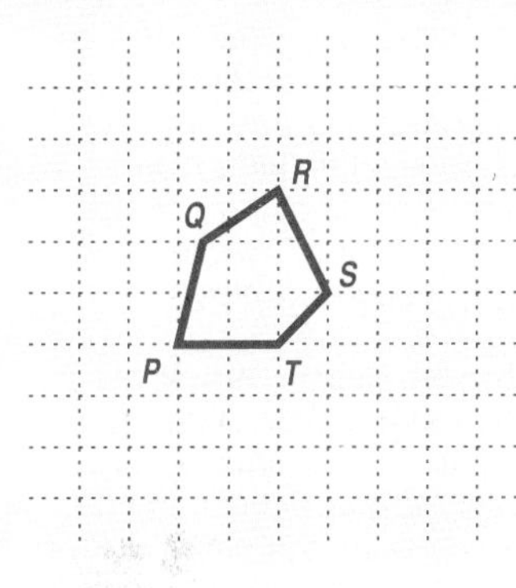

NAME

LESSON MASTER 5–8

QUESTIONS ON **SPUR** OBJECTIVES

■PROPERTIES *Objective E (See pages 256–259 for objectives.)*

In 1–3, x and y are corresponding sides of similar figures. So are a and b.

1. If $x = 4$, $y = 9$, and $a = 12$, then b = ? . **27**
2. If $x = 1.8$, $a = 0.6$, and $b = 1.1$, then y = ? . **3.3**
3. If $x = \frac{2}{3}$, $y = \frac{1}{2}$, and $b = \frac{3}{5}$, then a = ? . **$\frac{4}{5}$**
4. What property must be used to answer 1–3? **The Means-Extremes Property**

■REPRESENTATIONS *Objective K*

In 5–7, refer to the similar triangles. Corresponding sides are drawn with the same thickness.

5. Give one ratio of similitude. **$\frac{3}{4}$ or $\frac{4}{3}$**
6. Find x. **$x = 6$**
7. Find y. **$y = 10$**
8. A surveyor made the measurements in the diagram to find the length of a pond. $\overline{PQ}$ is parallel to $\overline{RS}$. Find RS. **106 yards 2 feet**

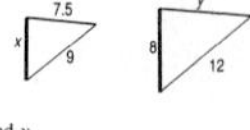

9. A building casts a shadow 51 feet long. At the same time, an 8-foot fence post casts a shadow 6 feet long. How high is the building? **68 feet**

NOTES ON QUESTIONS
Question 24: This problem should be solved mentally by thinking of paying \$7.00 each for the records, then receiving a 2¢ per record refund. The mathematical justification is the Distributive Property:

7(\$6.98) = 7(\$7.00 − 2¢) = 7(\$7.00) − 7(2¢) = \$49.00 − 14¢ = \$48.86

Question 25: The key to understanding this review question is in seeing this as a two-choice problem. You choose an entree, and you choose something else. There are 7 options (4 appetizers and 3 desserts) for your second choice.

Small Group Work for Question 30: Have students work in small groups while taking measurements. If you wish, the small groups may also solve the question.

FOLLOW-UP

MORE PRACTICE
For more practice on SPUR Objectives, use *Lesson Master 5-8,* shown on page 251.

EVALUATION
Alternative Assessment
Now that all four operations have been covered in Chapters 2–5, organize students into **small groups,** and have each group write a brief paper explaining what they have learned about the properties and uses of these operations.

19. Pixley is 38 kilometers by road from Mayberry. If a bicyclist stops at random on a trip between the two towns, what is the probability of her stopping within $\frac{1}{2}$ kilometer of the old barn? *(Lesson 5-5)* $\frac{1}{38}$

20. *Multiple choice* \$150.75, or 35%, of the yearbook committee's income comes from advertising. What equation describes the total income T of the committee? *(Lesson 5-4)* **(a)**

(a) $.35T = 150.75$ (b) $.35(150.75) = T$

(c) $.35 = 150.75T$ (d) $\frac{.35}{150.75} = T$

21. A sweater on sale costs \$17. It originally cost \$21. What is the percent of discount? *(Lesson 5-3)* **≈19%**

22. Jan walked 0.4 mile to the bus stop. She rode the bus to town and walked 0.7 mile to work. In the evening she took the same route home. If her round trip is 11.4 miles, how many miles does she ride on the bus each day? *(Lesson 2-7)* **9.2 miles**

23. Simplify: $\frac{3\pi}{y^2} \div \frac{\pi}{5}$. *(Lesson 5-1)* $\frac{15}{y^2}$

24. How much would you pay for 7 records at \$6.98 each? *(Lesson 4-5)* **\$48.86**

25. A menu includes 4 appetizers, 6 entrees, and 3 desserts. How many different meals are possible with one entree and either an appetizer or a dessert? *(Lesson (4-7)* **42**

26. Carla rode two dolphins for a distance of 100 yd. The trip took S seconds. What was their average rate of travel in ft/sec? *(Lesson 5-2)* $\frac{300}{S}\frac{\text{ft}}{\text{sec}}$

In 27–29, solve. *(Lessons 2-7, 3-3, 4-6)*

27. $3a \le 45$ $a \le 15$

28. $k + 7 > -25$ $k > -32$

29. $2b - b - 11 \le 58 + 6$ $b \le 75$

Exploration

30. Find the highest point of a tree, or a building, or some other object, using the shadow method described in this lesson. **Answers will vary.**

Summary

Division is closely related to multiplication. The definition of division states that to divide by a number is the same as multiplying by its reciprocal. This definition is directly applied to divide fractions. Because zero has no reciprocal, division by zero is impossible.

Rates and ratios are models for division. A rate compares quantities with different units; ratios compare quantities with the same units. An equation with two equal rates or ratios is called a proportion. The Means-Extremes Property can be used to find missing values in a proportion. One important use of proportions is in similar figures.

Percent, probability in geometry, and size changes are applications involving rates and ratios. It is possible to translate percent problems to equations of the form ab = c. Solving the equation then gives an answer to the problem. Since it is impossible to count the infinite number of points in a geometric region, a ratio of lengths or areas is used to compute probabilities in geometric situations. Size changes yield similar figures. If the magnitude is k, where $k > 1$ or $k < -1$, then the size change is an expansion. If $-1 < k < 1$, the size change is a contraction.

Vocabulary

Below are the most important terms and phrases for this chapter. You should be able to give a general description and a specific example of each.

Lesson 5-1
Algebraic Definition of Division

Lesson 5-2
Rate Model for Division
IF-THEN command

Lesson 5-3
ratio
Ratio Model for Division
percent of discount

Lesson 5-4
percent, %

Lesson 5-5
Probability Formula for Geometric Regions

Lesson 5-6
size change factor
Size Change Model for Multiplication
expansion, contraction
magnitude of a size change
similar figures

Lesson 5-7
proportion
means, extremes
Means-Extremes Property

Lesson 5-8
ratio of similitude

SUMMARY

The Summary gives an overview of the entire chapter and provides an opportunity for students to consider the material as a whole. Thus, the Summary can be used to help students relate the concepts presented in the chapter.

VOCABULARY

Terms, symbols, and properties are listed by lesson to provide a checklist of things a student must know. Emphasize to students that they should read the vocabulary list carefully before starting the Progress Self-Test. If students do not understand the meaning of a term, they should refer back to the indicated lesson.

Definitions or descriptions of all terms in the vocabulary list may be found in the Glossary.

We cannot overemphasize the importance of these end-of-chapter materials. It is at this point that the material "gels" for many students, allowing them to solidify skills and understanding. In general, student performance should be markedly improved after these pages.

Progress Self-Test

Take this test as you would take a test in class. You will need a calculator and graph paper. Then check your work with the solutions in the Selected Answers section in the back of the book.

In 1–4, simplify.

1. $15 \div -\frac{3}{2}$ $15 \cdot -\frac{2}{3} = -10$

2. $\frac{x}{9} \div \frac{2}{3}$ $\frac{x}{9} \cdot \frac{3}{2} = \frac{x}{6}$

3. $\frac{2b}{3} \div \frac{b}{3}$ $\frac{2b}{3} \cdot \frac{3}{b} = 2$

4. $\frac{\frac{4}{7}}{\frac{3}{m}}$ $\frac{4}{7} \cdot \frac{m}{3} = \frac{4m}{21}$

In 5 and 6, solve.

5. $\frac{y}{11} = \frac{2}{23}$ $23y = 22, y = \frac{22}{23}$

6. $\frac{10}{3y} = \frac{5}{6}$ $60 = 15y, y = 4$

7. If 14% of a number is 60, what is the number? $.14 \cdot b = 60, b \approx 428.6$

8. 4.5 is 25% of what number? $.25n = 4.5, n = 18$

9. $\frac{1}{2}$ is what percent of $\frac{4}{5}$? $\frac{1}{2} = x \cdot \frac{4}{5}; x = 62.5\%$

10. Dividing by 8 is the same as multiplying by what number? $\frac{1}{8}$

11. In $\frac{2}{3} = \frac{x}{10}$, which terms are the means? 3 and x

12. What value can v not have in the expression $\frac{10v}{v + 1}$? -1

13. *True or false* Using the Means-Extremes Property is an appropriate first step in solving the equation. False

$$d + \frac{4}{5} = \frac{2}{3}.$$

14. Horatio spent 36 minutes on his English homework. Mary Ellen spent a half hour on her English homework.

a. Horatio's time is what percent of Mary Ellen's time? $\frac{36}{30} = 1.2 = 120\%$

b. Horatio studied __?__ percent longer than Mary Ellen. 20%

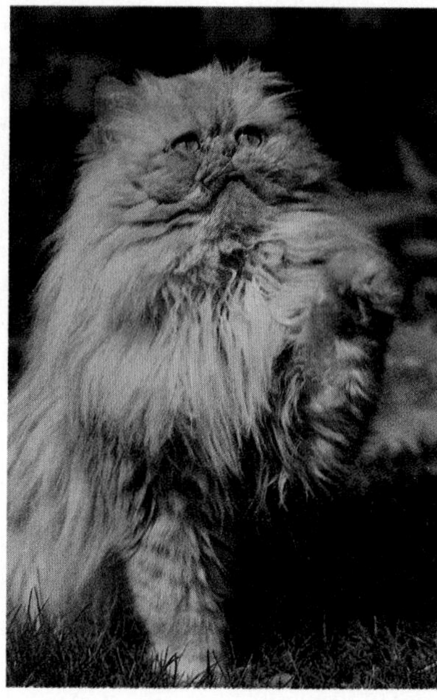

15. A cat has a life expectancy of c years. A dog has a life expectancy of d years. If $c < d$, then the life expectancy for a dog is how many times that of a cat? $n \cdot c = d, n = \frac{d}{c}$

16. Which is faster, reading p pages in $7y$ minutes or p pages in $8y$ minutes? p pages in $7y$ min

17. The profit on an item with a selling price of \$40 is \$16. What percent of the selling price is profit? $40p = 16, p = .4 = 40\%$

18. If the electricity goes out and a clock stops, what is the probability that the second hand stops between 2 and 3? $\frac{1}{12}$

19. Suppose your class covers three chapters of Algebra in 35 school days. At this rate, how many school days will it take to cover 13 chapters? 152 days

20. A car travels 250 miles on 12 gallons of gas. At this rate, about how far (to the nearest mile) can the car travel on 14 gallons of gasoline? **292 miles**

21. Here is a computer program. For what input value will the computer print 2? **B = 5**

```
10 INPUT B
11 IF B=0, PRINT "IMPOSSIBLE"
12 IF B <> 0, PRINT 10/B
13 END
```

22. a. Graph the triangle with vertices (2, 3), (-1, -3), and (3, 1). **See margin.**

b. Graph its image under a size change of -2.

23. The two triangles below are similar. Corresponding sides are parallel. Find z. **$5\frac{1}{3}$**

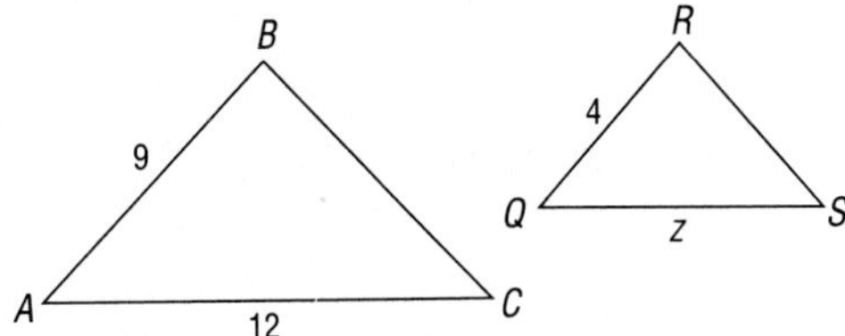

24. The pentagons below are similar. Corresponding sides are parallel. Find x. **$1\frac{3}{4}$**

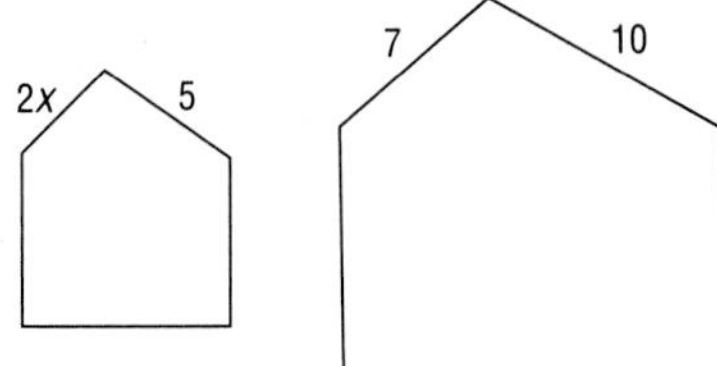

25. When Sasha stands in the back center of a tennis court she can cover (return the ball from) a rectangle 20 feet by 25 feet. Each side of the court is 27 feet by 39 feet. Find P(Sasha returns the ball), assuming her opponent's shot randomly bounces anywhere inside Sasha's side of the court. **$\frac{500}{1053} \approx .47$**

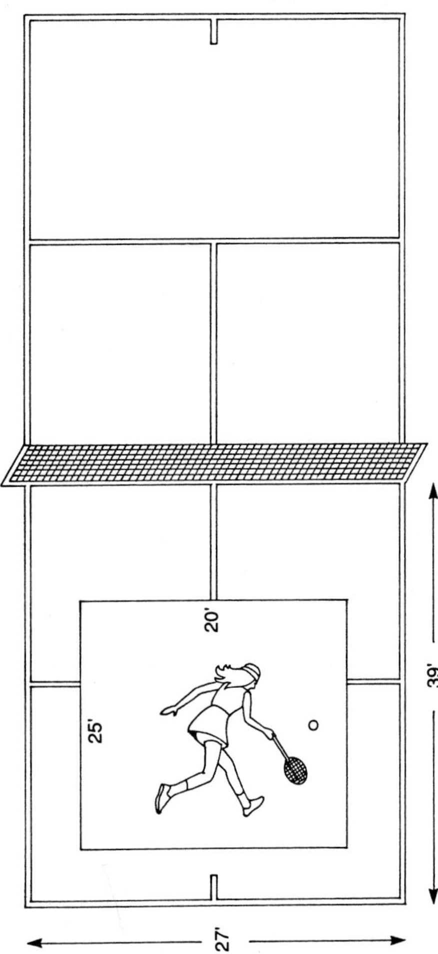

USING THE PROGRESS SELF-TEST

Assign the Progress Self-Test as a one-night assignment. Worked-out *solutions* for all questions are in the Selected Answers section at the back of the student book. Encourage students to take the Progress Self-Test honestly, grade themselves, and then be prepared to discuss the test in class.

Advise students to pay special attention to those Chapter Review questions (pages 256–259) which correspond to questions missed on the Progress Self-Test. A chart provided in the Selected Answers section in the student text keys the Progress Self-Test questions to the lettered SPUR Objectives in the Chapter Review or to the Vocabulary. It also keys the questions to the corresponding lessons where the material is covered.

ADDITIONAL ANSWERS

22a.

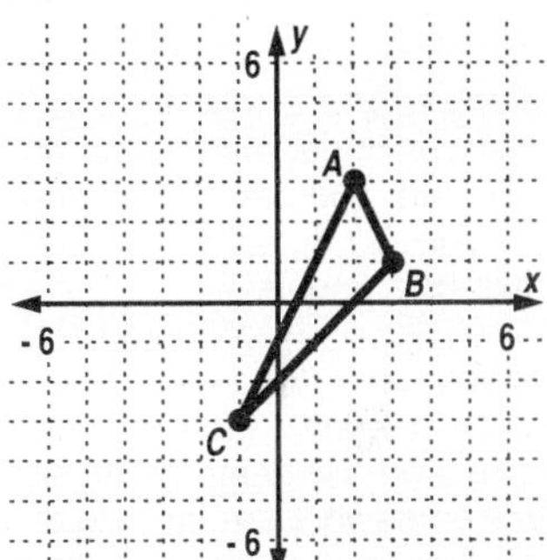

22b.

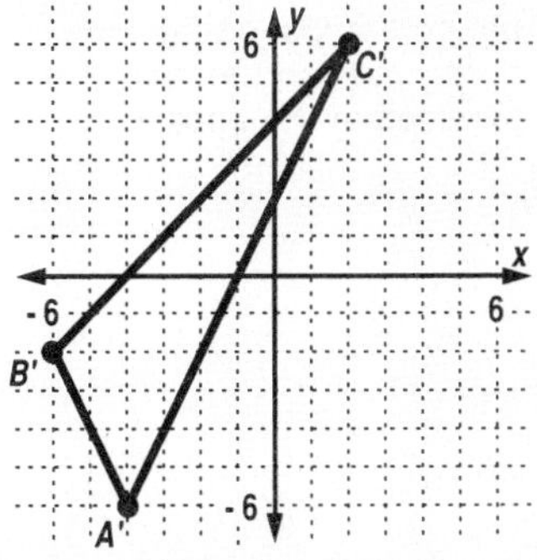

RESOURCES
- Chapter 5 Test, Form A
- Chapter 5 Test, Form B
- Chapter 5 Test, Cumulative Form

CHAPTER REVIEW

The main objectives for the chapter are organized here into sections corresponding to the four main types of understanding this book promotes: Skills, Properties, Uses, and Representations.

USING THE CHAPTER REVIEW
Whereas end-of-chapter material may be considered optional in some texts, in *Algebra* we have selected these objectives and questions with the expectation that they will be covered. Students should be able to answer these questions with about 85% accuracy after studying the chapter.

You may assign these questions over a single night to help students prepare for a test the next day, or you may assign the questions over a two-day period.

If you work the questions over two days, then we recommend assigning the *evens* for homework the first night so that students get feedback in class the next day, then assigning the *odds* the night before the test so the students can use the answers provided in the book.

Chapter Review

Questions on SPUR Objectives

SPUR stands for **S**kills, **P**roperties, **U**ses, and **R**epresentations. The Chapter Review questions are grouped according to the SPUR Objectives for this chapter.

SKILLS deal with the procedures used to get answers.

Objective A. *Divide real numbers and simplify division expressions.* (Lesson 5-1)

In 1–10, simplify.

1. $25 \div \frac{1}{5}$ **125**

2. $\dfrac{60}{\frac{1}{4}}$ **240**

3. $\frac{3}{4} \div \frac{7}{8}$ **$\frac{6}{7}$**

4. $\dfrac{a}{14} \div \dfrac{7}{2}$ **$\frac{a}{49}$**

5. $\dfrac{2\pi}{9} \div \dfrac{\pi}{6}$ **$\frac{4}{3}$**

6. $\dfrac{\frac{3}{2}}{-\frac{15}{16}}$ **$-\frac{8}{5}$**

7. $\dfrac{\frac{a}{b}}{\frac{c}{d}}$ **$\frac{ad}{cb}$**

8. $\dfrac{x}{-\frac{1}{4}}$ **-4x**

9. $\frac{4}{5} \div \frac{2}{5}$ **2**

10. $\dfrac{x}{z} \div \dfrac{x}{y}$ **$\frac{y}{z}$**

Objective B. *Solve percent problems using equations or in your head.* (Lesson 5-4)

11. What is 75% of 32? **24**

12. 10 is what percent of 5? **200%**

13. What is 20% of 18? **3.6**

14. 85% of what number is 170? **200**

15. 12 is what percent of 36? **33.33%**

16. 105% of 64 is what number? **67.2**

17. 30% of a number is $\frac{3}{4}$. What is the number? **$\frac{5}{2}$**

18. 1.2 is what percent of 0.8? **150%**

Objective C. *Solve proportions.* (Lesson 5-7)

In 19-24, solve.

19. $\dfrac{x}{130} = \dfrac{6}{5}$ **156**

20. $\dfrac{6}{25} = \dfrac{-10}{m}$ **$-\frac{125}{3}$**

21. $\dfrac{2w}{-5} = 3$ **$-\frac{15}{2}$**

22. $\dfrac{4}{x} = 7.5$ **$\frac{8}{15}$**

23. $\dfrac{-1.1}{y} = \dfrac{2.3}{0.4}$ **≈ -0.19**

24. $\dfrac{4}{12} = \dfrac{3b}{10}$ **$\frac{10}{9}$**

PROPERTIES deal with the principles behind the mathematics.

Objective D. *Identify restrictions on a variable in a division situation.* (Lesson 5-2)

In 25–28, what value(s) can the variable not have?

25. $\dfrac{3}{2y}$ **0**

26. $\dfrac{x+1}{x+4}$ **-4**

27. $\dfrac{15x}{x-.2}$ **.2**

28. $\dfrac{y}{y+\frac{1}{2}}$ **$-\frac{1}{2}$**

Objective E. *Use the language of proportions and the Means-Extremes Property.* (Lessons 5-7, 5-8)

29. In $\frac{5}{8} = \frac{15}{24}$, **a) 8 and 15; b) 5 and 24**
   a. Which numbers are the means?
   b. Which numbers are the extremes?

30. If $\dfrac{m}{n} = \dfrac{p}{q}$, then by the Means-Extremes Property __?__ = __?__. **mq = np**

31. If $\dfrac{2}{3} = \dfrac{x}{5}$, then $\dfrac{5}{x} =$ __?__. **$\frac{3}{2}$**

32. If $\dfrac{a}{b} = \dfrac{c}{d}$, then $\dfrac{b}{a} =$ __?__. **$\frac{d}{c}$**

Objective F. *Use the rate model for division.* (Lesson 5-2)

In 33–35, ask a question and calculate a rate to answer the question. **See margin.**

33. The Johnsons drove 30 miles in $\frac{3}{4}$ hours.

34. In d days Tony lost \$400.

35. Four weeks ago the puppy weighed 3 kilograms less.

In 36 and 37, assume a 22-mile bike trip took 2 hours. **36) 11 mph; 37) $\frac{1}{11}$ hours per mile**

36. What was the rate in miles per hour?

37. What was the rate in hours per mile?

38. A train travels from Newark to Trenton, a distance of 48.1 miles, in 30 minutes. At what average speed, in miles per hour, does the train travel? **96.2 mi per hr. 39) $\frac{1}{4}$ hr (15 min)**

39. Marlene worked $3\frac{1}{2}$ hours and earned \$14. How long did it take her to earn a dollar?

40. In one store a 46-ounce can of tomato juice costs \$1.03, and a 6-ounce can costs 23 cents. **46 oz: ≈ 2¢ per oz; 6 oz: ≈ 4¢ per oz**

a. Calculate the unit cost of each can.

b. Based on the unit cost, which is the better buy? **46-oz can; 41) 6*w* words in 2*m* min**

41. Which is faster, reading w words in m minutes or $6w$ words in $2m$ minutes?

42. *Multiple choice* Suppose s sweaters cost d dollars. At this rate how many sweaters can be bought for \$75? **(b)**

(a) $\frac{s}{75d}$ (b) $\frac{75s}{d}$

(c) $\frac{75d}{s}$ (d) $\frac{d}{75s}$

Objective G. *Use a ratio to compare two quantities.* (Lesson 5-3)

43. In the first period algebra class, there are 10 girls in a class of 27 students. Write the ratio of boys to girls. $\frac{17}{10}$

44. An item selling for \$36 is reduced by \$6. What is the percent of the discount? **≈17%**

45. The profit on an item selling for \$20 is \$8. What percent of the item's selling price is profit? **40%**

46. David paid k dollars for a tennis racket. Joe paid j dollars for the same racket on sale. How many times as much did David pay as Joe paid? $\frac{k}{j}$

47. Sue charges \$1.50 an hour to babysit. Lou charges \$2.00 an hour.

a. Lou charges what percent of Sue's price? **$133\frac{1}{3}$%**

b. Lou charges __?__ percent more than Sue. **$33\frac{1}{3}$%**

c. Sue charges __?__ less than Lou. **25%**

Objective H. *Solve percent and size change problems from real situations.* (Lessons 5-4, 5-6)

48. A sofa is on sale for \$450. It originally cost \$562.52. What percent of the original price is the sale price? **80%**

49. In 1983, 49% of all accidental deaths occurred in motor vehicle accidents. If 91,000 people died accidentally, how many were killed in motor accidents? **44,590**

50. In 1987, Kevin McHale from Boston had the highest field goal shooting percentage in professional basketball, 60.4%. If he attempted 1307 shots, how many did he make? **789**

51. A \$15.99 tape is on sale for \$11.99. To the nearest percent, what is the percent of discount? **25%**

52. A sales clerk at Clark's Department Store receives time-and-a-half for overtime. If normal time is \$9.00/hr, what is the overtime pay? **\$13.50/hr**

ADDITIONAL ANSWERS

33. Sample: What was their average speed? 40 miles per hour

34. Sample: How much did Tony lose per day? $\frac{-400}{d}$ dollars per day

35. Sample: How much weight did the puppy gain per week? $\frac{3}{4}$ kg per week

68.
EVALUATE AN EXPRESSION
ENTER VALUE OF A
?6

69.
```
10 PRINT "EVALUATE (K+1)/(K-2)"
20 PRINT "ENTER VALUE OF K"
30 INPUT K
40 IF K=2 THEN PRINT "IMPOSSIBLE"
50 IF K<>2 THEN PRINT (K+1)/(K-2)
60 END
```

53. Model trains of HO-gauge are $\frac{1}{87}$ actual size (no fooling!). If a model locomotive is 30 cm long, how long is the real locomotive it models? **2610 cm**

Objective I. *Solve problems involving proportions in real situations. (Lesson 5-7)*

54. Anne was saving for a class trip. For every \$35 that Anne earned her mother added an extra \$15. If Anne earned \$245, how much would her mother add? **\$105**

55. A $\frac{3}{4}$ cup of sugar is equivalent to 12 tablespoons of sugar. How many tablespoons are there in 3 cups of sugar? **48**

56. A family decided to keep track of the number of phone calls made. In the first seven days of November, 45 calls were made. At this rate, about how many calls will be made for the month? **193**

57. For every dollar, you could get 2.03 deutsche marks (the currency in West Germany) in 1986. If a crystal vase cost 120 deutsche marks in 1986, what would the cost be in dollars? **≈\$59.11**

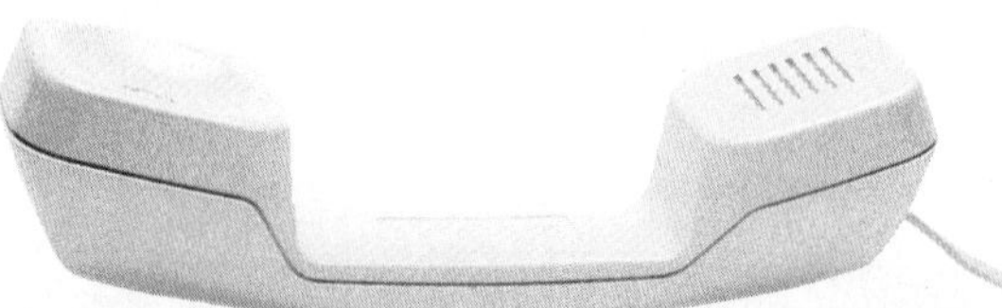

REPRESENTATIONS deal with pictures, graphs, or objects that illustrate concepts.

Objective J. *Find probabilities involving geometric regions. (Lesson 5-5)*

58. A 3-cm square inside a 4-cm square is drawn at the right. If a point is selected at random from the figure, what is the probability it lies in the shaded region? $\frac{7}{16}$

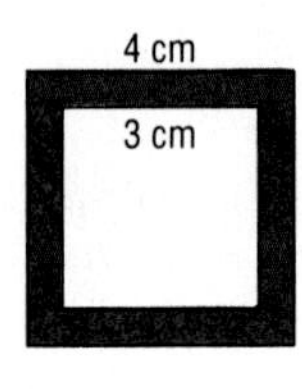

59. At the right is a picture of a spinner. Suppose any position of the spinner is equally likely. What is the probability that the spinner lands in region A or B? $\frac{150}{360} = \frac{5}{12}$

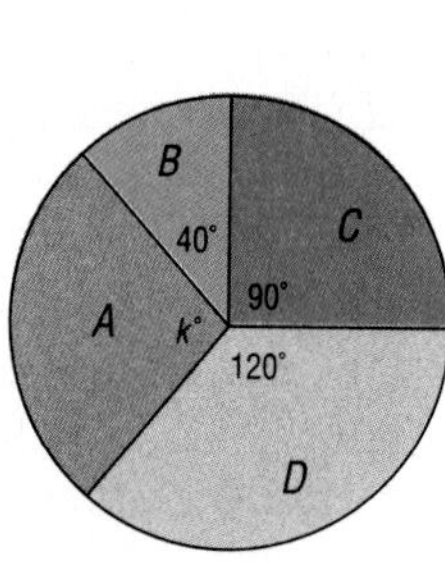

60. In a storm, the electricity went out. A clock stopped. What is the probability that its second hand stopped between the 5 and the 7? $\frac{1}{6}$

61. If accidents occur randomly on the roads from town A to town B as shown below, what is the probability that an accident on these roads occurs on the 8 km stretch of road shown in color? $\frac{1}{2}$

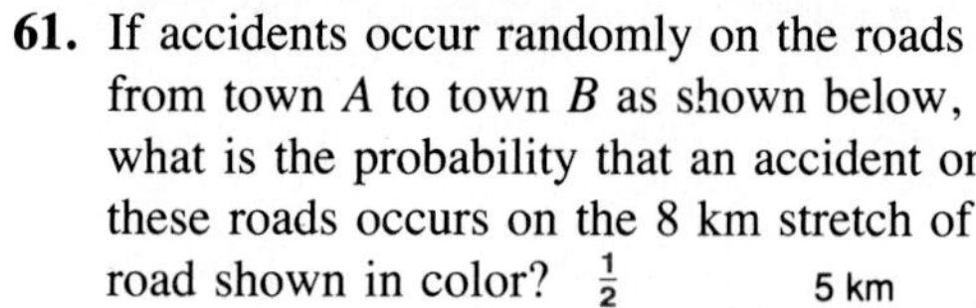

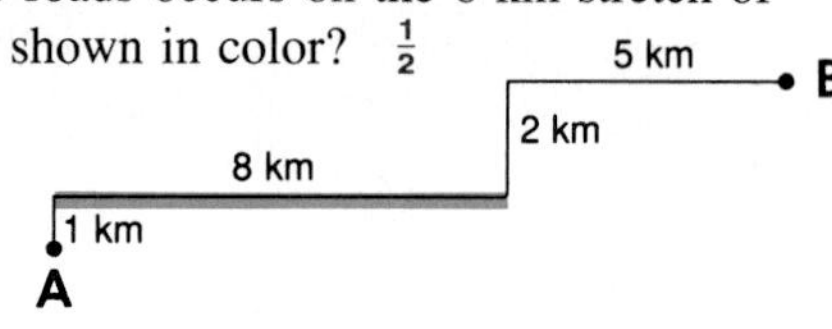

Objective K. *Find missing lengths in similar figures. (Lesson 5-8)*

In 62 and 63, refer to the similar figures below. Corresponding sides are parallel.

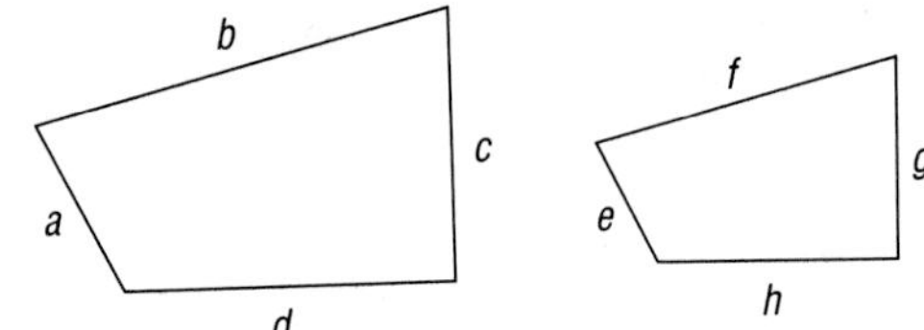

62. *Multiple choice* Which proportion is *incorrect*? **c**

(a) $\frac{d}{h} = \frac{c}{g}$ (b) $\frac{e}{a} = \frac{f}{b}$

(c) $\frac{g}{c} = \frac{a}{e}$ (d) $\frac{h}{d} = \frac{f}{b}$

258

63. If $a = 12$, $b = 15$, and $e = 10$, what is f? **12.5**

64. Refer to the similar triangles below. Corresponding sides are shown in the same color.

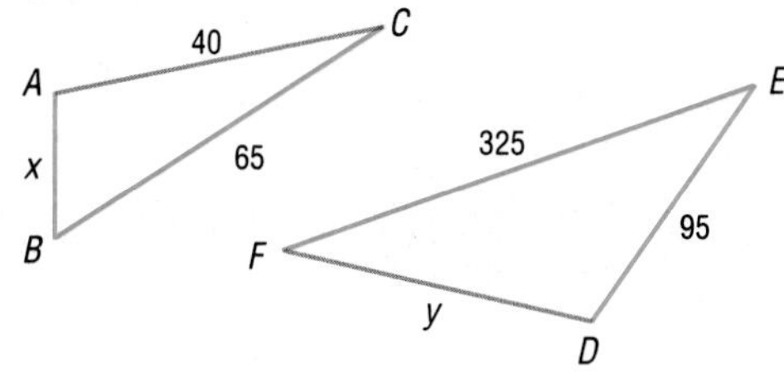

a. What is the ratio of similitude? **1/5**
b. Find the length of $\overline{AB}$. **19**
c. Find the length of $\overline{DF}$. **200**

65. The quadrilaterals below are similar. Corresponding sides are parallel.
a. Solve for y. **5.5**
b. Solve for x. **30**

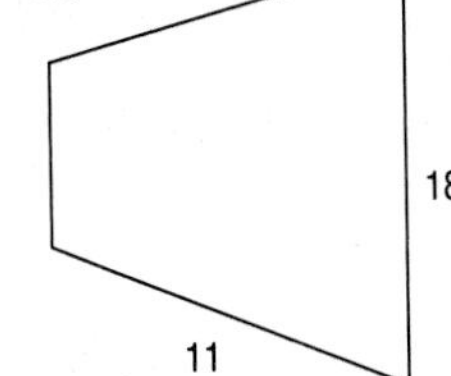

66. A man 6 feet tall casts a shadow 15 feet long. At the same time the shadow of a tree is 140 feet long. How tall is the tree? **56 ft**

67. A tree casts a shadow that is 9 feet long. A yardstick casts a shadow n feet long. How tall is the tree? $\frac{27}{n}$

Objective L. *Use the IF-THEN command in computer programs. (Lesson 5-2)*

68. What will be printed if the input for the program below is 8? **See margin.**

```
10 PRINT "EVALUATE AN EXPRESSION"
20 PRINT "ENTER VALUE OF A"
30 INPUT A
40 IF A = 0 THEN PRINT "IMPOSSIBLE"
50 IF A <> 0 THEN PRINT (40 + A)/A
60 END
```

69. Write a program to evaluate $\frac{k+1}{k-2}$ for any value of k that is entered. If the input makes the expression meaningless, the computer should print IMPOSSIBLE. **See margin.**

Objective M: *Apply the Size Change Model for Multiplication on the coordinate plane. (Lesson 5-6)*

70. Give the image of (2, 4) under a size change of magnitude 3. **(6, 12)**

71. Give the image of (-8, -12) under a size change of magnitude $-\frac{1}{4}$. **(2, 3)**

In 72 and 73, copy the figure below. Then draw its image under the size change with the given magnitude.

72. $\frac{1}{2}$ **See margin.**

73. -3 **See margin.**

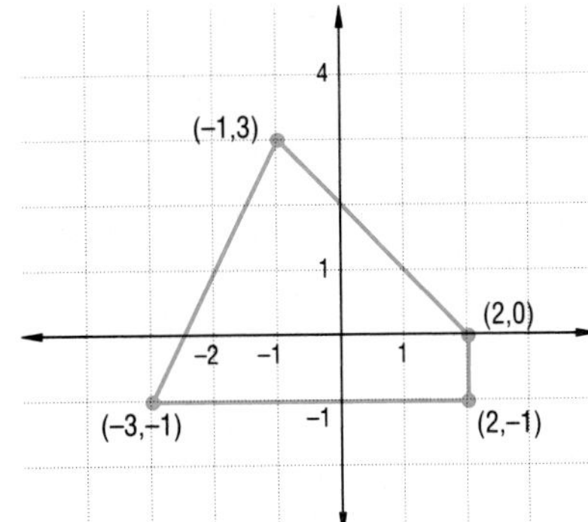

EVALUATION
Three tests are provided for this chapter in the Teacher's Resource File. Chapter 5 Test, Forms A and B, cover just Chapter 5. The third test is Chapter 5 Test, Cumulative Form. About 50% of this test covers Chapter 5, 25% covers Chapter 4, and 25% covers earlier chapters. For more information on grading, see *General Teaching Suggestions: Grading* on page T44 in the Teacher's Edition.

ASSIGNMENT RECOMMENDATION
On the day your students take the chapter test, we suggest you make an assignment in the first section of the next chapter.

72. vertices: (1, 0), $\left(1, -\frac{1}{2}\right)$, $\left(-\frac{3}{2}, -\frac{1}{2}\right)$, $\left(-\frac{1}{2}, \frac{3}{2}\right)$

73. vertices: (-6, 0), (-6, 3) (9, 3), (3, -9)

CHAPTER 6 ■ LINEAR SENTENCES

DAILY PACING CHART 6

DAILY PACING CHART ■ CHAPTER 6

Students in the Full Course should complete the entire text by the end of the year. Students in the Minimal Course spend more time to complete lessons that are combined with quizzes and more time to consider the Chapter Review. Therefore, these students may not complete all the chapters in the text.

DAY	MINIMAL COURSE	FULL COURSE
1	6-1	6-1
2	6-2	6-2
3	6-3	6-3
4	Quiz (TRF); Start 6-4.	Quiz (TRF); 6-4
5	Finish 6-4.	6-5
6	6-5	6-6
7	6-6	6-7
8	6-7	Quiz (TRF); 6-8
9	Quiz (TRF); Start 6-8.	6-9
10	Finish 6-8.	Progress Self-Test
11	6-9	Chapter Review
12	Progress Self-Test	Chapter Test (TRF)
13	Chapter Review	Comprehensive Test (TRF)
14	Chapter Review	
15	Chapter Test (TRF)	
16	Comprehensive Test (TRF)	

TESTING OPTIONS

TESTING OPTIONS

- ■ Quiz for Lessons 6-1 Through 6-3
- ■ Quiz for Lessons 6-4 Through 6-7
- ■ Chapter 6 Test, Form A
- ■ Chapter 6 Test, Form B
- ■ Chapter 6 Test, Cumulative Form
- ■ Comprehensive Test, Chapters 1–6

INDIVIDUAL DIFFERENCES

PROVIDING FOR INDIVIDUAL DIFFERENCES

The student text is written for the *average* student. The program, however, can be adapted for less capable and for more capable students.

For those students who need more practice, a blackline master (in the Teacher's Resource File) is provided for each lesson. The Teacher's Edition frequently provides Error Analysis and Alternate Approach features to provide additional instructional strategies for those students who do not readily grasp the material.

For students who require additional challenge, Extension activities are regularly provided in the Teacher's Edition.

OBJECTIVES ■ CHAPTER 6

Students should master the chapter objectives by the time they complete the chapter. To ensure objective mastery, there is continual review built into each set of lesson questions. After students complete the chapter lessons, they assess their mastery on the Progress Self-Test. Then they do the Chapter Review and pay special attention to those questions that match the objectives missed on the Progress Self-Test. Students can get extra practice on these objectives by using the master for each lesson in the Teacher's Resource File.

OBJECTIVES FOR CHAPTER 6 (Organized into the SPUR categories—Skills, Properties, Uses, and Representations)	**Progress Self-Test Questions**	**Chapter Review Questions**	**Lesson Master from Teacher's Resource File***
SKILLS			
A Use the Distributive Property to remove parentheses and collect like terms.	1 through 4	1 through 10	6-3, 6-8, 6-9
B Solve linear equations.	5 through 9, 12	11 through 24	6-1, 6-2, 6-5, 6-6, 6-8, 6-9
C Solve linear inequalities.	10, 11	25 through 32	6-7
PROPERTIES			
D Apply and recognize properties associated with linear sentences.	13, 25	33 through 40	6-1, 6-3, 6-6, 6-7, 6-8, 6-9
E Use the Distributive Property to perform calculations in your head.	14	41 through 44	6-3
USES			
F Answer questions involving markups or discounts.	15, 16	45 through 48	6-3
G Describe patterns and answer questions in repeated addition or repeated subtraction situations.	17, 18	49 through 54	6-4, 6-6
H Answer questions involving linear sentence formulas.	19, 24	55 through 58	6-2
I Answer questions about situations combining addition and multiplication.	20 through 22	59 through 62	6-3, 6-6
REPRESENTATIONS			
J Translate balance scale models and rectangle area models into expressions and equations.	23	63 through 66	6-1, 6-6, 6-8

*** The masters are numbered to match the lessons.**

OVERVIEW 6

OVERVIEW ■ CHAPTER 6

This chapter is devoted to linear sentences. These are perhaps the most important sentences in elementary algebra, and again, we are interested in the skills, properties, uses, and representations involving them.

The skills begin with equations of the form $ax + b = c$ (Lessons 6-1 and 6-2) and conclude with the sentences in which the variable is on both sides (Lessons 6-6 and 6-7). Because the former skill is necessary for the latter, a mid-chapter review (Lesson 6-5) is presented to help students achieve mastery. By the end of this chapter, we expect students to be able to solve linear equations and inequalities with any kind of coefficients.

The previous four chapters discussed the algebraic properties of the four basic operations of arithmetic. Although subtraction was related to addition and division to multiplication, in general, the operations were treated independently. This chapter brings all the operations together by relating multiplication and addition through the many forms of the Distributive Property. The forms

$$ac + bc = (a + b)c$$
$$ac - bc = (a - b)c$$

are considered in Lesson 6-3. The forms

$$c(a + b) = ca + cb$$
$$-(a + b) = -a + -b$$

are studied in Lessons 6-8 and 6-9.

Applications occur extensively throughout the chapter. Many of the applications come from combining uses of the operations. Others come from discounts and add-ons, explainable with the Distributive Property. The formula for the *n*th term in a linear (or arithmetic) sequence appears in Lesson 6-4. The patterning done in that lesson is a fundamental problem-solving skill.

Graphical representations of linear sentences are studied in the next two chapters. The representations here are more basic: concrete balance-scale representations for equations and the length-area representation for the Distributive Property.

PERSPECTIVES 6

PERSPECTIVES ■ CHAPTER 6

The Perspectives provide the rationale for the inclusion of topics or approaches, provide mathematical background, and make connections within UCSMP.

6-1

SOLVING $ax + b = c$

Combining the operations of multiplication and addition in equations can present a formidable challenge to students. It takes time for them to become accustomed to the patterns and algorithms. This lesson restricts the coefficients to integers; the next lesson is more general.

Even though there is substantial practice on equation solving in this chapter, students are not expected to achieve perfect mastery of all possible forms of equations. By Chapter 8, which discusses equations of lines, students should be very proficient at solving equations.

As students progress through the chapter, you will need to advise them about how many steps you want them to write down when solving an equation or inequality. It is best to keep in mind that the fundamental goal is getting the solution, not writing all the steps. There is research to indicate that the most capable problem solvers often skip steps and sometimes cannot even tell you what the intermediate steps would have been. Most teachers at first ask students to show the addition and multiplication to each side. But as student skill increases, these steps can be dropped.

6-2

MORE SOLVING $ax + b = c$

The last lesson covered $ax + b = c$, where *a, b* and *c* were integers and *a* was always positive. In this lesson, students will see fractions and decimals as well as negative values for *a*. Because of the more complicated coefficients, the generalized algorithm stated on page 267 is needed.

6-3

THE DISTRIBUTIVE PROPERTY

Although students have added like terms previously, the Distributive Property establishes a formal justification for the process. Here we apply the Distributive Property in only one direction: the change from the sum $ac + bc$ to the product $(a + b)c$. In Lesson 6-8 we do the reverse: converting the product $c(a + b)$ into the sum $ca + cb$.

The Distributive Property is used in applications about markup and discount. To calculate sale prices, the Distributive Property is used as follows:

$$S = R - D \times R = (1 - D) \times R,$$

where S = Sale price,
D = Discount rate (%), and
R = Regular price.

The preceding idea is directly applied in problems of growth and decay in Chapter 9.

6-4

REPEATED ADDITION AND SUBTRACTION

This lesson discusses the problem-solving strategy *making a table*. Here, tables are used to help find patterns and formulas for applications involving repeated addition and subtraction. Similar problems with arithmetic sequences are then considered.

The emphasis is on the linear expression that results from each situation. That expression is of the form $a + bx$ where a is the zeroth term and b is the constant difference. In Chapter 8, this same idea appears again but occurs with graphing of lines. The zeroth term becomes the y-intercept and the constant difference becomes the slope.

The technique of writing the formula for the nth term using the value of the zeroth term eliminates some of the problems students have in seeing patterns. It is best here to avoid writing the formulas in the form $a + (n - 1)d$, as this tends to confuse students. Note that in a real situation, the expression for the zeroth term may be artificial. For instance, in Example 1 you would not pay 70¢ to not park. This term is just an aid to establishing the pattern.

6-5

MID-CHAPTER REVIEW

This lesson is in a form quite like the SPUR Questions. The reason for this unique structure is that solving linear equations and solving the problems which lead to them constitute the most important ideas to be acquired in an algebra course, and we want to be sure that students become experts. Furthermore, the questions in the remainder of this chapter require that students have these ideas in hand, so a pause here is very helpful.

6-6

SOLVING $ax + b = cx + d$

In this lesson we deal with linear equations that have variable terms on both sides of the equal sign. In the next lesson the corresponding inequalities are treated. Once students master solving these sentences, our further work with equations will be about learning to simplify expressions on either side of the equal sign.

There are jumps in the equation-solving process that occur when the variable appears on both sides. No longer can equations be solved merely by undoing the operations. Also, it is possible to have a single variable on the left side but still not have the equation solved, as in $x = 2x + 3$. Each of these carries potential for errors by students.

The equation $ax + b = cx + d$ is also important because a category of applications leads to equations of this form. Suppose two quantities begin with values b and d and grow at rates a and c respectively. To find when the quantities are equal, we solve $ax + b = cx + d$. Example 3 is a classic example of this type.

6-7

SOLVING $ax + b < cx + d$

This lesson covers the solution of linear inequalities, but it accomplishes two other goals as well. It provides a second opportunity to practice sentence-solving skills, which are very similar for solving equations and inequalities. It also gives students more experience in writing sentences to describe real situations.

Because students have already encountered the Multiplication Properties of Inequality, there are no new properties needed for solving these inequalities. No additional steps are needed either.

6-8

WHY THE DISTRIBUTIVE PROPERTY IS SO NAMED

The Distributive Property is used here to multiply a polynomial by a monomial (terms we do not introduce until Chapter 10). Three settings for using the Distributive Property are given in the lesson:

(1) simplification of expressions,
(2) doing arithmetic mentally,
(3) solving equations.

The Area Model shows that rewriting $c(a + b)$ as $ca + cb$ (done in this lesson) and rewriting $ac + bc$ as $(a + b)c$ (in Lesson 6-3) involve the same property. But the feel of the two is quite different, and we give them different colloquial names: *removing parentheses* for the first; *adding like terms* for the second. The area representation will be used in later chapters for the multiplication of binomials and of all polynomials.

6-9

SUBTRACTING QUANTITIES

Two topics are discussed in this lesson. The first is the property that the opposite of a sum is the sum of the opposites of the terms. This allows us to express the opposites of quantities simply. This property is then used in the second topic, subtracting quantities.

Here we consider $\text{-}(a + b) = \text{-}a + \text{-}b$ as the special case of $c(a + b) = ca + cb$ when $c = \text{-}1$. Another approach avoids multiplication. You can think of $\text{-}(a + b)$ as that number which, when added to $a + b$, gives a sum of 0. Since $(a + b) + (\text{-}a + \text{-}b) = 0$, the opposite of the quantity $(a + b)$ is $\text{-}a + \text{-}b$. A third approach is somewhat in between: You think of the opposite sign as being distributed over the terms of the quantity. The latter view is mentioned in the lesson and comes closest to the idea of changing the signs of terms being subtracted.

CHAPTER 6

This chapter should take 9 or 11 days for the lessons and quizzes; 1 day for the Progress Self-Test; 1 or 2 days for the Chapter Review; and 1 day for testing. The total is 12 to 15 days. Allow an additional day for the Comprehensive Test.

CHAPTER 6

Linear Sentences

A linear sentence is one in which the variable or variables are all to the first power. Examples are

$$3x + 1000 = 1800$$
$$9a - 2(b - a) = 15$$
$$-\frac{2}{3}t \leq 12$$
$$m + n > 43.61$$

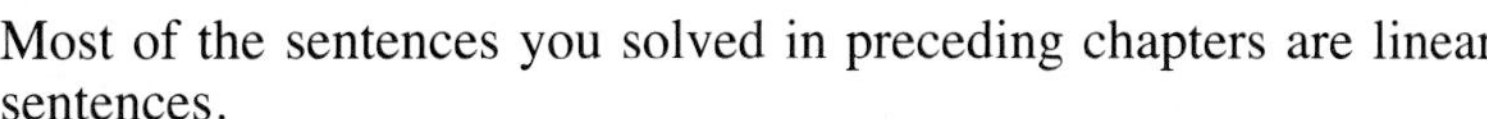

Most of the sentences you solved in preceding chapters are linear sentences.

An enormous variety of situations can lead to linear sentences. For instance, answers to all four questions below can be found by solving

$$3x + 1000 = 1800.$$

1. You want to go to Africa to see the wild animals. You can get \$1000 from your savings and your family, but you need \$1800. If you save \$3 a week, how many weeks will it take you to save up for the trip?
2. There is \$1000 in a school fund for a big dance. Tickets will be sold for \$3 apiece. How many tickets will need to be sold to cover the anticipated cost of \$1800 for the band, the food, the decorations, and the publicity?
3. There are 1000 students in a school in an area that is growing quickly. Each day it seems that about 3 more students are entering the school. The school building has a capacity of 1800. In about how many days will the school be at capacity?

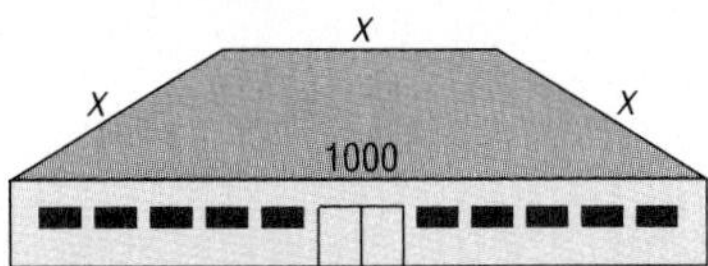

4. The perimeter of the roof line of the warehouse above is 1800 feet. If the front edge is 1000 feet and the other three edges have the same length, what is the length of each of the other edges?

In this chapter, you will learn methods which enable the solving of $3x + 1000 = 1800$ and many other linear sentences. This will give you the power to answer many questions about real situations.

USING PAGES 260-261
These pages should be used to stimulate student interest. It is not necessary to take the time to solve the problems now. The equation that is common to all four problems is solved in Example 2 of Lesson 6-1. Then the answer for one of the problems is given in the paragraph following Example 2.

The students are asked to provide the answers for the other three problems in Questions 16–18 of Lesson 6-1. As they will see, the answers to the problems are not all the same, even though they can all be solved by using the same equation. This occurs because the problem about the tickets requires a rounded result, the problem about the roof does not, and the other two can be answered either way, though most people would round those two answers.

LESSON 6-1

RESOURCES

- Lesson Master 6-1
- Visual for Teaching Aid 29: Balance Scales

OBJECTIVES

B Solve linear equations of the form $ax + b = c$ when the coefficients are integers.
D Apply and recognize the Addition and Multiplication Properties of Equality in solving linear sentences.
J Translate balance scale models into equations.

TEACHING NOTES

You might want to use a balance scale to illustrate solving equations. If you have no scale, *Teaching Aid 29* can be used to represent the steps pictorially. Use simple drawings, say, squares for variables and triangles for constants.

It is important for students to realize that there are only two major steps in solving $ax + b = c$ (as shown in **Example 1**) and that other steps (as in **Examples 2 and 3**) are to clarify the process.

Alternate Approach
Some teachers use the symbol A_k to mean adding k to both sides and M_k to mean multiplying both sides by k. Then the solution to **Example 3** would be written as

$$\begin{array}{lr} & 7x - 2 = -23 \\ A_2 & 7x = -21 \\ M_{\frac{1}{7}} & = -3. \end{array}$$

LESSON 6-1

Solving $ax + b = c$

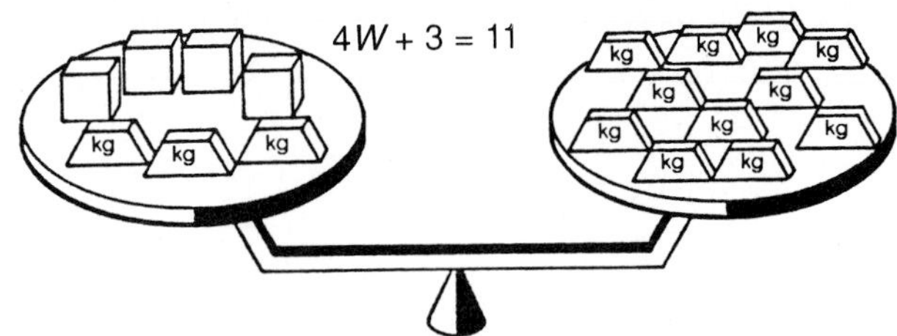

An equation is like a balance scale. Here is a picture of the equation $4W + 3 = 11$. On the left side of the scale are 4 boxes and 3 one-kilogram weights. They balance with the 11 kilograms on the right.

You can find the weight of one box in two steps. Each step keeps the scale balanced.

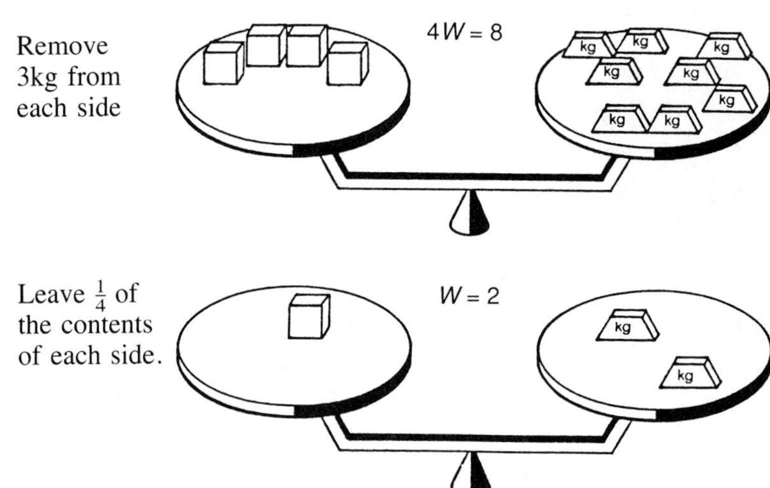

Example 1 shows the same steps without the balance scale.

Example 1 Solve: $4W + 3 = 11$

Solution $4W = 8$ Addition Property of Equality (added -3 to each side)
$W = 2$ Multiplication Property of Equality (multiplied both sides by $\frac{1}{4}$)

Check Substitute 2 for W in the original equation. Does $4 \cdot 2 + 3 = 11$? Yes.

Any equation like the one in Example 1 can be solved in two steps. First add a number to both sides. Then multiply both sides by a number. The only tasks are to determine the numbers and to do the arithmetic correctly. To help with these tasks, you may put in work steps showing what you did. Work steps are shown in Example 2, which is the equation for the situations on page 261.

Example 2 Solve: $3x + 1000 = 1800$

Solution Here is a work step, showing that -1000 is added to each side.

$$3x + 1000 + -1000 = 1800 + -1000$$
$$3x = 800$$

Another work step shows that both sides are multiplied by $\frac{1}{3}$.

$$\frac{1}{3} \cdot 3x = \frac{1}{3} \cdot 800$$
$$x = \frac{800}{3}$$
$$= 266\tfrac{2}{3}$$

Check Substitute $266\frac{2}{3}$ for x in the original equation.

Does $3 \cdot 266\frac{2}{3} + 1000 = 1800$? Yes, it does.

Using Example 2, you can answer the questions on page 261. For Question 2, 267 tickets will need to be sold. You are asked to answer the other questions yourself.

Equations involving subtraction are solved using the same two steps. Again we show work.

Example 3 Solve: $7x - 2 = -23$

Solution Add 2 to both sides. $7x - 2 + 2 = -23 + 2$

Simplify. $7x = -21$

Multiply both sides by $\frac{1}{7}$, or do the equivalent, divide by seven. $\frac{7x}{7} = \frac{-21}{7}$

$x = -3$

Check Substitute -3 for x in the original equation.

Does $7(-3) - 2 = -23$?

Yes, since $-21 - 2 = -23$.

Some teachers would prefer to have students begin by rewriting the preceding equation in terms of addition: $7x + -2 = -23$. We do not discourage this as part of the explanation, but the text does not employ that step.

The equation in **Example 2** helps to answer the four questions that appear in the chapter opener. Point out, however, that the solution to the equation is not necessarily the answer to the problem. Emphasize that, when equations are used to help solve real problems, the solution must be interpreted in the context of the real situation. For example, since it is impossible to sell a fraction of a ticket, the solution has to be rounded off.

ADDITIONAL EXAMPLES

In 1–3, solve.

1. $125 = 6m + 11$
19

2. $15x + 21 = 243$
$\frac{74}{5}$ **or 14.8**

3. $-20 - 4x = -12$
-2

NOTES ON QUESTIONS
Questions 2 and 3: These emphasize the process of solving an equation rather than the result.

Question 6: This is a simple one-step rather than two-step equation. Students should recognize that this problem is different (and easier) than **Questions 4, 5, and 7.** Of course, it can be viewed as an example of $ax + b = c$ with $a = 1$.

Questions 8, 9, and 12: Students sometimes have difficulty if the variable term is on the right side of the equation. Yet this is a common kind of equation to be solved when lines are given in the form $y = mx + b$. These questions lead students to recognize that solving $c = ax + b$ involves the same processes as solving $ax + b = c$.

Making Connections for Questions 16-18: These refer to the questions in the chapter opener. Students must consider whether answers other than integers make sense.

Making Connections for Question 24a: The complementary percents here help to prepare students for the percents involved in discounts in some of the questions of Lesson 6-3.

Question 27: Students should not forget that they can solve certain equations without writing any steps. This question serves that purpose.

Questions

Covering the Reading

1. The boxes are of equal weight. Each weight marked kg is 1 kilogram.

a. What equation is pictured by this balance scale? **See margin.**

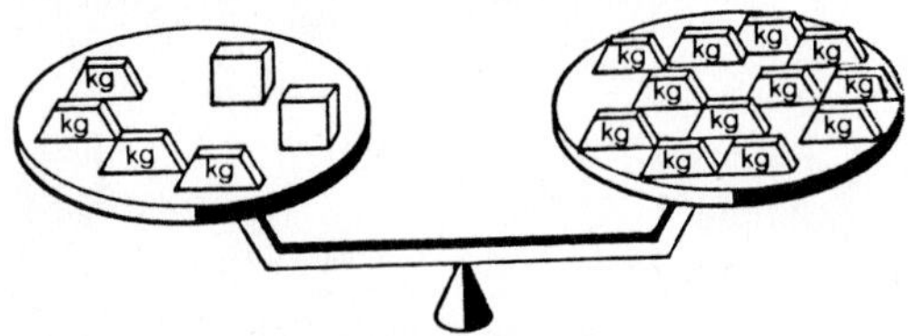

b. What two steps can be done with the weights on the scale to find the weight of a single box? **See margin.**

2. a. When solving $4n + 8 = 60$, first add _?_ to both sides. Then _?_ both sides by _?_. **-8, multiply, $\frac{1}{4}$**

b. Solve and check: $4n + 8 = 60$ **$n = 13$**

3. Here is an equation solved, but the work steps are not put in.

Given: $55v - 61 = 434$
Step 1: $55v = 495$
Step 2: $v = 9$

a. What was done to get Step 1? **Add 61 to each side.**
b. What was done to get Step 2? **Divide each side by 55.**

In 4–7, solve and check.

4. $8x + 15 = 47$ **$x = 4$**

5. $7y - 11 = 52$ **$y = 9$**

6. $n + 5 = -6$ **$n = -11$**

7. $2z + 32 = 288$ **$z = 128$**

8. *Multiple choice* Which equation does *not* have the same solution as $3x + 5 = 9$? **(c)**
(a) $5 + 3x = 9$
(b) $9 = 5 + 3x$
(c) $9 = 3 + 5x$
(d) All have same solutions.

In 9–12, solve and check.

9. $312 = 36w + 60$ **$w = 7$**

10. $22 + 11a = 66$ **$a = 4$**

11. $7 + 8t = 207$ **$t = 25$**

12. $-81 = 2x + 5$ **$x = -43$**

13. *Multiple choice* Which is the solution to $3a - 11 = -40$? **(b)**
(a) $-\frac{51}{3}$
(b) $-\frac{29}{3}$
(c) $\frac{51}{3}$
(d) $\frac{29}{3}$

In 14 and 15, solve and check.

14. $5y - 6 = 2$ **$y = \frac{8}{5}$**

15. $7x + 11 = -4$ **$x = -\frac{15}{7}$**

16. Answer Question 1 on page 261. **$266\frac{2}{3}$ weeks**

17. Answer Question 3 on page 261. $266\frac{2}{3}$ days

18. Answer Question 4 on page 261. $266\frac{2}{3}$ ft

Applying the Mathematics

In 19 and 20, use these formulas relating shoe size S and foot length L in inches.

$$\text{for men:} \quad S = 3L - 26$$
$$\text{for women:} \quad S = 3L - 22$$

19. If Sam wears a size 9 shoe, about how long are his feet? $11\frac{2}{3}$ in.

20. If Bernice wears a size 6 shoe, about how long are her feet? $9\frac{1}{3}$ in.

21. **a.** Simplify: $-2x + 5x + 16$. $3x + 16$
b. Solve: $-2x + 5x + 16 = 46$. $x = 10$

Review

22. To the nearest integer, what is the solution to $1.34m = 13.5$? *(Lesson 4-4)*
$m \approx 10$

23. Evaluate $(-7)^3 + (-6)^2 + (-5)^1$. *(Lesson 1-4)* -312

24. If a discount is 10%, then the sale price is 100% − 10% = 90% of the regular price.
a. Copy and complete the chart. *(Lesson 3-2)*

discount	sale price (as % of regular price)
10%	90%
25%	? 75%
50%	? 50%
? 70%	30%
n%	? $(100 - n)$ %

b. Graph the ordered pairs from the first four rows of part a. Label the horizontal axis "discount" and the vertical axis "sale price." *(Lesson 3-7)* See margin.

In 25 and 26, when $x = -4$ and $y = -5$, find the value of each expression. *(Lesson 1-4)*

25. $-5 - 4xy$ -85

26. $-4x + 5y^2$ 141

27. Solve in your head. *(Lesson 2-6)*
a. $20 = 35 + x$ $x = -15$
b. $20 + y = 35$ $y = 15$
c. $20 + (z - 30) = 35$ $z = 45$

28. There are 162 games in the major league baseball season. In 1987, Eric Davis of the Cincinnati Reds had 20 home runs after 55 games. If he continued at this rate, would he have broken the all-time record of 61 home runs set by Roger Maris of the New York Yankees in 1961? *(Lesson 5-7)* No

ADDITIONAL ANSWERS

1a. If B equals the weight of each box, then $2B + 4 = 12$.

1b. One: remove 4 kg from each side of the balance. Two: remove half the contents of each side of the balance.

24b.

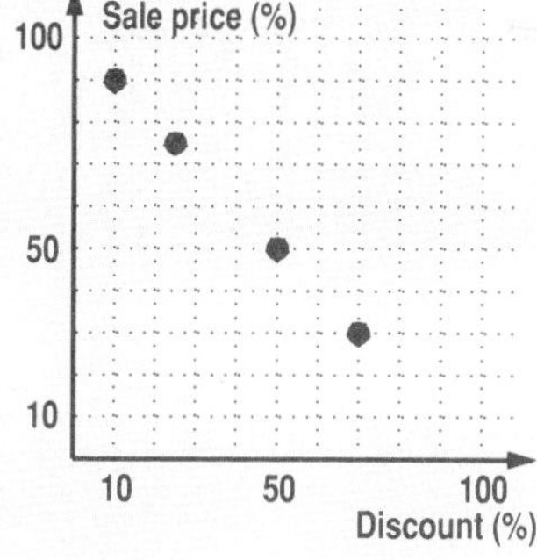

NAME ______

LESSON **MASTER 6–1**
QUESTIONS ON SPUR OBJECTIVES

■SKILLS *Objective B (See pages 308–311 for objectives.)*
In 1 and 2, solve and check.

1. $4y + 9 = -43$ $y = -13$; $4(-13) + 9 = -43$

2. $62 = 5n - 13$ $n = 15$; $62 = 5(15) - 13$

In 3–10, solve.

3. $13a - 72 = 58$ $a = 10$

4. $6k + 23 = 17$ $k = -1$

5. $3 + 2v = 17$ $v = 7$

6. $28 = 11w - 5$ $w = 3$

7. $-8 = -8 + 4c$ $c = 0$

8. $-2 = 13 + 3b$ $b = -5$

9. $6p - 16 = 23$ $p = 6.5$

10. $-34 = 5t - 18$ $t = -\frac{16}{5}$

■PROPERTIES *Objective D*
In 11–13, identify the property applied.

11. If $3x + 5 = 11$, then $3x = 6$. Add. Prop. of Equality

12. If $2y + 18 = 12$ then $y + 9 = 6$. Mult. Prop. of Equality

13. If $3t + 1 = 0$, then $6t + 2 = 0$. Mult. Prop. of Equality

■REPRESENTATIONS *Objective J*
14. In the picture, the boxes are of equal weight and each cylinder weighs 1 kg.

a. Write an equation representing this situation. $2b + 3 = 7$

b. What is the weight of one box? 2 kg

44

FOLLOW-UP

MORE PRACTICE

For more questions on SPUR Objectives, use *Lesson Master 6-1*, shown on page 265.

30. Female: longer than 10 in. but shorter than $10\frac{2}{3}$ in. male: longer than $11\frac{1}{3}$ in. but shorter than 12 in.

29. Joe is 5 feet tall. He stands so that the top of his shadow hits exactly the same place as the end of the flagpole's shadow. If his shadow is 8 feet long and the flagpole's shadow is 18 feet long, how high is the flagpole? *(Lesson 5-7)* **11.25 feet**

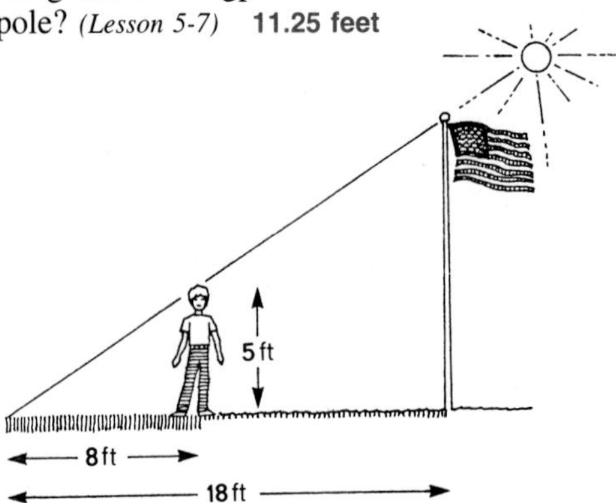

Exploration

30. A person usually wears shoes of the most comfortable size. Referring to the formula of Question 19, describe *all* the lengths of feet that would be best fit by a shoe of size 9. **See margin.**

266

LESSON

6-2

More Solving $ax + b = c$

The three examples of the last lesson are all of the same form.

$$4w + 3 = 11$$
$$3x + 1000 = 1800$$
$$7x - 2 = -23$$

The general form is $ax + b = c$

where the equation is to be solved for x. All equations of this type can be solved with the two major steps you used in the last lesson, even when a, b, and c are fractions or decimals.

Example 1 Solve: $\frac{2}{3}x - 16 = 11$

Solution Begin as you did in Lesson 6-1. Add 16 to both sides.

$$\frac{2}{3}x - 16 + 16 = 11 + 16$$
$$\frac{2}{3}x = 27$$

Multiply both sides by $\frac{3}{2}$. $\frac{3}{2} \cdot \frac{2}{3}x = \frac{3}{2} \cdot 27$

$$x = \frac{81}{2}$$
$$= 40\tfrac{1}{2}$$

Check Substitute 40.5 for x. Does $\frac{2}{3} \cdot 40\frac{1}{2} - 16 = 11$?

$$\frac{81}{3} - 16 = 11?$$
$27 - 16 = 11?$ Yes.

Example 1 and all the examples of the last lesson use the same two steps to solve equations of the form $ax + b = c$.

> To solve $ax + b = c$ for x, add $-b$ to both sides. Then multiply both sides by $\frac{1}{a}$.

Sometimes fractions and decimals occur in the same problem. Then it is convenient to convert all to either decimals or fractions.

Example 2 A formula relating Fahrenheit and Celsius temperatures is

$$F = \frac{9}{5}C + 32.$$

What is the Celsius equivalent of normal body temperature, 98.6°F?

LESSON 6-2

RESOURCES
■ Lesson Master 6-2

OBJECTIVES

B Solve linear equations of the form $ax + b = c$ when the coefficients are not integers.
H Answer questions involving linear sentence formulas.

TEACHING NOTES

The algorithm of this lesson for solving $ax + b = c$ (add $-b$, multiply by $1/a$) does not take into account all the variations produced by personal preference and special cases. For example, students should realize that it is often easier to divide both sides by a than to multiply by $1/a$. However, this algorithm gives a good general procedure: isolate the variable term on one side, then multiply by the reciprocal of its coefficient.

Discuss the check for **Example 3.** Point out that we did not check the equation. Rather, we went back to the application. This procedure checks the way the equation was written. If the check did not work, then one would go to the equation and check it. This would indicate whether the error is in solving the equation or in the translation to an equation.

ADDITIONAL EXAMPLES

1. Solve $\frac{5}{8}x + 20 = 85$.
104

2. Convert -19.3°F to degrees Celsius.
-28.5°C

3. The height of an office building is 117 feet. The height of the entrance level is $15\frac{1}{2}$ feet. If the building contains 11 floors of offices and the roof is $2\frac{1}{2}$ feet thick, what is the height of each floor of offices? (Your answer includes the thickness of the ceiling and floor.)
Let t = the height of each floor (in feet). Then $15\frac{1}{2} + 11t + 2\frac{1}{2} = 117$, so $t = 9$ feet.

4. Solve $594 = -18x - 72$.
-37

NOTES ON QUESTIONS
Questions 10 and 16: Students should write equations for these questions, even if they can determine the answer without an equation.

Questions 13 and 14: These can be solved with sentences that use the ≈ sign, but if students are more comfortable using equal signs, they may use them instead.

Solution Substitute 98.6 for F and solve for C.

$$98.6 = \frac{9}{5}C + 32$$

We change $\frac{9}{5}$ to a decimal because the decimal terminates. $\frac{9}{5} = 1.8$. So the problem becomes

$$98.6 = 1.8C + 32.$$

Add -32 to each side.

$$66.6 = 1.8C$$

Multiply both sides by $\frac{1}{1.8}$.

$$\frac{66.6}{1.8} = C$$

$$37° = C$$

Check Substitute 98.6 for F and 37 for C in the original formula.
Does $98.6 = \frac{9}{5} \cdot 37 + 32$?

$$= \frac{333}{5} + 32?$$

$$= 66.6 + 32? \text{ Yes.}$$

In fact, in almost the entire world, 37° is the value used for normal body temperature, not 98.6°, because the U.S. is the only major country that still measures temperature using the Fahrenheit scale.

Often equations are complicated but can be simplified into ones that you can solve. Simplifying each side is an important strategy for all equation solving.

Example 3 When Val works overtime at the zoo on Saturday she earns \$9.80 per hour. She is also paid \$8.00 for meals and \$3.00 for transportation. Last Saturday she was paid \$77.15. How many hours did she work?

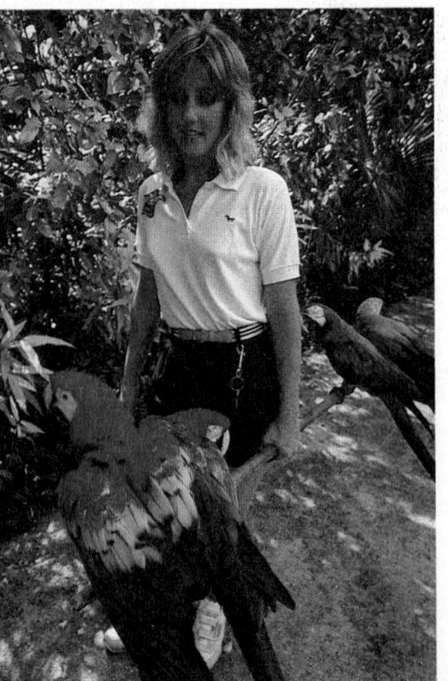

Solution Let h = the number of hours Val worked. She earned 9.80h dollars in those hours. So

$$9.80h + 8.00 + 3.00 = 77.15.$$

Simplify the left side and the equation looks more familiar.

$$9.80h + 11 = 77.15$$

$$9.80h + 11 + -11 = 77.15 + -11$$

$$9.80h = 66.15$$

$$\frac{9.80h}{9.80} = \frac{66.15}{9.80}$$

$$h = 6.75$$

Val worked $6\frac{3}{4}$ hours.

Check If she worked 6.75 hours at \$9.80 per hour, she earned $6.75 \cdot 9.80$ dollars. That comes to \$66.15. Now add \$8 for meals and \$3 for transportation. The total is \$77.15, as desired.

The coefficient of x in $ax + b = c$ can be negative. Still the equation is solved in the same way.

Example 4 Solve: $-5x + 1025 = 685$

Solution Add -1025 to each side. $-5x + 1025 + -1025 = 685 + -1025$

$$-5x = -340$$

Divide each side by -5. $\frac{-5x}{-5} = \frac{-340}{-5}$

$$x = 68$$

Check Does $-5 \cdot 68 + 1025 = 685$? Yes, $-340 + 1025 = 685$.

Questions

Covering the Reading

1. To solve an equation of the form $ax + b = c$, first add __?__ to both sides. Then __?__ both sides by __?__. **$-b$; multiply; $\frac{1}{a}$**

2. a. To solve $4 + 2.5x = 21.5$, what is an appropriate first step? **Add -4 to each side.**
b. Solve this equation. **$x = 7$**

In 3 and 4, solve and check.

3. $\frac{2}{3}x + 15 = 27$ **$x = 18$** **4.** $32 = 0.2y - 3$ **$y = 175$**

5. What is the Celsius equivalent of a room temperature of 68°F? **C = 20°**

6. If an equation is complicated, what important strategy of equation solving should you follow to solve it? **See margin.**

7. a. What should be the first step in solving $3.5 + 2x + 5.6 = 10$? **Add 3.5 and 5.6.**
b. Solve and check this sentence. **$x = .45$**

In 8 and 9, solve and check.

8. $8 + 27 + 4p + 1 = -44$ **$p = -20$** **9.** $6 - 30n - 18 = 69$ **$n = -2.7$**

10. Refer to Example 3. If Val's pay two Saturdays ago was \$89.40, how many hours did she work? **$h = 8$ hours**

In 11 and 12, solve and check.

11. $-4x + 12 = -100$ **$x = 28$** **12.** $2 = -8y - 1$ **$y = -\frac{3}{8}$**

ADDITIONAL ANSWERS

6. Simplify each side as the first step. Solve after the equation looks more familiar.

NAME ______

LESSON **MASTER 6–2**
QUESTIONS ON **SPUR** OBJECTIVES

SKILLS *Objective B (See pages 308–311 for objectives.)*
In 1–8, solve.

1. $2s + 1.5 = 5.5$ **$s = 2$**
2. $11.7 + 5.6k = 25.7$ **$k = 2.5$**
3. $-0.7 = 0.8 + .3x$ **$x = -5$**
4. $\frac{5v}{12} - \frac{2}{3} = \frac{1}{6}$ **$v = 2$**
5. $5 + 7y - 3 = 37$ **$y = 5$**
6. $\frac{3}{4} = \frac{5}{8} + 2a$ **$a = \frac{1}{16}$ or .0625**
7. $65 - 8x = 21$ **$x = 5.5$**
8. $\frac{7}{10} = 1 - \frac{3x}{5}$ **$x = \frac{1}{2}$**

USES *Objective H*

9. Freddie now weighs 260 pounds. To weigh 190 pounds in a half year (26 weeks), how much weight must he lose per week? **about 2.7 lb**

10. At the U-Pick Strawberry Farm, Susan paid a total of \$5.59 for the following: \$.55 for an empty basket and \$.48 a pound for the strawberries she picked. How many pounds of strawberries did she pick? **10.5 lb**

11. Ms. Gower sells stereos. She gets a salary of \$250 a week and a 5% commission on her total sales. If she earned a total of \$400 one week, what was the total of her sales? **\$3000**

12. As air rises, it cools by expansion according to the formula $T = t - \frac{H}{100}$, where t is the Celsius temperature at the earth's surface, and T is the Celsius temperature at altitude H. If the air temperature at the surface is 25°C, how high must the balloon go to reach a height where the temperature is -5°? **3000 feet**

 45

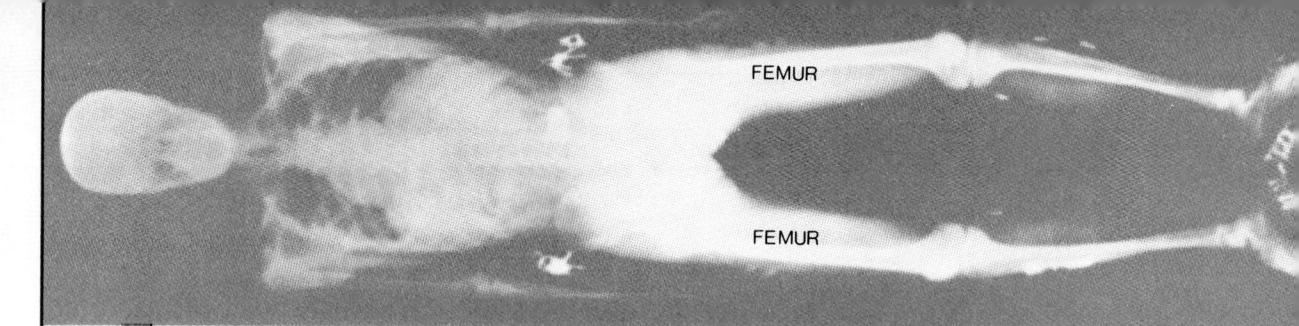

NOTES ON QUESTIONS
Small Group Work for Question 25: You may wish to have students work in small groups to research these vocations.

Question 26: This question reverses the typical question asked of students. You may wish to do this as a class exercise. A sample solution follows:

$$x = \frac{2}{3}$$
$$M_9 \quad 9x = 6$$
$$A_{-4} \quad 9x - 4 = 2$$

FOLLOW-UP

MORE PRACTICE
For more questions on SPUR Objectives, use *Lesson Master 6-2*, shown on page 269.

EXTENSION
After students have mastered the sequence of steps necessary for solving $ax + b = c$ where a, b, and c are given as numbers, ask them how to solve the literal equation $rx + t = s$ for x. (Students should be able to see the general solution from numerical examples.) Then, have students write the calculator steps for solving an equation like $3.1x + 2.8 = 7.3$
(7.3 [+] 2.8 [+/−] [=] [×] 3.1 [1/x] [=])

25. An archaeologist recovers and studies articles from past civilizations in order to learn about the people and culture of those times. A paleontologist studies fossils. A forensic scientist deals in legal proceedings, as in determining a cause of death.

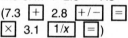

Applying the Mathematics

In 13 and 14, use this information. Lengths of human bones are related by linear sentences. These can be used to estimate heights of individuals if certain bones are found. Archaeologists, paleontologists, and forensic scientists all use these techniques. Here are formulas relating the length f of the femur (thigh bone) to the height h of a person, both in centimeters.

for men: $h \approx 69.089 + 2.238f$
for women: $h \approx 61.412 + 2.317f$

13. A 160-cm tall female has a femur of about what length? **$f \approx 42.5$ cm**

14. Clues from footprints show that a man was 180 cm tall. A partial skeleton is found in which the femur is 50 cm long. Could this be a matchup? **Yes, because $h \approx 181$ cm**

15. Solve for x: $ax + b = c$. **$x = \frac{c - b}{a}$**

16. A copy machine begins work with 1025 sheets of paper. It uses $5t$ sheets each second. After how many seconds will 685 sheets be left? **$\frac{68}{t}$ seconds**

Review

In 17–20, solve. Do at least one of these in your head. *(Lesson 6-1)*

17. $9x + 40 = 40$ **$x = 0$**
18. $2 + 5z = 3$ **$z = \frac{1}{5}$**
19. $-2y - 11 = 63$ **$y = -37$**
20. $100 = 20h + 160$ **$h = -3$**

21. When the singing group The Three Blungets goes on tour, they earn $1260 per concert. The group also gets $10 per mile for travel expenses. Their last tour covered 3500 miles.
a. How much did the group get for travel expenses? **$35,000**
b. If their earnings and money for travel expenses totaled $100,000, how many concerts did they give? *(Lesson 6-1)*
51 or 52 concerts

22. Simplify: **a.** $2y + y + 16 + y$ **b.** $(2y)(y)(16)(y)$ *(Lessons (2-2, 4-1)*
a) $4y + 16$; b) $32y^3$

23. Find the area of the right-angled figure at the left. *(Lesson 4-1)*
2.0625 in.^{2}

0.75 in.
0.75 in.
2 in.
1.5 in.

24. $\angle A$ and $\angle B$ are supplementary. $m\angle A = 20°$. Find $m\angle B$. *(Lesson 3-8)*
160°

Exploration

25. Three vocations are mentioned in Questions 13 and 14. What do these people do? **See margin.**

26. Give four linear sentences of the form $ax + b = c$ whose solution is $\frac{2}{3}$.
samples: $3x + 1 = 3$; $6x + 5 = 9$; $3x - 1 = 1$; $6x - 5 = -1$

LESSON

The Distributive Property

You know that $6x + 8x$ equals $14x$. This property, an instance of adding like terms, is one example of a more general property called the **Distributive Property.**

Distributive Property:

For any real numbers a, b, and c:

$$ac + bc = (a + b)c$$
$$ac - bc = (a - b)c.$$

The Distributive Property enables you to solve difficult-looking equations.

Example 1 Solve: $-3x + 4 + 5x = -6$

Solution First use the Commutative Property of Addition to put like terms next to each other.

$$-3x + 5x + 4 = -6$$

Now apply the Distributive Property.

$$(-3 + 5)x + 4 = -6$$
$$2x + 4 = -6$$

Now solve as usual.

$$2x + 4 + -4 = -6 + -4$$
$$2x = -10$$
$$x = -5$$

Recall the Multiplicative Identity Property of 1. For any real number n,

$$n = 1n.$$

When this property is combined with the Distributive Property, many expressions can be simplified. For instance, $k + 8k = 1k + 8k = 9k$. Here are some problems involving 1 as a coefficient.

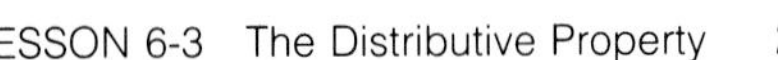

LESSON 6-3

RESOURCES

- Lesson Master 6-3
- Quiz on Lessons 6-1 Through 6-3

OBJECTIVES

A Use the Distributive Property to collect like terms.
D Apply and recognize the use of the Distributive Property and the Multiplicative Identity Property of 1 in solving linear sentences.
E Use the Distributive Property to perform calculations in your head.
F Answer questions involving markups or discounts.
I Answer questions about situations combining addition and multiplication.

TEACHING NOTES

Alternate Approach
Here are some images that can help your students to picture using the Distributive Property to combine like terms.

| a | a | | a | a | a |

$2a + 3a = 5a$

| n^2 | n^2 | n^2 | | n^2 | n^2 | n^2 | n^2 |

$3n^2 + 4n^2 = 7n^2$

The Distributive Property can also be shown with nongeometric examples. For instance, suppose Josie earns \$2.50 per hour babysitting. One week she babysat for 6 hours and the next week she baby-sat for 8 hours. Her pay can be figured by $6 \cdot 2.50 + 8 \cdot 2.50$ or by $(6 + 8) \cdot 2.50$. The results are equal.

If your students have trouble seeing how 1 is used as a coefficient in simplifying phrases like $m - .15m$, have them rewrite the phrase using the 1 before applying the Distributive Property.

ADDITIONAL EXAMPLES

1. Solve
$16 + -2x + -9x = 49$.
-3

In 2–4, write and solve an equation to answer the question.

2. Last week, Waverly Hardware had a sale on varnish. At the beginning of the week, there were 16 cans on the shelf. Those were sold, along with three cases containing cans of varnish. If a total of 112 cans were sold, how many cans of varnish does a case hold?
$16 + n + n + n = 112$,
$n = 32$ cans/case

Example 2 A $140,000 estate is to be split among three children and a grandchild. Each child gets the same amount and the grandchild gets one half as much. How much should each child receive?

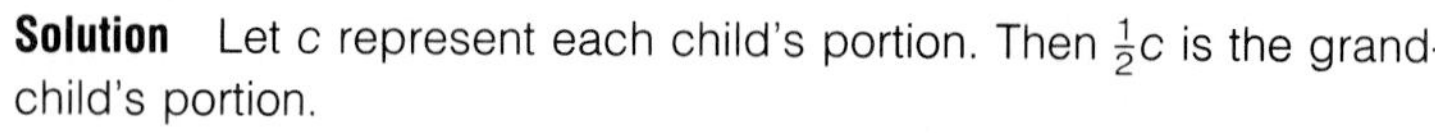

Solution Let c represent each child's portion. Then $\frac{1}{2}c$ is the grandchild's portion.

$$c + c + c + \tfrac{1}{2}c = 140{,}000$$

Use the Multiplication Property of 1.

$$1c + 1c + 1c + \tfrac{1}{2}c = 140{,}000$$

Use the Distributive Property and change $\frac{1}{2}$ to .5.

$$3.5c = 140{,}000$$

Divide each side by 3.5.

$$c = 40{,}000$$

Each child should receive $40,000.

Check The grandchild receives half as much as each child does, and so gets $20,000.
Does $40{,}000 + 40{,}000 + 40{,}000 + 20{,}000 = 140{,}000$? Yes.

The arithmetic in Example 2 could have been made easier by thinking of all amounts "in thousands." The equation would become $3\frac{1}{2}c = 140$. It would still be solved in the same way.

In Examples 3 and 4, the original price of an item is raised or lowered by a given percent. The idea of percent change can be generalized. If an item is 15% off, you pay 85%, which is 100% − 15%. The 15% is called a **discount.** If the item were 33% off, you would pay 100% − 33% or 67% of the price. If there is a 4% **tax,** you pay 104% of the price. If there is an 8% tax, you pay 108% of the price. The 4% or 8% is an example of a **markup.**

Example 3 A microwave oven is on sale for 15% off the regular price. The sale price is $279.65. What is the regular price?

Solution Let m be the regular price of the microwave.

sale price = regular price − 15% of regular price
$279.65 = m - .15m$

Remember $m = 1m$. $279.65 = (1 - .15)m$

$$279.65 = .85m$$
$$\frac{279.65}{.85} = \frac{.85m}{.85}$$
$$329 = m$$

The regular price is $329.

Check If the regular price is $329, the discount is 0.15 · $329, or $49.35.
The sale price is $329 – $49.35 = $279.65. This checks.

Example 4 The Richardsons bought a new van. The total amount they were charged was $11,864. Included in this amount was 4% sales tax and $60 for licenses. What was the cost of the van before the tax?

Solution Let V be the cost of the van. Then

$$\text{cost} + 4\% \text{ of cost} + \$60 = \$11864$$
$$V + .04V + 60 = 11864$$
$$1.04V + 60 = 11864$$
$$1.04V + 60 - 60 = 11864 - 60$$
$$1.04V = 11804$$
$$\frac{1.04V}{1.04} = \frac{11804}{1.04}$$
$$V = 11350$$

The cost of the van before tax and licenses was $11,350.

Check 4% of $11,350 is $454; 11,350 + 454 + 60 = 11,864

In general:

If an item is **discounted** x%, you pay $(100 - x)$% of the price.

If an item is **marked up** or **taxed** y%, you pay $(100 + y)$% of the price.

3. A football is on sale for $45.48, which is 20% off its regular price. What is the regular price?
$p - .20p = 45.48$ or $.80p = \$45.48$. The regular price is $56.85.

4. The Garcia family bought a new air conditioner. With 6% sales tax and a $40 installation fee, their bill was $385.03. What was the original price of the air conditioner?
$A + .06A + 40 = 385.03$ or $1.06A + 40 = 385.03$. The original price was $325.50.

NOTES ON QUESTIONS
Question 12: Students may not see that the percent of population growth is added to 100% like the percent of sales tax is. If the population grew 33.6%, then the 1984 population is 133.6% or 1.336 of the 1980 population.

Question 15: This can be solved by an equation. Let x = fraction of original price paid by the customer. Then $x \cdot 189 = 90$, so $x \approx .48$ = 48%. Since the customer pays 48% of the original price, the discount is 52%. Another method is to find the amount of discount: 189 − 90 = 99. Then the percent of discount is $\frac{99}{189} \approx$ 52%.

Error Analysis for Question 21: Some students may solve this question for $-c$ and think they are done. Note that this equation can be rewritten as $-1c + 3.4 = 6.21$. That may help students to realize that the job is not done until the equation is solved for c.

Making Connections for Question 28: Students will probably solve parts **a** and **b** by using repeated multiplication by .9, instead of using the expressions from part **c.** The situation is a decay situation of the type to be examined in detail in Chapter 9.

FOLLOW-UP

MORE PRACTICE
For more questions on SPUR Objectives, use *Lesson Master 6-3,* shown on page 275.

Questions

Covering the Reading

In 1–4, simplify one side of the equation. Then solve.

1. $h + h = 41$ **h = 20.5**

2. $.75y + y + 10 = 45$ **y = 20**

3. $g + .04g + 60 = 8796$ **g = 8400**

4. $x - .20x = \$35.00$ **x = $43.75**

5. $90,000 is to be divided among three heirs. Two of the heirs each receive equal amounts. The third heir receives one fourth that amount. Write an equation and find how much money each heir will receive. **See margin.**

6. In Question 5, suppose that $10,000 is given to charity before the heirs get any money. Write an equation and solve it to determine how much each heir will receive. **$h + h + \frac{1}{4}h = 80{,}000$**
Two heirs receive $35,555.56; third receives $8888.88.

7. In Example 3, suppose the sale price of another microwave is $350. What is the regular price? **$411.76**

8. *Multiple choice* The price of a bicycle is B. The total paid T includes 6% sales tax. Which equation describes this situation? **(c)**
(a) $B + .06 = T$ (b) $.06B = T$ (c) $1.06B = T$

9. Julian went out for dinner. The bill came to $11.55. Included in this amount was a 5% sales tax. What was the cost of the meal? **$11.00**

10. If a coat is discounted 30%, you pay __?__ of the original price. **70%**

Applying the Mathematics

11. Some taxicab companies allow their drivers to keep $\frac{3}{10}$ of all fares collected.The rest goes to the company. If a driver collects F dollars in fares, write an expression for how much the company gets. **$.7F$**

In 12–14, **a.** write an equation that can help answer the question and **b.** use your equation to answer the question.

12. The population of Arlington, Texas was about 214,000 in 1984 after a growth of 33.6% from 1980 to 1984. What was Arlington's population in 1980? **a) $p + .336p = 214{,}000$; b) 160,180 people**

13. Customers at Flo's Meat Market must pay 6% state sales tax. One day Flo takes in $2650, including tax. How much of the $2650 does Flo have left after sending the tax money to the state?
a) $s + .06s = 2650$; b) $2500

14. In a boxing match, $250,000 goes to the promoter and, of the rest, the loser will receive one fifth of what the winner will get. The total purse is $750,000. How much will each boxer receive?
a) $x + \frac{1}{5}x + 250{,}000 = 750{,}000$; b) winner $416,666.67; loser $83,333.33

15. A suit has a regular price of $189.00. The final discounted price is $90.00. What percent *discount* is this? **≈52%**

Review

In 16–21, solve. Do at least one of these in your head. *(Lessons 6-1, 6-2)*

16. $3a - 2 = 13$ **a = 5**

17. $7 + 5x = 24$ **$x = \frac{17}{5}$**

18. $\frac{1}{2}t + 4 = -2$ **t = -12**

19. $-4y + 30 = 12$ **y = 4.5**

20. $6B - \frac{2}{3} = \frac{3}{4}$ **$B = \frac{17}{72}$**

21. $-c + 3.4 = 6.21$ **c = -2.81**

22. You estimate that a trip to South America to see relatives will cost $1000 for air fare and $60 a day for living expenses.
- **a.** What will it cost to stay *n* days? **1000 + 60*n***
- **b.** How long can you stay for $1500? *(Lesson 6-1)* **over 8 days, but not over 9**

23. Use the formula $F = \frac{9}{5}C + 32$ to find the Celsius equivalent of 32°F. *(Lesson 6-2)* **C = 0°**

24. Simplify $-q \cdot -r \cdot -r$. *(Lesson 4-3)* **$-qr^2$**

25. The average mass of air molecules is $30 \cdot 1.66 \cdot 10^{-24}$ grams. Write this number in scientific notation. *(Appendix)* **4.98×10^{-23}**

26. Calculate in your head using the division fact 1625 ÷ 25 = 65. *(Previous course)*
- **a.** 162.5 ÷ 25 **6.5**
- **b.** 16.25 ÷ 25 **.65**
- **c.** 1.625 ÷ 25 **.065**

27. What are the coordinates of the point 2 units to the right and 4 units down from (*x*, *y*)? *(Lesson 2-5)* **(x + 2, y − 4)**

Exploration

28. In 1985, when IBM announced that it would no longer market the PC Jr. computer, *USA Today* reported:

> "Omni Computer Inc. of Des Moines, Iowa, cleared out its last 12 PC Jrs. in one day by announcing it would cut the price 10% (of the previous price) every hour, starting at the list of $1269, until the store closed at 5 P.M."

Suppose the store opened at 9 A.M. and the first price cut occurred at 10 A.M.
- **a.** What price would be charged at 1:15 P.M.? **$832.59**
- **b.** What price would be charged at 4:49 P.M.? **$606.96**
- **c.** Write an expression that gives the cost after *n* hours. **$.9^n \cdot 1269$**

EXTENSION

Have students use their calculators and the key sequence below to solve **Questions 28a and 28b.** Point out that the key sequence is based on the expression found in **Question 28c.**

.9 [y^x] *n* [×] 1269 [=]

EVALUATION

A quiz covering Lessons 6-1 through 6-3 is provided in the Teacher's Resource File.

Alternative Assessment
Have **small groups** of students write problems that can be solved by using an equation of the form $ax + b = c$. Then have them pose their problems to the class and solve them. Give extra points if the equation must first be simplified by using the Distributive Property in order to be changed to the form $ax + b = c$.

ADDITIONAL ANSWERS

5. $h + h + \frac{1}{4}h = 90{,}000$
Two heirs receive $40,000 each; third heir receives $10,000.

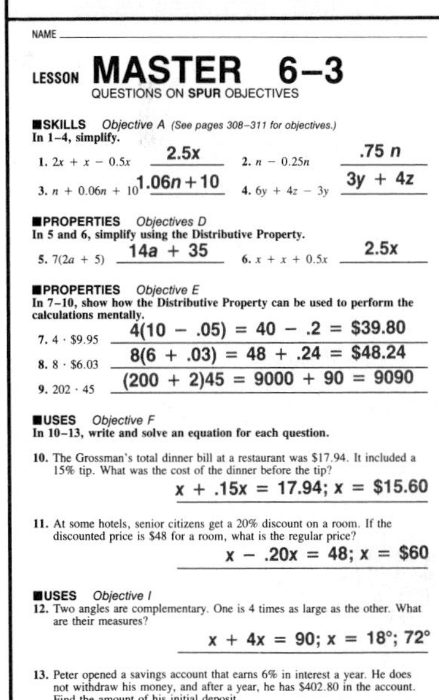

NAME ______

LESSON **MASTER 6–3**
QUESTIONS ON **SPUR** OBJECTIVES

■**SKILLS** *Objective A (See pages 308–311 for objectives.)*
In 1–4, simplify.

1. $2x + x - 0.5x$ **2.5x**
2. $n - 0.25n$ **.75 n**
3. $n + 0.06n + 10$ **1.06n + 10**
4. $6y + 4z - 3y$ **3y + 4z**

■**PROPERTIES** *Objectives D*
In 5 and 6, simplify using the Distributive Property.

5. $7(2a + 5)$ **14a + 35**
6. $x + x + 0.5x$ **2.5x**

■**PROPERTIES** *Objective E*
In 7–10, show how the Distributive Property can be used to perform the calculations mentally.

7. 4 · $9.95 **4(10 − .05) = 40 − .2 = $39.80**
8. 8 · $6.03 **8(6 + .03) = 48 + .24 = $48.24**
9. 202 · 45 **(200 + 2)45 = 9000 + 90 = 9090**

■**USES** *Objective F*
In 10–13, write and solve an equation for each question.

10. The Grossman's total dinner bill at a restaurant was $17.94. It included a 15% tip. What was the cost of the dinner before the tip?
x + .15x = 17.94; x = $15.60

11. At some hotels, senior citizens get a 20% discount on a room. If the discounted price is $48 for a room, what is the regular price?
x − .20x = 48; x = $60

■**USES** *Objective I*

12. Two angles are complementary. One is 4 times as large as the other. What are their measures?
x + 4x = 90; x = 18°; 72°

13. Peter opened a savings account that earns 6% in interest a year. He does not withdraw his money, and after a year, he has $402.80 in the account. Find the amount of his initial deposit.
x + .06x = 402.80; x = $380

46

LESSON 6-4

RESOURCES
- Lesson Master 6-4
- Visual for Teaching Aid 30: Graphs for **Questions 13 and 25**
- Computer Master 11

OBJECTIVE

G Describe patterns and answer questions in repeated addition or repeated subtraction situations.

TEACHING NOTES

The main topic of this chapter is equations, but this involves a lot of work with expressions also. You may have to help students distinguish between the two here. We look for an expression for the *n*th term of a sequence, then often use it to write an equation in order to answer a question.

For the parking example that opens the lesson, point out that to calculate the charge for parking 4 hours 10 minutes, the time would be rounded up to 5 hours.

Reading In **Example 2,** the words *sequence* and *term* may be unfamiliar. Instead of giving a definition first, you might ask students what they understood the words to mean from the reading.

LESSON

6-4 Repeated Addition and Subtraction

PARKING CHARGES

1 HOUR	$1.50
2 HOURS	2.30
3 HOURS	3.10
4 HOURS	3.90
5 HOURS	4.70

each additional hour $ .80

Equations of the form $ax + b = c$ often arise from situations of repeated addition or subtraction. For instance, consider the rates charged by a parking garage in a big city, as shown in the sign at the left. If a person left his car in the garage for a week, what would the parking charge be?

With 24 hours per day for 7 days, the person would be charged for 168 hours. Surely we don't want to add 80 cents each hour all these times.

A good strategy is to make a table to find the pattern. In this situation, we work back from the sign to figure out what 0 hours would cost. Then

Hours	Charges	Cost Pattern
0	.70 =	.70 + .80 · 0
1	.70 + .80 =	.70 + .80 · 1
2	.70 + .80 + .80 =	.70 + .80 · 2
3	.70 + .80 + .80 + .80 =	.70 + .80 · 3
4	.70 + .80 + .80 + .80 + .80 =	.70 + .80 · 4

Notice how the hours and cost pattern are related. The number on the far right is the number of hours. This signals an expression for the cost of parking t hours

$t \qquad .70 + .80t$

To find the charge for 168 hours, substitute 168 for t in the cost pattern.

$168 \qquad .70 + .80 \cdot 168 = \$135.10$

The pattern of costs can be used to answer questions about the parking situation.

Example 1 An uncle of yours parks in this garage and is charged $11.10 for parking. How many hours did he park?

Solution The cost is $.70 + .80t$ for parking t hours. So solve

$$.70 + .80t = 11.10.$$

You have solved equations like this in previous lessons. We omit the work steps.

Add -.70 to both sides.	$.80t = 10.40$
Divide both sides by .80.	$t = 13$

Your uncle parked there for 13 hours.

Check You should convince yourself that the answer is reasonable.

The method in Example 1 can be applied to find a formula for any situation involving repeated addition or subtraction of a constant quantity.

Example 2 Find the 88th term in the sequence below where each term is 6 more than the previous one.

7, 13, 19, 25, 31, 37, ...

Solution Make a table. We need a term before the first term, a row 0.

term number	term
0	1
1	$7 = 1 + 6$
2	$13 = 1 + 6 \cdot 2$
3	$19 = 1 + 6 \cdot 3$
4	$25 = 1 + 6 \cdot 4$
5	$31 = 1 + 6 \cdot 5$
6	$37 = 1 + 6 \cdot 6$
⋮	⋮

In the table, the number 6 is added n times to get the nth term. So

n $\qquad$ $1 + 6n$

To find the 88th term in the sequence, substitute 88 for n.

88 $\qquad$ $1 + 6 \cdot 88 = 529$

The 88th term is 529.

In Example 2, $1 + 6n$ is an expression for the nth term in the sequence. This expression enables you to answer some questions easily.

Computer You (or your students) may notice that line 20 in the program on page 279 could include a STEP command. For example,

```
20 FOR N = 1 TO 200
   STEP 6
```

Then the loop would be executed only for N = 1, 7, 13, 19, . . . , 199, computing only the first term of the sequence and every sixth term thereafter. We do not use STEP in order to focus on determining the formula for the *n*th term of the sequence.

ADDITIONAL EXAMPLES

1. Al opens a savings account with the $45 he has already saved. Then he deposits $4 each week in the account.

a. Write an expression for the amount Al has after *w* weeks.
45 + 4w

b. How long will it take Al to save $425 for a new racing bike?
95 weeks

2. Consider the sequence 83, 92, 101, 110, 119, ...

a. Write an expression for the *n*th term.
74 + 9n

b. Find the 25th term.
299

c. Tell which term is 569.

55th

3. The owner of a frozen-yogurt shop calculates that she pays $60 in wages and utilities for each day the store is open. On the average, for every serving sold, the owner receives $0.48 more than the price of its ingredients. Using -60 to represent her daily costs, write an expression for the owner's profit if *x* servings of frozen yogurt are sold in one day.
-60 + .48x

Example 3 In the sequence 7, 13, 19, 25, 31, 37, ..., of Example 2, what term is 595?

Solution The *n*th term is $1 + 6n$. Here,

$$1 + 6n = 595$$
$$6n = 594$$
$$n = 99.$$

595 is the 99th term.

In the next example, each term decreases by a certain amount. Since we know the beginning amount, no row 0 is needed.

Example 4 A newspaper publishing company buys paper by the boxcar load. It now has 8000 tons of paper. Each week the company uses 475 tons of paper. How much paper will be left *n* weeks from now?

Solution

End of week	Paper left (tons)
1	$8000 - 475 = 7525$
2	$8000 - 475 \cdot 2 = 7050$
3	$8000 - 475 \cdot 3 = 6575$
4	$8000 - 475 \cdot 4 = 6100$

The pattern is now easy to see.

n	$8000 - 475n$

After *n* weeks there will be $8000 - 475n$ tons of paper unless a new shipment comes in.

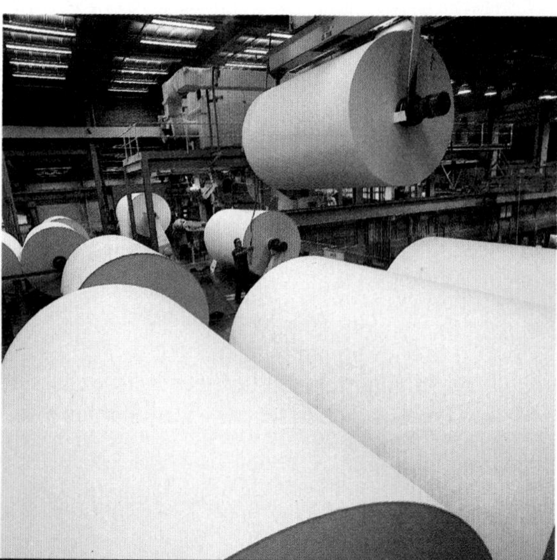

278

The examples in this lesson involve sequences in which a constant amount is repeatedly added or subtracted. Computers are most useful when jobs require speed or a lot of repetition. The following computer program will make a list of the first 200 terms of the sequence in Example 2. The program uses a **FOR/NEXT loop.** The FOR statement tells the computer the number of times to execute the loop. The first time through the loop, N is 1. Each time through, N increases by one. The NEXT statement sends the computer back to the FOR statement.

```
10 PRINT "TERMS OF A SEQUENCE"
20 FOR N = 1 TO 200      The loop will be executed 200 times.
30   LET T = 1 + 6 * N   The formula from Example 2 is evaluated.
40   PRINT T             Print the value of the term.
50 NEXT N                Go back to line 20 with a new value for N.
60 END
```

When the program is run, the computer will print 200 terms. The first three terms printed are:

7
13
19

The last three terms are:

1189
1195
1201

Questions

Covering the Reading

In 1–3, use the parking lot cost pattern $.70 + .80t$.

1. **a.** What does the t in the formula represent? **See margin.**
b. Where does .80 in the formula come from? **See margin.**
c. What would it cost to park 50 hours in this garage? **$40.70**

2. **a.** Does the formula work for parking one hour? **Yes**
b. Does it work for $2\frac{1}{2}$ hours? **No**
c. What is the domain for t in the formula? **positive integers**

3. A person is charged $35.10 for parking. How long did the person park? **43 hrs.**

In 4 and 5, refer to Example 2.

4. Find the 72nd term in the sequence. **433**

5. Which term is 493? **82nd**

NOTES ON QUESTIONS
Questions 10 and 11: Encourage students to write the table in the form at the beginning of the lesson, that is, without the arithmetic being done. For **Question 10,** that would be

1	5
2	5 + 9
3	$5 + 2 \cdot 9$
.	.
.	.
.	.

Question 12: The zeroth term is zero. (Running the buses no days means that no gas is used.) However, students can ignore this term and still write the formula.

ADDITIONAL ANSWERS
1a. ***t*** **is the number of hours the car is parked.**

1b. .80 is the charge for each additional hour beyond the first.

NOTES ON QUESTIONS
Making Connections for Question 13: Students are required to match the lesson examples with graphs of points on a line. This question lays a foundation for the graphing in Chapter 8.

Making Connections for Question 25: We want students to see that the greatest change corresponds to the steepest segment on the graph. This previews the idea of slope as rate of change.

Question 27c: Students can mentally convert $1\frac{3}{4}$ to $\frac{7}{4}$ and then multiply. A nicer method is to realize that $1\frac{3}{4}$ of 12 is equal to 12 plus $\frac{3}{4}$ of 12.
$1\frac{3}{4} \cdot 12 = 1 \cdot 12 + \frac{3}{4} \cdot 12 = 21.$
Thus the Distributive Property is exemplified.

12a.

Days	1	2
Gallons	7500	15,000

Days	3	4
Gallons	22,500	30,000

Days	5	6
Gallons	37,500	45,000

12d.
```
10 PRINT "GAS
   CONSUMPTION TABLE"
20 FOR N = 1 TO 20
30 LET G = 7500 * N
40 PRINT N, G
50 NEXT N
60 END
```

13d. They are discrete points which lie on a line.

28.
```
10 PRINT "SOLVE
   AX + B = C"
20 PRINT "GIVE VALUES
   OF A,B,C"
30 INPUT A,B,C
40 LET X = (C - B)/A
50 PRINT "X ="; X
60 END
```

In 6 and 7, refer to Example 4.

6. How many tons of paper are left at the end of the 10th week? **3250 tons**

7. The company orders new paper when down to 4000 tons. In what week will that occur? **9th**

In 8 and 9, refer to the computer program in this lesson.

8. Suppose line 20 read FOR N = 1 TO 99. How many times would the loop be executed? **99 times**

9. Find the value of T in line 30 for N = 86. **517**

Applying the Mathematics

10.

term number	term
1	5
2	14
3	23
4	32
5	41
6	50

a. What is the first term? **5**
b. How much larger is each term than the previous one? **9**
c. What is the 9th term? **77**
d. Write an expression for the nth term. **$5 + 9(n - 1)$**

11. 1000, 997, 994, 991, 988, 985,
a. Write an expression for the nth term of the sequence. (Hint: Begin with a row 0.) **$1000 - 3(n - 1)$**
b. Use your expression to find the 56th term of the sequence. **835**
c. 400 is which term of the sequence? **201st**

12. One large city school system with 140 school buses uses 7500 gallons of gas per day.
a. Make a chart showing gas consumption for 1, 2, 3, 4, 5 and 6 days. **See margin.**
b. Find a formula for gas consumed in n days. **$7500n$**
c. Calculate the number of gallons of gas consumed in 90 days. **675,000**
d. Write a computer program that will print a list of the gallons of gas consumed for 1 through 20 days. **See margin.**

13. These graphs picture situations discussed in the lesson.

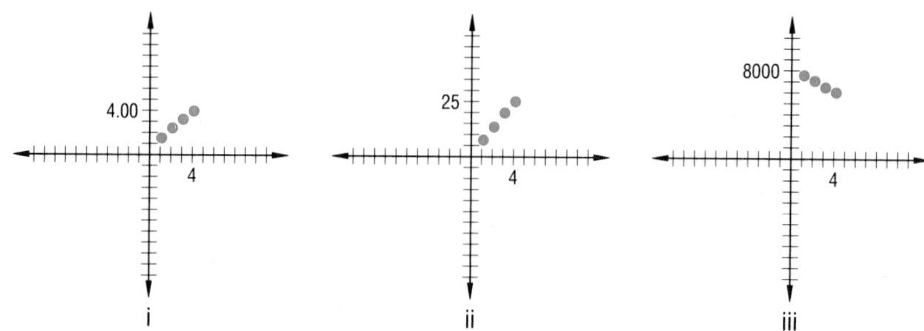

a. Which of these graphs represents the situation in Example 1? **i**
b. Which of these graphs represents the situation in Example 2? **ii**
c. Which of these graphs represents the situation in Example 4? **iii**
d. What do these graphs have in common? **See margin.**

280

Review

In 14 and 15, simplify. *(Lessons 2-2, 6-3)*

14. $3 + -2p + -2q - 7 - 3$ **$-2p - 2q - 7$**

15. $\frac{1}{5} - \frac{2}{3}p + \frac{5}{6}p$ **$\frac{1}{5} + \frac{1}{6}p$**

In 16 and 17, solve. *(Lessons 2-2, 6-3)*

16. $3x - 5x + 12 + -15 = -4$ **$x = .5$**

17. $x - .1x = 1.8$ **$x = 2$**

18. After a 15% discount, a suit costs $144.46. What was the original price? *(Lesson 6-3)* **$169.95**

19. In $\triangle ABC$, $m\angle A = x$, $m\angle B = 2x$, and $\angle C$ is a right angle. What are the measures of the three angles of the triangle? *(Lesson 3-8)* **$m\angle A = 30$; $m\angle B = 60$; $m\angle C = 90$**

In 20–23, solve. *(Lessons 2-7, 4-6, 6-1)*

20. $6 + 4t = -6$ **$t = -3$**

21. $\frac{5}{2}x - 1 = \frac{1}{2}$ **$x = \frac{3}{5}$**

22. $3 + y < 50$ **$y < 47$**

23. $3z < 231$ **$z < 77$**

24. Roberto traveled 53 mph for $2\frac{1}{2}$ hours. How many miles did he travel? *(Lesson 4-2)* **132.5**

25. Refer to the graph below. Douglas, Arizona is typical of a monsoon area, an area in which a wind system causes yearly rain to be concentrated in a few months. *(Lesson 2-4)*

a. During what months is the average rainfall in Douglas less than 1 in.? **January, February, March, April, May, June, October, November**

b. What months have the highest average rainfall? **July and August**

c. Give the average rainfall for April in Douglas. **zero inches**

d. Between which two consecutive months is there the greatest change in rainfall? **June and July**

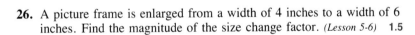

Average monthly rainfall in Douglas, Arizona (inches)

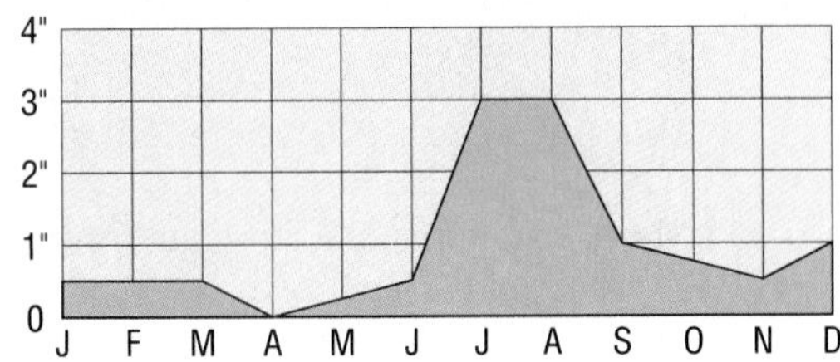

26. A picture frame is enlarged from a width of 4 inches to a width of 6 inches. Find the magnitude of the size change factor. *(Lesson 5-6)* **1.5**

27. Calculate in your head. *(Lesson 4-2)*

a. $4 \cdot \frac{3}{4}$ **3**

b. $12 \cdot \frac{3}{4}$ **9**

c. $12 \cdot 1\frac{3}{4}$ **21**

d. $12 \cdot \frac{4}{3}$ **16**

Exploration

28. Write a computer program to ask for the values of A, B, and C and then print the solution to $Ax + B = C$. **See margin.**

Computer for Question 28: To write this program, students are required to use the algorithm from Lesson 6-2. The program can be patterned after the program in **Question 31** of Lesson 2-6.

FOLLOW-UP

MORE PRACTICE

For more questions on SPUR Objectives, use *Lesson Master 6-4*, shown below.

EXTENSION

Computer Ask students to include a run-again option in the program they wrote for **Question 28.** For example,

```
60 PRINT "RUN AGAIN?
   (Y/N)"
70 INPUT R$
80 IF R$ = "Y" GOTO 10
90 END
```

NAME ______

LESSON **MASTER 6–4**
QUESTIONS ON **SPUR** OBJECTIVES

■USES *Objective G (See pages 308–311 for objectives.)*
In 1–4, find the difference between two successive terms. Then give a formula for the nth term.

	Difference	*n*th term
1. 2, 5, 8, 11, . . .	3	$2 + 3(n - 1)$
2. 15, 11, 7, 3, . . .	-4	$15 - 4(n - 1)$
3. -1.3, -1.1, -0.9, . . .	.2	$-1.3 + .2(n - 1)$
4. $\frac{1}{4}, \frac{1}{2}, \frac{3}{4}, 1, \ldots$	$\frac{1}{4}$	$\frac{1}{4}n$

5. In the sequence 3, 8, 13, 18, . . . , which term is 48? **the 10th**

6. In the sequence 14.8, 14.5, 14.2, 13.9, . . . , which term is 11.8? **the 11th**

7. In May, a store begins a closeout sale on coats by charging $34 per coat. The store reduces this price $5 per week until no coats remain. After how many weeks will remaining coats sell for $9 each? **5 weeks**

8. A taxi company charges $1.10 for the first 0.1 mile, and $.10 for each additional 0.1 mile. If a trip costs a total of $2.60, how many miles is the trip? **1.5 miles**

9. At 4 P.M. Jill must still drive 286 miles to reach her destination. She would like to stop for the night at 7 P.M. How fast must she drive to be 100 miles from her destination when she stops? **62 mph**

10. In a certain bank, the minimum balance you must have in a checking account to avoid paying a service charge is $100. Ruth has a balance of $638. If she withdraws $48 a month for a car payment and makes no deposits, how many payments can she make without having a service charge? **11 payments**

 47

LESSON 6-5

RESOURCES

■ Lesson Master 6-5

OBJECTIVE

B Solve linear equations with the variable on one side.

TEACHING NOTES

All the problems could be assigned as a night's homework. Then, in class, you could review those questions which caused difficulty. Or, you could assign all questions except those with numbers divisible by 5. This leaves **Questions 5, 10, 15, 20, 25, and 30** (one of each type) for in-class work.

Error Analysis Students often check by doing a problem over, a procedure which is more likely to repeat any error than to correct it. You may wish to introduce the line-by-line check, a procedure which enables students to analyze their work. For instance, suppose a student erroneously solves **Question 4** as follows:

$$-100 = 6D + 500$$
$$-400 = 6D$$
$$-\frac{400}{6} = D$$
$$-\frac{200}{3} = D$$

Now substitute -200/3 for D in each line. It will work in each step except the first. This shows that the error was made in going from the first step to the second.

LESSON

6-5 Mid-Chapter Review

You need to be able to solve equations of the form $ax + b = c$ in order to solve the equations of the next lessons. You also need to be able to translate situations into expressions of the form $ax + b$. This lesson gives you practice should you need it. There are no new ideas.

To solve equations of the form $ax + b = c$, add $-b$ to both sides. Then multiply both sides by $\frac{1}{a}$. Try these.

1. $7a + 40 = 33$ **a = -1**

2. $46 + 32b = 1230$ **b = 37**

3. $-3c - 2 = -4$ **c = $\frac{2}{3}$**

4. $-100 = 6D + 500$ **D = -100**

5. $0 = 7e + 3$ **e = $-\frac{3}{7}$**

6. $-f + 36 = 50$ **f = -14**

The same algorithm works if a, b, and c are decimals or fractions. Solve these.

7. $\frac{2}{3}g + \frac{1}{3} = \frac{7}{3}$ **g = 3**

8. $\frac{3}{5}h - 2 = 13$ **h = 25**

9. $8.8 + 3.1i = 42.9$ **i = 11**

10. $1024 = 1000 + .06j$ **j = 400**

11. $-\frac{1}{2}k + 3 = 4$ **k = -2**

12. $8L - 0.4 = 9.24$ **L = 1.205**

Sometimes one or both sides of an equation need to be simplified to get the equation in the form $ax + b = c$.

13. $11m + 12m + 13m + 14 = 15$ **m = $\frac{1}{36}$**

14. $31 = 2n - 3n + 4$ **n = -27**

15. $p + .2p = 120$ **p = 100**

16. $7.46 = q - .25q$ **q ≈ ~~0.0946~~** 9.946

17. $1000 + r + 3r + 3r = 9400$ **r = 1200**

18. $5s + 55 = 555 + 5555$ **s = 1211**

Many situations lead to equations of this form. For these, first write an equation. Then solve it.

19. With a 6% tax, a sofa cost $720.80. How much did the sofa cost without tax? **$680.00**

282

20. After a 30% discount, a compact disc player cost \$139.30. What was the original cost of the player? **\$199.00**

21. There is \$150 in a fund for a school dance. Tickets will be \$4.50 apiece. How many persons must attend in order to cover the estimated expenses of \$400? **56 persons**

22. The formula relating shoe size S and foot length L in women is $S = 3L - 22$. What is the approximate length of a foot of a woman who wears a size 7 shoe? **10 in.**

23. Connie babysat last weekend and earned \$8.50 for sitting for 4 hours. This included an extra \$1.50 because she took some long phone messages. What does she charge for sitting? **\$1.75**

24. If the height h of a man and the length f of his femur (both in centimeters) are approximately related by the formula $h = 69.089 + 2.238f$, what should be the length of a femur of a 6-ft man? (Note: Remember that 1 inch = 2.54 cm. You will have to first calculate the number of cm in 6 feet.)
50.84 cm; about 51 cm

25. The Judson family used 160 New Year's cards this year. Six cards were spoiled; the rest were mailed. Mrs. Judson addressed twice as many as her husband and three times as many as her son. How many cards did her son address? **28 cards**

26. If you work 40 hours a week for \$5.25 an hour and make time-and-a-half for overtime, how long must you work in order to earn \$250 in a week? (Hint: Let h be the number of hours of overtime.) **Total time = 5.08 + 40 = 45.08 hours**

Repeated addition and subtraction situations also lead to equations of the form $ax + b = c$. In these situations, first write a formula for a general term. Then use the formula to answer the question.

27. A sequence begins 3, 11, 19, 27, 35, ..., and every term is 8 more than the preceding. Which term of the sequence is 331?
$3 + 8(n - 1) = 331$; 42nd term

28. A parking garage charges \$.30 for the first hour and \$.20 each succeeding hour. How long was a car parked if the cost of parking is \$1.90? **$.30 + .20n = 1.90$; 9 hours**

29. If you began the school year with 1000 sheets of notebook paper and are using 6 sheets a day, in how many days will you have only 100 sheets left? **$1000 - 6n = 100$; 150 days**

30. The number of court cases in a city was 729 in 1985 and has been increasing by about 15 a year since then. In what year, if this trend continues, will the number of cases hit 1000? (Hint: Let the unknown n equal the number of years after 1985.)
$729 + 15n = 1000$; 2004

NOTES ON QUESTIONS

Questions 7-12: Now that the Distributive Property is available, students can solve these equations by first clearing the fractions.

Question 21: This can be answered by solving the inequality $150 + 4.50x \geq 400$ as well as an equation.

Question 26: The time-and-a-half salary is 1.50 • \$5.25/hr, or \$7.875/hr. If the rounding is done before solving the equation, the answer you get is slightly different than if the rounding is done afterwards.

FOLLOW-UP

MORE PRACTICE
For more review questions, use *Lesson Master 6-5*, shown below.

NAME ____________

LESSON **MASTER 6–5**
QUESTIONS ON **SPUR** OBJECTIVES

■**SKILLS** *Objective B* *(See pages 308–311 for objectives.)*
In 1–8, solve.

1. $3a + 20 = -31$ — **$a = -17$**
2. $-c + 4 = -24$ — **$c = 28$**
3. $-72 - 18k = 18$ — **$k = -5$**
4. $-1.3 - -1.1x = -0.9$ — **$x = \frac{4}{11}$ or $.\overline{36}$**
5. $\frac{1}{4}y + -\frac{1}{2} = \frac{3}{4}$ — **$y = 5$**
6. $15d + 3d - 26d = -64$ — **$d = 8$**
7. $.8m - 4.3m + 3.7m = -8.0$ — **$m = -40$**
8. $\frac{1}{2}n + -\frac{5}{4}n = \frac{1}{4}n + \frac{7}{8}$ — **$n = -\frac{7}{8}$**

9. The formula for finding the area of a triangle is $A = \frac{1}{2}bh$, where A is the area, b is the base, and h is the height. What is the height of a triangle that has a base of 3 cm and an area of 12 cm^2? **$h = 8$ cm**

10. In the sequence 3, 10, 17, 24, . . . , which term of the sequence is 52? **the 8th term**

11. Not including the 7% sales tax, a sweater cost \$28.42. How much did the sweater cost with tax? **\$30.41**

12. The Dennisons went to a Mexican restaurant and ordered tacos. Mr. Dennison ate twice as many tacos as Mrs. Dennison, and Greg Dennison ate three times as many tacos as his mother. If they ordered 12 tacos, how many did Greg eat? **6 tacos**

13. A gallon of gasoline costs \$1.02 at Bob's filling station. If you pay \$11.67 to fill your tank completely, how many gallons of gasoline did you buy? Round to the nearest hundredth. **11.44 gallons**

48

LESSON 6-6

RESOURCES
- ■ Lesson Master 6-6
- Visual for Teaching Aid 29: Balance Scales
- Visual for Teaching Aid 31: Sam Loyd Puzzle
- Computer Master 12

OBJECTIVES

B Solve equations of the form $ax + b = cx + d$.
D Apply and recognize properties associated with linear equations.
G Describe patterns and answer questions in repeated addition or repeated subtraction situations.
I Answer questions about situations combining addition and multiplication.
J Translate balance scale models into equations.

TEACHING NOTES

The algorithm for solving $ax + b = cx + d$ has just one more step than that for $ax + b = c$, and it is appropriate to talk about the famous Polya problem-solving strategy: *If you cannot solve a problem, try to reduce it to one that you can solve.* The balance scale representation that opens this chapter is useful for this purpose. In one step the equation is reduced to $3B + 6 = 18$, an equation whose solution has already been studied.

LESSON 6-6

Solving $ax + b = cx + d$

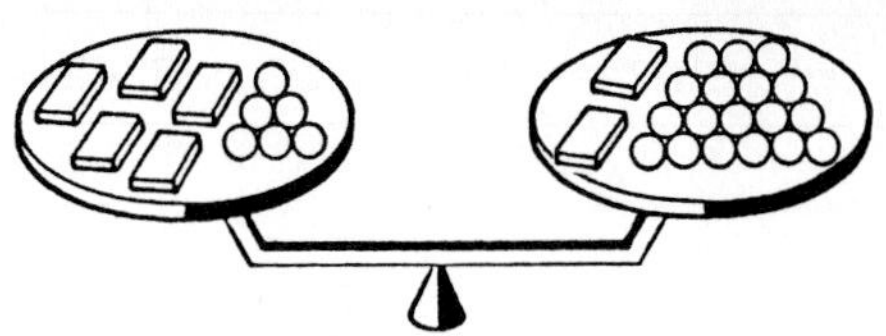

This diagram of a balance scale is similar to the one in Lesson 6-1. The circles represent one-kilogram weights and the weight of each box is unknown. If B is the weight of one box, then the situation is described by

$$5B + 6 = 2B + 18.$$

Notice that the variable B is on each side of the equation.

To solve this equation pictorially, remove 2 boxes from each pan.

$$3B + 6 = 18$$

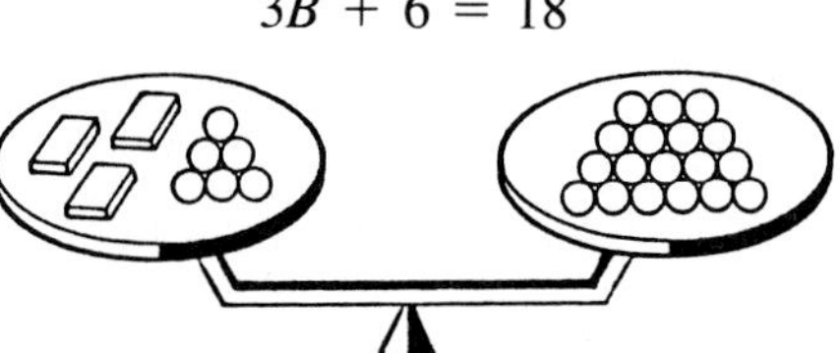

Remove 6 weights from each pan.

$$3B = 12$$

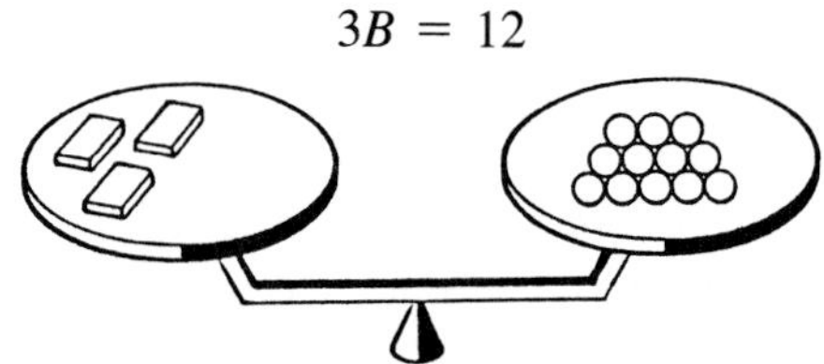

Then leave one third of the contents of each scale.

$$B = 4$$

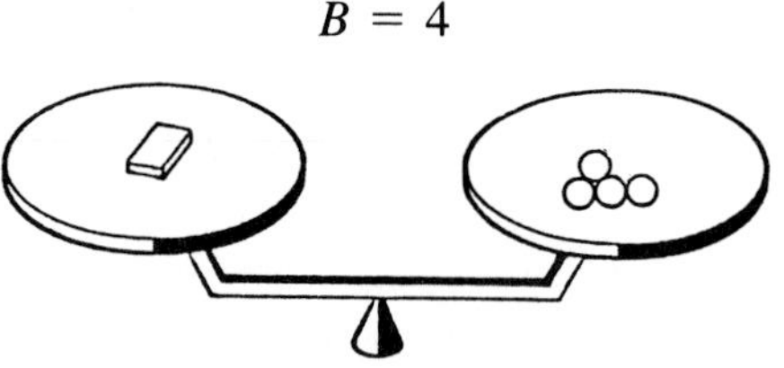

One box weighs 4 kilograms.

Example 1 shows this process algebraically. Work steps are put in. Reasons are given for the key steps.

Example 1 Solve: $5B + 6 = 2B + 18$

Solution $-2B + 5B + 6 = -2B + 2B + 18$ Addition Property of Equality (Remove 2 boxes.)

$3B + 6 = 18$

$3B + 6 + -6 = 18 - 6$ Addition Property of Equality (Remove 6 kg.)

$3B = 12$

$\frac{1}{3}(3B) = \frac{1}{3}(12)$ Multiplication Property of Equality

$B = 4$ (Leave $\frac{1}{3}$ of each side.)

Check Substitute 6 for B in the original equation.

Does $5 \cdot 4 + 6 = 2 \cdot 4 + 18$?

$20 + 6 = 8 + 18$? Yes.

The equation in Example 1 has the unknown variable on each side. It is of the form

$$ax + b = cx + d$$

and is called the **general linear equation.** To solve such equations, you need three key steps. In the first step, add either $-cx$ or $-ax$ to both sides. This removes a variable from one side and leaves an equation of the kind you have solved in previous lessons. Here is Example 1, written as an expert might, without the work steps.

Given	$5B + 6 = 2B + 18$
Step 1	$3B + 6 = 18$
Step 2	$3B = 12$
Step 3	$B = 4$

Example 2 Solve $-7y + 54 = 2y - 36$

Solution We could add either $7y$ or $-2y$ to both sides. We choose to add $-2y$.

$$-2y + -7y + 54 = -2y + 2y - 36$$

Adding like terms gives a simpler equation.

$$-9y + 54 = -36$$

Now add -54 to each side and simplify.

$$-9y + 54 + -54 = -36 + -54$$
$$-9y = -90$$

Finally, multiply both sides by $-\frac{1}{9}$ (or divide by -9).

$$y = 10$$

When solving these equations, students may collect the variable terms on either side. However, it is convenient to avoid coming up with a negative coefficient for the variable. You may want to have your students follow this rule: Eliminate the variable term that has the smaller coefficient.

Alternate Approach **Example 3** could be simplified by thinking of the populations in thousands. Then the equation becomes $565 + 2.5n = 636 - 8n$.

Making Connections In **Example 3,** the first two lines of the solution come from the repeated addition ideas of Lesson 6-3. Notice that the rounded answer is appropriate for this kind of situation.

ADDITIONAL EXAMPLES

1. Solve $14k - 20 = 21k - 43$.
9

2. Solve $-a + 11 = -6a - 4$.
-3

3. In a very tall office building, one elevator leaves the third floor and goes up at a speed of 2 floors per second. Another elevator leaves the 59th floor at exactly the same moment and descends at a speed of 2 floors per second. If the two do not stop, how long will it take them to pass? Write an equation, and answer the question.
$3 + 2t = 59 - 2t$; 14 seconds

4. At what floor will the elevators in the preceding example pass?
31st

Check Substitute 10 for y wherever y appears in the original equation.
Does $-7 \cdot 10 + 54 = 2 \cdot 10 - 36$?
$-70 + 54 = 20 - 36$?
Yes, both sides equal -16.

Many situations lead to the solving of equations with variables on both sides.

Example 3 The 1980 population of Columbus, Ohio was 565,000 people. In the 1970s it had been increasing at an average rate of 2500 people per year. In 1980, the population of Milwaukee, Wisconsin was 636,000. In the 70s it was decreasing at the rate of 8000 people a year. If these rates continued, in what year would the populations in Columbus and Milwaukee be the same?

Solution After n years the population in Columbus will be $565{,}000 + 2500n$. After n years the population in Milwaukee will be $636{,}000 - 8000n$. The populations would be the same when

$$565{,}000 + 2500n = 636{,}000 - 8000n.$$

Solve this equation for n. We add $8000n$ to each side.

$$\begin{aligned} 565{,}000 + 2500n + 8000n &= 636{,}000 - 8000n + 8000n \\ 565{,}000 + 10{,}500n &= 636{,}000 \\ -565{,}000 + 565{,}000 + 10{,}500n &= -565{,}000 + 636{,}000 \\ 10{,}500n &= 71{,}000 \\ n &\approx 6.76 \end{aligned}$$

At these rates, in 1986 or 1987 (that is, after 6.76 years), the populations would be the same.

Check The population of Columbus would be $565{,}000 + 6.76 \cdot 2500$, or 581,900. The population of Milwaukee would be $636{,}000 - 6.76 \cdot 8000$, or 581,920. These are close enough given the accuracy of the information.

286

Questions

Covering the Reading

1. The boxes are of equal weight. Each circle weighs 1 kg.
   a. What equation is pictured by this balance scale? **See margin.**

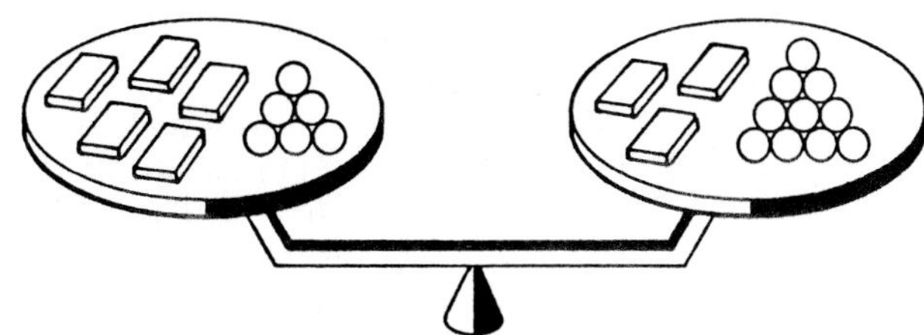

   b. What three steps can be done with the scale to find the weight of a box? **See margin**

2. **a.** To solve $8x + 7 = 2x + 9$, what could you add to both sides to collect all of the variables on one side of the equation? **-2x or -8x**
   b. Solve the equation in **a**. $x = \frac{1}{3}$

3. Solve the equation of Example 2 by adding $7y$ to both sides. $y = 10$

In 4–7, solve.

4. $12x + 1 = 3x - 8$ $x = -1$
5. $43 - 8w = 25 + w$ $w = 2$
6. $7y = 5y - 3$ $x = -\frac{3}{2}$
7. $2 - z = 3 - 4z$ $z = \frac{1}{3}$

8. Alaska has a population of 480,000 which has been increasing at a rate of 6000 people a year. Delaware's population of 606,000 has been increasing at a rate of 4000 people a year. If the rates of increase do not change, in how many years will the populations be equal? **63 years**

Applying the Mathematics

In 9–12, solve.

9. $\frac{1}{2}a + 3 = \frac{1}{3}a + 4$ $a = 6$
10. $3 - 8b + 2b = 4 + 2b - b$ $b = -\frac{1}{7}$
11. $1.5c + 17 = 0.8c - 32$ -70
12. $3d + 4d + 5 = 6d + 7d + 8$ $-\frac{1}{2}$

13. Kim has \$20 and is saving at a rate of \$6 per week. Jenny has \$150 but is spending at a rate of \$4 per week. **a.** After how many weeks will each have the same amount of money? **b.** After how many *days* will each have the same amount of money? **a) 13; b) 91**

14. Five more than twice a number is three more than four times the number. What is the number? **1**

NOTES ON QUESTIONS
Question 3: This shows that the variable terms can be collected on either side.

Questions 10 and 12: Make sure students see that simplifying is the first step in solving these equations.

Question 15: Explain that we are assuming that the rates of change will remain constant, which will probably not happen. This does allow us to make some predictions, but the quality of the prediction is only as good as the quality of the assumption.

ADDITIONAL ANSWERS
1a. Let *B* = weight of 1 box; then $5B + 6 = 3B + 10$

1b. Remove 3 boxes from both sides, remove 6 kg from both sides, divide the contents of both sides in half.

NOTES ON QUESTIONS
Questions 18-20: These require a better knowledge of the properties than just recognizing which property was used. Students may need to refer to previous lessons to refresh their memory.

Error Analysis for Question 21: A common error is to set up this question as $.95x = 10$ rather than as $1.05x = 10$. This is caused by wrongly thinking of deducting the 5% tax from the $10 rather than adding the 5% tax to the original cost. It should help understanding if you set the equation up as $x = 10 - .05x$, and change it to $1.05x = 10$.

Question 27: A diagram for the Sam Loyd puzzle is given on *Teaching Aid 31.*

FOLLOW-UP

MORE PRACTICE
For more questions on SPUR Objectives, use *Lesson Master 6-6,* shown on page 289.

EXTENSION
Students may enjoy doing other puzzles by Sam Loyd. His books are still being sold and may be available in your library. Many of his puzzles first appeared in newspapers and the books include discussions of readers' solutions.

EVALUATION
Alternative Assessment
Give students equations of the form $ax + b = cx + d$, for example, $5x + 3 = 3x + 7$. Have them use *Teaching Aid 29* to draw a diagram for each sentence. Then they should solve it using diagrams.

a) $54.73 - .33x$; b) $49.36 - .18x$

15. In 1988, the women's world record for the 100-m freestyle in swimming was 54.73 seconds. It had been decreasing at a rate of 0.33 seconds a year. The men's record was 49.36 seconds and had been decreasing at 0.18 seconds a year. Assume that these rates continued.
a. What would the women's 100-meter record be x years after 1988?
b. What would the men's 100-meter record be x years after 1988?
c. After how many years would the records be the same? $\approx$ **36 yr**

16. Stuart is offered two payment plans when he buys his new stereo. Under Plan A, he pays $100 down and x dollars a month for 4 months. In Plan B, he pays nothing down and $10 more per month than in Plan A for 6 months.
a. Write an equation to find x. $100 + 4x = 6(x + 10)$
b. What is the monthly payment under each plan? **See margin.**

Review

17. Evaluate these expressions in your head for $r = 4$. *(Lesson 1-4)*
a. r^2 16 **b.** $r^2 + r$ 20 **c.** $-10r^2$ -160

In 18–20, use the property named to write another expression equivalent to the one given.

18. $(5x + 5y) + 6$; Associative Property of Addition. *(Lesson 2-1)* $5x + (5y + 6)$

19. xyz; Commutative Property of Multiplication. *(Lesson 4-1)* **See margin.**

20. $13x - x$; Distributive Property. *(Lesson 6-3)* $(13 - 1)x$

21. A retailer wants to sell an item for exactly $10 including sales tax. If the sales tax is 5%, write an equation to find how much he or she should charge for the item without tax. *(Lesson 6-3)* $1.05c = 10$

22. During one week in Chicago in the spring, it rained on r days and was sunny the other days.
a. Write an expression in terms of r to tell how many days were sunny. $7 - r$
b. What is the probability that a randomly selected day from that week was sunny? *(Lessons 3-6, 1-7)* $\frac{7 - r}{7}$ or $1 - \frac{r}{7}$

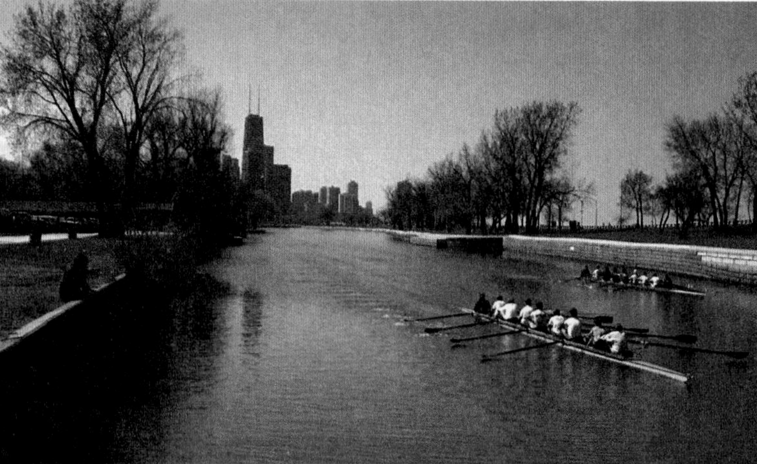

23. In a rectangular room, $\frac{2}{3}$ of the floor area is covered by a 9 ft by 12 ft rug.

a. Write an equation to find the area A of the floor. $\frac{2}{3}A = 9 \cdot 12$

b. Solve the equation. *(Lesson 2-6)* $A = 162$ **square feet**

In 24–26, solve. *(Lesson 4-4)*

24. $\frac{4}{3}y = -2$ $y = -\frac{3}{2}$

25. $\frac{4}{3}z - \frac{11}{3}z = -2$ $z = \frac{6}{7}$

26. $\frac{4}{3}w - \frac{11}{6}w = -2$ $w = 4$

Exploration

27. Here is a puzzle from the book *Cyclopedia of Puzzles*, written by Sam Loyd in 1914. If a bottle and a glass balance with a pitcher, a bottle balances with a glass and a plate, and two pitchers balance with three plates, can you figure out how many glasses will balance with a bottle? **5**

16b. $20 in plan A, $30 in plan B.

19. yxz, xzy, zyx, zxy, yzx

NAME ______

LESSON **MASTER 6–6**
QUESTIONS ON **SPUR** OBJECTIVES

■**SKILLS** *Objective B (See pages 308–311 for objectives.)*
In 1–12, solve.

1. $n + 2 = 3n - 8$ — $n = 5$

2. $6r - 7 = 3r - 22$ — $r = -5$

3. $22 - 5a = 47 - 3a$ — $a = -\frac{25}{2}$

4. $168 - 11t = 293 - 36t$ — $t = 5$

5. $1.9 + 1.8x = 8.2x - 6.9$ — $x = 1.375$

6. $.072v + .063 = .104v - .093$ — $v = 4.875$

7. $\frac{2h}{3} + \frac{1}{2} = \frac{5h}{6} - \frac{3}{4}$ — $h = \frac{15}{2}$

8. $\frac{9b}{5} - 3 = \frac{3b}{10} + 9$ — $b = 8$

9. $\frac{p + 3}{4} = \frac{p - 1}{6}$ — $p = -11$

10. $\frac{y - 8}{2} = \frac{y + 10}{5}$ — $y = 20$

11. $2x + 7 - 3x = 4x + 9 - 3x$ — $x = -1$

12. $16 - 3x - 9 = 28 - 2x + 4$ — $x = -25$

■**PROPERTIES** *Objective D*
In 13 and 14, identify the property being applied.

13. If $\frac{2}{A - 3} = \frac{3}{A + 1}$, then $2A + 2 = 3A - 9$. — **Means-Extremes Property**

14. If $3x + a = -2x + 4a$, then $5x = 3a$. — **Add. Prop. of Equality**

 Continued

NAME ______

LESSON **MASTER 6–6**
(page 2)

■**USES** *Objective G*

15. A magician says, "I am thinking of a number. Twenty-one less than three times the number is five more than the number." Find the number. **13**

16. A tank that contains 340 gallons of brine is being drained at a rate of 15 gallons per hour. Another tank which starts with 60 gallons is being filled at a rate of 20 gallons per hour. After how many hours will they both hold the same amount? **8 hours**

■**USES** *Objective I*

17. Janet has $105.00 and spends $5.00 every week. Marlene has $45.00 and saves $10.00 every week. In how many weeks will they have the same amount of money? **a.** Write an equation that describes this situation, and **b.** solve the problem.

a. $105 - 5w = 45 + 10w$

b. **4 weeks**

■**REPRESENTATIONS** *Objective J*
In 18–20, the boxes in each picture are of equal weight. Every cylinder weighs one pound. For each question, a. write an equation in which B represents the weight of one box, and b. find the weight of one box.

18. a. $2B + 9 = 5B + 3$
b. **2 pounds**

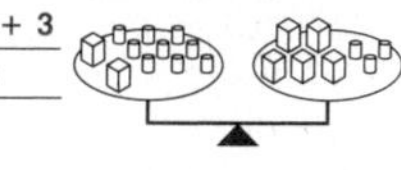

19. a. $3B + 4 = B + 6$
b. **1 pound**

20. a. $6B + 1 = 3B + 10$
b. **3 pounds**

LESSON 6-7

RESOURCES
- Lesson Master 6-7
- Quiz on Lessons 6-4 Through 6-7
- Computer Master 12

OBJECTIVES

C Solve linear inequalities.
D Apply and recognize properties associated with linear inequalities.

TEACHING NOTES

Students can forget to reverse the sense of the inequality when multiplying both sides by a negative. Therefore, it is advantageous to arrange to have the coefficient of the variable term be positive. In fact, this can be done even if there is only one term with a variable. For example,

$$\begin{aligned} -3x + 6 &\le 15 \\ 6 &\le 3x + 15 \\ -9 &\le 3x \\ -3 &\le x \end{aligned}$$

Keeping the coefficient positive requires the flexibility of solving sentences with the variable on the right side.

Error Analysis
Students often find sentences like $3n < 2n$ harder to solve than more complicated ones like $3n + 4 = 2n + 5$. They think that if you add $-2n$ to both sides of $3n < 2n$ there will be nothing left on the right side, forgetting about 0. Stress that zero is a perfectly legitimate number and is the answer to many calculations. Again, emphasize the two-step checking method for inequalities. The

LESSON

6-7 Solving $ax + b < cx + d$

The same steps for solving linear equations that you learned in Lesson 6-6 also work for solving inequalities of the form $ax + b < cx + d$. These are called **linear inequalities.**

Example 1 Graph all solutions to the inequality

$$13x + 18 > 10x + 12.$$

Solution The choice is to add either $-13x$ or $-10x$ to both sides. We add $-10x$.

$$-10x + 13x + 18 > -10x + 10x + 12$$
$$3x + 18 > 12$$

Now add -18. $\quad 3x > -6$

Multiply both sides by $\frac{1}{3}$. $\quad \frac{1}{3} \cdot 3x > \frac{1}{3} \cdot -6$

$$x > -2$$

Here is the graph.

Check Recall that checking an inequality requires two steps.

Step 1: Does $x = -2$ make both sides of the original sentence equal? Does $13 \cdot -2 + 18 = 10 \cdot -2 + 12$?

$-26 + 18 = -20 + 12$? Yes, each equals -8.

Step 2: Try a number that works in $x > -2$. We try 0. Does it work in the original sentence? You should verify that it does.

The reason that linear inequalities and linear equations can be solved with the same steps is that the Addition and Multiplication Properties of Inequality are just like the Addition and Multiplication Properties of Equality. Recall the only exception: multiplying by a negative number reverses the sense of the inequality. This is an important thing to remember, because it can happen in any linear inequality.

For instance, suppose you choose to add $-13x$ to both sides in Example 1. You would get

$$-13x + 13x + 18 > -13x + 10x + 12$$
$$18 > -3x + 12$$

Now add -12 to each side. The inequality remains >.

$$18 + -12 > -3x + 12 + -12$$
$$6 > -3x$$

To find x, multiply both sides by $-\frac{1}{3}$. This multiplication reverses the sense of the inequality.

$$-\tfrac{1}{3} \cdot 6 < -\tfrac{1}{3} \cdot -3x$$
$$-2 < x$$

This inequality is equivalent to that found in Example 1. Any number bigger than -2 works.

As always, many situations lead to these kinds of sentences. Example 2 gives an instance of such a situation.

Example 2 A crate weighs 6 kg when empty. A lemon weighs about 0.2 kg. For economical shipping the crate with lemons must weigh at least 45 kg. How many lemons should be put in the crate?

Solution First, let n be the number of lemons. Then the weight of n lemons is $0.2n$. The weight of the crate with n lemons is $0.2n + 6$, which must be at least 45 kg, so the question can be answered by solving the inequality

$$0.2n + 6 \geq 45.$$

This is of the form $ax + b \geq c$ and is solved like $ax + b = c$. First, add -6 to both sides and simplify.

$$0.2n + 6 + -6 \geq 45 + -6$$
$$0.2n \geq 39$$
$$\frac{0.2n}{0.2} \geq \frac{39}{0.2} \qquad \text{Multiply both sides by } \frac{1}{0.2} \text{ or divide by 0.2.}$$
$$n \geq 195$$

There must be at least 195 lemons in the crate.

Check Step 1: Does $0.2(195) + 6 = 45$?
$39 + 6 = 45$? Yes.
Step 2: Pick some value that works for $n \geq 195$. We choose 200.
Is $0.2(200) + 6 \geq 45$?
$40 + 6 \geq 45$? Yes.

more complicated the problem, the more likely there will be an error, so the more important it is to do a careful check.

ADDITIONAL EXAMPLES

1. Graph the solutions of $-2n - 16 \leq 9n + 17$.

2. Beth has $10.00 to spend for school supplies. She buys a notebook for $4.95 and with the rest she buys paper, which costs 79¢ per package. How many packages of paper can she buy? Write an inequality and answer the question.
$4.95 + .79p \leq 10.00$; She can buy at most 6 packages.

3. Nine times a number is less than the sum of 5 times that number and 13. What is the number? Write an inequality and answer the question.
$9n < 5n + 13$; The number could be any number less than $3\frac{1}{4}$.

NOTES ON QUESTIONS
Question 2: By working out both solutions, students see that the processes give the same result. Some students may prefer having a positive coefficient of k before the last step; other students may prefer having the variable on the left side.

Making Connections for Question 17: This question previews Lesson 6-9 by introducing the pattern that $a - b$ is the opposite of $b - a$.

The lemon crate question of Example 2 could be answered by solving $0.2n + 6 = 45$ and avoiding the inequality. This is true in many situations. But sometimes the inequality can help you determine if an answer is reasonable.

Example 3 Three times a number is less than two times the same number. Find the number.

Solution It may seem that there is no such number. But work it out to see. Let n be such a number. n must be a solution to

$$3n < 2n.$$

Solve this as you would any other linear inequality. Add $-2n$ to each side.

$$3n + -2n < 2n + -2n$$
$$n < 0$$

So if n is any negative number, 3 times it will be less than 2 times it.

Check Let $n = -5$; $3 \cdot -5$ is -15, $2 \cdot -5$ is -10, and -15 is less than -10.

Questions

Covering the Reading

1. The method for solving $ax + b < cx + d$ is like the method for solving the equation __?__. **$ax + b = cx + d$**

2. a. Solve $4k + 3 > 9k + 18$ by first adding $-4k$ to each side. **$-3 > k$**
b. Solve $4k + 3 > 9k + 18$ by first adding $-9k$ to each side. **$k < -3$**
c. Should you get the same solutions to parts a and b? **Yes**

In 3–6, solve and graph the solutions. **See margin for graphs.**

3. $3x + 4 < 19$ **$x < 5$**

4. $-48 + 10a < -8 + 20a$ **$a > -4$**

5. $6 \le 4b + 10$ **$-1 \le b$**

6. $0.12 - 0.03y > 0.27 + 0.07y$ **$-1.5 > y$**

7. A crate weighs 10 kg when empty. A grapefruit weighs about 0.5 kg. How many grapefruit can be put in the crate and still keep the total weight under 40 kg? **59**

8. Five times a number is less than three times the same number. Find the number. **$x < 0$; any number less than 0**

292

ADDITIONAL ANSWERS

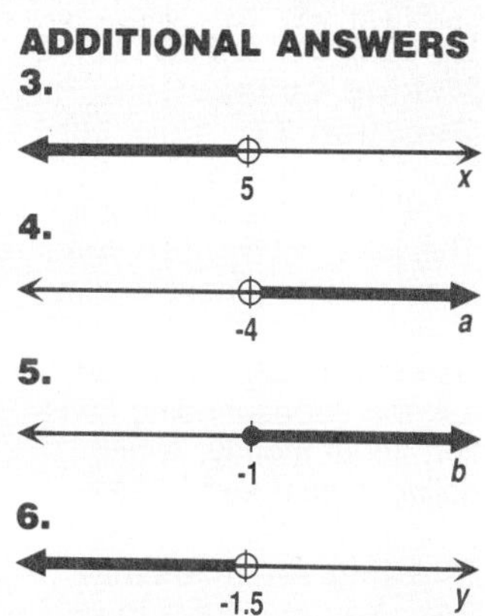

11. packages weighing more than 31.25 ounces

Applying the Mathematics

9. Suppose admission to a carnival is \$4.00. You allow \$3.00 for lunch and \$1.00 for a snack. Each ride is \$.80. You have \$15 to spend. How many rides can you go on? 8

10. A card printer charges \$5.00 to set up each job and an additional \$4.00 per box of 100 cards printed.

a. How much would it cost to print n boxes of cards? $5 + 4n$

b. What is the greatest number of boxes you could have printed for under \$100? 23

11. Sending a package by Fast Fellows Shipping costs \$3.50 plus 10 cents per ounce. Speedy Service charges \$4.75 plus 6 cents per ounce. What weight packages are cheaper at Speedy Service? See margin.

12. Find the two integers that satisfy both these properties.
(i) If you add six to it, the sum is greater than twice it.
(ii) If you add six to it, the sum is less than three times it. 4 and 5

Review

In 13–16, solve. *(Lesson 6-6)*

13. $4x + 12 = -2x - 6$ $x = -3$

14. $60t - 1 = 48t$ $t = \frac{1}{12}$

15. $109 - m = 18m - 5$ $m = 6$

16. $3n - n + 5 = 4n - n + 20$ $n = -15$

17. Three instances of a general pattern are given below. Write the pattern using two variables. *(Previous course)* $-(a - b) = b - a$

$$-(7 - 4) = 4 - 7$$
$$-(\tfrac{8}{3} - \tfrac{5}{6}) = \tfrac{5}{6} - \tfrac{8}{3}$$
$$-(1.2 - 2.1) = 2.1 - 1.2$$

18. Ten club members celebrate at a restaurant. Because it is a large group, the restaurant automatically adds on a 15% tip. If the bill is \$103.90 with the tip, what was the bill without the tip? *(Lesson 6-3)* ≈\$90.35

NOTES ON QUESTIONS
Making Connections for Question 21: Point out that 150% means "all of something plus a half of it." This idea will be used in an example in the next lesson.

Question 23: You can ask the corresponding question about money. A half dollar is what part of $2?

Reading for Question 24: You may have to explain what the word *commission* means.

19. In 1986, according to the Federal Communications Commission, 7.8% of all households in the U.S. were without a telephone. Of 100,000 households, how many would you expect to be without a phone? *(Lesson 5-4)*
7800

20. A car normally priced at $6990 is on sale for $6291. What percent discount is this? *(Lesson 5-3)* **10%**

In 21–23, try to answer the question in your head. If you cannot, then use an equation. *(Lesson 5-4)*

21. What is 150% of 6? **9**

22. 10% of what number is 12? **120**

23. $\frac{1}{2}$ is what percent of 2? **25%**

24. Mr. Roberts sells appliances. He earns $230 per month plus 5% commission on all he sells. He earns E dollars in a month when he sells S dollars worth of appliances. Write an equation that describes how E and S are related. *(Lesson 6-1)* **E = 230 + .05s**

25. The school lunch counter will make up sandwiches in three kinds of bread (white, rye, and whole wheat) and three fillings (ham, chicken, or tuna salad). How many different kinds of sandwiches are possible? *(Lesson 4-7)* **9**

26. What will a computer print on the screen when this program is run? *(Lesson 1-4)* **SOLVE 5 x + 3.4 = 10.18; x = 1.356**

```
10 PRINT "SOLVE 5X + 3.4 = 10.18"
20 LET A = 5
30 LET B = 3.4
40 LET C = 10.18
50 LET X = (C – B)/A
60 PRINT "X = "; X
70 END
```


294

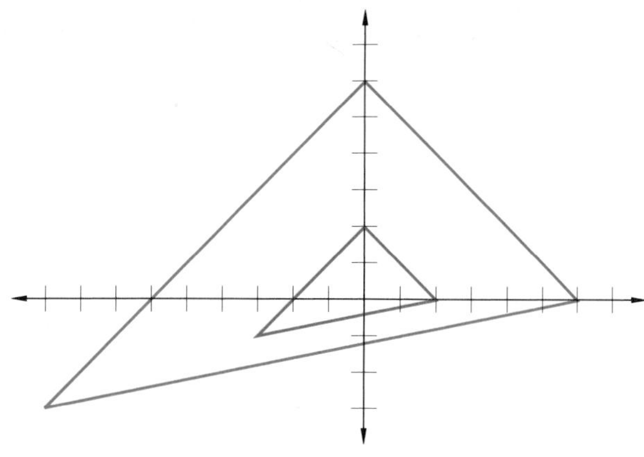

27. Give the magnitude for the size change shown. *(Lesson 5-6)* $\frac{1}{3}$

Preimage point	Image point
(-9, -3)	(-3, -1)
(0, 6)	(0, 2)
(6, 0)	(2, 0)

28. Use this diagram of mileage along Interstate 10. The distance from Los Angeles to New Orleans is 1946 miles. How far is it from San Antonio to Houston? *(Lessons 2-1, 2-6)* **201 miles**

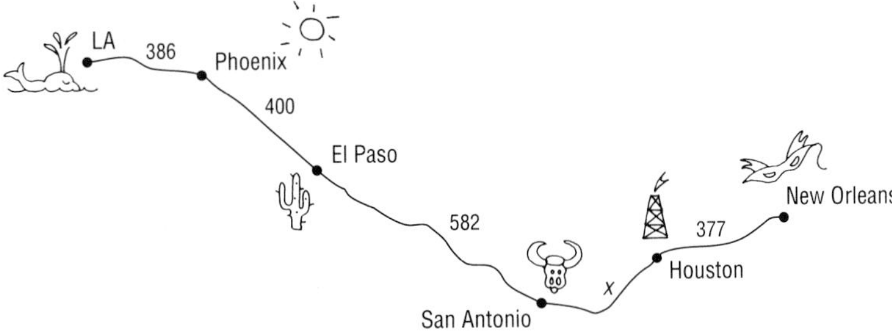

29. Write 725 billion in scientific notation. *(Appendix)* **7.25×10^{11}**

In 30–31, simplify. *(Lessons 2-3, 5-1)*

30. $\frac{x}{4} + \frac{x}{3}$ **$\frac{7x}{12}$**

31. $\frac{\frac{m}{4}}{\frac{12}{n}}$ **$\frac{mn}{48}$**

Exploration

32. There are certain numbers which are less than their squares.
a. Find one such number. **sample: 2, since $2 < 2^2$**
b. Find all such numbers. **All real numbers where $n < 0$ or $n > 1$**

FOLLOW-UP

MORE PRACTICE
For more questions on SPUR Objectives, use *Lesson Master 6-7,* shown below.

EXTENSION
Computer The computer program in **Question 26** can be adapted to solve all equations of the form AX + B = C or those of the form AX + B = CX + D. (sample: Change lines 10–40 as follows:

```
10 PRINT "SOLVE
   AX + B = C"
20 INPUT "WHAT IS A?";A
30 INPUT "WHAT IS B?";B
40 INPUT "WHAT IS C?";C
```

EVALUATION
A quiz covering Lessons 6-4 through 6-7 is provided in the Teacher's Resource File.

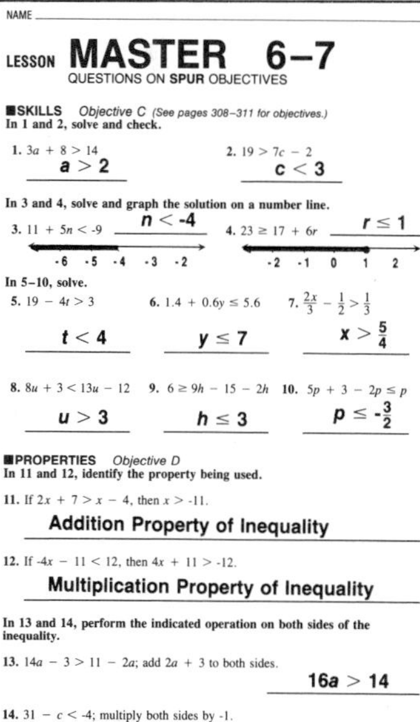

NAME ____________

LESSON **MASTER 6–7**
QUESTIONS ON **SPUR** OBJECTIVES

■SKILLS *Objective C (See pages 308–311 for objectives.)*
In 1 and 2, solve and check.

1. $3a + 8 > 14$ **$a > 2$**
2. $19 > 7c - 2$ **$c < 3$**

In 3 and 4, solve and graph the solution on a number line.

3. $11 + 5n < -9$ **$n < -4$**
4. $23 \geq 17 + 6r$ **$r \leq 1$**

In 5–10, solve.

5. $19 - 4t > 3$ **$t < 4$**
6. $1.4 + 0.6y \leq 5.6$ **$y \leq 7$**
7. $\frac{2x}{3} - \frac{1}{2} > \frac{1}{3}$ **$x > \frac{5}{4}$**
8. $8u + 3 < 13u - 12$ **$u > 3$**
9. $6 \geq 9h - 15 - 2h$ **$h \leq 3$**
10. $5p + 3 - 2p \leq p$ **$p \leq -\frac{3}{2}$**

■PROPERTIES *Objective D*
In 11 and 12, identify the property being used.

11. If $2x + 7 > x - 4$, then $x > -11$. **Addition Property of Inequality**
12. If $-4x - 11 < 12$, then $4x + 11 > -12$. **Multiplication Property of Inequality**

In 13 and 14, perform the indicated operation on both sides of the inequality.

13. $14a - 3 > 11 - 2a$; add $2a + 3$ to both sides. **$16a > 14$**
14. $31 - c < -4$; multiply both sides by -1. **$-31 + c > 4$**

 51

LESSON 6-8

RESOURCES
- Lesson Master 6-8
- Visual for Teaching Aid 32: Diagrams for **Questions 31 and 34**

OBJECTIVES

A Use the Distributive Property to remove parentheses.
B Solve linear equations.
D Apply and recognize the Distributive Property in linear sentences.
J Translate rectangle area models into expressions and equations.

TEACHING NOTES

Alternate Approach
Images can help in remembering this form of the Distributive Property. Write $a(b + c)$ and draw arcs connecting a with b and c.

$a(b + c)$

You may wish to draw a diagram for **Example 1:**

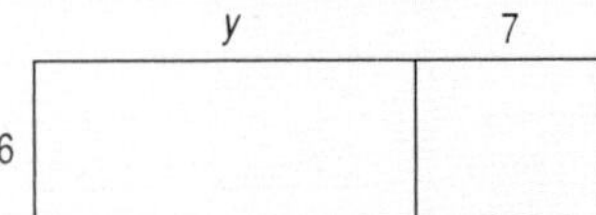

Ask: What is the total area? (Either it is the sum of the areas of the two smaller rectangles, $6y + 42$, or it is the length times the width, $6(y + 7)$, of the large rectangle.) Ask: How can this be checked? (Substitute some number for y and see if the values of the expressions are the same.)

Why the Distributive Property Is So Named

Two rectangles, each having width c, are placed end to end. What is the total area?

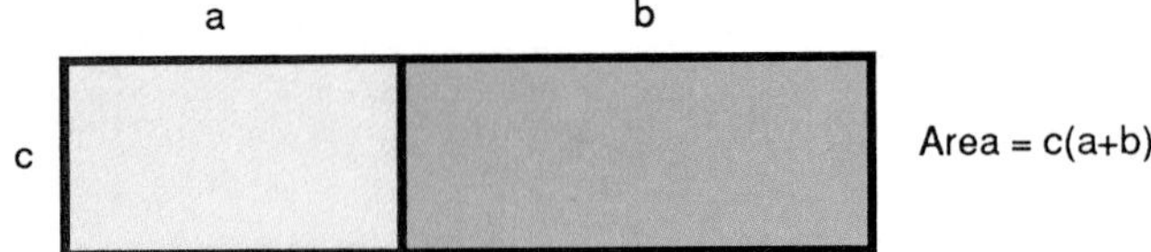

Since the length of this rectangle is $a + b$ and the width is c, the total area is $c(a + b)$. However, the area can also be expressed in a different way, by finding the areas of each smaller rectangle and adding.

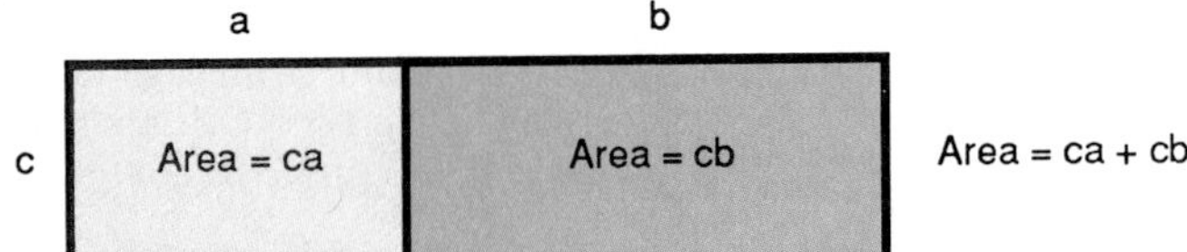

The area is the same, no matter which way it is calculated. This illustrates the pattern

$$c\,(a + b) = ca + cb.$$

This is not a new property. If the sides of this equation are switched and then each side is rearranged using the Commutative Property, the result is the familiar Distributive Property.

The property $c(a + b) = ca + cb$ is another form of the Distributive Property. It tells why the Distributive Property is so named. Multiplying by *c is distributed* over the terms in the sum. This form of the Distributive Property is used to **eliminate parentheses.** Here are some examples.

Examples

1. $6(y + 7) = 6y + 6 \cdot 7$
   $= 6y + 42$
2. $-60\left(\frac{x}{6} - \frac{y}{5}\right) = -60 \cdot \frac{x}{6} - -60 \cdot \frac{y}{5}$
   $= -10x + 12y$
3. $4a(3 + 2b - 5c) = 4a \cdot 3 + 4a \cdot 2b - 4a \cdot 5c$
   $= 12a + 8ab - 20ac$

This form of the Distributive Property shows how to perform some calculations mentally.

Example 4 Calculate in your head how much 5 records cost if they sell for \$8.97 each.

Solution Think of \$8.97 as \$9 − 3¢.

$$\left.\begin{aligned} \text{So } 5 \cdot \$8.97 &= 5(\$9 - 3¢) \\ &= 5 \cdot \$9 - 5 \cdot 3¢ \\ &= \$45 - 15¢ \\ &= \$44.85 \end{aligned}\right\} \text{Do all this in your head.}$$

Check Multiply 5(8.97) with pencil and paper or with your calculator. You should get 44.85.

This form of the Distributive Property also enables multiplication involving mixed numbers like $1\frac{1}{2}$.

Example 5 Monica's hourly wage as a carpenter is \$12.00. If she receives time-and-a-half for overtime, what is her overtime hourly wage?

Solution Time-and-a-half means $1\frac{1}{2}$ times the regular hourly wage. Since $1\frac{1}{2} = 1 + \frac{1}{2}$, use the Distributive Property to mentally calculate the wage.

$$\begin{aligned} 12 \cdot 1\tfrac{1}{2} = 12 \cdot (1 + \tfrac{1}{2}) &= 12 \cdot 1 + 12 \cdot \tfrac{1}{2} \\ &= 12 + 6 \\ &= 18 \end{aligned}$$

Monica receives \$18 as an hourly wage for overtime.

Check \$18 is halfway between her \$12 salary and double that, \$24.

The Distributive Property is *very important* in algebra. It may be used more than once in the same problem.

Most of the multiplication problems in this lesson involve a binomial. Point out that the Distributive Property can also be used with three or more terms, as in **Example 3.**

Just like pencil-and-paper skills, *mental calculations,* as in **Examples 4 and 5,** take practice.

ADDITIONAL EXAMPLES
In 1–3, remove parentheses.

1. $-4(5n + 2)$
$\mathbf{-20n - 8}$

2. $15\left(\frac{2}{3}x - \frac{4}{5}y\right)$
$\mathbf{10x - 12y}$

3. $2x(x - 11y + 8)$.
$\mathbf{2x^2 - 22xy + 16x}$

4. Stereo components sell for \$199 each. How much would three components cost?
3 · \$199 = 3 · (\$200 − \$1) = 3 · \$200 − 3 · 1 = \$597

5. The Indianapolis Motor Speedway is an oval $2\frac{1}{2}$ miles long. If a driver completed 32 laps before having a flat tire, how far had he driven?
$2\frac{1}{2}$ miles · 32 =
2 miles · 32 + $\frac{1}{2}$ mile · 32 =
64 miles + 16 miles =
80 miles

6. Solve $-4y + 7(y - 2) = 31$.
15

NOTES ON QUESTIONS
Question 2: You might ask what property is illustrated by each equation that does not show the Distributive Property.
(**b.** Commutative Property of Multiplication; **c.** Commutative Property of Addition)

Question 9: Having students write out the process they use makes them analyze their thinking more closely. However, some students will know how to do the mental arithmetic but not be able to write down the process.

Questions 19 and 20: Clearing the fractions makes the solution of some equations easier. This is a useful skill, one deserving some discussion.

ADDITIONAL ANSWERS
6. $-10abc + 10b^2c + 10bc^2$

9. 5(7.96) = 5(8.00) − 5(.04) = 40.00 − .20 = $39.80

19a. $\frac{1}{2}x = \frac{11}{15} - \frac{2}{3}$; $x = \frac{2}{15}$

19b. $15x + 20 = 22$; $x = \frac{2}{15}$

Example 6 Solve $-5(x + 2) + 3x = 8$.

Solution 1 We show reasons at the right.

$-5x + -5 \cdot 2 + 3x = 8$	Distributive Property (to eliminate parentheses)
$-5x + -10 + 3x = 8$	arithmetic
$-5x + 3x + -10 = 8$	Commutative Property of Addition
$-2x + -10 = 8$	Distributive Property (to add like terms)
$-2x + -10 + 10 = 8 + 10$	Addition Property of Equality
$-2x = 18$	arithmetic
$x = -9$	Multiplication Property of Equality

Solution 2 Experts do arithmetic and work steps mentally and may write down only a few steps:

$$-5x - 10 + 3x = 8$$
$$-2x - 10 = 8$$
$$-2x = 18$$
$$x = -9$$

Check Substitute -9 for x in the original sentence. Follow the order of operations.

Does $-5(-9 + 2) + 3 \cdot -9 = 8$?
$-5 \cdot -7 + 3 \cdot -9 = 8$?
$35 + -27 = 8$? Yes.

Questions

Covering the Reading

1. Fill in the blanks to express the area in two different ways.
c(a + b) = ca + cb
_?_ (_?_ + _?_) = _?_ + _?_

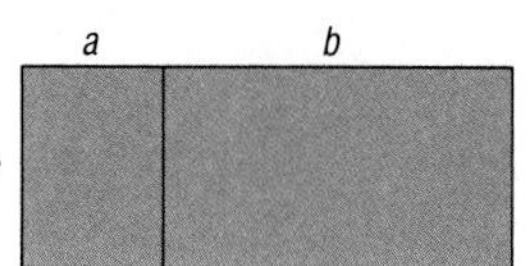

2. Which two of these true sentences are forms of the Distributive Property? **a, d**
a. $n(x + y) = nx + ny$ **b.** $n(x + y) = (x + y)n$
c. $nx + ny = ny + nx$ **d.** $nx + ny = n(x + y)$

In 3–8, use the Distributive Property to eliminate parentheses.

3. $12(k + 5)$ **12k + 60**
4. $2(y - 1.5)$ **2y − 3**
5. $7a(3 - 5b)$ **21a − 35ab**
6. $10bc(-a + b + c)$ **See margin.**
7. $\frac{1}{2}x(4y + 6)$ **2xy + 3x**
8. $-3(-2 + 2x)$ **6 − 6x**

9. Show how the Distributive Property can help you mentally compute the price of 5 records if each record costs $7.96. **See margin.**

10. Mentally compute the total cost of four gallons of milk at $2.07 each. **$8.28**

In Questions 11 and 12, mentally compute the overtime hourly wage (at time-and-a-half for overtime) if the normal hourly wage is the given amount.

11. $14.00 **$21.00**

12. $6.50 **$9.75**

In Questions 13–16, use the Distributive Property to simplify, then solve and check.

13. $4(m + 7) = 320$ **$m = 73$**

14. $11(3 - n) = 6(5 - 2n)$ **$n = -3$**

15. $2(x + 3.1) = 9.8$ **$x = 1.8$**

16. $6(4y - 1) - 2y = 82$ **$y = 4$**

Applying the Mathematics

17. Mentally compute 6 times 999,999. **5,999,994**

18. For each hour of television, there is an average of $8\frac{1}{2}$ minutes of commercials. If you watch 6 hours of television in a week, compute in your head how many commercial minutes you will see. **51 min.**

19. Solve the equation $\frac{1}{2}x + \frac{2}{3} = \frac{11}{15}$ in two ways: **See margin.**
   a. by first adding $-\frac{2}{3}$ to both sides and proceeding from that;
   b. by multiplying both sides by 30 and proceeding from that.

20. Solve $.05x - 1.03 = 2.92$ by first multiplying both sides by 100 to get an equation with no decimals. **$5x - 103 = 292$; $x = 79$**

21. The area A of a trapezoid with parallel bases b_1 and b_2 and height h is given by the formula

$$A = \frac{1}{2}h(b_1 + b_2).$$

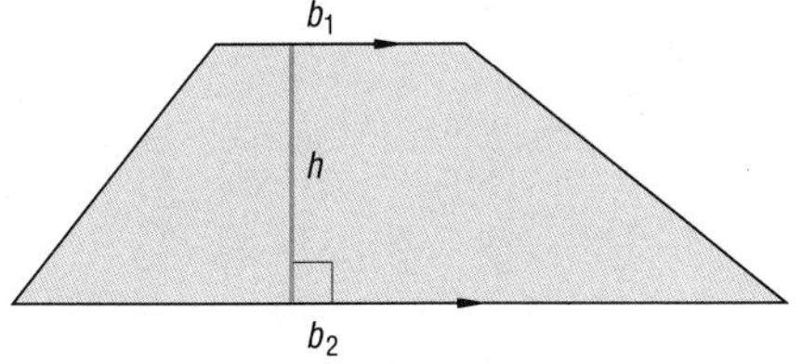

If a trapezoid has base $b_1 = 5$ cm, height 6 cm, and area 60 cm^2, what is the length of its other base? **$b_2 = 15$ cm**

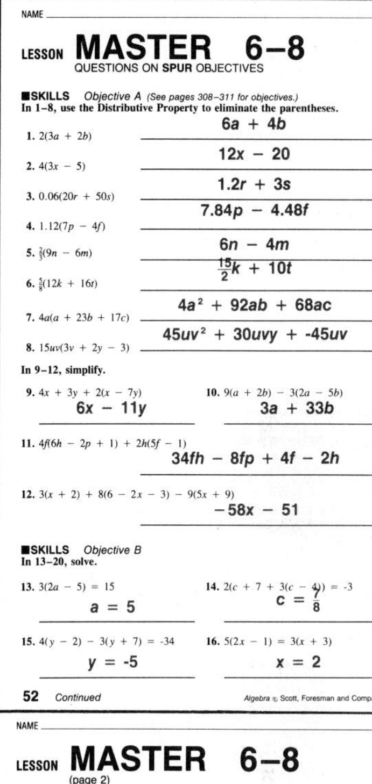

NAME ____

LESSON **MASTER 6–8**
QUESTIONS ON **SPUR** OBJECTIVES

■**SKILLS** *Objective A* *(See pages 308–311 for objectives.)*
In 1–8, use the Distributive Property to eliminate the parentheses.

1. $2(3a + 2b)$ **$6a + 4b$**
2. $4(3x - 5)$ **$12x - 20$**
3. $0.06(20r + 50s)$ **$1.2r + 3s$**
4. $1.12(7p - 4f)$ **$7.84p - 4.48f$**
5. $\frac{2}{3}(9n - 6m)$ **$6n - 4m$**
6. $\frac{5}{8}(12k + 16t)$ **$\frac{15}{2}k + 10t$**
7. $4a(a + 23b + 17c)$ **$4a^2 + 92ab + 68ac$**
8. $15uv(3v + 2y - 3)$ **$45uv^2 + 30uvy + -45uv$**

In 9–12, simplify.

9. $4x + 3y + 2(x - 7y)$ **$6x - 11y$**
10. $9(a + 2b) - 3(2a - 5b)$ **$3a + 33b$**
11. $4f(6h - 2p + 1) + 2h(5f - 1)$ **$34fh - 8fp + 4f - 2h$**
12. $3(x + 2) + 8(6 - 2x - 3) - 9(5x + 9)$ **$-58x - 51$**

■**SKILLS** *Objective B*
In 13–20, solve.

13. $3(2a - 5) = 15$ **$a = 5$**
14. $2(c + 7 + 3(c - 4)) = -3$ **$c = \frac{7}{8}$**
15. $4(y - 2) - 3(y + 7) = -34$ **$y = -5$**
16. $5(2x - 1) = 3(x + 3)$ **$x = 2$**

52 *Continued* *Algebra* © Scott, Foresman and Company

NAME ____

LESSON **MASTER 6–8**
(page 2)

17. $\frac{1}{2}(6k + 3) = 4\frac{1}{2}$ **$k = 1$**
18. $\frac{2}{3}(n + 10) = \frac{3}{4}(n + 9)$ **$n = -1$**
19. $0.04(p + 1.1) = 0$ **$p = -1.1$**
20. $0.8(2p - 3) = 0.6(p - 4)$ **$p = 0$**

■**PROPERTIES** *Objective D*
In 21–23, identify the property being applied.

21. If $2x + 7y = -5x - y$, then $7x = -8y$. **Add. Prop. of Equality**
22. $\frac{1}{2}(3 - 7x) = \frac{3}{2} - \frac{7x}{2}$ **Distributive Property**
23. If $3x = -8a$, then $x = \frac{-8a}{3}$. **Mult. Prop. of Equality**

■**REPRESENTATIONS** *Objective J*
In 24–26, write two different expressions that describe the total area of the two rectangles.

24. **$.2(.8 + .6)$ cm^2**
$(.16 + .12)$ cm^2
0.2 cm, 0.8 cm; 0.2 cm, 0.6 cm

25. **$16(a + b)$ in.^{2}**
$(16a + 16b)$ in.^{2}
16 in.; a in.; b in.

26. **$3(x + y)$ ft^2**
$(3x + 3y)$ ft^2
3 ft, x ft; 3 ft, y ft

Algebra © Scott, Foresman and Company 53

FOLLOW-UP

MORE PRACTICE
For more questions on SPUR Objectives, use *Lesson Master 6-8*, shown on page 299.

EXTENSION
A technique for *mentally calculating* a 15% tip uses the Distributive Property.

15% = 10% + 5% and
5% = 1/2 of 10%.
So 15% of bill =
10% of bill + 1/2 of 10% of bill.

For example:
15% of $25 =
$2.50 + 1/2 of $2.50 =
$2.50 + $1.25 = $3.75.

Have students use this technique to mentally calculate 15% of $10, $50, and $17. ($1.50, $7.50, $2.55)

34. sample:
ad + bc + ac + bd =
c(a + b) + d(a + b) =
(a + b)(c + d)

In Questions 22 and 23, solve.

22. $\frac{3x}{4} = \frac{3x + 1}{6}$ **$x = \frac{2}{3}$**

23. $2n + 3(5 + 2n) \leq 14$. **$n \leq -\frac{1}{8}$**

Review

24. The perimeter of triangle *TRI* is 120 units. Find the length of $\overline{RT}$. *(Lesson 6-2)*
30 units

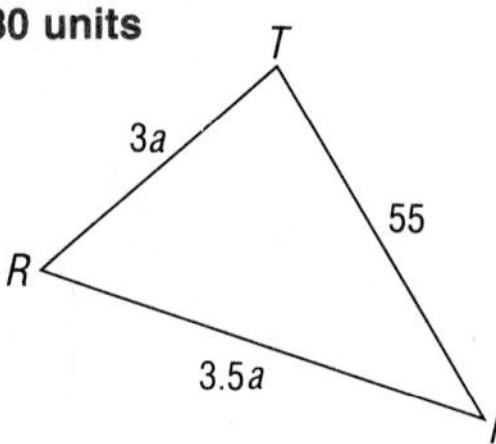

In Questions 25–27, solve. *(Lessons 6-1, 6-6, 6-7)*

25. $4x + 3 = 12$ **$\frac{9}{4}$** **26.** $3 - 4x = 12$ **$-\frac{9}{4}$** **27.** $5x + 2 < -x - 1$ **$x < -$**

In 28–30, simplify. *(Lessons 2-2, 4-1, 4-2)*

28. $-3(-\frac{2}{3}a)$ **2a** **29.** $4b - 6b + 8b - 2b$ **4b** **30.** $(3c)(2c)(-c)$ **$-6c^3$**

31. Here is a scale. On the left side, a $\frac{1}{8}$-lb weight together with 2 boxes balances with a $\frac{3}{4}$-lb weight and $\frac{1}{24}$-lb weight on the right. What is the weight of a box? *(Lessons 6-1,6-2)* **$\frac{1}{3}$ lb**

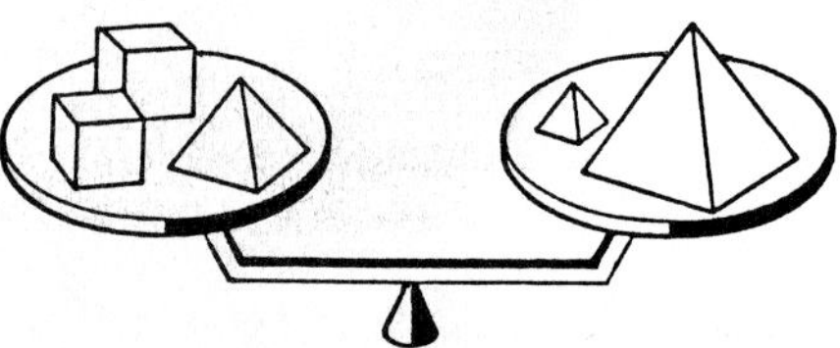

32. 6 is what percent of 45? *(Lesson 5-4)* **$13\frac{1}{3}$%**

33. In 1980, the population of Mississippi was 2,520,638 and was increasing at a rate of 27,400 people per year. If this rate continued, what was the population in 1985? *(Lesson 6-4)* **2,657,638**

Exploration

34. Write the area of the large rectangle in three different ways as the sum of the areas of smaller rectangles. **See margin.**

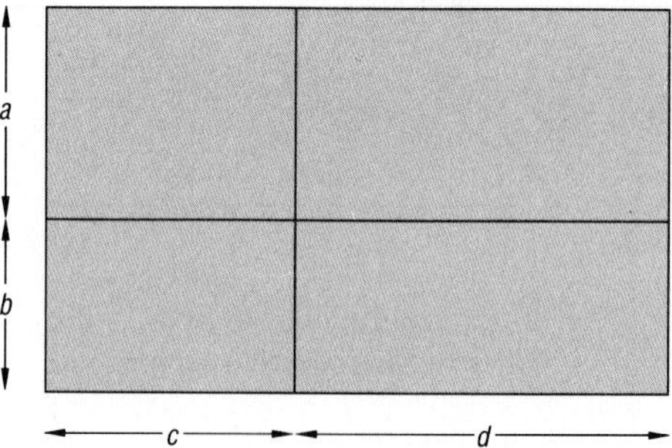

LESSON 6-9

Subtracting Quantities

The Distributive Property allows us to write

$$c(a + b) = ca + cb.$$

When $c = -1$ this means $-1(a + b) = -1a + -1b$.

Recall that the Multiplication Property of -1 states that for any real number n, $-1n = -n$. So the above property can be rewritten as

$$-(a + b) = -a + -b.$$

We say that *the opposite of the sum is the sum of the opposites of its terms.*

An algebraic expression in parentheses, like $a + b$ above, is called a **quantity.** You can think of the above discussion as showing that the opposite sign distributes over the terms of a quantity. The same idea holds if the quantity in parentheses has subtractions.

Example 1 Simplify $-(4a - 7)$.

Solution $-(4a - 7) = -1(4a - 7)$ Multiplication Property of -1
$= -4a + 7$ Distributive Property

Check Substitute some number for a. We substitute 5.

Does $-(4 \cdot 5 - 7) = -4 \cdot 5 + 7$?
$-(20 - 7) = -20 + 7$?
$-13 = -13$? Yes.

Remember that the definition of subtraction says that $x - y = x + -y$. In Example 2, y is the quantity $4a - 7$ found in Example 1. Example 2 is read "Subtract the quantity 4a − 7 from the quantity $10a + 6$."

Example 2 Simplify $(10a + 6) - (4a - 7)$.

Solution 1 Change the subtracting of $(4a - 7)$ to addition.

$$\begin{aligned} x \quad - \quad y \quad &= \quad x \quad + -y \\ (10a + 6) - (4a - 7) &= (10a + 6) + -(4a - 7) \\ &= 10a + 6 + -4a + 7 \\ &= 10a + -4a + 6 + 7 \\ &= 6a + 13 \end{aligned}$$

LESSON 6-9

RESOURCES

- Lesson Master 6-9

OBJECTIVES

A Use the Distributive Property to collect like terms.
B Solve linear equations involving subtracted quantities.
D Apply and recognize properties associated with linear sentences.

TEACHING NOTES

Reading The skills of this lesson are tricky. We recommend having students read the lesson in class; then going through each example in detail.

Chunking is required in **Example 2** to have full understanding. Students must view $(10a + 6) - (4a - 7)$ as the subtraction of two numbers, then rewrite it as the first number plus the opposite of the second.

Alternate Approach Your students might benefit from the following explanation of **Example 2:**

$(10a + 6)$ minus $(4a - 7) =$
$(10a + 6)$ plus the opposite of $(4a - 7) =$
$(10a + 6) + (-4a + 7)$

Example 3 gives a justification for the subtraction of a sum that involves an application. For some students, this example is quite illustrative.

Getting the correct signs when parentheses are removed will remain a problem for many students. Much practice is needed before mastery. Constant reminders are needed after mastery has seemingly been achieved. We encourage you to move to skip steps as quickly as is reasonable.

ADDITIONAL EXAMPLES

1. Simplify $-(6c - 5)$.
$-6c + 5$

2. Simplify $(3c + 8) - (2c - 7)$.
$c + 15$

3. Carrie had 27 almonds in a bag. On the way to school she ate x almonds. Then she gave y almonds to her friend. Express in two different ways the amount of almonds she had left.
$27 - x - y, 27 - (x + y)$

4. Solve $47z - (9 + 23z) = 3$.
$z = \frac{1}{2}$

5. Solve $5g = 2g - 3(g + 6)$.
$g = -3$

Solution 2 An expert might write the following.

$$\begin{aligned}(10a + 6) - (4a - 7) &= 10a + 6 - 4a + 7 \\ &= 6a + 13\end{aligned}$$

These ideas can be verified by considering a real situation in which a quantity is subtracted.

Example 3 Anton had \$500 in his savings account. He went to the bank and withdrew x dollars. Deciding that this was not enough, he went back and withdrew y more dollars. Express the amount of money left in his savings account in two different ways.

Solution Anton can subtract each amount from 500. This is written as

$$500 - x - y.$$

Anton could also add the two withdrawals and subtract the total. This is written as

$$500 - (x + y).$$

Check Pick some values for x and y. We pick 300 for x and 20 for y. Does $500 - 300 - 20 = 500 - (300 + 20)$? Always follow the order of operations. You should verify that each side equals 180.

CAUTION: Remember to distribute the opposite over each term of the sum or difference. For example, $-(a - b - c) = -a + b + c$. Notice the first step in Example 4.

Example 4 Solve: $3x - (2 + 4x) = 25$

Solution

$13x - 2 - 4x = 25$	Distributive Property (opposite of a sum)
$9x - 2 = 25$	Distributive Property (like terms)
$9x = 27$	Addition Property of Equality
$x = 3$	Multiplication Property of Equality

Check Does $13 \cdot 3 - (2 + 4 \cdot 3) = 25$?
$39 - (14) = 25$? Yes.

Example 5 Solve: $8t = 3t - 2(t + 14)$

Solution Simplify the right side. Because of order of operations, the multiplications come first, so the Distributive Property should be applied.

$$8t = 3t - (2t + 28)$$
$$8t = 3t - 2t - 28$$
$$8t = t - 28$$
$$7t = -28$$
$$t = -4$$

Check Does $8 \cdot -4 = 3 \cdot -4 - 2(-4 + 14)$?
Yes, $-32 = -12 - 2 \cdot 10$.

Questions

Covering the Reading

1. What property does this sentence illustrate? $-n = -1 \cdot n$
   Multiplication Property of -1
2. *Multiple choice* $-(x + 4) =$ **a**
   (a) $-x - 4$ (b) $x + -4$ (c) $-x + 4$
3. *Multiple choice* Which does *not* equal $-(x + y)$? **a**
   (a) $-x + y$ (b) $-1x + -1y$ (c) $-x - y$

In 4–7, simplify.

4. $-(x + 15)$ **$-x - 15$**
5. $-(4n - 3m)$ **$-4n + 3m$**
6. $x - (x + 2)$ **-2**
7. $3y - 5(y + 1)$ **$-2y - 5$**

In 8 and 9, simplify and check.

8. $(3k + 4) - (7k - 9)$
   $-4k + 13$
9. $-(5 + k) + (k - 18)$ **-23**
10. A clerk has a 20-yard bolt of cloth. She first cuts r yards of cloth from the bolt and then cuts t yards from the same bolt. **See margin.**
    a. Express the amount of cloth left in two different ways.
    b. Let $r = 3$ yards and $t = 7$ yards to check that the two expressions in part a are equal.
    $20 - (3 + 7) = 20 - 10 = 10$; $20 - 3 - 7 = 17 - 7 = 10$

ADDITIONAL ANSWERS
10a. $20 - (r + t)$, $20 - r - t$

303

NOTES ON QUESTIONS
Questions 10, 11, 18, and 19: Students must focus on the fact that $a - b - c$ and $a - (b + c)$ describe the same situation. These questions are similar to **Example 3.**

Error Analysis for Question 15: A solution of 13/3 means that a student multiplied 6.5 by 2, not by -2 as required. Changing the subtraction to addition may help. Then students would solve $4x = 3x + -2(x + 6.5)$.

Question 16: This question is easy to solve using chunking. Let $y = x + 9$. Then the equation becomes $3y - y + 6y = 80$. Then $8y = 80$, from which $y = 10$, from which $x = 1$.

Question 21: Here, a common mistake is pointed out to show the need to rewrite such expressions before combining terms.

Question 28: In proportions it is important to remember to use the Distributive Property when applying the Means-Extremes Theorem.

Making Connections for Question 29: Items like this one have been on National Assessment tests given to 11th graders with mediocre results. The question itself is to get students to think about graphing, the topic of the first lesson in the next chapter.

22b.

-3 n

34. samples: $-(b - a)$, $-(b + -a)$, $-(b + -1a)$, $1a - b$, $5a - 4a - 3b + 2b$

11. You begin the day with D dollars. You spend L dollars for lunch and $10 for a book. Write two expressions for the amount of money you have left. $D - (L + 10)$, $D - L - 10$

Applying the Mathematics

12. Rewrite without parentheses: $-(a + 2b - c)$. $-a + -2b + c$

13. a. Simplify the left side of $12 - (2y - 4) = 18$. $16 - 2y$
b. Solve. $y = -1$

In 14–17, solve.

14. $-(A - 9) = 11$ $A = -2$

15. $4x = 3x - 2(x + 6.5)$ $x = -\frac{13}{3}$

16. $3(x + 9) - (9 + x) + 6(x + 9) = 80$ $x = 1$

17. $\frac{3x}{2} - \frac{x + 1}{2} = 7$ $x = \frac{15}{2}$

15

18

Area A_1

Area A_2

18. Write an expression for the area of the colored part of this 15 by 18 rectangle at the left. $270 - (A_1 + A_2)$ or $270 - A_1 - A_2$

19. A carpenter has a board 96 inches long. He measures R inches, then another S inches and makes a cut. What is the length of the board after $R + S$ inches have been cut off? $96 - (R + S)$ or $96 - R - S$

20. Rayette had $400 in her savings account. She withdrew $37 Monday, and withdrew some more on Tuesday, but forgot to record the amount. The teller said she currently has $318 in her account.
a. Write an equation to describe the situation. $400 - 37 - x = 318$
b. Solve the equation to find out how much she withdrew on Tuesday. $45

21. Isaac thought himself an expert, so he wrote

$$13 - x + y - (x - 2 + y) = 11 - 2x + 2y.$$

Is Isaac right? No

22. a. Solve: $-(y - 7) - (-2) < 12$. $y > -3$
b. Graph the answer on a number line. See margin.

23. *Multiple choice* Which is *not* the opposite of $a + b$? (c)
(a) $-a + -b$ (b) $-(a + b)$ (c) $-a + b$ (d) $-1 \cdot a + -1 \cdot b$

Review

24. After a 10% raise, Myretta's salary was $8.80 an hour. What was her salary before the raise? *(Lesson 6-3)* $8.00 per hour

In 25–28, solve. *(Lessons 6-2, 6-7, 6-8)*

25. $\frac{1}{2}x - \frac{1}{3} = -\frac{5}{6}$ $x = -1$

26. $30 < 3n + 3$ $n > 9$

27. $8z + 2(z + 1) = 106$ $z = 10.4$

28. $\frac{x}{4} = \frac{x + 1}{6}$ $x = 2$

304

29. If the dots continue on a line in the graph below, how much would you pay for 20 tapes? *(Lesson 2-4)* $100

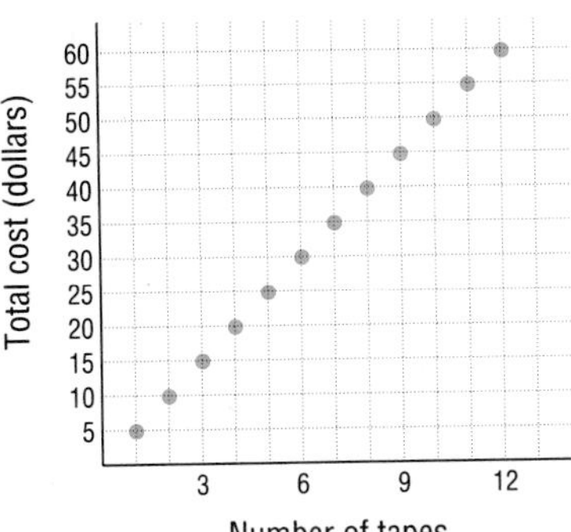

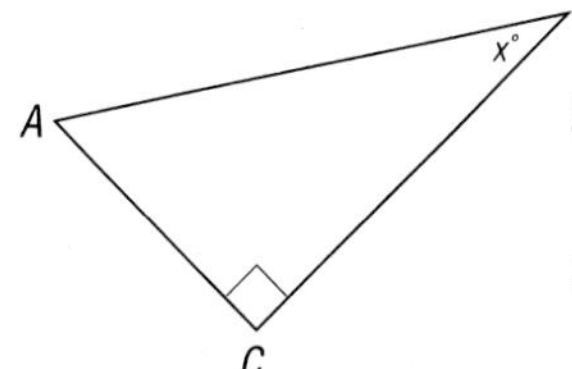

30. Triangle ADC is a right triangle. Write an expression for the measure of $\angle A$ in terms of x. *(Lesson 3-8)* $(90 - x)°$

31. *Skill sequence* Evaluate. *(Lesson 4-9)*

a. $6!$ 720 **b.** $\frac{6!}{3!}$ 120 **c.** $\frac{96!}{93!}$ 857,280

32. Carol Sue has 5 pairs of earrings, one pair of which is purple. If she picks two earrings at random, **a.** what is the probability that the first earring she picks will be purple, and **b.** what is the probability that both earrings are purple? *(Lesson 4-8)* a) $\frac{1}{5}$; b) $\frac{1}{45}$

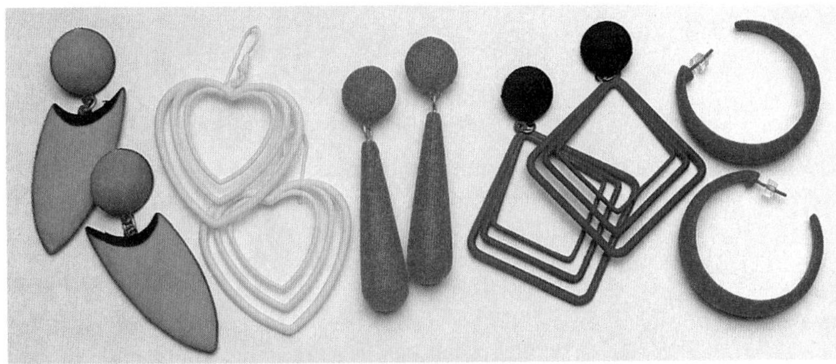

33. Estimate in your head. *(Previous course)*
    a. How much will 4 shirts cost at $19.95 each? $80
    b. If 3 VCR tapes sell for $17.95, how much does one cost? $6

Exploration

34. In this lesson, it was noted that $a - b$, $a + -b$, and $a + -1 \cdot b$ are all equal. Write five more expressions that are equal to $a - b$.
    See margin.

35. The difference of two numbers is subtracted from their sum. What can be said about the answer?
    The answer is equal to twice one of the numbers.

FOLLOW-UP

MORE PRACTICE

For more questions on SPUR Objectives, use *Lesson Master 6-9,* shown below.

NAME ______

LESSON **MASTER 6–9**
QUESTIONS ON **SPUR** OBJECTIVES

■SKILLS *Objective A* *(See pages 308–311 for objectives.)*
In 1–8, simplify.

1. $-(2x - 9)$ **$-2x + 9$**
2. $-(3a - 2b + 6c)$ **$-3a + 2b - 6c$**
3. $2 - (w + 4)$ **$-w - 2$**
4. $-(2a - 3) + (3a - 6)$ **$a - 3$**
5. $-3(4r + 3s) - (8r + s)$ **$-20r - 10s$**
6. $2.1d + 3.7 - (4.2d - 6.1)$ **$-2.1d + 9.8$**
7. $\frac{5m}{12} - \left(\frac{7m}{9} + 1\right)$ **$-\frac{13}{36}m - 1$**
8. $\frac{8k}{15} + \frac{7j}{30} - \left(\frac{7k}{15} + \frac{11j}{30}\right)$ **$\frac{k}{15} - \frac{2j}{15}$**

■SKILLS *Objective B*
In 9–12, solve.

9. $(8x - 3) - (5x + 6) = 6$ **$x = 5$**
10. $-(11x - 14) = -8$ **$x = 2$**
11. $2.6 = 1.8 - (0.2x - 1)$ **$x = 1$**
12. $7x - (2x + 1) = 7 - (x - 4)$ **$x = 2$**

■PROPERTIES *Objective D*
In 13 and 14, identify the property being applied.

13. If $12x + -4y = -15x - 3y$, then $27x = y$. **Add. Prop. of Equality**
14. $-2(3 - 7x) = -6 + 14x$. **Distributive Property**

54

SUMMARY

The Summary gives an overview of the entire chapter and provides an opportunity for students to consider the material as a whole. Thus, the Summary can be used to help students relate the concepts presented in the chapter.

VOCABULARY

Terms, symbols, and properties are listed by lesson to provide a checklist of things a student must know. Emphasize to students that they should read the vocabulary list carefully before starting the Progress Self-Test. If students do not understand the meaning of a term, they should refer back to the indicated lesson.

Definitions or descriptions of all terms in the vocabulary list may be found in the Glossary.

Summary

A linear sentence is one equivalent to a sentence of the form $ax + b = cx + d$ or $ax + b < cx + d$. An example is $3x + 4 = 5x - 2$; another example is $y = 4x + 5$. This chapter emphasizes how to solve linear sentences. In the next two chapters you will see why they are called "linear."

To solve linear sentences:
1. Simplify each side of the sentence, if possible.
2. Add a quantity to both sides to get all variables on one side, then simplify.
3. Add a quantity to both sides to get all numerical terms on the other side, then simplify.
4. Multiply both sides by a number that will get the variable alone.

A basic property needed in working with many linear sentences is the Distributive Property. The Distributive Property has many forms. As

$$ax + bx = (a + b)x,$$

it helps to combine like terms. In the form

$$c(a + b) = ca + cb,$$

it is used to remove parentheses. When $c = -1$, there is the special case $-(a+b) = -a + -b$, which is used when sums are subtracted. When $a = 1$ and b is a percent change, a special case arises which is useful in many practical situations such as markup and discounts: for example, $p + .05p = 1.05p$.

You have now studied how to solve virtually all linear equations or inequalities. The fundamental idea in solving is to change the given sentence into a simpler sentence. So, to solve an equation with the unknown on both sides, add something to change it to a sentence with the unknown on just one side. Then add to get an equation of the form $ax = b$. This last equation is one you know how to solve.

Vocabulary

Below are the most important terms and phrases for this chapter. You should be able to give a general description and a specific example for each.

Lesson 6-1
linear sentence

Lesson 6-3
Distributive Property
discount
markup, tax

Lesson 6-4
FOR/NEXT loop

Lesson 6-6
general linear equation

Lesson 6-7
linear inequality

Lesson 6-8
eliminate parentheses

Lesson 6-9
quantity (in parentheses)

Progress Self-Test

Take this test as you would take a test in class. You will need a calculator. Then check your work with the solutions in the Selected Answers in the back of the book.

In 1–4, simplify.

1. $m - 0.23m$ .77m
2. $k + 3(k + 3)$ 4k + 9
3. $\frac{5}{2}(4v + 100 - w)$ $10v + 250 - \frac{5}{2}w$
4. $6t - 2(9 - 4t)$ 14t − 18

In 5–12, solve.

5. $8r + 14 = 74$ r = 7.5
6. $-4q + 3 + 9q = -12$ q = -3
7. $6w - 37 = 8w + 35$ w = -36
8. $6(x + 2) = 3(x + 6)$ x = 2
9. $14m - 7(3 - m) = 21$ m = 2
10. $13 \leq 7 - x$ $x \leq -6$
11. $v - 3v > 2$ $v < -1$
12. $\frac{1}{5}(10h + 1) = 4h + \frac{1}{5}$ h = 0
13. If both sides of $\frac{1}{4}x + \frac{3}{20} = \frac{3}{5}$ are multiplied by 20, what equation results? 5x + 3 = 12
14. Irving bought 6 pairs of socks at $2.99 per pair. Show how Irving could calculate the total cost of the socks in his head. 6(3 − .01) = 17.94
15. A stereo system costs $385 after a 30% discount. What did it cost before the discount? $550
16. Some books cost a total of $20.41. If an 8% tax was included in this price, how much did the books originally cost? $18.90
17. A sequence begins 2, 14, 26, 38, 50, ... , and each term is 12 more than the preceding. Which term is 470? 40th
18. Each minute a computer printer prints 6 sheets of paper. Suppose the printer starts with 1100 sheets of paper and prints continuously. After how many minutes will 350 sheets be left? 125
19. If $F = \frac{9}{5}C + 32$, find the Celsius equivalent of a Fahrenheit temperature of 50°. C = 10°
20. A person's savings account has $137.25 and $2.50 is added each week. Disregarding interest, how much will there be after w weeks? 137.25 + 2.50w
21. Jack and Jill had a lemonade stand. Jack worked twice as long as Jill and so they decided to split their profits so that Jack received twice as much. If the total profits were $19.50, how much should Jill receive? $6.50
22. Town A has a population of 25,000 and is growing at a rate of 1200 people per year. Town B has a population of 37,000 and is declining at a rate of 200 people a year. If these rates continue, in how many years will the two towns have the same population? 8.6 yr
23. Explain how the picture below represents the Distributive Property. $c(a + b) = ca + cb$ See margin.

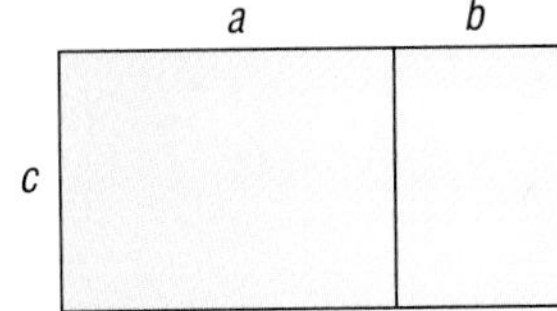

24. In the U.S., the life expectancy L of a 12- to 16-year-old white male is given by the formula
$$L - 60.7 = .95(A - 12).$$
where A is the age of the person. What is the life expectancy of a 14-year-old white male according to this formula? 62.6 years
25. From a roll of wallpaper y yards long, a decorator cuts off c yards for one wall and 15 more yards for another wall. Give two different expressions for how much is left. y − (c + 15); y − c − 15

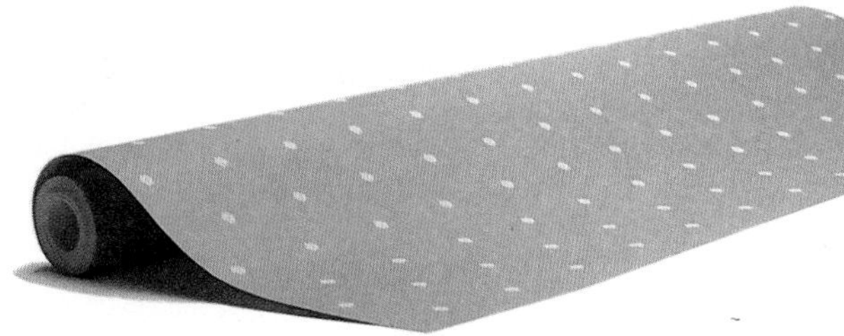

PROGRESS SELF-TEST

We cannot overemphasize the importance of these end-of-chapter materials. It is at this point that the material "gels" for many students, allowing them to solidify skills and understanding. In general, student performance should be markedly improved after these pages.

USING THE PROGRESS SELF-TEST

Assign the Progress Self-Test as a one-night assignment. Worked-out *solutions* for all these questions are in the Selected Answers section at the back of the student book. Encourage students to take the Progress Self-Test honestly, grade themselves, and then be prepared to discuss the test in class.

Advise students to pay special attention to those Chapter Review questions (pages 308-311) which correspond to questions missed on the Progress Self-Test. A chart provided in the Selected Answers section in the student text keys the Progress Self-Test questions to the lettered SPUR Objectives in the Chapter Review or to the Vocabulary. It also keys the questions to the corresponding lessons where the material is covered.

ADDITIONAL ANSWERS

23. The picture shows that the area can be calculated in two ways: c(a + b) or ca + cb

RESOURCES

- Chapter 6 Test, Form A
- Chapter 6 Test, Form B
- Chapter 6 Test, Cumulative Form
- Comprehensive Test, Chapters 1-6

CHAPTER REVIEW

The main objectives for the chapter are organized here into sections corresponding to the four main types of understanding this book promotes: Skills, Properties, Uses, and Representations.

USING THE CHAPTER REVIEW

Whereas end-of-chapter material may be considered optional in some texts, in *Algebra* we have selected these objectives and questions with the expectation that they will be covered. Students should be able to answer these questions with about 85% accuracy after studying the chapter.

You may assign these questions over a single night to help students prepare for a test the next day, or you may assign the questions over a two-day period.

If you work the questions over two days, then we recommend assigning the *evens* for homework the first night so that students get feedback in class the next day, then assigning the *odds* the night before the test so the students can use the answers provided in the book.

Chapter Review

Questions on SPUR Objectives

SPUR stands for **S**kills, **P**roperties, **U**ses, and **R**epresentations. The Chapter Review questions are grouped according to the SPUR Objectives for this chapter.

SKILLS deal with the procedures used to get answers.

Objective A. *Use the distributive property to remove parentheses and collect like terms.* *(Lessons 6-3, 6-8, 6-9)*

In 1–10, simplify.

1. $c + \frac{1}{2}c$ $\frac{3}{2}c$

2. $5w + 8z - 7w$ $-2w + 8z$

3. $m - .08m$ $.92m$

4. $.2x + x$ $1.2x$

5. $3(a + 2b)$ $3a + 6b$

6. $-\frac{2}{3}(6 - v)$ $-4 + \frac{2}{3}v$

7. $11(3x - 2) + 8(4 - 2x)$ $17x + 10$

8. $4(m - 1) - 5(2 + 3m)$ $-11m - 14$

9. $1 - (z - 1)$ $2 - z$

10. $3w + 2 + z - 4(w + 8 - z)$ $-w + 5z - 30$

Objective B. *Solve linear equations.* *(Lessons 6-1, 6-2, 6-5, 6-6, 6-8, 6-9)*

In 11–24, solve.

11. $4n + 3 = 15$ $n = 3$

12. $470 + 2n = 1100$ $n = 315$

13. $\frac{3}{4}x - 12 = 39$ $x = 68$

14. $66 = \frac{z}{5} + 2$ $z = 320$

15. $m - 3m = 10$ $m = -5$

16. $2x + 3(1 + x) = 18$ $x = 3$

17. $A + 5 = 9A - 11$ $A = 2$

18. $3n = 2n + 4$ $n = 4$

19. $216 = 2(w - 30) - 8$ $w = 142$

20. $(5x - 8) - (3x + 1) = 36$ $x = 22.5$

21. $2a - 6 = -2a$ $a = \frac{3}{2}$

22. $10e = 4e - 5(3 + 2e)$ $e = -\frac{15}{16}$

23. $\frac{5 + g}{3} = \frac{g + 2}{2}$ $g = 4$

24. $\frac{1}{x - 1} = \frac{3}{x - 2}$ $x = \frac{1}{2}$

Objective C. *Solve linear inequalities.* *(Lesson 6-7)*

In 25–32, solve.

25. $2x + 11 < 201$ $x < 95$

26. $11h + 71 \geq 13h - 219$ $h \leq 145$

27. $4 < 16g - 7g + 5$ $-\frac{1}{9} < g$

28. $4x - 1 < 2x + 1$ $x < 1$

29. $32 - y < 45$ $y > -13$

30. $\frac{3}{4}t + 21 > 12$ $t > -12$

31. $-4(2y - 1) \leq 12$ $y \geq -1$

32. $5(5 + z) < 3(2 + 2z)$ $z > 19$

PROPERTIES deal with the principles behind the mathematics.

Objective D. *Apply and recognize properties associated with linear sentences.*
Addition Property of Equality *(Lessons 6-1, 6-6)*
Addition Property of Inequality *(Lesson 6-7)*
Multiplication Property of Equality *(Lessons 6-1, 6-6)*
Multiplication Property of Inequality *(Lesson 6-7)*
Distributive Property *(Lessons 6-3, 6-8)*
Multiplication Property of 1 *(Lesson 6-3)*
Multiplication Property of -1 *(Lesson 6-9)*

In 33–36, identify the property being applied. See margin.

33. $4(x - y) = 4x - 4y$

34. $-(a + b + c) = -1(a + b + c)$

35. If $2x + 3 < 5$, then $2x < 2$.

36. Since $\frac{2m}{3} = 12$, $m = \frac{3}{2} \cdot 12$.

In 37–40, perform the indicated operation.

37. $a + 2 < 3a + 4$; add $-a$. $2 < 2a + 4$

38. $4000x + 300 = 11{,}000$; multiply on both sides by $\frac{1}{100}$. $40x + 3 = 110$

39. $B - 6B + 4(B + 2) \geq B - 5$; apply the Distributive Property See margin.

40. $-V \geq 3$; multiply on both sides by -1. $V \leq -3$

Objective E. *Use the Distributive Property to perform calculations in your head. (Lesson 6-3)*

In 41–44, show how the Distributive Property can be used to do the calculations mentally.

41. 7 · \$3.04 7(3 + .04) = \$21.28

42. 101 · 35 (100 + 1)35 = 3535

43. the cost of 9 shirts if each one costs \$19.99

44. 3 · 118 3(120 − 2) = 354

43) 9(20.00 − 0.01) = \$179.91

USES deal with applications of mathematics in real situations.

Objective F. *Answer questions involving markups or discounts. (Lesson 6-3)* \$55.50

45. The Jacobsons went out for dinner. The total amount they were charged was \$58.83. Included in this amount was a 6% sales tax. What was the cost of the meal before tax?

46. A stereo is on sale for a 25% discount. The sale price is \$325. What is the regular price? \$433.33

47. If phone rates have gone up 20% and you now pay \$10.80 a month, what was the previous rate? \$9.00

48. On sale at 40% off, a radio costs \$39.96. What was the original price? \$66.60

Objective G. *Describe patterns and answer questions in repeated addition or repeated subtraction situations. (Lessons 6-4, 6-6)* 50 weeks

49. Liz saves \$15 per week. She has \$750 in the bank and needs \$1500 in the bank before she can afford to go on vacation. For how many weeks must she save before she has the required amount? 50) 1406 + 2n

50. Mel adds 2 cards to his collection each week. If he has 1406 cards now, how many cards will he have n weeks from now?

51. Kate has \$1500 in an account and adds \$45 each month. Melissa has \$2000 and adds \$20 a month. When will they have the same amount of money in their accounts? 20 months

ADDITIONAL ANSWERS

33. Distributive Property

34. Multiplication Property of -1

35. Addition Property of Inequality

36. Multiplication Property of Equality

39. $B - 6B + 4B + 8 \geq B - 5$

62. visiting team $262
home team 5(262) = $1310

52. Len has $25 and is saving at the rate of $9 a week. Basil has $100 and is spending $5 a week. When will Len have more money than Basil? $n > 5.36$; after 6 weeks

53. A sequence begins 12, 17, 22, 27, ..., and each term is 5 more than the preceding.
   a. What is the 1100th term? 5507
   b. Which term is 182? 35th term

54. A sequence begins 10, 9.8, 9.6, 9.4, 9.2, ..., and each term is 0.2 less than the preceding. Which term is 3.4? 34th term

Objective H. *Answer questions involving linear sentence formulas. (Lesson 6-2)*

55. If $S = 3L - 26$ relates a man's shoe size S and foot length L (in inches), find the foot length of a man with a size 11 shoe. $12\frac{1}{3}$ in.

56. If $F = \frac{9}{5}C + 32$, find the Celsius equivalent of a Fahrenheit temperature of 100°. $37.\overline{7}°$

57. If the height h of a woman and the length f of her femur (in cm) are related by the formula $h \approx 61.412 + 2.317f$, estimate the length of the femur of a woman 150 cm tall. ≈38.2 cm

58. In a trapezoid, $A = \frac{1}{2}h(b_1 + b_2)$. If the area is 100 square feet, the height is 12.5 feet, and one base has length 7 feet. Find the length of the other base. 9 ft

Objective I. *Answer questions about situations combining addition and multiplication. (Lessons 6-3, 6-6)*

59. A hamburger bun has about 200 calories. One ounce of hamburger has about 80 calories. How large a plain hamburger with bun can you eat and still be under 600 calories? up to 5 ounces

60. Angle 2 has 3 times the measure of angle 1. What are their measures? 45°; 135°

61. If you work 35 hours a week for $4.50 an hour and receive time-and-a-half for overtime after that, how long must you work to earn over $200 in a week? more than 41.3

62. A home team is to get 5 times as much from gate sales as the visiting team. If the total receipts are $1572, how much should each team receive? See margin.

Objective J. *Translate balance scale models and rectangle area models into expressions and equations. (Lessons 6-1, 6-6, 6-8)*

63. Use the picture of a balance scale below. The boxes are equal in weight and the others are one-kilogram weights.

a. Write an equation describing the situation with B representing the weight of one box. **$3B + 2 = 8$**

b. What is the weight of one box? **2 kg**

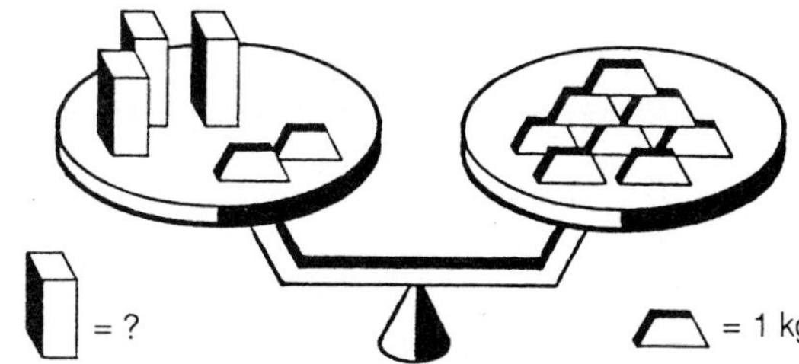

64. Use the picture below.

a. Write an equation to describe this situation with W representing the weight of one box. **$6W + 3 = 5W + 8$**

b. What is the weight of one box? **5 kg**

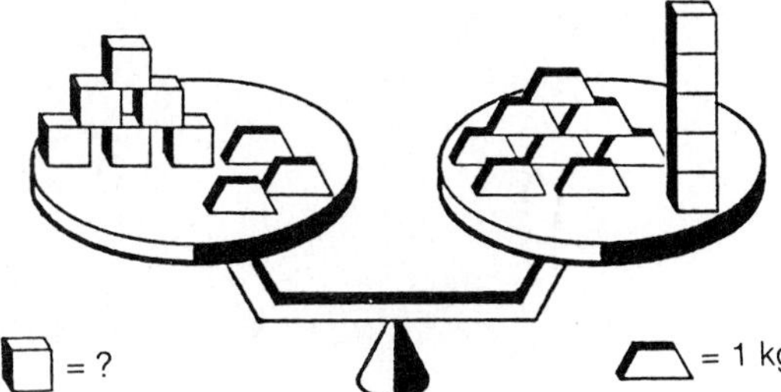

In 65 and 66, write two different expressions to describe the total areas of the rectangles.

65.

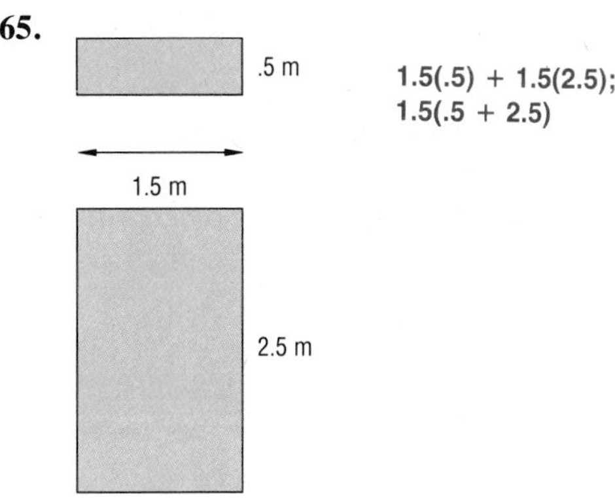

1.5(.5) + 1.5(2.5); 1.5(.5 + 2.5)

66.

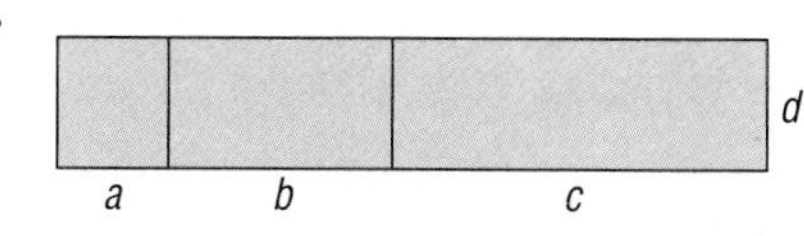

ad + bd + cd
(a + b + c)d

EVALUATION
Three tests are provided for this chapter in the Teacher's Resource File. Chapter 6 Test, Forms A and B, cover just Chapter 6. The third test is Chapter 6 Test, Cumulative Form. About 50% of this test covers Chapter 6; 25% covers Chapter 5, and 25% covers earlier chapters. A Comprehensive Test covering Chapters 1-6 is also included with this chapter. For more information on grading, see *General Teaching Suggestions: Grading* on page T44 in the Teacher's Edition.

ASSIGNMENT RECOMMENDATION
On the day your students take the chapter test, we suggest you make an assignment in the first section of the next chapter.

CHAPTER 7 ■ LINES AND DISTANCE

DAILY PACING CHART ■ CHAPTER 7

Students in the Full Course should complete the entire text by the end of the year. Students in the Minimal Course spend more time to complete lessons that are combined with quizzes and more time to consider the Chapter Review. Therefore, these students may not complete all the chapters in the text.

DAY	MINIMAL COURSE	FULL COURSE
1	7-1	7-1
2	7-2	7-2
3	7-3	7-3
4	7-4	7-4
5	Quiz (TRF); Start 7-5.	Quiz (TRF); 7-5
6	Finish 7-5.	7-6
7	7-6	7-7
8	7-7	7-8
9	7-8	Progress Self-Test
10	Progress Self-Test	Chapter Review
11	Chapter Review	Chapter Test (TRF)
12	Chapter Review	
13	Chapter Test (TRF)	

TESTING OPTIONS

TESTING OPTIONS

- Quiz for Lessons 7-1 Through 7-4
- Chapter 7 Test, Form A
- Chapter 7 Test, Form B
- Chapter 7 Test, Cumulative Form

INDIVIDUAL DIFFERENCES

PROVIDING FOR INDIVIDUAL DIFFERENCES

The student text is written for the *average* student. The program, however, can be adapted for less capable and for more capable students.

For those students who need more practice, a blackline master (in the Teacher's Resource File) is provided for each lesson. The Teacher's Edition frequently provides Error Analysis and Alternate Approach features to provide additional instructional strategies for those students who do not readily grasp the material.

For students who require additional challenge, Extension activities are regularly provided in the Teacher's Edition.

OBJECTIVES ■ CHAPTER 7

Students should master the chapter objectives by the time they complete the chapter. To ensure objective mastery, there is continual review built into each set of lesson questions. After students complete the chapter lessons, they assess their mastery on the Progress Self-Test. Then they do the Chapter Review and pay special attention to those questions that match the objectives missed on the Progress Self-Test. Students can get extra practice on these objectives by using the master for each lesson in the Teacher's Resource File.

OBJECTIVES FOR CHAPTER 7 (Organized into the SPUR categories— Skills, Properties, Uses, and Representations)	**Progress Self-Test Questions**	**Chapter Review Questions**	**Lesson Master from Teacher's Resource File***
SKILLS			
A Calculate absolute values.	1, 2	1 through 11	7-3
B Evaluate and simplify expressions involving square roots.	5, 7	12 through 18	7-4, 7-6
C Solve equations involving squares and square roots.	12 through 16	19 through 26	7-4
D Use chunking to evaluate expressions and solve equations.	11, 17 through 19	27 through 35	7-8
PROPERTIES			
E Apply the Square Root of a Product Property.	8 through 10	36 through 43	7-6
USES			
F Use squares and square roots in measurement problems.	6, 20	44 through 49	7-4, 7-5, 7-6
REPRESENTATIONS			
G Find distance on a number line.	3, 4	50 through 54	7-3
H Graph equations for straight lines by marking a table of values.	26 through 28	55 through 58	7-1
I Graph horizontal and vertical lines.	22	59 through 64	7-2
J Find the lengths of the sides of a right triangle using the Pythagorean Theorem.	21	65 through 68	7-5
K Calculate distances in the plane.	23 through 25	69 through 78	7-7
L Graph solutions to sentences of the form $\lvert x - a \rvert < b$, or $\lvert x - a \rvert > b$, where a and b are real numbers.	29	79 through 84	7-3

*** The masters are numbered to match the lessons.**

OVERVIEW ■ CHAPTER 7

This chapter covers a variety of topics relating algebra to geometry, including distance on the number line, distance in the coordinate plane, and the Pythagorean Theorem. It introduces two new operations: square root and absolute value. Equations involving these operations are then solved. Graphing lines by plotting points emphasizes the connection between an equation and its coordinate representation.

The first part of this chapter focuses on lines and distance in the coordinate plane. In Lesson 7-1, lines are graphed by plotting points. Then Lesson 7-2 looks at the equations $x = h$ and $y = k$ and the corresponding inequalities.

Most students know that they can subtract coordinates to find the length of a segment on a number line. Lesson 7-3 formalizes this intuition by introducing absolute value.

Understanding the distance formula in Lesson 7-7 requires the Pythagorean Theorem, which in turn necessitates some facility with radicals. Therefore, introductory work with square roots is found in Lesson 7-4, the Pythagorean Theorem is in Lesson 7-5, and more work with radicals is in Lesson 7-6.

Lesson 7-8 discusses an important problem-solving idea in algebra, chunking. This focuses student attention on use of an algebraic expression as a single number or variable. If students work at this technique, it makes solving some otherwise difficult equations, like absolute-value equations and certain quadratics, much easier.

PERSPECTIVES ■ CHAPTER 7

The Perspectives provide the rationale for the inclusion of topics or approaches, provide mathematical background, and make connections within UCSMP.

7-1

GRAPHING LINES

Students have graphed certain lines in Chapter 3, so the main idea of this lesson is largely review. Students need to know how to graph oblique lines before they graph horizontal and vertical lines in the next lesson.

The goals here are simple: from an equation students should be able to generate a table of values, and from the table they should be able to graph a line.

7-2

HORIZONTAL AND VERTICAL LINES

Students have difficulty with slopes of 0 and undefined slopes. One purpose of this lesson is to give students experience in graphing horizontal and vertical lines before the additional concepts of slope and intercept are introduced.

The distinction between graphing $y < -3$ on the number line versus the plane is explicit in this lesson. Later lessons and questions state whether the graph is on a number line or the coordinate plane.

Half-planes determined by lines which are not vertical or horizontal will be considered in Chapter 8. This lesson will set the groundwork, particularly with the ideas of when to dot the boundary, when to draw it solid, and which side to shade.

7-3

DISTANCE AND ABSOLUTE VALUE

The concept of absolute value is a topic which students will need for geometry. We introduce the ABS function in BASIC to give another representation of the absolute value idea.

The idea of absolute value is very important in computer work. For example, to avoid round off or truncation errors, computer programmers do not use a test like IF K = 3 THEN . . . . Instead they use absolute value: IF ABS(K − 3) < .001 THEN . . . . In this test, the number K is considered equal to 3 as long as it is within one-thousandth of 3.

Absolute value is also used in statistics. For example, if a set of data has a mean of 51, the *mean deviation* of any score x is $|x - 51|$. This statistic enables comparison of the "closeness" of scores to the mean.

Absolute values can be used to compute a range without distinguishing between the maximum and minimum values: "If a and b are extreme values of a set of data, then the range is $|a - b|$."

Still another use for absolute value is in stating rules for addition of positive and negative integers.

The calculation of distance along horizontal and vertical lines is discussed in this lesson. This concept is critical for calculating distance in the coordinate plane and is needed for Lesson 7-5.

7-4

SQUARE ROOTS

The idea of square root is a difficult one for students. It takes time to develop a good understanding. We strive here for an intuitive approach rather than a mechanical one. We solve problems and equations by referring back to the definition, which reinforces it. Using calculators to give decimal approximations for roots helps students develop a feel for them. It takes quite a bit of experience for students to firmly understand that $\sqrt{17}$ is not a number close to 17, but is approximately 4.

The definition of square root is motivated by the formula for the area of a square. This is the way the ancient Greeks thought of powers and roots (and the reason they did not deal with exponents greater than three, for which they saw no counterpart in the physical world).

The geometric interpretation, however, gives only the positive square root. The algebraic definition gives two square roots, and students must be alert to the two solutions of $A = s^2$.

7-5
PYTHAGOREAN THEOREM

Many students will have seen the Pythagorean Theorem before. This theorem is one of the most important relationships in mathematics. Teaching it here gives opportunities for students to practice working with squares and square roots. In the next section we apply it in the development of the formula for distance on a coordinate plane.

Pythagorean triples are useful in teaching the Pythagorean Theorem. This is such a fundamental idea that you might want to make some visual aids. A rope with 11 equally spaced knots makes a right triangle when you put the ends together and bend at the third knot and the seventh knot. This is also well illustrated, at least in the 3-4-5 case, by showing the squares on the sides of a right triangle.

7-6
SQUARE ROOTS OF PRODUCTS

With the advent of electronic calculators, simplifying radicals as an aid for calculating decimal approximations is passé. On a calculator, it is easier to evaluate $\sqrt{500}$ than to evaluate $10\sqrt{5}$. However, there still are situations where simplifying radicals is necessary. In some situations patterns do not become apparent unless the numbers are simplified. Other examples are the relationships in 30-60-90 and 45-45-90 triangles. (Sometimes, however, simplifying obscures patterns, as in the exploration question of Lesson 7-5.)

Another use of simplifying radicals is reconciling answers arrived at with different methods. We study simplifying here so students will have the skill when they get to geometry.

In this lesson we also solve simple quadratic equations like $2x^2 = 150$. Chapter 10 will introduce solving a quadratic equation when the factors are known, and Chapter 11 will show the Quadratic Formula.

7-7
DISTANCES IN THE PLANE

The distance between two points in a plane is one of the most important ideas for later work in coordinate geometry, and it provides wonderful practice in algebra.

Rather than skipping to the distance formula, we have students find the distance between two points by drawing a right triangle whose hypotenuse is the segment connecting the two points. Students will understand the traditional distance formula better for having worked problems with the actual triangle.

This lesson distinguishes between two types of distance—the street distance and the diagonal distance. This reinforces the Triangle Inequality Theorem. The distance "as the crow flies" is always shorter than the street distance, unless the two points are in a horizontal or vertical line.

7-8
CHUNKING

Chunking is the treatment of a group (the "chunk") of symbols as a single symbol. It is a fundamental problem-solving skill.

The term *chunking* comes from studies of psychology and information processing. Sometimes chunking is viewed as a part of substituting. However substitution usually involves putting numbers into expressions, whereas chunking involves treating expressions as single numbers or entities.

Here are some examples of chunking that students have already seen: $|x_1 - x_2|$ as a length important in calculating distance between two points; $\frac{2}{3}$ as representing a single number (when thought of as $2 \div 3$, the chunk is broken); (x, y) as being a single point.

Chunking is a tool many students have used to memorize the pledge of allegiance. Chunking is also often used to remember telephone numbers. In fact, it is difficult to start in the middle of a number, or of the pledge of allegiance, indicating that at times the brain stores chunks, not the individual digits or words.

The significance of chunking in algebra is that if a property holds for all values of a variable, then it holds also for expressions which have those values. For example, just as $2a + 3a = 5a$ is an instance of the Distributive Property, so $2(x + y) + 3(x + y) = 5(x + y)$ is also an instance.

Many algebra problems involving squares and square roots can be solved by students if they perceive the expressions involved as representing one number. For example, if $\sqrt{k + 3} = 10$, the chunk $(k + 3)$ equals 100 and $k = 97$.

Problems which have appeared on standardized tests illustrate chunking. For example, what is x if

$$2^{3x-1} = 2^{11} ?$$

The problem is easy if you see the expression $3x - 1$ as a chunk equal to 11.

CHAPTER 7

RESOURCES

Visual for Teaching Aid 33: Optical Illusions

This chapter should take 8 or 9 days for the lessons and quiz; 1 day for the Progress Self-Test; 1 or 2 days for the Chapter Review; and 1 day for testing. The total is 11 to 13 days.

CHAPTER 7

Lines and Distance

An *optical illusion* is something that looks one way but is actually another.

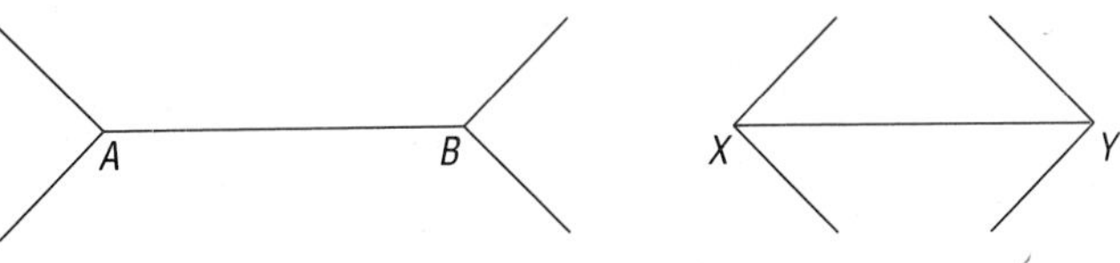

For instance, $\overline{AB}$ appears longer than $\overline{XY}$, but they are the same length. (If you don't believe this, measure them with a ruler!)

Most optical illusions rely on the fact that people have poor perceptions about distance and angle measure. The photograph at the left illustrates a real optical illusion. When the sun is seen near the horizon it appears larger than when it is higher in the sky. It is actually the same size both places since it is the same distance from the earth.

These illusions show that it is important to have more precise ways of computing lengths and distances. In this chapter you will learn more about lines and distance.

USING PAGES 312-313
Point out that our perceptions of lengths and distances are affected by the context in which the observations are made. Therefore, $\overline{AB}$ seems longer than $\overline{XY}$ because the V shapes at the ends of the segments cause us to compare the lengths of the two segments in relation to the overall lengths of the two diagrams.

Teaching Aid 33 provides six other optical illusions. The optical illusion regarding the size of the sun is similar to the optical illusion with the black dots on the Teaching Aid.

LESSON 7-1

RESOURCES
- Lesson Master 7-1
- Visual for Teaching Aid 34: Table and Graph for **Example 1**
- Computer Master 13

OBJECTIVE

H Graph equations for straight lines by making a table of values.

TEACHING NOTES

In discussing Beth's bank balance at the beginning of this lesson, we restrict the domain of w to nonnegative integers. Therefore, the graph is discrete. A more advanced view of this situation is given in the *Extension* activity.

In **Example 1,** the flood waters recede continuously, so the line is continuous. You might need to note that the points highlighted by dots on a continuous graph are there for convenience. They do not mean that the graph is partly discrete.

Computer If possible, run the computer program of **Example 2** in class. Explain that using a computer with complicated equations can save time and allow a more accurate graph to be drawn. You can have students change the constants in line 40 to experiment with different equations and see that changing the constants changes the graph. They can gain insight that will be helpful in the next chapter where slope and intercept are formally studied.

LESSON

7-1 Graphing Lines

Suppose Beth begins with \$10 in the bank and adds \$5 to her account each week. After w weeks she will have $10 + 5w$ dollars. If t represents the total amount in her account at the end of w weeks, Beth's bank balance can be described in three different ways:

(1) with an equation $\quad t = 10 + 5w$

(2) with a chart

w	t
0	10
1	15
2	20
3	25
4	30
⋮	⋮

(3) with a graph

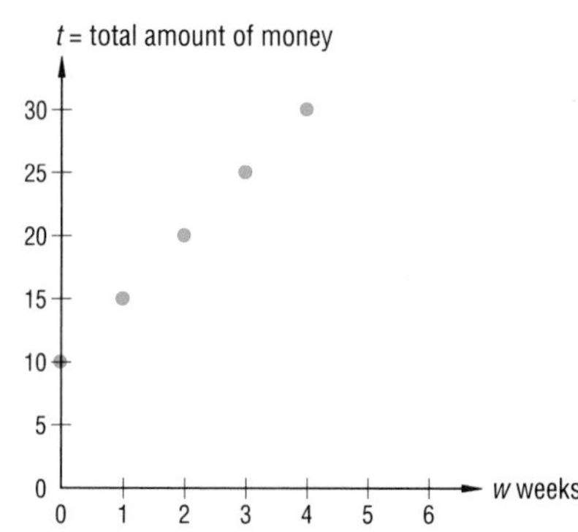

The chart lists the ordered pairs (0, 10), (1, 15), (2, 20), (3, 25) and (4, 30). All these pairs make the equation $t = 10 + 5w$ true. The equation $t = 10 + 5w$ is called a **linear equation** since the points of its graph lie on a line. Because Beth puts money into her account at specific intervals, it does not make sense to connect the points. The graph is *discrete*.

Whereas the equation $t = 10 + 5w$ uses the two variables w and t, the letters x and y are more commonly used to describe graphs. Many situations lead to straight-line graphs.

Example 1 A flooded stream is 14 inches above its normal level. The water level is dropping 2 inches per hour. Its height y above normal after x hours is given by $y = 14 - 2x$. Graph this relationship.

Solution Find the height at 0, 1, 2, 3, and 4 hours and make a table.

hour (x)	height ($y = 14 - 2x$)
0	$14 - 2 \cdot 0 = 14$
1	$14 - 2 \cdot 1 = 12$
2	$14 - 2 \cdot 2 = 10$
3	$14 - 2 \cdot 3 = 8$
4	$14 - 2 \cdot 4 = 6$

Graph the ordered pairs found in the table and draw the line through them.

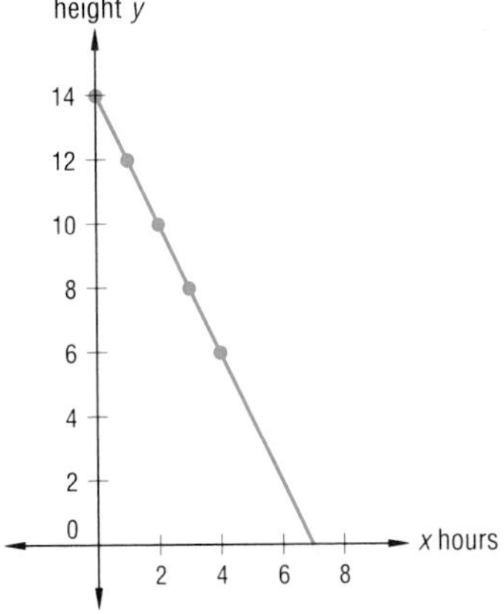

In Example 1, the points found are connected because the height is steadily decreasing. So the graph is *continuous*.

If you are not told the domain for a variable, assume that any number is allowed. The graph will be continuous. In later chapters you will see equations like $y = 3x^2 + 5$ and $y = 2^x$ whose graphs are not lines. They are not linear equations because both variables are not to the first power.

ADDITIONAL EXAMPLES

1. A frostbite victim's temperature was 11° below normal, but increased by 2° per hour. If t is the amount that the temperature is below normal after h hours, then $t = -11 + 2h$. Graph this relationship.

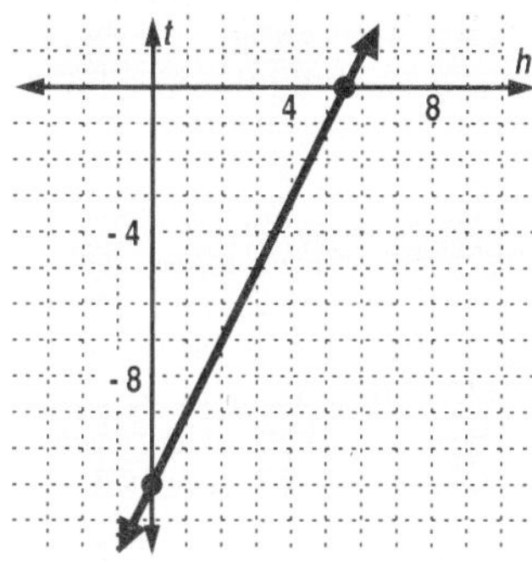

2. Draw the graph of $y = 3x - 4$.

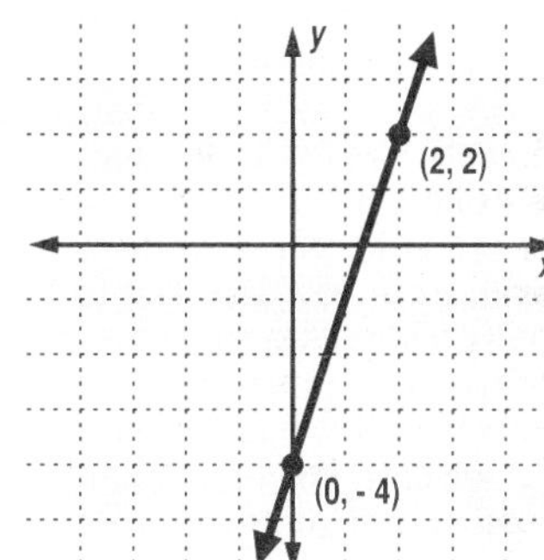

3. Write a computer program to print a table of values for $y = 3x - 4$ for $x = 0, 1, 2, 3$, and 4.

```
10 PRINT "TABLE OF (X,Y)
     VALUES"
20 PRINT "X VALUE", "Y
     VALUE"
30 FOR X = 0 TO 4
40 LET Y = 3*X-4
50 PRINT X, Y
60 NEXT X
70 END
```

NOTES ON QUESTIONS
Questions 4-6: These questions show the relationship between a table of values, an equation, and a graph. They can be answered by looking at the table or the graph or by solving an equation. Emphasize that all of these describe the same relationship and each has a special role. The table gives specific values. The equation allows you to rework the relationship between the variables. The graph gives a visual picture and can show pairs more compactly than a table.

Questions 11 and 13: These questions reinforce the understanding that if a point represented by an ordered pair is on the graph of an equation, its coordinates must make the equation true.

Small Group Work for Question 29: Use this question to stimulate discussion. You may wish first to have students work in small groups while analyzing the question. Allow any answer for which a student can provide an adequate rationale.

ADDITIONAL ANSWERS
2c.

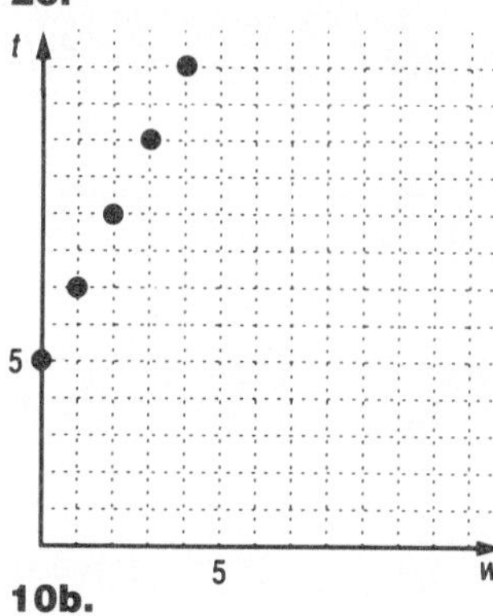

10b.

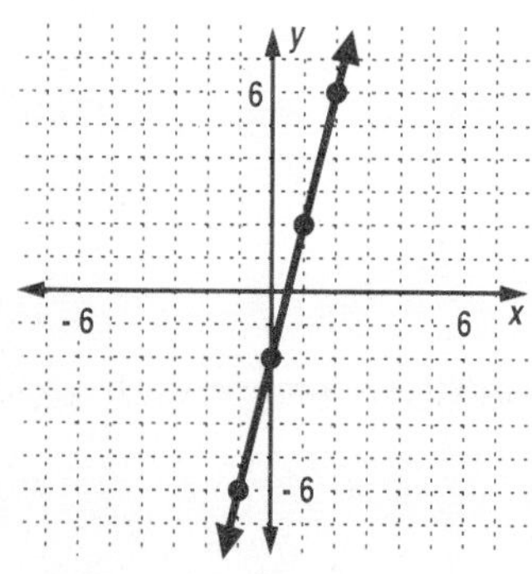

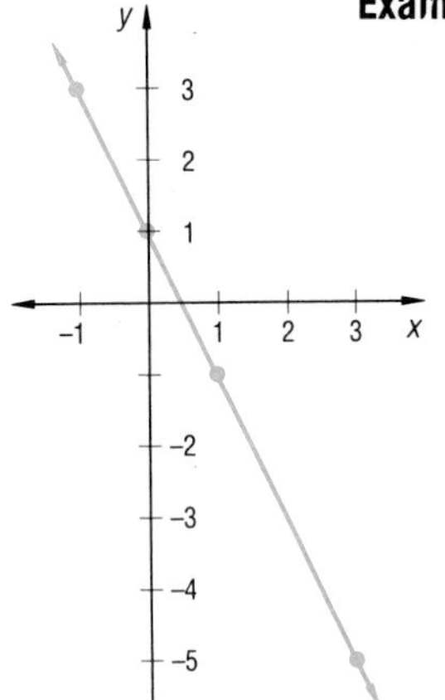

Example 2 Draw the graph of $y = -2x + 1$.

Solution 1 You can choose *any* values for x. We chose -1, 0, 1, 2, and 3. Make a table of solutions. Graph the points and connect them.

x	$y = -2x + 1$
-1	$-2 \cdot -1 + 1 = 3$
0	$-2 \cdot 0 + 1 = 1$
1	$-2 \cdot 1 + 1 = -1$
2	$-2 \cdot 2 + 1 = -3$
3	$-2 \cdot 3 + 1 = -5$

Solution 2 The following program will print a table of values similar to the one shown above. Lines 30–60 build the table for $x = -1, 0, 1, 2,$ and 3. From each x value, y is computed. The ordered pairs are printed in a table.

```
10 PRINT "TABLE OF (X,Y) VALUES"
20 PRINT "X VALUE", "Y VALUE"
30 FOR X = -1 TO 3
40    LET Y = -2 * X + 1
50    PRINT X,Y
60 NEXT X
70 END
-1   3
 0   1
 1  -1
 2  -3
 3  -5
```

You can change line 30 to specify a different set of points for your table. You can change line 40 to specify a different linear equation.

Questions

Covering the Reading

1. How much money will Beth have in her account after 3 weeks? **$25**

2. Suppose a person begins with \$5 and adds \$2 per week.
   a. Write an equation that represents t, the sum of money after w weeks. $t = 5 + 2w$
   b. Copy and complete this chart.
   c. Graph the ordered pairs (w, t). **See margin.**

weeks (w)	total (t)
0	5
1	7
2	9
3	11
4	13

3. The graphs in this lesson are graphs of __?__ equations. **linear**

In 4–6, refer to Example 1.

4. After how many hours will the stream be 10 inches above normal? **2 hr**
5. How high above normal will the stream be after 6 hours? **2 in.**
6. After how many hours will the stream level be back to normal? (Hint: y will be equal to zero.) **7 hr**
7. a. In Example 2, when $x = \frac{1}{2}$, what is y? **0**
   b. Will this point lie on the line that is graphed? **Yes**
8. Rewrite line 30 in the computer program so that ordered pairs are printed for x = 0, 1, 2, 3, 4, 5, 6, and 7 when the program is run. **30 FOR X = 0 TO 7**
9. Rewrite line 40 so the computer program will print a table of values for $y = 8x - 3$. **40 LET Y = 8 * X - 3**

Applying the Mathematics

10. a. Copy and complete the chart when $y = 4x - 2$.
    b. Graph the equation. **See margin.**

x	y
-1	-6
0	-2
1	2
2	6

11. For what value of x will $(x, 3)$ be on the line: $12x - 5 = y$? $\frac{2}{3}$

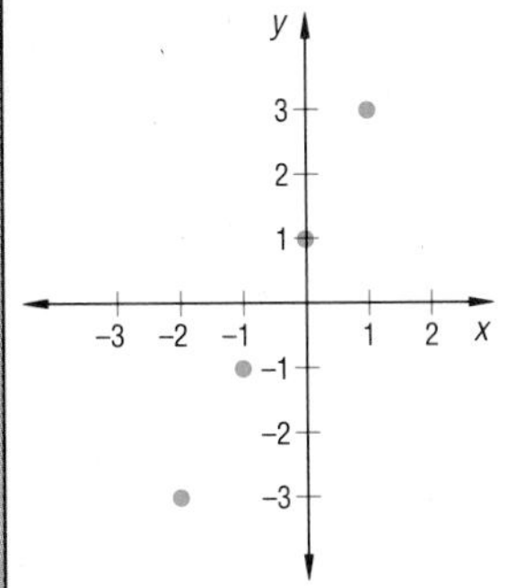

12. Copy and complete the chart for these graph at the left.

x	y
-2	-3
-1	-1
0	1
1	3

13. *Multiple choice* Which equation describes the ordered pairs? **(b)**

x	y
0	5
1	6
2	7
3	8

(a) $y = 5x$
(b) $y = x + 5$
(c) $y = x - 5$
(d) $y = \frac{x}{5}$

14. When a weight x is attached to a spring, the spring stretches y inches, where $y = 1.5x + 2$. Make a table of solutions and draw the graph. (Choose your own x values for the table.) **See margin**
15. a. Draw the graph of $y = 3x$. **See margin.**
    b. On the same grid as part a, draw the graph of $y = -3x$. **See margin.**
    c. What point(s) do the graphs of parts a and b have in common? **(0, 0)**
16. What is the minimum number of points needed to graph a straight line? **2**

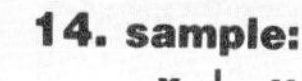

14. sample:

x	y
0	2
1	3.5
2	5

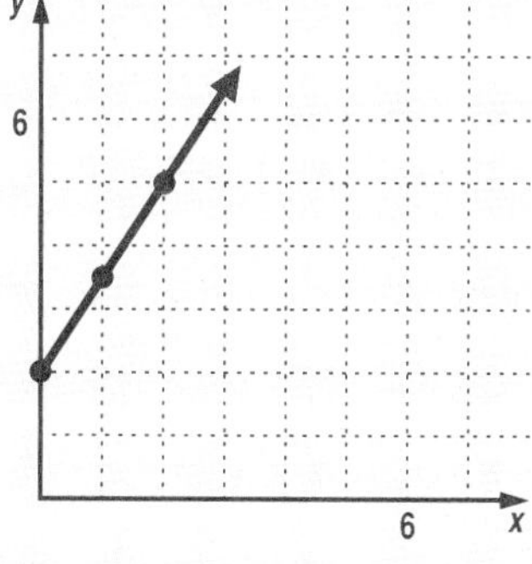

15a., b.

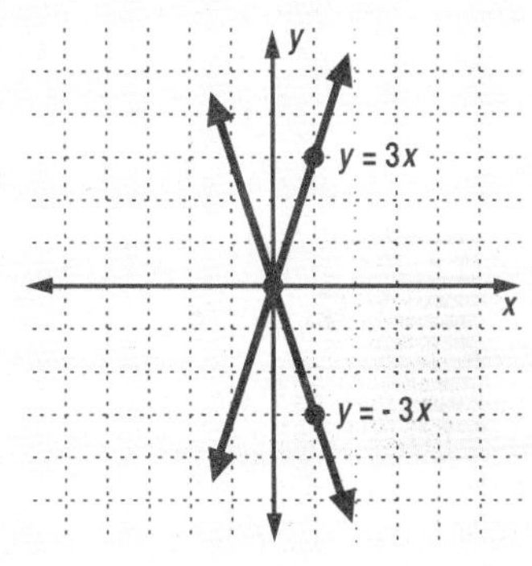

NAME ______

LESSON **MASTER 7–1**
QUESTIONS ON **SPUR** OBJECTIVES

■REPRESENTATIONS *Objective H* *(See pages 360–363 for objectives.)*
In 1 and 2, a. make a table of values, b. graph the line, and c. answer the question.

1. $y = 3x - 1$

a.

x	y
-1	-4
0	-1
1	2

b.

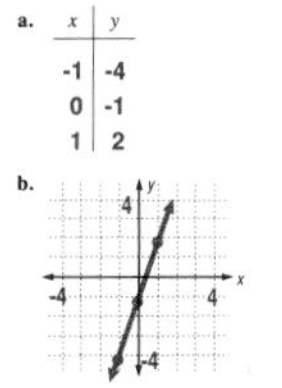

c. For what value of y will $(-2, y)$ be on the line? **y = -7**

2. $y = 2 - x$

a.

x	y
-1	3
0	2
1	1

b.

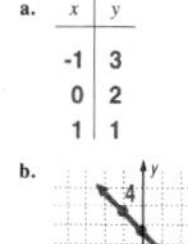

c. For what value of x will $(x, 4)$ be on the line? **x = -2**

3. Complete the chart for the graph.

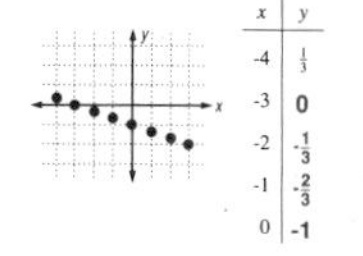

x	y
-4	$\frac{1}{3}$
-3	0
-2	$-\frac{1}{3}$
-1	$-\frac{2}{3}$
0	-1

4. *Multiple choice* Which equation describes the ordered pairs in the table below?

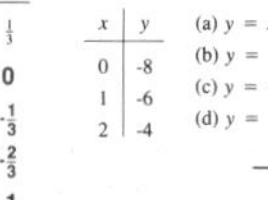

x	y
0	-8
1	-6
2	-4

(a) $y = x - 8$
(b) $y = 2x - 8$
(c) $y = -2x - 8$
(d) $y = 8 - 2x$

b

5. The difference d in dollars between the original price p of an item and its sale price of 14 dollars is given by $d = p - 14$. Complete the chart; then graph this relationship.

p	d
15	1
20	6
30	16

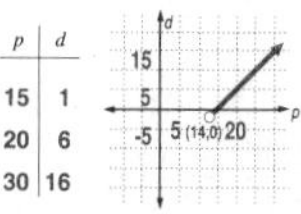

FOLLOW-UP

MORE PRACTICE
For more questions on SPUR Objectives, use *Lesson Master 7-1,* shown on page 317.

EXTENSION
For the situation regarding Beth's bank balance (see page 314), we can allow the domain of w to contain the nonnegative real numbers. Then the graph would consist of half-open segments as shown below. It would be described by the equation $t = 5[2 + w]$, where $[2 + w]$ is the greatest integer less than or equal to $2 + w$. For example, if $w = 1\frac{1}{4}$, then

$$\begin{aligned} t &= 5[2 + w] \\ &= 5\left[2 + 1\tfrac{1}{4}\right] \\ &= 5\left[3\tfrac{1}{4}\right] \\ &= 5 \cdot 3 \\ &= 15 \end{aligned}$$

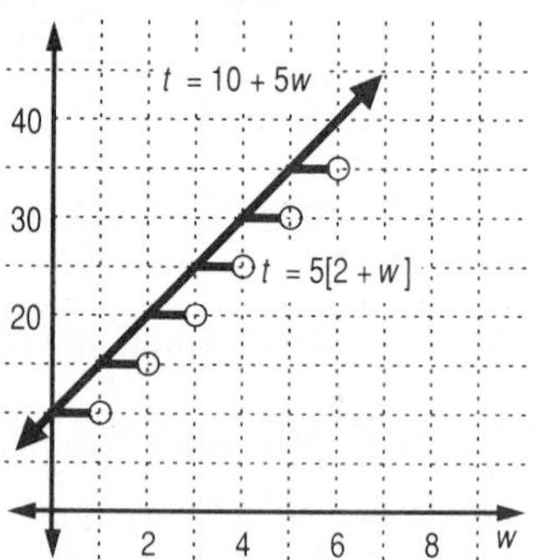

The equation $t = 10 + 5w$ gives points on the line containing the left-hand endpoints of these segments.

Explain the meaning of $t = 5[2 + w]$ to students and have them explore to discover the graph of this equation.

29. sample: sky diving. The diver initially picks up speed while falling, then reaches a terminal velocity. When the chute opens, velocity drops sharply; then the diver floats at a relatively constant rate until hitting the ground.

Review

17. Kristin worked at a hotel restaurant. She earned \$3.35 an hour but had to pay 14¢ for each dish she broke. Last week she worked h hours and broke a tray of y dishes. How much did she make last week? *(Lessons 3-2, 4-2)* **3.35h − .14y**

18. Calculate in your head. *(Previous course)*
a. 25% of 120 **30** **b.** 25% of 18 **4.5** **c.** 25% of 11 $\frac{11}{4}$

In 19–21, solve. *(Lessons 6-3, 6-6, 6-8)*

19. $x + .03x + 50 = 113.86$ $x = 62$ **20.** $3(w + 4) = 26 - 5(w + 12)$ $w = -\frac{23}{4}$

21. $4x + 9 = 2x$ $-\frac{9}{2}$

22. Six less than twice a number is equal to two more than the number. Find the number. *(Lesson 6-6)* **8**

23. Twenty-four is two fifths of what number? *(Lesson 4-4)* **60**

24. *Skill sequence* Simplify.
a. $\frac{3}{x} + \frac{12}{x}$ $\frac{15}{x}$ **b.** $\frac{x}{7} - \frac{2x}{5}$ $\frac{-9x}{35}$ **c.** $\frac{x}{y} + \frac{w}{z}$ *(Lesson 2-3)* $\frac{xz + wy}{yz}$

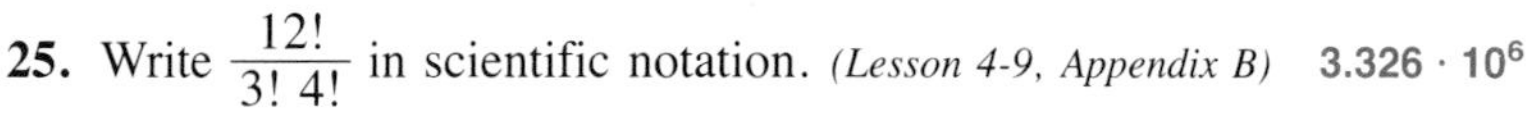

25. Write $\frac{12!}{3!\,4!}$ in scientific notation. *(Lesson 4-9, Appendix B)* $3.326 \cdot 10^6$

26. Recall that a formula for the area of a triangle is $A = \frac{1}{2}bh$. Find the area of $\triangle RST$ at the left. *(Lesson 1-5)* **46.2 sq in.**

27. Write as a decimal.
a. 1 divided by 4 **.25**
b. 1 divided by .4 **2.5**
c. 1 divided by .04 **25**
d. 1 divided by .000004 *(Previous course)* **250,000**

28. Consider the two equations:
i. $\frac{x + 2}{5} = \frac{x}{4}$ **ii.** $\frac{x}{3} + 5 = \frac{x + 1}{7}$
a. Which equation is a proportion? **i**
b. Solve the equation you chose in part a. *(Lesson 5-7)* **8**

Exploration

29. Which activity will produce a graph like this? **See margin.**

Choose the best answer from the following and explain how it fits the graph. **See margin.**

fishing	pole vaulting	100-meter sprint
sky diving	golf	archery
drag racing	javelin throwing	

LESSON

7-2

Horizontal and Vertical Lines

Consider the official temperature readings at the Chicago lakefront on October 27, 1985, as shown in the table below at the left. When the ordered pairs (1, 60), (2, 60), and (3, 60) are graphed, the points lie on a **horizontal** line.

time	temperature
1 A.M.	60°
2 A.M.	60°
3 A.M.	60°

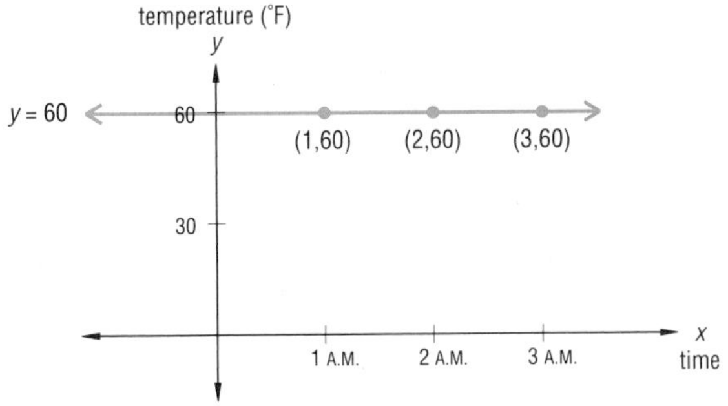

All the points have the same *y-coordinate*. The y-coordinate always equals 60. An equation for the line is therefore $y = 60$. Every horizontal line has an equation that is this simple. The equation says that the y-coordinate must be 60, but there are no restrictions on x. The line is parallel to the x-axis.

Every horizontal line has an equation of the form $\mathbf{y = k}$ where k is a fixed real number.

A **vertical** line is drawn below. Notice that each point on the line has the same *x-coordinate*, 2.5. Thus an equation for the line is $x = 2.5$. This means x is fixed at 2.5, but y can be any number. The line is parallel to the y-axis.

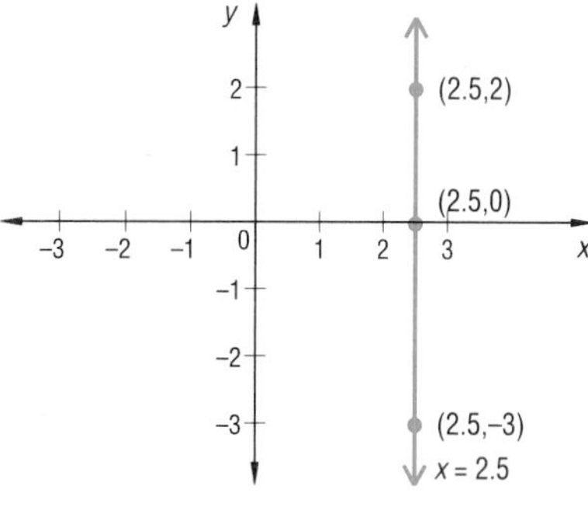

LESSON 7-2

RESOURCES

- Lesson Master 7-2
- Visual for Teaching Aid 35: Graph for **Question 33**

OBJECTIVE

I Graph horizontal and vertical lines.

TEACHING NOTES

Keep in mind that although the equations for horizontal and vertical lines are simple, these equations create problems for students. Also, be sure that your students know the difference between horizontal and vertical.

Discuss the equation $y = 60$ that opens the lesson. Emphasize that $y = 60$ is short for "y-coordinate equals 60." Note that the lack of any statement about x means that x could have any value. This should help to minimize difficulties.

Alternate Approach
Explain that $y = 60$ is equivalent to $y + 0 \cdot x = 60$ and ask for pairs of values that are solutions for the equation.

ADDITIONAL EXAMPLES

1. Graph $y \geq -4$

a. on a number line,

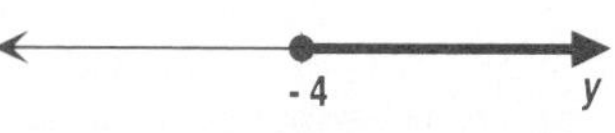

b. on a coordinate plane.

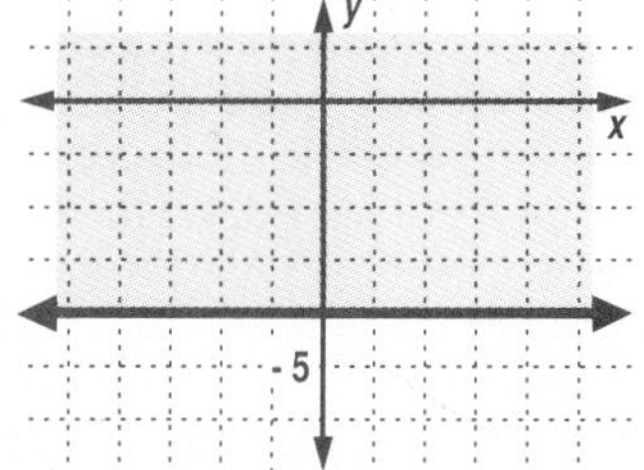

2. Give a sentence describing all points in each half-plane.

a. $x > 2$

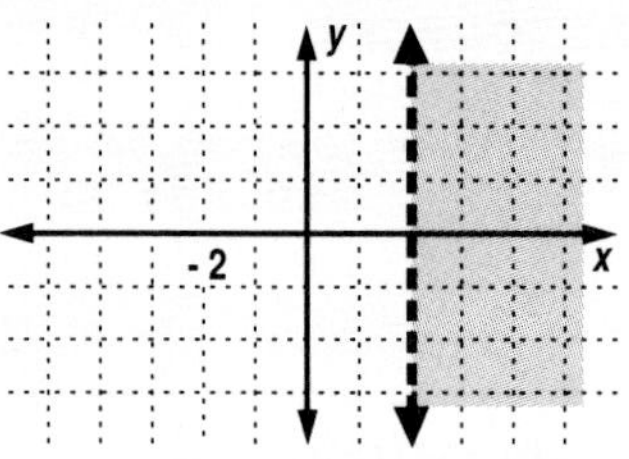

b. $y \le -3$

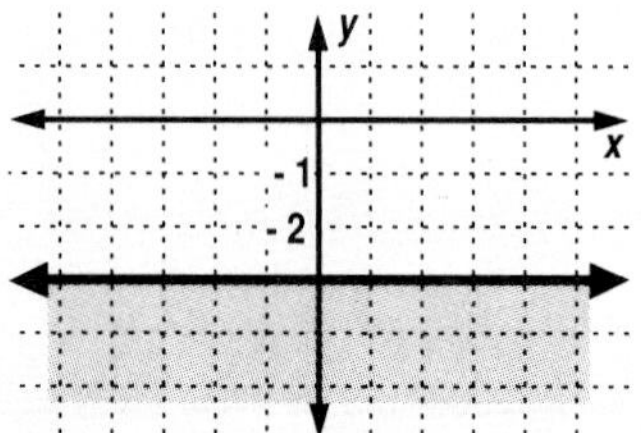

NOTES ON QUESTIONS

Question 13: Students must solve the inequality before they graph it.

Questions 14-16: Be sure students see that the equation of the line describes what remains constant. You may wish to use the term *constant* when describing these lines.

Questions 18 and 19: If students don't know how to proceed, suggest that they graph the lines first.

Computer for Question 21: Point out that a computer program is especially useful for an equation like the one given here.

ADDITIONAL ANSWERS

5a.

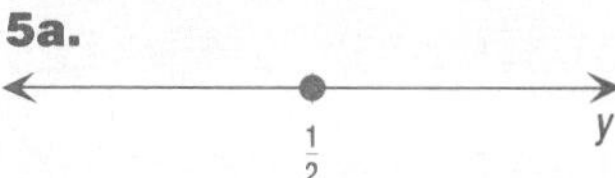

5b.

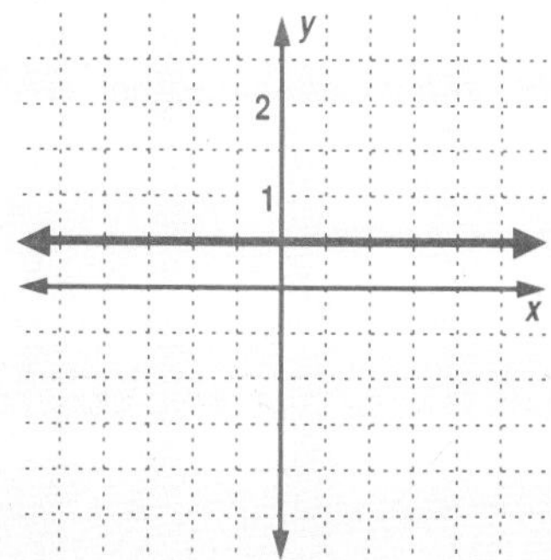

Every vertical line has an equation of the form $x = h$ where h is a fixed real number.

When you see an equation having only one variable, such as $x = -5$, you need to decide from the directions or the context of the problem whether it is graphed on a number line (in which case it is a point),

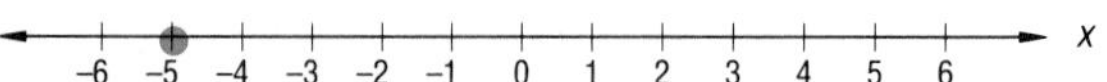

or on a coordinate plane (in which case it is a line).

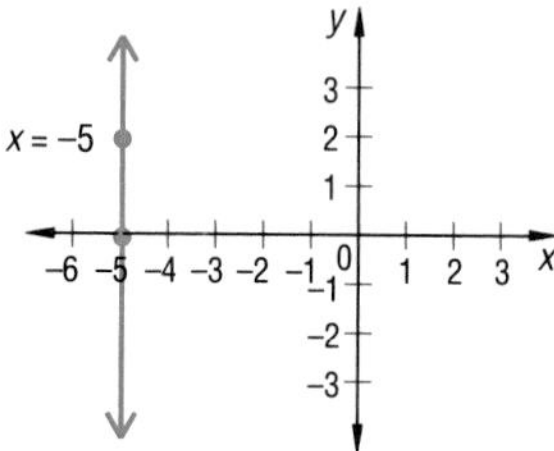

In a similar way, *inequalities* with one variable can be graphed on a number line or on a coordinate plane.

Example 1 Graph $y < 3$:
a. on a number line;
b. on a coordinate plane.

Solution

a.

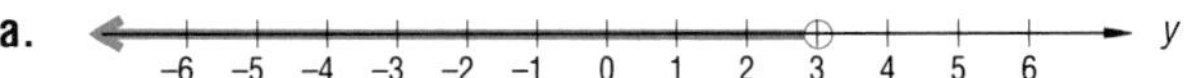

Recall that the *open circle* at 3 means that y is not equal to 3. The *ray* to the left of 3 is drawn. All points on this ray have a coordinate less than 3.

b.

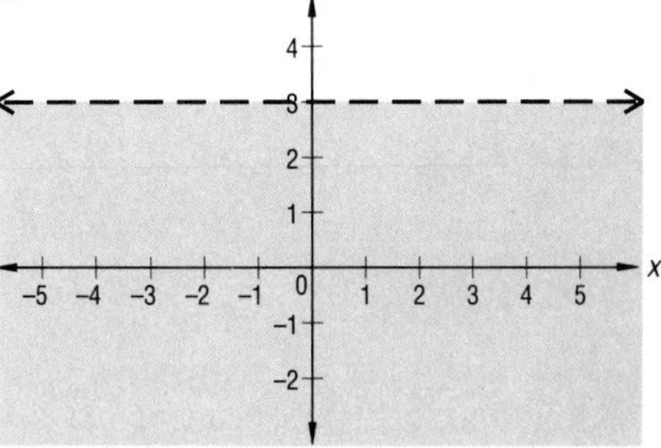

First graph the horizontal line $y = 3$. The line is *dotted* to indicate that the points having a y-coordinate of 3 are *not* to be included. Then the **half-plane** below the line is shaded. All points in the shaded half-plane have a y-coordinate which is less than 3.

320

When you graph an inequality on a number line, you use open and closed dots to show whether the boundary point is included. In a similar fashion, on a coordinate plane, use solid or dotted lines to show if the **boundary line** is included in the graph.

Example 2 Give a sentence describing all points in each shaded region.

a.

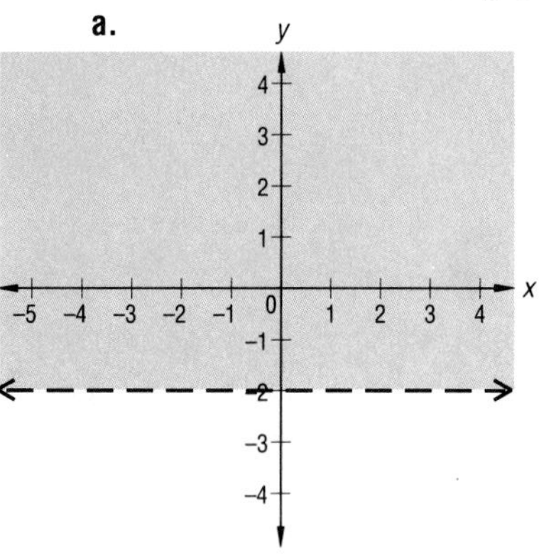

b.

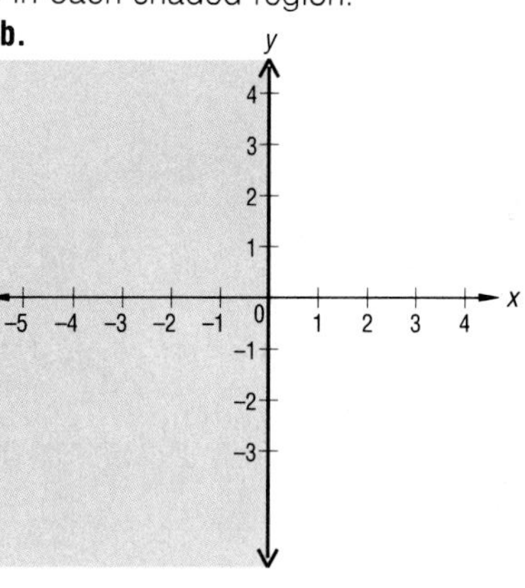

Solution

a. Every point in the shaded region has y-coordinate greater than -2. The dotted line shows that points with y-coordinate equal to -2 are not included. So a sentence describing this shaded region is $y > -2$.

b. Every point to the left of the y-axis has a negative x-coordinate. The solid line indicates that all points with x-coordinate equal to 0 are also to be included. So a sentence describing the shaded region is $x \leq 0$.

Questions

Covering the Reading

1. All points on a horizontal line have the same __?__. **y-coordinate**

2. All points on a vertical line have the same __?__. **x-coordinate**

3. *True or false* In the coordinate plane, points on the line y = 60 can have any real number for their x-coordinate. **True**

4. *True or false* The graph of all points in the coordinate plane satisfying $x = -.19$ is a vertical line. **True**

In 5–8, **a.** graph the points on a number line satisfying each equation; **b.** graph the points in the coordinate plane satisfying each equation. **See margin.**

5. $y = \frac{1}{2}$ **6.** $x = -15$

7. $y \geq 0$ **8.** $x < 5$

6a.

-15 x

6b.

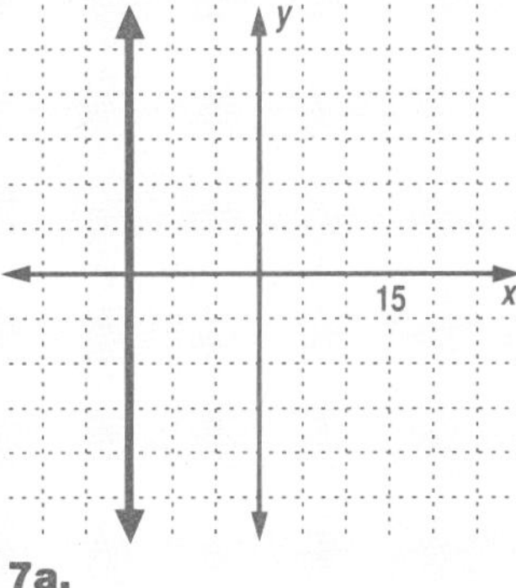

7a.

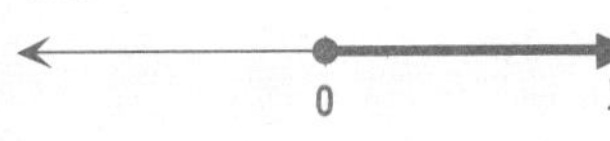

7b.

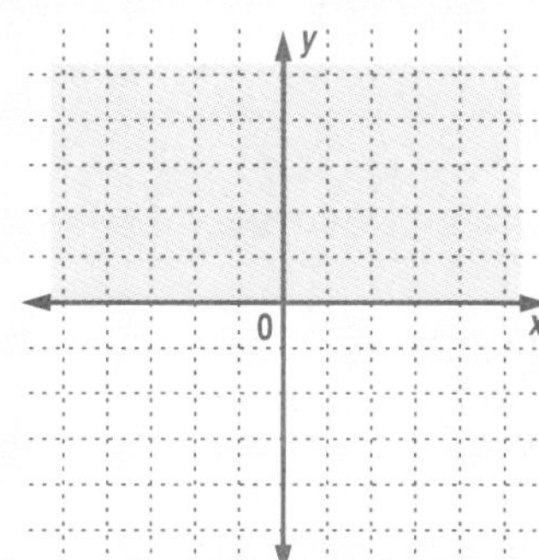

8a.

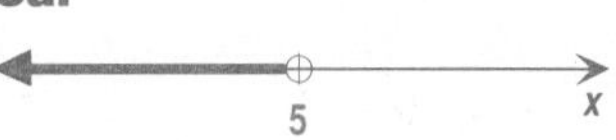

8b.

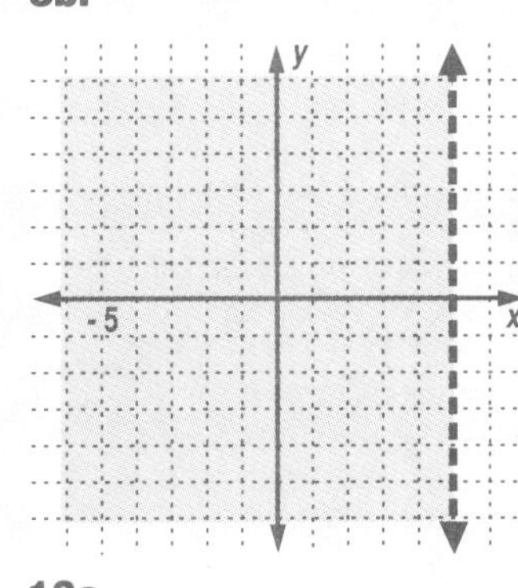

13a.

2 x

In 9–11, write an equation or inequality for each graph.

9.

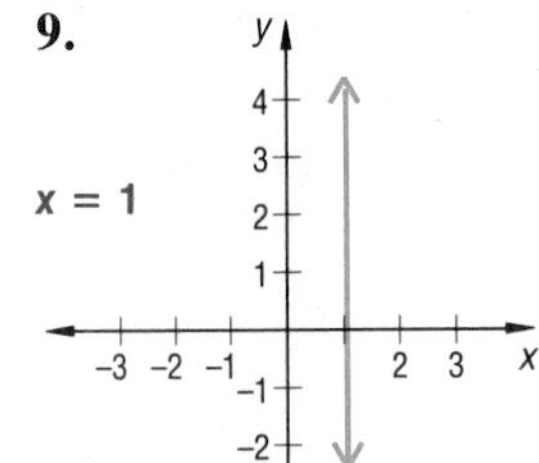

10.

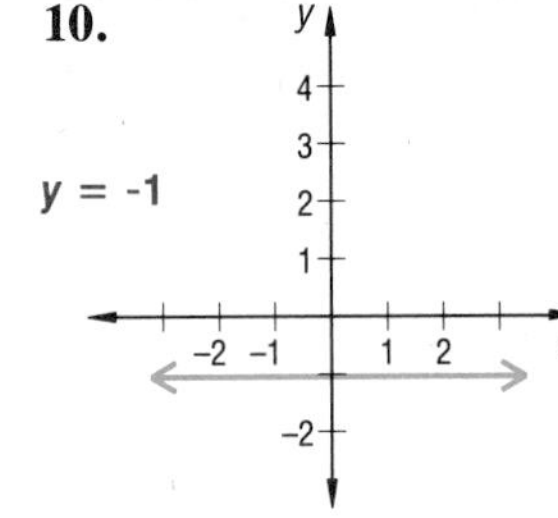

11.

x ≥ -3

12.

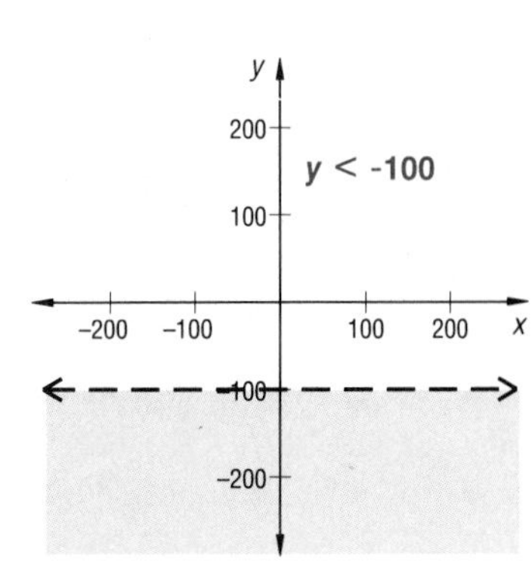

Applying the Mathematics

13. a. Graph all points on a number line satisfying $3x > 6$. **See margin.**

b. Graph all points in the coordinate plane satisfying $3x > 6$. **See margin.**

In 14–16, write an equation for the line containing the points. The equation will be of the form $y = k$ or $x = h$.

14. (-9, 12), (4, 12), (.3, 12) **y = 12** **15.** (-6, -3), (-6, 0), (-6, 200) **x = -6**

16. (4, m), (0, m), (-2, m) **y = m**

17. Graph the lines $y = -4$ and $x = 15$ and find the coordinates of the point of intersection. **See margin.**

18. a. Write an equation of the horizontal line through (7, -13). **y = -13**

b. Write an equation of the vertical line through (7, -13). **x = 7**

19. a. Write an equation for the x-axis. **y = 0**

b. Write an equation for the y-axis. **x = 0**

Review

20. a. Copy and complete the chart shown at the right for $y = -2x - 1$. **See margin.**

b. Graph $y = -2x - 1$. *(Lesson 7-1)*

x	y
-1	1
0	-1
1	-3
2	-5

21. Write a computer program to print a table of (x , y) values for the equation $y = -.63 + 19x$ where x is 0, 1, 2, 3, 4, and 5. *(Lesson 7-1)* **See margin.**

22. In your head, find y if $y = -x - 10$ and

a. $x = 15$; **-25** **b.** $x = 2$; **-12** **c.** $x = 4$. *(Lesson 1-4)* **-14**

13a. See margin, page 321.

13b.

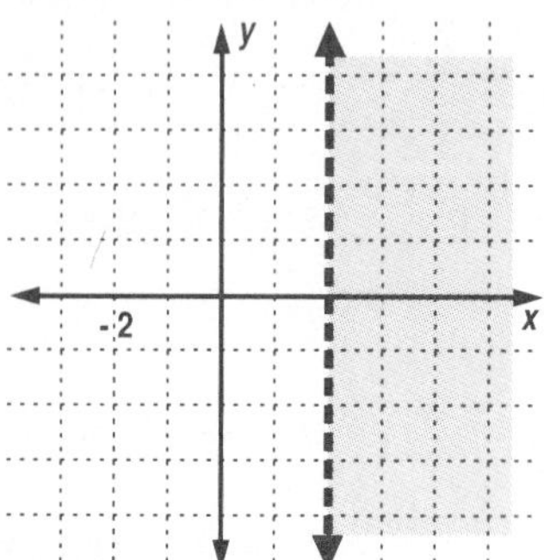

17.

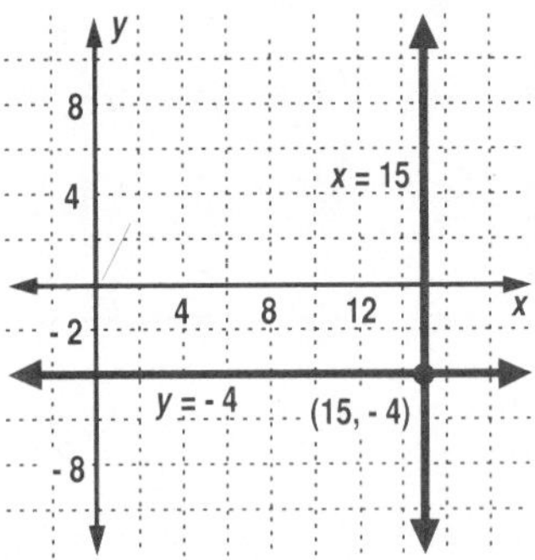

20b.

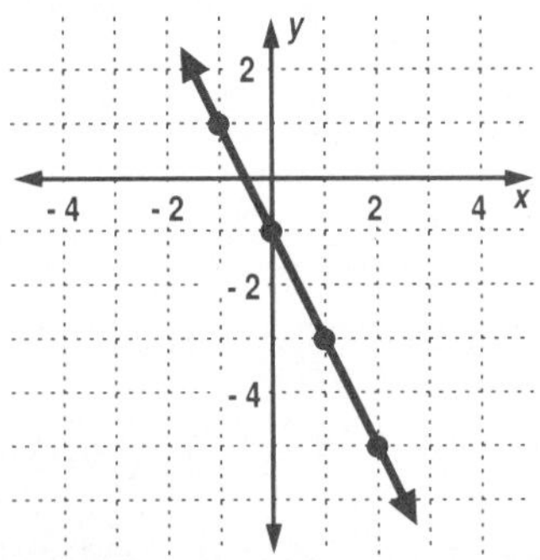

21.

```
10 PRINT "TABLE OF
   (X,Y) VALUES"
20 PRINT "X VALUES","Y
   VALUES"
30 FOR X=0 TO 5
40 LET Y=-0.63+19*X
50 PRINT X,Y
60 NEXT X
70 END
```

32.

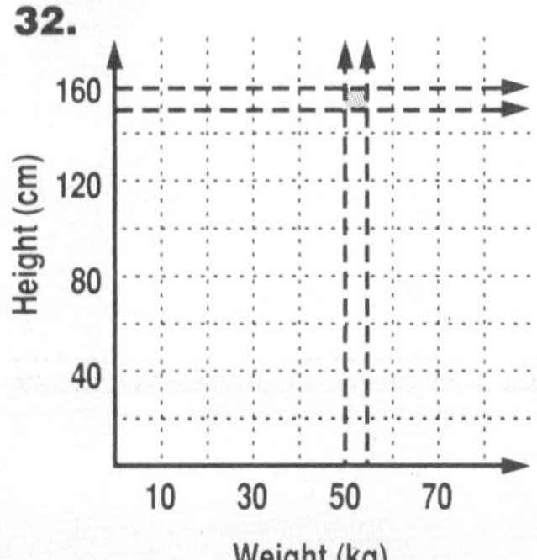

23. A glacier has already moved 25 inches and moves at a rate of 2 more inches per week. Let t be the total number of inches the glacier has moved after w weeks. Write a formula for t in terms of w. *(Lesson 6-4)*
$t = 25 + 2w$

24. A contractor estimates the cost of building a house at $85,000. His actual cost C is within $5,000 of his estimate. *(Lesson 1-3)*
   a. What are the endpoints of the interval in which C lies? **24a) $80,000 and $90,000**
   b. What is the length of the interval? **$10,000**

25. Simplify: $3(2x^2 + 15x - 11) + 10x^2$. *(Lessons 2-2, 6-3)* **$16x^2 + 45x - 33$**

26. Find the value of x in triangle ABC at left below. *(Lessons 3-8, 6-1)* **$x = 20$**

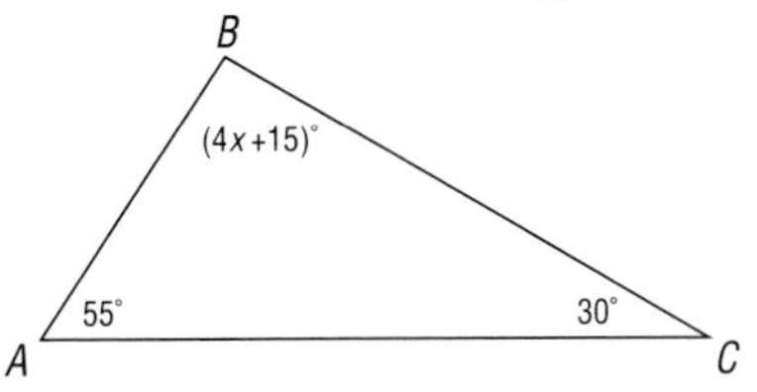

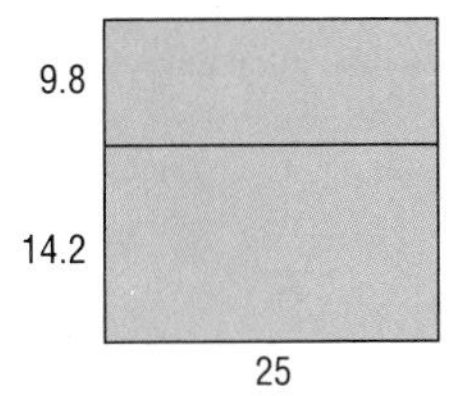

27. Show two ways to find the total area of the rectangles at right above. *(Lesson 6-8)* **$25 \cdot 9.8 + 25 \cdot 14.2$; $25(9.8 + 14.2)$**

In 28–31, solve. *(Lessons 4-4, 6-6)*

28. $-750y = 1350$ **$y = -1.8$**

29. $-7.5 = 10.7 - 1.35w$ **$w \approx 13.48$**

30. $y = 2.5y$ **$y = 0$**

31. $.4 + .7x = -2.1x + 2.5$ *(Lesson 6-6)* **$x = .75$**

Exploration

32. Marie is between 150 and 160 cm tall and weighs between 50 and 55 kg. Copy the graph on the right. Display all Marie's possible heights and weights on your graph.
See margin.

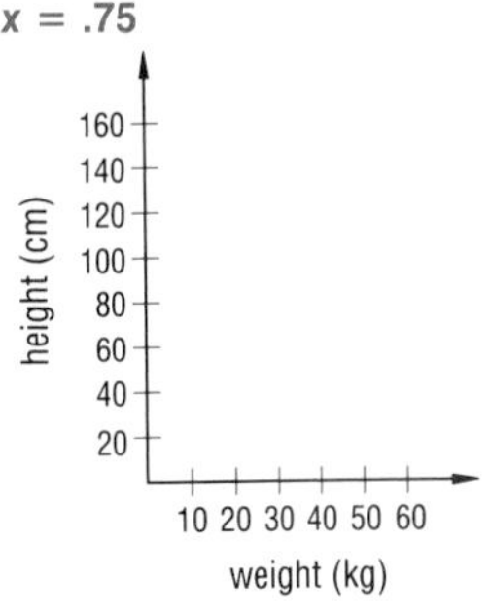

33. The robot below is described by the following inequalities:

Chest:	$2 \le x \le 6$	and $4 \le y \le 8$
Middle:	$3 \le x \le 5$	and $2 \le y \le 4$
Legs:	$3 \le x \le 3.5$	and $0 \le y \le 2$
	$4.5 \le x \le 5$	and $0 \le y \le 2$

Copy the diagram and put a head on the robot. Describe the head with inequalities.
sample: $3 \le x \le 5$ and $8 \le y \le 10$

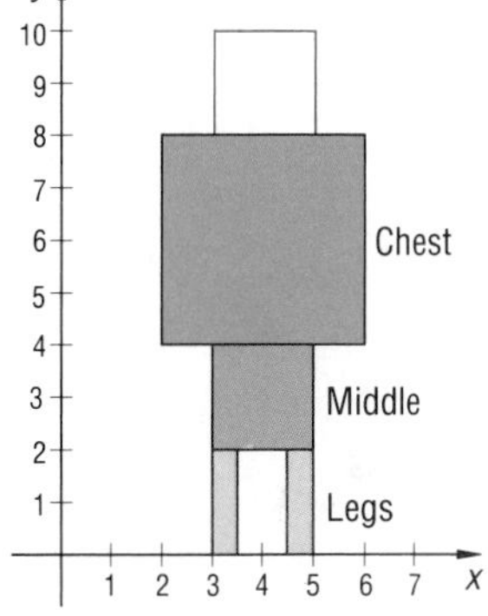

Making Connections for Question 32: This question reinforces the relationship between *and* and *intersection*. This is the two-dimensional extension of graphing intersections of solutions sets which was presented in Lesson 3-4.

FOLLOW-UP

MORE PRACTICE

For more questions on SPUR Objectives, use *Lesson Master 7-2,* shown below.

EXTENSION

Computer Have students adapt the computer program from Lesson 7-1 to compute (x, y) values for equations of the form $x = h$ or $y = k$. For $y = k$, only line 40 has to be changed. For example,

```
40 LET Y = -6
```

However, for $x = h$, lines 30, 40, and 60 have to be changed. For example,

```
30 FOR Y=0 TO 4
40 LET X=3
50 PRINT X,Y
60 NEXT Y
```

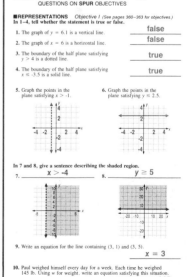

NAME ____________

LESSON **MASTER 7–2**
QUESTIONS ON **SPUR** OBJECTIVES

■**REPRESENTATIONS** *Objective I (See pages 360–363 for objectives.)*
In 1–4, tell whether the statement is true or false.

1. The graph of $y = 6.1$ is a vertical line. **false**
2. The graph of $x = 6$ is a horizontal line. **false**
3. The boundary of the half plane satisfying $y > 4$ is a dotted line. **true**
4. The boundary of the half plane satisfying $x \le -3.5$ is a solid line. **true**

5. Graph the points in the plane satisfying $x > -1$.

6. Graph the points in the plane satisfying $y \le 2.5$.

In 7 and 8, give a sentence describing the shaded region.

7. **$x > -4$**

8. **$y \ge 5$**

9. Write an equation for the line containing (3, 1) and (3, 5). **$x = 3$**

10. Paul weighed himself every day for a week. Each time he weighed 145 lb. Using w for weight, write an equation satisfying this situation. **$w = 145$**

56 *Algebra* © Scott, Foresman and Company

LESSON 7-3

RESOURCES

■ Lesson Master 7-3

OBJECTIVES

A Calculate absolute values.
G Find distance on a number line.
L Graph solutions to sentences of the form $|x - a| < b$, or $|x - a| > b$, where a and b are real numbers.

TEACHING NOTES

Reading Students are sometimes confused by their first exposure to a two-part definition such as the definition of *absolute value* in this lesson. Before assigning the reading, you may wish to discuss some two-part questions like the following:

If $h \geq 0$, let ⓗ $= h + 5$

If $h < 0$, let ⓗ $= h^2$

Ask students to find ⑥, ⓘ-2 + ⓪, ⓪(-3). (11, 9, 14)

LESSON

7-3

Distance and Absolute Value

Subtraction can be used to compare two numbers, to find out how much larger one is than another. 2000 is 45 larger than 1955 because $2000 - 1955 = 45$. In Lesson 3-2, we called this the Comparison Model for Subtraction.

Sometimes, when you compare, you do not care which number is larger. Suppose you are to guess the number of marbles in a large jar and the closest guess wins. Here are the guesses of five people: 350, 400, 382, 586, and 290. If the jar contains 487 marbles, then notice how the errors are calculated.

$$487 - 350 = 137$$
$$487 - 400 = 87$$
$$487 - 382 = 105$$
$$487 - 586 = -99$$
$$487 - 290 = 197$$

If the smallest error wins, then 586 is the winning guess because -99 is the smallest error, $-99 < 87$. But of course the guess with error 87 should win. If there were other guesses, then there might be other negative errors. What we would like is to change all the errors to positive numbers.

The operation which keeps positive numbers and zero the same and changes negatives to positives is called taking the **absolute value.**

Definition:

If a number is negative, its absolute value is its opposite. If a number is positive or zero, it equals its absolute value.

Taking the absolute value of a negative number changes it to a positive. The absolute value of -116 is 116. Taking the absolute value of a nonnegative number leaves it unchanged. The absolute value of 29 is 29. The absolute value of 0 is 0.

The symbol for absolute value is | |. So $|-116| = 116$, $|29| = 29$, and $|0| = 0$. With this symbol and algebra, you can make the definition shorter.

If $n < 0$, then $|n| = -n$.
If $n \geq 0$, then $|n| = n$.

Notice in the definition that $-n$ is positive because $n < 0$. The absolute value of a number cannot be negative.

Example 1 Solve and graph the solution set on a number line: $|x| = 5$.

Solution You can think: The absolute value of a number is 5. What is the number? The number could be 5 or -5. So $x = 5$ or $x = -5$. Here is the graph.

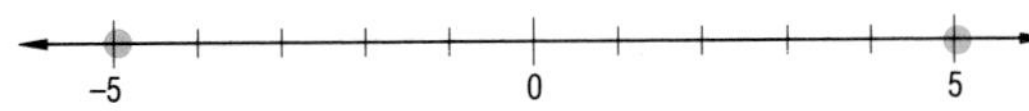

Check $|-5| = 5$; or $|5| = 5$.

The number line enables a geometric interpretation to be given to absolute value. *The absolute value of a number is its distance from the origin.*

This idea can be extended to find a formula for the distance between any two points on a number line. In the marble-guessing contest, the expression $|487 - G|$ gives the error between a guess G and the actual quantity of 487 marbles. On the number line, $|487 - G|$ represents the distance between 487 and G. The general formula for the distance between two points on a line is of the same form.

Distance Formula on a Number Line:

If two points on a line have coordinates x_1 and x_2, the distance between them is $|x_1 - x_2|$.

Instead of $|x_1 - x_2|$ you could use $|x_2 - x_1|$. Since $x_2 - x_1$ and $x_1 - x_2$ are opposites, they have the same absolute value. As an example, the distance between 72 and 92 is either $|72 - 92|$ or $|92 - 72|$. Either way you get 20.

In **Example 2,** point out that in solving $|487 - G| = 100$, we do not actually take the absolute value of anything, just as in solving $y + 3 = 18$ we do not add 3. Instead we undo the operation. To undo the absolute value operation in $|487 - G| = 100$, we transform it to $487 - G = 100$ or $487 - G = -100$.

ADDITIONAL EXAMPLES

1. Solve and graph on a number line: $|x - 8| = 25$.
$\mathbf{x = 33}$ **or** $\mathbf{x = -17}$

2. Write the interval $18 \le x \le 32$ using the absolute value symbol and one $\le$ sign.
$\mathbf{|x - 25| \le 7}$

3. Graph all solutions.
$|z - 10| \ge 20$

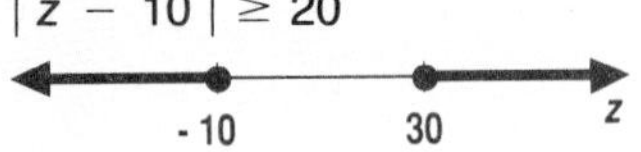

4. If $A = (-4, 6)$ and $B = (-9, 6)$, find the distance between A and B.
$\mathbf{|-4 - -9| = 5}$

Example 2 Solve and graph on a number line: $|487 - G| = 100$.

Solution 1 The number between the absolute value signs, $487 - G$, represents either 100 or -100.

$$487 - G = 100 \quad \text{or} \quad 487 - G = -100$$

Solve each equation.

$$G = 387 \quad \text{or} \quad G = 587$$

Solution 2 Think of $|487 - G| = 100$ as the error in the guess. Again the solutions are 387 or 587.

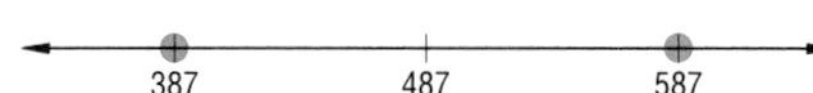

The description $4 \le x \le 14$ of an interval is not a simple sentence because there are two $\le$ signs. You can read this as "x is less than or equal to 14 *and* x is greater than or equal to 4." By using absolute value, intervals can be described using one $\le$ sign.

Example 3 Write the interval $4 \le x \le 14$ using the absolute value symbol and one $\le$ sign.

Solution First, calculate the midpoint of the interval. This is the mean of 4 and 14, which is 9.

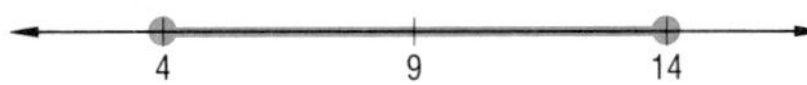

Now calculate the distance between the midpoint 9 and either endpoint using the distance formula (or in your head). That distance is found to be 5. Every other point on the interval is within 5 of the midpoint. Let x be a point on the interval.

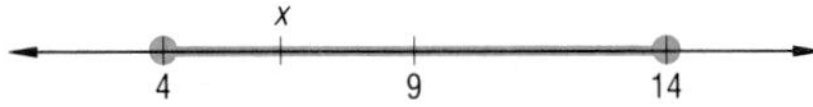

Then $|x - 9|$ is the distance from x to the midpoint. So the answer is

$$|x - 9| \le 5.$$

You can read this as "the absolute value of $x - 9$ is less than or equal to 5" or "the distance from x to 9 is less than or equal to 5."

Another way to describe an interval is with an error description. If the mean of the interval is 9, then $\pm$ 5 describes the amount of possible error.

You now have learned three ways to describe an interval such as the one from 4 to 14.

1. endpoint description: $4 \le x \le 14$
2. error description or tolerance: 9 ± 5
3. distance description: $|x - 9| \le 5$

The advantage of the distance description is that it lends itself to graphing sentences. Solutions to the three related sentences $|x - 9| = 5$, $|x - 9| < 5$, and $|x - 9| > 5$ are all related to the interval from 4 to 14. Think: The distance from x to 9 equals, is less than, or is greater than 5.

Example 4 Graph all solutions:

a. $|x - 9| = 5$
b. $|x - 9| < 5$
c. $|x - 9| > 5$

Solutions

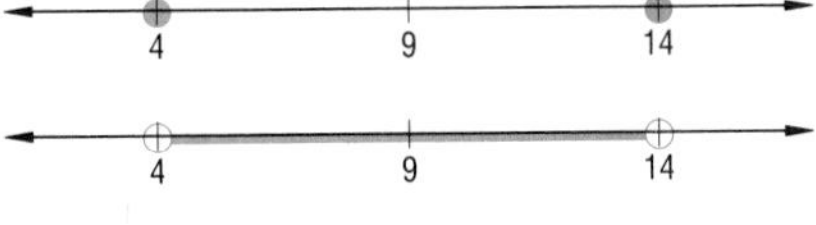

a. $|x - 9| = 5$

b. $|x - 9| < 5$

c. $|x - 9| > 5$

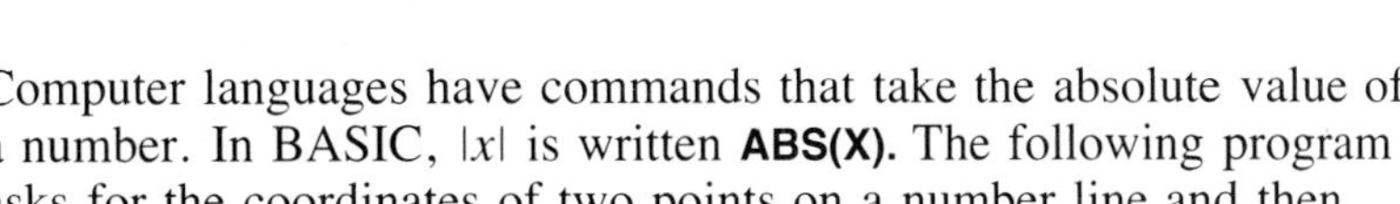

Computer languages have commands that take the absolute value of a number. In BASIC, $|x|$ is written **ABS(X).** The following program asks for the coordinates of two points on a number line and then finds the distance between them.

```
10 PRINT "ENTER THE FIRST COORDINATE"
20 INPUT X1
30 PRINT "ENTER THE SECOND COORDINATE"
40 INPUT X2
50 PRINT "THE DISTANCE IS "; ABS(X1 - X2)
60 END
```

On a coordinate plane, every horizontal or vertical line can be considered as being a number line. Therefore you can use the distance formula to find the distance between two points that are on the same horizontal or vertical line.

NOTES ON QUESTIONS
Questions 7, 8, and 18: These deal with the order of operations and absolute value. Inform students that the symbol | | acts as a grouping symbol; that is, it carries implicit parentheses |( )|. Thus we first operate inside the absolute value sign.

Question 11: Point out that often it is not wise to assume that because x is pictured to the right of 17.5, the value of x is larger. If it were larger, then the distance would be $x - 17.5$.

Making Connections for Question 33: This question introduces an idea which is covered in detail in Chapter 13.

ADDITIONAL ANSWERS
2a. If a number is negative, its absolute value is its opposite. If a number is positive or zero, it equals its absolute value.
2b. If $n < 0, |n| = -n$. If $n \geq 0, |n| = n$.

16.
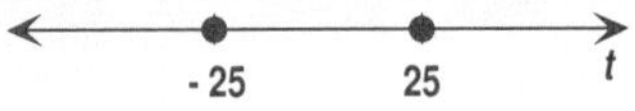

17.
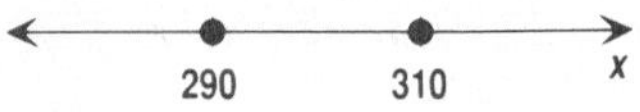

18a.
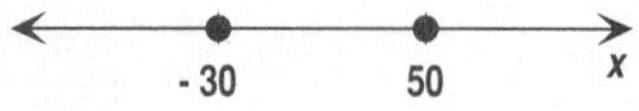

18b.
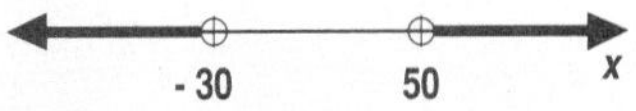

18c.

27.
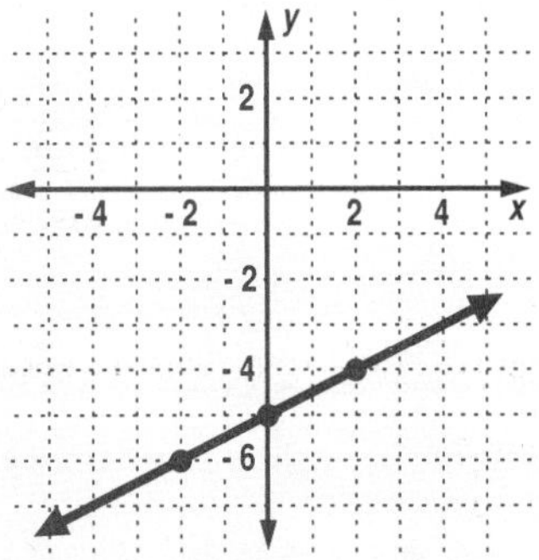

Example 5 $P = (-3, 5)$ and $Q = (-3, -2)$. Find the distance between P and Q.

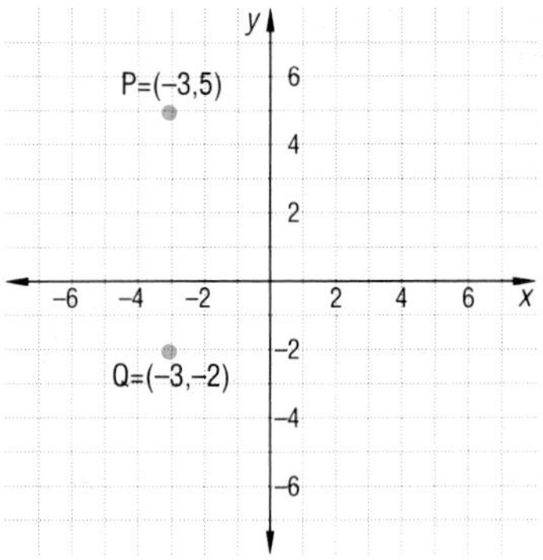

Solution The two points are on the same vertical line. All points on this line of the graph have x-coordinates of -3. Only the y-coordinates are different. Find the distance between the two points by using their y-coordinates and the distance formula. The distance is $|5 - (-2)| = 7$.

In Lesson 7-7, you will learn to find the distance between two points that are *not* on the same horizontal or vertical line.

Questions

Covering the Reading

1. A jar contains 487 marbles. Determine the error in your guess if you guess it contains:
a. 438 marbles; **49** **b.** 512 marbles; **25** **c.** G marbles. **|487 – G |**

2. Give the definition of absolute value: **See margin.**
a. in words;
b. in symbols.

In 3–5, give the absolute value of each number.

3. 72 **72** **4.** -3.4 **3.4** **5.** 0 **0**

In 6–8, simplify.

6. $|7\frac{1}{2}|$ $7\frac{1}{2}$ **7.** $|5 - 6|$ **1** **8.** $|5| - |6|$ **-1**

In 9–11, find the distance between the two points whose coordinates are given.

9.
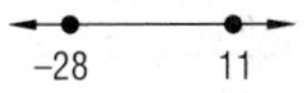

39

10.
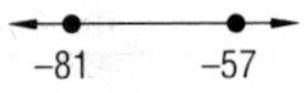

24

11.

|17.5 – x|

12. What will the computer print if the following line is entered?
PRINT ABS(-6 – 20) **26**

13. If the input for the program in this lesson is 30 and -8, what will the computer print in line 50? **THE DISTANCE IS 38**

328

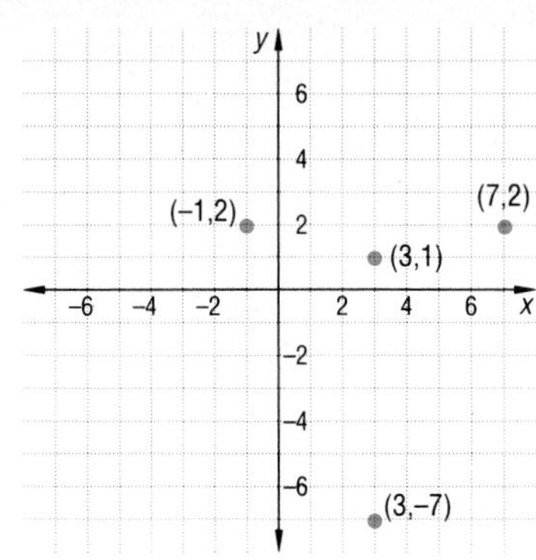

In 14 and 15, use the graph above. Find the distance between

14. (7, 2) and (-1, 2); **8**

15. (3, 1) and (3, -7). **8**

In 16 and 17, each equation has two solutions. Solve and graph on a number line.

16. $|t| = 25$
25, -25; see margin.

17. $|300 - x| = 10$
x= 290 or x = 310; see margin.

18. Graph all solutions to each sentence. **See margin.**
  a. $|x - 10| = 40$
  b. $|x - 10| > 40$
  c. $|x - 10| < 40$

Applying the Mathematics

19. Simplify. **a.** $|2| + |-2|$ **b.** $-3 \cdot |-2|$ **a. 4 b. -6**

In 20–22, make choices from these equations.
(a) $|n| = 0$ (b) $|n| = -6$ (c) $|n| = 31$

20. Which equation has two solutions? **(c)**

21. Which equation has one solution? **(a)**

22. Which equation has no solution? **(b)**

23. Find the perimeter of the rectangle at the left below. **36**

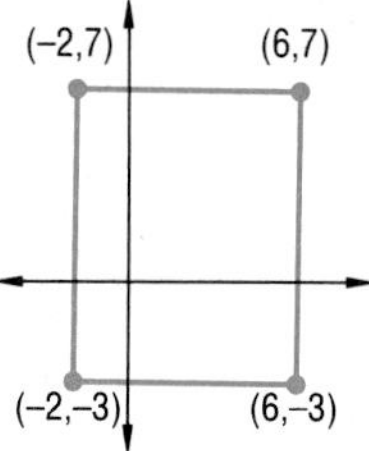

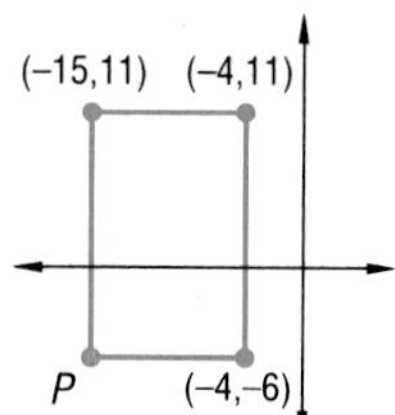

24. Find the coordinates of point P in the rectangle at the right above.
(-15, -6)

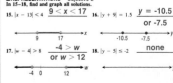

28.

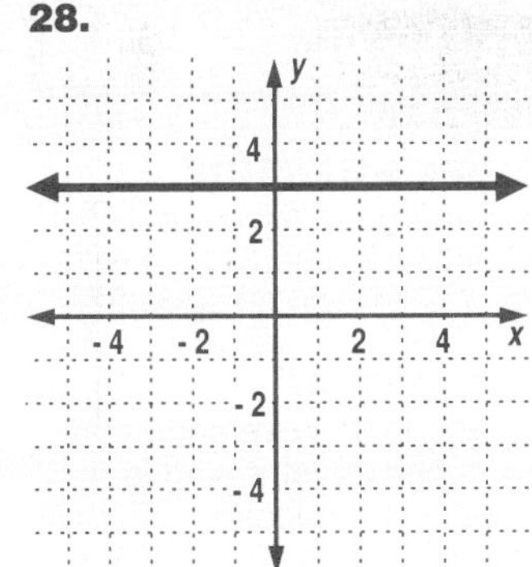

29.

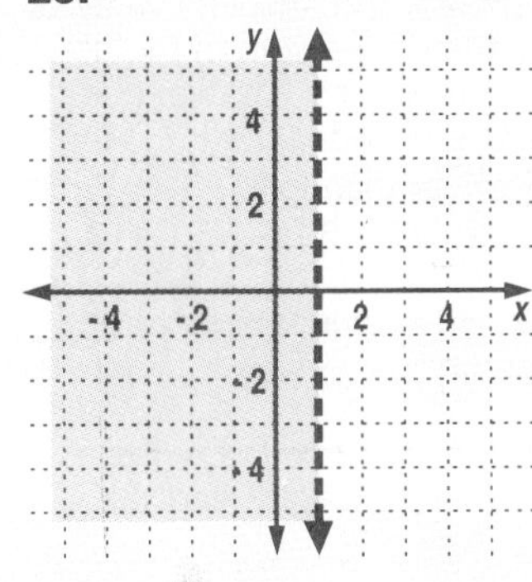

NAME ______

LESSON **MASTER 7–3**
QUESTIONS ON **SPUR** OBJECTIVES

■SKILLS *Objective A (See pages 360–363 for objectives.)*
In 1–6, simplify.

1. $|12 - 19|$ **7**
2. $|6 - 81|$ **75**
3. $|-219 - 31|$ **250**
4. $|-7| + |-2|$ **9**
5. $|18| - |-12|$ **6**
6. ABS(-1.8 + 0.6) **1.2**

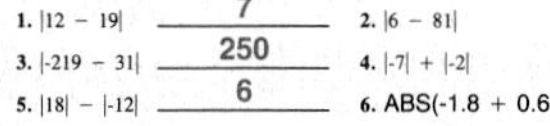

■REPRESENTATIONS *Objective G*
In 7–12, find the distance on a number line between the points with the given coordinates.

7. 237 and 182 **55**
8. 12 and -2 **14**
9. -32 and 14 **46**
10. -0.64 and -0.42 **.22**
11. $\frac{-1}{2}$ and $\frac{-3}{4}$ $\frac{1}{4}$
12. r and -25 $|r + 25|$
13. Find the perimeter of the rectangle at right. **44**

(-6, 5) (3, 5) (-6, -8) (3, -8)

14. The distance between two points on a number line with coordinates $8F - 3$ and $3F + 9$ is 15. Find all possible values of F. $\frac{27}{5}, -\frac{3}{5}$

■REPRESENTATIONS *Objective L*
In 15–18, find and graph all solutions.

15. $|x - 13| < 4$ **$9 < x < 17$**
16. $|y + 9| = 1.5$ **$y = -10.5$ or -7.5**

9 17 x   -10.5 -7.5 y

17. $|w - 4| > 8$ **$-4 > w$ or $w > 12$**
18. $|y - 5| \leq -2$ **none**

-4 0 12 w   y

Algebra © Scott, Foresman and Company 57

FOLLOW-UP

MORE PRACTICE
For more questions on SPUR Objectives, use *Lesson Master 7-3,* shown on page 329.

EXTENSION
1. Students have seen that the opposite of a sum is the sum of the opposites. For example, -(-3 + 5) = -(-3) + (-5). Have them determine whether the absolute value of a sum is the sum of the absolute values. That is, does $|a + b|$ equal $|a| + |b|$? (No; for example $|-3 + 5| = 2$, but $|-3| + |5| = 8$.)

2. Have students solve and graph.

a. $|x| \neq 2$ (x is any real number except 2 and -2)

b. $|x| \neq 0$ (x is any nonzero real number)

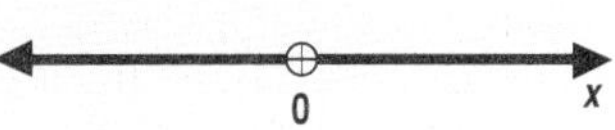

3. Have students answer *true or false:* The absolute value of every number is positive. (False; $|0|$ is not positive.)

27-29. See margin, page 329.

33a.

x	y
-10	13
-7	10
-4	7
-1	4
0	3
3	0
5	2
9	6

33b.

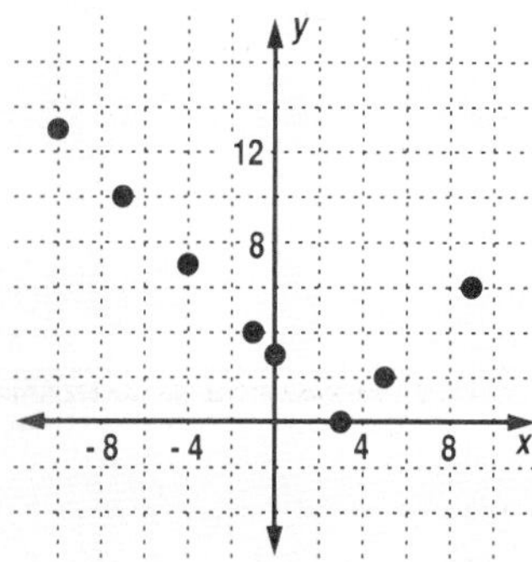

25. *M* is the midpoint of $\overline{PQ}$ and has coordinate *m*. The interval is described by $m \pm 4$.
a. Write an expression for the coordinate of *Q*. $m + 4$
b. Write an expression for the coordinate of *P*. $m - 4$
c. What is the distance between *P* and *M*? 4
d. What is the distance between *P* and *Q*? 8

P M Q
m

26. The distance between two points on a number line with coordinates $2v - 8$ and $4v + 1$ is 12. Find all possible values of *v*.
$v = -\frac{21}{2}$ or $v = \frac{3}{2}$

Review

In 27–29, graph in the plane.

27. $y = \frac{1}{2}x - 5$ *(Lesson 7-1)* **See margin.**

28. $y = 3$ *(Lesson 7-2)* **See margin.**

29. $x < 1$ *(Lesson 7-2)* **See margin.**

30. Give the property which justifies each step. *(Lessons 6-1, 6-3)*

$3(\frac{1}{2}x - 4) = 10$

a. $\frac{3}{2}x - 12 = 10$ **Distributive Property**
b. $\frac{3}{2}x = 22$ **Addition Property of Equality**
c. $x = \frac{44}{3}$ **Multiplication Property of Equality**

31. How many square centimeters are in a rectangle with width $9x$ cm and length $12x$ cm? *(Lesson 4-1)* $108x^2$ sq cm

32. Calculate in your head. *(Lesson 1-4)*
a. 4^2 16 **b.** $(\frac{1}{3})^2$ $\frac{1}{9}$ **c.** $(0.1)^2$ .01

Exploration

33. a. Make a table of various values for $y = |x - 3|$ where $-10 \leq x \leq 10$. **See margin.**
b. Graph the points you found in part a. **See margin.**
c. Describe the graph of *all* points for which $y = |x - 3|$.
The graph forms a "V," with the point of the "V" at (3, 0).

LESSON 7-4

Square Roots

In Lesson 7-3, you saw that the equation

$$|x| = 5$$

has two solutions, 5 and -5. Another equation with these same two solutions is $x^2 = 25$. We call the numbers 5 and -5 the **square roots** of 25.

Definition:

If $A = s^2$, then s is called a square root of A.

Because $16 = 4^2$, we say that 4 is a square root of 16. Similarly 20.25 is the square of 4.5, and 4.5 is a square root of 20.25. The term *square root* comes from the geometry of squares and their sides.

Pictured are the squares of 4 and of 4.5.

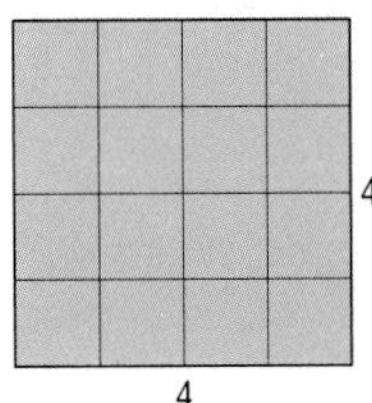

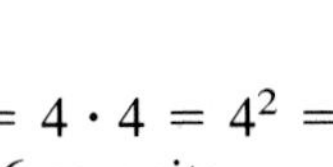

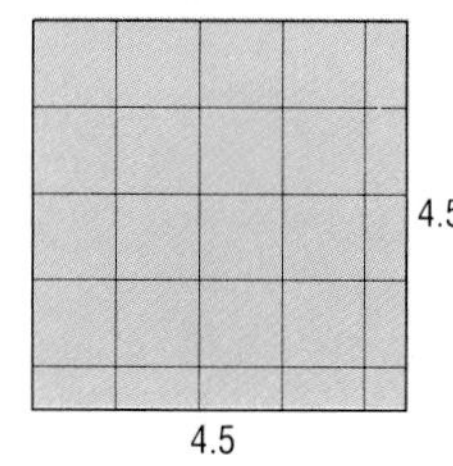

Area $= 4 \cdot 4 = 4^2 =$ 16 sq units

Area $= 4.5 \cdot 4.5 = 4.5^2 =$ 20.25 sq units

The symbol for square root is $\sqrt{}$ and is called a **radical sign.** From the above, $\sqrt{16} = 4$ and $\sqrt{20.25} = 4.5$.

You are familiar with squares of whole numbers. These are called **perfect squares.**

$0^2 = 0$ $\quad 1^2 = 1$ $\quad 2^2 = 4$ $\quad 3^2 = 9$ $\quad 4^2 = 16$ $\quad$ and so on.
$0 = \sqrt{0}$ $\quad 1 = \sqrt{1}$ $\quad 2 = \sqrt{4}$ $\quad 3 = \sqrt{9}$ $\quad 4 = \sqrt{16}$ $\quad$ and so on.

Some square roots are not whole numbers. You can get a rough estimate of the square root by placing it between whole numbers. A good approximation can be found using the calculator.

LESSON 7-4

RESOURCES

- ■ Lesson Master 7-4
- ■ Quiz on Lessons 7-1 Through 7-4

OBJECTIVES

B Evaluate and simplify expressions involving square roots.
C Solve equations involving squares and square roots.
F Use squares and square roots in measurement problems.

TEACHING NOTES

In the early portions of the lesson (through **Example 2**), concentrate on the meaning of *square root*. You may want to require students to know by heart the square roots of perfect squares through 144. Have students use calculators, as in **Examples 1 and 2,** to get a feel for the magnitude of the square roots of numbers that are not perfect squares.

In the remainder of the lesson make sure students understand the following:

(1) The symbol $\sqrt{}$ stands for the positive square root.

(2) $x^2 = a$ has two solutions (if a is positive), namely, $\sqrt{a}$ and $-\sqrt{a}$.

(3) $\sqrt{n} \cdot \sqrt{n}$ can be written as $(\sqrt{n})^2$, so $\sqrt{n} \cdot \sqrt{n} = n$.

Review the paragraph preceding **Example 3,** and indicate whether you want both exact solutions and decimal approximations for equations like $n^2 = 97$.

ADDITIONAL EXAMPLES

1. It took 130 square yards of tiles to cover a square floor. What is the approximate length of a side of the floor?
$\sqrt{130}$ yards ≈ 11.40 yards

2. If 10% of the 130 square yards used for the floor in Example 1 was waste, what is the approximate area of the floor?
$\sqrt{117}$ yards ≈ 10.82 yards

3. Solve $\frac{n}{3} = \frac{75}{n}$.
15 or -15

4. Solve $\sqrt{y} = 9$.
81

5. Multiply $4\sqrt{11} \cdot 5\sqrt{11}$.
220

Example 1 Estimate $\sqrt{2}$.

Solution 1 A rough estimate: since $\sqrt{1} = 1$ and $\sqrt{4} = 2$, $\sqrt{2}$ must be somewhere between 1 and 2.

Solution 2 A good approximation: use a calculator.

Key sequence:	2	$\sqrt{x}$
Display:	2.	1.4142136

The actual decimal for $\sqrt{2}$ is infinite and does not repeat. The number 1.4142136 is an estimate of $\sqrt{2}$.

Check Multiply 1.4142136 by itself. One calculator shows that $1.4142136 \cdot 1.4142136 \approx 2.0000001$

Example 2 The area of a square is 198 sq in. Give the length of a side: **a.** exactly, using a radical symbol; **b.** approximated to two decimal places.

Solution

a. Since the area is 198 sq in., the side is $\sqrt{198}$ in.

b. Use a calculator to evaluate $\sqrt{198}$. The side is approximately 14.07 in.

Check Does $14.07 \cdot 14.07 = 198$? $(14.07)^2 = 197.9649$, so it checks.

The check to Example 2 was approximate because 14.07 was used to approximate $\sqrt{198}$. But $\sqrt{198} \cdot \sqrt{198} = 198$ *exactly*, as does $\sqrt{2} \cdot \sqrt{2} = 2$. In general,

For any nonnegative number n, $\sqrt{n} \cdot \sqrt{n} = n$ and $(\sqrt{n})^2 = n$.

The equation $W^2 = 49$ has an obvious solution 7, because $7 \cdot 7 = 49$. However, $-7 \cdot -7 = 49$, so -7 is also a solution. Every positive number has *two* square roots, one positive and one negative. The radical sign symbolizes only the *positive* one. $\sqrt{49}$ means "the positive square root of 49" so $\sqrt{49} = 7$. The symbol for the *negative* square root of 49 is $-\sqrt{49}$. So $-\sqrt{49} = -7$.

The two square roots are opposites of each other. For example, the square roots of 97 are $\sqrt{97}$ and $-\sqrt{97}$, which are approximately 9.85 and -9.85, respectively. That is, $\sqrt{97} \cdot \sqrt{97} = 97$ and $-\sqrt{97} \cdot -\sqrt{97} = 97$.

332

When solving equations like $W^2 = 49$ or $97 = n^2$, you should give all solutions. When the solutions are not integers, your teacher may expect two versions: **a.** the exact solution and **b.** decimal approximations rounded to the nearest hundredth.

Example 3 Solve $\frac{2}{d} = \frac{d}{11}$. Express the solutions **a.** exactly and **b.** rounded to the nearest hundredth.

Solution Apply the Means-Extremes Property.

$$d^2 = 22$$

a. There is no integer whose square is 22. The solution is $d = \sqrt{22}$ or $d = -\sqrt{22}$.

b. A calculator shows $\sqrt{22} \approx 4.69$. The approximate solutions to the proportion are 4.69 and -4.69.

Check

a. Is $\frac{2}{\sqrt{22}} = \frac{\sqrt{22}}{11}$? Yes, since $\sqrt{22} \cdot \sqrt{22} = 22$.

b. Is $\frac{2}{4.69} \approx \frac{4.69}{11}$? Yes, since $\frac{2}{4.69} \approx 0.4264$ and $\frac{4.69}{11} \approx 0.4264$.

Suppose you were asked to solve the equation $x^2 = -4$. Your first guess might be that $x = -2$. But $-2 \cdot -2$ is 4, so -2 is not a solution. In the real number system, the equation $x^2 = -4$ has *no solution* because no number multiplied by itself gives -4. When n is negative, $\sqrt{n}$ is not a real number. To summarize:

Every positive number has *exactly two* real square roots. Every negative number has *no* real square roots. Zero has *exactly one* square root, itself. $\sqrt{0} = 0$

The equation $x^2 = k$ can be solved by taking square roots of each side. This results in $x = \pm\sqrt{k}$. The equation $\sqrt{y} = k$ can be solved for y by doing the reverse process, *squaring both sides*. This results in $y = k^2$.

Example 4 Solve $\sqrt{t} = 16$.

Solution Multiply the left side by $\sqrt{t}$, the right side by 16. Since they are equal, this can be done. The results are the squares of both sides.

$$(\sqrt{t})^2 = (16)^2$$
$$t = 256$$

NOTES ON QUESTIONS
Alternate Approach for Questions 10-15: You can point out the role of inverse operations in solving equations. Just as $x + a = b$ can be solved by subtracting and $x - a = b$ by adding, $x^2 = k$ can be solved by "taking the square root" and $\sqrt{x} = k$ by squaring. If positive numbers only are considered, then squaring and taking the square root are inverse operations.

Question 20: Remark that parts **a, b,** and **c** have different answers. This shows that you cannot "move" a number in and outside the radical sign without changing the value of the expression.

Questions 22 and 23: These involve simplifying expressions of the form $a\sqrt{n} \cdot b\sqrt{n}$. Encourage students to view this as four numbers being multiplied. Then have students regroup as in $(a \cdot b)(\sqrt{n} \cdot \sqrt{n})$.

Making Connections for Question 24: Point out that the radical sign acts as a grouping symbol. This question prepares students for calculations of the type to be found in the next lesson.

Check Does $\sqrt{256} = 16$? Yes, $16^2 = 256$.

You can also use the idea that $(\sqrt{x})^2 = \sqrt{x} \cdot \sqrt{x} = x$ to simplify expressions.

Example 5 Multiply $4\sqrt{10} \cdot \sqrt{10}$.

Solution Think of $4\sqrt{10}$ as being $4 \cdot \sqrt{10}$.

$$\begin{aligned} 4\sqrt{10} \cdot \sqrt{10} &= 4 \cdot \sqrt{10} \cdot \sqrt{10} \\ &= 4 \cdot (\sqrt{10})^2 \\ &= 4 \cdot 10 \\ &= 40 \end{aligned}$$

Check Convert to decimals. $\sqrt{10} \approx 3.16$, so $4\sqrt{10} \approx 12.64$. $4\sqrt{10} \cdot \sqrt{10} \approx 12.64(3.16) = 39.9424 \approx 40$. It checks.

A computer will also calculate square roots. In BASIC, **SQR(X)** is $\sqrt{x}$. Consider this program:

```
10 REM PROGRAM TO COMPUTE SQUARE ROOTS
20 INPUT "TYPE IN A NUMBER"; A
30 PRINT "CALCULATE SQUARE ROOTS"
40 IF A > 0 THEN PRINT SQR(A), -SQR(A)
50 IF A = 0 THEN PRINT A
60 IF A < 0 THEN PRINT "NO REAL SQUARE ROOTS"
70 END
```

Example 6 What will the computer print if $A = 39$?

Solution Since $39 > 0$, the computer will print:

```
TYPE IN A NUMBER ?39
CALCULATE SQUARE ROOTS
6.244997998      -6.244997998
```

Questions

Covering the Reading

1. Because $169 = 13 \cdot 13$, 13 is called a _?_ of 169. **square root**
2. $72.25 = 8.5 \cdot 8.5$; so _?_ is a square root of _?_. **8.5, 72.25**
3. When $A = s^2$, A is called the _?_ of s. **square**

4. Name the two square roots of 16. 4, -4

5. Compute in your head. **a.** $\sqrt{100}$ **b.** $-\sqrt{81}$ **c.** $16\sqrt{81}$
a. 10 b. -9 c. 144

6. **a.** Approximate $\sqrt{407}$ to the nearest hundredth using your calculator. 20.17
b. Check your answer. $(20.17)^2 \approx 406.8 \approx 407$

7. Between what two integers is $\sqrt{15}$? 3 and 4

289 m^2

8. The area of a square is 289m^2. What is the length of a side of the square? 17m

9. Every positive number has __?__ square root(s). two

In 10–15, find all solutions.

10. $x^2 = 121$ 11 or -11

11. $301 = b^2$ $\pm\sqrt{301} \approx \pm 17.35$

12. $\frac{9}{x} = \frac{x}{16}$ 12 or -12

13. $\sqrt{n} = 20$ 400

14. $\sqrt{t} = 9$ $t = 81$

15. $-16 = m^2$ no real solutions

In 16 and 17, what will the computer program in the lesson cause the computer to print for the inputted value of A?

16. $A = 0$ 0

17. $A = -13$ NO REAL SQUARE ROOTS

Applying the Mathematics

18. Find both solutions to $m^2 + 64 = 100$. 6, -6

19. Use a calculator to complete this table of three-place approximations to positive square roots of the whole numbers from 1 to 20.
See margin.

n	$\sqrt{n}$
1	1
2	1.414
3	
4	
5	
6	
7	
8	
9	
10	
11	
12	
13	
14	
15	
16	
17	
18	
19	
20	4.472

20. For clarity, the product of a number y and the square root of x is written $y\sqrt{x}$ instead of $\sqrt{x} \cdot y$. ($\sqrt{x} \cdot y$ can be mistaken for $\sqrt{xy}$.) When $x = 4$ and $y = 9$, evaluate
a. $y\sqrt{x}$ 18 **b.** $\sqrt{xy}$ 6 **c.** $x\sqrt{y}$ 12

21. Solve $\sqrt{r} = 0.81$. 0.6561

22. Simplify $2\sqrt{15} \cdot 8\sqrt{15}$. 240

23. Find the area of this rectangle. 90

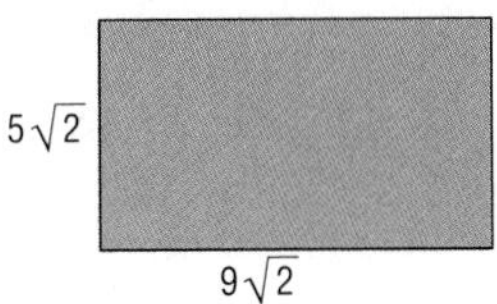

24. Evaluate: **a.** $\sqrt{3^2 + 4^2}$; 5 **b.** $\sqrt{3^2 \cdot 4^2}$. 12

ADDITIONAL ANSWERS

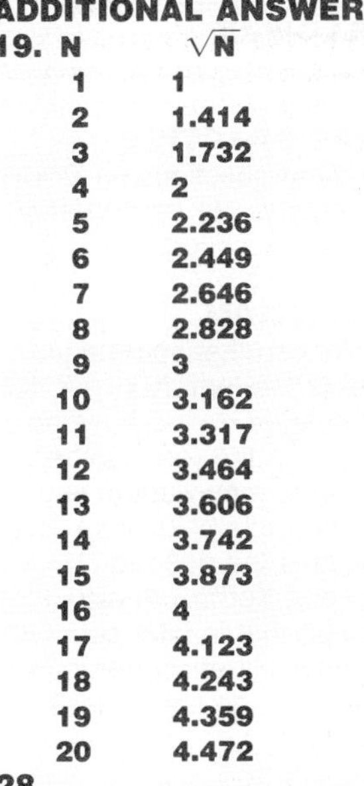

19.

N	$\sqrt{N}$
1	1
2	1.414
3	1.732
4	2
5	2.236
6	2.449
7	2.646
8	2.828
9	3
10	3.162
11	3.317
12	3.464
13	3.606
14	3.742
15	3.873
16	4
17	4.123
18	4.243
19	4.359
20	4.472

28.

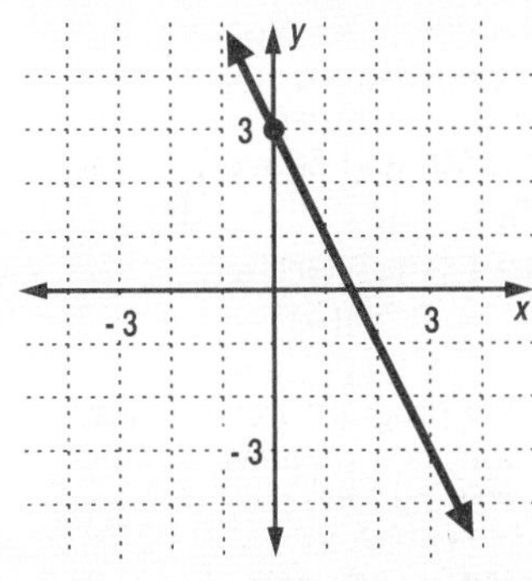

NAME ______

LESSON **MASTER 7–4**
QUESTIONS ON **SPUR** OBJECTIVES

SKILLS *Objective B* *(See pages 360–363 for objectives.)*
In 1 and 2, a. approximate the square root to the nearest hundredth using your calculator. b. Show a check of your answer.

1. $\sqrt{1357}$ a. 36.84 b. $(36.84)^2 = 1357.19$

2. $\sqrt{117}$ a. 10.82 b. $(10.82)^2 = 117.07$

In 3 and 4, find the two integers between which the square root lies.

3. $-\sqrt{87}$ -10 and -9

4. $\sqrt{103}$ 10 and 11

In 5–12, simplify.

5. $\sqrt{9 + 16}$ 5

6. $\sqrt{4 \cdot 9}$ 6

7. $\sqrt{9} + \sqrt{16}$ 7

8. $\sqrt{4} \cdot \sqrt{9}$ 6

9. $2 + \sqrt{\frac{18}{2}}$ 5

10. $7 - \sqrt{\frac{75}{3}}$ 2

11. $5\sqrt{8} \cdot \sqrt{8}$ 40

12. $-4\sqrt{13} \cdot \sqrt{13}$ -52

13. Evaluate $35 - \sqrt{1 + 4n}$ when $n = 30$. 24

14. Evaluate $4(7 + 2\sqrt{x})$ when $x = 25$. 68

15. Evaluate $3(\sqrt{x})^2$ when $x = 3$. 9

SKILLS *Objective C*
In 16–23, solve. Give the exact answer in simplified form.

16. $11n^2 = 187$ $n = \sqrt{17}$ or $-\sqrt{17}$

17. $-2a^2 = 32$ no solution

18. $\frac{7}{m} = \frac{m}{5}$ $m = \sqrt{35}$ or $-\sqrt{35}$

19. $\frac{k}{7} = \frac{13}{k}$ $k = \sqrt{91}$ or $-\sqrt{91}$

20. $\sqrt{y} - 9 = 25$ $y = 1156$

21. $4\sqrt{t} + 7 = 35$ $t = 49$

22. $2x^2 - 28 = 100$ $x = 8$ or -8

23. $3y^2 + 10 = 157$ $y = 7$ or -7

USES *Objective F*

24. A side of a square is $5\sqrt{13}$ cm. Find the area of the square. 325 cm^2

25. Four square tiles fit together to cover an area of 324 sq in. Find the length of the side of one tile. 9 in.

58 *Algebra* © Scott, Foresman and Company

FOLLOW-UP

MORE PRACTICE
For more questions on SPUR Objectives, use *Lesson Master 7-4,* shown on page 335.

EXTENSION
1. Mention that some equations of the form $\sqrt{x} = k$, for example, $\sqrt{x} = -5$ have no solution in the real numbers. (Students may want to suggest possible solutions.) This illustrates the need to check answers. You might also mention that in later courses students will encounter numbers which do solve these equations.

2. Computer Regarding the computer program on page 334, you might ask what would happen if lines 40, 50, and 60 were replaced by

```
40 PRINT SQR(A),
   -SQR(A)
```

(The program would fail as soon as a negative number were inputted.)

EVALUATION
A quiz covering Lessons 7-1 through 7-4 is provided in the Teacher's Resource File.

28. See margin, page 335.
34.

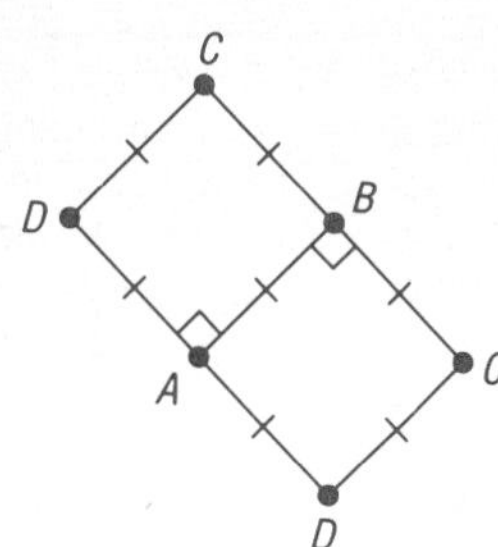

Review

25. Solve: $|x - 3| = 4$. *(Lesson 7-3)* $x = 7$ or $x = -1$

26. Write an expression for the distance between the points (p, m) and (a, m). *(Lesson 7-3)* $|p - a|$ or $|a - p|$

27. Here are three points: (0, -3), (0, 0), (0, 3).
a. Write an equation of the line containing the three points. $x = 0$
b. On which axis do they lie? *(Lesson 7-2)* y-axis

28. Graph all pairs of solutions to $y = -2x + 3$. *(Lesson 7-1)* See margin.

29. Solve for g. $\frac{g - 3}{5} = \frac{2g + 8}{3}$ *(Lessons 5-7, 6-6, 6-8)* -7

30. Solve $2p + 5k = 17k$ for p. *(Lesson 6-6)* $p = 6k$

31. If $x + 5 = 12$ and $8 + y + 3y = 0$, then find the value of $y - 2x$. *(Lesson 6-3)* -16

32. What value cannot replace y in this expression? *(Lessons 5-2, 6-1)*

$$\frac{9}{8 - 4y}$$ 2

33. A circle is inscribed in a square as shown at the right. If a point is selected at random from the square region, what is the probability it lies outside the circle? *(Lesson 5-5)* ≈ .215

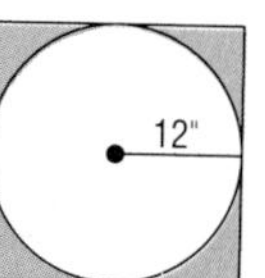

34. Trace $\overline{AB}$. Find points C and D so that $ABCD$ is a square. *(Previous course)* See margin.

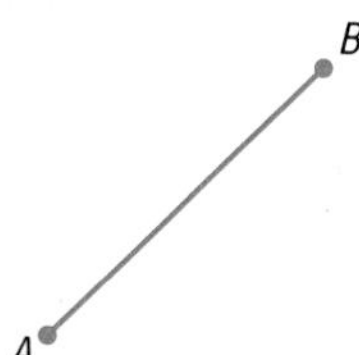

Exploration

35. Use your calculator to try to evaluate $\sqrt{-4}$.
a. Write the key sequence you are using. 4 [±] [√x]
b. What does your calculator display? E or error
c. Why does the calculator display what it does? Negative numbers have no real square roots.

LESSON

7-5

Pythagorean Theorem

A very famous statement in geometry, the Pythagorean Theorem, gets its name from the Greek mathematician Pythagoras, who lived about 2500 years ago. This formula relates the lengths of the three sides of a right triangle.

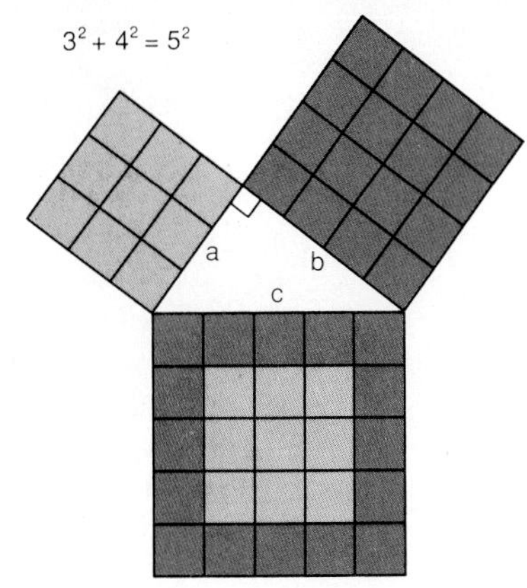

In a right triangle, one of the angles must be 90°. In the diagram the right angle is formed by the sides of length a and b. Those sides are called the **legs** of the right triangle. The longest side of the triangle is across from the right angle and is called the **hypotenuse.** The diagram shows that the square of the hypotenuse equals the sum of the squares of the squares of the two legs.

Pythagorean Theorem:

In a right triangle with legs a and b and hypotenuse c,
$$a^2 + b^2 = c^2.$$

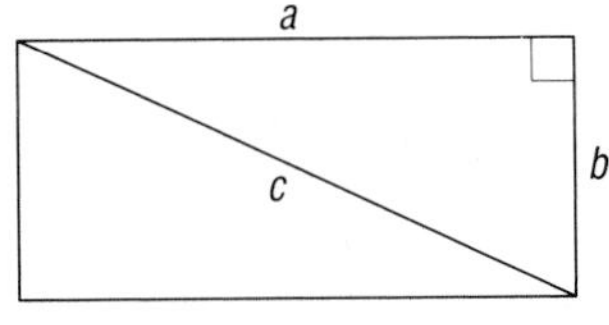

You can think of a right triangle as being formed by cutting a rectangle in half. Two sides of the rectangle become the triangle's legs and the diagonal becomes its hypotenuse.

Example 1 What is the length of the hypotenuse of the right triangle drawn at right?

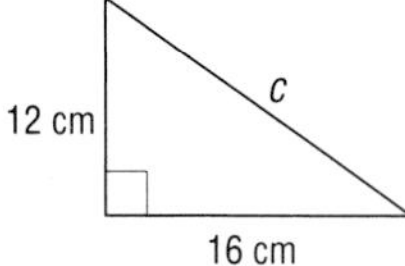

Solution Substitute the lengths of the legs of the triangle for a and b in the formula. The hypotenuse is c.

Substituting,
$$a^2 + b^2 = c^2$$
$$12^2 + 16^2 = c^2$$
$$144 + 256 = c^2$$
$$400 = c^2$$

The solution for c is either the positive or negative square root of 400.

$$c = 20 \text{ or } c = -20$$

However, c represents the length of the hypotenuse, and its length cannot be negative. So use only the positive solution. The hypotenuse is 20 cm.

LESSON 7-5

RESOURCES
- Lesson Master 7-5
- Visual for Teaching Aid 36: Diagram for **Question 30**

OBJECTIVES

F Use squares and square roots in measurement problems.
J Find the lengths of the sides of a right triangle using the Pythagorean Theorem.

TEACHING NOTES

Stress the equivalence of the two forms in which the Pythagorean Theorem can be stated:

$$c^2 = a^2 + b^2$$
$$c = \sqrt{a^2 + b^2}$$

Error Analysis With expressions like $\sqrt{a^2 + b^2}$, if a student simplifies wrongly to $a + b$, the student is taking square roots before performing the operation (addition) under the radical sign. Emphasize that the radical symbol acts as a grouping symbol. Computations under the radical symbol must be done *before* the root is taken. **Example 2** points out that $\sqrt{a + b} \neq \sqrt{a} + \sqrt{b}$.

Computer Point out that in the computer program on page 338 the hypotenuse is computed in line 60. The parentheses serve to group the expression for the SQR function. The program uses A * A for A^2. BASIC permits you to write A^2 for A^2, but that form will lead to approximations which will make it less likely you get an integer answer when you expect one.

In **Example 3,** emphasize that there are two algebraic solutions: $\sqrt{135}$ or $-\sqrt{135}$. But the geometric context of the problem requires that the length x be positive.

ADDITIONAL EXAMPLES

1.

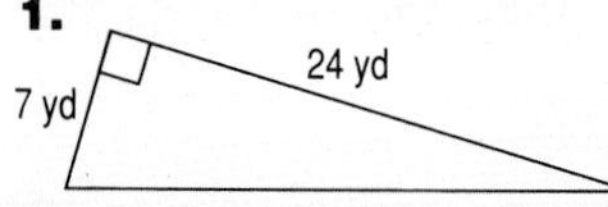

a. Find the length of the third side of this triangle.
25 yd

b. Have you found the length of a leg or hypotenuse?
hypotenuse

2.

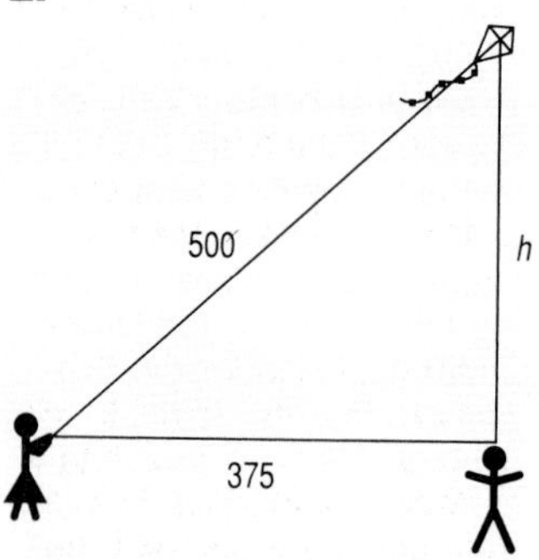

Ingrid is flying a kite on a 500-foot string. Ben is standing 375 feet from Ingrid and is directly under the kite. How far is the kite above Ben?
$375^2 + h^2 = 500^2$;
$h = \sqrt{109{,}375} \approx 330.72$ **feet**

NOTES ON QUESTIONS
Question 3: In any polygon which has a right angle ABC (where A, B, and C are consecutive vertices), the diagonal connecting A and C will form a right triangle ABC.

Take the square root of each side of the Pythagorean Theorem. You get

$$\sqrt{a^2 + b^2} = \sqrt{c^2}.$$

That is,

$$\sqrt{a^2 + b^2} = c.$$

To evaluate $\sqrt{a^2 + b^2}$, you must use the correct order of operations. The radical sign $\sqrt{\ }$ acts as a grouping symbol. The powers must be done first, and then the addition, before the square root is evaluated.

Example 2 Show that $\sqrt{3^2 + 4^2} \neq 3 + 4$.

Solution Follow the order of operations.

$$\begin{aligned}\sqrt{3^2 + 4^2} &= \sqrt{9 + 16}\\ &= \sqrt{25}\\ &= 5\end{aligned}$$

But $3 + 4 = 7$ and $5 \neq 7$. So $\sqrt{3^2 + 4^2} \neq 3 + 4$.

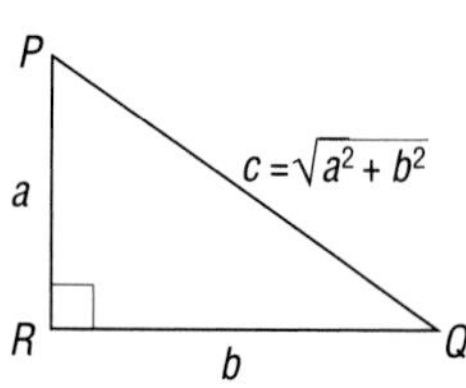

Notice that $\sqrt{3^2 + 4^2} < 3 + 4$. For *all* nonzero a and b, $\sqrt{a^2 + b^2} < a + b$. This fact can be visualized using the right triangle shown here. The hypotenuse is the direct path from P to Q and has length $\sqrt{a^2 + b^2}$. The sum $a + b$ is the length of the path from P to R to Q. The path with length $\sqrt{a^2 + b^2}$ is shorter than the path with length $a + b$.

The following program finds the length of the hypotenuse of a right triangle if the lengths of the legs are entered.

```
10 PRINT "FIND LENGTH OF HYPOTENUSE"
20 PRINT "GIVE LENGTH OF ONE LEG"
30 INPUT A
40 PRINT "GIVE LENGTH OF OTHER LEG"
50 INPUT B
60 LET C = SQR(A * A + B * B)
70 PRINT "LENGTH OF HYPOTENUSE IS"; C
80 END
```

Notice the parentheses for grouping in line 60. When 12 and 16 are entered for A and B, the computer calculates A * A + B * B to be 400. Then it takes just the positive square root of 400. So C = SQR(400)=20.

Sometimes you know the hypotenuse and one leg, and you want to find the length of the other leg of a right triangle.

Example 3 The bottom of a ladder is 3 feet from a wall. The ladder is 12 feet long. How far above the ground does the top of the ladder touch the wall?

Solution Let x stand for the distance (in feet) from the ground to the top of the ladder. This is one of the legs of the right triangle shown above. The other leg is 3 ft and the hypotenuse is 12 ft (the length of the ladder). According to the Pythagorean Theorem,

$$x^2 + 3^2 = 12^2$$
$$x^2 + 9 = 144$$
$$x^2 = 135$$
$$x = \sqrt{135} \text{ or } -\sqrt{135}$$

Length is positive; ignore the negative solution.
So the ladder touches the wall $\sqrt{135} \approx 11.62$ feet above the ground.

Questions

Covering the Reading

1. State the Pythagorean Theorem. **$a^2 + b^2 = c^2$, where a and b are the lengths of the legs of a right triangle and c is the length of the hypotenuse**

2. Examine the right triangle.
   a. Which sides are the legs?
   b. Which side is the hypotenuse?
   a) n and j; b) k

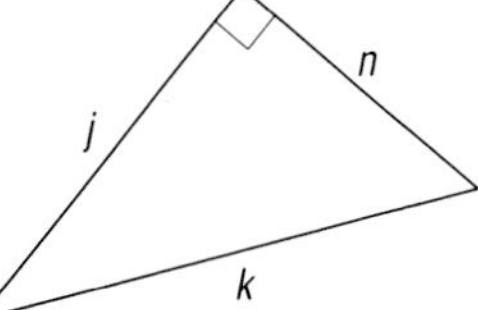

3. A right triangle can be formed by slicing what figure along its diagonal? **a rectangle**

4. *True or false* The longest side of a right triangle is always a leg. **False**

5. Evaluate when $x = 20$ and $y = 21$.
   a. $\sqrt{x^2 + y^2}$ **29** **b.** $x + y$ **41**

6. What will the computer program in this lesson print if 5 and 12 are entered for the values of A and B? **LENGTH OF HYPOTENUSE IS 13**

In 7 and 8, find the value of the variable. If the answer is not a whole number, find both its exact value and an approximation rounded to the nearest hundredth.

7.
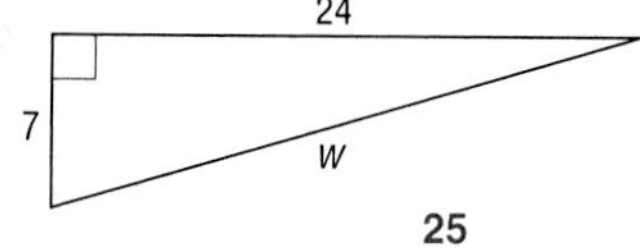

25

8.
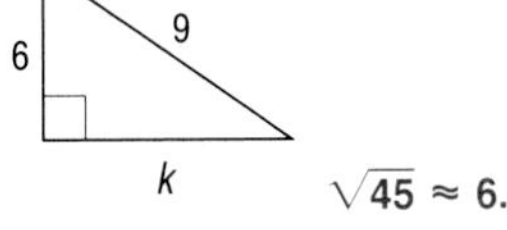

$\sqrt{45} \approx 6.7$

Question 5a: If students use a calculator here, they must be careful in sequencing their key strokes. You might want to have students evaluate $\sqrt{16 + 9}$ with their calculators to illustrate that. The key sequence 16 [+] 9 [$\sqrt{x}$] [=] will give the wrong answer 3 on many calculators. The key sequence [(] 16 [+] 9 [)] [$\sqrt{x}$] or 16 [+] 9 [=] [$\sqrt{x}$] will give the correct answer.

Question 11: Students can get an approximate answer by using an approximation for $\sqrt{13}$. However, to get the exact answer they must know how to square $\sqrt{13}$. They should be able to do both.

Computer for Question 14: Here is a situation for which solving a literal equation is needed. There is no BASIC command to solve $a^2 + b^2 = c^2$ for given values of b and c. However, once a has been expressed in terms of b and c, the computer can evaluate the resulting expression. You might point out that symbolic manipulation programs do have equation-solving capabilities, as do some calculators.

Making Connections for Question 23: Part **a** provides practice on a skill that is important in Chapter 8. This skill is not needed for part **b,** which can be done by choosing the obvious points (2,0) and (0,7).

Question 30: This shows that the square root of any integer can be represented as a length.

ADDITIONAL ANSWERS
10. Think of a and b as lengths of legs of a right triangle. Then $\sqrt{a^2 + b^2}$ is the length of the hypotenuse, and $a + b$ is the sum of the lengths of the legs. Using the Triangle Inequality, $a + b > \sqrt{a^2 + b^2}$.

FOLLOW-UP

MORE PRACTICE
For more questions on SPUR Objectives, use *Lesson Master 7-5,* shown on page 341.

EXTENSION
You can vary **Question 26** by changing the size of the overlap. Ask students to find the probabilities where the enclosing square has side 5″, 6″, 7″, 8″, 9″, and 10″. Is there a general formula? (Yes, if the enclosing square has side length s, with $5 \le s \le 8$, then the probability is $\frac{3^2 + 5^2 - (8 - s)^2}{s^2}$.)

10. See margin, page 339.
14b.

```
10 PRINT "FIND LENGTH
    OF SECOND LEG"
20 PRINT "GIVE LENGTH
    OF HYPOTENUSE"
30 INPUT C
40 PRINT "GIVE LENGTH
    OF ONE LEG"
50 INPUT B
60 LET A=SQR(C*C-
    B*B)
70 PRINT "LENGTH OF
    SECOND LEG IS ";A
80 END
```

23b.

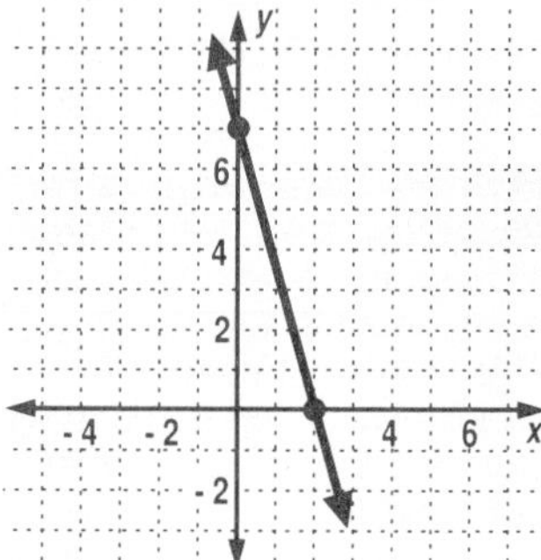

30b.

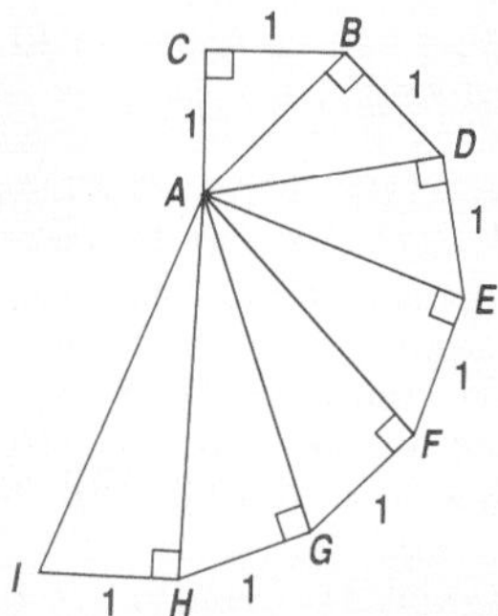

9. In Example 3, if the bottom of the ladder is moved out so that it is 5 feet away from the wall, how far up the building will the top of the ladder reach? **$\sqrt{119}$ ft ≈ 10.9 ft.**

10. Explain why $\sqrt{a^2 + b^2} < a + b$ whenever a and b are lengths. **See margin.**

11. Find x. **7**

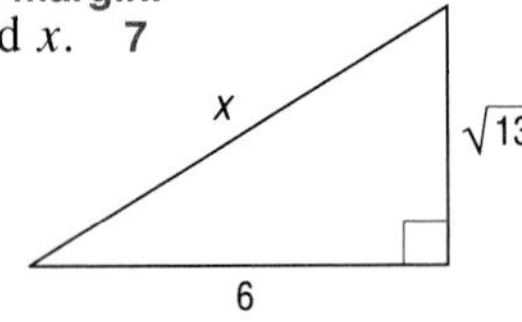

Applying the Mathematics

12. Some pedestrians want to get from point A to point B. The two roads shown at right meet at right angles. **a.** If they follow the roads, how far will they walk? **b.** Instead of walking along the road, they take the shortcut. Use the Pythagorean Theorem to find the length of the shortcut, rounded to the nearest tenth of a km. **c.** How much distance do they save?
a) 6 km; b) $\sqrt{20}$ ≈ 4.47 km; c) 6 − $\sqrt{20}$ ≈ 1.5 km

13. The area of a square is 81 square centimeters.
    a. Find the length of a side. **9 cm**
    b. Use the Pythagorean Theorem to find the length of the diagonal.
    $\sqrt{162}$ ≈ 12.73cm

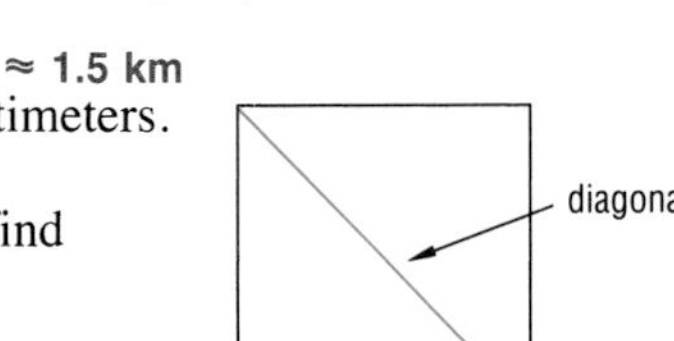

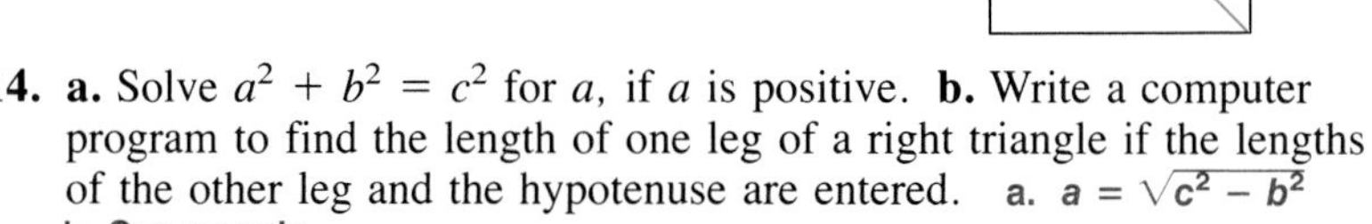

14. **a.** Solve $a^2 + b^2 = c^2$ for a, if a is positive. **b.** Write a computer program to find the length of one leg of a right triangle if the lengths of the other leg and the hypotenuse are entered. **a. $a = \sqrt{c^2 - b^2}$ b. See margin.**

Review

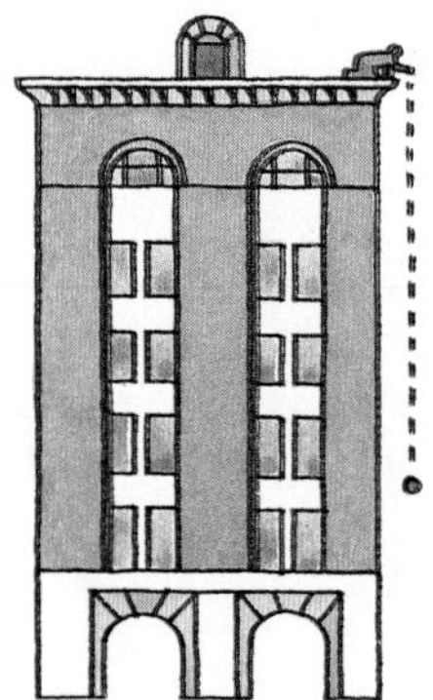

15. If an object is dropped, it takes about $\sqrt{\frac{d}{16}}$ seconds to fall d feet. If an object is dropped from a 100-foot building, about how long does it take to hit the ground? *(Lesson 7-4)* **$2\frac{1}{2}$ seconds**

16. Simplify in your head. *(Lesson 7-4)*
    a. $3\sqrt{25}$ **15** **b.** $10 + 4\sqrt{144}$ **58** **c.** $2\sqrt{9} + -6a\sqrt{100}$ **6 − 60a**

In 17 and 18, use your calculator. Fill in the blanks with <, =, or >. *(Lesson 7-4)*

17. $\sqrt{2} + \sqrt{8}$ __?__ $\sqrt{10}$ **>** 18. $\sqrt{2} \cdot \sqrt{8}$ __?__ $\sqrt{16}$ **=**

19. Sean guessed there were 823 beans in a jar. The actual number of beans was 1000. What is the error of Sean's guess? *(Lesson 7-3)* **177**

20. Which of these are perfect squares? *(Lesson 7-4)*
    a. 441 **Yes** **b.** 1030 **No** **c.** 1296 **Yes**

21. Solve. *(Lessons 7-3, 7-4)*
  a. $x^2 = 121$ **11 or -11** b. $\sqrt{y} = 121$ **14,641** c. $|z| = 121$ **121 or -121**

22. Find the distance between (80, 60) and (-200, 60). *(Lesson 7-3)* **280**

23. a. Solve $7x + 2y = 14$ for y. *(Lesson 6-1)* $y = -\frac{7}{2}x + 7$
  b. Graph $7x + 2y = 14$. *(Lesson 7-1)* **See margin.**

24. Beth begins with $10 in her account and saves $5 a week. Seth begins with $30 in his account and saves $3 a week. After how many weeks will they have the same amount of money in their accounts? *(Lesson 6-6)* **10 weeks**

25. Which is faster, reading w words in m minutes or reading $2w$ words in $3m$ minutes? *(Lesson 5-2)* **w words in m minutes**

26. In the figure to the left, a square is drawn around a 3″ square and a 5″ square which overlap in a 1″ square. What is the probability that a randomly selected point falls in a colored area? *(Lesson 5-5)* $\frac{33}{49}$

27. *Multiple choice* Which equation says that current sales C are 8% more than last year's sales y? *(Lesson 6-3)* **(b)**
  (a) $1.08C = y$ (b) $1.08y = C$
  (c) $.92C = y$ (d) $.92y = C$

28. The rectangles below are similar. *(Lesson 5-7)*
  a. Use a proportion to find a. **11**
  b. What is the perimeter of the smaller rectangle? **54**

29. Find the area of a square with side $10\sqrt{3}$. *(Lesson 7-4)* **300**

Exploration

30. Six of the segments in the figure below have length one unit.
  a. Find AB, AD, AE, AF, and AG.
  b. Copy the drawing and add to it to make a segment whose length is $\sqrt{8}$. **See margin.**
  $AB = \sqrt{2}$; $AD = \sqrt{3}$; $AE = 2$; $AF = \sqrt{5}$; $AG = \sqrt{6}$

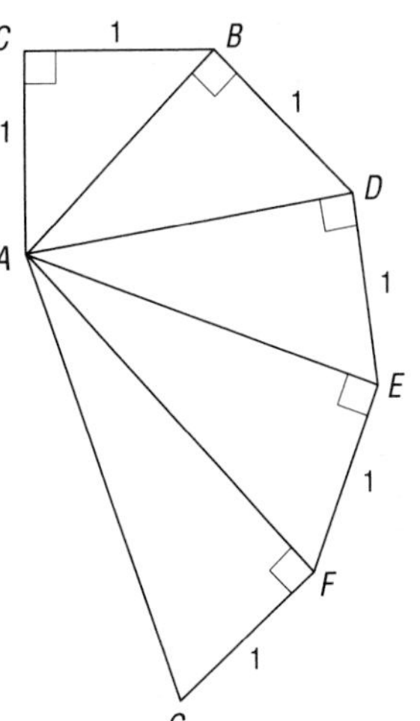

EVALUATION
Alternative Assessment
To evaluate student understanding of the Pythagorean Theorem, have **small groups** of students write a real-world problem that can be solved by using the Pythagorean Theorem. Then each group can pose its problem for the class and explain how to solve it.

NAME ______

LESSON **MASTER 7–5**
QUESTIONS ON **SPUR** OBJECTIVES

■**USES** *Objective F (See pages 360–363 for objectives.)*

1. A carpenter designs a brace for the corner of a frame as shown. Find the length c of the brace.
5 feet

2. A suitcase is 80 cm long and 50 cm wide. What is the length of the largest umbrella that can fit in the suitcase?
about 94 cm

3. Two boats leave a dock at the same time. One sails north at 9 mph, the other sails east at 10 mph. How far apart are they after 2 hours?
about 27 miles

4. Suppose you wanted to construct a ski lift that rises 50 m and extends a horizontal distance of 120 m. Ignoring the slack in the cable, what distance would the cable extend?
130 m

 Continued 59

NAME ______

LESSON **MASTER 7–5**
(page 2)

■**REPRESENTATIONS** *Objective J*

5. Examine the right triangle at the right.
  a. What variables represent the lengths of the legs? **v and t**
  b. What variable represents the length of the hypotenuse? **u**

6. Find the value of c in the triangle at the right.
37

7. Find the value of a in the triangle at the right.
$\sqrt{205}$

8. Find the length of the hypotenuse of the triangle at the right.
10.5

9. The diagonal of a rectangle is 26 and one side is 10. Find the lengths of all other sides.
24 **10** **24**

10. The diagonal of a square is $5\sqrt{2}$. Find the length of each side of the square.
5

60

LESSON 7-6

RESOURCES
- ■ Lesson Master 7-6
- Computer Master 14

OBJECTIVES

B Evaluate and simplify expressions involving square roots.
E Apply the Square Root of a Product Property.
F Use squares and square roots in measurement problems.

TEACHING NOTES

Reading Advise students that the terms *simplify, give the exact answer,* and *rewrite the expression with a smaller integer under the radical symbol,* mean that they should leave their answer as a radical. But, calculators can still be used to check answers. While reading the lesson, students should use a calculator to get decimal approximations for $\sqrt{12}$ and $2\sqrt{3}$. (See also **Question 7.**)

In **Example 3** a radical containing variables is simplified. We do not make a major issue regarding permissible values of variables. But, we do state that the variables represent positive numbers. Thus, instead of having to use $\sqrt{x^2} = |x|$, students can use $\sqrt{x^2} = x$.

LESSON

7-6 Square Roots of Products

Consider $\sqrt{ab}$, the positive square root of the product ab. Squaring gives

$$(\sqrt{ab})^2 = \sqrt{ab} \cdot \sqrt{ab} = ab.$$

Now consider $\sqrt{a} \cdot \sqrt{b}$, the product of two positive square roots. Squaring gives

$$\begin{aligned}(\sqrt{a} \cdot \sqrt{b})^2 &= (\sqrt{a} \cdot \sqrt{b}) \cdot (\sqrt{a} \cdot \sqrt{b})\\ &= \sqrt{a} \cdot \sqrt{b} \cdot \sqrt{a} \cdot \sqrt{b}\\ &= \sqrt{a} \cdot \sqrt{a} \cdot \sqrt{b} \cdot \sqrt{b}\\ &= ab.\end{aligned}$$

Since $\sqrt{ab}$ and $\sqrt{a} \cdot \sqrt{b}$ are positive numbers and have the same square, $\sqrt{ab} = \sqrt{a} \cdot \sqrt{b}$. This is a useful property, so we give it a name.

Square Root of a Product Property:

If $a \geq 0$ and $b \geq 0$, then

$$\sqrt{ab} = \sqrt{a} \cdot \sqrt{b}.$$

This property can easily be checked. For instance, let $a = 9$ and $b = 100$. Then the Square Root of a Product Property indicates

$$\sqrt{9 \cdot 100} = \sqrt{9} \cdot \sqrt{100}$$

or $\sqrt{900} = 3 \cdot 10$, which is known to be true.

For another example, let $a = 4$ and $b = 3$. Substituting in the property

$$\sqrt{4 \cdot 3} = \sqrt{4} \cdot \sqrt{3}$$

thus, $\sqrt{12} = 2\sqrt{3}$.

Check with a calculator. $3.464\ldots = 2 \cdot 1.732\ldots$

This example shows that $\sqrt{12}$ is twice $\sqrt{3}$. In this case $\sqrt{12}$ has been rewritten with a smaller integer under the radical sign. This is called **simplifying the radical.** The key to simplifying is to find a perfect square factor of the number under the radical sign.

Example 1 Simplify $\sqrt{50}$.

Solution A perfect square factor of 50 is 25.

$$\begin{aligned}\sqrt{50} &= \sqrt{25 \cdot 2} \\ &= \sqrt{25} \cdot \sqrt{2} && \text{Square Root of a Product Property} \\ &= 5\sqrt{2} && \text{since } \sqrt{25} = 5\end{aligned}$$

Check Use your calculator. 50 [√] gives 7.0710678.

5 [×] 2 [√] [=] gives 7.0710678.

Is $5\sqrt{2}$ really simpler than $\sqrt{50}$? It all depends. For most estimating and calculations, $\sqrt{50}$ is simpler. But for seeing patterns, $5\sqrt{2}$ may be easier. In the next example, the answer $8\sqrt{2}$ is related to the given information in a simple way. You would not see that without "simplifying" $\sqrt{128}$.

Example 2 Each leg of a right triangle is 8 inches long. Find the exact length of the hypotenuse.

Solution Use the Pythagorean Theorem to find the length of the hypotenuse.

$$\begin{aligned}c^2 &= 8^2 + 8^2 \\ c^2 &= 128 \\ c &= \sqrt{128} \\ c &= \sqrt{64 \cdot 2} && \text{64 is a perfect square factor of 128.} \\ &= \sqrt{64} \cdot \sqrt{2} \\ &= 8\sqrt{2}\end{aligned}$$

The exact length of the hypotenuse is $\sqrt{128}$ or $8\sqrt{2}$ inches. Can you see how the lengths of the legs and the hypotenuse are related? You are asked to generalize the pattern as an Exploration.

The Square Root of a Product Property applies to square roots containing variables.

Example 3 If x and y are both positive, simplify $\sqrt{9x^2y^2}$.

Solution

$$\begin{aligned}\sqrt{9x^2y^2} &= \sqrt{9} \cdot \sqrt{x^2} \cdot \sqrt{y^2} \\ &= 3 \cdot x \cdot y \\ &= 3xy\end{aligned}$$

Check Let $x = 2$, $y = 4$: $\sqrt{9(2)^2(4)^2} = \sqrt{9 \cdot 4 \cdot 16} = \sqrt{576} = 24$. Does this equal $3 \cdot 2 \cdot 4$? Yes.

ADDITIONAL EXAMPLES

1. Simplify $\sqrt{150}$.
$5\sqrt{6}$

2. Find the exact length of the hypotenuse.

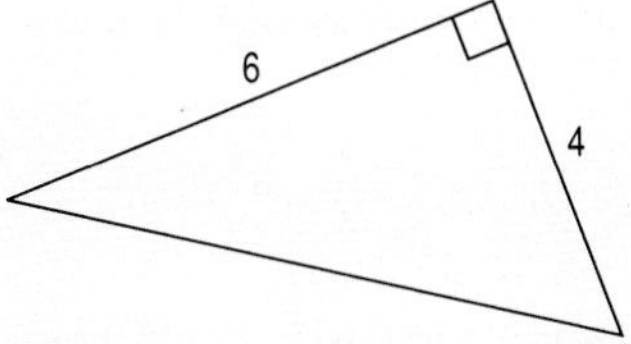

$2\sqrt{13}$

3. Simplify $\sqrt{11n^2}$, where n is positive.
$n\sqrt{11}$

4. Solve $y^2 + 9 = 33$.
$2\sqrt{6}$

NOTES ON QUESTIONS
Question 13: Two solution methods are possible. One is to transform the equation into $4a^2 = 24$ and solve. The other is to use $2a = \pm\sqrt{24}$, then simplify $\sqrt{24}$ and solve for a. You may wish to show both methods.

ADDITIONAL ANSWERS
13. Check: Does $(2 \cdot \sqrt{6})^2 = 24$? Yes
Does $(2 \cdot -\sqrt{6})^2 = 24$? Yes
14. Check: Does $\frac{9}{3\sqrt{6}} = \frac{3\sqrt{6}}{6}$?
Does $54 = (3\sqrt{6})(3\sqrt{6})$? Yes
Check: Does $\frac{9}{-3\sqrt{6}} = \frac{-3\sqrt{6}}{6}$?
Does $54 = (-3\sqrt{6})(-3\sqrt{6})$? Yes

Solutions to some equations can be rewritten by using the Square Root of a Product Property.

Example 4 Solve the equation $2x^2 = 150$.

Solution
$$2x^2 = 150$$
$$x^2 = 75$$
$$x = \sqrt{75} \text{ or } -\sqrt{75}$$

Now rewrite $\sqrt{75}$. A perfect square factor is 25.
$$\sqrt{75} = \sqrt{25 \cdot 3}$$
$$= \sqrt{25} \cdot \sqrt{3}$$
$$= 5\sqrt{3}$$

So the two solutions to the equation are $5\sqrt{3}$ and $-5\sqrt{3}$.

Check First check $5\sqrt{3}$.

Does
$$2(5\sqrt{3})^2 = 150?$$
$$2 \cdot 5\sqrt{3} \cdot 5\sqrt{3} = 150?$$
$$2 \cdot 5 \cdot 5 \cdot \sqrt{3} \cdot \sqrt{3} = 150?$$
$$50 \cdot 3 = 150? \text{ Yes, it checks.}$$

Now check $-5\sqrt{3}$.

Does
$$2(-5\sqrt{3})^2 = 150?$$
$$2 \cdot -5\sqrt{3} \cdot -5\sqrt{3} = 150?$$
$$2 \cdot -5 \cdot -5 \cdot \sqrt{3} \cdot \sqrt{3} = 150? \text{ Yes, it checks.}$$

Questions

Covering the Reading

1. By the Square Root of a Product Property, $\sqrt{p} \cdot \sqrt{q} =$ _?_. $\sqrt{pq}$

2. To use the Square Root of a Product Property to rewrite $\sqrt{ab}$, both a and b must be _?_. nonnegative

3. With a calculator, estimate to two decimal places:
a. $\sqrt{7}$ 2.65 **b.** $\sqrt{5}$ 2.24 **c.** $\sqrt{7} \cdot \sqrt{5}$ 5.92 **d.** $\sqrt{35}$ 5.92

In 4–6, **a.** find the perfect square factor of the number under the radical sign; **b.** simplify.

4. $\sqrt{20}$ $\sqrt{4} \cdot \sqrt{5}$; $2\sqrt{5}$
5. $\sqrt{50}$ $\sqrt{25} \cdot \sqrt{2}$; $5\sqrt{2}$
6. $\sqrt{700}$ $\sqrt{100} \cdot \sqrt{7}$; $10\sqrt{7}$

7. With your calculator, as a check to Example 2, verify that $\sqrt{128} = 8\sqrt{2}$. $\sqrt{128} \approx 11.314$; $8\sqrt{2} \approx 11.314$

8. If a and b are both positive, simplify $\sqrt{36a^2b^2}$. **6ab**

9. Each leg of a right triangle is 10 cm. Find the exact length of the hypotenuse. **$10\sqrt{2}$**

10. Solve $3x^2 = 2100$. **$\sqrt{700} = 10\sqrt{7}$; $-\sqrt{700} = -10\sqrt{7}$** , ± 26.46

Applying the Mathematics

In 11 and 12, find the exact value for the variable. Rewrite your answer so the number under the radical has no perfect square factors.

11. 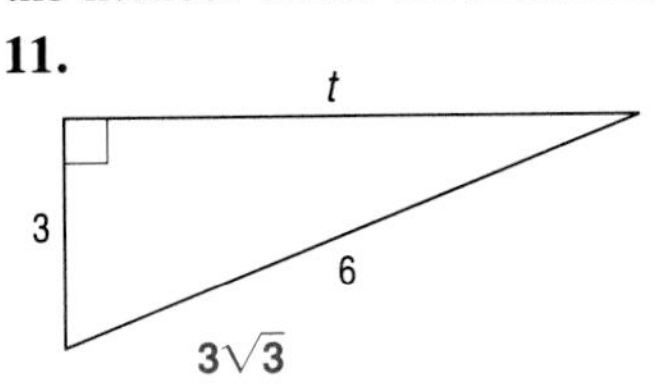

12. 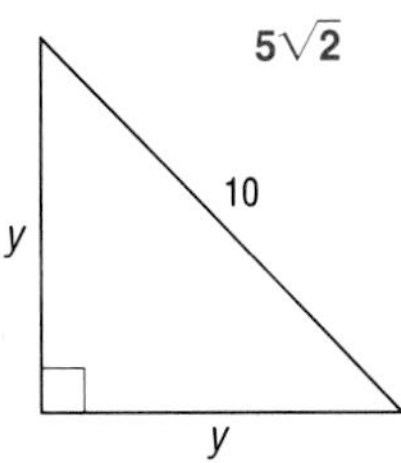

In 13 and 14, solve and check. Give your answer in simplified form.

13. $(2a)^2 = 24$ **$a = \sqrt{6}$ or $-\sqrt{6}$**

14. $\frac{9}{x} = \frac{x}{6}$ **$x = 3\sqrt{6}$ or $-3\sqrt{6}$**

15. Simplify each radical expression.
a. $\sqrt{75}$ **$5\sqrt{3}$** **b.** $\sqrt{12}$ **$2\sqrt{3}$** **c.** $\sqrt{75} + \sqrt{12}$ **$7\sqrt{3}$**

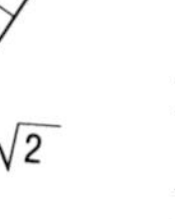

16. Find the area of the rectangle at the left. **30**

17. The area of a square is $20w^2$. Write the exact length of one side. **$2w\sqrt{5}$**

In 18 and 19, rewrite the numerator and simplify the fraction.

18. $\frac{\sqrt{175}}{5}$ **$\frac{5\sqrt{7}}{5} = \sqrt{7}$**

19. $\frac{\sqrt{300}}{5}$ **$\frac{10\sqrt{3}}{5} = 2\sqrt{3}$**

In 20 and 21, simplify in your head.

20. $\sqrt{5^2 \cdot 11^2}$ **55**

21. $\sqrt{100 \cdot 81 \cdot 36}$ **540**

Review

22. How high is the kite in the picture below? *(Lesson 7-5)* **16 ft**

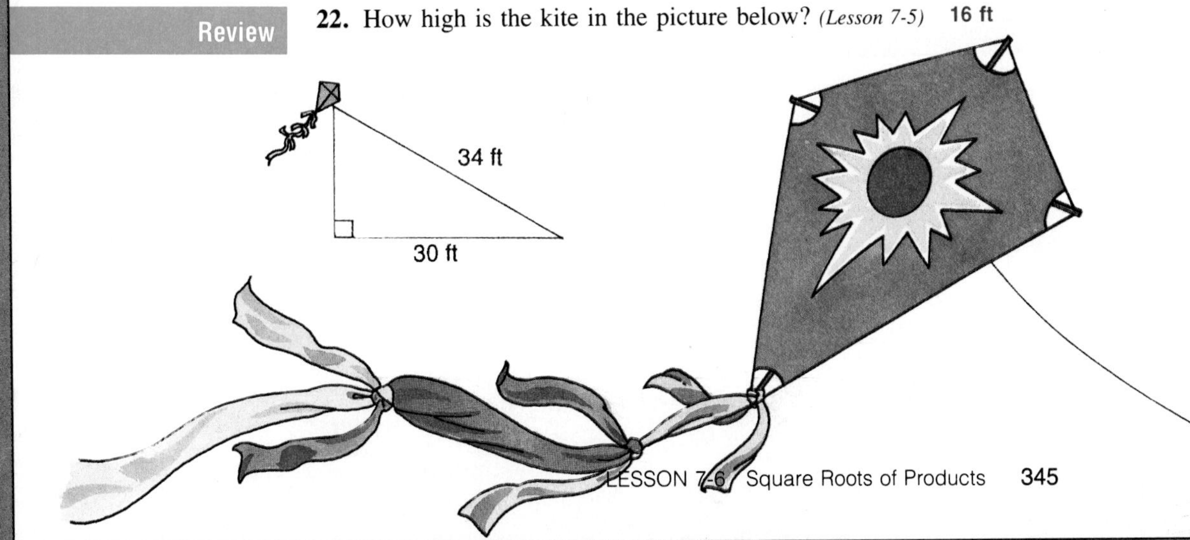

Question 15: The three parts show that $\sqrt{a} + \sqrt{b}$ is not in general equal to $\sqrt{a + b}$. You might ask students to give examples of other positive integers a, b, and c such that $\sqrt{a} + \sqrt{b} = \sqrt{c}$. (Begin with a sentence like $2\sqrt{5} + 4\sqrt{5} = 6\sqrt{5}$. Then reverse the usual simplification procedure to get $\sqrt{20} + \sqrt{80} = \sqrt{180}$.)

Making Connections for Questions 18 and 19: Students must reduce fractions involving radicals in the numerator. We do not expect complete mastery here. These questions are intended to point out situations in which simplifying radicals does lead to final answers that look simpler, and also to prepare for later simplifications involving the Quadratic Formula.

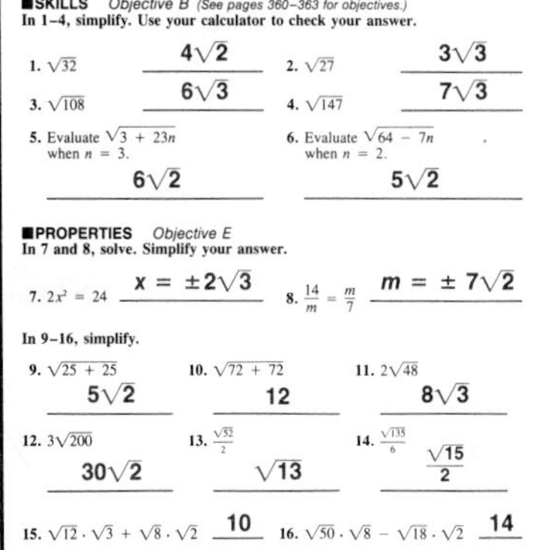

NAME ________

LESSON **MASTER 7–6**
QUESTIONS ON **SPUR** OBJECTIVES

■**SKILLS** *Objective B (See pages 360–363 for objectives.)*
In 1–4, simplify. Use your calculator to check your answer.

1. $\sqrt{32}$ **$4\sqrt{2}$** **2.** $\sqrt{27}$ **$3\sqrt{3}$**

3. $\sqrt{108}$ **$6\sqrt{3}$** **4.** $\sqrt{147}$ **$7\sqrt{3}$**

5. Evaluate $\sqrt{3 + 23n}$ when $n = 3$. **$6\sqrt{2}$**

6. Evaluate $\sqrt{64 - 7n}$ when $n = 2$. **$5\sqrt{2}$**

■**PROPERTIES** *Objective E*
In 7 and 8, solve. Simplify your answer.

7. $2x^2 = 24$ **$x = \pm 2\sqrt{3}$** **8.** $\frac{14}{m} = \frac{m}{7}$ **$m = \pm 7\sqrt{2}$**

In 9–16, simplify.

9. $\sqrt{25 + 25}$ **$5\sqrt{2}$** **10.** $\sqrt{72 + 72}$ **12** **11.** $2\sqrt{48}$ **$8\sqrt{3}$**

12. $3\sqrt{200}$ **$30\sqrt{2}$** **13.** $\frac{\sqrt{52}}{2}$ **$\sqrt{13}$** **14.** $\frac{\sqrt{135}}{6}$ **$\frac{\sqrt{15}}{2}$**

15. $\sqrt{12} \cdot \sqrt{3} + \sqrt{8} \cdot \sqrt{2}$ **10** **16.** $\sqrt{50} \cdot \sqrt{8} - \sqrt{18} \cdot \sqrt{2}$ **14**

In 17 and 18, simplify. Assume all variables are positive.

17. $\sqrt{25a^2b^2}$ **5ab** **18.** $\sqrt{81x^2y^2}$ **9xy**

■**USES** *Objective F*
19. Each side of a square is 9. Find the diagonal and simplify your answer. **$9\sqrt{2}$**

20. The sides of a rectangle are 6 and 15. Find the diagonal and simplify your answer. **$3\sqrt{29}$**

Question 28: Students may solve $x \cdot 18.62 = 20.35$, subtract 1 from the result x, and convert to a percent. Another way is to divide the amount of increase by the initial price.

Question 33: This presages a geometry theorem regarding isosceles right triangles.

FOLLOW-UP

MORE PRACTICE
For more questions on SPUR Objectives, use *Lesson Master 7-6,* shown on page 345.

EXTENSION
Have students use *trial-and-error* to find a special case for which $\sqrt{a + b} = \sqrt{a} + \sqrt{b}$. ($a = 0$ or $b = 0$)

ADDITIONAL ANSWERS
23a.

-13

23b.

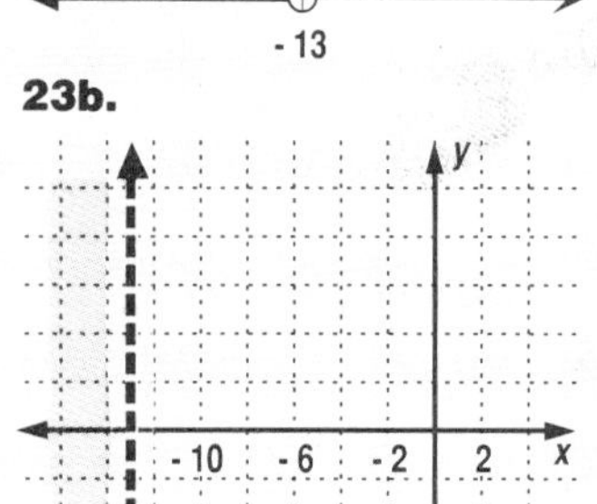

23. Graph $x < -13$ **a.** on a number line and **b.** on a coordinate plane. *(Lesson 7-2)* **a. See margin. b. See margin.**

24. Find both solutions of $|x + 2| = 14$. *(Lesson 7-3)* **12 or -16**

25. If $A = \{1, 2, 3, 4, 5, 6, 7, 8\}$, $B = \{2, 4, 6, 8, 10, 12\}$, and $C = \{1, 3, 5, 7, 9, 11\}$, find each of the following:
   a. $A \cup B$ **{1, 2, 3, 4, 5, 6, 7, 8, 10, 12}**
   b. $B \cap C$ **Ø**
   c. $A \cup (B \cap C)$ *(Lessons 3-4, 3-5)* **{1, 2, 3, 4, 5, 6, 7, 8}**

26. Refer to the graph below.
   a. ℓ is a _?_ line. **horizontal**
   b. m is a _?_ line. **vertical**
   c. The coordinates of $\ell \cap m$ are (_?_, _?_). *(Lesson 7-2)* **4; 3**

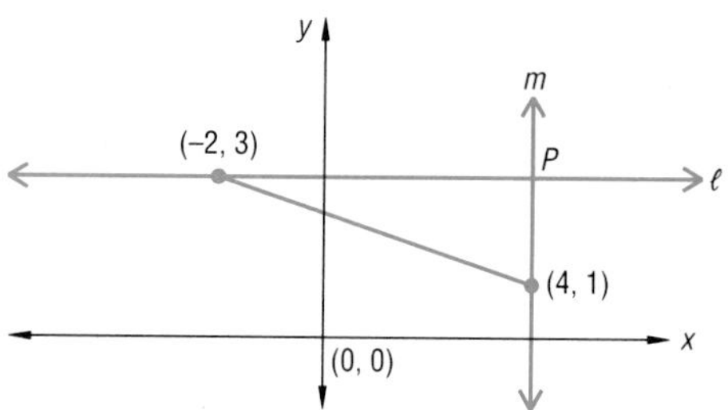

27. If $k = -3.5$ calculate **a.** k^2, **b.** $(-k)^2$, and **c.** $|k|^2$. *(Lessons 1-4, 7-3)*
   a) 12.25; b) 12.25; c) 12.25

28. From March 27, 1987 to June 29, 1987, the price of Texas intermediate crude oil went from \$18.62 to \$20.35 a barrel. Find the percent increase. *(Lesson 5-4)* **≈ 9.3%**

29. Betsy has q quarters and d dimes. She has at least \$5.20. Write an inequality that describes this situation. *(Lesson 6-7)* $.25q + .10d \geq 5.20$

In 30 and 31, solve. *(Lesson 6-6)*

30. $9y - 2 = 11y + 54$ **-28**

31. $50{,}000x - 10{,}000 = 30{,}000x + 50{,}000$ **3**

32. The diameter of a metal rod is to be 1.5 cm, with an allowable error of 0.05 cm. Is a rod with diameter 1.496 cm in the allowable range? *(Lesson 7-3)* **1.45 < 1.496 < 1.55; Yes**

Exploration

33. Generalize Example 2 on page 343 and Question 9 on page 345. **If the length of two legs are equal, then the length of the hypotenuse is equal to $\sqrt{2}$ times the length of a leg.**

LESSON

7-7

Distances in the Plane

Streets of many cities are laid out in a grid pattern like the coordinate plane. To get from point A to point C by car you have to travel along streets, so the shortest distance from A to C is not the hypotenuse of triangle ABC, but the sum of the legs $AB + BC$. But a bird or helicopter could go directly along segment $\overline{AC}$ **"as the crow flies."**

Example 1 **a.** How far is it from A to C traveling by car along $\overline{AB}$ and $\overline{BC}$? (Each unit is a city block.)

b. How far is it from A to C flying in a straight line?

Solution

a. Count the city blocks between points A and B. There are 4 blocks. Count the city blocks between B and C. There are 6 of them.

$$AB + BC = 4 + 6 = 10$$

Traveling by car, the distance between A and B is 10 blocks.

b. Use the Pythagorean Theorem.

$$\begin{aligned} AC^2 &= AB^2 + BC^2 \\ &= 4^2 + 6^2 \\ &= 16 + 36 \\ &= 52 \\ AC &= \sqrt{52} \\ &\approx 7.2 \end{aligned}$$

The flying distance from A to C is $\sqrt{52}$ blocks or approximately 7.2 blocks.

The map above looks like part of the coordinate plane. The idea used in Example 1 can be applied to find the distance between any points in the coordinate plane.

LESSON 7-7

RESOURCES
- Lesson Master 7-7
- Visual for Teaching Aid 7: Coordinate Grid
- Visual for Teaching Aid 37: Pythagorean Distance Formula
- Visual for Teaching Aid 38: Graphs for **Questions 6-9 and 11 and 12**

OBJECTIVE

K Calculate distances in the plane.

TEACHING NOTES

Some students may be confused by the fact that two triangles can be drawn in each example, one above the hypotenuse and one below. Note that each triangle is half of the same rectangle.

To build understanding, we start with specific examples using numbers, as in **Examples 1-3,** before going to the general case. Some students may continue to draw right triangles even after they know the formula. Emphasize that the formula avoids the need to draw a picture.

ADDITIONAL EXAMPLES

1. Let $C = (4, 2)$ and $K = (7, 11)$. Find CK as a simplified radical and a decimal.
$3\sqrt{10} \approx 9.49$

2. Let $N = (-5, 4)$ and $Q = (2, -2)$. Find NQ as a simplified radical and a decimal.
$\sqrt{85} \approx 9.22$

3. Tony and Alicea each left camp on a hike. Tony walked one mile north, then 5 miles west. Alicea went 6 miles east, then 2 miles south. Make a diagram and find the distance between Tony and Alicea.

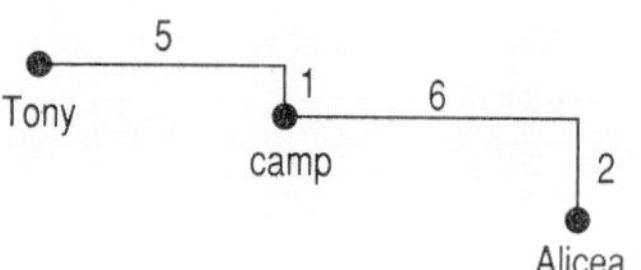

If Tony is at (0,0), then Alicea is at (11,-3). The distance between those points is $\sqrt{11^2 + 3^2} = \sqrt{130} \approx 11.4$ miles

Example 2 The streets in the Joneses' neighborhood are laid out in a grid oriented North-South and East-West. Suppose that a museum is 2 miles east and 4 miles south of the Joneses' house. A post office is 5 miles west and 3 miles north of the Joneses' house.

a. What is the street distance from the post office to the museum?

b. How far is it from the post office to the museum as the crow flies?

Solution Since the distances are given from the Joneses' house, make a graph with the Joneses' house J at (0, 0), the museum M at (2, -4), and the post office P at (-5, 3).

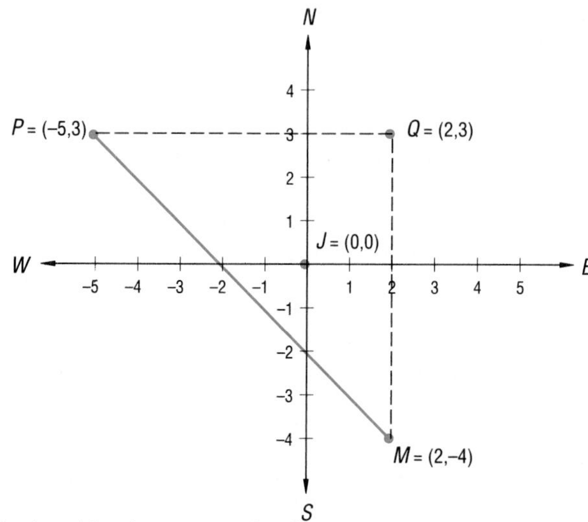

a. The key idea is to put point Q in the picture to form right triangle PQM.
$Q = (2, 3)$. The street distance is $PQ + QM$ miles.

$PQ = |-5 - 2| = 7$ $\qquad$ $QM = |3 - (-4)| = 7$

So the street distance from the post office to the museum is $7 + 7 = 14$ miles.

b. "As the crow flies" means the distance PM using the Pythagorean Theorem.

$$\begin{aligned} PM^2 &= PQ^2 + QM^2 \\ &= 7^2 + 7^2 \\ &= 98 \\ PM &= \sqrt{98} \\ &\approx 9.9 \text{ miles} \end{aligned}$$

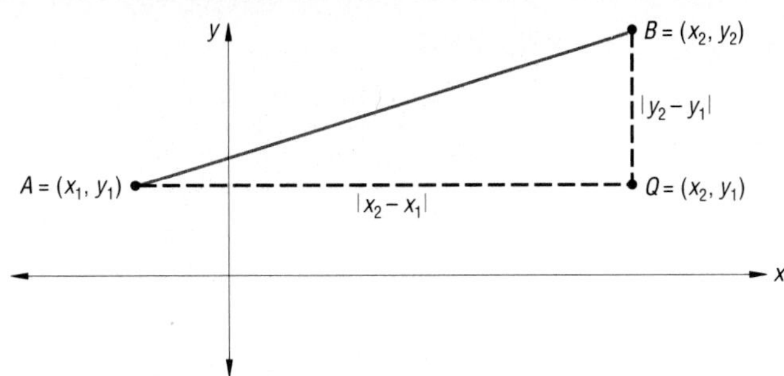

The calculations done in Example 2b can be generalized. To find the distance between $A = (x_1, y_1)$ and $B = (x_2, y_2)$, use $Q = (x_2, y_1)$ to form a right triangle ABQ.

Then $AQ = |x_2 - x_1|$
and $QB = |y_2 - y_1|$.

By the Pythagorean Theorem,

$$\begin{aligned}(AB)^2 &= (AQ)^2 + (QB)^2 \\ &= |x_2 - x_1|^2 + |y_2 - y_1|^2.\end{aligned}$$

Now take the square root of each side. The result is a formula for the distance between any two points in the plane.

Pythagorean Distance Formula:

The distance AB between points $A = (x_1, y_1)$ and $B = (x_2, y_2)$ is $AB = \sqrt{|x_2 - x_1|^2 + |y_2 - y_1|^2}$.

Example 3 Let $D = (4, 3)$ and $F = (6, -2)$. Find DF.

Solution Use the Pythagorean Distance Formula with $x_1 = 4$, $y_1 = 3$; $x_2 = 6$, $y_2 = -2$.

$$\begin{aligned}DF &= \sqrt{(4 - 6)^2 + (3 - -2)^2} \\ &= \sqrt{(-2)^2 + 5^2} \\ &= \sqrt{29} \approx 5.4\end{aligned}$$

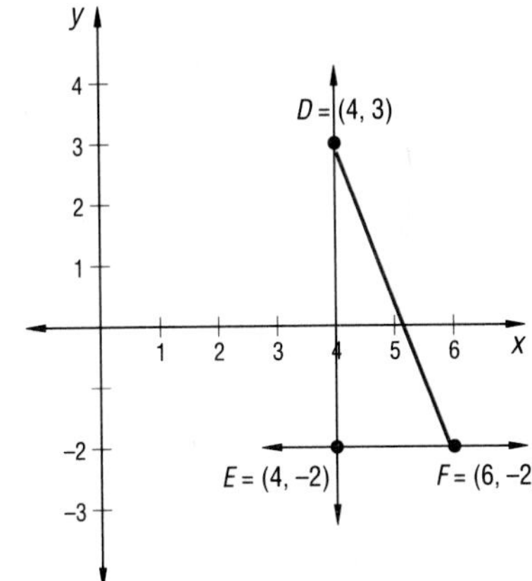

NOTES ON QUESTIONS
Questions 4 and 5: These are key questions, in which students must plot the points, draw the triangle, and find the lengths. Make sure that they understand how to do all the required steps, but then point out that by using the formula, the work can be shortened considerably.

Computer for Questions 13 and 14: Here, the BASIC program computes the Pythagorean ("as the crow flies") distance. You can add a line to give street (often called the "taxicab") distance:

```
105 PRINT "THE STREET
    DISTANCE IS";
    ABS(A) + ABS(B)
```

Questions

Covering the Reading

1. In the diagram below, each grid represents a city block.
   a. How many blocks does it take to go from P to Q by way of R? **11**
   b. Use the Pythagorean Theorem to find the distance from P to Q as the crow flies. **$\sqrt{73} \approx 8.5$**

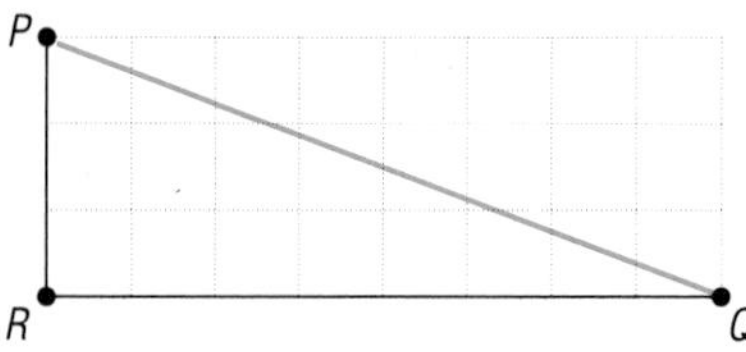

2. Find MN if $M = (40, 60)$ and $N = (40, 18)$. **42**

3. Use the graph at the right to:
   a. Find XY. **8**
   b. Find YZ. **5**
   c. Use the Pythagorean Distance Formula to find XZ. **≈ 9.4**

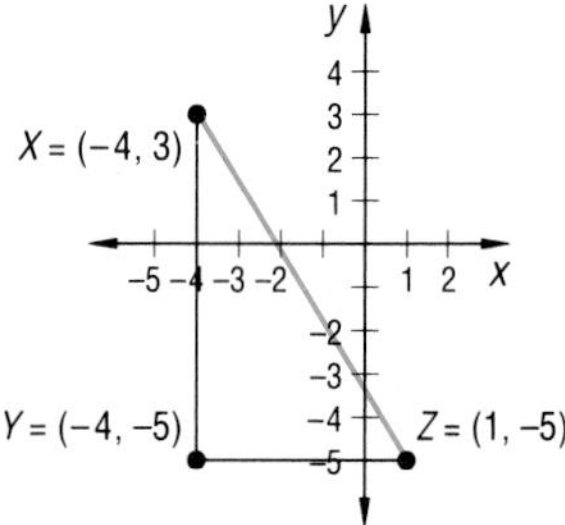

In 4 and 5, find DF.

4. $D = (5, 1)$; $F = (11, -7)$ **$DF = 10$**

5. $D = (-3, 5)$; $F = (-1, -8)$ **$DF = \sqrt{173} \approx 13.15$**

In 6–9, refer to Example 2. A school is at point S, which is 1 mile east and 2 miles north of the Joneses' house. Remember that $J = (0, 0)$.

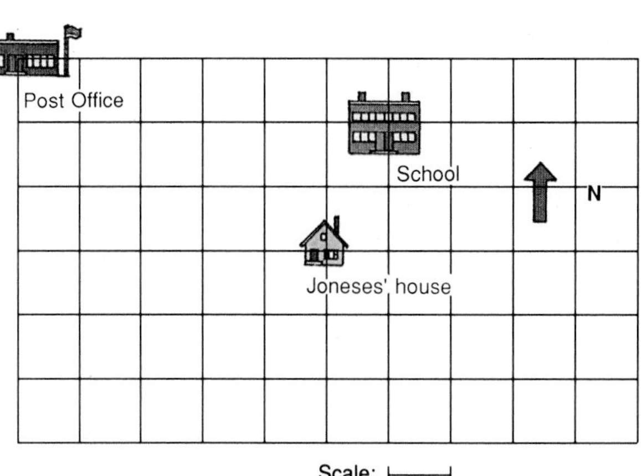

6. What are the coordinates of S? **(1, 2)**
7. Find the distance one would travel by car to get from the post office to the school. **7 miles**
8. Find the street distance from the Joneses' house to the school. **3 miles**
9. How far is it from the Joneses' house to the school as the crow flies? **$\sqrt{5} \approx 2.2$ miles**

10. What is the Pythagorean distance between (x_1, y_1) and (x_2, y_2)? **$\sqrt{|x_2 - x_1|^2 + |y_2 - y_1|^2}$**

Applying the Mathematics

In 11 and 12, use the diagram below. It shows part of a town laid out in a rectangular grid. Each block is 200 m long in an east-west direction and 100 m long in a north-south direction.

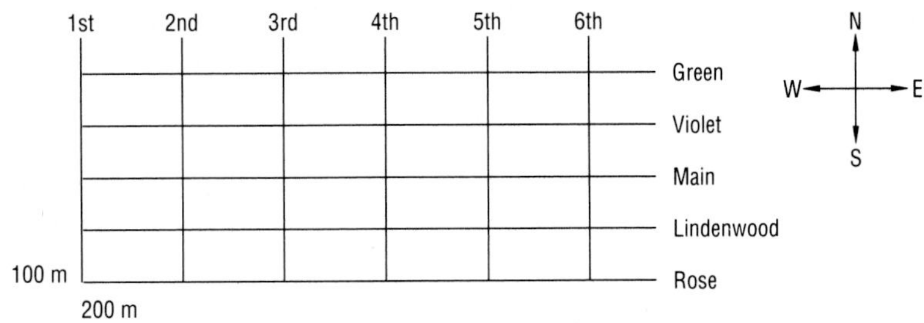

11. Locate the point at 5th and Green and the point at 2nd and Rose. What is the shortest street distance between these points? **1000 m**

12. As the crow flies, what is the distance from 5th and Green to 2nd and Rose? **≈ 721.1 m**

In 13 and 14, use this computer program that asks for coordinates of points in the coordinate plane, (x_1, y_1) and (x_2, y_2), and then calculates the distance between them.

```
10 PRINT "DISTANCE IN THE PLANE"
20 PRINT "BETWEEN (X1, Y1) AND (X2, Y2)"
30 PRINT "ENTER X1, Y1"
40 INPUT X1, Y1
50 PRINT "ENTER X2, Y2"
60 INPUT X2, Y2
70 LET HOZ = ABS(X1 - X2)
80 LET VERT = ABS(1 - Y2)
90 LET DIST = SQR(HOZ * HOZ + VERT * VERT)
100 PRINT "THE DISTANCE IS "; DIST
110 END
```

13. What value of DIST will the computer print when $(x_1, y_1) = (19, -5)$ and $(x_2, y_2) = (-3, 15)$? **29.732137**

14. What value of DIST will the computer print when $(x_1, y_1) = (0, 0)$ and $(x_2, y_2) = (1, 1)$? **1.4142136**

Review

15. *Skill sequence* If $y + 4 = 10$, find the value of each expression. *(Lessons 2-6, 7-4)*

a. $2y + 8$ **20**

b. $(y + 4)^2$ **100**

c. $2(y + 4)^2 - \frac{y + 4}{2}$ **195**

d. $(\sqrt{y + 4})^2$ **10**

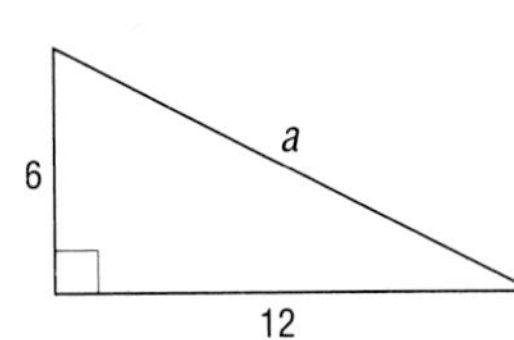

16. Simplify: **a.** $\sqrt{18}$; **b.** $\sqrt{50}$; **c.** $\sqrt{18} + \sqrt{50}$. *(Lesson 7-6)*
a) $3\sqrt{2}$; **b)** $5\sqrt{2}$; **c)** $8\sqrt{2}$

17. Find the exact value of the variable in the triangle at left. *(Lessons 7-5, 7-6)* $\sqrt{180}$ **or** $6\sqrt{5}$

NAME ____________

LESSON **MASTER 7–7**
QUESTIONS ON **SPUR** OBJECTIVES

■REPRESENTATIONS *Objective K* *(See pages 360–363 for objectives.)*
In 1–6, use the graph at the right. The midpoint of AC is M. Determine each length.

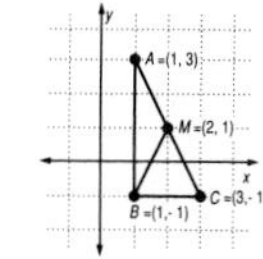

1. AB **4**
2. CB **2**
3. AC $2\sqrt{5}$
4. BM $\sqrt{5}$
5. MA $\sqrt{5}$
6. MC $\sqrt{5}$

In 7–10, find XY.

7. $X = (4, 9)$ and $Y = (1, 5)$ **5**
8. $X = (-3, 6)$ and $Y = (2, -6)$ **13**
9. $X = (-11, -16)$ and $Y = (0, -20)$ $\sqrt{137}$
10. $X = (1.8, -2.4)$ and $Y = (1.2, -1.6)$ **1**

In 11 and 12, use the diagram at the right. Each small square represents a city block.

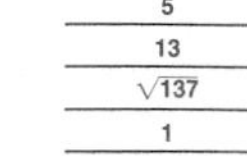

11. What is the street distance between R and N? **8 blocks**

12. How far is it from R to N as the crow flies? $\sqrt{34}$ **or about 5.8 blocks**

In 13–15, use the graph of the rectangle.

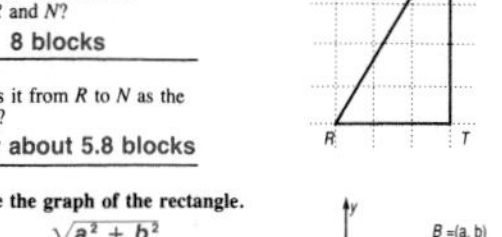

13. Find OB. $\sqrt{a^2 + b^2}$
14. Find AC. $\sqrt{a^2 + b^2}$
15. What can you conclude about the diagonals of a rectangle?

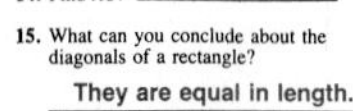

They are equal in length.

NOTES ON QUESTIONS
Small Group Work for Question 28: This is an example of taxicab (street-distance) geometry. You may wish to have students work in small groups to graph the points, giving each group a single coordinate grid.

FOLLOW-UP

MORE PRACTICE
For more questions on SPUR Objectives, use *Lesson Master 7-7,* shown on page 351.

ADDITIONAL ANSWERS
26.

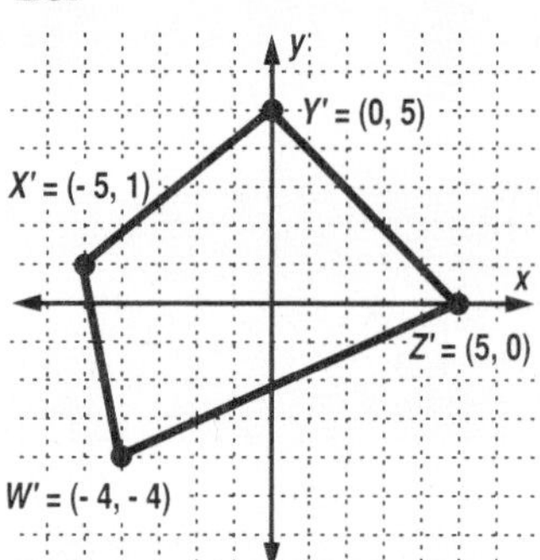

28.

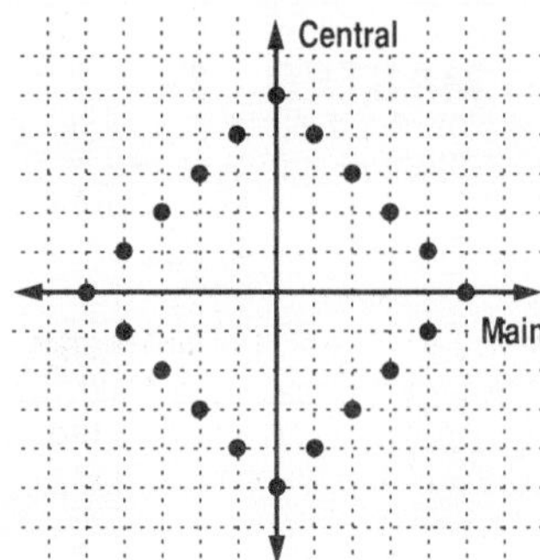

18. Simplify $(8\sqrt{10})^2$ without using a calculator. *(Lesson 7-4)* **640**

19. The distance from C to D on the number line below is twice the distance from A to B. Write an equation and solve to find x. (Assume that A is the point with the smallest coordinate.) *(Lesson 7-3)* **2(2x + 1 − x) = (4x + 6) − 20; 8**

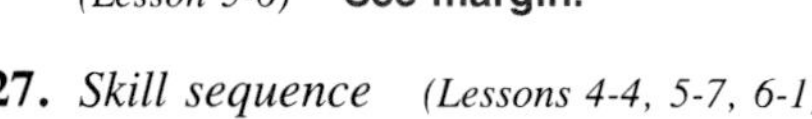

20. The bakery charges 70¢ for each croissant and 25¢ for a box. You have $5.00. At most how many croissants can you buy if you also want them in a box? *(Lesson 6-8)* **6**

(5x + 3)°
(3x)°
(7x + 13)°

21. In the triangle at the left, find the value of x. *(Lessons 3-8, 6-2)* **$\frac{164}{15}$ or $10\frac{14}{15}$**

In 22–25, solve without writing intermediate steps. *(Lessons 6-1, 6-6)*

22. $5y - 7 = 28$ **y = 7** **23.** $8a + 4a - 2a = 30$ **a = 3**

24. $10n = 8n - 30$ **n = -15** **25.** $-3m = -2m$ **m = 0**

26. Graph the image of quadrilateral $WXYZ$ under a size change of $-\frac{1}{2}$. *(Lesson 5-6)* **See margin.**

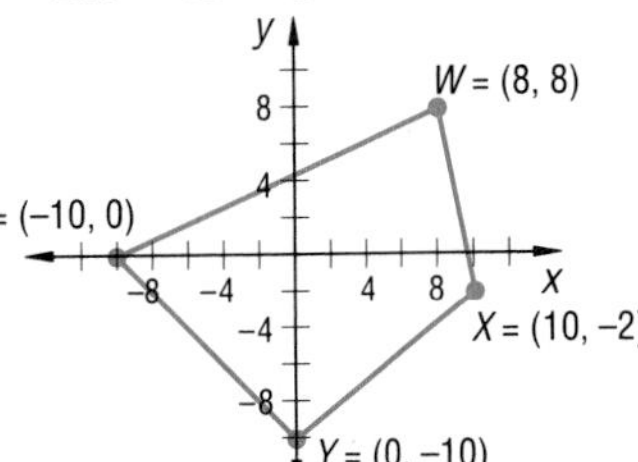

27. *Skill sequence* *(Lessons 4-4, 5-7, 6-1)*

a. Solve for m. $w = \frac{m}{a}$ **m = wa**

b. Solve for t. $z = \frac{s}{t}$ **t = $\frac{s}{z}$**

c. Solve for k. $x + 1 = \frac{k}{b}$ **k = b(x + 1)**

Exploration

28. The grid below pictures streets 1 unit apart in a city. Graph all points at a street distance of 5 units from the intersection of Main and Central. **See margin.**

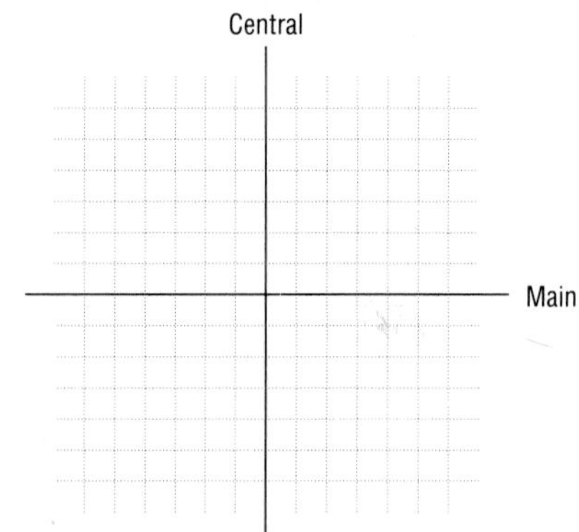

LESSON

7-8

Chunking

The following problem may look complex.

Solve $(k + 6)^2 = 81$.

However, it can be solved using *chunking*.

Chunking is the process of grouping some small bits of information into a single piece of information. For instance, when reading the word "store," you don't think "s, t, o, r, e." You chunk the five letters into one word. In algebra, chunking can be done by viewing an entire algebraic expression as one variable.

Example 1 If $3y = 8.5$, find $6y + 5$.

Solution This can be done without solving for y. Think of $3y$ as a chunk. Since you know $3y$, you can double it to get $6y$. Then add 5.

	$3y = 8.5$
Double it.	$6y = 17$
Add 5.	$6y + 5 = 22$

Check If $6y + 5 = 22$, then $6y = 17$, so $3y = 8.5$.

The equation at the beginning of the lesson is $(k + 6)^2 = 81$. To solve an equation like this, think what value the expression inside the parentheses must have. Also, remember that an equation like $x^2 = 81$ has two solutions.

Example 2 Solve $(k + 6)^2 = 81$.

Solution What number squared is 81? There are two such numbers, 9 and -9. So $k + 6$ can be 9 or -9.

$k + 6 = 9$ or $k + 6 = -9$

$k = 3$ or $k = -15$

There are two solutions, 3 and -15.

Check Check 3. Does $(3 + 6)^2 = 81$?

$9^2 = 81$? Yes, it checks.

Check -15. Does $(-15 + 6)^2 = 81$?

$(-9)^2 = 81$? Yes, it checks.

Equations in which the variable (or an expression involving the variable) is squared often have two solutions. You need to find both!

LESSON 7-8

RESOURCES

- Lesson Master 7-8
- Computer Master 16

OBJECTIVE

D Use chunking to evaluate expressions and solve equations.

TEACHING NOTES

Alternate Approach
One way to help students use chunking effectively is to focus their attention on the last operation to be performed in an expression rather than on the first. For example, to simplify

$5.3(3x - 7.2) + 9.7(3x - 7.2)$

one could perform the multiplications and then add like terms. However, if you focus on the last operation, the addition, you can perceive the problem as adding like expressions, the sum of which is $15(3x - 7.2)$. Then the final simplification is easier.

Using this idea, in **Example 2** you can emphasize the last operation by leaving the inside of the parentheses blank at first.

$(\quad)^2 = 81$
$(\quad) = 9$ or $(\quad) = -9$
$(k + 6) = 9$ or $(k + 6) = -9$

ADDITIONAL EXAMPLES

1. If $7n + 5y = 19$, find $70n + 50y + 3$.
193

2. Solve $(2n - 1)^2 = 49$.
4, -3

3. Solve $|26 - x| = 15$.
11, 41

4. Solve and graph. $|2x + 5| > 9$.
$x > 2$ or $x < -7$

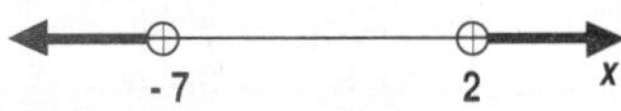

Another operation that often leads to equations with two solutions is absolute value.

Example 3 Solve $|6x - 3| = 21$.

Solution The absolute value of two numbers, 21 and -21, is 21. So $6x - 3$ can be 21 or it can be -21.

$$|6x - 3| = 21$$

$$\begin{aligned} 6x - 3 &= 21 \\ 6x &= 24 \\ x &= 4 \end{aligned} \qquad \text{or} \qquad \begin{aligned} 6x - 3 &= -21 \\ 6x &= -18 \\ x &= -3 \end{aligned}$$

Check Check 4. Does $|6 \cdot 4 - 3| = 21$?
$|24 - 3| = 21$?
$|21| = 21$? Yes, it checks.

Check -3. Does $|6 \cdot -3 - 3| = 21$?
$|-18 - 3| = 21$?
$|-21| = 21$? Yes, it checks.

In Lesson 7-3, you used the idea of distance to find and graph solutions to inequalities with absolute value. Chunking makes it possible to do this algebraically.

Example 4 Solve and graph $|x - 9| < 5$.

Solution Consider the easier problem of solving $|x| < 5$.
Its solution is $-5 < x < 5$.
Now think of $x - 9$ as a chunk. Put this chunk in place of x.

The solution to $|x - 9| < 5$ is $\quad -5 < x - 9 < 5.$

Add 9 to each part of the inequality. $\quad -5 + 9 < x - 9 + 9 < 5 + 9$

$$4 < x < 14$$

The graph is:

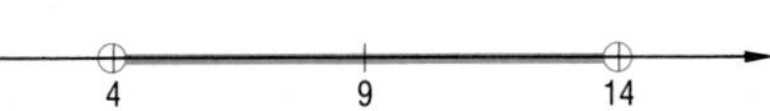

Check Try the endpoints 4 and 14 in the original sentence. They should make the sides equal.
Does $|4 - 9| = 5$?
$|-5| = 5$

You can also see that 14 works. Try a number between 4 and 14. We try 10.

Does $|10 - 9| < 5$?
$|1| < 5$? Yes. It checks.

Example 5 Solve $|y - 30| > .002$.

Solution Consider the easier problem $|y| > .002$.

Its solution is: $y < -.002$ or $y > .002$

Now think of $y - 30$ as a chunk.

$|y - 30| > .002$ has the solution $y - 30 < -.002$ or $y - 30 > .002$.

Solve each inequality. $y < 29.998$ or $y > 30.002$

Check Graph the solutions.

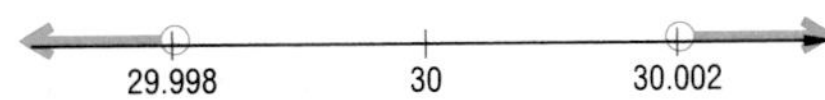

The graph pictures all points whose distance from 30 is greater than .002. This is exactly what is meant by $|y - 30| > .002$.

You have already used chunking to simplify expressions. For instance, consider the addition $\frac{4}{3x + 1} + \frac{3}{3x + 1}$. If you think of $(3x + 1)$ as a single chunk C, then the addition looks like $\frac{4}{C} + \frac{3}{C}$ and its sum is $\frac{7}{C}$. So the original sum is $\frac{7}{3x + 1}$.

Questions

Covering the Reading

1. What is chunking? **See margin.**
2. If $3x = 8.5$, find $6x - 1$. **16**
3. If $4y = 13$, find $12y + 7$. **46**
4. **a.** If $(m - 11)^2 = 64$, what two values can $m - 11$ have? **8, -8**
   b. Find both solutions to $(m - 11)^2 = 64$. **19, 3**
5. Find all solutions to $(p + 3)^2 = 225$. **12 or -18**
6. **a.** In $|.5a + 17| = 29$, what two values are possible for $.5a + 17$? **29, -29**
   b. Solve $|.5a + 17| = 29$. **24, -92**
7. Find both solutions to $|6y + 3| = 45$. **7, -8**

NOTES ON QUESTIONS
Questions 11-21: The variety of ideas here shows the power of chunking. When discussing these questions, emphasize the processes at least as much as the final answer.

Question 11: Students need to see that $18y - 12t$ is twice $9y - 6t$.

Question 15: This question shows the strategy which motivates completing the square to solve quadratic equations. Students can solve $x^2 = 57$. Now think of $d + 11$ in place of x.

ADDITIONAL ANSWERS
1. Chunking is the process of grouping small bits of information into a single piece of information.

NOTES ON QUESTIONS
Making Connections for Question 25: Students will see expressions like this one when working with the Quadratic Formula in Chapter 12.

Question 32: As mentioned previously on page 28, the world record for memorizing digits of pi is (as of 1987) held by a Japanese man, who memorized the first 40,000 digits. The first 100,000,000 decimal places of π have been calculated at the University of Tokyo using a supercomputer.

27.

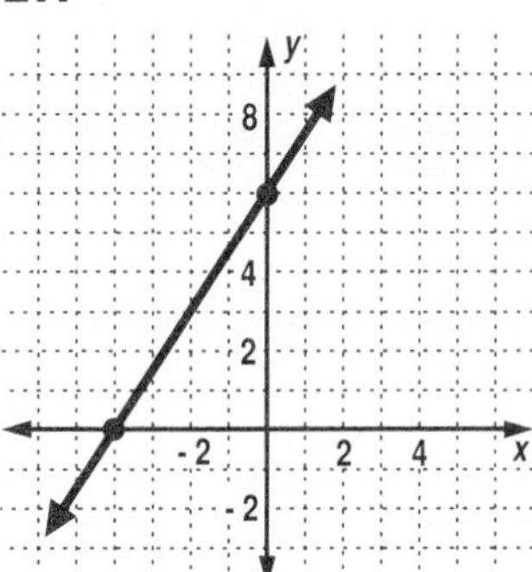

28.

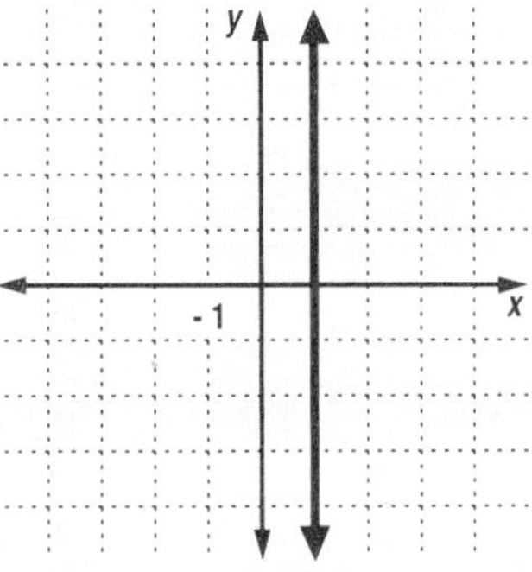

31a.

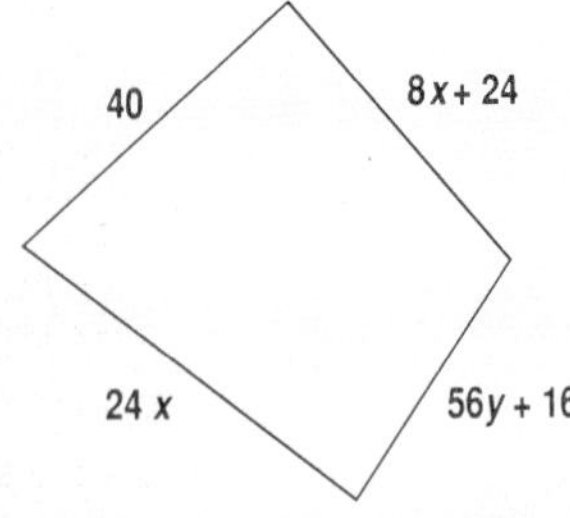

8. a. In adding $\frac{11}{2y - 6} + \frac{4}{2y - 6}$, what should you think of as a chunk?
b. Perform the addition. a) $2y - 6$; b) $\frac{15}{2y - 6}$

9. Simplify $\frac{x}{x + 8} - \frac{8}{x + 8}$. $\frac{x - 8}{x + 8}$

Applying the Mathematics

In 10–20, you may find chunking helpful.

10. Simplify $\frac{t + 4}{t + 3} + \frac{t + 2}{t + 3}$. 2

11. If $18y - 12t = 25$, find $9y - 6t$. $12\frac{1}{2}$

12. If $5x + 4y = 27$ and $2y = 1$, find $5x$. 25

13. Solve $(3x^2)^2 = 144$. 2, -2

14. Solve $|8n + 20| = 4$. -2, -3

15. Approximate the solutions of $(d + 11)^2 = 57$ to two decimal places. -3.45, -18.55

16. $AB = 7m + 1$ and $BC = 21m + 3$. Find the ratio of AB to BC. $\frac{1}{3}$

17. Simplify: $3\sqrt{5} + 6\sqrt{5} - 2\sqrt{5}$. $7\sqrt{5}$

18. If $\sqrt{3y + 1} = 3$, find **a.** $3y + 1$ 9 **b.** y $\frac{8}{3}$

19. If $\sqrt{2y + 8n} = 6$, find **a.** $2y + 8n$ **b.** $y + 4n$ **c.** $5y + 20n$
a) 36; b) 18; c) 90

20. Simplify $3(x^2 - 2y) + 6(x^2 - 2y) - 4(x^2 - 2y)$.
$5(x^2 - 2y)$ or $5x^2 - 10y$

21. Compute.
$\frac{8(x + 7)}{5a} \cdot \frac{3a}{2(x + 7)}$ $\frac{12}{5}$

Review

22. A mast on a sailboat is strengthened by a wire (called a *stay*) as shown at the left. The mast is 35 ft tall. The wire is 37 ft long. How far from the base of the mast does the wire reach? (Round to the nearest inch.) *(Lesson 7-5)* 12 ft

356

23. These two right triangles are similar. Corresponding sides are parallel.
a. Find x. **10**
b. Find y. *(Lesson 7-5)* **15**

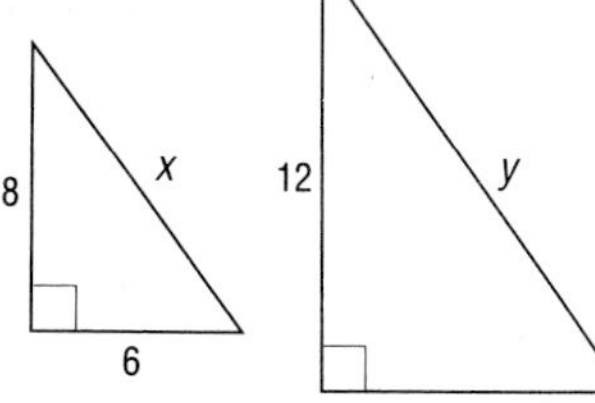

24. Find the distance between (-3, 2) and (11, 6). *(Lesson 7-7)*
$\sqrt{212} \approx 14.56$.

25. Evaluate $\frac{6 + 2\sqrt{16 - 9}}{3}$ to the nearest tenth. *(Lesson 7-4)* **3.8**

26. Simplify $(5\sqrt{3})^2$. *(Lesson 7-4)* **75**

27. Graph $2y - 3x = 12$. *(Lesson 7-1)* **See margin.**

28. Graph $x = 1$ in the coordinate plane. *(Lesson 7-2)* **See margin.**

29. You buy s sweaters at d dollars a sweater. The total cost is T dollars. Write an equation that relates s, d, and T. *(Lesson 4-2)* **$T = sd$**

30. Suppose a laser printer prints 3 pages/min. How long will it take to print 25 documents with 8 pages per document? *(Lesson 4-2)*
≈ 67 minutes

31. The figure at the left below is operated on by a size change of magnitude 8.
a. Find the length of each side of the image. *(Lesson 5-6)* **See margin.**

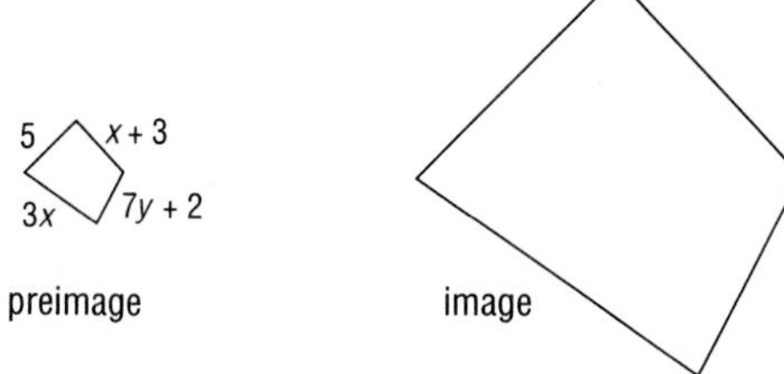

b. Find the perimeter of each figure. Put your answer in simplest form. *(Lesson 6-3)* **preimage: $4x + 7y + 10$, image: $32x + 56y + 80$**

Exploration

32. Often people use chunking as a help in memorization. Here are the first twenty decimal places of π.

3.14159265358979323846

Try memorizing these 20 digits by memorizing the following four chunks of five digits each.

14159   26535   89793   23846

students memorization by chunking

FOLLOW-UP

MORE PRACTICE

For more questions on SPUR Objectives, use *Lesson Master 7-8,* shown below.

EVALUATION

Alternative Assessment

To evaluate students' ability to chunk have them explain their solutions to the questions in the lesson.

NAME ____________

LESSON **MASTER 7–8**
QUESTIONS ON **SPUR** OBJECTIVES

■SKILLS *Objective D (See pages 360–363 for objectives.)*

1. If $4y = 5.1$, find $12y$. **15.3**
2. If $3n + 1 = 11$, find $9n + 3$. **33**
3. If $2x^2 = 9$, find $(2x^2)^2$. **81**
4. If $\sqrt{5p - 1} = 7$, find $5p - 1$. **49**
5. If $8k = 15$, find $16k - 1$. **29**
6. If $-6s = 19$, find $12s + 5$. **-33**
7. If $3t + 6u = -3$, and $2u = -3$, find $3t$. **6**
8. If $4f - 8g = 9$, and $2g = 1$, find $4f$. **13**

In 9–12, simplify.

9. $7\sqrt{3} + 4\sqrt{3} - 6\sqrt{3} - 3\sqrt{3}$ **$2\sqrt{3}$**
10. $4\sqrt{w + 5} + 13\sqrt{w + 5} - \sqrt{w + 5}$ **$16\sqrt{w + 5}$**
11. $12(x - 4) - 17(x - 4) - 2(x - 4)$ **$-7(x - 4)$**
12. $5(2y - 1)^2 - 8(2y - 1)^2 + 3(2y - 1)^2$ **0**

In 13–20, solve.

13. $(t + 3)^2 = 9$ **$t = 0$ or -6**
14. $(d - 4)^2 = 49$ **$d = 11$ or -3**
15. $\sqrt{3y - 2} = 5$ **$y = 9$**
16. $\sqrt{4p + 5} = 9$ **$p = 19$**
17. $|3w + 7| = 22$ **$w = 5$ or $\frac{-29}{3}$**
18. $|11q - 4| = 29$ **$q = 3$ or $\frac{-25}{11}$**
19. $\frac{x + 1}{2} = \frac{8}{x + 1}$ **$x = 3$ or -5**
20. $\frac{9}{3x - 3} = \frac{3x - 3}{4}$ **$x = 3$ or -1**

 63

SUMMARY

The Summary gives an overview of the entire chapter and provides an opportunity for students to consider the material as a whole. Thus, the Summary can be used to help students relate the concepts presented in the chapter.

VOCABULARY

Terms, symbols, and properties are listed by lesson to provide a checklist of things a student must know. Emphasize to students that they should read the vocabulary list carefully before starting the Progress Self-Test. If students do not understand the meaning of a term, they should refer back to the indicated lesson.

Definitions or descriptions of all terms in the vocabulary list may be found in the Glossary.

ADDITIONAL ANSWERS

27.

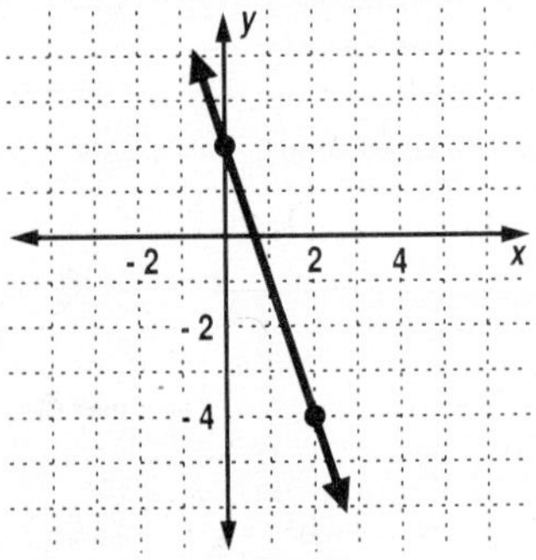

28.

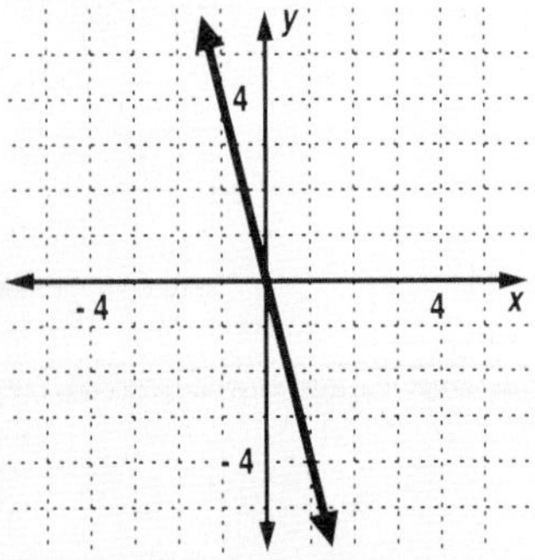

Summary

This chapter covers a variety of ideas related to lines and distance. Among them are absolute value, square root, and square. The absolute value of a number is its distance from the origin. If a square has area A, the positive square root of A, $\sqrt{A}$, is the length of a side of the square. The Pythagorean Theorem relates lengths of sides in a right triangle. If the legs have lengths a and b and the hypotenuse has length c, then

$$a^2 + b^2 = c^2.$$

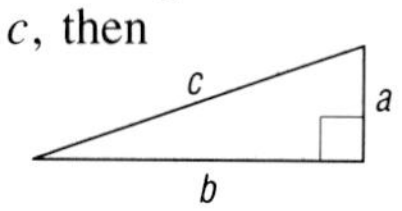

The distance between two points on a number line with coordinates x_1 and x_2 on a number line is $|x_2 - x_1|$. Using the Pythagorean Theorem, the distance between two points on the coordinate plane can be determined. If the points are (x_1, y_1) and (x_2, y_2), the Pythagorean distance is

$$\sqrt{(x_2 - x_1)^2 + (y_2 - y_1)^2}.$$

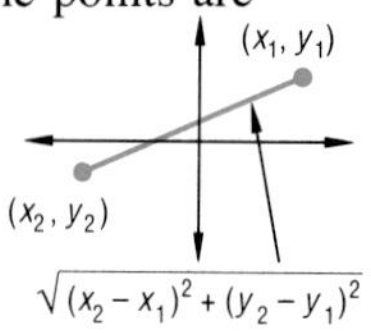

Square roots can be simplified using the Square Root of a Product Property:

$$\sqrt{ab} = \sqrt{a}\sqrt{b}$$

Here are the simplest equations involving these ideas, along with their solutions. Here $a > 0$.

Equation	Solution(s)
$\lvert x\rvert = a$	a, $-a$
$x^2 = a$	$\sqrt{a}$, $-\sqrt{a}$
$\sqrt{x} = a$	a^2

Here are the simplest sentences involving absolute value, along with their graphs. Again, $a > 0$.

Sentence	Graph
$\lvert x\rvert = a$	
$\lvert x\rvert < a$	
$\lvert x\rvert > a$	

Chunking is a problem-solving technique by which an expression is considered as a single number. Chunking allows equations like these to be solved when more complicated expressions are substituted for x.

Solutions to a linear equation in two variables may be graphed by making a table of values and plotting the resulting points. The result is a line. If the equation has only one variable, the graph is a horizontal line $y = k$ or a vertical line $x = h$.

Vocabulary

Below are the most important terms and phrases for this chapter. You should be able to give a definition or general description and a specific example of each.

Lesson 7-1
linear equation

Lesson 7-2
horizontal line $y = k$
vertical line $x = h$
boundary line
half-plane

Lesson 7-3
absolute value, $|x|$, ABS( )
Distance Formula on a number line

Lesson 7-4
square root
radical sign, $\sqrt{\ }$, SQR( )
perfect square

Lesson 7-5
leg of a right triangle
hypotenuse
Pythagorean Theorem

Lesson 7-6
Square Root of a Product Property
simplifying radicals

Lesson 7-7
"as the crow flies"
Pythagorean Distance Formula

Lesson 7-8
chunking

Progress Self-Test

Take this test as you would take a test in class. You will need graph paper and a calculator. Then check your work with the solutions in the Selected Answers section in the back of the book.

In 1 and 2, simplify.

1. $|-21| + |9|$ **30**
2. Evaluate $4\ |n - 17|$ if $n = 35$. **72**

In 3 and 4, find the distance between two points on a number line with coordinates:

3. -40 and -13. **27**
4. $5x$ and $-8x$. **$|13x|$ or $13\ |x|$**
5. Approximate $\sqrt{210}$ to the nearest hundredth using a calculator. **14.49**
6. The area of a square is 29 cm^2. What is the exact length of one side? **$\sqrt{29}$ cm** **7) 9**
7. Evaluate $\sqrt{\frac{x+y}{2}}$ if $x = 120$ and $y = 42$.
8. If a and b are positive, simplify $\sqrt{64a^2b^2}$.
9. Write $\sqrt{45}$ with a smaller integer under the radical sign. **$3\sqrt{5}$** **8) $8ab$**
10. Simplify $\sqrt{44}$. **$2\sqrt{11}$**
11. If $4y = 6.5$, find $12y - 5$. **14.5**

In 12–19 find all solutions.

12. $n^2 = 576$ **$n = 24$ or -24**
13. $-15 = k^2$ **no solutions**
14. $\sqrt{y} = 4$ **$y = 16$**
15. $3y^2 = 48$ **$y = 4$ or -4**
16. $\frac{7}{x} = \frac{x}{14}$ **$x = 7\sqrt{2}$ or $-7\sqrt{2}$**
17. $|4n - 18| = 22$ **10 or -1**
18. $|x - 3| > 7$ **$x < -4$ or $x > 10$**
19. $|y - 4| < 2$ **$2 < y < 6$**
20. How long is the ladder below? **17 ft**

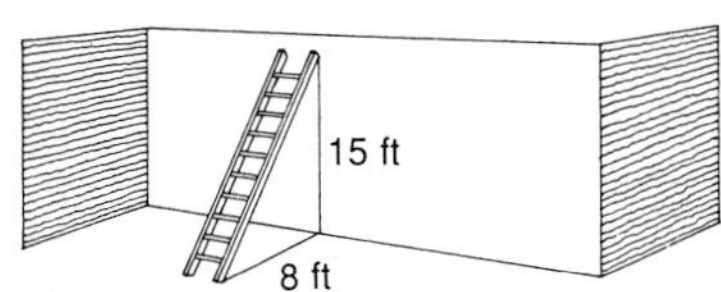

21. Find the value of y. **$\sqrt{609} \approx 24.7$**

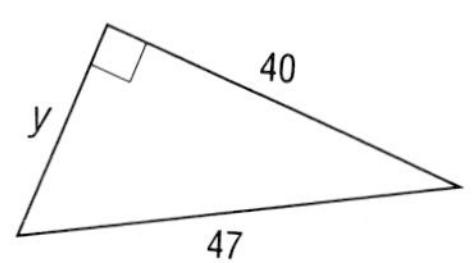

22. Write an equation for the line containing the points (-1, 6), (3, 6), and (0.5, 6). **$y = 6$**

24. $200\sqrt{10}$ m $\approx$ 632 m

In 23 and 24, use the diagram below. It shows part of a town laid out in a rectangular grid. The distance between consecutive streets is 200 meters for E-W streets and 100 meters for N-S streets.

23. What is the shortest street distance from 4th and Pine to 2nd and Olive? **800 m**
24. As the crow flies, what is the distance from 4th and Pine to 2nd and Olive?

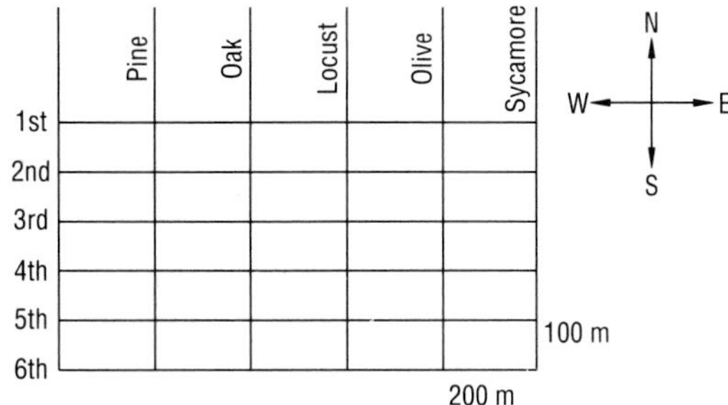

25. $A = (-3, 9)$ and $B = (6, 1)$. Find AB.
$AB = \sqrt{145}$

In 26 and 27, use the computer program below.

```
10 PRINT "TABLE OF (X,Y) VALUES"
20 PRINT "X VALUE", "Y VALUE"
30 FOR X = -2 TO 2
40 LET Y = 2 - 3 * X
50 PRINT X,Y
60 NEXT X
70 END
```

(-2, 8), (-1, 5), (0, 2), (1, -1), (2, -4)

26. What ordered pairs will the computer print?
27. Graph all solutions to the equation in line 40.
28. Graph $y = -4x$ in the coordinate plane.
29. Graph the points in the coordinate plane satisfying $y \leq 5$. **27–29) See margin.**

PROGRESS SELF-TEST

We cannot overemphasize the importance of these end-of-chapter materials. It is at this point that the material "gels" for many students, allowing them to solidify skills and understanding. In general, student performance should be markedly improved after these pages.

USING THE PROGRESS SELF-TEST

Assign the Progress Self-Test as a one-night assignment. Worked-out *solutions* for all questions are in the Selected Answers section at the back of the student book. Encourage students to take the Progress Self-Test honestly, grade themselves, and then be prepared to discuss the test in class.

Advise students to pay special attention to those Chapter Review questions (pages 360–363) which correspond to questions missed on the Progress Self-Test. A chart provided in the Selected Answers section in the student text keys the Progress Self-Test questions to the lettered SPUR Objectives in the Chapter Review or to the Vocabulary. It also keys the questions to the corresponding lessons where the material is covered.

29.

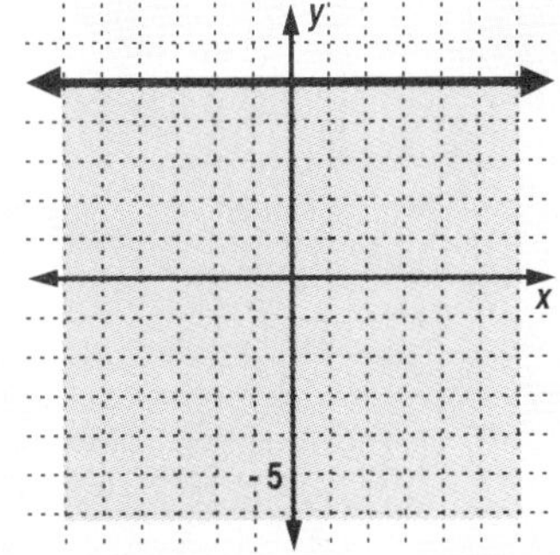

RESOURCES
- Chapter 7 Test, Form A
- Chapter 7 Test, Form B
- Chapter 7 Test, Cumulative Form

CHAPTER REVIEW

The main objectives for the chapter are organized here into sections corresponding to the four main types of understanding this book promotes: Skills, Properties, Uses, and Representations.

USING THE CHAPTER REVIEW
Whereas end-of-chapter material may be considered optional in some texts, in *Algebra* we have selected these objectives and questions with the expectation that they will be covered. Students should be able to answer these questions with about 85% accuracy after studying the chapter.

You may assign these questions over a single night to help students prepare for a test the next day, or you may assign the questions over a two-day period.

If you work the questions over two days, then we recommend assigning the *evens* for homework the first night so that students get feedback in class the next day, then assigning the *odds* the night before the test so the students can use the answers provided in the book.

ADDITIONAL ANSWERS
12b. Is $(10.25)^2 \approx 105$? 105.06 ≈ 105. Yes.

Chapter Review

Questions on SPUR Objectives

SPUR stands for **S**kills, **P**roperties, **U**ses, and **R**epresentations. The Chapter Review questions are grouped according to the SPUR Objectives for this chapter.

SKILLS deal with the procedures used to get answers.

Objective A: *Calculate absolute values.* (Lesson 7-3)

1. Give the absolute value of -43. **43**
2. Simplify $-|-1|$. **-1**

In 3–8, simplify.

3. $|13 - 19|$ **6**
4. $5 \cdot |4.2 - 3.8|$ **2**
5. $|3| - |-8|$ **-5**
6. ABS(3 − 8) **5**
7. $5\,|4 - 6|$ **10**
8. $|-20| - |15| + |-2|$ **7**

In 9–11, find all solutions.

9. $|d| = 16$ **$d = 16$ or -16**
10. $|k| = 0$ **$k = 0$**
11. $|300 - x| = 23$ **$x = 277$ or 323**

Objective B: *Evaluate and simplify expressions involving square roots.* (Lessons 7-4, 7-6)

12. a. Approximate $\sqrt{105}$ to the nearest hundredth using your calculator. **10.25**
    b. Check your answer. **See margin**
13. Between what two integers is $\sqrt{20}$? **4 and 5**
14. $4 + \sqrt{\frac{50}{2}}$ **9**
15. -SQR(100) **-10**
16. $\sqrt{\frac{20}{5}} + 5$ **3**
17. Evaluate $45 - \sqrt{4 + 2n}$ when $n = 70$. **33**
18. Evaluate $20 - 3(2 + 3\sqrt{x})$ when $x = 16$. **-22**

Objective C: *Solve equations involving squares and square roots.* (Lessons 7-4, 7-6)

In 19–26, solve. Give the exact answer, simplified.

19. $5x^2 = 200$ **$x = \pm 2\sqrt{10}$**
20. $q^2 = 121$ **$q = \pm 11$**
21. $\frac{16}{z} = \frac{z}{5}$ **$q = \pm 4\sqrt{5}$**
22. $\frac{2x}{5} = \frac{40}{x}$ **$x = \pm 10$**
23. $x^2 = -100$ **no solution**
24. $\sqrt{v} = 9$ **81**
25. $\sqrt{w} + 3 = 8$ **25**
26. $4\sqrt{t} = 1$ **$\frac{1}{16}$**

Objective D: *Use chunking to evaluate expressions and solve equations.* (Lesson 7-8)

27. If $7y = 21.2$, find $21y + 4$. **67.6**

In 28–35, solve.

28. $(m + 2)^2 = 64$ **6 or -10**
29. $(z - 4)^2 = 144$ **16 or -8**
30. $\sqrt{n + 5} = 25$ **620**
31. $\sqrt{3q + 2} = 11$ **$39\frac{2}{3}$**
32. $|2y - 3| = 9$ **6 or -3**
33. $-7 = |2 - x|$ **no solution**
34. $|6 - x| \geq 9$ **$x \geq 15$ or $x \leq -3$**
35. $|x - 3| < 4$ **$-1 < x < 7$**

PROPERTIES deal with the principles behind the mathematics.

■ **Objective E:** *Apply the Square Root of a Product Property.* (Lesson 7-6)

In 36–41, simplify.

36. $\sqrt{20^2 + 20^2}$ **$20\sqrt{2}$**

37. $\sqrt{500}$ **$10\sqrt{5}$**

38. $3\sqrt{72}$ **$18\sqrt{2}$**

39. $\frac{\sqrt{150}}{5}$ **$\frac{5\sqrt{6}}{5} = \sqrt{6}$**

40. $\frac{\sqrt{99}}{12}$ **$\frac{3\sqrt{11}}{12} = \frac{\sqrt{11}}{4}$**

41. $\sqrt{4} \cdot \sqrt{9} - \sqrt{3} \cdot \sqrt{48}$ **-6**

42. If a and b are positive, simplify $\sqrt{49a^2b^2}$. **$7ab$**

43. Simplify $\sqrt{5x^2}$ when $x > 0$. **$x\sqrt{5}$**

USES deal with applications of mathematics in real situations.

■ **Objective F:** *Use squares and square roots in measurement problems.* (Lessons 7-4, 7-5, 7-6)

44. The jacket for a record album is a square with area 150 sq in. Find the length of the side of the jacket, rounded to the nearest hundredth. **12.25 in.**

45. The area of a square is $147y^2$. Write the exact length of one side. **$7y\sqrt{3}$ if $y > 0$**

46. A side of a square is $3\sqrt{11}$. Find the area of the square. **99**

47. A rectangular field is 300 feet long and 100 feet wide. To the nearest foot, how far will you walk if you cut across the field diagonally? **≈316ft**

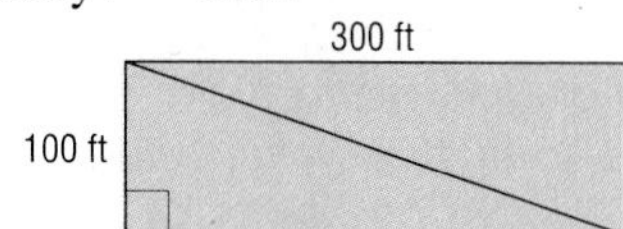

48. Ben uses a guy wire to support a young tree. He attaches it to a point 6 ft up the tree trunk. The wire is 10 ft long. How far away from the trunk will the wire reach? **8 ft**

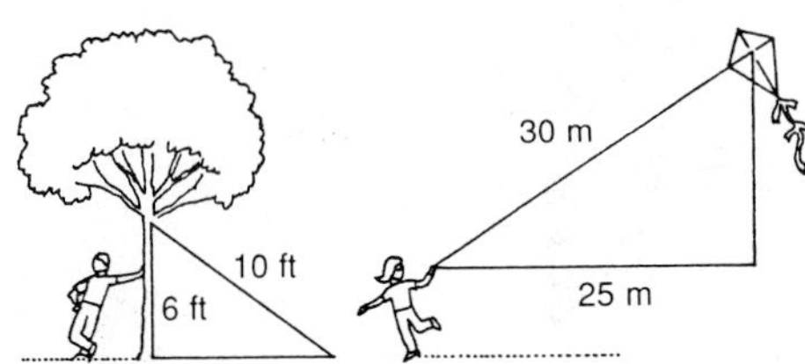

49. Megan is flying a kite. She has unrolled 30m of string and the kite is 25m from her along the ground. How high is the kite? **16.6 m + Megan's height**

55a.

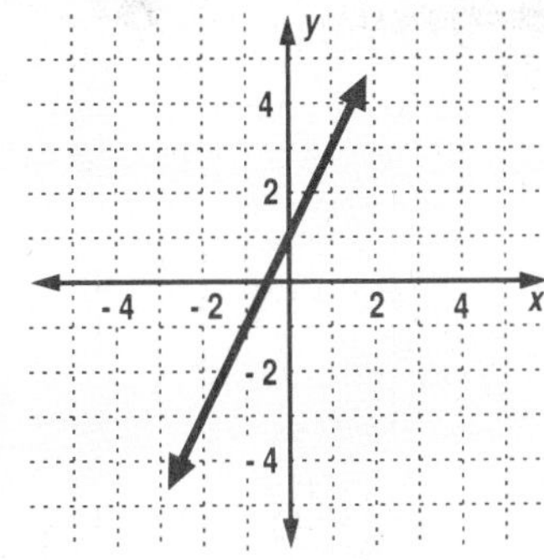

56.

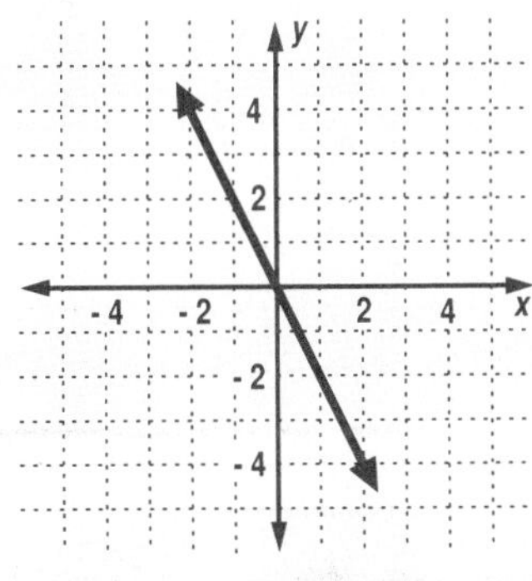

55a., 56. See margin, page 361.

57b.

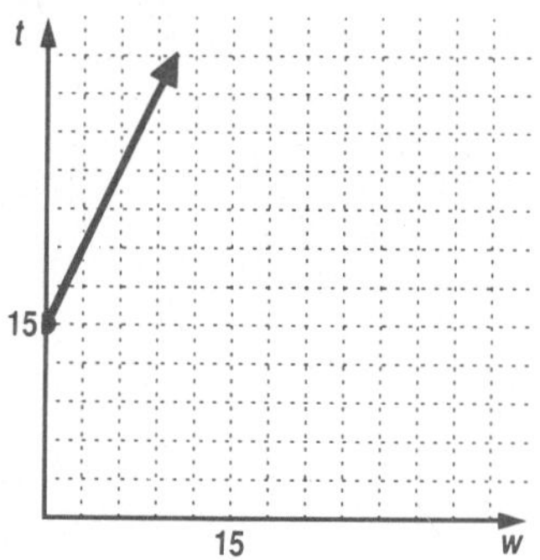

58.

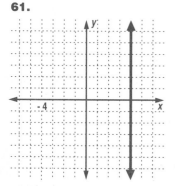

61.

62.

REPRESENTATIONS deal with pictures, graphs, or objects that illustrate concepts.

Objective G: *Find distance on a number line.* *(Lesson 7-3)*

In 50–52, find the distance between points with the given coordinates.

50. 72 and 18. 54

51. 13 and -11 24

52. 15 and s. $|15 - s|$

53. Find the distance between the two points with coordinates d and j. $|j - d|$ or $|d - j|$

54. Write a simplified expression for the distance between points with coordinates $5x - 3$ and $2x + 7$. $|3x - 10|$

Objective H: *Graph equations for straight lines by making a table of values.* *(Lesson 7-1)*

55. a. Draw the graph of $y = 2x + 1$. See margin.

b. For what value of y is $(-5, y)$ on this line? -9

56. Graph the set of points in the plane with $y = -2x$. See margin.

57. Suppose a person begins with \$15 and adds \$2 to an account each week.

a. Write an equation that represents the amount of money t in the account after w weeks. $t = 15 + 2w$

b. Draw the graph of the equation in part a. See margin.

58. The level in a swimming pool is dropping at the rate of 0.5 feet per hour. Suppose the level in the pool is at the 6 foot mark. The level L after h hours is given by $L = 6 - .5h$. Graph this relationship. See margin

Objective I: *Graph horizontal and vertical lines.* *(Lesson 7-2)*

In 59 and 60, answer true or false.

59. The graph of all points in the plane satisfying $x = -0.4$ is a vertical line. True

60. The graph of all points in the plane satisfying $y = 73$ is a horizontal line. True

In 61 and 62, graph the points satisfying each equation.

61. $x = 4$ See margin.

62. $y \geq 1$ See margin.

63. Give a sentence describing the colored region in the graph below. $y \leq -2$

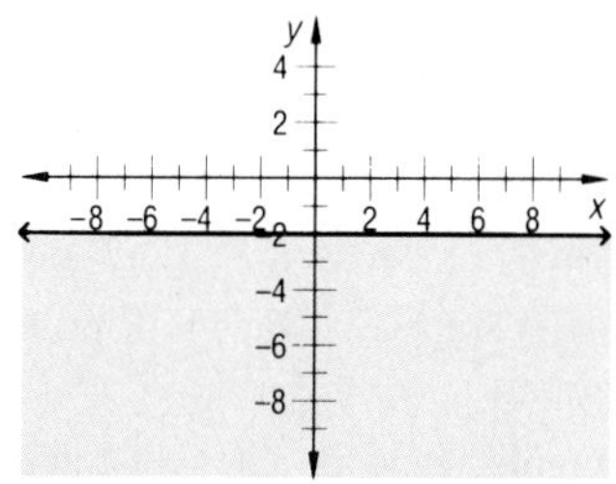

64. Write an equation for the line containing the points (5, 11), (5, 4), and (5, -7). $x = 5$

Objective J: *Find the lengths of the sides of a right triangle using the Pythagorean Theorem.* *(Lesson 7-5)*

65. Find the value of n. 37

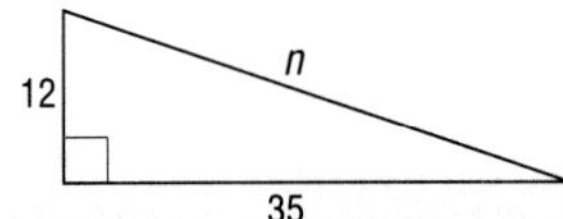

66. What is the length of the hypotenuse of the triangle on the left below? **$\sqrt{265} \approx 16.3$**

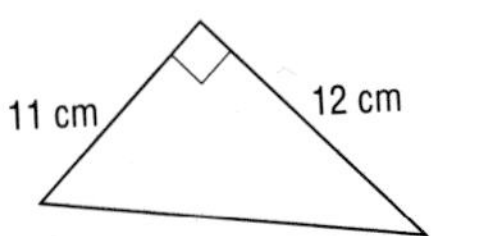

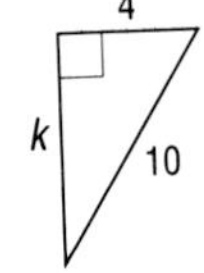

67. Find the value of k in the triangle at right above. **$2\sqrt{21} \approx 9.2$**

68. A diagonal of a rectangle has length 10 and one side has length 6. What are the lengths of the other sides of the rectangle? **8, 8, 6**

Objective K: *Calculate distances in the plane.* *(Lesson 7-7)* **69c) $\sqrt{185} \approx 13.6$**

In 69 and 70, use the graph below.

69. a. Find CB. **8**

b. Find AB. **11**

c. Find AC.

70. Find the distance from A to the origin. **5**

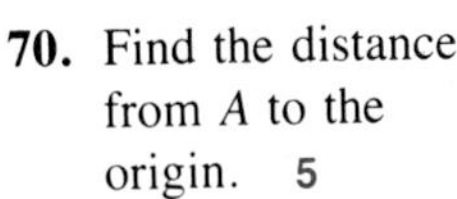

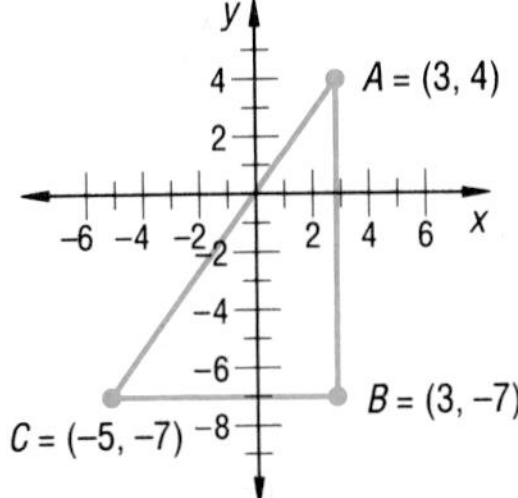

In 71–74, find AB.

71. $A = (50, 10)$ and $B = (50, 4)$ **6**

72. $A = (14, -20)$ and $B = (-2, -20)$ **16**

73. $A = (8, -3)$ and $B = (4, 12)$ **$\sqrt{241}$**

74. $A = (-2, 9)$ and $B = (-5, -1)$ **$\sqrt{109}$**

In 75 and 76, **a.** find the points on the line where $x = -2$ and $x = 8$. **b.** Find the distance between the points in part a.

75. $y = 2x - 3$ **a) (-2, -7); (8,13); b) $10\sqrt{5}$**

76. $\frac{1}{2}x - y = 5$ **a) (-2, -6); (8, -1); b) $5\sqrt{5}$**

In 77 and 78, suppose the school the Conners' children attend is 3 miles east and 5 miles south of their home. The library is 4 miles west and 2 miles north of the Conners' house. The streets in their neighborhood are laid out in a rectangular grid.

77. What is the street distance from the school to the library? **14 miles**

78. How far is it from the school to the library as the crow flies? **$7\sqrt{2} \approx 9.9$ miles**

Objective L: *Graph solutions to sentences of the form $|x - a| < b$, or $|x - a| > b$, where a and b are real numbers.* *(Lesson 7-3)*

In 79–84 graph all solutions on a number line. **See margin.**

79. $|x - 2| = 4$

80. $|y - 7| = 1\frac{1}{2}$

81. $|z + 5| \le 12$

82. $|a + 6| > 9$

83. $3 \ge |s - 2|$

84. $.03 < |r - 5|$

EVALUATION

Three tests are provided for this chapter in the Teacher's Resource File. Chapter 7 Test, Forms A and B, cover just Chapter 7. The third test is Chapter 7 Test, Cumulative Form. About 50% of this test covers Chapter 7; 25% covers Chapter 6, and 25% covers earlier chapters. For more information on grading, see *General Teaching Suggestions: Grading* on page T44 in the Teacher's Edition.

ASSIGNMENT RECOMMENDATION

On the day your students take the chapter test, we suggest you make an assignment in the first section of the next chapter.

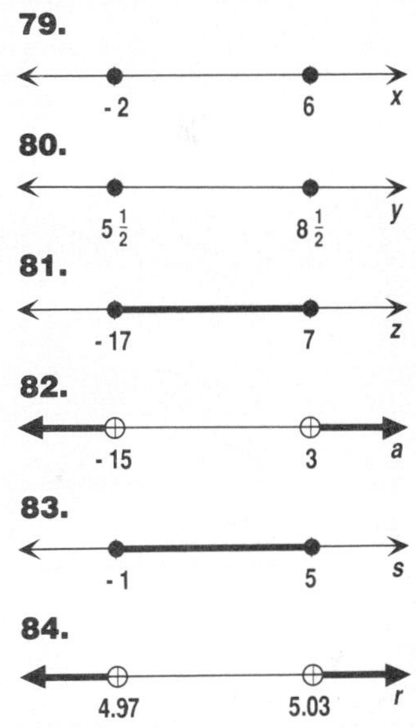

CHAPTER 8 ■ SLOPES AND LINES

DAILY PACING CHART 8

DAILY PACING CHART ■ CHAPTER 8

Students in the Full Course should complete the entire text by the end of the year. Students in the Minimal Course spend more time to complete lessons that are combined with quizzes and more time to consider the Chapter Review. Therefore, these students may not complete all the chapters in the text.

DAY	MINIMAL COURSE	FULL COURSE
1	8-1	8-1
2	8-2	8-2
3	8-3	8-3
4	8-4	8-4
5	Quiz (TRF); Start 8-5.	Quiz (TRF); 8-5
6	Finish 8-5.	8-6
7	8-6	8-7
8	8-7	Quiz (TRF); 8-8
9	Quiz (TRF); Start 8-8.	8-9
10	Finish 8-8.	Progress Self-Test
11	8-9	Chapter Review
12	Progress Self-Test	Chapter Test (TRF)
13	Chapter Review	
14	Chapter Review	
15	Chapter Test (TRF)	

TESTING OPTIONS

TESTING OPTIONS

- ■ Quiz for Lessons 8-1 Through 8-4
- ■ Quiz for Lessons 8-5 Through 8-7
- ■ Chapter 8 Test, Form A
- ■ Chapter 8 Test, Form B
- ■ Chapter 8 Test, Cumulative Form

INDIVIDUAL DIFFERENCES

PROVIDING FOR INDIVIDUAL DIFFERENCES

The student text is written for the *average* student. The program, however, can be adapted for less capable and for more capable students.

For those students who need more practice, a blackline master (in the Teacher's Resource File) is provided for each lesson. The Teacher's Edition frequently provides Error Analysis and Alternate Approach features to provide additional instructional strategies for those students who do not readily grasp the material.

For students who require additional challenge, Extension activities are regularly provided in the Teacher's Edition.

OBJECTIVES ■ CHAPTER 8

Students should master the chapter objectives by the time they complete the chapter. To ensure objective mastery, there is continual review built into each set of lesson questions. After students complete the chapter lessons, they assess their mastery on the Progress Self-Test. Then they do the Chapter Review and pay special attention to those questions that match the objectives missed on the Progress Self-Test. Students can get extra practice on these objectives by using the master for each lesson in the Teacher's Resource File.

OBJECTIVES FOR CHAPTER 8 (Organized into the SPUR categories— Skills, Properties, Uses, and Representations)	**Progress Self-Test Questions**	**Chapter Review Questions**	**Lesson Master from Teacher's Resource File***
SKILLS			
A Find the slope of the line through two given points.	1 through 3	1 through 4	8-2
B Find an equation for a line given its slope and any point on it.	6, 7	5 through 10	8-4, 8-5
C Find an equation for a line through two given points.	20	11, 12	8-6
PROPERTIES			
D Recognize slope as a rate of change.	9, 10	13 through 16	8-2, 8-3
E Rewrite an equation for a line in standard form or slope-intercept form.	8	17 through 20	8-4, 8-8
F Given an equation for a line, find its slope and *y*-intercept.	4, 5	21 through 24	8-2, 8-4
USES			
G Calculate rates of change from real data.	11, 12	25 through 28	8-1
H Use equations for lines to describe real situations.	13 through 15, 21	29 through 36	8-4, 8-5, 8-6, 8-8
REPRESENTATIONS			
I Graph a straight line given its equation, or given a point on it and its slope.	16	37 through 44	8-2, 8-3, 8-4
J Given data which approximates a linear graph, find a linear equation to fit the graph.	18, 19	45	8-7
K Graph linear inequalities.	17	46 through 51	8-9

*** The masters are numbered to match the lessons.**

OVERVIEW 8

OVERVIEW ■ CHAPTER 8

Graphing lines by using a table of values was covered in Chapters 3 and 7. The emphasis in this chapter is on equations of lines, which are tied in with the applications that give rise to them and with the geometry of the plane.

The chapter starts with rates, an idea from previous chapters. The goal is to have students interpret the slope of a line as a rate. In Lesson 8-2 a line emerges as a graph of a situation involving a constant rate of change, and the slope is defined in the traditional fashion. The results should remind students of their work with changes in Chapter 3 and with rates in Chapter 5. This preparation leads students to practice representing slope as a rate of change in Lesson 8-3 as well as to practice using the slope to draw a line.

There are four categories of applications covered. One, which leads to $y = mx + b$, involves an initial quantity and the rate at which it increases or decreases. These settings are covered in Lesson 8-4. In Lesson 8-5 there are problems in which a data point and the rate of change are known. In Lesson 8-6 two data points are known. The last type of application involves linear combination situations, which lead to sentences of the form $Ax + By = C$. These are covered in Lesson 8-8 as standard form for equations of lines.

Lesson 8-7 gives a method for finding a line which closely describes data. Many scattergrams of data do appear to be based on a linear relation, so the estimation of a line which fits the pattern of data opens up rich examples and problems on linear equations.

The chapter closes with a lesson on graphing linear inequalities.

The use of graph paper by students will be a time-saver and will aid understanding. For example, slope is illustrated better when students can accurately count squares to move on the graph.

PERSPECTIVES 8

PERSPECTIVES ■ CHAPTER 8

The Perspectives provide the rationale for the inclusion of topics or approaches, provide mathematical background, and make connections within UCSMP.

8-1

RATES OF CHANGE

In this lesson we use situations and graphs in which quantities change over time. The problems in this lesson result in graphs that are broken lines, and we talk about rate of change between pairs of points. In the next lesson we look at lines and introduce the term *slope*.

One reason to start with rate of change rather than slope is that no lines are needed, just two points. This is intuitively easier. Also, the subtraction and division in the formula come from change and rate, so the name *rate of change* is easily associated with the operations in the formula. This makes the formula easier to understand.

This applications approach helps students make sense of positive, negative, and zero rates of change. It is easy to picture population or height increasing, decreasing, or remaining constant.

8-2

CONSTANT RATES OF CHANGE

If the algebra of slope is divorced from its applications, students often wonder why slope is defined as $\frac{y_2 - y_1}{x_2 - x_1}$ rather than $\frac{x_2 - x_1}{y_2 - y_1}$. The approach in this lesson should make this clear. Many applications deal with things that change over time. Since time is usually graphed on the horizontal axis, the slope measures the rate of change in the quantity measured along the vertical axis.

The fact that the slope between any points on a line is constant is not obvious to students. In this lesson students find the slope of a line given two points. In Lesson 8-4 we will discuss the slope-intercept form of the equation.

8-3

PROPERTIES OF SLOPE

In this lesson we describe slope as the amount of change in the height as you go 1 unit to the right. At first, it may seem strange to graph a line with slope 1/4 by moving up 1/4 unit when going right 1 instead of going up 1 and over 4. However, use of this approach in field-test editions of this book has shown that it works very well. There are several advantages to this interpretation.

First, by stating that slope *always* measures the change in *height*, we eliminate one of the most common mistakes, reversing the horizontal and vertical motions. A slope of 5 means to move up 5. A slope of 1/4 means to move up 1/4.

The second advantage of this view of slope is that it fits naturally with the idea of rate that has been developed since Chapter 4. In this lesson, exercises deal with change in dollars/week, magazines/week and dollars/day. Notice these mean *per one unit.*

A third advantage is that it is easier to compare slopes, and to see that a larger slope means a faster increase (if both are positive).

Fourth, it is easier to make sense of positive, negative, and zero slopes. Since we always move to the right, a negative slope means to go down. Zero slope means that you don't change the height. Also, the fact that a vertical line has no slope is almost obvious. You can't measure change as you go to the right if you can't move to the right on the line.

Fifth, in the slope-intercept equation for a line, an increase of 1 in x means an increase of m in y. Thus thinking of increasing x by 1 offers a firm interpretation of this important parameter in the slope-intercept equation.

8-4

SLOPE-INTERCEPT EQUATIONS FOR LINES

Equations for lines are generally found in either of two common forms: the slope-intercept form $y = mx + b$ or the standard form $Ax + By = C$. The slope-intercept form has two major advantages: it is unique, in that a line has only one such equation; and it is akin to function notation $f(x) = mx + b$. Standard form also has advantages: every line, including each vertical line, has an equation in this form; and systems of linear equations in this form are often easier to analyze. There are applications for which each form is natural.

In this text, we call the *value* of b in the equation $y = mx + b$ the y-intercept. This fits well with the term *slope-intercept form.* In later courses, it extends easily to x-intercepts being solutions to equations of the form $f(x) = 0$. Some people call the *point* $(0, b)$, where the line crosses the y-axis, the y-intercept. Our definition is more common.

8-5

EQUATIONS FOR LINES WITH A GIVEN POINT AND SLOPE

In this lesson, an equation is found for a line having a given slope and containing any given point. Thus, in the applications in this lesson, the rate of change is described, along with information that corresponds to some point on the line other than the y-intercept or initial value.

Notice that we ask here for "an equation" for a line rather than "the equation" for a line. This is because a line has many equations. Be flexible at this point in what you consider an acceptable answer.

8-6

EQUATIONS FOR LINES THROUGH TWO POINTS

This lesson discusses the last in a three-problem sequence on finding equations of lines. Each problem requires one more step for its solution than the previous one.

(1) given slope and y-intercept (just substitute into $y = mx + b$)

(2) given slope and one point (reduce to type 1 by calculating b)

(3) given two points (reduce to type 2 by calculating slope)

8-7

FITTING A LINE TO DATA

Here, we cover the "eye-ball" fitting of a line to data. Lines are the simplest descriptors for trends in data arising in science, medicine, politics, psychology, economics, quality control, business, and so on. Many students don't study situations in which data fail to lie in a perfect line until later courses. Fitting a line to data, however, is a technique which is accessible to algebra students. In addition, it opens a rich source of applications for problems which will appear throughout this book.

Line-fitting is the simplest form of curve-fitting and begins an idea which is continued in later UCSMP texts. In *Advanced Algebra* students will study other types of graphs and discuss fitting a curve to data in situations of variation. Other curve-fitting is discussed in *Functions, Statistics and Trigonometry with Computers.*

8-8

EQUATIONS FOR ALL LINES

Linear combination situations naturally lead to equations in standard form. This is one of the reasons for studying this form. Another reason is that it works for all lines, whereas vertical lines do not have equations in slope-intercept form.

We do not insist that the coefficients in $Ax + By = C$ be integral or that A be positive, although you may do so if you wish. We feel that the context of the problem should determine the kinds of numbers used. Percent problems might best use decimals, and a problem about a recipe might use values which are fractions. If the situation involves first a loss, then a gain, the value of A might be negative.

8-9

GRAPHING LINEAR INEQUALITIES

Linear inequalities help with the understanding of lines. A student cannot fully understand what it means for a point to be on a line without understanding which points are not on the line.

Geometrically, linear inequalities allow one to easily describe half-planes. Intersections of half-planes are interiors of strips between parallel lines or interiors of angles or triangles and other polygons. Thus these sentences are quite useful in describing other figures. Graphing linear inequalities is important in business applications and is the foundation of the technique of linear programming.

CHAPTER 8

This chapter should take 9 to 11 days for the lessons and quizzes; 1 day for the Progress Self-Test; 1 or 2 days for the Chapter Review; and 1 day for testing. The total is 12 to 15 days.

CHAPTER 8

Slopes and Lines

Below is a graph of the population of Manhattan Island (part of New York) every ten years from 1790 to 1980. Coordinates of some of the points are shown.

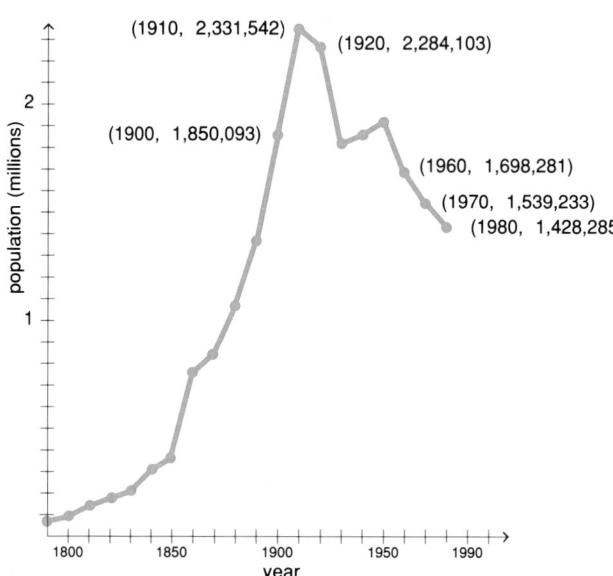

The slopes of the lines connecting the points tell how fast the population went up or down. In this chapter, you will study many examples of lines and slopes.

USING PAGES 364-365
Students may be familiar with the story that in 1626, Peter Minuit, governor of the Dutch West India Company, bought Manhattan Island from the Manhattan Indians for beads, cloth, and trinkets worth about $24.

Manhattan Island makes up most of the borough of Manhattan, one of the five boroughs that make up New York City. As its name implies, Manhattan Island is set off by water, primarily the Hudson and East rivers. It is the site of such famous landmarks and areas as the Empire State Building, Greenwich Village, Times Square, the U.N. headquarters, Wall Street, and Broadway.

The increase in the population of Manhattan Island up to 1910 reflects the historical growth, largely through immigration.

Students may wonder why the population decreased in the early 1900's. At that time, bridges and subways were built to provide convenient transportation to other boroughs. As the population of New York City spread out, the population of Manhattan decreased. The recent population decrease is typical of the movement of people out of the large cities of the industrial north to other areas.

LESSON 8-1

RESOURCES

- ■ Lesson Master 8-1
- Visual for Teaching Aid 7: Coordinate Grid
- Visual for Teaching Aid 39: Graph of Population of Manhattan Island for Page 364

OBJECTIVE

G Calculate rates of change from real data.

TEACHING NOTES

Because we emphasize the rate of change, students should label their answers with units of rate. The rate unit in the height example at the beginning of the lesson is *inches per year.*

Reading This entire chapter provides many opportunities to concentrate on careful reading of data presented graphically. For example, when discussing the graph on page 366, be careful to distinguish rate of change from amount of change. Point out that the faster the rate of growth, the steeper the incline of the segment. So, Karen's rate of growth was faster between ages 9 and 11. Between ages 11 and 14, there is greater growth but not faster growth because the time period is 3 years, not 2.

You may have to remind students that in the rate of change formula x_1 stands for the "first x-value" and x_2 stands for the "second x-value", and similarly for y_1 and y_2. Some students may still want to think of the 2 as being multiplied by x or as an exponent.

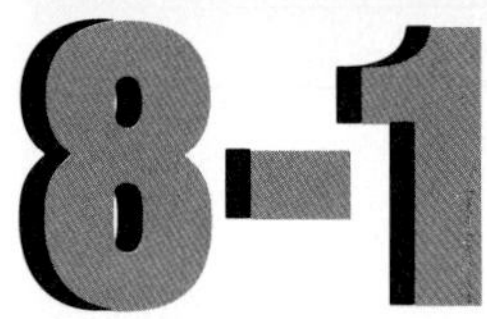

LESSON 8-1

Rates of Change

At age 9 Karen was 4′3″ tall. At age 11 she was 4′9″ tall. How fast did she grow from age 9 to age 11? To answer this question, we calculate the *rate of change* of Karen's height per year.

Rate of change in height per year (from age 9 to age 11)

$$= \frac{\text{change in height}}{\text{change in age}} = \frac{4'9'' - 4'3''}{(11 - 9)\text{ years}} = \frac{6''}{2\text{ years}} = 3\,\frac{\text{inches}}{\text{year}}.$$

At age 14 Karen was 5′4″ tall. How fast did she grow from age 11 to age 14? Again we calculate. Rate of change in height per year (from age 11 to age 14)

$$= \frac{\text{change in height}}{\text{change in age}} = \frac{5'4'' - 4'9''}{(14 - 11)\text{ years}} = \frac{7''}{3\text{ years}} = 2.\overline{3}\,\frac{\text{inches}}{\text{year}}.$$

Karen grew at a faster rate from age 9 to age 11 than from age 11 to 14.

The data can be graphed and points connected. The rate of change then measures how fast the graph goes up as you read from left to right along the x-axis.

The segment connecting (9, 4′3″) to (11, 4′9″) is steeper than the one connecting (11, 4′9″) and (14, 5′4″) since the rate of change is greater.

Example The graph on page 364 shows the population of Manhattan. Find the rate of change of the population (in people per year):

a. between 1900 and 1910;
b. between 1910 and 1920;
c. between 1960 and 1970.

Solution Every rate of change is found by dividing two changes.

a. Between 1900 and 1910:

$$\frac{2{,}331{,}542 - 1{,}850{,}093}{1910 - 1900} = \frac{481{,}449 \text{ people}}{10 \text{ years}}$$
$$= 48{,}144.9 \text{ people per year}$$

Notice that the population increased and the rate of change is positive. Between 1900 and 1910, from left to right, the graph slants up.

b. Between 1910 and 1920:

$$\frac{2{,}284{,}103 - 2{,}331{,}542}{1920 - 1910} = \frac{-47{,}439 \text{ people}}{10 \text{ years}}$$
$$= -4743.9 \text{ people per year}$$

c. Between 1960 and 1970:

$$\frac{1{,}539{,}233 - 1{,}698{,}281}{1970 - 1960} = \frac{-159{,}048 \text{ people}}{10 \text{ years}}$$
$$= -15{,}904.8 \text{ people per year}$$

In both parts b and c, the population decreased and therefore the rate of change is negative. Between those dates, from left to right, the graph slants down.

In Example 1, since a number of people is divided by a number of years, the unit of the rate of change is $\frac{\text{people}}{\text{year}}$. The unit of a rate of change is always a rate unit.

The following table summarizes the relationship between rates of change and their graphs.

Situation	Rate of Change	Graph (from left to right)
increase	positive	upward slant
no change	zero	horizontal
decrease	negative	downward slant

Another way of thinking of rate of change is in terms of coordinates. In the above example, the year is the x-coordinate and the population size is the y-coordinate. The **rate of change** between two points is calculated by dividing the difference in the y-coordinates by the difference in the x-coordinates.

The rate of change between points (x_1, y_1) and (x_2, y_2) is

$$\frac{y_2 - y_1}{x_2 - x_1}.$$

ADDITIONAL EXAMPLE

The chart below shows Tom's income for each week of a six-week period.

week	amount
1	$11
2	$15
3	$ 4
4	$21
5	$25
6	$18

a. Graph these points and connect them.

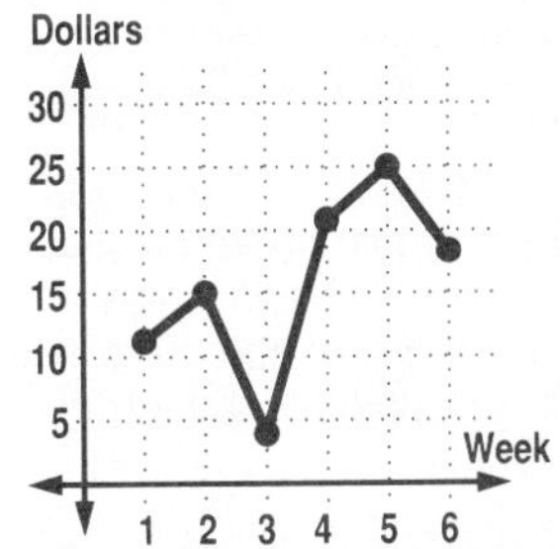

b. Find the rate of change of his income between weeks 1 and 6.

$\frac{\mathbf{18 - 11}}{\mathbf{6 - 1}} \frac{\textbf{dollars}}{\textbf{week}} =$

$\mathbf{1.40} \frac{\textbf{dollars}}{\textbf{week}}$ **= $1.40/wk.**

NOTES ON QUESTIONS
Question 2: The connection between steepness and rate of change is important. The steeper the segment, the greater the rate of change.

Questions 12-15: The graph for these questions provides many opportunities to compare different rates of change. During the swoop, the height is decreasing quickly, so the rate of change is negative. Then the vulture takes off and the height increases, so the rate of change becomes positive.

Question 16: Here you can also talk about positive, negative, and zero rates of change. From age 20 to age 55, Tim doesn't change in height.

Making Connections for Questions 20 and 26: These questions preview the two major types of applications that lead to linear equations in two variables. **Question 26** is the kind of application that has a starting quantity that is increased (or decreased) at a constant rate. **Question 20** is an example of a linear combination. It combines rate-factor multiplication (*p* pencils × 12 cents/pencil; *e* erasers × 20 cents/eraser) with the Putting-together Model for Addition.

Making Connections for Question 23: This *Skill Sequence* emphasizes manipulation skills which will be needed in later lessons of the chapter.

Making Connections for Question 24: Class discussion of this question will help students understand **Example 2** of the next lesson.

Small Group Work for Question 27: You may wish to have students work in small groups while researching this data.

Questions

Covering the Reading

1. The rate of change in height per year is the change in _?_ divided by the change in _?_. height, years

2. Which is steeper: the segment connecting (9, 4′3″) to (11, 4′9″) or the segment connecting (11, 4′9″) to (14, 5′4″)?
segment connecting (9, 4′3″) to (11, 4′9″)

In 3 and 4, suppose Karen in the lesson is 5′7″ tall at age 18 and 5′7″ tall at age 19.

3. **a.** What is the rate of change of her height from age 14 to age 18? .75 inches per year
b. Was the rate of change of Karen's height greater from age 9 to age 11 or from age 14 to age 18? from age 9 to 11

4. **a.** What is the rate of change of her height from age 18 to age 19? 0
b. What is the unit of the rate of change of her height from age 18 to age 19? inches/year

In 5–8, use the graph of the population of Manhattan on page 364.

5. If the rate of change in population is positive, does the population increase or decrease? increase

6. Between 1950 and 1960, did the population increase or decrease?
decrease

7. Find the rate of change in population between 1970 and 1980.
-11,094.8 people per year

8. Find the rate of change in population from 1900 to 1980.
-5272.6 people per year

9. In terms of coordinates, the rate of change between two points is the _?_ of the y-coordinates divided by the difference of the _?_.
difference, x-coordinates

10. Describe the graph of the segment connecting two points when the rate of change between them is **a.** positive; **b.** negative; **c.** zero.
a) slants upward from left to right; b) downward from left to right; c) horizontal

Applying the Mathematics

11. Below are heights (in inches) for a boy from age 9 to 15.

Age	9	10	11	12	13	14	15
Height	51″	53″	58″	61″	63″	64″	65″

a. Accurately graph these data and connect the points as was done in the lesson. See margin.
b. Using the graph, in which two-year period did the boy grow the fastest? from age 10 to 12
c. Calculate his rate of growth in that two-year period.
4 inches per year

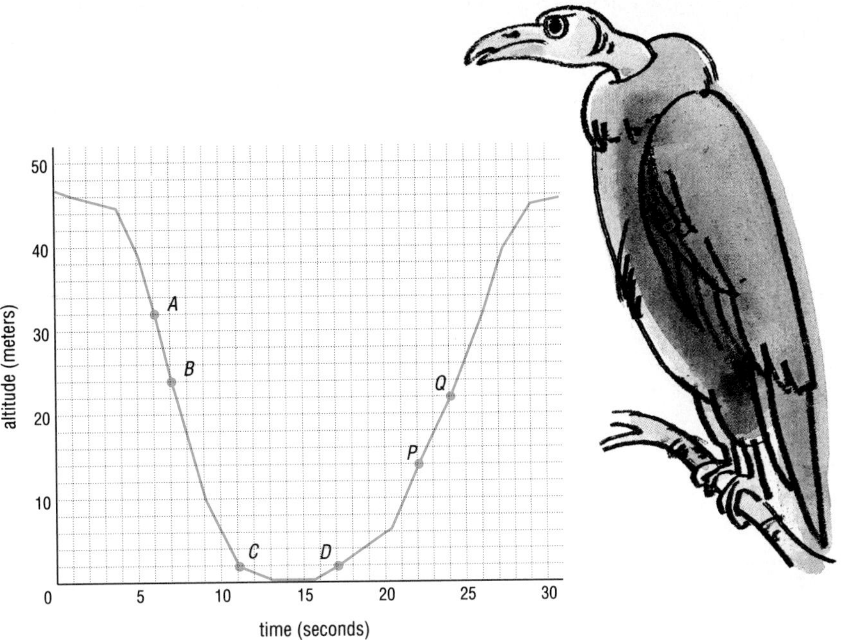

In 12–15, use the graph above. This graph shows the altitude of a vulture's flight over a period of time.

12. **a.** Give the coordinates of point A. **(6, 32)**
b. Give the coordinates of point B. **(7, 24)**
c. What is the rate of change of altitude (in meters per second) between points A and B? **-8 meters per second**

13. What is the rate of change of altitude in meters per second between points C and D? **0 meters per second**

14. After about how many seconds does the altitude of the vulture begin to increase? **15**

15. Is the rate of change between P and Q positive or negative? **positive**

16. Older people tend to lose height. Tim reached his full height at age 20, when he was 74″ tall. He stayed that height for 35 years, then started losing height. At age 65 his height is 73″. What was the rate of change of his height from age 55 to age 65? **-.1 inch per year**

17. Suppose Karen in the lesson was h inches tall at age 7. Write an expression for the rate of change in her height from age 7 to age 9.

18. In the graph at the right, find the rate of change in feet per minute.
$\frac{y}{4}$ **feet per minute**

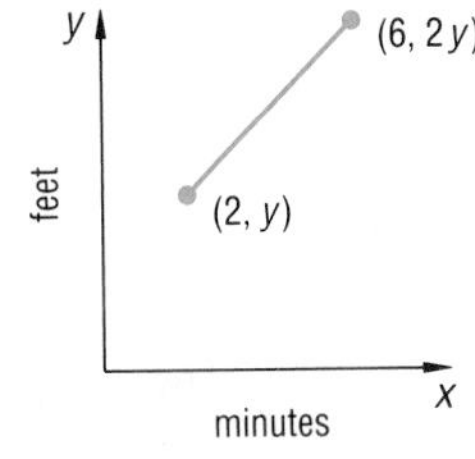

17) $\frac{4'3'' - h}{2 \text{ yr}}$

ADDITIONAL ANSWERS

11a.

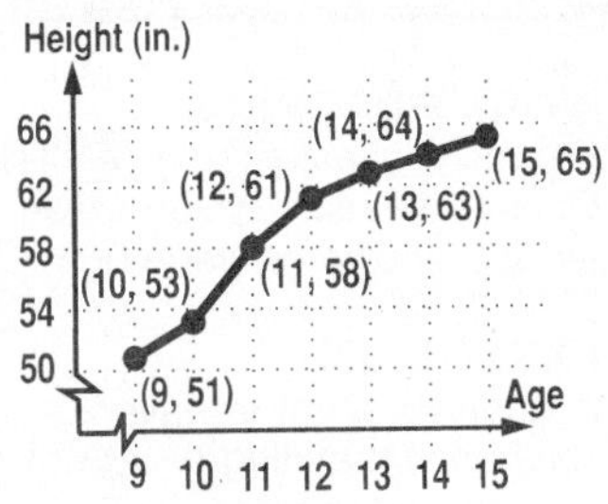

19a. and b.

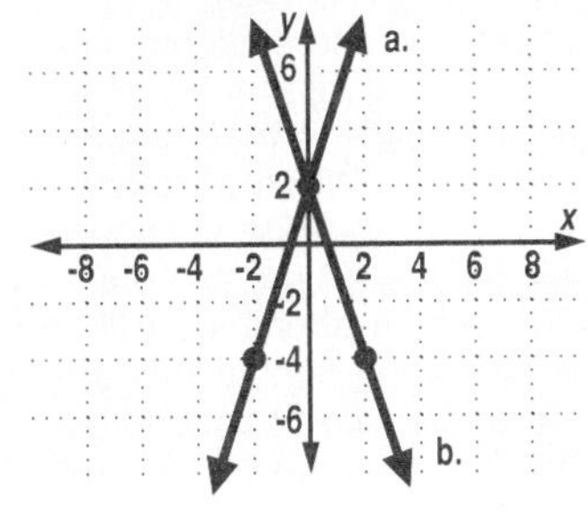

NAME ______

LESSON **MASTER 8–1**
QUESTIONS ON **SPUR** OBJECTIVES

■**USES** *Objective G (See pages 418–421 for objectives.)*
In 1–4, use the data given below on number of deaths in the U.S. caused by home fires.

Year	No. Deaths	Year	No. Deaths
1950	5000	1970	5600
1955	5400	1975	5000
1960	6350	1980	4400
1965	6100		

1. Graph the situation on the axes below.

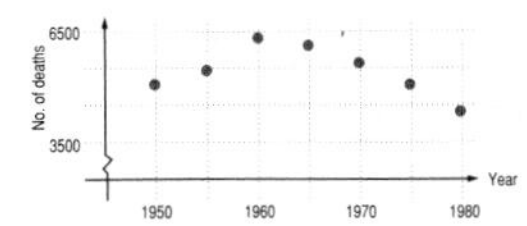

2. Find the rate of change of deaths per year from 1950 to 1955. **80 deaths per year**

3. **a.** In which five-year period did the number of deaths increase the most? **1955–1960**
b. What was the rate of change of deaths per year for that period? **190 deaths per year**

4. **a.** In which two five-year periods was the rate of change the same? **1970–1975, 1975–1980**
b. What was the average rate of change of deaths per year in those periods? **-120 deaths per year**

5. Using only the trend shown by the data for 1960–1980, predict an estimate for the number of deaths in the U.S. caused by home fires in 1985. **about 4000**

FOLLOW-UP

MORE PRACTICE
For more questions on SPUR Objectives, use *Lesson Master 8-1,* shown on page 369.

EXTENSION
If students seem to have a solid understanding of rate of change and percent, you may wish to compare rate of change with percent of change. (If the students' understanding seems tentative, the comparison may be too confusing.) When populations are small, the rate of change will generally be small but the percent of change will be large. When populations are large, the rate of change may be large, but the percent will be lower.

Have students calculate the percent of change of Manhattan Island's population each decade from 1790 on. The percent of change is calculated as

$$\frac{\text{new pop.} - \text{old pop.}}{\text{old pop.}}.$$

Year	Population (thousands)	Percent Change
1790	33	
1800	61	+85%
1810	96	+57%
1820	124	+29%
1830	203	+64%
1840	313	+54%
1850	516	+65%
1860	814	+58%
1870	942	+16%
1880	1165	+24%
1890	1441	+24%
1900	1850	+28%
1910	2332	+26%
1920	2284	-2%
1930	1867	-18%
1940	1890	+1%
1950	1960	+4%
1960	1698	-13%
1970	1539	-9%
1980	1428	-7%

19a. and b. See margin, page 369.

Review

19. a. Graph $y = 3x + 2$. **See margin.**
b. Graph $y = -3x + 2$ on the same axes. **See margin.**
c. Where do they intersect? *(Lesson 7-1)* **(0, 2)**

20. What is the total cost of p pencils at 12¢ each and e erasers at 20¢ each? *(Previous course)* **.12p + .20e dollars**

In 21 and 22, evaluate. *(Lesson 1-4)*

21. $\frac{y_2 - y_1}{x_2 - x_1}$ when $y_2 = 5$, $y_1 = 6$, $x_2 = -2$, and $x_1 = -4$ $-\frac{1}{2}$

22. $\frac{y_2 - y_1}{x_2 - x_1}$ when $y_2 = 8$, $y_1 = 4$, $x_2 = 2$, and $x_1 = \frac{1}{3}$ $\frac{12}{5}$ **or 2.4**

23. *Skill sequence* Solve for y. *(Lesson 6-6)*
a. $33 - 4y = 12$ $y = 5.25$
b. $3x - 4y = 12$ $y = \frac{3}{4}x - 3$
c. $ax - 4y = 12$ $y = \frac{a}{4}x - 3$

24. Simplify $\frac{-\frac{2}{5}}{4}$ *(Lesson 5-1)* $-\frac{1}{10}$

25. *Skill sequence* *(Lessons 2-2, 5-7, 7-8)*
a. Simplify $\frac{2}{a} - \frac{1}{a}$. $\frac{1}{a}$
b. Simplify $\frac{2}{3 + 4x} - \frac{1}{3 + 4x}$.
c. Solve $\frac{2}{3 + 4x} - \frac{1}{3 + 4x} = \frac{4}{x}$. $-\frac{4}{5}$ b) $\frac{1}{3 + 4x}$

26. Suppose a stamp collection now contains 10,000 stamps. If it grows at 1000 stamps a year, how many stamps will there be in x years? *(Lesson 6-4)* **10,000 + 1000x**

Exploration

27. a. What was the population of the town or city where you live (or nearest where you live) in 1940, 1950, 1960, 1970, and 1980?
b. In which 10-year period did the population grow the most?
a–b) Answers will depend on where students live.

370

LESSON 8-2

Constant Rates of Change

Consider the following situation. An ant is 12 feet high on a flagpole. The ant walks down the flagpole at a rate of 8 inches (which is $\frac{2}{3}$ foot) per minute.

This is a **constant decrease** situation. Each minute the height of the ant decreases by $\frac{2}{3}$ foot. You can see the constant decrease by graphing the height of the ant after 0, 1, 2, 3, and 4 minutes of walking. Below are the ordered pairs (time, height) charting the ant's progress.

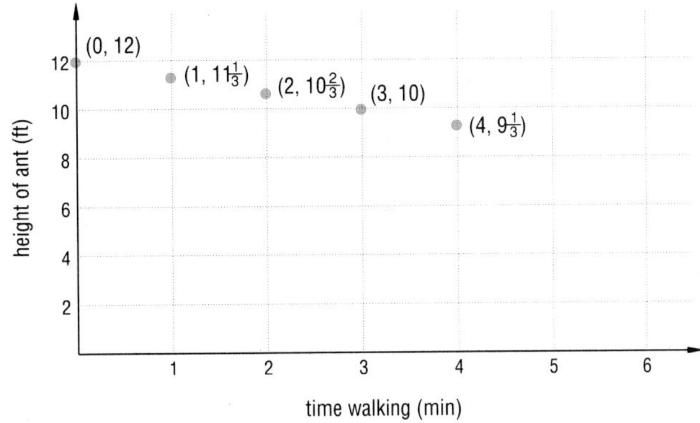

After 1 minute the ant is $11\frac{1}{3}$ feet high. After 4 minutes the ant is $9\frac{1}{3}$ feet high. Now calculate the rate of change of height between these points.

$$\frac{\text{change in height}}{\text{change in time}} = \frac{11\frac{1}{3}\text{ feet} - 9\frac{1}{3}\text{ feet}}{1\text{ minute} - 4\text{ minutes}} = -\frac{2\text{ feet}}{3\text{ minutes}}$$

The rate of change is $-\frac{2}{3}$ foot per minute, the same as the ant's rate. As long as the ant has a constant rate of walking, the rate of change in its height will always equal that constant rate.

Note that all the points on the graph of the ant's height lie on a line. In *any* situation when there is a constant rate of change between points, the points lie on a line. The constant rate of change is called the slope of the line.

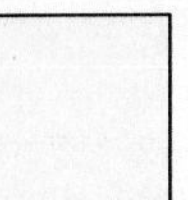

LESSON 8-2

RESOURCES
■ Lesson Master 8-2

OBJECTIVES

A Find the slope of the line through two given points.
D Recognize slope as a rate of change.
F Given an equation for a line, find two points on the line and its slope.
I Graph a straight line given its equation, or given a point on it and its slope.

TEACHING NOTES

In the introductory example the ant's speed is given in two ways:

$$-\frac{2\text{ feet}}{3\text{ minutes}} \text{ and } -\frac{2}{3}\frac{\text{foot}}{\text{minute}}.$$

Show each of these on the graph. The first is the change over three-minute intervals. The second is the change from one minute to the next.

In the previous lesson, there was no issue of which point was called (x_1, y_1) and which (x_2, y_2) because their assignment was naturally based on order of occurrence. Many of the problems in this lesson are abstract, though, and there is no natural order. Show your students why it is possible to interchange the points when calculating slope, first with any specific example (for instance with **Example 1**), then in general.

Example 2 uses the standard form of the equation of a line. Students should be reminded of why the sentences "If $x = 2$, then $y = 0$" and "if $x = 0$, then $y = 3/2$" are true. Stress that any two values for x can be chosen to find points to use in determining the slope.

Computer If you run the computer program in class, you might want to have students enter (2, 3) and (-1, 3), or (4, -1) and (4, 8). The first gives a slope of 0 (horizontal line) and the second gives an error message about division by zero (vertical line). These concepts relate to **Questions 15 and 16.**

ADDITIONAL EXAMPLES

1. Show that (1, 5), (3, 11), and (-3, -7) all lie on the same line. Find the slope of that line.

$\frac{11 - 5}{3 - 1} = 3; \frac{-7 - 11}{-3 - 3} = 3$

2. Find the slope of the line with equation $x - 4y = 8$.

$\frac{1}{4}$

Definition:

The slope of the line through (x_1, y_1) and (x_2, y_2) is

$$\frac{y_2 - y_1}{x_2 - x_1}.$$

Example 1

a. Show that (0, 3), (4, 1), and (-8, 7) lie on the same line.

b. Give the slope of that line.

Solution

a. Pick pairs of points and calculate the rate of change between them. The rate of change determined by (0, 3) and (4, 1) is

$$\frac{1 - 3}{4 - 0} = \frac{-2}{4} = -\frac{1}{2}.$$

The rate of change determined by (4, 1) and (-8, 7) is

$$\frac{7 - 1}{-8 - 4} = \frac{6}{-12} = -\frac{1}{2}.$$

The rate of change determined by (0, 3) and (-8, 7) is

$$\frac{7 - 3}{-8 - 0} = \frac{4}{-8} = -\frac{1}{2}.$$

Since the rate of change between any pair of the given points is $-\frac{1}{2}$, the points lie on the same line.

b. The slope of the line is the constant rate of change, $-\frac{1}{2}$.

Given an equation for a line, it is easy to find the slope of the line. Just find two points on it and calculate the rate of change between them.

Example 2 Find the slope of the line with equation $3x + 4y = 6$.

Solution Find two points on the line. If $x = 2$, then $y = 0$. If $x = 0$, then $y = \frac{3}{2}$. So find the rate of change between (2, 0) and $(0, \frac{3}{2})$.

$$\text{slope} = \frac{\frac{3}{2} - 0}{0 - 2} = \frac{\frac{3}{2}}{-2} = -\frac{3}{4}$$

372

Check Find another point on the line, say (10, -6) and calculate the rate of change between it and (2, 0). This gives $\frac{0 - -6}{2 - 10} = -\frac{3}{4}$. The slope is the same, so it checks. [You could have checked using (10, -6) and (0, $\frac{3}{2}$) as well.]

The program below determines the slope of a line given two points.

```
10 PRINT "DETERMINE SLOPE FROM TWO POINTS"
20 PRINT "GIVE COORDINATES OF FIRST POINT"
30 INPUT X1, Y1
40 PRINT "GIVE COORDINATES OF SECOND POINT"
50 INPUT X2, Y2
60 LET M = (Y2 – Y1)/(X2 – X1)
70 PRINT "THE SLOPE IS "; M
80 END
```

For instance, to compute the first slope in the solution to Example 1a, at line 30 you input 0, 3. At line 50 you input 4, 1.

Recall the population of Manhattan in Lesson 8-1. That population has been increasing and decreasing at different rates. Since the rate of change has not been constant, the points on the graph of the population are not on a straight line.

Questions

Covering the Reading

1. In a constant increase or decrease situation, all points lie on the same __?__. **line**

2. What is the constant rate of change between any two points on a line called? **slope**

3. An ant starts 5 feet from the base of a flagpole and climbs $\frac{1}{3}$ foot up the pole each minute. **See margin.**
   a. Graph the ant's progress using ordered pairs (time, height).
   b. Find the rate of change between any two points on the graph. **$\frac{1}{3}$ foot per minute**

4. a. Calculate the slope determined by (1, 2) and (6, 11). **$\frac{9}{5}$**
   b. Calculate the slope determined by (6, 11) and (-10, -16). **$\frac{27}{16}$**
   c. Do the points (1, 2), (6, 11), and (-10, -16) lie on the same line? **No**

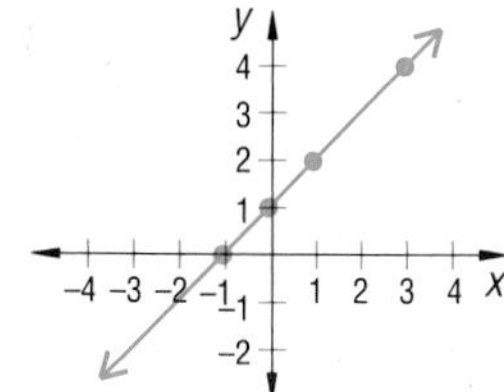

5. Using two different sets of points, show that the slope of the line at the left is 1. **See margin.**

6. Find the slope of the line with equation $5x - 2y = 10$. **$\frac{5}{2}$ or 2.5**

NOTES ON QUESTIONS
Making Connections for Questions 9-11: These questions help prepare students for the characterization of slope given in the next lesson.

Error Analysis for Questions 12-14 and 17: Here, students are led to think about positive, negative, and zero slopes without resorting to calculations. If students have difficulty with these, ask them to refer to Lesson 8-1 and to decide whether each case reflects a constant increase (positive slope), constant decrease (negative slope), or "no change" (zero slope) situation.

ADDITIONAL ANSWERS
3a.

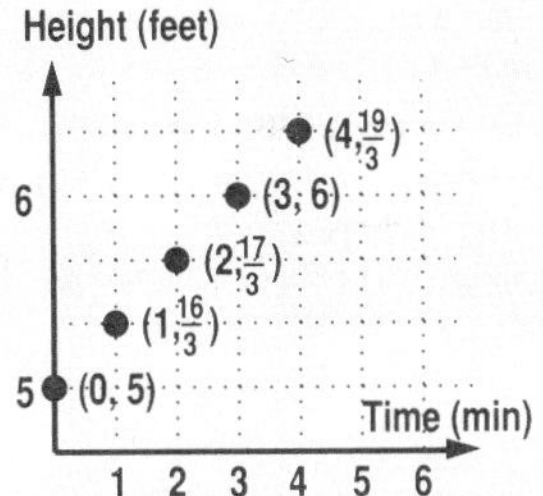

5. sample: using (1, 2) and (-1, 0), $\frac{0 - 2}{-1 - 1} = 1$

NOTES ON QUESTIONS

Question 18: This is an application in which a quantity is a function of height rather than time. The slope compares change in price divided by change in the level of the floor, which clarifies the idea.

Making Connections for Question 19d: The distinction between discrete and continuous situations is reviewed. You might have students critique the Manhattan Island population graph from this perspective.

Question 28: This question affords an opportunity to combine individual statistics and to look at average change in height for the whole class.

19d. The cost of stamps does not gradually rise over each 5-year period. For instance the cost was never 4.3 cents.

20.

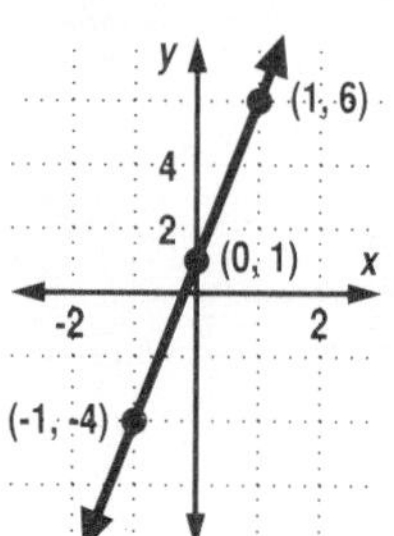

21.

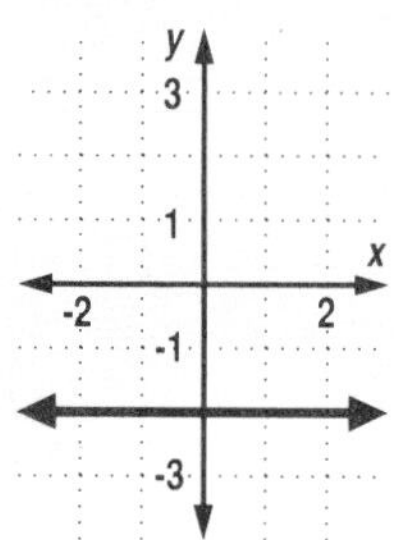

7. An equation for the height y of the ant in this lesson after x minutes is $y = -\frac{2}{3}x + 12$. **sample: (6, 8), (9, 6)**
 a. Find two points on this line not graphed in this lesson.
 b. Find the rate of change between those points. $-\frac{2}{3}$

8. Using the computer program from this lesson, what would you input at lines 30 and 50 to determine the slope of the line in Question 4a?
1, 2; 6, 11

Applying the Mathematics

In 9–11, the points (2, 5) and (3, y) are on the same line. Find y when the slope of the line is:

9. 3 **8** **10.** -2 **3** **11.** $\frac{1}{5}$ **$5\frac{1}{5}$ or 5.2**

In 12–14, use the figure at the right.

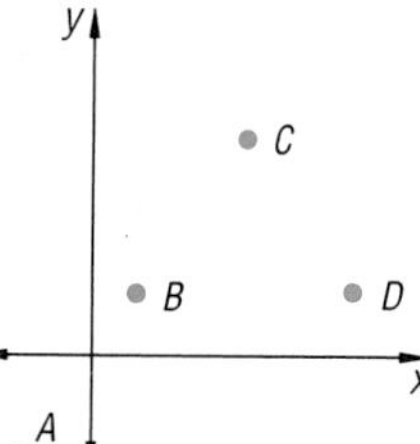

12. The slope determined by A and B seems to equal the slope determined by B and what other point? **C**

13. The slope determined by __?__ and __?__ is negative. **C; D**

14. The slope determined by __?__ and __?__ is zero. **B; D**

15. a. Find the slope of the horizontal line $y = 2$ below left. **0**
 b. Find the slope of the horizontal line $y = -3$ below left. **0**
 c. From parts a and b, what do you think can be said about the slope of all horizontal lines? **The slope is 0.**

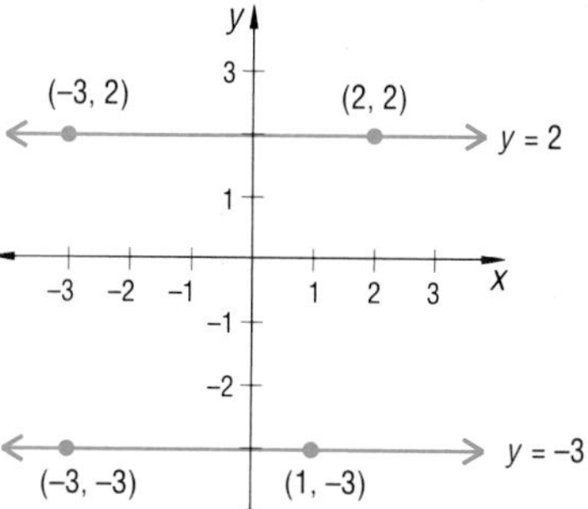

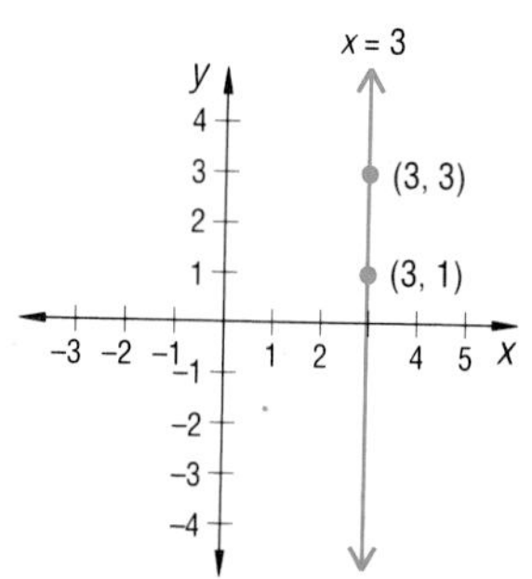

16. Consider the vertical line $x = 3$ graphed above right.
 a. What happens when you try to find its slope? **You divide by zero.**
 b. From your answer to part a, do you think that vertical lines have slope? **No**

17. Consider lines p, q, and r graphed at the right.
 a. Which line has slope $\frac{4}{3}$? ***r***
 b. Which line has slope $-\frac{4}{3}$? ***q***
 c. Which line has slope zero? ***p***

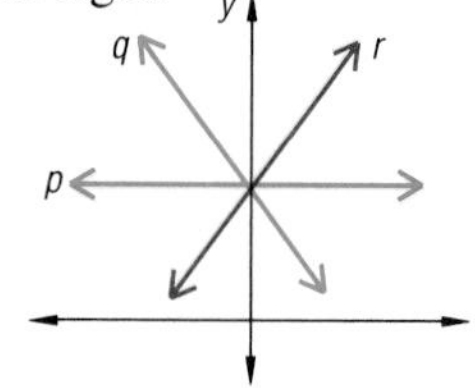

18. Consider the following set of points. High-rise apartment monthly rents: (13th floor, \$325), (17th floor, \$365), (19th floor, \$385).
 a. Calculate the slope of the line through these points. **10**
 b. What does the slope represent in this situation?
 a rise in rent of \$10 per floor

Review

19. Below is a graph showing the cost (in cents) of sending a one-ounce first-class letter. The graph is shown in 5-year intervals beginning in 1960. *(Lesson 8-1)*

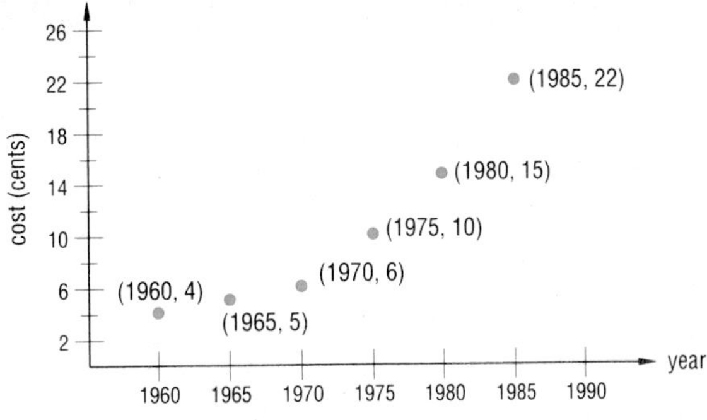

 a. During which 5-year period did the cost of postage increase the fastest? **1980–85**
 b. During which two 5-year periods was the increase in postage the same? **1960–65 and 1965–70**
 c. Calculate the average increase per year from 1965 to 1975. **.5 cent per year**
 d. Give a reason why the points on the graph are not connected.
 See margin.

In 20–22, graph the line. *(Lessons 7-1, 7-2)* **See margin.**

20. $y = 5x + 1$ 21. $y = -2$ 22. $x = -2$

In 23 and 24, write an expression for the amount of money the person has after x weeks. *(Lesson 6-4)*

23. Eddie is given \$100 and spends \$4 a week. **100 – 4x**

24. Gretchen owes \$350 on a stereo and is paying it off at \$5 a week.
 -350 + 5x

25. *Skill sequence* Solve. *(Lessons 5-7, 6-6, 7-4)*
 a. $\frac{w}{3} = \frac{5}{9}$ **$\frac{5}{3}$** b. $\frac{w+2}{3} = \frac{5}{9}$ **$-\frac{1}{3}$** c. $\frac{w}{3} = \frac{5}{w}$ **$\sqrt{15}, -\sqrt{15}$**

x + 1
9
3x
18

26. The two figures at the left are similar. Corresponding sides are parallel. Find the value of x. *(Lessons 5-7, 5-8)* **2**

27. Simplify. *(Lesson 7-6)*
 a. $\sqrt{3600}$ **60** b. $\sqrt{25b^2}$ **5b (if b ≥ 0)** c. $\sqrt{18}$ **$3\sqrt{2}$**

Exploration

28. Find a record of your height at some time over a year ago. Compare it with your height now. How fast has your height been changing from then until now? **Answers will vary.**

FOLLOW-UP

MORE PRACTICE

For more questions on SPUR Objectives, use *Lesson Master 8-2,* shown below.

EXTENSION

Refer to **Question 28.** You might ask students to think of other rates of change for themselves that might be calculated (change in weight over time; change in allowance over time; change in reading speed over time; and so on).

22.

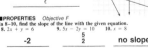

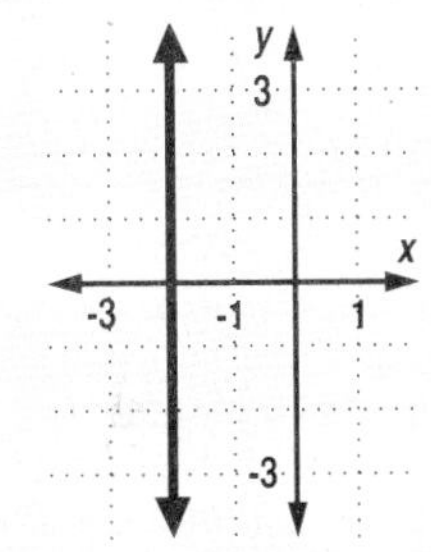

NAME

LESSON MASTER 8-2
QUESTIONS ON SPUR OBJECTIVES

■SKILLS Objective A (See pages 418–421 for objectives.)
In 1–4, find the slope of the line through the given points.
1. (2, -4), (5, -1) **1** 2. (12, 3), (2, 7) **$-\frac{2}{5}$**
3. (-5.2, 3.7), (7.2, 4.1) **$\frac{1}{31}$** 4. (4, k), (-2, k) **0**
5. Determine whether the points (3, -1), (5, 2), (9, 8) lie on the same line. If they do, give the slope of that line. **yes, $\frac{3}{2}$**

■PROPERTIES Objective D
6. If the slope of a line is __?__, then as x increases, y decreases. **negative**
7. Consider lines ℓ, m, and n graphed at right.
 a. Which line has slope -2? **n**
 b. Which line has slope $-\frac{1}{3}$? **m**
 c. Which line has slope 0? **ℓ**

■PROPERTIES Objective F
In 8–10, find the slope of the line with the given equation.
8. $2x + y = 6$ **-2** 9. $5x - 2y = 10$ **$\frac{5}{2}$** 10. $x = 8$ **no slope**

■REPRESENTATIONS Objective I
11. Graph the line which passes through (0, 1) and has a slope of -2.

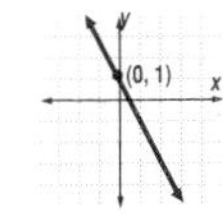

 65

LESSON 8-3

RESOURCES
- Lesson Master 8-3
- Visual for Teaching Aid 40: Graphs for **Questions 8, 9, and 20-22.**

OBJECTIVES

D Recognize slope as a rate of change.
I Graph a straight line given a point on it and its slope.

TEACHING NOTES

Alternate Approach
You may want to suggest that students plot more than two points before drawing the line through them. This gives more practice with the idea of slope and makes the graph more accurate.

Students often draw a line only long enough to connect the two points they plot. You can compare this to taking a snapshot of people and showing only their feet.

ADDITIONAL EXAMPLES
1. Graph the line with slope 3 which contains (-4, 0).

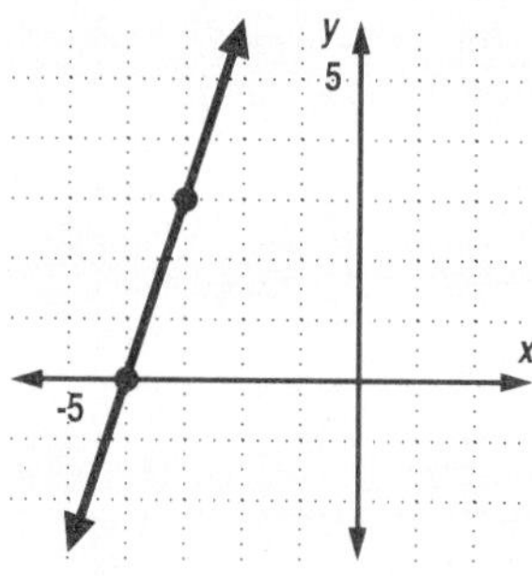

Properties of Slope

A General Motors test ramp for bulldozers goes down 0.6 foot for each foot it goes across, as illustrated at right.

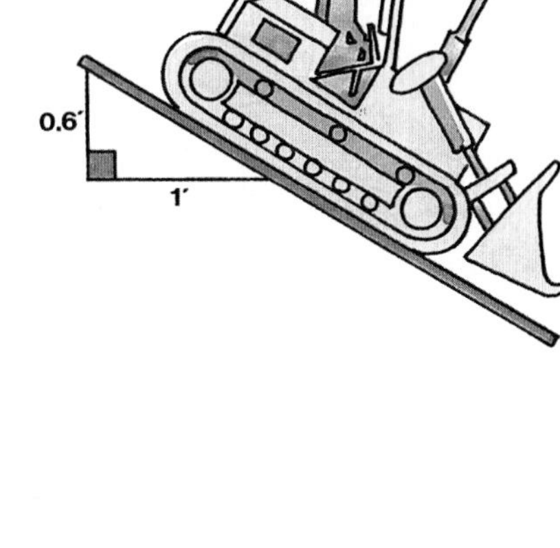

The part of the ramp with the triangle is enlarged and diagramed in the graph below.

There are two points shown on the graph. The rate of change between these points is the slope of the line.

$$\text{slope} = \frac{\text{change in height}}{\text{change in length}} = \frac{0 - 0.6}{1 - 0} = -0.6$$

This verifies an important property of slopes of lines.

> The slope of a line is the amount of change in the height of the line as you go 1 unit to the right.

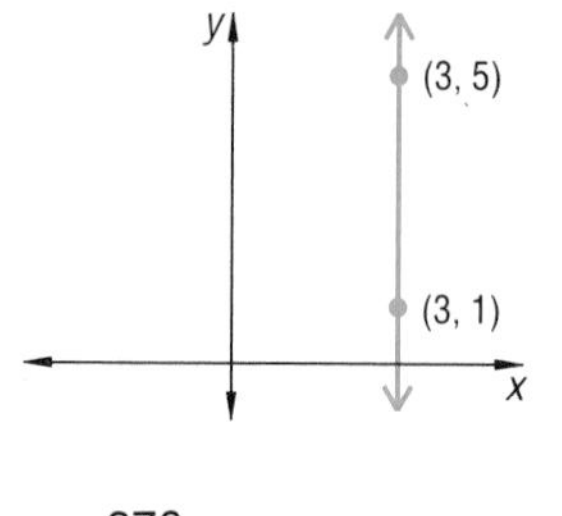

There is one kind of line for which this property of slopes does not apply. You cannot go to the right on a vertical line. Furthermore, if you try to calculate the slope, the denominator will be zero. At left, you would be calculating $\frac{5 - 1}{3 - 3}$. Thus the slope of a vertical line is not defined.

Example 1 Graph the line which passes through (3, -1) and has a slope of -2.

Solution 1 Plot point (3, -1). Since the line has slope -2, move from (3, -1) one unit to the right and two units down. Plot that point and draw the line.

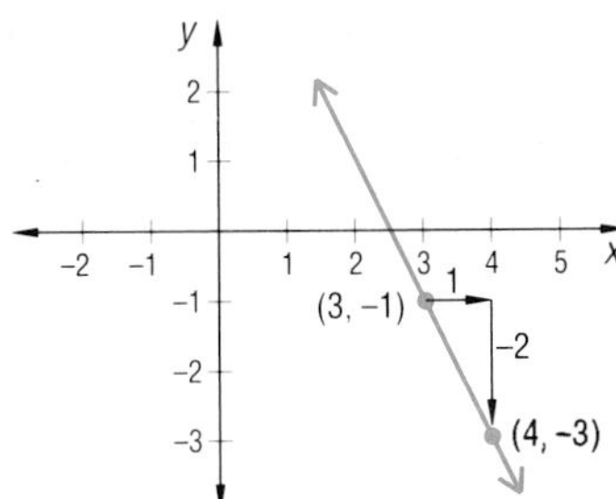

To graph lines having slopes that are given as fractions, it helps to make the unit intervals on the coordinate axes bigger.

Example 2 Graph the line through (-2, 1) with slope $\frac{1}{4}$.

Solution 1 Draw the axes with the unit interval split into fourths. Plot (-2, 1), then move right 1 unit and up $\frac{1}{4}$ unit. Plot the point $(-1, 1\frac{1}{4})$ and draw the line.

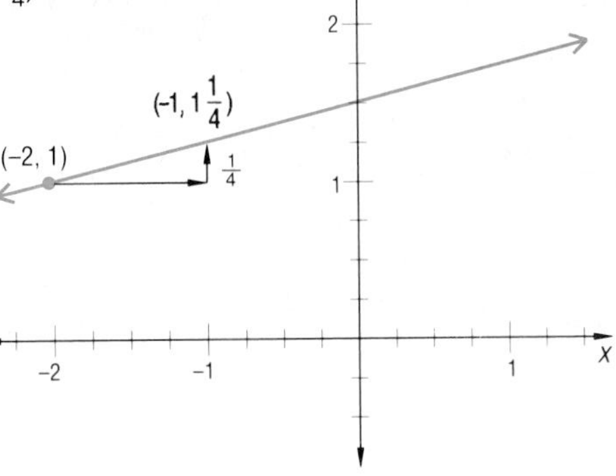

Solution 2 Plot (-2, 1) as in Solution 1. However, instead of going across 1 and up $\frac{1}{4}$, go across $4 \cdot 1$ and up $4 \cdot \frac{1}{4}$. That is, go across 4 and up 1 to the point (2, 2).

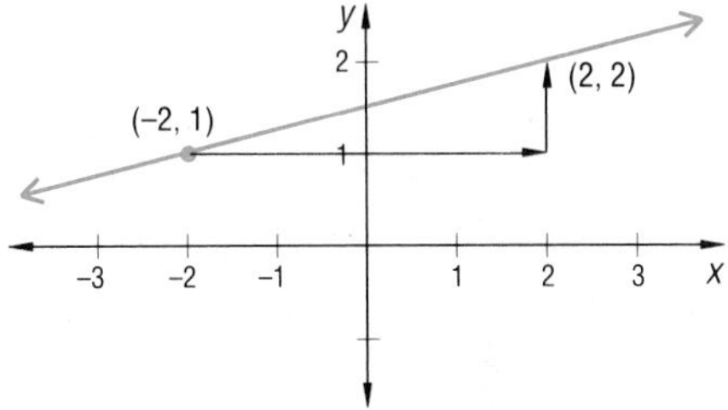

2. A line passes through the point (3, -5) and has slope $-\frac{1}{3}$. Graph the line.

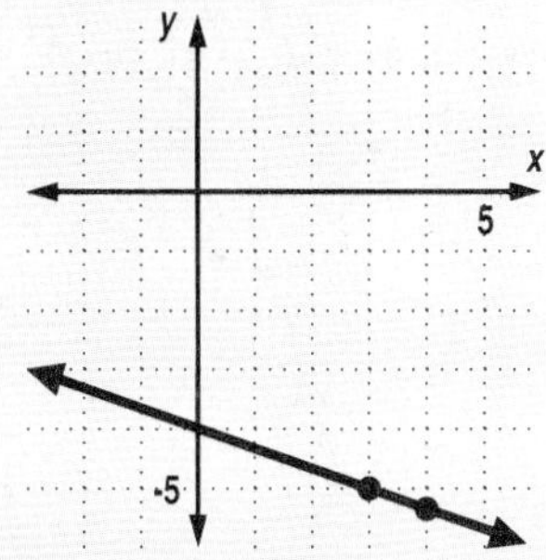

3. Ms. Wagner is draining her children's wading pool. The pool contained 10 inches of water, and it is draining at a rate of $\frac{1}{2}$ inch per minute. Graph the relationship between time and water height.

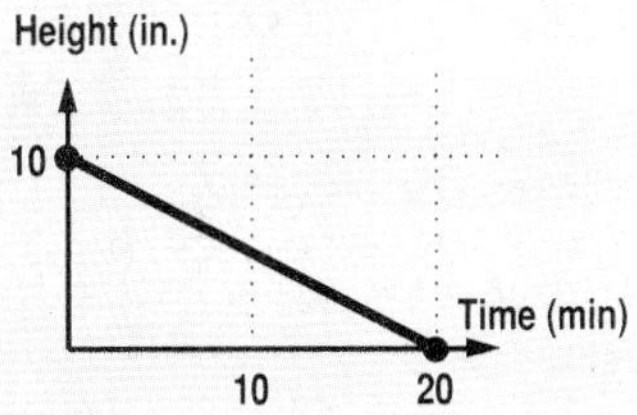

NOTES ON QUESTIONS

Questions 14-16: These questions are application parallels of **Questions 11-13.** That is, a point and the slope are given in each of these questions and another point must be found. In graphing these lines, students should be aware that an important decision is the size of the interval between tick marks on the axes.

Making Connections for Question 19: Students should use the method from the previous lesson. The next lesson discusses $y = mx + b$.

ADDITIONAL ANSWERS
3. The denominator in $\frac{y_2 - y_1}{x_2 - x_1}$ is 0. You cannot divide by 0.

4.

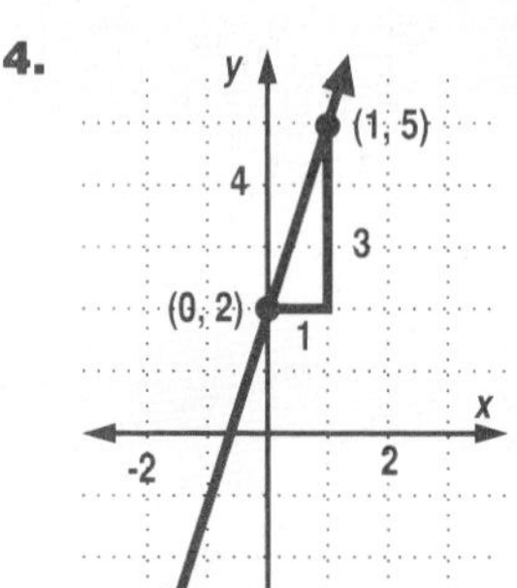

5.

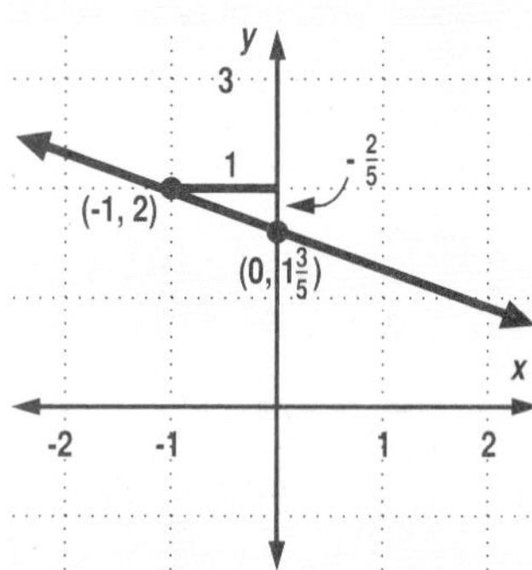

6.

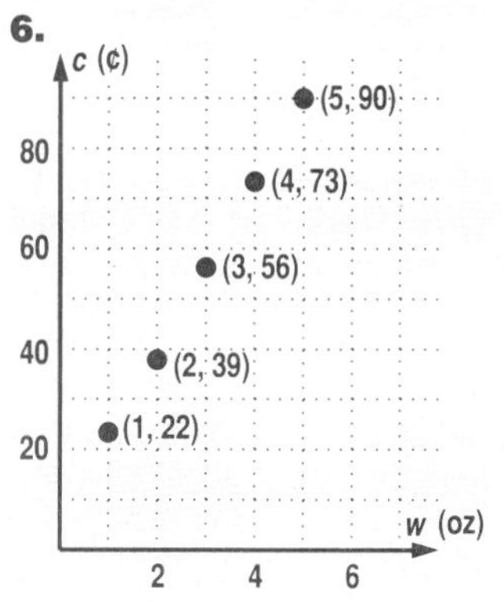

10.

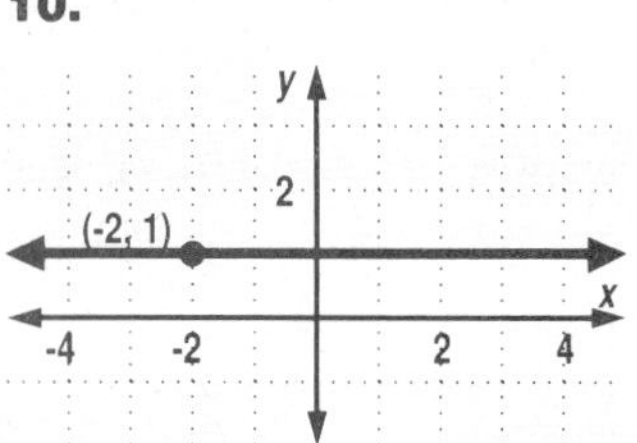

The idea in Examples 1 and 2 helps in drawing graphs of repeated addition situations.

Example 3 In 1988, postage rates for first-class mail were raised to \$.25 for the first ounce and \$.20 for each additional ounce. Graph the relation between weight and cost for whole number weights.

Solution The starting point is (1, .25). Because the rate goes up \$.20 for each ounce, the slope is \$.20/oz. The points are on a line because the situation is a constant increase situation.

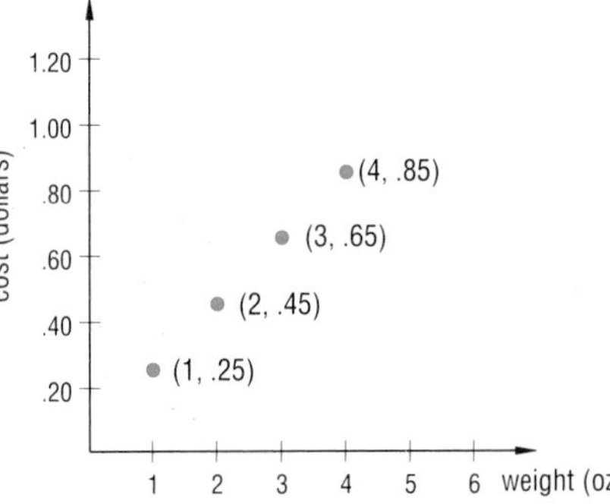

An equation for the cost C to mail a first-class letter weighing w whole ounces is $C = .25 + .20(w - 1)$. This is an equation for the line that contains the points graphed in Example 3. Notice that the given numbers .25 and .20 both appear in this equation. In the next lesson, you will learn how the slope can easily be seen from the equation.

Questions

Covering the Reading

1. A test track for bulldozers goes down 0.5 unit for each unit across. What is its slope? **-0.5**

2. Slope is the amount of change in the _?_ of a graph as you go _?_ unit to the right. **height, 1**

3. The slope of a vertical line is not defined. Why not? **See margin.**

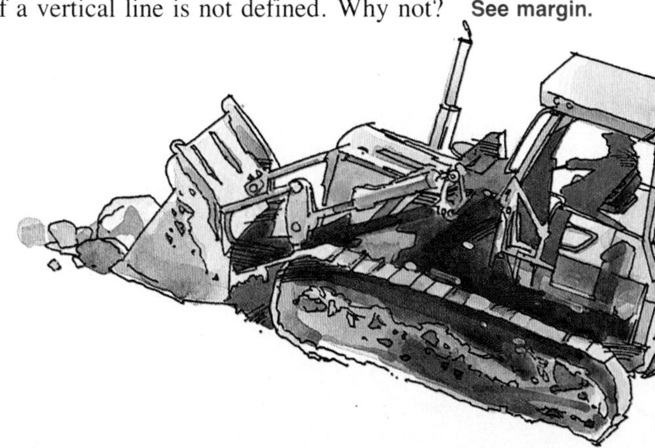

4. Graph the line which passes through (0, 2) and has slope 3. **See margin.**

5. Graph the line which passes through (-1, 2) and has slope $-\frac{2}{5}$. **See margin.**

6. In 1987, postal rates were 22¢ for the first ounce and 17¢ for each additional ounce. Graph the relation between weight and cost for whole number weights. **See margin.**

7. Using 1988 postal rates, what would it cost to mail a letter weighing 9 oz? **c = .25 + .20(9 − 1); c = 1.85**

In 8 and 9, give the slope of the line. **8) -3 9) 1**

8.

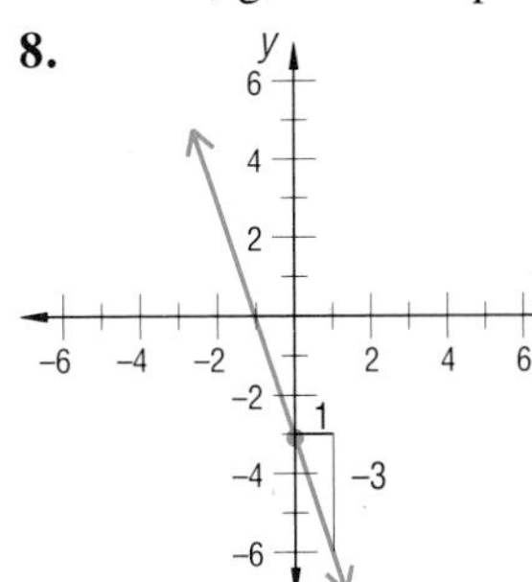

9.

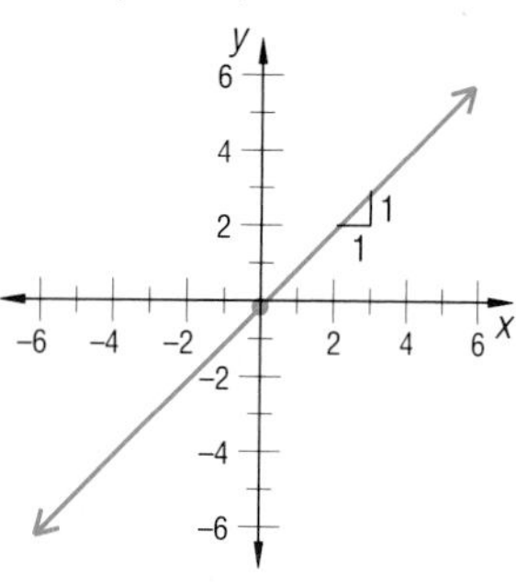

Applying the Mathematics

10. Graph the line through (-2, 1) with a slope of 0. **See margin.**

In 11–13, name one other point on the line.

11. through (-5, 2) with a slope of 7 **sample: (-4, 9)**

12. through (6, -11) with a slope of -8 **sample: (7, -19)**

13. through (0, 0) with a slope of $\frac{5}{4}$ **sample: (1, $\frac{5}{4}$) or (4, 5)**

14. Mae spends $65 a week on food. After 3 weeks she has $415 left in her food budget. Draw a graph to represent Mae's food budget as weeks go by. **See margin.**

15. Kareem collects magazines. He receives 3 magazines a week. This year, after 10 weeks he has 66 magazines in his collection. Draw a graph to represent the growth of Kareem's collection over the weeks. **See margin.**

Review

16. A rental truck costs $39 for a day plus $.25 a mile. After x miles, the total cost will be y dollars.
   a. Write an equation relating x and y. *(Lesson 6-4)* **y = .25x + 39**
   b. Graph the line. *(Lesson 7-1)* **See margin.**
   c. Find the rate of change between any two points on the graph. *(Lesson 8-2)* **.25**

In 17 and 18, calculate the slope determined by the two points. *(Lesson 8-2)*

17. (5, 3) and (8, -2) **$-\frac{5}{3}$**

18. (-6, -9) and (-13, 5) **-2**

19. Find the slope of the line $3x - y = 15$. *(Lesson 8-2)* **3**

14.

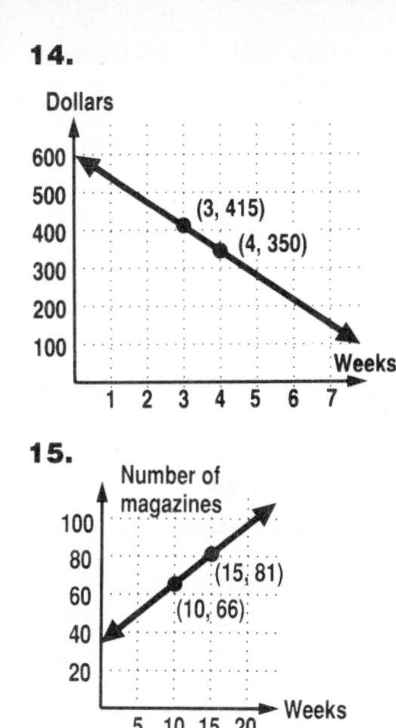

16b.

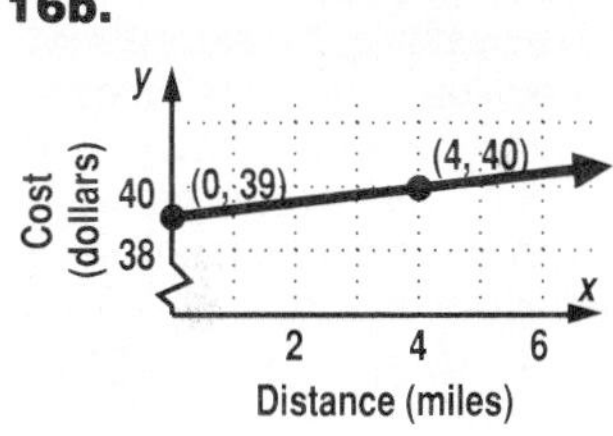

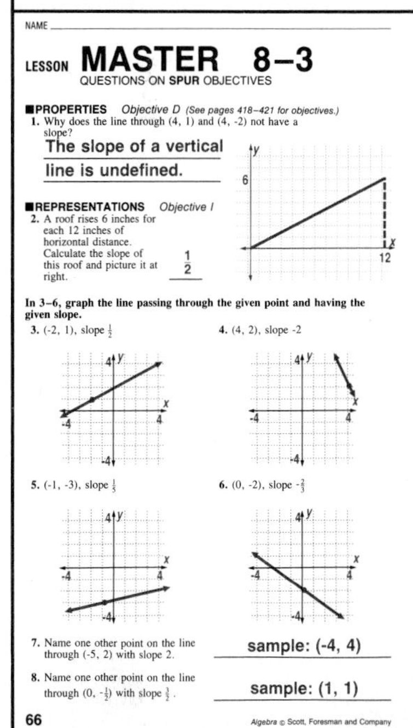

NAME

LESSON **MASTER 8–3**
QUESTIONS ON **SPUR** OBJECTIVES

■PROPERTIES *Objective D (See pages 418–421 for objectives.)*

1. Why does the line through (4, 1) and (4, -2) not have a slope? **The slope of a vertical line is undefined.**

■REPRESENTATIONS *Objective I*

2. A roof rises 6 inches for each 12 inches of horizontal distance. Calculate the slope of this roof and picture it at right. **$\frac{1}{2}$**

In 3–6, graph the line passing through the given point and having the given slope.

3. (-2, 1), slope $\frac{1}{2}$

4. (4, 2), slope -2

5. (-1, -3), slope $\frac{1}{5}$

6. (0, -2), slope $-\frac{2}{3}$

7. Name one other point on the line through (-5, 2) with slope 2. **sample: (-4, 4)**

8. Name one other point on the line through (0, $-\frac{1}{2}$) with slope $\frac{3}{2}$. **sample: (1, 1)**

66

NOTES ON QUESTIONS
Question 29: This puzzle relates to the subject matter of this lesson because Enrique is climbing at a rate of (3 feet − 2 feet)/day, or 1 foot/day. However, that rate changes to 3 feet/day on the last day, which is why the question seems to be a trick.

FOLLOW-UP

MORE PRACTICE
For more questions on SPUR Objectives, use *Lesson Master 8-3,* shown on page 379.

EVALUATION
Alternative Assessment
To evaluate students' understanding of slope, have them describe real situations in which the slope is positive, negative, or zero.

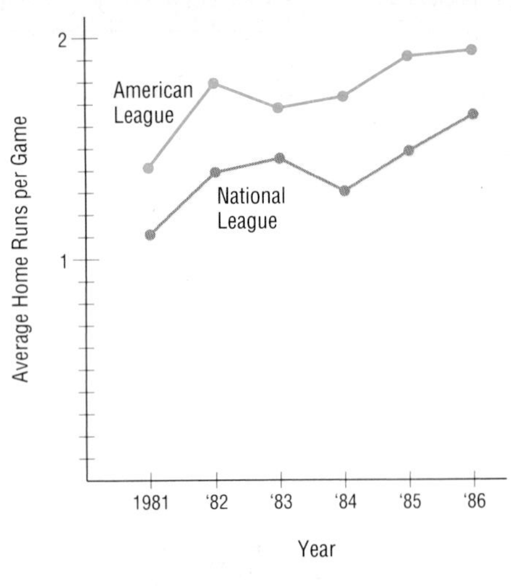

Average Home Runs per Game

Year	American League	National League
1981	1.42	1.12
1982	1.83	1.34
1983	1.68	1.44
1984	1.75	1.32
1985	1.92	1.47
1986	1.95	1.64

In 20–22, refer to the graph above. *(Lesson 8-1)*

20. Between what two consecutive years was there the biggest increase in average home runs per game for the
a. American League; **1981–1982** **b.** National League? **1981–1982**

21. Between what two consecutive years was there the biggest decrease in average home runs per game for the
a. American League; **1982–1983** **b.** National League? **1983–1984**

22. What is the rate of change from 1981 to 1986 in average home runs per game for the
a. American League; **about .11** **b.** National League? **about .10**

23. If $y = mx + b$ and $y = -4$, $m = 3$, and $x = 2$, find b. *(Lessons 1-5, 2-6)* **-10**

24. If the triangle at left has perimeter 38, what is z? *(Lesson 6-6)* $\frac{47}{8}$ **or 5.875**

25. Solve and check. $(y + 1)^2 = 64$ *(Lesson 7-8)* **7 or -9**

26. If $4a = 15$, find $12a - 5$. *(Lesson 7-8)* **40**

27. *Skill sequence* *(Lessons 2-2, 5-7, 6-9, 7-8)*
a. Simplify $(T - 3) - (5 - T)$. **b.** Simplify $\frac{T-3}{T} - \frac{5-T}{T}$.
c. Solve $\frac{T-3}{T} - \frac{5-T}{T} = \frac{4}{3}$. **a) $2T - 8$; b) $\frac{2T-8}{T}$; c) 12**

28. Calculate in your head. *(Lesson 5-4)*
a. 15% of \$8.00 **\$1.20** **b.** 200% of x dollars **2x dollars**

Exploration

29. Here is a famous puzzler. Beware of the trick. Enrique Escargot, a snail, is 30 feet deep in a well. Every day he climbs 3 feet up the walls of the well. At night the walls are damper and he slips down 2 feet. How many days will it take him to climb out of the well? **28 days**

LESSON

Slope-Intercept Equations for Lines

Quincy has \$225 saved for a used car and saves an additional \$8 a week. After 3 weeks, Quincy will have $225 + 3 \cdot 8$ dollars, or \$249. After x weeks, Quincy will have y dollars, where $y = 225 + 8x$.

The line $y = 225 + 8x$ is graphed at right. There are two key numbers in the equation for this line. The number 8 is the slope of the line. The number 225 indicates where the line crosses the y-axis. That number is called the ***y*-intercept** of the line.

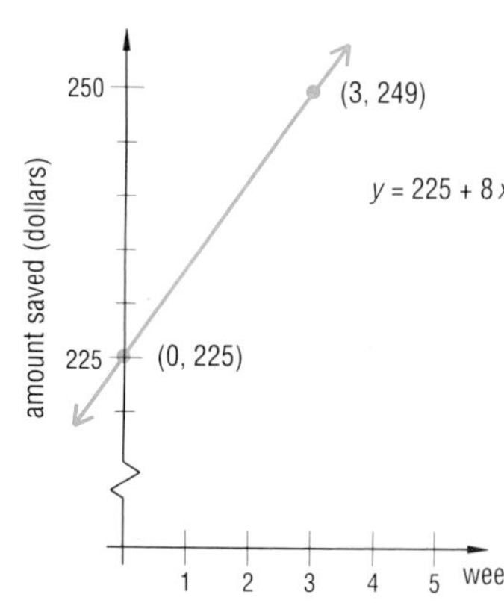

Definition:

When a graph intersects the y-axis at the point $(0, b)$, the number b is a y-intercept for the graph.

Quincy's situation, the graph of the line, and the equation $y = 225 + 8x$ are completely determined by the slope and y-intercept. When the equation is rewritten in the form $y = 8x + 225$, it is said to be in **slope-intercept form.**

Slope-Intercept Property:

The line with equation $y = mx + b$ has slope m and y-intercept b.

LESSON 8-4

RESOURCES

- Lesson Master 8-4
- Quiz on Lessons 8-1 Through 8-4
- Computer Master 15

OBJECTIVES

B Find an equation for a line given its slope and any point on it.
E Rewrite an equation for a line in slope-intercept form.
F Given an equation for a line, find its slope and y-intercept.
H Use equations for lines to describe real situations.
I Graph a straight line given its equation, or given a point on it and its slope.

TEACHING NOTES

Reading The zig-zag in the vertical axis in the graph for Quincy's auto purchase savings indicates that there is a gap. Leaving out a section of the graph makes it possible to fit the graph on the page. This practice is not used consistently in real-life graphs, so we do not use it consistently in this book. Yet, it is important that students know how to interpret the symbol.

Note that in **Example 3,** rather than dividing both sides by 4, it is just as easy to multiply both sides by 1/4. In converting equations of the form $by = ax + c$ to slope-intercept form, multiplication by the reciprocal of b usually results in fewer errors. If your students divide both sides by b, they must, of course, remember to divide *both* terms of $ax + c$ by b.

Example 1 Give the slope and y-intercept of $y = \frac{1}{2}x + 4$.

Solution The equation is already in slope-intercept form. Compare $y = \frac{1}{2}x + 4$ to $y = mx + b$. $m = \frac{1}{2}$ and $b = 4$. So the slope is $\frac{1}{2}$ and the y-intercept is 4.

Check A y-intercept of 4 means the line must contain (0, 4). Does (0, 4) satisfy $y = \frac{1}{2}x + 4$? Yes, because $4 = \frac{1}{2} \cdot 0 + 4$.

The advantage of slope-intercept form is that it tells you so much about the line. So it is often useful to convert other equations for lines into slope-intercept form.

Example 2 Give the slope and y-intercept of $y = -8 - 3x$.

Solution Rewrite $y = -8 - 3x$ in the form $y = mx + b$ using the Commutative Property of Addition and the definition of subtraction.

$$y = -3x + -8$$

The slope is -3 and the y-intercept is -8.

Example 3 Write the equation $3x + 4y = 9$ in slope-intercept form. Give the slope and y-intercept.

Solution Solve the given equation $3x + 4y = 9$ for y.

$$4y = -3x + 9$$
$$\frac{1}{4} \cdot 4y = \frac{1}{4}(-3x + 9)$$
$$y = -\frac{3}{4}x + \frac{9}{4}$$

The slope is $-\frac{3}{4}$. The y-intercept is $\frac{9}{4}$ or $2\frac{1}{4}$.

Equations for all nonvertical lines can be written in slope-intercept form.

Example 4 Write an equation for the line with slope 5 and y-intercept -1 and graph the line.

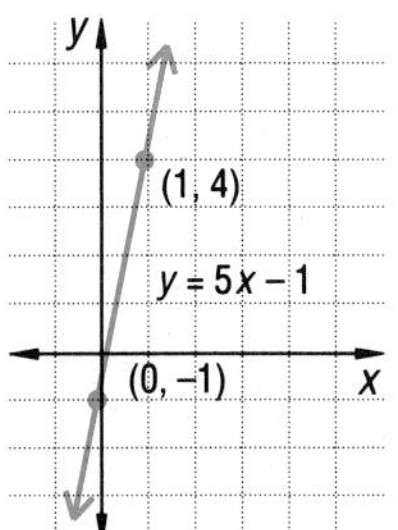

Solution Substitute 5 for m and -1 for b in $y = mx + b$.
So $y = 5x + -1$ or $y = 5x - 1$ is an equation for the line.
Since the intercept is -1, the graph contains (0, -1). Since the slope is 5, the graph goes up 5 units for each unit it goes to the right.

Check Find two points on $y = 5x - 1$. We find (0, -1) and (1, 4). The slope determined by the points is 5.

Every constant increase or constant decrease situation can be described by an equation whose graph is a line. The y-intercept of that line can be interpreted as the starting amount. The slope of that line is the amount of increase or decrease per unit.

Example 5 Pam received \$100 for graduation and spends \$4 of it a week.
a. Find an equation for the amount y she has after x weeks.
b. What is the slope and y-intercept of the graph?

Solution
a. The equation is found by methods you have learned in previous chapters.

$$y = 100 - 4x$$

b. Rewrite in slope-intercept form.

$$y = -4x + 100.$$

The slope is -4 and the y-intercept is 100.

Check A graph of $y = -4x + 100$ is shown at the left. In 25 weeks, she will have \$0, which agrees with the given information.

Recall that every vertical line has an equation of the form $x = h$ where h is a fixed number. Equations of this form clearly cannot be solved for y. Thus equations of vertical lines cannot be written in slope-intercept form. This confirms that the slope of vertical lines cannot be defined.

ADDITIONAL EXAMPLES
In 1 and 2, give **a.** the slope and **b.** the y-intercept.

1. $y = 16 + 4x$
a. 4; b. 16

2. $5x + 3y = 10$
a. $-\frac{5}{3}$; **b.** $\frac{10}{3}$

3. Write an equation of the line with y-intercept = 8 and slope = -6.
$y = -6x + 8$

4. The oven was at room temperature (70°). Just after it was turned on, the temperature rose 40° per minute.

a. Write an equation for the temperature y after x minutes.
$y = 70 + 40x$

b. Find the slope and y-intercept of the graph.
slope, 40; y-intercept, 70

5. Mr. Campbell's students asked him how much he weighs. He wouldn't say, but he gave them a hint. He picked up a bucket and told them to pour soup cans full of water into the bucket. When there were 6 canfuls of water in the bucket, Mr. Campbell (with bucket) stepped on the scale. He weighed 195 lb. With 33 canfuls of water he weighed 213 lb.

a. How much does Mr. Campbell weigh holding an empty bucket?
191 lb

b. How much does the water in one soup can weigh?
$\frac{2}{3}$ **lb**

NOTES ON QUESTIONS
Questions 18 and 19: Students are asked to notice how changes in the values of *m* and *b* affect the graphs of equations. Begin by asking what is the same in the graphs and equations for each problem. (In **Question 18** the lines are parallel. The equations have the same slope. In **Question 19** the lines all intersect the *y*-axis at (0, -2). The equations have the same *y*-intercept.)

Questions

Covering the Reading

1. What form of an equation of a line is $y = mx + b$? **slope-intercept**

2. Finish the check of Example 1. **sample: use (0, 4) and (2, 5); $m = \frac{4-5}{0-2} = \frac{1}{2}$**

In 3 and 4, give **a.** the slope and **b.** the *y*-intercept.

3. $y = 4x + 2$ **a) 4; b) 2**
4. $y = -\frac{1}{3}x + 6$ **a) $-\frac{1}{3}$; b) 6**

In 5–7, consider these three graphs. **a.** Match the situation with its graph. **b.** Give the slope of the line. **c.** Give the *y*-intercept.

(i)

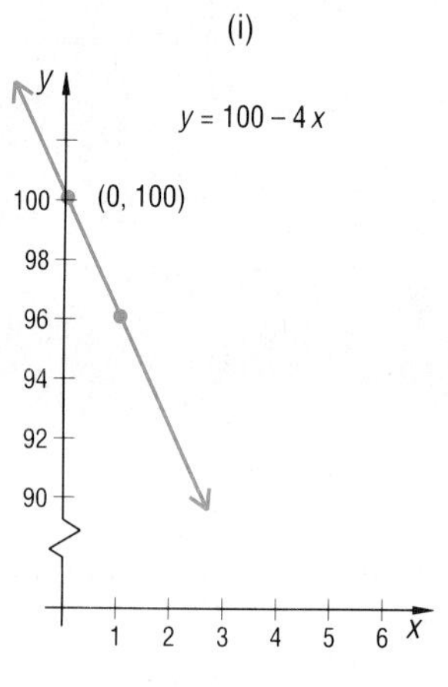

(ii)

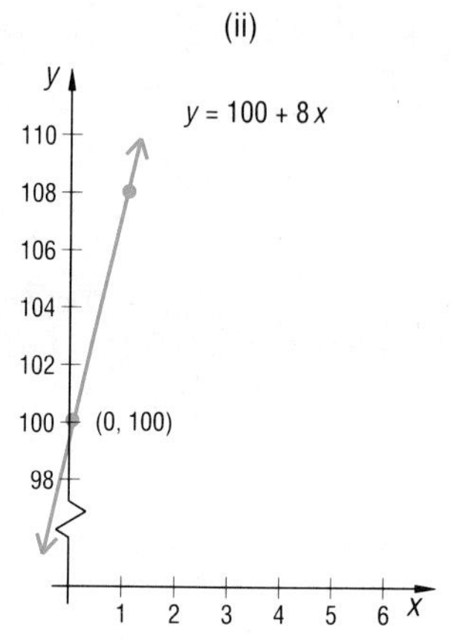

(iii)

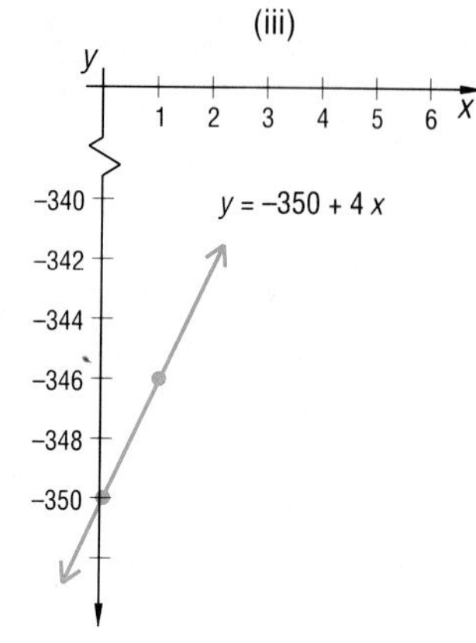

5. Quincy began with \$100 and earns \$8 a week. **a) ii; b) 8; c) 100**

6. Pam was given \$100 for graduation and spends \$4 a week. **a) i; b) -4; c) 100**

7. The Carter family owes \$350 on a refrigerator and is paying it off at \$4 a week. **a) iii; b) 4; c) -350**

8. When a constant increase situation is graphed, the *y*-intercept can be interpreted as the __?__. **starting point**

9. Equations of __?__ lines cannot be written in slope-intercept form. **vertical**

In 10 and 11, write an equation of the line with the given characteristics.

10. slope -3, *y*-intercept 5 **$y = -3x + 5$**
11. slope $\frac{2}{3}$, *y*-intercept -1 **$y = \frac{2}{3}x + -1$ or $y = \frac{2}{3}x - 1$**

In 12 and 13, **a.** write in slope-intercept form; **b.** give the slope.

12. $y = 7.3 - 1.2x$ **a) $y = -1.2x + 7.3$; b) -1.2**
13. $x + 6y = 7$ **a) $y = -\frac{1}{6}x + \frac{7}{6}$; b) $-\frac{1}{6}$**

In 14 and 15, give **a.** the slope and **b.** the *y*-intercept.

14. $3x + 2y = 10$ **a) $-\frac{3}{2}$ or -1.5; b) 5**
15. $y = x$ **a) 1; b) 0**

16. Write an equation of a horizontal line with *y*-intercept -4. **$y = -4$**

17. Graph $y = -\frac{1}{2}x + 5$ by using the slope and *y*-intercept. **See margin.**

Applying the Mathematics

18. Match each line n, p, q, and r with its equation below.

a. $y = x$ **q**
b. $y = x + 1$ **p**
c. $y = x + 3$ **n**
d. $y = x - 3$ **r**

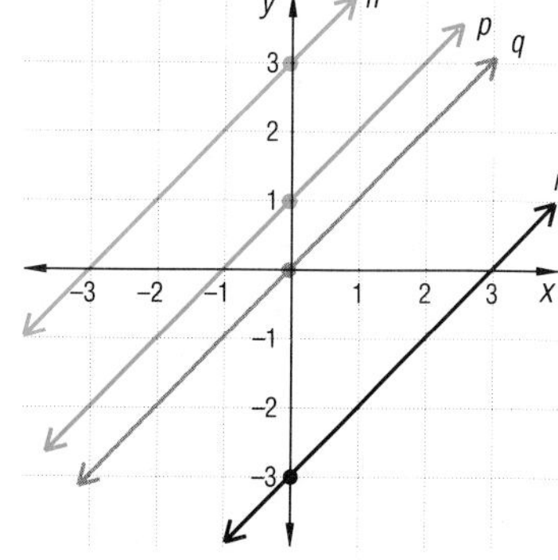

19. Match each line s, t, u, and v with its equation below.

a. $y = 2x - 2$ **u**
b. $y = \frac{2}{3}x - 2$ **v**
c. $y = -2x - 2$ **t**
d. $y = -\frac{2}{3}x - 2$ **s**

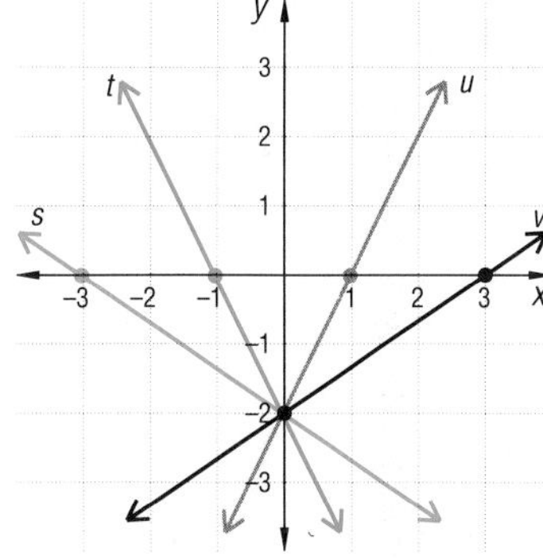

In 20 and 21, each situation naturally leads to an equation of the form $y = mx + b$. **a.** Give the equation. **b.** Graph the equation.

20. Begin with \$8.00. Collect \$.50 per day.
a) $y = .50x + 8$; b. See margin.

21. A sailboat is 9 miles from you. It travels towards you at a rate of 6 mph. **a) $y = 9 - 6x$; b. See margin.**

ADDITIONAL ANSWERS

17.

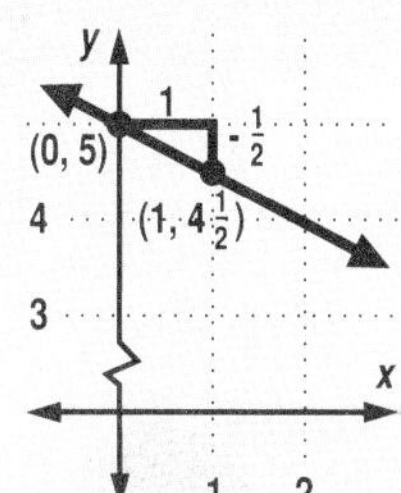

20b.

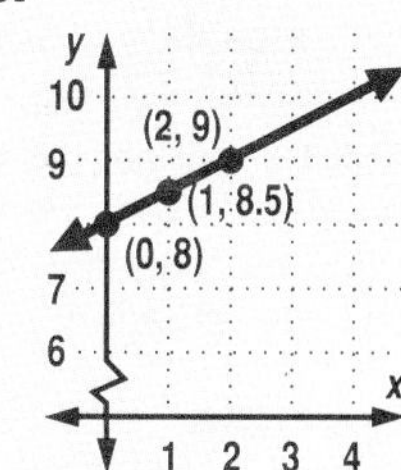

21b.

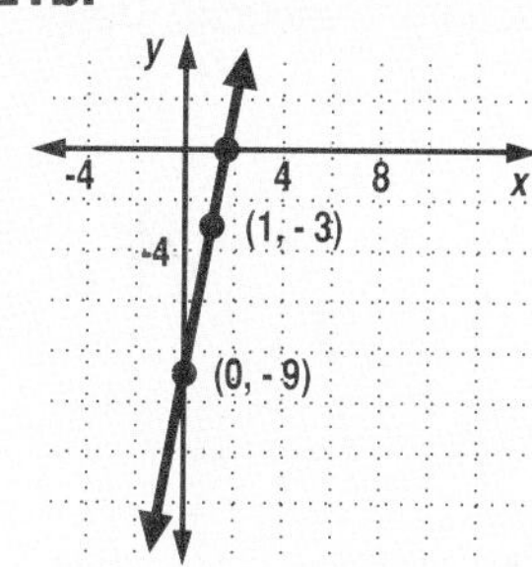

NAME __________

LESSON **MASTER 8–4**
QUESTIONS ON **SPUR** OBJECTIVES

■**SKILLS** *Objective B* *(See pages 418–421 for objectives.)*
In 1–4, write an equation for the line with the given slope m and y-intercept b.

1. $m = 3$, $b = -1$ **$y = 3x - 1$**
2. $m = 11.2$, $b = -3.9$ **$y = 11.2x - 3.9$**
3. $m = -3.2$, $b = 0$ **$y = -3.2x$**
4. $m = 4$, $b = p$ **$y = 4x + p$**

■**PROPERTIES** *Objective E*
In 5–8, write each equation in slope-intercept form.

5. $8x = 13 - 2y$ **$y = -4x + \frac{13}{2}$**
6. $5x + 3y = -2$ **$y = -\frac{5}{3}x - \frac{2}{3}$**
7. $x - y = 2$ **$y = x - 2$**
8. $y = 5$ **$y = 0x + 5$**

■**PROPERTIES** *Objective F*
In 9–11, find the slope and the y-intercept of the given line.

9. $y = -2$ slope **0** y-intercept **-2**
10. $2x - 8y = 11$ slope **$\frac{1}{4}$** y-intercept **$-\frac{11}{8}$**
11. $x = 23$ slope **undefined** y-intercept **none**

■**USES** *Objective H*

12. For an increase of one Kelvin (K), the Fahrenheit temperature (F) goes up 1.8 degrees. If $F = 32°$ when $K = 273.15$, write an equation for F in terms of K. **$F = 1.8K - 459.67$**

■**REPRESENTATIONS** *Objective I*

13. Graph the line which passes through (-2,4) and has a slope of -2.

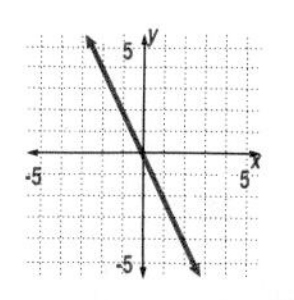

Algebra © Scott, Foresman and Company 67

FOLLOW-UP

MORE PRACTICE
For more questions on SPUR Objectives, use *Lesson Master 8-4,* shown on page 385.

EXTENSION
In Additional Example 5, if y is the total weight when Mr. Campbell is holding a bucket containing x canfuls of water, then $y = 191 + \frac{2}{3}x$. Your class might enjoy seeing or doing a similar experiment, and finding the equation that describes the situation.

EVALUATION
A quiz covering Lessons 8-1 through 8-4 is provided in the Teacher's Resource File.

32a.

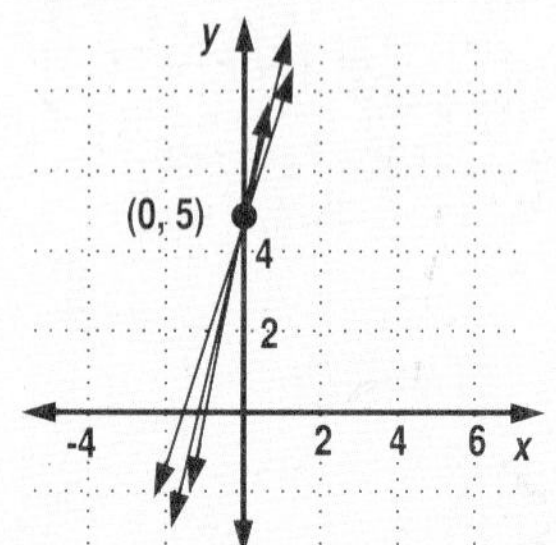

32b. a line that passes through (0, 5) with slope m

32c.

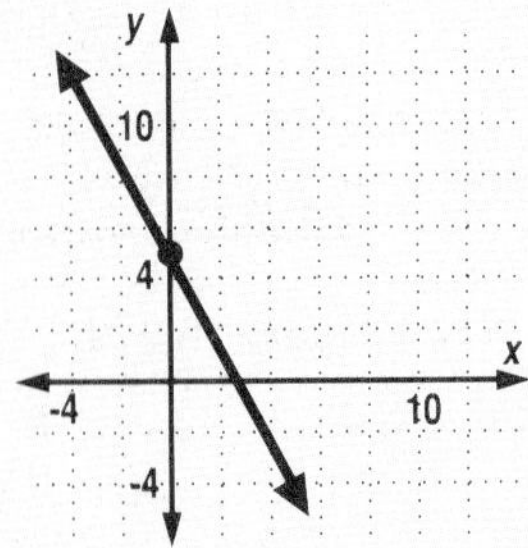

In 22 and 23, use this information: nonvertical lines are parallel if they have the same slope.

22. *True or false* The lines $y = \frac{1}{4}x + 7$ and $x + 4y = 2$ are parallel. **False**

23. Write an equation of a line with y-intercept -7 that is parallel to the line $y = 3x + 1$. **$y = 3x - 7$ or $y = 3x + -7$**

Review

24. Find the slope of the line through (5, -3) and (2, 7). *(Lesson 8-2)* **$-\frac{10}{3}$**

25. *Multiple choice* A line through which of the following pairs of points has no slope? *(Lesson 8-2)* **(b)**
(a) (4, 6), (6, 6)
(b) (3, -1), (3, 4)
(c) (0, 0), (5, 6)
(d) (0, 0), (5, 0)

26. Find the mean, median and range of each set. *(Lessons 1-2, 1-3)*
a. 34, 73, 21, 95, 86 **mean 61.8; median 73; range 74**
b. 3.4, 7.3, 2.1, 9.5, 8.6 **mean 6.18; median 7.3; range 7.4**

27. A brick wall is 20 feet high. How far away from the base of the wall will a 24-ft ladder be located when its top is at the top of the wall? *(Lesson 7-5)* **$\sqrt{176} \approx 13.3$ feet**

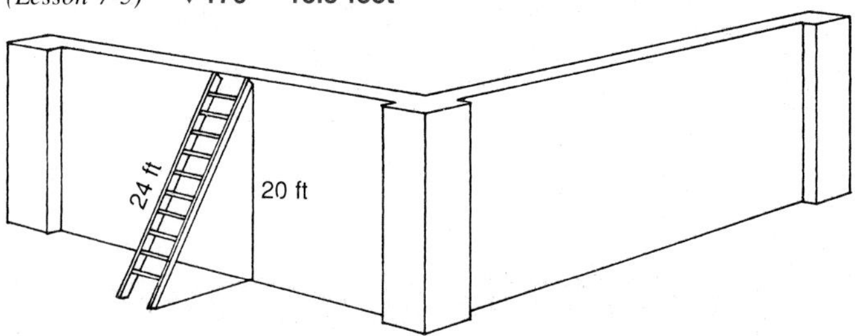

28. A rectangle is 5 cm longer than twice its width. Its perimeter is 58 cm.
a. Find its width and length. *(Lesson 6-1)* **8 cm; 21 cm**
b. What is its area? *(Lesson 4-1)* **168 cm^2**

In 29–31, solve. *(Lessons 5-7, 6-9)*

29. $\frac{3x + 5}{2 - 4x} = \frac{2}{3}$ **$-\frac{11}{17}$** **30.** $\frac{1}{2(1 + y)} = \frac{3}{y}$ **$-\frac{6}{5}$** **31.** $\frac{z + 2}{2} = 2z - 2$ **2**

Exploration

32. A graphing calculator or computer graphing program may be helpful in this question.
a. Graph the lines with equations $y = 3x + 5$, $y = 4x + 5$, and $y = 5x + 5$. **See margin.**
b. Describe the graph of $y = mx + 5$. **See margin.**
c. Graph $y = -2x + 5$. Is your description in part b true when m is negative? **See margin for graph; Yes**

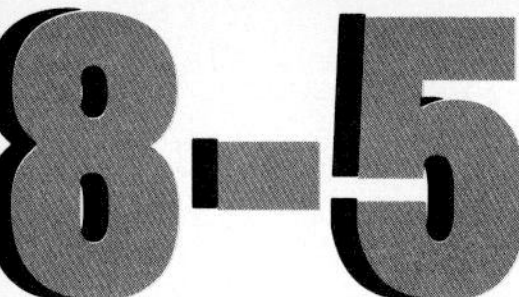

LESSON 8-5

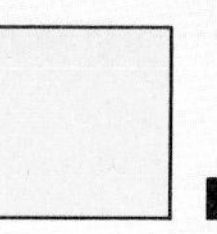

Equations for Lines with a Given Point and Slope

In Lesson 8-3, you graphed lines given the slope and any point on the line. In the last lesson you found an equation of a line given its slope and a particular point on the line, its y-intercept. You can, in fact, find an equation in slope-intercept form of a line given its slope and any point on the line, not necessarily the y-intercept.

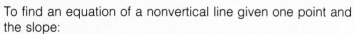

Example 1 Find an equation in slope-intercept form for the line through (-3, 5) with a slope of 2.

Solution You know that $y = mx + b$ is the slope-intercept equation of a line. In this case you are given $m = 2$. All that is needed is b.

1. Substitute $m = 2$ and the coordinates (-3, 5) into $y = mx + b$. This gives $5 = 2 \cdot -3 + b$.
2. Solve this equation for b. $5 = -6 + b$ so $b = 11$.
3. Substitute the values for m and b in $y = mx + b$. So the equation is $y = 2x + 11$.

Check Draw a rough graph of the line through (-3, 5) with slope 2. The graph shows that the y-intercept 11 seems reasonable.

If the line has a slope, the method of Example 1 will always work.

To find an equation of a nonvertical line given one point and the slope:
1. Substitute the slope m and the coordinates of the point (x, y) in the equation $y = mx + b$.
2. Solve the equation from step 1 for b.
3. Substitute the value for m and the value you found for b in $y = mx + b$.

LESSON 8-5

RESOURCES
- Lesson Master 8-5

OBJECTIVES

B Find an equation for a line given its slope and any point on it.
H Use equations for lines to describe real situations.

TEACHING NOTES

Reading The procedure for finding an equation for a line given one point and the slope is difficult for students to follow because the uses of the variables change during the problem. Here is an analysis, using **Example 1.** The slope m is a constant throughout the problem. In step **1,** x and y begin as variables in the equation $y = mx + b$ but end as constants, and b is an unknown. In step **2,** b becomes a constant. In step **3,** x and y return to their position as variables. It will be helpful to demonstrate the procedure step-by-step on the chalkboard or overhead projector.

Error Analysis When finding points on a line whose equation is in $y = mx + b$ form, some students put the y-coordinate in place of x because y comes first in the equation. It may help if students set the coordinates of the given point equal to (x, y) before substituting into the equation.

Example 3 assumes that the population of Ontario over time was a linear relationship, which is not true over the long term. However, this model can be used to describe short-term events. Some lively discussion can arise on this issue, paving the way for Lesson 8-7, which discusses fitting a line to data.

ADDITIONAL EXAMPLES

1. Write the equation in slope-intercept form of the line that has slope $\frac{1}{2}$ and contains (6, -5).
$y = \frac{1}{2}x - 8$

2. Write the equation in slope-intercept form of the line that contains (-4, 11) and has slope -1.
$y = -x + 7$

3. When Larry became president of a service organization, he decided to start a membership campaign with the goal of signing up 4 new members each week. He hoped that after 10 weeks the club's total membership would be 375. Write an equation to relate the desired number of members y to the number of weeks x that Larry would have been president.
$y = 335 + 4x$

NOTES ON QUESTIONS
Alternate Approach for Questions 7 and 8: It is often the case that applications are easier than theoretical problems because intuition can be used to find alternative strategies. For instance, in these questions the y-intercept can also be found by adding the amount of change to or subtracting it from the current value to find the initial value. This is equivalent to solving $y = mx + b$ for b. In **Question 7,** Marty has spent $3 \cdot 14 =$ \$42, so he began with $68 + 42 =$ \$110. In **Question 8,** at 10¢/min, the first three minutes cost 30¢, so the initial cost is $25 - 30 = -5$¢ (a 5¢ discount on the first three minutes).

Example 2 A line crosses the x-axis at (6, 0) and has slope -4. Find an equation for the line in slope-intercept form.

Solution Follow the steps above with $m = -4$, $x = 6$, and $y = 0$.

1. Substitute for m, x, and y. $0 = -4 \cdot 6 + b$
2. Solve for b. $24 = b$
3. Substitute for m and b. $y = -4x + 24$

This procedure is often useful for finding an equation to describe a real-life situation.

Example 3 The population of the province of Ontario in Canada was 8,543,000 in 1980. If the population is increasing at a rate of 80,000 people per year, find an equation relating the population y to the year x in Ontario.

Solution This is a constant increase situation so it can be described by a line with equation $y = mx + b$. The rate of 80,000 people per year is the slope, so $m = 80{,}000$. The population of 8,543,000 in 1980 is described by the point (1980, 8,543,000). You now have the slope and one point so you can follow the steps above.

1. Substitute for m, x, and y. $8{,}543{,}000 = 80{,}000 \cdot 1980 + b$
2. Solve for b. $8{,}543{,}000 = 158{,}400{,}000 + b$
   $-149{,}857{,}000 = b$
3. Substitute for m and b. $y = 80{,}000x - 149{,}857{,}000$

Check When $x = 1980$, does $y = 8{,}543{,}000$? Yes, so it checks.

Questions

Covering the Reading

1. Describe the steps for finding an equation for a line given the slope and one point on the line. **See margin.**

In 2–5, given the slope and one point, find an equation for the line.

2. point (2, 3), slope 4 **$y = 4x - 5$**
3. point (-10, 3), slope -2 **$y = -2x - 17$**
4. point (-6, 0), slope $\frac{1}{3}$ **$y = \frac{1}{3}x + 2$**
5. point (4, $-\frac{1}{2}$), slope 0 **$y = -\frac{1}{2}$**
6. The population of the province of Quebec in Canada was 6,398,000 in 1980. If the population is increasing at a rate of 40,000 people per year, find an equation relating the population of Quebec to the year. **$y = 40{,}000x - 72{,}802{,}000$**

Applying the Mathematics

7. Marty is spending money at the average rate of \$3 a day. After 14 days he has \$68 left. Write an equation relating the amount left y to the number of days x. **$y = -3x + 110$**

8. Diane knows a phone call to a friend costs 25¢ for the first 3 minutes and 10¢ for each additional minute. Write an equation to describe the cost y of a call of x-minutes duration. Check your answer. **See margin.**

9. Refer to Example 3. If the rate of population increase stays constant, what will be the population of Ontario in the year 2000? **10,143,000**

10. The *x-intercept* of a line is the point where the line crosses the x-axis. The slope of a line is -4 and its x-intercept is 7. Find an equation for the line. **$y = -4x + 28$**

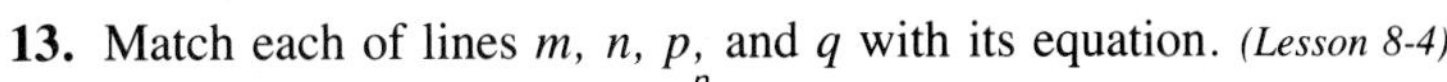

11. The slopes of two lines are reciprocals. The equation of one of the lines is $y = 2x + 1$.

a. Find the slope of the second line. **$\frac{1}{2}$**

b. Find an equation for the second line if it passes through the point (2, 3). **$y = \frac{1}{2}x + 2$**

12. Stephanie, a 4-week-old baby, weighs 142 oz. She is gaining weight at the rate of 3 oz per week. Give her weight y at age 15 weeks. **175 oz**

Review

13. Match each of lines m, n, p, and q with its equation. *(Lesson 8-4)*

a. $y = -\frac{1}{4}x$ **q**

b. $y = -\frac{1}{4}x + 3$ **n**

c. $y = -1 - \frac{1}{4}x$ **p**

d. $y = -4 - \frac{1}{4}x$ **m**

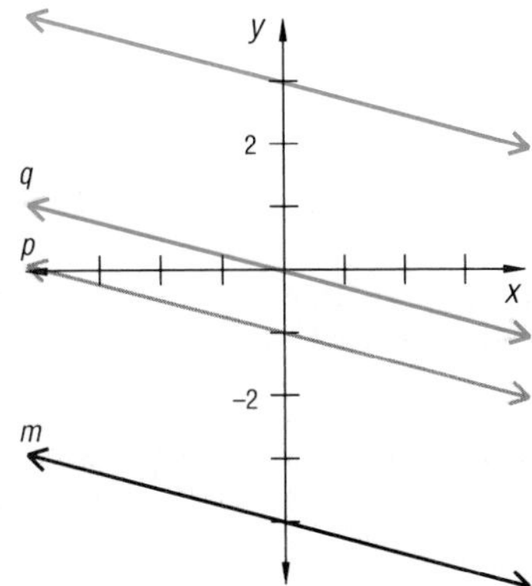

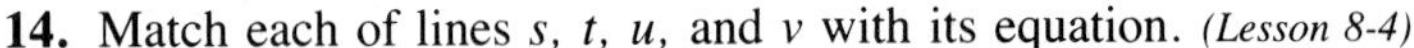

14. Match each of lines s, t, u, and v with its equation. *(Lesson 8-4)*

a. $y = x + 2$ **s**

b. $y = -x + 2$ **v**

c. $y = 2 - 3x$ **u**

d. $y = \frac{3}{2}x + 2$ **t**

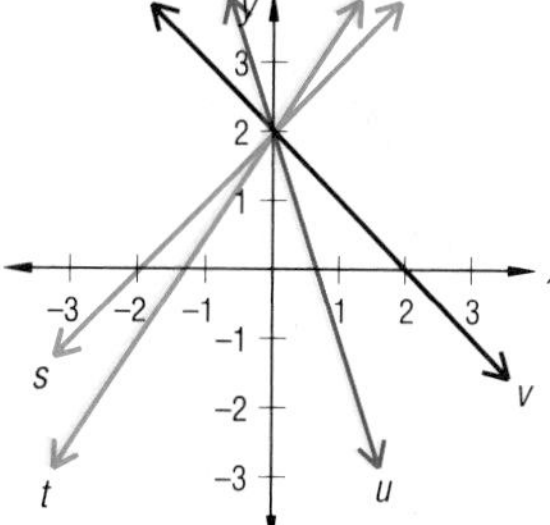

Question 10: Saying that the x-intercept is 7 is like saying that (7, 0) is a point on the line.

Reading for Question 11: Students may need a reminder of the meaning of *reciprocal*.

Making Connections for Questions 13 and 14: These questions are designed to continue the discussion of the effect on the graph of $y = mx + b$ of changing the values of m and b.

ADDITIONAL ANSWERS

**1. Step 1: Substitute the slope m and the coordinates of the point (x, y) in the equation $y = mx + b$.
Step 2: Solve the equation from step 1 for b.
Step 3: Substitute the values of m and b into $y = mx + b$.**

8. $y = .25$ if $0 < x < 3$, and
$y = .10(x - 3) + .25$ if $x \geq 3$ (y in dollars)
Let $x = 4$ minutes
$y = .10(4 - 3) + .25$
$y = .35$

NAME ____________

LESSON **MASTER 8–5**
QUESTIONS ON **SPUR** OBJECTIVES

■**SKILLS** *Objective B (See pages 418–421 for objectives.)*
In 1–8, given one point and slope, find an equation for the line.

1. point (4, -4), slope -3	**2.** point (-3, 1), slope $\frac{2}{3}$
$y = -3x + 8$	$y = \frac{2}{3}x + 3$
3. point (2.5, 6), slope 0.8	**4.** point (-15, 0), slope $-\frac{3}{5}$
$y = .8x + 4$	$y = -\frac{3}{5}x - 9$
5. point (5, -9), slope 0	**6.** point (5, 8), slope undefined
$y = -9$	$x = 5$
7. point (0, $\frac{1}{2}$), slope $-\frac{1}{8}$	**8.** point (0, -3), slope 4
$2x + 16y = 8$	$12x - 3y = 9$

■**USES** *Objective H*

9. A repairperson charges \$25 per hour plus an initial service-call charge. The bill for 3 hours was \$105. Give a linear equation which relates the cost y of having the repairperson work x hours. $y = 25x + 30$

10. Rich Nomore has been spending 65 cents on bus fare each day from a coin wallet. After 12 days, he has \$4.70 left. Write an equation giving the amount y he had left after x days. $y = -.65x + 12.50$

11. It costs \$1.25 for a 3-minute call and 30¢ for each additional minute. Give the cost c for a m-minute call, when $m > 3$. $c = .30(m - 3) + 1.25$

12. There are 100 days gone of the school year and 40,000 sheets of duplicating paper are left. If about 2,000 sheets are used each day, how many sheets s were left after d days of school? $s = -2000d + 240,000$

68

NOTES ON QUESTIONS
Question 21c: Students should solve the equation by *trial and error.*

Question 23: Part **b** generalizes part **a,** and part **c** further generalizes the first two parts.

Small Group Work for Question 24: You may wish to have students research population data while working in small groups.

FOLLOW-UP

MORE PRACTICE
For more questions on SPUR Objectives, use *Lesson Master 8-5,* shown on page 389.

18.

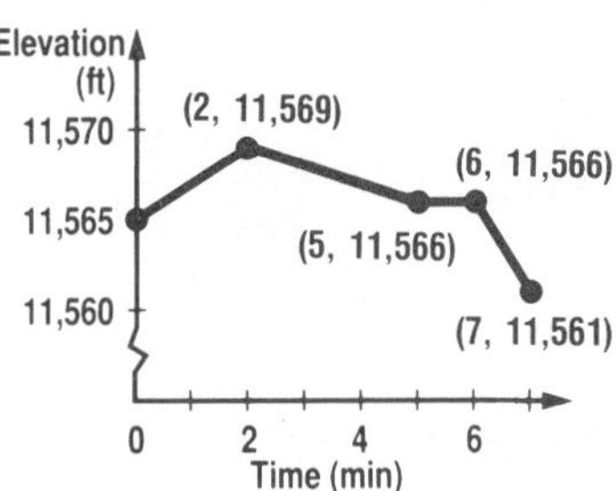

19.

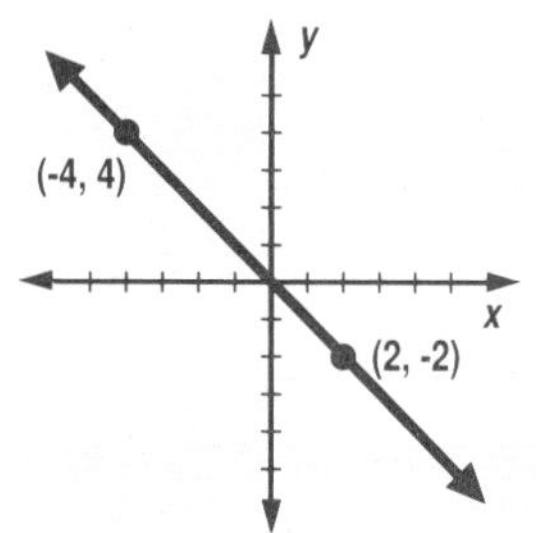

15. Do the points (1, 3), (-3, -5), and (3, 6) lie on the same line? *(Lesson 8-2)* **No**

16. The following two points give information about an overseas telephone call: (5 minutes, \$5.91), (10 minutes, \$10.86). Calculate the slope and describe what it stands for. *(Lesson 8-2)* **0.99; long-distance calls between 5 and 10 minutes long average \$.99 per minute**

17. Which section, or sections, of this graph shows: **a.** the fastest increase? **b.** the slowest decrease? **c.** no change? *(Lesson 8-1)*
a) A; b) C; c) All sections show some change.

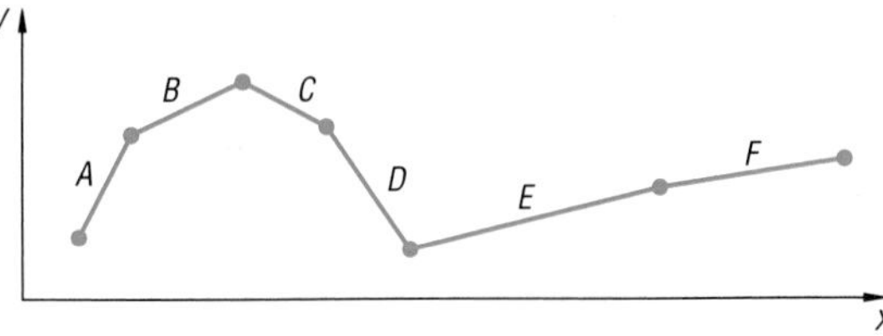

18. A rock climber starts at an elevation of 11,565 feet. He goes up 2 $\frac{\text{ft}}{\text{min}}$ for 2 minutes, then down 1 $\frac{\text{ft}}{\text{min}}$ for 3 minutes. He stands still for one minute, then descends 5 feet in one minute. Graph his elevation during this time. *(Lesson 8-1)* **See margin.**

19. Graph $y = -x$. *(Lesson 8-4)* **See margin.**

20. A survey showed that 7 out of 10 adults drink coffee in the morning. If 650 adults live in an apartment complex, how many of them would you expect to drink coffee in the morning? *(Lesson 5-7)* **455**

21. Solve for n. *(Lessons 4-9, 7-4)*
a. $n^2 = 24$ **$2\sqrt{6}$ or $-2\sqrt{6}$**
b. $\sqrt{n} = 24$ **576**
c. $n! = 24$ **$n = 4$**

22. Solve. *(Lessons 4-4, 7-3, 7-4, 7-8)*
a. $3x = 12$ **$x = 4$**
b. $3\sqrt{y} = 12$ **$y = 16$**
c. $3 \cdot |z - 5| = 12$ **$z = 9$ or 1**

23. Simplify. *(Lesson 5-1)*
a. $\frac{15}{2} \div \frac{15}{3}$ **$\frac{3}{2}$**
b. $\frac{a}{2} \div \frac{a}{3}$ **$\frac{3}{2}$**
c. $\frac{a}{b} \div \frac{a}{c}$ **$\frac{c}{b}$**

Exploration

24. Examine Example 3. **Answers will vary.**
a. Find the population at the last census of the state where you live.
b. Estimate or find out how fast your state is growing per year.
c. Using your estimate, find a linear equation relating the population y to the year x.
d. Use this equation to estimate what the population of your state will be when you are 50 years old.

390

LESSON

Equations for Lines Through Two Points

A phone book might tell you that a call to a friend some distance away costs 25¢ for the first 3 minutes and 10¢ for each additional minute. This is like being given the point (3, 25) and the slope 10. If you know an equation of the line through this point with this slope, then you have a formula which can help you know the cost of any phone call to that friend. In Lesson 8-5 you learned how to find such an equation.

Sometimes the given information does not include the slope, but includes two points. For instance, you might be told that a 5-minute call overseas costs $5.91 and a 10-minute call costs $10.86. You have two data points, (5, 5.91) and (10, 10.86). To obtain an equation for the line through these points, first calculate the slope. Then work as before.

Before finding this telephone cost equation, we work through an example with simpler numbers.

Example 1 Find an equation for the line through (5, -1) and (-3, 3).

Solution

1. First find the slope.

$$m = \frac{3 - -1}{-3 - 5} = \frac{4}{-8} = -\frac{1}{2}$$

Now you have the slope and two points. This is more information than you need. Pick one of these points. We pick (5, -1).

2. Substitute $-\frac{1}{2}$ and the coordinates of (5, -1) into $y = mx + b$.

$$-1 = -\tfrac{1}{2}(5) + b$$

3. Solve for b.

$$-1 = -\tfrac{5}{2} + b$$

$$\tfrac{3}{2} = b$$

4. Substitute the values of m and b into the equation.

$$y = -\tfrac{1}{2}x + \tfrac{3}{2}$$

LESSON 8-6

RESOURCES

■ Lesson Master 8-6

OBJECTIVES

C Find an equation for a line through two given points.

H Use equations for lines to describe real situations.

TEACHING NOTES

Some students may be uncomfortable with the number of choices they must make when solving these problems, while others may enjoy them. As you discuss these problems, reassure students who used different choices that the intermediate work shown in class might be different from theirs, but the slope-intercept equation of the line will be the same.

For example, you could show another solution for **Example 1.** The slope could be computed as $m = \frac{-1 - 3}{5 - -3} = -\frac{4}{8} = -\frac{1}{2}$. In step **2,** you could use (-3, 3) instead of (5, -1). Then $3 = -\frac{1}{2}(-3) + b$, and b is still $\frac{3}{2}$.

The lesson mentions Descartes. You might remind students that our coordinate system is called the Cartesian plane in his honor.

ADDITIONAL EXAMPLES

1. Find an equation for the line that contains (8, 7) and (-4, -2).

$y = \frac{3}{4}x + 1$

2. A printer charges $65 to print 100 copies of a booklet and $105 to print 500 copies. If the relationship between the number of copies and the cost is linear, write an equation relating the cost *y* and the number of copies *x*.

$y = .1x + 55$

Note: The unit for the slope 0.10 is cost/copy. This means that it costs 10¢ to print one more copy. In business, that cost is called *marginal cost*.

Check Substitute the coordinates of the point not used to see if they work.

Point (-3, 3): Does $3 = -\frac{1}{2}(-3) + \frac{3}{2}$?

Does $3 = \frac{3}{2} + \frac{3}{2}$? Yes.

The procedure involves just one more step than the procedure of Lesson 8-5.

To find an equation for a nonvertical line given two points on it:

1. Find the slope determined by the two points.
2. Substitute the slope m and the coordinates of one of the points (x, y) in the equation $y = mx + b$.
3. Solve for b.
4. Substitute the values you found for m and b in $y = mx + b$.

This method of finding the equation of a line was developed by René Descartes in the early 1600s. We now apply it to the telephone cost problem.

Example 2 If a 5-minute overseas call costs $5.91 and a 10-minute call costs $10.86, what is the cost *y* of a call of *x*-minutes duration? (Assume that this is a constant increase situation and *x* is a positive integer.)

Solution What you want is the line through (5, 5.91) and (10, 10.86).

1. Find the slope.

$$m = \frac{10.86 - 5.91}{10 - 5} = \frac{4.95}{5} = 0.99$$

2. Substitute 0.99 and one of the points into $y = mx + b$. We pick (5, 5.91).

$$5.91 = 0.99(5) + b$$

3. Solve for b.

$$5.91 = 4.95 + b$$
$$b = 0.96$$

4. Substitute the values for m and b into $y = mx + b$.

$$y = 0.99x + 0.96$$

392

Check Does this equation give the correct cost for a 10-minute call? Substitute 10 for x in the equation. Then $y = 0.99(10) + 0.96 = 9.9 + 0.96 = 10.86$, as needed.

The equation $y = 0.99x + 0.96$ of Example 2 says that a call costs 0.96 to make and then 0.99 for each minute. The letters x and y might be replaced by t (for time) and c (for cost), in which case the formula would become $c = 0.99t + 0.96$.

Linear relationships occur in many places. Some of them may surprise you.

Example 3 Biologists have found that the number of chirps some crickets make per minute is related to the temperature. The relationship is very close to being linear. When crickets chirp 124 times a minute, it is 68°F. When they chirp 172 times a minute, it is 80°F. Below is a graph of this information.

a. Find an equation for the line through the two points.

b. About how warm is it if you hear 100 chirps in a minute?

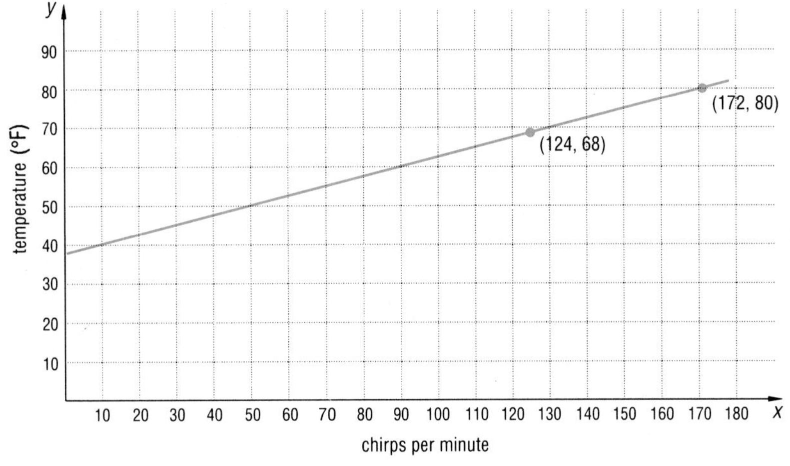

393

3. Blood pressure tends to increase with age. Suppose the normal blood pressure of a 20-year-old is 120 and that of 50-year-old is 135.

a. If the increase is at a constant rate, write an equation relating age x and normal blood pressure y.
$y = \frac{1}{2}x + 110$

b. According to this equation, what would be the normal blood pressure of a 60-year-old?
140

NOTES ON QUESTIONS
Question 11: Students can check their result by noting that the sum of the measures of the interior angles of a pentagon is 540°, and of a hexagon is 720°. The graph of the equation is discrete because polygons have integral numbers of sides.

Question 13: This application is a classic in that virtually every textbook uses it and virtually every student sees it. For this reason, it should be discussed in some detail. The given is information they should know; the result is an equation that may come in handy. Here we have arbitrarily selected the Fahrenheit temperature as x and the Celsius temperature as y. However, outside the classroom, students might see the formula solved for either variable.

Computer for Question 18: The method suggested by this computer program can always be used to find the y-intercept of an equation when the slope and a point are given. Your class may enjoy adding a line to the program so it will print the equation of the line.
40 PRINT "Y = " M "X + "B

Question 19a: Students can use two methods. One is to use the equation $(88 + 94 + 85 + 90 + x) \div 5 = 88$. The other is to work with the total points. If the average of the five scores is to be 88, the total points must be $5 \cdot 88 = 440$.

Solution
a. 1) First find the slope.

$$m = \frac{80 - 68}{172 - 124} = \frac{12}{48} = \frac{1}{4}$$

2) Substitute $\frac{1}{4}$ and the coordinates of (124, 68) into $y = mx + b$.

$$68 = \tfrac{1}{4}(124) + b$$

3) Solve for b.

$$68 = 31 + b$$
$$37 = b$$

4) Substitute for m and b.

An equation is $y = \frac{1}{4}x + 37$.

Check Substitute the coordinates of the point (172, 80) that was not used in finding the equation.

Does $80 = \frac{1}{4}(172) + 37$?
Does $80 = 43 + 37$? Yes.

Solution
b. Substitute 100 for x.

$$y = \tfrac{1}{4}(100) + 37$$
$$y = 25 + 37$$
$$y = 62$$

It is about 62° when you hear 100 chirps in a minute.

Check Plot (100, 62). It should lie on the line.

The equation in Example 3 enables you to find the temperature for any number of chirps. By solving for x in terms of y, you could get a formula for the number of chirps to expect at a given temperature. Formulas like these seldom work far from the data points. Crickets tend not to chirp at all below 50°F, yet the formula $y = \frac{1}{4}x + 37$ predicts about 52 chirps a minute at 50°F.

Questions

Covering the Reading

In 1–3, find an equation for the line through the two given points. Check your answer.

1. (1, 9), (7, 3) **$y = -x + 10$** **2.** (6, -3), (-8, -10) **$y = \frac{1}{2}x - 6$**

3. (0, 11), (13, 0) **$y = \frac{-11}{13}x + 11$**

394

4. Who developed the method used in this lesson for finding the equation of a line? **René Descartes**

5. In Example 2, what would an 8-minute call cost? **$8.88**

6. If a 5-minute overseas call to Bonn costs $4.50 and a 10-minute call costs $8.50, find a formula relating time and cost. **$y = 0.80x + 0.50$**

In 7–9, refer to Example 3.

7. The number of times a cricket chirps in a minute and the temperature is very close to what kind of relationship? **linear**

8. When the number of chirps is 90, about what is the temperature? Use the graph to find the answer. **about 60°F**

9. By substituting in the equation $y = \frac{1}{4}x + 37$, about how many chirps per minute would you expect if the temperature is 70°F? **about 132**

Applying the Mathematics

10. a. Show that $A = (-4, 7)$, $B = (1, 5)$, and $C = (16, -1)$ lie on the same line. **See margin.**
    b. Find an equation for the line. **$y = -\frac{2}{5}x + \frac{27}{5}$**

11. The sum of the measures of the angles in a triangle is 180°. In a quadrilateral, the sum is 360°. Find an equation relating n, the number of sides in a polygon, and the sum of its angles, S. (Hint: $S = mn + b$.) **$S = 180n - 360$**

12. It was reported in 1960 that the total length y and the tail length x of females of the snake species *Lampropeltis polyzona* have close to a linear relationship. When $x = 60$ mm, $y = 455$ mm. When $x = 140$ mm, $y = 1050$ mm.
    a. Find the slope of the relationship between x and y. (Approximate your answer to the nearest tenth.) **7.4**
    b. Find an equation for the relationship between x and y using (60, 455) and your slope from part a. **$y = 7.4x + 11$**
    c. Check your equation using (140, 1050). **See margin.**

ADDITIONAL ANSWERS

10a. $\frac{5 - 7}{1 - -4} = \frac{-1 - 5}{16 - 1} = \frac{-2}{5}$

12c. $7.4(140) + 11 = 1047 \approx 1050$

FOLLOW-UP

MORE PRACTICE
For more questions on SPUR Objectives, use *Lesson Master 8-6,* shown on page 397.

EXTENSION
In an application problem there is often a choice about which quantity will be represented by the independent variable *x* and which by the dependent variable *y*. Sometimes a problem will naturally lend itself toward one choice. In **Example 2** it makes sense to view the cost of the call as a function of its length.

However some problems, like **Example 3,** work well with the variables assigned in either order. Our solution has been stated with chirps per minute as the independent variable *x* and temperature as the dependent variable *y*. That is, we think of knowing the chirps and determining the temperature from that.

If the variables are reversed, then we think of the temperature as determining the number of chirps. The graph has temperature on the *x*-axis and chirps on the *y*-axis. The slope is 4 instead of 1/4. Interpreted as rates, the slope is 4 chirps per minute per degree instead of 1/4 degree per chirps per minute, The *y*-intercept is -148. The slope-intercept equation would be $y = \frac{1}{4}x - 148$. This is an equation for the inverse function of that graphed in **Example 3.**

Have students reverse the dependent and independent variables in **Example 3,** draw the graph, and find the equation.

13. The graph below shows the linear relationship between Fahrenheit and Celsius temperatures. The freezing point of water is 32 °F and 0 °C. The boiling point of water is at 212 °F and 100 °C.

a. Find an equation that relates Celsius and Fahrenheit temperatures. (Hint: $C = mF + b$.) $C = \frac{5}{9}F - \frac{160}{9}$

b. When it is 150 °F, what is the temperature in degrees Celsius? ≈65.6°C

c. When it is 150 °C, what is the temperature in degrees Fahrenheit? 302°F

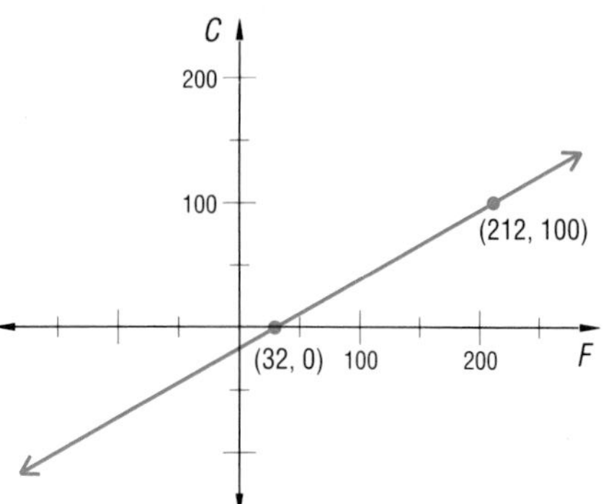

Review

14. A cab company charges a base rate plus \$1.10 a mile. A 12-mile cab ride costs \$14. Write an equation relating the number of miles driven to the cost of the cab ride. *(Lesson 8-5)* $C = 1.10m + 0.8$; C = cost of ride, m = miles driven

15. Graph $y = 4x - 3$ by using the slope and y-intercept. *(Lesson 8-4)* See margin.

16. A road leads from the town of Salida. There are signs every 5 miles that tell the elevation. *(Lesson 8-1)*

miles from Salida:	elevation (feet)
0	1744
5	1749
10	1749
15	1759
20	1757

a. Graph these data. See margin.

b. Calculate the rate of change of elevation for the entire distance. .65 foot per mile

17. Triangles *ABC* and *DEF* below are similar. Corresponding sides are parallel. **a.** Solve for x. $\frac{15}{2}$

b. What is the ratio of similitude? *(Lesson 5-8)* $\frac{2}{5}$ or $\frac{5}{2}$

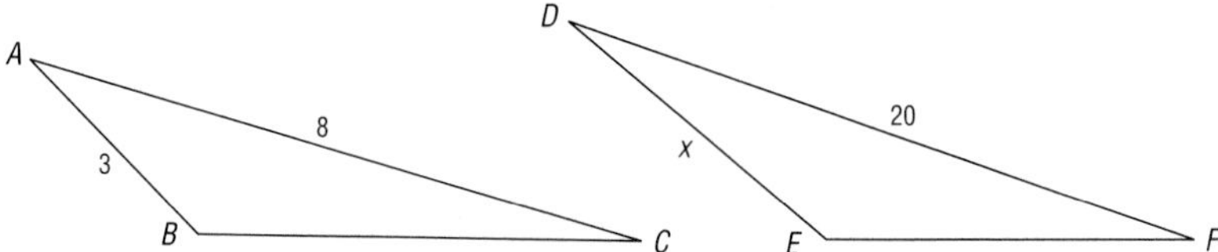

18. What question does the following computer program answer? *(Lesson 8-5)* **What is the y-intercept of the line with slope M through (X, Y)?**

```
10 INPUT M, X, Y
20 LET B = Y − M * X
30 PRINT B
```

19. A student has quiz scores of 88, 94, 85, and 80.
   a. What quiz score does the student need in order to average 88 for the five quizzes? **93**
   b. What quiz score is needed in order to have a median score of 88 for the five quizzes? **any score greater than or equal to 88**
   c. What quiz score is needed in order to have a mode score of 88 for the five quizzes? *(Lesson 1-2)* **88**

20. *Skill Sequence* Solve. *(Lessons 7-4, 7-8)*
   a. $x^2 = 64$ **-8 or 8**
   b. $(y - 7)^2 = 64$ **-1 or 15**
   c. $(3y - 7)^2 = 64$ **$-\frac{1}{3}$ or 5**

21. Simplify. *(Lesson 1-8)*
   a. $\frac{12}{144}$ **$\frac{1}{12}$**
   b. $\frac{3}{3^2}$ **$\frac{1}{3}$**
   c. $\frac{d}{d^2}$ **$\frac{1}{d}$**

Exploration

22. A ride in a taxicab costs a fixed number of dollars plus a constant charge per mile.
   a. Find a rate for taxi rides in your community.
   b. Graph your findings on coordinate axes like the ones at right.
   a–b) Answers will vary depending on the community.

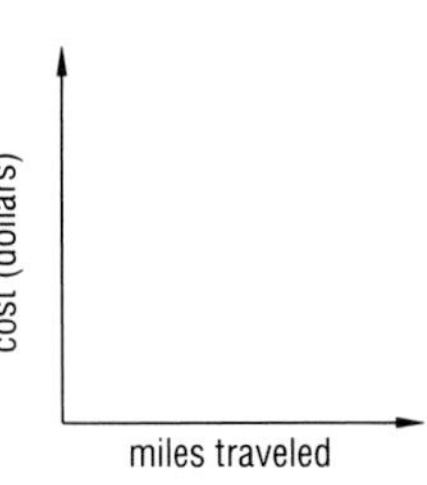

15.

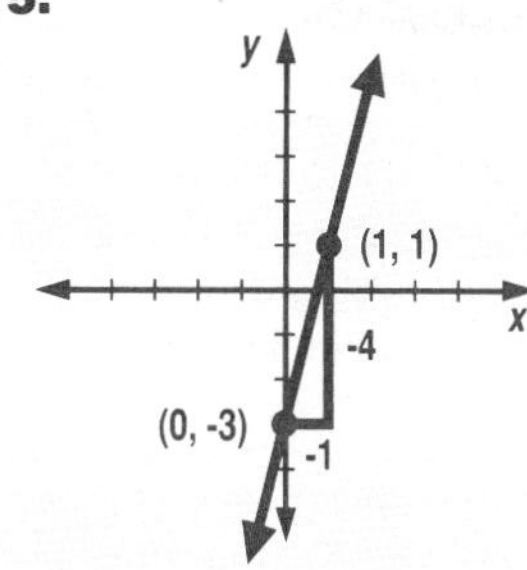

16a.

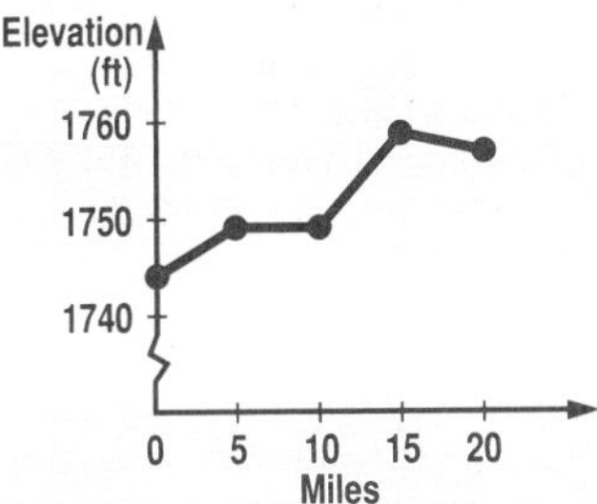

NAME ____________

LESSON MASTER 8–6

QUESTIONS ON **SPUR** OBJECTIVES

■SKILLS *Objective C (See pages 418–421 for objectives.)*
In 1–6, find an equation for the line through the two given points.

1. (4, -1), (7, 5) **$y = 2x - 9$**
2. (204, 358), (300, 406) **$y = \frac{1}{2}x + 256$**
3. (-0.43, 1.8), (0.57, -3.6) **$y = -5.4x - .522$**
4. $\left(\frac{2}{3}, \frac{3}{2}\right), \left(\frac{5}{6}, \frac{3}{4}\right)$ **$y = -\frac{9}{2}x + \frac{9}{2}$**
5. (0, 0), $(1, \sqrt{2})$ **$y = \sqrt{2}x$**
6. (a, 0), (0, b) **$y = -\frac{b}{a}x + b$**
7. a. Find an equation for the line through (-3, -8) and (1, 1). **$y = \frac{9}{4}x - \frac{5}{4}$**
   b. Does the point (9, 19) lie on the line? **yes**

■USES *Objective H*

8. A linear equation can be used to describe the length of a spring, y, when it is stretched by a weight, x. A spring is 4 cm long when a 50-g weight is attached, and 6 cm long when a 74-g weight is attached. Write an equation which relates x and y. **$y = \frac{1}{12}x - \frac{1}{6}$**

9. A man whose foot is 12 in. long wears a size 12 shoe. A man whose foot is 10 in. long wears a size 6 shoe. If the shoe size, S, and the foot length, F, are linearly related, write an equation which describes that relation. **$S = 3F - 24$**

10. a. Harvey began his diet when he weighed 260 pounds. After four weeks he weighed 246 pounds. If he lost weight at a constant rate, write an equation which relates his weight, W, and the number of weeks on the diet, n. **$W = 260 - 3.5n$**
   b. Why doesn't this relation work when n is large? **He would eventually have no weight or negative weight.**

LESSON 8-7

RESOURCES
- ■ Lesson Master 8-7
- ■ Quiz on Lessons 8-5 Through 8-7
- Visual for Teaching Aid 41: Table and Graph of Latitude and Temperature in Selected Cities for Pages 398–399
- Visual for Teaching Aid 42: Table and Graph for **Question 10**
- Visual for Teaching Aid 43: Table and Graph for Additional Example
- Computer Master 16

OBJECTIVE

J Given data which approximates a linear graph, find a linear equation to fit the graph.

TEACHING NOTES

You might want to bring a globe to class to explain what *latitude* and *longitude* are on the globe. You might also discuss temperature patterns and locate some of the cities in the lesson.

Students will need their calculators for the computations of slope and intercept in this lesson.

Because students are estimating the best-fitting line, they will get different slopes and intercepts as answers to some of the questions. The values they calculate should be quite close to each other, and you might ask if they can think of a way to choose the "best" values. This can be time consuming, however, so prepare accordingly. If class time is short, you might want to determine the best-fit line as a class.

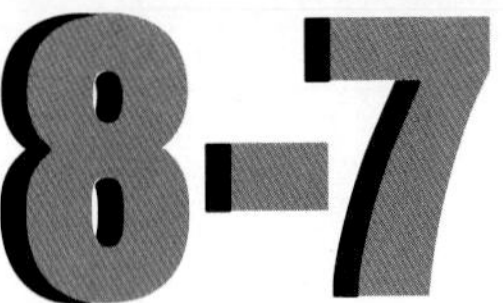

LESSON 8-7 Fitting a Line to Data

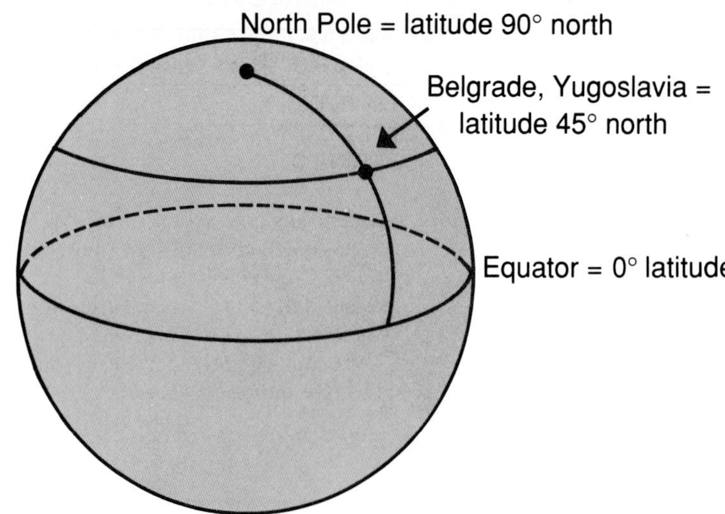

In many situations, there are more than two points. The points may not all lie on a line. Still an equation may be found that closely describes the coordinates. Finding that equation is the subject of this lesson.

The latitude of a place on the earth tells how far the place is from the equator. Latitudes in the Northern Hemisphere range from 0° at the equator to 90° at the North Pole.

In the table below are the latitude and mean high temperatures in April, for selected cities in the Northern Hemisphere. (The mean high temperature is the mean of all the high temperatures for the month.) Although in all of these cities temperature is measured in degrees Celsius, we have converted the temperatures to Fahrenheit for you.

Latitude and Temperature in Selected Cities

City	North Latitude	April Mean High Temperature (°F)
Lagos, Nigeria	6	89
San Juan, Puerto Rico	18	84
Calcutta, India	23	97
Cairo, Egypt	30	83
Tokyo, Japan	35	63
Rome, Italy	42	68
Belgrade, Yugoslavia	45	45
London, England	52	56
Copenhagen, Denmark	56	50
Moscow, USSR	56	47

To graph the data points in the table on page 398, let the latitude be the x-value. The y-value is the Fahrenheit temperature. Both units are degrees. For instance the data point for Tokyo is (35, 63). Here is the scattergram.

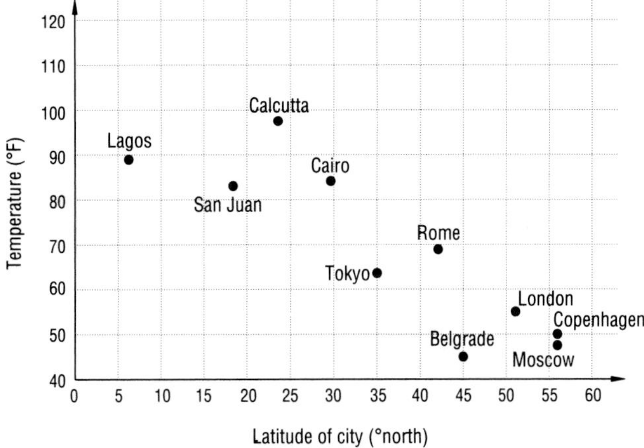

The points on the graph suggest that the higher the latitude, the lower the temperature. What does the data suggest for a city like Quito, Equador, at the equator (0° latitude)? What would you predict for the temperature at a city at 19° latitude, like Mexico City or Bombay?

To answer these questions, it helps to "fit a line" to the data. No line will pass through all the data points, but you can find a line that describes the trend of higher latitude, lower temperature. The simplest way is to take a ruler and draw a line that seems closest to all the points. This is called "fitting a line by eye," and one such line is graphed below.

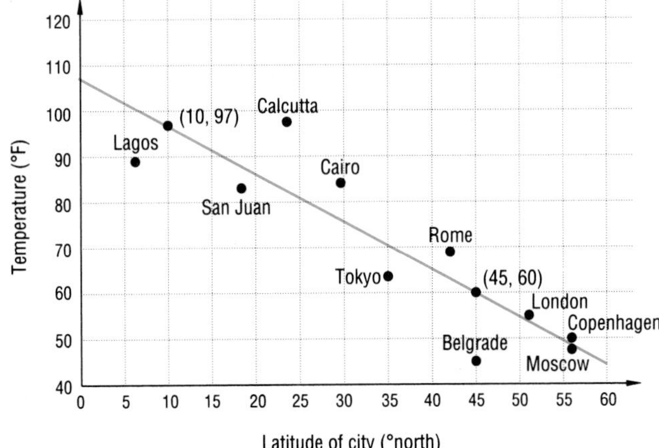

ADDITIONAL EXAMPLE
The chart below shows the number of U.S. travelers abroad for the years 1970 to 1983.

Year	Travelers (millions)
70	5.3
71	5.7
72	6.8
73	6.9
74	6.5
75	6.4
76	6.9
77	7.4
78	7.8
79	7.9
80	8.2
81	8.0
82	8.6
83	9.6

a. Draw a scattergram showing a point for each year.

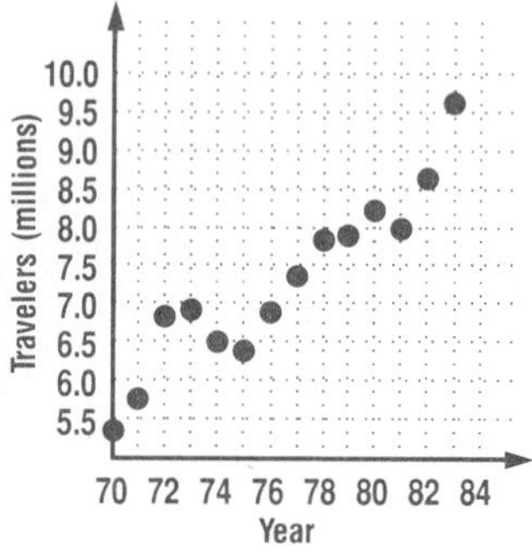

b. Use a ruler to fit a line to the data.
One such line passes through (77, 7.4) and (81, 8.0).

c. Write an equation for the line drawn in **b.**
The line through the two points named in b. is $y = .15x - 4.15$.

d. Use your equation to predict the number of U.S. travelers abroad in 1985.
9 million

Note: Actually the number of travelers in 1985 was 12.3 million. Foreign travel increased dramatically in 1983–86, then dropped in 1987–88. The value of the dollar in relation to other currencies has a substantial effect on the amount of foreign travel.

Once a line has been fitted to the data, the idea is to find an equation for the line and then use the equation to predict temperatures for different latitudes.

Example 1 Find a line to the latitude and temperature data points.

Solution We use the line from the previous page. It contains the points (10, 97) and (45, 60). First find the slope of the line.

$$\text{slope} = \frac{60 - 97}{45 - 10} = \frac{-37}{35} \approx -1.06$$

Now substitute this slope and the coordinates of one of the points into $y = mx + b$ and solve. We use (10, 97).

$$97 = -1.06 \cdot 10 + b$$
$$97 = -10.6 + b$$
$$107.6 = b$$

So an equation of the line is $y = -1.06x + 107.6$.

Check Substitute (45, 60) into the equation.
Does $60 = -1.06(45) + 107.6$?
$60 \approx 59.9$ so it checks.

The negative slope -1.06 means that as you move 1° north in latitude, the April mean high temperature is about 1°F lower. The y-intercept 107.6 means that the high temperature at the equator (0° latitude) should be about 108° Fahrenheit. Using the equation $y = -1.06x + 107.6$, you can estimate the temperature for cities not listed on the chart.

Example 2 Use the equation for the fitted line to predict the April mean high temperature for Madrid, Spain, which is at 40° north latitude.

Solution Use 40° for x in the equation.

$$y = -1.06 \cdot x + 107.6$$
$$y = -1.06 \cdot 40 + 107.6$$
$$y = 65.2$$

You can predict that Madrid would have an April mean high temperature of about 65°F.

Calahora Castle in Andalucia, Spain

The mean high temperature in April for Madrid is actually 64°. The predicted temperature is remarkably close. This is not always the case. For Mexico City, at a latitude of 19° north, the line predicts a temperature of 87°. The actual April mean temperature for Mexico City is 78°. The prediction is high because Mexico City is at an altitude of about one mile, and temperatures at high altitudes are lower.

Questions

Covering the Reading

1. What does the latitude of a place on earth signify? distance of the place from the equator
2. What is the latitude of the North Pole? 90° north
3. What is the latitude of the equator? 0°
4. Which city is farther north, Calcutta or Cairo? Cairo
5. What does it mean to "fit a line by eye" to a scattergram? Draw a line that seems closest to all of the points in the graph.
6. Use the graph of the fitted line in this lesson to predict the temperature in a city at 25° north latitude. about 81°F
7. Once a line is fitted, what is the first step toward getting an equation for the line? Estimate the coordinates of two points on the line.
8. **a.** Acapulco, Mexico, is at 17°N latitude. Use the equation in Example 2 to estimate its average April high temperature. ≈90°F
   b. The actual value for Acapulco is 87°. Give a reason why the answer in part a is closer to the actual value for Acapulco than the prediction was for Mexico City. Acapulco is at sea level.

NOTES ON QUESTIONS

Question 9: This question is important conceptually to demonstrate that not all sets of points are best fitted by a line. For **a,** a parabola might be appropriate. For **d,** there seems to be no particular pattern except that the points are rather evenly spaced within a circle.

Question 10: You could use an overhead transparency of the scattergram. (See *Teaching Aid 42.*) With a rubberband or thin rod set an estimated line for all students to use. They can discuss the best fit and establish the points in class before they do parts **d–g** on their own.

NOTES ON QUESTIONS

Question 11: This question raises some interesting issues. When can negative values make sense? If *h* is a measure of the distance a baseball is above your head when you throw it, then a negative value would mean the ball is below your head. If *t* is the number of seconds since an event happened, a negative value shows a time before it occurred. It makes sense to interpret negative latitudes as degrees south of the equator, but the temperature equation would not fit. However, in looking at the graph students may suggest that a graph for latitudes 0° to -90° could be made by reflecting the graph for positive values across the *y*-axis. Still another way to think of latitude is as a measure of distance from the equator, so the absolute value of the latitude might work in a temperature equation.

ADDITIONAL ANSWERS

10a. and b.

sample: through (6, 74) and (30, 47)

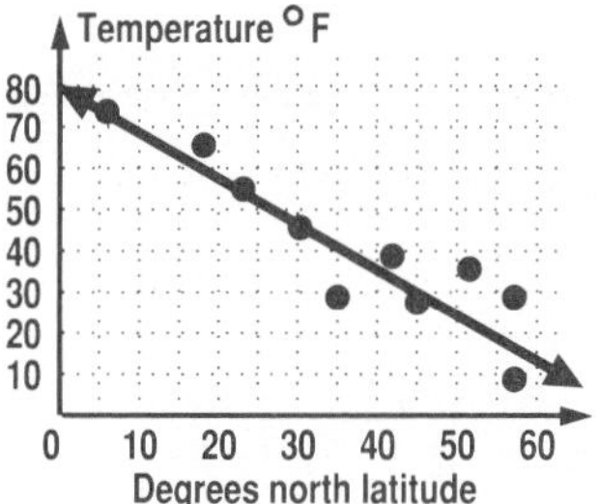

15a.

15b.

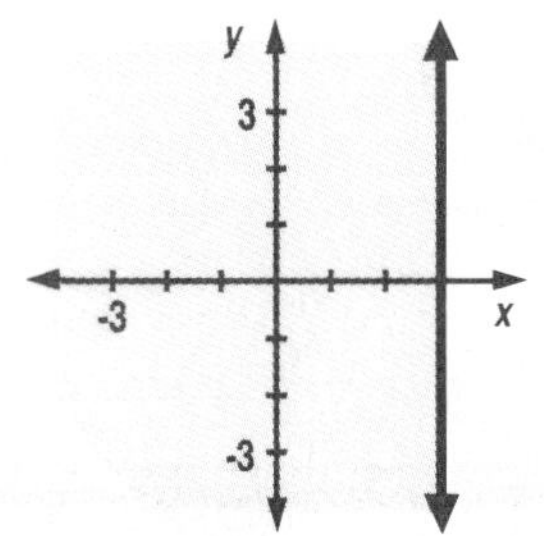

Applying the Mathematics

9. For which of the set of points below is fitting a line appropriate? **b, c**

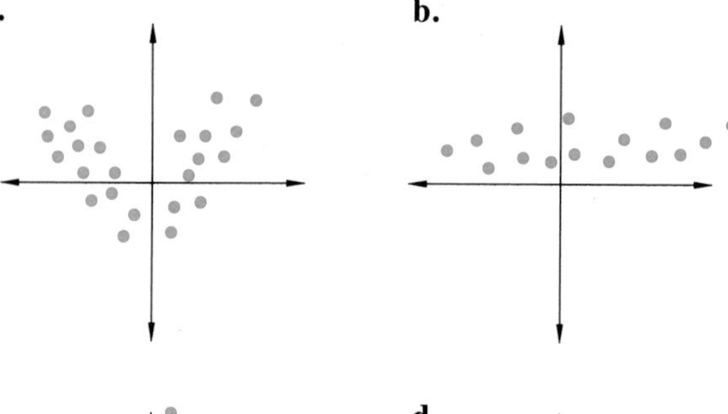

c.

d.

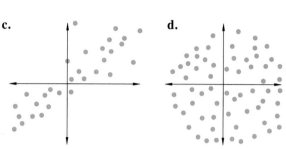

10. Use the following data. The temperatures are the mean low temperatures in January.

City	North Latitude	January Mean Low Temperature (°F)
Lagos, Nigeria	6	74
San Juan, Puerto Rico	18	67
Calcutta, India	23	55
Cairo, Egypt	30	47
Tokyo, Japan	35	29
Rome, Italy	42	39
Belgrade, Yugoslavia	45	27
London, England	52	35
Copenhagen, Denmark	56	29
Moscow, USSR	56	9

c) sample: (6, 74) and (30, 47); d) $y = -1.1x + 80$

a. Draw a scattergram showing a point for each city. **See margin.**

b. Use a ruler to fit a line to the data. **See margin.**

c. Estimate the coordinates of two points on the line you drew.

d. Find an equation for the line through the points in part c.

e. Complete the following sentence: "As you go one degree north, the January low temperature tends to __?__." **be about 1 degree colder**

f. What does the equation predict for a January mean low temperature at the equator? **about 80°F**

g. Use your equation to predict the January mean low temperature for Acapulco. (Note: the actual mean low is 70°.) **about 61°F**

h. Predict the January mean low temperature for the North Pole. **-19°**

11. *Yes or no* By using negative values of *x* in the equation in Example 1, would you expect to predict temperatures for cities south of the equator? **No**

Review

12. Give the slope and y-intercept of the line $3x + 5y = 2$. *(Lesson 8-4)* $-\frac{3}{5}, \frac{2}{5}$

13. Find an equation for the line through (3, 2) with a slope of $\frac{3}{5}$. *(Lesson 8-5)* $y = \frac{3}{5}x + \frac{1}{5}$

14. Find an equation for the line through (0, 7) and (4, 0). *(Lesson 8-6)* $y = -\frac{7}{4}x + 7$

15. Graph the points satisfying $x \leq 3$: **a.** on the number line; **b.** in the coordinate plane. *(Lessons 1-1, 7-2)* **See margin.**

16. An integer from 1 through 25 is chosen at random. Find the probability the integer is even or greater than 20. *(Lesson 3-6)* $\frac{12 + 5 - 2}{25} = \frac{3}{5}$

17. Seattle scored 17 points in the first nine minutes of a game. At that rate about how many points would they score in a 48-minute game? *(Lesson 5-7)* **about 91**

18. Solve for y. *(Lesson 6-6)*
    a. $8y = 2 + y$ $\frac{2}{7}$
    b. $By = C + y$ $\frac{C}{B - 1}$

19. Refer to the drawing below. About how far, to the nearest mile, is it from Marshall to Union? *(Lesson 7-5)* **≈74 miles**

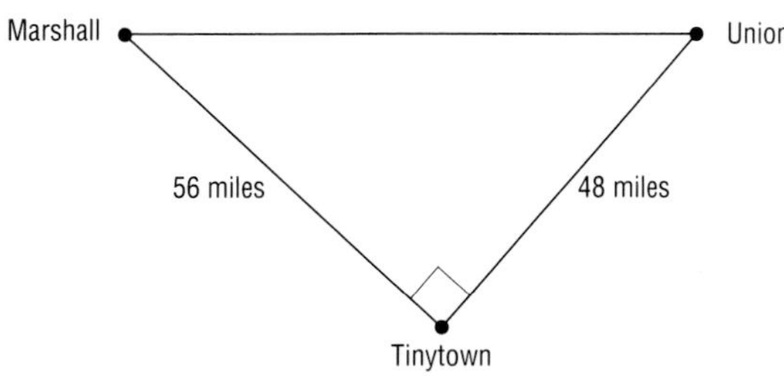

20. The scale on a map reads 1 inch = 2 miles. Two buildings are 3.6 miles apart. How far apart should they be on the map? *(Lesson 5-7)* **1.8 in.**

21. *Skill sequence* When $x = -4.2$ and $y = -0.7$, evaluate: *(Lesson 1-4)*
    a. $-\frac{-x}{y}$ 6 **b.** $\frac{-x}{-y}$ 6 **c.** $-\frac{-x}{-y}$ -6

22. The volume of a cube is 1000 cm^3. Calculate in your head. *(Lesson 4-1)*
    a. the length of an edge **10 cm**
    b. the area of a face **100 cm^2**

Exploration

23. **a.** Find the latitude of your school to the nearest degree. **Answers may vary.**
    b. Predict the April mean high temperature in °F for your latitude using the line in Example 1.
    c. Check your prediction in part b against some other source of the April mean high temperature. (Newspapers or TV weather records are possible sources.)

24. What is meant by *longitude*? **the distance east or west of the line from the North Pole to the South Pole through Greenwich, England.**

FOLLOW-UP

MORE PRACTICE
For more questions on SPUR Objectives, use *Lesson Master 8-7*, shown below.

EVALUATION
A quiz covering Lessons 8-5 through 8-7 is provided in the Teacher's Resource File.

NAME ____________

LESSON **MASTER 8–7**
QUESTIONS ON **SPUR** OBJECTIVES

■**REPRESENTATIONS** *Objective J (See pages 418–421 for objectives.)*

1. Below is a table showing the median height in cm of boys in the U.S. by age.

Age	Height (cm)	Age	Height (cm)	Age	Height (cm)
2	87	8	127	14	163
3	95	9	132	15	169
4	103	10	138	16	174
5	110	11	143	17	176
6	116	12	150	18	177
7	122	13	160		

a. Graph this data, and sketch a line to fit the data.

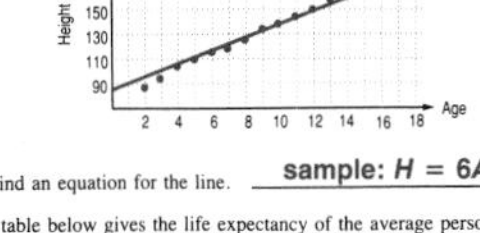

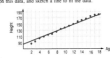

b. Find an equation for the line. **sample: $H = 6A + 80$**

2. The table below gives the life expectancy of the average person at birth in the U.S. for the years 1900–1980.

Year	Expectancy	Year	Expectancy
1900	47.3	1950	68.2
1910	50.0	1960	69.7
1920	54.1	1970	70.8
1930	59.7	1980	73.8
1940	62.9		

a. Graph this data, and sketch a line to fit the data.

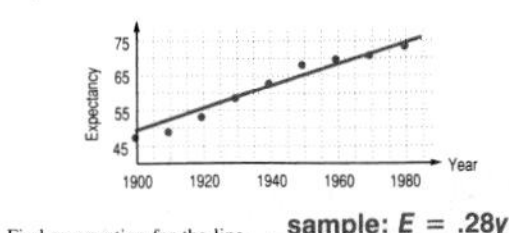

b. Find an equation for the line. **sample: $E = .28y - 481$**

c. What life expectancy would you predict in 1990? **about 76 years**

LESSON 8-8

RESOURCES
- ■ Lesson Master 8-8
- Computer Master 17

OBJECTIVES

E Rewrite an equation for a line in standard form.
H Use equations for lines to describe real situations.

TEACHING NOTES

In **Example 2** the given equation can be rewritten by multiplying both sides by 100 to clear the decimal.

Example 3 is important because it shows students an "easy" way of graphing lines in standard form. When $x = 0$, you get the y-intercept 8. When $y = 0$ you get the x-intercept 6. This is a particularly effective way to graph $Ax + By = C$ when A and B are factors of C, that is, when the intercepts are integers.

LESSON 8-8 Equations for All Lines

In this chapter, lines have been used to describe situations involving constant increase or decrease. They have also been used to fit a line to data. The slope-intercept form $y = mx + b$ arises naturally from these applications. All lines except vertical lines have equations in slope-intercept form.

Some situations naturally lead to equations of lines in a different form.

> The Ramirez family bought 4 adult and 3 children's tickets to the play. They spent \$24.00. If x is the cost of an adult ticket and y the cost of a children's ticket, then
>
> $$4x + 3y = 24.$$

The pairs of values of x and y that work in the equation above are possible costs of the ticket. For instance, since $3(4.50) + 4(2) = 24$, the adult tickets could have cost \$4.50 and the children's tickets \$2. This yields the point (4.50, 2).

This equation has the form

$$Ax + By = C.$$

All terms with variables are on one side of the equation. The constant term is on the other. This is the **standard form** for an equation of a line. Any equation for a line is either in standard form or can be rewritten in standard form.

Example 1 Rewrite $5y + 8 = 3x$ in standard form and find the values of A, B, and C.

Solution In standard form, the terms with variables are on the left side, so add $-3x$ to both sides.

$$-3x + 5y + 8 = -3x + 3x$$
$$-3x + 5y + 8 = 0$$

Now add -8 to both sides to get the constant on the right side.

$$-3x + 5y = -8.$$

This is standard form with $A = -3$, $B = 5$, and $C = -8$.

Some people prefer that the coefficient A be positive in standard form. To rewrite the equation in Example 1 with a positive A, you could multiply each side by -1.

$$-1(-3x + 5y) = -1(-8)$$
$$3x - 5y = 8$$

Both sides of this equation can be multiplied by any number. For instance, multiplying by 2 yields

$$6x - 10y = 16.$$

This is another equation for the same line. Every line has many equations in standard form. The equation $3x - 5y = 8$ is usually considered simplest because 3, 5, and 8 have no common factors.

Example 2 Rewrite $y = .25x$ in standard form with integer values of A, B, and C.

Solution Since $.25 = \frac{25}{100} = \frac{1}{4}$, multiply both sides by 4.

$$4y = x$$

Now, add $-x$ to get both variables on the left side.

$$-x + 4y = -x + x$$
$$-x + 4y = 0$$

Here $A = -1$, $B = 4$, and $C = 0$.

ADDITIONAL EXAMPLES

1. Rewrite $y = -7x - 2$ in standard form.
$7x + y = -2$

2. Rewrite $y = \frac{3}{8}x + \frac{1}{2}$ in standard form using integer values of A, B, and C.
$-3x + 8y = 4$; if you wish A to be positive, then $3x - 8y = -4$

3. Graph $5x - 2y = -20$.

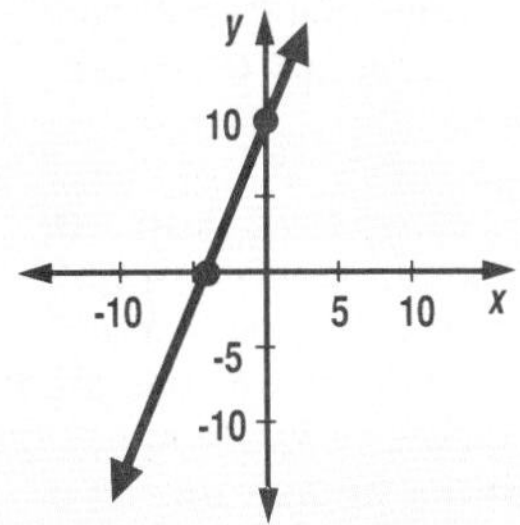

4. Day help kitchen workers at a restaurant earn $10 for each lunch meal and $15 for each dinner meal they work. If a worker earns $160, write an equation in standard form to describe the possible combinations of lunches and dinners.
$10x + 15y = 160$

NOTES ON QUESTIONS
Questions 6 and 7: The equations do not have convenient coefficients for the intercept method of graphing. On the other hand, the equations in **Questions 11 and 12** do have convenient coefficients.

Question 14d: To convince students that the equation is not the equation of a line, you might ask them to find three points and calculate the slopes between them.

Questions 19 and 20: These questions use data from the Olympics. You might want to discuss these problems *before* you assign them for homework. As a group, you might establish the points for a good fitting line so that students can work towards the same equations. Two convenient points to use are (1900, 35) and (1960, 60). Also, students should know why there is no data for 1916 (World War I) and 1940 and 1944 (World War II). Some students may know that the United States did not participate in the 1980 Moscow Olympics, and the Soviet block nations did not participate in the 1984 Los Angeles Olympics. Had all nations participated in the last two Olympics, the discus throw might have produced new records which would have followed the linear trend represented by most of the data. Here is a situation in which politics may have affected the data.

Making Connections for Questions 22-24: These questions prepare for the next lesson on graphing linear inequalities.

Making Connections for Question 28: This question helps to prepare students for the case of parallel lines in the discussion of systems, which they will encounter in Chapter 11.

Graphing a line is sometimes easier when its equation is given in standard form. This is particularly the case when A and B are factors of C. The strategy is to find the intercepts. Recall that the y-intercept is the value of y when $x = 0$. The ***x*-intercept** is the value of x when $y = 0$. It is the x-coordinate of the point of intersection of the graph and the x-axis.

Example 3 Graph $4x + 3y = 24$, the equation of the ticket costs of the Ramirez family.

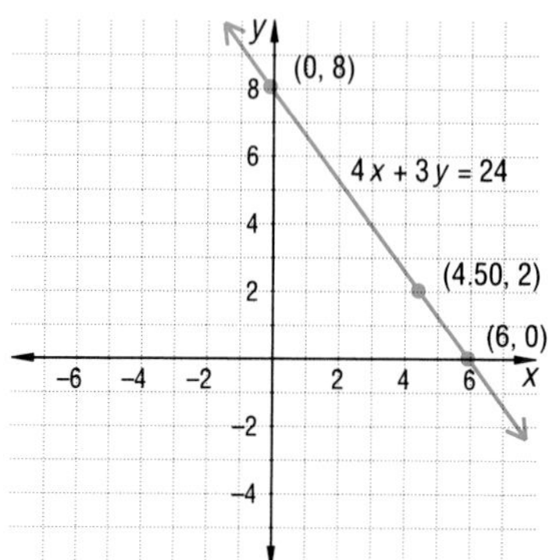

Solution Since 4 and 3 are factors of 24, it is easy to find the intercepts. When $x = 0$, $3y = 24$, so $y = 8$. This gives the point (0, 8). When $y = 0$, $4x = 24$, so $x = 6$. This gives the point (6, 0). Plot the points and connect them.

Check Find a third point satisfying the equation. Earlier we noted that (4.50, 2) satisfies the equation. Is it on the graph? Yes.

Lines in standard form often arise naturally from real situations.

Example 4 Roast beef sells for \$6 a pound. Shrimp is \$12 a pound. Andy has \$96 to buy beef and shrimp for a party. Write an equation in standard form to describe the different possible combinations Andy could buy.

Solution
Let x = pounds of roast beef bought, so $6x$ = cost of roast beef.
Let y = pounds of shrimp bought, so $12y$ = cost of shrimp.

$$\text{Cost of roast beef} + \text{cost of shrimp} = \text{total cost}$$
$$6x + 12y = 96$$

This equation on page 406 is in standard form. It can be further simplified by multiplying both sides by $\frac{1}{6}$.

$$\frac{1}{6}(6x + 12y) = \frac{1}{6} \cdot 96$$
$$x + 2y = 16$$

Check To check the equation, suppose Andy buys 6 pounds of roast beef. He will have spent 6 · \$6 = \$36. He will have \$96 − \$36 = \$60 left to spend on shrimp. At \$12 per pound he can buy $\frac{60}{12} = 5$ pounds of shrimp.

Does (6, 5) work in $x + 2y = 16$? Yes, $6 + 2 \cdot 5 = 16$.

The lines in all these Examples are *oblique,* meaning they are not horizontal or vertical. Recall from Lesson 7-2, if a line is vertical, then it has an equation of the form $x = h$. A horizontal line has an equation $y = k$. These are already in standard form. For example,

$x = 3$ is equivalent to $1 \cdot x + 0 \cdot y = 3$
$A = 1, B = 0, C = 3$

$y = -\frac{1}{2}$ is equivalent to $0 \cdot x + 1 \cdot y = -\frac{1}{2}$.
$A = 0, B = 1, C = -\frac{1}{2}$

Thus *every line* has an equation in the standard form $Ax + By = C$.

Questions

Covering the Reading

1. The equation $y = mx + b$ arises naturally from what two applications covered in this chapter?
constant increase/decrease situations and fitting a line to data

2. a. If each adult ticket cost the Ramirez family (at the beginning of the lesson) \$3.75, how much would a child's ticket have cost? \$3

b. Give the coordinates of the point. Can you find the point on the graph of Example 3? (3.75, 3)

3. The form of the equation $Ax + By = C$ is called __?__.
standard form

4. __?__ lines cannot be written in slope-intercept form. Vertical

5. Every line can be written in the form __?__. $Ax + By = C$

In 6 and 7, the line is in the form $Ax + By = C$. Give the values of A, B, and C.

6. $4x + 2y = 5$
$A = 4; B = 2; C = 5$

7. $x - 8y = 2$
$A = 1; B = -8; C = 2$

In 8–10, write the equation in standard form. Give values of A, B, and C.

8. $2x = 3y - 12$ **9.** $y = 4x$ **10.** $-4y = 20$

8) $2x - 3y = -12; A = 2, B = -3, C = -12$; 9) $-4x + y = 0; A = -4, B = 1, C = 0$

ADDITIONAL ANSWERS

10. $0x - 4y = 20; A = 0, B = -4, C = 20$ or $0x + 4y = -20: A = 0, B = 4, C = -20$

11.

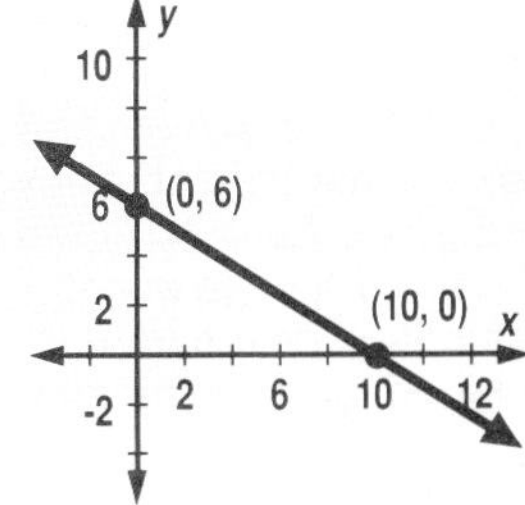

12.

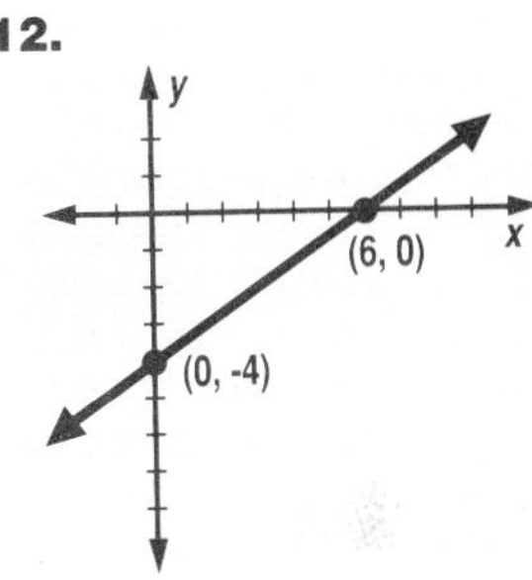

16a. $5f + s = 36$, where f = the number of fives and s = the number of singles.

16b.

f	s
0	36
1	31
2	26

16c.

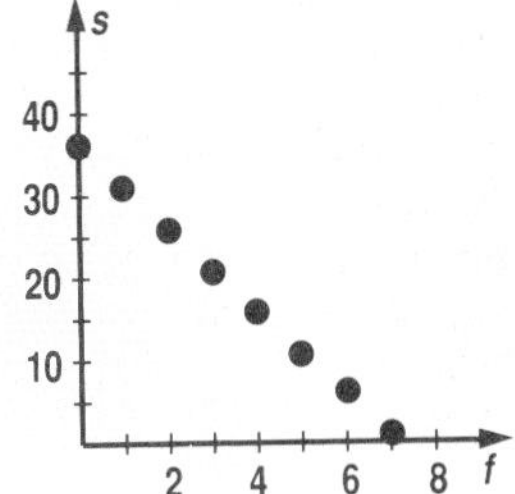

FOLLOW-UP

MORE PRACTICE
For more questions on SPUR Objectives, use *Lesson Master 8-8,* shown on page 409.

EXTENSION
Slope-intercept and standard forms are not the only forms of equations for lines. Any oblique line that does not contain the origin has a unique equation of the form

$$\frac{x}{a} + \frac{y}{b} = 1,$$

where a and b are its x-intercept and y-intercept, respectively. This is called the *intercept form* for the equation of a line. The intercept form is often used in later courses to describe asymptotes of hyperbolas. Ask students to consider the equations in Questions 6–12. Which lines are horizontal? (10) Which are vertical? (none) Which contain the origin? (9) For the rest, give the equation in intercept form.

6. $\frac{x}{\frac{5}{4}} + \frac{y}{\frac{5}{2}} = 1;$

7. $\frac{x}{2} + \frac{y}{-\frac{1}{4}} = 1;$

8. $\frac{x}{-6} + \frac{y}{4} = 1;$

11. $\frac{x}{10} + \frac{y}{6} = 1;$

12. $\frac{x}{6} + \frac{y}{-4} = 1.$

11, 12, 16, 19a. See margin, page 407.

19b. $y = .42x - 763$

19d. sample: The line is an estimate.

20. $\approx$ **226.4 ft**

In 11 and 12, graph using the method of Example 3. See margin.

11. $3x + 5y = 30$ **12.** $2x - 3y = 12$

13. Refer to Example 4. Find three different combinations of roast beef and shrimp Andy could buy. sample: (4, 6), (6, 5), (8, 4)

Applying the Mathematics

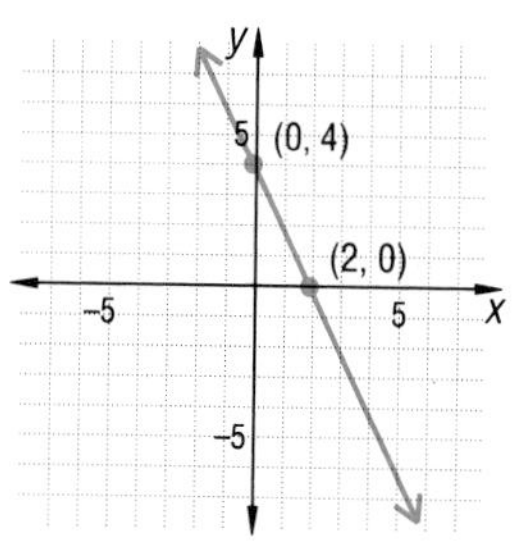

14. *Multiple choice* Which of the following is *not* an equation for a line?
(a) $x + 7y = 3$ (b) $y = x + 3$
(c) $5x = 3$ (d) $xy = 3$

15. A 100-point test has x questions worth 2 points apiece and y questions worth 4 points apiece. Write an equation that describes all possible numbers of questions. $2x + 4y = 100$

16. Carl has \$36 in five-dollar bills and singles. How many of each kind of bill does he have?
a. Write an equation to describe this situation. See margin.
b. Give three solutions. See margin.
c. Graph all possible solutions. (The graph will be discrete.) See margin.

17. Write an equation in standard form for the line through (0, 4) and (2, 0). $y + 2x = 4$

Review

18. Find an equation for the line through the points (-1, 7) and (1, 1). *(Lesson 8-6)* $y = -3x + 4$

19. The length of the winning toss in the men's discus throw has shown a steady increase since the first Olympics in 1896. The scattergram below shows the winning tosses in meters. *(Lesson 8-7)*

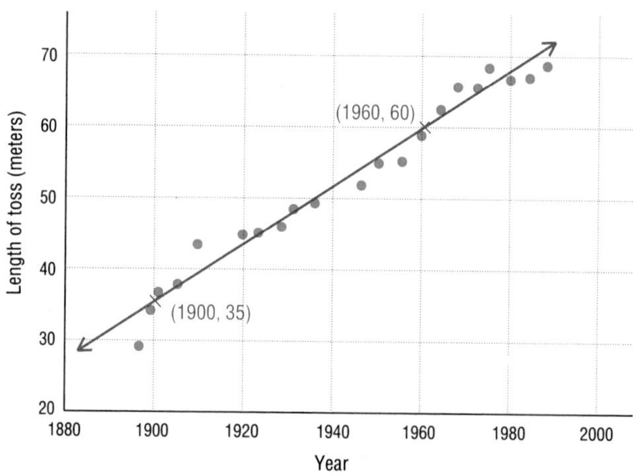

a. Trace the graph and fit a line to the data. See above.
b. Find an equation for the line in part a. sample: (1900, 35), (1960, 60)
c. Use your equation to predict the length of the winning toss in 1992. ≈74 meters
d. Why might the prediction for 1992 be incorrect? See margin.

408

20. Refer to Question 19. What is the length of the Olympic Record discus throw in feet? (Recall that 1 in. = 2.54 cm) *(4-2)* See margin.

21. Graph in the plane: $y < 17$. *(Lesson 7-2)* See margin.

In 22–24, determine whether (0, 0) is a solution to the sentence. *(Lesson 2-7)*

22. $x + y < -4$ No

23. $6x - y > -6$ Yes

24. $12x > y + 13$ No

25. A regular die is tossed once and a coin is flipped once. What is the probability of getting a 3 on the die and tails on the coin? *(Lesson 4-7)* $\frac{1}{12}$

26. *Skill sequence* Solve. *(Lessons 3-3, 4-5)*

a. $x - 4 = -1$ 3

b. $-y - 4 = -1$ -3

c. $-4 - z = -1$ -3

27.

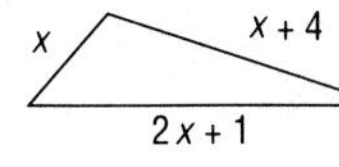

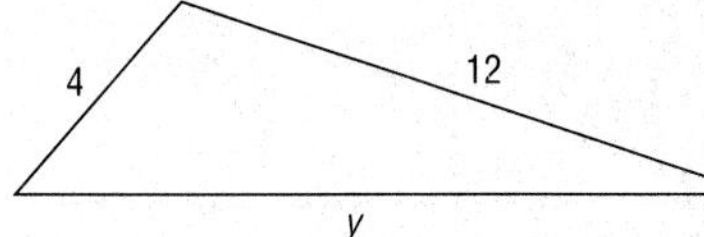

The triangles above are similar, with corresponding sides parallel. *(Lesson 5-8)*

a. Find x. 2

b. Find y. 10

c. Knowing the actual lengths, redraw the triangles to make them more accurate. See margin.

Exploration

28. A graphing calculator or computer graphing program may be useful in this question. See margin.

a. Graph the lines with equations:

$$3x + 2y = 6$$
$$3x + 2y = 12$$
$$3x + 2y = 18$$

b. What happens to the graph of $3x + 2y = C$ as C gets larger?

c. Try values of C that are negative. What can you say about the graphs of $3x + 2y = C$ then?

21.

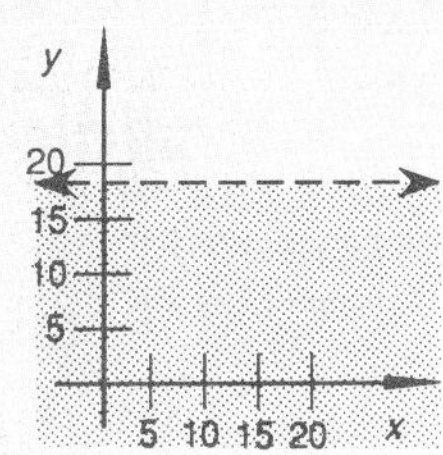

27c.

28a.

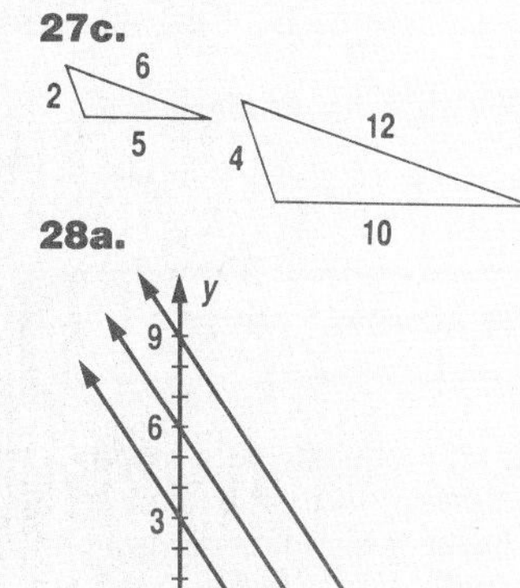

28b. The graph remains parallel to the first line, and slides to the upper-right.

28c. Sample: Try $3x + 2y = -6$. The graph is still parallel to the first line, but slides to the lower-left.

NAME ______

LESSON **MASTER 8–8**
QUESTIONS ON **SPUR** OBJECTIVES

■PROPERTIES *Objective E (See pages 418–421 for objectives.)*
In 1–6, rewrite the equation in slope-intercept form.

1. $5x + 2y = 10$ $y = -\frac{5}{2}x + 5$

2. $6x = 16 - 3y$ $y = -2x + \frac{16}{3}$

3. $-15x + 7y = 14$ $y = \frac{15}{7}x + 2$

4. $-7x = 6 - 13y$ $y = \frac{7}{13}x + \frac{6}{13}$

5. $2x + y = -6$ $y = -2x - 6$

6. $12x = -15 - 3y$ $y = -4x - 5$

In 7–12, rewrite the equation in standard form with integer coefficients.

7. $1.1x = .2y + 9$ $11x - 2y = 90$

8. $0.6y = 0.7x - 2$ $7x - 6y = 20$

9. $\frac{2}{3}x - \frac{3}{4}y - 1 = 0$ $8x - 9y = 12$

10. $y = -\frac{4}{3}x - 1$ $4x + 3y = -3$

11. $5.5x - 3y = 1.0$ $11x - 6y = 2$

12. $0.6x = 1.6 - 5.3y$ $6x + 53y = 16$

■USES *Objective H*

13. Tickets for the concert are \$6 and \$4. If s six-dollar tickets and f four-dollar tickets were sold and \$1000 was taken in, **a.** give a possible pair of values of s and f and **b.** write an equation relating s and f.

a. sample: $s = 50$, $f = 175$ **b.** $6s + 4f = 1000$

14. Paula worked for x hours at \$4 an hour and y hours at time and a half. She earned a total of \$48. Write an equation that relates x and y.

$4x + 6y = 48$

 71

LESSON 8-9

RESOURCES
■ Lesson Master 8-9

OBJECTIVE

K Graph linear inequalities.

TEACHING NOTES

If an inequality is in slope-intercept form, it is easy to decide which half-plane to shade. If $y > mx + b$, then you shade the upper half-plane. The y-coordinates of points shaded should be bigger than the y-coordinates of corresponding points on the line $y = mx + b$. If $y < mx + b$, shade the lower half-plane.

The reasoning in the paragraph above seems natural to adults, but the concept is a new one to students, so do not be surprised if your students feel that they have to check points by substituting. Checking is certainly necessary if the line is in standard form and is good verification of the fundamental idea of a solution to a sentence: an ordered pair is in the solution set of a sentence if and only if the corresponding point lies on the graph.

LESSON

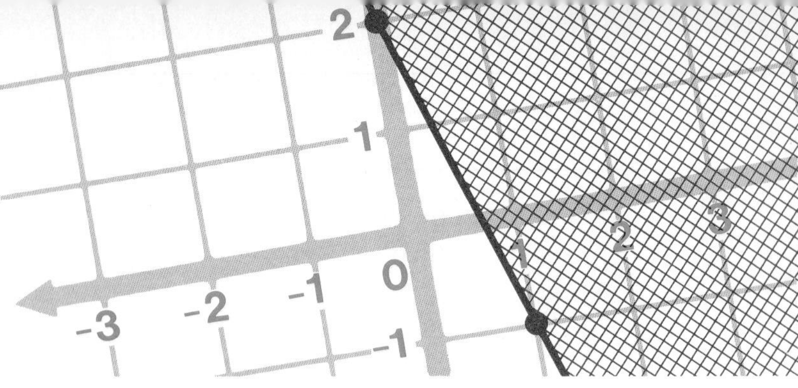

8-9 Graphing Linear Inequalities

You have graphed inequalities on the plane with horizontal and vertical lines in Lesson 7-2. This lesson extends linear inequalities to all lines in the plane.

Example 1 Draw the graph of $y \geq -3x + 2$.

Solution First graph the boundary line that separates the two regions. Here the boundary line is $y = -3x + 2$. Its y-intercept is 2. Then, since the slope is -3, plot the point 1 unit to the right and 3 units down. That point is (1, -1). Draw the line through (0, 2) and (1, -1).

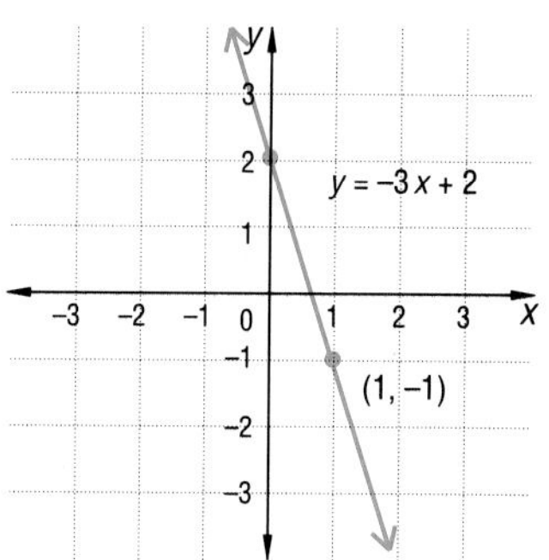

The $\geq$ sign in $y \geq -3x + 2$ indicates that points are desired whose y-coordinate is greater than or equal to the y values which satisfy $y = -3x + 2$. Since y values get larger as one goes higher, shade the entire region above the line.

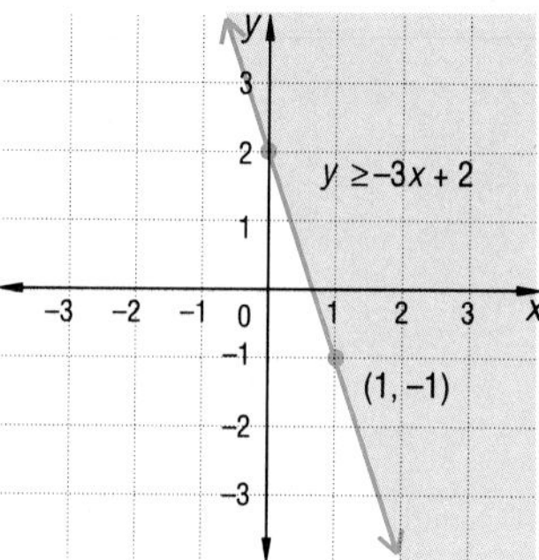

410

Check Try the point (0, 3), which is in the shaded region. Does it satisfy the inequality? Is $3 > -3 \cdot 0 + 2$? Yes, 3 is greater than 2. So the correct side of the line has been shaded.

The regions on either side of a line in a plane are called half-planes.

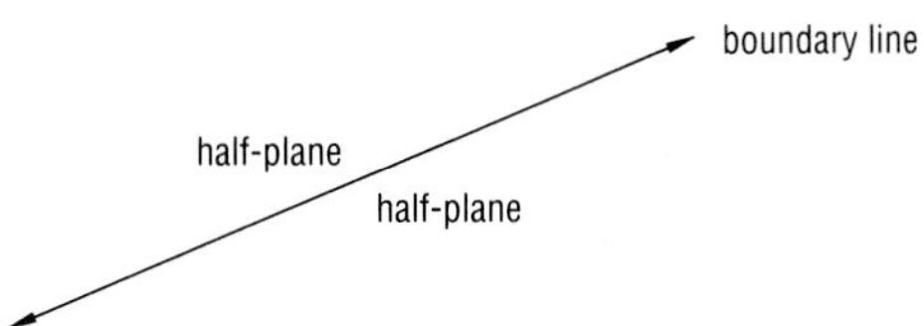

So the graph of $y \geq -3x + 2$ can be described as a line and one of its half-planes.

In general:
1. The graphs of $y > mx + b$ and $y < mx + b$ are the half-planes of the line $y = mx + b$.
2. The graphs of $Ax + By > C$ and $Ax + By < C$ are the half-planes of the line $Ax + By = C$.

When an inequality is in the standard form $Ax + By > C$, you cannot use the inequality sign to determine which side of the line to shade. A more direct method, the testing of a point, is usually used. The point (0, 0) is often chosen if it is not on the boundary line.

With the inequalities $\leq$ or $\geq$, the boundary line is drawn as a *solid* line as in Example 1. But with $<$ or $>$, the boundary is *not* part of the solution. It is not included in the graph. In this case, the boundary is drawn as a *dotted* line.

Example 2 Graph $3x - 4y > 12$.

Solution Since 3 and 4 are factors of 12, it is easy to find the intercepts of the boundary line $3x - 4y = 12$. They are (0, -3) and (4, 0). Plot these points and graph a dotted line through them. To determine which side of the line is to be shaded, substitute (0, 0) into the original equation. Is $3 \cdot 0 - 4 \cdot 0 > 12$? Is $0 > 12$? No. Since (0, 0) is in the upper half-plane and is *not* a solution, shade the lower half-plane. The finished graph is at the right.

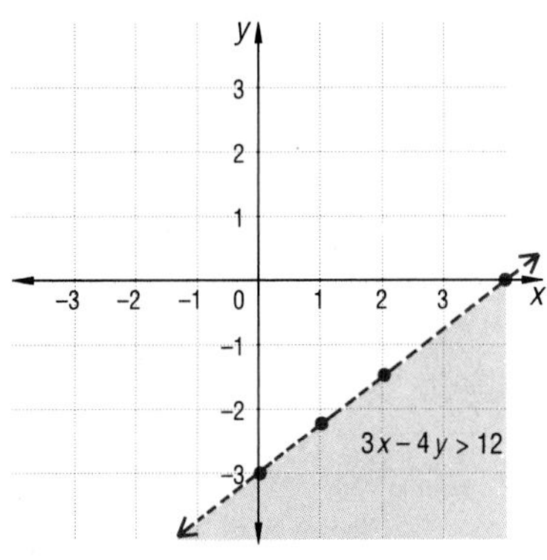

ADDITIONAL EXAMPLES

1. Graph $y < 3x - 4$.

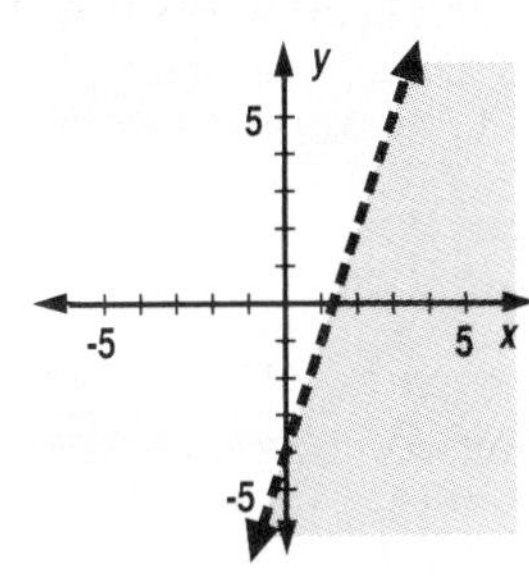

2. Graph $2x + 5y \geq 10$.

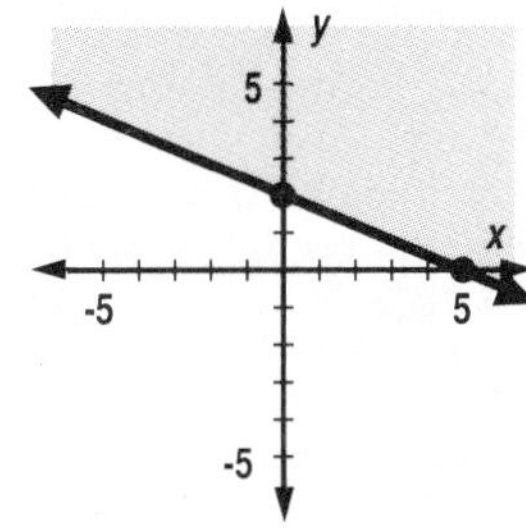

3. Suppose crepe paper costs $2.00 per package and balloons are $1.50 per pack. The decorations committee for the dance bought some of each and stayed within their $60 budget. Graph the possible numbers of packages of each they could have bought. (Let b be the number of packs of balloons and c be the number of packages of crepe paper.)
$1.50b + 2.00c \leq 60.00$, or $1.5b + 2c \leq 60$.

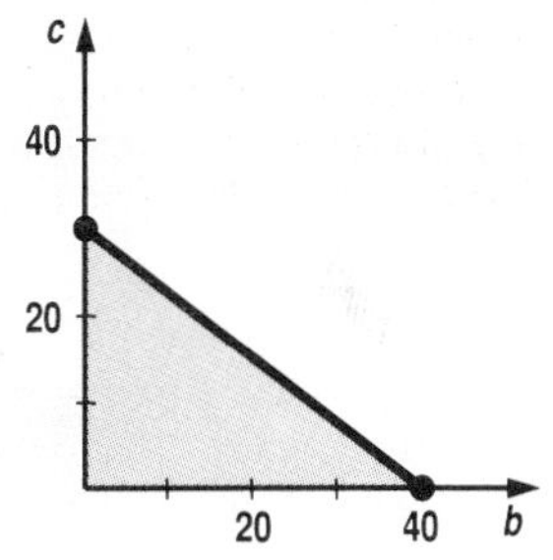

NOTES ON QUESTIONS
Question 11: This question, like **Question 12,** has a limited domain, but there are enough solutions to make graphing worthwhile.

Question 12: Here, it is easier to list the solutions than to graph them.

Making Connections for Question 13: Students may not realize that this question involves the intersection of two half-planes. You might compare the process used here with that of graphing solutions of $x > 5$ and $x < 8$ on a number line.

Questions 18b and 18c: These can be answered by chunking.

ADDITIONAL ANSWERS
3. Graph a dotted or solid line as the solution to the corresponding linear equation. Then shade the half-plane that satisfies the condition.

6.

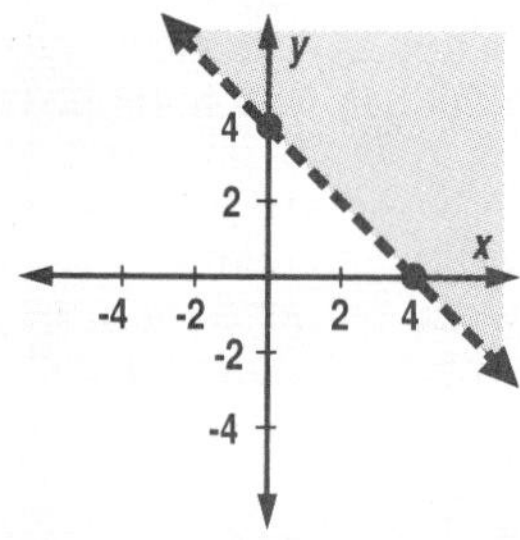

7.

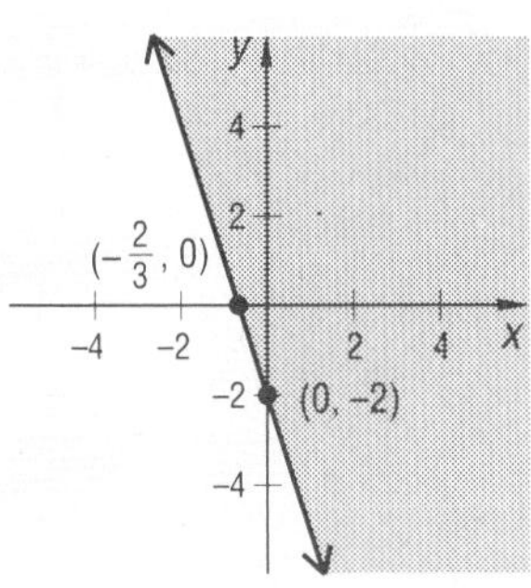

In summary, to graph any linear inequality:
1. Graph a dotted or solid line as the solution to the corresponding linear equation.
2. Shade the half-plane that satisfies the condition. [You may have to test a point. If possible, use (0, 0).]

Linear inequalities can help you to understand certain situations.

Example 3 Serena has less than $5.00 in nickels and dimes. How many nickels and dimes might she have?

Solution There are too many possibilities to list, so we graph them.
Let n = the number of nickels Serena has.
d = the number of dimes Serena has.
Since each nickel is worth .05 and each dime is worth .10,

$$.05n + .10d < 5.00.$$

Multiply both sides by 100 to make the sentence easier to work with.

$$5n + 10d < 500$$

This inequality is graphed below.

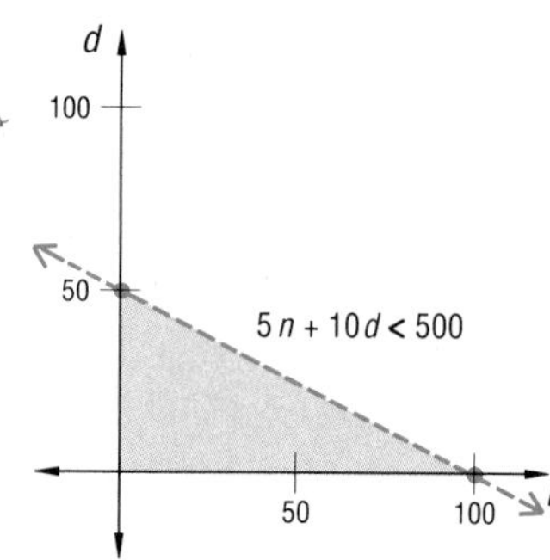

Since n and d cannot be negative, only the points in the first quadrant or on the axes are shaded. The graph is actually discrete, since n and d must be integers, but there are so many points that shading is easier. The graph thus shows that there are very many solutions.

Check (0, 0) is on the graph. If Serena has 0 nickels and 0 dimes, does she have less than $5.00? Of course.

Questions

Covering the Reading

1. The graphs of __?__ and __?__ are the half-planes of the line $y = mx + b$.
   $y > mx + b$; $y < mx + b$
2. The graphs of __?__ and __?__ are the half-planes of the line $Ax + By = C$.
   $Ax + By > C$; $Ax + By < C$
3. Name the two steps to graph any linear inequality. See margin.
4. In the graph of each inequality, tell whether the boundary line should be drawn as a solid or dotted line.
   a. $y > -4x - 7$ dotted **b.** $y \leq -4x - 7$ solid
   c. $4x + y < -7$ dotted **d.** $4x + y \geq -7$ solid
5. **a.** What point is usually chosen to test which half-plane is shaded? (0, 0)
   b. When would you not choose it? when it lies on the boundary line

In 6–9, graph the inequality. See margin.

6. $x + y > 4$
7. $y \geq -3x - 2$
8. $5x - y > 3$
9. $5x - y \leq 3$
10. Ted has less than \$4.00 in quarters and dimes. How many quarters and dimes does he have? $0.10d + 0.25q < 4.00$; samples: (25, 5), (15, 9), (5, 13), (0, 14); see margin.

Applying the Mathematics

11. "It will take at least 20 points to make the playoffs," the hockey team coach told the players. "We get 2 points for a win and 1 for a tie." Let W be the number of wins and T the number of ties.
    a. Write an inequality to describe the values of W and T that will enable the team to make the playoffs. $2W + T \geq 20$
    b. Graph these values. See margin.

8.

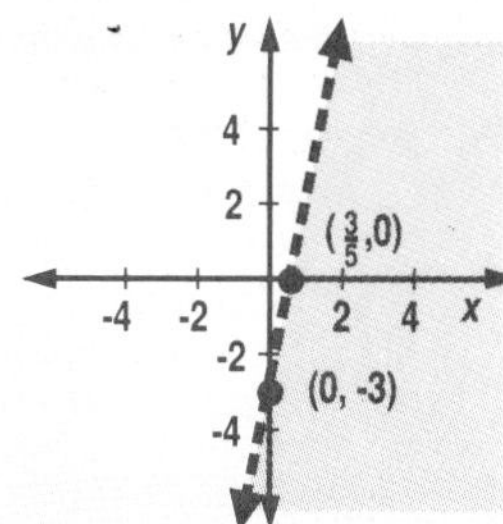

9.

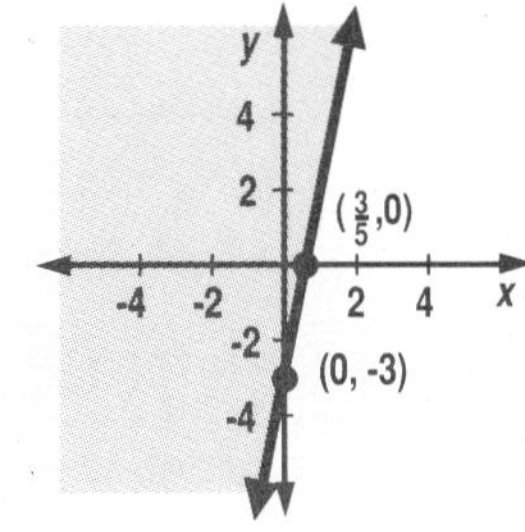

10. d and q must be whole numbers on the shaded part of the graph:

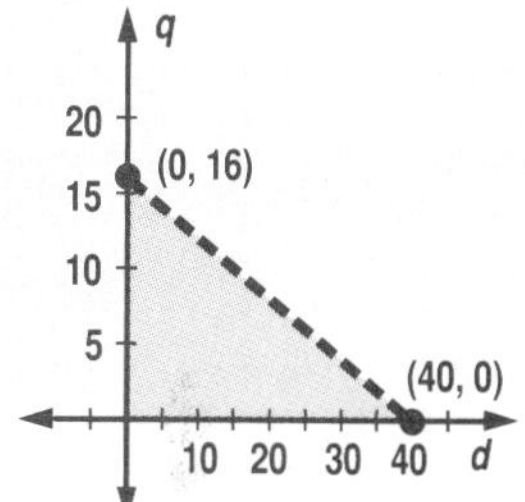

11b.

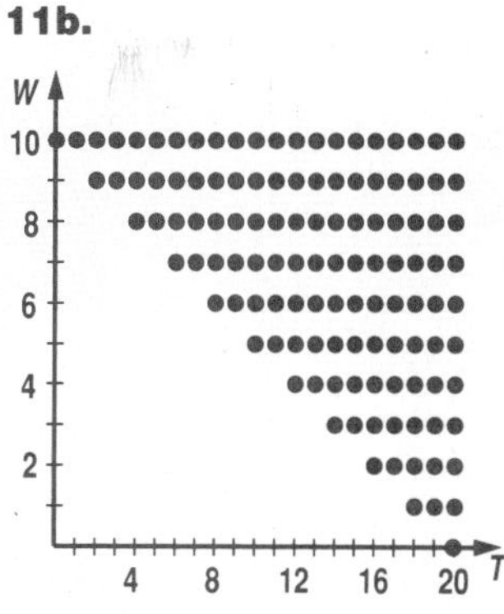

FOLLOW-UP

MORE PRACTICE
For more questions on SPUR Objectives, use *Lesson Master 8-9,* shown on page 415.

13a.

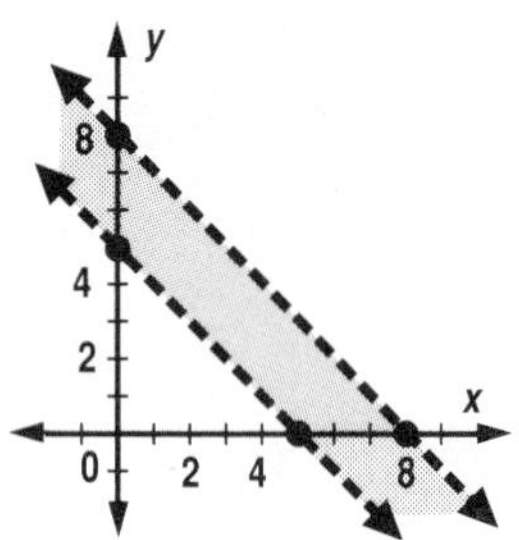

13b. The graph is the strip of infinite length that lies between the two boundary lines.

23.

No. of Dimes	No. of Nickels	No. of Ways
0	up to 99	100
1	up to 97	98
2	up to 95	96
3	up to 93	94
⋮	⋮	⋮
24	up to 51	52
25	up to 49	50
26	up to 47	48
⋮	⋮	⋮
47	up to 5	6
48	up to 3	4
49	up to 1	2

100 + 24(100) + 50 = 2550 ways to have up to $5.00.

12. Suppose m and n are positive integers. How many points (m, n) satisfy $m + n < 5$? **6**

13. a. Graph the points (x, y) for which $x + y > 5$ and $x + y < 8$. **See margin.**
b. Describe the graph. **See margin.**

Review

14. Write $4x - 28 = 3y$ in standard form. Give the values of A, B, and C. *(Lesson 8-8)* **4x − 3y = 28; A = 4, B = -3, C = 28**

15. A travel agency bought 25 coach tickets and 5 first-class tickets for a flight. If the agency spent $55,000, write an equation that describes all possible costs of the tickets. *(Lesson 8-8)* **25c + 5f = 55,000**

16. Find an equation for the line through (-6, 1) with slope 3. *(Lesson 8-5)* **y = 3x + 19**

17. A rectangular field is 100 yards wide by 300 yards long. **≈83.8 yds**

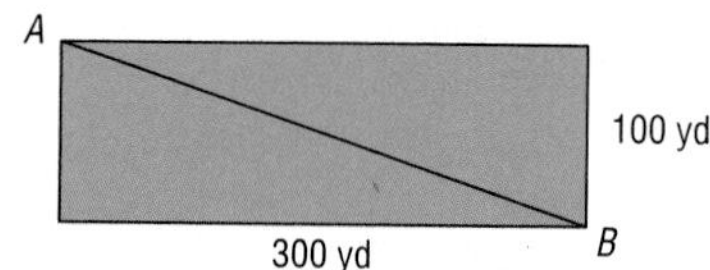

How much shorter is the distance from A to B if you walk diagonally across the field instead of around the outside edges? *(Lesson 7-5)*

18. *Skill sequence* Solve. *(Lessons 4-4, 7-8)*
a. $3x = 1987$ **$662.\overline{3}$**
b. $14y - 11y = 1987$ **$662.\overline{3}$**
c. $14(z - 3) - 11(z - 3) = 1987$ **$665.\overline{3}$**

19. Rewrite in decimal form. *(Appendix B)*
a. 10^{-1} **0.1**
b. $3 \cdot 10^{-2}$ **.03**
c. $2 \cdot 5 \cdot 10^{-6}$ **.00001**

20. Give the exact circumference. *(Lesson 1-5)*

a. **8π**

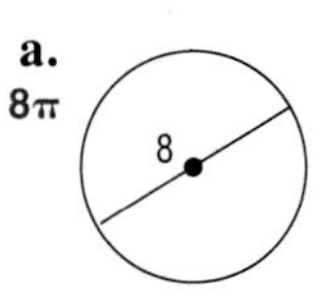

diameter = 8

b. **0.4π**

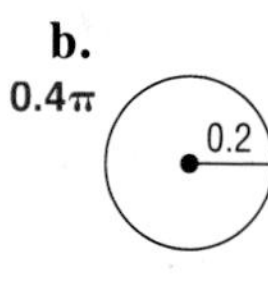

radius = 0.2

c. **6xπ**

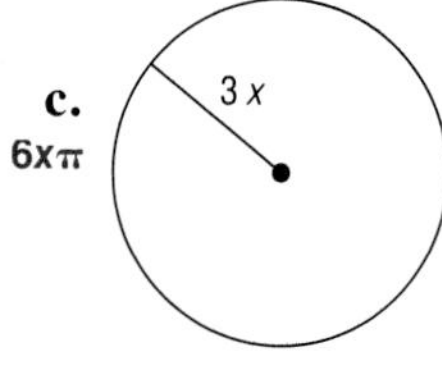

radius = 3x

In 21 and 22, use the graphs below.

21. Of the 10,886,000 males aged 25–29 in 1980 how many were single? *(Lesson 5-4)* **3,603,266**

22. What was the average yearly increase in the percentage of females aged 20–24 staying single?

a. from 1970 to 1980? **1.44%**

b. from 1980 to 1987? **1.51%**

c. Is the rate of increase constant from 1970 to 1987? *(Lesson 8-1)* **No**

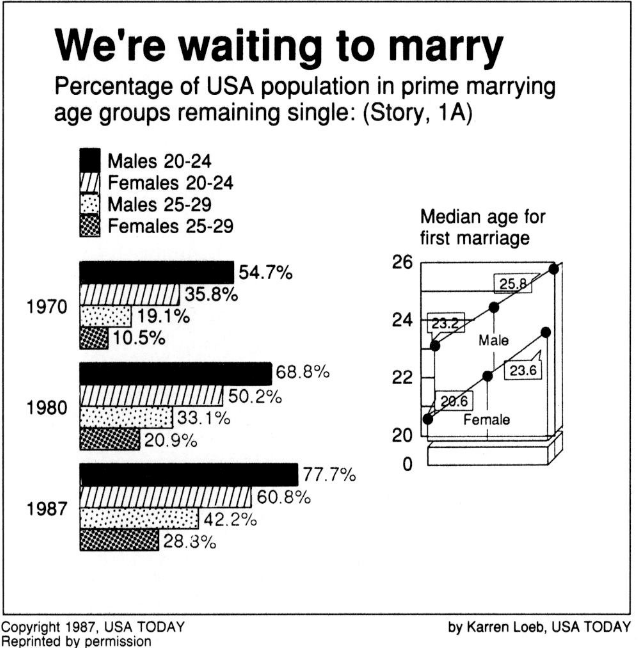

Copyright 1987, USA TODAY
Reprinted by permission

by Karren Loeb, USA TODAY

Exploration

23. Determine, any way you can, the number of solutions to Example 3. **See margin.**

EXTENSION

In **Example 3,** it is noted that there are too many possibilities to list. More accurately, there are too many possibilities for a *short* list. To calculate the total number of lattice points inside the triangle, Pick's Theorem can be used. That theorem gives the area A of a polygon whose vertices are lattice points (coordinates are integers) in terms of the number B of lattice points on the polygon itself and the number of lattice points I in its interior. $A = I + B/2 - 1$.

Solve the formula for I: $I = A + 1 - B/2$. In **Example 3,** the area of the right triangle is $50 \cdot 100/2$, or 2500. The number of points on the boundary is 51 on the y-axis, 100 more on the x-axis, and 49 more on the hypotenuse. Thus $B = 200$. And so the number of points inside is $2500 + 1 - 200/2$, or 2401.

You might wish to give students the formula and ask them to determine the number of interior lattice points as in the previous paragraph.

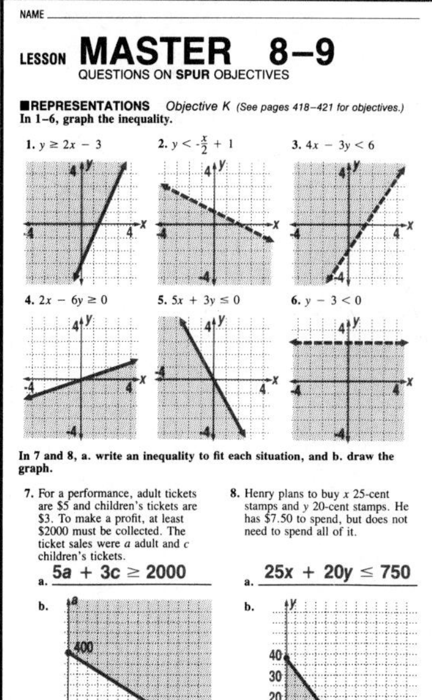

SUMMARY

The Summary gives an overview of the entire chapter and provides an opportunity for students to consider the material as a whole. Thus, the Summary can be used to help students relate the concepts presented in the chapter.

VOCABULARY

Terms, symbols, and properties are listed by lesson to provide a checklist of things a student must know. Emphasize to students that they should read the vocabulary list carefully before starting the Progress Self-Test. If students do not understand the meaning of a term, they should refer back to the indicated lesson.

Definitions or descriptions of all terms in the vocabulary list may be found in the Glossary.

ADDITIONAL ANSWERS

3. $\frac{1 - -5}{-2 - 4} = \frac{6}{-6} = -1$; $\frac{-20 - 1}{-20 - -2} = \frac{-21}{22}$

Since $-1 \neq \frac{-21}{22}$, the points do not lie on the same line.

11. Do a quick estimate. Between 1942 and 1944 the increase was from about 3 million to 8 million, or 5 million personnel. From 1943 to 1945 the increase was a little over 1 million. From 1944 to 1946 was a decrease. So the greatest 2-year increase was from 1942 to 1944.

16.

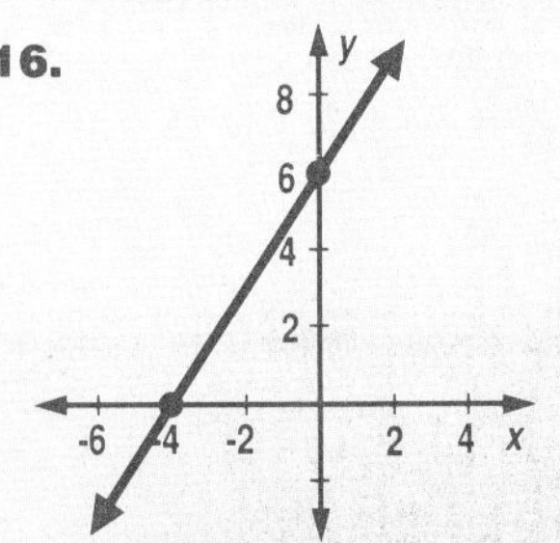

Summary

The rate of change between two points (x_1, y_1) and (x_2, y_2) is $\frac{y_2 - y_1}{x_2 - x_1}$. When points all lie on the same line, the rate of change between them is constant and is called the slope of the line. The slope tells how much the line rises or falls as you move one unit to the right. When it is positive, the line goes up to the right. When the slope is negative, the line falls to the right. When the slope is 0, the line is horizontal. The slope of vertical lines is not defined.

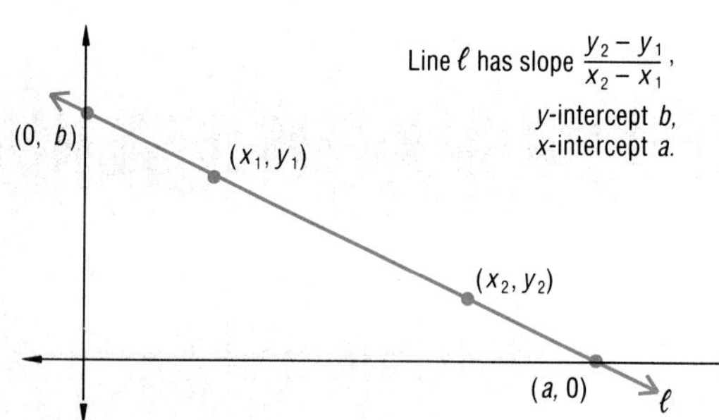

Constant increase or constant decrease situations lead naturally to linear equations of the form $y = mx + b$. The graph of the set of points (x, y) satisfying this equation is a line with slope m and y-intercept b. Other situations lead naturally to linear equations in the standard form $Ax + By = C$. When the = sign in these equations is replaced by $<$ or $>$, the graph of the resulting linear inequality is a half-plane, the set of points on one side of the line.

A line is determined by any point on it and its slope, and its equation can be found from this information. Likewise, an equation can be found for the line containing two given points. If more than two points are given, then there may be more than one line determined. You can then find two points on a line that comes close to all the points and use these points to determine an equation for the line.

Vocabulary

Below are the most important terms and phrases for this chapter. You should be able to give a definition or general description and a specific example of each.

Lesson 8-1
rate of change

Lesson 8-2
constant decrease
slope

Lesson 8-4
y-intercept
slope-intercept form
Slope-Intercept Property

Lesson 8-7
fitting a line to data

Lesson 8-8
standard form for an equation of a line
x-intercept

Progress Self-Test

Take this test as you would take a test in class. You will need graph paper, a ruler, and a calculator. Then check your work with the solutions in the Selected Answers section in the back of the book.

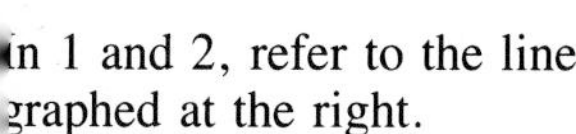

In 1 and 2, refer to the line graphed at the right.

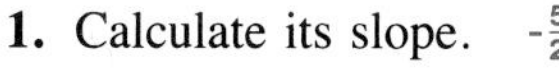

1. Calculate its slope. $-\frac{5}{2}$

2. a. Give its y-intercept. 5
b. Give its x-intercept. 2

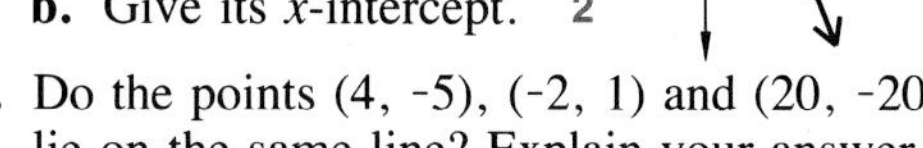

3. Do the points (4, -5), (-2, 1) and (20, -20) all lie on the same line? Explain your answer. See margin.

In 4 and 5, find the slope and y-intercept of the line. $-\frac{5}{2}, \frac{1}{2}$

4. $y = 8 - 4x$. -4; 8 **5.** $5x + 2y = 1$

6. Find an equation of the line with slope $\frac{3}{4}$ and y-intercept 13. $y = \frac{3}{4}x + 13$

7. Find an equation of the line with slope -2 containing the point (-5, 6). $y = -2x - 4$

8. Rewrite the equation $y = 5x - 2$ in standard form $Ax + By = C$ and give the values of A, B, and C. $-5x + y = -2$; $A = -5$, $B = 1$, $C = -2$

9. What is true about the slope of horizontal lines? Slope is 0.

10. If a line has a slope of $\frac{3}{5}$, how much will the graph change as you go one unit to the right? up $\frac{3}{5}$ units

In 11 and 12, use the following data of total U.S. Army personnel during and after World War II.

Year	Total Personnel
1942	3,074,184
1943	6,993,102
1944	7,992,868
1945	8,266,373
1946	1,889,690

11. In which two-year period was there the greatest increase in U.S. Army personnel? See margin

12. What is the rate of change for the entire period from 1942 to 1946? ≈ -296,123

$2x + y = 67$

13. A basketball team scored 67 points with x baskets worth 2 points each and y free throws worth 1 point each. Write an equation that describes all possible values of x and y.

14. A couple has already donated \$100 to a charity. Now they have decided to donate \$5 a week taken directly from their paycheck. After x weeks, they will have donated a total of y dollars. Give the slope and y-intercept of the line describing the relationship between x and y. slope = 5, y-intercept = 100

15. At age 12 Patrick weighed 43 kg; at 14 he weighed 50 kg. Find a linear equation relating Pat's weight y to his age x. $y = 3.5x + 1$

16. Graph $-3x + 2y = 12$. See margin.

17. Graph $y \le x + 1$. See margin.

In 18–21, the scattergram below illustrates the wingspan and length of 2-engine and 3-engine jet planes. 18) about 115 feet 19a) See sample line.

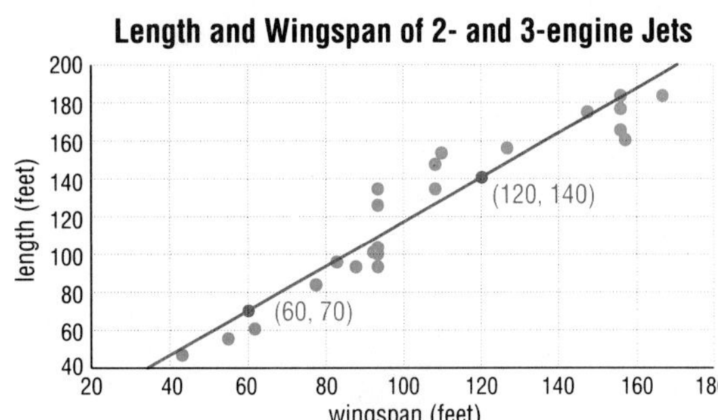

18. From the scattergram, about what length would you expect a jet to be if its wingspan is 100 feet?

19. a. Draw a line to fit the data and estimate the coordinates of two points on it.
b. Find the slope of your line. $\frac{140 - 70}{120 - 60} = \frac{7}{6}$

20. Write an equation for the line you have drawn in Question 19. $y = \frac{7}{6}x$

21. Use the equation from Question 20 to answer Question 18. about 117 ft

PROGRESS SELF-TEST

We cannot overemphasize the importance of these end-of-chapter materials. It is at this point that the material "gels" for many students, allowing them to solidify skills and understanding. In general, student performance should be markedly improved after these pages.

USING THE PROGRESS SELF-TEST

Assign the Progress Self-Test as a one-night assignment. Worked-out *solutions* for all these questions are in the Selected Answers section at the back of the student book. Encourage students to take the Progress Self-Test honestly, grade themselves, and then be prepared to discuss the test in class.

Advise students to pay special attention to those Chapter Review questions (pages 418–421) which correspond to questions missed on the Progress Self-Test. A chart provided in the Selected Answers section in the student text keys the Progress Self-Test questions to the lettered SPUR Objectives in the Chapter Review or to the Vocabulary. It also keys the questions to the corresponding lessons where the material is covered.

17.

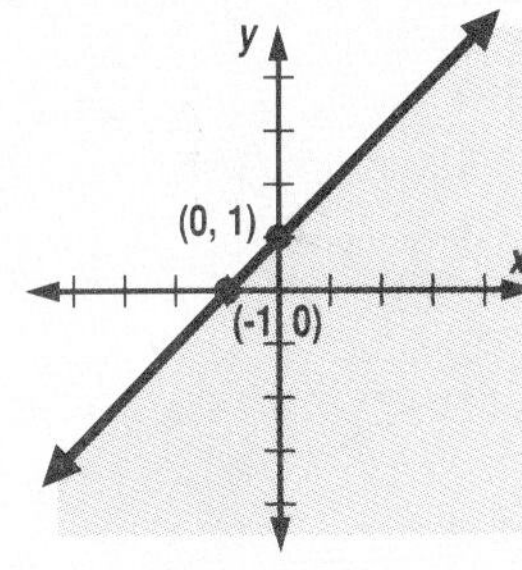

RESOURCES
- Chapter 8 Test, Form A
- Chapter 8 Test, Form B
- Chapter 8 Test, Cumulative Form

CHAPTER REVIEW

The main objectives for the chapter are organized here into sections corresponding to the four main types of understanding this book promotes: Skills, Properties, Uses, and Representations.

USING THE CHAPTER REVIEW

Whereas end-of-chapter material may be considered optional in some texts, in *Algebra* we have selected these objectives and questions with the expectation that they will be covered. Students should be able to answer these questions with about 85% accuracy after studying the chapter.

You may assign these questions over a single night to help students prepare for a test the next day, or you may assign the questions over a two-day period.

If you work the questions over two days, then we recommend assigning the *evens* for homework the first night so that students get feedback in class the next day, then assigning the *odds* the night before the test so the students can use the answers provided in the book.

ADDITIONAL ANSWERS
15a.

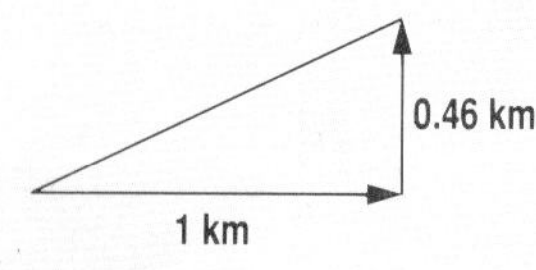

Chapter Review

Questions on SPUR Objectives

SPUR stands for **S**kills, **P**roperties, **U**ses, and **R**epresentations. The Chapter Review questions are grouped according to the SPUR Objectives for this chapter.

SKILLS deal with the procedures used to get answers

Objective A: *Find the slope of the line through two given points. (Lesson 8-2)*

1. Calculate the slope of the line containing (2, 4) and (6, 2). $-\frac{1}{2}$

2. Calculate the slope of the line through (1, 5) and (-2, -2). $\frac{7}{3}$

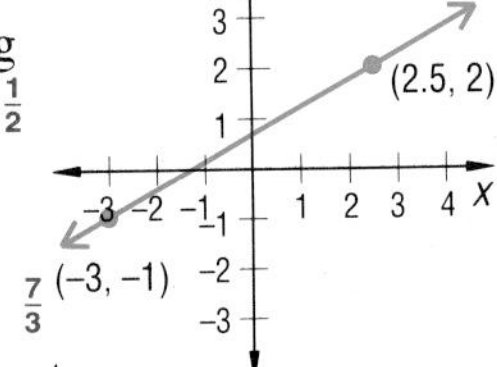

3. Find the slope of line *A* at the right. $\frac{3}{5.5} = .\overline{54}$

4. Using two different pairs of points, show that the slope of the line at the right is $-\frac{1}{2}$. **See margin.**

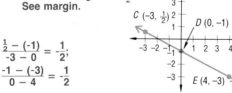

$\frac{\frac{1}{2} - (-1)}{-3 - 0} = -\frac{1}{2}$; $\frac{-1 - (-3)}{0 - 4} = -\frac{1}{2}$

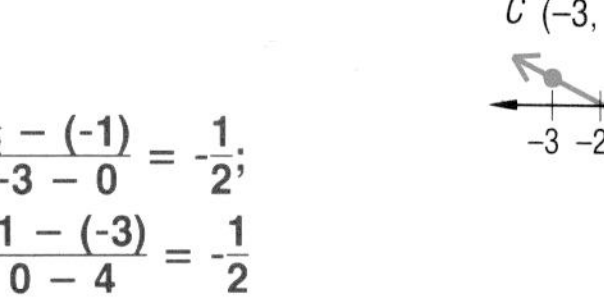

Objective B: *Find an equation for a line given its slope and any point on it. (Lessons 8-4, 8-5)*

5. Give an equation for the line with slope 4 and *y*-intercept 3. $y = 4x + 3$

6. What is an equation for the line with slope *p* and *y*-intercept *q*? $y = px + q$

In 7–10, find an equation for the line:

7. through (-4, 1) with slope -2 $y = -2x - 7$

8. through (6, 10) with slope 0 $y = 10$

9. through $(3, \frac{1}{4})$ with slope 30 $y = 30x - \frac{359}{4}$

10. through (3, -1) with undefined slope $x = 3$

Objective C: *Find an equation for a line through two given points. (Lesson 8-6)*

In 11 and 12, find an equation for the line through the two given points.

11. (5, -2), (-7, -8) $y = \frac{1}{2}x - \frac{9}{2}$

12. (0.5, 6), (0, 4) $y = 4x + 4$

PROPERTIES deal with the principles behind the mathematics.

Objective D: *Recognize slope as a rate of change. (Lessons 8-2, 8-3)*

13. Slope is the amount of change in the __?__ of the graph as you go one unit to the __?__. **height; right**

14. The slope determined by two points is the change in the __?__ coordinates divided by the __?__ in the *x*-coordinates. **y; change**

15. As it ascends, a jet aircraft climbs 0.46 km for each km it travels away from its starting point. **a) See margin. b) 0.46**

a. Draw a picture of this situation.

b. What is the slope of the ascent?

16. The slope of the line through (*a*, *b*) and (*c*, *d*) is __?__. $\frac{d - b}{c - a}$ or $\frac{b - d}{a - c}$

Objective E: *Rewrite an equation for a line in standard form or slope-intercept form.* (Lessons 8-4, 8-8)

In 17 and 18, write in the form $Ax + By = C$. Then give the values of A, B, and C.

17. $x - 22 = 5y$ **x − 5y = 22; A = 1, B = -5, C = 22**

18. $y = 2x + 7$ **-2x + y = 7; A = -2, B = 1, C = 7**

In 19 and 20, rewrite the equations in slope-intercept form.

19. $2x + y = 4$ **y = -2x + 4**

20. $x + 3y = 11$ $y = -\frac{1}{3}x + \frac{11}{3}$

Objective F: *Given an equation for a line, find its slope and y-intercept.* (Lessons 8-2, 8-4)

In 21–24, find the slope and y-intercept of the line.

21. $y = 7x - 3$ **m = 7, b = -3**

22. $4x + 5y = 1$ $m = -\frac{4}{5}, b = \frac{1}{5}$

23. $y = -x$ **m = -1, b = 0**

24. $48x - 3y = 30$ **m = 16, b = -10**

USES deal with applications of mathematics in real situations.

Objective G: *Calculate rates of change from real data.* (Lesson 8-1)

In 25 and 26, use the average weights (in kg) for girls between birth and age 14, as given below.

Age (yr)	kg
birth	4.4
1	9.1
2	11.3
3	13.6
4	15.0
5	17.2
6	20.4
7	22.2
8	25.4
9	28.1
10	31.3
11	34.9
12	39.0
13	45.5
14	48.5

25. Find the average rate of change of weight from age 10 to 14. **4.3 kg per yr**

26. a. According to these data, in which two-year period do girls gain weight fastest?

b. What is this rate of change?
a) 11 to 13 years; b) 5.3 kg per yr

In 27 and 28, use the temperatures (in °F) shown below recorded at O'Hare Airport in Chicago, starting at 10 P.M., November 21, 1985.

Temperatures Recorded at O'Hare Airport November 21, 1985

10 P.M.	20°	4 A.M.	14°
11 P.M.	18°	5 A.M.	13°
Mdnt.	17°	6 A.M.	13°
1 A.M.	16°	7 A.M.	14°
2 A.M.	15°	8 A.M.	17°
3 A.M.	15°	9 A.M.	20°

27. Find the average rate of change in temperature from 11 P.M. to 7 A.M. **-0.5° per hour**

28. a. During which three-hour period did the temperature decrease the most? **10 P.M. to 1 A.M.**

b. In that period, what was the average rate of change of the temperature? $\frac{-4°}{3}$ **per hour**

37.

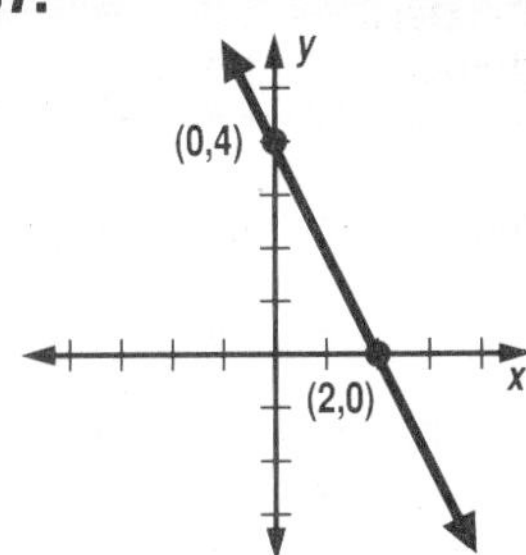

38.

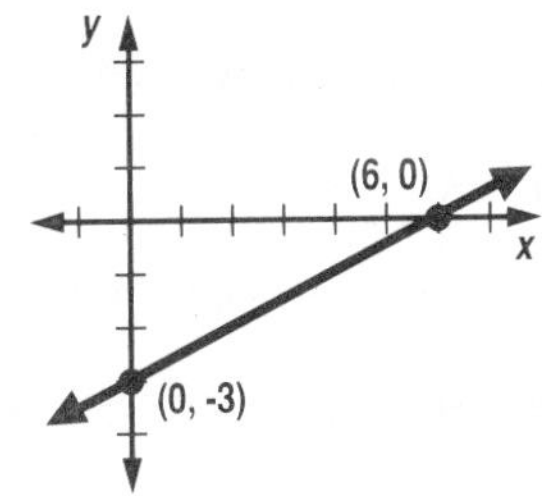

39.

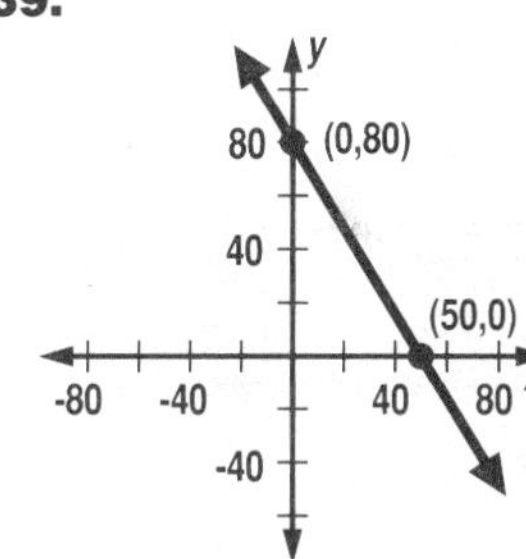

40.

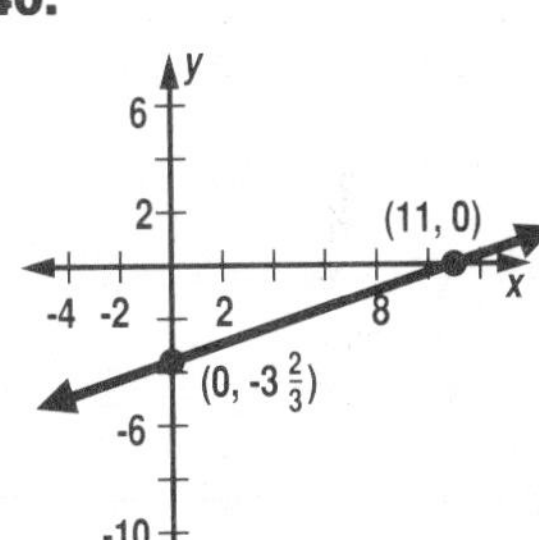

41.

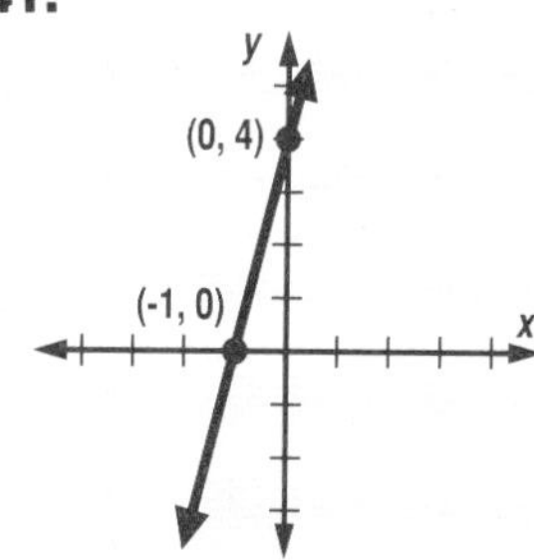

42.

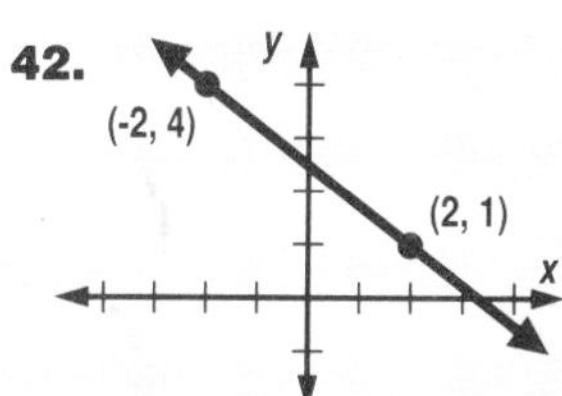

37–42. See margin, page 419.

43.

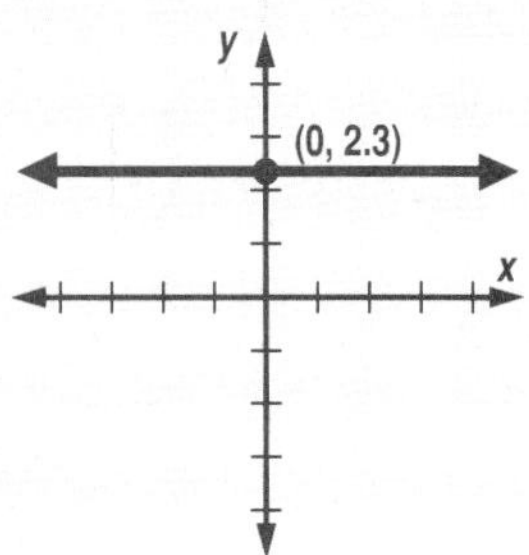

44.

y
x
(1, -2)
(0, -4)

45a.

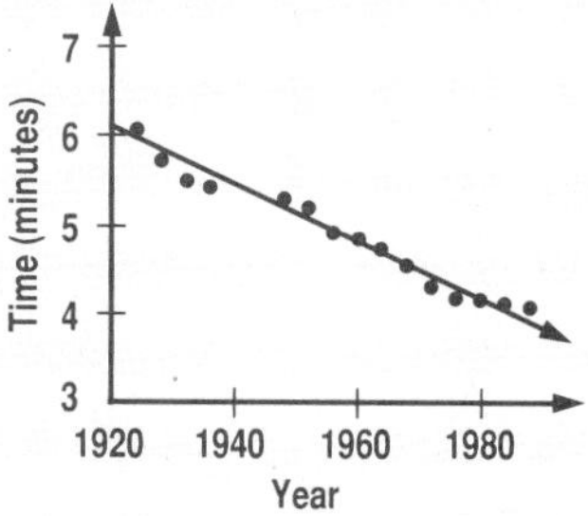

47.

y
10
(0, 8)
(40, 0)
x
40

48.

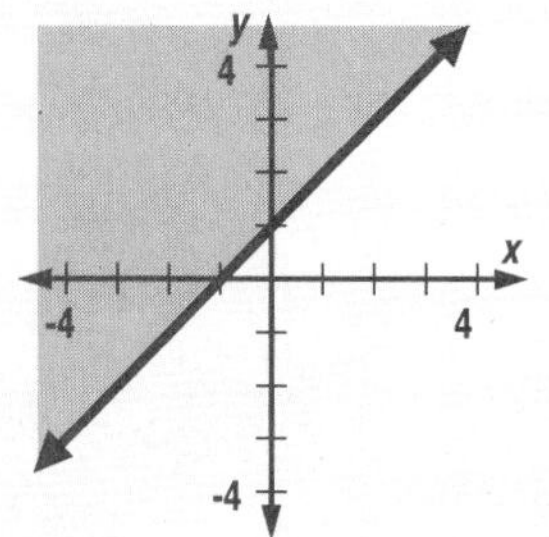

Objective H: *Use equations for lines to describe real situations. (Lessons 8-4, 8-5, 8-6, 8-8)*

In 29 and 30, each situation can be represented by a straight line. Give the slope and y-intercept of the line describing this situation.

29. Julie rents a truck. She pays an initial fee of \$15 and then \$0.25 per mile. Let y be the cost of driving x miles. **0.25, 15**

30. Nick is given \$50 to spend on a vacation. He decides to spend \$5 a day. Let y be the amount Nick has left after x days. **-5, 50**

In 31 and 32, each situation leads to an equation of the form $y = mx + b$. Find that equation.

31. A student takes a test and gets a score of 50. He gets a chance to take the test again. It is estimated that every hour of studying will increase his score by 3 points. Let x be the number of hours studied and y be his score. **$y = 3x + 50$**

32. A plane loses altitude at the rate of 5 meters per second. It begins at an altitude of 8500 meters. Let y be its altitude after x seconds. **$y = -5x + 8500$**

33. Julio plans a diet to gain 0.2 kg a day. After 2 weeks he weighs 40 kg. Write an equation relating Julio's weight w to the number of days d on his diet. **$w = .2d + 37.2$**

34. Each month about 50 new people come to live in a town. After 3 months the town has 25,500 people. Write an equation relating the number of months m to the number of people n in the town. **$n = 50m + 25{,}350$**

35. The games of the 21st Modern Olympiad were in 1976. The games of the 20th Olympiad were 4 years earlier. Let y be the year of the nth summer Olympic games. Give a linear equation which relates n and y. **using (21, 1976), (20, 1972); $y = 4n + 18$**

36. Robert babysat for \$2.50 an hour and mowed lawns for \$10 an hour. He earned a total of \$25. Write an equation that describes the possible babysitting hours B and lawnmowing hours L he could have spent at these jobs. **$2.5B + 10L = 25$**

REPRESENTATIONS deal with pictures, graphs, or objects that illustrate concepts.

Objective I: *Graph a straight line given its equation, or given a point on it and its slope. (Lessons 8-2, 8-3, 8-4)*

In 37–40, graph the line with the given equation. **See margin.**

37. $y = -2x + 4$ **38.** $y = \frac{1}{2}x - 3$

39. $8x + 5y = 400$ **40.** $x - 3y = 11$

41. Graph the line that passes through (0, 4) and has a slope of 4. **See margin.**

42. Graph the line that passes through (-2, 4) and has a slope of $-\frac{3}{4}$. **See margin.**

43. Graph the line with slope 0 and y-intercept 2.3. **See margin.**

44. Graph the line with slope 2 and y-intercept -4. **See margin.**

420

Objective J: *Given data which approximate a linear graph, find a linear equation to fit the graph.* (Lesson 8-7)

45. Olympic swimmers get faster and faster. The scattergram below shows the times for the winners of the Women's 400-meter freestyle for the years 1924 to 1988.

Women's 400-Meter Freestyle Olympic Winners

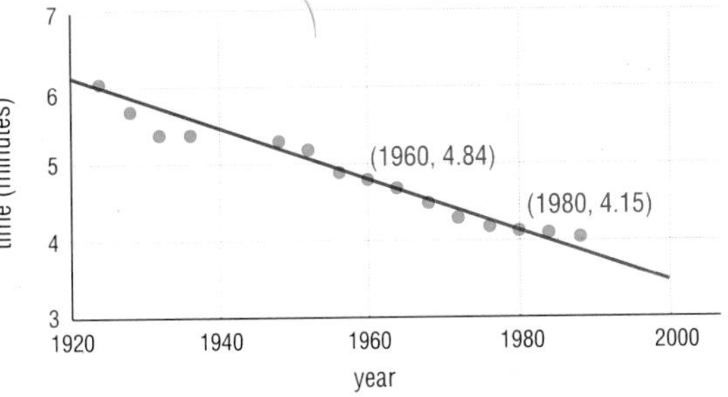

Year	Winner	Time	Converted Time
1924	Martha Norelius, U.S.	6:02.2	6.04
1928	Martha Norelius, U.S.	5:42.8	5.71
1932	Helene Madison, U.S.	5:28.5	5.48
1936	Hendrika Mastenbroek, Netherlands	5:26.4	5.44
1948	Anne Curtis, U.S.	5:17.8	5.30
1952	Valerie Gyenge, Hungary	5:12.1	5.20
1956	Lorraine Crapp, Australia	4:54.6	4.91
1960	Chris von Saltza, U.S.	4:40.6	4.84
1964	Virginia Duenkel, U.S.	4:43.3	4.72
1968	Debbie Meyer, U.S.	4:31.8	4.53
1972	Shane Gould, Australia	4:19.04	4.32
1976	Petra Thümer, E. Germany	4:09.89	4.17
1980	Ines Diers, E. Germany	4:08.76	4.15
1984	Tiffany Cohen, U.S.	4:07.10	4.12
1988	Janet Evans, U.S.	4:03.85	4.06

The times have been converted to decimal parts of a minute: 6:02.2 is graphed as 6.04 minutes. The result of converting all the times is listed in the table. Use the converted times to answer the questions.

a. Graph a line to fit the data. **See above.**

b. Find the slope of the fitted line. **b) Using (1960, 4.84) and (1980, 4.15), $m \approx -.035$;**

c. Find an equation for the line. **c) $y = -.035x + 73.45$;**

d. Predict the winning time in 1992. **d) 3.73 min or 3 min 43.8 sec**

Objective K: *Graph linear inequalities.* (Lesson 8-9)

46. The regions on either side of a line in a plane are called __?__. **half-planes**

47. If you have only x nickels and y quarters and a total of less than $2.00, graph all possible values of x and y. **See margin.**

In 48–51, graph. **See margin.**

48. $y \geq x + 1$

49. $y < -3x + 2$

50. $3x + 2y > 5$

51. $x - 8y \leq 0$

Janet Evans competing in the 1988 Olympics.

EVALUATION

Three tests are provided for this chapter in the Teacher's Resource File. Chapter 8 Test, Forms A and B, cover just Chapter 8. The third test is Chapter 8, Cumulative Form. About 50% of this test covers Chapter 8; 25% covers Chapter 7, and 25% covers earlier chapters. For more information on grading, see *General Teaching Suggestions: Grading* on page T44 in the Teacher's Edition.

ASSIGNMENT RECOMMENDATION

On the day your students take the chapter test, we suggest you make an assignment in the first section of the next chapter.

49.

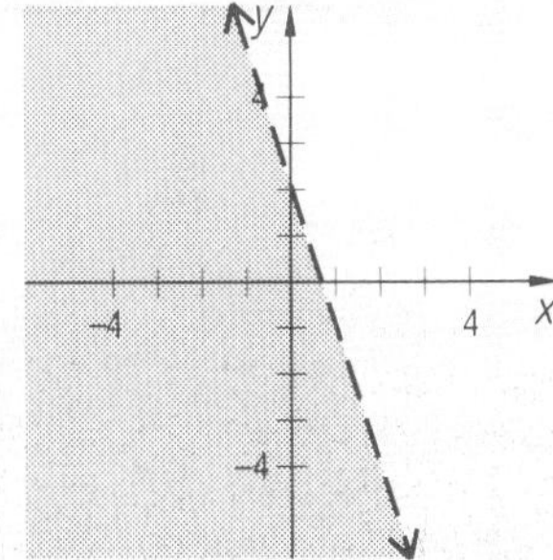

50.

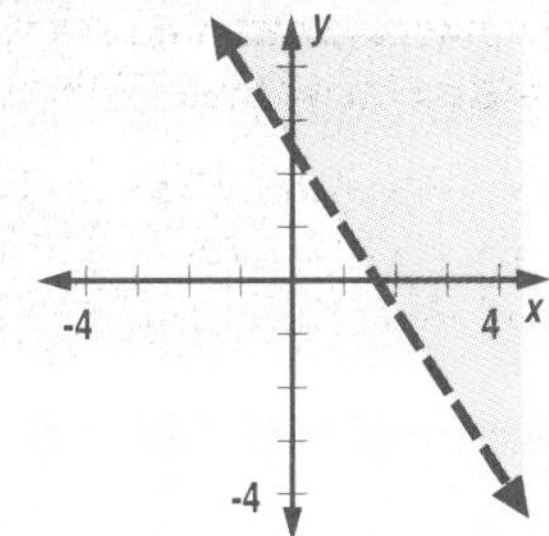

51.

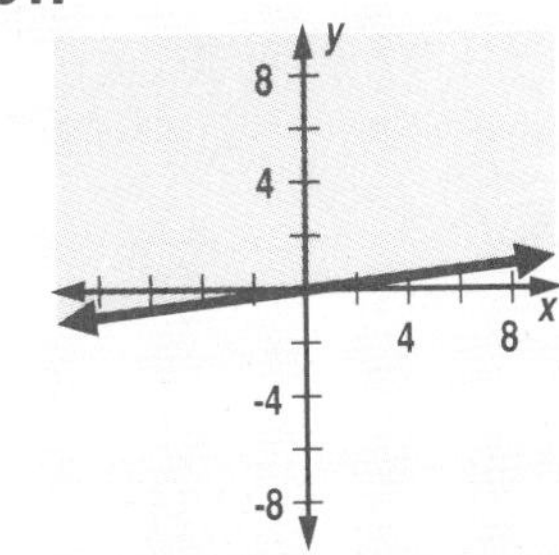

CHAPTER 9 EXPONENTS AND POWERS

DAILY PACING CHART 9

DAILY PACING CHART CHAPTER 9

Students in the Full Course should complete the entire text by the end of the year. Students in the Minimal Course spend more time to complete lessons that are combined with quizzes and more time to consider the Chapter Review. Therefore, these students may not complete all the chapters in the text.

DAY	MINIMAL COURSE	FULL COURSE
1	9-1	9-1
2	9-2	9-2
3	9-3	9-3
4	9-4	9-4
5	Quiz (TRF); Start 9-5.	Quiz (TRF); 9-5
6	Finish 9-5.	9-6
7	9-6	9-7
8	9-7	Quiz (TRF); 9-8
9	Quiz (TRF); Start 9-8.	9-9
10	Finish 9-8.	Progress Self-Test
11	9-9	Chapter Review
12	Progress Self-Test	Chapter Test (TRF)
13	Chapter Review	Comprehensive Test (TRF)
14	Chapter Review	
15	Chapter Test (TRF)	
16	Comprehensive Test (TRF)	

TESTING OPTIONS

TESTING OPTIONS

- Quiz for Lessons 9-1 Through 9-4
- Quiz for Lessons 9-5 Through 9-7
- Chapter 9 Test, Form A
- Chapter 9 Test, Form B
- Chapter 9 Test, Cumulative Form
- Comprehensive Test, Chapters 1–9

INDIVIDUAL DIFFERENCES

PROVIDING FOR INDIVIDUAL DIFFERENCES

The student text is written for the *average* student. The program, however, can be adapted for less capable and for more capable students.

For those students who need more practice, a blackline master (in the Teacher's Resource File) is provided for each lesson. The Teacher's Edition frequently provides Error Analysis and Alternate Approach features to provide additional instructional strategies for those students who do not readily grasp the material.

For students who require additional challenge, Extension activities are regularly provided in the Teacher's Edition.

OBJECTIVES ■ CHAPTER 9

Students should master the chapter objectives by the time they complete the chapter. To ensure objective mastery, there is continual review built into each set of lesson questions. After students complete the chapter lessons, they assess their mastery on the Progress Self-Test. Then they do the Chapter Review and pay special attention to those questions that match the objectives missed on the Progress Self-Test. Students can get extra practice on these objectives by using the master for each lesson in the Teacher's Resource File.

OBJECTIVES FOR CHAPTER 9 (Organized into the SPUR categories— Skills, Properties, Uses, and Representations)	**Progress Self-Test Questions**	**Chapter Review Questions**	**Lesson Master from Teacher's Resource File***
SKILLS			
A Evaluate integer powers of real numbers.	3, 6	1 through 12	9-2, 9-5, 9-6, 9-7, 9-8, 9-9
B Simplify products, quotients, and powers of powers.	1, 2, 4, 5	13 through 22	9-5, 9-7
C Rewrite powers of products and quotients.	7, 8	23 through 28	9-8
PROPERTIES			
D Test a special case to determine whether a pattern is true.	10, 11	29 through 32	9-9
E Identify properties of exponents.	9, 12	33 through 40	9-2, 9-5, 9-6, 9-7, 9-8
USES			
F Calculate compound interest.	13, 14	41 through 44	9-1
G Solve problems involving exponential growth and decay.	15, 16	45 through 50	9-2, 9-3
H Use and simplify expressions with powers in everyday situations.	19, 20	51 through 54	9-6, 9-7, 9-8
REPRESENTATIONS			
I Graph exponential growth and decay relationships.	18	55 through 60	9-4

*** The masters are numbered to match the lessons.**

OVERVIEW ■ CHAPTER 9

The first nonlinear graph in many algebra books is the parabola, which arises from a study of quadratic equations. However, among the most used mathematical concepts in modern business, finance, biology, physics, and sociology are exponential growth and decay, and so we discuss these concepts (and the corresponding nonlinear graphs) first.

Exponential growth and decay are introduced via biological and physical applications. These applications arise when there is a constant growth factor, as contrasted with situations of constant increase or decrease.

Because exponential growth problems give different values of y for different values of x, it is easier for students to study the problem "what x will produce a given value of y" in this context than it is with quadratics, where multiple and extraneous solutions may arise.

The first lesson introduces a topic—compound interest—that all high school students should study whether they take algebra or not. Problems involving compound interest can be solved by using a scientific calculator. (Historically, compound interest was not included in first-year algebra books because the computations used to require logarithms.)

The first four lessons stress the uses and representations that arise from exponential growth. This work builds strong ties between the idea of exponents and repeated multiplication. This leads to the properties of exponents that are discussed in the remaining sections of the chapter.

PERSPECTIVES ■ CHAPTER 9

The Perspectives provide the rationale for the inclusion of topics or approaches, provide mathematical background, and make connections within UCSMP.

9-1

COMPOUND INTEREST

The Compound Interest Formula is more important for students to know than the simple interest formula ($I = prt$). Few situations today involve $I = prt$ when $t > 1$.

According to federal law, investment advertisements must state both the interest rate and the annual yield. The interest rate determines the multiplier used when interest is calculated for each compounding period. The annual yield is the result of doing this over a year.

For instance, suppose an investment has a 8.25% *annual rate* compounded daily. We would expect the *annual yield* to be slightly higher. Each day the account would earn 1/365 of 8.25%, so the amount is multiplied by $1 + .0825/365$. When compounded 365 times, the multiplier is $(1 + .0825/365)^{365} \approx 1.086 =$ 108.6%. In effect, the account has grown by 8.6%. Thus the rate of 8.25% compounded daily equals a rate of 8.6% compounded yearly, and 8.6% is the annual yield.

9-2

EXPONENTIAL GROWTH

Exponential growth has the formula $y = b \cdot g^x$. The letter b was chosen because it serves the same purpose as in $y = mx + b$; namely, it represents the initial value. The letter g stands for the growth factor. Compound interest is an example of exponential growth. The major change for the Compound Interest Formula is in the replacement of the growth factor g with the expression $(1 + i)$. The "$y =$" in the formula does not appear in this lesson, but is postponed until Lesson 9-4. At this point, we do not want to confuse the student with the y on the $\boxed{y^x}$ key of the calculator.

Even though we use integral values for x and b in the examples, the formula holds for any real values of x and b. However, the growth factor g must be positive, and in this lesson g is always greater than 1.

This lesson contrasts exponential growth with linear growth. It is important that students understand the differences in the patterns $b + mx$ and $b \cdot g^x$.

It may take students several days to be convinced that quantities that grow exponentially will eventually increase *very* quickly. In this lesson, all situations involve growth. Situations in the next lesson involve decay.

When the only meaning that students have for powering is repeated multiplication, a zero exponent is not meaningful because one cannot repeat something 0 times. However, the idea of "zero time periods from now," namely the present, is meaningful. Thus, when $x = 0$, it is natural that $b \cdot g^x = b$, which implies that $g^x = 1$ for all nonzero g.

9-3

EXPONENTIAL DECAY

In the preceding lesson the growth factor g was greater than 1. This lesson deals with the exponential growth model $b \cdot g^x$ when g is a positive value less than 1. The result is decay. Students should realize that the growth factor affects whether there is growth or decay (just as slope of a line determines increase or decrease).

Linear increase/decrease and exponential growth/decay are mathematically *isomorphic;* that is, they have the same structure. The former is related to addition as the latter is related to multiplication. For instance, the additive identity 0 is the pivot in linear increase/decrease; a slope greater than 0 means increase whereas a slope less than 0 means decrease. Similarly, the multiplicative identity 1 is the pivot in exponential growth/decay; a growth factor greater than 1 means growth whereas a growth factor less than 1 signals decay.

9-4

GRAPHING EXPONENTIAL GROWTH AND DECAY

This lesson on graphing is included for several reasons. Students need to see many graphs of exponential growth and decay to see that they differ greatly from linear functions. In addition, the graphs allow you to ask questions which enable students to estimate solutions to equations. Students should be developing a feel for exponents, that if g is large, then g^x changes rapidly as x increases. The graphs help to make this clear.

Automatic graphers (computer software or graphing calculators) will simplify the job of graphing and enable you to cover this material more quickly.

Notice that now we use the complete equations $y = mx + b$ and $y = b \cdot g^x$ for descriptions and graphs. These are the convenient forms for automatic graphing.

All the graphs use $x \geq 0$ as the domain because we have not yet discussed negative exponents. Negative exponents are the topic of Lesson 9-6. To anticipate that lesson, you might want to extend some graphs, like Example 2, to negative values of x.

9-5

PRODUCTS OF POWERS

The rest of this chapter deals with the formal properties of exponents. When expressing these properties, we use the letter b for the base. Using x can be confusing because some calculators name their powering key [x^y] while others use the name [y^x].

The meanings for b^n (repeated multiplication and growth) are the most basic ideas about powers. From these we derive the Product of Powers property. Then that property can be used to explain the Power of a Power Property. If a property is forgotten, students should learn to go back to more primitive properties.

9-6

NEGATIVE EXPONENTS

In many books, the Negative Exponent Property $b^{-n} = 1/b^n$ is a definition. Here it is a theorem because the Growth Model of Powering gives meaning to negative exponents and we have assumed the Product of Powers Property for all exponents. The proof of the theorem is given in this lesson.

The Growth Model explains why even negative powers of a positive number should be positive, because going back in time does not mean that negative values are introduced. This is confirmed by evaluating negative powers.

9-7

QUOTIENTS OF POWERS

In this lesson, quotients of powers of the same number are simplified. Since negative exponents were covered in the previous section, we can say that $b^m/b^n = b^{m-n}$ for any values of n.

This is more efficient than the approach taken when negative exponents are avoided. That approach requires two rules.

9-8

POWERS OF PRODUCTS AND QUOTIENTS

Note the distinctions between the situations of this lesson and those of Lessons 9-6 and 9-7. We categorize expressions and name the properties in reverse order to the order of operations. For example, $(ab)^n$ is viewed as a power of a product. But $2^x \cdot 2^y$ is a product of powers. These distinctions may help students remember the names of properties. At this point, however, knowing the actual names of the properties is not important; being able to do the appropriate computation is.

9-9

REMEMBERING THE PROPERTIES

Of all the concepts that students need to learn in mathematics, there is none more important than the notion of the *consistency* of mathematics. Consistency allows us to *test special cases,* the problem solving strategy in this lesson. Consistency enables us to generalize, to prove, and to disprove.

Yet it is the case that students often see properties of powers as distinct independent facts to be memorized. The purpose of this lesson is to dissuade students from memorizing without understanding.

We want students to be able to test a simple case to verify their reasoning. As with the strategy of "chunking," *testing a special case* is used throughout the rest of the book. We take advantage of this powerful tool in many of the checks of problems involving quadratics and other polynomials. Another place that *testing a special case* is important is in calculator use—to test your key sequence.

CHAPTER 9

RESOURCES

Visual for Teaching Aid 44: Population Growth Graph for Page 422

This chapter should take 9 to 11 days for the lessons and quizzes; 1 day for the Progress Self-Test; 1 or 2 days for the Chapter Review; and 1 day for testing. The total is 12 to 15 days. Allow an additional day for the Comprehensive Test.

CHAPTER 9

Exponents and Powers

A city of 100,000 people is planning for the future. The planners want to know how many schools the town will need during the next 50 years. They test three assumptions.

(1) The population stays the same.
(2) The population increases by 2000 people per year. (increases by a constant amount)
(3) The population grows by 2% a year. (increases at a constant growth rate)

Here is a graph of what would happen under the three assumptions. P is the population n years from now.

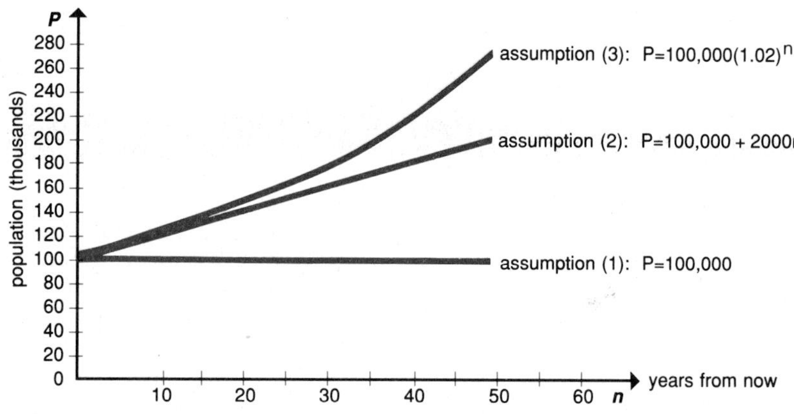

Assumption (3) is often considered the most reasonable of the three. Under this assumption, $P = 100{,}000(1.02)^n$. Because the variable n is an exponent, this equation is said to represent *exponential growth*. Exponential growth describes many other kinds of situations. To study exponential growth, you need to know how to compute and use powers and exponents.

USING PAGES 422-423
Since students have studied slopes of lines they should be able to appreciate a discussion of the graph.

For Assumption 1, for any 10-year period, say 20 − 10 = 10, the corresponding change in P is always 100,000 − 100,000 or 0. For Assumption 2, for any 10-year period, say 30 − 20 = 10, the corresponding change in P is always 20,000. (For the case chosen, 140,000 − 120,000 = 20,000) However, for Assumption 3, for each 10-year period the change in P is different. In fact, it is increasing with time as follows.

10-year period	Change in P (closest 1000)
10 − 0 = 10	122 − 100 = 22
20 − 10 = 10	149 − 122 = 27
30 − 20 = 10	181 − 149 = 32
40 − 30 = 10	221 − 181 = 40
50 − 40 = 10	269 − 221 = 48
60 − 50 = 10	328 − 269 = 59

The preceding can be seen intuitively from the graph. For Assumption 1, the graph is horizontal so P is not changing. For Assumption 2, the steepness of the graph does not change. So, for each change of 1 in n, the change in P is always 2000. For Assumption 3, the graph gets steeper as you move to the right. So, for each change of 1 as you move to the right, the change in P increases.

LESSON 9-1

RESOURCES
■ Lesson Master 9-1
Computer Master 18

OBJECTIVE

F Calculate compound interest.

TEACHING NOTES

The Compound Interest Formula need not be learned by rote, if compounding is thought of as a scale change of $1 + i$ repeated n times. Two ideas are fundamental to having students see this. One is the Distributive Property, as shown in **Example 1.** The other is expressing repeated products as powers, as in **Example 2.**

Alternate Approach
Instead of using the key sequence shown in **Example 3,** students may find it easier to evaluate $P(1 + i)^n$ by keying in $(1 + i)^n$ first and then multiplying by P. Parentheses are needed either way unless the student mentally adds 1 to the rate.

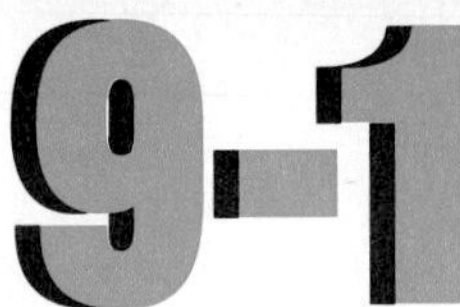

LESSON

9-1 Compound Interest

Recall that when n is a positive integer,

$$x^n = \underbrace{x \cdot x \cdot \ldots \cdot x}_{n \text{ factors}}.$$

The number x^n is the ***n*th power** of x and is read "x to the nth power" or just "x to the n." In x^n, x is the **base** and n is the **exponent**. In the expression $100{,}000(1.02)^n$ found on page 422, 1.02 is the base, n is the exponent, and 100,000 is the coefficient of 1.02^n. An important application of exponents and powers is *compound interest*.

When you save money, you have choices of where to put it. Of course, you can keep it at home. Banks, savings and loan associations, and credit unions will pay you to give them your money to save. The amount you give them is called the **principal.** The amount they pay you is called **interest.**

Interest is always a percent of the principal. The percent the money earns per year is called the **annual yield.**

Example 1 Suppose you deposit P dollars in a savings account upon which the bank pays an annual yield of 5.5%. If the account is left alone, how much money will be in it at the end of a year?

Solution 1 Total = principal + 5.5% of principal
$= P + .055P$
$= (1 + .055)P$
$= 1.055P$

Solution 2 Total = 100% of principal + 5.5% of principal
= 105.5% of principal
$= 1.055P$

So, if you deposited \$1000 in a savings account for a year with an annual yield of 5.5%, a bank would pay you 5.5% of \$1000, or \$55 interest. Banks and other savings institutions pay you interest because they want money to loan to other people. They might charge someone 12% on a loan. Thus, if the bank could loan your \$1000 (perhaps to someone buying a car or a house) at 12%, the bank would receive 12% of \$1000, or \$120 from that person. So the bank would earn \$120 − \$55 = \$65 on your money. Part of that \$65 goes for salaries to the people who work at the bank, part for other bank costs, and part as profit to the owners of the bank.

Savings accounts pay **compound interest,** which means that the interest earns interest.

Example 2 Suppose you deposit \$100 in a savings account upon which the bank pays an annual yield of 5.5%. If the account is left alone, how much money will be in it at the end of *three* years?

Solution Each year the amount in the bank is multiplied by $1 + .055 = 1.055$.

End of first year:

$$100(1.055) = 100(1.055)^1 = 105.50$$

End of second year:

$$100(1.055)(1.055) = 100(1.055)^2 \approx 111.3025 \approx 111.30$$

End of third year:

$$100(1.055)(1.055)(1.055) = 100(1.055)^3 \approx 117.4241 \approx 117.42$$

At the end of three years there will be \$117.42 in your account.

Examine the pattern in the solution to Example 2. At the end of n years there will be

$$100(1.055)^n$$

dollars in the account. The general formula for compound interest uses this expression, but variables replace the principal and annual yield.

Compound Interest Formula:

If a principal P earns an annual yield of i, then after n years there will be a total T, where

$$T = P(1 + i)^n.$$

The compound interest formula is read "T equals P times the quantity 1 plus i, that quantity to the nth."

ADDITIONAL EXAMPLES

1. If P dollars is invested at 9.2% annual yield, what will the value of the account be at the end of one year?
1.092*P*

2. Suppose \$500 is deposited at 7% annual yield. How much will be in the account after 8 years?
$500(1.07)^8 \approx$ \$859.09

3. A baby's grandparents invest \$1000 for her on the day the baby is born.

a. How much is the investment worth on her 18th birthday if it earns 10.3% interest?
$1000(1.103)^{18} \approx$ \$5,839.28

b. How much interest was earned?
\$4839.28

NOTES ON QUESTIONS
Error Analysis for Questions 9a, 11, and 12: For these questions and many others in this chapter, students need to derive an expression and then evaluate it on the calculator. We suggest that you require students to write both the expression and the result. For example, $500(1.07)^8 \approx$ \$859.09. In this way, they can determine whether an error is due to having an incorrect expression or to incorrect use of the calculator.

Alternate Approach for Question 15: Students are expected to solve this problem by using *trial and error.* Another way to answer this question is to use a rule of thumb called the *Rule of 72.* If money is invested at x% annual yield, it will double in about $72/x$ years. Your class can test this rule with several interest rates.

Questions 16-18: These are important for class discussion. Employing correct order of operations in expressions involving exponents is critical for this chapter. Many students multiply by coefficients before taking the power, whether they use calculators or not.

Example 3 \$1500 is deposited in a savings account. What will be the total amount of money in the account after 10 years at an annual yield of 6%?

Solution Here P = \$1500, i = 6%, and n = 10.
Substitute the values into the compound interest formula. 6% = .06

$$T = P(1 + i)^n$$
$$= 1500(1 + .06)^{10}$$

Use the calculator key sequence

1500 [×] 1.06 [y^x] 10 [=].

Displayed will be 2686.2716, which is approximately \$2686.27. In 10 years, at an annual yield of 6%, \$1500 will increase to \$2686.27.

Example 4 How much interest will be earned on a principal of \$800 after 5 years if there is an annual yield of 5.8%?

Solution The question asks for the *interest*, not the total, so first find the total amount. Then, to find the interest, subtract the original amount from the total.

Use the formula, with P = \$800, i = 5.8%, and n = 5.

$$T = P(1 + i)^n$$
$$= 800(1 + 0.058)^5$$
$$= 800(1.058)^5$$
$$= 1060.52$$

The total amount in the savings account is \$1060.52. The amount of interest earned is \$1060.52 − \$800, or \$260.52.

Questions

Covering the Reading

1. Name three kinds of savings institutions. **sample: banks, savings and loan associations, credit unions**

In 2–4, match each term with its description.

2. money you deposit **C**
3. interest paid on interest **B**
4. yearly percentage paid on amount in a savings account **A**

A. annual yield
B. compound interest
C. principal

In 5 and 6, write an expression for the amount in the bank after one year if P dollars are in an account with an annual yield as given.

5. 6% **P(1.06)** **6.** 7.2% **P(1.072)**

7. Write a calculator key sequence to evaluate $573(1.063)^{24}$.
See margin.

8. In Question 7, identify the base, coefficient, and exponent of the number evaluated. **base: 1.063; coefficient: 573; exponent: 24**

9. Consider the situation of Example 2. **a.** How much money will you have in your savings account at the end of 4 years? **b.** How much interest will you have earned? **a. $123.88 b. $23.88**

10. a. Write the compound interest formula. $T = P(1 + i)^n$
b. What does T represent? **total amount in account**
c. What does P stand for? **principal**
d. What is i? **annual yield**
e. What does n represent? **number of years invested**

11. How much interest will be earned in 7 years on a principal of $500 at an annual yield of 5.6%? **$232.18**

12. A bank advertises an annual yield of 6.8% on a 6-year CD (certificate of deposit). If the CD's original amount was $2000, how much will it be worth after 6 years? **$2967.96**

Applying the Mathematics

Susan, $10.25; Jake, $21.00

13. Susan invests $100 at an annual yield of 5%. Jake invests $100 at an annual yield of 10%. They leave the money in the bank for 2 years.
a. How much interest does each person earn?
b. Does Jake earn exactly twice the interest that Susan does? **No**

14. Which yields more money, **a.** an amount invested for 5 years at an annual yield of 6%, or **b.** the same amount invested for 3 years at an annual yield of 10%? **a**

15. Use your calculator. If a principal of $1000 is saved at an annual yield of 8% and the interest is kept in the account, in how many years will it double in value? **in about 9 years**

Review

In 16–18, evaluate. *(Lesson 1-4)*

16. $-4x^5$ when $x = \frac{1}{2}$ **$-\frac{1}{8}$**

17. $5m^2 - y^2$ when $m = 4$ and $y = -1$ **79**

18. $2(cy)^3$ when $c = 0.8$ and $y = 0.5$ **.128**

ADDITIONAL ANSWERS

7. 573 [×] 1.063 [y^x] 24 [=]

NAME ____________

LESSON **MASTER 9–1**
QUESTIONS ON **SPUR** OBJECTIVES

■USES *Objective F (See pages 471–473 for objectives.)*
In 1–4, find the amount for each of the following bank accounts after one year for the given principal and annual yield.

1. $100, 5.5% **$105.50**

2. $240, 6% **$254.40**

3. $1200, 7.5% **$1290.00**

4. $2500, 8.4% **$2710.00**

5. Suppose P dollars is invested in a Certificate of Deposit (CD) with an annual yield of 7.2% for 3 years. Write an expression for the amount received when the CD matures. **1.23P**

6. Petra opened a savings account by depositing $800. If the annual yield is 5.8%, write an expression for the amount in the account after n years. **$\$800(1.058)^n$**

In 7 and 8, find the amount in an account from the given information.

7. $400 at 5.7% after 3 years **$472.37**

8. $2200 at 7.8% after 2 years **$2556.58**

In 9 and 10, find the interest earned from the given information.

9. $180 at 5% for 2 years **$18.45**

10. $1 at 6% for 4 years **$.26**

11. a. Which will earn more interest, $120 at 4% for 2 years or $120 at 8% for 1 year? **$120 at 4% for 2 yr**

b. By how much do the earnings differ? **by 19 cents**

12. If $200 is deposited in an account with an annual yield of 10%, in how many years will the amount double? **a little over 7 yr**

13. In 1626, Peter Minuit bought Manhattan Island from the Manhattan Indians for beads, clothing, and trinkets worth about $24. If that money had been invested at 5% annual yield, what would the amount be in 1988? **about $1,240,000,000**

 73

NOTES ON QUESTIONS
Making Connections for Question 22: Problems like this appear throughout the chapter. At this point, *trial and error* with or without a calculator is an appropriate method of solution. Students will learn about problem solving and about exponents.

Making Connections for Question 24: This question deals with the Zero Exponent Property, which is discussed in the next lesson.

FOLLOW-UP

MORE PRACTICE
For more questions on SPUR Objectives, use *Lesson Master 9-1,* shown on page 427.

19b.

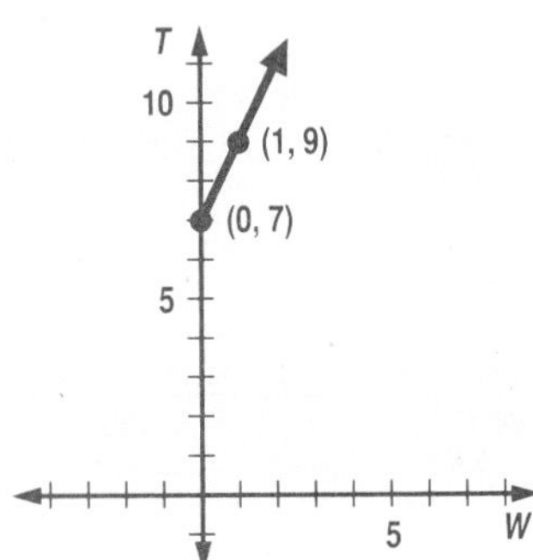

19. Lonnie puts \$7.00 in his piggy bank. Each week thereafter he puts in \$2.00. (The piggy bank pays no interest.) **a.** Write an equation showing the total amount of dollars T after W weeks. **b.** Graph the equation. *(Lesson 8-2)* **a) $T = 7 + 2W$; b) See margin.**

20. *Skill sequence* Simplify. *(Lessons 4-1, 6-3)*
a. $12(3n)$ **$36n$**
b. $12(3n - 7)$ **$36n - 84$**
c. $-12(3n - 7)$ **$-36n + 84$**
d. $n(3n - 7)$ **$3n^2 - 7n$**

21. Solve: $(1 + x)^2 = 1.664$. *(Lesson 7-8)* **≈.29, ≈-2.29**

22. Find t: $2^t = 64$. *(Previous course)* **6**

Exploration

23. Find out the yield for a savings account in a bank or other savings institution near where you live. (Often these yields are in newspaper ads.) **Answers will vary.**

24. **a.** Enter 25 [y^x] 0 [=] on your calculator. What is displayed? **1**
b. Enter 0 [y^x] 0 [=] on your calculator. What is displayed? **error**
c. Enter -1 [y^x] 0 [=] on your calculator. What is displayed? **error**
d. Try other numbers and generalize what happens.
Answers may vary, depending on the calculator.
b [y^x] 0 [=] displays 1 if $b > 0$. For $b \le 0$, an error message appears.

LESSON 9-2

Exponential Growth

Another important application of powers and exponents is population growth. The next example concerns rabbit populations, which can grow quickly. Rabbits are not native to Australia, and in 1859, 22 rabbits were imported from Europe as a new source of food. Australia's conditions were ideal for rabbits, and they flourished. Soon, there were so many rabbits that they damaged grazing land. By 1887, the government was offering a reward for a population control technique.

Example 1 Twenty-five rabbits are introduced to an area. Assume that the rabbit population doubles every six months. How many rabbits are there after 5 years?

Solution Since the population doubles twice each year, in 5 years it will double 10 times. The number of rabbits will be

$$25 \cdot \underbrace{2 \cdot 2 \cdot 2 \cdot 2 \cdot 2 \cdot 2 \cdot 2 \cdot 2 \cdot 2 \cdot 2}_{\text{10 factors}}.$$

To evaluate this expression on a calculator rewrite it as

$$25 \cdot 2^{10}.$$

Use the y^x key. After 5 years there will be 25,600 rabbits.

The rabbit population in Example 1 is said to grow exponentially. In **exponential growth,** the original amount is repeatedly *multiplied* by a nonzero number called the **growth factor.**

Growth model for powering:

When an amount is multiplied by g, the growth factor, in each of x time periods, then after the x periods, the original amount will be multiplied by g^x.

LESSON 9-2

RESOURCES
- Lesson Master 9-2
- Visual for Teaching Aid 45: Comparison of Linear Increase to Exponential Growth

OBJECTIVES

A Evaluate integer powers of real numbers.
E Identify the Zero Exponent Property.
G Solve problems involving exponential growth.

TEACHING NOTES

Stress **Example 2** in order to help students recognize the differences between linear increase and exponential growth. You could ask what the percent of increase is in each time period in **Example 2.** (Since the multiplier is 1.5, the percent of increase is 50%.)

The word *rate* is often used in discussing both constant increase and exponential growth. In the former, it is a rate of change; in the latter it is a growth rate. This dual use of *rate* can confuse students. We suggest using the word *growth* when referring to change under *exponential growth,* and *increase* when referring to *linear increase.*

Whenever a growth rate, say 6%, is given, it can be changed to the growth factor simply by adding 1. Thus, compound interest problems from the previous lesson can be handled with the growth model. The Compound Interest Formula is not necessary.

ADDITIONAL EXAMPLES

1. The population of South America is growing 2.4% per year. In 1986 its population was 279 million. If this growth continues, what will the population of South America be in the year 2000?
$279(1.024)^{14} \approx$ 389 million

2. Company A earned $1000 profit this month; its profits are increasing by $40 each month. Company B also earned $1000 profits this month; its profits are growing 2% per month. If these trends continue, after 3 years, which company would have the greater monthly profit?
Company A:
$1000 + 40 \cdot 36 = \$2440$,
Company B:
$1000(1.02)^{36} = \$2039.89$.
Company A earns more.

3. Evaluate
$3 \cdot 10^5 + 2 \cdot 10^2 + 7$.
300,207

In Lesson 6-4, you studied linear increase, in which a number is repeatedly *added* to the original amount. If the growth factor g is greater than 1, exponential growth always overtakes linear increase.

Example 2 Suppose you have $10. Your rich uncle agrees either to (1) increase each day by $50 what you had the previous day, or (2) multiply what you had the previous day by 1.5. Which is the better choice?

Solution Make a table to compare the two options.

	Linear increase: add 50	Exponential growth: multiply by 1.5
1st day	$10 + 50 \cdot \mathbf{1} = \$\ 60$	$10 \cdot 1.5^1 = \$15$
2nd day	$10 + 50 \cdot \mathbf{2} = \$110$	$10 \cdot 1.5^2 = \$22.50$
3rd day	$10 + 50 \cdot \mathbf{3} = \$160$	$10 \cdot 1.5^3 = \$33.75$
4th day	$10 + 50 \cdot \mathbf{4} = \$210$	$10 \cdot 1.5^4 = \$50.63$
5th day	$10 + 50 \cdot \mathbf{5} = \$260$	$10 \cdot 1.5^5 = \$75.94$
6th day	$10 + 50 \cdot \mathbf{6} = \$310$	$10 \cdot 1.5^6 = \$113.91$
7th day	$10 + 50 \cdot \mathbf{7} = \$360$	$10 \cdot 1.5^7 = \$170.86$
nth day	$10 + 50\mathbf{n}$	$10 \cdot 1.5^n$

As you can see, on the 7th day, you begin having your money grow faster with choice (2). By the end of 2 weeks (14 days) the options are as follows.

14th day $10 + 50 \cdot \mathbf{14} = \$710$ $10 \cdot 1.5^{\mathbf{14}} = \$2919.29$

Here is how linear increase and exponential growth compare, in general.

Linear Increase	Exponential Growth
1. Begin with an amount b.	1. Begin with an amount b.
2. *Add* m (the slope) for x time periods.	2. *Multiply* by g (the growth factor) for x time periods.
3. After the x time periods, there will be $b + mx$.	3. After the x time periods, there will be $b \cdot g^x$.

The growth model applies even when $x = 0$. If there are no time periods, the original amount is unchanged, so $b \cdot g^0 = b$. That means $g^0 = 1$, regardless of the value of the growth factor g.

Zero Exponent Property:

If g is any nonzero real number, then $g^0 = 1$.

In words, the zero power of any nonzero number equals 1. For example, $4^0 = 1$, $(-2)^0 = 1$, and $(\frac{5}{7})^0 = 1$.

430

Example 3 Evaluate $4 \cdot 10^2 + 5 \cdot 10^1 + 7 \cdot 10^0$.

Solution Apply the correct order of operations. Do powers first.

$$= 4 \cdot 100 + 5 \cdot 10 + 7 \cdot 1$$
$$= 400 + 50 + 7$$
$$= 457$$

Putting it altogether, $4 \cdot 10^2 + 5 \cdot 10^1 + 7 \cdot 10^0 = 457$. Notice that the coefficient of the second power of 10 becomes the hundreds digit, the coefficient of the first power of 10 becomes the tens digit, and the coefficient of the zero power of 10 becomes the units digit.

The Compound Interest Formula is an application of the growth model of powering. In

$$T = P(1 + i)^n$$

the growth factor is $1 + i$. If $100 is invested for 0 years at 5%, then $P = 100$, $i = 0.05$, and $n = 0$. But there is no time for the money to earn anything. So $T = 100$. Substituting all these values,

$$100 = 100(1.05)^0.$$

So $1.05^0 = 1$. The yield of 5% has no effect. Again the Zero Exponent Property is confirmed.

Questions

Covering the Reading

In 1–3, refer to Example 1.

1. After 7 years, **a.** how many times has the rabbit population doubled? **b.** How many rabbits are there? **a) 14; b) 409,600**

2. How many rabbits will there be after 10 years? **26,214,400**

3. If the rabbit population triples in 6 months, rather than doubles, how many rabbits will there be after 5 years? **1,476,225**

4. Give the general formula for **a.** linear growth; **b.** exponential growth. **a) $b + mx$; b) bg^x**

5. Refer to Example 2. After one month (30 days), how much would you have with choice (1)? with choice (2)? **1) $1510; 2) $1,917,510.60**

6. State the growth model for powering. **See margin.**

NOTES ON QUESTIONS
Error Analysis for Questions 1-3: A common error is not to realize that the number of time periods is twice the number of years. Thus, if students got 3200 as the answer to **Question 1,** they have used 7 as the number of time periods. Have students reread the problem. Ask: What is the time period? (6 months) How many such periods are in 7 years? (14)

ADDITIONAL ANSWERS
6. When an amount is multiplied by g in each of x time periods, then after the x periods, the original amount will be multiplied by g^x.

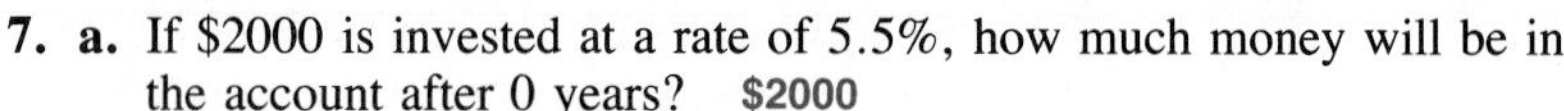

NOTES ON QUESTIONS
Questions 12 and 13: Town A is growing linearly and town B is growing exponentially. To get the growth factor, students must add 1 to the percent of growth to get 1.04.

Making Connections for Question 19: This problem should be done by using the meaning of exponents. You can use this question to anticipate the Product of Powers Property, which is covered in Lesson 9-5.

Questions 22 and 23: Students can use the pattern $b \cdot g^x$ rather than the Compound Interest Formula. Either way is all right.

Alternate Approach for Question 32: Some students may be interested in a shorter way to solve this problem than calculating each power of 2 and then adding the results. One approach follows: If S is the sum of the number of kernels of wheat on all the squares, then

$S = 1 + 2 + 2^2 + 2^3 + \ldots + 2^{62} + 2^{63}$.

Multiply both sides by 2:
$2S = 2 + 2^2 + 2^3 + 2^4 + \ldots + 2^{63} + 2^{64}$.

Subtract the first from the second:

$S = 2^{64} - 1$

$\approx 1.84 \cdot 10^{19} =$
18,400,000,000,000,000,000.

Still another way to do this problem is to begin calculating the sums

$1 = 1$
$1 + 2 = 3$
$1 + 2 + 4 = 7$
$1 + 2 + 4 + 8 = 15$
$1 + 2 + 4 + 8 + 16 = 31$

Notice that the sum in each row is one less than the last addend in the next row. So if 2^{63} is the number of grains in the last square on the chessboard, then the sum of all grains until that time will be $2^{64} - 1$.

7. a. If \$2000 is invested at a rate of 5.5%, how much money will be in the account after 0 years? \$2000
b. What is the significance of part a?
There is no time for the money to earn interest.

8. If b is any nonzero real number, then b to what power equals 1? 0

In 9 and 10, simplify.

9. $6 \cdot 10^2 + 3 \cdot 10^1 + 8 \cdot 10^0$ 638 **10.** $9 \cdot 10^4 + 4 \cdot 10^2 + 10^0$ 90,401

Applying the Mathematics

11. The following chart describes the exponential growth of a colony of bacteria. You can see that this strain of bacteria grows very fast. In only one hour it grows from 2000 to 54,000 bacteria.

Time Intervals from now	Time (min)	Number of Bacteria
0	0	2000
1	20	$6000 = 2000 \cdot 3^1$
2	40	$18{,}000 = 2000 \cdot 3^2$
3	60	$54{,}000 = 2000 \cdot 3^3$

a. How long does it take the population to triple? 20 minutes
b. How many times will the population triple in two hours? 6
c. How many bacteria will be in the colony after two hours?
d. How many bacteria will be in the colony after four hours?
1,062,882,000 c) 1,458,000

In 12 and 13, town A has 20,000 people and is adding 800 people each year. Town B has 20,000 people and is growing exponentially by 4% each year.

12. After 1 year, how many more people will live in town B than town A? No more; populations are equal.

13. After 10 years, how many more people will town B have than town A? 1605

14. The gross income of a company is growing at the rate of 15% per year. The company's gross income this year is \$2,000,000. If the growth rate remains constant, what will be the company's gross income at the end of 3 years? \$3,041,750

15. In 1986 the U.S. national debt was about 1.7 trillion dollars and was growing at a rate of about 7% per year. At this rate, find the national debt in 1994. ≈\$2.92 trillion

16. Jamaica's population of 2,347,000 in 1986 was expected to grow exponentially by 1.2% each year for the next twenty years.
a. With this growth, what will the population be in 1989? 2,432,510
b. With this growth, what will the population be in 2006? 2,979,362

432

17. Calculators and computers are getting smaller and smaller. It has been estimated that the amount of information that can be stored on a silicon chip is doubling every 18 months. If today's chips have 5000 memory locations, how many might the same size chip have in 6 years? **80,000**

In 18–21, simplify.

18. $(4y)^0$ when $y = \frac{1}{2}$ **1**

19. $7^0 \cdot 7^1 \cdot 7^2$ **343**

20. $(x + y)^0$ when $x = 3$ and $y = -8$ **1**

21. $(\frac{1}{2})^0 + (\frac{2}{3})^2$ **$1\frac{4}{9}$**

Review

22. \$2200 is deposited in a savings account.
    a. What will be the total amount of money in the account after 6 years at an annual yield of 6%? **\$3,120.74**
    b. How much interest will have been earned in those 6 years? *(Lesson 9-1)* **\$920.74**

23. Jeremy invests x dollars for 2 years at an annual yield of 7%. At the end of the 2 years he has \$915.92 dollars in his account.
    a. Write an equation describing this situation. **$x \cdot 1.07^2 = 915.92$**
    b. Find x. *(Lesson 9-1)* **\$800**

24. A card is drawn randomly from a deck of 52 playing cards. Find **a.** P(a three); **b.** P(a king or an ace). *(Lessons 1-7, 3-5)* **a) $\frac{1}{13}$; b) $\frac{2}{13}$**

25. Suppose a letter from the alphabet is chosen randomly. What is the probability that it is in the first half of the alphabet and is a vowel? *(Lesson 4-8)* **$\frac{3}{26}$**

26. *Skill sequence* Solve. *(Lessons 7-4, 7-8)*
    a. $y^2 = 144$ **12 or -12**
    b. $(4y)^2 = 144$ **3 or -3**
    c. $(4y - 20)^2 = 144$ **8 or 2**
    d. $y^2 + 80 = 144$ **8 or -8**

In 27–30, simplify. *(Lessons 1-5, 6-9)*

27. $6(n + 8) + 4(2n - 1)$ **$14n + 44$**

28. $13 - (2 - x)$ **$11 + x$**

29. $4s^9$ when $s = \frac{1}{2}$ **$\frac{1}{128}$**

30. $t^2 \cdot t^3$ when $t = 11$ **161,051**

31. *Skill sequence* Simplify. *(Lesson 5-1)*
    a. $\frac{2}{3} \div \frac{4}{3}$ **$\frac{1}{2}$**
    b. $\frac{x}{15} \div \frac{x}{5}$ **$\frac{1}{3}$**
    c. $\frac{a}{b} \div \frac{c}{b}$ **$\frac{a}{c}$**

Exploration

32. An old story is told about a man who did a favor for a king. The king wished to reward the man and asked how he could do so. The man asked for a chessboard with one kernel of wheat on the first square of the chessboard, two kernels on the second square, four on the third square, eight on the fourth square, and so on for the entire sixty-four squares of the board. Find how many grains of wheat would be on the whole chessboard. (The answer may amaze you. It is about 500 times the total present yearly wheat production of the world.) **about $1.84 \cdot 10^{19}$**

FOLLOW-UP

MORE PRACTICE

For more questions on SPUR Objectives, use *Lesson Master 9-2,* shown below.

EXTENSION

Computer The following program can be used to solve **Question 32.** (Note that this program uses the BASIC symbol ^, which is introduced in the next lesson.)

```
10 FOR N=1 TO 63
20 LET X=2^N
30 LET S=S+X
40 NEXT N
50 PRINT "THE SUM IS:"
   1+S
60 END
```

NAME ______

LESSON **MASTER 9–2**
QUESTIONS ON **SPUR** OBJECTIVES

■SKILLS *Objective A (See pages 471–473 for objectives.)*
In 1–9, evaluate.

1. 2^4 **16**
2. -2^4 **-16**
3. $(-2)^4$ **16**
4. $4 \cdot 17^0$ **4**
5. -5^3 **-125**
6. $(-5)^3$ **-125**
7. If $x = -4$, then $10 + x^0 =$ **11**.
8. $3 \cdot 10^2 + 6 \cdot 10^1 + 8 \cdot 10^0$ **368**
9. $8 \cdot 10^0 + 2 \cdot 10^1 + 1 \cdot 10^2$ **128**

■PROPERTIES *Objective E*
In 10 and 11, tell whether the statement is true or false. If false, correct the statement by changing the right side of the equation.

10. $12 + x^0 = 12$ **false; $12 + x^0 = 13$**
11. If $x = 3$ and $y = 2$, then $(x + y)^0 = 1$. **true**

■USES *Objective G*

12. Suppose that 10 squirrels are introduced to an area. If their population doubles every three months, how many squirrels are there in 1 year? **160 squirrels**

13. The number of people who ride skateboards in a town is growing at the rate of 20% per year. If 400 ride skateboards now and the growth rate remains constant, how many will ride skateboards in 3 years? **691 people**

14. A gray filter lets in only $\frac{2}{5}$ of the light that hits it. What fraction (or portion) of the light would pass through a series of 3 of these filters? **$\frac{8}{125}$ of light**

15. A copy machine can make an enlargement 1.2 times as large as the original. If you make copies of copies, enlarging each time, how many times as large as the original will the fourth copy be? **about 2.1 times as large**

LESSON 9-3

RESOURCES
■ Lesson Master 9-3

OBJECTIVE

G Solve problems involving exponential decay.

TEACHING NOTES

The formula for exponential decay is the same as the formula for exponential growth, namely $b \cdot g^x$. In the **Example,** the starting amount is 67,000 and the growth factor $g = 1 - .05 = .95$, which is less than 1, so there is decay.

Making Connections
To emphasize the last paragraph of the lesson, you might graph the population of the town over time. Not only does this emphasize the drop in population, but prepares students for Lesson 9-4 on graphing.

If you do not assign the Exploration question, at least explain to your students why this lesson is so named.

ADDITIONAL EXAMPLE
When calculators were first introduced they were quite expensive, but their price dropped dramatically as technology improved. For a certain type of calculator that cost \$350 in 1973, the price dropped about 19% each year. What was the price 15 years later?
$350(.81)^{15} \approx$ \$14.84

LESSON

Exponential Decay

bonjour	vous	avec
au revoir	étudie	mais
salut	je suis	mal
voici	français	oui
voilà	anglais	non
franc	parle	est-ce que
aujourd'hui	bien	pourquoi
mercredi	très	ils sont

A student crams for a Friday French test, learning 100 vocabulary words Thursday night. Each day the student expects to forget 10% of the words known. If the test is delayed from Friday to Monday, what will happen if the student does not review?

To answer this question, a table is convenient. Since 10% of the words are forgotten, 90% are remembered.

Day	Day Number	Words Known
Thursday	0	100
Friday	1	$100(.90) = 90$
Saturday	2	$100(.90)(.90) = 100(.90)^2 = 81$
Sunday	3	$100(.90)(.90)(.90) = 100(.90)^3 = 72.9 \approx 73$
Monday	4	$100(.90)(.90)(.90)(.90) = 100(.90)^4 = 65.61 \approx 66$

The pattern is just like that of the growth model or compound interest. After d days, this student will know about $100(.90)^d$ words. Because the growth factor .90 is less than 1, the number of known words decreases. The situation is of a type called **exponential decay.**

Exponential decay can occur when populations are decreasing.

Example A town with population 67,000 is losing 5% of its population each year. At this rate, how many people will be left in the town after 10 years?

Solution If 5% of the population is leaving, 95% is staying. Every year, the population is multiplied by 0.95.

$$\begin{aligned} \text{population} &= 67{,}000 \cdot (0.95)^{10} \\ &\approx 40{,}115 \end{aligned}$$

After ten years, the population will be about 40,115.

Exponential decay is similar to compound interest. If the town starts with P people and loses $r\%$ of its population each year, then after n years there will be $P(1 - r\%)^n$ people. The percent loss is like an annual yield loss.

Questions

Covering the Reading

1. In the French test situation of this lesson, if the test is delayed a week until the next Friday, about how many words will the student know? **≈48**
2. Evaluate $100x^5$ when $x = .90$ **59.049**

In 3 and 4, refer to the Example.

3. What is the population of this town after 1 year? **63,650**
4. What is the population of this town after n years? **$67{,}000(.95)^n$**
5. If the population of a town declines by 6.3% each year, by what number would you multiply to find the population each year? **.937**
6. A school has 2500 students. The number of students is decreasing by 3% each year.
   a. By what number would you multiply to find the number of students after each year? **.97**
   b. If this rate continues, write an expression for the number of students after n years. **$2500 \cdot (.97)^n$**
   c. If this rate continues, how many students will the school have after 10 years? **≈1844**

Applying the Mathematics

7. The original size of a diagram is 8 inches by 10 inches. It is put through a photocopy machine six times. Each time it is reduced to 75% of its previous dimensions. What is its final size? **≈1.4 in. by 1.8 in.**
8. Bertha Bigbucks had 12 children. In her will she left her first child \$300,000. The second child got $\frac{1}{4}$ of what the first child did. The third child got $\frac{1}{4}$ of what the second child did, and so on. How much did the last child get? **about 7¢**

NOTES ON QUESTIONS
Question 7: The copier reduces the picture to 75% of its dimensions. You might want to ask what happens to the area. (The area is reduced to $.75^2$ of the original area.)

Error Analysis for Question 8: Some students may mistakenly evaluate $300{,}000(\frac{1}{4})^{12}$ rather than $300{,}000(\frac{1}{4})^{11}$. You could give two explanations. In one method, look at the sequence $300{,}000$, $300{,}000 \cdot \frac{1}{4}$, $300{,}000 \cdot (\frac{1}{4})^2, \ldots$. The exponent is one less than the child's position in the family. Another method parallels our treatment of arithmetic sequences in Lesson 6-4. Consider the first child's inheritance as $\$1{,}200{,}000 \cdot \frac{1}{4}$. To answer the question, evaluate $1{,}200{,}000(\frac{1}{4})^{12}$.

NOTES ON QUESTIONS
Computer for Question 9: The BASIC notation ↑ or ^ for powering is introduced. The expression g^t is typed as G↑T (or G^T). This is a nice program to have handy when students graph exponential growth and decay. They need many points to plot the exponential curves. This will reduce the amount of time needed to prepare a table of points. You or a student could easily build in a FOR/NEXT loop to calculate several values during one run of the program.

Question 19: Ask students to describe the methods they used. It is possible, if not likely, that students will have used different methods.

Question 22: Students should use *trial and error* or repeated multiplication by 3.

ADDITIONAL ANSWERS
15.

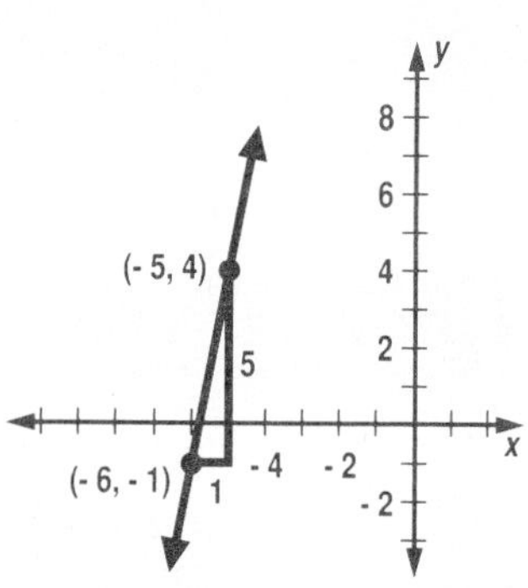

9. The following program finds the result when an amount grows or decays exponentially. The BASIC statement for n^x is N ^ X or N ↑ X.

```
10 PRINT "EXPONENTIAL GROWTH"
20 PRINT "WHAT IS THE AMOUNT AT BEGINNING?"
30 INPUT B
40 PRINT "WHAT ARE YOU MULTIPLYING BY?"
50 INPUT G
60 PRINT "HOW MANY TIME PERIODS?"
70 INPUT T
80 LET AMT = B * G ^ T
90 PRINT "TOTAL AMOUNT IS "
100 PRINT AMT
110 END
```

a. What will the total be if 8, 3, and 6 are entered? 5832
b. What will the total be if 8, 0.33, and 6 are entered? ≈.01
c. What should be entered to find the amount to which a city of 100,000 will grow in 10 years if the growth rate is 2% a year? 100,000, 1.02, and 10

Review

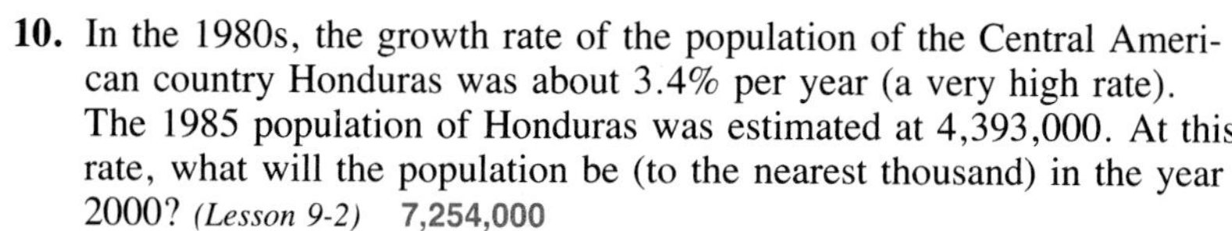

10. In the 1980s, the growth rate of the population of the Central American country Honduras was about 3.4% per year (a very high rate). The 1985 population of Honduras was estimated at 4,393,000. At this rate, what will the population be (to the nearest thousand) in the year 2000? *(Lesson 9-2)* 7,254,000

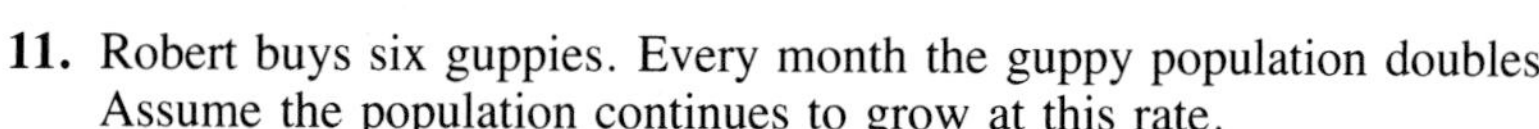

11. Robert buys six guppies. Every month the guppy population doubles. Assume the population continues to grow at this rate.
a. How many guppies will there be after 4 months? 96
b. How many will there be after a year? *(Lesson 9-2)* 24,576

12. Calculate the interest paid on \$500 at a 6.1% annual yield for 5 years. *(Lesson 9-1)* \$172.27

13. When $n = 3$ and $x = 4$, which is larger, x^n or n^x? *(Lesson 9-1)* n^x

14. Given the equation $y = -\frac{1}{2}x + 20$, find the slope and the y-intercept. *(Lesson 8-4)* slope $= -\frac{1}{2}$, y-intercept $= 20$

15. Graph the line which passes through (-6, -1) with slope 5. *(Lesson 8-2)* See margin.

16. If $a + b = 75$, find $(a + b)^2$. *(Lesson 7-8)* 5625

17. The sum of two numbers is 36. One of the numbers is k. Write an expression for the product of the numbers. *(Lesson 4-1)* $k(36 - k)$

18. Calculate 230% of 60. *(Lesson 5-4)* **138**

19. Calculate in your head. *(Lesson 6-3)*
a. The total cost of 6 cans of beans at \$.98 per can. **\$5.88**
b. The total cost of 4 tickets at \$15.05 per ticket. **\$60.20**
c. A 15% tip for a \$40.00 dinner bill. **\$6.00**

20. Write an expression for the volume of the box pictured at the right. *(Lesson 4-1)*
$y \cdot 2y \cdot 3y = 6y^3$

In 21 and 22, solve.

21. $2x = 512$ *(Lesson 4-4)* **256**

22. $486 = 18 \cdot 3^t$ *(Lessons 1-4, 4-4)*
3

23. *Skill sequence* Lesson 2-3)
a. Simplify $\frac{2}{9} + \frac{5}{9}$. **$\frac{7}{9}$** **b.** Simplify $\frac{2}{3} + \frac{5}{9}$. **$\frac{11}{9}$**
c. Solve $\frac{2}{3}x + \frac{5}{9}x = 33$. **27**

24a) length of time it takes half the atoms of a radioactive substance to disintegrate

Exploration

24. Exponential decay gets its name from the decay of elements in nature, called radioactive decay. Radioactive decay is used to approximate the age of archaeological objects that were once alive. This can be done because all living things contain radioactive carbon_{14}, which has a half-life of 5600 years.
a. What is meant by the half-life of an element?
b. A fossil animal bone is found to have $\frac{1}{16}$ of the carbon_{14} that it had as living animal bone. How old is the bone? **22,400 years**

The age of this Tyrannosaurus rex was determined to be about 70 million years.

FOLLOW-UP

MORE PRACTICE
For more questions on SPUR Objectives, use *Lesson Master 9-3,* shown below.

EXTENSION
Computer Have students add a FOR/NEXT loop to the program in **Question 9** so that it will calculate a table of values. sample: Replace lines 80–110 with the following:

```
80  PRINT "TIME PERIODS", "TOTAL AMOUNT"
90  FOR T=1 TO T
100 LET AMT=B*G^T
110 PRINT T,AMT
120 NEXT T
130 END
```

NAME ______________________

LESSON **MASTER 9–3**
QUESTIONS ON **SPUR** OBJECTIVES

■USES *Objective G (See pages 471–473 for objectives.)*

1. A 6″ by 4″ drawing is reduced three times by using a photocopy machine. Each time it is reduced to 90% of its previous dimensions. What is its final size? **≈4.4″ by 2.9″**

2. Suppose a radioactive substance loses $\frac{1}{2}$ of its remaining mass each second. How much of a 36 g sample will remain after 6 seconds? **0.5625 g**

3. Each year an automobile depreciates in value by 25%. Find the value after five years of a car which cost \$4800 new. **\$1139.06**

4. Because of the use of an antibiotic, 15% of the bacteria die each hour. After how many hours will less than 50% of the original bacteria remain alive? **5 hours**

5. The population of a large city has been decreasing 2% each year. At this rate, what will be the percent of loss in a decade? **≈18.3% less**

6. The enrollment at a certain college is increasing at the rate of 2% per year. If there are presently 1752 students, how many will there be in 10 years? **2136 students**

LESSON 9-4

RESOURCES
- Lesson Master 9-4
- Quiz on Lessons 9-1 Through 9-4
- Visual for Teaching Aid 46: Linear and Exponential Increase and Decrease
- Visual for Teaching Aid 47: Graph for **Example 4**
- Computer Master 19

OBJECTIVE

I Graph exponential growth and decay relationships.

TEACHING NOTES

Make sure students realize that when the growth factor g is greater than 1 as in **Examples 1-3,** exponential growth occurs. But when $0 < g < 1$ as in **Example 4,** exponential decay occurs. *Teaching Aid 46* provides a good summary.

Computer The second solution of **Example 1** involves a graphing calculator or computer program. These tools make it easy to examine many functions.

Example 3 asks students to work in two directions. In part **a,** they are given a nonintegral x and asked to estimate y, which in this case is denoted as N. In part **b,** they are given a value for y and asked to find the value of x associated with it. In both cases, the calculator is used to check the answer.

About the check for part **b,** which of the following values might be a better answer for x: 3.15, 3.28, 3.32, or 3.5? Since the function is increasing, the last two answers would give values greater

LESSON 9-4 Graphing Exponential Growth and Decay

The situations of the preceding lessons can all be graphed. In Lesson 9-2, you saw linear increase and exponential growth contrasted. In linear increase a constant amount is added and in exponential growth a constant amount is multiplied. In exponential growth, the multiplier is greater than one, and so such growth will eventually overtake linear increase. The difference can be seen in the graph of each type.

Linear Increase
$y = mx + b,\ m > 0$

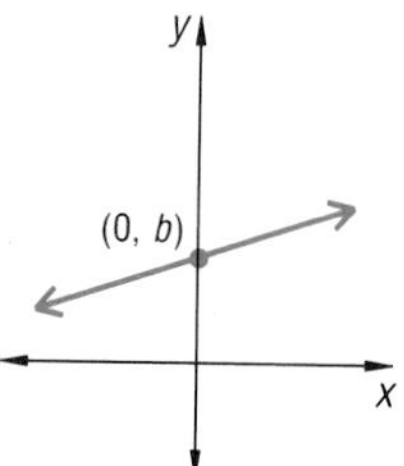

Exponential Growth
$y = b \cdot g^x,\ g > 1$

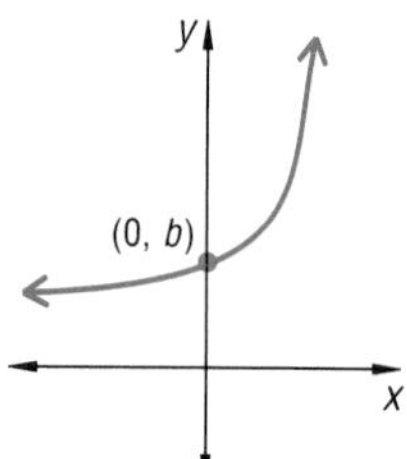

Example 1 You invest \$100 at an annual yield of 6%. **a.** Graph your savings if you take the interest out of the bank and put it in a piggy bank each year. **b.** On the same set of axes graph your savings if you leave the interest in the bank. Use values at the end of 0, 5, 10, 15, 20, 25, and 30 years.

Solution 1

a. 6% of the original \$100 (or \$6) is earned in interest each year. If y is the amount after x years, $y = 100 + 6x$. Make a table.

number of years	0	5	10	15	20	25	30
value	\$100	\$130	\$160	\$190	\$220	\$250	\$280

b. Make a table for the amount saved at 6% compound interest. Use the formula $y = 100(1.06)^x$.

number of years	0	5	10	15	20	25	30
value	\$100	\$134	\$179	\$240	\$321	\$429	\$574

Plot the points and connect them for each graph. In the graph at right, the piggy bank graph (blue) is linear. The compound interest graph (green) is exponential.

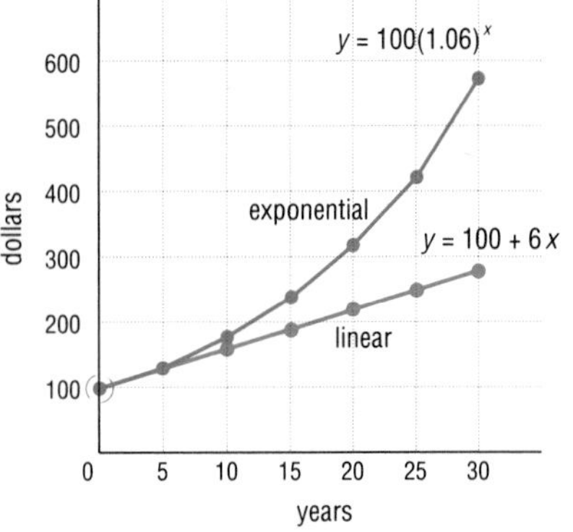

Solution 2 Use a graphing calculator or a computer with a function grapher. Set the domain from 0 to 30 and the range from 0 to 600. First graph $y = 100 + 6x$, then $y = 100(1.06)^x$. You should get graphs like those in Solution 1.

As you can see in the graph in Example 1, exponential growth graphs curve upward. They do not follow a straight line.

Example 2 The number of bacteria per square millimeter in a certain culture doubles every 6 hours. There are 100 bacteria per square millimeter at first count. So 6 hours later there are 200, 12 hours later there are 400, and so on. After x 6-hour intervals, there will be B bacteria in the culture, where $B = 100 \cdot 2^x$. Draw 5 points on the graph of this equation and connect them with a smooth curve.

Solution Let the 5 values of x be 0, 1, 2, 3, and 4. This leads to the points (0, 100), (1, 200), (2, 400), (3, 800), (4, 1600). These are graphed at the right.

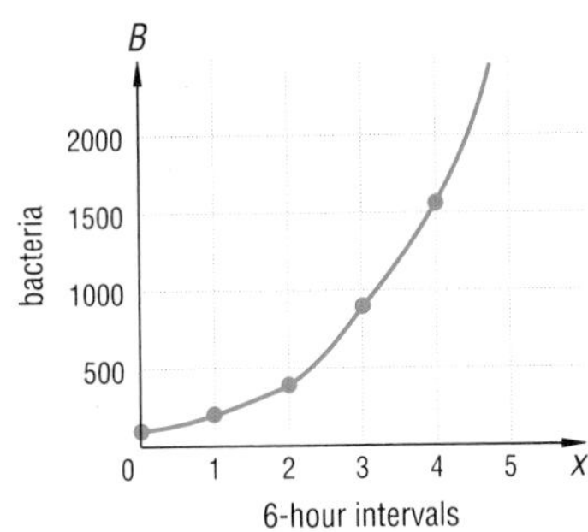

Example 3 Use the graph in Example 2. **a.** Estimate the number of bacteria per square millimeter at the end of 15 hours. **b.** Estimate how long it takes for the number of bacteria to grow to 1000 per square millimeter.

Solution **a.** The number of 6-hour intervals in 15 hours is $\frac{15}{6} = 2.5$. Read where $x = 2.5$ on the graph. At this point $N \approx 550$.
b. On the graph find where $N = 1000$. At this point $x \approx 3.3$ intervals, so it should take about $3.3 \cdot 6 \approx 20$ hours.

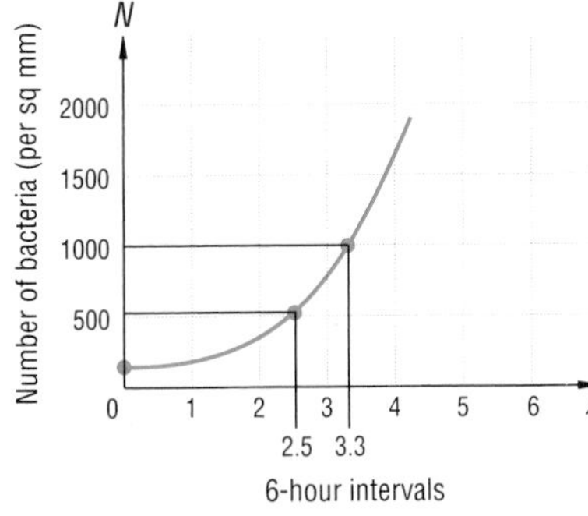

than 985, and hence have a chance of being closer to 1000. The 3.5 is overly large, however, according to the graph.

Thanks to the calculator, we are able to work with nonintegral exponents easily. We would like students to see that $2^{1.5}$ is between 2^1 and 2^2.

Students are often intrigued by the fact that the graph of an exponential decrease situation approaches the x-axis (as an *asymptote*) but never touches it. This can be shown by extending the graph from **Example 4.** (*Teaching Aid 47* can be used.)

ADDITIONAL EXAMPLES

1. Two villages each have 50 inhabitants. The first village grows by 20 people each year. The second one grows 20% each year. Graph the populations of the two villages over the next 10 years.
1st village: $y = 50 + 20x$
2nd village: $y = 50(1.20)^x$

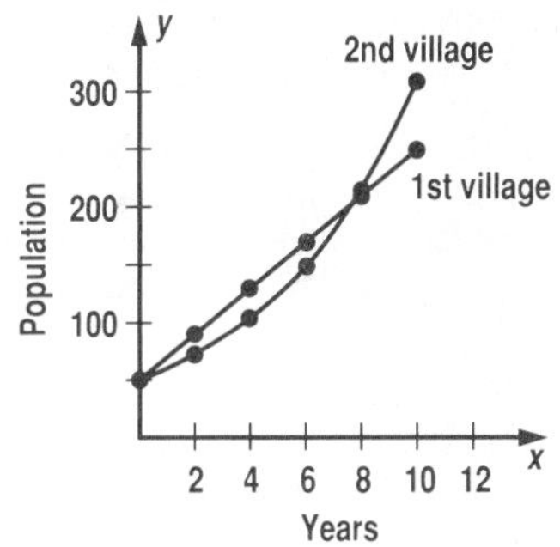

1st village		**2nd village**	
2	**90**	**2**	**72**
4	**130**	**4**	**104**
6	**170**	**6**	**149**
8	**210**	**8**	**215**
10	**250**	**10**	**310**

2. A biologist is raising white mice under special conditions. The mouse population doubles every 5 weeks. At the beginning of the experiment there are 10 mice. Graph the mouse population for 25 weeks.

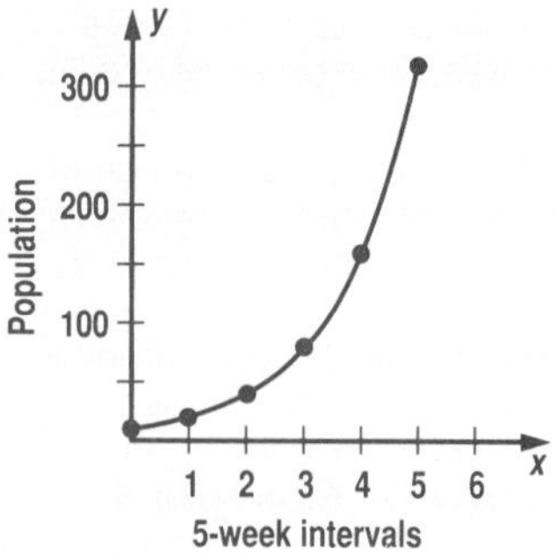

x	y
0	**10**
1	**20**
2	**40**
3	**80**
4	**160**
5	**320**

3. Use the graph from Additional Example 2 to estimate the number of mice after 18 weeks.
≈120

4. Use the graph from Additional Example 2 to estimate how long it takes for the mouse population to reach 250.
≈4.6 intervals or 23 weeks

Check Use $N = 100 \cdot 2^x$ and your calculator.

a. 100 [×] 2 [y^x] 2.5 [=] 566 is close to 500 on the graph.

b. 100 [×] 2 [y^x] 3.3 [=] 985 is close to 1000.

The next example deals with an exponential decay situation found in Lesson 9-3.

Example 4 A student memorizes 100 words and then forgets 10% of those words each day. If w is the number of words known after d days, then $w = 100(.90)^d$. Graph this equation for values of d between 0 and 10.

Solution From the formula, obtain the coordinates of points.

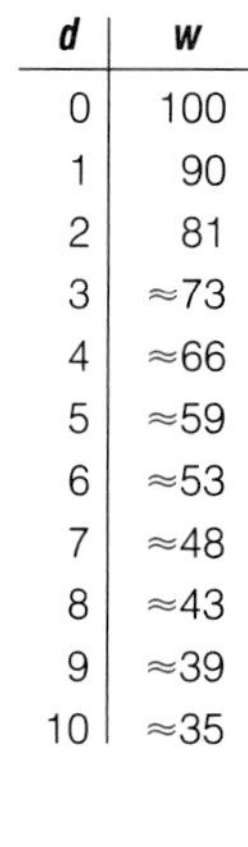

d	w
0	100
1	90
2	81
3	≈73
4	≈66
5	≈59
6	≈53
7	≈48
8	≈43
9	≈39
10	≈35

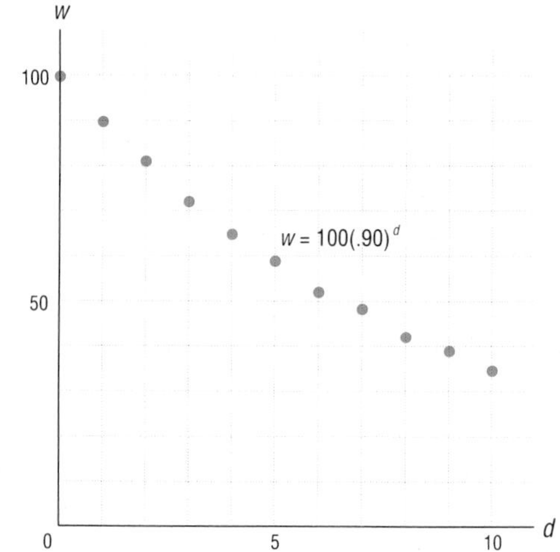

The graph of Example 4 differs from those in the previous examples. It goes down as x increases. The others go up as x increases.

Linear Decrease
$y = mx + b,\ m < 0$

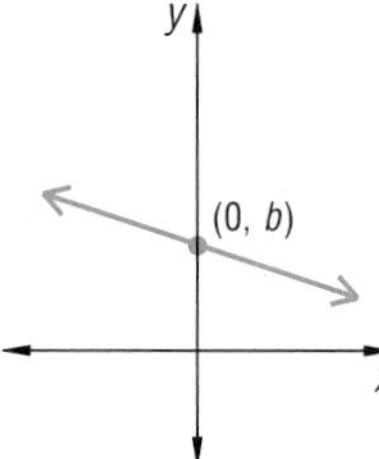

Exponential Decay
$y = b \cdot g^x,\ 0 < g < 1$

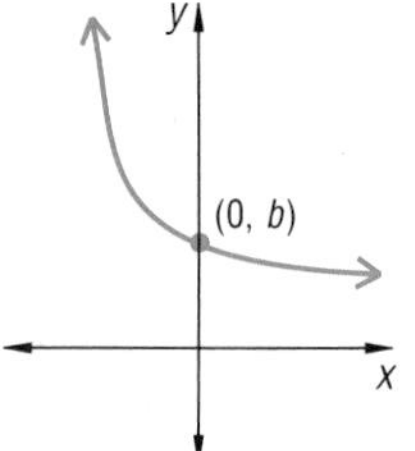

440

Questions

Covering the Reading

1. In linear increase, a constant amount is __?__ to the total, while in exponential growth, a constant amount is __?__ by the total. **added; multiplied**
2. As x increases, which increases more rapidly, $y = 100 + 6x$ or $y = 100(1.06)^x$? **$y = 100 \cdot (1.06)^x$**
3. What is the difference in shape of the graphs of linear decrease and exponential decay? **The graph of linear decrease is a line. The graph of exponential decay is a curve.**

In 4 and 5, refer to Example 1.

4. How much more will the amount be in 30 years at compound interest than with the piggy bank? **$294**
5. Use the graph to estimate when the investment will be worth $500. **after about 27 years**
6. If you start with 100 bacteria per square millimeter and they double every 6 hours, what is the growth formula? **See margin.**
7. From the graph in Example 2, estimate the number of bacteria at the end of 21 hours. **≈1300**
8. From the graph in Example 2, estimate the number of hours it takes to produce 2000 bacteria. **≈26**
9. Refer to Example 4.
   a. About how many words did the student forget the first 3 days? **27**
   b. About how many more words did the student forget the second 3 days? **20**

Applying the Mathematics

10. Tell whether each of the following graphs is linear or exponential.
    a. $y = 3x - 2$ **linear**
    b. $y = 3x$ **linear**
    c. $y = 200(1.05)^x$ **exponential**
    d. $2y = x + 1$ **linear**
11. The graph of which of the following equations goes up to the right?
    a. $y = 5^x$
    b. $y = .075^x$
    c. $y = 100 \cdot (2.3)^x$
    d. $y = \frac{1}{2}(10)^x$
    a, c, d
12. If the growth rate of the 1980s continues, the U.S. population will double every 75 years. Since the U.S. population was 226.5 million in 1980, the number of people y (in millions) in the U.S. after x 75-year periods from 1980 is given by the formula $y = 226.5 \cdot 2^x$.
    a. Graph six points on the graph, letting x equal the integers 0 to 5, and connect them with a smooth curve. **See margin.**
    b. Estimate the value of x when the U.S. population is one billion. **≈2.14**
    c. In what year is the U.S. population expected to be one billion? **≈2141**

5. Mr. Scrooge is such a cruel boss that each year 40% of his employees quit. If 300 people work for Mr. Scrooge now, graph the number of these employees that will still be working for him n years from now. Use $n = 1, 2, 3, 4,$ or 5.

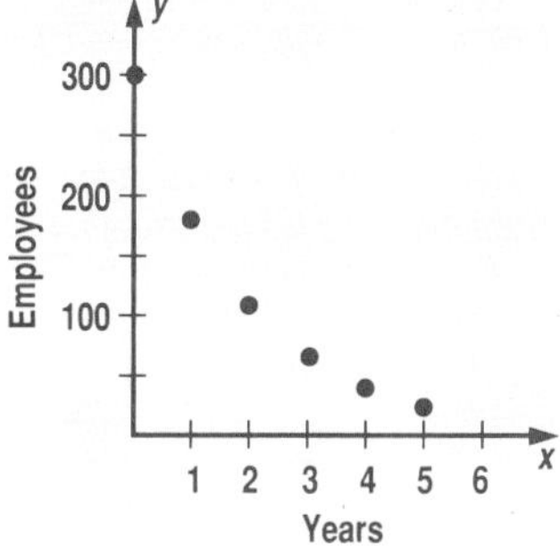

Years	Employees
0	300
1	180
2	108
3	65
4	39
5	23

NOTES ON QUESTIONS

Question 9: Using the chart from **Example 4** may be an easier way to find the answers than using the graph.

ADDITIONAL ANSWERS

6. $N = 100 \cdot 2^x$, **where x is the number of 6-hour intervals.**

12a.

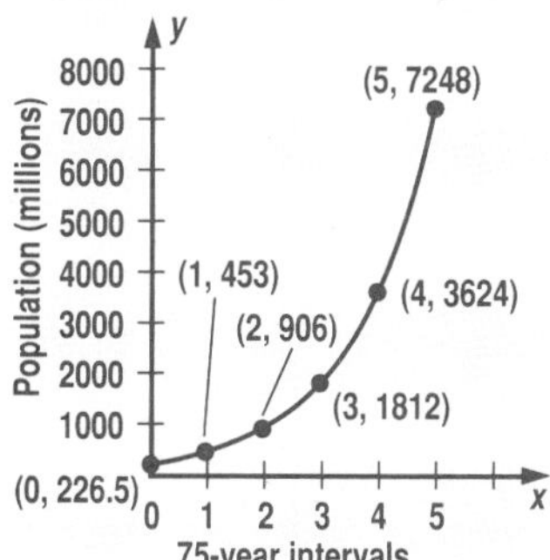

NOTES ON QUESTIONS
Question 14c: This question asks "Can $(\frac{1}{2})^x$ ever be zero?" in a graphical context.

Question 20: Before assigning this question you might want to establish common choices for points which will determine the estimated line.

Making Connections for Questions 23 and 24: Aspects of the Distributive Property are reviewed in preparation for the study of polynomials in the next chapter.

13. sample:

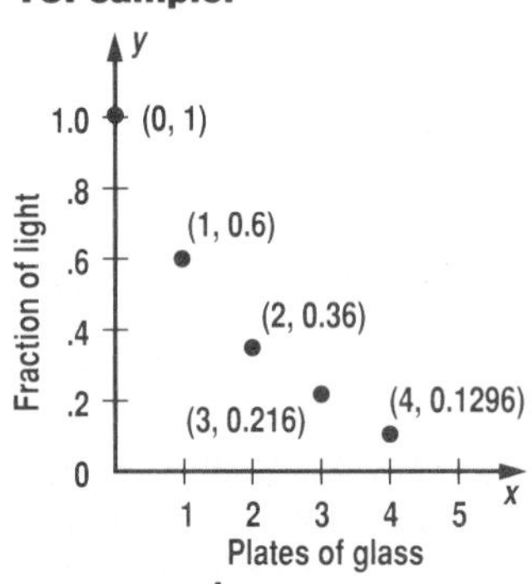

14a. 1, 1; $\frac{1}{8}$, .125; $\frac{1}{1024}$, .00098; $\frac{1}{1,048,576}$, .00000095 or .000001 (depending on calculator).

14b.

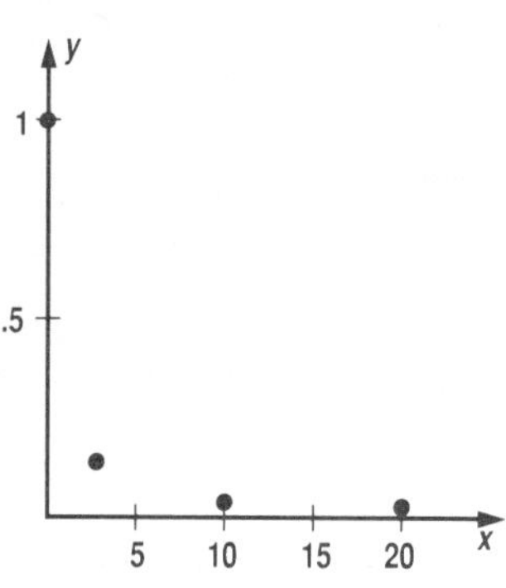

13. When one plate of glass allows 60% of the light through, the amount of light y passing through x panes of tinted glass is described by the formula $y = (.6)^x$. Draw 5 points on the graph of this equation. See margin.
14. Consider the equation $y = (\frac{1}{2})^x$.
    a. Find the value of y as both a fraction and a decimal when x takes on each value in this replacement set: {0, 3, 10, 20}. See margin.
    b. Draw the graph using the points from part a. See margin.
    c. Does the graph ever touch the x-axis? No

Review

15. Forgottonia's population of 680,000 is decreasing at a rate of 25% per year. What will the town's population be in 20 years? *(Lesson 9-3)* ≈2156

In 16 and 17, consider the equations $k = 30 + 1.05n$ and $k = 30(1.05)^n$. *(Lesson 9-2)*

16. In which equation does k increase more rapidly? $k = 30(1.05)^n$
17. Which equation could represent the value of $30 invested at 5% compound interest for n years? $k = 30(1.05)^n$
18. Evaluate $4x^n$
    a. when $x = 1.2$ and $n = 3$; 6.912
    b. when $x = 1.2$ and $n = 0$. *(Lessons 1-4, 9-2)* 4
19. Evaluate $(2x)^2(3y)^3$ when $x = 4$ and $y = -2$. *(Lesson 1-4)* -13,824

442

a-b) See margin; c) y = -4.5x + 45.5

20. The graph at the right shows the average diameter of rocks in a stream at half-mile intervals from the stream's source.
a. Fit a line to the data.
b. Give two points on your line in part a.
c. Find the equation of your line using the points in part b.
d. Predict the average diameter of rocks 7.5 miles from the stream's source. *(Lesson 8-7)*
about 11.75 inches

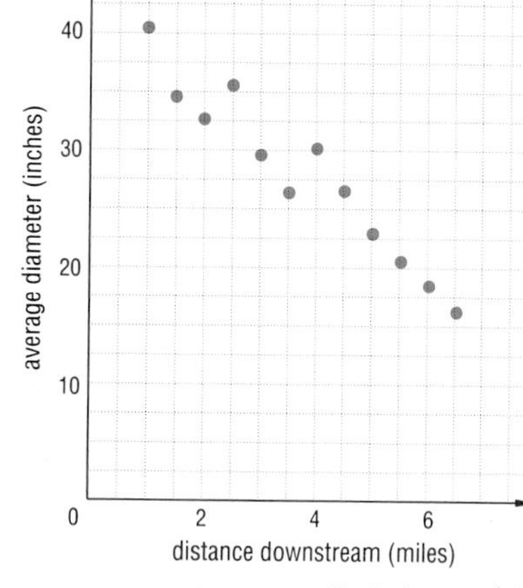

21. a. Copy and complete the computer program below to find the total T in the bank when \$100 is invested at an annual yield of 6% for x years. 100 * 1.06 ^ YEAR

```
10 PRINT "$100 AT 6 PERCENT"
20 PRINT "YEARS", "AMOUNTS"
30 FOR YEAR = 0 TO 20
40    LET AMOUNT = _?_
50    PRINT YEAR, AMOUNT
60 NEXT YEAR
70 END
```

20   320.71355
b. When this program is run, write the last line that will be printed.
c. How would you modify line 30 to print the table for $x = 1, 2, 3, \ldots, 100$? 30 FOR YEAR = 1 TO 100
d. After the change in part c is made, what will be the last line printed when the program is run? *(Lesson 9-1)* 100   33930.208

22. *Skill sequence* Add and simplify. *(Lesson 2-3)*
a. $\frac{4}{x} + \frac{5}{x}$ $\frac{9}{x}$
b. $\frac{4}{y} + \frac{5}{2y}$ $\frac{13}{2y}$
c. $4 + \frac{5}{2z}$ $\frac{8z + 5}{2z}$

In 23 and 24, simplify. *(Lesson 6-3)*

23. $4a^2(a + 3) + 2a(a^2 - 1)$ $6a^3 + 12a^2 - 2a$

24. $b(b + 3) - b(b + 1)$ 2b

25. Recall that if an item is discounted x%, you pay $(100 - x)$% of the original price. Calculate in your head the amount you pay for a jacket originally costing \$200 and discounted.
a. 10%. \$180
b. 20%. \$160
c. 33%. *(Lesson 5-4)* \$134

Exploration

26. Calculate values of $y = 100(1.06)^x$ when $x = -5$ and $x = -10$. Refer to Example 1. What do the answers mean? See margin.

FOLLOW-UP

MORE PRACTICE
For more questions on SPUR Objectives, use *Lesson Master 9-4,* shown below.

EVALUATION
A quiz covering Lessons 9-1 through 9-4 is provided in the Teacher's Resource File.

20a. Answers will vary.

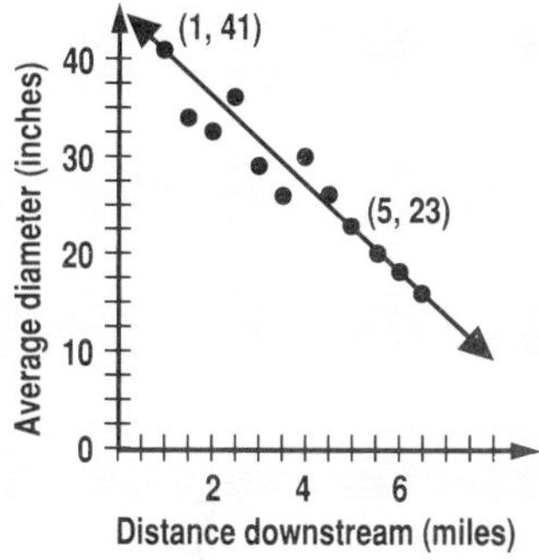

20b. sample: (1, 41) and (5, 23).

26. (-5, 74.7), (-10, 55.8), the answers can be viewed as amounts in the account 5 and 10 years ago.

NAME

LESSON **MASTER 9–4**
QUESTIONS ON SPUR OBJECTIVES

REPRESENTATIONS *Objective I (See pages 471–473 for objectives.)*
In 1–4, tell whether the graph of each equation is linear or exponential.

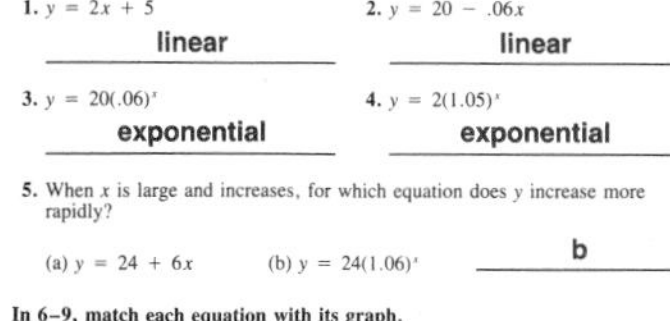

1. $y = 2x + 5$ linear
2. $y = 20 - .06x$ linear
3. $y = 20(.06)^x$ exponential
4. $y = 2(1.05)^x$ exponential

5. When x is large and increases, for which equation does y increase more rapidly?
(a) $y = 24 + 6x$ (b) $y = 24(1.06)^x$ b

In 6–9, match each equation with its graph.
6. $y = 10 - 5x$ d
7. $y = 10(1.5)^x$ a
8. $y = 10 + 5x$ b
9. $y = 10(0.5)^x$ c

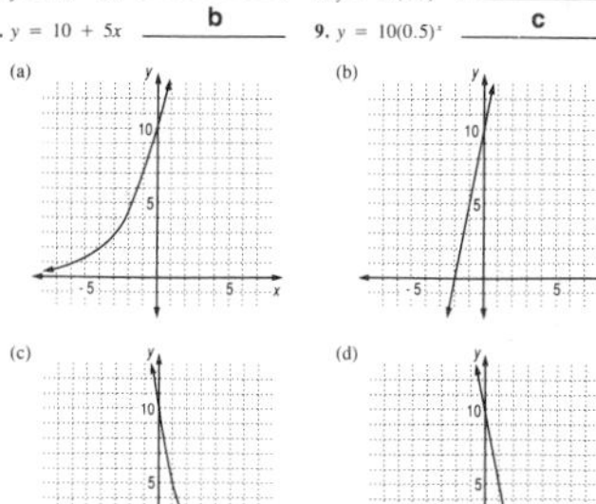

76 *Continued*

LESSON 9-5

RESOURCES
■ Lesson Master 9-5

OBJECTIVES

A Evaluate integer powers of real numbers.
B Simplify products and powers of powers.
E Identify the Product of Powers Property and the Power of a Power Property.

TEACHING NOTES

Not all algebra students are ready to use the properties of exponents. Some must solve these problems by going back to the meaning of powers as repeated multiplication. If some of your students are more comfortable with this approach, it is probably best to not discourage them. They are using their understanding of the operations involved.

The problem-solving strategy *testing a special case* is used in the checks of **Examples 1, 3, and 4.** It is very useful and helps students avoid errors with properties of exponents. It will be used in the rest of the chapter, especially Lesson 9-9. You might discuss wise choices of numbers to test. One and zero should be avoided because they have special properties. Two can also cause trouble because squaring it gives the same result as doubling it.

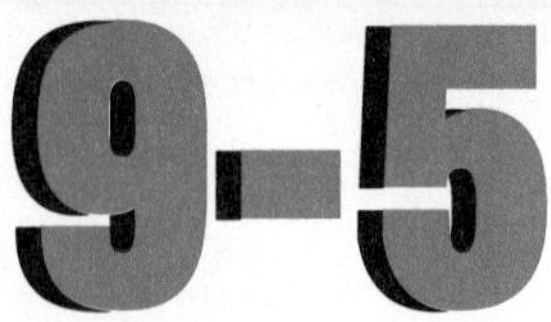

LESSON

9-5 Products of Powers

You already know two meanings for b^n.

(1) Repeated multiplication: $b^n = \underbrace{b \cdot b \cdot \ldots \cdot b}_{n \text{ factors}}$

(2) Growth: b^n is the growth factor after n years if there is growth by a factor b in each one-year interval.

Each meaning shows that powers are closely related to multiplication.

Example 1 Multiply $x^7 \cdot x^5$.

Solution Use the repeated multiplication meaning of x^n.

$$x^7 \cdot x^5 = \underbrace{x \cdot x \cdot x \cdot x \cdot x \cdot x \cdot x}_{7 \text{ factors}} \cdot \underbrace{x \cdot x \cdot x \cdot x \cdot x}_{5 \text{ factors}}$$

$$= \underbrace{x \cdot x \cdot x \cdot x \cdot x \cdot x \cdot x \cdot x \cdot x \cdot x \cdot x \cdot x}_{12 \text{ factors}}$$

$$= x^{12}$$

So, $x^7 \cdot x^5 = x^{7+5} = x^{12}$.

Check Test a special case. Let $x = 3.2$.
Does $(3.2)^7 \cdot (3.2)^5 = (3.2)^{12}$? Try it with a calculator.
The key sequences

3.2 [y^x] 7 [=] [×] 3.2 [y^x] 5 and 3.2 [y^x] 12 [=] give the same value.

Example 2 Suppose a colony of bacteria doubles every hour. Then, if there were 2000 bacteria in the colony at the start, after h hours there will be T bacteria, where

$$T = 2000 \cdot 2^h.$$

How many bacteria will there be after the 5th hour? How many bacteria will there be 3 hours after that?

Solution 1 There will be $2000 \cdot 2^5$ bacteria at the end of the 5th hour. Three hours later the bacteria will have doubled three more times. There will be $(2000 \cdot 2^5) \cdot 2^3$ bacteria. This equals $2000 \cdot (2^5 \cdot 2^3)$ bacteria.

444

Solution 2 Three hours after the 5th hour is the 8th hour. There will be $2000 \cdot 2^8$ bacteria.

These examples suggest the Product of Powers Property.

Product of Powers Property:

When b^m and b^n are defined,

$$b^m \cdot b^n = b^{m+n}.$$

The Product of Powers Property tells how to multiply two powers with the *same base*. An expression with different bases like $a^3 \cdot b^4$ usually cannot be simplified.

Example 3 Simplify $r^4 \cdot s^3 \cdot r^5 \cdot s^8$.

Solution Use the properties of multiplication to group factors with the same base.

$$r^4 \cdot s^3 \cdot r^5 \cdot s^8 = r^4 \cdot r^5 \cdot s^3 \cdot s^8$$

Apply the Product of Powers Property. $= r^9 \cdot s^{11}$.

$r^9 \cdot s^{11}$ cannot be simplified further because the bases are different.

Check Look at the special case when $r = 2$, $s = 3$.
Does $2^4 \cdot 3^3 \cdot 2^5 \cdot 3^8 = 2^9 \cdot 3^{11}$?
Does $16 \cdot 27 \cdot 32 \cdot 6561 = 512 \cdot 177{,}147$?
Yes, they each equal 90,699,264.

Chunking is useful for simplifying an expression in which a power is raised to a power.

Example 4 Simplify $(x^3)^4$.

Solution Think of x^3 as a single number, that is, chunk x^3.

$$\begin{aligned}(x^3)^4 &= x^3 \cdot x^3 \cdot x^3 \cdot x^3 \\ &= x^{3+3+3+3} \\ &= x^{12}\end{aligned}$$

Check Use a special case. Let $x = 3$. $(x^3)^4 = (x^3)^4 = 27^4 = 531{,}441$. $3^{12} = 531{,}441$. Since the two expressions are equal, it checks.

ADDITIONAL EXAMPLES

1. Simplify $k^4 \cdot k^2$.
k^6

2. A population of guinea pigs is tripling every year.

a. If there were 6 guinea pigs to start, how many would there be after 5 years?
1458

b. Four years after that?
118,098

3. Simplify $a^4 \cdot x^3 \cdot a \cdot x^{10}$.
a^5x^{13}

4. Simplify $(x^5)^2$.
x^{10}

5. Verify the answer to Additional Example 4 by testing a special case.
sample: Let $x = 3$. $(3^5)^2 = 243^2 = 59{,}049$, and $3^{10} = 59{,}049$.

NOTES ON QUESTIONS

Question 14: Point out that $b^0 \cdot b^9$ can be simplified by adding exponents or by substituting 1 for b^0.

Questions 15 and 16: These expressions show the difference between multiplying by two and squaring. Writing the expressions as $2 \cdot x^3 \cdot x^4$ and $x^3 \cdot x^4 \cdot x^3 \cdot x^4$ may help in making the distinction.

Question 23b: If students evaluate $(-1)^{100}$ on their calculators, different answers may result. Some newer calculators can handle integral powers of negative bases. Some older ones do not, but give an error message instead.

NOTES ON QUESTIONS
Making Connections for Questions 30, 31, and 33: These questions involve negative exponents with 10 as a base, which students have seen in their work with scientific notation. These questions help prepare the students for the next lesson.

FOLLOW-UP

MORE PRACTICE
For more questions on SPUR Objectives, use *Lesson Master 9-5,* shown on page 447.

EXTENSION
As indicated in the paragraph following the statement of the Power of a Power Property, $(b^m)^n = (b^n)^m$. Have students derive this in general. [sample:
$(b^n)^m = b^{mn}$ Power of a Power Prop.
$= b^{nm}$ Commutative Property of Multiplication
$= (b^n)^m$ Power of a Power Prop.]

ADDITIONAL ANSWERS
1b. x^6 is the growth factor after 6 years if there is growth by a factor x in each one-year interval.

7. When $b > 0$, for all m and n, $(b^m)^n = b^{mn}$.

23a. -1, 1, -1, 1, -1, 1, -1, 1

25.

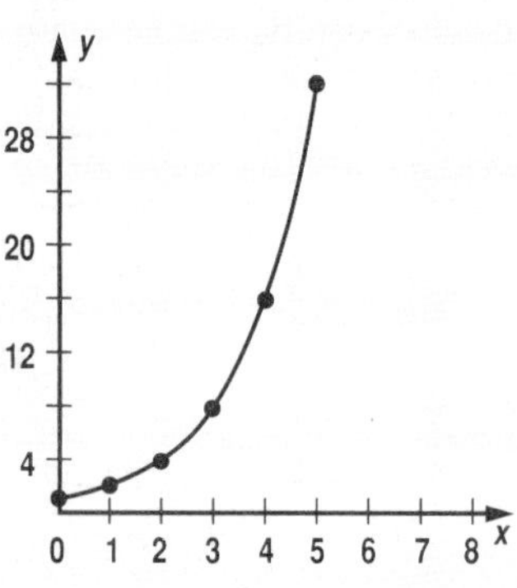

Example 4 is an instance of the Power of a Power Property:

Power of a Power Property:

When $b > 0$, for all m and n,
$$(b^m)^n = b^{mn}.$$

For instance, $(b^0)^3 = b^{0 \cdot 3} = b^0 = 1$. This checks, because $1^3 = 1$. The Power of a Power Property implies that $(b^m)^n = (b^n)^m$. So the square of x^{10} is the same as the 10th power of x^2.

Questions

Covering the Reading

1. Explain the meaning of x^6:
  a. using repeated multiplication; $x^6 = x \cdot x \cdot x \cdot x \cdot x \cdot x$
  b. using growth. **See margin.**

2. State the Product of Powers Property. **If b^j and b^k are defined, then $b^j \cdot b^k = b^{j+k}$.**

3. Why can't $x^8 \cdot y^2$ be simplified? **The expression has two different bases.**

4. a. Simplify $a^2 \cdot a^3$. a^5
  b. Check your answer by letting $a = -2$. $(-2)^2 \cdot (-2)^3 = 4(-8) = -32$; $(-2)^5 = -32$

5. Refer to Example 2. Give answers in exponential form.
  a. How many bacteria will there be after 11 hours? $2000 \cdot 2^{11}$
  b. How many bacteria will there be 6 hours after that? $(2000 \cdot 2^{11}) \cdot 2^6$, or $2000 \cdot 2^{17}$

6. Suppose a population P of bacteria triples each day.
  a. Write an expression for the number of bacteria after 5 days. $P \cdot 3^5$
  b. How many days after the fifth day will the bacteria population be $P \cdot 3^{17}$? 12

7. State the Power of a Power Property. **See margin.**

In 8–19, simplify.

8. $(k^{10})^3$ k^{30} **9.** $(n^2)^6$ n^{12} **10.** $(x^2)^3 - (x^3)^2$ 0

11. $x^5 \cdot x^{50}$ x^{55} **12.** $13^{12} \cdot 17^{10}$ $13^{12} \cdot 17^{10}$ **13.** $(1.5)^8 \cdot (1.5)^2$ $(1.5)^{10}$

Applying the Mathematics

14. $a^3 \cdot a^5 \cdot b^0 \cdot a^2 \cdot b^9$ $a^{10}b^9$ **15.** $2(x^3 \cdot x^4)$ $2x^7$ **16.** $(x^3 \cdot x^4)^2$ x^{14}

17. $3m^4 \cdot 5m^2$ $15m^6$ **18.** $b^3(a^3b^5)$ a^3b^8 **19.** $12 \cdot 12^{100}$ 12^{101}

20. a. Simplify $2^3 \cdot 2^x$. 2^{3+x} b) $2^3 \cdot 2^4 = 8 \cdot 16 = 128$; $2^{3+4} = 2^7 = 128$
  b. Check your answer by letting $x = 4$.

In 21 and 22, use the Distributive Property, then simplify. Recall that unlike terms cannot be combined.

21. $a^2(a^3 + 4a^4)$ **$a^5 + 4a^6$** **22.** $y(y^7 - y^2)$ (Remember, $y = y^1$.) **$y^8 - y^3$**

23. a. Calculate $(-1)^n$ for $n = 1, 2, 3, 4, 5, 6, 7$, and 8. **See margin.**
b. What is $(-1)^{100}$? **1**

24. You are descended from two natural parents each of whom had two natural parents, each of whom had two natural parents, and so on.
a. If you traced your family tree back through ten generations of natural parents, at most how many ancestors would you have? **$2^{10} = 1024$**
b. Suppose you marry, and you and your spouse have a child. At most how many ancestors could your child have back through eleven generations? **$2^{11} = 2048$**

Review

25. Graph $y = 2^x$ for values of x from 0 to 5. *(Lesson 9-4)* **See margin.**

26. Write an expression for the population of a city y years from now whose current population is 2,500,000 when
a. the population is growing at 4.5% per year, **$2{,}500{,}000(1.045)^y$**
b. the population is decreasing 3% per year, **$2{,}500{,}000(.97)^y$**
c. the population is decreasing by 2500 people each year. *(Lessons 6-4, 9-2, 9-3)* **$2{,}500{,}000 - 2500y$**

27. Rewrite $7y - 2x - 7 = 19 - 9x$
a. in standard form. *(Lesson 8-8)* **$7x + 7y = 26$ or $-7x - 7y = -26$**
b. in slope-intercept form. *(Lesson 8-4)* **$y = -x + \frac{26}{7}$**

In 28–31, write in scientific notation. *(Appendix B)*

28. 4,000,000,000 **4×10^9** **29.** 2,439,000 **2.439×10^6**

30. 0.00036 **3.6×10^{-4}** **31.** 0.897 **8.97×10^{-1}**

32. *Skill sequence* *(Lessons 2-2, 6-9, 7-8)*
a. Simplify $x - (4x + 6)$ **$-3x - 6$**
b. Simplify $\frac{x}{2 - x} - \frac{4x + 6}{2 - x}$ **$\frac{-3x - 6}{2 - x}$**
c. Solve $\frac{x}{2 - x} - \frac{4x + 6}{2 - x} = 1$ **-4**

Exploration

33. Metric measures involving powers of 10^3 have special names. For instance, 10^3 meters is one kilometer. Find the name of each of the following expressions.
a. 10^6 grams **megagram** **b.** 10^{-6} meters **micron**
c. 10^{-3} seconds **millisecond** **d.** 10^9 watts **gigawatt**

NAME ______

LESSON **MASTER 9–5**
QUESTIONS ON **SPUR** OBJECTIVES

■**SKILLS** *Objective A* *(See pages 471–473 for objectives.)*

1. Evaluate $3^2 \cdot 3^3$. **243**
2. Evaluate $(3^2)^3$. **729**
3. Find the value of $x^3 \cdot x^4$ when $x = 2$. **128**
4. Find the value of $(2y)^5$ when $y = -1$. **-32**

■**SKILLS** *Objective B*
In 5–18, simplify.

5. $a^5 \cdot a^7$ **a^{12}**
6. $2n^0 \cdot n^8$ **$2n^8$**
7. $6t^6 \cdot 3t^2$ **$18t^8$**
8. $0.7b^3 \cdot 0.4b^9$ **$0.28b^{12}$**
9. $u^7 \cdot v^2 \cdot u^6 \cdot v^4$ **$u^{13}v^6$**
10. $g^5 \cdot k^3 \cdot g^8 \cdot k^9$ **$g^{13}k^{12}$**
11. $(b^6c^5)(b^2c^6)$ **b^8c^{11}**
12. $(w^5)^2$ **w^{10}**
13. $3(h^4)^3$ **$3h^{12}$**
14. $(3h^4)^3$ **$27h^{12}$**
15. $(x^4)^2(x^4)^2$ **x^{16}**
16. $(x^2)^4 + (x^4)^2$ **$2x^8$**
17. $(a + b)^4(a + b)^5$ **$(a + b)^9$**
18. $(2s - 3t)^3(2s - 3t)^8$ **$(2s - 3t)^{11}$**

■**PROPERTIES** *Objective E*
In 19–22, name the property or properties which justify each statement.

19. $r^9r^6 = r^{15}$ **Product of Powers Property**
20. $(4d^3)d^2 = 4d^5$ **Associative Property of Multiplication and Product of Powers Property**
21. $(a^8)^4 = a^{32}$ **Power of a Power Property**

In 22–25, tell whether the statement is true or false. If false, correct the statement by changing the right side of the equation.

22. $(p^3)^4 = p^7$ **false; $(p^3)^4 = p^{12}$**
23. $q^5 \cdot q^3 = q^8$ **true**
24. $(5^3)^0 = 0$ **false; $(5^3)^0 = 1$**
25. $3x^2 \cdot 2x^3 = 5x^5$ **false; $3x^2 \cdot 2x^3 = 6x^5$**

LESSON 9-6

RESOURCES

- Lesson Master 9-6

OBJECTIVES

A Evaluate integer powers of real numbers.
E Identify the Negative Exponent Property.
H Use and simplify expressions with powers in everyday situations.

TEACHING NOTES

You might wish to begin by noting that 10^{-n} and 10^n are reciprocals. Then help students to see how this lesson simply generalizes that idea to other bases.

Referring to the graph of $y = 2^x$ can help students avoid the most common pitfall of negative exponents: assuming that b^{-n} is a negative number. The entire graph of $y = 2^x$ lies above the x-axis because 2^x is always positive, even for negative values of x.

The graph of $y = 2^x$ can also be related to exponential growth situations. Suppose you are doubling your money every year. If now you have \$1 million, moving to the right on the graph shows what will happen in the future; moving to the left shows the past. Each time you move left one, you multiply by $2^{-1} = \frac{1}{2}$, which is equivalent to dividing by 2.

LESSON 9-6 Negative Exponents

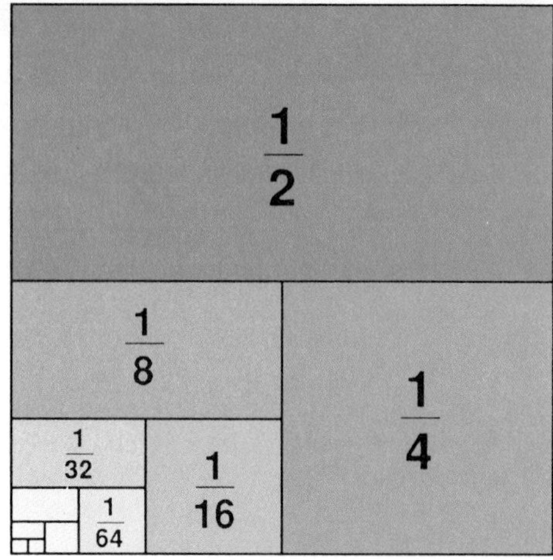

You have used the base 10 with a negative exponent to represent small numbers in scientific notation.

$$10^{-1} = 0.1,\ 10^{-2} = 0.01,\ 10^{-3} = 0.001, \text{ and so on}$$

Now consider other bases with negative exponents:

What is the value b^{-n}?

The following pattern of the powers of 2 helps to answer this question.

$$2^5 = 32$$
$$2^4 = 16$$
$$2^3 = 8$$
$$2^2 = 4$$

Each exponent is one less than the one above it and each number on the right is half the number above. This pattern continues.

$$2^1 = 2$$
$$2^0 = 1$$
$$2^{-1} = \frac{1}{2}$$
$$2^{-2} = \frac{1}{4} = \frac{1}{2^2}$$
$$2^{-3} = \frac{1}{8} = \frac{1}{2^3}$$
$$2^{-4} = \frac{1}{16} = \frac{1}{2^4}$$
$$2^{-5} = \frac{1}{32} = \frac{1}{2^5}$$

The pattern is simple: $2^{-n} = \frac{1}{2^n}$. That is, 2^{-n} is the reciprocal of 2^n. We call the general property the **Negative Exponent Property.**

448

Negative Exponent Property:

For any nonzero b,

$b^{-n} = \frac{1}{b^n}$, the reciprocal of b^n.

The Negative Exponent Property can be deduced by multiplying b^n and b^{-n}.

$$\begin{aligned} b^n \cdot b^{-n} &= b^{n+-n} && \text{Product Property of Powers} \\ &= b^0 \\ &= 1 && \text{Zero Exponent Property} \end{aligned}$$

Since the product of b^n and b^{-n} is 1, b^{-n} must be the reciprocal of b^n.

Example 1 Write 3^{-4} as a simple fraction.

Solution Using the Negative Exponent Property, $3^{-4} = \frac{1}{3^4} = \frac{1}{81}$.

Notice that 3^{-4} is a positive number. This surprises many people, but it fits the pattern of all applications. For instance, examine this graph of $y = 2^x$, extended to include negative values of x.

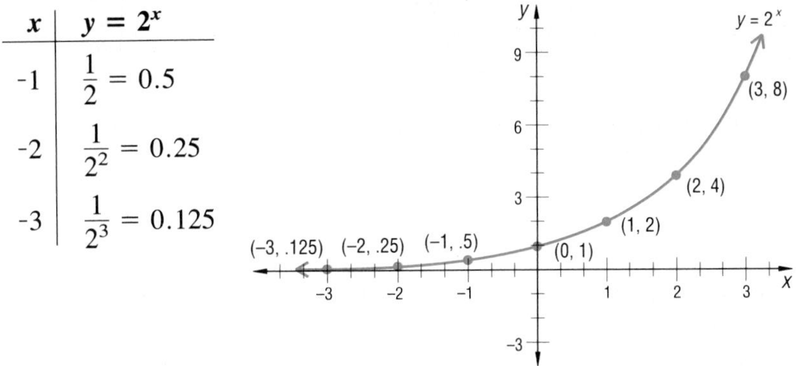

x	$y = 2^x$
-1	$\frac{1}{2} = 0.5$
-2	$\frac{1}{2^2} = 0.25$
-3	$\frac{1}{2^3} = 0.125$

Even when x is negative, the number 2^x is still positive. *All* powers of positive numbers are positive.

The Negative Exponent Property also agrees with the negative powers of 10 you already know.

$$10^{-6} = .000001 = \frac{1}{1{,}000{,}000} = \frac{1}{10^6}$$

ADDITIONAL EXAMPLES

1. Write 7^{-3} as a simple fraction.
$\frac{1}{343}$

2. Simplify $n^5 \cdot n^{-6}$ and write your answer without negative exponents.
$\frac{1}{n}$

3. The viruses in a culture are quadrupling in number each day. Right now, the culture contains about 1,000,000 viruses. About how many viruses did the culture have 6 days ago?
$1{,}000{,}000 \cdot 4^{-6} \approx 244$

NOTES ON QUESTIONS

Question 4: Some calculators will give the denominator 729 exactly if students evaluate 3^{-6} and then find the reciprocal of the result.

Questions 14, 19-22: A graphing calculator or function plotter can be used to display the graphs of the equations.

Question 18: This base-10 pattern is perhaps the pattern that, more than any other, convinces students of the reasonableness of the properties of negative exponents.

Questions 20-22: Negative exponents must be used for years prior to 1985.

Questions 27-29: A graphing calculator or function plotter can be used to check the answers.

Also, as a special case $b^{-1} = \frac{1}{b}$. That is, the -1 power of a number equals its reciprocal. You can use the Negative Exponent Property to rewrite expressions so they have no negative exponents.

Example 2 Rewrite $q^5 \cdot t^{-3}$ without negative exponents.

Solution Substitute $\frac{1}{t^3}$ for t^{-3}.

$$q^5 \cdot t^{-3} = q^5 \cdot \frac{1}{t^3} = \frac{q^5}{t^3}$$

Negative exponents work in the growth model for powering. They stand for time years ago.

Example 3 Recall the compound interest formula

$$T = P(1 + i)^n.$$

Three years ago, Mr. Cabot put money in a CD at an annual yield of 7%. If the CD is worth $3675 now, what was it worth then?

Solution Here $P = 3675$, $i = .07$, and $n = -3$ (for three years ago). Use a calculator.

3675 [×] 1.07 [y^x] 3 [±] [=]

gives 2999.8947.
So Mr. Cabot probably started with $3000.

Questions

Covering the Reading

1. Write the next three equations in this pattern:
$4^3 = 64$ $4^{-1} = \frac{1}{4}$
$4^2 = 16$ $4^{-2} = \frac{1}{16}$
$4^1 = 4$ $4^{-3} = \frac{1}{64}$
$4^0 = 1$

2. *Multiple choice* $x^{-n} =$ **(d)**

(a) $-x^n$ (b) $(-x)^n$ (c) $\frac{1}{x^{-n}}$ (d) $\frac{1}{x^n}$

In 3–5, write as a simple fraction.

3. 5^{-2} $\frac{1}{25}$ **4.** 3^{-6} $\frac{1}{729}$ **5.** 7^{-1} $\frac{1}{7}$

6. b^{-1} is the __?__ of b. **reciprocal**

In 7–9, write without negative exponents.

7. x^5y^{-2} $\frac{x^5}{y^2}$ **8.** $3a^{-2}b^{-4}$ $\frac{3}{a^2b^4}$ **9.** 2^{-n} $\frac{1}{2^n}$

10. Refer to the graph of $y = 2^x$.
a. Can the value of x be negative? **b.** Can the value of y be negative?
a) Yes b) No

11. Write 10^{-9} **a.** as a decimal; **b.** as a simple fraction.
a) 0.000000001 b) 1/1,000,000,000

12. *True or false* If x is positive, x^{-4} is positive. **True**

13. Refer to Example 3. Find what Mr. Cabot's CD was worth
a. one year ago; **b.** two years ago. **a) \$3434.58 b) \$3209.89**

Applying the Mathematics

14. Theresa has \$1236.47 in a savings account that has had an annual yield of 5.25% since she opened the account. Assuming no withdrawals or deposits were made, how much was in the account 8 years ago?
\$821.12

15. If the reciprocal of $(1.06)^{11}$ is $(1.06)^n$, what is n? **-11**

In 16 and 17, simplify.

16. $c^j \cdot c^{-j}$ **1** **17.** $t^{-2} \cdot t^{-4}$ t^{-6}

18. **a.** Evaluate $3 \cdot 10^4 + 5 \cdot 10^2 + 6 \cdot 10^1 + 2 \cdot 10^0 + 4 \cdot 10^{-1} + 7 \cdot 10^{-3}$
30,562.407
b. Evaluate $9 \cdot 10^3 + 8 \cdot 10^2 + 7 \cdot 10^1 + 6 \cdot 10^0 + 5 \cdot 10^{-1} + 4 \cdot 10^{-2} + 9 \cdot 10^{-4}$ **9876.5409**

19. Consider the equation $y = 3^x$.
a. Complete the table. **b.** Graph $y = 3^x$. **See margin.**

x	y
2	9
1	3
0	1
-1	$\frac{1}{3}$
-2	$\frac{1}{9}$
-3	$\frac{1}{27}$

In 20–22, use this information. The human population P of the earth, x years from 1985, can be estimated by the formula

$$y = 5 \text{ billion } (1.017)^x.$$

Use this formula to estimate the earth's population in

20. 1990; **≈5.44 billion** **21.** 1980; **≈4.60 billion** **22.** 1970. **≈3.88 billion**

ADDITIONAL ANSWERS

19b.

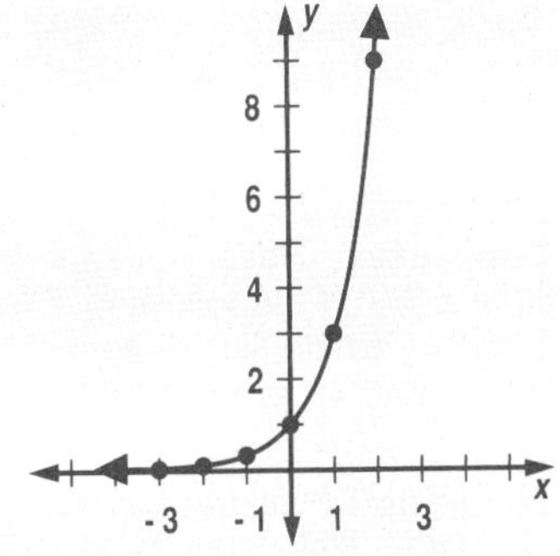

NAME ____________________

LESSON **MASTER 9–6**
QUESTIONS ON **SPUR** OBJECTIVES

■SKILLS *Objective A (See pages 471–473 for objectives.)*
In 1–6, evaluate.

1. 5^{-1} $\frac{1}{5}$ 2. 10^{-4} $\frac{1}{10,000}$ 3. $7 \cdot 4^{-3}$ $\frac{7}{64}$
4. $-9 \cdot 3^{-3}$ $-\frac{1}{3}$ 5. -2^{-6} $-\frac{1}{64}$ 6. $(-2)^{-6}$ $\frac{1}{64}$

In 7–10, simplify.

7. $3 \cdot 10^1 + 1 \cdot 10^0 + 4 \cdot 10^{-1}$ **31.4**
8. $7 \cdot 10^0 + 2 \cdot 10^{-1} + 6 \cdot 10^{-3}$ **7.206**
9. $8 \cdot 10^4 + 5 \cdot 10^0 + 9 \cdot 10^{-1}$ **80,005.9**
10. $8^{17} \cdot 8^{-17}$ **1**

■SKILLS *Objective B*
In 11–18, rewrite without a negative exponent.

11. xy^{-3} $\frac{x}{y^3}$ 12. $2a^{-4}$ $\frac{2}{a^4}$ 13. $3t^{-5}$ $\frac{3}{t^5}$
14. $(b^7)^{-2}$ $\frac{1}{b^{14}}$ 15. $(4y)^{-1}$ $\frac{1}{4y}$ 16. m^6n^{-3} $\frac{m^6}{n^3}$
17. $a^3b^{-2}c^4$ $\frac{a^3c^4}{b^2}$ 18. $w^{-6}x^2y^{-5}$ $\frac{x^2}{w^6y^5}$

■PROPERTIES *Objective E*
In 19 and 20, name the property or properties which justify each statement.

19. $x^5y^{-1} = \frac{x^5}{y}$ **Negative Exponent Property**
20. $(a^3)^{-2} = \frac{1}{a^6}$ **Power of a Power and Negative Exponent Properties**

■USES *Objective H*

21. The population of a town is 25,194. It has been gaining 8% for each of the last three years. What was the population three years ago? **20,000 people**
22. Hakeem has \$2917 in a Certificate of Deposit which has an annual yield of 5%. How much was it worth 4 years ago? **\$2399.82**

FOLLOW-UP

MORE PRACTICE
For more questions on SPUR Objectives, use *Lesson Master 9-6,* shown on page 451.

EXTENSION
Computer Have students input and run the following program, which illustrates that x^n and x^{-n} are reciprocals.

```
10  PRINT "WHAT
    NONZERO BASE X
    DO YOU WANT TO
    USE?"
20  INPUT X
30  PRINT "WHAT
    VALUES (N,-N)
    DO YOU
    WANT TO USE?"
40  INPUT N,M
50  PRINT X"^"N "=
    "X^N
60  PRINT X"^"M "=
    "X^M
70  PRINT X"^"N "*"X
    "^"M "=" X^N*X^M
80  PRINT "RUN AGAIN?
    (Y/N)"
90  INPUT A$
100 IF A$="Y" GOTO 10
110 END
```

28c.

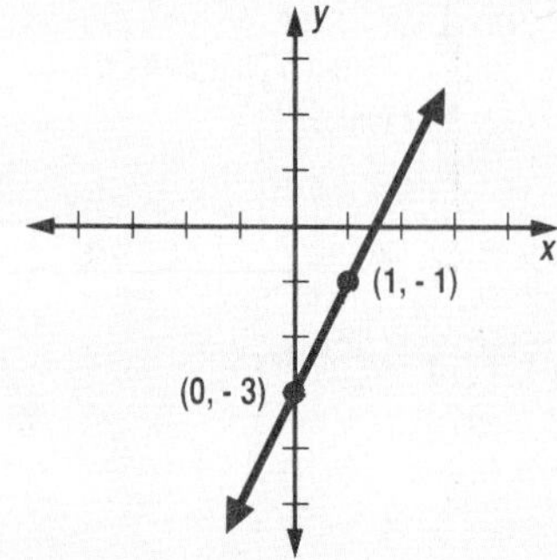

Review

In 23–25, simplify. *(Lesson 9-5)*

23. $a^2 \cdot a^5$ **a^7**   **24.** $(b^3)^{10}$ **b^{30}**   **25.** $3c^3 \cdot 4c^4$ **$12c^7$**

26. A certain kind of virus doubles its population every 3 hours.
a. In two days, how many times does the population double? **16**
b. If a biologist begins an experiment with 25 virus organisms, how many does he or she have after two days? *(Lesson 9-2)* **1,638,400**

27. *Multiple choice* The graph at the right is the graph of points on
(a) $y = 0.3^x$.
(b) $y = -0.3^x + 1$
(c) $y = 0.8^x$.
(d) $y = -0.8^x + 1$
(Lesson 9-4) **(c)**

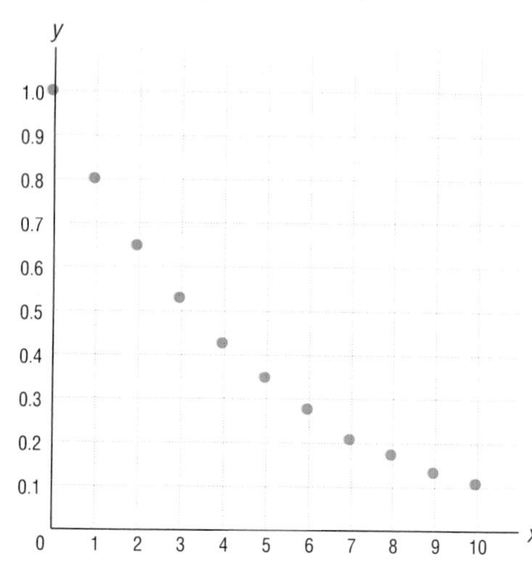

28. Consider the line $y = 2x - 3$.
a. Give its slope. **2**
b. Give its y-intercept. **-3**
c. Graph the line. *(Lesson 8-4)* **See margin.**

29. Write an equation for the line with slope -5 that passes through the point (2, -1). *(Lesson 8-5)* **$y = -5x + 9$**

30. *Skill sequence (Lessons 6-1, 6-9)*
a. Simplify $4(7a - 2)$. **$28a - 8$**
b. Simplify $4(7a - 2) - 3(5a + 1)$. **$13a - 11$**
c. Solve $4(7a - 2) - 3(5a + 1) = 15$. **2**

31. Simplify $\frac{3x + 6x}{12x}$. *(Lesson 6-3)* **$\frac{3}{4}$**

In 32 and 33, a number n is chosen at random from {-10, -9, -8, ..., -1, 0, 1, 2, ..., 8, 9, 10}. Find the probability that

32. $n > -4$; *(Lesson 1-7)* **$\frac{2}{3}$**

33. $n \le -9$ or $n \ge 9$. *(Lesson 3-6)* **$\frac{4}{21}$**

Exploration

34. $(\frac{1}{2})^2 = \frac{1}{2} \cdot \frac{1}{2} = \frac{1}{4}$. Find other positive and negative integer powers of the number $\frac{1}{2}$. **Powers of $\frac{1}{2}$ are reciprocals of the same power of 2.**
a. How do the powers of $\frac{1}{2}$ compare with the powers of 2?
b. Generalize to other pairs of reciprocal bases. **$\left(\frac{1}{x}\right)^n = x^{-n}$**

452

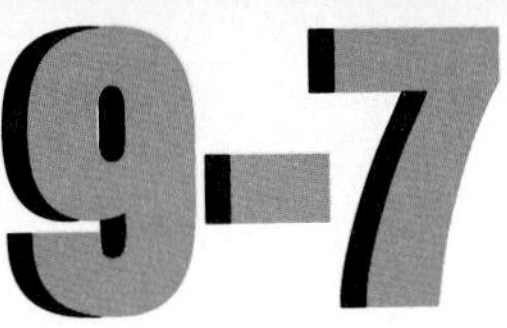

LESSON 9-7

Quotients of Powers

Here is part of a list of the positive integer powers of 2.

2, 4, 8, 16, 32, 64, 128, 256, 512, 1024, 2048, 4096, ...

Multiply any two of these numbers and you will find that the product is on the list. For instance,

$$32 \cdot 128 = 4096.$$

This can be explained using the Product of Powers Property.

$$2^5 \cdot 2^7 = 2^{12}$$

It may surprise you that if you *divide* any number on the list, the quotient is on the list. For instance, consider 512 and 16.

	Dividing larger by smaller	*Dividing smaller by larger*
	$\frac{512}{16} = 32$	$\frac{16}{512} = \frac{1}{32}$
As powers,	$\frac{2^9}{2^4} = 2^5,$	$\frac{2^4}{2^9} = \frac{1}{2^5} = 2^{-5}$

These examples illustrate the Quotient of Powers Property.

Quotient of Powers Property:

When b^m and b^n are defined and $b \neq 0$, then

$$\frac{b^m}{b^n} = b^{m-n}$$

When simplifying $\frac{b^m}{b^n}$, if the larger power is in the numerator, the result is a positive power of b. If the larger power is in the denominator, then the result is a negative power of b.

Example 1 Simplify $\frac{y^{12}}{y^5}$

Solution Use the Quotient of Powers Property.

$$\frac{y^{12}}{y^5} = y^{12-5} = y^7$$

Check Use repeated multiplication,

$$\frac{y^{12}}{y^5} = \frac{\cancel{y}\cdot\cancel{y}\cdot\cancel{y}\cdot\cancel{y}\cdot\cancel{y}\cdot y\cdot y\cdot y\cdot y\cdot y\cdot y\cdot y}{\cancel{y}\cdot\cancel{y}\cdot\cancel{y}\cdot\cancel{y}\cdot\cancel{y}} = y^7$$

LESSON 9-7

RESOURCES
- Lesson Master 9-7
- Quiz on Lessons 9-5 Through 9-7

OBJECTIVES

A Evaluate integer powers of real numbers.
B Simplify quotients of powers.
E Identify the Quotient of Powers Property.
H Use and simplify expressions with powers in everyday situations.

TEACHING NOTES

Alternate Approach
Some of your students may prefer to do the problems in this lesson by rewriting them as repeated multiplication, as in the check of **Example 1.** This method works well since most of the exponents in the problems are small. Such rewriting can also be used to explain why the properties hold.

Show students that the Quotient of Powers Property is consistent with the Zero Exponent Property. That is, $\frac{b^n}{b^n} = b^{n-n} = b^0$, but also $\frac{b^n}{b^n}$ obviously equals 1.

ADDITIONAL EXAMPLES
In 1-4, simplify.

1. $\frac{12x^7}{3x^2}$
$4x^5$

2. $\frac{a^5}{a^8}$
$\frac{1}{a^3}$

3. $\frac{28 \cdot 10^{14}}{7 \cdot 10^{17}}$
$4 \cdot 10^{-3} = .004$

4. $\frac{30x^2y^{10}}{25xy^{15}}$
$\frac{6x}{5y^5}$

5. In 1986, there was a total of 183.6 billion dollars in U.S. currency in circulation. The U.S. population was about 241.5 million. How much currency per person was in circulation?
about $760.25

Example 2 Simplify $\frac{3^{16}}{3^{27}}$.

Solution
$$\frac{3^{16}}{3^{27}} = 3^{16-27} = 3^{-11} = \frac{1}{3^{11}}$$

Either 3^{-11} or $\frac{1}{3^{11}}$ can be considered simpler than the given fraction.

Check Use a calculator. Does $\frac{3^{16}}{3^{27}} = \frac{1}{3^{11}}$?
Yes, 3 [y^x] 16 [÷] 3 [y^x] 27 [=] gives 0.0000056.
3 [y^x] 11 [±] [=] also gives 0.0000056.

To use the Quotient of Powers Property, both bases must be the same. For instance, $\frac{a^9}{b^4}$ cannot be simplified.

Example 3 In 1985, there were approximately 3.6 billion one-dollar bills in circulation and about 227 million people in the U.S. How many dollar bills was this per person?

Solution Since dollars per person is a rate unit, the answer is found by division.

$$\frac{\text{number of dollar bills}}{\text{number of persons}} = \frac{3.6 \text{ billion}}{227 \text{ million}}$$

Change the words to their power of 10 equivalents. $= \frac{3.6 \cdot 10^9}{227 \cdot 10^6}$

This is a product of fractions. $= \frac{3.6}{227} \cdot \frac{10^9}{10^6}$

By the Quotient of Powers Property $\approx 0.0158 \cdot 10^3$

$\approx 16 \frac{\text{dollar bills}}{\text{person}}$

Check Change the numbers to decimals and simplify the fraction.

$$\frac{3{,}600{,}000{,}000}{227{,}000{,}000} = \frac{3{,}600}{227} \approx 16$$

454

In Example 3, it was easier to rewrite the fraction $\frac{3.6 \cdot 10^9}{227 \cdot 10^6}$ as the product of two fractions before using the Quotient of Powers Property. This technique can be especially helpful when an expression with several bases is involved.

Example 4 Simplify $\frac{7a^3b^2c^6}{28a^2b^5c}$.

Solution

$$\frac{7a^3b^2c^6}{28a^2b^5c} = \frac{7}{28} \cdot \frac{a^3}{a^2} \cdot \frac{b^2}{b^5} \cdot \frac{c^6}{c}$$

$$= \frac{1}{4} \cdot a^{3-2} \cdot b^{2-5} \cdot c^{6-1} \text{ (Recall that } c = c^1.)$$

$$= \frac{1}{4} \cdot a \cdot b^{-3} \cdot c^5$$

$$= \frac{1}{4} \cdot a \cdot \frac{1}{b^3} \cdot c^5$$

$$= \frac{ac^5}{4b^3}$$

Experts do all of this work in one step.

NOTES ON QUESTIONS
Questions 11 and 12: Students need to look back to **Example 3** to find the population of the U.S. So, they are actually calculating the consumption per person for 1985.

Alternate Approach for Question 18: We expect students to use the Quotient of Powers Property. $\frac{x^{-2}}{x^{-3}} = x^{-2--3} = x^1$. An alternate approach is to multiply both numerator and denominator by x^3.

ADDITIONAL ANSWERS

2. When b^j and b^k are defined and $b \neq 0$, then $\frac{b^j}{b^k} = b^{j-k}$.

3. $\frac{9.29 \cdot 10^8}{2.27 \cdot 10^8} = \frac{9.29}{2.27} \approx$ **4.1** $\frac{\text{five-dollar bills}}{\text{person}}$

Questions

Covering the Reading

1. Rewrite the multiplication problem $64 \cdot 256 = 16{,}384$ using powers of 2. $2^6 \cdot 2^8 = 2^{14}$

2. State the Quotient of Powers Property. **See margin.**

3. In 1985, there were approximately 929 million five-dollar bills in circulation and 227 million people in the U.S. Convert these words to powers of 10 and find the number of five-dollar bills per person. **See margin.**

In 4–8, use the Quotient of Powers Property to simplify the fraction.

4. $\frac{y^5}{y^5}$ $y^0 = 1$

5. $\frac{3^2}{3^8}$ $\frac{1}{3^6} = \frac{1}{729}$

6. $\frac{9.5 \cdot 10^{12}}{1.9 \cdot 10^4}$ $5 \cdot 10^8$

7. $\frac{w^2z^6}{42w^2z^3}$ $\frac{z^3}{42}$

8. $\frac{4abc^{10}}{28a^2b^5c}$ $\frac{c^9}{7ab^4}$

9. $\frac{r^{10}}{s^7}$ cannot be simplified because __?__. **bases are different**

10. If $m = n$, $\frac{b^m}{b^n} =$ __?__. **1**

NOTES ON QUESTIONS

Question 20: Students can write a proportion or reason that since Alpha Centauri is $\frac{6.2 \cdot 10^{12}}{2.4 \cdot 10^5}$ times as far away as the moon, it should take that many times as long to travel there.

Question 21: Students can convert to $\frac{1}{64}$, then divide. They can also use the y^x key on the calculator.

Error Analysis for Question 22: Some students may say that $4^x \cdot 4^y = 16^{x+y}$. Point out that when the properties of exponents are applied, they are used instead of the arithmetic computations, not in addition to them. Show examples that can be worked both ways. For instance, $2^3 \cdot 2^4 = 8 \cdot 16 = 128$; 128 is 2^7, not 4^7.

Making Connections for Question 28: Students should find the volumes of the two boxes and then form the ratio. Emphasize that, although each dimension of the first box is twice the corresponding dimension of the second box, the volume is not two times as great. This relates to the first example in the next lesson.

25. $3^5 \cdot 3^5 \cdot 3^5 = 243 \cdot 243 \cdot 243 = 14{,}348{,}907$; and $3^{15} = 14{,}348{,}907$

30b.

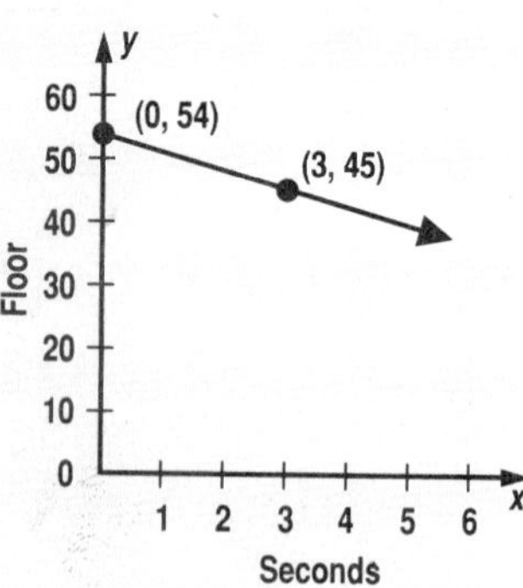

Applying the Mathematics

© 1987 King Features Syndicate, Inc.

11. $4 \cdot 10^6$ pounds of plastic are used each year in the U.S. to produce dry cleaning bags, plastic cups, plates and the like. About how many pounds of plastic are used per person? **$\approx .018 \frac{\text{pound}}{\text{person}}$**

12. About $1.13 \cdot 10^6$ pounds of spinach are consumed per year in the United States. How much is this per person? **$\frac{1.13 \cdot 10^6}{2.27 \cdot 10^8}$ $\approx .005 \frac{\text{pound}}{\text{person}}$**

In 13–18, simplify.

13. $\frac{x^{12n}}{x^{3n}}$ **x^{9n}**

14. $\frac{(7m)^2}{(7m)^3}$ **$\frac{1}{7m}$**

15. $\frac{(x+3)^6}{(x+3)^6}$ **1**

16. $\frac{3x^2}{y^3} \cdot \frac{y^5}{x^9}$ **$\frac{3y^2}{x^7}$**

17. $\frac{3p^5 + 2p^5}{p^4}$ **5p**

18. $\frac{x^{-2}}{x^{-3}}$ **x**

19. Alaska has a population of $4.79 \cdot 10^5$ and an area of $1.48 \cdot 10^6$ square km. Find Alaska's population per square km. **$\approx .32 \frac{\text{people}}{\text{sq km}}$**

20. Other than the sun, the star nearest to us, Alpha Centauri, is about $6.2 \cdot 10^{12}$ miles away. Earth's moon is about $2.4 \cdot 10^5$ miles from us. If it took astronauts about 3 days to get to the moon in 1969, at that speed how long would it take to get to Alpha Centauri? **7.75×10^7 days**

Review

21. Write 2^{-6} as a decimal. *(Lesson 9-6)* **.015625**

In 22–24, simplify. *(Lessons 9-5, 9-6)*

22. $4^x \cdot 4^y$ **4^{x+y}**

23. $(y^4)^3$ **y^{12}**

24. $(y^4)^3 \cdot y^4$ **y^{16}**

25. Simplify $x^5 \cdot x^5 \cdot x^5$. Check by letting $x = 3$. *(9-5)* **x^{15}; see margin.**

26. In 1976, Milo invested \$6000 for 10 years at 5% compound interest. In 1981, Sylvia invested \$6000 for 5 years at 10%. By the end of 1986, who had more? *(Lesson 9-1)* **Milo**

27. In your head, find the ratio of the areas of two squares, the first with a side of length 2 and the second with a side of length 3. *(Lesson 5-3)* **$\frac{4}{9}$**

28. A box with dimensions 4 by 6 by 8 will hold how many times as much as one with dimensions 2 by 3 by 4? *(Lesson 5-6)* **8 times**

29. a. Find the perimeter of the rectangle at the right. *(Lesson 2-1)* **4x + 32**

b. Write a simplified expression for the area of this rectangle. *(Lesson 6-3)*

c. If the area is 312, find the value of x. *(Lesson 6-1)* **11** **29b) 24x + 48**

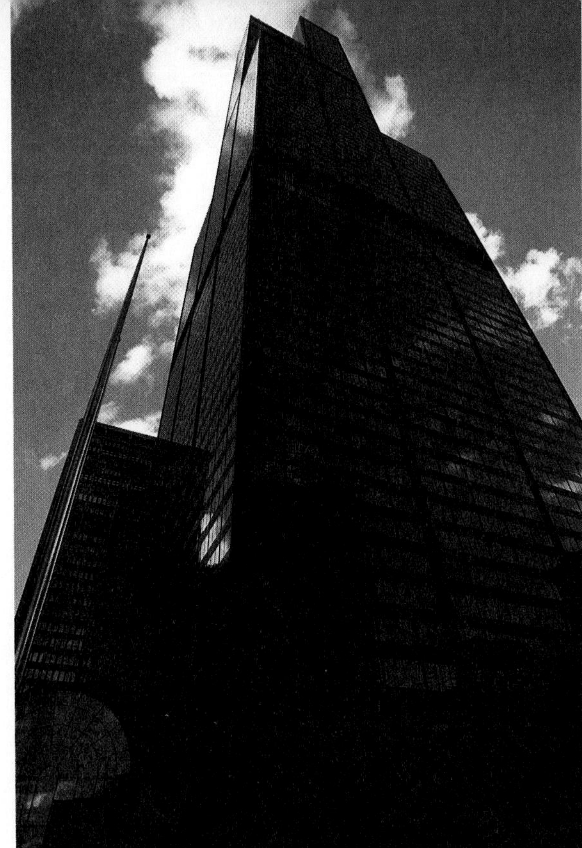

30. An elevator is y floors high in a tall building. After x seconds, $y = 54 - 3x$.

a. Give the slope and y-intercept of $y = 54 - 3x$ and describe what they mean in this situation.

b. Graph the line. *(Lesson 8-4)* **See margin.**

In 31–33, solve. *(Lessons 4-6, 6-7)* **30a) slope = -3, y-intercept = 54; elevator descends at 3 floors per second and started at the 54th floor.**

31. $-4x \leq 25$ **$x \geq -\frac{25}{4}$**

32. $-4x > 6x + 25$ **$x < -\frac{5}{2}$**

33. $5x - 6 \geq 9(x + 2)$ **$x \leq -6$**

Exploration

34. The average 8th grader has a volume of about 3 cubic feet.

a. If you took all the students in your school, would their volume be more or less than the volume of one classroom that is 10 feet high, 30 feet long, and 30 feet wide? **Answers will vary.**

b. Assume the population of the world to be 5 billion people. Is the volume of all the people more or less than the volume of a cubic mile? How much more or less? Assume the average volume of a person equals $\frac{4}{3}$ the average volume of an eighth grader. (There are 5280^3 cubic feet in a cubic mile.) **less by about $1.3 \cdot 10^{11}$ cubic ft**

FOLLOW-UP

MORE PRACTICE

For more questions on SPUR Objectives, use *Lesson Master 9-7,* shown below.

EXTENSION

Have students derive the Quotient of Powers Property from other properties. (sample:

$\frac{b^m}{b^n} = b^m \cdot \frac{1}{b^n}$	Definition of Division
$= b^m \cdot b^{-n}$	Negative Exponent Property
$= b^{m+-n}$	Product of Powers Prop.
$= b^{m-n}$	Definition of Subtraction)

EVALUATION

A quiz covering Lessons 9-5 through 9-7 is provided in the Teacher's Resource File.

NAME ____________

LESSON **MASTER 9–7**
QUESTIONS ON **SPUR** OBJECTIVES

■SKILLS *Objective A (See pages 471–473 for objectives.)*
In 1–6, evaluate.

1. $\frac{3^5}{3^8}$ **$\frac{1}{27}$**
2. $\frac{7^{12}}{7^8}$ **7^4**
3. $\frac{2^x}{2^x}$ **1**
4. $\frac{6^{-8}}{6^{-9}}$ **6**
5. $\frac{5.6 \cdot 10^{15}}{3.2 \cdot 10^{10}}$ **$1.75 \cdot 10^5$**
6. $\frac{1.21 \cdot 10^6}{8.8 \cdot 10^9}$ **$1.375 \cdot 10^{-4}$**
7. Rewrite $\frac{2187}{27} = 81$ using positive powers of 3. **$\frac{3^7}{3^3} = 3^4$**

■SKILLS *Objective B*
In 8–17, simplify.

8. $\frac{8a^8b^3}{2a^4b^2}$ **$4a^4b$**
9. $\frac{15r^4s}{25r^2s^5} \cdot r^3$ **$\frac{3r^5}{5s^4}$**
10. $\frac{(h + 2k)^5}{(h + 2k)^2}$ **$(h + 2k)^3$**
11. $\frac{(y - 8)^6}{(y - 8)^8}$ **$\frac{1}{(y - 8)^2}$**
12. $\frac{w^{18n}}{w^{22n}}$ **$\frac{1}{w^{4n}}$**
13. $\frac{z^{12k} \cdot z^{3k}}{z^{8k}}$ **z^{7k}**
14. $\frac{t^7}{t^{-2} \cdot t^0}$ **t^9**
15. $\frac{v^{-5}}{v^{-10}}$ **v^5**
16. $\frac{4x^6 + 3x^6}{x^6}$ **7**
17. $\frac{9y^3 - 3y^3}{3y^3}$ **2**

■PROPERTIES *Objective E*
In 18 and 19, tell whether the statement is true or false.

18. $\frac{a^{16}}{a^8} = a^2$ **false**
19. $\frac{c^{9n}}{c^{3n}} = c^{6n}$ **true**

■USES *Objective H*

20. In 1981, there were about $1.6 \cdot 10^8$ registered vehicles (autos, buses, trucks) in the U.S. If there were $1.12 \cdot 10^{11}$ gallons of fuel consumed, how many gallons per vehicle was this? **700 gallons**

21. In 1986, $1.93 \cdot 10^{10}$ pounds of beef were consumed in the U.S. If at the end of 1986 the U.S. population was 242.2 million people, how many pounds per person was this? **79.8 lb**

80

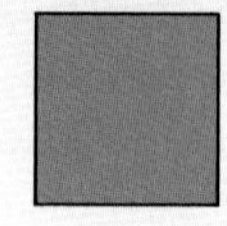

LESSON 9-8

RESOURCES

- Lesson Master 9-8

OBJECTIVES

A Evaluate integer powers of real numbers.
C Rewrite powers of products and quotients.
E Identify the Power of a Product Property and the Power of a Quotient Property.
H Use and simplify expressions with powers in everyday situations.

TEACHING NOTES

Reading Some students may need help in reading **Examples 1 and 2.** You can go through the solutions step by step, highlighting where the properties of exponents are applied.

Practice is needed on questions like **Examples 3 and 4.** It is easy to compose questions by using bases that can be written in different forms. For instance, $(1.2)^9 = \left(\frac{6}{5}\right)^9$. Now write $\left(\frac{6}{5}\right)^9$ without parentheses. The answer is $\frac{6^9}{5^9}$. Does it equal $(1.2)^9$? (Yes, since we simply wrote the same number in different forms.)

LESSON

9-8 Powers of Products and Quotients

$(3x)^4$ is an example of a **Power of a Product.** It can be rewritten without parentheses using repeated multiplication.

$$\begin{aligned}(3x)^4 &= (3x)\cdot(3x)\cdot(3x)\cdot(3x) & \\ &= 3\cdot x\cdot 3\cdot x\cdot 3\cdot x\cdot 3\cdot x & \text{Associative Property}\\ &= 3\cdot 3\cdot 3\cdot 3\cdot x\cdot x\cdot x\cdot x & \text{Commutative Property}\\ &= 3^4\cdot x^4 & \text{meaning of } x^n\\ &= 81x^4\end{aligned}$$

You can check this. Consider the special case when $x = 2$. Then

$$(3x)^4 = 6^4 = 1296 \text{ and } 81x^4 = 81\cdot 2^4 = 81\cdot 16 = 1296.$$

When you want a positive integer power of a product, you can always use repeated multiplication.

$$\begin{aligned}(ab)^n &= \underbrace{(ab)\cdot(ab)\cdot\ldots\cdot(ab)}_{n\text{ factors}}\\ &= \underbrace{a\cdot a\cdot\ldots\cdot a}_{n\text{ factors}}\cdot\underbrace{b\cdot b\cdot\ldots\cdot b}_{n\text{ factors}}\\ &= a^n\cdot b^n\end{aligned}$$

This result holds when n is any integer, positive, negative or zero.

Power of a Product Property:

For all nonzero a and b, and any integer n,

$$(ab)^n = a^n \cdot b^n$$

Example 1 Suppose one cube has edges twice the size of another. The volume of the second cube is how many times the volume of the first?

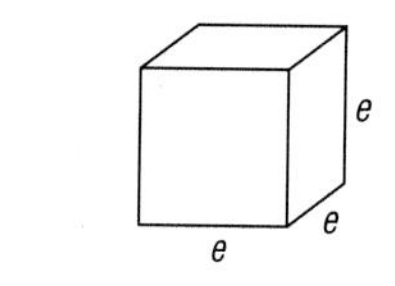

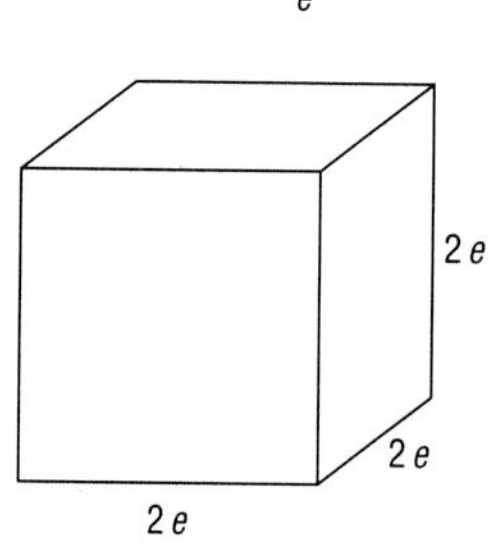

Solution The volume of a cube is the cube of its edge.

$$\begin{aligned}\text{Volume of larger cube} &= (2e)^3\\ &= 2^3e^3\\ &= 8e^3\\ &= 8\cdot\text{volume of the smaller cube}\end{aligned}$$

So the larger cube has eight times the volume of the smaller.

458

The Power of a Product Property is quite convenient when taking powers of numbers written in scientific notation.

Example 2 The radius of the earth is approximately $6.36 \cdot 10^3$ km. The volume of a sphere of radius r is given by the formula

$$V = \frac{4}{3}\pi r^3.$$

Calculate the approximate volume of the earth.

Solution Substitute $6.36 \cdot 10^3$ for r.

$$V = \frac{4}{3}\pi(6.36 \cdot 10^3)^3$$

Apply the Power of a Product Property.

$$\begin{aligned} V &= \frac{4}{3}\pi(6.36)^3 \cdot (10^3)^3 \\ &\approx \frac{4}{3}\pi(257.26) \cdot 10^9 \\ &\approx 1077.60 \cdot 10^9 \quad \text{(Note: } (10^3)^3 = 10^3 \cdot 10^3 \cdot 10^3 = 10^9\text{)} \\ &\approx 1.08 \cdot 10^{12} \text{ km}^3 \text{ in scientific notation} \\ &\approx 1{,}080{,}000{,}000{,}000 \text{ km}^3 \text{ written as a decimal} \end{aligned}$$

The Power of a Quotient Property is very similar to the Power of a Product Property. It enables powers of fractions to be easily found.

Power of a Quotient Property:

For all a and nonzero b, and any integer n,

$$\left(\frac{a}{b}\right)^n = \frac{a^n}{b^n}.$$

Example 3 Write $(\frac{2}{3})^5$ as a simple fraction.

Solution Use the Power of a Quotient Property.

$$\left(\frac{2}{3}\right)^5 = \frac{2^5}{3^5} = \frac{32}{243}$$

Check Change the fractions to decimals. $\left(\frac{2}{3}\right)^5 \approx (.\overline{6})^5 \approx 0.1316872\ldots$ $\frac{32}{243} \approx 0.1316872\ldots$also.

ADDITIONAL EXAMPLES

1. Simplify $(4y^2)^3$.
$64y^6$

2. The sun's radius is about $6.96 \cdot 10^5$ km. Find its volume.
$\frac{4}{3}\pi \cdot (6.96 \cdot 10^5)^3 \approx 1.41 \cdot 10^{18}$ km³

3. Write $\left(\frac{4}{5}\right)^4$ as a simple fraction.
$\frac{256}{625}$

4. Rewrite $\frac{2x}{5y} \cdot \left(\frac{7}{xy}\right)^3$ as a single fraction.
$\frac{686}{5x^2y^4}$

Example 4 Rewrite $3 \cdot \left(\frac{x}{2y}\right)^4$ as a single fraction.

Solution First rewrite the power using the Power of a Quotient Property.

$$3 \cdot \left(\frac{x}{2y}\right)^4 = 3 \cdot \frac{x^4}{(2y)^4}$$

Now use the Power of a Product Property.

$$= 3 \cdot \frac{x^4}{2^4y^4}$$
$$= \frac{3x^4}{16y^4}$$

Check By repeated multiplication,

$$3 \cdot \left(\frac{x}{2y}\right)^4 = 3 \cdot \frac{x}{2y} \cdot \frac{x}{2y} \cdot \frac{x}{2y} \cdot \frac{x}{2y} = \frac{3 \cdot x^4}{16y^4}.$$

The properties in this lesson help to calculate powers of negative numbers. You know that $(-1)^2 = 1$, $(-1)^3 = -1$, $(-1)^4 = 1$, and so on. Think of $-x$ as $-1 \cdot x$. Here are some examples.

$(-3)^4$	$(-\frac{4}{5})^7$	$(-xy)^6$
$= (-1 \cdot 3)^4$	$= (-1 \cdot \frac{4}{5})^7$	$= (-1 \cdot x \cdot y)^6$
$= (-1)^4 \cdot 3^4$	$= (-1)^7 \cdot (\frac{4}{5})^7$	$= (-1)^6 \cdot x^6 \cdot y^6$
$= 1 \cdot 3^4$	$= -1 \cdot \frac{4^7}{5^7}$	$= 1 \cdot x^6 \cdot y^6$
$= 81$	$= -\frac{4^7}{5^7}$	$= x^6y^6$

Experts remember that odd powers of negatives are negative. Even powers of negatives are positive. They do all of the intermediate steps at once.

Caution: Powers take precedence over opposites. Although $(-b)^2 = b^2$, it happens that when $b \neq 0$, $-b^2 \neq b^2$. The number $-b^2$ is negative, whereas b^2 is positive.

Questions

Covering the Reading

1. a. Rewrite $(5x)^3$ without parentheses. **$125x^3$**

b. Check your answer by letting $x = 2$.
$(5 \cdot 2)^3 = 10^3 = 1000$; $125(2)^3 = 125 \cdot 8 = 1000$

2. Calculate $(1.3 \cdot 10^4)^5$. **$\approx 3.7 \cdot 10^{20}$**

3. In Example 1, suppose the length of each side of the smaller cube is 12.5 feet.
   a. Find the volume of the cube. **1953.125 cu ft**
   b. Find the volume of the larger cube. **15,625 cu ft**

4. What happens to the volume of a cube when each edge is doubled? **It is multiplied by a factor of 8.**

5. The radius of Earth's moon is approximately $(1.773 \cdot 10^3)$ km. Calculate its approximate volume. Give your answer **a.** as a decimal, and **b.** in scientific notation. **a) $\approx$23,350,000,000 km^3; b) $\approx 2.335 \cdot 10^{10}$ km^3**

In 6–8, write as a simple fraction.

6. $(\frac{1}{2})^4$ **$\frac{1}{16}$** 7. $(\frac{7}{10})^3$ **$\frac{343}{1000}$** 8. $(\frac{2}{3})^6$ **$\frac{64}{729}$**

In 9–11, rewrite each expression without parentheses.

9. $(8y)^3$ **$512y^3$** 10. $\left(\frac{m}{n}\right)^2$ **$\frac{m^2}{n^2}$** 11. $4L \cdot \left(\frac{k}{2L}\right)^2$ **$\frac{k^2}{L}$**

Applying the Mathematics

In 12 and 13, answer *true or false*.

12. $-5^2 = (-5)^2$ **False** 13. $(-7)^2 = 7^2$ **True**

In 14–19, first choose the property from this list needed to simplify the expression, then simplify.
a. Product of Powers **b.** Quotient of Powers **c.** Power of a Power
d. Power of a Product **e.** Power of a Quotient

14. $(ab)^3$ **d; a^3b^3** 15. x^5x^8 **a; x^{13}** 16. $\left(\frac{I}{S}\right)^3$ **e; $\frac{I^3}{S^3}$**

17. $\frac{k^{12}}{k^9}$ **b; k^3** 18. $y \cdot y^3$ **a; y^4** 19. $(v^{-2})^3$ **c; v^{-6}**

In 20–25, rewrite without parentheses and simplify.

20. $(\frac{2}{7}z)^4$ **$\frac{16z^4}{2401}$ or $\frac{16}{2401}z^4$** 21. $\left(\frac{a^{-1}}{b^5}\right)^3$ **$\frac{a^{-3}}{b^{15}}, \frac{1}{a^3b^{15}}$** 22. $\frac{1}{2}(6x)^2$ **$18x^2$**

23. $(pqr)^0$ **1** 24. $\left(\frac{u}{3}\right)^t$ **$\frac{u^t}{3^t}$** 25. $2(kq)^5(3kq^4)^2$ **$18k^7q^{13}$**

26. If $x = 4$, what is the value of $\frac{(4x)^8}{(4x)^5}$? **4096**

27. The edge of one cube is k in. The edge of a second cube is 5 times as long.
   a. Write an expression for the volume of the first cube. **k^3 in.^{3}**
   b. Write a simplified expression for the volume of the second cube. **$125k^3$ in.^{3}**

NOTES ON QUESTIONS

Questions 2 and 5: These illustrate that knowing how to calculate the power of a product is most useful for dealing with numbers in scientific notation.

Questions 14-19: Ask students to give an algebraic statement of each property.

Question 26: Students can substitute 4, then evaluate, or they can simplify the fraction first, then substitute. It is interesting to ask students which they think is easier.

Question 35: This is an excellent calculator exercise.

NAME ____________

LESSON **MASTER 9–8**
QUESTIONS ON **SPUR** OBJECTIVES

■SKILLS *Objective A (See pages 471–473 for objectives.)*
In 1–4, evaluate.

1. 2^3 **8** 2. 3^2 **9** 3. $(-2)^4$ **16** 4. -2^4 **-16**

■SKILLS *Objective C*
In 5–24, simplify.

5. $(2a)^3$ **$8a^3$** 6. $(3x^3)^2$ **$9x^6$**
7. $5(4y)^2$ **$80y^2$** 8. $7(b^5)^3$ **$7b^{15}$**
9. $\left(\frac{t}{2}\right)^4$ **$\frac{t^4}{16}$** 10. $\left(\frac{2w^2}{3}\right)^5$ **$\frac{32w^{10}}{243}$**
11. $\left(\frac{k^5}{3}\right)^4$ **$\frac{k^{20}}{81}$** 12. $\left(\frac{2b^4c^7}{5}\right)^2$ **$\frac{4b^8c^{14}}{25}$**
13. $(2.5y^2)^3$ **$15.625y^6$** 14. $0.61(3c^5)^4$ **$49.41c^{20}$**
15. $(r^m)^n$ **r^{mn}** 16. $(2x^a)^0$ **1**
17. $\left(\frac{a}{b}\right)^n$ **$\frac{a^n}{b^n}$** 18. $\left(\frac{x^n}{y^2}\right)^3$ **$\frac{x^{3n}}{y^6}$**

■PROPERTIES *Objective E*
In 19 and 20, name the property which justifies the statement.

19. $\left(\frac{x}{y}\right)^5 = \frac{x^5}{y^5}$ **Power of a Quotient**
20. $(a^mb^n)^3 = a^{3m}b^{3n}$ **Power of a Product**

■USES *Objective H*

21. A square section of land is one mile on a side. (Recall that there are $5.28 \cdot 10^3$ feet in a mile.) What is the area of the section in square feet? **2.79×10^7 sq ft**

22. The planet Mercury, shaped nearly like a sphere, has a diameter of about 3031 miles. What is the volume of Mercury in cubic miles? (Recall that the volume of a sphere is $\frac{4}{3}\pi r^3$.) **about 1.46×10^{10} cubic miles**

 81

FOLLOW-UP

MORE PRACTICE
For more questions on SPUR Objectives, use *Lesson Master 9-8,* shown on page 461.

EXTENSION
There is a legend associated with the situation in **Example 1.** The Greeks called this legend the problem of duplicating (or doubling) the cube. When his son died, King Minos had a tomb built in the shape of a cube. When it was finished, he thought it was too small and ordered it to be rebuilt twice as large. His engineers interpreted this to mean twice as long in each dimension. But Minos meant twice the volume. The new tomb that the engineers built had 8 times the volume of the old and had to be rebuilt again.

The Greeks searched in vain for a ruler and compass construction that would show how to duplicate the cube; not until over 2000 years later was such a construction shown to be impossible. Ask students to explore with their calculator to find the length of a cube that would give a volume close to 2 cubic units. ($\sqrt[3]{2} \approx 1.26$; thus, a cube with edge 1.26*e* has about twice the volume of a cube with edge *e*.)

ADDITIONAL ANSWERS
32a.

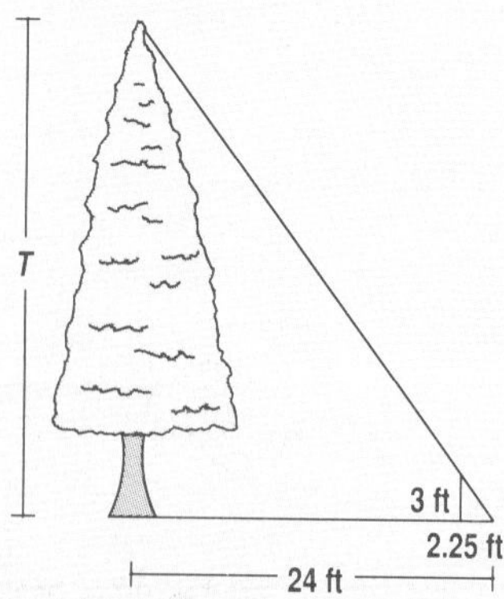

34. 1, 4, 9, 16, 25, 36, 49, 64, 81, 100, 121, 144

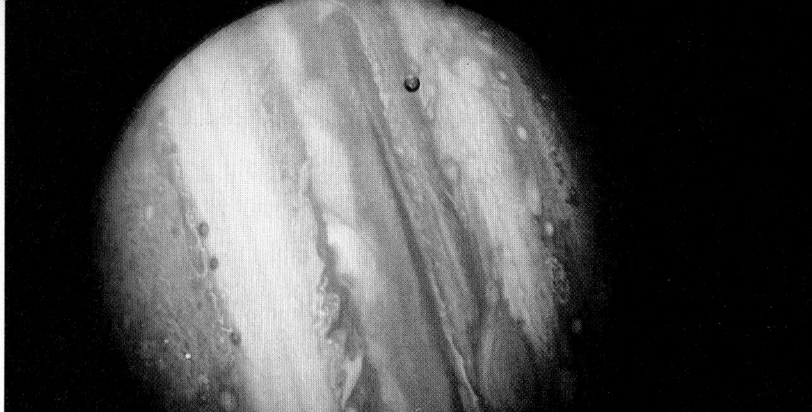

28. The radius of Jupiter is 11 times that of Earth. The volume of Jupiter is how many times the volume of Earth? **11^3 or 1331**

Review

29. Simplify $\frac{5n^2 - 3n^2}{10n^2}$. *(Lesson 9-7)* **$\frac{1}{5}$ or .2**

30. Which is larger, $(5^4)^3$ or $5^4 \cdot 5^3$? *(Lesson 9-5)* **$(5^4)^3$**

31. *Skill sequence* Simplify. *(Lesson 9-5)*
a. $2(x \cdot x^4)$ **$2x^5$**
b. $x \cdot (x^4)^2$ **x^9**
c. $(x \cdot x^4)^2$ **x^{10}**

32. A tree casts a shadow 24 ft long. A yardstick casts a shadow 2.25 ft long. **a) See margin.**
a. Draw a diagram illustrating this situation.
b. Write a proportion that describes this situation. **b. sample: $\frac{T}{24} = \frac{3}{2.25}$**
c. How tall is the tree? *(Lesson 5-8)* **32 ft**

33. A store advertises a sweater for \$45 dollars for the first 2 months it is in stock, then discounts the price 8% in each 2-month period thereafter. What is the selling price of the sweater after 10 months? *(Lesson 9-3)* **\$29.66**

34. List all the perfect squares under 150. *(Lesson 7-4, Previous course)*
1, 4, 9, 16, 25, 36, 49, 64, 81, 100, 121, 144

35. Find the area of the colored region at the right. (Recall that for a triangle, Area = $\frac{1}{2} \cdot$ base $\cdot$ height.) *(Lessons 3-2, 4-1)* **414 sq units**

Exploration

36. Each of these numbers can be written in more than one way in the form a^n, where a and n are positive integers from 2 to 20. For each, find two pairs of values of a and n.
a. 81 **b.** 256 **c.** 32,768 **d.** 43,046,721
samples: a) 3^4 or 9^2; b) 16^2 or 2^8; c) 32^3 or 2^{15}; d) 3^{16} or 9^8

LESSON 9-9

Remembering the Properties

Seven properties of powers have been studied in this chapter. They are, for all integers n and nonzero a and b:

Zero Exponent	$b^0 = 1$
Negative Exponent	$b^{-n} = \frac{1}{b^n}$
Product of Powers	$b^m \cdot b^n = b^{m+n}$
Quotient of Powers	$\frac{b^m}{b^n} = b^{m-n}$
Power of a Power	$(b^m)^n = b^{mn}$
Power of a Product	$(ab)^n = a^n b^n$
Power of a Quotient	$\left(\frac{a}{b}\right)^n = \frac{a^n}{b^n}$

It is easy to confuse these properties. Fortunately, mathematics is *consistent*. As long as you apply properties correctly, the results you get using some properties will not disagree with the results you get using other properties. We begin with what may look like a new problem: a negative power of a fraction.

Example 1 Write $\left(\frac{2}{3}\right)^{-4}$ as a simple fraction.

Solution 1: Think: The problem asks for the power of a quotient. So use that property.

$$\left(\frac{2}{3}\right)^{-4} = \frac{2^{-4}}{3^{-4}}$$

Now evaluate the numerator and denominator.

$$= \frac{\frac{1}{2^4}}{\frac{1}{3^4}} = \frac{\frac{1}{16}}{\frac{1}{81}} = \frac{1}{16} \cdot 81 = \frac{81}{16}$$

Solution 2: Think: The problem asks for a negative exponent. So use the Negative Exponent Property.

$$\left(\frac{2}{3}\right)^{-4} = \frac{1}{\left(\frac{2}{3}\right)^4}$$

Now use the Power of a Quotient Property.

$$= \frac{1}{\frac{2^4}{3^4}} = \frac{3^4}{2^4} = \frac{81}{16}$$

LESSON 9-9

RESOURCES
- Lesson Master 9-9
- Visual for Teaching Aid 48: Properties of Powers

OBJECTIVES

A Evaluate integer powers of real numbers.
D Test a special case to determine whether a pattern is true.

TEACHING NOTES

Example 1 gives three methods for simplifying a negative power of a fraction. Your students may be more comfortable sticking to one method.

Emphasize again that negative powers mean reciprocals, not negative numbers. But if students forget this or any other property, they can test a special case.

Testing a special case is a strategy that is quite useful on multiple-choice tests. It can be used both to verify properties and to find counterexamples.

Small Group Work
Have students work in small groups to give counterexamples of generalizations that are not equations, such as:

(1) All prime numbers are odd. (2 is the only even prime.)

(2) The square of a number is greater than the number itself. (If $0 \le x \le 1$, then $x^2 \le x$.)

(3) A polygon has more diagonals than sides. [A quadrilateral has two diagonals, a pentagon has five; a n-gon has $\frac{1}{2}n(n - 3)$ diagonals, and $\frac{1}{2}n(n - 3) > n$ for $n > 5$.]

Solution 3: Think: $-1 \cdot 4 = -4$. Use the Power of a Power Property.

$$\left(\frac{2}{3}\right)^{-4} = \left(\left(\frac{2}{3}\right)^{-1}\right)^4$$

Now use the Negative Exponent Property.

$$= \left(\frac{3}{2}\right)^4 = \frac{3^4}{2^4} = \frac{81}{16}$$

Check Use a calculator. 2 [÷] 3 [=] [y^x] 4 [±] [=] gives 5.0625, which is $\frac{81}{16}$.

Before the days of hand-held calculators (before the early 1970s), problems with large exponents could not be approached in a first-year algebra course. So it would be difficult to check some answers. With a calculator, a strategy called **testing a special case** is often useful.

Example 2 Norm was asked to simplify $x^8 \cdot x^6$. He forgot whether the answer should be x^{14}, x^{48}, or $2x^{14}$. How can he be helped by a special case?

Solution Let $x = 3$. That is a special case. Now calculate $3^8 \cdot 3^6$ (with a calculator) and see if it equals 3^{14} or 3^{48} or $2 \cdot 3^{14}$. A calculator shows

$$\begin{aligned} 3^8 \cdot 3^6 &= 4{,}782{,}969 \\ 3^{14} &= 4{,}782{,}969 \\ 3^{48} &= 7.9766 \cdot 10^{22} \\ 2 \cdot 3^{14} &= 9{,}565{,}938. \end{aligned}$$

The answer is 3^{14}. So $x^8 \cdot x^6 = x^{14}$.

In the test of a special case, the number tested must not be too special. A pattern may work for a few numbers, but not for all. A **counterexample** is a special case for which a pattern is false. To show that a pattern is not always true, it is enough to find *one* counterexample.

Example 3 Ali noticed that $2^3 = 2^2 + 2^2$ since $8 = 4 + 4$. She guessed that, in general, there is a property

$$x^3 = x^2 + x^2.$$

She tested a second case by letting $x = 0$. She found that $0^3 = 0^2 + 0^2$. She concluded that her *property* was always true. Is Ali right?

Solution No. Try a different number. Let $x = 5$.

$$\text{Does } 5^3 = 5^2 + 5^2?$$
$$\text{Is } 125 = 25 + 25? \text{ No.}$$

$x = 5$ is a counterexample which shows that Ali's *property* does not *always* hold.

Two is a very special number. It has properties that other numbers do not. For instance, squaring it gives the same result as doubling it. So beware of using 2 as a special case. Also avoid 0 and 1. Some patterns are true for whole numbers but not fractions. Some patterns are true for positive numbers, but not negative numbers.

You can test a special case even in applications. In the next example, a special case is used to solve a problem involving compound interest.

Example 4 In 1985, Monica wanted to invest some money for 10 years. She had two choices. Either (1) invest it all at 7% annual yield, or (2) invest half at 6% and half at 8%. Would she earn the same amount each way?

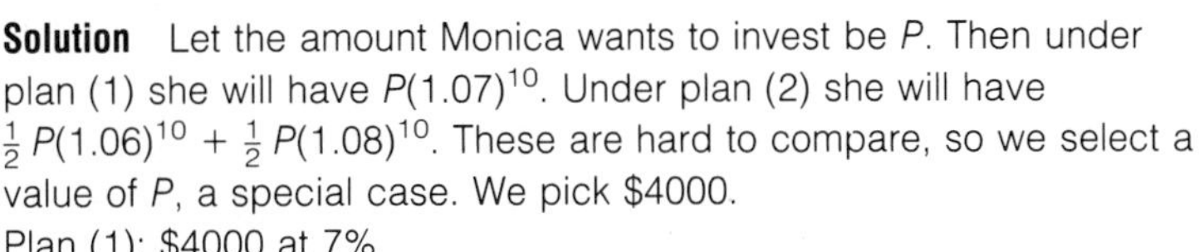

Solution Let the amount Monica wants to invest be P. Then under plan (1) she will have $P(1.07)^{10}$. Under plan (2) she will have $\frac{1}{2}P(1.06)^{10} + \frac{1}{2}P(1.08)^{10}$. These are hard to compare, so we select a value of P, a special case. We pick \$4000.
Plan (1): \$4000 at 7%

$$T = 4000(1.07)^{10}$$
$$\approx 7868.61$$

Plan (2): \$2000 at 6% and \$2000 at 8%

$$T = 2000(1.06)^{10} + 2000(1.08)^{10}$$
$$\approx 3581.70 + 4317.85$$
$$= 7899.55$$

Monica would earn \$7868.61 under the first plan and \$7899.55 under the second. The yield on the plans is not the same. Splitting her money between the investments gives in plan (2) a greater return.

In the questions, if you have trouble remembering a property or are not certain that you have simplified an expression correctly, try this technique of testing a special case.

ADDITIONAL EXAMPLES

1. Simplify $\left(\frac{7}{8}\right)^{-2}$.
$\frac{64}{49}$

2. Simplify $x^{-4} \cdot x^{10}$ and test a special case to check your answer.
sample: x^6; if $x = 2$, then $2^{-4} \cdot 2^{10} = \frac{1}{16} \cdot 1024 = 64 = 2^6$, as desired.

3. Use a counterexample to show that $\sqrt{a + b} \neq \sqrt{a} + \sqrt{b}$.
sample: Let $a = 4$ and $b = 9$. Then $\sqrt{4 + 9} = \sqrt{13} \approx 3.6$ but $\sqrt{4} + \sqrt{9} = 2 + 3 = 5$.

4. Ann works at a dress shop and gets 20% off anything she buys. Winter merchandise is on sale for 30% off. If Ann buys something, does it make any difference if the 20% discount is figured before or after the employee discount?
No. This can be answered by testing a special case or examining .8(.7x) and .7(.8x).

NOTES ON QUESTIONS
Questions 10, 11 and 13: You might discuss algebraic methods of determining the truth or falsity of the patterns. Mathematicians often use special cases to suggest properties that may be true; then they use deductive reasoning to prove them.

Question 19: The numbers are too large to evaluate on a calculator. However, if students realize that the power of 2 with the greatest exponent is the largest, they can use calculators to examine the exponents.

Question 23d: Ask why the restriction $a \neq 0$ is included. (It allows you to divide both sides by a.) Would the answer to the problem be different if $a = 0$? (Yes. All ordered pairs would solve the equation. The problem solving technique *try a simpler case* may help to explain this. Compare the solutions of $5ax = 10$ when $a = 0$ and when $a \neq 0$.)

Question 29: Students should be expected to memorize the small powers in the table.

Questions

Covering the Reading

1. a. Write $(\frac{5}{2})^{-3}$ as a fraction. $\frac{8}{125}$
b. Check your answer using a calculator. .064

In 2–4, *choose* the correct choice and check by testing a special case.

2. $\frac{x^6}{x^3} =$ (b); sample: $\frac{3^6}{3^3} = \frac{729}{27} = 27$; $3^3 = 27$

(a) x^2 (b) x^3 (c) 2 (d) 1

3. $\left(\frac{m}{n}\right)^2 =$ (d); sample: $\left(\frac{3}{4}\right)^2 = \frac{9}{16}$; $\frac{3^2}{4^2} = \frac{9}{16}$

(a) $\frac{2m}{n}$ (b) $\frac{m}{n}$ (c) $\frac{2m}{2n}$ (d) $\frac{m^2}{n^2}$

4. $\left(\frac{3x}{y}\right)^{-2} =$ (c); sample: $\left(\frac{3(3)}{5}\right)^{-2} = \left(\frac{9}{5}\right)^{-2} = \frac{25}{81}$; $\frac{5^2}{9(3)^2} = \frac{25}{81}$

(a) $\frac{y^2}{3x^2}$ (b) $-6x^2y^2$ (c) $\frac{y^2}{9x^2}$ (d) $\frac{-6x^2}{y^2}$

5. Consider the equation $x^4 = 4x^2$. Tell if the equation is true for the special case indicated.
a. $x = 0$ Yes **b.** $x = 2$ Yes **c.** $x = -2$ Yes **d.** $x = 3$ No

6. *True or false* If more than two special cases of a pattern are true, then the pattern is true. False, you can't be certain.

7. Define counterexample. A counterexample is a special case for which a pattern is false.

8. *True or false* If one special case of a pattern is not true, then the general pattern is not true. True

9. Suppose Monica can invest money at (1) 10% annual yield for 5 years or at (2) 5% annual yield for 10 years. Let her principal be \$4000. Will the two investments give the same total amount?
No, plan (2) yields more.

Applying the Mathematics

10. Consider the pattern $\frac{1}{z} + \frac{1}{y} = \frac{y+z}{yz}$.
a. Is the pattern true when $y = 3$ and $z = 4$? Yes
b. Test a special case when $y = z$. See margin.
c. Test another special case. Let $y = 5$ and $z = 2$. Convert the fractions to decimals to check. $\frac{1}{5} + \frac{1}{2} = \frac{7}{10}$; Does $.2 + .5 = .7$?; Yes
d. Do you think this pattern is true? Yes

11. Find a counterexample for the pattern $(2x)^3 = 2x^3$. The pattern is false. Sample: let $x = 0$: $(2 \cdot 0)^3 = 0^3 = 0$, $2 \cdot 0^3 = 2 \cdot 0 = 0$, and the pattern holds. Let $x = 1$: $(2 \cdot 1)^3 = 2^3 = 8$, $2 \cdot 1^3 = 2 \cdot 1 = 2$, and the pattern does not hold.

12. Consider the pattern $a^2 + b^2 = (a + b)^2$. Test special cases to decide whether this pattern is true. **sample: $a = 2$, $b = 3$; Does $2^2 + 3^2 = (2 + 3)^2$? Does $13 = 25$? No**

13. *Multiple choice* Use a special case to answer. Suppose a, b, and c are all positive numbers. **(b); sample: $a = 25$; $\frac{25}{b} = b$; $b^2 = 25$, $b = 5$; Does $\sqrt{25} = 5$? Yes**

If $\frac{a}{b} = c$ and $b = c$, then b equals which of the following:

(a) $\frac{a}{2}$ (b) $\sqrt{a}$ (c) a (d) $2a$ (e) a^2

14. Use special cases to answer. If a price is discounted 30% and then the sale price is discounted 10%, what percent of the original price is the sale price? **63%; x = original price, (x(.70))(.90) = .63x**

Review

In 15–17, simplify. *(Lessons 9-7, 9-8)*

15. $\left(\frac{3}{5x}\right)^4 \cdot \left(\frac{2}{3}\right)^2$ $\frac{36}{625x^4}$ 16. $(7ny)^3$ $343n^3y^3$ 17. $x^2 \cdot \left(\frac{3}{x}\right)^2$ 9

18. If $\frac{6n^5}{x} = 3n$, what is x? *(Lesson 9-7)* $2n^4$

19. Which is largest: 2^{1492}, $(2^{14})^{92}$, or $2^{((14)^{92})}$? *(Lesson 9-5)* $2^{((14)^{92})}$

20. John bought a used car for \$1700. It lost 10% of its value each year for the first 5 years. Then its value stayed the same for 5 years. At this point it became a collector's item and increased in value 20% each year. Find the value of the car 20 years after John bought it. *(Lessons 9-2, 9-3)* **\$6215.47**

21. Use the Pythagorean Theorem to find the length of the longest segment that can be drawn on a 3-inch by 5-inch card. Check by measuring an index card. *(Lesson 7-5)* **See margin.**

22. The rectangle below is enlarged to a size twice as long and 3 times as wide.

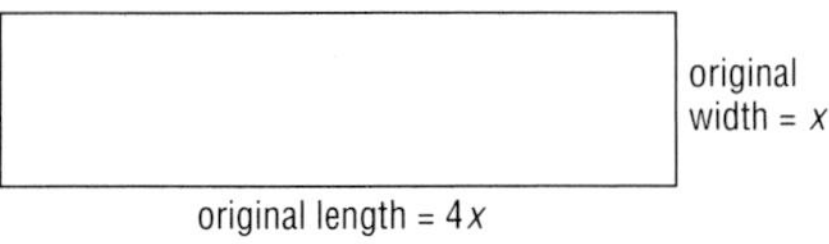

a. What is the new length? **8x**
b. What is the new width? **3x**
c. What is the new area? **$24x^2$**
d. The new area is how many times as big as the old area? *(Lessons 4-1, 5-3)* **6**

23. *Skill sequence* Solve for y. *(Lesson 6-8)* **a-d) $y = -\frac{2}{3}x + \frac{4}{3}$**

a. $2x + 3y = 4$ b. $4x + 6y = 8$
c. $6x + 9y = 12$ d. $2ax + 3ay = 4a$, $(a \neq 0)$.

ADDITIONAL ANSWERS

10b. sample: let $y = z = 2$, then $\frac{1}{2} + \frac{1}{2} = \frac{2 + 2}{2 \cdot 2} = \frac{4}{4} = 1$.

21. The longest segment connects opposite corners of the card. If its length is d, then $d^2 = 3^2 + 5^2$, $d^2 = 9 + 25$, $d^2 = 34$, $d = \sqrt{34} \approx 5.8$ in.

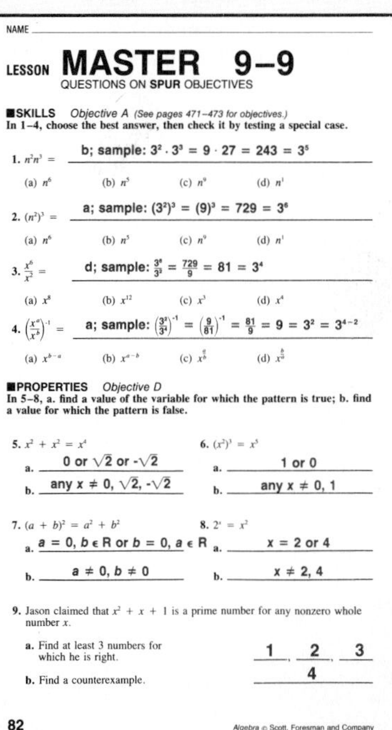
NAME ____

LESSON **MASTER 9–9**
QUESTIONS ON **SPUR** OBJECTIVES

■SKILLS *Objective A (See pages 471–473 for objectives.)*
In 1–4, choose the best answer, then check it by testing a special case.

1. $n^2n^3 =$ **b; sample: $3^2 \cdot 3^3 = 9 \cdot 27 = 243 = 3^5$**
(a) n^6 (b) n^5 (c) n^9 (d) n^1

2. $(n^2)^3 =$ **a; sample: $(3^2)^3 = (9)^3 = 729 = 3^6$**
(a) n^6 (b) n^5 (c) n^9 (d) n^1

3. $\frac{x^6}{x^2} =$ **d; sample: $\frac{3^6}{3^2} = \frac{729}{9} = 81 = 3^4$**
(a) x^8 (b) x^{12} (c) x^3 (d) x^4

4. $\left(\frac{x^a}{x^b}\right)^{-1} =$ **a; sample: $\left(\frac{3^2}{3^4}\right)^{-1} = \left(\frac{9}{81}\right)^{-1} = \frac{81}{9} = 9 = 3^2 = 3^{4-2}$**
(a) x^{b-a} (b) x^{a-b} (c) $x^{\frac{a}{b}}$ (d) $x^{\frac{b}{a}}$

■PROPERTIES *Objective D*
In 5–8, a. find a value of the variable for which the pattern is true; b. find a value for which the pattern is false.

5. $x^2 + x^2 = x^4$
a. **0 or $\sqrt{2}$ or $-\sqrt{2}$**
b. **any $x \neq 0, \sqrt{2}, -\sqrt{2}$**

6. $(x^2)^3 = x^5$
a. **1 or 0**
b. **any $x \neq 0, 1$**

7. $(a + b)^2 = a^2 + b^2$
a. **$a = 0, b \in R$ or $b = 0, a \in R$**
b. **$a \neq 0, b \neq 0$**

8. $2^x = x^2$
a. **$x = 2$ or 4**
b. **$x \neq 2, 4$**

9. Jason claimed that $x^2 + x + 1$ is a prime number for any nonzero whole number x.
a. Find at least 3 numbers for which he is right. **1, 2, 3**
b. Find a counterexample. **4**

82 *Algebra* © Scott, Foresman and Company

FOLLOW-UP

MORE PRACTICE
For more questions on SPUR Objectives, use *Lesson Master 9-9,* shown on page 467.

EXTENSION
Additional Example 4 indicates that successive discounts can be calculated in either order. A similar situation exists for a discount combined with a sales tax rate. For example, for an $80 item with a 10% discount and a 6% sales tax, the final cost is the same with both of the following calculations:

1. $(80 \times 1.06) \times .90 =$ $\$84.80 \times .90 = \$76.32$

2. $(80 \times .90) \times 1.06 =$ $\$72.00 \times 1.06 = \$76.32$

Ask students if the amount of tax and the amount the merchant receives would be the same with both calculations above? (No; in the first case the tax is $4.80, so the merchant receives 76.32 − 4.80 or $71.52; in the second case the tax is $4.32, so the merchant receives 76.32 − 4.32 or $72.00. In practice the tax is computed on the sale price as in computation 2 above.)

EVALUATION
Alternative Assessment
Evaluate students' understanding of the properties of powers as follows: Have students write and verify two special cases for each property listed on *Teaching Aid 48*. Then have them state each property in words.

24. In a studio audience, there are m men and w women. Suppose one contestant is chosen at random from the audience. Find P(the contestant is a woman). *(Lesson 1-7)* $\frac{w}{m + w}$

25. There is a $6 profit on an item selling for $20. What percent of the selling price is the profit? *(Lesson 5-4)* **30%**

26. A motorist used 8 gallons of gas in traveling 275.5 miles. At this rate, how far could the motorist travel on 10 gallons of gas? *(Lesson 5-7)* **≈ 344.4 miles**

27. If a point from the square at right is picked at random, what is the probability that it is not in the colored rectangle? *(Lesson 5-5)* $\frac{193}{225} \approx .86$

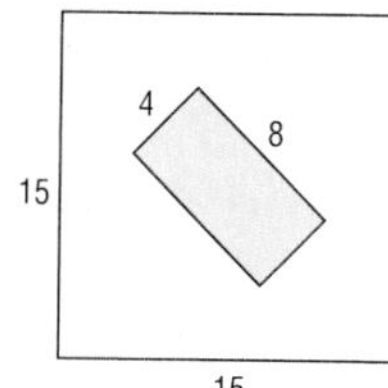

28. *Skill sequence* Evaluate $\frac{4}{3}\pi r^3$ for the given r. Leave your answer in terms of π. *(Lessons 9-5, 9-8)*
a. $r = 3$ 36π
b. $r = 3k$ $36\pi k^3$
c. $r = 3k^2$ $36\pi k^6$

Exploration

29. If you do not have a calculator, testing a special case can be difficult. So it helps to know the small positive integer powers of 2, 3, 4, 5, and 6. Copy and fill in this table of values of x^n.

$n =$	2	3	4	5	6	7	8	9	10
$x = 2$	4	8	16	32	64	128	256	512	1024
3	9	27	81	243	729				
4	16	64	256	1024					
5	25	125	625						
6	36	216							

How can you use the properties of powers to make it easier to remember these powers? **Answers will vary.**

Summary

The nth power of x is written x^n. The number n is called the exponent. Thus, whenever there is an exponent, there is a power. The expression x^n may mean $x \cdot x \cdot \ldots \cdot x$, where there are n factors. Because powers are related to multiplication, the basic properties of powers involve multiplication and division. For all integers m and n and all nonzero x and y,

$$x^m \cdot x^n = x^{m+n} \qquad \frac{x^m}{x^n} = x^{m-n}$$

$$(xy)^n = x^n y^n \qquad \left(\frac{x}{y}\right)^n = \frac{x^n}{y^n}$$

x^n can also be the growth factor in a time interval of length n, when the growth factor in the unit interval is x. Important applications of exponential growth and decay are population growth and compound interest. In compound interest, the growth factor is the quantity $1 + i$, where i is the annual yield. So at an annual yield of i, after n years an amount P grows to $P(1 + i)^n$. When the growth factor is between 0 and 1, the amount gets smaller, and exponential decay occurs.

The growth model allows x^n to be interpreted when n is not a positive integer. The number x^0 is a growth factor in 0 time, so x^0 is the identity under multiplication. Thus $x^0 = 1$. The number x^{-n} is a growth factor going back in time, and $x^{-n} = \frac{1}{x^n}$.

Vocabulary

Below are the most important terms and phrases for this chapter. You should be able to give a general description and a specific example of each.

Lesson 9-1
nth power, base, exponent
principal
interest
annual yield
compound interest
Compound Interest Formula

Lesson 9-2
exponential growth
growth factor
growth model for powering
Zero Exponent Property

Lesson 9-3
exponential decay

Lesson 9-5
Product of Powers Property
Power of a Power Property

Lesson 9-6
Negative Exponent Property

Lesson 9-7
Quotient of Powers Property

Lesson 9-8
Power of a Product Property
Power of a Quotient Property

Lesson 9-9
testing a special case
counterexample

SUMMARY

The Summary gives an overview of the entire chapter and provides an opportunity for students to consider the material as a whole. Thus, the Summary can be used to help students relate the concepts presented in the chapter.

VOCABULARY

Terms, symbols, and properties are listed by lesson to provide a checklist of things a student must know. Emphasize to students that they should read the vocabulary list carefully before starting the Progress Self-Test. If students do not understand the meaning of a term, they should refer back to the indicated lesson.

Definitions or descriptions of all terms in the vocabulary list may be found in the Glossary.

ADDITIONAL ANSWERS

11a. sample:
Does $3^2 - 2^2 = (3 - 2)(3 + 2)$?
$9 - 4 = 1 \cdot 5$? Yes.
Does $(-4)^2 - (3)^2 = (-4 - 3)(-4 + 3)$?
$16 - 9 = (-7)(-1)$? Yes.
Does $(-10)^2 - (-9)^2 = (-10 + 9)(-10 - 9)$?
$100 - 81 = (-1)(-19)$? Yes.

12. Product of a Power Property, or $b^j \cdot b^k = b^{j+k}$

PROGRESS SELF-TEST

We cannot overemphasize the importance of these end-of-chapter materials. It is at this point that the material "gels" for many students, allowing them to solidify skills and understanding. In general, student performance should be markedly improved after these pages.

USING THE PROGRESS SELF-TEST

Assign the Progress Self-Test as a one-night assignment. Worked-out *solutions* for all questions are in the Selected Answers section at the back of the student book. Encourage students to take the Progress Self-Test honestly, grade themselves, and then be prepared to discuss the test in class.

Advise students to pay special attention to those Chapter Review questions (pages 471–473) which correspond to questions missed on the Progress Self-Test. A chart provided in the Selected Answers section in the student text keys the Progress Self-Test questions to the lettered SPUR Objectives in the Chapter Review or to the Vocabulary. It also keys the questions to the corresponding lessons where the material is covered.

11, 12. See margin, page 469.

18.

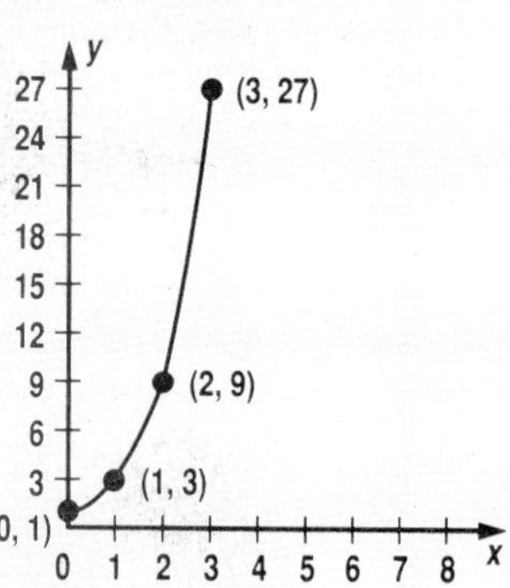

Progress Self-Test

Take this test as you would take a test in class. You will need graph paper and a calculator. Then check your work with the solutions in the Selected Answers section in the back of the book.

In 1–6, simplify.

1. $b^7 \cdot b^{11}$ **b^{18}**

2. $\frac{5x^2y}{15x^{10}}$ **$\frac{y}{3x^8}$**

3. $7 \cdot 10^1 + 3 \cdot 10^0 + 6 \cdot 10^{-1}$ **73.6**

4. $(-8)^{-5}$ **$-\frac{1}{32768}$**

5. $\frac{3z^6}{12z^4}$ **$.25z^2$, or $\frac{z^2}{4}$**

6. -5^4 **-625**

7. Rewrite $\left(\frac{3}{x}\right)^2 \cdot \left(\frac{x}{3}\right)^4$ as a simple fraction. **$\frac{x^2}{9}$**

8. Write $(3y^2)^4$ without parentheses. **$81y^8$**

9. If $q = 11$, then $6q^0 =$ __?__. **6; 10) $3^{-1} = \frac{1}{3} \neq -3$**

10. Find a counterexample to the pattern $x^{-1} = -x$.

11. Consider the pattern $x^2 - y^2 = (x - y)(x + y)$.

a. Test three special cases with positive and negative numbers. **See margin.**

b. Does it appear the pattern is true? **Yes**

12. Name the general property that justifies the simplification $2^{10} \cdot 2^3 = 2^{13}$. **See margin.**

13. Felipe invests $6500 in an account with an annual yield of 5.71%. Without any withdrawals or more deposits, how much will be in the account after 5 years? **≈ $8580.13**

14. Darlene invests $1900 for three years at an annual yield of 5.8%. At the end of the three years, how much interest has she earned? **≈ $350.15**

In 15 and 16, the present population P of a city has been growing exponentially at 3% a year.

15. What will the population be in fifteen years? **$P(1.03)^{15} \approx 1.56P$**

16. If $P = 100{,}000$, what was the population 2 years ago? **≈ 94,260 people**

17. Which of the following equations are exponential? **a. and d.**

a. $y = (\frac{1}{3})^x$ **b.** $y = 27 + 14x$

c. $y = \frac{1}{3}x$ **d.** $y = 27 \cdot 14^x$

18. Graph $y = 3^x$ for $0 \leq x \leq 3$. **See margin.**

19. A duplicating machine enlarges a picture 30%. If that enlarger is used 3 times, how many times as large as the original picture will the final picture be? **$(1.30)^3 = 2.197$ times as large**

20. Recall that the volume V of a sphere with radius r is $V = \frac{4}{3}\pi r^3$. The radius of the sun (roughly a sphere of gas) is about $4.33 \cdot 10^5$ miles. Estimate the volume of the sun. **$\approx 3.4 \times 10^{17}$ miles^3**

Chapter Review

Questions on SPUR Objectives

SPUR stands for **S**kills, **P**roperties, **U**ses, and **R**epresentations. The Chapter Review questions are grouped according to the SPUR Objectives for this chapter.

SKILLS deal with the procedures used to get answers.

Objective A: *Evaluate integer powers of real numbers.* (Lessons 9-2, 9-5, 9-6, 9-7, 9-8, 9-9)

1. Evaluate. **a.** 3^4 81 **b.** -3^4 -81 **c.** $(-3)^4$ 81
2. Simplify $-2^5 \cdot (-2)^5$. 1024
3. If $y = 7$, then $4y^0 =$ _?_. 4
4. If $x = 2$, then $3x^3 - x^2 =$ _?_. 20

In 5 and 6, simplify.

5. $7 \cdot 10^2 + 3 \cdot 10^0 + 4 \cdot 10^{-2}$ 703.04
6. $3 \cdot 10^1 + 8 \cdot 10^0 + 9 \cdot 10^{-1}$ 38.9

In 7 and 8, rewrite without an exponent.

7. -5^{-3} $-\frac{1}{125}$
8. 2^{-5} $\frac{1}{32}$

In 9–12, write as a simple fraction.

9. $(\frac{2}{7})^3$ $\frac{8}{343}$
10. $(-\frac{4}{3})^4$ $\frac{256}{81}$
11. $(\frac{1}{3})^{-4}$ 81
12. $10 \cdot (\frac{2}{5})^{-3}$ $\frac{625}{4}$

Objective B: *Simplify products, quotients, and powers of powers.* (Lessons 9-5, 9-7)

In 13–18, simplify.

13. $x^4 \cdot x^7$ x^{11}
14. $r^3 \cdot t^5 \cdot r^8 \cdot t^2$ $r^{11}t^7$
15. $y^2(x^3y^{10})$ x^3y^{12}
16. $\frac{3a^4c}{3a^5}$ $\frac{c}{a}$
17. $\left(\frac{2^{19}}{2^{19}}\right)^2$ 1
18. $(x^5)^3 + (x^3)^5$ $2x^{15}$
19. Rewrite $\frac{4m^6}{20m^2}$ without fractions. $5^{-1}m^4 = .2m^4$
20. Simplify $\frac{(x+8)^5}{(x+8)^2}$. $(x+8)^3$
21. Rewrite xy^{-2} without a negative exponent. $\frac{x}{y^2}$
22. Rewrite $2m^{-1}n^4p^2$ without a negative exponent. $\frac{2n^4p^2}{m}$

Objective C: *Rewrite powers of products and quotients.* (Lesson 9-8)

In 23–28, rewrite without parentheses.

23. $\left(\frac{y}{x}\right)^3$ $\frac{y^3}{x^3}$
24. $(4x)^m$ 4^mx^m
25. $\left(\frac{a}{b}\right)^5$ $\frac{a^5}{b^5}$
26. $(3m^2n)^3$ $27m^6n^3$
27. $4 \cdot \left(\frac{k}{3}\right)^3$ $\frac{4k^3}{27}$
28. $2(4x)^2$ $32x^2$

PROPERTIES deal with the principles behind the mathematics.

Objective D: *Test a special case to determine whether a pattern is true.* (Lesson 9-9)

29. For which of the following special cases is the pattern $x = x^2$ true? a; b
    a. $x = 0$ **b.** $x = 1$
    c. $x = 2$ **d.** $x = -1$
30. Consider the pattern $(x^2)^y = x^{2y}$.
    a. Is the pattern true when $x = 3$ and $y = 4$? Yes
    b. Is the pattern true when $x = 5$ and $y = 1$? Yes
    c. Based on your answers to parts a and b is the pattern true? Yes

RESOURCES
- Chapter 9 Test, Form A
- Chapter 9 Test, Form B
- Chapter 9 Test, Cumulative Form
- Comprehensive Test, Chapters 1–9

CHAPTER REVIEW

The main objectives for the chapter are organized here into sections corresponding to the four main types of understanding this book promotes: Skills, Properties, Uses, and Representations.

USING THE CHAPTER REVIEW

Whereas end-of-chapter material may be considered optional in some texts, in *Algebra* we have selected these objectives and questions with the expectation that they will be covered. Students should be able to answer these questions with about 85% accuracy after studying the chapter.

You may assign these questions over a single night to help students prepare for a test the next day, or you may assign the questions over a two-day period.

If you work the questions over two days, then we recommend assigning the *evens* for homework the first night so that students get feedback in class the next day, then assigning the *odds* the night before the test so the students can use the answers provided in the book.

ADDITIONAL ANSWERS

31. Does $(3 + 4)^3 = 3^3 + 4^3$? Does $7^3 = 27 + 64$? No.

32. Does $(5^3)^2 = 5^{(3^2)}$? Does $125^2 = 5^9$? Does $15625 = 1,953,125$? No.

47b. After 4 hours there will be 128,000 bacteria.

48b. The bacteria count was 1000 three hours earlier.

55.

x	y
-4	$\frac{1}{16}$
-3	$\frac{1}{8}$
-2	$\frac{1}{4}$
-1	$\frac{1}{2}$
0	1
1	2
2	4
3	8
4	16

56.

x	y
-3	$\frac{1}{64}$
-2	$\frac{1}{16}$
-1	$\frac{1}{4}$
0	1
1	4
2	16
3	64

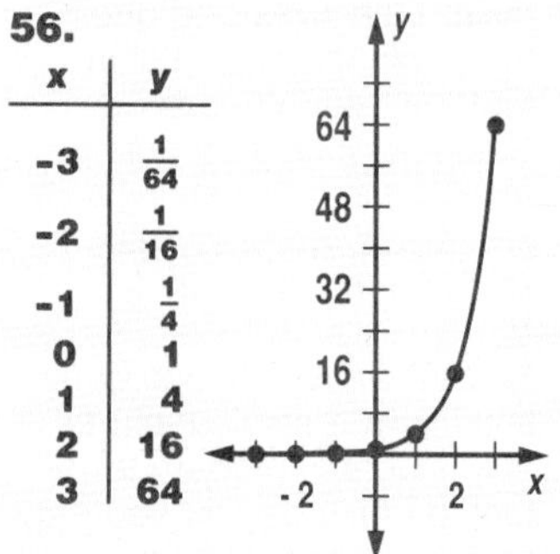

59a.

Year	Amount
0	200
5	200
10	200
15	200

59b.

Year	Amount
0	200
5	255.26
10	325.78
15	415.79

In 31 and 32, find a counterexample to the pattern. **See margin.**

31. $(a + b)^3 = a^3 + b^3$

32. $(x^3)^2 = x^{(3^2)}$

Objective E: *Identify properties of exponents.* (*Lessons 9-2, 9-5, 9-6, 9-7, 9-8*)

Here is a list of the power properties in this chapter. For all integers m and n and nonzero a and b:

Zero Exponent Property:	$b^0 = 1$
Product of Powers Property:	$b^m \cdot b^n = b^{m+n}$
Power of a Product Property:	$(ab)^n = a^n \cdot b^n$
Negative Exponent Property:	$b^{-n} = \frac{1}{b^n}$
Quotient Property of Powers:	$\frac{b^m}{b^n} = b^{m-n}$
Power of a Power Property:	$(b^m)^n = b^{mn}$
Power of a Quotient Property:	$\left(\frac{a}{b}\right)^n = \frac{a^n}{b^n}$

In 33–40, name the general property or properties that justify the simplification.

33. $a^7 \cdot b^7 = (ab)^7$ **Power of a Product**

34. $a^7 \div a^2 = a^5$ **Quotient of Powers**

35. $(4.36)^0 = 1$ **Zero Exponent**

36. $4^6 \cdot 4^9 = 4^{15}$ **Product of Powers**

37. $\left(\frac{7}{g}\right)^y = \frac{7^y}{g^y}$ **Power of a Quotient**

38. $6^3 \cdot 2^0 = 6^3$ **Zero Exponent**

39. $14^{-2} = \frac{1}{14^2}$ **Negative Exponent**

40. $\left(\frac{x}{y}\right)^{-2} = \frac{y^2}{x^2}$ **Negative Exponents; Power of a Quotient**

USES deal with applications of mathematics in real situations.

Objective F: *Calculate compound interest.* (*Lesson 9-1*)

In 41 and 42, use the advertisement below.

41. Using the annual yield, calculate how much money there will be in your account if you deposit $2500 for 3 years. **$3123.11**

42. Using the annual yield, calculate how much interest $3000 will earn if deposited for 4 years. **$1036.31**

43. Susan invested $1200 in a bank at an annual yield of 6%. Without any withdrawals, how much money would she have in the account after 2 years? **$1348.32**

44. *Multiple choice* Which yields more money? **(b)**
(a) an amount invested for 2 years at an annual yield of 10%
(b) the same amount invested for 10 years at an annual yield of 2%

Objective G: *Solve problems involving exponential growth and decay.* (*Lessons 9-2, 9-3*)

45. Jennifer earns $7.25 an hour. She gets a 12% raise each year. How much will she earn per hour after 4 years on the job? **$11.41**

46. In 1986, the United States had an inflation rate of about 4% per year. That means an article costing $100 in 1986 would cost $104 in 1987. Consider a hardcover book that sells for $16.95 in 1986. At the rate of inflation above, how much would the same book cost in 1990? **$19.83**

In 47 and 48, after a few hours a colony of bacteria that doubles every hour has 8000 bacteria. After n more hours there will be T bacteria where

$$T = 8000 \cdot 2^n.$$

47. a. Find the value of T when $n = 4$. **128,000**

b. In words describe the meaning of your answer to part a. **See margin.**

48. a. Find T when $n = -3$. **1000**

b. Describe the meaning of your answer to part a. **See margin.**

In 49 and 50, the population in a city of 1,500,000 is decreasing exponentially at a rate of 3% per year. The population P in n years can be described by

$$P = 1{,}500{,}000 \cdot (0.97)^n.$$

49. What will the population be in 10 years' time? **1,106,136**

50. What is the population when $n = 0$? What does your answer mean? **1,500,000; the population now at year 0**

■ **Objective H:** *Use and simplify expressions with powers in everyday situations.* *(Lessons 9-6, 9-7, 9-8)*

51. A certain photographic enlarger can make any picture $\frac{3}{2}$ times its original size. By how many times will a picture be enlarged if the enlarger is used

a. twice $\frac{9}{4}$ **b.** 5 times? $\frac{243}{32}$

52. Water blocks out light. (At a depth of 10 meters it is not as bright as on the surface.) Suppose 1 meter of water lets in $\frac{9}{10}$ of the light. How much light will get through x meters of water? $\left(\frac{9}{10}\right)^x$ **or** $(.9)^x$

53. In 1987, there were about $5 \cdot 10^9$ people on earth. The land area of the earth is about $1.46 \cdot 10^8$ sq km. How many people are there per sq km? **≈ 34**

54. The moon is nearly a sphere with radius of $1.05 \cdot 10^3$ miles. The volume of a sphere is $\frac{4}{3}\pi r^3$. To the nearest billion cubic miles, what is the volume of the moon? $5 \cdot 10^9$ **miles**^{3}

REPRESENTATIONS deal with pictures, graphs, or objects that illustrate concepts.

■ **Objective I:** *Graph exponential growth and decay relationships.* *(Lesson 9-4)*

55. Graph $y = 2^x$ for $-4 \le x \le 4$. **See margin.**

56. Graph $y = 4^x$ for $-3 \le x \le 3$. **See margin.**

57. When x is large, the graph of which equation increases faster, $y = 56 + .04x$ or $y = 56 \cdot (1.04)^x$? $y = 56 \cdot (1.04)^x$

58. Tell whether the graph of each equation is linear or exponential.

a. $y = 4x$ **linear** **b.** $y = 4^x$ **exponential**

c. $y = 100 \cdot (3.4)^x$ **exponential;** **d.** $y = \frac{3}{4}x + 100$ **d) linear**

59. Suppose $200 is invested in a bank at a 5% annual yield. Make a table for the amount in the bank after 0, 5, 10, and 15 years if

a. the interest is removed each year; **See margin.**

b. the interest is kept in the bank and compounded. **See margin.**

c. Graph smooth curves through the amounts in parts a and b on the same set of axes. **See margin.**

60. Match each graph with its description.

a. constant increase **ii**

b. constant decrease **iv**

c. exponential growth **i**

d. exponential decay **iii**

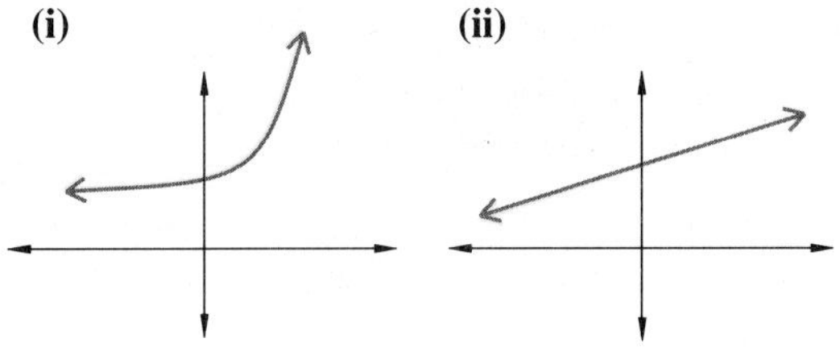

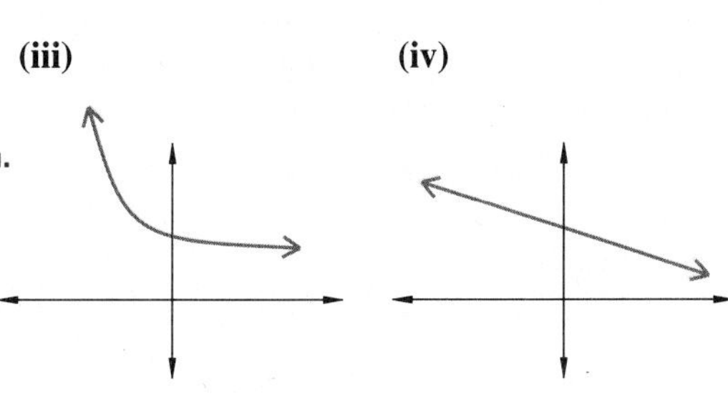

EVALUATION
Three tests are provided for this chapter in the Teacher's Resource File. Chapter 9 Test, Forms A and B, cover just Chapter 9. The third test is Chapter 9 Test, Cumulative Form. About 50% of this test covers Chapter 9; 25% covers Chapter 8, and 25% covers earlier chapters. A Comprehensive Test covering Chapters 1-9 is also included with this chapter. For more information on grading, see *General Teaching Suggestions: Grading* on page T44 in the Teacher's Edition.

ASSIGNMENT RECOMMENDATION
On the day your students take the chapter test, we suggest you make an assignment in the first section of the next chapter.

59c.

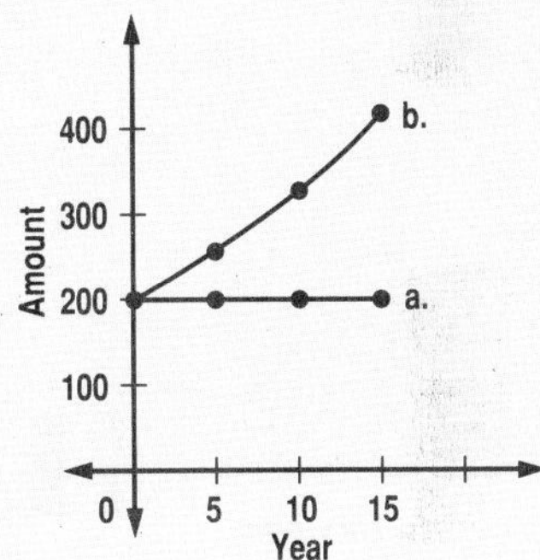

CHAPTER 10 ■ POLYNOMIALS

DAILY PACING CHART 10

DAILY PACING CHART ■ CHAPTER 10

Students in the Full Course should complete the entire text by the end of the year. Students in the Minimal Course spend more time to complete lessons that are combined with quizzes and more time to consider the Chapter Review. Therefore, these students may not complete all the chapters in the text.

DAY	MINIMAL COURSE	FULL COURSE
1	10-1	10-1
2	10-2	10-2
3	10-3	10-3
4	10-4	10-4
5	Quiz (TRF); Start 10-5.	Quiz (TRF); 10-5
6	Finish 10-5.	10-6
7	10-6	10-7
8	10-7	10-8
9	10-8	Quiz (TRF); 10-9
10	Quiz (TRF); Start 10-9.	10-10
11	Finish 10-9.	10-11
12	10-10	Progress Self-Test
13	10-11	Chapter Review
14	Progress Self-Test	Chapter Test (TRF)
15	Chapter Review	
16	Chapter Review	
17	Chapter Test (TRF)	

TESTING OPTIONS

TESTING OPTIONS

- ■ Quiz for Lessons 10-1 Through 10-4
- ■ Quiz for Lessons 10-5 Through 10-8
- ■ Chapter 10 Test, Form A
- ■ Chapter 10 Test, Form B
- ■ Chapter 10 Test, Cumulative Form

INDIVIDUAL DIFFERENCES

PROVIDING FOR INDIVIDUAL DIFFERENCES

The student text is written for the *average* student. The program, however, can be adapted for less capable and for more capable students.

For those students who need more practice, a blackline master (in the Teacher's Resource File) is provided for each lesson. The Teacher's Edition frequently provides Error Analysis and Alternate Approach features to provide additional instructional strategies for those students who do not readily grasp the material.

For students who require additional challenge, Extension activities are regularly provided in the Teacher's Edition.

OBJECTIVES ■ CHAPTER 10

Students should master the chapter objectives by the time they complete the chapter. To ensure objective mastery, there is continual review built into each set of lesson questions. After students complete the chapter lessons, they assess their mastery on the Progress Self-Test. Then they do the Chapter Review and pay special attention to those questions that match the objectives missed on the Progress Self-Test. Students can get extra practice on these objectives by using the master for each lesson in the Teacher's Resource File.

OBJECTIVES FOR CHAPTER 9 (Organized into the SPUR categories— Skills, Properties, Uses, and Representations)	**Progress Self-Test Questions**	**Chapter Review Questions**	**Lesson Master from Teacher's Resource File***
SKILLS			
A Add and subtract polynomials.	1–3	1 through 8	10-1, 10-2
B Multiply polynomials.	4–9, 11	9 through 22	10-3, 10-5, 10-6, 10-7, 10-9
C Recognize perfect squares and perfect square trinomials.	12	23 through 28	10-8
D Find common monomial factors of polynomials.	13, 14, 17	29 through 34	10-4
E Factor perfect square trinomials and the difference of squares into a product of two binomials.	15, 16	35 through 40	10-8, 10-9
PROPERTIES			
F Apply $(a + b)^2 = a^2 + 2ab + b^2$, $(a - b)^2 = a^2 - 2ab + b^2$, and $(a + b)(a - b) = a^2 - b^2$ to multiply numbers in your head.	18, 10	41 through 44	10-7, 10-9
G Recognize and use the Zero Product Property to solve equations.	20, 21	45 through 51	10-10
H Recognize factors of polynomials using the properties of algebra, testing a special case and ruling out possibilities.	19	52 through 55	10-11
USES			
I Translate real situations into polynomials.	22, 23	56 through 61	10-1, 10-2, 10-3, 10-6, 10-10
REPRESENTATIONS			
J Represent areas of figures in terms of polynomials.	24, 25	62 through 67	10-2, 10-3, 10-5

*** The masters are numbered to match the lessons.**

OVERVIEW ■ CHAPTER 10

This chapter covers the basic operations of addition, subtraction, and, multiplication of polynomials. Polynomials are developed from uses. For example, the concepts of exponential growth from the last chapter are used to generate situations which lead to polynomial expressions.

The Area Model for Multiplication forms the basis of the lessons on multiplication of binomials. This representation of an algebraic technique with a geometric model provides a way for students to reconstruct the algorithms for multiplication of polynomials.

The Distributive Property plays a major role in all the algorithms of this chapter. Also, the Zero Product Property is introduced as a way to solve equations involving products of polynomials. Evaluation of polynomials is repeated in lessons throughout the chapter to emphasize that properties of polynomial operations arise from real number properties. Emphasis on evaluation leads to an important problem solving strategy, namely, *ruling out possibilities*.

The goal of the chapter is to have students become skillful in the addition, subtraction, and multiplication of polynomials. Practice throughout the chapter focuses on these important manipulations.

This chapter touches on factoring trinomials as reversing the process of multiplication of binomials. The emphasis is on two special forms—difference of two squares and perfect-square trinomials. We want students to become proficient in these special forms because they are critical for understanding mathematical patterns and they occur in applications. General trinomial factoring is covered in Chapter 12.

PERSPECTIVES ■ CHAPTER 10

The Perspectives provide the rationale for the inclusion of topics or approaches, provide mathematical background, and make connections within UCSMP.

10-1

HOW POLYNOMIALS ARISE

Polynomials arise in mathematics from many considerations: any continuous function can be approximated by a polynomial function; there is a polynomial function for any finite sequence; the set of polynomials with real coefficients under the usual operations forms the structure called a ring. These considerations are beyond the level of this book.

Fortunately, the extensive work students have done on compound interest and exponential growth in Chapter 9 can be immediately applied. The application is to *annuities*. Annuities are investments which involve periodic deposits or withdrawals. Thus the principal amounts in an annuity can be different (have different coefficients in the compound interest formula) and grow for different lengths of time (have different exponents in the compound interest formula). For instance, if x is $1 + r$, where r is the annual yield, the polynomial

$$ax^2 + bx + c$$

can stand for the total when an amount a has been invested for 2 time periods, an amount b has been in the annuity for 1 time period, and the amount c has just been deposited.

A nice characteristic of this application is that each component of the polynomial has a clear meaning. It is a rich application, and it is used throughout the chapter.

10-2

ADDING AND SUBTRACTING POLYNOMIALS

The annuity application introduced in Lesson 10-1 is used in this lesson to establish a situation involving addition of polynomials. Just add the amounts in two annuities! Students have been adding like terms since Chapter 4, so addition should not be a problem.

For subtraction, the representation of polynomials with areas is used. This introduces area as a way of picturing multiplication, an idea applied often in this chapter. When situations involve subtraction or negatives, students are more likely to make errors.

10-3

MULTIPLYING A POLYNOMIAL BY A MONOMIAL

The Area Model for Multiplication introduced in Chapter 4 is employed in this lesson to multiply a polynomial by a monomial. The skill is easy and will be generalized in Lesson 10-5 to the multiplication of any polynomials, and later to the multiplication of binomials.

10-4

COMMON MONOMIAL FACTORING

There are many times in mathematics that you work with ideas in two directions and therefore understand them better. Common monomial factoring is a different way of viewing the Distributive Property.

In this lesson, the factoring is applied immediately to exhibit division by a monomial.

10-5

MULTIPLYING POLYNOMIALS

The Area Model for Multiplication is extended here to multiplying a polynomial by a polynomial. Many books discuss multiplication of binomials before multiplication of polynomials. That order was also used in early field-test versions of *Algebra*. But, apparently, the case $(a + b)(c + d)$ is too special, and some students develop poor habits. By first focusing on the general case, we emphasize the notion that each term of one sum is multiplied by every term of the other.

In each example, before the multiplication is done, a note is made of the number of terms that will be in the result. This helps students to check their work and also provides an example of the Multiplication Counting Principle discussed in Chapter 4.

10-6

MULTIPLYING BINOMIALS

After covering the general case of multiplying polynomials using the Extended Distributive Property in the last lesson, in this lesson we discuss the more specific case of multiplying a binomial by a binomial. Because this is done so often, an efficient method is needed. We employ the FOIL (First terms, Outside terms, Inside terms, Last terms) algorithm. FOIL is a useful mnemonic for remembering the skill. It does not substitute for knowing the properties, for using the ideas, or for their representation.

10-7

SQUARES OF BINOMIALS

Two patterns of polynomial multiplication occur often in mathematics. They are the square of a binomial (covered in this lesson and the next) and the difference of two squares (covered in Lesson 10-9). These are patterns which every algebra student should master and are far more important than trinomial factoring.

The lesson includes some mental arithmetic shortcuts based on the square of a binomial.

10-8

RECOGNIZING PERFECT SQUARES

This lesson begins with a topic already covered in Chapter 7, but now students should look at patterns they get when squaring whole numbers. Why can't a number which ends in 3, for example, be a perfect square? (The unit digit of a number determines the unit digit of its square.) Similarly, the first and last terms of a perfect square trinomial must have a certain form. If the trinomial is a perfect square, then the sign of the middle term of the trinomial determines the operation in the binomial.

10-9

DIFFERENCE OF SQUARES

The difference of two squares is the second factoring pattern which students should master. This lesson covers a variety of examples of the pattern and, like Lesson 10-7, has some applications to mental arithmetic.

10-10

THE ZERO PRODUCT PROPERTY

The Zero Product Property gives a reason for factoring of all kinds. In the problems, either the factored form is given or the problem requires only common monomial factoring.

This lesson also anticipates work with projectile motion in Chapter 12 by considering the special case $0 = vt - \frac{1}{2}gt^2$ of the formula $h = vt - \frac{1}{2}gt^2$. This formula gives the height h of a projectile at time t if its initial upward velocity is v. The g in the formula stands for the gravitational constant.

Measurements show that g is about 32 ft/sec^2 or 9.8 m/sec^2 in a vacuum at the surface of the earth. Air resistance changes the amount somewhat and altitude changes it quite a bit. Furthermore, because the earth is not perfectly spherical the gravitational constant varies several percent depending on your position on the earth's surface. In the preceding formulas if g is in ft/sec^2, then h is in feet, v in ft/sec, and t in seconds. However, if g is in m/sec^2, then h is in meters and v in m/sec.

10-11

RECOGNIZING FACTORS OF POLYNOMIALS

The problem-solving strategy called *ruling out possibilities* is used here to establish connections between polynomials and multiplication problems.

It is important that students see a wide variety of multiplication problems before they are taught general factoring. Too often students in algebra classes try to learn algorithms for factoring trinomials and lose sight of the relationship to multiplication. We want to emphasize the multiplication in this lesson. More work on factoring will be done in Chapter 12.

The use of a special case to check results emphasizes the idea that factoring should give an identity. $x^2 - y^2 = (x - y)(x + y)$ because the sentence is true for every pair of values for x and for y. This is a method which is used in sophisticated computer programs to solve engineering problems. Checking values takes students back to the basics, the meaning of expressions.

Problems like the multiple-choice questions in this lesson are often on standardized tests. The methods of this lesson apply to far more situations than factoring.

CHAPTER 10

This chapter should take 11 to 13 days for the lessons and quizzes; 1 day for the Progress Self-Test; 1 or 2 days for the Chapter Review; and 1 day for testing. The total is 14 to 17 days.

CHAPTER 10

Polynomials

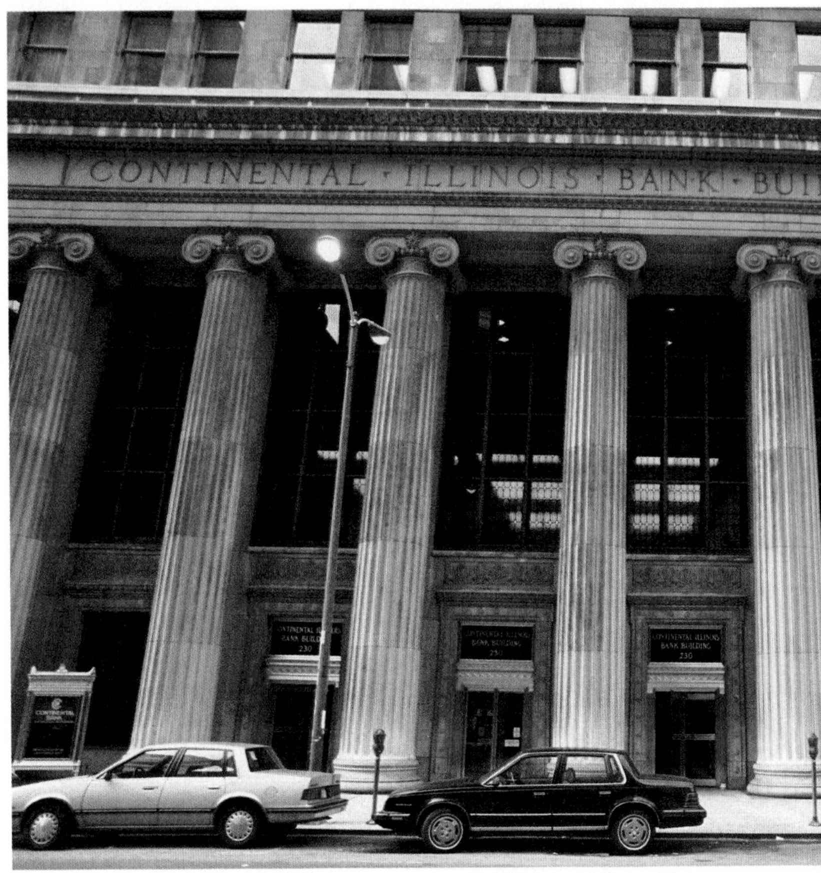

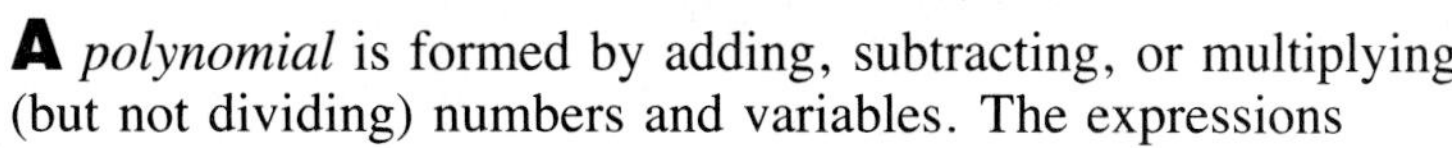

A *polynomial* is formed by adding, subtracting, or multiplying (but not dividing) numbers and variables. The expressions

$$3x^2$$
$$3a + 4a^2 - 5c$$
$$\frac{1}{2}y^2zt^5 - 17$$

are polynomials. Many of the algebraic expressions you have studied in this book are polynomials.

Polynomials arise naturally in certain situations. In this chapter you will learn that polynomial

$$Ax^3 + By^2 + Cz$$

tells how much you would have if you invested A dollars 3 years ago at a yield $x - 1$, added B dollars to it 2 years ago at a yield $y - 1$, and added C dollars 1 year ago at a yield $z - 1$.

Polynomials also can approximate other expressions. Here is a graph of the polynomial equation

$$y = x - \frac{1}{5}x^3 + \frac{1}{120}x^5.$$

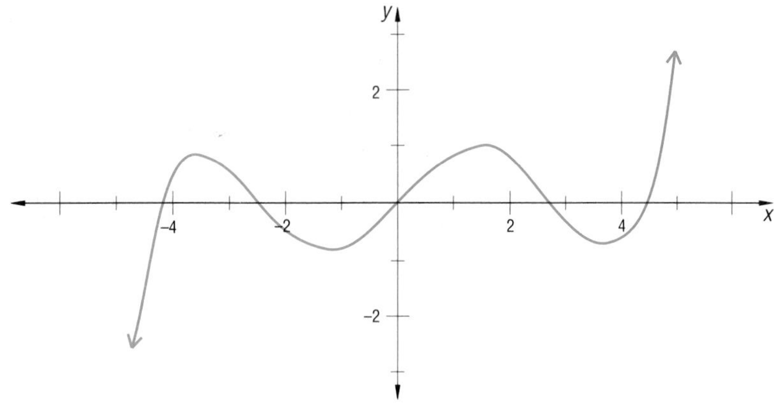

For values of x from -4 to 4, it approximates the motion of a wave.

In this chapter you will learn about situations that give rise to polynomials, and how to add, subtract, and multiply them.

USING PAGES 474-475
You may wish to point out that the first expression on page 475 is a monomial. A monomial is a constant or a variable or a product of a constant and one or more variables. The first three expressions are all polynomials. A polynomial is a monomial or a sum (or difference) of two or more monomials.

You might also wish to point out that in a polynomial any exponent applied to a variable must be a nonnegative integer. Then ask why

$$\frac{3}{x} \text{ and } 4\sqrt{y}$$

are not monomials. (The first involves division by the variable, and is equivalent to $3x^{-1}$; the second involves taking the square root of the variable.) Point out that, therefore,

$$\frac{3}{x} + 5x^2 \text{ (or } 3x^{-1} + 5x^2\text{)}$$

and

$$4\sqrt{y} - 6abc$$

are not polynomials.

When discussing $Ax^3 + By^2 + Cz$, you might ask why the annual yields are stated as $x - 1$, $y - 1$, and $z - 1$. (x, y, and z are growth factors like 1.07; therefore, to express the annual yield, we must subtract 1.)

LESSON 10-1

RESOURCES
- Lesson Master 10-1
- Visual for Teaching Aid 49: Patterns for **Questions 1-4**
- Visual for Teaching Aid 50: Graphs for **Question 26**
- Visual for Teaching Aid 51: Polynomials from Mortgage Payments (for use with Extension)
- Computer Master 20

OBJECTIVES

A Add and subtract polynomials.

I Translate real situations into polynomials.

TEACHING NOTES

Example 1 illustrates the value of writing uncalculated arithmetic expressions to describe situations. Were students to compute every step of the argument with their calculators, they would not see the pattern. However, students should check the values of the "Total" column with their calculator. The calculator memory can be very helpful when doing these evaluations. You may have to help your students learn to use it.

LESSON

How Polynomials Arise

The largest money matters most adults deal with are

salary or wages,
savings,
payments on loans for cars or trips or other items,
insurance,
social security payments and benefits, and
home mortgages or rent.

Each of these items involves paying or receiving money each month or every few months or every year. But what is the total amount paid or received? The answer is not easy to calculate because interest is involved. Here is an example of this kind of situation.

Example 1 Each birthday, from age 12 on, Mary has received \$50 from her grandparents. She saves the money and can get an annual yield of 7%. How much will she have by the time she is 16?

Solution It helps to write down how much Mary has on each birthday. On her 12th birthday she has \$50. She then receives interest on that \$50 and an additional \$50 on her 13th birthday.

$$50(1.07) + 50 = \$103.50$$

Each year interest is paid on all the money previously accumulated and each year another \$50 gift is added. The totals for her 12th through 16th birthdays are summarized below.

Birthday		Total
12th	50	= \$50
13th	$50(1.07) + 50$	= \$103.5
14th	$50(1.07)^2 + 50(1.07) + 50$	= \$160.7
15th	$50(1.07)^3 + 50(1.07)^2 + 50(1.07) + 50$	= \$222.0
16th	$50(1.07)^4 + 50(1.07)^3 + 50(1.07)^2 + 50(1.07) + 50$	= \$287.5
	↑ from 12th birthday; ↑ from 13th birthday; ↑ from 14th birthday; ↑ from 15th birthday; ↑ from 16th birthday	

The total of \$287.54 she has by her 16th birthday is \$37.54 more than the total \$250 she received as gifts because of the interest earned.

476

Letting $x = 1.07$, you can write the amount of money Mary has with the expression

$$50x^4 + 50x^3 + 50x^2 + 50x + 50 \text{ dollars.}$$

This expression is useful because if the interest rate changes, you only have to substitute a different value for x. We call x a **scale factor**.

Example 2 Suppose Erin's parents gave her \$50 on her 12th birthday, \$60 on her 13th, \$70 on her 14th, and \$80 on her 15th. If she invests all the money in an account with a yearly scale factor x, how much will she have on her 15th birthday?

Solution The money from her 12th birthday will earn three years worth of interest, from her 13th, two years of interest, and from her 14th, one year. So the total is

$$50x^3 + 60x^2 + 70x + 80.$$

The expression $50x^3 + 60x^2 + 70x + 80$ is a **polynomial in the variable x.** Recall that a term is a number or a number multiplied by a variable. So this polynomial has four terms. The 80 is a **constant term.** All other terms consist of a number, called the *coefficient*, multiplied by a variable. Sometimes the variable has an exponent. Almost always the coefficient of a term is written first.

The largest exponent in a polynomial with one variable is the **degree of the polynomial**. For instance, the polynomial $17y^3 + 8y^5 - y + 6$ is a polynomial in y with degree 5. It is common practice to arrange terms of a polynomial in descending order of exponents ending with the constant term. If the terms are arranged in descending order of exponents, the polynomial is

$$8y^5 + 17y^3 - y + 6.$$

The coefficient of y^5 is 8. Since there is no y^4 term, we say that the coefficient of y^4 is 0. The coefficient of y^3 is 17. The coefficient of y^2 is 0. The coefficient of y is -1. The constant term is 6.

Polynomials with 1, 2, or 3 terms have special names.

Name	Number of terms	Examples
monomial	1 term	$3x^2$, $\frac{1}{2}xy^3$, $-500m^{14}$
binomial	2 terms	$c - 7d$, $4x^2 - 1$, $w + 2$
trinomial	3 terms	$b^2 + 2b + 1$
		$9y^2 + 30yz + 25z^2$
		$-4x^4 - 7.2x^3 + .019$

In **Example 1** the amounts (coefficients) are the same. **Example 2** develops a polynomial with different coefficients by varying information in the situation.

Point out to your students that the polynomial

$$8y^5 + 17y^3 - y + 6$$

on page 477 can be written

$$8y^5 + 0y^4 + 17y^3 + 0y^2 - y + 6$$

to show the terms with coefficients of 0.

ADDITIONAL EXAMPLES

1. As a New Year's Resolution, Bert has decided to deposit \$100 in a savings account every January 2. The account yields 8% annually. How much will his savings be worth after he makes his fourth deposit?
$100(1.08)^3 + 100(1.08)^2 + 100(1.08) + 100 = \$450.61$

2. Janice has a savings account that has a scale factor of x. She makes deposits at regular yearly intervals. The first year she deposits \$800, the second year \$300, the third year \$450 and the fourth year \$775. What is her balance immediately after the fourth deposit?
$800x^3 + 300x^2 + 450x + 775$

NOTES ON QUESTIONS

Questions 1-5: You will probably need to go through these questions in detail with your students. *Teaching Aid 49* includes partially completed solutions for **Questions 1-4.**

Question 11: Students should begin by calculating the number of cords of wood in the trees that are planted each year. These are the quantities that are growing exponentially.

Question 12: Students may need help interpreting the formula. Show them a few more instances of the pattern.

$1 + 2 + 3 + 4 = \frac{1}{2} \cdot 4^2 + \frac{1}{2} \cdot 4$

$1 + 2 + 3 + 4 + 5 = \frac{1}{2} \cdot 5^2 + \frac{1}{2} \cdot 5$

Computer for Question 13: The square of x has been written as X * X rather than X^2. The power symbol ^ signals the computer to use a computational technique which involves logarithms. As a result, input of integer values may produce output which is nonintegral. If you write powers as multiplications, you can be sure that within the accuracy of your computer, integral input will produce integral output.

Making Connections for Question 19: Students are required to subtract binomials, a skill they have seen before, in Lesson 6-9. As preparation for the work in Lesson 10-2, emphasize the subtraction step.

$(9x + 8) - (6x - 5) = 9x + 8 - 6x + 5.$

Making Connections for Question 22: This question provides practice in the Distributive Property which is needed for the multiplication of binomials starting with Lesson 10-3.

Questions

Covering the Reading

1. Mary's grandfather will receive \$200 on each of his birthdays from age 61 on. If he saves the money and can get an annual yield of 7%, how much will he have by the time he retires at age 65? \$1150.15

In 2–5, Huey, Dewey and Louie are triplets. They received the following cash presents on their birthdays.

	H	D	L
In 1982	\$10	\$15	\$5
In 1983	\$20	\$15	\$40
In 1984	\$15	\$15	nothing

Each year they put all their money into a bank account which paid a 6% annual yield.

2. How much money did Huey have on his 1983 birthday? \$30.60

3. How much did Dewey have on his 1984 birthday? \$47.75

4. How much did Louie have on his 1984 birthday? \$48.02

5. In 1985, Huey received \$30 on his birthday. If he had invested all the money received from years 1982–85 into an account with scale factor x, how much would he have had by his birthday in each of the following years? a) 10 dollars; b) $10x + 20$ dollars
a. 1982 **b.** 1983 **c.** 1984 **d.** 1985
c) $10x^2 + 20x + 15$ dollars; d) $10x^3 + 20x^2 + 15x + 30$ dollars

6. For the polynomial $2m^2 - 5m^4 + m - 80$, give the coefficient of:
a. m^4 -5 **b.** m^3 0 **c.** m^2 2 **d.** m 1

7. a. Write the polynomial $3 - 90x^3 + 4x^2 + x^5$ in descending order of exponents. $x^5 - 90x^3 + 4x^2 + 3$
b. Give its degree. 5

8. How many terms does each of the following have?
a. trinomial 3 **b.** monomial 1 **c.** binomial 2

9. *True or false* $7xy$ is a trinomial. False

Applying the Mathematics

10. Give the value of $x^3 + 2x^2 - 9x + 2$ when x is:
a. 1 -4 **b.** $\frac{1}{2}$ $-\frac{15}{8} = -1.875$ **c.** -1 12 **d.** 0 2

11. A wood harvester plants trees each spring in a forest. The first spring 16,000 trees were planted. The second spring 22,000 trees were planted, the third spring 18,000, and the fourth spring 25,000. Suppose that each tree contains $\frac{1}{100}$ of a cord of wood when it is planted. Then suppose each year the amount of wood grows by a scale factor y. How many cords of wood are in the forest the fourth spring?
$160y^3 + 220y^2 + 180y + 250$

12. The formula below gives the sum of the consecutive integers from 1 to n.

$$1 + 2 + 3 + \ldots + n = \frac{1}{2}n^2 + \frac{1}{2}n$$

For instance, when $n = 6$,

$$\begin{aligned} 1 + 2 + 3 + 4 + 5 + 6 &= \frac{1}{2} \cdot 6^2 + \frac{1}{2} \cdot 6 \\ &= \frac{36}{2} + \frac{6}{2} \\ &= 21. \end{aligned}$$

Use the formula to find the sum of the integers from 1 to 100. **5050**

13. The computer program below can be used to evaluate the polynomial $x^2 + 2x - 3$ for integer values of x from -3 to 3.

```
10 PRINT "VALUES OF POLYNOMIAL X ^ 2 + 2X - 3"
20 PRINT "X", "VALUE"
30 FOR X = -3 TO 3
40 LET V = X * X + 2 * X - 3
50 PRINT X, V
60 NEXT X
70 END
```

X	VALUE
-3	0
-2	-3
-1	-4
0	-3
1	0
2	5
3	12

a. Write the table that this program will produce.
b. Rewrite the program to evaluate $x^2 - 8x + 16$ for integer values of x from -6 to 6. **See margin.**

14. Suppose that in 1985 Barry received \$100 on his birthday. From 1986–1989 he received \$150 on his birthday. He put the money in a shoebox. The money is still there.
a. How much money did Barry have after his 1989 birthday? **\$700**
b. How much more would he have had if he had invested his money at an annual yield of 8% each year? **\$111.97**

ADDITIONAL ANSWERS
13b. Change line 10 to
PRINT "VALUES OF POLYNOMIAL X^2 − 8X + 16"
Change line 30 to
FOR X = -6 TO 6
Change line 40 to
LET V = X*X − 8*X + 16

NAME ____________

LESSON **MASTER 10–1**
QUESTIONS ON **SPUR** OBJECTIVES

■**SKILLS** *Objective A (See pages 527–529 for objectives.)*
In 1–3, classify each polynomial as a monomial, binomial, or trinomial.
1. $4 - 3x$ **binomial**
2. $3ab$ **monomial**
3. $4n^2 - 3n + 2$ **trinomial**

In 4–6, give the degree of each polynomial.
4. $17 - 6y$ **1**
5. $3t^2 - 5t + 7t^3 - 10$ **3**
6. $4x^2$ **2**

In 7 and 8, write the polynomial in descending order of exponents.
7. $12 + 2x^3 - 4x^2 + x^5$ **$x^5 + 2x^3 - 4x^2 + 12$**
8. $8y - 6y^2 + 5 + 3y^3$ **$3y^3 - 6y^2 + 8y + 5$**

In 9 and 10, evaluate.
9. $6x^2 - 2x + 1$ when $x = -3$ **61**
10. $8a^3 - 4a^2 + 3a - 2$ when $a = \frac{1}{2}$ **$-\frac{1}{2}$**

■**USES** *Objective I*
11. For three consecutive years, Mr. Sandberg's annual deposits in his Individual Retirement Account (IRA) were \$1000, \$1500, and \$2000. If the account had an annual yield of 8%, how much did he have in his account at the end of the third year? **\$5169.31**

12. At each annual baseball card show, Tim buys baseball cards. The first year he spent \$20, the second, \$30, the third, \$50, and the fourth, \$50. If the value of the cards in his collection increases by 10% each year, how much will the collection be worth at the end of the fourth year? **\$184.71**

13. If a ball is thrown upward at 57 ft/sec from a height of 3 ft, its distance s above the ground after t seconds is given by the formula $s = -16t^2 + 57t + 3$. How far above the ground will it be
a. after 2 seconds? **53 feet**
b. after 3 seconds? **30 feet**
c. Why is it lower after 3 seconds than after 2 seconds? **At some point, it stopped rising and began to fall.**

NOTES ON QUESTIONS
Question 26: This can be answered by picking points from the graphs (say those where $x = 0$ or $x = 2$) and testing their coordinates in the equation. *Teaching Aid 50* may be used for this question.

FOLLOW-UP

MORE PRACTICE
For more questions on SPUR Objectives, use *Lesson Master 10-1,* shown on page 479.

EXTENSION
Polynomials also arise from mortgages. Suppose that you have a 30-year mortgage for \$50,000 at 10% interest and that payments each month are set at \$439. Each month the interest rate is $\frac{10\%}{12} \approx$ .0083. Before your monthly payment is recorded, interest is assessed.

The following polynomial can be used to calculate the principal p remaining on the mortgage after monthly payment n is recorded:

$50{,}000\,(1.0083)^n -$
$439\,(1.0083)^{n-1} -$
$439\,(1.0083)^{n-2} - \ldots -$
$439\,(1.0083)^2 -$
$439\,(1.0083) - 439$

Teaching Aid 51 shows how this polynomial can be derived.

Notice that most of the first amounts paid go for interest. Only \$24.00 of the first month's payment, \$24.20 of the second month's, \$24.40 of the third month's, and \$24.60 of the fourth month's go towards reducing the principal.

Have students write the polynomials for months 5 and 6 and compute the principal remaining in each case.

Review

15. a. The price of a \$100 object is marked up 10%. What is the new price? *(Lesson 6-3)* **\$110**
b. The price from part a. is discounted 10%. What is the new price? *(Lesson 6-3)* **\$99**

16. *Multiple choice* Which is a pair of like terms? *(Lesson 2-2)* **(a)**
(a) $50x^3$ and $50x^3$ (b) $50x^2$ and $50y^2$
(c) $50x^4$ and $50x$ (d) $50x$ and 50

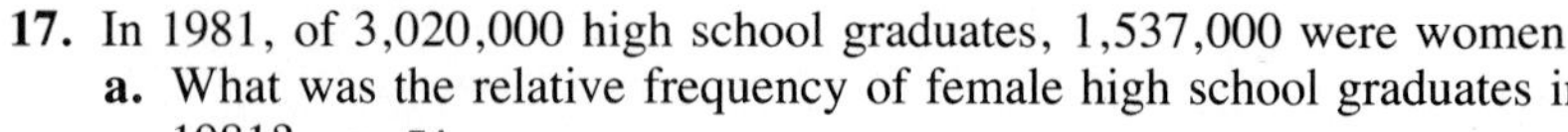

17. In 1981, of 3,020,000 high school graduates, 1,537,000 were women.
a. What was the relative frequency of female high school graduates in 1981? **≈ .51**
b. What is the probability that a randomly chosen high school graduate will be male? *(Lesson 1-8)* **≈ .49**

18. Simplify $-5n + 2n + k + k + 10n$. *(Lesson 2-2)* **$7n + 2k$**

19. Simplify $(9x + 8) - (3x - 5)$. *(Lesson 6-9)* **$6x + 13$**

20. Solve $-(x - 6.5) = 13.4$. *(Lesson 6-9)* **-6.9**

21. If the area of the colored part of the larger rectangle below is 20, what is x? *(Lessons 4-1, 6-3)* $\frac{1}{2}$

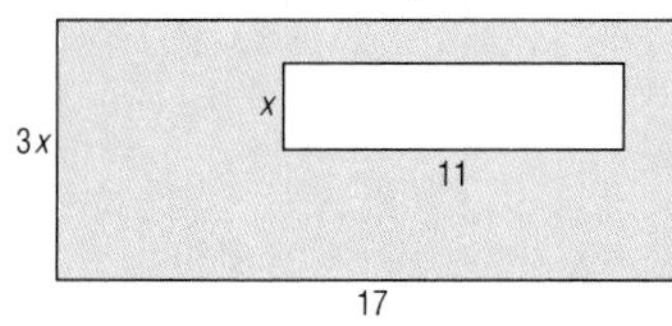

22. *Skill sequence* Simplify. *(Lesson 6-3)* **b) $24y + 56$; c) $24y + 56 - 32x$**
a. $8(3y)$ **$24y$** **b.** $8(3y + 7)$ **c.** $8(3y + 7 - 4x)$

In 23–25, solve in your head. *(Lessons 3-3, 4-4)*

23. $x - \frac{1}{2} = \frac{5}{2}$ **3** **24.** $\frac{1}{2}y = \frac{5}{2}$ **5** **25.** $2z = \frac{2}{5}$ $\frac{1}{5}$

Exploration

26. *Multiple choice* One of the graphs has the equation

$$y = x^4 - 4x^3 + 3x^2 + 4x - 4.$$

a. Which one is it? **(ii)**

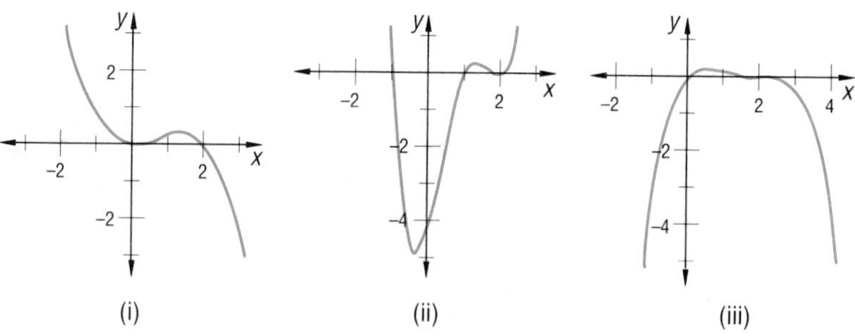

b. Explain how you determined your answer to part a. **For $x = 0$, $y = -4$, graph (ii) was the only graph containing this point.**

480

LESSON

10-2

Adding and Subtracting Polynomials

In the previous lesson, Erin's parents gave her \$50, \$60, \$70 and \$80 for her 12th, 13th, 14th, and 15th birthdays. She put the money into a savings account with a scale factor x. The polynomial

$$50x^3 + 60x^2 + 70x + 80$$

expresses the amount she had on her 15th birthday. Suppose Erin's aunt gave her \$20 on each of these 4 birthdays. If she put this money into the same account, the amount from the aunt's gifts would be

$$20x^3 + 20x^2 + 20x + 20.$$

The total amount she would have from all these gifts is found by adding these two polynomials.

$$(50x^3 + 60x^2 + 70x + 80) + (20x^3 + 20x^2 + 20x + 20)$$

This new expression contains some like terms. Recall that like terms are terms that have identical powers on identical variables. $50x^3$ and $20x^3$ are like terms, $60x^2$ and $20x^2$ are like terms, and so on. Polynomials can be simplified by using the Distributive Property to add like terms.

Example 1 Simplify $(50x^3 + 60x^2 + 70x + 80) + (20x^3 + 20x^2 + 20x + 20)$.

Solution 1 Use the Associative and Commutative Properties of Addition to rearrange the polynomials so that like terms are together.

$$(50x^3 + 20x^3) + (60x^2 + 20x^2) + (70x + 20x) + (80 + 20)$$

Use the Distributive Property to add like terms.

$$= (50 + 20)x^3 + (60 + 20)x^2 + (70 + 20)x + (80 + 20)$$
$$= 70x^3 + 80x^2 + 90x + 100$$

LESSON 10-2

RESOURCES

- Lesson Master 10-2
- Visual for Teaching Aid 52: Diagrams for **Question 26**

OBJECTIVES

A Add and subtract polynomials

I Translate real situations into polynomials.

J Represent areas of figures in terms of polynomials.

TEACHING NOTES

In this lesson, it is best to move on even if you sense students are uncertain about the situations leading to polynomials or about their skills. There is practice in the following lessons. If you want to spend another day on skills in this chapter, we suggest that you wait until after Lesson 10-6 or 10-7.

Both solutions to **Example 1** are important. Solution 1 emphasizes the use of properties. Solution 2 emphasizes the algorithm.

The area setting in **Example 2** provides a brushup on the Distributive Property and prepares for the use of area to illustrate more complex multiplication problems.

Note the checking with a special case in **Example 2.** You can use this to remind students that in spite of its complex appearance, a polynomial still represents a number.

Solution 2 Experts add the pairs of like terms without rearranging them on paper. Here is an expert solution after two steps. The like terms are underlined after they have been combined so no term will be overlooked.

$$(\underline{50x^3} + \underline{60x^2} + 70x + 80) + (\underline{20x^3} + \underline{20x^2} + 20x + 20)$$
$$70x^3 + 80x^2 +$$

After two more combinations, all the original terms are accounted for.

$$= \underline{50x^3} + \underline{60x^2} + \underline{70x} + \underline{80} + \underline{20x^3} + \underline{20x^2} + \underline{20x} + \underline{20}$$
$$= 70x^3 + 80x^2 + 90x + 100$$

Check Think of the answer in relation to Erin's birthday presents. The first year she got \$70 (\$50 from her parents, \$20 from her aunt). The \$70 has 3 years to earn interest. The \$80 from her next birthday earns interest for 2 years. And so on.

Polynomials can be subtracted as well as added. Differences are also simplified by collecting like terms, but special care must be taken with signs.

Example 2 Find the colored area in the figure below.

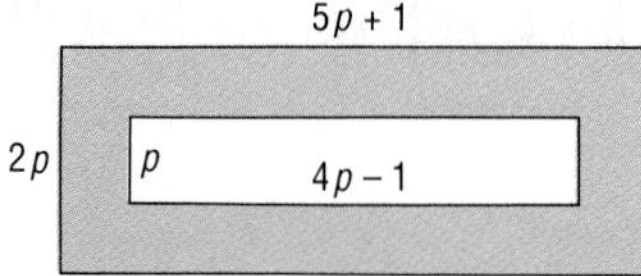

Solution 1 The colored area is the difference of the areas of the rectangles.

$$2p(5p + 1) - p(4p - 1)$$

Here we put in many steps.

$= (10p^2 + 2p) - (4p^2 - p)$
$= (10p^2 + 2p) + (-4p^2 + p)$ recalling that $-(a - b) = -a + b$
$= 10p^2 + -4p^2 + 2p + p$
$= 6p^2 + 3p$

Solution 2 An expert may write the following.

$2p(5p + 1) - p(4p - 1)$
$= 10p^2 + 2p - 4p^2 + p$ remembering to distribute $-p$
$= 6p^2 + 3p$

Check Test a special case. Let $p = 10$. The dimensions of the figure are now as follows.

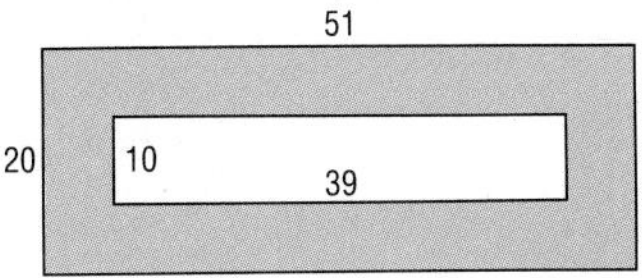

The colored area $= 51 \cdot 20 - 10 \cdot 39 = 1020 - 390 = 630$.
When $p = 10$, $6p^2 + 3p = 6(10)^2 + 3(10) = 6 \cdot 100 + 30 = 630$.
So the answer checks.

Example 3 Simplify $(12y^2 + 6y^3 - 5) - (2 + 6y^3)$.

Solution To combine the expressions, add the opposite of the terms in the second polynomial.

$$12y^2 + 6y^3 - 5 + -2 + -6y^3$$

Arrange in descending order.

$$= 6y^3 + -6y^3 + 12y^2 - 5 + -2$$

Combine the like terms.

$$= 12y^2 - 7$$

Check Pick a value for y. We let $y = 3$.
Does $(12(3)^2 + 6(3)^3 - 5) - (2 + 6(3)^3) = 12(3)^2 - 7$?
$(108 + 162 - 5) - (2 + 162) = 108 - 7$?
$265 - 164 = 101$?
Yes, it checks.

Questions

Covering the Reading

In 1 and 2, refer to Example 1.

1. Consider the polynomial $70x^3 + 80x^2 + 90x + 100$. What coefficient indicates the amount Erin received on her 14th birthday? **90**

2. Suppose Erin gets \$15, \$25, \$35, and \$45 from cousin Lilly on her four birthdays. She also puts this money into her account.
   a. By her 15th birthday, how much money will Erin have from just her cousin? $\mathbf{15x^3 + 25x^2 + 35x + 45}$
   b. What is the total Erin will have received and saved from all of her birthday presents? $\mathbf{85x^3 + 105x^2 + 125x + 145}$

ADDITIONAL EXAMPLES

1. In the figure below, all angles are right angles. Find the area.

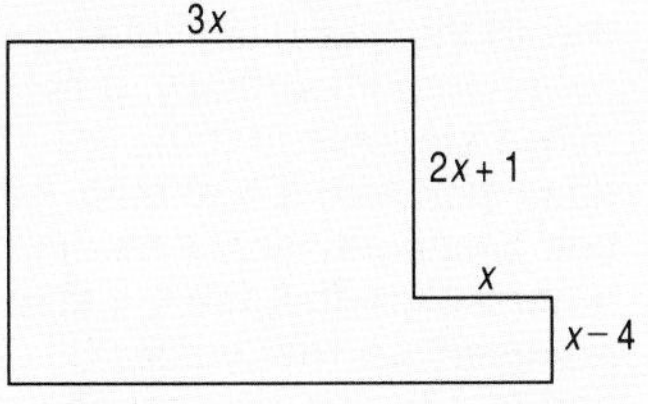

$\mathbf{10x^2 - 13x}$

2. Simplify
$(m^3 - 2m + 16) - (-4m^3 - 2m^2 + 4m - 20)$.
$\mathbf{5m^3 + 2m^2 - 6m + 36}$

3. Simplify
$3(2x^2 + 5x) - 7(x^2 + x)$.
$\mathbf{-x^2 + 8x}$

NOTES ON QUESTIONS

Making Connections for Question 12: This question provides practice on order of operations and on use of the calculator. But even more importantly, it reminds students that the *y* does stand for a real number. Students should develop a perception that the variable represents a real number and that the polynomial can be evaluated for a specific value of the variable.

Question 17: Students should begin by reasoning that there are 14 youngsters and 7 adults.

Question 19: Students need to use the problem solving strategy *work backwards*. Let $m = 3$. What value does t then have?

Question 21: Advise students to *draw pictures,* another useful problem-solving strategy.

Small Group Work for Question 26: This question provides a *trial-and-error* activity suitable for small group work. *Teaching Aid 52* provides several repetitions of the diagram.

ADDITIONAL ANSWERS

20.

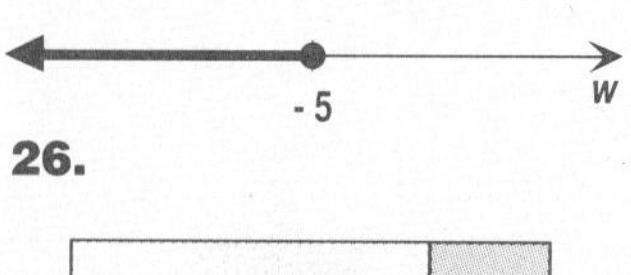

26.

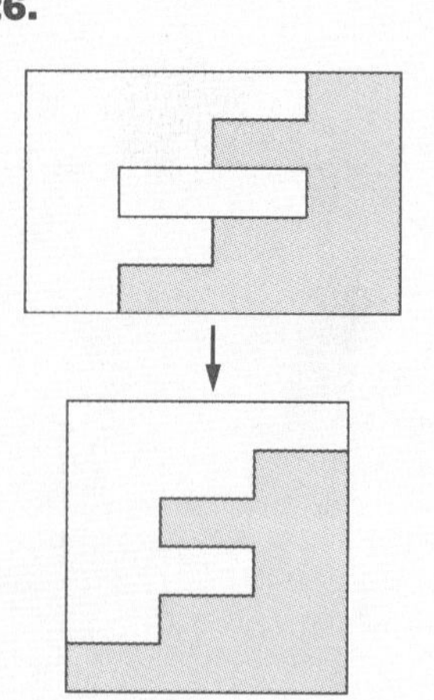

In 3–6, simplify the expressions.

3. $(12y^2 + 3y - 7) + (4y^2 - 2y - 10)$ $16y^2 + y - 17$

4. $(6w^2 - w + 14) - (4w^2 + 3)$ $2w^2 - w + 11$

5. $(3 + 5k^2 - 2k) + (2k^2 - 3k - 10)$ $7k^2 - 5k - 7$

6. $(x^3 - 4x + 1) - (5x^3 + 4x - 8)$ $-4x^3 - 8x + 9$

7. A rectangle with dimensions $3p$ and $p + 1$ is contained in a rectangle with dimensions $8p$ and $4p + 2$, as in the figure below.

a. Write an expression for the area of the big rectangle.

b. Write an expression for the area of the little rectangle.

c. Write a simplified expression for the area of the colored region.
$29p^2 + 13p$

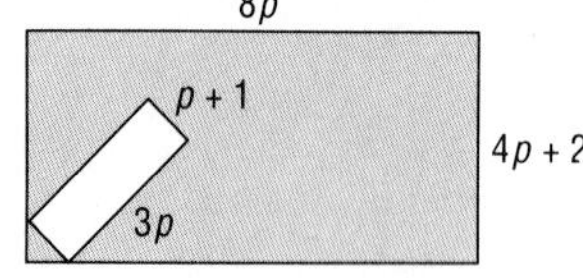

7a) $8p(4p + 2) = 32p^2 + 16p$

7b) $3p(p + 1) = 3p^2 + 3p$

Applying the Mathematics

In 8 and 9, simplify.

8. $(12y^4 - 3y^3 + y) + (5y^3 - 7y^2 - 2y + 1) + (2y - 3y^2 + 6)$
$12y^4 + 2y^3 - 10y^2 + y + 7$

9. $(x^2 - 4x + 1) - (3x^2 - 2x) - 2(7x + 4)$ $-2x^2 - 16x - 7$

In 10–12, Ashok, Barbara and Cam have the following amounts of money:

Ashok:	$90y^3 + 20y^2 + 60y + 100$
Barbara:	$60y^4 + 25y^3 + 80y^2 + 75y + 12$
Cam:	$50y^2 + 100y + 150$

10. How much do Ashok and Barbara have together?
$60y^4 + 115y^3 + 100y^2 + 135y + 112$

11. If Betsy has the same amount of money as Barbara, how much do the two girls have together? $120y^4 + 50y^3 + 160y^2 + 150y + 24$

12. If $y = 1.08$, who has more, Ashok or Cam? Cam

13. The total surface area T of a prism with a square base is given by the formula $T = 2s^2 + 4sh$, where s is the length of a side of the base and h is the height. Prism Q has a square base with side of length n and height 5. Prism R has a square base with edge $3n$ and height 10.

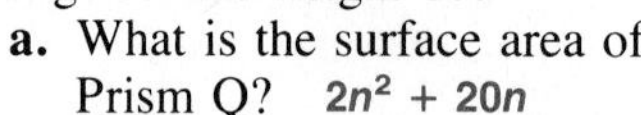

a. What is the surface area of Prism Q? $2n^2 + 20n$

b. What is the surface area of Prism R? $18n^2 + 120n$

c. Find the difference of the surface areas of Prism Q and Prism R.
$16n^2 + 100n$

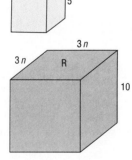

484

Review

14. After five years of birthdays, Wanda has received and saved

$$80x^4 + 60x^3 + 70x^2 + 45x + 50$$

dollars, having put the money in a savings account at a scale factor x.

a. How much did Wanda get on her most recent birthday? **$50**

b. How much did Wanda get on the first birthday? **$80**

c. Give an example of a reasonable value for x in this problem. **sample: 1.06**

d. If $x = 1$, how much has Wanda saved? **$305**

e. What does a value of 1 for x mean? *(Lesson 10-1)* **She received no interest.**

15. *Skill sequence* Simplify. *(Lessons 2-2, 9-5, 9-7)*
a. $x^m + x^n$ **simplified** **b.** $x^m \cdot x^n$ x^{m+n} **c.** $x^m \div x^n$ x^{m-n}

16. Four consecutive integers (like 7, 8, 9, 10) can be represented by the expressions n, $n + 1$, $n + 2$, and $n + 3$. The sum of four consecutive integers is 250. What are the integers? *(Lesson 6-1)* **61, 62, 63, and 64**

17. There are 6 girls, 8 boys, 4 women, and 3 men on a community youth board. How many leadership teams consisting of one adult and one youngster could be formed from these people? *(Lesson 4-7)* **98**

18. *Skill sequence* Solve for y. *(Lesson 6-1)*
a. $x - y = 5$ $x - 5$ **b.** $x - 2y = 5$ $\frac{x-5}{2}$ **c.** $x - ay = 5$ $\frac{x-5}{a}$

19. In the equation $8m + 5m = 4(6 + tm)$, what is the value of t when m is equal to 3? *(Lesson 6-1)* $\frac{5}{4}$

20. Solve and graph on a number line: $4.6 - 3.1w \geq 20.1$. *(Lesson 6-7)*
$w \leq -5$; **see margin.**

21. The length and width of a rectangle are integers. The area is 18. What are the possible perimeters? *(Lesson 4-1)* **38, 22, or 18**

22. *Skill sequence* *(Lesson 7-5)*

a. The area of a square is 49 in.^{2}. Find the length of a side. **7 in.**

b. The area of a square is 49 in.^{2}. Find the length of a diagonal. **≈ 9.9 in.**

c. The area of a square is 50 in.^{2}. Find the length of a diagonal. **10 in.**

b) $\sqrt{98}$ **or** $7\sqrt{2}$ **in.; c) 10 in.**

In 23–25, simplify. Assume $a \geq 0$, $b \geq 0$, and $c \geq 0$. *(Lesson 7-4)*

23. $\sqrt{400}$ **20** **24.** $\sqrt{9 \cdot 25}$ **15** **25.** $\sqrt{a^2b^4c^2}$ ab^2c

Exploration

26. At the right is a 5-by-8 rectangle with a hole in the center in the shape of a 1-by-4 rectangle. With a single cut (not necessarily straight), divide the colored shape into two pieces that, when rearranged, can form a 6-by-6 square. **See margin.**

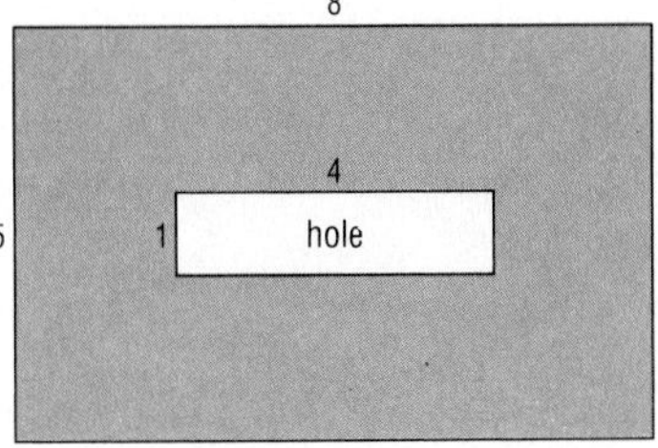

FOLLOW-UP

MORE PRACTICE

For more questions on SPUR Objectives, use *Lesson Master 10-2,* shown below.

NAME ______

LESSON **MASTER 10–2**
QUESTIONS ON **SPUR** OBJECTIVES

■SKILLS *Objective A* *(See pages 527–529 for objectives.)*
In 1–8, simplify.

1. $(h - 3) + (2h + 6)$ **3h + 3**

2. $(3h^2 + 7h - 6) + (4h - 9)$ $3h^2 + 11h - 15$

3. $(16 - 7x^2) + (9 - 4x + 2x^2)$ $25 - 4x - 5x^2$

4. $(4t - 9) - (3t + 8)$ $t - 17$

5. $(9r - 7) - (3r - 4) - (r - 6)$ $5r + 3$

6. $(11 - 5w^2) - (18 - 8w^2)$ $3w^2 - 7$

7. $(10k^2 - 5k + 32) - (2k^2 - 3k + 6)$ $8k^2 - 2k + 26$

8. $(4y^4 + 6y^3 - 5y^2 - 11y) + (y^4 - y^3 + 12y)$ $5y^4 + 5y^3 - 5y^2 + y$

■USES *Objective I*

9. Jack has two accounts, each with an annual scale factor of y. In one account he deposits $150 a year, and in the other account he deposits $250 a year.

a. How much does he have in both accounts combined after four years?
$\$(400y^4 + 400y^3 + 400y^2 + 400y)$

b. If each account pays 7% interest, what is the total after four years?
$1900.30

10. If a rocket is shot upward from the surface of the earth at 500 ft/sec, its distance s above the ground after t seconds is given by $s = 500t - 16t^2$. If a rocket is shot upward from the surface of the moon, then $s = 500t - 2.7t^2$. For the times that the rocket is actually in flight, how many feet higher will it go on the moon than on the earth after t seconds?
$13.3t^2$ **feet**

■REPRESENTATIONS *Objective J*
In 11 and 12, write an expression for the shaded area. Each quadrilateral shown is a rectangle.

11.

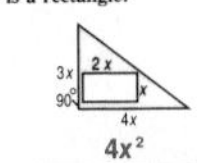

$4x^2$

12. $6x + 20y$

84 *Algebra* © Scott, Foresman and Company

LESSON 10-3

RESOURCES

- Lesson Master 10-3
- Visual for Teaching Aid 53: Tiles for Representing Polynomials

OBJECTIVES

B Multiply polynomials.
I Translate real situations into polynomials.
J Represent areas of figures in terms of polynomials

TEACHING NOTES

It is important that students understand the area example at the beginning of the lesson. You can clarify it by drawing the diagram two ways. First, draw it as a single large rectangle as follows:

h	$h(L_1 + L_2 + L_3 + L_4)$
	$L_1 + L_2 + L_3 + L_4$

Next draw it as the union of smaller rectangles as follows:

h	hL_1	hL_2	hL_3	hL_4
	L_1	L_2	L_3	L_4

Testing a special case, as used in **Example 1,** is a problem-solving skill that is emphasized through the chapter. It also reminds students that x stands for a real number and that the polynomial has a single real value for a given x.

LESSON

10-3 Multiplying a Polynomial by a Monomial

The pictures show a view of a section of storefronts at a shopping mall. The displays in the windows are used to attract shoppers, so store owners and mall managers are interested in the areas of storefronts. The total area of the four windows can be computed in two ways.

The first way is to consider the union of the windows, one big rectangle with length $(L_1 + L_2 + L_3 + L_4)$ and height h. Thus,

$$\text{Area} = h \cdot (L_1 + L_2 + L_3 + L_4).$$

The second way is to compute the area of each storefront and add the results. Thus,

$$\text{Area} = hL_1 + hL_2 + hL_3 + hL_4.$$

These areas are equal, so

$$h \cdot (L_1 + L_2 + L_3 + L_4) = hL_1 + hL_2 + hL_3 + hL_4.$$

Note that h is a monomial while $(L_1 + L_2 + L_3 + L_4)$ is a polynomial. Multiplying a monomial by a polynomial is simply an extension of the Distributive Property.

Example 1 Multiply $7x(x^2 + 2x - 1)$.

Solution Multiply each term in the polynomial by the monomial.

$$= 7x \cdot x^2 + 7x \cdot 2x - 7x \cdot 1$$

Simplify using the Product of Powers Property.

$$= 7x^3 + 14x^2 - 7x$$

Check Test a special case. We let $x = 3$.

Does $7 \cdot 3(3^2 + 6 - 1) = 7 \cdot 3^3 + 14 \cdot 3^2 - 7 \cdot 3$?
$21 \cdot 14 = 189 + 126 - 21$?
Yes, $294 = 294$.

When multiplying with polynomial expressions, care must be taken with the signs.

Example 2 Multiply $-4x^2(2x^3 + y - 5)$.

Solution: Distribute the $-4x^2$ over each term of the polynomial.

$$= \mathbf{-4x^2} \cdot 2x^3 + \mathbf{-4x^2} \cdot y - \mathbf{-4x^2} \cdot 5$$
$$= -8x^5 - 4x^2y - -20x^2$$

Simplify to avoid opposites when possible.

$$= -8x^5 - 4x^2y + 20x^2$$

In the last lesson you saw how the birthday gift polynomials were added and subtracted. Example 3 shows how the birthday situation can illustrate multiplying a monomial by a polynomial.

Example 3 Anwar received \$50 on his 16th birthday, \$70 on his 17th birthday, and \$60 on his 18th birthday, which he was able to invest at a scale factor x. He received no more gifts, but continued to invest this money at the same scale factor for 3 more years. How much money did he have then?

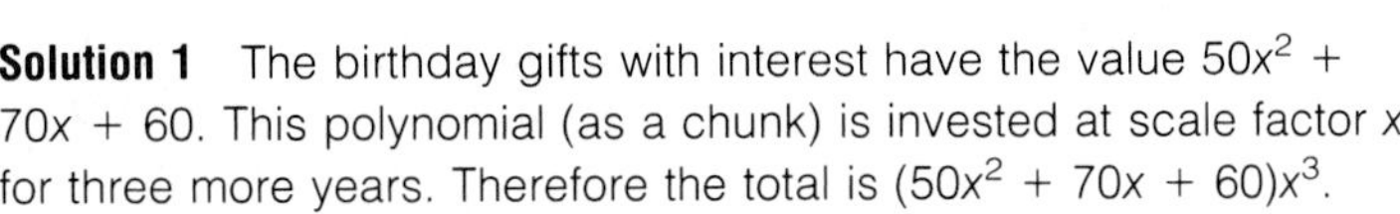

Solution 1 The birthday gifts with interest have the value $50x^2 + 70x + 60$. This polynomial (as a chunk) is invested at scale factor x for three more years. Therefore the total is $(50x^2 + 70x + 60)x^3$.

Solution 2 Look at how long each gift individually earned interest: \$50 for five years; \$70 for four years; and \$60 for three years. This leads to the polynomial $50x^5 + 70x^4 + 60x^3$.

Check The two solutions must be equal. $(50x^2 + 70x + 60)x^3 = 50x^5 + 70x^4 + 60x^3$. This is exactly what you would expect using the Distributive Property.

Questions

Covering the Reading

1. Suppose the height of the stores at the beginning of this lesson is $2h$. Write the area of the complete section of storefronts in two different ways. $\mathbf{2h(L_1 + L_2 + L_3 + L_4), 2hL_1 + 2hL_2 + 2hL_3 + 2hL_4}$

2. Using the Distributive Property, $a(b + c + d) =$ _?_. **ab + ac + ad**

ADDITIONAL EXAMPLES
In 1 and 2, apply the Distributive Property.

1. $-5y(y^3 - 6y^2 + 2y + 6)$.
$\mathbf{-5y^4 + 30y^3 - 10y^2 - 30y}$

2. $k^4(k^2 - 16km)$.
$\mathbf{k^6 - 16k^5m}$

3. For 3 years in a row Ms. Wilson received an end-of-year bonus, \$500 the first year and \$1000 each of the next two years. She invested the money at a scale factor of x. For the next 5 years she did not get a bonus. Give two expressions for the amount in her investment account after that period of time.
$\mathbf{500x^7 + 1000x^6 + 1000x^5}$ **or** $\mathbf{(500x^2 + 1000x + 1000)x^5}$

NOTES ON QUESTIONS
Question 8: In many applications, the scale factor changes, so this is not a contrived situation.

Making Connections for Question 26: This question illustrates that the value of $50x^2 + 70x + 60$ varies, depending upon the value of x. This previews some of the ideas in Chapter 12.

FOLLOW-UP

MORE PRACTICE
For more questions on SPUR Objectives, use *Lesson Master 10-3,* shown on page 489.

EXTENSION
Teaching Aid 53 can be used to illustrate multiplication (and factoring) of polynomials in x by arranging squares and rectangles. Such activities can be used throughout the chapter. For this lesson, you can ask students to illustrate the following.

1. $x(x + 5)$

2. $2x(2x + 4)$

Answers:
1. First use x by x squares and 1 by x strips to build a rectangle that has height x and length $x + 5$.

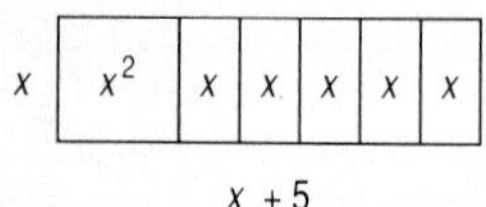

Then use the markings on the tiles to find the area.

x^2 x x x x x

$= x^2 + 5x$

So $x(x + 5) = x^2 + 5x$

In 3–6, multiply.

3. $z(q + r - 13)$ $zq + zr - 13z$

4. $5x^2(x^2 - 9x + 2)$ $5x^4 - 45x^3 + 10x^2$

5. $-3wy(4y - 2w - 1)$ $-12wy^2 + 6w^2y + 3wy$

6. $-rt(r^2 - t^2)$ $-r^3t + rt^3$

In 7 and 8, refer to Example 3.

7. Suppose Anwar kept his money invested at a scale factor x for 6 years after his 18th birthday. How much money would he have at the end of this period?
$50x^8 + 70x^7 + 60x^6$ dollars

Applying the Mathematics

8. Suppose that after his 18th birthday, Anwar took the total amount and invested it at a new scale factor y for 4 years. How much money would he have after this?
$50x^2y^4 + 70xy^4 + 60y^4$ or $(50x^2 + 70x + 60)y^4$ dollars

In 9–12, simplify.

9. $2(x^2 + 3x) - 3x^2$ $-x^2 + 6x$

10. $a(y^2 - 2y) + y(a^2 + 2a)$ $ay^2 + a^2y$

11. $m^3(m^2 - 3m + 2) - m^2(m^3 - 5m^2 - 6)$ $2m^4 + 2m^3 + 6m^2$

12. $v(v + 1) - v(v + 2) + v(v + 3) - v(v + 4)$ $-2v$

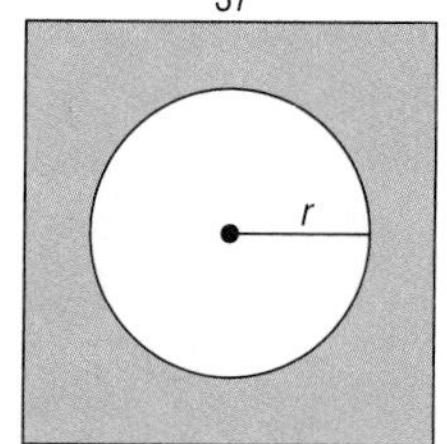

13. At the right is a circle in a square.
a. What is the area of the square? $9r^2$
b. What is the area of the circle? πr^2
c. What is the area of the colored region? $9r^2 - \pi r^2$
d. If a person had 5 copies of the colored region, how much area would be colored? $5(9r^2 - \pi r^2)$ or $45r^2 - 5\pi r^2$

14. Maryalice is now 21. She received \$120 on her 19th birthday, \$125 on her 20th birthday, and \$200 on her 21st birthday.
a. If she invested this amount at a scale factor x, how much does she have now? $120x^2 + 125x + 200$ dollars
b. If she keeps the amount in part a invested at the same scale factor for two more years, how much will she have at age 23?
c. If she invests the amount in part b at a different scale factor y, how much will she have at age 28?
$120x^4y^5 + 125x^3y^5 + 200x^2y^5$ dollars

14b) $120x^4 + 125x^3 + 200x^2$ dollars

Review

In 15–18, simplify. *(Lesson 10-2)*

15. $(4n^4 + 6n^3 - 9n^2 + 12) + (9n^3 + 7n^2 - 9n + 13)$
$4n^4 + 15n^3 - 2n^2 - 9n + 25$

16. $(21y^2 - 3y + 1) - (4y^2 + 5y - 14) - 3y^2$ $14y^2 - 8y + 15$

17. $\frac{20x^2y}{2xy}$ *(Lesson 2-3)* $10x$

18. $\frac{3}{2v} + \frac{4v}{2v}$ *(Lesson 9-7)* $\frac{3 + 4v}{2v}$

19. On each of three successive birthdays, Mary received \$25 from her grandparents. Mary also received \$17 from other relatives on the first of these birthdays, \$24 on the second and \$31 on the third. Mary invested all the money at a scale factor of x each year. On the last of these birthdays,
   a. how much money did Mary have from her grandparents' gifts? *(Lesson 10-1)* **$25x^2 + 25x + 25$ dollars**
   b. How much money did she have from the gifts of her other relatives? *(Lesson 10-1)* **$17x^2 + 24x + 31$ dollars**
   c. How much money did she have in all? *(Lesson 10-2)* **$42x^2 + 49x + 56$ dollars**

20. a. Three years ago you invested A dollars at a rate of $x - 1$. How much would you have now? **Ax^3**
   b. Two years ago you invested B dollars in a different investment at a rate of $y - 1$. Including the investment in part a, how much would you have now? *(Lesson 10-1)* **$Ax^3 + By^2$**

In 21–23 write an equation for the line with the following characteristics:

21. slope -2, y-intercept 5 *(Lesson 8-4)* **$y = -2x + 5$**

22. slope -4, contains the point (-1, 6) *(Lesson 8-5)* **$y = -4x + 2$**

23. contains the points (-5, 8), and (-1, 16) *(Lesson 8-6)* **$y = 2x + 18$**

24. Calculate the speed of the object and identify a possible object. *(Lesson 5-2)*
   a. It flew 200 miles in $\frac{1}{2}$ hour. **400 mph or $\frac{1}{400}$ hour per mile; plane**
   b. It slithered 14 meters in 7 seconds. **2 meters per second or 0.5 second per meter; snake**
   c. It took 3 days to creep 15 inches. **5 inches per day or 0.2 days per inch; snail**

25. *Skill sequence* Simplify. *(Lesson 2-3)*
   a. $\frac{c}{3} + \frac{5c}{13}$ **$\frac{28c}{39}$**
   b. $\frac{c}{13q} + \frac{5c}{13}$ **$\frac{c + 5cq}{13q}$**
   c. $\frac{c}{13q} + \frac{5c}{12}$ **$\frac{12c + 65cq}{156q}$**

Exploration

26. In Example 3, Anwar has $50x^2 + 70x + 60$ dollars on his 18th birthday. Suppose this amount equals \$200. By trial and error, determine the value of x to the nearest hundredth. **$x \approx 1.11$**

27. With a function grapher or graphing calculator, graph the equation $y = 50x^2 + 70x + 60$ and estimate where it crosses the horizontal line $y = 200$, and thus answer Question 26. **See margin.**

2.

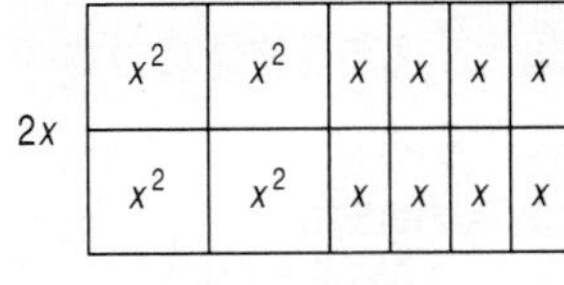

$= 4x^2 + 8x$

Note: It is possible to use tiles to illustrate a multiplication such as $x(2x - 3)$ which involves subtraction. However, it is necessary to overlap the tiles to show subtraction, and this procedure would be confusing to most students. So, we do not introduce it.

ADDITIONAL ANSWERS

27. $x \approx 1.11$

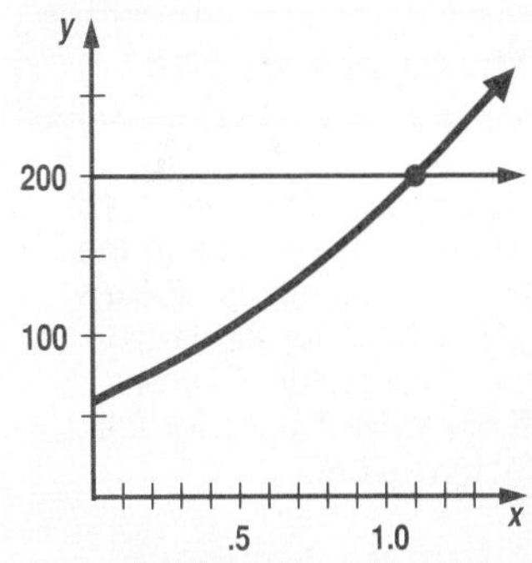

NAME ______

LESSON **MASTER 10–3**
QUESTIONS ON **SPUR** OBJECTIVES

■**SKILLS** *Objective B (See pages 527–529 for objectives.)*

In 1–6, multiply.

1. $6(x - 3x^2)$ **$6x - 18x^2$**
2. $4r(r^2 + 2r + 3)$ **$4r^3 + 8r^2 + 12r$**
3. $(4y - 11)(-3x)$ **$-12xy + 33x$**
4. $-5a(2a^2 - 3a - 10)$ **$-10a^3 + 15a^2 + 50a$**
5. $\frac{1}{6}a^2(2a^2 - 3b^2)$ **$\frac{1}{3}a^4 - \frac{1}{2}a^2b^2$**
6. $-6xy(2x - 8y^3)$ **$-12x^2y + 48xy^4$**

■**USES** *Objective I*

7. Gilbert received \$110 on his 16th birthday, \$140 on his 17th birthday, and \$155 on his 18th birthday, which he invested after every birthday at a scale factor x. He kept his money invested at the same scale factor for 3 more years after his 18th birthday. How much money did he have at the end of this period? **$\$(110x^5 + 140x^4 + 155x^3)$**

8. If Gilbert invests the amount in Question 7 at a different scale factor y, how much will he have after three more years? **$\$(110x^5y^3 + 140x^4y^3 + 155x^3y^3)$**

■**REPRESENTATIONS** *Objective J*

Refer to the diagram at the right.

9. a. Find the area of the shaded region. **$21x^2 - 5x$**

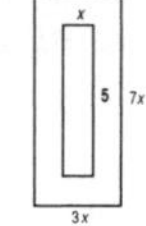

   b. The shaded region is the amount of usable space on each floor of a building. If a company rents three full floors, how much space will the company have? **$63x^2 - 15x$**

LESSON 10-4

RESOURCES
- Lesson Master 10-4
- Quiz on Lessons 10-1 Through 10-4
- Visual for Teaching Aid 53: Tiles for Representing Polynomials

OBJECTIVE

D Find common monomial factors of polynomials.

TEACHING NOTES

Reading Emphasize the different instructions in the first two examples. **Example 1** asks for the largest common factor; whereas, **Example 2** asks for the factorization.

Alternate Approach Although the examples and exercises deal with finding the *largest* common factor, any problem of this type can be done by simply finding *some* common factor and factoring until you are finished. For instance, consider

$-30x^3y + 20x^4 + 50x^2y^5$

from **Example 2.** A student could factor out x first, then factor out 10, then factor out x again. It's more efficient, however, to find the largest common factor $10x^2$.

LESSON

10-4 Common Monomial Factoring

The process that reverses multiplication is called factoring.

Multiplication: Begin with $37 \cdot 3$, end up with 111.
Factoring: Begin with 111, end up with $37 \cdot 3$.

The same idea is used with polynomials.

Multiplication: Begin with $50(x^4 + x^3 + x^2 + x + 1)$, end up with $50x^4 + 50x^3 + 50x^2 + 50x + 50$.
Factoring: Begin with $50x^4 + 50x^3 + 50x^2 + 50x + 50$, end up with $50(x^4 + x^3 + x^2 + x + 1)$.

Factoring a number or polynomial provides flexibility. The factored form may be easier to evaluate or use.

For instance, the expression $50x^4 + 50x^3 + 50x^2 + 50x + 50$ arose in Lesson 10-1 from a compound interest situation. To evaluate this expression on a calculator for a given value of x, you need to enter 11 numbers and perform 11 operations: 3 powerings, 4 multiplications, and 4 additions. A calculator key sequence shows this; the operations are shown below in the first 11 squares and the total number of steps is 23.

50 [×] x [y^x] 4 [+] 50 [×] x [y^x] 3 [+] 50 [×] x [x^2] [+] 50 [×] x [+] 50 [=]

In the above sequence, 50 has been entered five times. That is unnecessary. The factored form $50(x^4 + x^3 + x^2 + x + 1)$ contains 50 only once and only has 1 multiplication. This reduces the work to 8 operations and the total number of steps is 19.

50 [×] [(] x [y^x] 4 [+] x [y^x] 3 [+] x [x^2] [+] x [+] 1 [)] [=]

The number 50 is a monomial factor of each term in the original polynomial. So the rewriting of $50x^4 + 50x^3 + 50x^2 + 50x + 50$ as $50(x^4 + x^3 + x^2 + x + 1)$ is called **common monomial factoring**. The idea in common monomial factoring is to isolate the largest common factor from each individual term.

Example 1 Find the largest common factor of $-30x^3y$, $20x^4$, and $50x^2y^5$.

Solution First find the largest common factor of the coefficients -30, 20, and 50. That factor is 10. Since each term has the variable x in it, the largest common factor will include an x. The lowest exponent of x in any of the terms is x^2, so x^2 is part of the largest common factor. The variable y does not appear in all terms so y does not appear in the largest common factor. Thus, the largest common factor is $10x^2$.

Example 2 Factor out the largest common monomial factor in $-30x^3y + 20x^4 + 50x^2y^5$.

Solution In Example 1, the largest common monomial factor of the three terms of this polynomial was found to be $10x^2$. Thus

$$-30x^3y + 20x^4 + 50x^2y^5 = 10x^2(\underline{?} + \underline{?} + \underline{?}).$$

Now divide to get the terms in the parentheses.

$$\frac{-30x^3y}{10x^2} = -3xy \qquad \frac{20x^4}{10x^2} = 2x^2 \qquad \frac{50x^2y^5}{10x^2} = 5y^5$$

So $-30x^3y + 20x^4 + 50x^2y^5 = 10x^2(-3xy + 2x^2 + 5y^5)$.

To generalize from Examples 1 and 2, the largest common factor of an expression will include the largest common factor of the coefficients of the terms. It will also include any common variable raised to the *lowest* exponent of that variable found in any of the terms.

Example 3 Factor $24x^2y + 6x$.

Solution The largest common factor of $24x^2y$ and $6x$ is $6x$ itself.

$$24x^2y + 6x = 6x(\underline{?} + \underline{?})$$

Now divide each term by $6x$ to fill in the factors.

$$= 6x(4xy + 1).$$

Check Test a special case. Let $x = 3$, $y = 4$. Follow the order of operations.

$24x^2y + 6x = 24 \cdot 3^2 \cdot 4 + 6 \cdot 3 = 864 + 18 = 882$.
$6x(4xy + 1) = 6 \cdot 3(4 \cdot 3 \cdot 4 + 1) = 18(49) = 882$. It checks.

Factoring provides an alternate way of simplifying some fractions.

Example 4 Simplify $\frac{5n^2 + 3n}{n}$.

Solution 1 Factor the numerator and simplify the fraction.

$$\frac{5n^2 + 3n}{n} = \frac{n(5n + 3)}{n}$$
$$= 5n + 3$$

Just as rectangles can be used to show multiplication, they can illustrate factoring. For example, the diagram below illustrates **Example 3.**

Area = $24x^2y + 6x$

$4xy$ + 1
$6x$

Point out that a rectangle of area 12 could have integer dimensions 1 × 12, 2 × 6, or 3 × 4. Similarly, there may be more than one way to factor a polynomial. By stating that the common factor must be as large as possible, we limit ourselves to just one way.

ADDITIONAL EXAMPLES

1. Find the largest common factor of $16a^5m$, $-12a^3m^3$, and $4a^2m^5$.
$4a^2m$

2. Factor $18y^3 - 6y^2 - 15y$.
$3y(6y^2 - 2y - 5)$

3. Factor $28c^2d - 14d^5$.
$14d(2c^2 - d^4)$

4. Simplify $\frac{-10z^2 - 5z}{5z}$.
$-2z - 1$

NOTES ON QUESTIONS
Error Analysis for Question 7: Some students may not know how to factor $23a^3 + a^2$ because they fail to realize that $a^2 = 1a^2$. Stress that if they use the procedure of this lesson, such problems will be easy. First, find the largest common factor (a^2). Now find the polynomial factor by dividing $23a^3 + a^2$ by a^2.

Questions 12b and 13: The geometrical approach discussed in the Teaching Notes is used in these questions.

Question 15: The answer is found by factoring $n^2 + n$ into $n(n + 1)$. You might mention that since either n or $n + 1$ must be an even number, this shows that, when n is an integer, $n^2 + n$ is always even.

Question 18: Two forms of the answer are possible. Factoring the numerator, then reducing, gives

$$\frac{4n^2 + 6n + 1}{2}$$

Rewriting the given expression as the sum of three fractions gives $2n^2 + 3n + \frac{1}{2}$. Have students check by substituting some number for n. If $n = 3$, each expression has the value 27.5. Ask students which expression is easier to evaluate, the given expression or the answer. Making expressions easier to evaluate is one reason for factoring.

Solution 2 Separate the given expression into the sum of two fractions.

$$\frac{(5n^2 + 3n)}{n} = \frac{5n^2}{n} + \frac{3n}{n}$$

Divide. $= 5n + 3$

Check The solutions give the same answer, so they check each other.

Questions

Covering the Reading

1. a. How many operations are needed to calculate $40x^4 + 40x^3 + 40x^2 + 40x + 40$? **11**

b. How many operations are needed to calculate $40(x^4 + x^3 + x^2 + x + 1)$? **8**

c. Which is more efficient, part a or part b? **b**

d. The process that converts the expression in part a to the expression in part b is called __?__. **common monomial factoring**

2. What factoring question and answer are suggested by $3t(t^2 + 4) = 3t^3 + 12t$? **Factor $3t^3 + 12t$; answer $3t(t^2 + 4)$.**

In 3–5, copy and complete.

3. $8x^3 + 40x = 8x(\underline{?} + \underline{?})$. **$x^2$; 5**

4. $4p^2 - 3p = p(\underline{?} - \underline{?})$. **4p; 3**

5. $7x^2y - 3x - x^3 = (\underline{?} - \underline{?} - \underline{?}) \cdot x$. **7xy; 3; x^2**

In 6–9, **a.** find the largest common factor of the terms of the polynomials; **b.** factor the polynomial.

6. $27b^3 - 27c^3 + 27bc$
a) 27 b) $27(b^3 - c^3 + bc)$

7. $23a^3 + a^2$
a) a^2; b) $a^2(23a + 1)$

8. $15x^2 - 21xy$
a) 3x; b) 3x(5x − 7y)

9. $30xy^4 - 12y^3 + 18x^3y^5$
a) $6y^3$; b) $6y^3(5xy - 2 + 3x^3y^2)$

In 10 and 11, simplify.

10. $\frac{4x^2 - 2x}{x}$ **4x − 2**

11. $\frac{12n^2 + 15n}{3n}$ **$\frac{3n(4n + 5)}{3n} = 4n + 5$**

Applying the Mathematics

12. a. Factor $3y^2 + 5y$. **y(3y + 5)**

b. If a rectangle has area $3y^2 + 5y$, and its length is y, what is its width? **3y + 5**

5y | Area = $100y^3 - 55y^2 + 30y$

L

13. The area of the rectangle above is $100y^3 - 55y^2 + 30y$. Write an expression for the length L of the rectangle. **$20y^2 - 11y + 6$**

14. *Multiple choice* One factor of $6n^2 + 12n$ is $6n$. The other factor is a **(b)**
(a) monomial (b) binomial (c) trinomial.

15. *True or false* If n is an integer, $n^2 + n$ can be written as the product of two consecutive integers. **True**

16. Computers often have to do millions of calculations, so anything that reduces the number of calculations saves money. The following program asks the computer to evaluate

$$50x^4 + 50x^3 + 50x^2 + 50x + 50$$

for the 20,000 values of x from 1.00001 to 1.20000, increasing by steps of 0.00001.

```
10 FOR X = 1.00001 TO 1.2 STEP 0.00001
20    LET P = 50 * X ^ 4 + 50 * X ^ 3 + 50 * X ^ 2 + 50 * X + 50
30 NEXT X
40 END
```

Comment: We ignore other statements that would analyze or print values, but which are not necessary for this question.

a. If, on the average, each operation takes the computer a millionth of a second, how long will it take this program to run? **.22 second**

b. If the expression in line 20 is rewritten in factored form, how long will it take the program to run? **.16 second**

c. If each second of running time costs \$.25, how much will factoring save? **\$.015**

In 17 and 18, simplify.

17. $\dfrac{-3x^2y + 6xy - 9xy^2}{3xy}$ **$-x + 2 - 3y$**

18. $\dfrac{28n^2 + 42n + 7}{14}$ **$\dfrac{4n^2 + 6n + 1}{2}$**

NAME ______

LESSON **MASTER 10–4**
QUESTIONS ON **SPUR** OBJECTIVES

■SKILLS *Objective D (See pages 527–529 for objectives.)*
In 1–5, fill in the blanks.

1. $6x^2 + 18x = 6x($ **x** $+$ **3** $)$

2. $4y^2 - 6y = 2y($ **2y** $-$ **3** $)$

3. $-8a^3 - 4a = -4a($ **$2a^2$** $+$ **1** $)$

4. $-9n^4 - 6n^2 = -3n^2($ **$3n^2$** $+$ **2** $)$

5. $12n^3 - 21n^2 + 27n = 3n($ **$4n^2$** $-$ **7n** $+$ **9** $)$

In 6 and 7, find the largest common factor.

6. $-24b^3x, 32b^4x, 48b^2$ **$8b^2$**

7. $14r^2s^2, 63r^3s, -42r^2s^3$ **$7r^2s$**

In 8–13, factor.

8. $2k^5 + 3k^3$ **$k^3(2k^2 + 3)$**

9. $6x^2 + 3$ **$3(2x^2 + 1)$**

10. $12c^3 - 15ac^2 - 18c$ **$3c(4c^2 - 5ac - 6)$**

11. $x^3y^2 - x^2y^3 + x^2y^2$ **$x^2y^2(x - y + 1)$**

12. $-3y^2z - 9yz - 12z$ **$-3z(y^2 + 3y + 4)$**

13. $25p^4q^3 + 20p^3q^4 - 35p^2q^3$ **$5p^2q^3(5p^2 + 4pq - 7)$**

In 14–17, simplify.

14. $\dfrac{3a^2 + a}{a}$ **$3a + 1$**

15. $\dfrac{16t^2 - 8t}{4t}$ **$4t - 2$**

16. $\dfrac{4d^3 - 6d^2 + 2d}{2d}$ **$2d^2 - 3d + 1$**

17. $\dfrac{9f^3 + 6f^2}{3f^2}$ **$3f + 2$**

86

NOTES ON QUESTIONS
Question 31: The program might run for 5–20 minutes, depending on how fast and powerful your microcomputer is. Here is a way of rewriting the expression which uses even fewer operations:
(((50*X+50)*X+50)*X+50)*X+50

FOLLOW-UP

MORE PRACTICE
For more questions on SPUR Objectives, use *Lesson Master 10-4,* shown on page 493.

EXTENSION
Students can use *Teaching Aid 53* to illustrate common monomial factoring. For example, to factor $2x^2 + 3x$, first build a rectangle with that area:

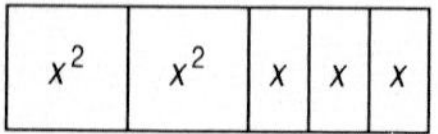

Then label the height and length.

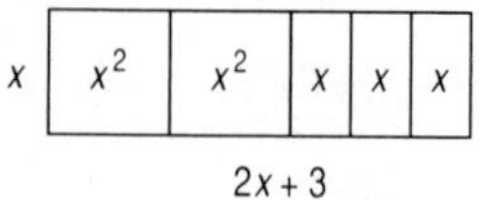

So, $2x^2 + 3x = x(2x + 3)$

EVALUATION
A quiz covering Lessons 10-1 through 10-4 is provided in the Teacher's Resource File.

Review

19. On each birthday from age 16, Kate receives \$75 from her parents. She saves the money and gets 8% interest a year. How much will she have when she turns 21? *(Lesson 10-1)* **\$550.19**

20. Add $3x^2 + 2x - 5$ to $8x^2 + 4 + 3x$. *(Lesson 10-2)* **$11x^2 + 5x - 1$**

21. Subtract $3x^2 + 2x - 5$ from $8x^2 + 4 + 3x$. *(Lesson 10-2)* **$5x^2 + x + 9$**

In 22–24, multiply and simplify. *(Lesson 10-3)*

22. $(3x + 5) \cdot x + (3x + 5) \cdot 2$ **$3x^2 + 11x + 10$**

23. $8v^2(v + 1) - 4v(v^2 - 1)$ **$4v^3 + 8v^2 + 4v$**

24. $4(x^2 - 3x + 1) - 2(x^2 + 5x + 3)$ **$2x^2 - 22x - 2$**

In 25 and 26, find x if $AB = 12$. *(Lesson 2-6)* **25) 9; 26) 2**

25.

26.

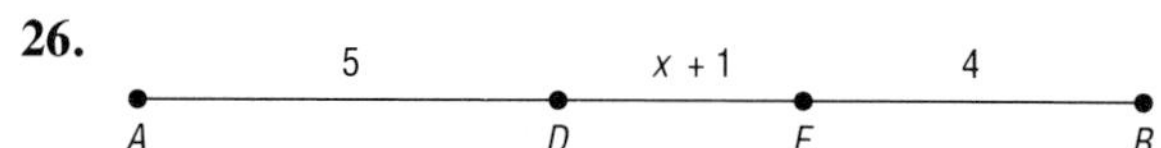

27. On the third day of a diet, a person weighs 93.4 kg. On the 10th day, the person weighs 91.2 kg. What has been the average rate of change in weight per day? *(Lesson 8-1)* **≈ -.31 kg per day**

In 28–30, solve for b.

28. $y = mx + b$ *(Lesson 2-6)* **$b = y - mx$**

29. $bx + c = d$ *(Lesson 6-1)* **$b = \frac{d - c}{x}$**

30. $ax + by = c$ *(Lesson 6-1)* **$b = \frac{c - ax}{y}$**

Exploration

31. Insert the following lines in the program of Question 16.

```
23  IF ABS(X-1.1)<0.00001 THEN PRINT X, P
26  IF ABS(X-1.2)<0.00001 THEN PRINT X, P
```

a. Run the program, timing how long it takes to run to the nearest tenth of a second. **Student's computer run time**

b. Change line 20 to factored form and time the modified program.
20 LET P = 50 * (X ^ 4 + X ^ 3 + X ^ 2 + X + 1)

c. Powering takes longer for computers to do than multiplication. Rewrite line 20 as follows:

```
20  LET P = 50 * (X * X * X * X + X * X * X + X * X + X + 1)
```

Run this modified program and time it. **student's computer run time**

d. Which is fastest and by how much? **Answers depend on a.–c.**

Multiplying Polynomials

The Area Model for Multiplication provides a way of picturing multiplication. In this lesson, the area model is used to illustrate how to multiply two polynomials with many terms. For instance, to multiply $a + b + c + d$ by $x + y + z$, draw a rectangle with length $a + b + c + d$ and width $x + y + z$.

	a	b	c	d
x	ax	bx	cx	dx
y	ay	by	cy	dy
z	az	bz	cz	dz

The area of the biggest rectangle equals the sum of the areas of the twelve little rectangles.

Total area =
$ax + ay + az + bx + by + bz + cx + cy + cz + dx + dy + dz$

But the area of the biggest rectangle also equals the product of its length and width.

$= (a + b + c + d) \cdot (x + y + z)$

The Distributive Property can be used to justify this same result. Distribute the chunk $(x + y + z)$ over $(a + b + c + d)$ to get:

$(a + b + c + d) \cdot (x + y + z) =$

$a(x + y + z) + b(x + y + z) + c(x + y + z) + d(x + y + z)$

Four more applications of the Distributive Property lead to the same expansion found above.

$= ax + ay + az + bx + by + bz + cx + cy + cz + dx + dy + dz$

Because of the multiple use of the Distributive Property we call this an instance of the **Extended Distributive Property.**

Extended Distributive Property:

To multiply two sums, multiply each term in the first sum by each term in the second sum.

LESSON 10-5

RESOURCES
- Lesson Master 10-5
- Visual for Teaching Aid 54: Representation of the Extended Distributive Property
- Visual for Teaching Aid 55: Diagrams for **Questions 1, 3-6, 9, and 10**

OBJECTIVES

B Multiply polynomials.
J Represent areas of figures in terms of polynomials.

TEACHING NOTES

The multiplication problem that opens this lesson is included in *Teaching Aid 54*. You will probably need to show your students how each term in the first polynomial is multiplied by each term in the second one, both in the diagram and in the algebraic manipulation.

Error Analysis As the number of multiplications increases, it is easy to lose one of the products. In our examples, we have always distributed each term from the first polynomial over all terms of the second. Students are not so organized. They may, for instance, start a problem like **Example 1** by distributing the $5x^2$ over the $(x + 7)$, and then distribute the x over the $(5x^2 + 4x + 3)$! Colored chalk helps to emphasize a correct pattern.

Also, you may want to have students show some of their work in a rectangle pattern. The diagram on page 496 is for **Example 1.**

	$5x^2$	$4x$	3
x	$5x^3$	$4x^2$	$3x$
7	$35x^2$	$28x$	21

Each small rectangle should be filled in as the products of terms are computed.

Reading Point out that the subtractions are handled differently in **Examples 2 and 3.** In **Example 2,** all subtractions are first converted to additions. This method may be less prone to error, but the method of **Example 3,** in which subtractions are distributed, is more efficient.

ADDITIONAL EXAMPLES

1. Multiply $2a + 10b + 1$ by $4a + b + 11$.
$\mathbf{8a^2 + 42ab + 26a + 10b^2 + 111b + 11}$

2. Multiply $(n - 5)(2n^2 - 3n + 7)$.
$\mathbf{2n^3 - 13n^2 + 22n - 35}$

3. Multiply $3j - 5k + 6$ by $3j + 5k - 8$.
$\mathbf{9j^2 - 6j - 25k^2 + 70k - 48}$

NOTES ON QUESTIONS

Questions 1, 3-6, 9 and 10: *Teaching Aid 55* provides rectangle patterns that may be used to organize the work. Note that for **Question 10** the simplified result from step 1 must be written across the top of the rectangle used in step 2.

Question 15b: The answer can be obtained in a variety of ways. One method is to solve the equation $(5x + 3)(5x - 2) = 25x^2 - 6$. This yields $15x - 10x = 0$, so $x = 0$. Another possible method is *trial and error.* Zero is a simple number to test. A third method is to use the fact that $25x^2 - 6$ and the expanded form of $(5x + 3)(5x - 2)$ are identical except that the latter has a term $5x$. The desired value of x must make $5x$ drop out.

If one polynomial has m terms and the second n terms, there will be mn terms in their product. When possible, you should simplify the product by combining like terms.

Example 1 Multiply $(5x^2 + 4x + 3)(x + 7)$.

Solution Multiply each term in the first polynomial by each in the second. There will be six terms in the product.

$$= \mathbf{5x^2} \cdot x + \mathbf{5x^2} \cdot 7 + \mathbf{4x} \cdot x + \mathbf{4x} \cdot 7 + \mathbf{3} \cdot x + \mathbf{3} \cdot 7$$
$$= 5x^3 + 35x^2 + 4x^2 + 28x + 3x + 21$$

Now simplify by adding or subtracting like terms.

$$= 5x^3 + 39x^2 + 31x + 21$$

Check Let $x = 2$. The check is left to you as Question 7.

In these long problems it helps if you are neat and precise. Be extra careful with problems involving negatives or several variables.

Example 2 Multiply $(3x + y - 1)(x - 5y + 8)$.

Solution Each term of $x - 5y + 8$ must be multiplied by $3x$, y, and -1. There will be nine terms.

$$= \mathbf{3x} \cdot x + \mathbf{3x} \cdot -5y + \mathbf{3x} \cdot 8 + \mathbf{y} \cdot x + \mathbf{y} \cdot -5y + \mathbf{y} \cdot 8 + \mathbf{-1} \cdot x + \mathbf{-1} \cdot -5y + \mathbf{-1} \cdot 8$$

Watch the signs!

$$= 3x^2 - 15xy + 24x + xy - 5y^2 + 8y - x + 5y - 8$$
$$= 3x^2 - 14xy + 23x - 5y^2 + 13y - 8$$

Check A quick check of the coefficients can be found by letting all variables equal 1.
Does $(3 + 1 - 1)(1 - 5 + 8) = 3 - 14 + 23 - 5 + 13 - 8$?
Does $3 \cdot 4 = 12$? Yes.
A better check requires using different values for both x and y, but if you have made an error, this quick check may find it.

After simplifying, the product of two polynomials can be a polynomial with fewer terms than one or both factors.

Example 3 Multiply $x^2 - 2x + 2$ by $x^2 + 2x + 2$.

Solution Each term of $x^2 + 2x + 2$ must be multiplied by x^2, $-2x$, and 2. Again there will be nine terms.

$$\begin{aligned}&(x^2 - 2x + 2)(x^2 + 2x + 2)\\ &= x^2(x^2 + 2x + 2) - 2x(x^2 + 2x + 2) + 2(x^2 + 2x + 2)\\ &= x^4 + 2x^3 + 2x^2 - 2x^3 - 4x^2 - 4x + 2x^2 + 4x + 4\\ &= x^4 + 4\end{aligned}$$

Check Let $x = 10$. Then $x^2 - 2x + 2 = 82$ and $x^2 + 2x + 2 = 122$. Now $82 \cdot 122 = 10{,}004$, which is $x^4 + 4$. Ten is a nice value to use in checks, because powers of 10 are so easily calculated.

Questions

Covering the Reading

1. a. What multiplication is pictured below? **$(w^2 + 5w + 4)(w + 6)$**
   b. Do the multiplication. **$w^3 + 11w^2 + 34w + 24$**

	w^2	$5w$	4
w			
6			

2. State the Extended Distributive Property. **To multiply two sums, multiply each term in the first sum by each term in the second sum and then simplify.**

In 3–6, multiply and simplify.

3. $(y^2 + 7y + 2)(y + 6)$ **$y^3 + 13y^2 + 44y + 12$**
4. $(5c - 4d + 1)(c - 7d)$ **$5c^2 - 39cd + 28d^2 + c - 7d$**
5. $(m^2 + 10m + 3)(3m^2 - 4m - 2)$ **$3m^4 + 26m^3 - 33m^2 - 32m - 6$**
6. $(x + 1)(2x + 3)$ **$2x^2 + 5x + 3$**
7. Finish the check of Example 1. **$(5 \cdot 2^2 + 4 \cdot 2 + 3)(2 + 7) = 31 \cdot 9 = 279$; $5 \cdot 2^3 + 39 \cdot 2^2 + 31 \cdot 2 + 21 = 40 + 156 + 62 + 21 = 279$**
8. Check Example 2 by letting $x = 10$ and $y = 2$. **See margin.**
9. Multiply $x^2 + 4x + 8$ by $x^2 - 4x + 8$. **$x^4 + 64$**
10. Multiply $(n - 3)(n + 4)(2n + 5)$ by first multiplying $n - 3$ by $n + 4$, then multiplying their product by $2n + 5$. **$2n^3 + 7n^2 - 19n - 60$**

Applying the Mathematics

In 11–13, multiply and simplify.

11. $(7 - 3x)(7 + 3x)$. **$49 - 9x^2$**
12. $(a + b + c)(a + b - c)$ **$a^2 + 2ab + b^2 - c^2$**
13. $(x + 4)(x + 4) - (8x - 16)$ **$x^2 + 32$**

Making Connections for Questions 24b and 24c: These can be solved by chunking. Encourage your students to do this. In Lesson 10-10 students are asked to solve $3m(4m - 1) = 0$ by the Zero Product Property; either the chunk $3m$ is zero, or the chunk $4m - 1$ is zero.

Question 28: This question should be discussed. It gives a reason to think about the degree of a polynomial. Generalization is a very important skill; good problem solvers try to generalize what they are doing as much as they can.

ADDITIONAL ANSWERS

8. $[3(10) + 2 - 1][10 - 5(2) + 8] \stackrel{?}{=} 3(10^2) - 14(10)(2) + 23(10) - 5(2^2) + 13(2) - 8.$
$(30 + 1)(18 - 10) \stackrel{?}{=} 3(100) - 280 + 230 - 5(4) + 26 - 8.$
$31(8) \stackrel{?}{=} 300 - 32 - 20.$
$248 = 248$ (check)

NAME ____________

LESSON **MASTER 10–5**
QUESTIONS ON **SPUR** OBJECTIVES

■**SKILLS** *Objective B* (See pages 527–529 for objectives.)
In 1–12, multiply and simplify.

1. $(x + 4)(x - 6)$ **$x^2 - 2x - 24$**
2. $(2a - 8)(a - 5)$ **$2a^2 - 18a + 40$**
3. $(5r + 4)(3r + 2)$ **$15r^2 + 22r + 8$**
4. $(11k - 3)(2k + 9)$ **$22k^2 + 93k - 27$**
5. $(7x + 2y)(3x + 4y)$ **$21x^2 + 34xy + 8y^2$**
6. $(x^2 + 2)(x^2 - 3)$ **$x^4 - x^2 - 6$**
7. $(2y - 1)(y^2 - 3y - 1)$ **$2y^3 - 7y^2 + y + 1$**
8. $(a + b + 1)(a - b - 1)$ **$a^2 - b^2 - 2b - 1$**
9. $(2x - y + 3)(x - y - 1)$ **$2x^2 + y^2 - 3xy + x - 2y - 3$**
10. $(t^2 - 1)(t^4 + t^2 + 1)$ **$t^6 - 1$**
11. $(P^3 - 2)(P^3 - 1)$ **$P^6 - 3P^3 + 2$**
12. $(a + 1)(a - 3)(a + 4)$ **$a^3 + 2a^2 - 11a - 12$**

■**REPRESENTATIONS** *Objective J*
In 13 and 14, write the area of the largest rectangle as a. the sum of terms and b. as the product of two polynomials.

13. a. **$x^2 + xy + 4x + 3y + 3$**
    b. **$(x + y + 1)(x + 3)$**

	x	3
x		
y		
1		

14. a. **$ba + ca + 2a + b^2 + cb + 4b + 2c + 4$**
    b. **$(b + c + 2)(a + b + 2)$**

	a	b	2
b			
c			
2			

FOLLOW-UP

MORE PRACTICE

For more questions on SPUR Objectives, use *Lesson Master 10-5,* shown on page 497.

EXTENSION

1. Follow up on **Questions 14 and 28.** Ask students how many digits will be in their product if an m-digit number x is multiplied by an n-digit number y. The question can be explored by using special cases, but it is answered by examining polynomials. For instance, if $m = 4$ and $n = 3$, then the numbers could be written as

$$x = a \cdot 10^3 + b \cdot 10^2 + c \cdot 10 + d$$

$$y = e \cdot 10^2 + f \cdot 10 + g.$$

This leads us to believe that xy will have six digits (since $10^3 \cdot 10^2 = 10^5$ and a number whose leading digit is in the 10^5 place has six digits). But it is possible that ae itself will have two digits, and thus result in a seven-digit answer. In general, there will be either $m + n - 1$ or $m + n$ digits in the product.

2. Ask students to find the perimeter of the rectangle in the Teaching Notes. This gives practice in addition of polynomials. The formula for perimeter would give rise to the expression $2(5x^2 + 4x + 3) + 2(x + 7)$, so the perimeter is $10x^2 + 10x + 20$.

14. A first degree polynomial in x is of the form $ax + b$. A second degree polynomial in x is of the form $cx^2 + dx + e$. When these are multiplied, $ax \cdot cx^2 = acx^3$ and this is the highest power of x in the product. So the product is a third degree polynomial.

22.

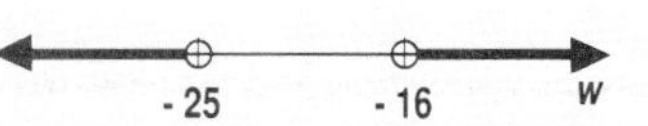

14. In Example 1, a 2nd degree polynomial is multiplied by a 1st degree polynomial. The product is a 3rd degree polynomial. Explain why this will always happen. **See margin.**

15. a. Show by a check that this multiplication is wrong.

Sample: $(5x + 3)(5x - 2) = 25x^2 - 6$
Let $x = 1$; Does $(5 + 3)(5 - 2) = 25 - 6$? Does $8(3) = 19$? No

b. Is there any value of x for which the multiplication in part a is correct? **0**

Review

16. Suppose x is either 7, 6, 5, 3, -2, or -8. Find x given the clues. **-2 or 7**
Clue 1: $x > -3$.
Clue 2: x is not the degree of $a^3 + 4a^2 + 7$.
Clue 3: x is not the coefficient of b^2 in the polynomial $4b^4 + 6b^2 - 3b + 9$.
Clue 4: x is not the number of terms in $2a^2 + a - 3b + c - 5f$.
(Lesson 10-1)

In 17–20, factor. *(Lesson 10-4)*

17. $4v^2 - 2v$ **$2v(2v - 1)$** **18.** $11x^3 + 33x^2 + 22x$ **$11x(x^2 + 3x + 2)$**

19. $3x^2y^3 + 3xy^3$ **$3xy^3(x + 1)$** **20.** $8m^2 - 4$ **$4(2m^2 - 1)$**

21. Subtract $3x^2 + 5$ from $2x^2 - 3x + 40$. *(Lesson 10-2)* **$-x^2 - 3x + 35$**

22. Graph $A \cup B$ on a number line where A = set of solutions to $-4w > 100$, and B = set of solutions to $3w + 8 > -40$. *(Lessons 3-5, 6-7)* **See margin.**

23. If the area of a square is 64 square kilometers, find the length of a diagonal. *(Lesson 7-5)* **$\sqrt{128}$ or $8\sqrt{2}$ km**

24. *Skill sequence* Solve. *(Lesson 6-7)*
a. $4z - 7 = 13$ **5**
b. $4(z + 8) - 7 = 13$ **-3**
c. $5(z + 8) - 7 = (z + 8) + 13$ **-3**

In 25 and 26, simplify. *(Lesson 9-7)*

25. $\frac{14a^3b}{6ab^2}$ **$\frac{7a^2}{3b}$** **26.** $\frac{-150m^5n^8}{100m^6n^3}$ **$\frac{-3n^5}{2m}$**

Exploration

27. Multiply each of the following polynomials by $x + 1$.
a. $x - 1$ **$x^2 - 1$**
b. $x^2 - x + 1$ **$x^3 + 1$**
c. $x^3 - x^2 + x - 1$ **$x^4 - 1$**
d. $x^4 - x^3 + x^2 - x + 1$ **$x^5 + 1$**
e. Look for a pattern and use it to multiply $(x + 1)(x^8 - x^7 + x^6 - x^5 + x^4 - x^3 + x^2 - x + 1)$. **$x^9 + 1$**

28. Generalize the idea of Question 14. **Let n = the degree of the first polynomial and m = the degree of the second polynomial. Then the degree of the product is $m + n$.**

LESSON

10-6

Multiplying Binomials

In the last lesson, the Area Model for Multiplication was used to represent multiplying two polynomials. Recall that a polynomial with two terms is a binomial. You will multiply binomials often enough that we examine this as a special case.

The rectangle below has length $(a + b)$ and width $(c + d)$.

	a	b
c		
d		

The area of the rectangle = length · width = $(a + b) \cdot (c + d)$. But the area of the rectangle also must equal the sum of the areas of the four small rectangles inside it.

	a	b
c	ac	bc
d	ad	bd

The sum of the areas of the four small rectangles = $ac + ad + bc + bd$. So,

$$(a + b) \cdot (c + d) = ac + ad + bc + bd.$$

Another way to show the pattern above is true is to chunk $(c + d)$ and distribute it over $(a + b)$ as follows:

$$(a + b) \cdot (c + d) = a(c + d) + b(c + d).$$

Now apply the Distributive Property twice more.

$$= ac + ad + bc + bd$$

This pattern shows how to multiply two binomials. The result has four terms. To get them, multiply each term in the first binomial by each term in the second binomial. The binomials $(a + b)$ and $(c + d)$ are each factors of the polynomial $ac + ad + bc + bd$.

LESSON 10-6

RESOURCES

- Lesson Master 10-6
- Visual for Teaching Aid 53: Tiles for Representing Polynomials
- Visual for Teaching Aid 56: Diagrams for **Questions 3-10**

OBJECTIVES

B Multiply binomials.
I Translate real situations into polynomials.

TEACHING NOTES

The multiplication which starts the lesson uses four variables. Then there are no like terms after the FOIL algorithm has been employed. However, when the factors being multiplied involve the same variable, it is quite likely that some terms will combine. You might show **Example 1** in the rectangle format:

	m	4
m	m^2	$4m$
3	$3m$	12

Error Analysis The most common error that students make in multiplying two binomials is to miss the two middle terms. For example, some students say $(x + 3)(x + 7) = x^2 + 21$. Emphasize that the four letters in FOIL suggest that they should find four terms. But it may be possible to combine some of these terms. Also, have students show their work in a rectangle pattern as above.

Making Connections When considering **Examples 1-4,** you might inform students that in a later chapter they will be expected to work backwards to determine the factors from the product. In this regard, **Example 4** is particularly important. Its pattern is the subject of Lesson 10-9.

ADDITIONAL EXAMPLES

1. Multiply $(y + 5)(y - 8)$.
$\mathbf{y^2 - 3y - 40}$

2. Multiply $(3n + 10)(7n + 2)$.
$\mathbf{21n^2 + 76n + 20}$

3. Multiply $(5a - 6x)(3a - 2x)$.
$\mathbf{15a^2 - 28ax + 12x^2}$

4. Multiply $(7m + 2y)(7m - 2y)$.
$\mathbf{49m^2 - 4y^2}$

Here is a way to remember which multiplications you have done. The name of the algorithm and the face might help.

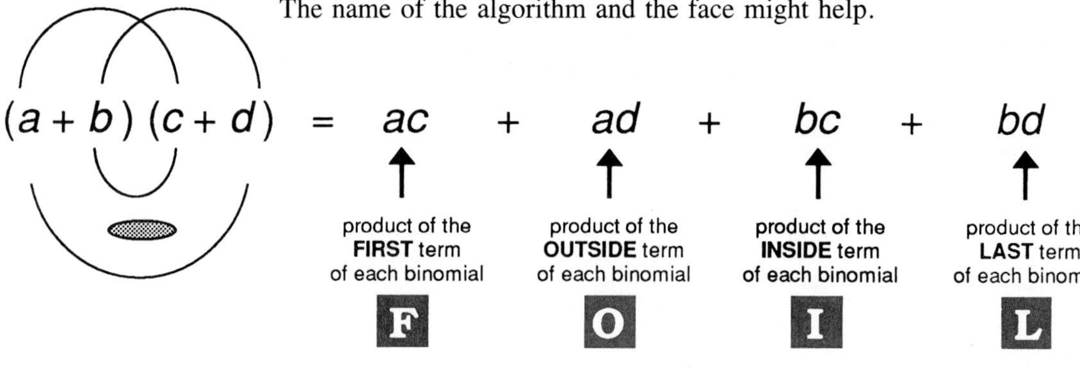

Example 1 Multiply $(m + 4)(m + 3)$.

Solution F O I L

$$(m + 4)(m + 3) = m \cdot m + m \cdot 3 + 4 \cdot m + 4 \cdot 3$$
$$= m^2 + 3m + 4m + 12$$
$$= m^2 + 7m + 12$$

Check Let $m = 10$. Then $m + 4 = 14$, $m + 3 = 13$, and $m^2 + 7m + 12 = 182$.
It checks, because $14 \cdot 13 = 182$.

After multiplying two binomials, you should simplify the product whenever possible by adding like terms. This was the last step in Example 1. If the binomials themselves involve expressions with like terms, then you will always be able to simplify the product. This happens even when subtraction is involved. You must, however, be careful with signs.

Example 2 Multiply $(2x - 5)(6x + 1)$.

Solution Recall that $2x - 5 = 2x + -5$.

$$(2x - 5)(6x + 1) \quad \text{FOIL algorithm}$$
$$= 2x \cdot 6x + 2x \cdot 1 - 5 \cdot 6x - 5 \cdot 1$$
$$= 12x^2 + 2x - 30x - 5$$
$$= 12x^2 - 28x - 5.$$

Check We let $x = 3$ this time.
Does $(2 \cdot 3 - 5)(6 \cdot 3 + 1) = 12 \cdot 3^2 - 28 \cdot 3 - 5$?
Yes, each side equals 19.

Examples 1 and 2 illustrate an important property. The product of two first degree polynomials in a single variable is a polynomial of the second degree. This is true even when there is more than one variable in the polynomial, as Example 3 shows.

Example 3 Multiply $(7x + 5y)(x - 4y)$.

Solution F O I L

$$(7x + 5y)(x - 4y) = 7x \cdot x + 7x \cdot -4y + 5y \cdot x + 5y \cdot -4y$$
$$= 7x^2 - 28xy + 5yx - 20y^2$$

Notice that $-28xy$ and $5yx$ are like terms.

$$= 7x^2 - 23xy - 20y^2$$

Check Let $x = 2$ and $y = 3$.
Does $(7 \cdot 2 + 5 \cdot 3)(2 - 4 \cdot 3) = 7 \cdot 2^2 - 23 \cdot 2 \cdot 3 - 20 \cdot 3^2$?
Does $29 \cdot -10 = 28 - 138 - 180$?
Yes, each side equals -290.

You have seen that the product of two binomials generally has four terms, as in FOIL. After simplifying, the products in Examples 1–3 have three terms. Sometimes, after simplifying, there are only two terms.

Example 4 Multiply $4x - 3$ by $4x + 3$.

Solution F O I L

$$(4x - 3)(4x + 3) = 4x \cdot 4x + 4x \cdot 3 - 3 \cdot 4x - 3 \cdot 3$$
$$= 16x^2 + 12x - 12x - 9$$
$$= 16x^2 - 9$$

Questions

Covering the Reading

1. a. What multiplication is pictured at the right?
   $(2w + 6)(w + 7)$
   b. Do the multiplication.
   $2w^2 + 20w + 42$

	2w	**6**
w		
7		

2. In the FOIL algorithm, what do the letters F, O, I, and L stand for?
   First; Outside; Inside; Last

NOTES ON QUESTIONS

Questions 3-10: *Teaching Aid 56* provides rectangle patterns that may be used to organize the work. Note that for **Question 5** the simplified result from step 1 must be written across the top of the rectangle used in step 2.

Question 11: This question applies the Multiplication Counting Principle. Number of twosomes = (number of students in the freshman and sophomore class) • (number of students in the junior and senior class). Part **a** does not appear to have anything to do with binomials, but the answer to part **b** is very instructive. Either the answer is $(f + p)(j + s)$, using the Multiplication Counting Principle just once, or the answer is $fj + pj + fs + ps$ (that is, number of freshman-junior pairs + number of sophomore-junior pairs + . . .), using that principle four times.

NOTES ON QUESTIONS
Question 24b: You might ask students how they would respond if the rocket were launched at the edge of a cliff or fired from a plane. Then the height at 7 seconds (-106 feet) could represent the rocket's position below the point of firing.

Making Connections for Question 28: This question previews the Zero Product Property which is covered in Lesson 10-10. Students should solve these questions mentally, realizing that a factor must equal zero in order for the product to be equal to zero.

Small Group Work for Question 29: This question is similar to **Question 11** in that the idea is to emphasize the different ways of expressing the same quantity, and then see these ways as exemplifying the multiplication of binomials. You might have small groups of students build a model for the figure in **Question 29.** They can use paper, cardboard, or plastic foam. If it is made of eight parts, each labeled to show its volume, the model will illustrate $(a + b)(c + d)(e + f)$.

FOLLOW-UP

MORE PRACTICE
For more questions on SPUR Objectives, use *Lesson Master 10-6,* shown on page 503.

In 3–10, multiply. Then simplify, if possible.

3. $(a + b)(c + d)$
$ac + ad + bc + bd$

4. $(2x - 3)(4y - 4)$
$8xy - 8x - 12y + 12$

5. $(y + 5)(y + 6)$
$y^2 + 11y + 30$

6. $(3x + 2)(5x - 1)$
$15x^2 + 7x - 2$

7. $(k - 3)(9k + 8)$
$9k^2 - 19k - 24$

8. $(3m + 2n)(7m - 6n)$
$21m^2 - 4mn - 12n^2$

9. $(a + b)(a - b)$ **$a^2 - b^2$**

10. $(2x - 3y)(2x + 3y)$ **$4x^2 - 9y^2$**

Applying the Mathematics

11. a. One student is selected from the freshman or sophomore class as co-chairperson for the school dance committee. A second student is selected from the junior or senior class as co-chairperson. How many such twosomes are possible in a school with
550 freshmen,
500 sophomores,
450 juniors,
and 400 seniors? **892,500**

b. Repeat part a, if there are f freshmen, p sophomores, j juniors, and s seniors. **$(f + p)(j + s)$ or $fj + fs + pj + ps$**

12. a. Complete the following multiplication by using the FOIL algorithm. Simplify your answer. **$36 + 3 + 4\frac{1}{2} + \frac{3}{8} = 43\frac{7}{8}$**

$$4\tfrac{1}{2} \cdot 9\tfrac{3}{4} = (4 + \tfrac{1}{2})(9 + \tfrac{3}{4})$$

b. Check by converting to decimals and using a calculator. **See margin.**

13. a. Multiply $(x^2 + 2)(x^3 - 1)$. **$x^5 + 2x^3 - x^2 - 2$**

b. Check your answer by letting $x = 4$. **$(4^2 + 2)(4^3 - 1) = 18 \cdot 63 = 1134$; $4^5 + 2 \cdot 4^3 - 4^2 - 2 = 1024 + 128 - 16 - 2 = 1134$**

In 14–16, multiply. Then simplify, if possible.

14. $(5c + 2)^2$ [Hint: $(5c + 2)^2 = (5c + 2)(5c + 2)$] **$25c^2 + 20c + 4$**

15. $n(n + 1)(n + 2)$ [Hint: Multiply $n + 1$ by $n + 2$ first] **$n^3 + 3n^2 + 2n$**

16. $(2x - 3)(2x - 4)(2x - 5)$ **$8x^3 - 48x^2 + 94x - 60$**

Review

In 17–20, multiply and then simplify. *(Lessons 6-3, 10-5)*

17. $75(4q - 3r)$ **$300q - 225r$**

18. $y(4y^2 - 3y + 2)$ **$4y^3 - 3y^2 + 2y$**

19. $wz^3(4w^2z - 3wz^2 + 2)$
$4w^3z^4 - 3w^2z^5 + 2wz^3$

20. $(x^2 - 2)(x^2 + 3x + 2)$
$x^4 + 3x^3 - 6x - 4$

21. Simplify $5(x^2 - 7) - 3(x^2 - 2x - 1) + 4(3x^2 + x - 7)$. *(Lesson 10-3)*
$14x^2 + 10x - 60$

22. a. Simplify $(4x^2 - 7x - 8) + (6x^2 + 2x - 9)$. **$10x^2 - 5x - 17$**

b. Simplify $(4x^2 - 7x - 8) - (6x^2 + 2x - 9)$. *(Lesson 10-2)*
$-2x^2 - 9x + 1$

In 23 and 24, use this formula for the height h reached by a rocket after t seconds, when fired straight up from a launching pad 6 feet off the ground,

$$h = 6 + 96t - 16t^2.$$

23. The rocket reaches its maximum height at 3 seconds. What is its maximum height? *(Lesson 10-1)* **150 feet**

24. a. Find the height of the rocket after 7 seconds. **-106 feet**

b. What does this answer mean? *(Lesson 10-1)* **The rocket hit the ground before 7 seconds elapsed.**

3

3

10

10

25. Factor $3x^3y + 2xy^3$. *(Lesson 10-4)* $\mathbf{xy(3x^2 + 2y^2)}$

26. A point is selected at random from the big square at the left. Find the probability that the selected point is in the colored area. *(Lesson 5-5)* **.91**

27. Write an equation for the line which passes through the points (-3, 7) and (-9, 4). *(Lesson 8-6)* $y = \frac{1}{2}x + \frac{17}{2}$

28. Solve in your head. *(Lesson 7-8)*

a. $3(k + 5) = 0$ **-5**

b. $6(m - \frac{1}{2}) = 0$ $\frac{1}{2}$

c. $42(512 - x) = 0$ **512**

Exploration

29. The largest rectangular solid at right has length $(a + b)$, width $(c + d)$, and height $(e + f)$. Give at least two ways of expressing the volume of the box.
sample: $(a + b)(c + d)(e + f) = ace + bce + ade + bde + acf + bcf + adf + bdf$

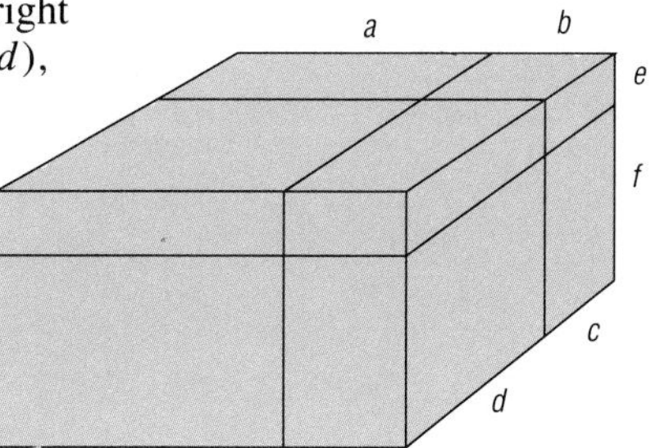

EXTENSION

Students can use *Teaching Aid 53* to illustrate multiplication of binomials in x. Examples follow:

1. $(x + 1)(x + 2)$

$x + 1$ (across), $x + 2$ (down)

x^2	x
x	1
x	1

$= x^2 + 3x + 2$

2. $(2x + 1)(x + 5)$

$2x + 1$ (across), $x + 5$ (down)

x^2	x^2	x
x	x	1
x	x	1
x	x	1
x	x	1
x	x	1

$= 2x^2 + 11x + 5$

ADDITIONAL ANSWERS

12b. Does 4.5 · 9.75 = 43.875? Yes.

NAME ______

LESSON MASTER 10–6

QUESTIONS ON **SPUR** OBJECTIVES

■**SKILLS** *Objective B (See pages 527–529 for objectives.)*

In 1–14, multiply and simplify.

1. $(x + 4)(x + 1)$ — $\mathbf{x^2 + 5x + 4}$

2. $(a - 4)(a - 3)$ — $\mathbf{a^2 - 7a + 12}$

3. $(2w - 3)(w + 5)$ — $\mathbf{2w^2 + 7w - 15}$

4. $(5t + 3)(3t - 5)$ — $\mathbf{15t^2 - 16t - 15}$

5. $(9a + 2b)(3a + b)$ — $\mathbf{27a^2 + 15ab + 2b^2}$

6. $(7x - y)(x - y)$ — $\mathbf{7x^2 - 8xy + y^2}$

7. $(x + y)(x + y)$ — $\mathbf{x^2 + 2xy + y^2}$

8. $(2y - z)(2y - z)$ — $\mathbf{4y^2 - 4yz + z^2}$

9. $(r + s)(r - s)$ — $\mathbf{r^2 - s^2}$

10. $(4d - 1)(4d + 1)$ — $\mathbf{16d^2 - 1}$

11. $(x^2 + 1)(x^2 - 2)$ — $\mathbf{x^4 - x^2 - 2}$

12. $(A^2 + 4)(A^2 + 3)$ — $\mathbf{A^4 + 7A^2 + 12}$

13. $2y(2y - 1)(y - 3)$ — $\mathbf{4y^3 - 14y^2 + 6y}$

14. $(a - 2)(a + 2)(a + 1)$ — $\mathbf{a^3 + a^2 - 4a - 4}$

■**USES** *Objective I*

15. Cindy can wear any of s sweaters or b blouses, with j jeans or k skirts. How many outfits are possible?

$\mathbf{(s + b)(j + k)}$

16. On a restaurant menu, you may select one item from m meats and f fish. You may also select one item from a second list of v vegetables and p potatoes. How many different meals can you order?

$\mathbf{(m + f)(v + p)}$

LESSON 10-7

RESOURCES

- Lesson Master 10-7
- Visual for Teaching Aid 53: Tiles for Representing Polynomials

OBJECTIVES

B Multiply polynomials.

F Apply $(a + b)^2 = a^2 + 2ab + b^2$ and $(a - b)^2 = a^2 - 2ab + b^2$ to multiply numbers in your head.

TEACHING NOTES

You can show the partitioning of the square in **Example 1** with the following drawing.

	$5n$	4
$5n$	$25n^2$	$20n$
4	$20n$	16

There are two squares, and also two rectangles with equal areas, in this picture.

Reading The lesson uses the term *expand* without actually defining it. Generally, expanding the power of a polynomial means to put that power in the standard form for a polynomial. The following everyday use of the word *expand* may help your students remember its mathematical meaning: *Expand* means "to express in full or write out in greater detail."

LESSON

10-7 Squares of Binomials

The expression $(a + b)^2$ (read "a plus b, the quantity squared") is the square of the binomial $(a + b)$. So it can be written as the product $(a + b)(a + b)$. This product can be **expanded** using the Extended Distributive Property or its special case, the FOIL algorithm.

$$\begin{aligned}(a + b)(a + b) &= a^2 + ab + ba + b^2\\ &= a^2 + 2ab + b^2 \text{ (}ab\text{ and }ba\text{ are like terms.)}\end{aligned}$$

Example 1 The area of a square with side $5n + 4$ is $(5n + 4)^2$. Expand this binomial.

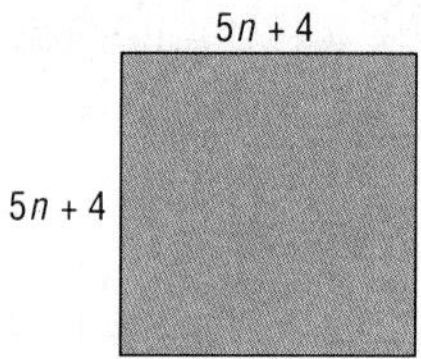

Solution 1 Change the square to multiplication.

$$\begin{aligned}(5n + 4)^2 &= (5n + 4)(5n + 4)\\ &= 25n^2 + 20n + 20n + 16\\ &= 25n^2 + 40n + 16\end{aligned}$$

Solution 2 Use the pattern for the square of $a + b$ with $a = 5n$ and $b = 4$.

$$\begin{aligned}(a + b)^2 &= a^2 + 2ab + b^2\\ (5n + 4)^2 &= (5n)^2 + 2 \cdot 5n \cdot 4 + 4^2\\ &= 25n^2 + 40n + 16\end{aligned}$$

The square of a difference, $(a - b)^2$, can be expanded in the same way.

$$\begin{aligned}(a - b)^2 &= (a - b)(a - b)\\ &= a^2 - ab - ba + b^2\\ &= a^2 - 2ab + b^2\end{aligned}$$

Notice that after simplifying, the square of a binomial has three terms. It is a trinomial. Trinomials of the form $a^2 + 2ab + b^2$ and $a^2 - 2ab + b^2$ are called **perfect square trinomials** because each is the result of squaring a binomial.

Perfect Square Trinomial Patterns:

$$(a + b)^2 = a^2 + 2ab + b^2$$
$$(a - b)^2 = a^2 - 2ab + b^2$$

You need to know these patterns, and you should realize that they can be derived from the multiplication of binomials.

The algebraic description is short but many people remember these patterns in words.

The square of a binomial is the sum of
(1) the square of its first term
(2) twice the product of its terms
and (3) the square of its last term.

Example 2 Expand $(w - 3)^2$.

Solution 1 Follow the Perfect Square Trinomial Pattern. Here $a = w$ and $b = 3$.

$$(w - 3)^2 = w^2 - 2 \cdot w \cdot 3 + 3^2$$
$$= w^2 - 6w + 9$$

Solution 2 Change the square to multiplication of $w - 3$ by itself.

$$(w - 3)^2 = (w - 3)(w - 3)$$
$$= w^2 - 3w - 3w + 9$$
$$= w^2 - 6w + 9$$

Check Test a special case. Let $w = 5$. Then

$$(w - 3)^2 = (5 - 3)^2 = 2^2 = 4.$$
$$w^2 - 6w + 9 = 5^2 - 6 \cdot 5 + 9 = 25 - 30 + 9 = 4$$

It checks.

ADDITIONAL EXAMPLES

1. Write the area of the square below in $(a + b)^2$ form and in expanded form.

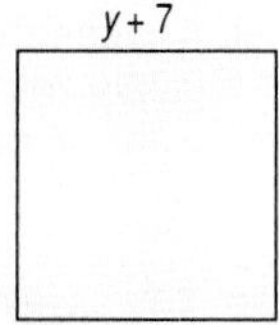

$(y + 7)^2, y^2 + 14y + 49$

2. Expand $(2n - 5)^2$.
$4n^2 - 20n + 25$

3. Compute in your head:

a. 51^2
$(50 + 1)^2 = 50^2 + 2 \cdot 50 \cdot 1 + 1^2 = 2601$

b. 98^2
$(100 - 2)^2 = 100^2 - 2 \cdot 2 \cdot 100 + 2^2 = 9604$

c. $(8.01)^2$.
$(8 + .01)^2 = 8^2 + 2 \cdot 8 \cdot .01 + .01^2 = 64.1601$

NOTES ON QUESTIONS
Questions 6 and 7: These questions can be answered very quickly by using the pattern for the square of a binomial. It takes much longer to multiply with FOIL and examine the middle terms.

Question 14: Have students check by substituting numbers for *a* and *b*. The result may surprise some students. It works!

Question 16: Ask students to generalize: For all *a* and *b*, $(a - b)^2 = (b - a)^2$.

ADDITIONAL ANSWERS
15a. $(2 + 7)^2 = 81$, $2^2 + 7^2 = 53$

The Perfect Square Trinomial Patterns can be applied to find squares of certain numbers without a calculator. With practice, you can do these computations in your head.

Example 3 Compute: **a.** 43^2; **b.** 79^2; **c.** $(1.08)^2$.

Solution **a.** Think of 43 as 40 + 3.

$$\begin{aligned} 43^2 &= (40 + 3)^2 \\ &= 40^2 + 2 \cdot 40 \cdot 3 + 3^2 \\ &= 1600 + 240 + 9 \\ &= 1849 \end{aligned}$$

b. Think of 79 as 80 − 1.

$$\begin{aligned} 79^2 &= (80 - 1)^2 \\ &= 80^2 - 2 \cdot 80 \cdot 1 + 1^2 \\ &= 6400 - 160 + 1 \\ &= 6241 \end{aligned}$$

c. Think of 1.08 as 1 +.08.

$$\begin{aligned} (1.08)^2 &= (1 + .08)^2 \\ &= 1^2 + 2 \cdot 1 \cdot .08 + (.08)^2 \\ &= 1 + .16 + .0064 \\ &= 1.1664 \end{aligned}$$

Questions

Covering the Reading

1. What is a perfect square trinomial? **the square of a binomial**

2. Expand $(x + y)^2$. $\mathbf{x^2 + 2xy + y^2}$

3. Write an expression for the area of a square with side $3x + 7$,
a. as the square of a binomial. $\mathbf{(3x + 7)^2}$
b. as a perfect square trinomial. $\mathbf{9x^2 + 42x + 49}$

4. a. Expand $(m - 6)^2$. $\mathbf{m^2 - 12m + 36}$
b. Check your answer by letting $m = 10$. **Does $(10 - 6)^2 = 10^2 - 12(10) + 36$? Does $16 = 100 - 120 + 36$? Yes**

5. Write $(x - y)^2$ as a perfect square trinomial. $\mathbf{x^2 - 2xy + y^2}$

In 6 and 7, give the middle term after expanding the binomials.

6. $(w + 5)^2$ **10w** **7.** $(4p - 3)^2$ **-24p**

In 8–11, compute as in Example 3.

8. $(41)^2$
$(40 + 1)^2 = 1600 + 80 + 1 = 1681$;

9. $(1.02)^2$
$(1 + .02)^2 + 1 + .04 + .0004 = 1.0404$

10. $(29)^2$
$(30 - 1)^2 = 900 - 60 + 1 = 841$;

11. $(37)^2$
$(40 - 3)^2 = 1600 - 240 + 9 = 1369$

Applying the Mathematics

In 12–14, expand and simplify.

12. $(1 - x)^2$
$1 - 2x + x^2$

13. $4(9 + y)^2$
$324 + 72y + 4y^2$

14. $(a + b)^2 - (a - b)^2$
$4ab$

15. a. Evaluate $(x + y)^2$ and $x^2 + y^2$ for $x = 2$ and $y = 7$. See margin.
b. By how much do the values in part a differ? 28
c. Evaluate $2xy$ for $x = 2$, $y = 7$. Compare the answer with part b.
28; it's the same.

16. Show that $(x - 3)^2$ and $(3 - x)^2$ have the same expansion.
$(x - 3)^2 = x^2 - 6x + 9$; $(3 - x)^2 = 9 - 6x + x^2$

17. An object is falling at a rate of $32t + 20$ feet per second. If it falls for $t + 3$ seconds, write an expression for how far it drops.
$(32t + 20)(t + 3)$ or $32t^2 + 116t + 60$ feet

18. Expand $(x + 2)^3$ by multiplying $(x + 2)(x + 2)(x + 2)$.
$x^3 + 6x^2 + 12x + 8$

Review

In 19 and 20, multiply and simplify. *(Lesson 10-6)*

19. $(z - 11)(z + 8)$
$z^2 - 3z - 88$

20. $(2c - 7d)(c + 5d)$ $2c^2 + 3cd - 35d^2$

21. *Skill sequence* Multiply and simplify. *(Lessons 6-3, 10-2, 10-3)*
a. $4x^3(13x - 2)$ $52x^4 - 8x^3$
b. $(4x^3 + 6x + 1)(13x - 2)$ $52x^4 - 8x^3 + 78x^2 + x - 2$
c. $4x^2(13x - 2) - (4x^2 - 7x + 1)$ $52x^3 - 12x^2 + 7x - 1$

22. Simplify $(3x^2 + 7x - 2) - 3(x^2 - 3x + 1)$ and give the degree of your answer. *(Lessons 10-1, 10-3)* $16x - 5$; 1

23. Factor $60x^2y + 60xy^2 + 60xy$. *(Lesson 10-4)* $60xy(x + y + 1)$

24. *Multiple choice* It was reported in *USA Today* on July 12, 1985 that the Federal National Mortgage Association's first quarter earnings increased 363% to 11.1 million in the second quarter. Which equation can be used to find the first quarter earnings E in millions? *(Lesson 5-4)*
(a) $3.63(11.1) = E$ (b) $4.63(11.1) = E$ (d)
(c) $3.63E = 11.1$ (d) $4.63E = 11.1$

25. Solve $2x + 1 = 0$ in your head. *(Lesson 6-1)* $-\frac{1}{2}$

Exploration

26. The square of 41 is 81 more than the square of 40.
The square of 51 is 101 more than the square of 50.
The square of 61 is 121 more than the square of 60.
Describe the general pattern using variables by filling in the blanks.
The square of _?_ is _?_ more than the square of $10x$.
$10x + 1$; $20x + 1$

FOLLOW-UP

MORE PRACTICE
For more questions on SPUR Objectives, use *Lesson Master 10-7,* shown below.

EXTENSION
Students can illustrate the square of a binomial with tiles, using *Teaching Aid 53.* Example:

2x + 3 (across); 2x + 3 (down)

x^2	x^2	x	x	x
x^2	x^2	x	x	x
x	x	1	1	1
x	x	1	1	1
x	x	1	1	1

$= 4x^2 + 12x + 9$

NAME ____________

LESSON MASTER 10–7
QUESTIONS ON **SPUR** OBJECTIVES

■SKILLS *Objective B (See pages 527–529 for objectives.)*
In 1–8, expand and simplify.

1. $(t + 3)^2$ $t^2 + 6t + 9$
2. $(r - 5)^2$ $r^2 - 10r + 25$
3. $(3x + 4)^2$ $9x^2 + 24x + 16$
4. $(10x - y)^2$ $100x^2 - 20xy + y^2$
5. $(7 - 2a)^2$ $49 - 28a + 4a^2$
6. $3(2k - 1)^2$ $12k^2 - 12k + 3$
7. $2x(x + 3)^2$ $2x^3 + 12x^2 + 18x$
8. $y^2 - (y - 6)^2$ $12y - 36$

9. Show that $(a - 5)^2$ and $(5 - a)^2$ are equal.

$(a - 5)^2$	$(5 - a)^2$
$= (a - 5)(a - 5)$	$= (5 - a)(5 - a)$
$= a^2 - 10a + 25$	$= 25 - 10a + a^2$
	$= a^2 - 10a + 25$

■PROPERTIES *Objective F*
In 10–15, show how to calculate in your head by using the square of a binomial.

10. 51^2 $(50 + 1)^2 = 2601$
11. 19^2 $(20 - 1)^2 = 361$
12. $(1.02)^2$ $(1 + .02)^2 = 1.0404$
13. $(0.98)^2$ $(1 - .02)^2 = .9604$
14. 201^2 $(200 + 1)^2 = 40,401$
15. 103^2 $(100 + 3)^2 = 10,609$

LESSON 10-8

RESOURCES

- Lesson Master 10-8
- Quiz on Lessons 10-5 to 10-8
- Visual for Teaching Aid 53: Tiles for Representing Polynomials

OBJECTIVES

C Recognize perfect squares and perfect square trinomials.
E Factor perfect square trinomials into a product of two binomials.

TEACHING NOTES

We do not intend that students should memorize the number patterns at the beginning of the lesson. Recognizing and factoring perfect square trinomials is the main thrust of the lesson. It is the latter patterns that should be learned.

Demonstrate the link between perfect square numbers and perfect square trinomials by substituting integers for m and n in **Example 2.** For instance, when $m = 5$ and $n = 8$, $9m^2 - 12mn + 4n^2 = 225 - 480 + 256 = 1$, which is exactly the square of $3m - 2n$, which in this case is $3 \cdot 5 - 2 \cdot 8$ or -1.

Alternate Approach The idea in the preceding paragraph can be used to check whether a trinomial is a perfect square. For instance in **Example 3,** let $m = 1$. Then $m^2 + 4m + 36 = 41$, which is not a perfect square, so the trinomial

LESSON

10-8 Recognizing Perfect Squares

Here is a table of the first twenty perfect square whole numbers.

n	1	2	3	4	5	6	7	8	9	10
n^2	1	4	9	16	25	36	49	64	81	100

n	11	12	13	14	15	16	17	18	19	20
n^2	121	144	169	196	225	256	289	324	361	400

You are probably able to recognize many of the numbers in the second row as perfect squares the moment you see them, but what about numbers you don't recognize? Are 528 and 3325 perfect squares? A calculator can help you answer these questions, but it can be handy to recognize perfect squares in your head—or at least to recognize numbers which cannot be perfect squares.

Look at the table above. All the perfect square numbers end with one of these digits:

$$1, 4, 5, 6, 9, 0.$$

It can be shown that *all* perfect square whole numbers end with one of these digits. So any whole number ending with 2, 3, 7, or 8 *cannot* be a perfect square.

There is another pattern hinted at in the table above. Note that $5^2 = 25$ and $15^2 = 225$. Here are some other squares of numbers ending in 5.

25^2	35^2	125^2
625	1225	15,625

All of these perfect squares end with 25. Also, the part of the number before the last two digits is always even and is the product of two consecutive whole numbers.

In 625, $6 = 2 \cdot 3$.
In 1225, $12 = 3 \cdot 4$.
In 15,625 $156 = 12 \cdot 13$.

Example 1 Determine if each number is a perfect square.
a. 528 **b.** 3325 **c.** 4225

Solution
a. Since 528 ends in 8, it cannot be a perfect square.
b. 3325 ends in 25, but 33 is odd, so 3325 is not a perfect square.
c. 4225 ends in 25, and $42 = 6 \cdot 7$, so 4225 is a perfect square. It is the square of 65.

Recognizing perfect square trinomials can also be a useful skill. If you switch the sides of each equation in the perfect square trinomial pattern, you get $a^2 + 2ab + b^2 = (a + b)^2$ and $a^2 - 2ab + b^2 = (a - b)^2$. The binomials $a + b$ and $a - b$ in the pattern are square roots of the original trinomials.

Recall, whenever a binomial is squared, the result is a trinomial in which:

(1) The first and last terms are the squares of the terms of the binomial.
(2) The middle term is twice the product of the terms of the binomial.

Example 2 Write the perfect square trinomial $9m^2 - 12mn + 4n^2$ as the square of a binomial.

Solution The first and last terms are the squares of 3m and $2n$. Since the middle term of the trinomial is subtracted, each factor will be a difference. So $9m^2 - 12mn + 4n^2 = (3m - 2n)^2$.

Check Expand $(3m - 2n)^2$.

$$\begin{aligned}(3m - 2n)(3m - 2n) &= 9m^2 - 6mn - 6mn + 4n^2 \\ &= 9m^2 - 12mn + 4n^2\end{aligned}$$

It checks.

You must be sure to check your answers to be certain that all the signs are correct. The Perfect Square Trinomial Pattern will also tell you when a trinomial is *not* a perfect square.

is not one either. (However, this is not a sure method. When $m = 0$ or $m = 5$, the value of the trinomial is a perfect square.)

In the solution of **Example 3,** students should also realize that the middle term of $m^2 + 4m + 36$ can be checked by comparing it to the pattern $a^2 + 2ab + b^2$. Here $a = m$ and $b = 6$. Since $4m \neq 2 \cdot m \cdot 6$, the expression $m^2 + 4m + 36$ is not a perfect square trinomial.

ADDITIONAL EXAMPLES
1. Determine if each number is a perfect square.

a. 7225
Yes

b. 427
No

c. 3328
No

2. Write $25y^2 + 70y + 49$ as the square of a binomial.
$\mathbf{(5y + 7)^2}$

3. Is $100x^2 + 60x + 9$ a perfect square?
Yes

4. Solve $k^2 + 18k + 81 = 144$.
$\mathbf{k = 3}$ **or** $\mathbf{k = -21}$

NOTES ON QUESTIONS
Question 9: You might remind students that, except under restricted circumstances, testing special cases can never prove that a statement is true for all numbers, although it may suggest that it is. However, one counterexample is enough to prove that a generalization is false.

Making Connections for Questions 17 and 18: These are preparation for the next lesson.

FOLLOW-UP

MORE PRACTICE
For more questions on SPUR Objectives, use *Lesson Master 10-8,* shown on page 511.

EXTENSION
1. Students can demonstrate the difference between a perfect square trinomial and an ordinary one using *Teaching Aid 53.* An area of $x^2 + 6x + 9$ can be rearranged to form a square with sides $x + 3$, while one of $x^2 + 6x + 8$ cannot (without cutting the pieces). Yet $x^2 + 6x + 8$ can be the area of a rectangle with sides $x + 2$ and $x + 4$, but $x^2 + 6x + 1$ cannot be represented as a rectangle, illustrating a prime polynomial.

2. If your students are intrigued by the number patterns at the beginning of the lesson, they may enjoy seeing how algebra can be used to prove that patterns hold. Here is an example from elementary number theory.

Theorem: If a number is the square of a whole number, then it is either a multiple of 4 or one more than a multiple of 4.

Example 3 Is the trinomial $m^2 + 4m + 36$ a perfect square?

Solution The first and third terms are the perfect squares of m and 6. If the trinomial could be factored using the method in Example 2, it would equal $(m + 6)^2$. But checking,

$$(m + 6)^2 = m^2 + 12m + 36.$$

This does not equal $m^2 + 4m + 36$, so $m^2 + 4m + 36$ is not a perfect square trinomial.

Recognizing perfect squares can make solving some equations a simple task.

Example 4 Solve $x^2 + 6x + 9 = 2025$.

Solution Recognize that $x^2 + 6x + 9$ is a perfect square trinomial, the square of $x + 3$. Also note that 2025 is a perfect square, the square of 45. So the equation is

$$(x + 3)^2 = 2025.$$

Take a square root of each side. This gives two possibilities:

$$x + 3 = 45 \quad \text{or} \quad x + 3 = -45$$
$$x = 42 \quad \text{or} \quad x = -48$$

There are two solutions, 42 and -48.

Check Does $42^2 + 6 \cdot 42 + 9 = 2025$?
Yes. $1764 + 252 + 9 = 2025$

Does $(-48)^2 + 6 \cdot -48 + 9 = 2025$?
Yes. $2304 - 288 + 9 = 2025$

Questions

Covering the Reading

1. All perfect square whole numbers end with one of the digits __?__, __?__, __?__, __?__, __?__, or __?__. **1; 4; 5; 6; 9; 0**

In 2–5, determine if the number is a perfect square.

2. 324 **Yes**

3. 2125 **No**

4. 7225 **Yes**

5. 3063 **No**

6. Write $4m^2 - 4mn + n^2$ as the square of a binomial. **$(2m - n)^2$**

7. a. $x^2 + 10x + 25$ is a perfect square trinomial. What binomial squared equals $x^2 + 10x + 25$? **$(x + 5)$**
   b. Solve $x^2 + 10x + 25 = 9$. **-2 or -8**

8. Solve $(t - 5)^2 = 361$. **24 or -14**

Applying the Mathematics

9. Refer to the table at the beginning of the lesson. The number in the tens place of the perfect squares ending with 6 is *odd*. It can be shown that no perfect square ending in 6 can have an even number in the tens place.
   a. Use this fact to decide which of the following might be perfect squares.
   (i) 576 (ii) 686 (iii) 776 **i or iii**
   b. Test your answers to part a in order to decide if *all* whole numbers ending in 6 with an odd digit in the tens place are perfect squares.
   No, $576 = 24^2$, but 776 is not a perfect square.

In 10 and 11, determine whether or not the trinomial is a perfect square.

10. $4x^2 + 24x + 9$ **No** 11. $9w^2 + 18wz + 9z^2$ **Yes**

12. Solve $9t^2 - 12t + 4 = 100$ by rewriting the left side as the square of a binomial and then chunking. **$t = 4$ or $-\frac{8}{3}$**

13. This computer program uses a special case to test if $(4x - 2y)^2 = 16x^2 - 8xy + 4y^2$.

```
10 PRINT "ENTER VALUES FOR X AND Y"
20 INPUT X,Y
30 LET S = (4*X - 2*Y)*(4*X - 2*Y)
40 LET T = 16*X*X - 8*X*Y + 4*Y*Y
50 PRINT "S =" S, "T =" T
60 IF S = T THEN PRINT "THEY ARE EQUAL."
70 IF S<>T THEN PRINT "THEY ARE NOT EQUAL."
80 END
```

(Comment: S<>T means S<T or S>T.)

   a. What binomial does the program test? **$4x - 2y$**
   b. What will the computer print if you run the program for $x = 1$ and $y = 5$? **S = 36, T = -4 THEY ARE NOT EQUAL.**

Review

In 14–16, expand and simplify. *(Lesson 10-7)*

14. $(2p - q)^2$ **$4p^2 - 4pq + q^2$** 15. $\frac{1}{2}(m + 3n)^2$ **$\frac{1}{2}m^2 + 3mn + \frac{9}{2}n^2$** 16. $(x^2 - y^2)^2 + 2x^2y^2$ **$x^4 + y^4$**

In 17 and 18, multiply. *(Lesson 10-6)*

17. $(a - b)(a + b)$ **$a^2 - b^2$** 18. $(2c - 3d)(2c + 3d)$ **$4c^2 - 9d^2$**

Proof: Any whole number can be expressed as $2n$ (even) or $2n + 1$ (odd) where n is a whole number. If the number is even, its square is $(2n)^2 = 4n^2$, a multiple of 4. If the number is odd, its square is $(2n + 1)^2 = 4n^2 + 4n + 1 = 4(n^2 + n) + 1$, which is one more than a multiple of 4.

Students can check this result in the chart at the beginning of the lesson.

A second theorem is that the square of an odd number is always one more than a multiple of 8. Here's a proof:

Any odd number is of the form $2n + 1$. Now $(2n + 1)^2 = 4n^2 + 4n + 1$, which equals $4n(n + 1) + 1$. Since $n(n + 1)$ is even (recall the comment on Question 15 of Lesson 10-4), $4n(n + 1)$ is divisible by 8.

EVALUATION
A quiz covering Lessons 10-5 through 10-8 is provided in the Teacher's Resource File.

NAME ____________

LESSON MASTER 10–8
QUESTIONS ON **SPUR** OBJECTIVES

■SKILLS *Objective C (See pages 527–529 for objectives.)*
In 1–4, determine if the number is a perfect square.

1. 262 **no** 2. 289 **yes** 3. 123 **no** 4. 200 **no**

In 5–10, state whether the trinomial is a perfect square trinomial.

5. $x^2 + 4x + 4$ **yes** 6. $2y^2 - 6y + 9$ **no** 7. $36a^2 - 30a + 25$ **no**

8. $49t^2 + 42t - 9$ **no** 9. $4n^2 - 36nk + 81k^2$ **yes** 10. $144x^2 + 24xy + y^2$ **yes**

■SKILLS *Objective E*
In 11–18, write each perfect square trinomial as the square of a binomial. Otherwise, write "not a perfect square."

11. $w^2 + 18w + 81$ **$(w + 9)^2$** 12. $9a^2 - 12a + 4$ **$(3a - 2)^2$**

13. $100h^2 + 30h + 9$ **not a per. sq.** 14. $x^2 + 22xy + 121y^2$ **$(x + 11y)^2$**

15. $25a^2 - 80ab + 64b^2$ **$(5a - 8b)^2$** 16. $16u^2 + 56uv + 49v^2$ **$(4u + 7v)^2$**

17. $x^4 + 2x^2 + 1$ **$(x^2 + 1)^2$** 18. $d^2 + 4cd - 4c^2$ **not a per. sq.**

In 19–22, solve.

19. $(x - 2)^2 = 9$ **$x = 5$ or -1** 20. $(n + 7)^2 = 361$ **$n = 12$ or -26**

21. $(3t - 5)^2 = 225$ **$t = \frac{20}{3}$ or $-\frac{10}{3}$** 22. $3025 = (9 - d)^2$ **$d = 64$ or -46**

90

NOTES ON QUESTIONS
Question 25: The answer is a nice application of square roots where one might not expect it.

19. Write a simplified expression for the total area of the rectangles at the right. *(Lesson 10-3)* **$6x^2 + 8x$**

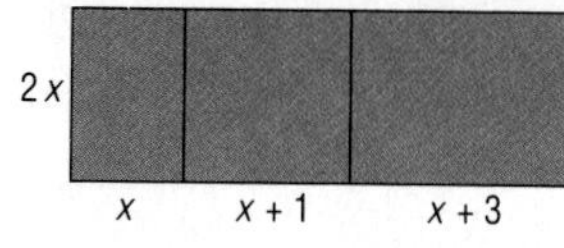

20. The formula $d = 0.042s^2 + 1.1s$ gives the approximate number of feet d needed to stop a car on a dry concrete road (including both reaction distance and braking distance) if the speed of the car is s miles per hour. How much farther will a car travel before stopping, if it is going 65 miles per hour instead of 55 miles per hour? *(Lesson 10-2)* **61.4 ft**

21. Jules bought 2 raffle tickets, one for a boat and one for a stereo. 5000 raffle tickets for the boat and 2250 tickets for the stereo were sold. What is the probability that Jules will win both the boat and the stereo? *(Lesson 4-8)* **$\approx 8.9 \cdot 10^{-8}$**

22. If Aurora invested \$1200 for three years at an annual yield of 5.7%, how much would she have at the end of three years? *(Lesson 9-1)* **\$1417.12**

23. Match each equation with its graph. *(Lesson 8-6)*

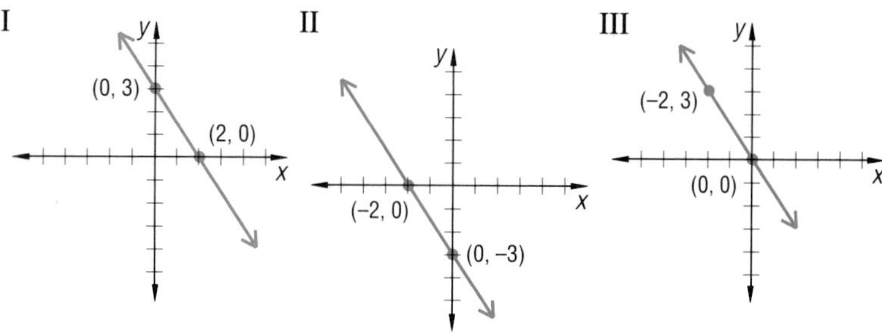

a. $3x + 2y + 6 = 0$ **II**
b. $3x + 2y = 6$ **I**
c. $3x + 2y = 0$ **III**

24. Which holds more: a cube with edges of length 4 or a box with dimensions 3 by 4 by 5? *(Lesson 4-1)* **the cube**

Exploration

25. a. How many perfect square whole numbers are there under 100? (Include zero.) **10**
b. How many perfect square whole numbers are there under 500? **23**
c. How many perfect square whole numbers are there under any given number n?
$\sqrt{n}$; if $\sqrt{n}$ is not a whole number, round up to whole number.

LESSON 10-9

Difference of Squares

Consider two numbers n and 6. Multiply their sum $n + 6$ by their difference $n - 6$.

$$(n + 6)(n - 6) = n^2 + 6n - 6n - 36$$

The two middle terms are opposites, so add to 0.

$$= n^2 - 6^2$$

You have seen this pattern before. In words, the product of the sum and difference of two numbers is the **difference of squares** of the two numbers.

Difference of Two Squares Pattern:

$$(a + b)(a - b) = a^2 - b^2.$$

Example 1 Multiply $(3y + 7)(3y - 7)$.

Solution The binomial factors are the sum and difference of the same terms. Use the difference of squares pattern with $a = 3y$ and $b = 7$.

$$\begin{aligned}(3y + 7)(3y - 7) &= (3y)^2 - 7^2 \\ &= 9y^2 - 49\end{aligned}$$

Check Let $y = 4$.
$(3 \cdot 4 + 7)(3 \cdot 4 - 7) = 19 \cdot 5 = 95$.
Does $9 \cdot 4^2 - 49 = 95$? Yes

The Difference of Squares pattern can help you find the product of some pairs of numbers in your head.

Example 2 Compute $53 \cdot 47$.

Solution Find the mean of 53 and 47, which is 50.
Write 53 and 47 as a sum and difference involving 50.

$$53 \cdot 47 = (50 + 3)(50 - 3)$$

Notice that 3 is the other number involved in both cases. Use the Difference of Squares Pattern to do the binomial multiplication.

$$\begin{aligned}(50 + 3)(50 - 3) &= 50^2 - 3^2 \\ &= 2500 - 9 \\ &= 2491\end{aligned}$$

LESSON 10-9

RESOURCES
■ Lesson Master 10-9

OBJECTIVES

B Multiply polynomials.
E Factor the difference of squares into a product of two binomials.
F Apply $(a + b)(a - b) = a^2 - b^2$ to multiply numbers in your head.

TEACHING NOTES

Alternate Approach
Your class may enjoy the following visual interpretation of the Difference of Two Squares Pattern. You begin with a square of side a and remove from one corner a square of side b. Then cut the remaining part in two and rearrange to make a rectangle with sides $a - b$ and $a + b$.

Step 1

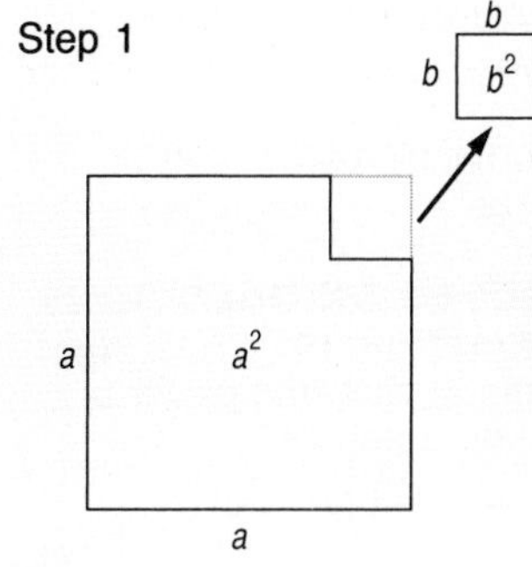

Step 2

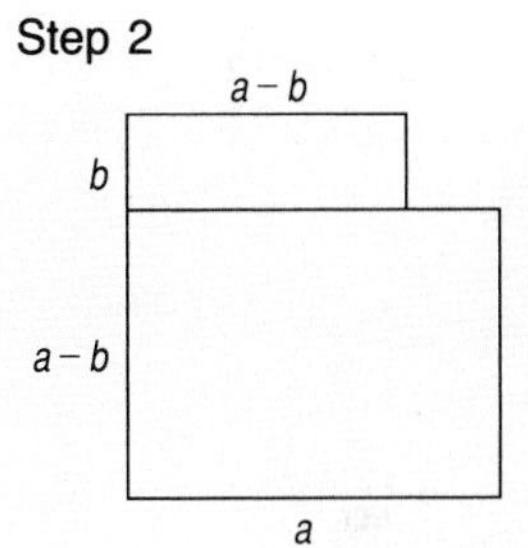

Step 3

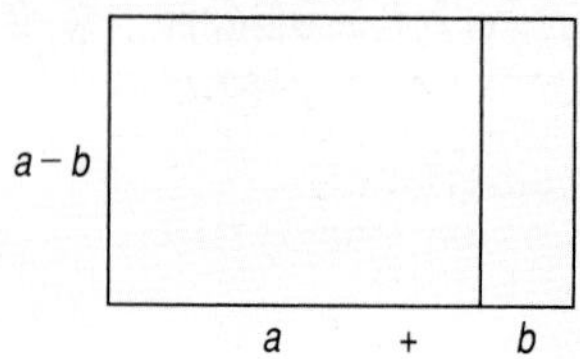

So, $a^2 - b^2 = (a - b)(a + b)$.

Making Connections
To preview Lesson 10-10, you might show students how to solve $x^2 = 9$ by a method other than taking square roots. Subtract 9 from each side.

$$x^2 - 9 = 0$$

Factor.

$$(x - 3)(x + 3) = 0$$

The product can be zero if and only if one of the factors is zero, from which $x = 3$ or $x = -3$.

ADDITIONAL EXAMPLES

1. Multiply $(10n - 7)(10n + 7)$.
$\mathbf{100n^2 - 49}$

2. Compute $16 \cdot 24$ in your head.
$\mathbf{(20 - 4)(20 + 4) = 20^2 - 4^2 = 384}$

3. Write $81x^2 - 4$ as the product of two binomials.
$\mathbf{(9x - 2)(9x + 2)}$

4. Factor $144a^2 - 49y^2$.
$\mathbf{(12a - 7y)(12a + 7y)}$

NOTES ON QUESTIONS
Question 14: Take some time to show the power of using a pattern.

$$(x + \sqrt{11})(x - \sqrt{11}) = x^2 - (\sqrt{11})^2$$

is much easier than

$$(x + \sqrt{11})(x - \sqrt{11}) = x^2 - x\sqrt{11} + x\sqrt{11} - (\sqrt{11})^2$$

The shortcut in Example 2 works best when you can find the mean with little work and when the mean is easy to square. For example, to multiply 41 by 39:

(1) The mean is 40.
(2) 41 and 39 are both 1 away from 40.
(3) The product is $40^2 - 1^2 = 1600 - 1 = 1599$.

The shortcut uses the idea that $(40 + 1)(40 - 1) = 40^2 - 1^2$.

By reversing the pattern for the difference of squares you can factor a binomial in which one perfect square term is *subtracted* from another.

Example 3 Write the difference of squares $r^2 - 9s^2$ as the product of two binomials.

Solution Use the Difference of Two Squares Pattern with $a = r$ and $b = 3s$.

$$\begin{aligned} r^2 - 9s^2 &= r^2 - (3s)^2 \\ &= (r + 3s)(r - 3s) \end{aligned}$$

Check 1 Multiply. $(r + 3s)(r - 3s) = r^2 - 3rs + 3rs - 9s^2 = r^2 - 9s^2$

Check 2 Let $r = 5$, $s = 4$. Then

$$(r + 3s)(r - 3s) = (5 + 3 \cdot 4)(5 - 3 \cdot 4) = 17 \cdot -7 = -119.$$
$$r^2 - 9s^2 = 5^2 - 9 \cdot 4^2 = 25 - 9 \cdot 16 = 25 - 144 = -119.$$

It checks.

Example 4 Factor the difference of squares $25p^2q^2 - 1$.

Solution $25p^2q^2$ is a perfect square: $25p^2q^2 = (5pq)^2$.
1 is a perfect square: $1 = 1^2$
So, $25p^2q^2 - 1 = (5pq)^2 - 1^2 = (5pq + 1)(5pq - 1)$.

Check Multiply. $(5pq + 1)(5pq - 1) = 25p^2q^2 - 5pq + 5pq - 1 = 25p^2q^2 - 1$

Questions

Covering the Reading

1. Fill in the blank: $a^2 - b^2 = (a - b) \cdot$ __?__. **(a + b)**

In 2–4, multiply and simplify.

2. $(x + 13)(x - 13)$ **$x^2 - 169$**

3. $(5y - 7)(5y + 7)$ **$25y^2 - 49$**

4. $(w + kq)(w - kq)$ **$w^2 - k^2q^2$**

5. *Multiple choice* Which is *not* the difference of two squares? **(b)**
(a) $9 - w^2$
(b) $25k^2 + 36$
(c) $x^2y^2 - 1$
(d) $121m^2 - n^2$

In 6 and 7, compute using the method in Example 2.

6. $69 \cdot 71$

7. $85 \cdot 95$

$(70 - 1)(70 + 1) = 70^2 - 1^2 = 4899$; $(90 - 5)(90 + 5) = 90^2 - 5^2 = 8075$

8. *Multiple choice* Which cannot be written as a product of two binomial factors? **(a)**
(a) $x^2 + y^2$
(b) $x^2 - y^2$
(c) $x^2 + 2xy + y^2$
(d) $x^2 - 2xy + y^2$

In 9–12, write each difference of squares as the product of two binomials.

9. $x^2 - 1$ **$(x + 1)(x - 1)$**

10. $a^2 - 64b^2$ **$(a - 8b)(a + 8b)$**

11. $36m^2 - 25n^2$ **$(6m - 5n)(6m + 5n)$**

12. $16p^2q^2 - 100$ **$(4pq - 10)(4pq + 10)$**

Applying the Mathematics

13. Compute $8\frac{1}{2} \cdot 9\frac{1}{2}$ using the idea of Example 2. **$9^2 - (\frac{1}{2})^2 = 80\frac{3}{4}$**

14. Multiply $(x + \sqrt{11})(x - \sqrt{11})$. **$x^2 - 11$**

15. Multiply and simplify $(\frac{1}{2} + 3m^2)(\frac{1}{2} - 3m^2)$. **$\frac{1}{4} - 9m^4$**

16. A rectangle has 3 units more length and 3 units less width than the side of the colored square below.
a. Which has larger area, the square or the rectangle? **square**
b. How much larger is that area? **9 square units**

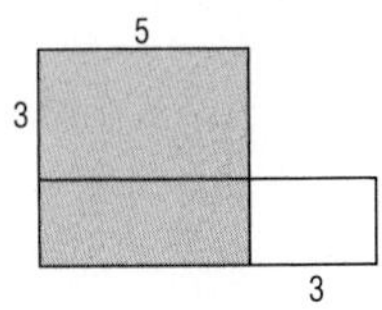

17. a. Write $x^4 - 81$ as the product of two binomials. **$(x^2 - 9)(x^2 + 9)$**
b. Write $x^4 - 81$ as the product of three binomials. **$(x - 3)(x + 3)(x^2 + 9)$**

18. Write $(x + y)^2 - 16$ as the product of two trinomials. **$(x + y - 4)(x + y + 4)$**

Alternate Approach for Question 16: This question can be answered algebraically or arithmetically, but there is also a geometric explanation. Begin with a 2×8 rectangle.

Step 1

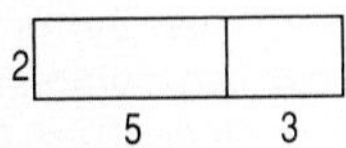

Step 2

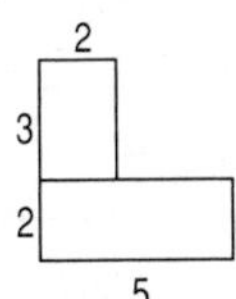

Step 3

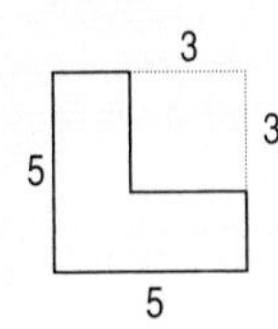

The area of the square is 25 but the area of the L-shape is 25 − 9 or 16.

NAME ______

LESSON **MASTER 10–9**
QUESTIONS ON **SPUR** OBJECTIVES

■SKILLS *Objective B* *(See pages 527–529 for objectives.)*
In 1–8, multiply and simplify.

1. $(x + 5)(x - 5)$ **$x^2 - 25$**
2. $(2y - 3)(2y + 3)$ **$4y^2 - 9$**
3. $(9a + 4b)(9a - 4b)$ **$81a^2 - 16b$**
4. $(2pr - 7)(2pr + 7)$ **$4p^2r^2 - 49$**
5. $(y - \sqrt{10})(y + \sqrt{10})$ **$y^2 - 10$**
6. $\left(a - \frac{1}{b}\right)\left(a + \frac{1}{b}\right)$ **$a^2 - \frac{1}{b^2}$**
7. $x(3x + 2)(3x - 2)$ **$9x^3 - 4x$**
8. $2y(y - 6)(y + 6)$ **$2y^3 - 72y$**

■SKILLS *Objective E*
In 9–14, write each difference of squares as the product of two binomials. Otherwise, write "not a difference of squares."

9. $t^2 - 24$ **not a diff. of sq.**
10. $9w^2 - 64$ **$(3w + 8)(3w - 8)$**
11. $144b^2 - 25c^2$ **$(12b + 5c)(12b - 5c)$**
12. $z^2 - 0.01$ **$(z + 0.1)(z - 0.1)$**
13. $0.16x^2 - 81$ **$(0.4x + 9)(0.4x - 9)$**
14. $\frac{4}{9}p^2 - 49q^2$ **$\left(\frac{2}{3}p + 7q\right)\left(\frac{2}{3}p - 7q\right)$**

■PROPERTIES *Objective F*
In 15–18, show how to calculate mentally by multiplying binomials.

15. $19 \cdot 21$ **$(20 - 1)(20 + 1) = 399$**
16. $7.8 \cdot 8.2$ **$(8 - 0.2)(8 + 0.2) = 63.96$**
17. $100.1 \cdot 99.9$ **$(100 + 0.1)(100 - 0.1) = 9999.99$**
18. $6\frac{1}{2} \cdot 7\frac{1}{2}$ **$\left(7 - \frac{1}{2}\right)\left(7 + \frac{1}{2}\right) = 48\frac{3}{4}$**

 91

NOTES ON QUESTIONS
Question 30: This question can be used to develop the notion that at times it is more useful to write 3 consecutive integers as $n - 1$, n, $n + 1$ than as n, $n + 1$, $n + 2$. If we choose the former representation, then the square of the middle number is one more than the product of the other two numbers because $n^2 - 1 = (n - 1)(n + 1)$.

FOLLOW-UP

MORE PRACTICE
For more questions on SPUR Objectives, use *Lesson Master 10-9,* shown on page 515.

ADDITIONAL ANSWERS
27.

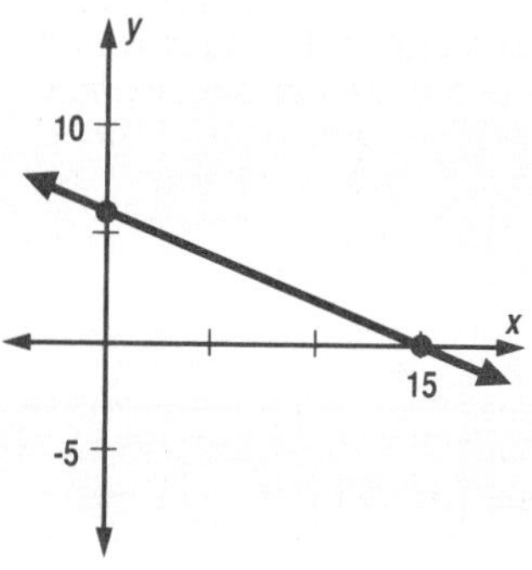

Review

19. *True or false* $49a^2 - 112a + 16$ is a perfect square trinomial. *(Lesson 10-8)* **False**

20. The area of a square is $4b^2 + 4b + 1$. Find the length of its side. *(Lesson 10-8)* **$2b + 1$**

21. Calculate in your head. *(Lesson 10-7)*
a. 21^2 **441** **b.** $(1.1)^2$ **1.21**

22. Multiply and simplify $(2x - y)(4x + 5y)$. *(Lesson 10-6)* **$8x^2 + 6xy - 5y^2$**

23. Factor $-9x^2 + 24x^3 + 18x^4$. *(Lesson 10-4)* **$3x^2(-3 + 8x + 6x^2)$**

24. Expand $(a + b + c)^2$. *(10-5)* **$a^2 + 2ab + 2ac + b^2 + 2bc + c^2$**

25. a. Simplify $3(4 - 5x^2 + 2x) - 8(2x^2 + 1) + 3(x^2 - 4)$. *(Lesson 10-3)* **a) $-28x^2 + 6x - 8$**
b. Give the degree of the polynomial from part a. *(Lesson 10-1)* **2**

26. Multiply $3b^2(4b^3 - 2by + 7)$. *(Lesson 10-3)* **$12b^5 - 6b^3y + 21b^2$**

27. Graph the line $2x + 5y = 30$. *(Lesson 8-8)* **See margin.**

28. Westinghouse Electric Corporation's second quarter earnings rose 12.3% to \$143.9 million. What were the company's first quarter earnings? *(Lessons 5-4, 6-3)* **≈\$128.14 million**

29. Solve **a.** $x = 2x$; **b.** $x > 2x$. *(Lessons 6-6, 6-7)* **a) $x = 0$; b) $x < 0$**

Exploration

30. a. Write down three consecutive integers. **sample: 1, 2, 3**
b. Square the second number. **sample: $2^2 = 4$**
c. Find the product of the first and the third. **sample: $1 \cdot 3 = 3$**
d. Do this with three more sets of consecutive integers. **See below.**
e. What do you notice? **See below.**
f. Explain why this will always happen. **See below.**

30d) 6, 7, 8; $7^2 = 49$; $6 \cdot 8 = 48$;
9, 10, 11; $10^2 = 100$, $9 \cdot 11 = 99$;
-3, -4, -5; $(-4)^2 = 16$, $-3 \cdot -5 = 15$
30e) The second number squared is one more than the product of the first and third numbers.
30f) Let n, $n + 1$, and $n + 2$ be the three consecutive numbers.
$(n + 1)^2 = n^2 + 2n + 1$
$n(n + 2) = n^2 + 2n$
$n^2 + 2n + 1$ is one more than $n^2 + 2n$

LESSON

10-10

The Zero Product Property

Suppose a baton is thrown upward from ground level at a speed of 35 feet per second. If there were no pull of gravity, the distance above the ground after t seconds would be $35t$, and the baton would never come down. Gravity pulls the baton down $16t^2$ feet in t seconds. So the distance d above the ground after t seconds is given by

$$d = 35t - 16t^2.$$

In this situation, how long before the baton hits the ground? At ground level the distance d is zero, so to answer this question you need to solve the equation $35t - 16t^2 = 0$. This equation can be solved using common monomial factoring and the **Zero Product Property.**

Zero Product Property:

For any real numbers a and b, if the product of a and b is 0, then $a = 0$ or $b = 0$.

Numbers may be represented by expressions. So in words, the Zero Product Property is: If two *expressions* multiply to zero, one or the other (or both) must be zero. This property is often combined with chunking to solve equations involving products of binomials or products of a monomial with binomials. Here are three examples.

Example 1 Solve for x: $5(x - 3) = 0$.

Solution 1 Use the Zero Product Property. Either $5 = 0$ or $x - 3 = 0$. We know $5 \neq 0$. So $x - 3 = 0$, which means $x = 3$.

Solution 2 Use the Distributive Property.

$$5x - 15 = 0$$
$$5x = 15$$
$$x = 3$$

LESSON 10-10

RESOURCES

■ Lesson Master 10-10

OBJECTIVES

G Recognize and use the Zero Product Property to solve equations.

I Translate real situations into polynomials.

TEACHING NOTES

Reading Emphasize the last paragraph of the lesson. We can only use the method of this lesson to determine the value of numbers if their product is *zero.* To illustrate this, you can ask your students for many solutions to $ab = 6$.

You might point out that generally second-degree equations have two solutions. Equations with one solution, like $(x + 6)(x + 6) = 0$ can also be discussed. Remind students that they have already seen some second-degree equations that have no solution, like $x^2 = -4$.

ADDITIONAL EXAMPLES

1. Solve for y: $11(2y - 8) = 0$.
4

2. For what values of k does $(k - 4)(5k - 3) = 0$?
4, $\frac{3}{5}$

3. Solve for x: $7x(9 + x) = 0$.
0, -9

4. A model rocket is launched into the air at a speed of 160 feet per second. Its distance d above the ground is given by $d = 160t - 16t^2$. After how many seconds will the rocket have fallen back to the ground?
$160t - 16t^2 = 0$, which has solutions 0 and 10; the former is when the rocket left the ground, the latter is when it hits, so the answer is 10 seconds.

NOTES ON QUESTIONS

Question 12: This question can be answered by factoring $ax^2 + bx$ or by *trial and error*. If the latter method is used, students will see that substituting 0 for x yields $0 + 0 = 0$.

Question 13: You can reinforce the idea that there is not enough information by giving two additional clues.

Clue 1: x and y are both positive.

Clue 2: x is even and y is odd.

There still is not enough information! However, if the following two clues are added, then x and y are determined.

Clue 3: $x + y = 7$.

Clue 4: $x > y$.

By including these, we know that $x = 6$ and $y = 1$.

Making Connections for Questions 14 and 15: These questions show how to solve some quadratic equations by the Zero Product Property. When students learn the Quadratic Formula in Chapter 12, they should be careful not to forget these simpler methods.

Example 2 For what values of y does $(y + 3)(y - 2) = 0$?

Solution Using the Zero Product Property, either the chunk $(y + 3)$ equals zero, or the chunk $(y - 2)$ equals zero. Solve each equation for y.

$$y + 3 = 0 \quad \text{or} \quad y - 2 = 0$$
$$y = -3 \quad \text{or} \quad y = 2$$

So y is either 2 or -3.

Check Let $y = 2$: $(2 + 3)(2 - 2) = 5 \cdot 0 = 0$.
Let $y = -3$: $(-3 + 3)(-3 - 2) = 0 \cdot -5 = 0$.

Example 3 Solve for m: $3m(4m - 1) = 0$.

Solution Either the monomial $3m = 0$ or the binomial $(4m - 1) = 0$. Solving each equation for m,

$$3m = 0 \quad \text{or} \quad 4m - 1 = 0$$
$$m = 0 \quad \text{or} \quad 4m = 1$$
$$m = \tfrac{1}{4}.$$

So $m = 0$ or $\frac{1}{4}$.

Check Let $m = 0$. $3 \cdot 0(4 \cdot 0 - 1) = 0 \cdot -1 = 0$
Let $m = \frac{1}{4}$. $3 \cdot \frac{1}{4}(4 \cdot \frac{1}{4} - 1) = \frac{3}{4} \cdot 0 = 0$

Common monomial factoring turns a polynomial into a product of factors. If the product of factors is zero, then the Zero Product Property can be used.

Example 4 Refer to the baton toss at the beginning of this lesson. How long was the baton in the air?

Solution We need to solve $35t - 16t^2 = 0$.
Factoring, $t(35 - 16t) = 0$.
By the Zero Product Property,

$$\text{either } t = 0 \quad \text{or} \quad 35 - 16t = 0.$$
$$t = 0 \quad \text{or} \quad -16t = -35$$
$$t = 0 \quad \text{or} \quad t = \tfrac{-35}{-16} \approx 2.19.$$

The solution $t = 0$ means the baton was at ground level at the start. The solution $t \approx 2.19$ means that it hit the ground again after about 2.19 seconds. So it was in the air for about 2.19 seconds.

A word of caution: to use the Zero Product Property, the product must be *zero*. This property does *not* work for an equation such as $(x + 3)(x - 2) = 1$.

Questions

Covering the Reading

1. State the Zero Product Property. **For any real numbers a and b, if the product of a and b is 0, then $a = 0$ or $b = 0$**

2. For what values of k does $(k + 4)(k - 1) = 0$? **-4, 1**

In 3–6, solve.

3. $2x(3x - 5) = 0$ **$0, \frac{5}{3}$**

4. $-18x(12 - 5x) = 0$ **$0, \frac{12}{5}$**

5. $(y - 15)(9y - 8) = 0$ **$15, \frac{8}{9}$**

6. $(p - 3)(2p + 4) = 0$ **3, -2**

7. A ball is thrown upward from ground level at 45 feet per second. The distance d above the ground after t seconds is $d = 45t - 16t^2$. After how many seconds will the ball hit the ground? **2.8125**

8. Why can't the Zero Product Property be used on the equation $(w + 1)(w + 2) = 3$? **It only applies to products equal to 0.**

Applying the Mathematics

In 9 and 10, solve.

9. $4x(x - 11)(2x + 7) = 0$ **$0, 11, -\frac{7}{2}$**

10. $0 = (.4y - 2.1)(y - 18.62)(5.2 - .3y)$ **$5.25, 18.62, 17.\overline{3}$**

11. A human cannonball in the circus is fired upward from the cannon at 80 feet per second. In t seconds, the cannonball will be $80t - 16t^2$ feet above where it was fired. In how many seconds will the cannonball reach a net that is the same height as the cannon? **5**

12. *Multiple choice* In the equation $ax^2 + bx = 0$, one solution for x is always **(d)**

(a) 1 (b) a (c) b (d) 0.

13. *Multiple choice* If $xy = 6$, then **(c)**

(a) $x = 6$ or $y = 6$. (b) $x = 3$ and $y = 2$.

(c) there is not enough information to tell.

14. Consider the equation $2v^2 = 3v$.

a. subtract $3v$ from both sides; **$2v^2 - 3v = 0$**

b. solve using the Zero Product Property. **$0, \frac{3}{2}$**

15. Given the equation $t^2 - 6t + 9 = 9$, **See margin.**

a. add -9 to both sides and solve using the Zero Product Property;

b. recognize the left side as a perfect square and solve by taking square roots.

Question 26b: This question can be answered by calculating $11 \div 1/3$ or by substituting zero for y in the equation.

FOLLOW-UP

MORE PRACTICE
For more questions on SPUR Objectives, use *Lesson Master 10-10,* shown below.

ADDITIONAL ANSWERS

15.a. $t^2 - 6t = 0$
$t(t - 6) = 0$
$t = 0$ or 6
b. $(t - 3)^2 = 9$
$t - 3 = 3$ or $t - 3 = -3$
$t = 6$ or 0

NAME ______________________

LESSON **MASTER 10–10**
QUESTIONS ON **SPUR** OBJECTIVES

■PROPERTIES *Objective G (See pages 527–529 for objectives.)*

1. In which of the following can the Zero Product Property be used to solve the equation?

(a) $(x + 5)(x - 1) = 4$ (b) $(3y + 4)(2y - 5) = 9$
(c) $c^2 - 4c = 0$ (d) $t(t - 8)(4t + 6) = 0$ **c, d**

In 2–13, solve.

2. $x(x - 8) = 0$ **$x = 0$ or 8**

3. $-3y(2y - 8) = 0$ **$y = 0$ or 4**

4. $(L - 7)(4L + 9) = 0$ **$L = 7$ or $-\frac{9}{4}$**

5. $(2W + 12)(3W + 21) = 0$ **$W = -6$ or -7**

6. $0 = (a - 0.4)(a + 0.9)$ **$a = 0.4$ or -0.9**

7. $(3b - 2.1)(2b + 4.6) = 0$ **$b = 0.7$ or -2.3**

8. $0 = x(3x + 18)(2x - 9)$ **$x = 0, -6,$ or $\frac{9}{2}$**

9. $0 = -3a(a + 15)(2a - 7)$ **$a = 0, -15,$ or $\frac{7}{2}$**

10. $(z - 4)(z + 14)(z + 23) = 0$ **$z = 4, -14,$ or -23**

11. $0 = (3k + 7)(5k - 8)(4k - 13)$ **$k = -\frac{7}{3}, \frac{8}{5},$ or $\frac{13}{4}$**

12. $4x^2 - 8x = 0$ **$x = 0$ or 2**

13. $5v^2 = 35v$ **$v = 0$ or 7**

■USES *Objective I*

14. An arrow is shot into the air at 120 feet per second. The distance d above the ground after t seconds is $d = 120t - 16t^2$. After how many seconds will the arrow hit the ground? **7.5 seconds**

15. An arrow is shot up on Mars at 120 feet per second. The distance d above the ground after t seconds is $d = 120t - 6t^2$. After how many seconds will the arrow hit the surface of Mars? **20 seconds**

92

EXTENSION
Question 12 leads to other questions. Ask students to find one number that is a solution to an equation like $3x^3 - 7x^2 + 4x = 0$ or even $5x^7 - 24x^2 + 3x = 0$. (0) Also, you can ask what can be determined about $ax^2 + bx = 0$ if you know that 1 is a solution. ($a = -b$)

ADDITIONAL ANSWERS
25.

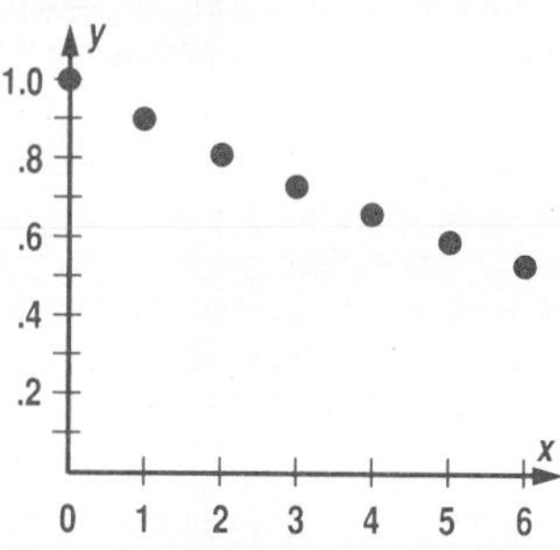

x = Number of panes of glass
y = Fraction of light

31b.

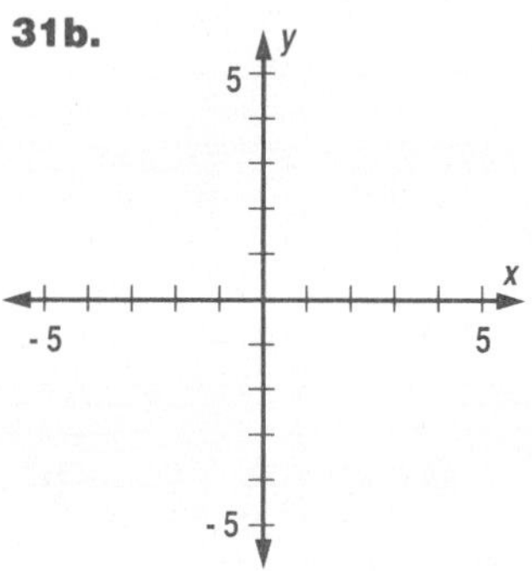

The graph of $xy = 0$ is the union of the coordinate axes.

31c.

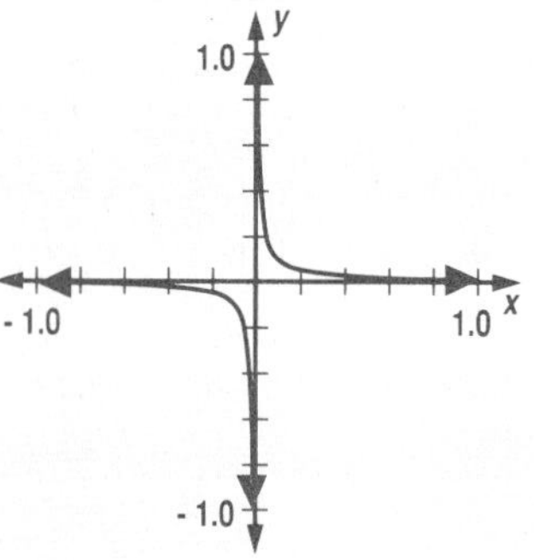

The graph of $xy = \frac{1}{100}$ is the union of two curves (a hyperbola) that approximate the coordinate axes.

16. If $a \neq 0$, solve for x: $ax^2 - ax = 0$. **0, 1**

17. The product of four consecutive integers is zero. Find all possible values for the smallest of these integers. **-3, -2, -1, 0**

Review

In 18 and 19, factor. *(Lessons 10-4, 10-9)*

18. $14x^2 - 7xy + 28x^3$. **$7x(2x - y + 4x^2)$**

19. $49p^2 - q^2$. **$(7p - q)(7p + q)$**

In 20–22, multiply and simplify. *(Lessons 6-3, 10-5, 10-9)*

20. $4y(3y - 7)$ **$12y^2 - 28y$**

21. $(3x + 7)(3x - 7)$ **$9x^2 - 49$**

22. $(3z + 7)(5z + q - 8)$ **$15z^2 + 11z + 3zq + 7q - 56$**

23. Find the area of a square which is $4e + 1$ units on a side. *(Lesson 10-7)* **$(4e + 1)^2$ or $16e^2 + 8e + 1$**

24. Simplify $\frac{13x^2 - 14x}{x}$. *(Lesson 10-4)* **$13x - 14$**

25. A certain glass allows $\frac{9}{10}$ of the light hitting it to pass through. The fraction of light y passing through x thickness of glass is then

$$y = \left(\frac{9}{10}\right)^x.$$

Draw a graph of this equation for $0 \leq x \leq 6$. *(Lesson 9-4)* **See margin.**

26. An inchworm starts at a height of 11 ft on the trunk of an apple tree and crawls down at a constant rate of 4 inches ($\frac{1}{3}$ ft) per hour. After x hours, the inchworm will be y feet above the ground, where $y = -\frac{1}{3}x + 11$. **slope = $-\frac{1}{3}$, y-intercept = 11**

a. Give the slope and y-intercept of this equation. *(Lesson 8-2)*

b. How long will it take the inchworm to reach the ground? *(Lesson 6-1)* **33 hours if it doesn't fall or isn't eaten**

In 27–29, solve. *(Lessons 5-7, 7-4)*

27. $\frac{3}{5} = \frac{x}{15}$ **9**

28. $1 = \frac{0.6}{m}$ **0.6**

29. $\frac{d}{9} = \frac{4}{d}$ **6 or -6**

30. In 1986, World Wide Wrench Company increased all their prices by 12% across the board. Their basic wrench now sells for \$9.25. What did it sell for in 1985? *(Lessons 5-4, 6-3)* **\$8.26**

Exploration

31. Given the equation $xy = 0$, **sample: (0, 0), (0, 1), (-1,0), (0, -2), (2, 0)**

a. give five different ordered pairs (x, y) that work in this equation.

b. Graph this equation on a coordinate plane. Describe this graph in words. **See margin.**

c. Compare the graph in part b with the graph of $xy = \frac{1}{100}$. **See margin.**

LESSON 10-11 Recognizing Factors of Polynomials

Is $x^2 - 7x + 12$ equal to $(x - 3)(x - 4)$?

It is hard to answer this question just by looking because the trinomial $x^2 - 7x + 12$ has a different appearance than the product of the two binomials $(x - 3)$ and $(x - 4)$.

There are several ways of determining whether expressions are equal. In this lesson, you will study two of these methods, both of which are familiar to you. The first is simply to use the properties of algebra on one expression to make it look like the other. The second is to test a special case.

Example 1 Is $x^2 - 7x + 12$ equal to $(x - 3)(x - 4)$?

Solution 1 Multiply the binomials.

$$(x - 3)(x - 4) = x^2 - 4x - 3x + 12$$
$$= x^2 - 7x + 12$$

The expressions are equal, thus $(x - 3)$ and $(x - 4)$ are factors of $x^2 - 7x + 12$.

Solution 2 Test special cases. Substitute 5 for x in each expression.

$$(5)^2 - 7(5) + 12 = 25 - 35 + 12 = 2$$
$$(5 - 3)(5 - 4) = 2 \cdot 1 = 2$$

Let $x = -2$.

$$(-2)^2 - 7(-2) + 12 = 4 + 14 + 12 = 30$$
$$(-2 - 3)(-2 - 4) = -5 \cdot -6 = 30$$

The special cases work so it appears that the expressions are equal.

Testing a special case can easily show when expressions are *not* equal. Recall that if two expressions are not equal for only one special case, then you have found a *counterexample*. This means the expressions are not equal. But if you can't find a counterexample, it is likely (but not certain) that the expressions are equal.

When faced with a multiple choice question, it is sometimes possible to arrive at the right answer by eliminating wrong ones. This is called **ruling out possibilities**. When you have ruled out all answers but one, then that one is the correct choice. Many people like multiple-choice tests because even if you don't know the correct answer to a question you still have a chance of getting it right.

LESSON 10-11

RESOURCES
- Lesson Master 10-11
- Visual for Teaching Aid 53: Tiles for Representing Polynomials
- Visual for Teaching Aid 57: Graph and Table for **Question 14**

OBJECTIVE

H Recognize factors of polynomials using the properties of algebra, testing a special case and ruling out possibilities.

TEACHING NOTES

Students should find this lesson to be a relatively easy one. It allows a review of multiplication of polynomials and the special patterns from Lessons 10-7 and 10-9. Students should recognize perfect square trinomials and the difference of two squares.

Point out that **Example 2** and many of the questions in this lesson are multiple-choice items. Some students believe that it is not ethical to rule out possibilities on a multiple-choice test. All students should be made aware that the makers of such tests often purposely design the choices so that certain ones can be ruled out easily and only a couple of choices remain. Occasionally only one choice remains. Not only is it fair to rule out possibilities in such tests, it is expected.

ADDITIONAL EXAMPLES

1. Is $3x^2 + 2x + 10$ equal to $(3x + 5)(x - 2)$?
No

2. Multiple choice. Which expression equals $x^2 - x - 6$?
(a) $(x - 6)(x + 1)$
(b) $(x - 1)(x + 6)$
(c) $(x - 3)(x + 2)$
(d) $(x - 2)(x + 3)$
c

Example 2 *Multiple choice* Which expression equals $x^2 + y^2$?
(a) $(x + y)^2$ (b) $(x + y)(x - y)$ (c) $(x - y)^2$ (d) none of (a)–(c)

Solution 1 Rule out answers by evaluating each of the choices using the FOIL algorithm.
(a) $(x + y)^2 = x^2 + 2xy + y^2$ (by the Perfect Square Trinomial Pattern). This does not equal $x^2 + y^2$.
(b) $(x + y)(x - y) = x^2 - y^2$ (by the Difference of Squares Pattern). This does not equal $x^2 + y^2$.
(c) $(x - y)^2 = x^2 - 2xy + y^2$ (again by the Perfect Square Trinomial Pattern). This does not equal $x^2 + y^2$.

None of the expressions equals $x^2 + y^2$, therefore (d) is the correct choice.

Solution 2 Test a special case. Let $x = 2$ and $y = 3$. Then $x^2 + y^2 = 4 + 9 = 13$ and the choices equal
(a) $(2 + 3)^2 = 25$ (b) $(2 + 3)(2 - 3) = -5$
(c) $(2 - 3)^2 = 1$ (d) none of (a)–(c).

Since none of (a)–(c) yields 13, (d) is the correct choice.

Questions

Covering the Reading

1) Use the properties of algebra on one expression to make it look like the other, or test a special case.

1. Name two ways of determining whether expressions are equal.

2. What are the factors of $x^2 - 7x + 12$? **(x − 3) and (x − 4)**

3. Determine if $x^2 + 9x - 10$ is equal to $(x + 10)(x - 1)$ by **a.** multiplying the binomials; **b.** testing two special cases.
a) $(x + 10)(x - 1) = x^2 + 9x - 10$; b) See margin.

4. When is testing a special case very useful?
if it leads to a counterexample

5. In Example 2, why is only one special case needed?
Each case gave a counterexample.

Applying the Mathematics

Questions 6–13 are *multiple choice*.

6. $ax + bx + ay + by =$ **(a)**
(a) $(a + b)(x + y)$ (b) $(a + x)(b + y)$
(c) $a(x + b + y)$ (d) none of (a)–(c)

7. $3x^2 - 5x - 2 =$ **(c)**
(a) $(3x - 1)(x + 2)$ (b) $(3x - 5)(x - 2)$ (c) $(3x + 1)(x - 2)$
(d) $(3x - 2)(x + 1)$ (e) none of (a)–(d)

8. $2x^4 + x^3y + 2xy^2 + y^3 =$ **(b)**
(a) $(2x^2 + y)(x^2 + y^2)$ (b) $(x^3 + y^2)(2x + y)$
(c) $(x + y^2)(2x + y)$ (d) none of (a)–(c)

522

9. $x^4 - 10x^2 + 18 =$ **(e)**
(a) $(x - 3)(x - 6)$ (b) $(x - 2)(x - 9)$ (c) $(x^2 - 3)(x^2 - 6)$
(d) $(x^2 - 2)(x^2 - 9)$ (e) none of (a)–(d)

10. $4y^2 + 12y + 9 =$ **(d)**
(a) $(4y + 1)(y + 9)$ (b) $(4y + 9)(y + 1)$ (c) $(2y + 1)(2y + 9)$
(d) $(2y + 3)^2$ (e) none of (a)–(d)

11. $25x^2 - 81 =$ **(c)**
(a) $(5x - 9)^2$ (b) $(25x - 1)(x + 81)$ (c) $(5x - 9)(5x + 9)$
(d) $(25x - 81)(x + 1)$ (e) none of (a)–(d)

12. Which expression equals $m + n$? **(d)**
(a) $\sqrt{m^2 + n^2}$ (b) $(\sqrt{m} + \sqrt{n})^2$
(c) $\dfrac{m^2 + n^2}{m + n}$ (d) none of (a)–(c)

13. Sylvia was working on a physics project and had to calculate several estimates using the formula $y^2 - 6y - 7$. She knew that the calculations would go faster if this expression was factored. Which of the following is equal to $y^2 - 6y - 7$? **(b)**
(a) $(y - 1)(y - 7)$ (b) $(y + 1)(y - 7)$ (c) $(y + 1)(y + 7)$
(d) $(y - 1)(y + 7)$ (e) none of (a)–(d)

Review

Diameter	Volume
8.3	10.3
8.6	10.3
8.8	10.2
10.5	16.4
10.7	18.8
11.0	15.6
11.0	18.2
11.1	22.6
11.2	19.9
11.3	24.2
11.4	21.0
11.4	21.4
11.7	21.3
12.0	19.1
12.9	22.2
12.9	33.8
13.3	27.4
13.7	25.7
13.8	24.7
14.0	34.5
14.2	31.7
14.5	36.3
16.3	42.6
17.3	55.4
17.5	55.7
17.9	58.3
18.0	51.0
18.0	51.5
20.6	77.0

14. Foresters in the Allegheny National Forest were asked to estimate the volume of timber in the black cherry trees in the forest. They had to do it without cutting all the black cherry trees down. They did cut down 29 trees of varying sizes. They measured the diameter of each tree and the volume (in cubic feet) of wood that the tree produced.
  a. Fit a line to the data by eye. **See graph.**
  b. Is it a good fit? **Yes**
  c. Find an equation for your line. **Using (11, 20) and (18, 60), $y = 5.7x - 42.9$**
  d. Estimate the volume of a black cherry tree with diameter 15 inches. *(Lesson 8-7)* **using the equation from part c, 42.6 ft³**

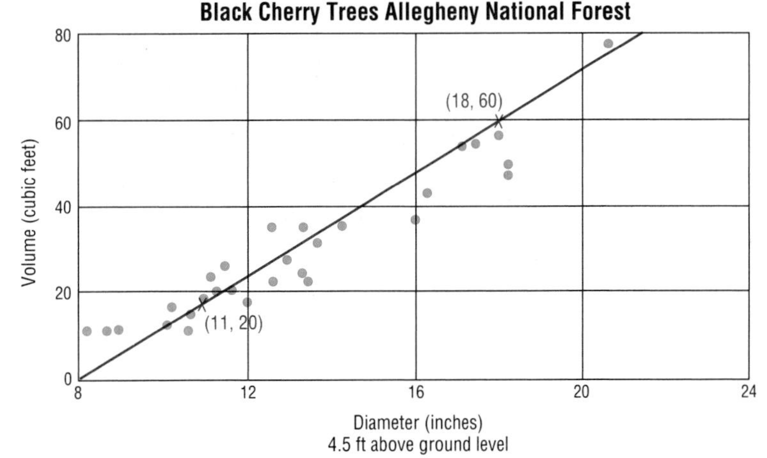

NOTES ON QUESTIONS

Question 12: The easiest way to answer this question is to test a special case. However, some good review can be done by discussing how each answer can be tested algebraically. For choice (a), check whether the square of $m + n$ gives the expression under the radical. In choice (b), expand $(\sqrt{m} + \sqrt{n})^2$. In choice (c), check to see if $m + n$ multiplied by the denominator produces the numerator.

Question 14: *Teaching Aid 57* can be used for this question.

ADDITIONAL ANSWERS

3b. Sample: let $x = 3$; $(13)(2) = 26$, and $3^2 + 9(3) - 10 = 26$. Let $x = -4$; $(6)(-5) = -30$, and $(-4)^2 + 9(-4) - 10 = -30$.

NAME ______

LESSON MASTER 10–11
QUESTIONS ON **SPUR** OBJECTIVES

■**PROPERTIES** *Objective H (See pages 527–529 for objectives.)*
In 1 and 2, answer the question by a. multiplying the binomials, b. testing two special cases.

1. Is $x^2 - 4x + 3$ equal to $(x - 3)(x - 1)$?
a. **yes** b. **sample: x = 1; 1 − 4 + 3 = (-2)(0)**
sample: x = 0; 3 = (-3)(-1)

2. Is $2a^2 - 3a - 20$ equal to $(2a + 5)(a - 4)$?
a. **yes** b. **sample: a = 1; 2 − 3 − 20 = (7)(-3)**
sample: a = 0; -20 = (5)(-4)

In 3–8, choose the best answer or write none.

3. $t^2 - 5t - 14 =$? **b**
(a) $(t + 7)(t - 2)$ (b) $(t - 7)(t + 2)$
(c) $(t + 7)(t + 2)$ (d) $(t - 7)(t - 2)$

4. $4b^2 + 27b + 18 =$? **c**
(a) $(2b + 9)(2b + 2)$ (b) $(2b + 6)(2b + 3)$
(c) $(4b + 3)(b + 6)$ (d) $(4b + 6)(b + 3)$

5. $6x^2 + 5x - 6 =$? **none**
(a) $(3x + 2)(2x + 3)$ (b) $(3x - 2)(2x - 3)$
(c) $(3x + 2)(2x - 3)$ (d) $(6x + 1)(x - 6)$

6. $x^2 - 2xy + 3x - 6y =$? **a**
(a) $(x + 3)(x - 2y)$ (b) $(x - 3)(x + 2y)$
(c) $(x + 3y)(x - 2)$ (d) $(x - 3y)(x + 2)$

7. $ac - bc + ad - bd =$? **d**
(a) $(a + b)(c - d)$ (b) $(a + d)(b - c)$
(c) $(a - d)(b + c)$ (d) $(a - b)(c + d)$

8. $x^3 - x^2 - 6x =$? **c**
(a) $(x^2 - 3)(x + 2)$ (b) $(x^2 + 2)(x - 3)$
(c) $x(x - 3)(x + 2)$ (d) $x(x + 3)(x - 2)$

NOTES ON QUESTIONS
Question 18: *Teaching Aid 53* can be used for this question.

FOLLOW-UP

MORE PRACTICE
For more questions on SPUR Objectives, use *Lesson Master 10-11,* shown on page 523.

EVALUATION
Alternative Assessment
Have students draw area diagrams which illustrate each of the following: (1) subtracting one polynomial from another, (2) multiplying a polynomial by a monomial, (3) common monomial factoring, (4) multiplying a trinomial by a binomial, and (5) multiplying a binomial by a binomial.

15. *Skill sequence* Solve. *(Lesson 10-10)*
a. $3(y - 2) = 0$ **2**
b. $3y(y - 2) = 0$ **0, 2**
c. $(3y + 4)(y - 2) = 0$ $\frac{-4}{3}$**, 2**
d. $(y - 5)(3y + 4)(y - 2) = 0$ **5,** $\frac{-4}{3}$**, 2**

16. Solve $15t^2 - 55t = 0$. *(Lesson 10-10)* **0,** $\frac{11}{3}$

17. Factor $100x - 100y + 100w - 100z$. *(Lesson 10-4)* $100(x - y + w - z)$

Exploration

18. The following diagram uses area to show the factoring of $x^2 + 4x + 3$.

$$x^2 + 4x + 3 = (x + 1)(x + 3)$$

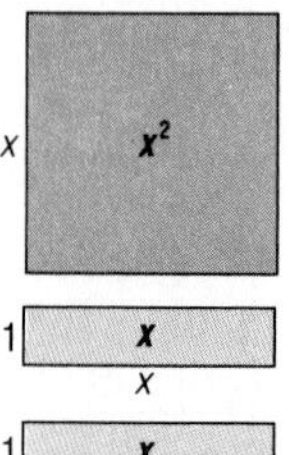

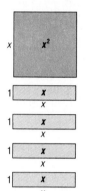

rearranged as

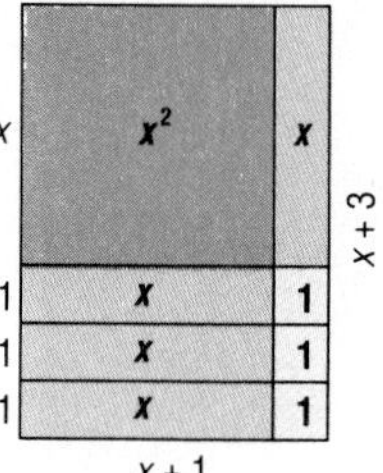

Make a drawing to show the factoring of
a. $x^2 + 7x + 10 = (x + 2)(x + 5)$;
b. $2x^2 + 9x + 4 = (2x + 1)(x + 4)$.

a.

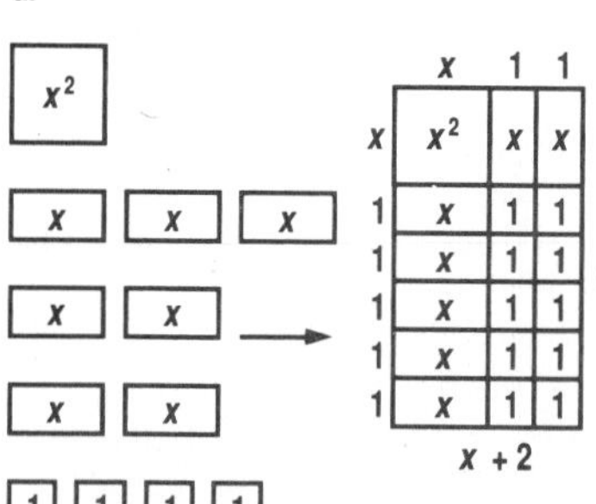

b.

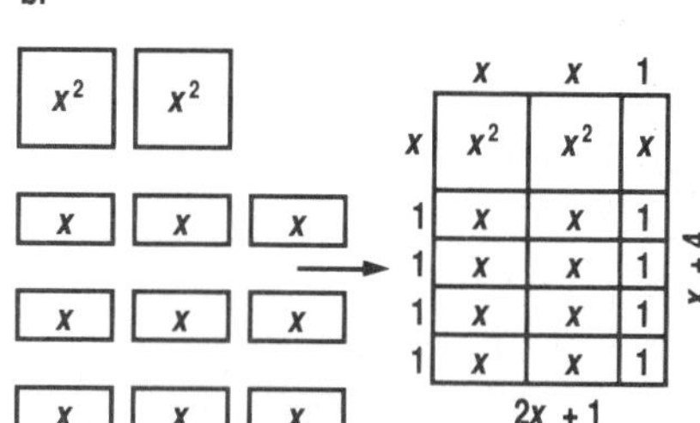

Summary

A term is a number, a product of numbers and variables, or a product of powers of numbers and variables. Polynomials are sums of terms and are classified by the number of terms. Polynomials arise from many situations. This chapter emphasizes situations where money is invested at the same rate but for different lengths of times. It also covers the use of polynomials in some formulas for areas, acceleration, and counting.

Like all algebraic expressions, polynomials can be added, subtracted, multiplied, and divided. All of these operations except division are studied in this chapter. Adding or subtracting polynomials is done by collecting like terms. Multiplying polynomials is done by multiplying each term of one polynomial by each term of the other, and then adding the products. Multiplication of polynomials can be represented by the area model.

Multiplication of binomials is a special case of multiplication of all polynomials and follows a pattern called FOIL.

$$(a + b)(c + d) = ac + ad + bc + bd$$

Certain special cases of this pattern are particularly important.

$$(a + b)(a + b) = a^2 + 2ab + b^2$$
$$(a - b)(a - b) = a^2 - 2ab + b^2$$
$$(a + b)(a - b) = a^2 - b^2$$

Reversing this process is called factoring. When the product of two or more factors is zero, then one of the factors must be zero. This Zero Product Property helps in solving certain equations.

Vocabulary

Below are the important new terms and phrases for this chapter. You should be able to give a general description and a specific example of each.

Lesson 10-1
polynomial
scale factor
polynomial in the variable x
constant term
degree of a polynomial
monomial, binomial, trinomial

Lesson 10-4
common monomial factoring

Lesson 10-5
Extended Distributive Property

Lesson 10-6
FOIL algorithm

Lesson 10-7
expanding a power of a polynomial
perfect square trinomial
Perfect Square Trinomial Patterns

Lesson 10-9
difference of squares
Difference of Two Squares Pattern

Lesson 10-10
Zero Product Property

Lesson 10-11
ruling out possibilities

SUMMARY

The Summary gives an overview of the entire chapter and provides an opportunity for students to consider the material as a whole. Thus, the Summary can be used to help students relate the concepts presented in the chapter.

VOCABULARY

Terms, symbols, and properties are listed by lesson to provide a checklist of things a student must know. Emphasize to students that they should read the vocabulary list carefully before starting the Progress Self-Test. If students do not understand the meaning of a term, they should refer back to the indicated lesson.

Definitions or descriptions of all terms in the vocabulary list may be found in the Glossary.

PROGRESS SELF-TEST

We cannot overemphasize the importance of these end-of-chapter materials. It is at this point that the material "gels" for many students, allowing them to solidify skills and understanding. In general, student performance should be markedly improved after these pages.

USING THE PROGRESS SELF-TEST
Assign the Progress Self-Test as a one-night assignment. Worked-out *solutions* for all questions are in the Selected Answers section at the back of the student book. Encourage students to take the Progress Self-Test honestly, grade themselves, and then be prepared to discuss the test in class.

Advise students to pay special attention to those Chapter Review questions (pages 527–529) which correspond to questions missed on the Progress Self-Test. A chart provided in the Selected Answers section in the student text keys the Progress Self-Test questions to the lettered SPUR Objectives in the Chapter Review or to the Vocabulary. It also keys the questions to the corresponding lessons where the material is covered.

ADDITIONAL ANSWERS
24.

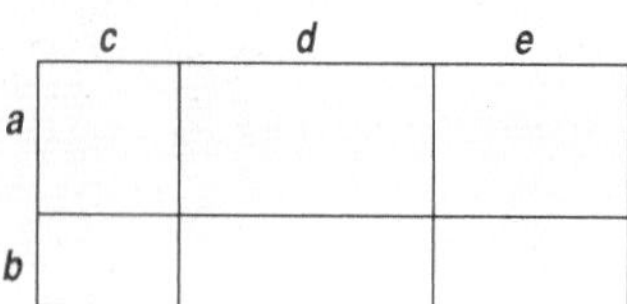

Progress Self-Test

Take this test as you would take a test in class. You will need a calculator. Then check your work with the solutions in the Selected Answers section in the back of the book. **$13x^2 - 7x - 23$**

1. a. Simplify $4x^2 - 7x + 9x^2 - 12 - 11$.
   b. Give the degree of this polynomial. **2nd**

In 2–11, perform the indicated operations and simplify. **$11k^3 - 5k^2 + 6k + 6$**

2. Add $4k^3 - k^2 + 8$ and $7k^3 - 4k^2 + 6k - 2$.
3. Subtract $2v^2 + 5$ from $9v^2 + 2$. **$7v^2 - 3$**
4. Multiply $3v^2 - 9 + 2v$ by 4. **$12v^2 - 36 + 8v$**
5. $6(3x^2 - 2x + 1) - 4(3x - 8)$ **$18x^2 - 24x + 38$**
6. $-5z(z^2 - 7z + 8)$ **$-5z^3 + 35z^2 - 40z$**
7. $(x - 7)(x + 9)$ **$x^2 + 2x - 63$**
8. $(4y - 2)(3y - 16)$ **$12y^2 - 70y + 32$**
9. $(q - 7)^2$ **$q^2 - 14q + 49$**
10. $(3x - 8)(3x + 8)$ **$9x^2 - 64$**
11. $(2a - 3)(a^2 + 5ab + 7b^2)$
    $2a^3 + 10a^2b + 14ab^2 - 3a^2 - 15ab - 21b^2$
12. Is $4x^2 - 10x + 25$ a perfect square trinomial? If so, of what binomial is it the square?
    No; $(2x - 5)^2 = 4x^2 - 20x + 25$, not $4x^2 - 10x + 25$.

In 13–16, factor.

13. $12m^3 - 2m^5$ **$2m^3(6 - m^2)$**
14. $500x^2y + 100xy + 50y$ **$50y(10x^2 + 2x + 1)$**
15. $z^2 - 81$ **$(z + 9)(z - 9)$**
16. $y^2 + 12y + 36$ **$(y + 6)(y + 6)$**
    18) $(30 - 1)(30 + 1) = 900 - 1 = 899$
17. Simplify $\frac{8c^2 + 4c}{c}$. **$4(2c + 1)$**
18. Show how you can compute $29 \cdot 31$ mentally.
19. *Multiple choice* $3y^2 - 17y - 6 =$ **(a)**
    (a) $(3y + 1)(y - 6)$ (b) $(3y - 17)(y - 6)$
    (c) $3y(y - 17)$ (d) $(3y - 6)(y + 1)$
    (e) none of (a)–(d).

In 20 and 21, solve.

20. $7z(5z - 2) = 0$ **$0, \frac{2}{5}$**
21. $(x - 13)(2x + 15) = 0$ **$13, -\frac{15}{2}$**
    $80x^2 + 60x + 90$
22. On his 18th birthday, Hank received \$80. He received \$60 on his 19th birthday and \$90 on his 20th birthday. If he had invested all this money at a scale factor x, how much total money would he have on his 20th birthday?
23. A tennis ball bounces up from ground level at 8 meters per second. An equation that estimates the distance d above ground (in meters) after t seconds is $d = 8t - 5t^2$. After how many seconds will the ball return to the ground? **$\frac{8}{5}$ sec**
24. Represent the product $(a + b)(c + d + e)$ using areas of rectangles. **See margin.**
25. Write a simplified polynomial expression for the volume of the figure below.
    $10y^3 + 84y^2 - 54y$

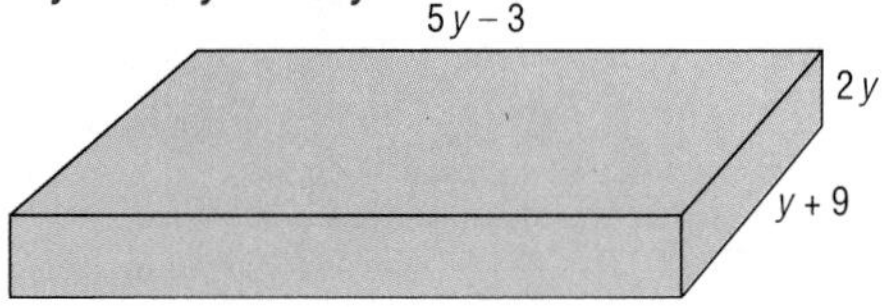

Chapter Review

Questions on SPUR Objectives

SPUR stands for **S**kills, **P**roperties, **U**ses, and **R**epresentations. The Chapter Review questions are grouped according to the SPUR Objectives for this chapter.

SKILLS deal with the procedures used to get answers.

Objective A. *Add and subtract polynomials.* *(Lessons 10-1, 10-2)* **1a) $7x^2 + 4x + 1$; 1b) 2**

In 1–2, **a.** simplify the expression; **b.** give its degree. **2a) $8m^4 + 10m^3 - 6m^2 - 3m$; 2b) 4**

1. $5x^2 - 3x + 2x^2 + 7x + 1$

2. $(8m^4 - 2m^3) + (12m^3 - 6m^2 - 3m)$

3. Add $1.3x^2 + 14$, $4.7x - 1$, and $2.6x^2 - 3x + 6$. **$3.9x^2 + 1.7x + 19$**

4. Subtract $3y^5 - 2y^3 + 8y$ from $4y^5 - 6y^3 + 4y + 2$. **$y^5 - 4y^3 - 4y + 2$**

In 5–8, simplify.

5. $(k - 4) - (k^2 + 1)$ **$-k^2 + k - 5$**

6. $(5p^2 - 1) - (6p^2 - p)$ **$-p^2 + p - 1$**

7. $2(4x^2 - x - 4) + 4(3x - 7)$

8. $6(3x^2 + 4x - 7) - 5(2x^2 - x + 11)$
7) $8x^2 + 10x - 36$ 8) $8x^2 + 29x - 97$

Objective B. *Multiply polynomials.* *(Lessons 10-3, 10-5, 10-6, 10-7, 10-9)*

In 9–22, multiply and simplify, if possible.

9. $4(x - x^3)$ **$4x - 4x^3$**

10. $3k(k^2 + 4k - 1)$ **$3k^3 + 12k^2 - 3k$**

11. $-2mn(3m - 2n + 4)$ **$-6m^2n + 4mn^2 - 8mn$**

12. $5xy(x + 3y^2)$ **$5x^2y + 15xy^3$**

13. $(x - 3)(x + 7)$ **$x^2 + 4x - 21$**

14. $(y + 1)(y - 13)$ **$y^2 - 12y - 13$**

15. $(a - b)(c - d)$ **$ac - ad - bc + bd$**

16. $(4z + 1)(-z - 1)$ **$-4z^2 - 5z - 1$**

17. $(d - 1)^2$ **$d^2 - 2d + 1$**

18. $(2t + 3)^2$ **$4t^2 + 12t + 9$**

19. $(a + 15)(a - 15)$ **$a^2 - 225$**

20. $(12b + m)(12b - m)$ **$144b^2 - m^2$**

21. $(a - 1)(a^2 + a + 1)$ **$a^3 - 1$**

22. $(x^2 + 3x - 2)(2x^2 + 5x + 4)$
$2x^4 + 11x^3 + 15x^2 + 2x - 8$

Objective C. *Recognize perfect squares and perfect square trinomials.* *(Lesson 10-8)*

In 23 and 24, use a calculator to determine if the number is a perfect square.

23. 5625 **Yes** **24.** 138,627 **No**

In 25–28, state whether the trinomial is a perfect square trinomial.

25. $16x^2 + 36x + 25$ **No** **26.** $16y^2 - 8y + 1$ **Yes**

27. $4z^2 + 49$ **No** **28.** $x^2 + 2x - 1$ **No**

Objective D. *Find common monomial factors of polynomials.* *(Lesson 10-4)*

29. Copy and complete: $7x^4 + 49x = 7x(\underline{?} + \underline{?})$. **$x^3$; 7**

30. Find the largest common factor of $20ay^3$, $-15y^4$, $35a^2y^6$. **$5y^3$**

In 31 and 32, factor.

31. $14m^4 + m^2$ **$m^2(14m^2 + 1)$**

32. $18b^3 - 21ab + 3b$ **$3b(6b^2 - 7a + 1)$**

In 33 and 34, simplify.

33. $\frac{6z^3 - z}{z}$ **$6z^2 - 1$** **34.** $\frac{14x^2 + 12x}{2x}$ **$7x + 6$**

RESOURCES
- Chapter 10 Test, Form A
- Chapter 10 Test, Form B
- Chapter 10 Test, Cumulative Form

CHAPTER REVIEW

The main objectives for the chapter are organized here into sections corresponding to the four main types of understanding this book promotes: Skills, Properties, Uses, and Representations.

USING THE CHAPTER REVIEW

Whereas end-of-chapter material may be considered optional in some texts, in *Algebra* we have selected these objectives and questions with the expectation that they will be covered. Students should be able to answer these questions with about 85% accuracy after studying the chapter.

You may assign these questions over a single night to help students prepare for a test the next day, or you may assign the questions over a two-day period.

If you work the questions over two days, then we recommend assigning the *evens* for homework the first night so that students get feedback in class the next day, then assigning the *odds* the night before the test so the students can use the answers provided in the book.

ADDITIONAL ANSWERS

45. For any two numbers a and b, if $ab = 0$, then $a = 0$ or $b = 0$.

52. Rewrite the expressions using the properties of algebra or test special cases.

53b. sample: $3^2 + 5 \cdot 3 - 6 = 18$, $(3 + 6)(3 - 1) = 9 \cdot 2 = 18$. $4^2 + 5 \cdot 4 - 6 = 30$, $(4 + 6)(4 - 1) = 10 \cdot 3 = 30$.

62.

	d	e	f
a			
b			
c			

Objective E. *Factor perfect square trinomials and the difference of squares into a product of two binomials.* (Lessons 10-8, 10-9)

In 35 and 36, write each perfect square trinomial as the square of a binomial.

35. $m^2 + 16m + 64$ $(m + 8)^2$

36. $9a^2 - 24ab + 16b^2$ $(3a - 4b)^2$

In 37–40, write each difference of squares as the product of two binomials.

37. $a^2 - 4$ $(a + 2)(a - 2)$

38. $b^2 - 81m^2$ $(b + 9m)(b - 9m)$

39. $4x^2 - 1$ $(2x + 1)(2x - 1)$

40. $25t^2 - 25$ $25(t + 1)(t - 1)$ or $(5t + 5)(5t - 5)$

PROPERTIES deal with the principles behind the mathematics.

Objective F. *Apply $(a + b)^2 = a^2 + 2ab + b^2$, $(a - b) = a^2 - 2ab + b^2$, and $(a + b)(a - b) = a^2 - b^2$ to multiply numbers in your head.* (Lessons 10-7, 10-9)

In 41–44, calculate in your head.

41. 41^2 1681

42. $(.95)^2$ .9025

43. $63 \cdot 57$ 3591

44. $88 \cdot 92$ 8096

Objective G. *Recognize and use the Zero Product Property to solve equations.* (Lesson 10-10)

45. What is the Zero Product Property? See margin.

In 46 and 47, why can't the Zero Product Property be used on the given equation?

46. $(x + 3)(x + 4) = 5$ The product is not zero.

47. $(x + 3) + (x - 4) = 0$ There is no product.

In 48–51, solve.

48. $5q(2q - 7) = 0$ $0, \frac{7}{2}$

49. $(m - 3)(m - 1) = 0$ 3, 1

50. $(2w - 3)(3w + 5) = 0$ $\frac{3}{2}, -\frac{5}{3}$

51. $(y - 3)(2y - 1)(2y + 1) = 0$ $3, \frac{1}{2}, -\frac{1}{2}$

Objective H. *Recognize factors of polynomials using the properties of algebra, testing a special case and ruling out possibilities.* (Lesson 10-11)

52. Name two ways of determining whether expressions are equal. See margin.

53. Determine if $x^2 + 5x - 6$ is equal to $(x + 6)(x - 1)$ by

a. multiplying the binomials; $x^2 + 5x - 6$

b. testing two special cases. See margin.

Questions 54 and 55 are *multiple choice*.

54. $11a^2 + 26a - 21 =$ (c)

(a) $(11a - 7)(a - 3)$ (b) $(11a + 7)(a - 3)$
(c) $(11a - 7)(a + 3)$ (d) $(11a + 7)(a + 3)$
(e) none of (a)–(d)

55. $x^2 - 2xy + 13x - 26y =$ (b)

(a) $(x - 13)(x + 2y)$ (b) $(x + 13)(x - 2y)$
(c) $(x + 13y)(x - 2)$ (d) $(x - 13y)(x + 2)$
(e) none of (a)–(d)

USES deal with applications of mathematics in real situations.

Objective I. *Translate real situations into polynomials.* (Lessons 10-1, 10-2, 10-3, 10-6, 10-10)

In 56 and 57, use the following information: Each birthday from age 11 on Katherine has received \$250. She puts the money in a savings account with a scale factor of x.

56. Write an expression which shows how much Katherine will have after her 15th birthday.
$250x^4 + 250x^3 + 250x^2 + 250x + 250$

57. If the bank pays 8% interest a year, calculate how much Katherine will have after her 13th birthday. \$811.60

58. Recall that $d = .042s^2 + 1.1s$ gives the number of feet d needed to stop a car traveling at s mph on a concrete road. How much farther will a car travel before stopping, if it is going 50 mph instead of 30 mph? 89.2 feet

528

59. José received \$25 on his 12th birthday, \$50 on his 13th birthday and \$75 on his 14th birthday, which he invested at a scale factor x. He kept this money in the same account at the same scale factor for 4 more years. How much money did he have in this account? **$25x^6 + 50x^5 + 75x^4$**

60. At a family reunion there are b boys, m men, g girls, and w women. If each dance couple includes one male and female, how many different couples are possible?

61. An orange is thrown upward from ground level at 50 feet per second. Gravity pulls the orange down $16t^2$ feet in t seconds. An equation that gives the distance d above the ground after t seconds is $d = 50t - 16t^2$. After how many seconds will the orange hit the ground? $\frac{25}{8}$

60) $(b + m)(g + w)$ or $bg + bw + mg + mw$

REPRESENTATIONS deal with pictures, graphs, or objects that illustrate concepts.

Objective J. *Represent areas of figures in terms of polynomials. (Lessons 10-2, 10-3, 10-5)*

62. Represent $(a + b + c)(d + e + f)$ using areas of rectangles **See margin.**

63. a. Write the area of rectangle $ABCD$ below as the sum of 4 terms.

b. Write the area of $ABCD$ as the product of 2 binomials. **$(x + 3)(y + 2)$**

c. Are the answers to parts a and b equal? **Yes**

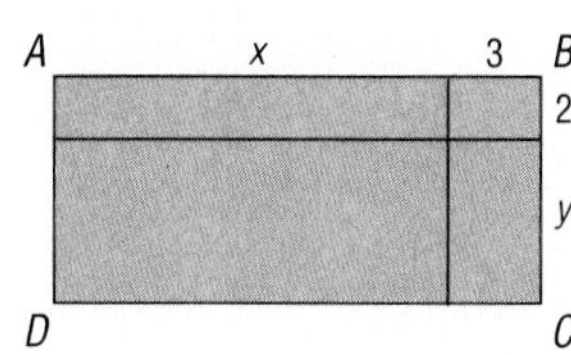

63a) $xy + 3y + 2x + 6$

In 64 and 65, write a simplified expression for the area of the region in color.

64. **$45x - 4x^2$**

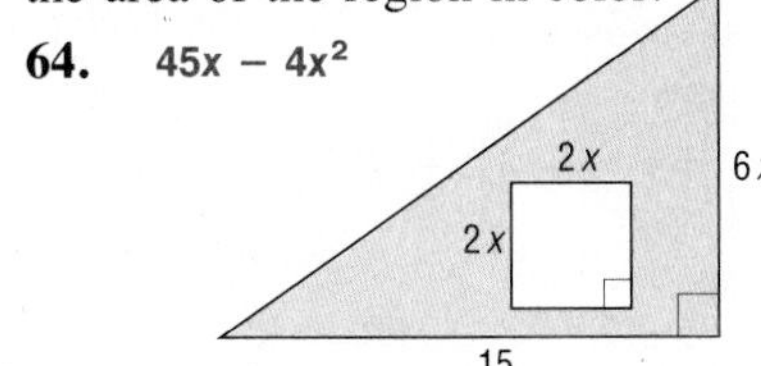

65.

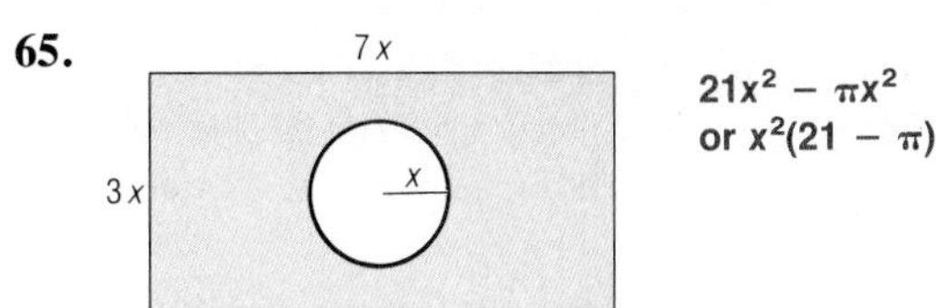

$21x^2 - \pi x^2$ or $x^2(21 - \pi)$

66. Write a polynomial for the volume of the figure below. **$24x^3 + 291x^2 + 36x$**

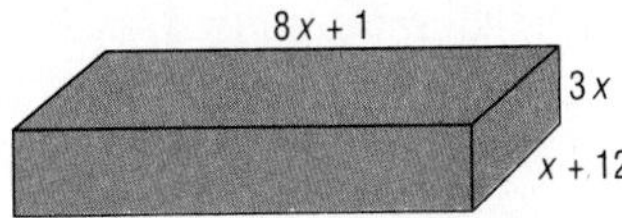

67. A box has dimensions x, $x + 1$, and $x - 1$. Write its volume as a polynomial. **$x^3 - x$**

EVALUATION

Three tests are provided for this chapter in the Teacher's Resource File. Chapter 10 Test, Forms A and B, cover just Chapter 10. The third test is Chapter 10 Test, Cumulative Form. About 50% of this test covers Chapter 10; 25% covers Chapter 9, and 25% covers earlier chapters. For more information on grading, see *General Teaching Suggestions: Grading* on page T44 in the Teacher's Edition.

ASSIGNMENT RECOMMENDATION

On the day your students take the chapter test, we suggest you make an assignment in the first section of the next chapter.

CHAPTER 11 ■ SYSTEMS

DAILY PACING CHART 11

DAILY PACING CHART ■ CHAPTER 11

Students in the Full Course should complete the entire text by the end of the year. Students in the Minimal Course spend more time to complete lessons that are combined with quizzes and more time to consider the Chapter Review. Therefore, these students may not complete all the chapters in the text.

DAY	MINIMAL COURSE	FULL COURSE
1	11-1	11-1
2	11-2	11-2
3	11-3	11-3
4	Quiz (TRF); Start 11-4.	Quiz (TRF); 11-4
5	Finish 11-4.	11-5
6	11-5	11-6
7	11-6	11-7
8	11-7	Quiz (TRF); 11-8
9	Quiz (TRF); Start 11-8.	11-9
10	Finish 11-8.	11-10
11	11-9	Progress Self-Test
12	11-10	Chapter Review
13	Progress Self-Test	Chapter Test (TRF)
14	Chapter Review	
15	Chapter Review	
16	Chapter Test (TRF)	

TESTING OPTIONS

TESTING OPTIONS

- Quiz for Lessons 11-1 Through 11-3
- Quiz for Lessons 11-4 Through 11-7
- Chapter 11 Test, Form A
- Chapter 11 Test, Form B
- Chapter 11 Test, Cumulative Form

INDIVIDUAL DIFFERENCES

PROVIDING FOR INDIVIDUAL DIFFERENCES

The student text is written for the *average* student. The program, however, can be adapted for less capable and for more capable students.

For those students who need more practice, a blackline master (in the Teacher's Resource File) is provided for each lesson. The Teacher's Edition frequently provides Error Analysis and Alternate Approach features to provide additional instructional strategies for those students who do not readily grasp the material.

For students who require additional challenge, Extension activities are regularly provided in the Teacher's Edition.

OBJECTIVES ■ CHAPTER 11

Students should master the chapter objectives by the time they complete the chapter. To ensure objective mastery, there is continual review built into each set of lesson questions. After students complete the chapter lessons, they assess their mastery on the Progress Self-Test. Then they do the Chapter Review and pay special attention to those questions that match the objectives missed on the Progress Self-Test. Students can get extra practice on these objectives by using the master for each lesson in the Teacher's Resource File.

OBJECTIVES FOR CHAPTER 11 (Organized into the SPUR categories—Skills, Properties, Uses, and Representations)	**Progress Self-Test Questions**	**Chapter Review Questions**	**Lesson Master from Teacher's Resource File***
SKILLS			
A Solve systems using substitution.	1–3	1 through 10	11-2, 11-3
B Solve systems by addition.	4	11 through 14	11-4
C Solve systems by multiplying.	5, 6	15 through 20	11-5
PROPERTIES			
D Recognize sentences with no solutions, one solution, or all real numbers as solutions.	9, 10, 13, 14	21 through 24	11-9
E Determine whether a system has 0, 1, or infinitely many solutions.	7, 8	25 through 28	11-8
USES			
F Use systems of equations to solve real world problems involving linear combinations.	11, 12	29 through 36	11-2, 11-3, 11-4, 11-5, 11-8, 11-9
G Calculate and use weighted averages.	15, 16	37 through 42	11-6, 11-7
REPRESENTATIONS			
H Find solutions to systems of equations by graphing.	17	43 through 48	11-1, 11-8
I Graphically represent solutions to systems of linear inequalities.	18	49 through 53	11-10

*** The masters are numbered to match the lessons.**

OVERVIEW ■ CHAPTER 11

The graphical approach to solving systems of equations starts the chapter (Lesson 11-1). Then algebraic methods are covered—first substitution (Lessons 11-2 and 11-3), then addition and multiplication (Lessons 11-4 and 11-5). Among the most important applications of systems are problems which are classified as weighted average problems (Lesson 11-6). Many of the classic word problems can be set up and solved as weighted average problems. This concept is used to organize lessons on further applications of linear systems (Lesson 11-7). The chapter concludes with special systems which are related to ideas of graphing. Parallel lines are related to systems of linear equations which have no solutions or an infinite number of solutions (Lessons 11-8 and 11-9). Systems of inequalities are solved by finding overlapping regions (Lesson 11-10).

PERSPECTIVES ■ CHAPTER 11

The Perspectives provide the rationale for the inclusion of topics or approaches, provide mathematical background, and make connections within UCSMP.

11-1

AN INTRODUCTION TO SYSTEMS

In this lesson, the emphasis is on what constitutes a system and the graphical meaning of a solution to the system. A system has two or more sentences or conditions which must be satisfied simultaneously. They are assumed to be linked with the word *and,* so the idea of a solution to a system relates to the intersection of sets.

Although this chapter emphasizes using algorithms to solve systems, students should be continually reminded that they can use the graphical interpretation for indicating numbers of solutions and approximating the solutions. Advances in computers make solving systems from graphs an important technique.

11-2

SOLVING SYSTEMS USING SUBSTITUTION

In this lesson we begin solving systems algebraically. The work that students have done on chunking should make the replacement of one variable with an expression easier to see.

11-3

MORE WITH SUBSTITUTION

In the previous lesson, the systems were written in such a way that one of the possible substitution choices was obviously the easiest. In this lesson, both equations are given in slope-intercept form. Students often see the substitution step in these systems more easily because an entire side of an equation is being replaced.

11-4

SOLVING SYSTEMS BY ADDITION

The systems in this lesson have one variable for which the coefficient in one of the equations is either the opposite of or equal to the coefficient in the other equation. In the former case, "adding the equations," which is short for "adding the sides of one equation to the sides of the other equation" yields an equation in one variable and thus solves the system quite easily.

In the latter case, we multiply one of the equations by -1 and then add. Some teachers prefer to avoid the multiplication step and subtract one equation from the other. Others feel that this leads to too many sign errors. Some teachers like to teach both methods.

11-5

MULTIPLYING TO SOLVE SYSTEMS

This lesson again demonstrates the following problem-solving strategy: *If you cannot solve a problem, transform it into one you can solve.* In one step, any system can be transformed into a system in which the addition process of the previous lesson can be utilized.

The multiplication method is a very powerful way to solve systems which have integer coefficients. Even systems with noninteger coefficients can be solved with the multiplication approach.

11-6

WEIGHTED AVERAGES AND MIXTURES

Consider the following mixture problem: How much pure alcohol should be added to 8 ounces of a 30% solution in order to obtain a 50% solution? To solve, we let $x =$ the number of ounces of pure alcohol to be added. Then $x + 8(.30) = (x + 8).50$. It seems simple enough, but for many students this equation is purely symbolic. They have no way to check the problem, for they do not understand the situation. The purpose of this lesson is to provide the arithmetical grounding for such algebra mixture problems.

We think of the above problem as a mixture of a 100% solution with a 30% solution. Students should realize that any mixture will result in a solution whose percent of alcohol is somewhere between 100% and 30%. Depending on the relative amounts (the *weights*) of 100% and 30% solutions, the result will be nearer one percentage or the other. If the weights are equal, the percentage will be 65%, in the middle. If there is twice as much 100% solution as 30% solution, then the weights are 2/3 and 1/3, and the mixture will be twice as close to 100% as to 30%.

In general, if the two weights are equal, each must be 1/2 of the total. Then

$$W_1x_1 + W_2x_2 = \tfrac{1}{2}x_1 + \tfrac{1}{2}x_2 = \frac{x_1 + x_2}{2},$$

the mean of the two numbers x_1 and x_2. The traditional average is a special case of weighted averages.

Weighted averages are found in probability, in the concept of *expected value*. For instance, suppose you enter a sweepstakes with two prizes. If the probability of winning the $100 first prize is 0.3%, and the probability of winning one of the $50 second prizes is 2%, then the expected value, the average amount you would expect to win per try if you made attempt after attempt, is $100 • .003 + $50 • .02 = $1.30.

11-7

MORE WITH MIXTURES

In this section we look at problems in which the weighted average of two quantities is known but either one of the weights (Example 1) or one of the quantities (Example 2) is missing. In the missing quantity situation a system of equations can be used.

The weighted average idea enables answers to be estimated. For instance, with 400 shirts at $10 and 250 at $*S*, as in Example 1, we think of $10 and $*S* as weights, giving a weighted average of $9. Now *S* must be less than 9. (Otherwise, the weighted average of 10 and *S* would be greater than $9.) This small amount of intuition can be useful in solving such problems.

In Example 2, the quantities are time and the weights are rates. The clue to the second equation comes from the fact that the average is a rate between the given rates of 35 mph and 55 mph.

11-8

PARALLEL LINES

This lesson returns to the representation of equations as lines. The slope-intercept form of the equation is stressed in two ways: It is useful for graphing and for discussing the relationships between slopes (or intercepts) of parallel lines.

Our use of the term *parallel* includes identical lines as parallel. This is very common in higher mathematics; for example, (1) equivalent vectors are those with the same length lying on parallel lines; (2) under a translation, lines are parallel to their images.

Our definition allows us to say simply: If two lines have the same slope, then they are parallel.

The familiar postulates and theorems of geometry still hold with this broader notion of parallel. Two lines perpendicular to the same line are parallel. (The lines could be the same line or not.)

The algebra is simplified as well. Lines in a plane either intersect in one point or are parallel.

11-9

SITUATIONS WHICH ALWAYS OR NEVER HAPPEN

In this lesson, we return to equations and inequalities in a single variable. There are three reasons for doing so. First, the single variable situation is often harder for students than the two variable systems in which these special cases appear. The representation of the ways that two lines can be related has a vividness that cannot be duplicated with single-variable equations. In Lesson 11-8 there are simple ways to identify the special cases of no solution or an infinite number of solutions. These ways are not used for one-dimensional equations and inequalities.

Second, we wish to return to inequalities, and by focusing on familiar inequalities in one variable, students are more ready for the inequalities in two variables.

Third, we wish students to realize that not only can algebraic methods give solutions when there indeed are solutions, but algebraic methods can also tell you when there are *no solutions*. This is an important idea which is often missed by students.

11-10

SYSTEMS OF INEQUALITIES

Graphing systems of inequalities gives another visual image for the idea that solutions of systems must satisfy all the conditions. Systems of inequalities are used in linear programming, a topic studied in some detail in *Advanced Algebra*, a later text in this program.

The discrete situation in Example 4 is shown because applications often involve discrete quantities. Recall that the points whose coordinates are integers are called *lattice points*.

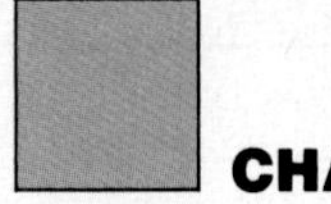

CHAPTER 11

This chapter should take 10 to 12 days for the lessons and quizzes; 1 day for the Progress Self-Test; 1 or 2 days for the Chapter Review; and 1 day for testing. The total is 13 to 16 days.

CHAPTER 11

Systems

530

Here are the men's and women's winning times in the Olympic 100-meter freestyle swimming race for all Olympic years from 1912 to 1988.

100-Meter Freestyle
Olympic Winning Time (seconds)

Year	Men's	Women's	Year	Men's	Women's
1912	63.2	72.2	1960	55.2	61.2
1920	61.4	73.6	1964	53.4	59.5
1924	59.0	72.4	1968	52.2	60.0
1928	58.6	71.0	1972	51.22	58.59
1932	58.2	66.8	1976	49.99	55.65
1936	57.6	65.9	1980	50.40	54.79
1948	57.3	66.3	1984	49.80	55.92
1952	57.4	66.8	1988	48.63	54.93
1956	55.4	62.0			

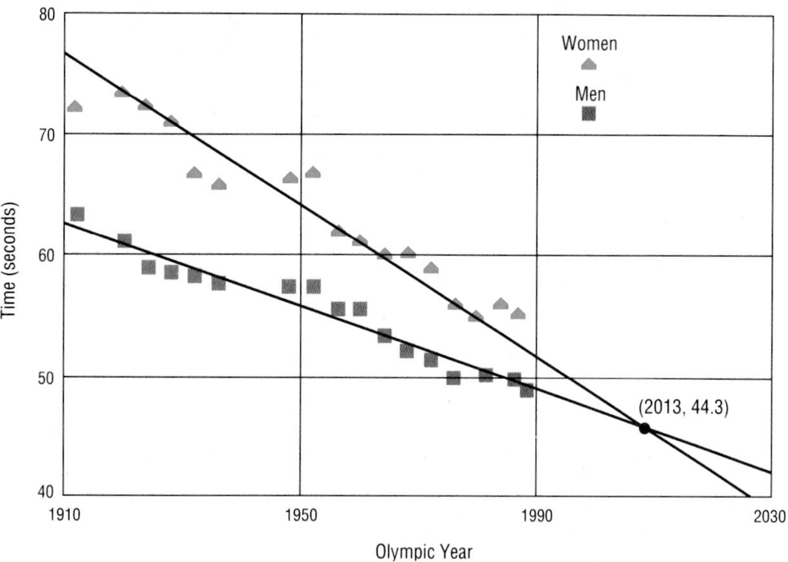

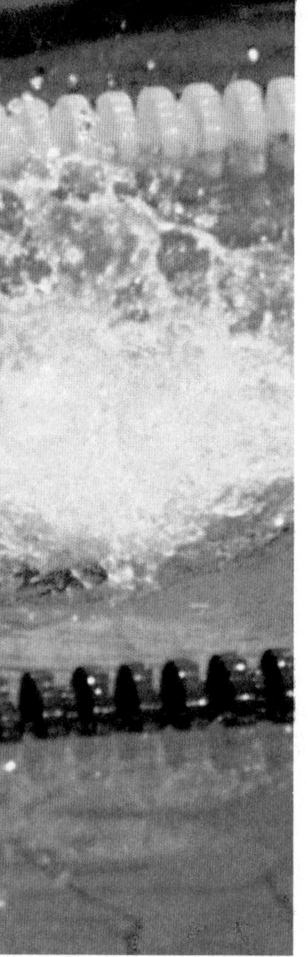

Matt Biondi, 1988 Olympic winner in men's 100-meter free-style

The graph shows that the women's winning time has been decreasing faster than the men's. Lines have been fitted to the data. The lines intersect near (2013, 44.3). This means that if the times continue to decrease at a constant rate, the women's time would be faster than the men's in the Olympic year 2016. The winning times would each be about 44 seconds.

The finding of points of intersection of lines and other curves on the coordinate plane is called *solving a system.* In this chapter you will learn various ways of solving systems.

USING PAGES 530-531
Use the discussion about Olympic swimming times to introduce some important ideas of the chapter. Point out that the two lines in the graph represent the following two situations: the separate trends in winning times for men's and women's Olympic 100-meter freestyle swimming champions. An equation can be found for each of the lines. (The equations are given in Lesson 11-1.) The two equations form a *system of equations*. The solution to this system is given by the point in the graph where the two lines intersect. The coordinates of the point are the year, 2013, when the men's time and women's time will be the same (if the trends continue) and the time itself, namely, 44.3 seconds.

LESSON 11-1

RESOURCES
- Lesson Master 11-1
- Visual for Teaching Aid 7: Coordinate Grid
- Visual for Teaching Aid 58: Graph for page 531
- Visual for Teaching Aid 59: Graph for Additional Example and Extension
- Computer Master 21

OBJECTIVE

H Find solutions to systems of equations by graphing.

TEACHING NOTES

Alternate Approach If your desks are in rows and columns, introduce systems of equations as follows. Assign each student in the class a point (x, y) with $-3 \le x \le 3$ and $-3 \le y \le 3$. Have someone near the center of the room be (0, 0) and base the other coordinates on their relationship to the origin. Write the following equations on the board.

a. $x + y = 3$ **b.** $x - y = 1$
c. $y = 2x$ **d.** $x + y = -3$

Ask students to stand if their point is a solution to equation **a.** Then ask students to stand if their point is a solution to equation **b.** Who stood both times? This helps to reinforce the meaning of *and.* To solve the system, the ordered pair must be a solution of both equations. Repeat with the other pairs of equations.

LESSON

11-1 An Introduction to Systems

On page 531, if the time is y seconds in year x, equations of the lines are as follows:

Men: $y = -0.185x + 416.70$
Women: $y = -0.313x + 674.41$

The graphs of these lines give you a way of estimating the point of intersection. The point of intersection indicates the year when the men's and women's Olympic winning times in the 100-meter freestyle will be the same. It also indicates the winning time. We now seek a way of finding the coordinates of this point.

The numbers in the equations above are quite complicated, so consider a simpler situation.

> The sum of two numbers is 22 and their difference is 8. What are the numbers?

To answer this question, first note that there are two numbers to be found. It is customary to name them x and y. The given information contains two *conditions* separated by the word *and*. Each condition can be translated into an equation.

Condition 1: The sum of the two numbers is 22.

$$x + y = 22$$

Condition 2: Their difference is 8.

$$x - y = 8$$

A **system** is a set of conditions each separated from the others by the word "and." In algebra systems, the conditions are usually equations and the word "and" is often signified with a single brace {. The system immediately above can be written

$$\begin{cases} x + y = 22 \\ x - y = 8. \end{cases}$$

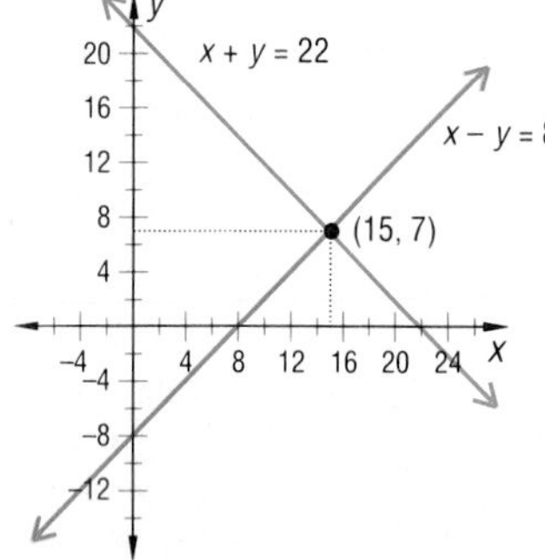

The *solution* to this system is the particular ordered pair (x, y) which satisfies both $x + y = 22$ and $x - y = 8$. The solution can be found by graphing the two lines. It is (15, 7), the point of intersection shown at the left.

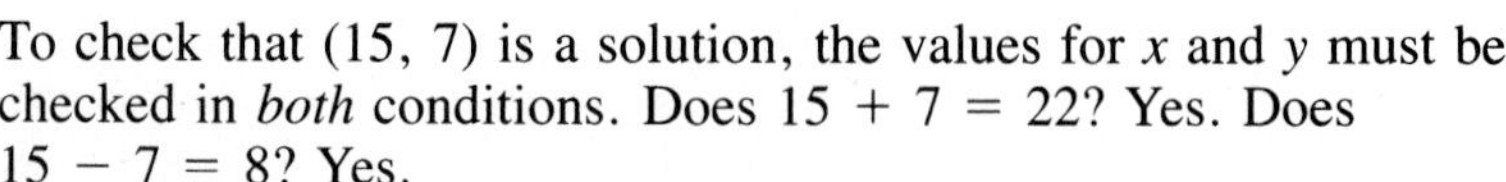

To check that (15, 7) is a solution, the values for x and y must be checked in *both* conditions. Does $15 + 7 = 22$? Yes. Does $15 - 7 = 8$? Yes.

In general, the **solution set to a system** is the intersection of the solution sets for each of the conditions in the system.

Here are four ways to indicate the solution to the system graphed on the previous page.

as an ordered pair:	(15, 7)
as an ordered pair identifying the variables:	$(x, y) = (15, 7)$
by naming the variables individually:	$x = 15$ and $y = 7$
as a set of ordered pairs:	{(15, 7)}

When the sentences in a system have no solutions in common, there is no solution to the system. The solution set is the set with no elements, Ø.

Example Find all solutions to the system $\begin{cases} y = 2x + 1 \\ y = 2x - 3. \end{cases}$

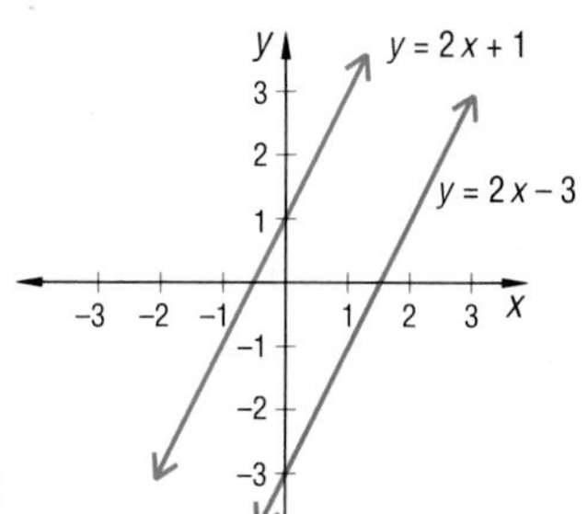

Solution Draw the graph of each equation. Look for all intersection points.

Since these lines have the same slope and different y-intercepts, they are parallel and do not intersect. There is no solution to the system since there are no pairs of numbers that make both equations true.

Check Twice a number plus one $(2x + 1)$ could never give the same value as twice the same number minus three $(2x - 3)$.

The systems discussed in this chapter all involve sentences whose graphs are lines. Accordingly, they are called **linear systems**. Graphing linear systems can help you find exact solutions, as in the solution to $\begin{cases} x + y = 22 \\ x - y = 8 \end{cases}$. If solutions do not have integer coordinates, however, it is likely that reading a graph will only give you an estimate. In the next lessons you will use algebra to find exact solutions to linear systems.

Emphasize the last paragraph of the lesson to your students. Use it to explain the situation at the beginning of the lesson. When the intersection point does not have integer coordinates, you can estimate the coordinates from a graph, but it may be impossible to read the exact solution from the graph.

ADDITIONAL EXAMPLE
Find all solutions to the system.
$\begin{cases} y = -3x + 1 \\ -2x + 2y = -14 \end{cases}$

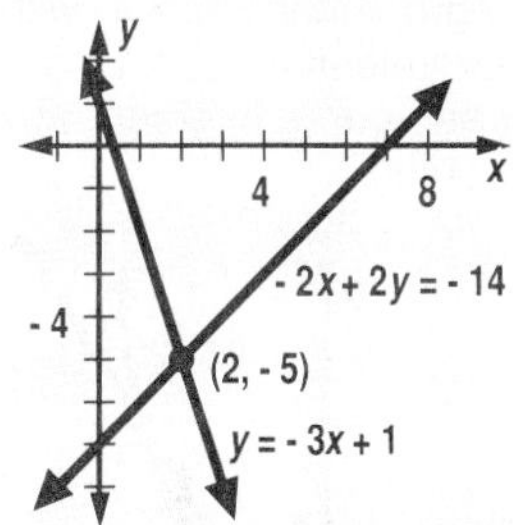

NOTES ON QUESTIONS
Question 26: The mean of each set of three numbers can be found by sight because the data is symmetric about it. One number is smaller, and another is larger than the mean by the same amount.

Question 27: This question provides another way of looking at the swimming data. This helps point out that data sets can often be interpreted in many ways. *Teaching Aid 58* may be used when discussing this question.

ADDITIONAL ANSWERS
7b.

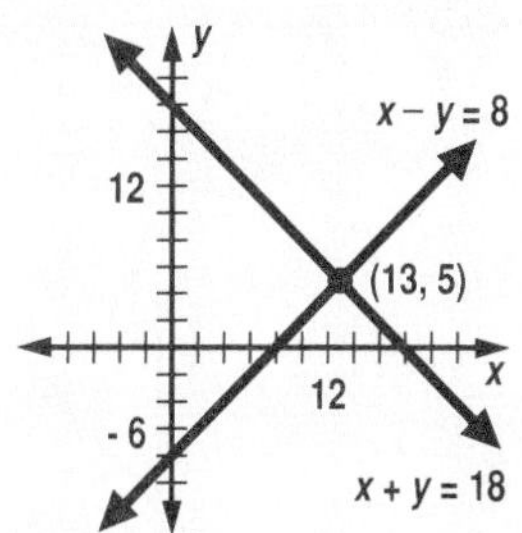

9. Any two of: $(x, y) = (-1, -9)$; $x = -1$ and $y = -9$; or {(−1, −9)}.

FOLLOW-UP

MORE PRACTICE
For more questions on SPUR Objectives, use *Lesson Master 11-1*, shown on page 535.

EXTENSION
In this chapter we consider systems of linear equations. But students can be informed that systems may involve any equations. In Chapter 9, students compared linear growth with exponential growth. Here is a graph comparing a linear function with an exponential function. The line and curve intersect at two points.

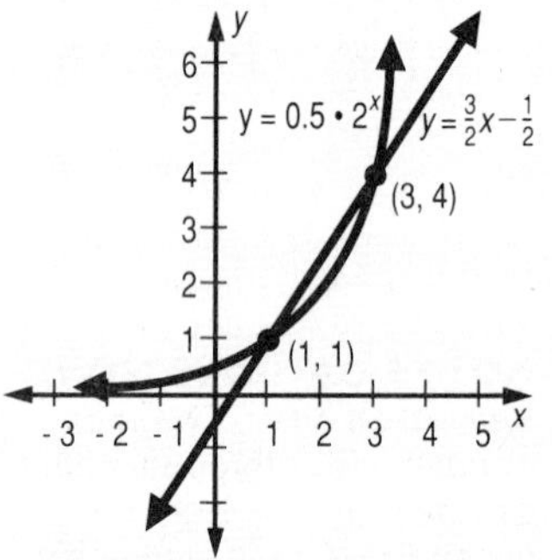

The solutions (1, 1) and (3, 4) can be seen from the graph. Have students check the solutions with a calculator.

7b, 9. See margin, page 533.

11.

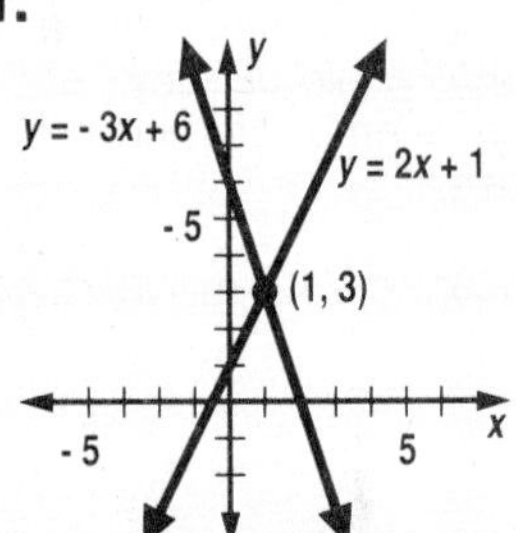

12.

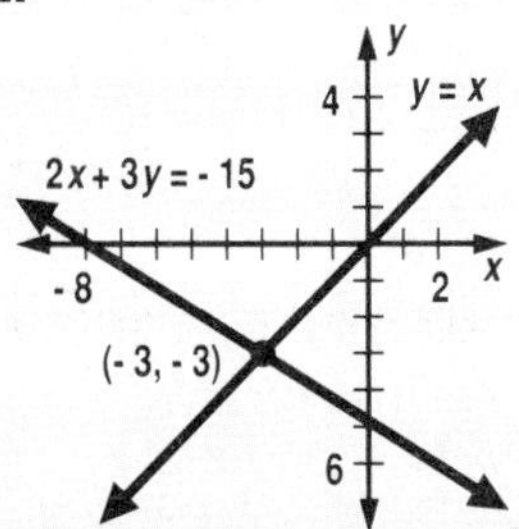

Questions

Covering the Reading

1. Define: system. **A set of conditions each separated from the others by the word "and."**
2. In algebra systems, the conditions are usually __?__ and the word __?__ is denoted by a brace. **equations; "and"**
3. Define: the solution set to a system. **the intersection of the solution sets for each condition in the system**
4. When a system has two variables, each solution is an __?__. **ordered pair**
5. Refer to the graph at the right. **$y = 2x + 4$, $x + 2y = 3$**
   a. What system is being graphed?
   b. What is the solution to the system? **(-1, 2)**

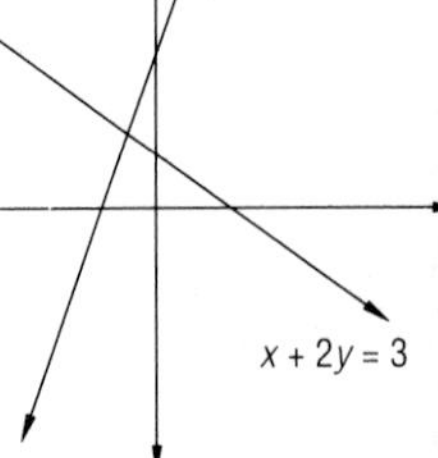

6. Is (4, 8) a solution to the following system? **Yes**
$$\begin{cases} 10x - y = 32 \\ y - x = 4 \end{cases}$$
7. The sum of two numbers is 18 and their difference is 8.
   a. If the numbers are x and y, translate the two conditions of the sentence above into two equations. **$x + y = 18$; $x - y = 8$**
   b. Graph both of these equations on the same coordinate system.
   c. What are the numbers? **13 and 5; b) See margin.**
8. Find all solutions to the system $\begin{cases} y = 4x - 2 \\ y = 4x + 5. \end{cases}$ **no solution**
9. The solution to the system $\begin{cases} y = 9x \\ y = 2x - 7 \end{cases}$ is (-1, -9). Write this solution in two other ways. **See margin.**
10. Why are the systems of Questions 8 and 9 called *linear systems*? **The graph of each equation is a line.**

Applying the Mathematics

In 11 and 12, solve each system by graphing. **See margin.**

11. $\begin{cases} y = 2x + 1 \\ y = -3x + 6 \end{cases}$
12. $\begin{cases} y = x \\ 2x + 3y = -15 \end{cases}$

13. Use the equations, on page 532, of the system of the 100-meter freestyle times graphed on page 531. Verify that (2013, 44.3) is the solution to the system. **$-0.185(2013) + 416.7 \approx 44.3$; $-0.313(2013) + 674.41 \approx 44.3$**

Review

14. Solve $2x + y = 7$ for y. *(Lesson 8-4)* **$y = 7 - 2x$**
15. Solve $3x + 5(2x - 2) = 16$. *(Lesson 6-8)* **$x = 2$**
16. If a country has population P now and is increasing by I people per year, what will its population be in Y years? *(Lesson 6-4)* **$P + IY$**

17. Multiply $4x - y$ by 3. *(Lesson 6-3)* **12x − 3y**

18. Eight more than three times a number is two more than six times the number. What is the number? *(Lesson 6-6)* **x = 2**

19. a. How many quarts are there in 5 gallons? **20 quarts**
b. How many quarts are there in n gallons? *(Previous course)* **4n quarts**

20. Simplify $7\pi \div \left(\frac{2\pi}{3}\right)$. *(Lesson 5-1)* $\frac{21}{2}$

21. In 1985, the cost for a large computer to process a typical data processing job was 4¢. The job took 0.4 seconds. What is the cost per second? *(Lesson 5-2)* **10¢ per second**

22. a. Evaluate $\frac{y_2 - y_1}{x_2 - x_1}$ where $y_2 = 7$, $y_1 = -1$, $x_2 = 8$, and $x_1 = 10$. *(Lesson 1-5)* **-4**
b. What have you calculated in part a? *(Lesson 8-2)* **The slope of the segment between the points (10, -1) and (8, 7).**

23. On a map, 1 inch represents 325 miles. The map distance from Los Angeles to Houston is $4\frac{3}{4}$ inches. Suppose you want the distance in miles from Los Angeles to Houston.
a. Write a proportion that will help solve the problem. **sample:** $\frac{325}{1} = \frac{x}{4\frac{3}{4}}$
b. Find the distance in miles. *(Lesson 5-7)* **≈1544**

24. In the similar figures below, corresponding sides are parallel.

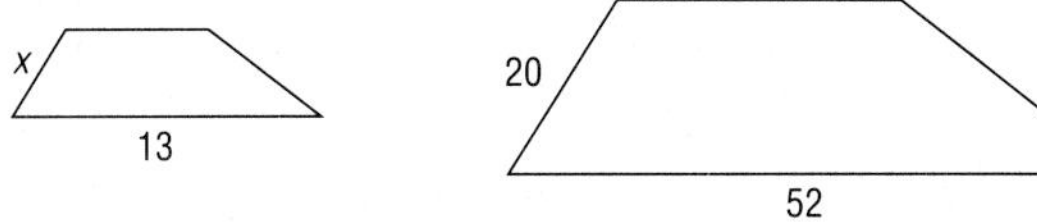

a. What is the ratio of similitude? $\frac{1}{4}$ **or 4**
b. Find the value of x. *(Lesson 5-6)* **5**

25. *Skill sequence* Solve. *(Lessons 6-1, 6-6, 6-8)*
a. $3x + 8 = -12$ $-\frac{20}{3} = -6\frac{2}{3}$
b. $3x + 8 = x - 12$ **-10**
c. $3(x + 8) = -4(x - 12)$ $\frac{24}{7} = 3\frac{3}{7}$

26. Find the mean of the three numbers. Calculate in your head. *(Lesson 1-2)*
a. 3, 4, 5 **4**
b. 7, 10, 13 **10**
c. $20n$, $25n$, $30n$ **25n**

Exploration

27. Some experts believe that even though the women's swim times are decreasing faster than the men's, it is the ratio of the times that is the key to predictions. **See margin.**
a. Compute the ratio of the men's time to the women's time for the 100-meter freestyle for each Olympic year.
b. Graph your results. (Plot Olympic year on the horizontal axis and the ratio of times on the vertical axis.)
c. What do you think the ratio will be in 2016? Does this agree with the prediction on page 531?

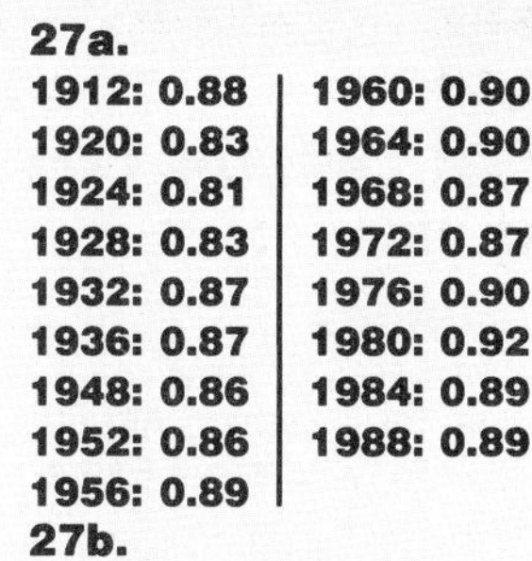

27a.

1912: 0.88	**1960: 0.90**
1920: 0.83	**1964: 0.90**
1924: 0.81	**1968: 0.87**
1928: 0.83	**1972: 0.87**
1932: 0.87	**1976: 0.90**
1936: 0.87	**1980: 0.92**
1948: 0.86	**1984: 0.89**
1952: 0.86	**1988: 0.89**
1956: 0.89	

27b.

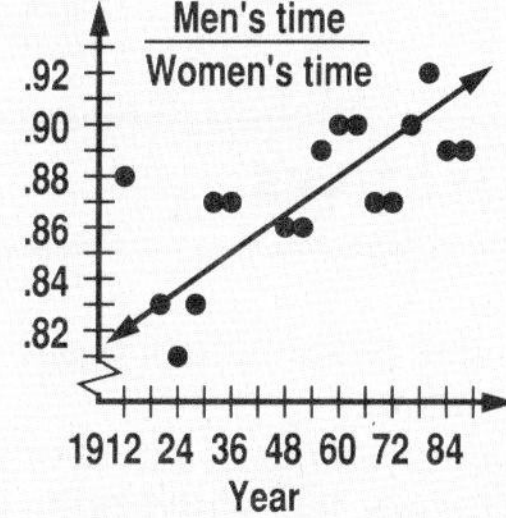

27.c. Fitting a line through (1920, .83) and (1976, .90) gives y = .00125x − 1.57. When x = 2016, y = .95. This does not agree with the prediction on the first page of the chapter. For women's time to be faster than men's time, the ratio y must be greater than 1. However, depending on where the line is drawn, some student answers may agree with the text.

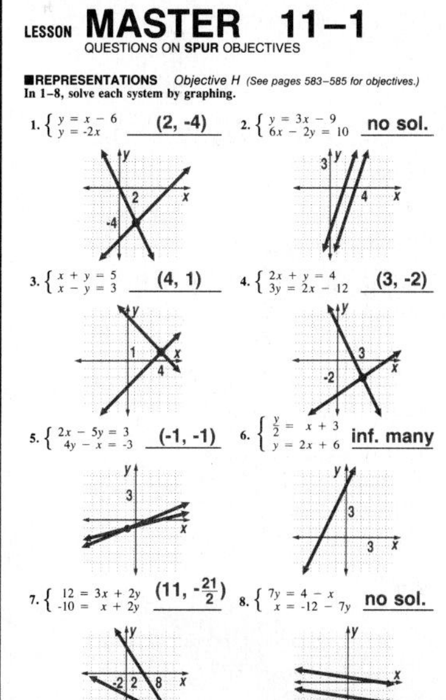

LESSON 11-2

RESOURCES

- Lesson Master 11-2
- Visual for Teaching Aid 60: Graph for Additional Example 3

OBJECTIVES

A Solve systems using substitution.
F Use systems of equations to solve real world problems involving linear combinations.

TEACHING NOTES

Reading You may have to spend extra time explaining the examples in this lesson. Some students find the algebraic manipulations difficult to understand by reading. The process may be easier to follow if they see it unfolding. In **Example 1,** you can illustrate substituting $2B$ for G by writing $B + G = 109$ on the board, then erasing G and writing $2B$ in its place.

The lesson mentions that students may have been able to answer **Examples 1 and 2** without algebra. You might ask them to suggest ways of doing this. In **Example 1** you can reason that the girls received 2/3 of \$109, while the boys got 1/3. In **Example 2,** 2/5 of the 24 quarts are orange juice and 3/5 are ginger ale.

Students may ask, "I substituted for x, not y. Does it matter?" Of course it doesn't matter, but sometimes one choice of substitution will ease the work in solving.

LESSON

11-2 Solving Systems Using Substitution

Graphing is a useful technique, but it does not always show exact solutions to a system. However, exact solutions for some systems can be found algebraically. **Substitution** is a common method.

Example 1

From a car wash a service club made \$109 that was to be divided between the Boy Scouts and the Girl Scouts. There were twice as many girls as boys so a decision was made to give the girls twice as much money. How much did each group receive?

Solution Translate each condition into an equation. Suppose the Boy Scouts receive B dollars and the Girl Scouts receive G dollars. We number the equations in the system for reference.

The sum of amounts is \$109. Girls get twice as much as boys.
$$\begin{cases} B + G = 109 & (1) \\ G = 2B & (2) \end{cases}$$

Since $G = 2B$ in equation (2), you can substitute $2B$ for G in equation (1).

$$\begin{aligned} B + 2B &= 109 \\ 3B &= 109 \\ B &= 36\tfrac{1}{3} \end{aligned}$$

To find G, substitute $36\frac{1}{3}$ for B in either equation. We use equation (2).

$$\begin{aligned} G &= 2B \\ &= 2 \cdot 36\tfrac{1}{3} \\ &= 72\tfrac{2}{3} \end{aligned}$$

So the solution is $(B, G) = (36\frac{1}{3}, 72\frac{2}{3})$. The Boy Scouts will receive $\$36\frac{1}{3} \approx \$36.33$, and the Girl Scouts will get $\$72\frac{2}{3} \approx \$72.67$.

Check Are both conditions satisfied? Will the groups receive a total of \$109? Yes, \$36.33 + \$72.67 = \$109. Will the girls get twice as much as the boys? Yes, it is as close as possible.

In the equation $G = 2B$, G is in terms of B. Substitution is a good method to use when one variable is given in terms of others. In the next example, two different variables are given in terms of a third.

Example 2 An orange punch is made by mixing two parts orange juice with three parts ginger ale. Six gallons of punch are needed. How many quarts of orange juice and how many quarts of ginger ale will it take?

Solution First, identify the unknowns.

Let J = the number of quarts of orange juice in the punch.
Let G = the number of quarts of ginger ale in the punch.
Let P = the number of quarts in one "part" of juice.

Remember that one gallon equals four quarts, so six gallons is twenty-four quarts. This problem has three given conditions.

Two parts are orange juice.	$J = 2P$ (1)
Three parts are ginger ale.	$G = 3P$ (2)
The total is 24 (quarts).	$J + G = 24$ (3)

To solve the system, substitute $2P$ for J and $3P$ for G in equation (3).

$$\begin{aligned} 2P + 3P &= 24 \\ 5P &= 24 \\ P &= 4.8 \end{aligned}$$

Each part contains 4.8 quarts of liquid.
To find J, substitute 4.8 for P in equation (1).

$$J = 2P = 2 \cdot 4.8 = 9.6$$

To find G, substitute 4.8 for P in equation (2).

$$G = 3P = 3 \cdot 4.8 = 14.4$$

So it takes 9.6 quarts of orange juice and 14.4 quarts of ginger ale to make six gallons of this punch.

You might have been able to answer the questions of Examples 1 and 2 without algebra. Doing the algebra is then a check. But in the next example, algebra is necessary.

Throughout the chapter, stress the importance of the checking process. Since solving a system involves several steps, it is very easy to make a mistake. Also, each time the check is done, students use the idea that the solution works in both equations. One way to emphasize the check is to give partial credit for a wrong solution if the student recognizes that it is wrong because it doesn't check.

ADDITIONAL EXAMPLES

1. The Wolff family bought two chairs. One cost \$15 less than the other. Together they cost \$374. Find the price of each chair.
\$179.50, \$194.50

2. The recipe for a sauce for vegetables calls for 5 parts mayonnaise to 1 part mustard. To make 16 ounces of sauce, how many ounces of each ingredient should be used?
$13\frac{1}{3}$ oz mayonnaise, $2\frac{2}{3}$ oz mustard

3. Find the point where the lines $7x - 2y = -3$ and $y = 6x - 1$ intersect. (*Teaching Aid 60* provides the graph.)
(1, 5)

NOTES ON QUESTIONS
Questions 9 and 10: For systems of equations that use variables other than x and y, it is customary to write ordered pairs with the variables in alphabetical order.

Question 17: This question involves substitution in a slightly different setting. Students should substitute $x - 1$ for y; then expand the resulting expression.

Making Connections for Question 18: This question reviews a skill which will be needed when students use the addition and multiplication methods for solving systems in Lesson 11-4 and 11-5.

Making Connections for Question 23: This question relates to **Example 1.** Cities replace Scouts. The concept of weighting the cities' costs by their populations previews Lessons 11-6 and 11-7 on weighted averages.

FOLLOW-UP

MORE PRACTICE
For more questions on SPUR Objectives, use *Lesson Master 11-2,* shown on page 539.

EXTENSION
The following example uses substitution to solve a system involving a quadratic.

Solve $\begin{cases} y = x^2 \\ 2x + y + 1 = 4 \end{cases}$

Use x^2 in place of y in the second equation.

$$\begin{aligned} 2x + x^2 + 1 &= 4 \\ x^2 + 2x + 1 &= 4 \\ (x + 1)^2 &= 4 \end{aligned}$$

So $x + 1 = 2$ or $x + 1 = -2$. The two solutions are $x = 1$ and $x = -3$. The corresponding y values are $y = 1$ and $y = 9$. Final solution set: $\{(1, 1), (-3, 9)\}$.

Example 3 Two lines have equations $3x + 2y = 10$ and $y = 4x + 1$. Where do they intersect?

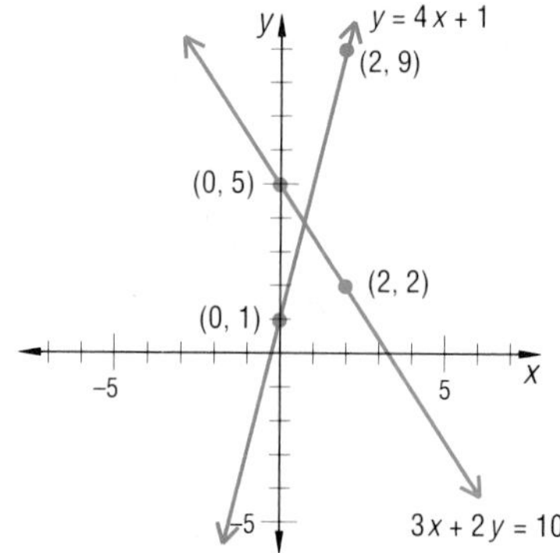

Solution The coordinates of the point of intersection are not integers, so reading the solution from the graph is difficult. Notice that the line $y = 4x + 1$ is in slope-intercept form. This makes substitution a natural method for solving the system. Substitute $4x + 1$ for y in the first equation and solve.

$$\begin{aligned} 3x + 2(4x + 1) &= 10 \\ 3x + 8x + 2 &= 10 \\ 11x + 2 &= 10 \\ 11x &= 8 \\ x &= \tfrac{8}{11} \end{aligned}$$

You have found the x-coordinate of the point of intersection. To find y, substitute for x in the second equation.

$$\begin{aligned} y &= 4 \cdot \tfrac{8}{11} + 1 \\ &= \tfrac{32}{11} + 1 \\ &= \tfrac{43}{11} \end{aligned}$$

The lines intersect at $(\frac{8}{11}, \frac{43}{11})$.

Check This seems correct on the graph. You should substitute $\frac{8}{11}$ for x and $\frac{43}{11}$ for y in both equations to produce an exact check.

Does $3(\frac{8}{11}) + 2(\frac{43}{11}) = 10$?

Does $4(\frac{8}{11}) + 1 = \frac{43}{11}$?

You should verify that they do.

Questions

Covering the Reading

1. In Example 1 suppose the service club made \$180. Also suppose the boys were to get three times as much money as the girls. How much would each group receive? **\$135 for the boys, \$45 for the girls**

2. a. Solve the system. **$t = 5, B = 35$**

$$\begin{cases} B = 7t \\ B - t = 30 \end{cases}$$

b. Check your answer. **Does $35 = 7 \cdot 5$? Yes. Does $35 - 5 = 30$? Yes.**

3. Suppose the orange punch of Example 2 was made by mixing 3 parts orange juice to 1 part ginger ale. If 5 gallons of punch are made, how many quarts of orange juice and how many quarts of ginger ale will it take? **15 quarts of orange juice and 5 quarts of ginger ale**

4. Solve for A, B, and K. **$A = 800, B = 600, K = 20$**

$$\begin{cases} A = 40K \\ B = 30K \\ A + B = 1400 \end{cases}$$

5. Complete the check of Example 3. **Does $\frac{24}{11} + \frac{86}{11} = \frac{110}{11} = 10$? Yes. Does $\frac{32}{11} + \frac{11}{11} = \frac{43}{11}$? Yes.**

In 6–10, **a.** find the point of intersection of the lines algebraically, and **b.** check your answer. **See margin.**

6. $\begin{cases} y = x - 2 \\ -4x + 7y = 10 \end{cases}$ **(8, 6)**

7. $\begin{cases} 12x - 5y = 30 \\ y = 2x - 6 \end{cases}$ **(0, -6)**

8. $\begin{cases} x + y = 14 \\ x = 6y \end{cases}$ **(12, 2)**

9. $\begin{cases} 2m - 3n = -15 \\ m = 4n \end{cases}$ **(-12, -3)**

10. $\begin{cases} 3a + 4b = -15 \\ b = 2a - 3 \end{cases}$ **$\left(-\frac{3}{11}, -\frac{39}{11}\right)$**

Applying the Mathematics

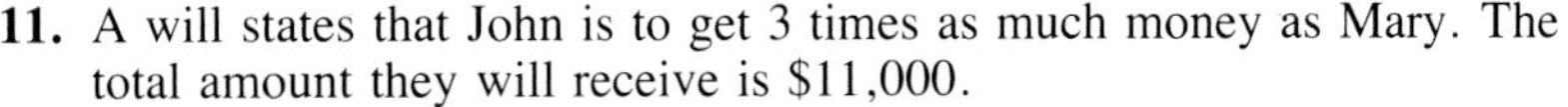

11. A will states that John is to get 3 times as much money as Mary. The total amount they will receive is \$11,000.

a. Write a system of equations describing this situation. **See margin.**

b. Solve to find the amounts of money John and Mary will get. **Mary gets \$2750 and John gets \$8250.**

12. A homemade sealer to use after furniture is stained can be made by mixing one part shellac with five parts denatured alcohol. To make a pint (16 fluid ounces) of sealer, how many fluid ounces of shellac and how many of denatured alcohol are needed? **$2\frac{2}{3}$ oz shellac and $13\frac{1}{3}$ oz alcohol**

Solutions of systems involving quadratics are usually left to an advanced algebra course. The problems that students should master in this course are certainly those involving linear relationships. However, you may wish to show your class the preceding problem, to point out the power of the substitution method and to reinforce their ability to chunk terms.

ADDITIONAL ANSWERS

6b. Does $6 = 8 - 2$? Yes. Does $-4(8) + 7(6) = 10$? Yes.

7b. Does $12(0) - 5(-6) = 30$? Yes. Does $-6 = 2(0) - 6$? Yes.

8b. Does $12 + 2 = 14$? Yes. Does $12 = (6)(2)$? Yes.

9b. Does $2(-12) - 3(-3) = -15$? Yes. Does $-12 = 4(-3)$? Yes.

10b. Does $3\left(-\frac{3}{11}\right) + 4\left(-\frac{39}{11}\right) = -15$? Yes. Does $-\frac{39}{11} = 2\left(-\frac{3}{11}\right) - 3$? Yes.

11a. $\begin{cases} J = 3M \\ J + M = 11{,}000 \end{cases}$

NAME ____________

LESSON MASTER 11–2
QUESTIONS ON **SPUR** OBJECTIVES

■SKILLS *Objective A (See pages 583–585 for objectives.)*
In 1–8, solve each system of equations.

1. $\begin{cases} y = 2x - 7 \\ y = 5 - x \end{cases}$ **$x = 4, y = 1$**

2. $\begin{cases} b = 2a - 1 \\ 2a - 3b = 7 \end{cases}$ **$a = -1, b = -3$**

3. $\begin{cases} r = 2t \\ 3r - 5t = 2 \end{cases}$ **$r = 4, t = 2$**

4. $\begin{cases} m = 3n - 5 \\ n + 4m = 6 \end{cases}$ **$m = 1, n = 2$**

5. $\begin{cases} x = 3n \\ y = 4n \\ 2x + y = 120 \end{cases}$ **$n = 12, x = 36, y = 48$**

6. $\begin{cases} x = 5p \\ y = -2p \\ x - 4y = 52 \end{cases}$ **$p = 4, x = 20, y = -8$**

7. $\begin{cases} h = 4k \\ 3h + 2k = 21 \end{cases}$ **$h = 6, k = \frac{3}{2}$**

8. $\begin{cases} x = 2 - y \\ x = 5 + 3y \end{cases}$ **$x = \frac{11}{4}, y = -\frac{3}{4}$**

■USES *Objective F*

9. A boat can travel r mph in still water. This is three times as fast as the current, c, in a river. The boat can go downstream at 12 mph. What is the speed of the boat and the speed of the current? **$r = 9$ mph, $c = 3$ mph**

10. Helen earned \$240 in the summer by working at a fast food restaurant and baby-sitting. If she earned five times as much in the restaurant as she did baby-sitting, how much did she earn at each job? **\$200 at the restaurant, \$40 baby-sitting**

11. In 14-carat gold, there are 14 units of gold for every 10 units of other metal. If a 14-carat gold pendant weighs 0.72 ounces, how much pure gold is in it? **0.42 ounces**

14a.

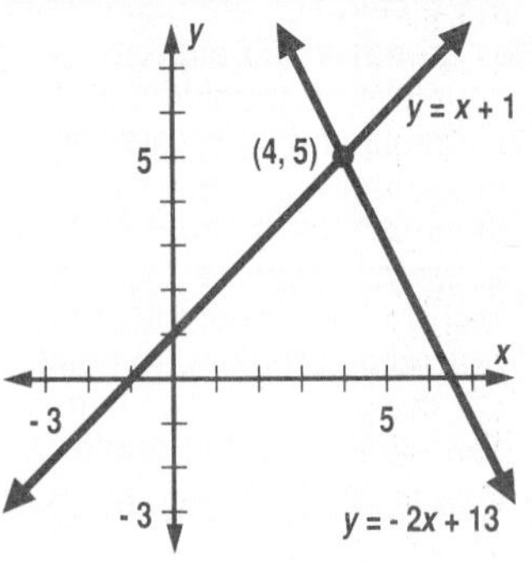

14b. $5 \stackrel{?}{=} 4 + 1$; $5 \stackrel{?}{=} -2(4) + 13$

15a.

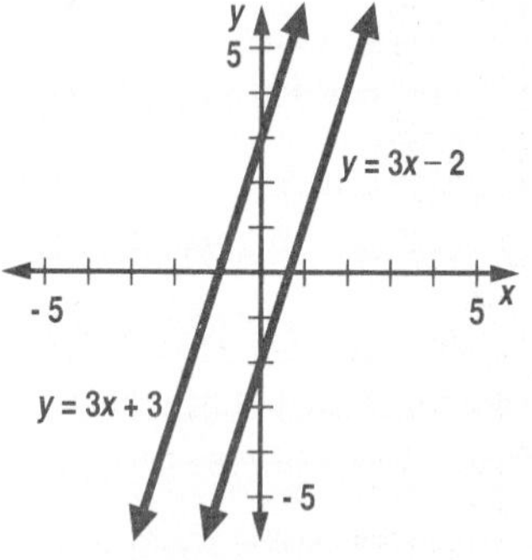

15b. There is no answer to check.

19.

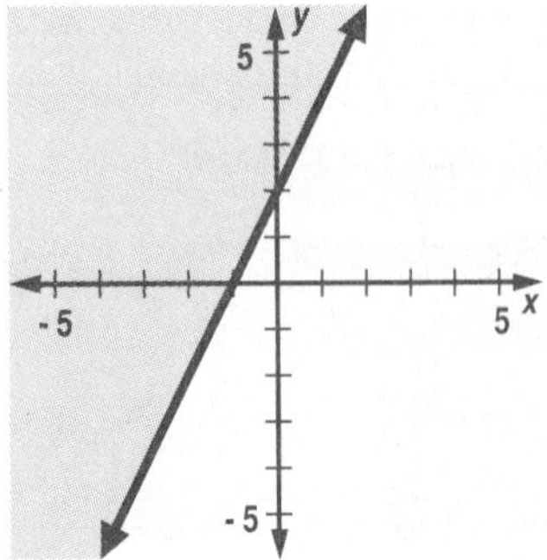

13. Profits of a company were up $200,000 this year over last year. This was a 25% increase. If T and L the profits in dollars for this year and last year, then:

$$\begin{cases} T = L + 200{,}000 \\ T = 1.25L. \end{cases}$$

Find the profits for this year and last year.
L = $800,000 and T = $1,000,00

Review

In 14 and 15, **a.** graph to find the solution to the system. **b.** Check your answer. *(Lesson 11-1)* **See margin.**

14. $\begin{cases} y = x + 1 \\ y = -2x + 13 \end{cases}$ **15.** $\begin{cases} y = 3x - 2 \\ y = 3x + 3 \end{cases}$

16. Solve $5x + 9y = 7$ for y. *(Lesson 8-4)* $y = \frac{-5}{9}x + \frac{7}{9}$

17. Expand and simplify $x^2 + y^2$ when $y = x - 1$. *(Lessons 10-2, 10-5)*
$2x^2 - 2x + 1$

18. Subtract $a + b + 7$ from $3a + b - 2$. *(Lesson 6-9)* $2a - 9$

19. Graph $y \geq 2x + 2$ on a coordinate plane. *(Lesson 8-9)* **See margin.**

In 20–22, solve. *(Lesson 6-6)*

20. $3x + 11 = -2x - 1$ $\frac{-12}{5}$

21. $-4y + 18 = 81 - 7y$ 21

22. $15z - 3(4 + 8z) = 21$ $\frac{-11}{3}$

Exploration

23. Sister cities Lovely and Elylov are building a joint conference center that will cost $10 million. Lovely's population in the last census was 35,729. Elylov's population was 74,212. How would you suggest they split the costs? **E: $6,750,323.52; L: $3,249,909.84**

540

LESSON 11-3

More with Substitution

Substitution is a good way to solve a system of two equations if both are solved for the same variable. This is the case if you have equations of two lines in slope-intercept form and want the exact intersection.

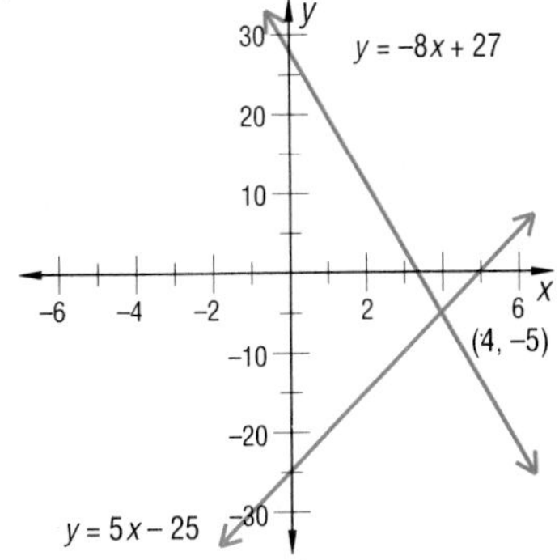

Example 1 In the graph above, two lines have equations $y = 5x - 25$ and $y = -8x + 27$. Where do they intersect? (Note that the units shown on the x-axis and y-axis are different.)

Solution Solve the system.

$$\begin{cases} y = 5x - 25 & (1) \\ y = -8x + 27 & (2) \end{cases}$$

Substitute $-8x + 27$ for y in equation (1).

$-8x + 27 = 5x - 25$

Now solve for x as usual.

$$\begin{aligned} 27 &= 13x - 25 \\ 52 &= 13x \\ 4 &= x \end{aligned}$$

To find y, substitute 4 for x in either equation. We use equation (1).

$$y = 5 \cdot 4 - 25 = -5$$

The point of intersection is (4, -5).

Check The point is on both lines, as substitution shows.

$-5 = 5 \cdot 4 - 25$ and $-5 = -8 \cdot 4 + 27$

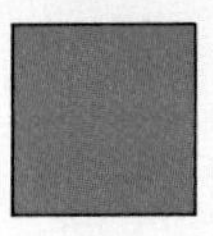

LESSON 11-3

RESOURCES

- Lesson Master 11-3
- Quiz on Lessons 11-1 Through 11-3

OBJECTIVES

A Solve systems using substitution.
F Use systems of equations to solve real world problems involving linear combinations.

TEACHING NOTES

The solutions of the examples are justified by substitution. You could also say that

$$-8x + 27 = 5x - 25$$

in **Example 1** is justified by the Symmetric and Transitive Properties of Equality. That is, from the given $y = A$ and $y = B$, the Symmetric Property of Equality allows $A = y$, and then the Transitive Property of Equality allows $A = B$. Some attention to these properties will serve as a precursor to the next lesson, which generalizes the Addition Property of Equality.

ADDITIONAL EXAMPLES

1. Solve $\begin{cases} y = 5x + 9 \\ y = -3x + 37 \end{cases}$
(3.5, 26.5)

2. Mrs. Janeski wants to have a clown deliver balloons to her daughter's birthday party. Two companies offer this service. Company A charges 25¢ per balloon, plus a $6 delivery fee. Company B charges 40¢ per balloon, but does not have a delivery fee. For what number of balloons would the cost be the same? (Let x = number of balloons. Let y = cost of x balloons.)
$\begin{cases} y = .25x + 6 \\ y = .40x \end{cases}$ **; 40 balloons**

NOTES ON QUESTIONS
Alternate Approach for Questions 6 and 7: A graph of the equations in **Example 2** provides an alternate way of answering these questions. Still another way is to test a distance other than .8 miles (where the costs are equal.) This test is similar to testing a point to decide which side of the boundary to shade when graphing an inequality.

Question 15: You might wish to get data for one or two large cities near you. The situation is perhaps most dramatic when one city is losing population (common in older cities) and a second is gaining population.

Question 23: Solving part **a** should alert students to the fact that in parts **b** and **c** it is wise to divide through by 2 first.

Small Group Work for Question 24: This question lends itself well to small group work.

ADDITIONAL ANSWERS
9.

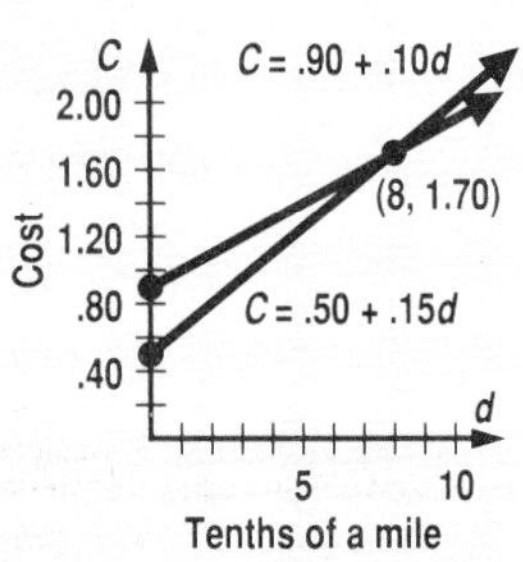

Suppose two quantities are increasing or decreasing at different constant rates. You may want to know when they are equal. The answer can be found by solving a system.

Example 2 A taxi ride in Burford costs 90¢ plus 10¢ each $\frac{1}{10}$ mile. In Spotswood, taxi rides cost 50¢ plus 15¢ each $\frac{1}{10}$ mile. For what distance do the rides cost the same?

Solution Let d = the distance of a cab ride, in *tenths* of a mile. Let C = the cost of a cab ride of distance d.

In Burford: $C = .90 + .10d$ (1)
In Spotswood: $C = .50 + .15d$ (2)

The rides cost the same when the values of C and d in Burford equal the values in Spotswood. So there is a system to solve. Since both equations are expressed in terms of C, substitute $.90 + .10d$ for C in equation (2).

$$.90 + .10d = .50 + .15d$$

Now solve as usual.

$$.05d = .40$$
$$d = 8$$

So a ride of 8 tenths of a mile will cost the same in either city.

Check Check to see if the cost will be the same for a ride of 8 tenths of a mile.

The cost in Burford is $.90 + .10 \cdot 8 = .90 + .80 = 1.70$.
The cost in Spotswood is $.50 + .15 \cdot 8 = .50 + 1.20 = 1.70$.
The cost is $1.70 in each city, so it checks.

Questions

Covering the Reading

1. *True or false* Solving a system by substitution only approximates the answer. **False**

In 2 and 3, find the point of intersection of the two lines.

2. $\begin{cases} y = 3x - 19 \\ y = x + 1 \end{cases}$ **(10, 11)** **3.** $\begin{cases} y = 12x + 50 \\ y = 10x - 60 \end{cases}$ **(-55, -610)**

In 4–8, refer to Example 2.

4. What would it cost for a 3-mile taxi ride in Burford? (Hint: convert to tenths of a mile) **\$3.90**

5. What would it cost for a 2.5-mile taxi ride in Spotswood? **\$4.25**

6. At what distances are taxi rides more expensive in Burford than in Spotswood? **distances less than 8 tenths of a mile**

7. At what distances are taxi rides more expensive in Spotswood than in Burford? **distances greater than 8 tenths of a mile**

8. Suppose that in Manassas, a taxi ride costs \$.70 plus 10¢ each $\frac{1}{10}$ mile.

a. What does it cost to ride d tenths of a mile? **.70 + .10*d* dollars**

b. At what distance does a ride in Manassas cost the same as a ride in Spotswood? **4 tenths of a mile**

Applying the Mathematics

9. Check the answer to Example 2 by graphing the lines $C = .90 + .10d$ and $C = .50 + .15d$ on the same axes. (Let d be the first coordinate and C be the second coordinate.) **See margin.**

In 10–12, solve each system. Check your answers. **See margin.**

10. $\begin{cases} y = 21 - x \\ y = 3 + x \end{cases}$ **(9, 12)**

11. $\begin{cases} a = 2b + 3 \\ a = 3b + 20 \end{cases}$ **(-31, -17)**

12. $\begin{cases} y = \frac{1}{2}x - 5 \\ y = -\frac{3}{4}x + 10 \end{cases}$ **(12, 1)**

13. Jana has \$290 and saves \$5 a week. Dana has \$200 and saves \$8 a week.

a. After how many weeks will they each have the same amount of money? **30**

b. How much money will each one have? **\$440**

 **14.** One plumbing company charges \$45 for the first half-hour of work and \$23 for each additional half-hour. Another company charges \$35 for the first half-hour and then \$28 for each additional half-hour. For how many hours will the cost of each company be the same? **1.5**

10. Does 12 = 21 − 9? Yes. Does 12 = 3 + 9? Yes.

11. Does -31 = 2(-17) + 3? Yes. Does -31 = 3(-17) + 20? Yes.

12. Does 1 = $\frac{1}{2}$(12) − 5? Yes. Does 1 = -$\frac{3}{4}$(12) + 10? Yes.

21.

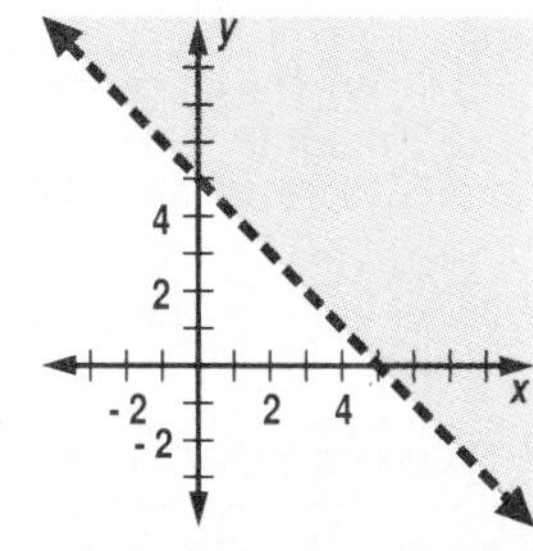

NAME ____________

LESSON **MASTER 11–3**
QUESTIONS ON **SPUR** OBJECTIVES

■**SKILLS** *Objective A (See pages 583–585 for objectives.)*
In 1–8, find the point of intersection of the lines with the given equations.

1. $\begin{cases} y = 3x + 1 \\ y = x - 9 \end{cases}$ **x = -5, y = -14**

2. $\begin{cases} r = 11 - s \\ r = -3s + 9 \end{cases}$ **r = 12, s = -1**

3. $\begin{cases} p = 0.4q + 1.6 \\ p = 0.2q - 1.8 \end{cases}$ **p = -5.2, q = -17**

4. $\begin{cases} u = 0.6v - 3.2 \\ u = 0.3v - 3.1 \end{cases}$ **u = -3, v = $\frac{1}{3}$**

5. $\begin{cases} y = \frac{1}{2}x - \frac{1}{3} \\ y = \frac{1}{6}x + \frac{1}{4} \end{cases}$ **x = $\frac{7}{4}$, y = $\frac{13}{24}$**

6. $\begin{cases} a = \frac{2}{3}b + \frac{1}{2} \\ a = \frac{1}{6}b + \frac{1}{3} \end{cases}$ **a = $\frac{5}{18}$, b = -$\frac{1}{3}$**

■**USES** *Objective F*

7. A tortoise and a hare are racing. The tortoise goes one foot per second and the hare runs 13 feet per second. The tortoise has a 24 ft head start. (The hare must travel 24 ft more than the tortoise.) How many feet will the hare have to run to catch up with the tortoise? **26 feet**

8. For a certain call one long distance phone company charges \$2 for the first three minutes and 60 cents for each additional minute. Another company charges \$1.50 for the first three minutes and 70 cents for each additional minute for the same call. After how many minutes beyond three minutes will the total charge be the same for both companies? **5 minutes**

96

FOLLOW-UP

MORE PRACTICE
For more questions on SPUR Objectives, use *Lesson Master 11-3,* shown on page 543.

EXTENSION
Computer Both of the examples in this lesson relate to the slope-intercept form of the equations of two intersecting lines. The following computer program asks for equations in slope-intercept form and gives the solution. It requires that the slopes of the two lines be different, so that there is a unique solution. Students can use this program for the examples and questions in this lesson.

```
10  PRINT "FIND
    INTERSECTION OF
    LINES"
20  PRINT "ENTER
    SLOPE, INTERCEPT
    OF FIRST LINE"
30  INPUT M1,B1
40  PRINT "ENTER
    SLOPE, INTERCEPT
    OF SECOND LINE"
50  INPUT M2,B2
60  PRINT "SYSTEM IS"
70  PRINT "Y=";M1;
    "X + ";B1
80  PRINT "Y=";M2;
    "X + ";B2
90  LET X=(B2-B1)/
    (M1-M2)
100 LET Y=M1*X+B1
110 PRINT "SOLUTION IS
    X="; X;"AND Y=";Y
120 END
```

EVALUATION
A quiz covering Lessons 11-1 through 11-3 is provided in the Teacher's Resource File.

21. See margin, page 543.

15. In 1980, the population of Pittsburgh was about 424,000 and was decreasing by about 10,000 people a year. The 1980 population of Phoenix, Arizona, was about 790,000 and was increasing by 20,000 people a year.
 a. If these trends had been going on for some time, how many years before 1980 did each city have the same population? **12.2 years**
 b. What was this population? **546,000**

16. Frank weighs 160 lb and is on a diet to gain 2 lb a week so that he can make the football team. John weighs 208 lb and is on a diet to lose 3 lb a week so that he can be on the wrestling team at a lower weight. If they can meet these goals with their diets, when will Frank and John weigh the same, and how much will they weigh?
9.6 weeks, 179.2 pounds

Review

17. Solve this system by substitution. *(Lesson 11-2)* **$b = -1.9$; $a = -4.6$**

$$\begin{cases} a = 4b + 3 \\ 2b - 3a = 10 \end{cases}$$

18. Suppose 8 pounds of peanuts cost \$15.90. At that rate, what is the cost of 10 pounds of peanuts? *(Lesson 4-2)* **\$19.88**

19. Calculate the y-intercept in your head. *(Lesson 8-4)*
 a. $y = 7x - 2$ **-2** **b.** $2x + y = 7$ **7** **c.** $7 + y = 2x$ **-7**

20. Factor $3a^2b - 12ab^3 + 27ab$. *(Lesson 10-10)* **$3ab(a - 4b^2 + 9)$**

21. Graph all points for which $y > -x + 5$. *(Lesson 8-9)* **See margin.**

22. Simplify $\frac{7m^4n^5}{343m^3n^6}$. *(Lesson 9-8)* **$\frac{m}{49n}$**

23. *Skill sequence* Solve for x. *(Lessons 6-1, 7-6, 10-10)*
 a. $2x - 18 = 0$ **9**
 b. $2x^2 - 18 = 0$ **3 or -3**
 c. $2x^2 - 18x = 0$ **0 or 9**

Exploration

24. Find the taxi rates where you live or in a nearby community. How do these rates compare to the cities in Example 2? **Answers will vary.**

LESSON 11-4

Solving Systems by Addition

The numbers $\frac{3}{4}$ and 75% are equal even though they do not look equal. So are $\frac{1}{5}$ and 20%. If you add these numbers (as seen below), the sums are equal.

$$\frac{3}{4} = 75\%$$

$$\frac{1}{5} = 20\%$$

So $$\frac{3}{4} + \frac{1}{5} = 75\% + 20\%.$$

Simplifying each side, $$\frac{19}{20} = 95\%.$$

This is one instance of the following generalization of the Addition Property of Equality.

Generalized Addition Property of Equality:

For all numbers or expressions a, b, c, and d:

If $a = b$
and $c = d$,
then $a + c = b + d$.

The Generalized Addition Property of Equality is quite useful in solving some systems. Consider the system

$$\begin{cases} 3x + 2y = 1 & (1) \\ x - 2y = 107 & (2). \end{cases}$$

If x and y satisfy both equations, they will satisfy the equation that results from adding the left and right sides. In this case $2y$ and $-2y$ add to 0, so the sum has only one variable.

$$\begin{array}{rl} 3x + 2y = 1 & (1) \\ \underline{x - 2y = 107} & (2) \\ 4x \quad\quad = 108 & (1) + (2) \end{array}$$

The line below equation (2) indicates the addition. Adding equation (1) and equation (2) gives equation (1) + (2). Solve $4x = 108$ as usual.

$$x = 27$$

To find y, substitute 27 for x in equation (1).

$$\begin{aligned} 3(27) + 2y &= 1 \\ 81 + 2y &= 1 \\ 2y &= -80 \\ y &= -40 \end{aligned}$$

Since (27, -40) checks in both equations, it is the solution. This **addition method** is an easy way to solve systems when coefficients of the same variable are opposites.

LESSON 11-4

RESOURCES

- Lesson Master 11-4
- Visual for Teaching Aid 61: Diagram for Additional Example 3

OBJECTIVES

B Solve systems by addition.
F Use systems of equations to solve real world problems involving linear combinations.

TEACHING NOTES

Compare the Generalized Addition Property of Equality to the original Addition Property of Equality presented in Lesson 2-6 (page 85). There, the same expression was added to both sides of an equation. Here, equal expressions are added.

It is easy to follow the steps in this algorithm in the lesson because the equal signs are aligned and the variables are written in neat columns. Tell students they will avoid errors if they do the same. To emphasize the benefit of the variables and symbols being properly organized, you might want to show a system slightly more complicated than those in the examples. For instance, use the system

$$\begin{cases} 4x - 3y = 20 \\ -4y + 36 + x = 2x \end{cases}$$

None of the systems in the questions are as complicated as the one above. The exercises are set up so that students should not have to perform extensive transformations on the equations. The only transformation needed is illustrated in **Example 2**—multiplication of both sides of the equation by -1.

Example 1 Mr. Robinson flew his small plane the 80 miles from Tampa to Orlando in 40 minutes ($\frac{2}{3}$ hour) against the wind. He returned to Tampa in 32 minutes ($\frac{32}{60}$ hour) with the wind at his back. How fast was he flying? What was the speed of the wind?

Solution Let A be the average speed of the airplane without wind and W be the speed of the wind, both in miles per hour. His total speed against the wind is then $A - W$, and his speed with the wind is $A + W$. There are two conditions given on these total speeds.

From Tampa to Orlando his rate was $\frac{80 \text{ miles}}{\frac{2}{3} \text{ hour}}$ or $120 \frac{\text{miles}}{\text{hour}}$.

This was against the wind, so $A - W = 120$.

From Orlando to Tampa his rate was $\frac{80 \text{ miles}}{\frac{32}{60} \text{ hour}}$ or $150 \frac{\text{miles}}{\text{hour}}$.

This was with the wind, so $A + W = 150$.
Now solve the following system. Since the coefficients of W are opposites (1 and -1), add the equations.

$$\begin{aligned} A - W &= 120 \quad (1) \\ A + W &= 150 \quad (2) \\ \text{Adding,} \quad 2A \quad &= 270 \quad (1) + (2) \\ A &= 135 \end{aligned}$$

Substitute 135 for A in either equation. We choose (2).

$$\begin{aligned} 135 + W &= 150 \\ W &= 15 \end{aligned}$$

So the average speed of the airplane was 135 mph and the speed of the wind was 15 mph.

Check Refer to the original question. Against the wind, he flew at $135 - 15$ or 120 mph. In 40 minutes ($\frac{2}{3}$ of an hour) he would travel 80 miles, as desired. With the wind he was flying $135 + 15$ or 150 mph. At that rate he flew 80 miles in 32 minutes, which checks with the given conditions.

Sometimes the coefficients of the same variable are equal. In this case, use the Multiplication Property of Equality to multiply both sides of one of the equations by -1. This changes all the numbers in that equation to their opposites. Then you can use the addition method to find solutions to the system. Alternatively, you may subtract one equation from the other.

Example 2 Solve this system.

$$\begin{cases} 4x + 13y = 40 & (1) \\ 4x + 3y = -40 & (2) \end{cases}$$

Solution 1 Notice that the coefficients of x in (1) and (2) are equal. Multiply (2) by -1. Call this equation (3).

$$-4x - 3y = 40 \quad (3)$$

Now use the addition method with (1) and (3).

$$\begin{array}{rcll} 4x + 13y &=& 40 & (1) \\ -4x - 3y &=& 40 & (3) \\ \hline 10y &=& 80 & (1) + (3) \\ y &=& 8 & \end{array}$$

Substitute 8 for y in (1) to find the value for x.

$$\begin{aligned} 4x + 13(8) &= 40 \\ 4x + 104 &= 40 \\ 4x &= -64 \\ x &= -16 \end{aligned}$$

So $(x, y) = (-16, 8)$.

Solution 2 Subtract the second equation from the first. This again gives $10y = 80$ and you can continue as in Solution 1.

Check Substitute in both equations.

(1) Does $4 \cdot -16 + 13 \cdot 8 = 40$? Yes.
(2) Does $4 \cdot -16 + 3 \cdot 8 = -40$? Yes.

ADDITIONAL EXAMPLES

1. A blimp flies 360 miles to an air show going with the wind. The trip takes 4 hours. The return trip, flying against the wind, takes 9 hours. How fast is the blimp in still air? How fast is the wind? [Let the speed of the blimp with the wind be $(b + w)$, and let the speed of the blimp against the wind be $(b - w)$.]
$\begin{cases} b + w = 90 \\ b - w = 40 \end{cases}$;
65 mph, 25 mph

2. Solve $\begin{cases} 2x - 5y = 18 \\ 4x - 5y = -4 \end{cases}$
(-11, -8)

3. The system below comes from a Denny's restaurant in California (found coincidentally during the 1987 Annual Meeting of the National Council of Teachers of Mathematics). On each table was the following menu card (reproduced on *Teaching Aid 61*).

Multiple Choice
2 or more entrées

Choose 1 from Column *A* and 1 from columm *B*—$5.49
Choose 1 from Column *A* and 2 from column *B*—$6.99

A	***B***
• Chicken Dijon	• Fried Chicken (2 pieces)
• Top Sirloin Steak	• Battered Cod
• Steak Dijon	• Shrimp
• Fried Chicken	• Chicken Strips

$$A + B = \$5.49$$
$$A + 2B = \$6.99$$

Yes, they did show the system on the bottom of the menu card. So the question for your class is, "How much did each item in *A* cost, and how much did each item in *B* cost?"
$A = \$3.99$; $B = \$1.50$

NOTES ON QUESTIONS
Error Analysis for Questions 11 and 12: Both systems have the variables in reverse order. Students who commute the addition in the second equation of each system will probably solve the problems correctly. You will need to make sure that students who have commuted in the first equations have not equated $2x - 3y$ with $3y - 2x$ or $4z - 5w$ with $5w - 4z$.

Alternate Approach for Questions 13 and 14: Students may be able to solve **Question 13** without algebra by reasoning that the extra egg costs \$1.35 − \$.90 = \$.45, so bacon costs \$.90 − \$.45 = \$.45. **Question 14** can be answered by similar reasoning. It is worthwile to discuss these methods and then relate them to the algebra, which does the same steps abstractly.

Questions 15 and 16: While students may be able to guess the solution to **Question 15,** most will need to write a system for **Question 16.**

ADDITIONAL ANSWERS
8. Does 3(32.50) + 6(5.75) = 132? Does 97.50 + 34.50 = 132? Yes. Does 3(32.50) + 2(5.75) = 109? Does 97.50 + 11.50 = 109? Yes.

Example 3 A resort hotel offers two weekend specials.

Plan (1): 3 nights with 6 meals \$132
Plan (2): 3 nights with 2 meals \$109

At these rates, what is the cost of one nights lodging and what is the average cost per meal? (Assume there is no discount for 6 meals.)

Solution Let N = price of one nights lodging.
Let M = average price of one meal.

From Plan (1): $3N + 6M = 132$
From Plan (2): $3N + 2M = 109$

The coefficients of N are the same so subtract.

Subtract (2) from (1). $4M = 23$
$M = 5.75$

Substitute 5.75 for M in either equation. We select equation (1).

$$3N + 6(5.75) = 132$$
$$3N + 34.50 = 132$$
$$3N = 97.50$$
$$N = 32.50$$

Thus, $(N, M) = (32.50, 5.75)$.
One nights' lodging costs \$32.50 and a meal averages \$5.75.

Check In Question 8, you are asked to check that at these rates the totals for Plans (1) and (2) are correct.

Questions

Covering the Reading

1. What is the goal in adding equations to solve systems?
to eliminate one variable
2. Which property allows you to add corresponding sides of two equations to get a new equation?
the Generalized Addition Property of Equality
3. Solve. $\begin{cases} 3x + 8y = 2 \\ -3x - 4y = 6 \end{cases}$ $(-\frac{14}{3}, 2)$
4. Solve. $\begin{cases} a + b = 11 \\ a - b = 4 \end{cases}$ $(a, b) = (\frac{15}{2}, \frac{7}{2})$
5. In Example 1, suppose it took 50 minutes ($\frac{50}{60}$ hour) to fly to Orlando against the wind and 40 minutes ($\frac{2}{3}$ hour) for the return flight with the wind. Find the speed of the plane and the speed of the wind in miles per hour under these conditions.
plane speed is 108 mph; wind speed is 12 mph
6. When is it appropriate to multiply an equation by -1 or subtract the two equations as a first step in solving a system?
when coefficients of the same variable are equal

7. Solve. $\begin{cases} 2x - 3y = 5 \\ 5x - 3y = 11 \end{cases}$ **(2, $-\frac{1}{3}$)**

8. Check Example 3. **See margin.**

9. A hotel offers the following specials: Plan (1) is two nights and one meal for \$106. Plan (2) is 2 nights and 4 meals for \$130. What price is the hotel charging per night and per meal?
\$49 per night and \$8 per meal

Applying the Mathematics

10. As you know, $\frac{3}{4} = 75\%$ and $\frac{1}{5} = 20\%$. Is it true that $\frac{3}{4} - \frac{1}{5} = 55\%$?
Yes

In 11 and 12, solve.

11. $\begin{cases} 2x - 3y = 17 \\ 3y + x = 1 \end{cases}$ **(6, $-\frac{5}{3}$)** 12. $\begin{cases} 4z - 5w = 15 \\ 2w + 4z = -6 \end{cases}$ **$z = 0$; $w = -3$**

13. Two eggs with bacon cost \$1.35. One egg with bacon costs \$.90. At these rates, what should bacon alone cost? **45¢**

14. Five gallons of unleaded gas plus eight gallons of regular cost \$13.87. Five gallons of unleaded plus two gallons of regular cost \$7.93. Find the cost per gallon of each kind of gasoline. **Regular is \$.99 per gallon; unleaded is \$1.19 per gallon.**

15. Find two numbers whose sum is -1 and whose difference is 5.
2 and -3

16. Find two numbers whose sum is 4386 and whose difference is 2822.
782 and 3604

Review

In 17 and 18, solve. *(Lessons 11-2, 11-3)*

17. $\begin{cases} y = 2x - 1 \\ y = 9x + 6 \end{cases}$ **(-1, -3)** 18. $\begin{cases} Q = 4z \\ R = -5z \\ 4R + Q = 40 \end{cases}$ **$z = -\frac{5}{2}$, $Q = -10$, and $R = \frac{25}{2}$**

19. Ida is playing with toothpicks. It takes 5 toothpicks to make a pentagon and 6 toothpicks to make a hexagon. She has 100 toothpicks. She wants to make P pentagons and H hexagons. Give three different possible values of P and H that use up all the toothpicks. *(Lesson 8-9)*
sample: $P = 20$, $H = 0$; $P = 14$, $H = 5$; $P = 8$, $H = 10$

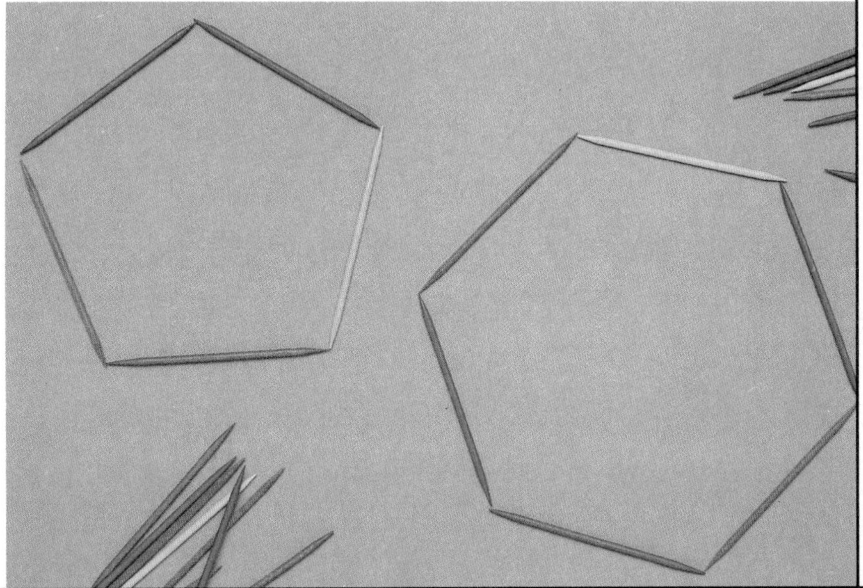

NAME ______

LESSON MASTER 11–4
QUESTIONS ON **SPUR** OBJECTIVES

■SKILLS *Objective B (See pages 583–585 for objectives.)*
In 1–10, solve each system of equations.

1. $\begin{cases} 2x - y = 7 \\ x + y = 5 \end{cases}$ **$x = 4$, $y = 1$**

2. $\begin{cases} 3h - k = 7 \\ 2h + k = 8 \end{cases}$ **$h = 3$, $k = 2$**

3. $\begin{cases} 3u + 2v = 18 \\ 5u - 2v = 14 \end{cases}$ **$u = 4$, $v = 3$**

4. $\begin{cases} 2a + b = 9 \\ 2a - 3b = 5 \end{cases}$ **$a = 4$, $b = 1$**

5. $\begin{cases} 2r - 3s = 1 \\ 2r - 4s = 2 \end{cases}$ **$r = -1$, $s = -1$**

6. $\begin{cases} 4x - 3y = 30 \\ 7x - 3y = 48 \end{cases}$ **$x = 6$, $y = -2$**

7. $\begin{cases} \frac{5}{6}c - d = 2 \\ \frac{2}{3}c + d = 16 \end{cases}$ **$c = 12$, $d = 8$**

8. $\begin{cases} \frac{3}{4}a + \frac{1}{3}b = 6 \\ \frac{1}{2}a - \frac{1}{3}b = 4 \end{cases}$ **$a = 8$, $b = 0$**

9. $\begin{cases} .04x + .02y = 1.8 \\ .04x - .01y = 1.5 \end{cases}$ **$x = 40$, $y = 10$**

10. $\begin{cases} .7y + .2z = 11 \\ .4y - .2z = 11 \end{cases}$ **$y = 20$, $z = -15$**

■USES *Objective F*

11. The sum of two numbers is 79 and their difference is 5. What are the numbers?
37 and 42

12. Three hamburgers and two orders of fries cost \$6.10. Four hamburgers and two orders of fries cost \$7.60. At these rates, what is the cost h of one hamburger and the cost f of one order of fries?
$h = \$1.50$, $f = \$.80$

13. Marianne has two investments. The first pays 4% interest and the second pays 5%. The total annual interest is \$130. If the first investment paid 6%, her annual interest would be \$170. How much does she have invested at each rate?
at 4%: \$2000; at 5%: \$1000

 97

3F—Algebra Spur. p. 97

NOTES ON QUESTIONS
Making Connections for Questions 25-27: These questions review rewriting an equation in standard form. You can mention that sometimes this is a useful step when solving a system. Problems involving this idea appear in the next lesson.

Question 28: Students must change a repeating decimal to a fraction. Ask students to use this process to write $.\overline{9}$ as a fraction. They will be surprised at the result. As further verification, they can do $.\overline{3} + .\overline{6} = .\overline{9}$ by converting to fractions. But $.\overline{4} + .\overline{7} \neq 1.\overline{1}$.

FOLLOW-UP

MORE PRACTICE
For more questions on SPUR Objectives, use *Lesson Master 11-4,* shown on page 549.

EXTENSION
Ask students to solve (or demonstrate the solution for them) the following nonlinear system, which can be solved with addition.

$$\begin{cases} 2x - y^2 = -2 \\ x + y^2 = 14 \end{cases}$$

[Adding gives $3x = 12$; $x = 4$. Substituting in the first equation gives $8 - y^2 = -2$ or $10 = y^2$. So $y = \pm\sqrt{10}$. The points $(4, \sqrt{10})$ and $(4, -\sqrt{10})$ are where two parabolas intersect.]

23.

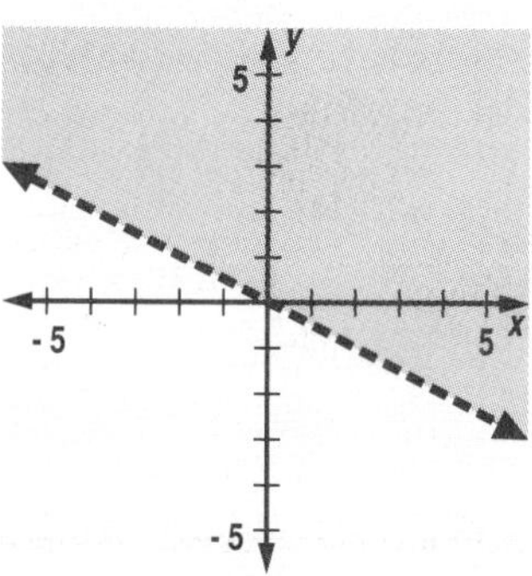

In 20 and 21, simplify by removing parentheses.

20. $3(2a^2 - 5)$ *(Lesson 6-3)* **$6a^2 - 15$**

21. $b^2(2b^2)$ *(Lesson 9-5)* **$2b^4$**

22. Suppose a 30-gram necklace is 14K gold. This means $\frac{14}{24}$ of the necklace is gold and the rest is other materials. How many grams of gold are in the necklace? *(Lesson 5-3)* **17.5 grams**

23. Graph the half-plane $x + 2y > 0$. *(Lesson 8-9)* **See margin.**

24. *Skill Sequence* Simplify. *(Lessons 2-2, 6-9, 7-8)*
a. $100 - (80 - 4p) + 2(p + 5)$ **$30 + 6p$**
b. $\frac{100}{p+2} - \frac{80 - 4p}{p+2} + \frac{2(p+5)}{p+2}$ **$\frac{30 + 6p}{p + 2}$**

In 25–27, rewrite in the form $Ax + By = C$. *(Lesson 8-8)*

25. $-15 - 8x = y$ **$8x + y = -15$ or $-8x - y = 15$**

26. $2x + y = 17 - 7y$ **$2x + 8y = 17$ or $-2x - 8y = -17$**

27. $9y - 15 = 4x + 2y - 7$ **$4x - 7y = -8$ or $-4x + 7y = 8$**

Exploration

28. Multiplying equations by 100 can be used to find simple fractions for repeating decimals. For instance, to find a fraction for $.\overline{39}$, first let $d = .\overline{39}$. Then

	$100d = 39.\overline{39}$	(1)
	$d = .\overline{39}$	(2)
Subtract (2) from (1).	$99d = 39$	(1) − (2)
Solve for d.	$d = \frac{39}{99}$	
Simplify the fraction.	$d = \frac{13}{33}$	

A calculator shows that $\frac{13}{33}$ has a decimal equivalent 0.393939...
a. Use this process to find a simple fraction equal to $.\overline{81}$. **$\frac{9}{11}$**
b. Modify the process to find a simple fraction equal to $.\overline{003}$. **$\frac{1}{333}$**
c. Find a simple fraction equal to $3.89\overline{5}$. **$\frac{3506}{900}$**

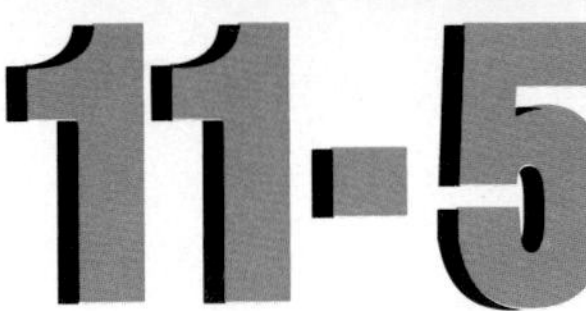

LESSON

11-5

Multiplying to Solve Systems

Recall that there are two common forms for equations of lines.

standard form: $Ax + By = C$
slope-intercept form: $y = mx + b$

The substitution method described in Lesson 11-3 is convenient for solving systems in which one or both equations are in slope-intercept form. The **multiplication method** outlined in the following example provides a way to solve any system where both equations are in standard form. The idea is to multiply one of the equations by a number chosen so that the addition method can be used on the result.

Example 1 Solve the following system.

$$\begin{cases} 5x + 8y = 21 & (1) \\ 10x - 3y = -15 & (2) \end{cases}$$

Solution 1 Multiply equation (1) by -2. This makes the coefficients of x opposites of one another. The code (3) = -2 · (1) in the solution below shows what has been done; equation (3) is found by multiplying both sides of equation (1) by -2. The solutions are unchanged because of the Multiplication Property of Equality.

$$\begin{cases} -10x - 16y = -42 & (3) = -2 \cdot (1) \\ 10x - 3y = -15 & (2) \end{cases}$$

Add the equations. $-19y = -57$ (3) + (2)
Solve for y. $y = 3$
Substitute $y = 3$ in (1) to find x.

$$5x + 8 \cdot 3 = 21$$
$$5x + 24 = 21$$
$$5x = -3$$
$$x = -\frac{3}{5}$$

So the solution is $(x, y) = (-\frac{3}{5}, 3)$.

Solution 2 Multiply equation (2) by $-\frac{1}{2}$. This also makes the coefficients of x opposites.

$$\begin{cases} 5x + 8y = 21 & (1) \\ -5x + 1.5y = 7.5 & (3) = -\frac{1}{2} \cdot (2) \end{cases}$$

Add. $9.5y = 28.5$ (1) + (3)
$y = 3$

LESSON 11-5

RESOURCES
■ Lesson Master 11-5

OBJECTIVES

C Solve systems by multiplying.
F Use systems of equations to solve real world problems involving linear combinations.

TEACHING NOTES

Example 1 shows students that either equation can be multiplied to eliminate the variable x. The solution is the same either way the problem is solved. You might want to also show students that this system can be solved by first eliminating the variable y. Multiply equation (1) by 3 and equation (2) by 8. Then

$$\begin{array}{rcr} 15x + 24y & = & 63 \\ 80x - 24y & = & -120 \\ \hline 95x & = & -57 \end{array}$$

$$x = -\frac{57}{95} = -\frac{3}{5}$$

Very frequently there is a best choice of multiplication—one which will keep the products small and minimize the arithmetic needed for the rest of the solution. Do not expect your students to make the ideal choice of multiplication every time. Students need experience with the algorithm before they become skilled at selecting the most efficient multipliers.

In **Example 3,** emphasize that the multiplication method will always find a solution to the *system* if one exists, but the *situation* in **Example 3** requires that the solution be an integer. You can modify the situation slightly by asking whether the band and pompon people can form hexagons and squares if one of the band members is sick and can't march. The system can still be solved, but the number of hexagons is 180/23. You might ask students how many band members should be sent to the sidelines if a band member is ill. This question is related to **Questions 25 and 26.**

The solution would proceed as in Solution 1 to find x. Again $(x, y) = (-\frac{3}{5}, 3)$.

Check Does $5 \cdot -\frac{3}{5} + 8 \cdot 3 = 21$? Yes, $-3 + 24 = 21$.

Does $10 \cdot -\frac{3}{5} - 2 \cdot 3 = -12$? Yes, $-6 - 6 = -12$.

Example 1 shows that the solution is the same no matter which equation is multiplied by a number. The goal is to obtain coefficients of one variable which are opposites. Then add the resulting equations to eliminate one of the variables.

Sometimes you must multiply *each* equation by a number before adding.

Example 2 Solve the system.

$$\begin{cases} 3a + 5b = 8 & (1) \\ 2a + 3b = 4.6 & (2) \end{cases}$$

Solution To make the coefficients of a opposites, multiply equation (1) by 2 and equation (2) by -3.

$$\begin{cases} 6a + 10b = 16 & (3) = 2 \cdot (1) \\ -6a - 9b = -13.8 & (4) = -3 \cdot (2) \end{cases}$$

Now add. $$b = 2.2 \quad (3) + (4)$$

Substitute in equation (1) to find the value of a.

$$\begin{aligned} 3a + 5(2.2) &= 8 \\ 3a + 11 &= 8 \\ 3a &= -3 \\ a &= -1 \end{aligned}$$

Therefore, $(a, b) = (-1, 2.2)$.

Check Does $3(-1) + 5(2.2) = 8$? Yes, $-3 + 11 = 8$.
Does $2(-1) + 3(2.2) = 4.6$? Yes, $-2 + 6.6 = 4.6$.

Many situations lead naturally to linear equations in standard form. This results in a linear system that can be solved using the multiplication method.

Example 3 A marching band has 52 members and there are 24 in the pompon squad. They wish to form hexagons and squares like those diagrammed below. Can it be done with no people left over?

HEXAGON *pompon person in center*	SQUARE *band member in center*	
Ⓑ Ⓑ Ⓑ P Ⓑ Ⓑ Ⓑ	P P Ⓑ P P	B = band member P = pompon person

Solution Consider the entire formation to include h hexagons and s squares. There are two conditions in the system: one for band members and one for pompon people.

There are 6 $\frac{\text{band members}}{\text{hexagon}}$ and 1 $\frac{\text{band member}}{\text{square}}$, so $6h + s = 52$. (1)

There is 1 $\frac{\text{pompon person}}{\text{hexagon}}$ and 4 $\frac{\text{pompon people}}{\text{square}}$, so $h + 4s = 24$. (2)

To solve the system, multiply equation (1) by -4 and add to equation (2).

$$\begin{aligned} -24h - 4s &= -208 \\ h + 4s &= 24 \\ \hline -23h \quad &= -184 \\ h &= 8 \end{aligned}$$

Substitute 8 for h in (1).

$$\begin{aligned} 6 \cdot 8 + s &= 52 \\ 48 + s &= 52 \\ s &= 4 \end{aligned}$$

Since h and s are both positive integers, the formations can be done with no people left over.

Check 8 hexagons would use 48 band members and 8 pompon people. 4 squares would use 4 band members and 16 pompon people. This setup uses exactly 52 band members and 24 pompon people.

ADDITIONAL EXAMPLES

1. Solve $\begin{cases} 5x + 2y = 11 \\ x + 6y = 19 \end{cases}$
(1, 3)

2. Solve $\begin{cases} 5a + 3b = -15 \\ a - .5b = -3 \end{cases}$
(-3, 0)

3. The accounting department of a company bought 4 staplers and 5 boxes of paper for $51.50. The planning department bought 10 staplers and one box of paper for $65.50. What is the cost of a stapler? of a box of paper?
$\begin{cases} \mathbf{4x + 5y = 51.50} \\ \mathbf{10x + y = 65.50} \end{cases}$;
stapler: $6, box of paper: $5.50

NOTES ON QUESTIONS
Question 5: This question emphasizes that a system can be solved by eliminating either variable.

Question 13: This situation should be familiar to teachers who have had to make up exams worth a particular number of points.

FOLLOW-UP

MORE PRACTICE
For more questions on SPUR Objectives, use *Lesson Master 11-5,* shown on page 555.

EXTENSION
Computer The following program is similar to the one in the Extension for Lesson 11-3. It works for equations written in standard form. It does not test situations in which there are no solutions or an infinite number of solutions. Have students use the program to solve the systems in this lesson.

```
10  PRINT "SOLVE A SYSTEM OF EQUATIONS"
20  PRINT "FIRST EQUATION AX + BY = C"
30  PRINT "ENTER A, B, AND C."
40  INPUT A,B,C
50  PRINT "SECOND EQUATION DX + EY = F"
60  PRINT "ENTER D, E, AND F"
70  INPUT D,E,F
80  DT = A*E-D*B
90  PRINT "X =";(C*E-B*F)/DT
100 PRINT "Y =";(A*F-D*C)/DT
110 END
```

A system can involve equations that are not in standard or slope-intercept form. Then it is wisest to rewrite the equations in one of these forms before proceeding. For example, to solve the system

$$\begin{cases} 5b = 8 - 3a & (1) \\ 2a + 3b = 4.6 & (2) \end{cases}$$

you could add $3a$ to both sides of equation (1). The result is the system that was solved in Example 2.

Questions

Covering the Reading

1. Which property allows you to multiply both sides of an equation in a system by a number without changing the solutions?
the Multiplication Property of Equality
2. What is the goal of multiplying one or both equations in a system?
to obtain coefficients of one variable that are opposites
3. Consider this system. $\begin{cases} 6u - 5v = 2 & (1) \\ 12u - 8v = 5 & (2) \end{cases}$
   a. If equation (1) is multiplied by __?__, then adding the equations will eliminate u. **-2**
   b. Solve the system. **$(u, v) = (\frac{3}{4}, \frac{1}{2})$**

4. In Example 2, equation (1) could have been multiplied by 3 and equation (2) could have been multiplied by -5. Use this procedure to verify the solution. **See margin.**

5. Consider this system. $\begin{cases} 3a - 2b = 20 & (1) \\ 9a + 4b = 40 & (2) \end{cases}$
   a. If equation (1) is multiplied by -3, and the equations are added, what is the resulting equation? **$10b = -20$**
   b. If equation (1) is multiplied by 2, and the equations are added, what is the resulting equation? **$15a = 80$**
   c. Use one of these methods to solve the system. **$(\frac{16}{3}, -2)$**

6. Use the hexagon and square formations of Example 3. Will there be an exact fit if the marching band consists of 100 band members and 42 pompon people? **No**

In 7–10, solve the system.

7. $\begin{cases} 6m - 7n = 6 \\ 7m - 8n = 15 \end{cases}$ **$(m, n) = (57, 48)$**

8. $\begin{cases} 3x = 4y + 2 \\ 9x - 5y = 7 \end{cases}$ **$(x, y) = (\frac{6}{7}, \frac{1}{7})$**

9. $\begin{cases} 5x + y = 30 \\ 3x - 4y = 41 \end{cases}$ **$(x, y) = (7, -5)$**

10. $\begin{cases} 3a = 2b + 5 \\ a - 4b = 6 \end{cases}$ **$(a, b) = (0.8, -1.3)$**

Applying the Mathematics

11. A marching band has 67 band members and 47 pompon people. They wish to form pentagons and rectangles like those diagrammed below. Will every person have a spot? If so, how?

```
  B   B          B   P   B
B   P   B        P   P   P
    B            B   P   B
```

Yes; make 7 pentagons and 8 rectangles.

12. The sum of two numbers is 45. Three times the first number plus seven times the second is 115. Find the two numbers. **(50, -5)**

13. A test has m multiple-choice questions and t true-false questions. If multiple-choice questions are worth 7 points each and the true-false questions 2 points each, the test will be worth a total of 185 points. If multiple-choice and true-false questions are each worth 4 points each, the test will be worth a total of 200 points. Find m and t.
$m = 17$ and $t = 33$

In 14 and 15, solve the system. **14. $(m, n) = (0, 0)$ 15. $(x, y) = (1, -1)$**

14. $\begin{cases} 2m - 5n = 0 \\ 6m + n = 0 \end{cases}$

15. $\begin{cases} 4x - 3y = 2x + 5 \\ 8y = 5x - 13 \end{cases}$

Review

In 16 and 17, solve the system. **16. $(11, -\frac{78}{5})$ 17. $(x, y) = (-30, -12)$**

16. $\begin{cases} 10x + 5y = 32 \\ 8x + 5y = 10 \end{cases}$ *(Lesson 11-4)*

17. $\begin{cases} y = \frac{1}{2}x + 3 \\ y = \frac{1}{3}x - 2 \end{cases}$ *(Lesson 11-3)*

18. Molly has \$400 and saves \$25 a week. Vince has \$1400 and spends \$25 a week.
    a. How many weeks from now will they each have the same amount of money? **20 weeks**
    b. What will this amount be? *(Lesson 11-3)* **\$900**

In 19 and 20, solve each equation or inequality.

19. $x^2 + 5 = 13$ *(Lesson 7-4)* **$\pm\sqrt{8} = \pm 2\sqrt{2}$**

20. $3y - 2(4 + 2y) = 0$ *(Lesson 6-5)* **-8**

21. In December 1986, Jeana Yeager and Dick Rutan flew the Voyager airplane nonstop around the earth without refueling. The average rate for the 25,012-mile trip was 115 mph. How many days was this flight? *(Lesson 5-2)* **≈ 9 days**

ADDITIONAL ANSWERS

4. $9a + 15b = 24$
$-10a - 15b = -23$
So $a = -1$. To find b: $3(-1) + 5b = 8$, $5b = 11$, and $b = \frac{11}{5} = 2.2$. It checks.

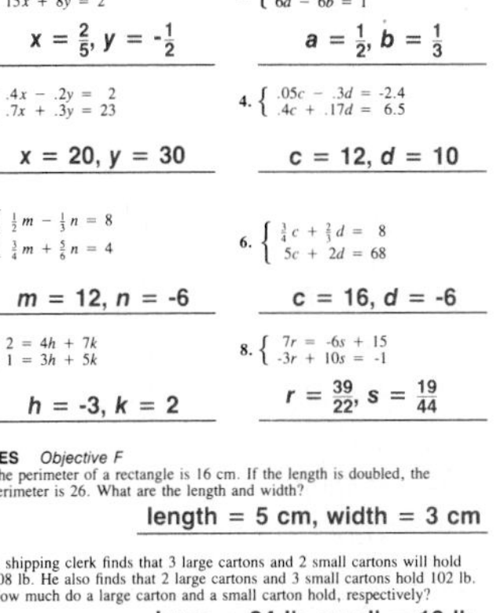

NAME ______

LESSON **MASTER 11–5**
QUESTIONS ON **SPUR** OBJECTIVES

■**SKILLS** *Objective C (See pages 583–585 for objectives.)*
In 1–8, solve each system of equations.

1. $\begin{cases} 5x - 2y = 3 \\ 15x + 8y = 2 \end{cases}$ **$x = \frac{2}{5}, y = -\frac{1}{2}$**

2. $\begin{cases} 2a + 3b = 2 \\ 6a - 6b = 1 \end{cases}$ **$a = \frac{1}{2}, b = \frac{1}{3}$**

3. $\begin{cases} .4x - .2y = 2 \\ .7x + .3y = 23 \end{cases}$ **$x = 20, y = 30$**

4. $\begin{cases} .05c - .3d = -2.4 \\ .4c + .17d = 6.5 \end{cases}$ **$c = 12, d = 10$**

5. $\begin{cases} \frac{1}{2}m - \frac{1}{3}n = 8 \\ \frac{3}{4}m + \frac{5}{6}n = 4 \end{cases}$ **$m = 12, n = -6$**

6. $\begin{cases} \frac{3}{4}c + \frac{2}{3}d = 8 \\ 5c + 2d = 68 \end{cases}$ **$c = 16, d = -6$**

7. $\begin{cases} 2 = 4h + 7k \\ 1 = 3h + 5k \end{cases}$ **$h = -3, k = 2$**

8. $\begin{cases} 7r = -6s + 15 \\ -3r + 10s = -1 \end{cases}$ **$r = \frac{39}{22}, s = \frac{19}{44}$**

■**USES** *Objective F*

9. The perimeter of a rectangle is 16 cm. If the length is doubled, the perimeter is 26. What are the length and width? **length = 5 cm, width = 3 cm**

10. A shipping clerk finds that 3 large cartons and 2 small cartons will hold 108 lb. He also finds that 2 large cartons and 3 small cartons hold 102 lb. How much do a large carton and a small carton hold, respectively? **large = 24 lb, small = 18 lb**

11. For a school play, the eighth graders sold 220 adult tickets and 100 children's tickets. They took in \$410 altogether. The ninth graders collected \$366 from the sale of 180 adult tickets and 120 children's tickets. What was the price of an adult ticket and a child's ticket? **adult = \$1.50, child = \$.80**

98

22a. PYTHAGOREAN TRIPLES
ENTER M
5
ENTER N
3
A = 16
B = 30
C = 34

22b. PYTHAGOREAN TRIPLES
ENTER M
7
ENTER N
1
A = 48
B = 14
C = 50

22c. Does $16^2 + 30^2 = 34^2$? Does $256 + 900 = 1156$? Yes.
Does $48^2 + 14^2 = 50^2$? Does $2304 + 196 = 2500$? Yes.

26. sample:

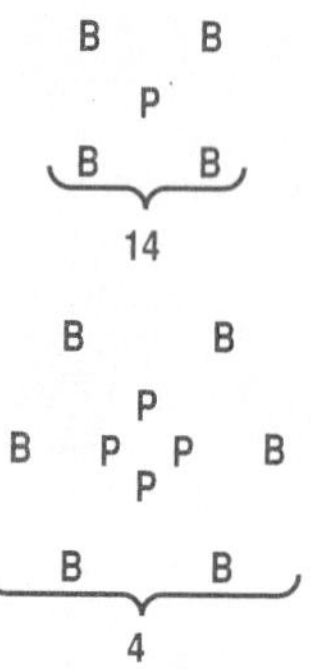

22. *Pythagorean triples* are three whole numbers A, B, and C, such that $A^2 + B^2 = C^2$. Here is a program that will generate a Pythagorean triple from two positive integers M and N where $M > N$. *(Lesson 7-5)*

```
10 PRINT "PYTHAGOREAN TRIPLES"
20 PRINT "ENTER M"
30 INPUT M
40 PRINT "ENTER N"
50 INPUT N
60 LET A = M * M - N * N
70 LET B = 2 * M * N
80 LET C = M * M + N * N
90 PRINT "A = ";A
100 PRINT "B = ";B
110 PRINT "C = ";C
120 END
```

a. What will the program print when M = 5 and N = 3?
b. What will the program print when M = 7 and N = 1?
c. Verify that the triples in part a and part b satisfy the Pythagorean Theorem. See margin.

23. Two dice are tossed once. What is the probability of getting a sum of 8? *(Lesson 1-7)* $\frac{5}{36}$

24. *True or false* *(Lesson 1-8)*
a. Probabilities are numbers between 0 and 1, inclusive. True
b. A probability of 1 means that an event must occur. True
c. A relative frequency of -1 cannot occur. True

Exploration

25. If your school has a band and pompon squad, determine if all members could fit exactly into the formations of Example 3.
Answers will vary.

26. Create formations that a band of 80 and pompon squad of 30 would fit exactly. See margin.

556

LESSON

11-6

Weighted Averages and Mixtures

Mrs. Counts, a mathematics teacher at Eastwestern H.S., told her class that the final exam was worth 2 tests. Before the final exam she had given 6 tests.

Dennis averaged 91 on the 6 tests and got 84 on the final exam. He computed his average for the course by using a **weighted average.**

$$\frac{6}{8} \cdot 91 + \frac{2}{8} \cdot 84 = 89.25$$

Notice that 91 and 84 are scores per test. They are rates. The quantity $\frac{6}{8} \cdot 91$ comes from the fact that 6 tests out of a total of 8 averaged 91. The quantity $\frac{2}{8} \cdot 84$ comes from the fact that 2 tests (the final) out of a total of 8 scored 84. The ratios $\frac{6}{8}$ and $\frac{2}{8}$ are called weights. A **weight** is the part or percent of the total accounted for by each score.

Suppose two rates x_1 and x_2 have weights W_1 and W_2, with $W_1 + W_2 = 1$. Then the weighted average of the rates is

$$W_1x_1 + W_2x_2.$$

For Dennis's weighted average, his average scores $x_1 = 91$ and $x_2 = 84$ had weights $W_1 = \frac{6}{8}$ and $W_2 = \frac{2}{8}$. The weighted average 89.25 is closer to x_1 than to x_2. This is because x_1's weight is greater than x_2's weight.

LESSON 11-6

RESOURCES

- Lesson Master 11-6
- Computer Master 22

OBJECTIVE

G Calculate weighted averages.

TEACHING NOTES

The opening paragraphs involve grading, an example of weighted averages with which students are probably familiar. Many teachers use weighted grading scales. You might want to use the following to introduce this lesson. "A test had 100 points and a quiz had 10 points. George's teacher averaged the 60% George got on the test with the 90% he got on the quiz to get 63%. George thinks he should have gotten (60 + 90)/2 = 75%. Why is he wrong?" [George didn't weight his percents by the number of points on the test and the quiz in taking the average. The test has a weight of $\frac{100}{110} \approx .9$, and the quiz has a weight of $\frac{10}{110} \approx .1$. So his grade is .60(.9) + .90(.10) or 63%, which is the weighted average.]

Examples 1 and 3 use the actual procedure of formulating a mixture. This contrasts with the traditional mixture problem where the mixture has already been formed and evaluated as to price or percentage.

Example 2 explores the difficult and often confusing concept of average speed. What is surprising is that the distance between the cities is unnecessary information: If a car averages 60 mph from A to B and 40 mph on the way back, the average speed is always 48 mph. Because of the surprise, this example needs to be discussed carefully. The answer is in miles/hour. The common denominator of 2/5 and 3/5 measures time so these weights show the fraction of the total time spent in each part of the trip.

Weighted averages are found when two or more quantities are mixed or put together to produce a new quantity.

Example 1 A store owner mixes 12 pounds of peanuts worth \$1.59 per pound with 8 pounds of cashews worth \$4.99 per pound. What is the resulting mixture worth per pound?

Solution Here, x_1 and x_2 are the rates \$1.59/pound and \$4.99/pound Now compute the weights in the mixture. There are altogether 12 + 8 = 20 pounds of nuts, so the weight for peanuts is $\frac{12}{20}$ and the weight for cashews is $\frac{8}{20}$. Compute the total value:

$$\begin{array}{ccccc} \text{value of peanuts} & + & \text{value of cashews} & = & \text{worth of mix} \\ \frac{12}{20} \cdot 1.59 & + & \frac{8}{20} \cdot 4.99 & = & 2.95 \end{array}$$

The mixture is worth \$2.95 per pound.

If you know speeds going and returning on a trip, the average speed for the entire trip is a *weighted* average of the speeds used on the trip. The weights are the amount of time traveled, not distance.

Example 2 Suppose towns A and B are 120 miles apart. If a car averages 60 mph from A to B and 40 mph on the way back, what is the average speed for the round trip?

Solution The rates are easy: 60 mph and 40 mph. To find the weights, determine the *time* traveled at each speed.

From A to B, $t = \frac{d}{r} = \frac{120}{60} = 2$ hours.

From B to A, $t = \frac{d}{r} = \frac{120}{40} = 3$ hours.

The entire round trip took 5 hours. Since 2 out of the 5 hours were at 60 mph and 3 out of the 5 hours were at 40 mph, the weights are $\frac{2}{5}$ and $\frac{3}{5}$. The average speed is

$$\tfrac{2}{5}(60) + \tfrac{3}{5}(40) = 48.$$

The average speed is 48 mph.

Check The round trip takes 5 hours. The distance traveled is 240 miles. This gives an average speed of 48 mph.

Pharmacists and other chemists often face situations involving weighted averages.

Example 3 Five ounces of a 30% alcohol solution are mixed with ten ounces of a 50% alcohol solution. What is the percent of alcohol in the result?

Solution Here the rates are 30% and 50% (alcohol/total). The result is a solution with 15 ounces. The percent of alcohol in it is a weighted average of 30% alcohol and 50% alcohol.

$$\frac{5}{15} \cdot 30\% + \frac{10}{15} \cdot 50\%$$
$$= 10\% + 33\tfrac{1}{3}\%$$
$$= 43\tfrac{1}{3}\%$$

The resulting mixture is $43\frac{1}{3}\%$ alcohol.

Check The 30% solution has 30% · 5 ounces, or 1.5 ounces of alcohol. The 50% solution has 50% · 10 ounces, or 5 ounces of alcohol. The resulting $43\frac{1}{3}\%$ solution has $43\frac{1}{3}\%$ · 15 ounces of alcohol. This should compute to 6.5 ounces of alcohol, which it does.

The weighted average of more than two quantities is found just like other weighted averages.

Example 4 In Mr. Vollmer's class, 3 students have no siblings (brothers or sisters), 8 students have 1 sibling per student, 10 have 2 siblings, 4 have 3 siblings, and 1 has 4 siblings. What is the average number of siblings per student?

Solution The rates are the siblings per students. There are 26 students. Use a weighted average of 5 quantities.

$$\frac{3}{26} \cdot 0 + \frac{8}{26} \cdot 1 + \frac{10}{26} \cdot 2 + \frac{4}{26} \cdot 3 + \frac{1}{26} \cdot 4$$
$$= \frac{44}{26}$$
$$\approx 1.7$$

The students average 1.7 siblings.

ADDITIONAL EXAMPLES

1. A cologne manufacturer mixes 5 ounces of perfume oil worth $25 per ounce with 25 ounces of alcohol worth $.10 per ounce. How much is the resulting mixture worth per ounce?
$\frac{5}{30} \cdot 25 + \frac{25}{30} \cdot 0.10 = \$4.25$

2. To pass a test to qualify to be a lifeguard Mary must swim 500 feet out into the lake, "rescue" the instructor, and swim back with him. Her swimming speed must average at least 80 feet/minute. If Mary swims out at a speed of 125 feet/minute and back at a speed of 64 feet/minute, does she pass the test?
$\frac{4}{11.8125} \cdot 125 + \frac{7.8125}{11.8125} \cdot 64 \approx$ **84.7 feet/minute; yes**

3. The cabin of a rocket holds 400 cubic feet of air. Shortly after it landed on Venus, the cabin developed a leak and $\frac{1}{4}$ of the air leaked and was replaced by Venusian air. If the cabin's air had been 2% carbon dioxide and the atmosphere of Venus is 90% carbon dioxide, what was the percent of carbon dioxide in the cabin after the leak?
$\frac{300}{400} \cdot .02 + \frac{100}{400} \cdot .90 = 24\%$

4. In Mr. Vollmer's class, the families of 5 students subscribe to no magazines, 11 subscribe to one magazine, 8 subscribe to two, and 2 subscribe to three. What is the average number of magazine subscriptions per family?
$\frac{5}{26} \cdot 0 + \frac{11}{26} \cdot 1 + \frac{8}{26} \cdot 2 + \frac{2}{26} \cdot 3 \approx$ **1.3 subscriptions per family**

NOTES ON QUESTIONS

Question 4: The proportion of peanuts to cashews is the same as the proportion in **Example 1.** So the solution to the question is the same as the one in the example. You might show students how

$\frac{12}{20} \cdot 1.59 + \frac{8}{20} \cdot 4.99$ and

$\frac{15}{25} \cdot 1.59 + \frac{10}{25} \cdot 4.99$

both simplify to

$\frac{3}{5} \cdot 1.59 + \frac{2}{5} \cdot 4.99.$

Question 12: Encourage students to view this situation as a weighted average. The number of courses (4, 5, or 6) is weighted by the relative frequency with which each course occurs. So the weighted average is

$\frac{4}{17} \cdot 4 + \frac{7}{17} \cdot 5 + \frac{6}{17} \cdot 6.$

Questions 14, 15 and 22: These questions explore grade point average, the topic with which this lesson was introduced.

Example 4 illustrates the following generalization of the definition of weighted average.

> Suppose n quantities $x_1, x_2, \ldots, x_n$ have weights $W_1, W_2, \ldots, W_n$ with $W_1 + W_2 + \ldots + W_n = 1$. Then the weighted average of the quantities is $W_1x_1 + W_2x_2 + \ldots + W_nx_n$.

Questions

Covering the Reading

1. Denise is a student in Mrs. Counts's class. She received a 75 average on the 6 tests and an 88 on the final.
   a. Fill in the missing weights in Denise's weighted average.
   $\underline{\ ?\ } \cdot 75 + \underline{\ ?\ } \cdot 88$ **$\frac{6}{8}, \frac{2}{8}$**
   b. Compute her average for the course. **78.25**
2. What is the weighted average of quantities x_1 and x_2 with weights W_1 and W_2? **$W_1x_1 + W_2x_2$**
3. What is the weighted average of quantities $x_1, x_2, \ldots, x_n$ with weights $W_1, W_2, \ldots, W_n$? **$W_1x_1 + W_2x_2 + \ldots + W_nx_n$**
4. Refer to Example 1. Suppose the store owner mixes 15 pounds of peanuts with 10 pounds of cashews. What is the resulting mixture worth per pound? **\$2.95**
5. Another store owner mixes 6 pounds of almonds worth \$3.99 per pound with 9 pounds of peanuts worth \$1.79 per pound. What is the resulting mixture worth per pound? **\$2.67**
6. When average speeds are computed, what is the unit of the weights used? **time**
7. Suppose towns A and B are 275 miles apart. If a car averages 55 mph from A to B and 25 mph on the way back, what is the average speed for the whole trip? **≈34.4 mph**
8. Six liters of a 10% alcohol solution are mixed with three liters of a 100% solution (that is, pure alcohol). What is the percent of alcohol in the resulting solution? **40%**
9. Refer to Example 4. A new student enrolled in Mr. Vollmer's class. This student has a brother and no sisters. Compute the average number of siblings per student in Mr. Vollmer's class including this new student. (Answer to the nearest tenth.) **≈1.7 siblings**

Applying the Mathematics

10. A company puts out a party mix using 11 pounds of cereal at \$.79 per pound, 6 pounds of raisins at \$2.29 per pound and 13 pounds of sunflower seeds at \$4.19 per pound. What is the resulting mixture worth per pound? **≈\$2.56**

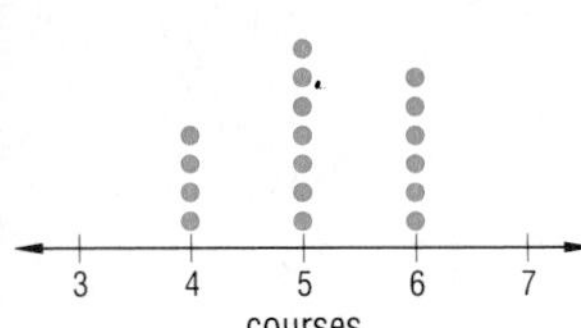

11. A plane makes a trip of 600 miles each way. Going, it travels at 400 mph, while returning it travels at 500 mph. What is the average speed for the round trip? **≈444 mph**

12. At left is a dot frequency diagram that shows the number of students in Mr. Roosevelt's homeroom who take various numbers of courses. What is the average number of courses taken by a student? **≈5.1 courses**

13. a. Five nights a week I get 7 hours of sleep. The other two nights I get 9 hours of sleep. What is my average number of hours of sleep a night in a week? **≈7.6 hours**

b. Five nights a week I get x hours of sleep. The other two nights I get y hours of sleep. What is my average number of hours of sleep a night in a week? **$(\frac{5}{7}x + \frac{2}{7}y)$ hours**

In 14 and 15, use this information. School grade point averages often use the following scale.

A = 4.0 B = 3.0 C = 2.0 D = 1.0 F = 0.0

14. Carla has the following transcript: 3A's, 6B's, 4C's, and 1D. What is her grade point average? (Answer to the nearest hundredth.) **2.79**

15. Maurice needs a 2.0 grade point average to remain eligible for football. He has 2A's, 1B, 4C's, 4D's and 1F. Does he qualify? **No**

Review

16. *Skill sequence* Solve. *(Lessons 5-7, 6-1)*

a. $\frac{3}{4}x + \frac{1}{4} = 15$ **$x = \frac{59}{3}$**

b. $\frac{3}{4y} + \frac{1}{4y} = 15$ **$y = \frac{1}{15}$**

c. $\frac{3}{z} \cdot 4 + \frac{1}{z} \cdot 4 = 15$ **$z = \frac{16}{15}$**

In 17 and 18, solve the system. *(Lessons 11-4, 11-5)*

17. $\begin{cases} 4x + 9y = -11 \\ -4x + y = -19 \end{cases}$ **(4, -3)**

18. $\begin{cases} 3x - 6y = 15 \\ 2x + 5y = 0 \end{cases}$ **$(\frac{25}{9}, -\frac{10}{9})$**

19. Twice one number plus 3 times a second number is 22. The first number minus the second number is 31.

a. Write a system describing the problem. **$\begin{cases} 2n + 3m = 22 \\ n - m = 31 \end{cases}$**

b. Find the values of the two numbers. *(Lesson 11-5)* **23 and -8**

20. Three events have probabilities of 0.75, 0.192, and 0.4. Which of these events is most likely to happen? *(Lesson 1-7)* **The one with probability 0.75.**

21. Solve $10x^2 = 320$. *(Lessons 7-4, 7-6)* **$\pm\sqrt{32}$ or $\pm 4\sqrt{2}$**

Exploration

22. a. What grading scale is used in your school?

b. Compute your grade point average for last semester on this scale. (If your school has no grading scale, use that given in Questions 14–15.) **a–b) Answers will vary depending on school and students.**

FOLLOW-UP

MORE PRACTICE

For more questions on SPUR Objectives, use *Lesson Master 11-6*, shown below.

NAME ________

LESSON **MASTER 11–6**
QUESTIONS ON **SPUR** OBJECTIVES

■USES *Objective G (See pages 583–585 for objectives.)*

1. Two large towns are 60 miles apart. For 20 miles the speed limit is 55 mph. For the rest of the distance the speed limit is 65 mph. If I travel at the speed limit for the entire trip, what will be my average speed? **$61\frac{2}{3}$ mph**

2. Mark earned the following grades in high school: 6 A's, 7 B's, 4 C's, and 1 D. What is his grade point average? (Assume A = 4, B = 3, C = 2, D = 1.) **3.0**

3. A final exam consists of two parts: multiple choice questions worth 100 points, and essay questions worth 150 points. Sally got 75 points on the multiple choice section and 95 points on the essay section. What is her average for the whole test? **87 points**

4. "Slugger" Miller had a batting average of .220 in 120 times at bat on natural grass, and an average of .310 in 180 times at bat on artificial turf. What was his overall batting average? **.274**

5. Pure gold is 24 carat. A jeweler mixes 1.2 oz of 14-carat gold with 1.8 oz of 18-carat gold. What is the carat value (purity) of the mixture? **16.4 carat**

6. A meat manufacturer makes up packages of lunchmeat containing 10 slices of ham worth $.15 each, 8 slices of chicken worth $.12 each and 6 slices of bologna worth $.10 each. How much should he sell the mixture for so as not to lose money? **$3.06**

7. A boat travels 12 miles downstream at 4 mph, and returns upstream the same distance at 3 mph. What is the average speed for the whole trip? **$3\frac{3}{7}$ mph**

 99

LESSON 11-7

RESOURCES
- Lesson Master 11-7
- Quiz on Lessons 11-4 Through 11-7

OBJECTIVE

G Use weighted averages.

TEACHING NOTES

This is a lesson in which the questions hold the key. The more questions the student does, the more he or she internalizes the idea of mixture. However, emphasize estimating answers before solving the problems. **Question 1** exemplifies the kind of question to ask about any of these problems.

In **Example 2,** there are 4 hours at 35 mph. There is an unknown number of hours at 55 mph. Since the weighted average is 50 mph, ask students if the time at 55 mph should be more or less than 4 hours. [It should be more since the weighted average is closer to 55 mph than to 35 mph. (In fact, it is 3 times closer to 55 mph than to 35 mph, which gives a way of doing this entire problem by mental calculations.)]

LESSON

11-7 More with Mixtures

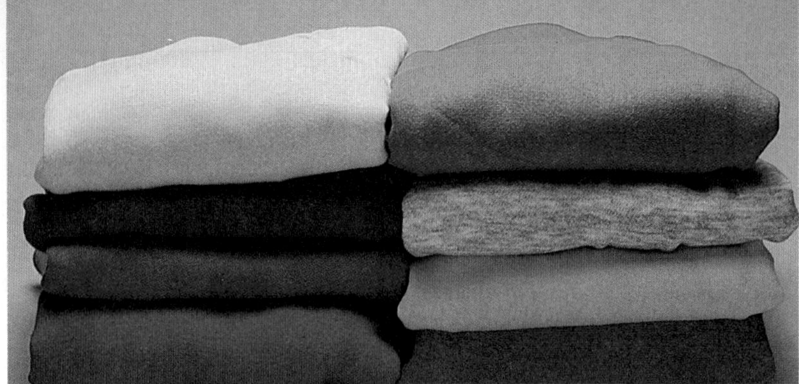

In the previous lesson you computed a weighted average when you knew weights and quantities. Often, you may be presented with a reverse situation. You know the average and want to find the amount of one of the quantities or weights.

Example 1 A retailer sold 400 sweatshirts at \$10 retail and has 250 sweatshirts left. For what sale price should each of the remaining sweatshirts be sold to have an overall average price of \$9 a sweatshirt?

Solution Let the sale price be S dollars per shirt. There are a total of 650 sweatshirts to start with. Think of the \$10, \$$S$, and \$9 as weights. Because the average is to be \$9, S must be less than 9. Calculate the sales from each price.

$$\begin{pmatrix}\text{sales from}\\ \$10 \text{ shirts}\end{pmatrix} + \begin{pmatrix}\text{sales from}\\ \$S \text{ shirts}\end{pmatrix} = \begin{pmatrix}\text{sales from}\\ \$9 \text{ shirts}\end{pmatrix}$$

$$400 \cdot 10 + 250 \cdot S = 650 \cdot 9$$

$$4000 + 250S = 5850$$

$$250S = 1850$$

$$S = \frac{1850}{250} = 7.4$$

The sale price should be \$7.40.

Check 400 sweatshirts at \$10 is \$4000, and 250 sweatshirts at \$7.40 is \$1850; so the total sales are \$5850. Does this equal 650 sweatshirts sold at \$9? Yes, since $650 \cdot 9 = 5850$.

In Example 1, you were asked to find the amount of a weight in a weighted average situation. Example 2 is a similar kind of problem in which a system is used to find a missing quantity.

Example 2 A truck averages 35 mph for the first four hours of a trip. How long must the truck travel at 55 mph to have an overall average speed of 50 mph?

Solution You can use a system.
Let x = number of hours at 55 mph.
Let y = total number of hours for the trip.
Since the total number of hours is 4 more than the number of hours at 55 mph,

$$y = 4 + x. \qquad (1)$$

The other equation in the system comes from the total distance.

Because 4 out of a total y hours are traveled at 35 mph and x hours are traveled at 55 mph, the total distance is

$$4 \cdot 35 + x \cdot 55$$

The weighted average speed is given as 50 mph. So, in all, the driver traveled $50y$ miles.

$$140 + 55x = 50y \qquad (2)$$

Now the system is set up for solution.

$$\begin{cases} y = 4 + x & (1) \\ 140 + 55x = 50y & (2) \end{cases}$$

We use substitution. Substitute $4 + x$ for y in equation (2).

$$140 + 55x = 50(4 + x)$$
$$140 + 55x = 200 + 50x$$
$$5x = 60$$
$$x = 12$$

The truck must travel 12 hours at 55 mph to average 50 mph for the trip. (Notice that you did not need to find y for this solution.)

Check 4 hours at 35 mph is 140 miles, and 12 hours at 55 mph is 660 miles; so the total trip is 800 miles. Does this equal 16 hours at 50 mph? Yes, since $16 \cdot 50 = 800$.

ADDITIONAL EXAMPLES

1. Shortly before the election, polls had estimated that 60% of the voters had decided on a candidate. Of these, 55% plan to vote for Mr. Smith. What percent of the undecided voters must vote for Smith for him to at least tie with the other candidate?
$.6(.55) + .4x \geq .5$, at least 42.5%

2. This year the nine members of the Math Team had decided that their goal was to average 90 at the end-of-the-year contest. After seven members' scores had been reported, the team average was 88. What must be the average of the last two members' scores if the team is to meet its goal?
$7 \cdot 88 + 2 \cdot x = 9 \cdot 90$; 97

3. A research scientist needs an 8% solution of a chemical for an experiment. She has a 50 mL container of 10% solution as well as some 4% solution. How much of the 4% solution must she add to dilute the 10% solution to the proper strength?
$y = 50 + x$, $.10 \cdot 50 + .04 \cdot x = .08 \cdot y$; 25 mL

NOTES ON QUESTIONS
The following are estimates students might give before answering the questions.

Question 7: The car stops for less than 2 hours because the average is closer to 55 mph than to 0 mph.

Question 8: The average must be over 3.1 to overcome the lower weight of the 14 courses.

Question 9: Cyril can score below 79 and still maintain the average of 81.

Question 10: Janice can score below 88 and still maintain her average.

Question 11: Since $2.59 is closer to $1.79 than it is to $3.99, there will be more than 10 pounds of peanuts at $1.79.

Question 12: Since the 12 pounds of cashews and pecans combined are at quite high prices, there will need to be more than 12 pounds of peanuts at $1.79 in the mixture.

ADDITIONAL ANSWERS
16a.

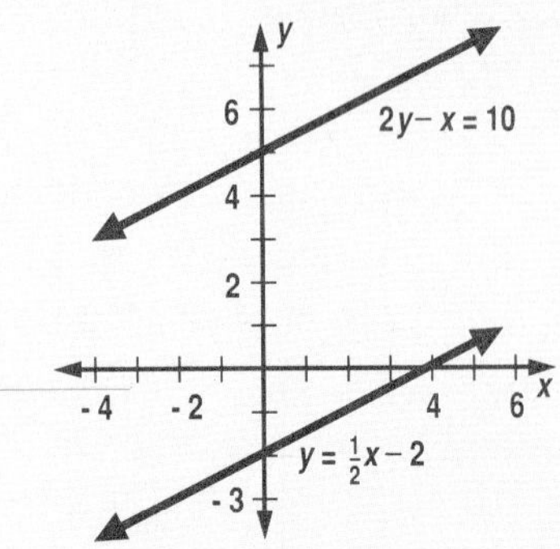

Questions

Covering the Reading

1. In Example 1, how do you know the sale price must be less than $9? **With a $9 average, more than half are $10, balance must be less than 9.**

2. If the retailer of Example 1 sold 400 sweatshirts at $10 retail and had 150 sweatshirts left, at what sale price should the remaining sweatshirts be sold to have an overall average price of $9 a sweatshirt? **$6.33**

3. A retailer sold 130 pairs of sunglasses at $15 retail and has 70 pairs left. At what sale price should the remaining sunglasses be sold to have an overall average price of $13 a pair? **$9.29**

In 4 and 5, solve.

4. $\begin{cases} y = x + 8 \\ 200 + 12x = 20y \end{cases}$ **(5, 13)**

5. $\begin{cases} q = z + 9 \\ 27z + 423 = 36q \end{cases}$ **(q, z) = (20, 11)**

6. A truck averages 40 mph for the first 4 hours of a trip. How long must the truck travel at 55 mph to have an overall average speed of 50 mph? **8 hours**

Applying the Mathematics

7. A car averages 55 mph for the first 2 hours of a trip. How long can the car stop (travel at 0 mph) and still have an average speed of 40 mph when it returns to the road? **0.75 hours or 45 minutes**

8. After 18 courses, Mahesh has a grade point average of 3.1. What must he average over the next 14 courses to have an overall grade point average of 3.25? **≈3.4**

9. After 8 tests, Cyril has an 83 average. The final is worth 3 tests. What must he score on the final to have an overall average of 81? **76**

10. After 6 tests, Janice has a 92 average. What can she average on the 4 remaining tests and still maintain a 90 overall average? **87**

11. How many pounds of peanuts at $1.79 per lb must be mixed with 10 pounds of cashews at $3.99 per lb to produce a mixture worth $2.59 per lb? **17.5**

12. How many pounds of peanuts at $1.79 per lb must be mixed with 10 pounds of cashews at $3.99 per lb and 2 pounds of pecans at $3.59 per lb to produce a mixture worth $2.59 per lb? **20**

Review

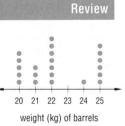

13. Suppose 12 liters of a 40% alcohol solution are mixed with 3 liters of an 80% alcohol solution. What is the percent of alcohol in the new solution? *(Lesson 11-6)* **48%**

14. At the left is a diagram of numbers of barrels of various weights in a storehouse. What is the average weight of a barrel? *(Lesson 11-6)* **≈22.3 kg**

20 21 22 23 24 25
weight (kg) of barrels

564

15. A band has 94 members (B) with an additional 28 flag bearers (F). They plan to form the following formations:

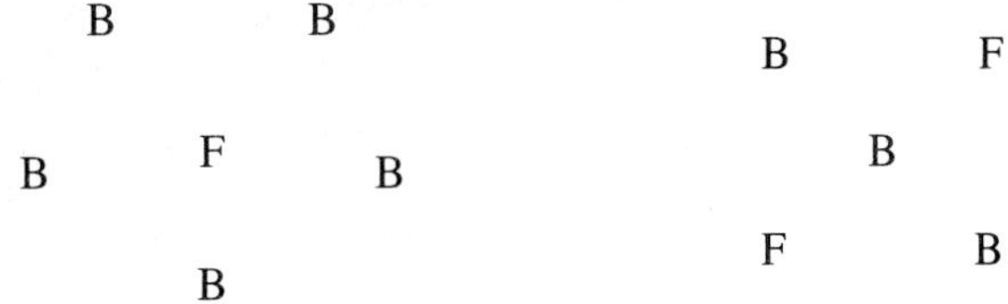

Will they exactly fit these formations? *(Lesson 11-5)* **No**

16. On the same set of coordinate axes, **a.** graph $y = \frac{1}{2}x - 2$ and $2y - x = 10$ and **b.** give the coordinates of their point of intersection. *(Lessons 7-1, 11-1, 11-4)*
a) See margin. b) No points of intersection; lines are parallel.

17. A point is selected at random from $\overline{AE}$ below. What is the probability that the point is on $\overline{AB}$? *(Lesson 5-5)* $\frac{8}{30} = \frac{4}{15}$

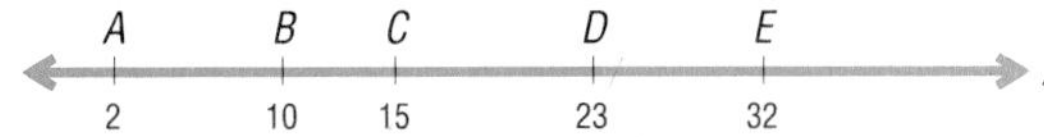

18. A die is tossed once. What is the probability of tossing a number that is
a. even and less than 3? $\frac{1}{6}$
b. odd and greater than 6? *(Lessons 1-7, 3-4)* **0**

19. Write an inequality describing all numbers x such that $x > 0$ and $x < 12$. *(Lesson 3-4)* **$0 < x < 12$**

20. Calculate in your head. *(Lesson 5-4)*
a. 5% of 200 **b.** 10% of 32 **c.** 200% of .5 **a) 10; b) 3.2; c) 1**

Exploration

21. Weighted averages may be used to compare opinions about things. Cities are sometimes rated on the following factors:
(1) climate
(2) attractions (sports, museums, etc.)
(3) cost of living
(4) availability of good jobs.

a. Assign positive weights adding to 1 to these factors by how important each factor is to you. For instance, you could assign 30% to climate, 40% to attractions, 10% to cost of living, and 20% to jobs.
b. Ask an adult in your family what weights he or she would assign.
c. Rate your home town from 1 to 10 in each category.
d. Compute the weighted average.
e. We gave New York the following category ratings:
(1) 4 (2) 9 (3) 2 (4) 6.
Does your hometown do better on your ratings?
Answers will vary depending on student's opinion

FOLLOW-UP

MORE PRACTICE

For more questions on SPUR Objectives, use *Lesson Master 11-7,* shown below.

EVALUATION

A quiz covering Lessons 11-4 through 11-7 is provided in the Teacher's Resource File.

NAME ____

LESSON **MASTER 11-7**
QUESTIONS ON SPUR OBJECTIVES

USES *Objective G (See pages 583–585 for objectives.)*

1. At the Math Club bake sale, 20 slices of date-nut bread were sold for 25 cents a slice. There were 10 slices left over. How much should members pay for a leftover slice so that the overall average price per slice is 21 cents? **13 cents**

2. After 8 tests Mario has an average of 78. The final exam is worth 2 tests. The minimum average for a B is 80. What minimum grade does he have to make on the final in order to make a B? **88**

3. Because of heavy traffic a bus averages 20 mph for the first 2 hours of a trip. How long must the bus travel at 60 mph in order to average 40 mph for the entire trip up to that point? **2 hours**

4. In 15 basketball games, Ken has been averaging 18 points a game. How many more games must he play at 25 points per game in order to have an overall average of 20 points per game? **6 games**

5. How many liters of 60% acid solution must be added to 8 liters of a 40% acid solution to make a mixture that is 50% acid? **8 liters**

6. Harry has $1200 invested at 5%. How much more money must he invest at 8% to have an overall investment of 6%? **$600**

7. In a large city, there has been an average of 16 auto accidents a day for 110 days. How many consecutive accident free days must there now be in order to bring the average down to 10 per day? **66 days**

100

LESSON 11-8

RESOURCES
- ■ Lesson Master 11-8
- Visual for Teaching Aid 7: Coordinate Grid
- Visual for Teaching Aid 62: Slopes of Perpendicular Lines

OBJECTIVES

E Determine whether a system has 0, 1, or infinitely many solutions.
F Use systems of equations to solve real world problems involving linear combinations.
H Find solutions to systems of equations by graphing.

TEACHING NOTES

Reading The lesson mentions that 0 = 36 is an equation with no solution. It may not be clear to your students that a tautology like 0 = 0 in the **Example** does have solutions. Ask them to think of that sentence as $0x = 0x$, and ask which values of x work.

Emphasize the table following the **Example** because the ideas it presents are later extended to oblique lines.

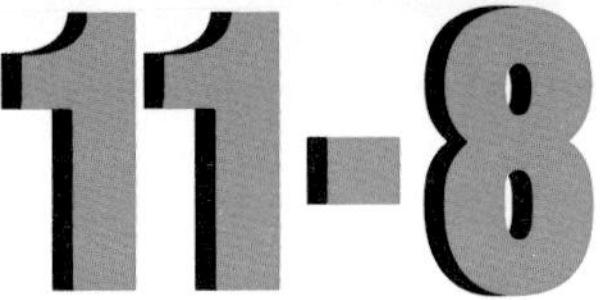

LESSON

11-8

Parallel Lines

The idea behind parallel lines is that they "go in the same direction." All vertical lines are parallel to each other. So are all horizontal lines. But not all oblique lines are parallel. For oblique lines to be parallel, they must have the same slope.

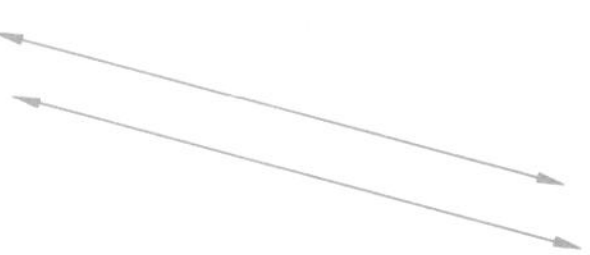

If two lines have the same slope, then they are parallel.

You have learned that when two lines intersect in exactly one point, the coordinates of the point of intersection can be found by solving a system. But what happens when the lines are parallel? Consider this linear system.

$$\begin{cases} 2x + 3y = -6 & (1) \\ 4x + 6y = 24 & (2) \end{cases}$$

As usual, you can solve the system by multiplying the top equation by -2.

$$\begin{array}{rll} -4x - 6y = 12 & (3) = -2 \cdot (1) \\ 4x + 6y = 24 & (2) \\ \hline 0 = 36 & (3) + (2) \end{array}$$

If you add you get 0 = 36

which is impossible. This signals that the system has no solution, or no point of intersection. To check, graph the lines. The graph shows that the lines are parallel with no points in common.

As another check, put the equations for the lines in slope-intercept form.

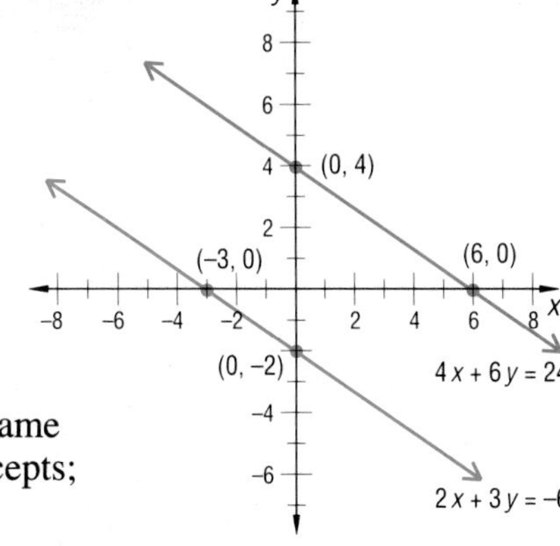

line (1) $2x + 3y = -6$
$3y = -2x - 6$
$y = -\frac{2}{3}x - 2$

line (2) $4x + 6y = 24$
$6y = -4x + 24$
$y = -\frac{2}{3}x + 4$

Both lines (1) and (2) have the same slope of $-\frac{2}{3}$, but different y-intercepts; thus they are parallel.

When an equation with no solution (such as $0 = 36$) results from correct work with equations, then the original conditions must also be impossible. There are no pairs of numbers that work in *both* equations (1) and (2).

In the example below, just the opposite occurs. A situation results that is always true.

Example Solve. $\begin{cases} 8x - 7y = 3 & (1) \\ 16x - 14y = 6 & (2) \end{cases}$

Solution Multiply the top equation by -2.

$$-16x + 14y = -6 \quad (3) = -2 \cdot (1)$$
$$16x - 14y = 6 \quad (2)$$

Now add.

$$0 = 0 \quad (3) + (2)$$

This is always true, so any ordered pair that is a solution to equation (1) is also a solution to equation (2). There are infinitely many points that are on both lines.

You can check that (1) and (2) have the same slope and same y-intercept. So the graphs of equations (1) and (2) are the same line as shown at the right. Because the graphs coincide, the lines are called **coincident**. They too are parallel because they go in the same direction and have the same slope.

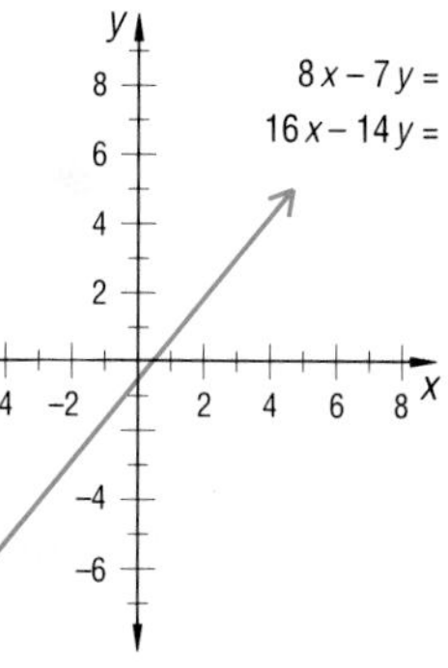

Error Analysis Emphasize that if combining the two equations in a system results in a statement that is false, there are no solutions. If it results in a statement that is always true, there are infinitely many solutions. But caution students to be careful in the latter case—if one sentence in a system is subtracted from itself, then $0 = 0$ arises. That would normally signify that the lines coincide, but the other sentence was not used. *All sentences in a system* must contribute in order for these signals to have meaning.

ADDITIONAL EXAMPLES

1. Solve $\begin{cases} 4x + 6y = -2 \\ 10x + 15y = -5 \end{cases}$
infinitely many solutions

2. Solve $\begin{cases} y = 5x - 7 \\ 20x - 4y = 9 \end{cases}$
no solution

NOTES ON QUESTIONS
Alternate Approach for Question 14: Students should write a system of equations. They do not have to solve the system; they can just look at the graphs or at the slopes and intercepts. You might wish to go over the problems and show how, by dividing the given numbers in the first equation by 3 and in the second by 4, one could answer the question without solving a system.

NOTES ON QUESTIONS
Making Connections for Question 20: This question reviews a skill that will be needed in Lesson 11-10.

ADDITIONAL ANSWERS

1. sample: $\begin{cases} 2x + 3y = -6 \\ 4x + 6y = 24 \end{cases}$

2. sample: $\begin{cases} 8x - 7y = 3 \\ 16x - 14y = 6 \end{cases}$

5b.

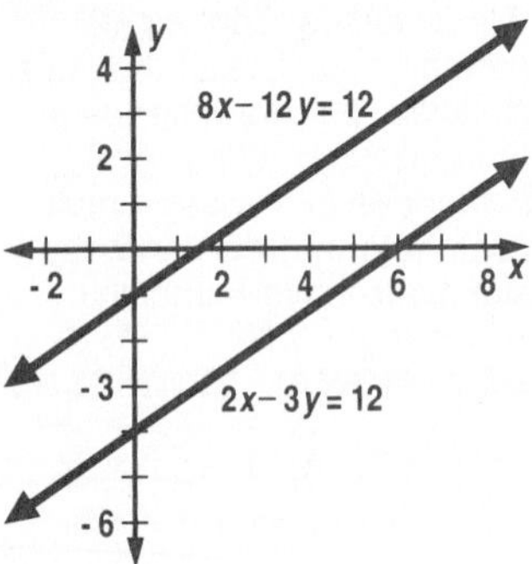

6b.

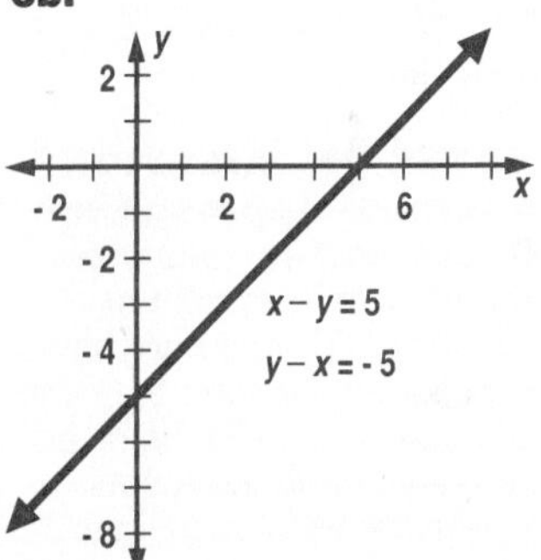

20.

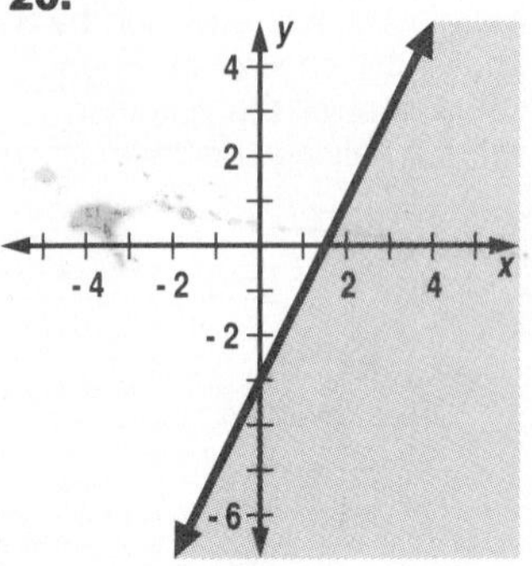

25. sample: $A_1x + B_1y = C_1$ and $A_2x + B_2y = C_2$, if $\frac{A_1}{A_2} = \frac{B_1}{B_2} = \frac{C_1}{C_2}$, the lines coincide. If $\frac{A_1}{A_2} = \frac{B_1}{B_2}$ but $\frac{A_1}{A_2} \neq \frac{C_1}{C_2}$, the lines are parallel. If $\frac{A_1}{A_2} \neq \frac{B_1}{B_2}$, the lines intersect.

You have now studied all the possible number of points in common that two lines in the plane can have.

Number of solutions to system	Line	Slopes
one (the point of intersection)	intersecting	different
zero (no points of intersection)	parallel and nonintersecting	equal
infinitely many (same line)	parallel and coincident	equal

Questions

Covering the Reading

1. Give an example of a system of two nonintersecting lines. See margin.

2. Give an example of a system of two coincident lines. See margin.

3. Parallel lines have the same _?_. slope

4. Which two lines are parallel? a and c

a. $y = 3x + 5$ **b.** $y = 2x + 5$
c. $y = 3x + 6$ **d.** $x = 2y + 5$

In 5 and 6, **a.** determine whether the system includes nonintersecting or coincident lines, and **b.** check by graphing.

5. $\begin{cases} 2x - 3y = 12 \\ 8x - 12y = 12 \end{cases}$ a) nonintersecting; b) See margin.

6. $\begin{cases} x - y = 5 \\ y - x = -5 \end{cases}$ a) coincident b) See margin.

In 7–9, match the orientation with the solution.

7. lines intersect c — **a.** no solution
8. lines nonintersecting a — **b.** infinitely many solutions
9. lines coincident b — **c.** one solution

Applying the Mathematics

In 10–13, determine whether the system includes nonintersecting, intersecting, or coincident lines.

10. $\begin{cases} 3u + 2t = 7 \\ 14 - 2t = 6u \end{cases}$ intersecting

11. $\begin{cases} 6a + 2b = 9 \\ 9a + 3b = 12 \end{cases}$ nonintersecting

12. $\begin{cases} 2x - 5y = -3 \\ -4x + 10y = 6 \end{cases}$ coincident

13. $\begin{cases} \frac{1}{2}x - \frac{3}{2} = y \\ 2x + y = 3 \end{cases}$ intersecting

In 14 and 15, could the given situation have happened?

14. A pizza parlor sold 39 pizzas and 21 gallons of soda for \$396. The next day, at the same prices, they sold 52 pizzas and 28 gallons of soda for \$518. No

15. In an all-school survey of 900 students altogether 10% of the boys and 15% of the girls voted yes. In a different survey of 1080 students in the same school, 12% of the boys and 18% of the girls voted yes. **Yes**

Review

16. Suppose 30 liters of a solution with an unknown percentage of alcohol is mixed with 5 liters of a 90% alcohol solution. If the resulting mixture is a 62% alcohol solution, what is the percentage of alcohol in the first solution? *(Lesson 11-7)* **≈57.3%**

17. A car travels at an average speed of 25 mph for an hour through a construction zone. How long must the car travel at 55 mph to achieve an overall average speed of 45 mph? *(Lesson 11-7)* **2 hours**

18. If 12 pounds of lettuce at \$.79 per pound are mixed with 4 pounds of celery at \$.59 per pound and 2 pounds of croutons at \$1.69 per pound, how much is the mixed salad worth per pound? *(Lesson 11-6)* **≈\$.85 per pound**

19. Solve by any method. $\begin{cases} 4x + 3y = 7 \\ x - 1.5y = 7 \end{cases}$ *(Lessons 11-1, 11-3, 11-5)* **$(\frac{7}{2}, -\frac{7}{3})$**

20. Draw the graph of $y \le 2x - 3$. *(Lesson 8-9)* **See margin.**

21. Write as the square of a binomial: $x^2 - 14x + 49$. *(Lesson 10-8)* **$(x - 7)^2$**

22. Write as the product of two binomials: $4t^2 - 81u^2$. *(Lesson 10-9)* **$(2t - 9u)(2t + 9u)$**

23. **a.** Give an equation of the horizontal line through (8, -12). **y = -12**
    b. Give an equation of the vertical line through (8, -12). *(Lesson 7-2)* **x = 8**

24. A sweater costs a store owner \$15.50. If the profit is to be 40% of the cost, what is the selling price? *(Lessons 5-4, 6-3)* **\$21.70**

Exploration

25. Here are more examples of parallel lines. **See margin.**

Nonintersecting	Coincident
$\begin{cases} 3x + 6y = -2 \\ 4x + 8y = 4 \end{cases}$	$\begin{cases} -2x + 8y = 30 \\ 5x - 20y = -75 \end{cases}$
$\begin{cases} 9x + 3y = 5 \\ 6x + 2y = 1 \end{cases}$	$\begin{cases} 12x - 4y = 80 \\ 15x - 5y = 100 \end{cases}$

Compare the ratios of the coefficients of x, the coefficients of y, and the constant terms. Use the pattern to find a way to recognize parallel lines directly from their equations.

FOLLOW-UP

MORE PRACTICE
For more questions on SPUR Objectives, use *Lesson Master 11-8,* shown below.

EXTENSION
This lesson shows that parallel lines have the same slope. Have students investigate oblique perpendicular lines to discover how their slopes are related. *Teaching Aid 62* may be used. [For oblique perpendicular lines, the slope of one line is the opposite (additive inverse) of the reciprocal (multiplicative inverse) of the slope of the other line. That is, if $y = m_1x + b_1$ and $y = m_2x + b_2$ are equations of oblique perpendicular lines, then $m_1m_2 = -1$.]

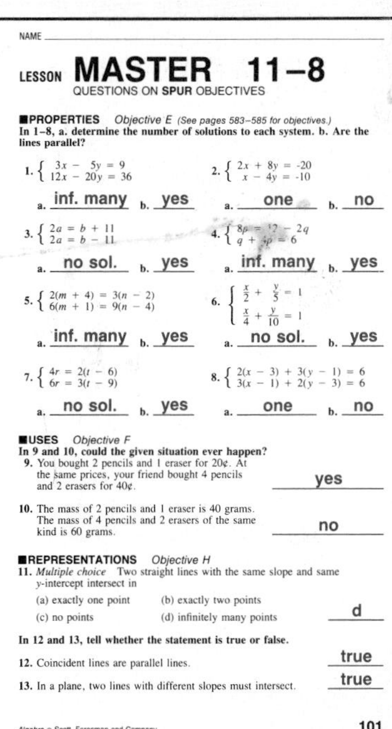
NAME ____

LESSON **MASTER 11–8**
QUESTIONS ON **SPUR** OBJECTIVES

■**PROPERTIES** *Objective E (See pages 583–585 for objectives.)*
In 1–8, a. determine the number of solutions to each system. b. Are the lines parallel?

1. $\begin{cases} 3x - 5y = 9 \\ 12x - 20y = 36 \end{cases}$ a. **inf. many** b. **yes**

2. $\begin{cases} 2x + 8y = -20 \\ x - 4y = -10 \end{cases}$ a. **one** b. **no**

3. $\begin{cases} 2a = b + 11 \\ 2a = b - 11 \end{cases}$ a. **no sol.** b. **yes**

4. $\begin{cases} 8p = 12 - 2q \\ q + 4p = 6 \end{cases}$ a. **inf. many** b. **yes**

5. $\begin{cases} 2(m + 4) = 3(n - 2) \\ 6(m + 1) = 9(n - 4) \end{cases}$ a. **inf. many** b. **yes**

6. $\begin{cases} \frac{x}{2} + \frac{y}{5} = 1 \\ \frac{x}{4} + \frac{y}{10} = 1 \end{cases}$ a. **no sol.** b. **yes**

7. $\begin{cases} 4r = 2(t - 6) \\ 6r = 3(t - 9) \end{cases}$ a. **no sol.** b. **yes**

8. $\begin{cases} 2(x - 3) + 3(y - 1) = 6 \\ 3(x - 1) + 2(y - 3) = 6 \end{cases}$ a. **one** b. **no**

■**USES** *Objective F*
In 9 and 10, could the given situation ever happen?

9. You bought 2 pencils and 1 eraser for 20¢. At the same prices, your friend bought 4 pencils and 2 erasers for 40¢. **yes**

10. The mass of 2 pencils and 1 eraser is 40 grams. The mass of 4 pencils and 2 erasers of the same kind is 60 grams. **no**

■**REPRESENTATIONS** *Objective H*

11. *Multiple choice* Two straight lines with the same slope and same y-intercept intersect in
    (a) exactly one point (b) exactly two points
    (c) no points (d) infinitely many points **d**

In 12 and 13, tell whether the statement is true or false.

12. Coincident lines are parallel lines. **true**

13. In a plane, two lines with different slopes must intersect. **true**

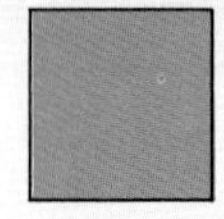

LESSON 11-9

RESOURCES
■ Lesson Master 11-9
Computer Master 23

OBJECTIVES

D Recognize sentences with no solutions, one solution, or all real numbers as solutions.
F Use systems of equations to solve real world problems involving linear combinations.

TEACHING NOTES

In the two real life choices in this lesson, the answers are obvious. Thus algebra is not very useful in these cases. However, the point of this lesson is to show that the real life obviousness has a counterpart in the algebraic solution. Algebra can tell you whether there is no solution, whether there is exactly one solution, or whether there are infinitely many solutions. It covers all the possibilities.

Example 3 could be solved as a system, in which the equation for town 1 is $P = 23{,}000 + 1000t$ and the equation for town 2 is $P = 23{,}000 + 1200t$. Solving the system, we see that the lines intersect when $t = 0$.

Reading The distinction between 0 solutions and a solution of 0 which is discussed at the close of **Example 3** should be emphasized to students. Since the students have seen the ∅ notation for the null set in Chapter 1, you might use that here to make sure that students realize the difference between {0} and ∅.

LESSON

11-9

Situations Which Always or Never Happen

Which job would you take?

Job 1	*Job 2*
Starting wage \$5.60/hour; every 3 months the wage increases \$.10/hour.	Starting wage \$5.50/hour; every 3 months the wage increases \$.10/hour.

Of course, the answer is obvious. Job 1 will always pay better than Job 2. But what happens when this is solved mathematically? Let n = number of 3-month periods worked.

Wage in Job 1	*Wage in Job 2*
$5.60 + .10n$	$5.50 + .10n$

When is the pay in Job 1 better than the pay in Job 2? The corresponding mathematical problem is to solve this inequality:

$$5.60 + .10n > 5.50 + .10n$$

Add $-.10n$ to each side.

$$5.60 + .10n - .10n > 5.50 + .10n - .10n$$
$$5.60 > 5.50$$

As was the case in solving systems of parallel lines, the variable has disappeared. Since $5.60 > 5.50$ is always true, n can be any real number. Job 1 will always pay a better wage than Job 2, as expected. So for any equations or inequalities we can now make the following generalization.

If, in solving a sentence, you get a sentence which is *always* true, then the original sentence is always true.

When does Job 1 pay *less* than Job 2? To answer this, you could solve:

$$5.60 + .10n < 5.50 + .10n$$
$$5.60 + .10n - .10n < 5.50 + .10n - .10n$$
$$5.60 < 5.50$$

It is never true that 5.60 is less than 5.50. So Job 1 never pays less than Job 2, something which was obvious from the pay rates.

If, in solving a sentence, you get a sentence which is *never* true, then the original sentence is never true.

Example 1 Solve: $5 + 3x = 3(x - 2)$

Solution

$$5 + 3x = 3x - 6$$
$$5 + 3x + -3x = -3x + 3x + -6$$
$$5 = -6$$

This is never true, so the original sentence has no solution. Write: *no solution*.

Example 2 Solve: $8(2y + 5) < 16y + 60$

Solution

$$16y + 40 < 16y + 60$$
$$-16y + 16y + 40 < -16y + 16y + 60$$
$$40 < 60$$

This is always true, so the original sentence is true for every possible value of y. Write: *y may be any real number*.

CAUTION: Here is a problem that looks like the one at the beginning of the lesson but is different.

Example 3 When will the population of the towns be the same?

Town 1	*Town 2*
Present population 23,000	Present population 23,000
Growing 1000 a year	Growing 1200 a year

Solution In t years:

Population of Town 1	*Population of Town 2*
$23{,}000 + 1000t$	$23{,}000 + 1200t$

The populations will be the same when

$$23{,}000 + 1000t = 23{,}000 + 1200t$$
$$23{,}000 = 23{,}000 + 200t$$
$$0 = 200t$$
$$0 = t$$

The solution $t = 0$ means their populations are the same *now. Having zero for a solution is different from having no solution at all.*

ADDITIONAL EXAMPLES

1. Solve $9x - 5x - 2(2x + 1) = 15$.
no solution

2. Solve $(20x + 17) - (6 + 20x) = 11$.
x may be any real number

3. Town A has a population of 50,000 and is growing at a rate of 3000 people a year. Town B has a population of 40,000 and is growing at a rate of 3000 people a year. When will these towns have the same population?
$50{,}000 + 3000t = 40{,}000 + 3000t$; never

NOTES ON QUESTIONS
Questions 2 and 3: Asking students to write the resulting sentence in part **a** emphasizes its importance.

Questions 8-11: If students are alert, they will not need algebra to recognize that in **Question 8** the cities have the same population now and that in **Questions 9-11** apartment B is always cheaper. Again, the point is to show how algebra mirrors the real situation, not necessarily to use algebra to answer the question.

ADDITIONAL ANSWERS
1b. Let y = number of years employed.
$6.20 + 1.00y > 6.00 + 1.00y$
$6.20 > 6.00$
Any value of y works.

14.

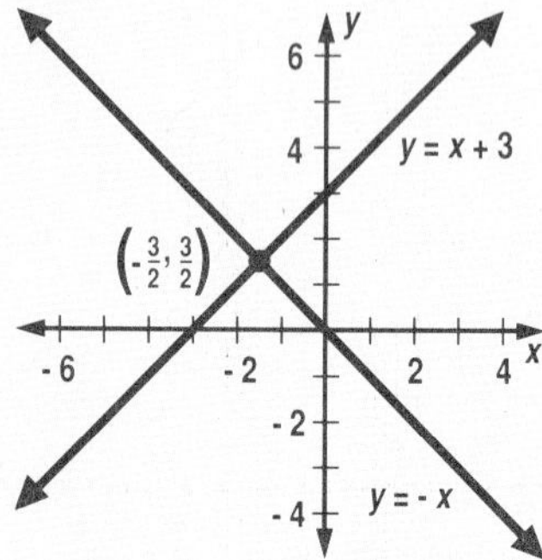

Questions

Covering the Reading

1. Job A pays a starting salary of \$6.20 an hour and each year increases \$1.00 an hour. Job B starts at \$6.00 an hour and also increases \$1.00 an hour per year.
a. When does Job A pay more? always
b. Show how algebra can be used to represent this situation. See margin.

2. a. Add $-2x$ to both sides of the sentence $2x + 10 < 2x + 8$. What sentence results? $10 < 8$
b. What should you write to describe the solutions to this sentence? no solution

3. a. Add $5y$ to both sides of the sentence $-5y + 9 = 3 - 5y + 6$. What sentence results? $9 = 3 + 6$
b. What should you write to describe the solutions to this sentence? y may be any real number.

In 4–7, solve.

4. $2(2y - 5) \leq 4y + 6$ y may be any real number.

5. $3x + 5 = 5 + 3x$ x may be any real number.

6. $-2m = 3 - 2m$ no solution

7. $2A - 10A > 4(1 - 2A)$ no solution

8. The population of City 1 is about 200,000 and growing at about 5000 people a year. City 2 has a population of about 200,000 and is growing at about 4000 people a year. $200{,}000 + 5000y$
a. In y years, what will be the population of City 1?
b. In y years what will be the population of City 2? $200{,}000 + 4000y$
c. When will their populations be the same? They are the same now.

Applying the Mathematics

In 9–11, consider the following information. Apartment A rents for \$375 per month with a \$500 security deposit. Apartment B rents for \$315 per month with a \$400 security deposit, but the renter must pay \$60 per month for utilities.

9. a. What sentence would you solve to find out when apartment A is cheaper? $375m + 500 < 315m + 400 + 60m$
b. Solve this sentence. $500 < 400$; Apartment A is never cheaper.

10. a. What sentence would you solve to find out when apartment B is cheaper? $375m + 500 > 315m + 400 + 60m$
b. Solve this sentence. $500 > 400$; Apartment B is always cheaper.

11. If Naomi wanted to rent an apartment for two years, which one is cheaper? B

Review

12. Solve $\begin{cases} 4x - 3y = 12 \\ 8x - 6y = 24 \end{cases}$. *(Lesson 11-8)* Infinitely many solutions; the lines are coincident.

13. A retailer sold 220 records at \$10 each. What can the sale price be of the 110 remaining records to have an overall average price of \$8? *(Lesson 11-7)* \$4.00

572

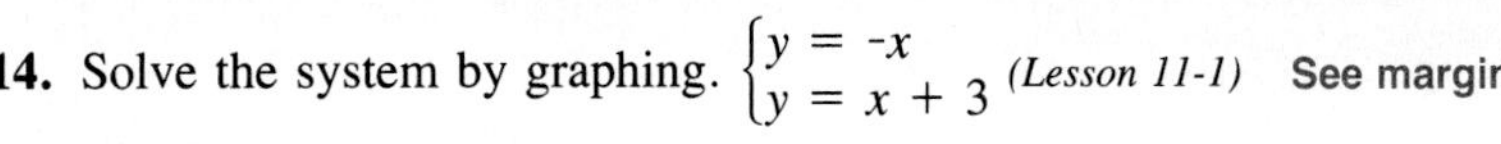

14. Solve the system by graphing. $\begin{cases} y = -x \\ y = x + 3 \end{cases}$ *(Lesson 11-1)* See margin.

15. Solve: $-(a - 4) = 2a + 3$. *(Lessons 6-5, 6-6)* $\frac{1}{3}$

16. Anna spends \$1.30 on breakfast, then d dollars on lunch, then \$2 on flowers. *(Lessons 2-1, 3-3)*
  a. How much does she spend altogether? $3.30 + d$ dollars
  b. She had \$10 to start with, and now has \$1.25 left. If she spent no other money that day, how much did she spend on lunch? \$5.45

17. A book has an average of 25 lines per page, w words per line, and 21 pages per chapter. Estimate the number of words per chapter in this book. *(Lesson 4-2)* $525w$

18. Simplify in one step. *(Lesson 9-8)*
  a. $\left(\frac{2}{3}\right)^2$ $\frac{4}{9}$ **b.** $(5d^2g)^2$ $25d^4g^2$ **c.** $\frac{1}{4}\left(\frac{c}{a}\right)^2$ $\frac{c^2}{4a^2}$

19. A person wants 10,000 square meters of floor space for a store. Walking by a set of vacant stores he wonders if the 4 stores together will meet his requirements. It is possible to measure their widths, and they are given in the floor plan below. How deep must these stores be to give the required area? *(Lessons 4-1, 4-4)* ≈ 143 m

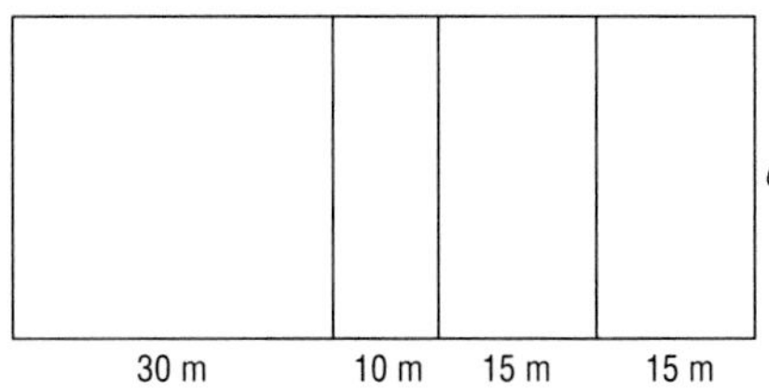

20. *Skill sequence* Solve. *(Lesson 5-7)*
  a. $\frac{x}{2} = \frac{7}{8}$ $\frac{7}{4}$
  b. $\frac{3.5}{y} = \frac{2}{y + 2}$ $-4.\overline{6}$
  c. $\frac{z + 2}{2} = 4$ 6

Exploration

21. When solving the equation $ax + b = cx + d$ for x, there may be no solution, exactly one solution, or infinitely many solutions. What must be true about a, b, c, and d to guarantee that there is exactly one solution? $a \neq c$

FOLLOW-UP

MORE PRACTICE
For more questions on SPUR Objectives, use *Lesson Master 11-9,* shown below.

NAME ______

LESSON **MASTER 11–9**
QUESTIONS ON **SPUR** OBJECTIVES

■PROPERTIES *Objective D (See pages 583–585 for objectives.)*
In 1–8, solve.

1. $3t + 1 < 3t + 4$ — t is any real number
2. $6(x - 3) = 2(3x + 2)$ — no solution
3. $8x + 7 > 4(2x + 2)$ — no solution
4. $-4b + 8b < 4(b + 3)$ — b is any real number
5. $5q - 2 = 3q - 2$ — $q = 0$
6. $12w + 10 = 5(3w + 2)$ — $w = 0$
7. $2(r - 3) > r - 6$ — $r > 0$
8. $d + 7 = d - 7$ — no solution

■USES *Objective F*

9. Sara deposited \$500 in Bank A paying 5% interest. At the same time, she also deposited \$500 in Bank B paying 5.5% interest. She withdrew only the interest each year and made no more deposits.
  a. What sentence could you solve to find out when the account in Bank A would have earned more money?
  $500(.05)t > 500(.055)t$
  b. Solve the sentence to answer the question. no sol.; The account in Bank A will never earn more money.

10. Car rental Company X charges \$29.95 a day plus \$.15 per mile. Car rental Company Y charges \$29.95 a day plus \$.20 a mile.
  a. What sentence could you solve to find out after how many miles the charges would be the same?
  $29.95 + .15m = 29.95 + .20m$
  b. Solve the sentence to answer the questions. $m = 0$; They are the same now.

102 *Algebra* © Scott, Foresman and Company

LESSON 11-10

RESOURCES
- Lesson Master 11-10
- Visual for Teaching Aid 7: Coordinate Grid
- Visual for Teaching Aid 63: Graphs for Example 1
- Visual for Teaching Aid 64: Graphs for Example 2
- Visual for Teaching Aid 65: Graph for Example 4

OBJECTIVE

I Graphically represent solutions to systems of linear inequalities.

TEACHING NOTES

Graphing systems of inequalities is not easy for many students. Transparencies are very useful in showing the overlap on an overhead projector. Shade the graphs of two inequalities differently. Show them separately to make sure that students understand which half-plane should be shaded for each inequality. Then place them both on the overhead so that students can see that the region where the individual graphs overlap is the solution region. *Teaching Aids 63 and 64* can be used to show the graphs involved in **Examples 1 and 2.** (Cut the teaching aids in two so you can overlap the individual graphs.)

You might point out to students that the figures drawn in computer games are often described by giving inequalities; this is how the computer knows to shade regions rather than just use stick figures.

LESSON

11-10 Systems of Inequalities

In Lesson 7-2, you graphed linear inequalities like $x > -5$ and $y \leq 6$ on a plane. These sentences describe half-planes with boundary lines that are horizontal or vertical. In Lesson 8-9, you went on to graph half-planes with boundaries that are oblique lines. Now you will graph regions described by two or more inequalities. Solving a **system of inequalities** involves finding the common solutions of two or more linear inequalities.

Recall that the graph of $Ax + By < C$ is a half-plane. It lies on one side of the boundary line $Ax + By = C$. When systems involve linear inequalities, their solutions are intersections of half-planes.

Example 1 Graph all solutions to the system

$$\begin{cases} y \geq -3x + 2 & (1) \\ y < x - 2 & (2) \end{cases}$$

Solution First graph the boundary line $y = -3x + 2$ for the first inequality. This line contains (0, 2) and (1, -1). The graph of $y \geq -3x + 2$ consists of points on or above the line with equation $y = -3x + 2$.

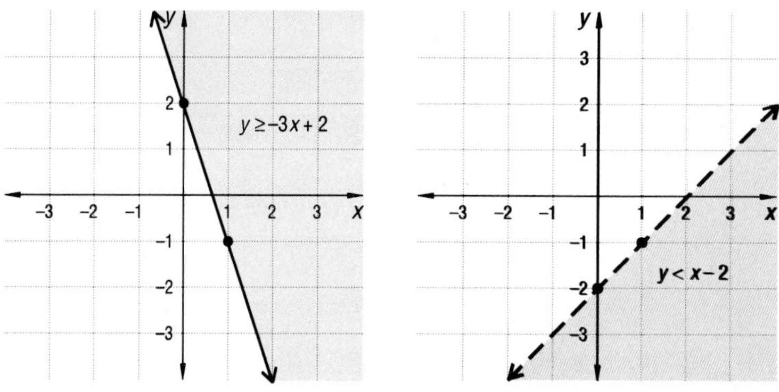

Next graph the boundary line $y = x - 2$ for the second inequality. Two parts on this line are (0, 2) and (1, -1). The graph of $y < x - 2$ consists of points below the line with equation $y = x - 2$. Points on the line are excluded.

We have drawn the half-planes on different axes only to make it easier to see them. You should draw them on the same axes. The part of the plane marked with both types of shading is the solution set for the system. Geometrically, it can be described as the interior of an angle with vertex (1, -1).

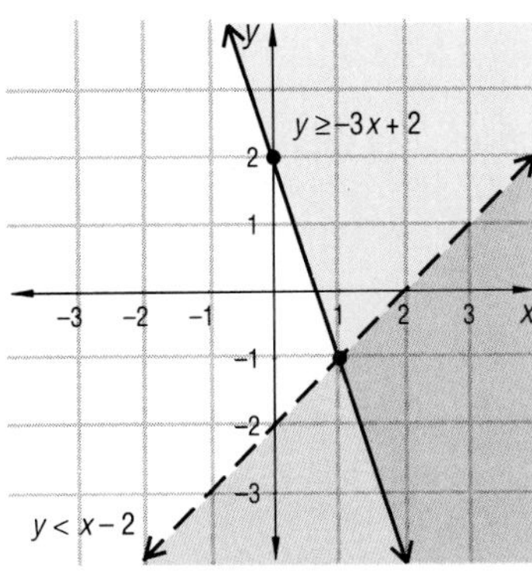

What your paper should look like

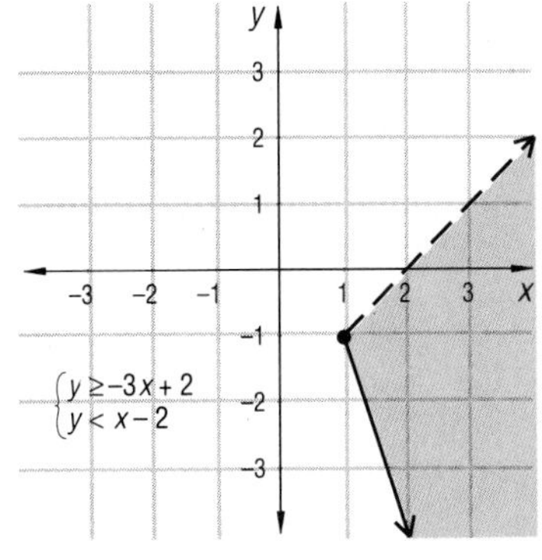

The solutions to the system

Example 2 involves a system of inequalities quite often seen in applications.

Example 2 Graph all solutions to the system

$$\begin{cases} x > 0 \\ y > 0 \end{cases}$$

Solution The graph of the solution to the system is the intersection of the left and center sets graphed below. It is the part of the right graph that has both colors.

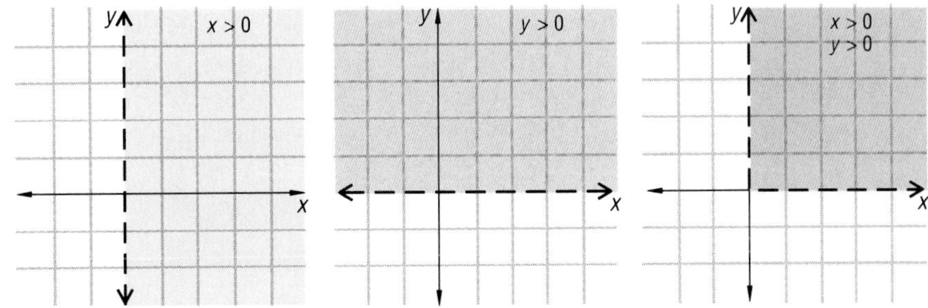

In **Example 4** we have not considered the possibility of a three-point shot, now used in professional and college basketball and in some states for high school basketball. The three-point shot would require a third variable and hence a third dimension. For simplicity, we choose to stay with two variables.

ADDITIONAL EXAMPLES

1. Graph all solutions to the system

$$\begin{cases} x - y \le -3 \\ 2x - 2y > 4 \end{cases}$$

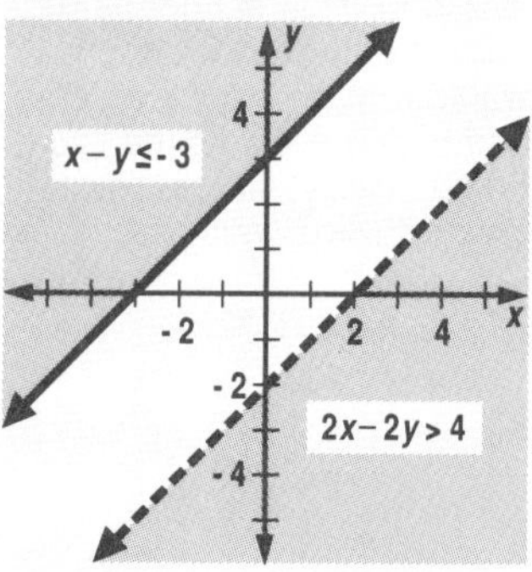

There are no solutions.

2. Miss Moffat is planning refreshments for a party. She decides to have from 10 to 15 pounds of salad—some potato salad and some fruit salad. She wants to have at least 4 times as much fruit salad as potato salad. Graph the number of pounds of each she can have. (Let p and f be the numbers of pounds of potato salad and fruit salad.) The inequalities are: $p \ge 0$, $f \ge 0$, $10 \le p + f$, $p + f \le 15$, and $f \ge 4p$.

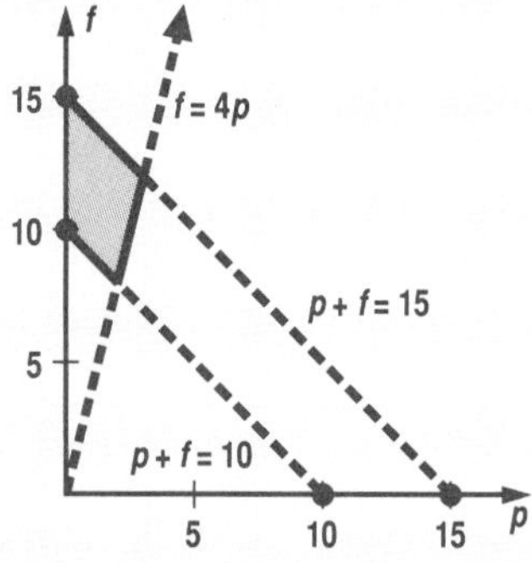

The vertices of the shaded region are (0, 10), (0, 15), (2, 8), and (3, 12). She can have 3 pounds of potato salad and 10 pounds of fruit salad, for instance.

Example 3 Suppose the sum of two positive numbers x and y is less than 50 and greater than 25. The desired numbers are the solution to this system of inequalities.

$$\begin{cases} x > 0 \\ y > 0 \\ x + y < 50 \\ x + y > 25 \end{cases}$$

Solution The graph of the solution to the system is the intersection of the four sets graphed below.

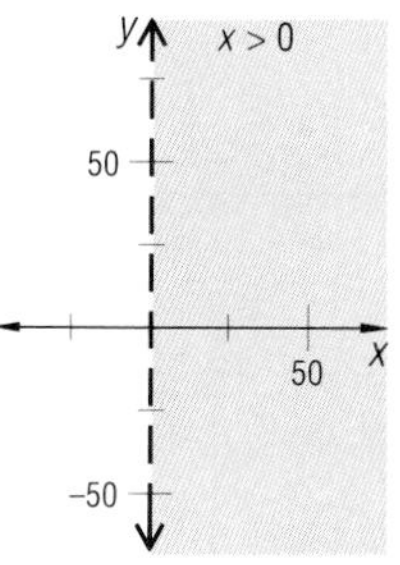

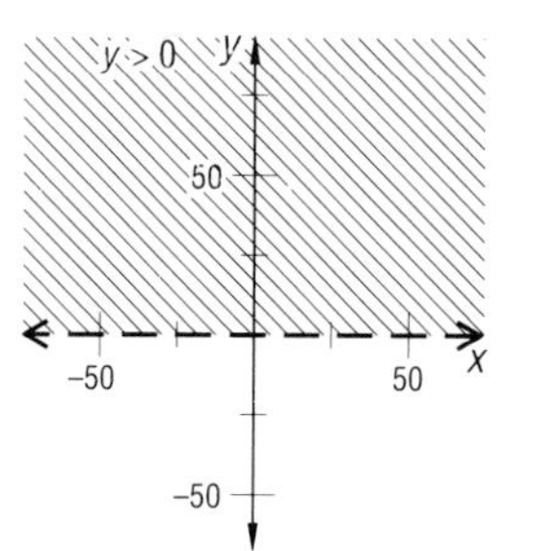

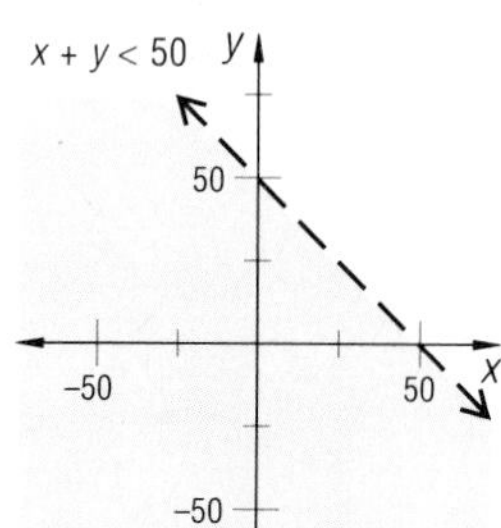

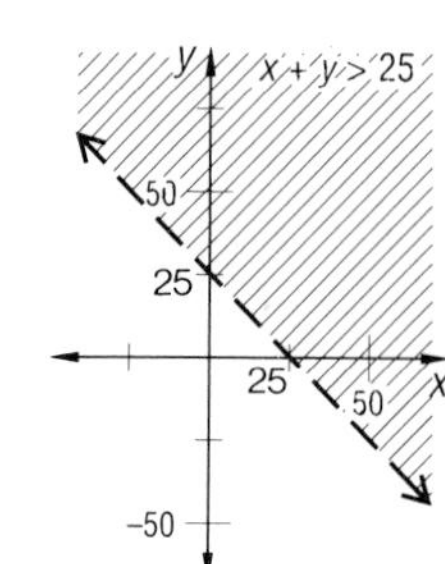

The result below shows only the intersection of the four graphs drawn on the same set of axes.

Graph of all solutions to the system.

$$\begin{cases} x > 0 \\ y > 0 \\ x + y < 50 \\ x + y > 25 \end{cases}$$

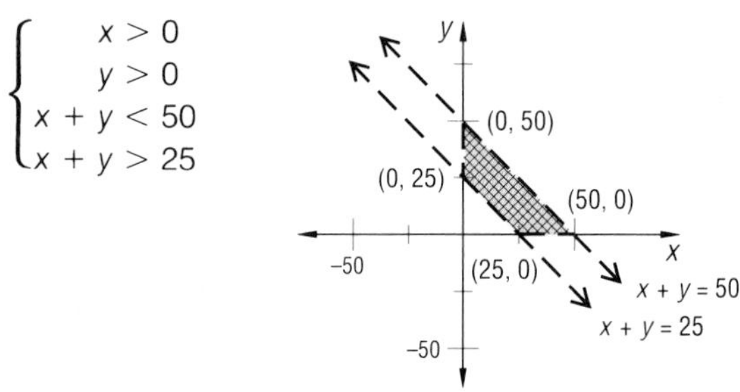

Notice that there are infinitely many solutions to the system, so they cannot be listed. But the graph is easy to describe. It is the interior of the quadrilateral with vertices (0, 50), (50, 0), (25, 0), and (0, 25).

Systems of inequalities arise from many different kinds of situations. Here is one.

Example 4 In basketball a player scores 2 points for a basket and 1 point for a free throw. Suppose a player has scored no more than 20 points in a game. How many baskets b and free throws f could the player have made?

Solution You could answer this question by trial and error, but there are a lot of possibilities. It is much easier to show the answers on a graph. The numbers b and f must be positive integers or zero.

$$b \geq 0 \text{ and } f \geq 0$$

Since the total number of points is less than or equal to 20,

$$2b + f \leq 20.$$

Since this is a discrete situation, only the dotted points on or above the b-axis, on or to the right of the f-axis, and on or below $2b + f = 20$ are possible solutions.

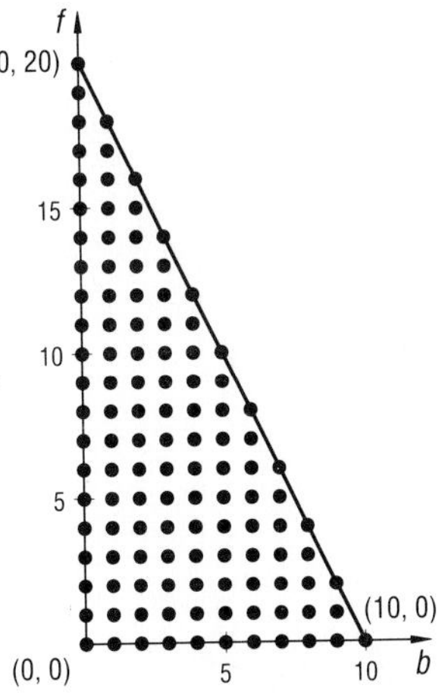

For example, the point (5, 3) represents the possibility of the player making 5 baskets and 3 free throws. Altogether there are 121 possibilities. The above graph is the solution to this system of inequalities.

$$\begin{cases} b \geq 0 \\ f \geq 0 \\ 2b + f \leq 20 \end{cases}$$

If the situation allowed fractions, the entire triangle above would be shaded in.

NOTES ON QUESTIONS
Question 12: By limiting the number of baskets, it becomes reasonable to count the possibilities from the graph. Use *Teaching Aid 65* to show your students how the graph is affected by adding the condition that $b > 5$.

ADDITIONAL ANSWERS
6.

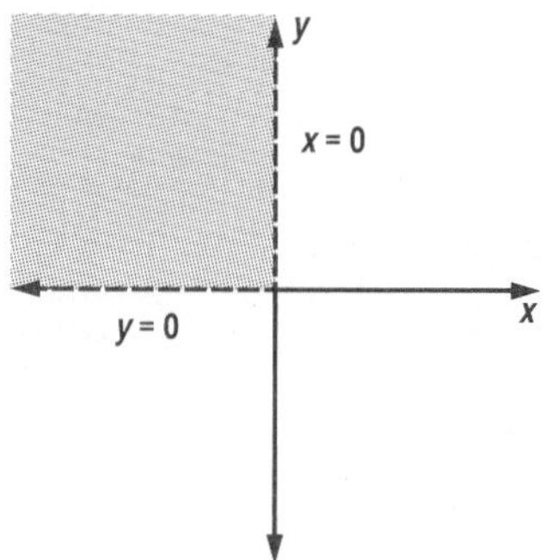

15.

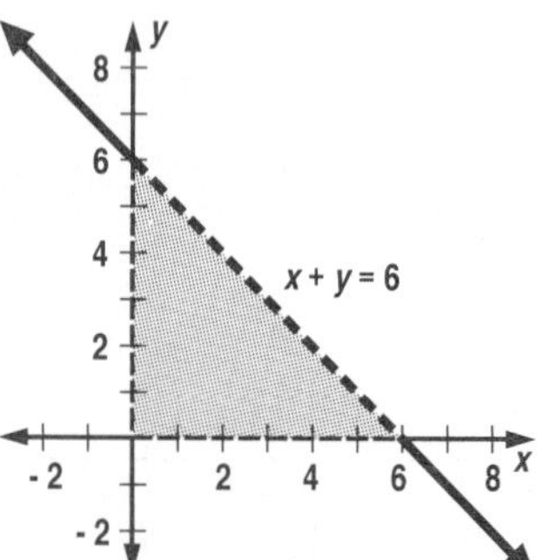

16.

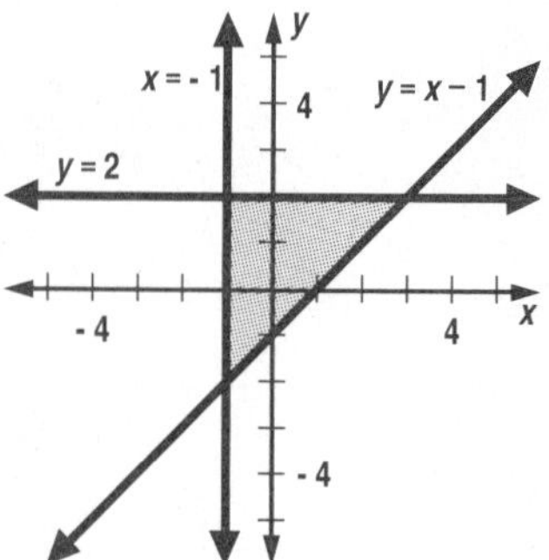

Questions

Covering the Reading

In 1–4, refer to Example 1.

1. The graph of all solutions to the system
$$\begin{cases} y \geq -3x + 2 \\ y < x - 2 \end{cases}$$
is the __?__ of the graphs of $y \geq -3x + 2$ and $y < x - 2$. **intersection**

2. The graph of $y < x - 2$ is a __?__. **half-plane**

3. Why does the graph of $y \geq -3x + 2$ include its boundary line?
An equal sign means the boundary is included.

4. Is (2, 1) a solution to this system? **No**

5. The graph of $\begin{cases} x > 0 \\ y > 0 \end{cases}$ consists of all points in which quadrant? **first**

6. Graph the system $\begin{cases} x < 0 \\ y > 0 \end{cases}$. **See margin.**

In 7 and 8 consider the system of Example 3.
$$\begin{cases} x > 0 \\ y > 0 \\ x + y < 50 \\ x + y > 25 \end{cases}$$

7. The graph of all solutions to this system is the interior of a quadrilateral with what vertices? **(0, 50), (50, 0), (25, 0), and (0, 25)**

8. Is (25, 25) a solution to the system? **No**

In 9–12, refer to Example 4. **9. samples: (0, 20), (1, 18), (2, 16), (3, 14), (4, 12), (8, 4), (9, 2), (10, 0)**

9. Give at least three possible combinations of baskets and free throws that would total exactly 20 points.

10. For which part of the plane is $b \geq 0$? **on or to the right of the *f*-axis**

11. For which part of the plane is $f \geq 0$? **on or above the *b*-axis**

12. Suppose the player made at least five baskets. How many possibilities are there for $2b + f \leq 20$? **36**

578

Applying the Mathematics

In 13 and 14, describe the system graphed.

13. **14.**

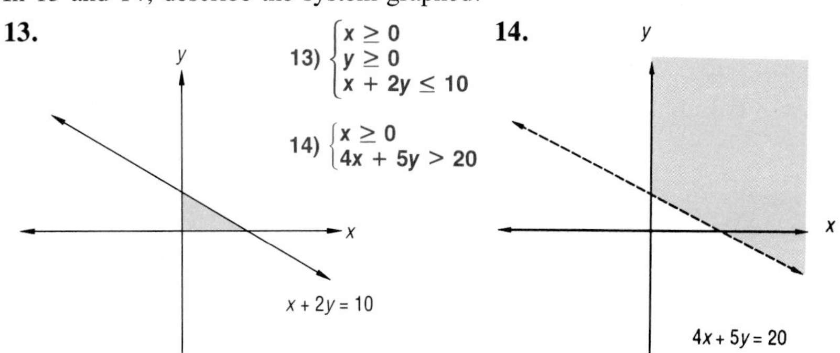

13) $\begin{cases} x \geq 0 \\ y \geq 0 \\ x + 2y \leq 10 \end{cases}$
14) $\begin{cases} x \geq 0 \\ 4x + 5y > 20 \end{cases}$
y
x
x + 2y = 10
4x + 5y = 20

In 15 and 16, graph the solution set. **See margin.**

15. $\begin{cases} x > 0 \\ y > 0 \\ x + y < 6 \end{cases}$ **16.** $\begin{cases} x \geq -1 \\ y \leq 2 \\ y \geq x - 1 \end{cases}$

In 17 and 18, accurately graph the set of points that satisfies each situation.

17. It takes a good typist about 10 minutes to type a letter of moderate length and about 8 minutes to type a normal double-spaced page. About how many letters L and how many pages P will keep a typist busy for 1 hour or less? **See margin.**

18. A hockey team estimates that it needs at least 16 points to make the playoffs. A win is worth 2 points and a tie is worth 1 point. How many wins w and ties t will get the team into the playoffs? **See margin.**

17.

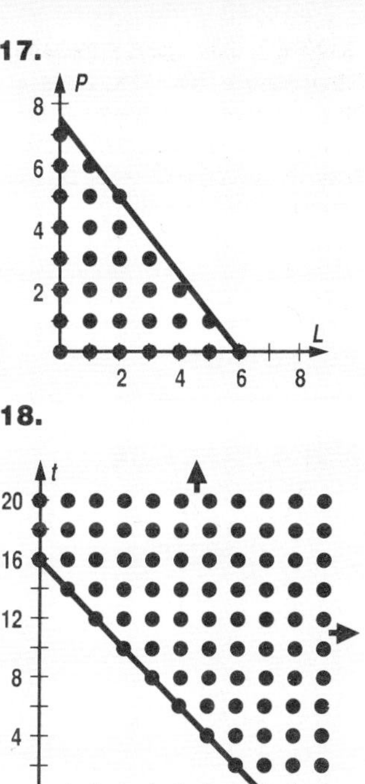

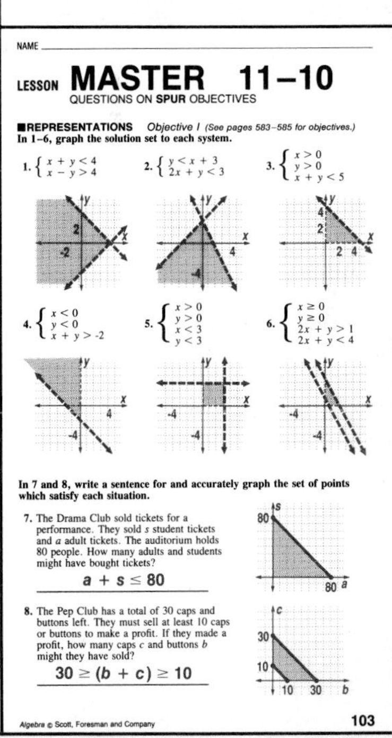

NAME

LESSON **MASTER 11–10**
QUESTIONS ON SPUR OBJECTIVES

REPRESENTATIONS *Objective I* (See pages 583–585 for objectives.)
In 1–6, graph the solution set to each system.

1. $\begin{cases} x + y < 4 \\ x - y > 4 \end{cases}$ 2. $\begin{cases} y < x + 3 \\ 2x + y < 3 \end{cases}$ 3. $\begin{cases} x > 0 \\ y > 0 \\ x + y < 5 \end{cases}$

4. $\begin{cases} x < 0 \\ y < 0 \\ x + y > -2 \end{cases}$ 5. $\begin{cases} x > 0 \\ y > 0 \\ x < 3 \\ y < 3 \end{cases}$ 6. $\begin{cases} x \geq 0 \\ y \geq 0 \\ 2x + y > 1 \\ 2x + y < 4 \end{cases}$

In 7 and 8, write a sentence for and accurately graph the set of points which satisfy each situation.

7. The Drama Club sold tickets for a performance. They sold s student tickets and a adult tickets. The auditorium holds 80 people. How many adults and students might have bought tickets?
a + s ≤ 80

8. The Pep Club has a total of 30 caps and buttons left. They must sell at least 10 caps or buttons to make a profit. If they made a profit, how many caps c and buttons b might they have sold?
30 ≥ (b + c) ≥ 10

 103

NOTES ON QUESTIONS
Question 20: Students can answer this question by simplifying the left side of the equation to get 3 = 3, or by using a proportion.

FOLLOW-UP

MORE PRACTICE
For more questions on SPUR Objectives, use *Lesson Master 11-10,* shown on page 579.

Review

19. Solve. *(Lesson 11-9)*
a. $6(3 - 2x) = -12(x - 3)$ no solution
b. $6(3 - 2y) = -12(y - \frac{3}{2})$ y may be any real number

20. Consider the equation $\frac{6(z - 3)}{2(z - 3)} = 3$.
a. What value can z not have? z cannot be 3
b. Solve for z. *(Lesson 11-9)* z can be any value but 3

In 21 and 22, determine whether the lines are parallel, coincident, or intersecting. *(Lesson 11-8)*

21. $\begin{cases} 4x - y = 8 \\ 8x - y = 8 \end{cases}$ intersecting

22. $\begin{cases} y = 3x + 9 \\ 6x - 2y = -27 \end{cases}$ parallel

23. Solve the system using any method you wish. $\begin{cases} 3x + 5y = 4 \\ 2x - 3y = 9 \end{cases}$ *(Lessons 1-3, 11-1, 11-5)* (3, -1)

24. Given the system $\begin{cases} w = -9z & (1) \\ z - 2w = 323 & (2) \end{cases}$, a student substituted $-9z$ for w in equation (2). The student wrote $z - 18z = 323$. See margin.
a. Is this result correct? No
b. If it is correct, finish solving the system. If not, describe what is wrong with it. *(Lessons 11-2, 11-3)* $-2(-9z) = +18z$

25. For what value of c will $x^2 + 6x + c$ be a perfect square? *(Lesson 10-7)* 9

26. If $x^2 = 121$, then x = __?__ or __?__. *(Lesson 7-4)* 11, -11

27. Suppose a bank offers an 8.5% annual yield. What would be the amount in an account after 5 years if $1000 is invested? *(Lesson 9-1)* $1503.66

28. Maureen has an ID number that consists of two letters followed by four single-digit numbers. How many different possible ID numbers can be made this way? *(Lesson 4-7)* 6,760,000

Exploration

29. The graph of the solution to the system of inequalities on page 576 is a special type of quadrilateral called an *isosceles trapezoid.* Look in a dictionary or geometry book for a definition of isosceles trapezoid. An isosceles trapezoid is a quadrilateral with at least one pair of parallel sides and the other two sides are congruent.

Summary

A system is a set of sentences in which you want to find all the solutions common to each sentence in the set. Thus the solution set for a system is the intersection of the solutions for the individual sentences.

One way to solve a system is by graphing. By looking for intersection points on a graph you can quickly tell if there are any solutions to the system. There are as many solutions as intersection points. Graphing is also a way to describe solutions to systems that have infinitely many solutions. For instance, graphs show the solutions to systems of linear inequalities.

However, graphing does not always yield exact solutions. In this chapter you studied three strategies for finding exact solutions to systems of linear equations. They are substitution, addition, and multiplication. Substitution is a good method to use if an equation is given in $y = mx + b$ form. Addition works if opposite terms are in two equations. Multiplication is a good method when both equations are in $Ax + By = C$ form.

Any kind of situation that leads to a linear equation can lead to a linear system. All that is needed is more than one condition to be satisfied. Problems involving mixtures were solved using weighted averages.

The graph of all solutions to a system of inequalities can be found by graphing each inequality on the same axes. The solution is the intersection of all the individual graphs.

Vocabulary

Below are the new terms and phrases for this chapter. You should be able to give a general description and a specific example for each.

Lesson 11-1
system
solution set for a system
linear systems

Lesson 11-2
substitution method for solving a system

Lesson 11-4
Generalized Addition Property of Equality
addition method for solving a system

Lesson 11-5
multiplication method for solving a system

Lesson 11-6
weighted average
weight

Lesson 11-8
coincident lines

Lesson 11-10
system of inequalities

SUMMARY

The Summary gives an overview of the entire chapter and provides an opportunity for students to consider the material as a whole. Thus, the Summary can be used to help students relate the concepts presented in the chapter.

VOCABULARY

Terms, symbols, and properties are listed by lesson to provide a checklist of things a student must know. Emphasize to students that they should read the vocabulary list carefully before starting the Progress Self-Test. If students do not understand the meaning of a term, they should refer back to the indicated lesson.

Definitions or descriptions of all terms in the vocabulary list may be found in the Glossary.

ADDITIONAL ANSWERS
17.

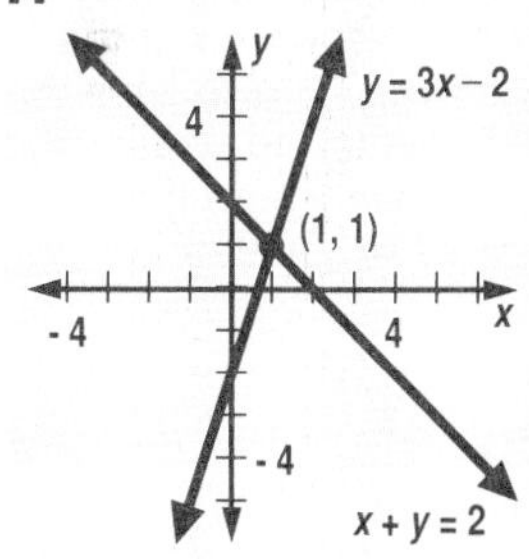

PROGRESS SELF-TEST

We cannot overemphasize the importance of these end-of-chapter materials. It is at this point that the material "gels" for many students, allowing them to solidify skills and understanding. In general, student performance should be markedly improved after these pages.

USING THE PROGRESS SELF-TEST

Assign the Progress Self-Test as a one-night assignment. Worked-out *solutions* for all questions are in the Selected Answers section at the back of the student book. Encourage students to take the Progress Self-Test honestly, grade themselves, and then be prepared to discuss the test in class.

Advise students to pay special attention to those Chapter Review questions (pages 583–585) which correspond to questions missed on the Progress Self-Test. A chart provided in the Selected Answers section in the student text keys the Progress Self-Test questions to the lettered SPUR Objectives in the Chapter Review or to the Vocabulary. It also keys the questions to the corresponding lessons where the material is covered.

17. See margin, page 581.

18.

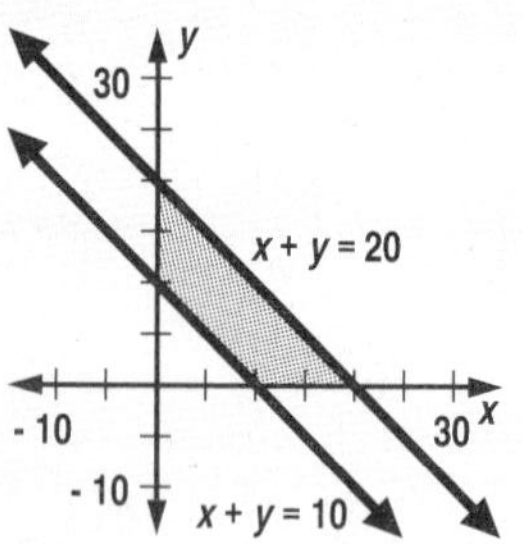

Progress Self-Test

Take this test as you would take a test in class. Then check your work with the solution in the Selected Answers section in the back of the book.

In 1 and 2, solve.

1. $\begin{cases} a - 3b = -8 \\ b = 3a \end{cases}$ **(a, b) = (1, 3)**

2. $\begin{cases} p = 5r + 80 \\ p = -7r - 40 \end{cases}$ **(p, r) = (30, -10)**

3. Line 1 has equation $y = -5x - 15$. Line 2 has equation $y = x - 3$. Find the point of intersection. **(x, y) = (-2, -5)**

In 4–6, solve.

4. $\begin{cases} m - n = -1 \\ -m + 2n = 4 \end{cases}$ **(m, n) = (2, 3)**

5. $\begin{cases} 2x + y = -6 \\ 2x + 3y = 10 \end{cases}$ **(x, y) = (-7, 8)**

6. $\begin{cases} 7x + 3y = 1 \\ 4x - y = 6 \end{cases}$ **(x, y) = (1, -2)**

In 7 and 8, determine whether the lines coincide, intersect, or are parallel and nonintersecting.

7. $\begin{cases} 5 = 2A + 7B \\ 10 = 4A + 14B \end{cases}$ **coincident**

8. $\begin{cases} y = 2x + 7 \\ y - 2x = 3 \end{cases}$ **parallel**

In 9 and 10, solve and check.

9. $12z + 8 = 12z - 3$ **no solution**

10. $-19p < 22 - 19p$ **p may be any real number.**

11. Lisa weighs 4 times as much as her baby sister. Together they weigh 92 pounds. How much does each person weigh? **Lisa weighs 73.6 pounds and the baby weighs 18.4 pounds.**

13) The situation could not happen.
12) s = $2.70

12. The Reid family goes to a restaurant and orders 3 hamburgers and 4 small salads. Without tax the bill comes to $21.30. At the same restaurant the Millers order 5 burgers and 2 small salads. Their bill without tax is $22.90. What is the cost of a small salad?

13. If the cost per unit is constant, could the following situation have happened?
    10 roses and 15 daffodils were sold for $35.
    2 roses and 3 daffodils were sold for $8.

14. South Carolina had a 1980 population of about 3,100,000 and was growing at a rate of 55,000 people each year. Louisiana had a 1980 population of about 4,200,000 and was growing at a rate of 55,000 people each year. If these rates continue, in how many years after 1980 will these two states have the same population? **never**

15. Suppose 14 liters of a 40% salt solution are mixed with 6 liters of an 80% salt solution. What is the percent of salt in the resulting mixture? **52% salt**

16. A car averages 55 mph for the first 3 hours of a trip. How long can it travel at 40 mph and still maintain an overall average speed of 45 mph? **It can travel 6 hours at 40 mph.**

In 17 and 18, solve the system by graphing.

17. $\begin{cases} y = 3x - 2 \\ x + y = 2 \end{cases}$ **See margin.**

18. $\begin{cases} x \ge 0 \\ y \ge 0 \\ x + y \le 20 \\ x + y \ge 10 \end{cases}$ **See margin.**

Chapter Review

Questions on SPUR Objectives

SPUR stands for **S**kills, **P**roperties, **U**ses, and **R**epresentations. The Chapter Review questions are grouped according to the SPUR Objectives for this chapter.

SKILLS deal with the procedures used to get answers.

Objective A. *Solve systems using substitution.* *(Lessons 11-2, 11-3)*

1. Determine (a, b).
$\begin{cases} b = 3a \\ 60 = a + b \end{cases}$ **(a, b) = (15, 45)**

2. Determine (x, y).
$\begin{cases} x - y = 13 \\ x = 6y - 7 \end{cases}$ **(x, y) = (17, 4)**

3. Solve for c, p, and q.
$\begin{cases} p = 2c \\ q = 3c \\ p + 6q = 200 \end{cases}$ **c = 10, p = 20, q = 30**

4. Solve the system.
$\begin{cases} 10y = 20x + 20 \\ 2x + 4y = 29 \end{cases}$ **(x, y) = (2.1, 6.2)**

In 5–8, solve.

5. $\begin{cases} y = x + 5 \\ 300 + 10x = 35y \end{cases}$ **(x, y) = (5, 10)**

6. $\begin{cases} q = z + 8 \\ 14z + 89 = 13q \end{cases}$ **(q, z) = (23, 15)**

7. $\begin{cases} a = 2b + 3 \\ a = 3b + 20 \end{cases}$ **(a, b) = (-31, -17)**

8. $\begin{cases} 16 - 2x = y \\ x + 4 = y \end{cases}$ **(x, y) = (4, 8)**

In 9 and 10, two lines have the given equations. Find the point of intersection.

9. Line 1: $y = 7x + 20$
Line 2: $y = 3x - 16$ **(x, y) = (-9, -43)**

10. Line 1: $y = \frac{2}{3}x - \frac{1}{6}$
Line 2: $y = \frac{1}{3}x + \frac{1}{3}$ **(x, y) = $(\frac{3}{2}, \frac{5}{6})$**

Objective B. *Solve systems by addition.* *(Lesson 11-4)*

In 11–14, solve.

11. $\begin{cases} 3m + b = 11 \\ -4m - b = 11 \end{cases}$ **(m, b) = (-22, 77)**

12. $\begin{cases} 6a + 2c = 200 \\ 9a - 2c = 25 \end{cases}$ **(a, c) = (15, 55)**

13. $\begin{cases} .6x - .4y = 1.1 \\ .2x - .4y = 2.3 \end{cases}$ **(x, y) = (-3, -7.25)**

14. $\begin{cases} \frac{1}{2}x + 3y = -6 \\ \frac{1}{2}x + y = 2 \end{cases}$ **(x, y) = (12, -4)**

Objective C. *Solve systems by multiplying.* *(Lesson 11-5)*

In 15 and 16, **a.** multiply one of the equations by a number which makes it possible to solve the system by adding. **b.** Solve the system.

15. $\begin{cases} 5x + y = 30 \\ 3x - 4y = 41 \end{cases}$ **15b) (x, y) = (7, -5)**

16. $\begin{cases} 5u + 6v = -295 \\ u - 9v = 400 \end{cases}$ **16b) (u, v) = (-5, -45)**

In 17–20, solve the system.

17. $\begin{cases} 3y - 2z = 3 \\ 2y + 5z = 21 \end{cases}$ **(y, z) = (3, 3)**

18. $\begin{cases} 7m - 4n = 0 \\ 9m - 5n = 1 \end{cases}$ **(m, n) = (4, 7)**

19. $\begin{cases} a + b = 3 \\ 5b - 3a = -17 \end{cases}$ **(a, b) = (4, -1)**

20. $\begin{cases} 46 = 2t + u \\ 20 = 8t - 4u \end{cases}$ **(t, u) = $(\frac{51}{4}, \frac{41}{2})$**

15a) sample: Multiply equation (1) by 4 to give 20x + 4y = 120
16a) sample: Multiply equation (2) by -5 to give -5u + 45v = -2000

RESOURCES
- Chapter 11 Test, Form A
- Chapter 11 Test, Form B
- Chapter 11 Test, Cumulative Form

CHAPTER REVIEW

The main objectives for the chapter are organized here into sections corresponding to the four main types of understanding this book promotes: Skills, Properties, Uses, and Representations.

USING THE CHAPTER REVIEW
Whereas end-of-chapter material may be considered optional in some texts, in *Algebra* we have selected these objectives and questions with the expectation that they will be covered. Students should be able to answer these questions with about 85% accuracy after studying the chapter.

You may assign these questions over a single night to help students prepare for a test the next day, or you may assign the questions over a two-day period.

If you work the questions over two days, then we recommend assigning the *evens* for homework the first night so that students get feedback in class the next day, then assigning the *odds* the night before the test so the students can use the answers provided in the book.

ADDITIONAL ANSWERS
43.

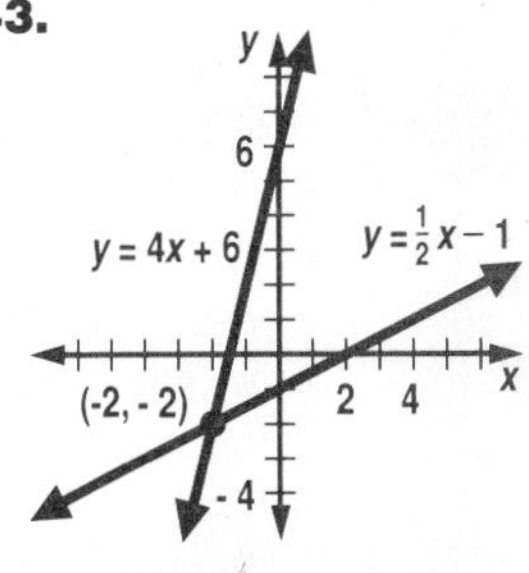

43. See margin, page 583.

44.

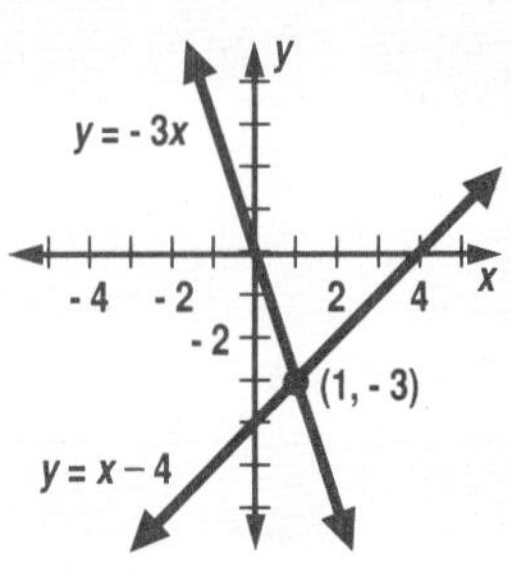

45.

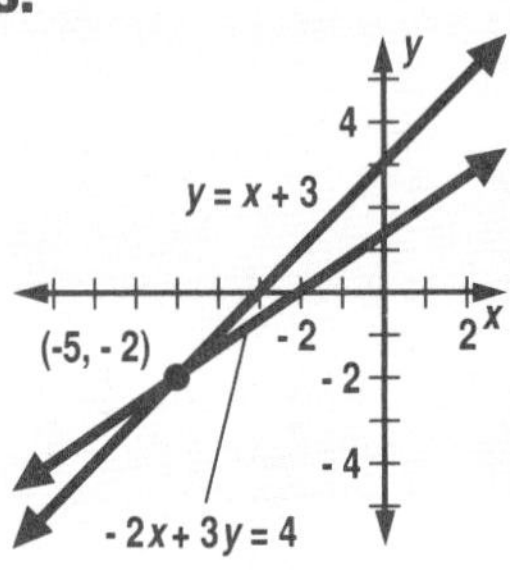

46. coincident, infinitely many solutions

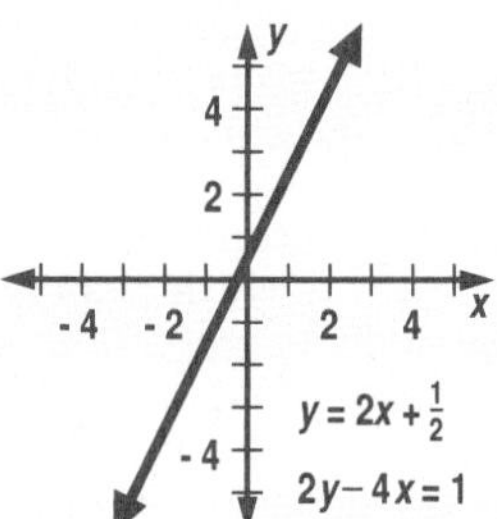

49.

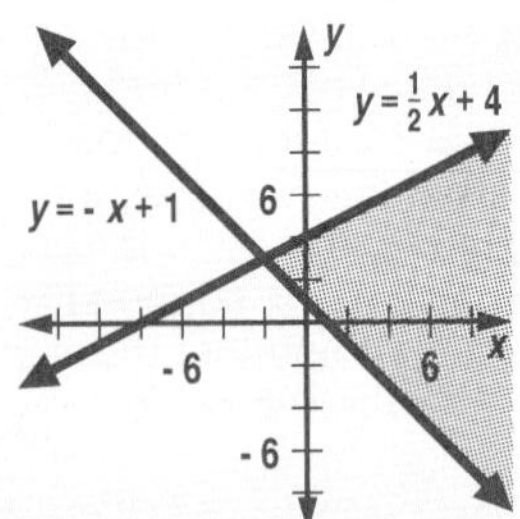

50.

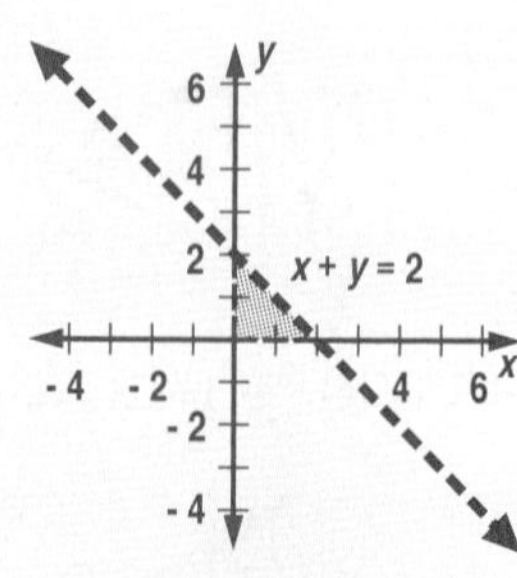

PROPERTIES deal with the principles behind the mathematics.

Objective D. *Recognize sentences with no solutions, one solution, or all real numbers as solutions.* (*Lesson 11-9*)

In 21–24, solve.

21. $2a + 4 < 2a + 3$ **no solutions**

22. $12c < 6(3 + 2c)$ **all real numbers**

23. $7x - x = 12x$ **0 (one solution)**

24. $-10x = 15 - 10x$ **no solution**

Objective E. *Determine whether a system has 0, 1, or infinitely many solutions.* (*Lesson 11-8*)

In 25–28, determine whether each system describes lines that coincide, intersect, or are parallel.

25. $\begin{cases} 2x + 4y = 7 \\ 10x + 20y = 35 \end{cases}$ **coincide**

26. $\begin{cases} y - 2x = 5 \\ y = 2x + 4 \end{cases}$ **parallel**

27. $\begin{cases} 6 = m - n \\ -6 = n - m \end{cases}$ **coincide**

28. $\begin{cases} a - 3b = 2 \\ a - 4b = 2 \end{cases}$ **intersect**

USES deal with applications of mathematics in real situations.

Objective F. *Use systems of equations to solve real world problems involving linear combinations.* (*Lessons 11-2, 11-3, 11-4, 11-5, 11-8, 11-9*)

29. Suppose Joe earned three times as much as Marty during the summer. Together they earned \$210. How much did each person earn? **See below.**

30. A punch is made by mixing 4 parts cranberry juice to 1 part club soda. If 8 gallons of punch are to be made, how many gallons of cranberry juice and how many gallons of club soda will it take? **See below.**

31. In her restaurant, Charlene sells 2 eggs and a muffin for \$1.80. She sells 1 egg with a muffin for \$1.35. At these rates, how much is she charging for the egg and how much for the muffin? **See below.**

32. A hotel offers two weekend packages. Plan A which costs \$315, gives one person 3 nights lodging and 2 meals. Plan B gives 2 nights lodging and 1 meal and costs \$205. At these rates, what is the charge for a room for one night? **\$95**

29) Marty earned \$52.50. Joe earned \$157.50.
30) juice, 6.4 gal; soda, 1.6 gal
31) \$.45 for an egg and \$.90 for a muffin

33. If the cost per unit is constant, could the given situation have happened?

16 pencils and 5 erasers were bought for \$8.00.

32 pencils and 10 erasers were bought for \$16.00. **Yes**

34) 107 miles

34. Renting a car from company (1) costs \$39 plus \$.10 a mile. Renting a car from company (2) costs \$22.95 plus \$.25 a mile. At what distance do the cars cost the same?

35. The starting salary on Job (1) is \$7.00 an hour and every 6 months increases \$0.50 an hour. For Job (2) the starting salary is \$7.20 an hour and every 6 months increases \$0.50 an hour. When does Job (2) pay more than Job (1)? **always**

36. The Lorain, Ohio, area had a 1980 population of about 276,000 people and was growing at a rate of 1800 people each year. The Virginia Beach, Virginia, area had a 1980 population of about 262,000 people and was growing at a rate of 1950 people each year. If these rates continue, in how many years after 1980 will these two areas have the same population? **about 93**

Objective G. *Calculate and use weighted averages.* (*Lessons 11-6, 11-7*)

37. Suppose towns A and B are 300 miles apart. If a car averages 50 mph from A to B and 40 mph on the way back, what is the average speed for the whole trip? **≈ 44.4 mph**

38. Linda had the following transcript: 4 A's, 9 B's, and 2 C's. What is her grade point average? (Assume A = 4.0, B = 3.0, C = 2.0, D = 1.0, F = 0.0) **≈3.13**

39. Suppose 6 liters of a 25% alcohol solution are mixed with 4 liters of a 100% solution (pure alcohol). What is the percent of alcohol in the resulting mixture? **55%**

40. A retailer sold 250 T-shirts at $8 retail and has 150 left. For what sale price should the remaining T-shirts be sold to have an overall average price of $7 a T-shirt? **≈$5.33**

41. How many pounds of granola at $.99 per pound must be mixed with 5 pounds of raisins at $1.79 per pound to produce a trail mix worth $1.19 per pound? **15 pounds**

42. A car averages 30 mph for the first 3 hours of a trip. How long must the car travel at 55 mph to have an overall average speed of 45 mph? **4.5 hours**

REPRESENTATIONS deal with pictures, graphs, or objects that illustrate concepts.

Objective H. *Find solutions to systems of equations by graphing.* (*Lessons 11-1, 11-8*)

In 43–46, solve each system by graphing. **See margin.**

43. $\begin{cases} y = 4x + 6 \\ y = \frac{1}{2}x - 1 \end{cases}$

44. $\begin{cases} y = x - 4 \\ y = -3x \end{cases}$

45. $\begin{cases} y = x + 3 \\ -2x + 3y = 4 \end{cases}$

46. $\begin{cases} 2y - 4x = 1 \\ y = 2x + \frac{1}{2} \end{cases}$

47. *Multiple choice* Two straight lines *cannot* intersect in **(c)**
(a) exactly one point
(b) no points
(c) exactly two points
(d) infinitely many points.

48. Parallel nonintersecting lines have the same _?_ but different y-intercepts. **slope**

Objective I. *Graphically represent solutions to systems of linear inequalities.* (*Lesson 11-10*)

49. Graph the solution set of this system. **See margin.**
$\begin{cases} y \le \frac{1}{2}x + 4 \\ y \ge -x + 1 \end{cases}$

50. Graph the solution set of this system. **See margin.**
$\begin{cases} x > 0 \\ y > 0 \\ x + y < 2 \end{cases}$

51. Graph all solutions to this system. **See margin.**
$\begin{cases} x \ge 0 \\ y \ge 0 \\ x + y \le 6 \\ x + y \ge 4 \end{cases}$

In 52 and 53, accurately graph the set of points that satisfies each situation.

52. A small elevator in a building only has a capacity of 280 kg. If a child averages 40 kg and an adult 70 kg, how many children C and adults A can you have in the elevator without its being overloaded? **See margin.**

53. A person wants to buy x pencils at 5¢ each and y erasers at 15¢ each and cannot spend more than 60¢. **See margin.**

EVALUATION
Three tests are provided for this chapter in the Teacher's Resource File. Chapter 11 Test, Forms A and B, cover just Chapter 11. The third test is Chapter 11 Test, Cumulative Form. About 50% of this test covers Chapter 11; 25% covers Chapter 10, and 25% covers earlier chapters. For more information on grading, see *General Teaching Suggestions: Grading* on page T44 in the Teacher's Edition.

ASSIGNMENT RECOMMENDATION
On the day your students take the chapter test, we suggest you make an assignment in the first section of the next chapter.

51.

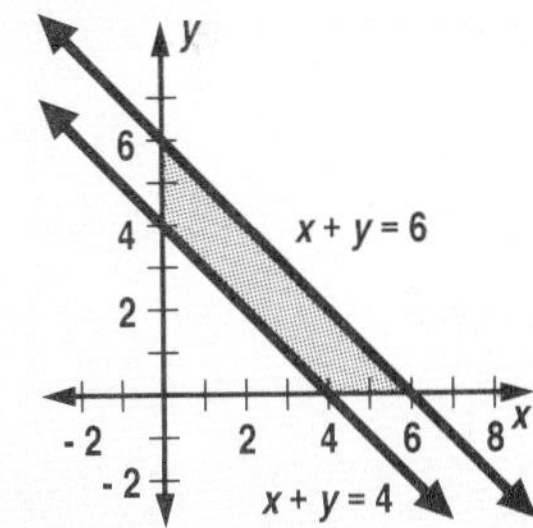

52.

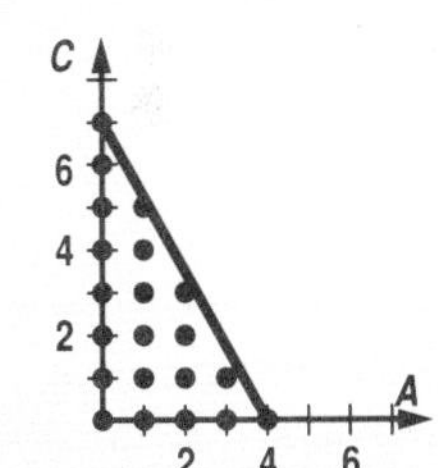

53.

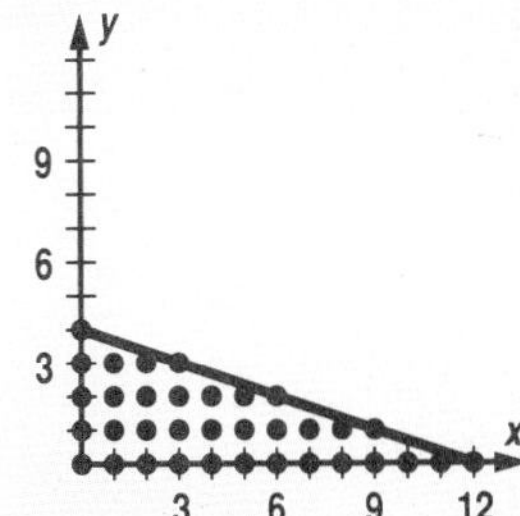

CHAPTER 12 ■ PARABOLAS AND QUADRATIC EQUATIONS

DAILY PACING CHART 12

DAILY PACING CHART ■ CHAPTER 12

Students in the Full Course should complete the entire text by the end of the year. Students in the Minimal Course spend more time to complete lessons that are combined with quizzes and more time to consider the Chapter Review. Therefore, these students may not complete all the chapters in the text.

DAY	MINIMAL COURSE	FULL COURSE
1	12-1	12-1
2	12-2	12-2
3	12-3	12-3
4	Quiz (TRF); Start 12-4.	Quiz (TRF); 12-4
5	Finish 12-4.	12-5
6	12-5	12-6
7	12-6	Quiz (TRF); 12-7
8	Quiz (TRF); Start 12-7.	12-8
9	Finish 12-7.	12-9
10	12-8	Progress Self-Test
11	12-9	Chapter Review
12	Progress Self-Test	Chapter Test (TRF)
13	Chapter Review	
14	Chapter Review	
15	Chapter Test (TRF)	

TESTING OPTIONS

TESTING OPTIONS

- Quiz for Lessons 12-1 Through 12-3
- Quiz for Lessons 12-4 Through 12-6
- Chapter 12 Test, Form A
- Chapter 12 Test, Form B
- Chapter 12 Test, Cumulative Form

INDIVIDUAL DIFFERENCES

PROVIDING FOR INDIVIDUAL DIFFERENCES

The student text is written for the *average* student. The program, however, can be adapted for less capable and for more capable students.

For those students who need more practice, a blackline master (in the Teacher's Resource File) is provided for each lesson. The Teacher's Edition frequently provides Error Analysis and Alternate Approach features to provide additional instructional strategies for those students who do not readily grasp the material.

For students who require additional challenge, Extension activities are regularly provided in the Teacher's Edition.

OBJECTIVES ■ CHAPTER 12

Students should master the chapter objectives by the time they complete the chapter. To ensure objective mastery, there is continual review built into each set of lesson questions. After students complete the chapter lessons, they assess their mastery on the Progress Self-Test. Then they do the Chapter Review and pay special attention to those questions that match the objectives missed on the Progress Self-Test. Students can get extra practice on these objectives by using the master for each lesson in the Teacher's Resource File.

OBJECTIVES FOR CHAPTER 12 (Organized into the SPUR categories— Skills, Properties, Uses, and Representations)	**Progress Self-Test Questions**	**Chapter Review Questions**	**Lesson Master from Teacher's Resource File***
SKILLS			
A Solve quadratic equations using the Quadratic Formula.	1, 2, 4–6	1 through 14	12-4, 12-5
B Factor quadratic trinomials.	3, 7, 10, 12	15 through 22	12-7, 12-9
C Solve quadratic equations by factoring.	13	23 through 26	12-8
PROPERTIES			
D Recognize properties of the parabola.	9	27 through 30	12-1, 12-5
E Recognize properties of quadratic equations.	8, 11	31 through 38	12-4, 12-5, 12-6
F Determine whether a number is rational or irrational.	19, 20	39 through 44	12-6
USES			
G Use the parabola and quadratic equations to solve real world problems.	14, 15	45 through 48	12-3, 12-4, 12-8
REPRESENTATIONS			
H Graph parabolas.	16–18	49 through 56	12-1, 12-2

*** The masters are numbered to match the lessons.**

OVERVIEW 12

OVERVIEW ■ CHAPTER 12

This chapter has three themes, each of which occupies three lessons. The first theme is the graphing of parabolas. The second is the Quadratic Formula. The last is the factoring of quadratics. The order in which these themes appear is the reverse of the order in many books, but it is the most natural.

This order enables us to begin with applications of quadratics by picturing them with graphs. Then we introduce the Quadratic Formula to solve quadratics and to further the work with applications. This leads into using the Quadratic Formula to determine whether a quadratic trinomial is factorable.

Extensive use of technology is appropriate with this chapter and automatic graphers are specifically introduced. We encourage students and teachers to utilize this technology.

Calculators are also very much needed in this chapter. The numbers which arise from actual data are not always amenable to hand calculation. A decimal estimate may have more meaning in the context of the original problem than an exact value written with radicals. It is easier to understand that a solution to a motion problem is -4.3 meters or 6.3 meters than it is to understand $1 \pm 2\sqrt{7}$ as the solutions.

The chapter also provides practice in factoring trinomials by trial and error. This topic is introduced so that in the following lessons we can link factoring and solutions to quadratics through the Factor Theorem. The Factor Theorem is important in the theory of equations, makes it easier to handle applications of quadratics, and dispenses with the need for an exhaustive study of factoring of trinomials. Students should aim for understanding this theorem. However, proficiency in factoring general trinomials is a topic whose applicability even within elementary mathematics seems limited to the mathematics classroom.

PERSPECTIVES 12

PERSPECTIVES ■ CHAPTER 12

The Perspectives provide the rationale for the inclusion of topics or approaches, provide mathematical background, and make connections within UCSMP.

12-1

GRAPHING $y = ax^2 + bx + c$

At this point students have worked with graphs of linear and exponential functions. This lesson introduces quadratic functions and initiates the student into graphing parabolas. The functions which start the lesson are in the form $y = ax^2$. After examining the graphs, we move on to parabolas generated by $y = ax^2 + bx + c$.

In all the examples, the effect of *a* is studied only in relation to its sign. If students conclude that the value of *a* also determines how "wide" the parabola looks, that is fine, but in this lesson this observation is a bonus.

12-2

USING AN AUTOMATIC GRAPHER

Graphing calculators and computer programs can be very useful tools in studying parabolas. They make it quick and easy to graph several functions and compare them, helping students see relationships between the equations and the graphs. Automatic graphers also make it as easy to graph functions with "messy" coefficients as those with "nice" numbers, so they are a great convenience when dealing with applications.

In this lesson we deal with how to use automatic graphers. The equipment you have available (in the classroom or in a computer lab) will affect how you approach this lesson and how you use automatic graphers in the lessons that follow. Any function plotter that displays multiple graphs should be appropriate. If you are using one computer for demonstration, you can spend class time showing different graphs.

Most automatic graphers require that the equation to be graphed be given either in the form "$y =$ __" or "$f(x) =$ __." Be prepared for the latter. You may wish to explain $f(x)$ notation (it is found in Lesson 13-1), or simply tell students to think of $f(x)$ as y.

12-3

APPLICATIONS OF PARABOLAS

Parabolas describe the path of a projectile. This fact was not obvious to our mathematical predecessors. However, our students have some things not available even to the best minds of those earlier times. Virtually all students have seen slow motion pictures of baseballs, basketballs, and footballs in flight.

In many books, the first equations for parabolas are like those in Example 2. They relate the height of the projectile to the *time* it has been in the air. This graph, while a parabola, is not the graph of the path of the projectile. The graph of the path relates the height of the projectile to its *horizontal distance along the ground*.

12-4

THE QUADRATIC FORMULA

Lessons 12-3, 12-4, and 12-5 are very closely related. In Lesson 12-3 students use a graph to find what x-coordinates will produce a given y-coordinate for a quadratic function. In Lesson 12-4, the Quadratic Formula is used to answer the same question algebraically. Lesson 12-5 relates the two approaches and examines the cases in which a quadratic equation has one or no solutions.

The Quadratic Formula is derived in the next lesson. The first concern is that students understand what it does; for this, they must be able to use it. This skill should be mastered by all first-year algebra students. We suggest that students memorize the Quadratic Formula as quickly as possible.

Because they have calculators, we expect students to carry out their computations to get decimal approximations of nonintegral solutions. We do not expect students to use simple radical form. A solution of $1 \pm 2\sqrt{7}$ meters does not convey meaning and cannot be related to a graph or picture without a decimal approximation.

12-5

ANALYZING THE QUADRATIC FORMULA

This lesson has three purposes. The first is to explain that a quadratic equation may have zero, one, or two solutions. This idea is related not just to the Quadratic Formula and the discriminant, but also to the graph of the parabola and to the application of the diver. The ties between these various representations are important.

The second purpose of the lesson is to present a derivation of the Quadratic Formula. We feel that algebra students should see this and realize that the algebraic processes they have learned can produce powerful and useful results. The derivation presented here differs from that found in many books. Its advantage is that it avoids fractions until the last step. Most students are not ready to repeat this derivation themselves. That is best deferred to the second year of algebra.

The third purpose is to provide another day of practice in using the Quadratic Formula.

12-6

RATIONAL AND IRRATIONAL NUMBERS

The terms *rational* and *irrational* have not been used until now. Here, another use of the discriminant comes into play. It can discriminate between rational and irrational solutions to quadratic equations.

Perhaps the most common confusion about this topic is between the words *rational* and *fraction*. Any number can be expressed as a fraction; for instance, $\pi = 2\pi/2$. But only rational numbers can be expressed as simple fractions, that is, as fractions with integers as both the numerator and denominator.

As examples of irrational numbers we give π and $\sqrt{2}$. Another type of irrational number includes those whose decimal expansions have a pattern but do not repeat. An example is 0.050050005 . . . , where the number of zeros between the 5's increases by one each time.

12-7

FACTORING QUADRATIC TRINOMIALS

This lesson recalls the work from Chapter 10 which included multiplication of binomials and factoring of the special cases of common monomial factors, perfect square trinomials and difference of squares. We did not expect students to master factoring of other trinomials.

Here we introduce the idea of factoring any trinomial. We don't give a general algorithm for factoring $ax^2 + bx + c$ in this lesson. We want students to see the relationship of coefficients in the binomial factors of $ax^2 + bx + c$ to the values a, b, and c. The strategy presented is: (1) Make a good guess based on information from a and c. (2) Check your guess by multiplication. If it does not check, repeat step 1.

12-8

SOLVING SOME QUADRATIC EQUATIONS BY FACTORING

The Quadratic Formula is the primary method for solving quadratic equations because it applies in all cases, even those that are impossible or inconvenient to factor. However, students should also be able to solve equations by factoring when the factoring is easy.

Also, the topic of the next lesson is the Factor Theorem. Experience with solving by factoring helps to explain the relationship between the signs of the factors and the roots. If $x - r$ is a factor of $ax^2 + bx + c$, then r is a solution. (Equivalently, when $x + r$ is a factor, then $-r$ is a solution.) This apparent reversal of signs would be difficult to explain without the work in this lesson.

12-9

THE FACTOR THEOREM

The Factor Theorem is a very important theorem, with applications in the theory of equations, in computational mathematics, and in real-world situations.

The Factor Theorem tells you that if r and s are solutions of $ax^2 + bx + c = 0$, then $(x - r)$ and $(x - s)$ are the binomial factors of the quadratic trinomial. However, the theorem doesn't give the constant (or scaling) factor of the expression. In Example 3 this constant is 12. In general, if r and s are solutions of a quadratic equation $ax^2 + bx + c = 0$, then $a(x - r)(x - s)$ is a factorization of the trinomial $ax^2 + bx + c$.

CHAPTER 12

This chapter should take 9 to 11 days for the lessons and quizzes; 1 day for the Progress Self-Test; 1 or 2 days for the Chapter Review; and 1 day for testing. The total is 12 to 15 days.

CHAPTER 12

Parabolas and Quadratic Equations

Many situations can be described by second degree polynomial equations. These are called quadratic equations.

For instance, suppose an insurance company finds that the number y of accidents per 50 million miles driven is related to a driver's age x in years for $16 \leq x \leq 74$ by the formula

$$y = .4x^2 - 36x + 1000.$$

Below is a graph of this equation.

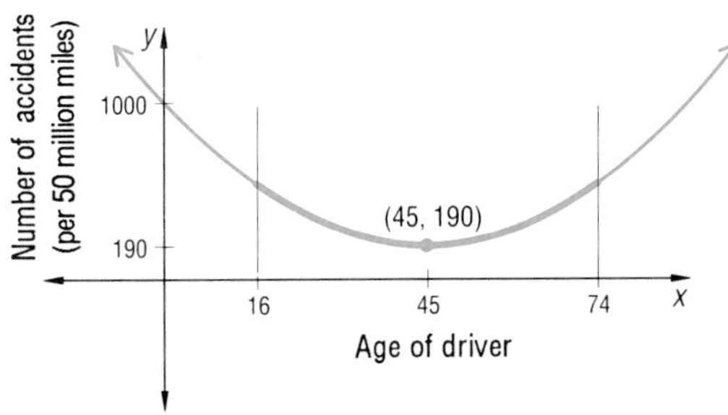

The graph shows that the insurance company predicts 45-year-olds to have the least number of accidents (190 per 50 million miles driven) while drivers both younger and older than 45 are predicted to have more. The shape of the graph is a curve called a **parabola**.

Parabolas occur often both in nature and in manufactured objects. A parabola is the shape of the path of a basketball tossed into a hoop as shown at left, the path of a football kicked for a field goal,

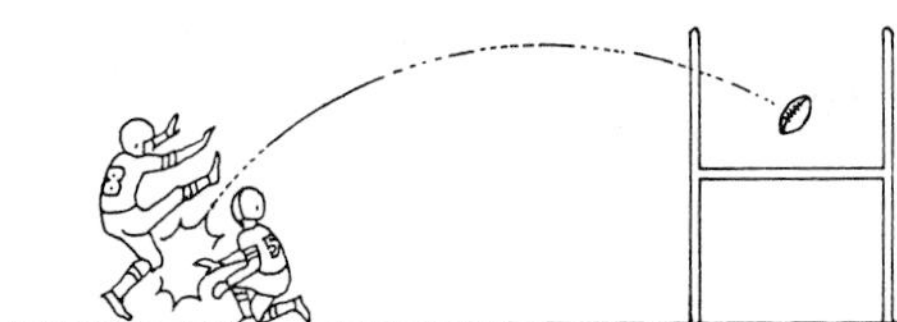

and the spray of water in a fountain.

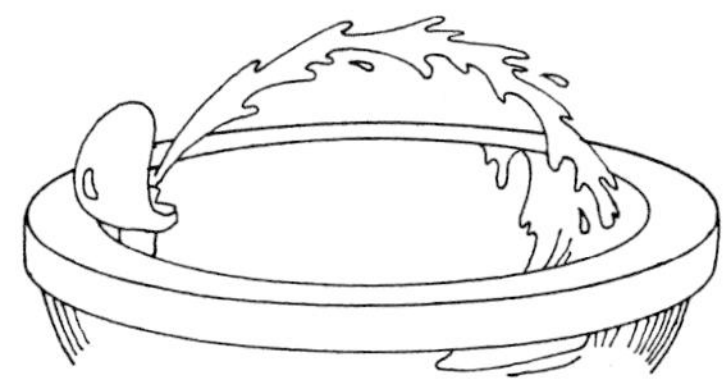

USING PAGES 586-587
The text mentions some real-life situations in which parabolas may occur. Students may be able to suggest others. [samples: Various antennas for receiving radio or TV signals have a parabolic cross section. Archways and arched supports in architecture are often parabolic. The cross section of some contact lenses is also parabolic.]

Note: The Gateway Arch in St. Louis, Missouri, resembles a parabola, but it was actually designed by using the equation $y = \frac{1}{2}a(e^{x/a} + e^{-x/a})$, where e is the base of natural logarithms. Cables on suspension bridges approximate parabolas, though most are more closely approximated by the curve called a catenary, which is represented by $y = a\cosh(x/a)$, where cosh denotes the hyperbolic cosine function.

LESSON 12-1

RESOURCES
- Lesson Master 12-1
- Visual for Teaching Aid 7: Coordinate Grid
- Visual for Teaching Aid 66: Graph of $y = x^2$
- Visual for Teaching Aid 67: Graphs for Question 13
- Computer Master 24

OBJECTIVES

D Recognize properties of the parabola.
H Graph parabolas.

TEACHING NOTES

The graph of $y = x^2$ is on *Teaching Aid 66* so you can easily display it when discussing the lesson. Focus on some essential characteristics of the parabola. Emphasize that students should make smooth curves. You might plot points close to the vertex to show that a parabola really is quite rounded, not pointed, at the vertex. Point out the symmetry of a parabola about its axis. Make sure that students understand that the sign of the coefficient *a* determines whether a parabola opens up or down. You might mention that if the parabola opens up, the vertex is the minimum point. If it opens down, the vertex is the maximum.

Computer The computer program in **Example 2** makes it easier to generate values. For each run of the program, lines 10 and 40 must be changed to reflect the different coefficients and line 30 must be changed to accommodate different

LESSON

12-1

Graphing $y = ax^2 + bx + c$

At the right is a square with side of length s. The area is described by the familiar property $A = s^2$. It is possible to graph all possibilities for s and A on the coordinate plane as shown at the left below.

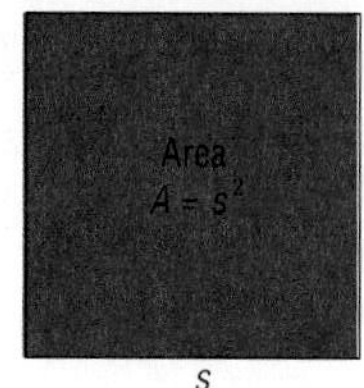

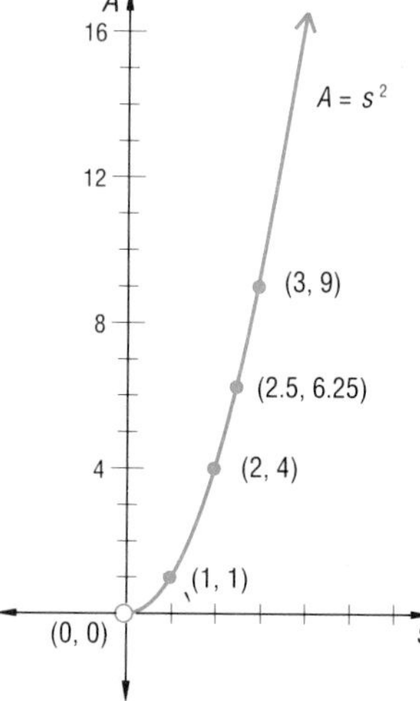

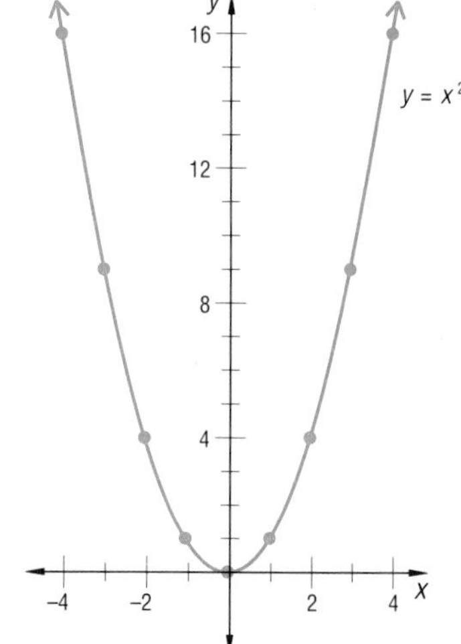

At the right above is the graph of the equation $y = x^2$. The graph has the same equation as $A = s^2$ except for the letters. In the area situation, A and s can only be positive because they are measures of area and length. In $y = x^2$, x is not limited to positive numbers. A table of values for $y = x^2$ is given below.

x	-4	-3	-2	-1	0	1	2	3	4
y	16	9	4	1	0	1	4	9	16

The graph of $y = x^2$ is a parabola that opens up. The y-axis separates the parabola into two halves. The right half is the exact same graph as the graph for the side and area of a square. The left half is a reflection or mirror image of the right half. If the parabola is folded along the y-axis, the two halves will coincide. For every point to the left of the y-axis, there is a matching point to the right. For this reason we say the parabola is **symmetric** to the y-axis. The y-axis is called the **axis of symmetry** of the parabola.

$A = s^2$ and $y = x^2$ are both equations of the form $y = ax^2$, with $a = 1$. Equations of this form all yield parabolas with the y-axis as the axis of symmetry. When a is negative, the parabola opens down.

Example 1 Graph $y = -\frac{1}{5}x^2$.

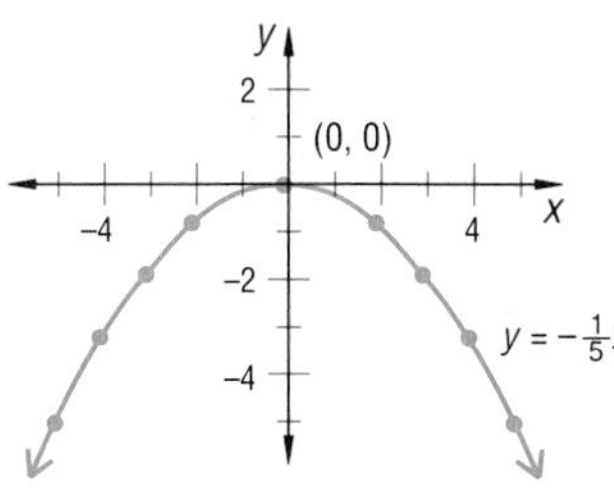

Solution Make a table of values.

x	-5	-4	-3	-2	-1	0	1	2	3	4	5
y	-5	$-\frac{16}{5}$	$-\frac{9}{5}$	$-\frac{4}{5}$	$-\frac{1}{5}$	$-\frac{0}{5}$	$-\frac{1}{5}$	$-\frac{4}{5}$	$-\frac{9}{5}$	$-\frac{16}{5}$	-5

Except when $x = 0$, $-\frac{1}{5}x^2$ is negative.

So except for the origin, the parabola lies below the x-axis.

The intersection of a parabola with its axis of symmetry is called the **vertex** of the parabola. In Example 1, the vertex is also (0, 0). In summary:

The graph of $y = ax^2$ is a parabola with the following properties:

1. (0, 0) is the vertex.
2. It is symmetric to the y-axis.
3. If $a > 0$, the parabola opens up.
   If $a < 0$, the parabola opens down.

A parabola can be positioned so that the vertex is some other point in the plane. If the axis of symmetry is vertical, then it has an equation of the form $y = ax^2 + bx + c$ (with $a \neq 0$). The values of a, b, and c determine where the parabola is positioned in the plane and whether it opens up or down.

Example 2 **a.** Write a computer program to print a table of values for $y = 2x^2 - 8x + 6$. Use the x-values 0, 0.5, 1, 1.5, ..., 4.
b. Draw the graph.

Solution **a.** x must take on values from 0 to 4, but must increase by 0.5 each time, instead of by 1. The command **STEP** tells the computer how much to add to x each time through the FOR/NEXT loop. The value of x increases in "steps" of 0.5.

```
10 PRINT "VALUES FOR Y = 2X^2 - 8X + 6"
20 PRINT "X", "Y"
30 FOR X = 0 TO 4 STEP .5
40    LET Y = 2 * X * X - 8 * X + 6
50    PRINT X, Y
60 NEXT X
70 END
```


choices of x-values. A more general program that may be useful throughout the chapter is given in the Extension which follows.

Reading We have used the term *y-intercept* for lines and exponential curves, and here we reintroduce the term *x-intercept*. The x-intercepts are symmetric to the axis of the parabola. They will be seen again after the Quadratic Formula is introduced. You might ask students how to find the y-intercept of a parabola. (Substitute 0 for x, and evaluate to find y.)

ADDITIONAL EXAMPLES

1. Graph $y = 2x^2$.

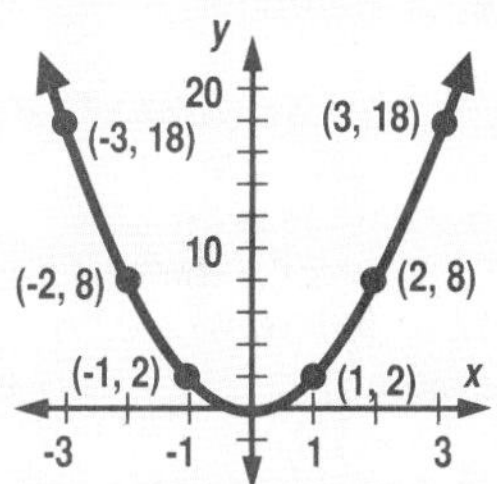

Note: Use symmetry to show students how to find the points at (-1, 2), (-2, 8), and (-3, 18).

2. Write a computer program to print values for $y = x^2 + 8x + 13$ for $x = -7, -6, -5, \ldots 2$.

```
10 PRINT "TABLE OF
   VALUES FOR A
   PARABOLA"
20 PRINT "X", "Y"
30 FOR X= -7 TO 2 STEP 1
40 LET Y=X*X+8*X+13
50 PRINT X, Y
60 NEXT X
70 END
```

3. Graph $y = .5x^2 - 2x$.

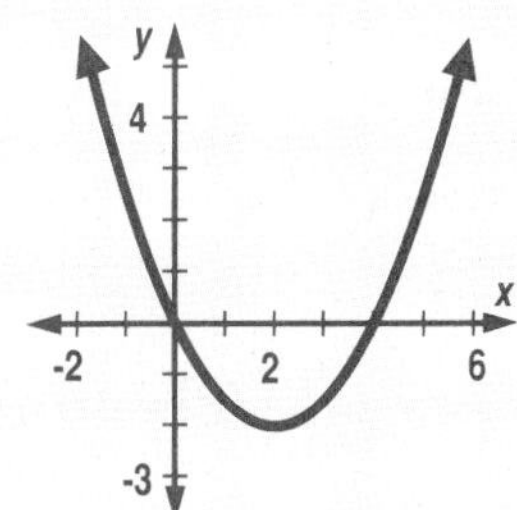

NOTES ON QUESTIONS
Computer for Questions 7-9: You might use the program in **Example 2** or the one in the Extension to generate one or two tables for these questions. Having the tables will speed up the homework in this lesson for your students. However, leave some of the problems to be done value by value by your students.

Question 11: The area formula for the circle is viewed as an equation to be graphed. In part **a,** the context of the problem restricts the graph to the right "half" of a parabola (radius ≥ 0). In part **b,** all values of *x* are possible, so students should get a full parabola.

ADDITIONAL ANSWERS

1. samples: path of a basketball tossed at a hoop, path of a kicked ball, spray of water in a fountain

4.

```
10 PRINT "VALUES FOR Y
   =  7X^2 - 3X + 5"
30 FOR X=0 TO 4 STEP
   .25
40 LET Y=7*X*X-3*X+5
```

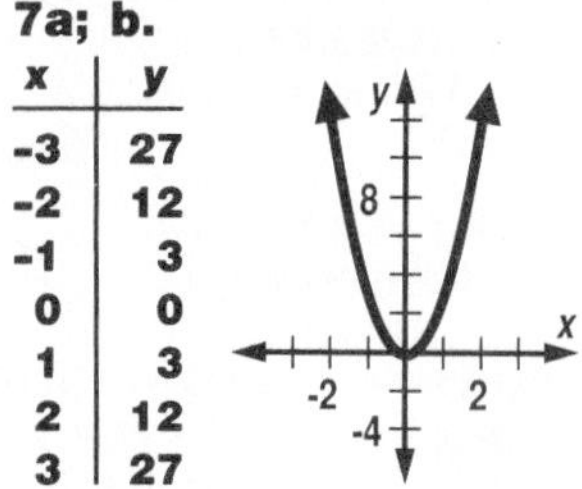

7a; b.

x	y
-3	27
-2	12
-1	3
0	0
1	3
2	12
3	27

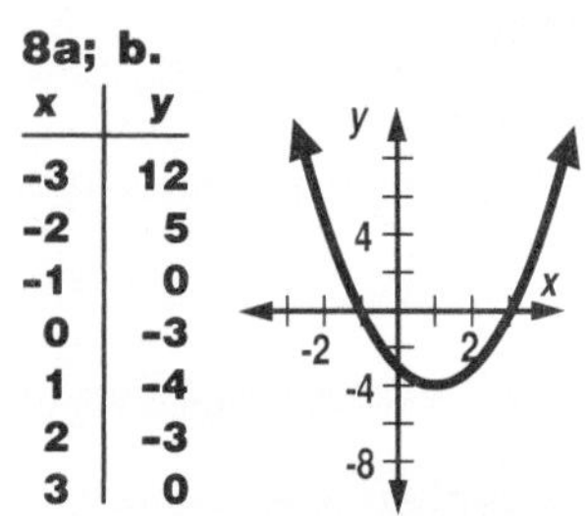

8a; b.

x	y
-3	12
-2	5
-1	0
0	-3
1	-4
2	-3
3	0

b. At the left below is what the computer would print if the program is run. At the right below, the points are plotted and connected to show the parabola.

VALUES FOR Y = 2X^2 − 8X + 6

X	Y
0	6
.5	2.5
1	0
1.5	-1.5
2	-2
2.5	-1.5
3	0
3.5	2.5
4	6

The vertex of the parabola in Example 2 is at (2, -2). The graph is symmetric to the line $x = 2$, its axis of symmetry. Except for (2, -2), there are pairs of points with the same *y*-value. (1, 0) and (3, 0) are both on the *x*-axis. (1.5, 2) and (3.5, 2) are both on the horizontal line $y = 2$. There are two points where the *y*-coordinate is 6.

In the form $y = ax^2 + bx + c$, as with the form $y = ax^2$, if $a > 0$ the parabola opens up, and if $a < 0$ the parabola opens down.

Example 3 Graph $y = -x^2 - 12$.

Solution Form a table of values and plot.

x	-2	-1	0	1	2
y	-16	-13	-12	-13	-16

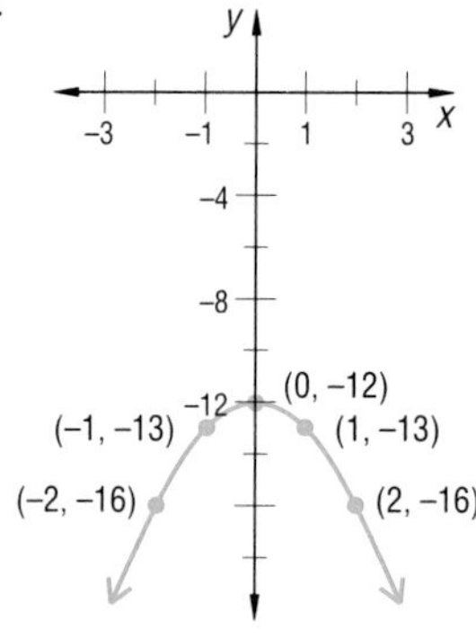

Recall that an *x-intercept* is a point where a curve crosses the *x*-axis. Look back at the parabolas in the examples of this lesson. Notice that a parabola can have two *x*-intercepts (Example 2), one *x*-intercept (Example 1) or no *x*-intercept (Example 3).

Questions

Covering the Reading

1. Name three instances in nature or in synthetic objects where parabolas occur. **See margin.**

2. The graph of $y = x^2$ is symmetric to the _?_. **y-axis**

3. What shape is the graph of $y = 47x^2$? **a parabola**

4. Refer to Example 2. Change lines in the computer program to print values for x and y for $y = 7x^2 - 3x + 5$, where x has values 0, .25, .50, .75, ... , 4. **See margin.**

In 5 and 6, consider the graph of the equation $y = ax^2$.

5. What is the vertex of this parabola? **(0, 0)**

6. a. If a is positive, the parabola opens _?_. **up**
b. If a is negative, the parabola opens _?_. **down**

In 7–9, **a.** make a table of values for values of x between -3 and 3; **b.** graph the equation. **See margin.**

7. $y = 3x^2$ **8.** $y = x^2 - 2x - 3$ **9.** $y = -3x^2 - 5$

10. Write the table of the values that this program will print.

```
10 PRINT "VALUES FOR X * X - 2X"
20 PRINT "X", "Y"
30 FOR X = -1 TO 3 STEP.5
40   LET Y = X * X - 2 * X
50   PRINT X, Y
60 NEXT X
70 END
```

x	-1	-0.5	0	0.5	1	1.5	2	2.5	3
y	3	1.25	0	-0.75	-1	-0.75	0	1.25	3

Applying the Mathematics

See margin.

11. a. In a circle of radius r, the area is described by $A = \pi r^2$. Graph all possibilities for r and A on a coordinate plane.

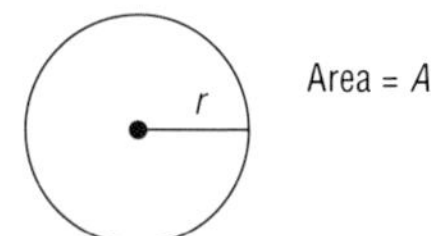

b. Graph $y = \pi x^2$. **See margin.**

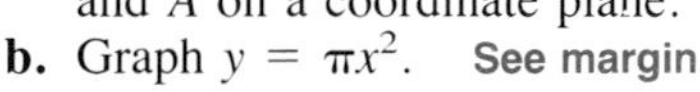

12. On the parabola at below, points A and B are symmetric to the y-axis. What are the coordinates of B? **(6, 10)**

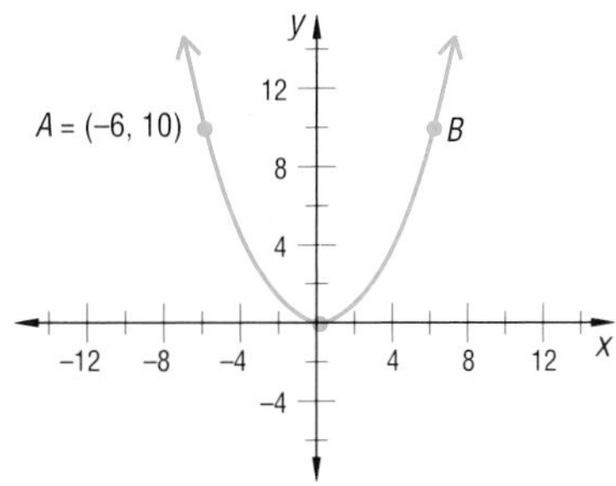

9a; b.

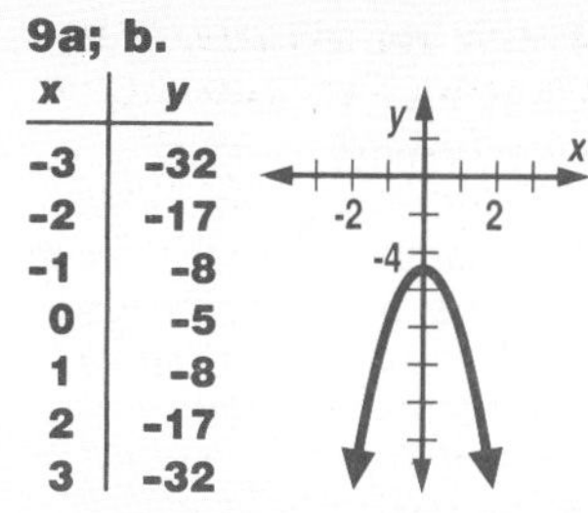

x	y
-3	-32
-2	-17
-1	-8
0	-5
1	-8
2	-17
3	-32

11a.

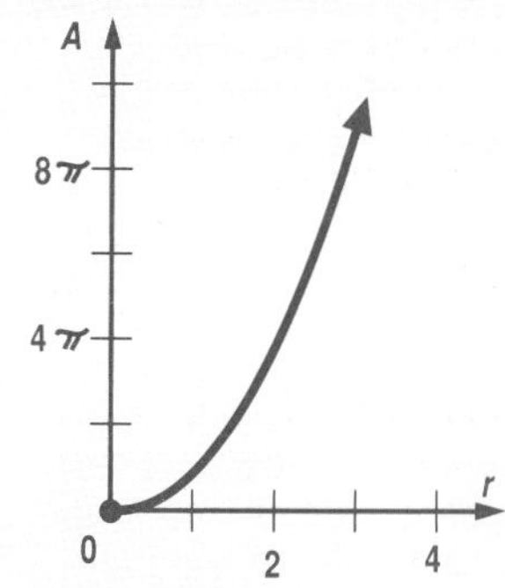

11b.

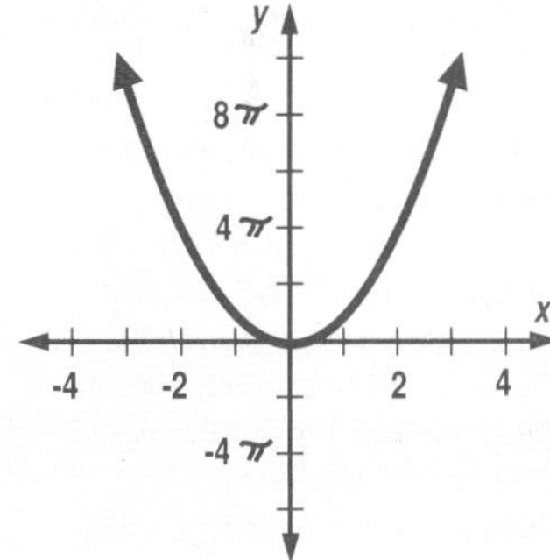

NOTES ON QUESTIONS
Questions 13 and 14: Students must compute a few values and then deduce which parabolas match which equations. It is often convenient to examine the vertex, the x-intercept, or the y-intercept. *Teaching Aid 67* may be used.

Making Connections for Questions 16 and 17: The standard form of the quadratic equation is reviewed here because it will be important in the discussion of the Quadratic Formula in Lesson 12-4.

Making Connections for Questions 26b and 26c: These questions involve the discriminant of a quadratic and its square root; both are expressions students will need to evaluate later in this chapter.

Small Group Work for Question 27: This exploration is suitable for small group work. Good quality flashlights have parabolic reflectors. Some inexpensive models don't. So be aware that some students may doubt the statement in the problem.

13. Match each graph with its equation. a) iii b) iv c) i d) ii

(i) $y = x^2$ (ii) $y = x^2 + 1$

(iii) $y = x^2 - 1$ (iv) $y = -x^2 - 1$

a.

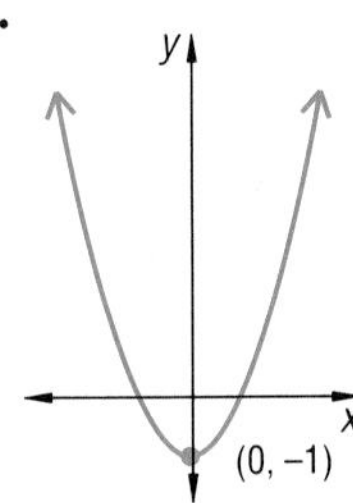

b.

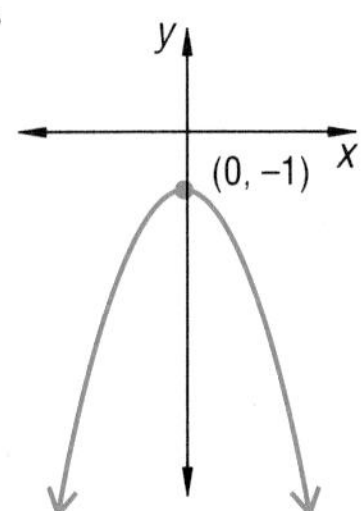

c.

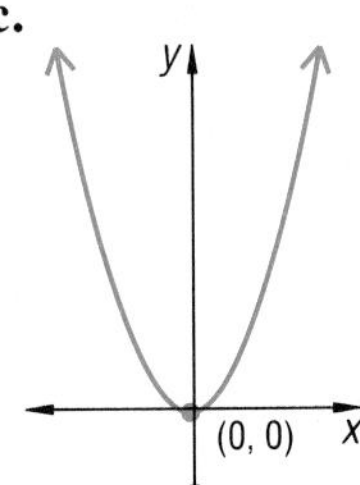

d.

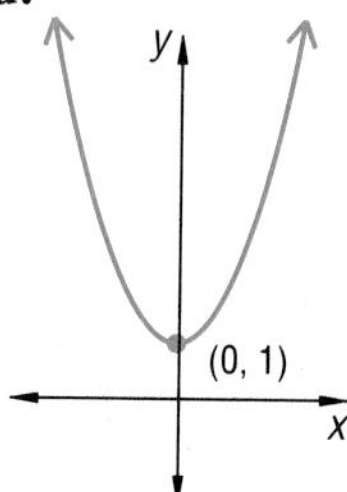

14. Which of these could be the graph of $y = x^2 - 6x + 8$? b

a.

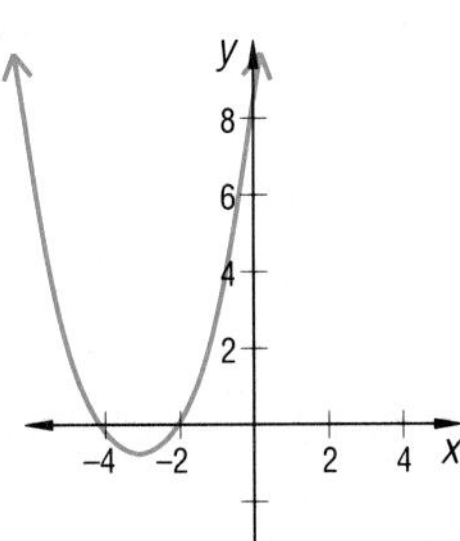

b.

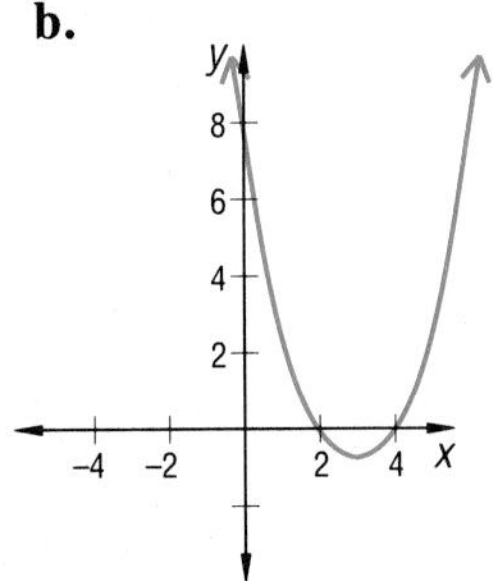

15. If (5, -11) is the vertex of a parabola with a vertical symmetry line and one of its x-intercepts is 2, find the other x-intercept. 8

Review

In 16 and 17, write in the form $ax^2 + bx + c = 0$. *(Lesson 10-1)*

16. $18 = 7x - 10x^2$ $-10x^2 + 7x - 18 = 0$ or $10x^2 - 7x + 18 = 0$

17. $3x + 8 = 4x^2 - 7x$ $4x^2 - 10x - 8 = 0$ or $-4x^2 + 10x + 8 = 0$

In 18–21, simplify.

18. $x^4 \cdot y \cdot x^3 \cdot y^3$ *(Lesson 9-5)* x^7y^4

19. $\frac{a^9}{a^6}$ *(Lesson 9-7)* a^3

20. $\left(\frac{2a}{5}\right)^3$ *(Lesson 9-8)* $\frac{8a^3}{125}$

21. $\frac{-4 + 6x}{2}$ *(Lesson 10-4)* $-2 + 3x$

22.

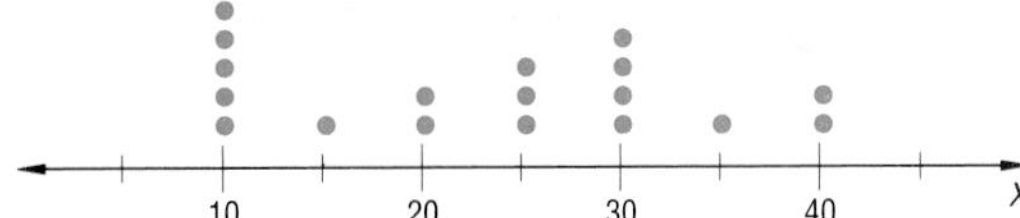

Multiple choice Which is correct for the data in the dot frequency diagram above? *(Lesson 1-2)* **(d)**

(a) The mean is 4.15, median is 20, mode is 25.
(b) The mean is 24.4, median is 25, mode is 10.
(c) The mean is 25, median is 20, mode is 30.
(d) The mean is 23.05, median is 25, mode is 10.

23. *Multiple choice* The graph below is of all solutions to which inequality? *(Lesson 2-7)* **(c)**

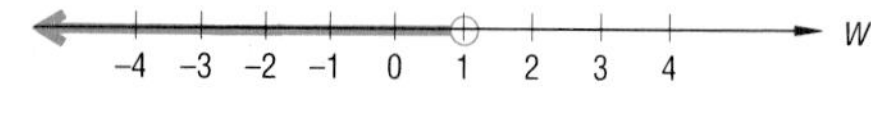

(a) $w + 6 < 5$ (b) $w - 6 < 5$
(c) $w + 5 < 6$ (d) $w - 5 < 6$

24. Calculate in your head. *(Lesson 10-9)*
a. $(20 - 1)(20 + 1)$ 399 **b.** $(100 - 5)(100 + 5)$ 9975
c. $(1 - 0.1)(1 + 0.1)$ .99

25. A house with 1800 square feet is being built on a 7500-square foot lot. The driveway will cover k square feet. Write an expression for the area left for the lawn. *(Lesson 3-2)* $7500 - 1800 - k$ or $5700 - k$

26. *Skill sequence* If $a = -7$, $b = 6$, $c = 15$, find the value of each expression.
a. $-4ac$ 420 **b.** $b^2 - 4ac$ 456 **c.** $\sqrt{b^2 - 4ac}$ ≈ 21.35 *(Lessons 1-4, 7-4)*

Exploration

27. Draw a set of axes on graph paper. Hold a lighted flashlight at the origin so the light is centered on an axis as shown. What is the shape of the lighted area? Keep the lighted end of the flashlight in the same position and raise the other end. How does the shape change? **Parabola; the parabola becomes wider.**

FOLLOW-UP

MORE PRACTICE

For more questions on SPUR Objectives, use *Lesson Master 12-1,* shown below.

EXTENSION

Computer You may prefer to have students use the following program instead of the one in **Example 2,** since it is more general and emphasizes the coefficients *a, b,* and *c.*

```
10 PRINT "GIVE THE
   COEFFICIENTS A,B,C"
12 INPUT A,B,C
15 PRINT "GIVE THE
   STARTING AND
   ENDING VALUES
   FOR X"
18 INPUT ST,ED
20 PRINT "GIVE THE
   INCREMENT FOR X"
22 INPUT IX
30 FOR X=ST TO ED
   STEP IX
40 LET Y=A*X*X+B*X+C
```

The rest of the program is the same as given in **Example 2.**

NAME ______

LESSON **MASTER 12–1**
QUESTIONS ON **SPUR** OBJECTIVES

■PROPERTIES *Objective D (See pages 633–635 for objectives.)*

1. What is the shape of the graph of $y = -x^2 + 6x + 8$? parabola

In 2–4, tell whether the graph of the equation opens up or down.

2. $y = 3x^2$ up **3.** $y = 9 - x^2$ down

4. $y = 4 - 2x + x^2$ up

■REPRESENTATIONS *Objective H*
In 5–8, a. make a table of values and b. graph the equation.

5. $y = 2x^2$

a.

x	y
0	0
1	2
-1	2
2	8
-2	8

b.

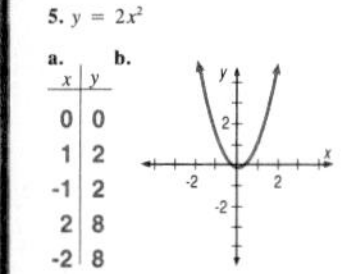

6. $y = -\frac{1}{4}x^2$

a.

x	y
0	0
2	-1
-2	-1
4	-4
-4	-4

b.

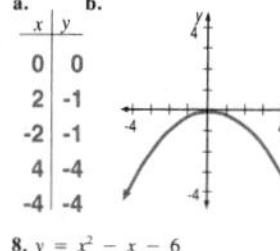

7. $y = -x^2 + 3$

a.

x	y
0	3
1	2
-1	2
2	-1
-2	-1

b.

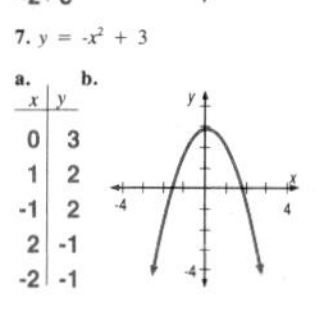

8. $y = x^2 - x - 6$

a.

x	y
0	-6
3	0
-2	0
4	6
-3	6

b.

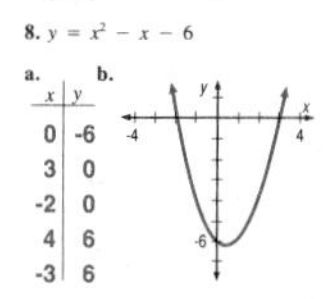

9. *Multiple choice* Which could be the graph of $y = x^2 + 2x + 1$? c

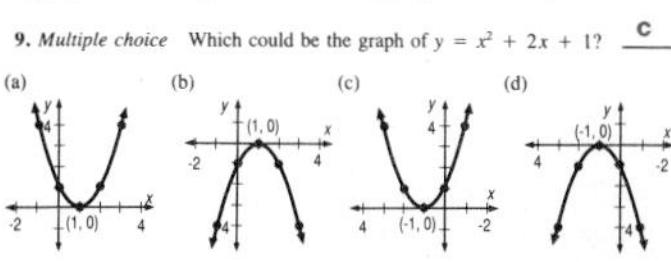

LESSON 12-2

RESOURCES
- ■ Lesson Master 12-2
- Visual for Teaching Aid 7: Coordinate Grid
- Visual for Teaching Aid 68: Graph for Additional Example
- Computer Master 24

OBJECTIVE

H Graph parabolas.

TEACHING NOTES

Alternate Approach If you do not have automatic graphers available, all the work in this lesson can still be done with graph paper. The instructions about window setting also apply to graph paper.

Even if students draw their graphs on a calculator or computer, you may want to require them to sketch the results on paper. Parabolas are a new topic to them and they need lots of experience with the shape. Also, in sketching the graph, they should note the key points: the *x*- and *y*-intercepts and the vertex.

Expect your students to have difficulty with the idea that the two graphs in **Example 1** have the same shape. An analogy can help. Adjusting the window on a graph can be likened to taking a photograph of a person. The photographer controls how big the image is by moving forward and backward, and the photographer controls the portion of the subject shown by aiming the camera.

LESSON

12-2

Using an Automatic Grapher

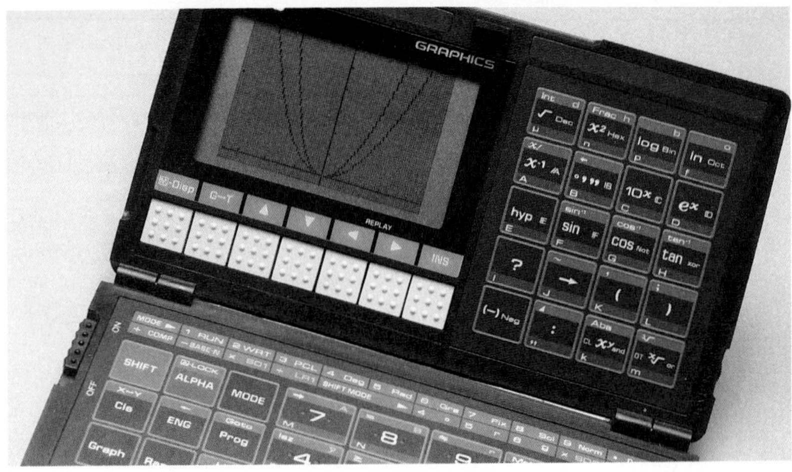

Graphs of equations are so helpful to have that there exist calculators that will automatically display part of a graph. Also, there are programs for every personal computer that will display graphs. Because computer screens are larger than calculator screens, they can more clearly show more of a graph, but graphing calculators are less expensive and more convenient.

Graphing calculators and computer graphing programs work in much the same way, and so we call them **automatic graphers** and do not distinguish them. Of course, no grapher is completely automatic. Each has particular keys to press that you must learn from a manual. Here we discuss what you need to know in order to use any of them.

The part of the coordinate grid that is shown is called a **window**. The screen at the right displays a window in which

$$-2 \le x \le 12$$
$$\text{and} \quad -3 \le y \le 7.$$

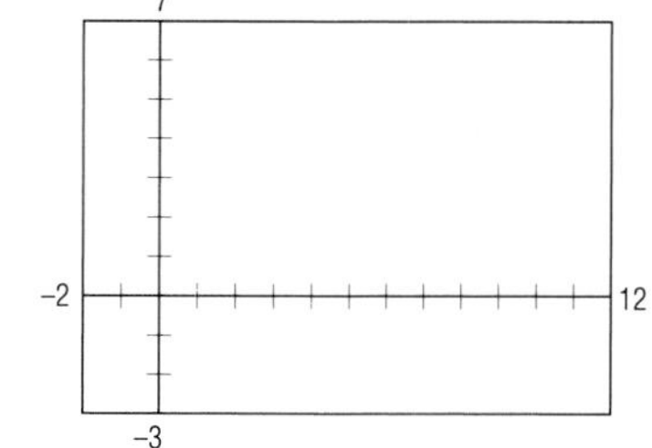

On calculators, the intervals for x and y may be left unmarked. Usually you need to pick the x-values at either end of the window. Some graphers automatically adjust and pick y-values so your graph will fit, but often you need to pick the y-values. If you don't do this, the grapher will usually pick a **default window** (perhaps $-10 \le x \le 10$, $-6 \le y \le 6$) and your graph may not appear on the screen.

On almost all graphers, the equation to be graphed must be a formula for y in terms of x.

$y = 3x^2 + 4x - 2$	can be handled.
$x = 4y$	cannot be handled.

In order to determine a reasonable window for your graph, you may have to do some calculations, but nothing else is needed. The steps, then, are

1. Put the equation you wish to graph in y = __?__ form.
2. Calculate (perhaps by hand) the coordinates of some points you want on the graph.
3. Determine a window and key it in.
4. Give instructions to graph.

Example 1 Graph $y = 3x^2 + 4x - 2$ using an automatic grapher.

Solution 1

1. The equation is already solved for y. Key in
   y [=] 3 [×] [x^2] [+] 4 [×] [x] [−] 2 for a calculator or
   y = 3*x*x + 4*x − 2 for a computer.
2. To determine a window, you can find some points on the graph by hand. To begin it is useful to pick values of x not so close to each other.

x	y
0	-2
10	338
5	93
-5	53
1	5
-1	-3

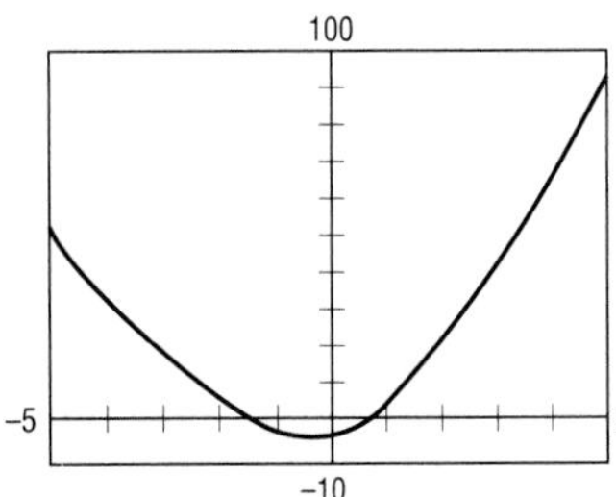

The values suggest a window from -5 to 5 for x-values and a window of -10 to 100 for the y-values. Key these values in. (Keying is different on different machines.)

3. Key in what is needed to tell the computer or calculator to graph and see a result like that shown above.

Solution 2 If you neglect step 2, the automatic grapher uses a default window (or perhaps the window of the last problem graphed). Below, the *same* equation is graphed with the default window

$-10 \le x \le 10$
$-6 \le y \le 6$.

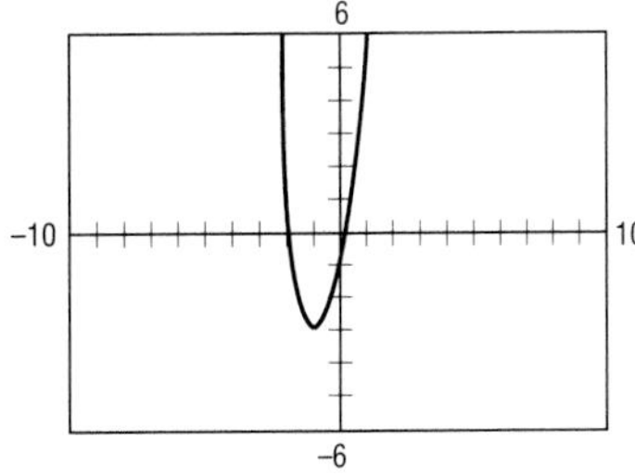

ADDITIONAL EXAMPLE
Graph $y = (x - d)^2$ when d = -8, and then when d = 0, and finally when d = 5. Use the window $-15 \le x \le 15$ and $-5 \le y \le 25$. What happens as d increases?

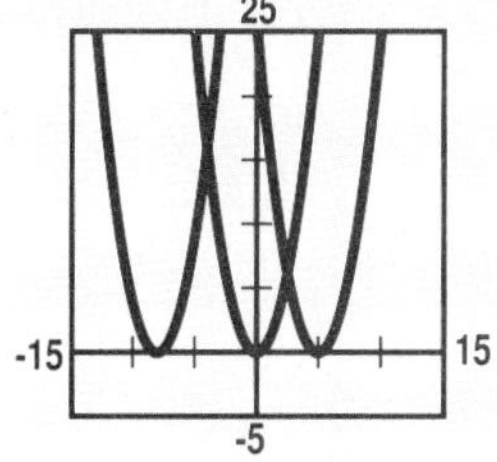

The parabola moves to the right.

NOTES ON QUESTIONS
Questions 6 and 9: As you discuss windows, note that the description is a natural use for inequalities.

Questions 17 and 18: You may want the class to decide ahead of time on a convenient window to use. If students use different windows, the shapes of their graphs may appear different. However, the answers to **17b** and **18b** will be the same.

Question 19: Students should recall from Lesson 7-4 that $\sqrt{-23}$ is not a real number.

Question 25: This problem can be solved with an equation ($3x$ = distance) or by converting the rate to $\frac{1}{3}\frac{\text{min}}{\text{ft}}$, then multiplying by the number of feet.

Making Connections for Question 28: A companion to this question can be found in Lesson 12-3 (Question 26), where students are asked to vary the value of the constant.

ADDITIONAL ANSWERS

14.

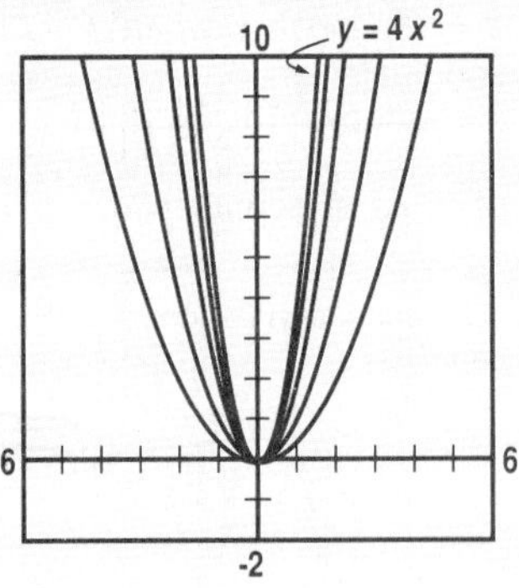

15a.

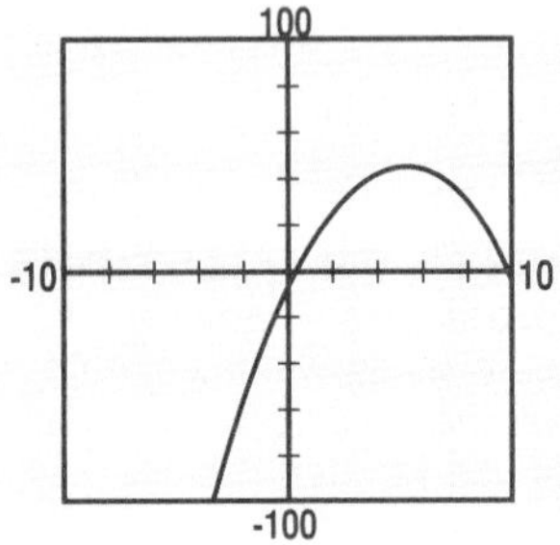

15b.

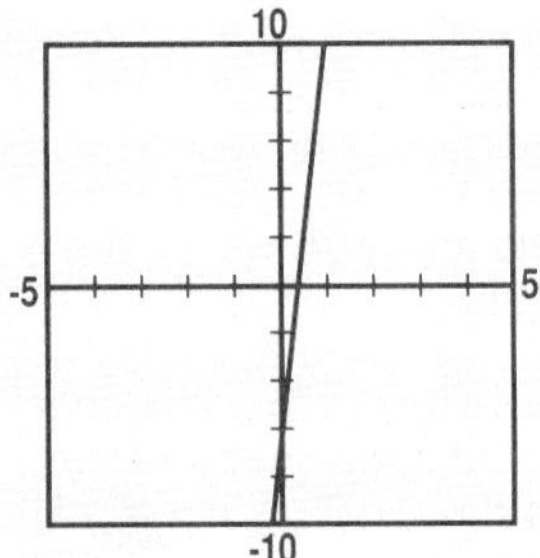

15c. The graph in part a gives you a "bigger" picture. It lets you see what is happening over more points. The graph in part b zooms into the graph in part a. You see more detail.

16a.

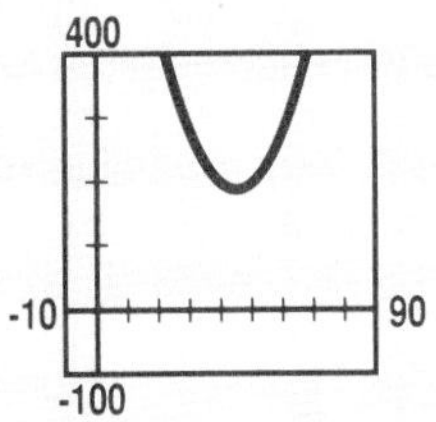

Some graphers have a **zoom** feature like those found on cameras. This feature enables you to change the window of a graph without retyping in the intervals for x and y. With such a feature, for Example 1 you could begin with Solution 2 and use it to suggest a better window for seeing the graph. In general a good window for a parabola is one in which you can estimate the coordinates of the vertex, the values of the x-intercepts (if any), and any other points you need in the problem. For these purposes, Solution 1 to Example 1 is better. The vertex seems to be at about (-.7, -3.3) and the x-intercepts are near .4 and -1.7. In the next lesson you will see why these values are important.

With most graphers more than one graph can be displayed on the same screen. This enables you to explore what happens when values in the equation are changed in some way.

Example 2 **a.** Graph $y = ax^2$ when $a = \frac{1}{2}$, 1, 2, and 3.
b. What happens to the graph as a gets larger?

Solution **a.** The question asks to graph

$y = \frac{1}{2}x^2$
$y = x^2$
$y = 2x^2$
$y = 3x^2$

Normally, this would be quite time-consuming, but with a function grapher, it is not too difficult. We use the window $-6 \le x \le 6$ knowing that these parabolas are symmetric to the y-axis. The interval $-2 \le y \le 10$ is reasonable for comparing.

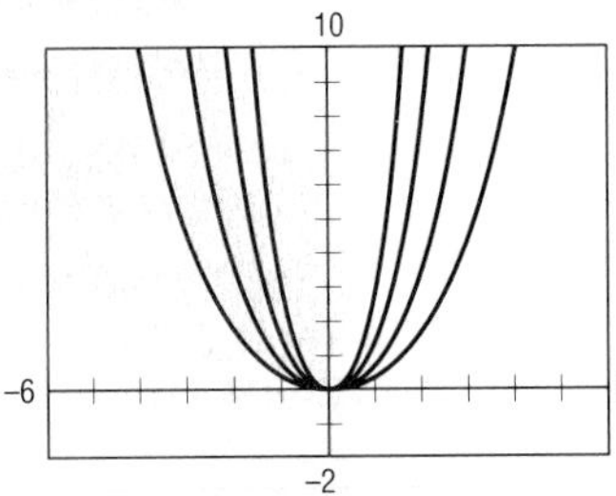

b. The parabola that looks widest is $y = \frac{1}{2}x^2$. As the value of a increases, the parabola looks thinner and thinner. The thinnest parabola is $y = 3x^2$.

596

Questions

Covering the Reading

1. On an automatic grapher, to what does the *window* refer? **part of the coordinate grid that is shown**

2. Describe the window in Solution 1 to Example 1. **$-5 \le x \le 5$; $-10 \le y \le 100$**

In 3–5, decide whether the equation is in a form in which it can be graphed with a grapher.

3. $x = 3y - 10$ **No** 4. $y = 1.3x^2 + 2.7x$ **Yes** 5. $y = 4 + 3x^2$ **Yes**

In 6–8, refer to Example 1.

6. Describe the default window. **$-10 \le x \le 10$; $-6 \le y \le 6$**

7. Estimate the coordinates of the vertex of the parabola. **$\approx (-.7, -3.3)$**

8. Estimate the larger x-intercept. **.4**

In 9–11, refer to the parabola graphed at right.

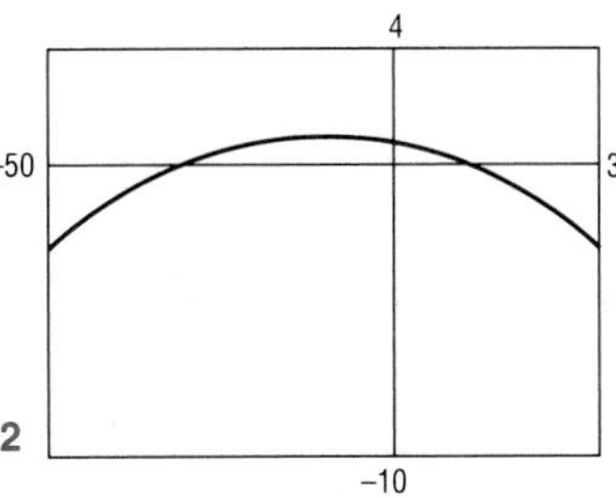

9. Describe the window. **$-50 \le x \le 30$; $-10 \le y \le 4$**

10. Estimate the coordinates of the vertex of the parabola. **$\approx (-18, 1.7)$**

11. Estimate the x-intercepts. **≈ -35 and 12**

In 12–14, refer to Example 2.

12. Which value of a gives the widest parabola? **$\frac{1}{2}$**

13. Which value of a gives the thinnest parabola? **3**

14. Copy the graphs and add a sketch of the graph of $y = 4x^2$ to them. **See margin.**

Applying the Mathematics

15. a. Graph $y = -2x^2 + 20x - 6$ using the window $-10 \le x \le 10$ and $-100 \le y \le 100$. **See margin.**
    b. Graph $y = -2x^2 + 20x - 6$ using the window $-5 \le x \le 5$ and $-10 \le y \le 10$. **See margin.**
    c. Explain the difference between parts a and b. **See margin.**

16. a. Graph the equation $y = .4x^2 - 36x + 1000$ given on page 587, using the window $-10 \le x \le 90$ and $-100 \le y \le 400$. **See margin.**
    b. Use the graph to estimate the values of x for which $y = 400$.
    c. At about what ages are there 400 accidents per 50 million miles driven? **b-c) about 22 and 68**

17. a. Graph $y = ax^2$ when $a = -\frac{1}{2}, -1, -2$, and -3. **See margin.**
    b. What happens to the graph as a gets smaller? **As a gets smaller, the parabola appears thinner.**

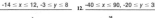

17a.

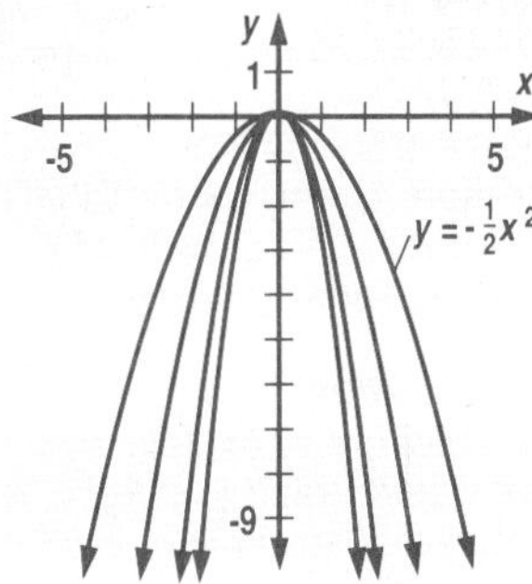

18a.

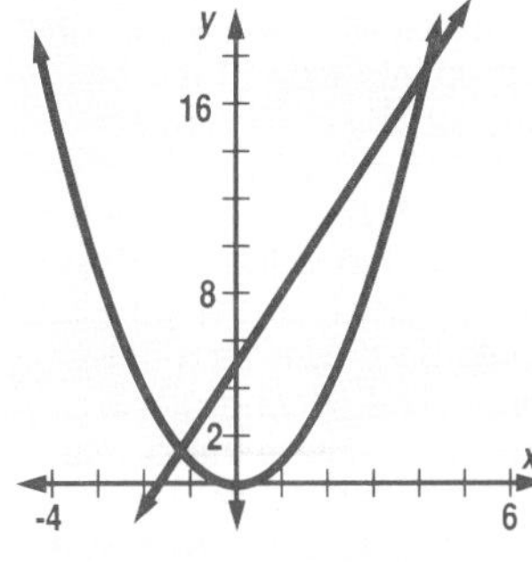

NAME ____________

LESSON **MASTER 12-2**
QUESTIONS ON **SPUR** OBJECTIVES

■**REPRESENTATIONS** *Objective H (See pages 633–635 for objectives.)*
In 1–4, put the equation in a form in which it can be graphed with an automatic grapher.

1. $2x + y = 6$ $y = -2x + 6$
2. $6x + 2y = x^2$ $y = \frac{1}{2}x^2 - 3x$
3. $x^2 + y - 3x = 0$ $y = -x^2 + 3x$
4. $3x^2 - 6x - 2y = 0$ $y = \frac{3}{2}x^2 - 3x$

In 5–8, give a suitable window that will give a graph that includes the vertex.

vertex: sample window:

5. $y = 2x^2 + x - 1$ $(-\frac{1}{4}, -1\frac{1}{8})$; $-2 \le x \le 2$, $-2 \le y \le 10$
6. $y = x^2 - 6x + 8$ $(3, -1)$; $1 \le x \le 5$, $-2 \le y \le 4$
7. $y = x^2 - 3x + 16$ $(1\frac{1}{2}, 13\frac{3}{4})$; $0 \le x \le 3$, $12 \le y \le 18$
8. $y = 9x - x^2$ $(4\frac{1}{2}, 20\frac{1}{4})$; $3 \le x \le 7$, $17 \le y \le 21$

In 9 and 10, graph the equation and estimate the vertex.

9. $y = 3x^2 + 6x - 1$ $(-1, -4)$ 10. $y = 2x^2 - 8x + 3$ $(2, -5)$

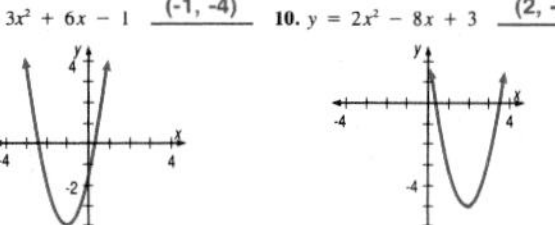

In 11 and 12, describe the window.

11. $-14 \le x \le 12$, $-3 \le y \le 8$ 12. $-40 \le x \le 90$, $-20 \le y \le 35$

Algebra © Scott, Foresman and Company 105

FOLLOW-UP

MORE PRACTICE
For more questions on SPUR Objectives, use *Lesson Master 12-2,* shown on page 597.

EXTENSION
Ask students to explain how they would graph $y \le x^2$. (Graph the parabola $y = x^2$. Test a point on one side of the parabola to see whether it makes $y < x^2$ true or false. Based on the test, shade the appropriate side of the parabola.) Next ask how the graph of $y \le x^2$ would differ from that of $y < x^2$. (The first graph includes the points on the parabola, so the parabola would be drawn as a solid curve. The second graph does not include the points on the parabola, so the parabola would be drawn as a dashed curve.)

18a. See margin, page 597.

28a.

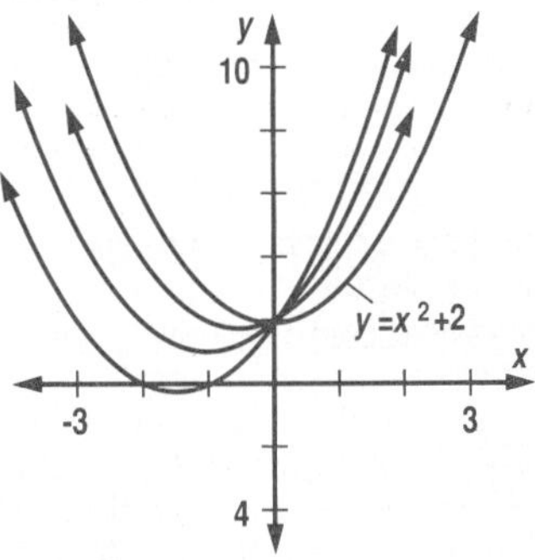

28b. sample: As *b* increases, the vertex shifts down and to the left. The vertex is always at $\left(\frac{-b}{2}, 2 - \frac{b^2}{4}\right)$.

c. sample: (-50, -2498)

18. **a.** Graph $y = 3x + 5$ and $y = x^2$ on the same axes. **See margin.**
b. Estimate the two points of intersection of these graphs. These are the solutions to the system $\begin{cases} y = x^2 \\ y = 3x + 5. \end{cases}$
nearest tenth: (-1.2,1.4); (4.2, 17.6); estimates will vary.

Review

19. *Skill sequence* When $a = 2$, $b = 3$, and $c = 4$, give the value of each expression. *(Lessons 1-4, 7-4)*
a. $-4ac$ **-32** **b.** $b^2 - 4ac$ **-23** **c.** $\sqrt{b^2 - 4ac}$ $\sqrt{-23}$

20. If $\sqrt{20} = 2\sqrt{k}$, what is the value of k? *(Lesson 7-6)* **5**

21. Calculate the distance between the origin and (-2, -4). *(Lesson 7-7)*
≈ 4.47

In 22–24, simplify. *(Lesson 10-4)*

22. $\frac{3x + 6}{3}$ **$x + 2$** **23.** $\frac{4 - 2\sqrt{5}}{2}$ **$2 - \sqrt{5}$** **24.** $\frac{3x^2 + 4x^3 - 5x^4}{x}$ **$3x + 4x^2 - 5x^3$**

25. A tortoise is walking at a rate of 3 $\frac{\text{feet}}{\text{minute}}$. Assume this rate continues.
a. How long will it take the tortoise to travel 20 feet? **≈ 6.67 min**
b. How long will it take the tortoise to travel f feet? *(Lesson 5-2)* **$\frac{f}{3}$ min**

Dallas skyline

26. Refer to the table below. If the populations of Dallas and San Antonio continue increasing at the rate of increase from 1970 to 1984, when will they have the same population and what will that population be? *(Lessons 6-6, 11-3)* **2015; 1,262,600**

Populations	1970	1984
Dallas	844,000	974,000
San Antonio	654,000	843,000

27. **a.** Multiply $(2x + 3)$ by $(3x + 2)$. **$6x^2 + 13x + 6$**
b. Multiply $(6x - 1)$ by $(x - 6)$. *(Lesson 10-6)* **$6x^2 - 37x + 6$**

Exploration

28. **a.** Graph $y = x^2 + bx + 2$ when $b = 0$, 1, 2, and 3. **See margin.**
b. How does the value of b affect the graph? **See margin.**
c. From your answer to part b, predict where the graph of $y = x^2 + 100x + 2$ would be located. **See margin.**
d. Explore the negative values of b. **Same pattern as b, except vertex is shifted to the right and down**

LESSON

12-3 Applications of Parabolas

The path of a tossed ball is a part of a parabola. Consider a quarterback who tosses a football to a receiver 40 yards downfield. If the ball is thrown and caught 6 feet above the ground, and is 16 ft above the ground at the peak of the throw (the vertex), then the path of the ball can be graphed as it is below.

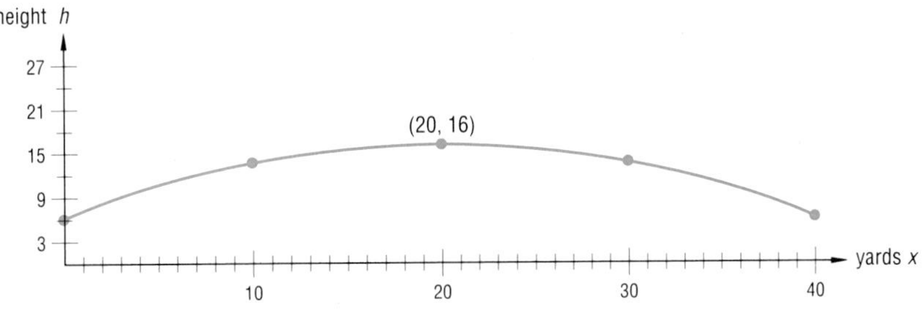

This parabola is symmetric to the vertical line $x = 20$. So the ball is at its peak 20 yards downfield. If the ball is at a height of h feet when it is x yards downfield, its path is a piece of the parabola described by the equation

$$h = -\frac{1}{40}(x - 20)^2 + 16.$$

Suppose there is a defender 3 yards in front of the receiver. This means the defender is 37 yards from the quarterback. Would he be able to deflect or catch the ball?

Example 1 Refer to the above situation. What is the height of the ball 37 yards downfield from the quarterback?

Solution Substitute 37 for x into the equation.

$$\begin{aligned} h &= -\frac{1}{40}(x - 20)^2 + 16 \\ &= -\frac{1}{40}(37 - 20)^2 + 16 \\ &= -\frac{1}{40}(17)^2 + 16 \\ &= -7.225 + 16 \\ &= 8.775 \end{aligned}$$

The ball will be 8.775 feet above the ground. This is approximately 8 feet 9 inches.

To deflect or intercept the ball, the defender would have to reach a height of 8 feet 9 inches. With a tall defender and a well-timed jump, this is quite possible.

LESSON 12-3

RESOURCES
- Lesson Master 12-3
- Quiz on Lessons 12-1 Through 12-3
- Visual for Teaching Aid 69: Graph for **Example 1**
- Visual for Teaching Aid 70: Graph for **Examples 2 and 3**
- Visual for Teaching Aid 71: Graphs for Additional Examples 1 and 2
- Computer Master 25

OBJECTIVE

G Use the parabola to solve real world problems.

TEACHING NOTES

If you have a long blackboard in your room, partition it into rectangles by drawing with chalk a few reference lines that are approximately equally spaced. Have one student toss a ball from one end of the board to another student at the other end. The ball should be tossed so that it goes just to the top of the board. With a little experimentation, your students should see a very broad parabolic path.

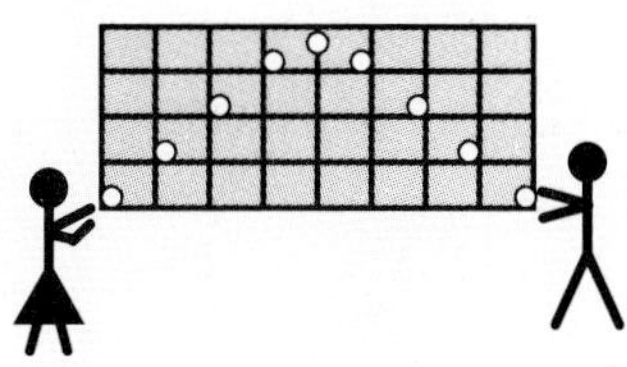

That path is used in the first figure of the lesson, the football graph. This graph is provided on *Teaching Aid 69*. The second parabola of the lesson (*Teaching Aid 70*) is a plot of the height of a ball against time.

Making Connections
The two preceding situations are repeated throughout this chapter. The last paragraph of the lesson emphasizes the difference.

Each of the parabolas in this lesson is given in the form $y = a(x - h)^2 + k$. At this point, we don't expect students to relate the numbers h and k to the vertex. This form is easier to use in the preparation of tables for the questions.

ADDITIONAL EXAMPLES
A model rocket is shot into the air at an angle.

1. Its height h when it is horizontally x feet from the launch pad is given by $h = -.163x^2 + 11.43x$.

a. Graph this equation.

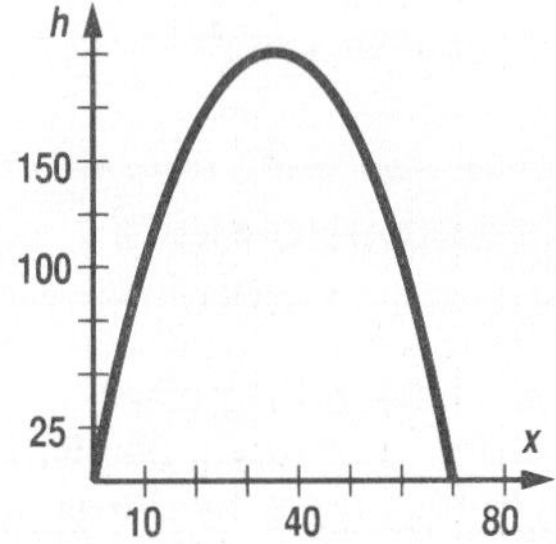

b. How high is the rocket when it has traveled 10 feet horizontally?
98 feet

2. The rocket's height h at t seconds after the launch is given by $h = -22.2t^2 + 133t$.

a. Graph this equation.

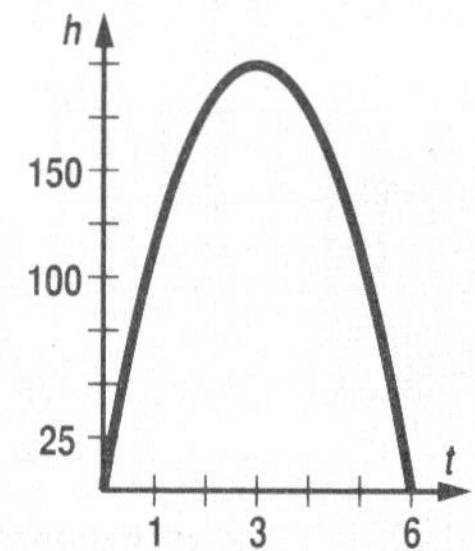

b. How high will the rocket be after 2 seconds?
177.2 feet

A different parabola represents the height of a throw against the time the ball has been in the air. The throw on page 599 reaches a height of h feet after t seconds, where $h = -10(t - 1)^2 + 16$. A graph of this parabola is shown below.

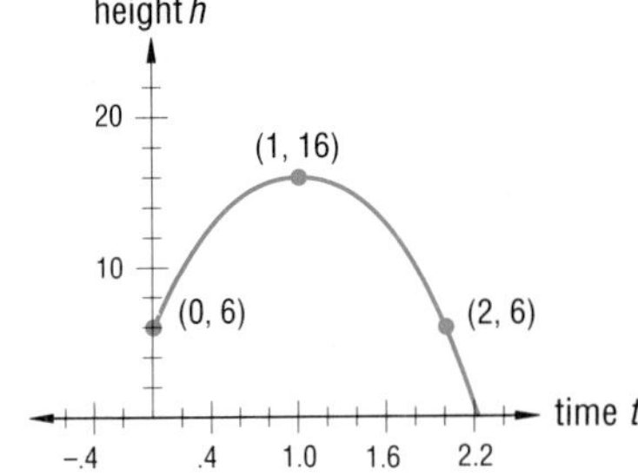

Example 2 Refer to the above situation. How high will the ball be after half a second?

Solution Substitute $t = .5$.

$$\begin{aligned} h &= -10(.5 - 1)^2 + 16 \\ &= -10(-.5)^2 + 16 \\ &= -10 \cdot .25 + 16 \\ &= -2.5 + 16 \\ &= 13.5 \end{aligned}$$

In half a second, the ball will be at a height of 13.5 feet.

Example 3 Again refer to the above situation. Estimate from the graph when the ball would reach a height of 9 feet.

Solution Draw a horizontal line at $h = 9$ feet. The ball reaches this height at two points, at about 0.2 seconds and at about 1.8 seconds.

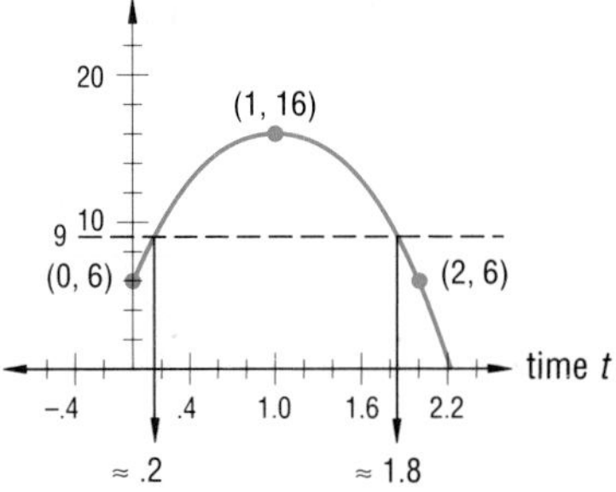

Notice that both these times are 0.8 seconds away from 1 second, where the vertex of the parabola is located.

You have seen that some parabolas describe the actual path of an object, the height at a given *distance* from the start. Other parabolas describe an object's height at a specific *time*. It is essential to read the labels of the axes to know what a graph is representing.

Questions

Covering the Reading

1. What is the shape of the path of a tossed ball? **a parabola**

In 2 and 3, refer to the tossed football at the beginning of the lesson.

2. If a defender is 5 yards in front of the receiver, how far is he from the quarterback? **35 yards**

3. What is the height of the ball 39 yards downfield from the quarterback? Write the answer: a. in feet; b. in feet and inches.
a) 6.975 feet; b) about 6 feet $11\frac{7}{10}$ inches

In 4 and 5, a quarterback throws the ball to a receiver 60 yards downfield. The ball is at a height of h feet, x yards downfield where $h = -\frac{1}{45}(x - 30)^2 + 25$.

4. At what height does the receiver catch the ball? **5 feet**

5. A defender is 5 yards in front of the receiver. How high would he have to reach to deflect the ball? **≈ 11.1 feet**

6. When the height of a toss is plotted against time, what shape is the graph? **a parabola**

In 7–11, refer to the graph at right. It shows h, the height in yards of a football t seconds after it is kicked into the air.

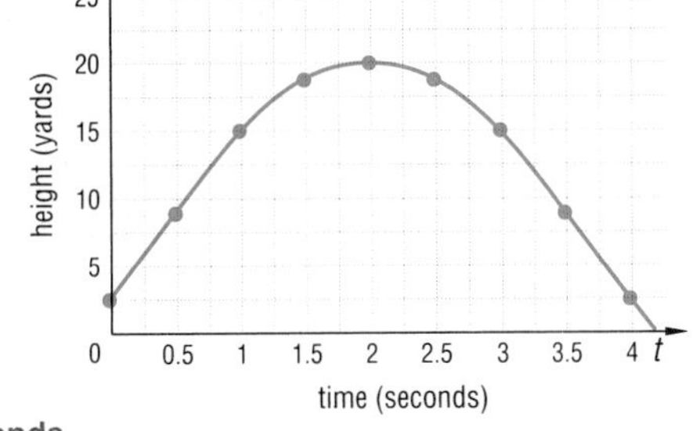

7. What is the greatest height the football reaches?
20 yards

8. How high is the ball 1 second after it is kicked?
15 yards

9. At what times is the height 18 yards? **≈ 1.5 and 2.5 seconds**

10. How long is the football in the air? **a little more than 4 seconds**

11. For how many seconds is the football more than 15 yards above the ground? **2 seconds**

c. Use the graph to estimate how many seconds it takes the rocket to reach its maximum height.
3 seconds

NOTES ON QUESTIONS

Question 15: This situation gives meaning to a negative height. The graph continues down past the point where $x = 6$. However, it does not make sense to include negative heights which occur before time zero in this problem.

Making Connections for Question 19: This question reviews the Zero Product Property, which is used in Lesson 12-7.

Making Connections for Question 20: The ± notation is reviewed here, since it is used in the next lesson, which is about the Quadratic Formula. Be sure that your students remember the meaning of this symbol.

NAME ______

LESSON **MASTER 12–3**
QUESTIONS ON **SPUR** OBJECTIVES

USES *Objective G (See pages 633–635 for objectives.)*

1. A baseball crosses home plate at a height of 4 ft. The batter hits the ball into the air. The path of the ball is described by the equation below where h is the height of the ball in feet and x is the number of feet the ball is downfield.

$$h = -\frac{1}{729}(x - 162)^2 + 40.$$

The outfield wall is 6 ft high and 318 ft from home plate. Will the ball go over the wall for a home run? If so, by how many feet will it clear the wall?
yes **≈.6 ft**

2. Suppose the outfield wall in Question 1 was 324 feet from home plate. Would it be possible for an outfielder to catch the ball? If so, at what height above the ground would the ball be when he caught it with his back against the wall?
yes **4 ft**

3. A ball is thrown upward from the surface of Mars with an initial velocity of 36 feet per second. Its approximate height h above the surface after a time of t seconds is given by the equation: $h = 36t - 6t^2$.
a. What is its height after 2 seconds? **48 ft**
b. What is its height after 6 seconds? **0 ft**
c. From the answer in part **b.**, after how many seconds will it reach its highest point, and how high will it be? **3 sec** **54 ft**

4. Refer to the graph at the right. It shows the height of a ball at a time of t seconds after it is thrown upward with an initial velocity of 30 meters per second.
a. Estimate from the graph its height h after 1 second. **25 m**
b. Estimate from the graph when it will reach a height of 30 meters. **$1\frac{1}{3}$ sec and $4\frac{2}{3}$ sec**
c. What is the maximum height? **45 m**

106

FOLLOW-UP

MORE PRACTICE
For more questions on SPUR Objectives, use *Lesson Master 12-3,* shown on page 601.

EVALUATION
A quiz covering Lessons 12-1 through 12-3 is provided in the Teacher's Resource File.

ADDITIONAL ANSWERS
17a; b. sample:

x	y
-2	2
-1	$\frac{1}{2}$
0	0
1	$\frac{1}{2}$
2	2

18a; b. sample:

x	y
0	0
1	5
2	8
3	9
4	8
5	5
6	0

25. sample: A baseball is not a sphere, so air currents do not evenly pass over its surface. Also, a pitcher can affect the travel of the ball—giving it a spin, etc.

26a. sample: for c = -3, 0, 3, 5

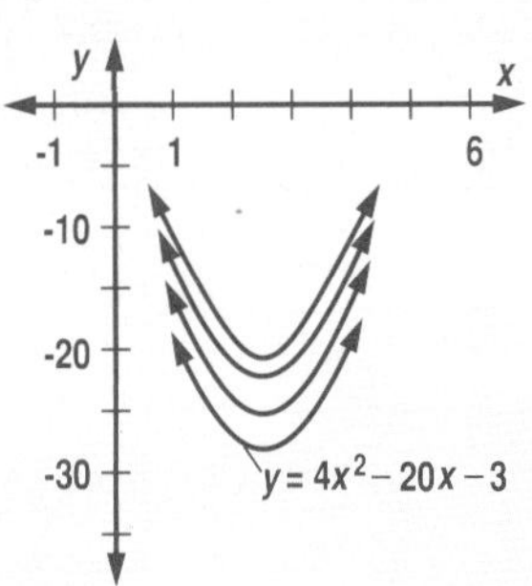

26b. c shifts graph up or down; if positive, up; if negative, down.

Applying the Mathematics

In 12–15, a projectile is shot from the edge of a cliff. The projectile is y meters above the cliff after x seconds where $y = 30x - 5x^2$. This equation is graphed at right.

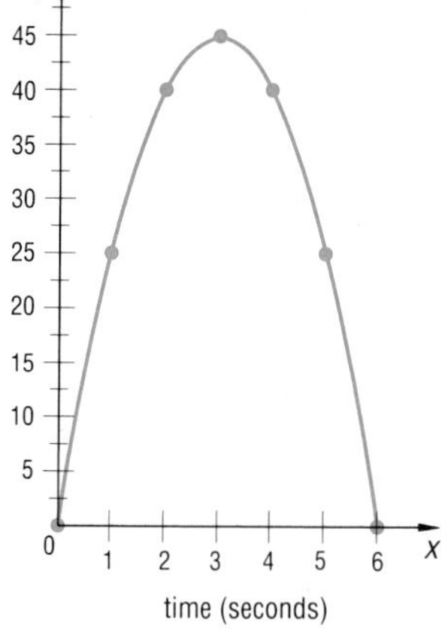

12. What is the greatest height reached? **45 meters**

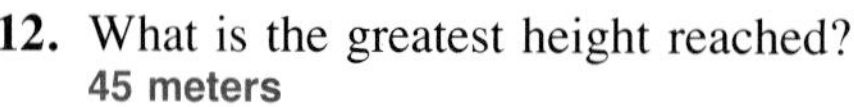

13. How far above the cliff edge is the projectile after 5 seconds? **25 meters**

14. When is the projectile 40 meters above the cliff edge? **after 2 and 4 seconds**

15. How far below the edge of the cliff would the projectile be after 7 seconds? **35 meters**

Review

16. *True or false* The graph of $y = 6x^2$ has a vertex at (0, 0). *(Lesson 12-1)* **True**

In 17 and 18, **a.** make a table of values; **b.** graph the equation. *(Lessons 12-1, 12-2)* **See margin.**

17. $y = \frac{1}{2}x^2$ **18.** $y = 6x - x^2$

19. Solve in your head: $2x(x - 4)(x - 3) = 0$. *(Lesson 10-10)* **0, 4, 3**

20. Find the endpoints of the interval 8 ± 1.27. *(Lesson 1-3)* **6.73 and 9.27**

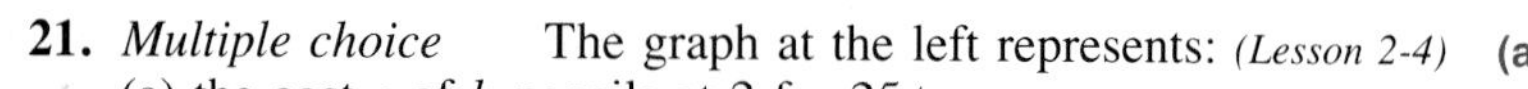

21. *Multiple choice* The graph at the left represents: *(Lesson 2-4)* **(a)**
(a) the cost c of h pencils at 2 for 25¢;
(b) the cost c of h pencils at 25¢ each;
(c) the cost c of h pencils at 50¢ each.

22. *Multiple choice* Which of the following is not equivalent to ab^2? *(Lessons 9-5, 9-8)* **(c)**
(a) $a \cdot b \cdot b$ (b) $a \cdot (b^2)$
(c) $(a \cdot b)^2$ (d) $a \cdot (b)^2$

23. What is the image of (-6, 0) after a slide 3 units to the right and 5 units down? *(Lesson 2-5)* **(-3, -5)**

24. *Skill sequence* Write as a single fraction. *(Lessons 2-2, 7-8)*
a. $2 + \frac{7}{11}$ **$\frac{29}{11}$**
b. $2 + \frac{x}{y}$ **$\frac{2y + x}{y}$**
c. $a + \frac{b - 1}{c + 1}$ **$\frac{ac + a + b - 1}{c + 1}$**

Exploration

25. A pitched ball in baseball does not always follow the path of a parabola. Why not? **See margin.**

26. a. Graph $y = 4x^2 - 20x + c$ for four different values of c of your own choosing. **See margin.**
b. How does the value of c affect the graph? **See margin.**

LESSON

12-4

The Quadratic Formula

A cliff diver in Acapulco, Mexico dives from a height of approximately 27 meters to the waters below "La Quebrada" ("the break in the rocks"). If the diver is x meters away from the cliff and y meters above the water, then under certain conditions $y = -x^2 + 2x + 27$ describes the path of the dive.

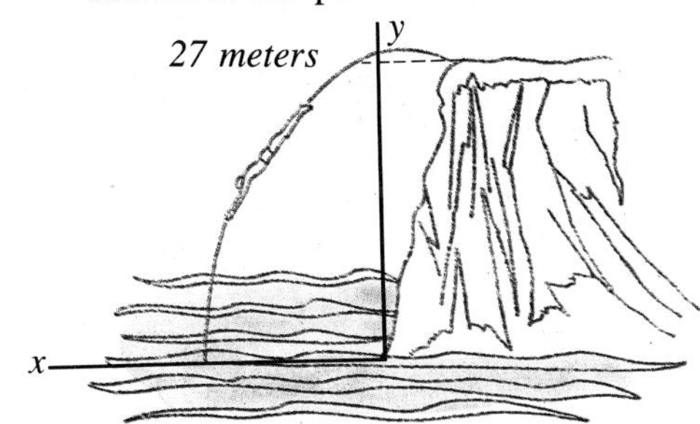

When the diver enters the water, the height $y = 0$. So solving

$$0 = -x^2 + 2x + 27$$

or, equivalently,

$$-x^2 + 2x + 27 = 0$$

will give the number of meters from the cliff the diver enters the water.

The equation $-x^2 + 2x + 27 = 0$ is an example of a quadratic equation. A **quadratic equation** is an equation that can be simplified into the form $ax^2 + bx + c = 0$. Solutions to *any* quadratic equation can be found by using the Quadratic Formula.

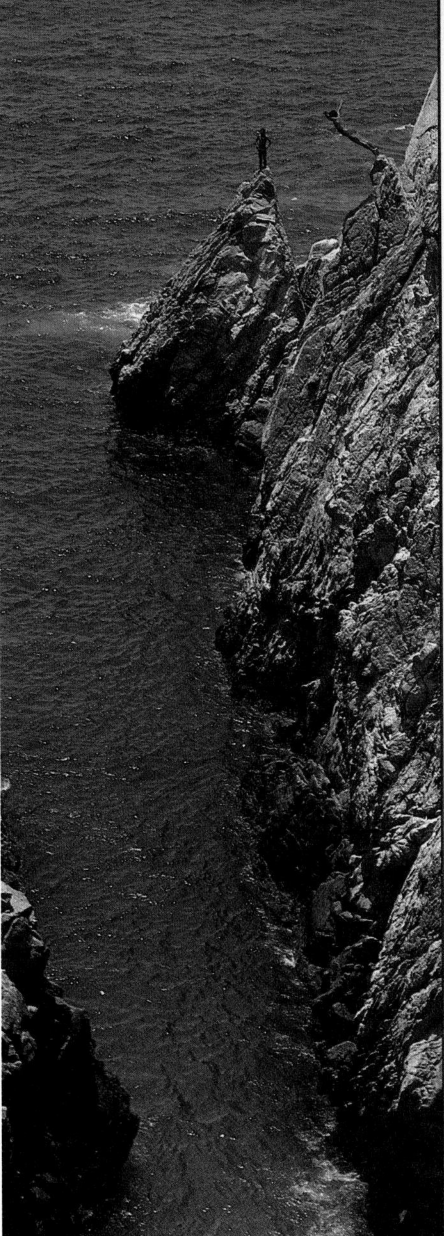

Quadratic Formula:

If $ax^2 + bx + c = 0$ and $a \neq 0$, then

$$x = \frac{-b \pm \sqrt{b^2 - 4ac}}{2a}.$$

The Quadratic Formula is one of the most famous formulas in all of mathematics. *You should memorize it today.*

LESSON 12-4

RESOURCES

- Lesson Master 12-4
- Computer Master 26

OBJECTIVES

A Solve quadratic equations using the Quadratic Formula.
E Recognize properties of quadratic equations.
G Use quadratic equations to solve real world problems.

TEACHING NOTES

The motivation to solve a quadratic equation is given here by asking the question, "If we know how high the diver is, how can we find his location?" For some heights there are two values of x, the distance from the cliff. The diver actually starts his dive by leaping up. Students will believe this more readily if you ask them why a swimming pool diving board has spring to it. In the case of the Acapulco divers, the vertex is reached very quickly because they are leaping from rocks, not from a springboard.

Making Connections To give your students more understanding of the situation, you might wish to refer to the graph of

$$y = -x^2 + 2x + 27$$

found in the next lesson. (You could use *Teaching Aid 72* from that lesson.) The negative solution to **Example 2** can be related to the graph. The path of the diver is only part of the parabola. He does not follow the portion for which $x < 0$.

Error Analysis Students should check their work, even when they have decimal approximations for answers. The check for decimal approximations will not come out exactly and may require some discussion. Checking 5.53 in $m^2 - 3m = 14$ yields $13.9909 \approx 14$.

Students may need some additional practice in identifying the *a, b,* and *c* values in quadratic equations, and in recognizing that the standard form of the quadratic has zero on one side. You can give practice in identifying the values without actually solving the equations.

The Quadratic Formula uses the shorthand symbol ± means "plus or minus." That symbol signifies that there are possibly two solutions to any quadratic equation:

$$x = \frac{-b + \sqrt{b^2 - 4ac}}{2a} \text{ or } x = \frac{-b - \sqrt{b^2 - 4ac}}{2a}.$$

Caution: Many calculators have a [+/-] key. That key takes the opposite of a number. It does *not* perform the two operations + and − required in the Quadratic Formula.

To apply the Quadratic Formula, notice that a is the coefficient of x^2, b is the coefficient of x, and c is the constant term. One side of the equation *must* be 0. Rearrange the other side in descending order of exponents. $ax^2 + bx + c = 0$ is called the **standard form of a quadratic equation**.

Example 1 Solve $3x^2 - 6x - 45 = 0$ by using the Quadratic Formula.

Solution In general, $x = \frac{-b \pm \sqrt{b^2 - 4ac}}{2a}$.

Here $a = 3$, $b = -6$ and $c = -45$.

So $$x = \frac{-(-6) \pm \sqrt{(-6)^2 - 4 \cdot 3 \cdot -45}}{2 \cdot 3}$$

Use the order of operations. Do the work inside the radical sign, first powers, then multiplications then subtractions.

$$= \frac{6 \pm \sqrt{36 - (-540)}}{6}$$

$$= \frac{6 \pm \sqrt{576}}{6}$$

$$= \frac{6 \pm 24}{6}.$$

Now translate the shorthand.

$$x = \frac{6 + 24}{6} = \frac{30}{6} = 5 \quad \text{or} \quad x = \frac{6 - 24}{6} = \frac{-18}{6} = -3.$$

Check Substitute 5 for x. $3(5)^2 - 6(5) - 45 = 75 - 30 - 45 = 0$. Substitute -3 for x. $3(-3)^2 - 6(-3) - 45 = 27 + 18 - 45 = 0$. It checks.

Working with an equation before applying the Quadratic Formula can occasionally make the calculations simpler. In Example 1, the numbers could have been made smaller by multiplying both sides of the original equation by $\frac{1}{3}$. The resulting equation, $x^2 - 2x - 15 = 0$, has the same solutions, $x = 5$ or $x = -3$.

When the term under the radical sign in the formula is not a perfect square, a calculator will give approximations.

Example 2 Solve $-x^2 + 2x + 27 = 0$ to find the distance of the diver from the cliff when he enters the water.

Solution Recall that $-x^2 = -1x^2$. So rewrite the equation as

$$-1x^2 + 2x + 27 = 0.$$

Since the left side is in descending order of exponents, apply the Quadratic Formula with $a = -1$, $b = 2$, and $c = 27$.

$$x = \frac{-2 \pm \sqrt{2^2 - 4 \cdot -1 \cdot 27}}{2 \cdot -1}$$

$$= \frac{-2 \pm \sqrt{4 - (-108)}}{2}$$

$$= \frac{-2 \pm \sqrt{112}}{-2}$$

So $x = \frac{-2 + \sqrt{112}}{-2}$ or $x = \frac{-2 - \sqrt{112}}{-2}$

These are exact answers to the equation. Using a calculator gives approximations.

$x \approx \frac{-2 + 10.6}{-2}$ or $x \approx \frac{-2 - 10.6}{-2}$

So $x \approx -4.3$ or $x \approx 6.3$

The diver cannot land a negative number of meters from the cliff, so the solution $x \approx -4.3$ does not make sense in this situation. The diver will enter the water about 6.3 meters away from the cliff.

Check Does 6.3 work in the equation $-x^2 + 2x + 27 = 0$? Substitute 6.3 for x. $-(6.3)^2 + 2(6.3) + 27 = -39.69 + 12.6 + 27 = -.09$. This is close enough to zero, given that 6.3 is an approximation.

ADDITIONAL EXAMPLES

1. Solve $2x^2 - 11x + 12 = 0$.
1.5, 4

2. Solve $10 = -x^2 + 2x + 27$ to find out how far the diver is away from the cliff when he is 10 meters above the water.
about 5.2 meters

3. Solve $5k^2 + 5k - 2 = 2k^2 - 2k$.
$\frac{-7 \pm \sqrt{73}}{6} \approx$ **0.26 or -2.59**

NOTES ON QUESTIONS
Making Connections for Question 8: Asking students for both the exact and approximate solutions helps them distinguish between the two. This leads up to Lesson 12-6 when irrational numbers will be discussed.

Questions 12 and 13: You could have students check their answers by graphing the functions with an automatic grapher.

Question 17b: There is a physical interpretation of negative values of y. The rock would be below the level of the cliff-top.

In Example 3, the equation has to be put into $ax^2 + bx + c = 0$ form before the formula can be applied.

Example 3 Solve $m^2 - 3m = 14$. Give m to the nearest hundredth.

Solution To apply the Quadratic Formula, one side of the equation must be 0. Add -14 to both sides.

$$m^2 - 3m - 14 = 0$$

Now the formula can be easily applied with $a = 1$, $b = -3$, $c = -14$.

$$m = \frac{-(-3) \pm \sqrt{(-3)^2 - 4 \cdot 1 \cdot -14}}{2 \cdot 1} = \frac{3 \pm \sqrt{9 - (-56)}}{2}$$

$$= \frac{3 \pm \sqrt{65}}{2}$$

$$\text{Thus } m = \frac{3 + \sqrt{65}}{2} \quad \text{or} \quad m = \frac{3 - \sqrt{65}}{2}$$

$$m \approx \frac{3 + 8.06}{2} \quad \text{or} \quad m \approx \frac{3 - 8.06}{2}$$

So $m \approx 5.53$ or $m \approx -2.53$.

Check The check is left to you as Question 7.

Questions

Covering the Reading

1. State the Quadratic Formula. **See margin.**

2. *True or false* The Quadratic Formula can be used to solve any quadratic equation. **True**

3. Refer to Example 1. Verify that $x = 5$ or $x = -3$ are solutions to $x^2 - 2x - 15 = 0$. **See margin.**

4. Give the two solutions to the sentence $x^2 + x - 1 = 0$, using the "±" symbol. $\mathbf{\frac{-1 \pm \sqrt{5}}{2}}$

In 5 and 6, each sentence is equivalent to a quadratic equation of the form $ax^2 + bx + c = 0$. **5a) $a = 12$, $b = 7$, $c = 1$; b) $-\frac{1}{4}$ or $-\frac{1}{3}$**

a. Give the values of a, b, and c. **6a) $a = 3$, $b = 1$, $c = -2$; b) $\frac{2}{3}$ or -1**

b. Give the exact solutions to the equation.

5. $12x^2 + 7x + 1 = 0$

6. $3n^2 + n - 2 = 0$

7. Check both decimal answers to Example 3. See margin.

8. Suppose the cliff diver at the beginning of the lesson dove from a cliff 22 meters high. Then, under certain conditions, solving the equation $0 = -x^2 + 2x + 22$ gives the number of meters the diver is from the cliff when entering the water. a) $a = -1$, $b = 2$, $c = 22$;
   a. Give the values of a, b, and c for use in the quadratic formula.
   b. Apply the Quadratic Formula to give the exact solutions to the equation. $1 + \sqrt{23}$ or $1 - \sqrt{23}$
   c. Approximate the solutions to the nearest tenth. -3.8 or 5.8
   d. How far away from the cliff does the diver enter the water? about 5.8 meters

9. a. Find a simpler equation that has the same solutions as $4m^2 - 16m - 64 = 0$. $m^2 - 4m - 16 = 0$
   b. Solve the simpler equation using the Quadratic Formula. $2 \pm 2\sqrt{5} \approx -2.47, 6.47$

In 10 and 11, put each equation in the form $ax^2 + bx + c = 0$. Then solve the equation using the Quadratic Formula. Round solutions to the nearest hundredth. 10) $a = 20$, $b = -6$, $c = -2$; $\frac{1}{2}$ or $-\frac{1}{5}$. 11) $a = 3$, $b = -1$, $c = -5$; 1.47 or -1.14

10. $20w^2 - 6w = 2$

11. $3w^2 - w = 5$

Applying the Mathematics

In 12 and 13, use this information. The solutions to $ax^2 + bx + c = 0$ are the x-intercepts of the graph of $y = ax^2 + bx + c$. Find the x-intercepts of the graph of the given equation.

12. $y = 2x^2 + 3x - 2$ $\frac{1}{2}$, -2

13. $y = 12x^2 - 12x + 1$ $\frac{12 \pm \sqrt{96}}{24} \approx$ .908 or .092

14. A square has a side of length x. If the sum of the area and the perimeter of the square is 86.25, find x. 7.5

15. When a ball on the moon is thrown upward with an initial velocity of 6 meters per second, its approximate height y after t seconds is given by $y = -0.8t^2 + 6t$.
   a. At what *two* times will it reach a height of 10 m? Give your answers to the nearest tenth of a second. 2.5, 5.0 b) See margin.
   b. Graph $y = -0.8t^2 + 6t$. Let t take on values from 0 to 7.5.
   c. Use the graph to check your answer to part a. See margin.

16. Solve by multiplying the binomials and then using the Quadratic Formula: $(w - 11)(w + 5) = 37$. $\frac{6 \pm \sqrt{404}}{2} = 3 \pm \sqrt{101} \approx 13$ or -7

Review

17. A rock is tossed up from a cliff with upward velocity of 10 meters per second. $h = 10t - 5t^2$ relates the height h of the rock *above the cliff* after t seconds. a) 5 meters above;
   a. How high above the cliff is the rock 1 second after it is tossed?
   b. Where will the rock be after 3 seconds? *(Lesson 12-2)* 15 meters below the cliff

18. The x-coordinate of the vertex of a parabola is the mean of the x-intercepts of the parabola. If the x-intercepts of a parabola are 3 and -1, what is the x-coordinate of the vertex? *(Lessons 1-2, 10-1)* 1

ADDITIONAL ANSWERS

1. If $ax^2 + bx + c = 0$ and $a \neq 0$, then $x = \frac{-b \pm \sqrt{b^2 - 4ac}}{2a}$

3. Substitute $x = 5$; does $5^2 - 2 \cdot 5 - 15 = 0$? Yes. Substitute $x = -3$; does $(-3)^2 - 2 \cdot -3 - 15 = 0$? Yes.

7. Substitute 5.53 for m. $(5.53)^2 - 3(5.53) = 13.9909 \approx 14$. Substitute -2.53 for m. $(-2.53)^2 - 3(-2.53) = 13.9909 \approx 14$. Both values check.

15b; c.

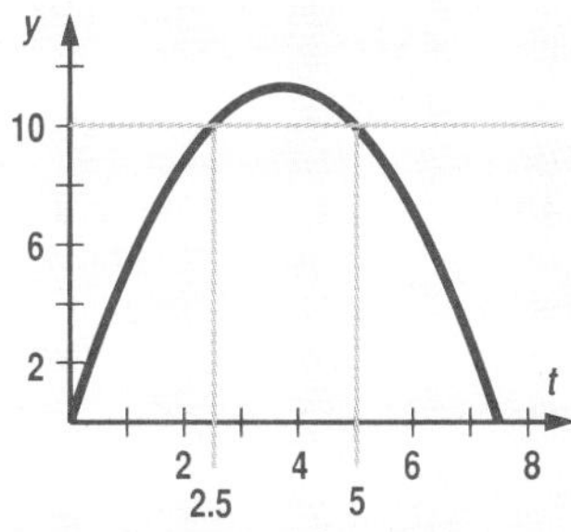

NAME ____________

LESSON **MASTER 12–4**
QUESTIONS ON **SPUR** OBJECTIVES

■SKILLS *Objective A (See pages 633–635 for objectives.)*

In 1–6, give the exact solutions to the equation.

1. $3x^2 - 10x + 8 = 0$ $x = \frac{4}{3}$ or $x = 2$
2. $14a^2 + 13a + 3 = 0$ $a = -\frac{1}{2}$ or $a = -\frac{3}{7}$
3. $t^2 - 10t = -25$ $t = 5$
4. $(n + 2)(n - 4) = 7$ $n = -3$ or $n = 5$
5. $4r - r^2 = -21$ $r = -3$ or $r = 7$
6. $10p - p^2 = 24$ $p = 4$ or $p = 6$

In 7 and 8, a. find a simpler equation that has the same solution. b. Then solve the equation.

7. $3x^2 - 27x + 54 = 0$
   a. $x^2 - 9x + 18 = 0$
   b. $x = 3$ or $x = 6$
8. $16y^2 + 28y - 8 = 0$
   a. $4y^2 + 7y - 2 = 0$
   b. $y = -2$ or $y = -\frac{1}{4}$

In 9 and 10, solve. Approximate solutions to the nearest tenth.

9. $x^2 + 3x - 5 = 0$ $x \approx -4.2$ or $x \approx 1.2$
10. $(2c - 1)(c + 2) = 5$ $c \approx -2.8$ or $c \approx 1.3$

■PROPERTIES *Objective E*

In 11 and 12, tell whether the statement is true or false.

11. Some quadratic equations cannot be solved using the Quadratic Formula. false
12. To apply the Quadratic Formula, one side of a quadratic equation must be zero. true

■USES *Objective G*

13. The height h in feet of a ball thrown upward on Mars after a time of t seconds is given by $h = 48t - 6t^2$. At what times was the ball 30 feet above the surface? at about .7 and 7.3 seconds

14. The side of a square is n cm. If the length is increased by 5 cm and the width is decreased by 4 cm, the resulting rectangle has an area of 112 square cm. What was the length of the side of the square? 11 cm

NOTES ON QUESTIONS
Making Connections for Question 24: The derivation of the Quadratic Formula in the next lesson relies on factoring a perfect square trinomial. This question is intended to remind students of that pattern.

FOLLOW-UP

MORE PRACTICE
For more questions on SPUR Objectives, use *Lesson Master 12-4,* shown on page 607.

EXTENSION
The idea in **Question 18** can be used to determine a general method for finding the vertex of a parabola $y = ax^2 + bx + c$. The two x-intercepts are

$$\frac{-b + \sqrt{b^2 - 4ac}}{2a} \text{ and } \frac{-b - \sqrt{b^2 - 4ac}}{2a}$$

The x-coordinate of the vertex is their mean, $-b/(2a)$. Once the x-coordinate is known, the y-coordinate can be found by evaluating $ax^2 + bx + c$ for that value of x.

Your students may enjoy using this method to find maximum or minimum points of parabolas. The formula for the height of a ball thrown vertically with an initial velocity of v ft/sec is $y = vx - 16x^2$. You could ask students to find the maximum heights for different initial velocities.

20.

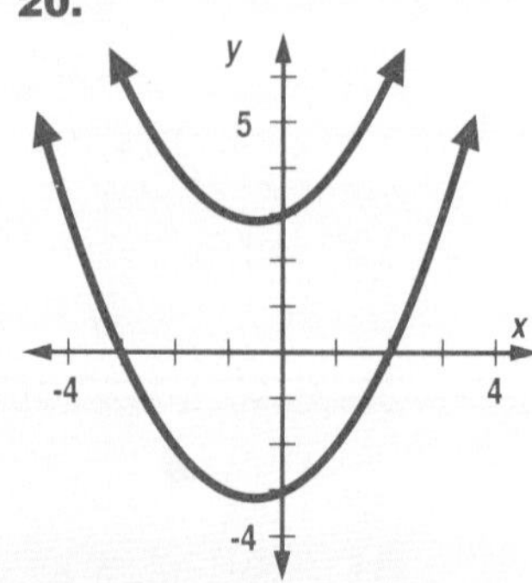

19. *Multiple choice* The graph below is the graph of (d)
(a) $y = 2x$
(b) $y = 2x^2$
(c) $y = 2x^2 + 1$
(d) $y = 2x^2 - 1$. *(Lesson 12-1)*

20. On the same coordinate axes, graph $y = \frac{1}{2}x^2 + \frac{1}{2}x + 3$ and $y = \frac{1}{2}x^2 + \frac{1}{2}x - 3$. *(Lessons 12-1, 12-2)* See margin.

21. A school begins the year with 200 reams of paper. (A ream contains 500 sheets.) The teachers are using 12 reams a week. How many reams will be left after 18 weeks? *(Lesson 6-2)* none

22. Find the volume of a box that is $15a$ inches in length, $8b$ inches in width, and $6c$ inches in height. *(Lesson 4-7)* $720abc$ cubic inches

23. Mr. Robinson is ordering a new car. He can choose from 5 models, 12 exterior colors, and 9 interior colors. How many combinations of models, interiors, and exteriors are possible? *(Lesson 4-6)* 540

24. Factor $x^2 - 2x + 1$. *(Lesson 10-11)* $(x - 1)^2$ or $(x - 1)(x - 1)$

25. *Skill sequence* Expand. *(Lesson 10-7)*
a. $(x + 1)^2$ $x^2 + 2x + 1$
b. $(3x - 2)^2$ $9x^2 - 12x + 4$
c. $(2ax + b)^2$ $4a^2x^2 + 4abx + b^2$

Exploration

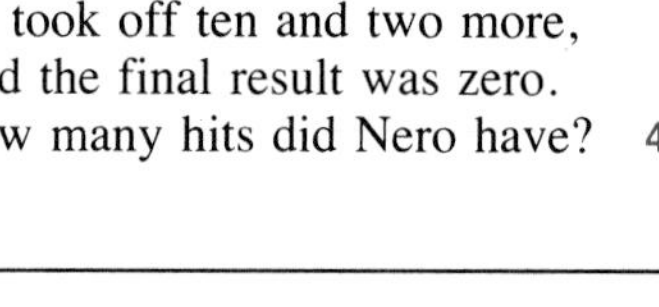

26. A team's opening batter named Nero
Squared his number of hits, the hero!
After subtracting his score,
He took off ten and two more,
And the final result was zero.
How many hits did Nero have? 4

LESSON

12-5

Analyzing the Quadratic Formula

In the previous lesson, we introduced the Quadratic Formula without telling you why it works. There is no mystery. The formula can be found by solving the general equation

$$ax^2 + bx + c = 0$$

using only properties you already know. The idea used below was first written by the Arab mathematician al-Khowarizmi in A.D. 825 in a book entitled *Hisab al-jabr w'al muqabalah*. This book was very influential. From the second word in that title comes our modern word "algebra." From his name comes our word "algorithm." The Quadratic Formula provides an algorithm for solving any quadratic equation.

The idea is to work with the equation $ax^2 + bx + c = 0$ until the left side is a perfect square. Then the equation will have the form $t^2 = k$, which you know how to solve for t.

If $k > 0$, then $t^2 = k$ has two real solutions, namely $t = \sqrt{k}$ or $t = -\sqrt{k}$.
If $k = 0$, then $t^2 = 0$ and there is only one solution, $t = 0$.
If $k < 0$, then $t^2 = k$ has no real solutions.

Examine the argument in the next paragraph closely. See how each equation follows from the preceding equation.

Multiply both sides of $ax^2 + bx + c = 0$ by $4a$. This makes the le term equal to $4a^2x^2$, the square of $2ax$.

$$4a^2x^2 + 4abx + 4ac = 0$$

When the quantity $2ax + b$ is squared, it equals $4a^2x^2 + 4abx + b$ The left and center terms of this trinomial match what is in the equa tion. We add b^2 to both sides of the equation to get all three terms into our equation.

$$4a^2x^2 + 4abx + b^2 + 4ac = b^2$$

The first three terms are the square of $2ax + b$.

$$(2ax + b)^2 + 4ac = b^2$$

Add $-4ac$ to both sides.

$$(2ax + b)^2 = b^2 - 4ac$$

Now the equation has the form $t^2 = k$, with $t = 2ax + b$ and $k = b^2 - 4ac$. At this point we need to ask: Is $b^2 - 4ac$ greater than, equal to, or less than 0?

LESSON 12-5

RESOURCES
- Lesson Master 12-5
- Visual for Teaching Aid 72: Graph for **Example 4**
- Visual for Teaching Aid 73: Graph for **Questions 24 and 25**
- Computer Master 26

OBJECTIVES

A Solve quadratic equations using the Quadratic Formula.
D Recognize properties of the parabola.
E Recognize properties of quadratic equations.

TEACHING NOTES

Reading Point out three sections of the derivation of the Quadratic Formula, each with a different goal. First, the equation must be expressed so that x appears just once. This is accomplished by factoring. The next goal is to "liberate" x from being squared. Taking the square root does that. Then the third goal is to isolate x.

You can trace the argument with an example.

Solve $3x^2 - 2x - 2 = 0$.
$36x^2 - 24x - 24 = 0$
(multiply by $4a = 12$)
$36x^2 - 24x + 4 - 24 = 4$
(add b^2)
$(6x + -2)^2 - 24 = 4$
$(6x - 2)^2 = 28$
$6x - 2 = \sqrt{28}$ or
$6x - 2 = -\sqrt{28}$
$x = \frac{2 + \sqrt{28}}{6}$ or $x = \frac{2 - \sqrt{28}}{6}$

A knowledge of the parabola of the diver's path helps students see why **Example 3** has only one solution and why **Example 4** has no solution. The parabola is shown following **Example 4.** Note that the horizontal lines for $y = 29$ and $y = 28$ have been shown. Here is a place where students are, in effect, solving for the intersection of a line and a parabola. *Teaching Aid 72* can be used to display the graph.

Making Connections
Solution 2, using factoring, is included in **Example 3** to remind students of the Zero Product Property in anticipation of the next few lessons.

Emphasize a limitation of the discriminant. Though it allows you to determine how many solutions a quadratic equation has, it doesn't tell whether the solutions make sense in the situation which gave rise to the quadratic equation.

If $b^2 - 4ac > 0$, then there are two real solutions. They are found by taking the square roots of both sides.

$$2ax + b = \pm \sqrt{b^2 - 4ac}$$

It is beginning to look like the formula. Now add $-b$ to each side.

$$2ax = -b \pm \sqrt{b^2 - 4ac}$$

Dividing both sides by $2a$ results in the solutions given by the Quadratic Formula.

$$x = \frac{-b \pm \sqrt{b^2 - 4ac}}{2a}$$

If $b^2 - 4ac = 0$, then you can still take the square roots, but the formula reduces to

$$x = \frac{-b \pm 0}{2a} = \frac{-b}{2a}.$$

This verifies that there is exactly one solution.

If $b^2 - 4ac < 0$, then the quadratic equation has no real number solutions. The formula still works, but you have to take square roots of negative numbers to get solutions. You will study these nonreal solutions in a later course.

Because the value of $b^2 - 4ac$ discriminates between the various possible numbers of real number solutions to a quadratic equation, it is called the **discriminant** of the equation.

Discriminant Property:

Suppose $ax^2 + bx + c = 0$ and a, b, and c are real numbers. Let $D = b^2 - 4ac$. Then

when $D > 0$, the equation has exactly two real solutions.
when $D = 0$, the equation has exactly one solution.
when $D < 0$, the equation has no real solutions.

Example 1 How many real solutions does the equation $8x^2 - 5x + 2 = 0$ have?

Solution Find the value of the discriminant $b^2 - 4ac$.
Here $a = 8$, $b = -5$, and $c = 2$.
So $b^2 - 4ac = (-5)2 - 4 \cdot 8 \cdot 2$
$= 25 - 64$
$= -39$.
Since $b^2 - 4ac$ is negative, there are no real solutions.

The discriminant can quickly give information about a situation. Recall from Lesson 12-4 that the cliff diver's height y above the water at a distance x meters from the cliff was described by the formula $y = -x^2 + 2x + 27$. Remember that the diver starts 27 meters above the water.

Example 2 Will the diver ever reach a height of 27.5 meters above the water?

Solution Let $y = 27.5$ in the equation $y = -x^2 + 2x + 27$.

$$27.5 = -x^2 + 2x + 27$$

Add -27.5 to both sides to put the equation in standard form.

$$0 = -x^2 + 2x - 0.5$$

Now calculate the discriminant. $b^2 - 4ac = 2^2 - 4 \cdot (-1) \cdot (-0.5) = 2$. Since the discriminant is positive, there are two solutions. Use the Quadratic Formula to find them. Notice that the calculation is easy since $b^2 - 4ac$ has been found.

$$x = \frac{-2 \pm \sqrt{2}}{-2}$$

$$x \approx \frac{-2 + 1.414}{-2} \text{ or } x = \frac{-2 - 1.414}{-2}$$

$$\approx 0.293 \text{ or } x \approx 1.707$$

The diver reaches the height of 27.5 meters twice, at about 0.3 meters from the cliff (on the way up) and about 1.7 meters from the cliff (on the way down).

Example 3 Will the diver ever reach a height of 28 meters above the water?

Solution 1 Let y be 28 in the equation $y = -x^2 + 2x + 27$.

$$28 = -x^2 + 2x + 27$$

Put the equation in general form by adding -28 to both sides.

$$0 = -x^2 + 2x - 1$$

The discriminant is $2^2 - 4 \cdot (-1) \cdot (-1) = 0$. Because the discriminant is 0, there is exactly one solution. The diver will be 28 meters above the water once. This must be the vertex of the parabolic path of the dive.

ADDITIONAL EXAMPLES

1. How many real solutions does $25x^2 - 10x + 1 = 0$ have?
one

2. Suppose that a ball is thrown into the air and its height h (in feet) after t seconds is given by $h = -8t^2 + 16t + 6$.

a. After how many seconds is the ball 12 feet in the air?
0.5, 1.5

b. When will the ball reach a height of 14 feet?
after 1 second

c. Will the ball ever reach a height of 20 feet?
No

NOTES ON QUESTIONS
Question 5: This question requires students to look carefully at the explanation of the derivation of the Quadratic Formula.

Question 16: Point out the difference between the quadratic in this question and the quadratic which has been used to describe the path of the Acapulco diver. The quadratic here gives height as a function of *time*. The Acapulco-diver quadratic gives height as a function of *distance from the cliff*. The latter parabola is a picture of the actual path of the diver. If students want to graph the parabola for this question, that is fine. The parabola will keep the physical meaning of the problem close to the student's computations.

Solution 2 The equation $-x^2 + 2x - 1 = 0$ from Solution 1 can be solved without using the Quadratic Formula. Multiply both sides by -1. Then the left side is a perfect square trinomial that can be factored.

$$x^2 - 2x + 1 = 0$$

Factor. $$(x - 1)(x - 1) = 0$$

Use the Zero Product Property.

$$x - 1 = 0 \quad \text{or} \quad x - 1 = 0$$
$$x = 1 \quad \text{or} \quad x = 1$$

This verifies that there is exactly one solution.

Example 4 Will the diver ever reach a height of 29 meters?

Solution Solve $29 = -x^2 + 2x + 27$

Add -29 to both sides to put into standard form,

$$0 = -x^2 + 2x - 2.$$

Here $a = -1$, $b = 2$, and $c = -2$. $-b^2 - 4ac = 2^2 - 4 \cdot (-1) \cdot (-2) = -4$. The discriminant is negative. Since negative numbers have no square roots in the real number system, this equation has no real solution. The diver will never reach a height of 29 meters.

Examples 2, 3, and 4 can be verified by looking at the graph of $y = -x^2 + 2x + 27$.

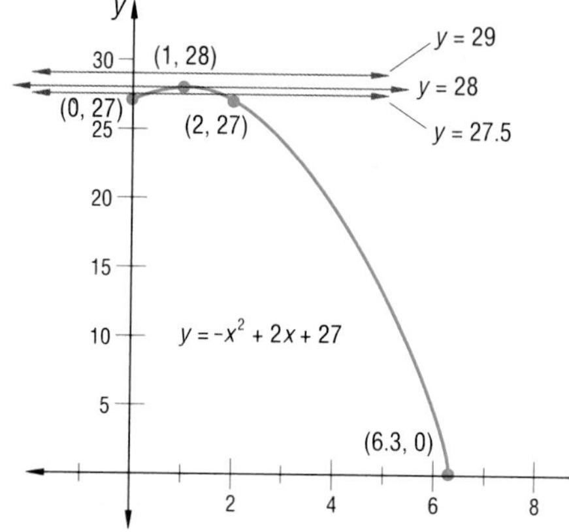

Here is a summary of the examples.

diver height	equation	discriminant	number of real solutions	graph intersects line
27.5 meters	$-x^2 + 2x + 27 = 27.5$	positive	2	$y = 27.5$ twice
28 meters	$-x^2 + 2x + 27 = 28$	zero	1	$y = 28$ once
29 meters	$-x^2 + 2x + 27 = 29$	negative	0	$y = 29$ never

Questions

Covering the Reading

1. The first person to write down an algorithm for solving quadratic equations was _?_ in the year _?_. **al-Khowarizmi; A.D. 825**

In 2–4, give all real solutions to the equation.

2. $x^2 = 10$ **$\pm\sqrt{10}$**
3. $y^2 = 0$ **0**
4. $z^2 = -81$ **no real solution**

5. Here are steps in the derivation of the Quadratic Formula. Tell what was done to get each step.

$$ax^2 + bx + c = 0$$

a. $4a^2x^2 + 4abx + 4ac = 0$ **multiplied by 4a**

b. $4a^2x^2 + 4abx + b^2 = b^2 - 4ac$ **subtracted 4ac and added b^2 to both sides**

c. $(2ax + b)^2 = b^2 - 4ac$ **grouped $4a^2x^2 + 4abx + b^2$ as $(2ax + b)^2$**

d. $2ax + b = \pm\sqrt{b^2 - 4ac}$ **took square roots of both sides**

e. $2ax = -b \pm \sqrt{b^2 - 4ac}$ **subtracted b from both sides**

f. $x = \dfrac{-b \pm \sqrt{b^2 - 4ac}}{2a}$ **divided by 2a on both sides**

6. Define: discriminant. **$b^2 - 4ac$**

7. Give the number of real solutions to a quadratic equation when its discriminant is
   a. positive **two** b. negative **none** c. zero. **one**

In 8–11, **a.** give the value of the discriminant; **b.** give the number of real solutions; **c.** find all the real solutions. **See margin.**

8. $w^2 - 16w + 64 = 0$
   a) 0; b) 1; c) 8
9. $4x^2 - 3x + 8 = 0$
   a) -119; b) 0; c) no real solution
10. $25y^2 = 10y - 1$
   a) 0; b) 1; c) $\frac{1}{5}$
11. $13z = 5z^2 + 9$
   a) -11; b) 0; c) no real solution

12. What equation can be solved to determine how far away from the cliff the diver in this lesson will be when he is 28 meters above the water? **$28 = -x^2 + 2x + 27$**

13. When will the diver of this lesson reach a height of 30 meters above the water? **never**

14. When will the diver of this lesson be 10 meters above the water? **after $\frac{2 + \sqrt{72}}{2}$ seconds ($\approx$5.24 sec)**

Applying the Mathematics

15. a. Solve $4x^2 + 8x = 5$ **$\frac{1}{2}, -\frac{5}{2}$** b. Solve $4x^2 + 8x = -1$. **$\frac{-8 \pm \sqrt{48}}{8} \approx -.13$ or -1.9**
   c. Solve $4x^2 + 8x = -10$. **no real solution**

16a) 20 feet; b) 1 sec

16. Suppose an equation that describes a diver's path when diving off of a platform is $d = -5t^2 + 10t + 20$, where d is the distance above the water (feet) and t is the time from the beginning of the dive (seconds).
   a. How high is the diving platform? (Hint: let $t = 0$ seconds).
   b. After how many seconds is the diver 25 feet above the water?
   c. After how many seconds does the diver enter the water? (Round your answer to the nearest tenth.) **3.2 sec**

NAME ____________

LESSON MASTER 12–5
QUESTIONS ON **SPUR** OBJECTIVES

SKILLS *Objective A (See pages 633–635 for objectives.)*
In 1 and 2, give the exact solutions to the equation.

1. $2x^2 + 13x - 7 = 0$ **$\frac{1}{2}, -7$**
2. $x^2 - 7x - 3 = 0$ **$\frac{-7 \pm \sqrt{61}}{2}$**

PROPERTIES *Objective D*
In 3–6, tell how many times the graph of the equation intersects the x-axis.

3. $y = 2x^2 - 5x - 7$ **2**
4. $y = 7x^2 + 6x + 2$ **none**
5. $y = 4x^2 - 4x + 1$ **1**
6. $y = x^2 - 9x - 22$ **2**

PROPERTIES *Objective E*
In 7–9, let D be the discriminant of the equation $ax^2 + bx + c = 0$. Match the answers.

7. $D > 0$ **b** (a) no real solutions
8. $D = 0$ **c** (b) two real solutions
9. $D < 0$ **a** (c) one real solution

In 10–15, a. find the value of the discriminant, and b. determine the number of real solutions to the equation.

10. $5x^2 - x + 2 = 0$ a. **-39** b. **none**
11. $a^2 - 6a = 8$ a. **68** b. **2**
12. $1 + 6n + 9n^2 = 0$ a. **0** b. **1**
13. $0.6k^2 - 1.39k + 2 = 0$ a. **$\approx$-2.87** b. **none**
14. $1.1p^2 + 3.2p - 1.2 = 0$ a. **15.52** b. **2**
15. $\frac{1}{4}x^2 + \frac{1}{2}x + \frac{1}{3} = 0$ a. **$-\frac{1}{12}$** b. **none**

NOTES ON QUESTIONS
Making Connections for Question 17: Similar questions appear in the next two lessons.

Question 26: This *Skill sequence* culminates with the sum of the roots of the general quadratic. The fact that the sum of the roots is $-b/a$ can be employed to check solutions. This can be related to the parabola. The average of the roots gives the x-value of the vertex of the parabola. (See the Extension for Lesson 12-4.)

FOLLOW-UP

MORE PRACTICE
For more questions on SPUR Objectives, use *Lesson Master 12-5,* shown on page 613.

ADDITIONAL ANSWERS
27.

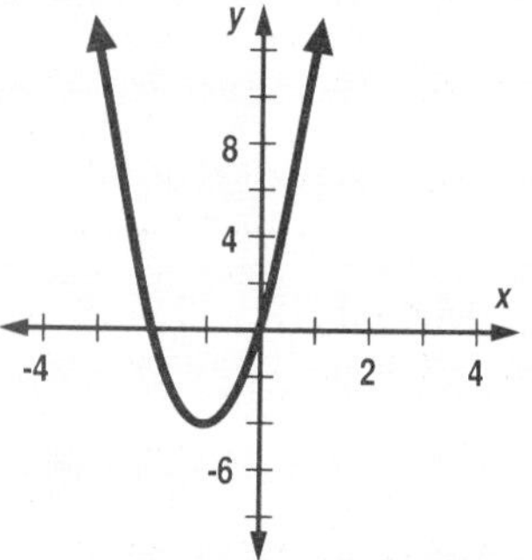

For this parabola, when $y = 5$, $x = \frac{1}{2}$ or $-\frac{5}{2}$; when $y = -1$, $x \approx -.13$ or -1.9; there is no x value associated with $y = -10$.

17. For what value of h does $x^2 + 3x + h = 0$ have exactly one solution? **2.25**

Review

18. Solve $60x^2 - 190x - 110 = 0$. *(Lesson 12-4)* **$3\frac{2}{3}$ or $-\frac{1}{2}$**

19. Alan receives \$50 a year on each birthday and invests it with a scale factor of z. After 3 years, he knows he has $50z^2 + 50z + 50$ dollars. He also knows he has \$160.
a. Find z. *(Lesson 12-3)* **≈1.07**
b. What is the interest rate on his investment? *(Lesson 9-1)* **about 7%**

20. Calculate $\frac{15!}{8!7!}$. *(Lesson 4-9)* **6435**

In 21 and 22, state whether the parabola opens up or down. *(Lesson 12-1)*

21. $y = -\frac{1}{5}x^2 - 3x + 2$ **down**
22. $x^2 + x = y$ **up**

23. Solve. *(Lesson 6-7)*
a. $a - \frac{1}{3} < 0$ **$a < \frac{1}{3}$**
b. $\frac{1}{3} - b < 0$ **$b > \frac{1}{3}$**
c. $\frac{1}{3}c < 0$ **$c < 0$**

In 24 and 25, a softball pitcher tosses a ball in practice to her catcher 50 ft away. The ball is at a height of h ft, x feet from the pitcher where

$$h = -\frac{1}{62.5}(x - 25)^2 + 12.$$

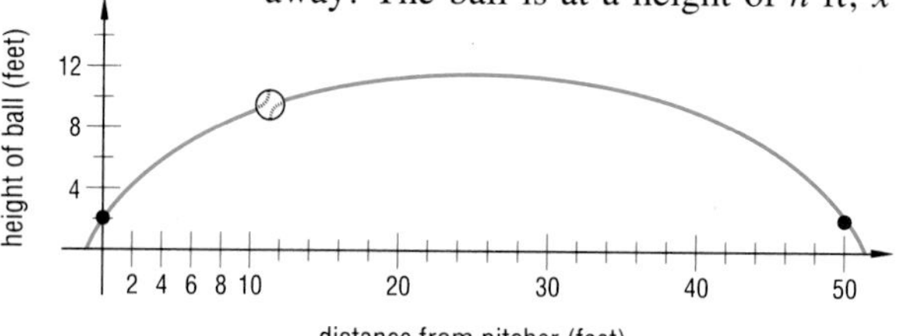

24. How high is the ball at its peak? *(Lesson 12-2)* **12 feet**

25. a. If the batter is 2 ft in front of the catcher, how far is she from the pitcher? **48 feet**
b. How high is the ball when it reaches the batter? *(Lesson 12-2)* **≈3.5 feet**

26. *Skill sequence* Add and simplify. *(Lessons 7-4, 7-6)*
a. $\frac{-5 + x}{2a} + \frac{-5 - x}{2a}$ **$\frac{-5}{a}$**
b. $\frac{-b + y}{2a} + \frac{-b - y}{2a}$ **$\frac{-b}{a}$**
c. $\frac{-b + \sqrt{z}}{2a} + \frac{-b - \sqrt{z}}{2a}$ **$\frac{-b}{a}$**
d. $\frac{-b + \sqrt{b^2 - 4ac}}{2a} + \frac{-b - \sqrt{b^2 - 4ac}}{2a}$ **$\frac{-b}{a}$**

Exploration

27. Graph the parabola $y = 4x^2 + 8x$ as accurately as you can. Explain the answers you get to Question 15 by referring to this parabola. **See margin.**

LESSON

12-6

Rational and Irrational Numbers

A number that can be written as a ratio of two integers is called a **rational number**. Here are some examples.

$\frac{1}{2}$ is rational. It is the ratio of the integers 1 and 2.

$\frac{-6}{5}$ is rational. It is the ratio of the integers -6 and 5.

$3\frac{1}{7}$ is rational. It equals $\frac{22}{7}$, the ratio of the integers 22 and 7.

0 is rational. It is the ratio of 0 and any other integer n.

149 is rational. It equals $\frac{149}{1}$, the ratio of 149 and 1.

18.89 is rational. It equals $\frac{1889}{100}$.

$-4.\overline{2}$ is rational. It equals $-4\frac{2}{9}$, or $-\frac{38}{9}$.

In general, any integer, simple fraction, mixed number, finite decimal, or repeating decimal, whether positive or negative, represents a rational number.

Real numbers that are not rational are called **irrational**. Every infinite decimal that does not repeat represents an irrational number. Examples are

$$\pi \approx 3.141592653 \ldots$$
$$\text{and } \sqrt{2} = 1.414213562 \ldots$$

In fact, any square root of an integer that is not itself an integer is irrational. Namely, $\sqrt{3}$, $\sqrt{5}$, $\sqrt{6}$, $\sqrt{7}$, $\sqrt{8}$, $\sqrt{10}$, ... , are all irrational. (But $\sqrt{4}$ is rational, for it equals $\frac{2}{1}$.)

Thus, if a number is rational, it has a finite or repeating decimal. But if a number is irrational, you can only approximate it by a decimal.

All of this is useful in solving quadratic equations by the Quadratic Formula. Under the square root sign in the formula is the discriminant. When a, b, and c are integers, the discriminant $b^2 - 4ac$ will be an integer. If $b^2 - 4ac$ is a perfect square, then the solutions are rational. If $b^2 - 4ac$ is positive but not a perfect square, then $\sqrt{b^2 - 4ac}$ will be irrational and you can only write a decimal approximation to the roots.

If a, b, and c are integers and $b^2 - 4ac$ is a positive number but not a perfect square, then the equation $ax^2 + bx + c = 0$ has two irrational solutions.

LESSON 12-6

RESOURCES
- Lesson Master 12-6
- Quiz on Lessons 12-4 Through 12-6

OBJECTIVES

E Recognize properties of quadratic equations.
F Determine whether a number is rational or irrational.

TEACHING NOTES

Make sure students realize that, due to the Equal Fractions Property, any rational number can be expressed as the ratio of two integers in infinitely many ways. They may need to be reminded of how to express a number like 18.89 as a simple fraction.

The rule stated before **Example 1** describes the situation in which a quadratic equation has two irrational solutions. You might explain that it is impossible for an equation with integer coefficients to have one rational and one irrational root.

ADDITIONAL EXAMPLES

1. Determine whether the solutions to $2x^2 - 7x - 4 = 0$ are rational or irrational.
rational

2. Are the solutions to $4x^2 + 8x = x^2 - 2$ rational or irrational?
irrational

NOTES ON QUESTIONS

Question 18: The test in this lesson is stated so it applies to equations for which *a, b,* and *c* are integers. In answering this question, first multiply through to eliminate the fractions. Not only does this make it possible to use the discriminant test for equations with rational but nonintegral coefficients, but it also makes the calculations involved with the Quadratic Formula easier.

Questions 19 and 20: Have students write expressions for the discriminant and then use trial and error to find values of *k* for which that expression will equal a perfect square.

Question 31: Let *c* be the product of two integers whose sum is *b*, and there will be integer solutions.

ADDITIONAL ANSWERS

19. sample: $k = \frac{21}{4}$ **or** $k = \frac{13}{4}$

20. $k = 6$ **or** $k = -6$

31a. sample: $c = 8$

31b. infinitely many

Example 1 Determine whether the solutions to $6x^2 + 5x - 4 = 0$ are rational or irrational.

Solution Calculate the discriminant when $a = 6$, $b = 5$, and $c = -4$.

$$b^2 - 4ac = 5^2 - 4 \cdot 6 \cdot -4 = 25 + 96$$
$$= 121$$

121 is a perfect square, so the solutions are rational.

Check By the Quadratic Formula,

$$x = \frac{-5 \pm \sqrt{121}}{12}$$
$$= \frac{-5 \pm 11}{12}$$
$$x = \frac{-5 + 11}{12} \text{ or } x = \frac{-5 - 11}{12}.$$

Thus,

$$x = \frac{6}{12} \qquad \text{or } x = \frac{-16}{12}$$
$$x = \frac{1}{2} \qquad \text{or } x = \frac{-4}{3}.$$

These are rational numbers.

Example 2 Are the solutions to $x^2 + 8x - 5 = 0$ rational?

Solution Here $a = 1$, $b = 8$, and $c = -5$.

$$b^2 - 4ac = 8^2 - 4 \cdot 1 \cdot -5 = 64 + 20$$
$$= 84$$

84 is not a perfect square, so the solutions are irrational.

Check Using the Quadratic Formula, $x = \frac{-8 \pm \sqrt{84}}{2} \approx \frac{-8 \pm 9.165}{2}$.

Thus $x \approx 0.582$ or $x \approx -8.582$. These both approximate infinite decimals.

Questions

Covering the Reading

1. Define: rational number. **A number than can be written as a ratio of two integers.**

In 2–9, **a.** decide whether the number is rational or irrational. **b.** If it is rational, find a ratio of integers equal to it.

2. $\sqrt{13}$ **3.** $\frac{6}{8}$ $\frac{3}{4}$ **4.** 1.5 $\frac{3}{2}$ **5.** -1.5 $-\frac{3}{2}$

2 and 6) irrational; 3–5, 7–9) rational; samples are shown.

6. π **7.** $\frac{1}{3}$ $\frac{2}{6}$ **8.** 0.004 $\frac{4}{1000}$ **9.** $\sqrt{16}$ $\frac{4}{1}$

10. If a, b, and c are integers, when does $ax^2 + bx + c = 0$ have rational solutions? **when $b^2 - 4ac$ is a perfect square**

In 11–18, use the discriminant to determine the number of rational solutions the equation has. Then solve.

11. $6x^2 + 13x + 6 = 0$
    2 rational; $-\frac{2}{3}$ or $-\frac{3}{2}$
12. $2x^2 - 7x - 10 = 0$
    no rational; ≈4.589 or ≈-1.089
13. $y^2 - 2 = 0$
    no rational; ≈1.414 or ≈-1.414
14. $5t^2 + 3t = 0$
    2 rational; 0 or -.6
15. $10x^2 = 3x + 1$
    two rational; .5 or -.2
16. $400v^2 + 100 = 400v$
    1 rational; $\frac{1}{2}$
17. $t(t + 9) = 5$
    no rational; ≈.525 or ≈-9.525
18. $x^2 + \frac{1}{4}x - \frac{1}{8} = 0$
    two rational; .25 or -.5

Applying the Mathematics

19. Find two different values for k that will make $3x^2 + 8x + k = 0$ have rational solutions.
    See margin.

20. Find a value for k so that $x^2 + kx + 5 = 0$ has rational solutions.
    See margin.

Review

21. Find the x-intercepts of $y = x^2 + 9x - 5$. *(Lesson 12-3)*
    ≈-9.525 or ≈.525

22. Solve $4x^2 - 12x + 9 = 0$ by factoring and using the Zero Product Property. *(Lessons 10-5, 10-10)* **$x = \frac{3}{2}$**

In 23–25, in a vacuum chamber on Earth an object will drop d meters in approximately t seconds, where $d = 4.9t^2$. *(Lesson 12-2)*

23. How far will the object drop in 3 seconds? **44.1 ft.**

24. Write an expression for how far an object would drop in $n + 1$ seconds. **$d = 4.9(n + 1)^2$**

25. **a.** Write an equation that could be used to find the number of seconds it takes an object to drop 10 meters. **$d = 4.9t^2$**
    b. Solve the equation in part a. **$1.43 \approx t$**

26. In how many ways can you draw two prize tickets from a jar with 30 tickets? (Assume the tickets are not replaced.) *(Lesson 4-7)*
    870 ways

27. *Skill sequence* Simplify. All variables represent positive numbers. *(Lesson 7-6)*
    a. $\sqrt{169x^2}$ **13x** **b.** $\sqrt{25y^4}$ **$5y^2$** **c.** $\sqrt{169x^2 \cdot 25y^4}$ **$65xy^2$**

In 28–30, calculate in your head. *(Lessons 4-2, 5-4)*

28. one third of a dozen **4**

29. $33\frac{1}{3}\%$ of 900 **300**

30. $\frac{2}{6}$ of 30 **10**

Exploration

31. **a.** Find an integer value of c so that the equation $x^2 + 6x + c = 0$ has rational solutions. **See margin.**
    b. How many possible values of c are there? **See margin.**

FOLLOW-UP

MORE PRACTICE

For more questions on SPUR Objectives, use *Lesson Master 12-6*, shown below.

EXTENSION

You may want to discuss fractions and decimals that are perfect squares like $\frac{25}{9}$ or 0.0625, so that $\sqrt{\frac{25}{9}}$ and $\sqrt{0.0625}$ are rational even though they don't look it.

A fraction is a perfect square if, when it is expressed in lowest terms, its numerator and denominator are perfect squares. Decimals are perfect squares if they can be written as perfect square fractions.

EVALUATION

A quiz covering Lessons 12-4 through 12-6 is provided in the Teacher's Resource File.

NAME ______

LESSON **MASTER 12–6**
QUESTIONS ON **SPUR** OBJECTIVES

■**PROPERTIES** *Objective E (See pages 633–635 for objectives.)*

1. *Multiple choice* If its discriminant is a nonzero perfect square, a quadratic equation has:
   (a) one real solution (b) two irrational solutions
   (c) two rational solutions (d) none of these **c**

In 2–7, a. use the discriminant to determine the number of real solutions. b. Tell whether the real solutions are rational or irrational.

2. $x^2 - 8x + 3 = 0$
   a. **2**
   b. **irrational**
3. $16a^2 + 8a + 1 = 0$
   a. **1**
   b. **rational**
4. $13y^2 - 4 = 0$
   a. **2**
   b. **irrational**
5. $t(t + 2) = 4$
   a. **2**
   b. **irrrational**
6. $4b(b + 2) = 5$
   a. **2**
   b. **rational**
7. $9r^2 + 16 = 0$
   a. **none**
   b. **—**

■**PROPERTIES** *Objective F*
In 8–13, tell whether the number is rational or irrational.

8. $\sqrt{32}$ **irrational**
9. 19.031 **rational**
10. $-\frac{2}{3}$ **rational**
11. $\frac{3\pi}{2}$ **irrational**
12. $\sqrt{144}$ **rational**
13. $6.\overline{4}$ **rational**

LESSON 12-7

RESOURCES
■ Lesson Master 12-7

OBJECTIVE

B Factor quadratic trinomials.

TEACHING NOTES

Emphasize that students should always ask themselves whether a quadratic trinomial is factorable first, before they try to factor it. Why waste time trying to factor if it is not factorable?

Error Analysis Point out that multiplying is not a good way to check a factoring problem because multiplication was probably the way the factors were found in the first place. Students should use the arithmetic check shown in **Example 2.** It relates factoring of trinomials to factoring of integers.

LESSON

12-7

Factoring Quadratic Trinomials

In Chapter 10, you studied how differences of squares and perfect square trinomials can be factored into a product of two binomials. For instance,

$$x^2 - y^2 = (x + y)(x - y)$$
$$x^2 + 6x + 9 = (x + 3)(x + 3)$$
$$x^2 - 2x + 1 = (x - 1)(x - 1).$$

Other quadratic trinomials can be factored.

$$x^2 + 5x + 6 = (x + 2)(x + 3)$$
$$3m^2 + 5m - 12 = (3m - 4)(m + 3)$$
$$4y^2 - 4y - 3 = (2y - 3)(2y + 1)$$

In all the examples and questions of this lesson, we are looking for factors with integer coefficients, as in the examples above. If a, b, and c are integers, then $ax^2 + bx + c$ is factorable if and only if the discriminant $b^2 - 4ac$ is a perfect square. You will learn why this is so in the following lessons. First we discuss how to factor.

Notice the general pattern. On the left side of each equal sign is a quadratic trinomial. On the right side are two binomials. Here is the form.

$$ax^2 + bx + c = (dx + e)(fx + g)$$

The product of d and f, the first terms of the binomials, is a. The product of e and g, the last terms of the binomials, is c.

So, if you need to factor the quadratic trinomial

$$ax^2 + bx + c$$

and you know it is factorable, first write the parentheses and the variables.

$$ax^2 + bx + c = (\ x \qquad)(\ x \qquad).$$

The coefficients of the x's must multiply to a and the constant terms must multiply to c. The problem is to find them so that the rest of the multiplication gives b.

Example 1 Is $x^2 + 9x + 14$ factorable?

Solution Here $a = 1$, $b = 9$, and $c = 14$. So $b^2 - 4ac = 81 - 4 \cdot 1 \cdot 14 = 25$. Since the discriminant is a perfect square, $x^2 + 9x + 14$ is factorable.

Example 2 Factor $x^2 + 9x + 14$.

Solution The idea is to rewrite the expression as a product of two binomials.

$$x^2 + 9x + 14 = (dx + e)(fx + g).$$

Look for integers d, e, f, and g.
The coefficient of x^2 is 1, so $df = 1$. Thus $d = 1$ and $f = 1$. Now you know

$$x^2 + 9x + 14 = (x + e)(x + g).$$

The product of e and g is 14. Try each possibility.
Can $e = 1$ and $g = 14$?

$(x + 1)(x + 14) = x^2 + 15x + 14$. No, you want $b = 9$, not 15.

Can $e = 2$ and $g = 7$?
$(x + 2)(x + 7) = x^2 + 9x + 14$. This does it. The answer is $(x + 2)(x + 7)$.

Check The problem is already checked by multiplication. Another check is to substitute a value for x, say 4. Then does

$$x^2 + 9x + 14 = (x + 2)(x + 7)?$$
$$4^2 + 9 \cdot 4 + 14 = (4 + 2)(4 + 7)?$$
$$16 + 36 + 14 = 6 \cdot 11?$$

Yes. Each side equals 66.

In Example 2, because the coefficient of x^2 is 1, and all numbers are positive, there are only a few possible factors. Example 3 has more possibilities, but the idea is still the same. Try factors until you find the correct ones.

ADDITIONAL EXAMPLES

1. Is $2x^2 + 5x + 3$ factorable? If so, factor it. If not, tell why not.
Yes, $(2x + 3)(x + 1)$

2. Factor $2n^2 - 3n - 20$.
$(2n + 5)(n - 4)$

3. Factor $6y^2 - 29y + 5$ if possible.
not possible

NOTES ON QUESTIONS
Questions 4-11: Using the discriminant to test for "factorability" prevents the frustration and uncertainty caused by unsuccessfully searching for factors.

Questions 4-11 and 14-16: Students use the discriminant in several ways in these problems. They use it in **Questions 4-11** to determine whether an expression is factorable, in **Questions 14 and 15** to distinguish between rational and irrational roots, and in **Question 16** to determine the number of real solutions.

Example 3 Factor $6y^2 - 7y - 5$. (Assume it is factorable.)

Solution First put down the form.
$6y^2 - 7y - 5 = (\_y + \_)(\_y + \_)$.
The coefficients of y will multiply to 6. Thus either there is $3y$ and $2y$, or y and $6y$. The constant terms will multiply to -5. So they are either 1 and -5, or -1 and 5.

Here are all the possibilities with $3y$ and $2y$.

$$(3y + 1)(2y - 5)$$
$$(3y - 1)(2y + 5)$$
$$(3y - 5)(2y + 1)$$
$$(3y + 5)(2y - 1)$$

Here are all the possibilities with y and $6y$.

$$(y + 1)(6y - 5)$$
$$(y - 1)(6y + 5)$$
$$(y - 5)(6y + 1)$$
$$(y + 5)(6y - 1)$$

At most, you need to do these eight multiplications. If one of them gives $6y^2 - 7y - 5$, then that is the correct factoring.

We show all eight multiplications. You can see that the desired one is third.

$$(3y + 1)(2y - 5) = 6y^2 - 13y - 5$$
$$(3y - 1)(2y + 5) = 6y^2 + 13y - 5$$
$$(3y - 5)(2y + 1) = 6y^2 - 7y - 5$$
$$(3y + 5)(2y - 1) = 6y^2 + 7y - 5$$
$$(y + 1)(6y - 5) = 6y^2 + y - 5$$
$$(y - 1)(6y + 5) = 6y^2 - y - 5$$
$$(y - 5)(6y + 1) = 6y^2 - 29y - 5$$
$$(y + 5)(6y - 1) = 6y^2 + 29y - 5$$

So the correct answer is $(3y - 5)(2y + 1)$.

In Example 3, notice that each choice of factors gives a product that differs only in the coefficient of y (the middle term). If the problem was to factor $6y^2 - 100y - 5$, this process would show that no factors with integer coefficients will work.

Factoring quadratic trinomials using trial and error is a skill people learn to do in their heads. But it takes practice. This skill can save you time in solving some quadratic equations, as the next lesson explains.

Questions

Covering the Reading

1. If a, b, and c are integers, when is $ax^2 + bx + c$ factorable? **when the discriminant, $b^2 - 4ac$, is a perfect square**

2. Consider $ax^2 + bx + c = (dx + e)(fx + g)$ for all values of x.
   a. The product of d and f is __?__. **a**
   b. The product of __?__ and __?__ is c. **e, g**

3. How can you check the factors of a quadratic trinomial? **Multiply the two binomials or substitute a number.**

In 4–11, **a.** determine whether the trinomial can be factored; **b.** if so, factor it. **a) See margin.**

4. $x^2 + 7x + 10$ **(x + 2)(x + 5)**
5. $x^2 + 21x + 110$ **(x + 10)(x + 11)**
6. $x^2 + 2x + 3$ **not factorable**
7. $y^2 + 10y + 9$ **(y + 9)(y + 1)**
8. $n^2 + 4n - 12$ **(n + 6)(n − 2)**
9. $t^2 - t - 30$ **(t + 5)(t − 6)**
10. $4x^2 - 12x - 7$ **(2x − 7)(2x + 1)**
11. $3x^2 + 11x - 4$ **(3x − 1)(x + 4)**

Applying the Mathematics

12. **a.** Factor $x^3 - 5x^2 + 6x$ into the product of a monomial and a trinomial. **x(x² − 5x + 6)**
    b. Complete the factoring by finding factors of the trinomial in part a. **x(x − 2)(x − 3)**

13. Find k if $8x^2 + 10x - 25 = (2x + k)(4x - k)$. **k = 5**

Review

In 14 and 15, determine whether the solutions to the equation are rational numbers. *(Lesson 12-7)*

14. $13x^2 - 63x - 10 = 0$ **Yes**
15. $x^2 + x = 1$ **No**

16. *Multiple choice* Which equation has more than one real solution? *(Lesson 12-6)* **(c)**
    (a) $x^2 - 22x + 121 = 0$
    (b) $9p^2 + 14p + 16 = 0$
    (c) $64z^2 - 32 = 0$
    (d) $w^2 + 1 = 0$

17. Solve $3x^2 - 5x + 1 = 0$ **a.** exactly; **b.** to the nearest tenth. *(Lesson 12-4)* **a) $\frac{5 \pm \sqrt{13}}{6}$; b) 1.4 or 0.2**

18. *Multiple choice* Which equation has the graph below? *(Lesson 12-1)* **(c)**
    (a) $y = \frac{1}{2}x^2$
    (b) $y = 2x^2$
    (c) $y = -2x^2$
    (d) $y = -\frac{1}{2}x^2$

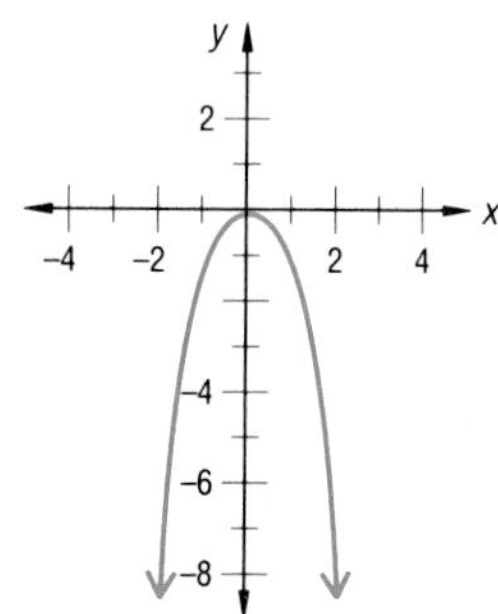

ADDITIONAL ANSWERS

4a. $7^2 - 4 \cdot 1 \cdot 10 = 9$ is a perfect square; yes

5a. $21^2 - 4 \cdot 1 \cdot 110 = 1$ is a perfect square; yes

6a. not factorable

7a. $10^2 - 4 \cdot 1 \cdot 9 = 64$ is a perfect square; yes

8a. $4^2 - 4 \cdot 1 \cdot (-12) = 64$ is a perfect square; yes

9a. $(-1)^2 - 4 \cdot 1 \cdot (-30) = 121$ is a perfect square; yes

10a. $(-12)^2 - 4 \cdot 4 \cdot (-7) = 256$ is a perfect square; yes

11a. $11^2 - 4 \cdot 3 \cdot (-4) = 169$ is a perfect square; yes

NAME ____________

LESSON **MASTER 12–7**
QUESTIONS ON **SPUR** OBJECTIVES

■**SKILLS** *Objective B (See pages 633–635 for objectives.)*
In 1–12, a. use the discriminant to determine which quadratic trinomials are factorable. b. If possible, factor.

1. $t^2 + t - 12$ (t + 4)(t − 3)
2. $r^2 + 16r + 15$ (r + 15)(r + 1)
3. $3x^2 - 7x + 4$ (3x − 4)(x − 1)
4. $n^2 - 7n - 18$ (n − 9)(n + 2)
5. $y^2 + 9y + 20$ (y + 4)(y + 5)
6. $24a^2 + 10a - 21$ (6a + 7)(4a − 3)
7. $12c^2 + 7c - 45$ (4c + 9)(3c − 5)
8. $3x^2 - 10x + 3$ (3x − 1)(x − 3)
9. $2x^2 - x - 10$ (2x − 5)(x + 2)
10. $5x^2 - 14 - 3x$ (5x + 7)(x − 3)
11. $6 - 25t + 4t^2$ (4t − 1)(t − 6)
12. $6y^2 - 4y - 3$ not factorable

In 13–18, a. factor the trinomial into the product of a monomial and a trinomial. b. Complete the factoring by finding the factors of the trinomial.

13. $x^3 - 3x^2 + 2x$
    a. x(x² − 3x + 2)
    b. x(x − 2)(x − 1)
14. $y^3 + 8y^2 + 12y$
    a. y(y² + 8y + 12)
    b. y(y + 6)(y + 2)
15. $2a^3 - 6a^2 - 8a$
    a. 2a(a² − 3a − 4)
    b. 2a(a − 4)(a + 1)
16. $r^4 + 8r^3 + 12r^2$
    a. r²(r² + 8r + 12)
    b. r²(r + 6)(r + 2)
17. $3t^3 - 12t^2 + 12t$
    a. 3t(t² − 4t + 4)
    b. 3t(t − 2)²
18. $5a^4 + 10a^3 + 5a^2$
    a. 5a²(a² + 2a + 1)
    b. 5a²(a + 1)²

110

NOTES ON QUESTIONS

Making Connections for Question 22: In stating the Zero Product Property, students are preparing for the next lesson.

FOLLOW-UP

MORE PRACTICE
For more questions on SPUR Objectives, use *Lesson Master 12-7,* shown on page 621.

EXTENSION
Extend **Example 2** by asking students to factor $x^2 + 9xy + 14y^2$. $[(x+2y)(x+7y)]$ Then ask: In general, if $ax^2 + bx + c = (dx + e) \cdot (fx + g)$, what will be the factors of $ax^2 + bxy + cy^2$? $[(dx + ey)(fx + gy)]$

EVALUATION
Alternative Assessment
You might wish to split the class into **small groups** and have each group make up factoring questions by multiplying two binomials. The other groups then try to figure out the factoring from the quadratic expression. This activity will give students practice in deduction of values as well as multiplication of binomials and will enable you to assess their understanding.

22. For any real numbers *a* and *b*, if the product of *a* and *b* is 0, then *a* = 0 or *b* = 0.

19. Here are 3 instances of a pattern. Describe the pattern using variables. *(Lesson 10-7)* **$(2a + 2b)(a - b) = 2(a^2 - b^2)$**

$$(72 + 100)(36 - 50) = 2(36^2 - 50^2)$$
$$(30 + 20)(15 - 10) = 2(15^2 - 10^2)$$
$$(2 + 1)(1 - 0.5) = 2(1^2 - 0.5^2)$$

In 20 and 21, give the slope and y-intercept for each line. *(Lesson 8-4)*

20. $y = \frac{1}{2}x$ **$m = \frac{1}{2}, b = 0$**

21. $8x - 5y = 1$ **$m = \frac{8}{5}, b = \frac{-1}{5}$**

22. State the Zero Product Property. *(Lesson 10-10)* **See margin.**

In 23–26, calculate the area of the shaded region. *(Lessons 4-1, 7-4)*

23. **$2x^2$**

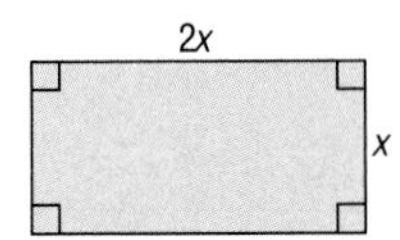

24. **24**

10
6
8

25. **5**

3
2
2
3

26. **$\sqrt{14}$**

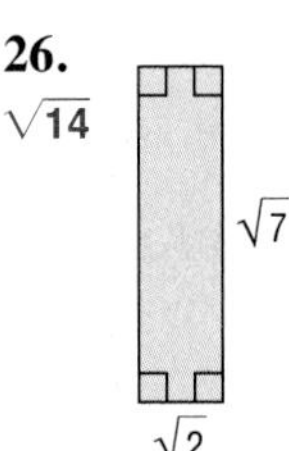

Exploration

27. The polynomial $x^3 + 6x^2 + 11x + 6$ can be factored into the form

$$(x + a)(x + b)(x + c).$$

Find a, b, and c. Hint: What is abc? **$abc = 6$; $(x + 1)(x + 2)(x + 3)$**

LESSON

12-8

Solving Some Quadratic Equations by Factoring

You already know that the Quadratic Formula will give you solutions to any quadratic equation you encounter — or show that the equation has no real solutions. There are lots of calculations involved in using the formula, however, so if you can factor a quadratic by sight and use the Zero Product Property to find solutions, you can save time and effort.

Example 1 Solve $x^2 - 6x - 27 = 0$.

Solution Since the coefficient of x^2 is 1, it is worth trying factoring. $1 \cdot 1 = 1$, so $x^2 - 6x - 27 = (x + \quad)(x + \quad)$. It is easy to see that 3 and -9 in the blanks yield the -6x and -27 needed. Thus,

$$(x + 3)(x - 9) = 0$$

Use the Zero Product Property and solve.

$$(x + 3) = 0 \quad \text{or} \quad (x - 9) = 0.$$
$$x = -3 \quad \text{or} \quad x = 9.$$

The solutions are -3 or 9.

Check
Substitute -3. Does $(-3)^2 - 6(-3) - 27 = 0$? $9 + 18 - 27 = 0$.
Substitute 9. Does $(9)^2 - 6(9) - 27 = 0$? $81 - 54 - 27 = 0$.
It checks.

Keep in mind that some equations have common monomial factors. By first factoring out the monomial, you can further factor the remaining expression.

LESSON 12-8

RESOURCES
■ Lesson Master 12-8

OBJECTIVES

C Solve quadratic equations by factoring.
G Use quadratic equations to solve real world problems.

TEACHING NOTES

Emphasize these two points: (1) one side of the equation must be zero before the Zero Product Property can be used, and (2) students should look for a common factor first.

Reading In **Example 3** the term *round-robin tournament* is used. In such a tournament each contestant (player or team) meets every other contestant in turn.

Alternate Approach You might ask students to write a quadratic equation when they are given its solutions. For instance, if the solutions are -5 and 7, an equation is $(x + 5)(x - 7) = 0$ or $x^2 - 2x - 35 = 0$. If the only solution is $-\frac{3}{4}$, an equation is $\left(x + \frac{3}{4}\right)\left(x + \frac{3}{4}\right) = 0$ or $16x^2 + 24x + 9 = 0$. By adding the same number to both sides of these equations or multiplying both sides by the same number, they can achieve other equivalent equations with the same solutions.

ADDITIONAL EXAMPLES

1. Solve $x^2 - 14x + 33 = 0$.
3, 11

2. Solve $10x^3 + 80x^2 - 200x = 0$.
0, 2, -10

3. In a sports league involving n teams, if every team is to play each other team twice (once on its field, once on theirs), there must be $n^2 - n$ games played. If a baseball league finds that it has time slots available for 72 games, how many teams can be formed?
$n^2 - n = 72$; 9 teams

Example 2 Solve $4x^3 - 18x^2 + 8x = 0$.

Solution This trinomial is not a quadratic, so in this form even the Quadratic Formula is of no use. Inspection shows, however, that $2x$ is a common monomial factor.

$$4x^3 - 18x^2 + 8x = 0$$
$$2x(2x^2 - 9x + 4) = 0$$

Now factor the quadratic expression. $(x - 4)$ and $(2x - 1)$ work out, so the equation can be rewritten as

$$2x(x - 4)(2x - 1) = 0.$$

Apply the Zero Product Property. The factor 2 cannot be 0, but any of the other three could be. So,

$$x = 0 \text{ or } (x - 4) = 0 \text{ or } (2x - 1) = 0.$$
$$x = 0 \text{ or } \quad x = 4 \text{ or } \quad 2x = 1$$
$$x = \tfrac{1}{2}.$$

The equation has three solutions: 0, 4, or $\frac{1}{2}$.

Check The check is left to you as Question 6.

The shortcut of solving equations by factoring may even help you answer some application questions more quickly.

Example 3 In a round robin chess tournament with n players, $\frac{n^2 - n}{2}$ names are needed. If there is time for 55 games, how many players can be entered in the tournament?

World Champion chess player Gary Kasparov

624

Solution You must solve $\frac{n^2 - n}{2} = 55$.

This is a quadratic equation, but it is not in standard form. Multiply both sides by 2 and then subtract 110 from both sides.

$$n^2 - n = 110$$
$$n^2 - n - 110 = 0$$

The quadratic expression can be factored.

$$(n - 11)(n + 10) = 0$$

Use the Zero Product Property and solve.

$$n - 11 = 0 \quad \text{or} \quad n + 10 = 0$$
$$n = 11 \quad \text{or} \quad n = -10$$

A negative number of players does not make sense in this situation. So 11 players can be entered.

Check Substitute. Does $\frac{11^2 - 11}{2} = 55$? Yes, it does.

Questions

Covering the Reading

1. To solve quadratic equations by factoring, first make sure the equation is in standard form. Then __?__ the quadratic and apply the __?__ Property to solve. **factor, Zero Product**

In 2 and 3, solve by factoring.

2. $x^2 + 2x - 3 = 0$ -3, 1
3. $y^2 - 4y - 5 = 0$ 5, -1

In 4 and 5, **a.** factor out the common monomial factor; **b.** solve the equation.

4. $7x^2 + 7x - 84 = 0$
5. $9x^3 + 12x^2 - 12x = 0$;

4a. $7(x^2 + x - 12) = 0$; b) -4, 3 5a. $3x(3x^2 + 4x - 4 = 0)$; b) 0, $\frac{2}{3}$, -2

6. Check each solution to Example 2. **See margin.**
7. In Example 3, if there is time for 66 games, how many players can be entered? 12

Applying the Mathematics

In 8–11, solve by factoring.

8. $a^2 - 5a = 50$ 10, -5
9. $26 + b^2 = -15b$ -13, -2
10. $x^2 + 620x = 0$ 0, -620
11. $20y^3 - 95y^2 - 25y = 0$ 0, $-\frac{1}{4}$, 5

NOTES ON QUESTIONS
Question 7: Students may be surprised at the answer. They may assume that the number of games is proportional to the number of players. Examining the formula should show that the rate is more complex than a simple proportion.

Error Analysis for Questions 8-11: Students may have difficulty because they are concentrating on factoring trinomials and overlook common monomial factoring.

ADDITIONAL ANSWERS
6. Does $4(0)^3 - 18(0)^2 + 8(0) = 0$? $0 - 0 + 0 = 0$; yes. Does $4(4)^3 - 18(4)^2 + 8(4) = 0$? $256 - 288 + 32 = 0$; yes. Does $4\left(\frac{1}{2}\right)^3 - 18\left(\frac{1}{2}\right)^2 + 8\left(\frac{1}{2}\right) = 0$? $\frac{4}{8} - \frac{18}{4} + \frac{8}{2} = 0$, $\frac{1}{2} - \frac{9}{2} + \frac{8}{2} = 0$; yes.

NAME ____________

LESSON **MASTER 12–8**
QUESTIONS ON **SPUR** OBJECTIVES

SKILLS *Objective C* *(See pages 633–635 for objectives.)*
In 1–14, solve by factoring.

1. $x^2 + 14x + 24 = 0$ $x = -12$ or $x = -2$
2. $a^2 - 4a - 21 = 0$ $a = -3$ or $a = 7$
3. $2y^2 + 5y - 3 = 0$ $y = -3$ or $y = \frac{1}{2}$
4. $2r^2 - 17r + 21 = 0$ $r = \frac{3}{2}$ or $r = 7$
5. $c^2 - 16 = 0$ $c = -4$ or $c = 4$
6. $k^2 - 64 = 0$ $k = -8$ or $k = 8$
7. $4t^2 + 15t = 4$ $t = -4$ or $t = \frac{1}{4}$
8. $6x^2 = x + 35$ $x = -\frac{7}{3}$ or $x = \frac{5}{2}$
9. $y^3 + 9y^2 + 20y = 0$ $y = -5$ or $y = -4$ or $y = 0$
10. $(n - 2)(n + 3) = 6$ $n = -4$ or $n = 3$
11. $(b + 1)(b + 5) = 45$ $b = -10$ or $b = 4$
12. $4d^3 + 11d^2 - 3d = 0$ $d = -3$ or $d = 0$ or $d = \frac{1}{4}$
13. $p^2 - 8p = 0$ $p = 0$ or $p = 8$
14. $a^3 - 9a^2 = 0$ $a = 0$ or $a = 9$

USES *Objective G*

15. In a round-robin tournament, 66 games were played. The expression
$$\frac{n^2 - n}{2}$$
gives the number of games played in the tournament for n teams. How many teams were in the tournament? 12 teams

16. One formula for finding the approximate stopping distance d (in feet) of an automobile going x mph on a wet road is
$$d = \frac{10x + x^2}{10}.$$
If it took 20 ft to stop a car, how fast was it going? 10 mph

111

NOTES ON QUESTIONS

Making Connections for Question 15: One approach is to express 20 as $5 \cdot 4$, then multiply $5(x - \frac{1}{5})$ and $4(x - \frac{1}{4})$ before using FOIL. This question is important to prepare students for the manipulation in Example 3 of Lesson 12-9.

Question 16(i): Students may be tempted to expand $(x - 1)^2$ before working with the equation. You might point out that it is easier to calculate values from the factored form.

Question 28: This question calls on students' notions of chunking.

FOLLOW-UP

MORE PRACTICE
For more questions on SPUR Objectives, use *Lesson Master 12-8,* shown on page 625.

In 12 and 13, solve by any method.

12. $4t^2 + 4t + 1 = 0$ $t = -\frac{1}{2}$ **13.** $9v = 2v^2 - 35$ $v = -\frac{5}{2}$ or 7

14. The height h in feet of a projectile after t seconds is given by $h = -16t^2 + 128t$. a) at 2 and 6 seconds
a. When is the projectile 192 feet above the ground?
b. When is the projectile on the ground? (Think: what is the value of h at ground level?) at 0 and 8 seconds

Review

15. Multiply: $20(x - \frac{1}{5})(x + \frac{1}{4})$. *(Lesson 10-4)* $20x^2 + x - 1$

16. Match each graph with its equation. *(Lessons 12-1, 7-1)*
(i) $y = (x - 1)^2$ (ii) $y - x = 1$ (iii) $-1 + x^2 = y$

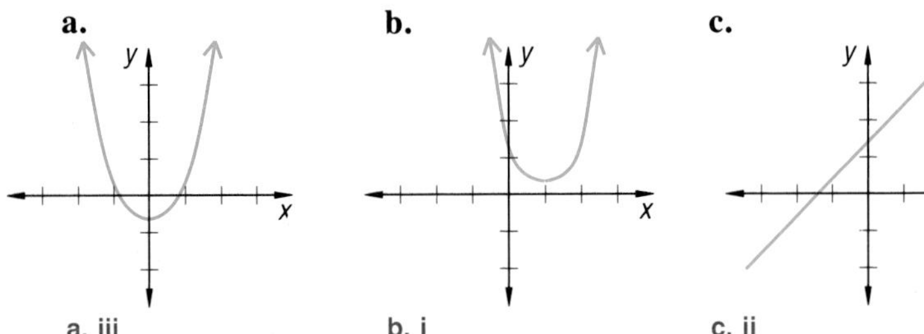

a. iii b. i c. ii

17. *True or false* $x^2 + x + 100 = 0$ has no real solutions. *(Lesson 12-4)* True

In 18–23, tell whether the number is rational or irrational. *(Lesson 12-6)*

18. $\sqrt{81}$ rational **19.** $3 + \sqrt{2}$ irrational **20.** 7.984 rational

21. $\sqrt{80}$ irrational **22.** $\sqrt{\frac{4}{9}}$ rational **23.** 0 rational

In 24–26, write the reciprocal. *(Lesson 4-3)*

24. $\frac{2x}{3y}$ $\frac{3y}{2x}$ **25.** $\frac{a + b}{5}$ $\frac{5}{a + b}$ **26.** $2.8q^2$ $\frac{1}{2.8q^2}$

27. Factor $\frac{1}{4}y^2 - 9$. *(Lesson 10-9)* $(\frac{1}{2}y - 3)(\frac{1}{2}y + 3)$

Exploration

28. Some trinomials that are not quadratics can be rewritten as quadratics and solved by the method of this lesson. For example, $x^4 - 3x^2 - 4 = (x^2)^2 - 3(x^2) - 4 = (x^2 - 4)(x^2 + 1)$. Use this idea to solve the following equations.
a. $x^4 - 10x^2 + 9 = 0$ 3, -3, 1, -1 **b.** $m^4 - 13m^2 + 36 = 0$ -2, 2, -3, 3

29. Make up some examples of quadratic equations of the form $ax^2 + bx + c = 0$ that can be solved by factoring and some that cannot.

Samples:

by factoring:	not by factoring:
$x^2 - x - 2 = 0$	$x^2 + 4x + 2 = 0$
$x^2 - 3x + 2 = 0$	$x^2 - 5x + 1 = 0$
$2x^2 - x - 15 = 0$	$x^2 + 5x + 1 = 0$

LESSON

12-9

The Factor Theorem

In the last two lessons you have been factoring $ax^2 + bx + c$ by trial and error. There is another way, using the Quadratic Formula. The idea is to compare the solutions to $ax^2 + bx + c = 0$ with the factors of $ax^2 + bx + c$.

The equation	The expression
$x^2 - 13x + 40 = 0$	$x^2 - 13x + 40$
has solutions 5 and 8.	has factors $x - 5$ and $x - 8$.

Factor Theorem for Quadratic Expressions:

If r is a solution of $ax^2 + bx + c = 0$, then $(x - r)$ is a factor of $ax^2 + bx + c$.

The Factor Theorem is true for any quadratic expression.

Example 1 6 and -19 are solutions to $x^2 + 13x - 114 = 0$. Write the factors of $x^2 + 13x - 114$.

Solution Since 6 and -19 are solutions, $(x - 6)$ and $(x - -19)$ are factors of $x^2 + 13x - 114$. These simplify to $(x - 6)$ and $(x + 19)$. That is, $x^2 + 13x - 114 = (x - 6)(x + 19)$.

Check $(x - 6)(x + 19) = x^2 + 19x - 6x - 114 = x^2 + 13x - 114$

Example 2 Factor $x^2 + 2x - 15$.

Solution Solve $x^2 + 2x - 15 = 0$ using the Quadratic Formula.
$a = 1, b = 2, c = -15$.

$$x = \frac{-2 \pm \sqrt{(2)^2 - 4 \cdot 1 \cdot -15}}{2 \cdot 1} = \frac{-2 \pm \sqrt{64}}{2} = \frac{-2 \pm 8}{2}$$

$$\frac{-2 + 8}{2} = \frac{6}{2} = 3 \text{ and } \frac{-2 - 8}{2} = \frac{-10}{2} = -5.$$

Because the solutions are 3 and -5, the Factor Theorem gives $(x - 3)$ and $(x - -5)$ as factors. So $x^2 + 2x - 15 = (x - 3)(x + 5)$.

Check $(x - 3)(x + 5) = x^2 - 3x + 5x - 15 = x^2 + 2x - 15$.

LESSON 12-9

RESOURCES
- Lesson Master 12-9
- Computer Master 27

OBJECTIVE

B Factor quadratic trinomials.

TEACHING NOTES

Your students may be puzzled at first that $x - r$, not $x + r$, is a factor of $ax^2 + bx + c = 0$ when r is a solution. Use a simple example at first; for instance, the solutions of $(x - 2)(x - 3) = 0$ are 2 and 3.

Making Connections Lesson 12-7 states that an expression of the form $ax^2 + bx + c$ is factorable if an only if $b^2 - 4ac$ is a perfect square. By that we mean "factorable over the set of integers." You may want to relate that idea to the Factor Theorem. If the discriminant is a perfect square, then the roots are rational. With the choice of the proper constant factor, the factors then can be expressed with integral coefficients.

ADDITIONAL EXAMPLES

1. 12 and 23 are the solutions of $x^2 - 35x + 276 = 0$. Use this information to factor $x^2 - 35x + 276$.
$(x - 12)(x - 23)$

2. Factor $x^2 + 21x - 270$.
$(x + 30)(x - 9)$

3. Factor $8x^2 + 18x - 5$.
$(4x - 1)(2x + 5)$

NOTES ON QUESTIONS

Question 6: The Factor Theorem is particularly useful because 24 and 36 have so many factors. The trial-and-error method would be particularly tedious.

Questions 7 and 8: Your students may ask when the property given here holds. The proof follows for the case where $a \geq c$. If $a < c$, the method is similar, but $c - a$ is the value of the square root.

Since $a + b + c = 0$, we know $b = -a - c$. Substituting into the quadratic formula gives

$$x = \frac{a + c \pm \sqrt{(-a - c)^2 - 4ac}}{2a}$$

$$= \frac{a + c \pm \sqrt{a^2 - 2ac + c^2}}{2a}$$

$$= \frac{a + c \pm \sqrt{(a - c)^2}}{2a}$$

$$= \frac{a + c \pm (a - c)}{2a}$$

Thus $x = \frac{2a}{2a} = 1$ or $x = \frac{2c}{2a}$. So 1 is a solution.

Questions 13-15: Some related problems are those in which a quadratic equation and one solution are given, and students are asked to find the other solution. For instance, one solution of $2x^2 - 13x + 15 = 0$ is 5; find the other. $(\frac{3}{2})$

Questions 19 and 20: The path of a cannonball is an important topic in the history of mathematics. When cannons were introduced during the Renaissance, it became important to be able to predict the paths of their projectiles. Galileo was the first to establish that the path is approximately a parabola. Tartaglia and other important mathematicians also studied this path.

Of course you could have factored the quadratic in Example 2 in your head using the method of Lesson 12-7. For some quadratics, however, there are many possible factors and the Factor Theorem may save time.

When the coefficient of x^2 is not 1, the process requires a step to multiply by this coefficient. This step is seen in Example 3.

Example 3 Factor $12x^2 - x - 6$.

Solution Both 12 and 6 have many pairs of factors. So solve $12x^2 - x - 6 = 0$ and use the Factor Theorem.

$$x = \frac{-(-1) \pm \sqrt{(-1)^2 - 4 \cdot 12 \cdot -6}}{2 \cdot 12}$$

$$= \frac{1 \pm \sqrt{1 + 288}}{24}$$

$$= \frac{1 \pm \sqrt{289}}{24}$$

$$= \frac{1 \pm 17}{24}$$

$$x = \frac{1 + 17}{24} = \frac{18}{24} = \frac{3}{4} \text{ or } x = \frac{1 - 17}{24} = \frac{-16}{24} = \frac{-2}{3}$$

Notice that $x - \frac{3}{4}$ and $x + \frac{2}{3}$ are factors but there is a constant factor also.

$$12x^2 - x - 6 = 12(x - \tfrac{3}{4})(x + \tfrac{2}{3})$$

Factor the 12 into $4 \cdot 3$ to match the denominators. (This is always possible.)

$$= 4(x - \tfrac{3}{4}) \cdot 3(x + \tfrac{2}{3})$$
$$= (4x - 3)(3x + 2)$$

Questions

Covering the Reading

1. State the Factor Theorem for quadratic expressions. **If r is a solution of $ax^2 + bx + c = 0$, then $(x - r)$ is a factor of $ax^2 + bx + c$.**

2. -8 and 13 are solutions to $x^2 - 5x - 104 = 0$.
   a. Write the factors of $x^2 - 5x - 104$. **$(x + 8)(x - 13)$**
   b. Check your work using the FOIL algorithm. **$(x + 8)(x - 13) = x^2 - 13x + 8x - 104 = x^2 - 5x - 104$**

In 3–6, factor by first solving the corresponding quadratic equation.

3. $x^2 - 7x + 10$ **$(x - 2)(x - 5)$**
4. $y^2 - 11y - 60$ **$(y - 15)(y + 4)$**
5. $5k^2 - 8k - 4$ **$(5k + 2)(k - 2)$**
6. $24t^2 + 59t + 36$ **$(3t + 4)(8t + 9)$**

Applying the Mathematics

In 7 and 8, use this information. Whenever the coefficients a, b, and c of the quadratic equation $ax^2 + bx + c = 0$ sum to zero, then 1 is a solution to the equation.

7. If 1 is a solution to $ax^2 + bx + c = 0$, then what is a factor? $(x - 1)$

8. Factor $98x^2 - 99x + 1$. $(x - 1)(98x - 1)$

In 9–12, factor using any method.

9. $x^2 + 16x + 64$ $(x + 8)^2$

10. $y^2 + 3y - 700$ $(y + 28)(y - 25)$

11. $16m^3 - 44m^2 + 120m$ $4m(4m^2 - 11m + 30)$

12. $12 + 25a + 12a^2$ $(4a + 3)(3a + 4)$

In 13–15, a quadratic expression is given with one of its factors. Find the other factor.

13. $x^2 + 7x + 6$; $(x + 1)$ $x + 6$

14. $2x^2 - 17x + 8$; $(2x - 1)$ $x - 8$

15. $3x^2 - 7x + 4$; $(x - 1)$ $3x - 4$

Review

In 16 and 17, solve. *(Lesson 12-7)*

16. $x^2 - 15x + 14 = 0$ 1, 14

17. $5x^3 + 15x^2 = 50x$ 0, -5, 2

18. How many real solutions does $x^2 - 2x + 2 = 0$ have? *(Lesson 12-4)* none

In 19 and 20, a cannon is set so that the path of its cannonball is described by the equation $y = -136x^2 + 54x + 5$ where y is the cannonball's distance above the ground (in meters) and x is the corresponding distance along the ground (in kilometers).

19. How high is the cannonball when it is 300 m along the ground from the point of firing? *(Lesson 12-5)* 8.96 meters high

20. How far will the cannonball travel before it hits the ground? $\approx$.475 kilometers = 475 meters

NAME ______

LESSON **MASTER 12–9**
QUESTIONS ON **SPUR** OBJECTIVES

■**SKILLS** *Objective B (See pages 633–635 for objectives.)*
In 1–4, given that p and q are solutions to the quadratic equation, write the factors of the quadratic expression.

1. $x^2 - 11x - 42 = 0$; $p = 14$, $q = -3$ $(x - 14)(x + 3)$
2. $y^2 - 28y + 96 = 0$; $p = 4$, $q = 24$ $(y - 4)(y - 24)$
3. $2a^2 - a - 36 = 0$; $p = -4$, $q = \frac{9}{2}$ $(a + 4)(2a - 9)$
4. $3c^2 + 22c + 24 = 0$; $p = -6$, $q = -\frac{4}{3}$ $(c + 6)(3c + 4)$

In 5–8, a quadratic equation is given with one of its solutions. Use this information to factor.

5. $x^2 - 39x + 108 = 0$; 3 $(x - 3)(x - 36)$
6. $t^2 - 48t + 540 = 0$; 18 $(t - 18)(t - 30)$
7. $4a^2 - 11a - 45 = 0$; $-\frac{9}{4}$ $(4a + 9)(a - 5)$
8. $12x^2 - 43x + 36 = 0$; $\frac{4}{3}$ $(3x - 4)(4x - 9)$

In 9–11, factor the expression as much as possible.

9. $2y^3 - 3y + y^2$ $y(y - 1)(2y + 3)$
10. $15x^3 + 41x^2 + 14x$ $x(5x + 2)(3x + 7)$
11. $c^4 - 36c^3 + 320c^2$ $c^2(c - 20)(c - 16)$

FOLLOW-UP

MORE PRACTICE
For more questions on SPUR Objectives, use *Lesson Master 12-9,* shown on page 629.

EXTENSION
1. You could show your students how the Factor Theorem can be used to factor an expression like $x^2 - 5x + 3$ that cannot be factored over the integers. Solving $x^2 - 5x + 3 = 0$ by using the Quadratic Formula gives $x = \frac{5 \pm \sqrt{13}}{2}$. The expression factors into $\left(x - \frac{5 + \sqrt{13}}{2}\right)\left(x - \frac{5 - \sqrt{13}}{2}\right)$.

2. You could ask your students to graph $y = a(x - d)(x - e)$ holding a constant but using different values of d and e. Ask what relation d and e have to the graph. (They are the x-intercepts.) This is another instance in which the factored form is most convenient, not just for yielding information but also for calculation.

ADDITIONAL ANSWERS
27a.

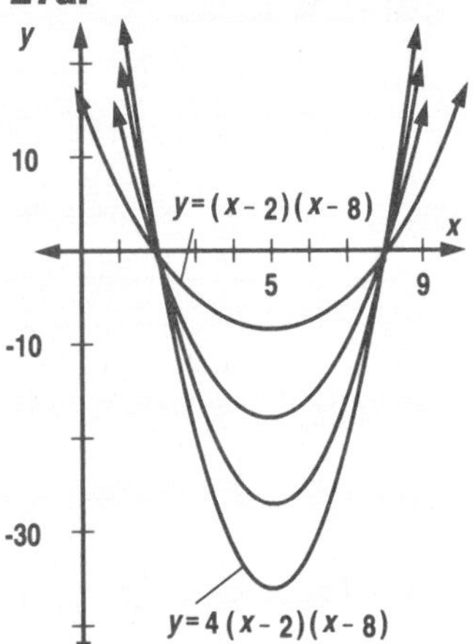

All these parabolas open up, all have axis of symmetry $x = 5$, all contain (2, 0) and (8, 0).

27b. Same as above, except parabolas open down.

In 21 and 22, a thermometer is taken from a room temperature of 70°F to a point outside where it is 45°F. After t minutes, the thermometer reading D is approximated by $D = 24(1 - .04t)^2 + 45$.

21. What temperature will the thermometer read after 10 minutes? *(Lesson 12-2)* **≈53.6°F**

22. How long will it take the thermometer to get down to 45°F? *(Lessons 12-2, 7-6)* **25 minutes**

23. The total cost of a car is $3869 including 6% sales tax. What is the cost of the car before tax? *(Lesson 6-3)* **$3650**

24. Simplify $(7b + 8) - (2 - 3b)$. *(Lesson 6-5)* **$10b + 6$**

25. Donna has $75 and is saving $5 per week. Her brother has $48 and is saving $8 per week. In how many weeks will her brother have saved more money? *(Lesson 6-7)* **as soon as he passes 9 weeks**

26. *Multiple choice* Choose the equation of the line graphed below. *(Lesson 7-2)* **(a)**
(a) $y = x - 2$
(b) $y = x + 2$
(c) $y = 2 - x$
(d) $y = 2x$

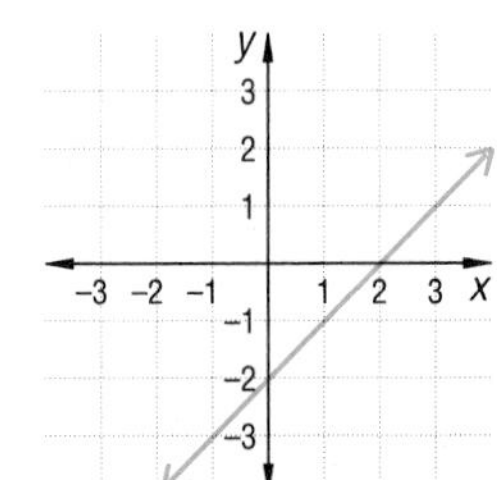

Exploration

27. Graph $y = a(x - 2)(x - 8)$ for $a = 1, 2, 3,$ and 4.
a. What do these parabolas have in common? **See margin.**
b. Explore whether the same property holds when a is negative. **See margin.**

630

Summary

This chapter discusses graphs and equations involving quadratic expressions. A quadratic expression is an expression that can be put in the form $ax^2 + bx + c$. These expressions describe the shapes of trajectories and are found in area and other formulas.

A quadratic equation is an equation equivalent to $ax^2 + bx + c = 0$. The solutions to that equation are found by the Quadratic Formula.

$$x = \frac{-b \pm \sqrt{b^2 - 4ac}}{2a}$$

The discriminant of a quadratic equation $ax^2 + bx + c = 0$ is $b^2 - 4ac$. If the discriminant is positive, there are two real solutions; if zero, there is one solution; if negative, there are no real solutions. If a, b, and c are integers and $b^2 - 4ac$ is a perfect square, then the solutions are rational and the expression $ax^2 + bx + c$ can be factored.

If r is a solution of $ax^2 + bx + c = 0$, then $(x-r)$ is a factor. Thus knowing the roots, you can find the factors of a quadratic expression.

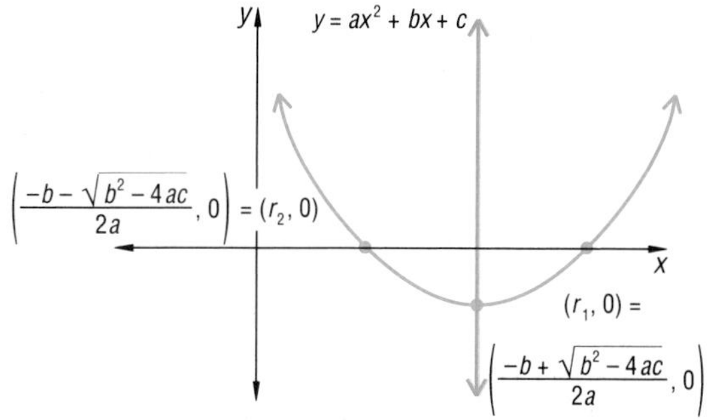

The graph of $y = ax^2 + bx + c$ is a parabola. This parabola is symmetric through the vertical line through the vertex. If $a > 0$, the parabola opens up. If $a < 0$, the parabola opens down. The Quadratic Formula gives the x-intercepts of the parabola if there are any.

Vocabulary

Below are the most important terms and phrases for this chapter. You should be able to give a general description and a specific example of each.

Lesson 12-1
parabola
symmetric
axis of symmetry
vertex
STEP command

Lesson 12-2
automatic grapher
window, default window
zoom feature

Lesson 12-4
quadratic equation
Quadratic Formula
standard form of a quadratic equation

Lesson 12-5
discriminant
Discriminant Property

Lesson 12-6
rational number, irrational number

Lesson 12-9
Factor Theorem for Quadratic Expressions

SUMMARY

The Summary gives an overview of the entire chapter and provides an opportunity for students to consider the material as a whole. Thus, the Summary can be used to help students relate the concepts presented in the chapter.

VOCABULARY

Terms, symbols, and properties are listed by lesson to provide a checklist of things a student must know. Emphasize to students that they should read the vocabulary list carefully before starting the Progress Self-Test. If students do not understand the meaning of a term, they should refer back to the indicated lesson.

Definitions or descriptions of all terms in the vocabulary list may be found in the Glossary.

ADDITIONAL ANSWERS
16a. sample:

x	-2	-1	0	1	2
y	-8	-2	0	-2	-8

16b.

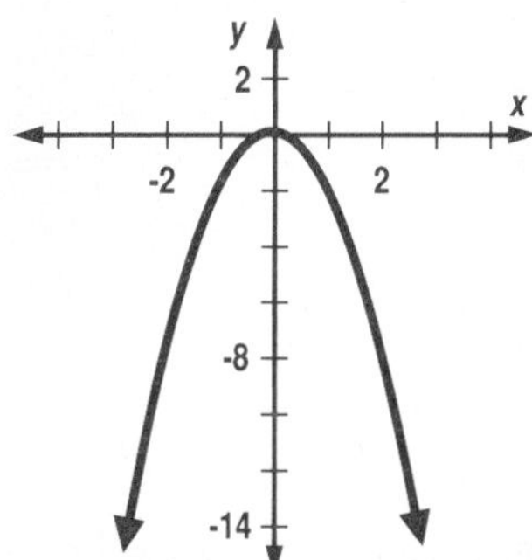

17a. sample:

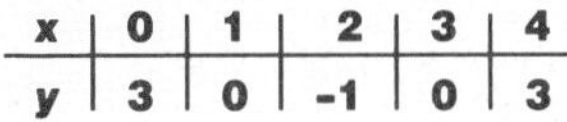

x	0	1	2	3	4
y	3	0	-1	0	3

We cannot overemphasize the importance of these end-of-chapter materials. It is at this point that the material "gels" for many students, allowing them to solidify skills and understanding. In general, student performance should be markedly improved after these pages.

USING THE PROGRESS SELF-TEST

Assign the Progress Self-Test as a one-night assignment. Worked-out *solutions* for all questions are in the Selected Answers section at the back of the student book. Encourage students to take the Progress Self-Test honestly, grade themselves, and then be prepared to discuss the test in class.

Advise students to pay special attention to those Chapter Review questions (pages 633–635) which correspond to questions missed on the Progress Self-Test. A chart provided in the Selected Answers section in the student text keys the Progress Self-Test questions to the lettered SPUR Objectives in the Chapter Review or to the Vocabulary. It also keys the questions to the corresponding lessons where the material is covered.

16a, b, 17a. See margin, page 631.

17b.

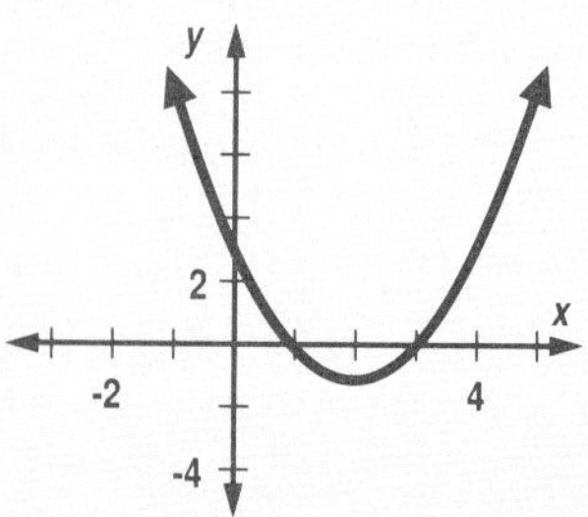

19. a number that can be written as the ratio of two integers

Progress Self-Test

Take this test as you would take a test in class. Then check your work with the solution in the Selected Answers section in the back of the book.

In 1 and 2, give the exact solutions to the equation.

1. $x^2 - 9x + 20 = 0$ $x = 4$ or $x = 5$

2. $5y^2 - 3y = 11$ $\frac{3 \pm \sqrt{229}}{10}$

3. Find a simpler equation that has the same solutions as $18z^2 - 3z + 24 = 0$. $6z^2 - z + 8 = 0$

In 4–7, find all real solutions. Approximate answers to the nearest hundredth.

4. $k^2 - 6k - 3 = 0$ $k = 6.46$ or $k = -0.46$

5. $3r^2 + 15r + 8 = 0$ $r = -0.61$ or $r = -4.39$

6. $8x^2 - 7x = -11$ no real solution

7. $z^2 = 16z - 64$ $z = 8$

8. *True or false* The solutions to $8x^2 - 18x - 5 = 0$ are rational. True

9. *True or false* The parabola $y = 3x^2 - 7x - 35$ opens down. False

10. If -2 and 18 are solutions to $x^2 - 16x - 36 = 0$, what are the factors of $x^2 - 16x - 36$? $(x + 2)(x - 18)$

In 11 and 12, factor.

11. $x^2 + 8x + 19$ The equation has no solutions and the expression does not factor.

12. $x^2 - 12x + 35$ $(x - 7)(x - 5)$

13. Solve $x^2 - x - 42 = 0$ by factoring. $x = 7$ or $x = -6$

In 14 and 15, Harry tosses a ball to Ferdinand who is 20 yards away. At x yards away from Harry, the ball is at height h feet, where

$$h = -.07(x - 10)^2 + 12.$$

14. If Melody is 2 yards in front of Ferdinand, how high is the ball when it passes by her? ≈7.5 ft

15. Ferdinand misses the ball and it falls to the ground. To the nearest yard, how far did it go? ≈23.09 yds

In 16 and 17, **a.** make a table of values; **b.** graph the equation.

16. $y = -2x^2$ See margin.

17. $y = x^2 - 4x + 3$ See margin.

18. *Multiple choice* Which of these is the graph of $y = 2.5x^2$? (a)

(a)

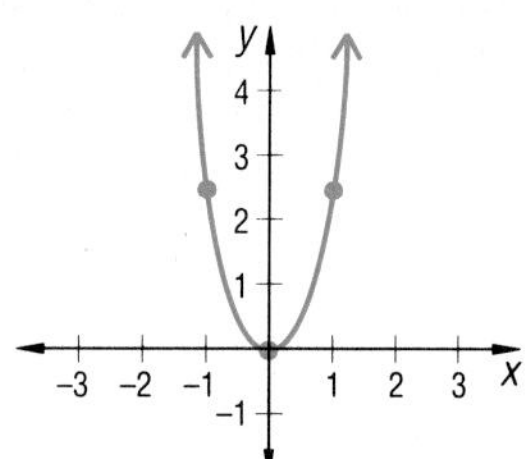

(b)

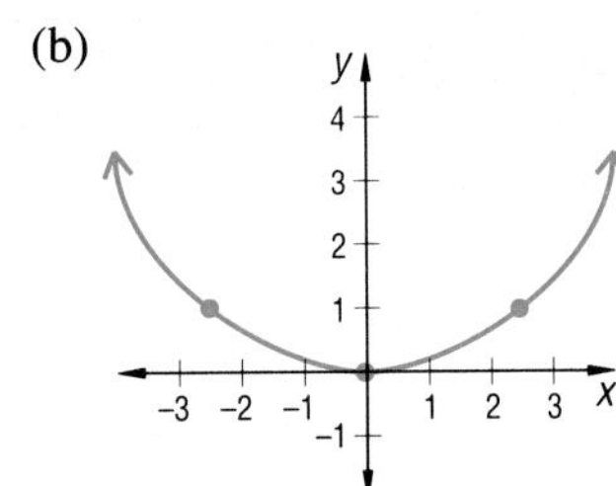

19. Define: rational number. See margin.

20. *Multiple choice* Which number is rational?
(a) $\sqrt{23}$ (b) $\sqrt{24}$ (c) $\sqrt{25}$ (d) $\sqrt{26}$ (c)

Chapter Review

Questions on SPUR Objectives

SPUR stands for **S**kills, **P**roperties, **U**ses, and **R**epresentations. The Chapter Review questions are grouped according to the SPUR Objectives for this chapter.

SKILLS deals with the procedures used to get answers.

Objective A. *Solve quadratic equations using the Quadratic Formula.* *(Lessons 12-4, 12-5)*

In 1–4, give the exact solutions to the equation.

1. $6y^2 + 7y - 20 = 0$ $-\frac{5}{2}, \frac{4}{3}$
2. $x^2 + 7x + 12 = 0$ -3, -4
3. $4a^2 - 13a = 12$ 4, $-\frac{3}{4}$
4. $-q^2 - 6q + 12 = -4$ -8, 2

In 5 and 6, find a simpler equation that has the same solutions as the given equation. Then solve. **See below.**

5. $10m^2 - 50m + 30 = 0$
6. $20y^2 + 14y - 24 = 0$

In 7–14, solve when possible. Approximate irrational answers to the nearest hundredth.

7. $k^2 - 7k - 2 = 0$ 7.27, -0.27
8. $2m^2 + m - 3 = 0$ 1, $-\frac{3}{2}$
9. $22a^2 + 2a + 3 = 0$ no real solution
10. $0 = x^2 + 10x + 25$ -5
11. $13k^2 + k = 2$ 0.36, -0.43
12. $16x^2 + 8x = -5$ no real solutions
13. $z^2 = 9z - 14$ 2, 7
14. $14y - 3 = 2y^2$ 6.78, 0.22

5a) $m^2 - 5m + 3 = 0$; b) $\frac{5 \pm \sqrt{13}}{2}$, ≈4.3 or ≈.7
6a) $10y^2 + 7y - 12 = 0$; b) $\frac{4}{5}$ or $-\frac{3}{2}$

Objective B. *Factor quadratic trinomials.* *(Lessons 12-7, 12-9)*

In 15–20, factor.

15. $x^2 + 5x - 6$ $(x + 6)(x - 1)$
16. $3y^2 + 2y - 8$ $(3y - 4)(y + 2)$
17. $10a^2 - 19a + 7$ $(5a - 7)(2a - 1)$
18. $12m^3 + 117m^2 + 81m$ $3m(4m + 3)(m + 9)$
19. $x + 5x^2 - 6$ $(5x + 6)(x - 1)$
20. $-3 - 2k + 8k^2$ $(4k - 3)(2k + 1)$
21. Given that -3 and 17 are solutions to $x^2 - 14x - 51 = 0$, write the factors of $x^2 - 14x - 51$. $(x + 3)(x - 17)$
22. Factor $x^2 + 5x + 4$ by first solving $x^2 + 5x + 4 = 0$. Solutions −1 and -4; factors: $(x + 1)(x + 4)$

Objective C. *Solve quadratic equations by factoring.* *(Lesson 12-8)*

In 23–26, solve by factoring.

23. $6y^2 + y - 2 = 0$ $\frac{1}{2}, -\frac{2}{3}$
24. $z^2 + 7z = -12$ -3, -4
25. $x^2 - 2x = 0$ 0, 2
26. $0 = 16m^2 - 8m + 1$ $\frac{1}{4}$

PROPERTIES deal with the principles behind the mathematics.

Objective D. *Recognize properties of the parabola.* *(Lessons 12-1, 12-5)*

27. What shape is the graph of $y = -6x^2$? a parabola
28. *True or False* The parabola $y = -2x^2 + 3x + 1$ opens down. True
29. What equation must you solve to find the x-intercepts of the parabola $y = ax^2 + bx + c$? $ax^2 + bx + c = 0$
30. *True or false* The graph of $y = x^2 + 2x + 2$ intersects the x-axis twice. False

RESOURCES
- Chapter 12 Test, Form A
- Chapter 12 Test, Form B
- Chapter 12 Test, Cumulative Form

CHAPTER REVIEW

The main objectives for the chapter are organized here into sections corresponding to the four main types of understanding this book promotes: Skills, Properties, Uses, and Representations.

USING THE CHAPTER REVIEW

Whereas end-of-chapter material may be considered optional in some texts, in *Algebra* we have selected these objectives and questions with the expectation that they will be covered. Students should be able to answer these questions with about 85% accuracy after studying the chapter.

You may assign these questions over a single night to help students prepare for a test the next day, or you may assign the questions over a two-day period.

If you work the questions over two days, then we recommend assigning the *evens* for homework the first night so that students get feedback in class the next day, then assigning the *odds* the night before the test so the students can use the answers provided in the book.

ADDITIONAL ANSWERS

49a. sample:

x	y
-2	12
-1	3
0	0
1	3
2	12

49a. See margin, page 633.
49b.

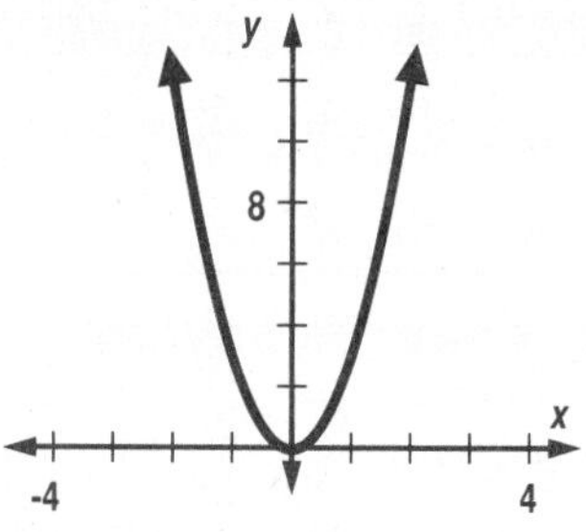

50a. sample:

x	y
-2	-2
-1	$-\frac{1}{2}$
0	0
1	$-\frac{1}{2}$
2	-2

50b.

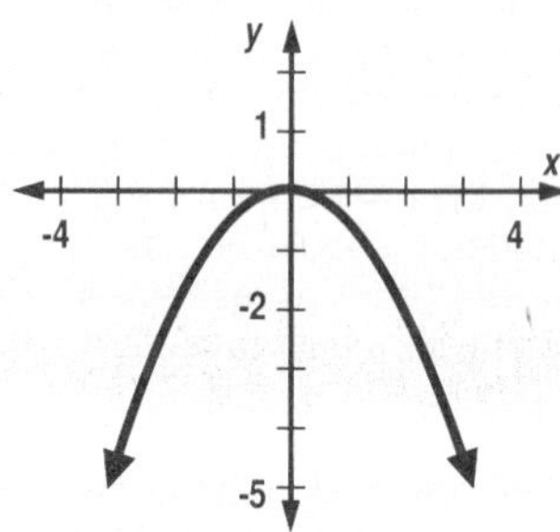

51a. sample:

x	y
-4	2
-3	0
-2	0
-1	2
0	6

51b.

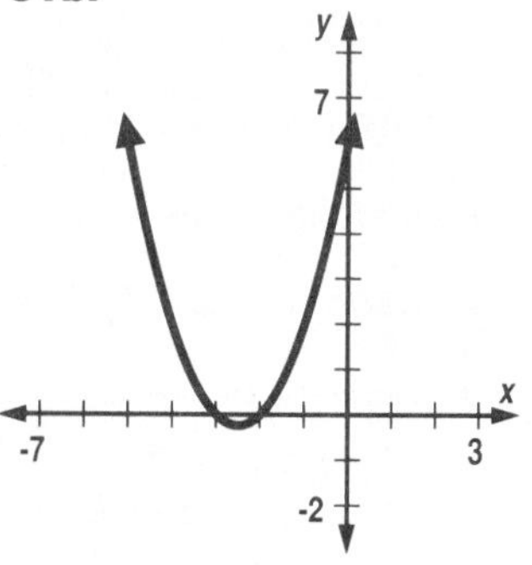

52a. sample:

x	y
-2	0
-1	-3
0	-4
1	-3
2	0

Objective E. *Recognize properties of quadratic equations. (Lessons 12-4, 12-5)*

31. Give two solutions to the sentence $ax^2 + bx + c = 0$. $\frac{-b \pm \sqrt{b^2 - 4ac}}{2a}$

32. *True or false* Some quadratic equations have no real solutions. True

33. *True or false* Any quadratic equation can be solved using the Quadratic Formula.

34. If a quadratic equation has solutions which are rational, the discriminant is a _?_.
33) True; 34) perfect square

In 35–38, use the discriminant to determine the number of real solutions to the equation.

35. $2x^2 - 3x + 4 = 0$ no real solution

36. $a^2 = 3a + 8$ two real solutions

37. $9d = 40 + 8d^2$ no real solution

38. $n(n + 1) = -5$ no real solution

Objective F. *Determine whether a number is rational or irrational. (Lesson 12-6)*

In 39–44, tell whether the number is rational.

39. $\sqrt{2}$ irrational **40.** 7.0707 rational

41. $\frac{1}{3}$ rational **42.** -86 rational

43. $\pi + 1$ irrational **44.** $\sqrt{9}$ rational

USES deal with applications of mathematics in real situations.

Objective G. *Use the parabola and quadratic equations to solve real world problems. (Lesson 12-2, 12-3, 12-8)*

45. Consider again the quarterback in Lesson 12-2 who tosses a football to a receiver 40 yards downfield. The ball is at height h feet, x yards downfield where $h = -\frac{1}{40}(x - 20)^2 + 16$. If a defender is 6 yards in front of the receiver, 34 yards
a. how far is he from the quarterback?
b. Would the defender have a chance to deflect the ball? Yes

46. When a ball is thrown into the air with initial upward velocity of 20 meters per second, its approximate height y above the ground after x seconds is given by $y = 20x - 5x^2$. When will the ball hit the ground? 4 seconds

47. A golf ball was hit on the moon. Suppose that the height h meters of the ball t seconds after it was hit is described by $h = -.8t^2 + 10t$. At what times was the ball at a height of 20 meters? 2.5 and 10 sec

48. Refer to the graph below. It shows the height h in feet of a ball, t seconds after it is thrown from ground level at a speed of 64 feet per second.
a. Estimate from the graph at what height the ball will be after 1 second. ≈45 feet
b. Estimate from the graph when the ball will reach a height of 35 feet.
≈0.8 or ≈3.2 seconds

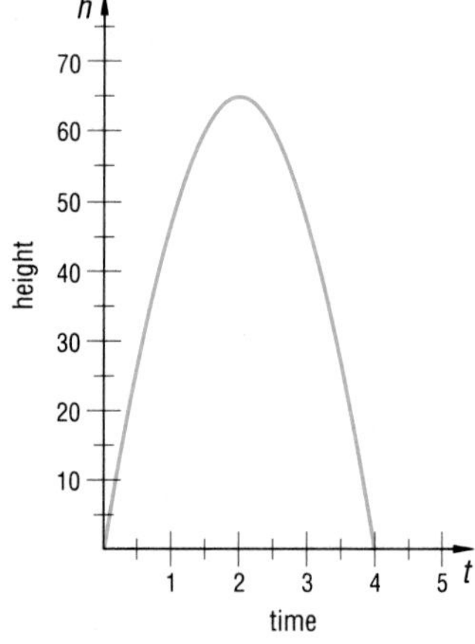

REPRESENTATIONS deal with pictures, graphs, or objects that illustrate concepts.

Objective H. *Graph parabolas. (Lessons 12-1, 12-2)*

In 49–52, **a.** make a table of values; **b.** graph the equation. **See margin.**

49. $y = 3x^2$

50. $y = -\frac{1}{2}x^2$

51. $y = x^2 + 5x + 6$

52. $y = x^2 - 4$

53. *Multiple choice* Which equation has the given graph? **(b)**

(a) $y = -4x^2$

(b) $y = \frac{-1}{4}x^2$

(c) $y = 4x^2$

(d) $y = \frac{1}{4}x^2$

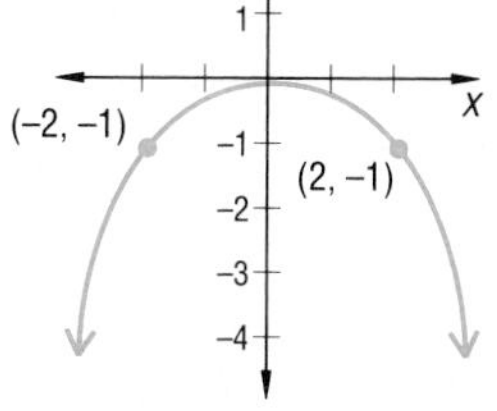

54. *Multiple choice* Which of these is the graph of $y = x^2 + 4x + 3$? **(a)**

(a)

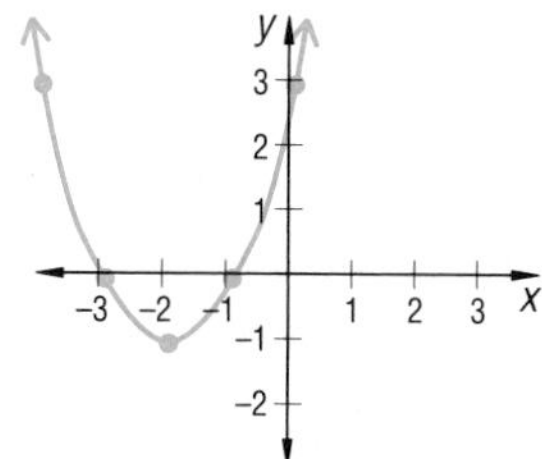

(b)

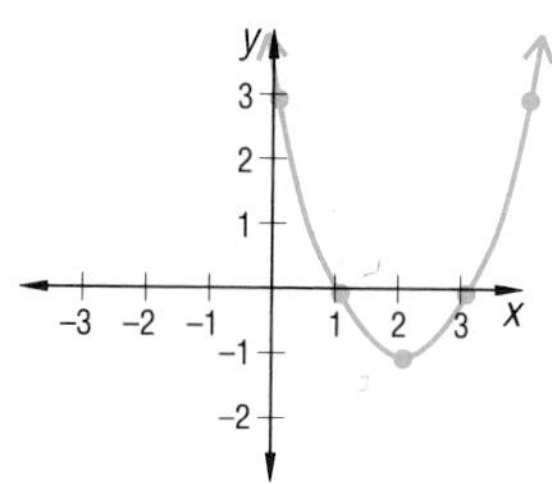

55. Describe the graphing window shown below. **$-35 \le x \le 35$; $-20 \le y \le 10$**

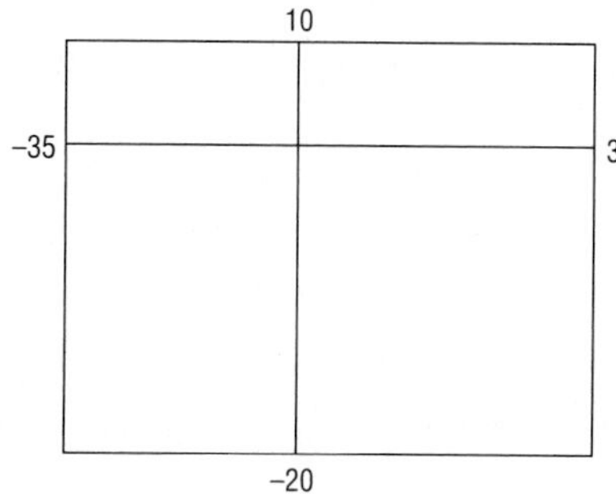

56. Consider $y = 2x^2 - 11.8x + 17$. **See margin.**

a. Graph this parabola using an automatic grapher.

b. Estimate the coordinates of its vertex.

c. Estimate the values of its x-intercepts.

EVALUATION

Three tests are provided for this chapter in the Teacher's Resource File. Chapter 12 Test, Forms A and B, cover just Chapter 12. The third test is Chapter 12 Test, Cumulative Form. About 50% of this test covers Chapter 12; 25% covers Chapter 11, and 25% covers earlier chapters. For more information on grading, see *General Teaching Suggestions: Grading* on page T44 in the Teacher's Edition.

ASSIGNMENT RECOMMENDATION

On the day your students take the chapter test, we suggest you make an assignment in the first section of the next chapter.

52b.

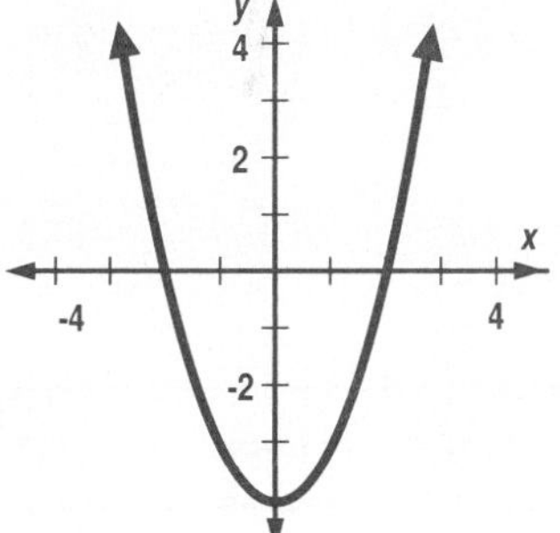

56a.

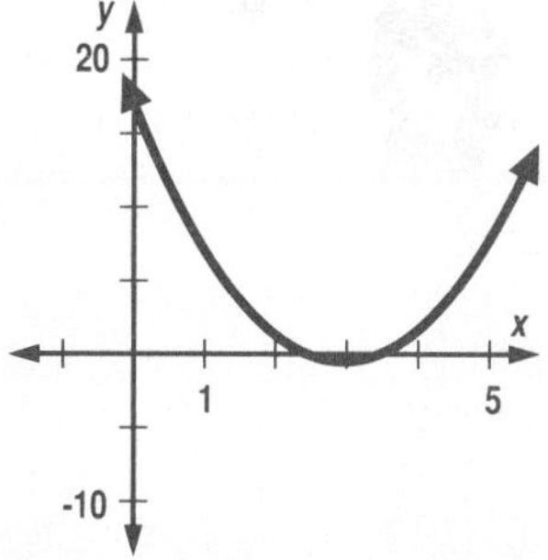

56b. (3, -.5) [Actual = (2.95, -.405).]

56c. (2.5, 0), (3.4, 0)

CHAPTER 13 FUNCTIONS

DAILY PACING CHART 13

DAILY PACING CHART CHAPTER 13

Students in the Full Course should complete the entire text by the end of the year. Students in the Minimal Course spend more time to complete lessons that are combined with quizzes and more time to consider the Chapter Review. Therefore, these students may not complete all the chapters in the text.

DAY	MINIMAL COURSE	FULL COURSE
1	13-1	13-1
2	13-2	13-2
3	13-3	13-3
4	13-4	13-4
5	Quiz (TRF); Start 13-5.	Quiz (TRF); 13-5
6	Finish 13-5.	13-6
7	13-6	13-7
8	13-7	Progress Self-Test
9	Progress Self-Test	Chapter Review
10	Chapter Review	Chapter Test (TRF)
11	Chapter Review	Comprehensive Test (TRF)
12	Chapter Test (TRF)	
13	Comprehensive Test (TRF)	

TESTING OPTIONS

TESTING OPTIONS

- Quiz for Lessons 13-1 Through 13-4
- Chapter 13 Test, Form A
- Chapter 13 Test, Form B
- Chapter 13 Test, Cumulative Form
- Comprehensive Test, Chapters 1–13

INDIVIDUAL DIFFERENCES

PROVIDING FOR INDIVIDUAL DIFFERENCES

The student text is written for the *average* student. The program, however, can be adapted for less capable and for more capable students.

For those students who need more practice, a blackline master (in the Teacher's Resource File) is provided for each lesson. The Teacher's Edition frequently provides Error Analysis and Alternate Approach features to provide additional instructional strategies for those students who do not readily grasp the material.

For students who require additional challenge, Extension activities are regularly provided in the Teacher's Edition.

OBJECTIVES ■ CHAPTER 13

Students should master the chapter objectives by the time they complete the chapter. To ensure objective mastery, there is continual review built into each set of lesson questions. After students complete the chapter lessons, they assess their mastery on the Progress Self-Test. Then they do the Chapter Review and pay special attention to those questions that match the objectives missed on the Progress Self-Test. Students can get extra practice on these objectives by using the master for each lesson in the Teacher's Resource File.

OBJECTIVES FOR CHAPTER 13 (Organized into the SPUR categories—Skills, Properties, Uses, and Representations)	**Progress Self-Test Questions**	**Chapter Review Questions**	**Lesson Master from Teacher's Resource File***
SKILLS			
A Find values of functions from their formulas.	1, 2	1 through 8	13-2, 13-3
B Find and analyze values of functions.	4	9 through 20	13-6, 13-7
PROPERTIES			
C Determine whether a set of ordered pairs is a function.	5	21 through 27	13-1
D Classify functions.	6	28 through 33	13-1, 13-3
E Find the domain and range of a function from its formula, graph, or rule.	8	34 through 39	13-4
USES			
F Determine values of probability functions.	11, 13	40 through 43	13-5
G Find lengths and angle measures in triangles using the tangent function.	3, 15	44 through 47	13-6
REPRESENTATIONS			
H Determine whether or not a graph represents a function.	9, 10	48 through 51	13-1
I Graph functions.	7, 12, 14, 16, 17	52 through 57	13-2, 13-3, 13-5

*** The masters are numbered to match the lessons.**

OVERVIEW 13

OVERVIEW ☐ CHAPTER 13

The idea of a function is one of the unifying themes in mathematics. Similarly, in this chapter functions summarize many of the ideas that have been covered in this book.

Lessons 13-1, 13-2, and 13-4 discuss functions whose graphs students have already studied, namely linear, exponential, and quadratic functions. The language and symbolism of functions make it easier to communicate ideas about them.

Earlier chapters covered probability and absolute value. In Lessons 13-3 and 13-5 functions related to those topics are treated. This causes us to look at them somewhat differently. The function idea particularly lends itself to a graphical representation.

Lesson 13-6 introduces the tangent function. Lesson 13-7 concludes the book with a quick look at some of the functions that students will see in later courses.

PERSPECTIVES 13

PERSPECTIVES ☐ CHAPTER 13

The Perspectives provide the rationale for the inclusion of topics or approaches, provide mathematical background, and make connections within UCSMP.

13-1

WHAT ARE FUNCTIONS?

This lesson discusses the distinction between a function and a relation. In the examples, graphs and equations are examined to determine whether they describe functions.

The key idea in a function is the notion that the first coordinate of the ordered pair determines the second. But this does not have to be causal determination; there is a function consisting of the set of ordered pairs (name, age) for people, but a person's name does not cause his or her age.

13-2

FUNCTION NOTATION

Function notation is not completely new to students, for they have seen P(*E*) used to describe the probability of an event and N(*S*) used to represent the number of elements in a set. They have also used this symbolism in some BASIC commands.

It is natural for students to wonder why $f(x)$ notation is needed. After all, they have graphed $y = x^2$, and it seems that $s(x) = x^2$ is just a more complicated way of saying the same thing. Quite obviously, there must be very good reasons for having this notation, for it is so commonly used. (1) The notation clearly tells us the dependence of the second value on the first; that is, $s(x)$ depends on x. (2) The use of $s(x)$ rather than y allows the introduction of a letter which describes the situation, in this case squaring. This use is found particularly with computer functions, where more than one letter is used, as in ABS(X). (3) When two or more quantities depend on x, they can be handled as $a(x)$, $b(x)$, and so on.

Before 1960 it was common in all mathematics books to call $f(x)$ a function. Nowadays it is more common to distinguish the function f from the value $f(x)$.

13-3

ABSOLUTE VALUE FUNCTIONS

In Lesson 7-3, absolute value was introduced and used in two settings—measuring error and finding distances on a number line. These same two common applications of absolute value are used in this lesson. Here, however, instead of using absolute value to find the error or distance for specific values, we use absolute value functions to graph all possible errors or distances.

13-4

FUNCTION LANGUAGE

Chapter 1 began an important theme: choosing a reasonable replacement set for a variable. Those questions involved a single variable. Here we extend the issue to problems involving two variables. The situations are familiar ones: applications and variables in divisors and radicands.

The lesson allows another day to look at some special functions.

13-5

PROBABILITY FUNCTIONS

Probability is another topic that students have studied earlier in this course and that can be fit into the language and symbolism of functions. In fact, the symbolism P(*E*) has been used ever since probability was introduced in Lesson 1-7. Here, however, the probabilities of all the possible outcomes are considered. A graph is a natural way to summarize the information.

A bonus is that the probability function for the sum of the numbers that appear when two fair dice are tossed is an absolute value function as well. This provides a wonderful illustration of the ways in which diverse topics in mathematics can come together.

13-6

THE TANGENT OF AN ANGLE

A lesson on a trigonometric function is included for a number of reasons. (1) It ties together much of the mathematics the students have encountered in this book. (2) It explains a key on the calculator which students may have wondered about. (3) It helps to take away some of the fear students have of trigonometric functions and will make it far easier for them when they study these functions in a later course.

The tangent is defined as a ratio. A calculator is the most common way to find tangents or to solve equations involving tangents. You can use your calculator to find situations in which the function is not defined. Equations with tangents arise from problems involving right triangles. The tangent of the angle formed by a line and the positive ray of the *x*-axis is the slope of the line. Thus this trigonometric idea relates to slope, graphing, angles, ratios, triangles, equations, calculators, and domains of functions.

Between the reading and the questions, the student works in all four dimensions of understanding: representations (the line as a representation of a linear equation); uses (the use of tangents to calculate unknown distances as in Examples 2 and 3); properties (the relation between measures of the two acute angles in a right triangle); and skills (calculating tangents and solving equations.)

13-7

FUNCTIONS ON CALCULATORS

Having just been introduced to a new key on their calculators, students are naturally curious about the other keys on their calculators. Here we give a very brief explanation of the roles of some of them, while emphasizing the importance of functions.

As in the preceding lesson, the goal is to stimulate curiosity and lessen the fear students have of these keys which are mysterious to them.

The idea of domain is also important when using a calculator or computer. An error message will result if a person tries to evaluate a function with a calculator for a value outside its domain. This provides a nice reason for introducing the idea.

CHAPTER 13

This chapter should take 7 to 8 days for the lessons and quiz; 1 day for the Progress Self-Test; 1 or 2 days for the Chapter Review; and 1 day for testing. The total is 10 to 12 days. Allow an additional day for the Comprehensive Test.

CHAPTER 13

Functions

Fahrenheit-Celsius temperatures

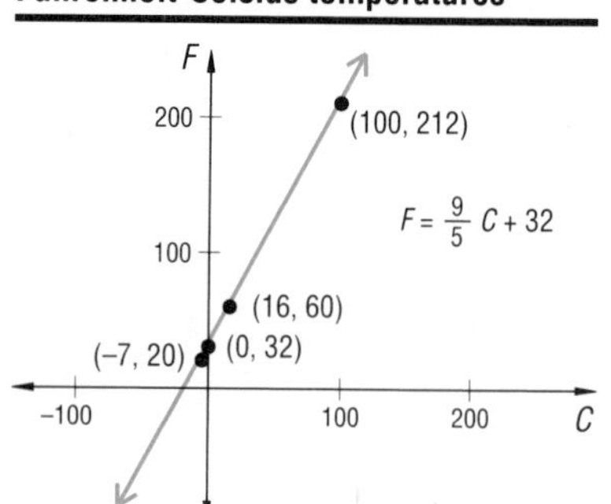

636

In earlier chapters, you have seen many types of graphs. Below are four of them.

These graphs picture situations that have much in common.
(1) There are two variables. (The first variable is indicated horizontally; the second vertically.)
(2) Every value of the first variable determines exactly one value of the second variable.

For instance, in the La Quebrada graph, the first variable stands for the distance from the cliff. The second variable stands for the height above the water. The distance from the cliff determines the height above the water. (But the height above the water does not always determine exactly the diver's distance from the cliff.)

Look at the graph of temperatures. If you were at the base of Mount Rainier, near Seattle, (shown on page 636), the temperature could be 60°F, or about 16°C. If you were close to the summit, the temperature could be 20°F, or about -7°C. The Fahrenheit-Celsius relationship is a linear one.

When a situation has two variables, it is natural to think of describing the situation using ordered pairs. The general name given to sets of ordered pairs like those above is *function*. You can think of a function as a particular kind of relationship between variables. The analysis of functions is extremely important in mathematics. Entire courses are often devoted to this. In this chapter, you will review many of the ideas of the earlier chapters using the language of functions, and you will encounter some functions you have not seen before.

Women's Olympic 400-meter freestyle

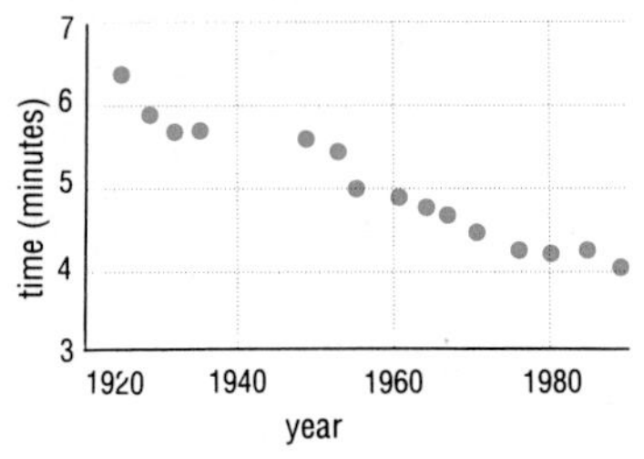

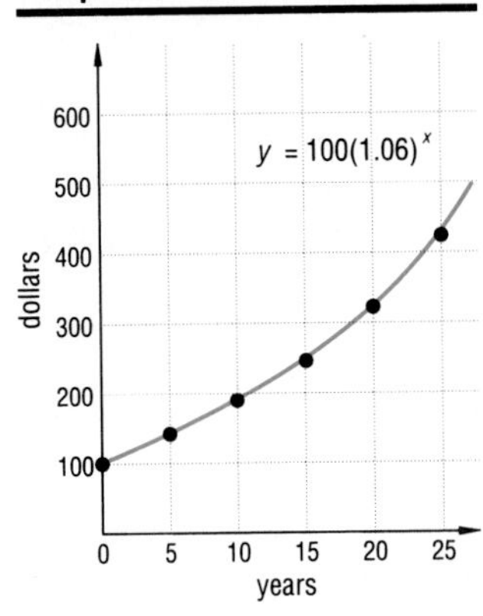

La Quebrada cliff diver

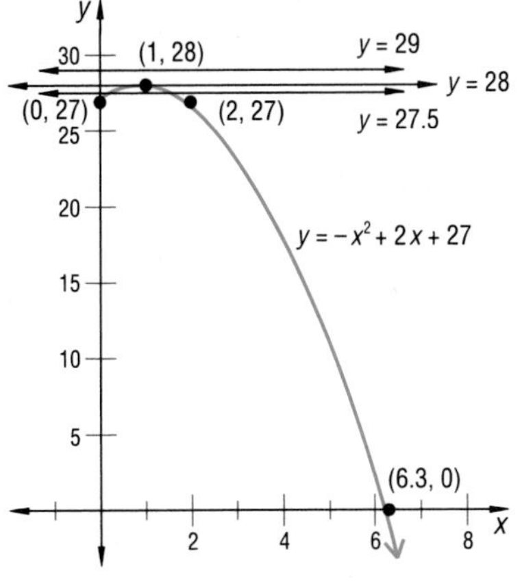

USING PAGES 636-637
As these pages point out, students have been studying functions throughout this course. The *word* might be new but the *idea* is not. *Teaching Aid 74* reproduces the graphs on these pages, and may be used with Lesson 13-1 since that lesson frequently refers to these examples.

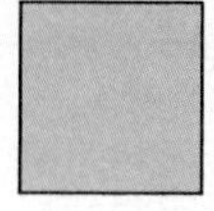

LESSON 13-1

RESOURCES
- Lesson Master 13-1
- Visual for Teaching Aid 74: Graphs for pages 636–637
- Visual for Teaching Aid 75: Graphs for **Example 1** and Additional Example 2

OBJECTIVES

C Determine whether a set of ordered pairs is a function.
D Classify functions.
H Determine whether or not a graph represents a function.

TEACHING NOTES

Discuss the familiar examples of the chapter opener. These situations from everyday life can help students understand the definition of a function.

You might ask: Is there a function relating a person with his or her age? (Yes.) Is there a function relating an age with a person? (No, each age may relate to many people.)

You might mention to your students that a calculator allows people to easily find the values of some functions. In particular, most calculators have keys for square roots, reciprocals, and opposites. When these operations are applied to a number, there is just one result. The value of the function is found by pressing the appropriate key. The functions have the equations

$y = \sqrt{x}$, $y = \frac{1}{x}$, and $y = -x$.

LESSON

13-1

What Are Functions?

On pages 636 and 637, four functions are graphed. Below, a set of ordered pairs is graphed that is *not* a function.

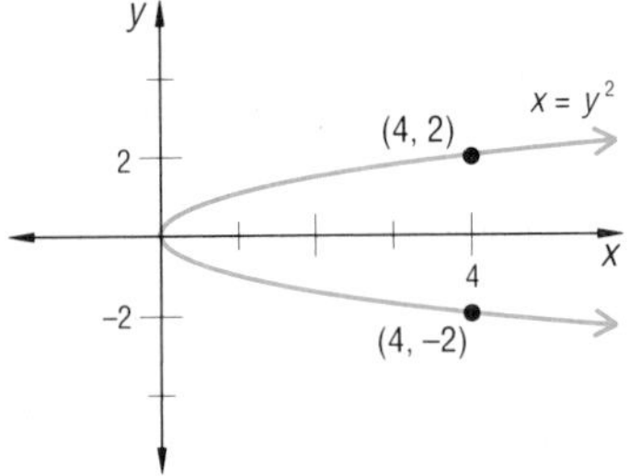

The distinction between this graph and the four on the previous pages has to do with the number of y-values determined by each x-value. The four previous graphs have the characteristic that a value of x gives you exactly one value of y. For example, there is only one Women's Olympic winning freestyle swimming time in 1972, 4.32 minutes. On the graph above, however, the value $x = 4$ corresponds to two possible values for y; $y = 2$ or -2.

Since the points (4, 2) and (4, -2) are on the graph, the set of ordered pairs satisfying $x = y^2$ is not a function.

Definition:

A function is a set of ordered pairs in which each first coordinate appears with exactly one second coordinate.

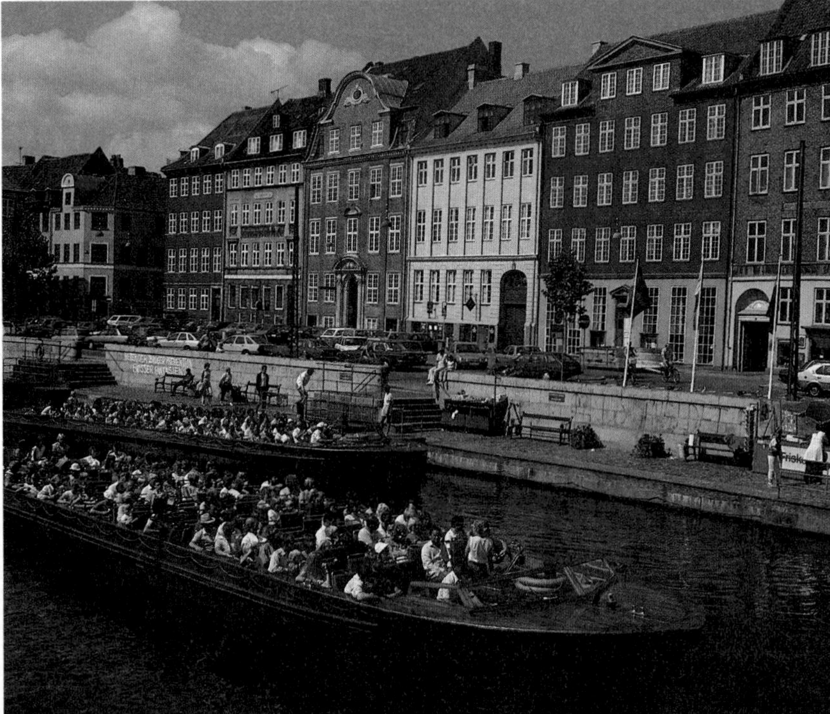

Canal in Copenhagen, Denmark

Red Square, Moscow, U.S.S.R.

Example 1 On page 399, latitudes and April mean high temperatures (°F) for 10 selected cities are graphed. Here that graph is repeated. Does the graph describe a function?

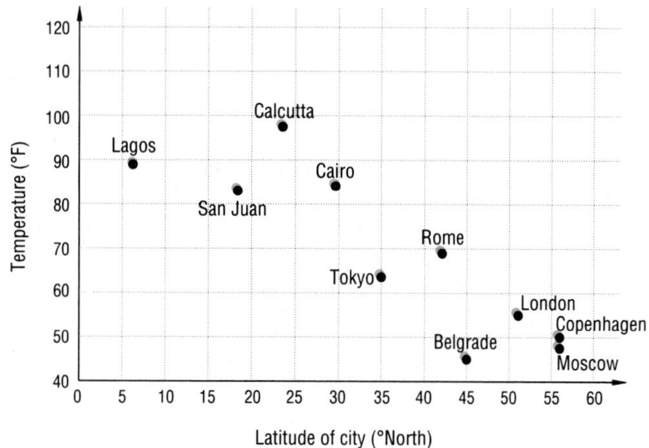

Solution No. The latitudes for Copenhagen and Moscow are the same, but the temperatures are different. These ordered pairs have the same first coordinate but different second coordinates. The graph pictures a relation, but not a function.

In a function, the first variable determines the second. If you know the value of the first variable (often called x), then there is only one value for the second (often called y). A value of the second variable is called a **value of the function.** Many equations you have studied describe functions.

Students can use the "vertical line test" to determine whether a graph describes a function. If it is possible to draw a vertical line through a graph and intersect more than one point of the graph, it is *not* the graph of a function. You can illustrate the idea with **Example 1;** *Teaching Aid 75* can be used.

ADDITIONAL EXAMPLES

1. The chart below is used to describe the severity of hurricanes.

Category	Sustained Winds (mph)	Damage
1	74–95	Minimal
2	96–110	Moderate
3	111–130	Extensive
4	131–155	Extreme
5	≥ 156	Catastrophic

Does the following set of ordered pairs describe a function?

a. (category, wind speed)
No

b. (wind speed, damage)
Yes

c. (damage, category)
Yes

2. The graph below shows the number of bacteria per square millimeter in a biologist's culture. Is this the graph of a function?

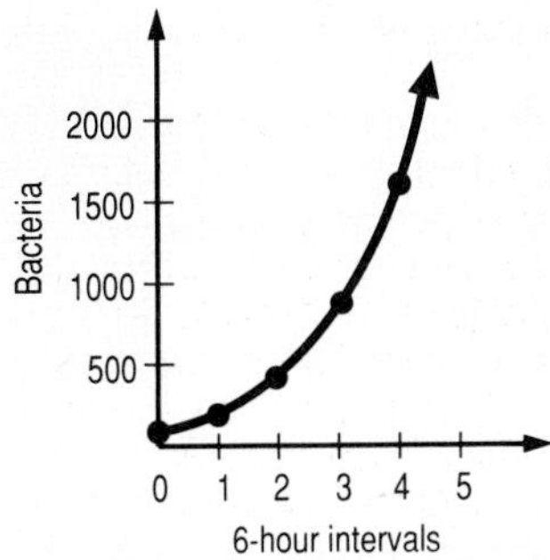

Yes

NOTES ON QUESTIONS
Question 11: This question involves the one type of linear relation that is not a function.

ADDITIONAL ANSWERS
1. A function is a set of ordered pairs in which each first coordinate appears with exactly one second coordinate.

7. One positive value for x will give two different values for y.

8. (1) by a graph, (2) by an equation, (3) by listing all the ordered pairs, (4) by a written rule

9. $y = \frac{1}{3}x - 2$**; Each value of x corresponds to one value of y, so the equation describes a function.**

11. One x value is paired with infinitely many y values.

To determine whether an equation describes a function, solve it for the second variable. For instance, $y^2 = x$ becomes $y = \pm\sqrt{x}$. It is clear in $y = \pm\sqrt{x}$ that every positive value of x corresponds to two values of y. So $y^2 = x$ does *not* describe a function. It describes a relation. A **relation** is any set of ordered pairs. So a function is always a relation, but not all relations are functions.

Example 2 Does the equation $3x + 4y = 12$ describe a function?

Solution 1 Solve the equation for y.

$$4y = -3x + 12$$

$$y = \frac{-3}{4}x + 3$$

Since each value of x corresponds to one value of y, the equation describes a function.

Solution 2 Graph $3x + 4y = 12$. Since the graph does not contain two points with the same first coordinate, the graph describes a function.

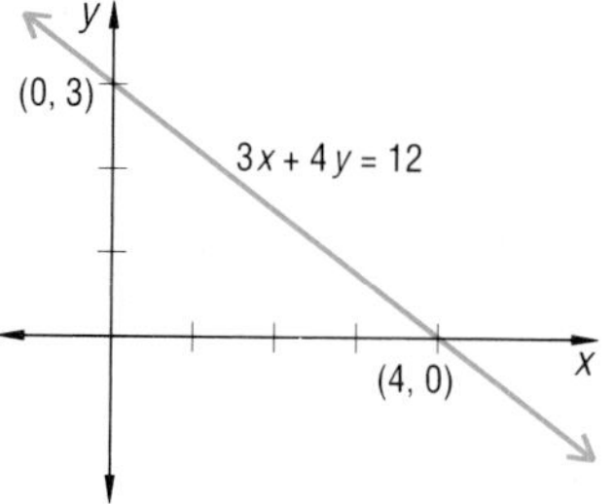

The function of Example 2 is a **linear function.** Linear functions have equations of the form $y = mx + b$. Another example is the Fahrenheit-Celsius relationship graphed on page 636. A **quadratic function** has an equation of the form $y = ax^2 + bx + c$ and its graph is a parabola. The La Quebrada graph on page 637 is a graph of a quadratic function. You studied exponential functions with the form $y = ab^x$ in Chapter 9. The compound interest graph on page 637 is a graph of an exponential function.

Functions are found in every branch of mathematics and are extremely important in applications. As a result, there are many ways to describe them:

(1) by a graph
(2) by an equation
(3) by listing all the ordered pairs (only possible if there are finitely many pairs)
(4) by a written rule.

For instance, a written rule for the Fahrenheit-Celsius function on page 637 is: To find the Celsius temperature, subtract 32 from the Fahrenheit temperature and then multiply the difference by $\frac{5}{9}$.

Questions

Covering the Reading

1. Define: function. **See margin.**

2. Define: relation. **A relation is any set of ordered pairs.**

In 3–6, two first coordinates of the relation are given. **a.** Find all corresponding second coordinates. **b.** Is the relation also a function?

3. Fahrenheit-Celsius relation on page 636; $F = 32°$, $F = 212°$.
a) $C = 0$ °C, $C = 100$ °C; b) Yes

4. Women's Olympic 400-meter freestyle swimming champion times on page 637; 1984, 1988. **a) $T = 4.2$ min, $T = 4.06$ min; b) Yes**

5. La Quebrada cliff diver on page 637; $x = 27$, $x = 28$.
a) $y = -648$, $y = -701$; b) Yes

6. Latitude-high temperature relation on page 639; latitude = 6, latitude = 56. **a) $T = 89$°F, $T = 46$°F, 50°F; b) No**

7. Why is $x = y^2$ not an equation for a function? **See margin.**

8. Name four ways in which a function can be described. **See margin.**

9. Explain why the graph of $x - 3y = 6$ describes a function.
See margin.

Applying the Mathematics

10. *Multiple choice* Which set of ordered pairs is *not* a function? **(c)**
(a) $\{(0, 0), (1, 1), (2, 2)\}$ (b) $\{(3, 5), (5, 3), (4, 4)\}$
(c) $\{(0, 0), (1, 0), (0, 1)\}$ (d) $\{(\frac{1}{2}, 1), (\sqrt{7}, \sqrt{8}), (6, \frac{-9}{23})\}$

11. Explain why a vertical line cannot be the graph of a function.
See margin.

In 12–14, can the graph be a graph of a function?

12. **No** 13. **Yes** 14. **Yes**

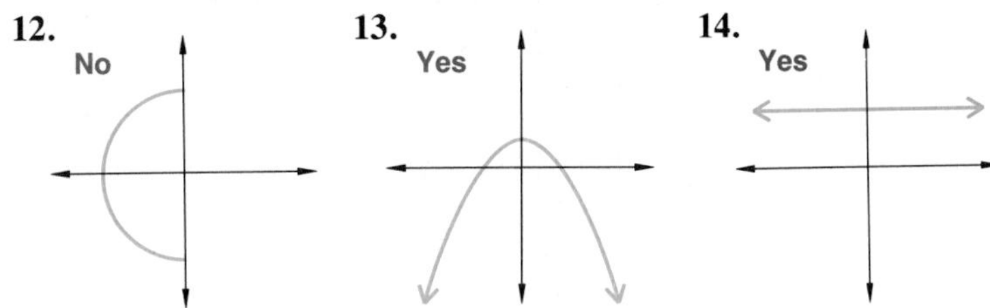

NAME ____________

LESSON **MASTER 13–1**
QUESTIONS ON **SPUR** OBJECTIVES

■**PROPERTIES** *Objective C* *(See pages 673–675 for objectives.)*
In 1–6, tell whether or not the equation determines a function.

1. $x = 2y + 5$ **yes** 2. $y = |2x - 5|$ **yes**
3. $x^2 = y - 4$ **yes** 4. $x = |y - 3|$ **no**
5. $y^2 = x$ **no** 6. $y = 100(1.06)^x$ **yes**

In 7–10, tell whether or not the set of ordered pairs is a function.

7. $\{(1, 3), (2, 4), (3, 5)\}$ **yes** 8. $\{(2, 5), (3, 5), (4, 5)\}$ **yes**
9. $\{(\pi, 5), (\pi, 4), (0, 0)\}$ **no** 10. $\{(a, b), (b, c), (c, d)\}$ **yes**

■**PROPERTIES** *Objective D*
In 11–14, classify the function as (a) linear, (b) quadratic, or (c) exponential.

11. $y = x(x + 2)$ **b** 12. $y = 2^2 - x$ **a**
13. $y = 2^x$ **c** 14. $y = x^2$ **b**

■**REPRESENTATIONS** *Objective H*
In 15–20, tell whether or not the set of ordered pairs graphed is a function.

15. **yes** 16. **no** 17. **yes**

18. **yes** 19. **yes** 20. **no**

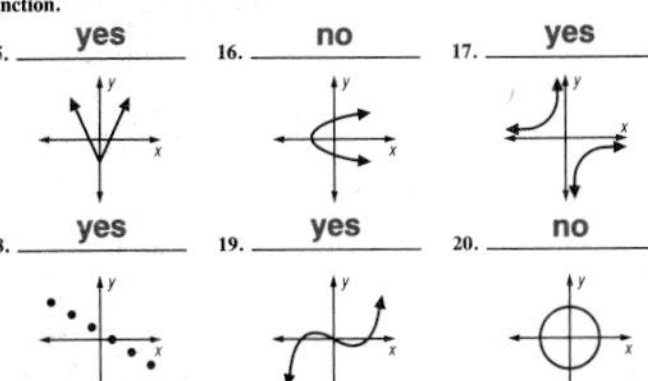

21. *True or False* Any vertical line passing through the graph of a function will intersect the graph in no more than one point. **true**

NOTES ON QUESTIONS
Error Analysis for Question 21: If students have difficulty understanding, tell them to imagine a pie. The numbers $1/m$ and $1/n$ are the fraction of the pie each person gets when it is shared equally with m or n people, respectively. Then ask: When you share with more people, do you get more or less pie?

FOLLOW-UP

MORE PRACTICE
For more questions on SPUR Objectives, use *Lesson Master 13-1,* shown on page 641.

15. sample: (-2, 5), (0, 3), (2, 5)

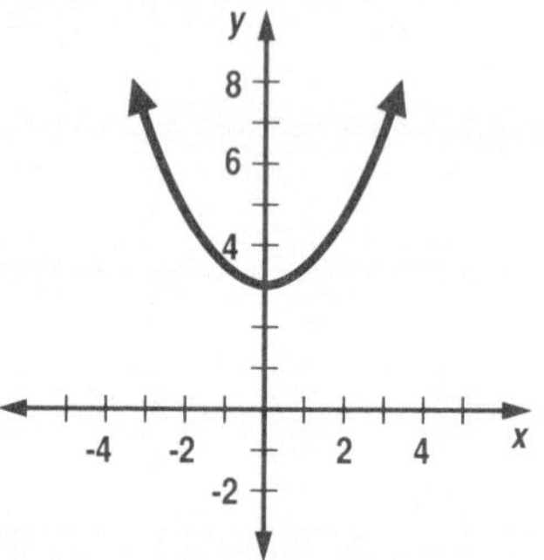

16. sample: (400, 0), (0, -400), 200, -200)

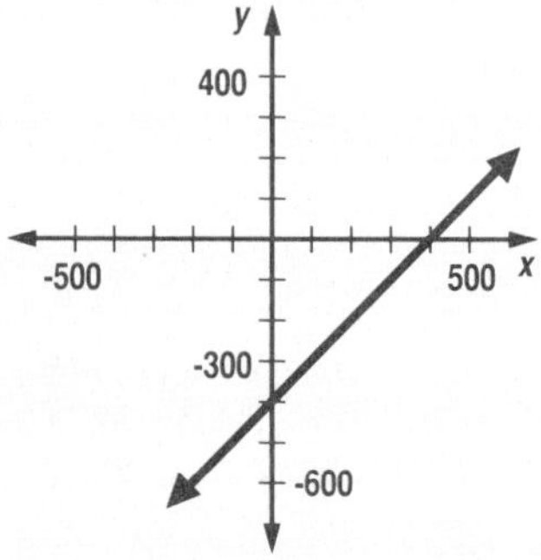

In 15 and 16, name three points of the function with the given equation. Then graph the function. **See margin.**

15. $y = \frac{1}{2}x^2 + 3$ **16.** $x = y + 400$

In 17 and 18, a written rule for a function is given. Name three ordered pairs of the function.

17. The cost of wrapping and mailing a particular package is three dollars plus fifty cents a pound. **See below.**

18. To find the volume of a sphere, multiply the cube of the radius by $\frac{4}{3}\pi$. **See below.**

Review

19. *Skill sequence* Write as a single fraction. *(Lessons 2-3, 7-8)*
a. $\frac{1}{2} + \frac{1}{3}$ **$\frac{5}{6}$** **b.** $\frac{1}{x} + \frac{1}{y}$ **$\frac{x+y}{xy}$** **c.** $\frac{1}{a+1} + \frac{1}{b-2}$ **$\frac{a+b-1}{(a+1)(b-2)}$**

20. A class of 24 students contains 3% of all the students in the school. How many students are in the school? *(Lesson 5-4)* **800 students**

21. When $m > n > 0$, which is larger, $\frac{1}{m}$ or $\frac{1}{n}$? *(Lesson 4-3)* **$\frac{1}{n}$**

22. *True or false* The slope of the line through (x_1, y_1) and (x_2, y_2) is the opposite of the slope of the line through (x_2, y_2) and (x_1, y_1). *(Lesson 8-2)* **False**

23. Write $2^{-3} + 4^{-3}$ as a simple fraction. *(Lesson 9-6)* **$\frac{9}{64}$**

Exploration

24. A function contains the ordered pairs (1, 1) and (2, 4).
a. Find a possible equation describing this function.
b. Find a second possible equation describing this function.
c. Find a third possible equation describing this function. (The equations should not be equivalent.)
samples: a) $y = x^2$; b) $y = 3x - 2$; c) $y = (-x)^2$

17. $y = 3.00 + .50x$
Samples:

x	y	
0	3.00	3.00 + .50(0)
1	3.50	3.00 + .50(1)
2	4.00	3.00 + .50(2)

(0, 3.00), (1, 3.50), (2, 4.00)

18. $y = \frac{4}{3}\pi x^3$
Samples:

x	y	
1	$\frac{4}{3}\pi$	$\frac{4}{3}\pi(1)^3$
2	$\frac{32}{3}\pi$	$\frac{4}{3}\pi(2)^3$
3	36π	$\frac{4}{3}\pi(3)^3$

$(1, \frac{4}{3}\pi)$, $(2, \frac{32}{3}\pi)$, $(3, 36\pi)$

642

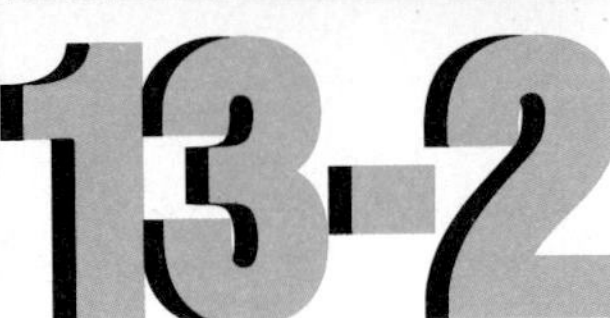

LESSON 13-2 Function Notation

Ordered pairs in functions need not be numbers. You are familiar with the abbreviation P(*E*), read "the probability of E," or even shorter, "P of *E*." In P(*E*), the letter *E* names an event and P(*E*) names the probability of that event. An event can have only one probability, so any set of events and their probabilities is a function. For instance, in the tossing of a fair coin, P(heads) = $\frac{1}{2}$ and P(tails) = $\frac{1}{2}$. The function *P* is {(heads, $\frac{1}{2}$), (tails, $\frac{1}{2}$)}.

This kind of abbreviation is used for all functions. For instance, we could use the shorthand $s(x)$, read "*s* of *x*," to stand for the *square of x*. Then for each number *x*, there is a value of the function $s(x)$, its square. The function is named *s* and called the *squaring function*. In the abbreviation $s(x)$, as in P(*E*), the parentheses do *not* mean multiplication. $s(x)$ stands for the square of *x*. When $x = 3$, $s(x) = 3^2 = 9$. Here are some pairs of values.

x	$s(x)$
3	9
-4	16
-13	169
$\frac{1}{5}$	$\frac{1}{25}$
1.7	2.89

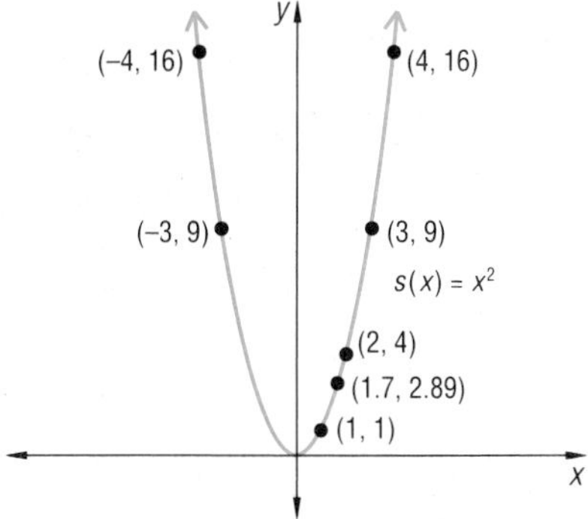

An equation or formula for this function is $s(x) = x^2$. You are familiar with this function. In previous lessons it was named $y = x^2$. Its graph is a parabola.

Example 1 Suppose $A(n)$ is the average number of accidents per 50 million miles driven by a driver who is *n* years old. Using function notation, the formula on page 587 becomes

$$A(n) = 0.4n^2 - 36n + 1000.$$

Find $A(16)$ and $A(40)$.

Solution To find $A(16)$, substitute 16 for *n* in the formula.

$A(16) = 0.4 \cdot 16^2 - 36 \cdot 16 + 1000$
$= 102.4 - 576 + 1000$
$= 526.4$

$A(16)$ is shorthand for the average number of accidents per 50 million miles driven by 16-year-olds. $A(16)$ is about 500.

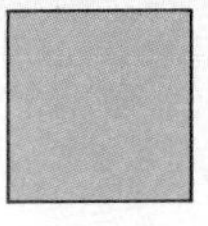

LESSON 13-2

RESOURCES
- Lesson Master 13-2

OBJECTIVES

A Find values of functions from their formulas.
I Graph functions.

TEACHING NOTES

Reading Students have seen P(*E*) and N(*S*) notation as precursors to *f*(*x*) notation. It is much easier for students to understand *f*(*x*) notation when they have seen the notation in other contexts before. Nevertheless, *f*(*x*) notation can be more difficult than P(*E*) or N(*S*) notation because both *f* and *x* are variables, and *f* stands for something the students have never before encountered. You may wish to emphasize that a function *f* is a *correspondence,* and that *f*(*x*) is the number that corresponds to *x*.

Error Analysis Some students may confuse function notation with multiplication. This is a logical mistake to make since previously an expression like *n*(2) was meant to indicate a product. Refer again and again to N(*S*) and ABS(*T*) and other instances they have seen in which the notation was not multiplication.

We suggest going through all the questions in order. There are a variety of functions included, and the notation should be clear by the time you finish.

ADDITIONAL EXAMPLES
1. The average height in inches of boys at age a can be approximated with the formula $h(a) = -0.1a^2 + 4.3a + 24.6$.

a. Find $h(5)$.
43.6 in.

b. Find $h(10)$.
57.6 in.

c. Find the amount an average boy grows between the ages of 5 and 10.
14 in.

Note: If you have a function grapher, you might wish to graph this function to determine on what interval it seems accurate.

2a. What kind of function is described with the equation $f(x) = 4x^2 + 6x - 8$?
quadratic function

b. What is its graph called?
parabola

NOTES ON QUESTIONS
Reading for Questions 1-3: Students must learn to read these symbols correctly in order to use them well and communicate effectively.

Question 10: Asking students to interpret the result will help them give meaning to the symbols.

Questions 19 and 20: The goal is to give students a feel for the notation by using reasonable abbreviations. If f is always used for the name of the function, this goal is lost.

Error Analysis for Question 21: Your students may have difficulty understanding what this function does. It may help to have them evaluate a value like $SS(4)$ two ways, once with the formula and once by calculating $1^2 + 2^2 + 3^2 + 4^2$. The answer to **21b** can be found by adding 12^2 to the answer to **21a.**

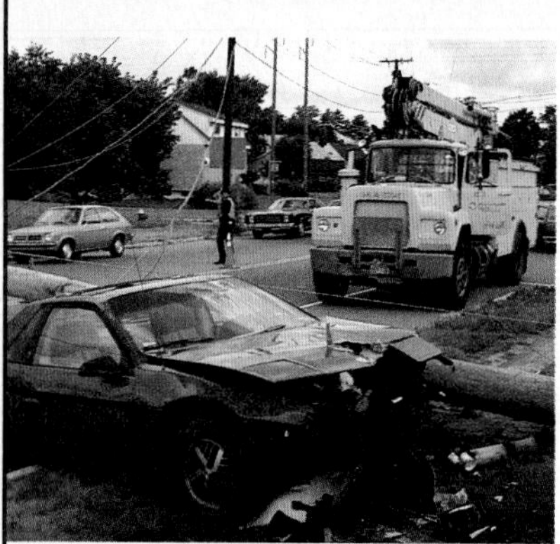

To find $A(40)$, substitute 40 for n in the formula.

$$\begin{aligned} A(40) &= 0.4 \cdot 40^2 - 36 \cdot 40 + 1000 \\ &= 640 - 1440 + 1000 \\ &= 200 \end{aligned}$$

Thus the average number of accidents per 50 million miles driven by 40-year-olds is about 200. That is quite a bit lower than the number for 16-year-olds.

In Chapter 12, we described the relationship of Example 2 with the equation $y = 0.4x^2 - 36x + 1000$. So why use function notation? One advantage of function notation is that it is shorter to write.

$A(16) > A(40)$ means the number of accidents per 50 million miles for 16-year-olds is greater than the number for 40-year olds.

Another advantage is that the letters x and y do not always convey any meaning. But the letter A, which stands for the function, is the first letter of "accident" and could be easier to remember.

Computer programs take advantage of function notation. Remember from Chapter 7 that in BASIC,

SQR(X)	means	the square root of x.
ABS(X)	means	the absolute value of x.

In this way, BASIC uses function notation. The names of the functions are SQR and ABS.

When there is no application, the most common letter used to name a function is f.

Example 2 What kind of function is described with the equation $f(x) = -5x + 40$?

Solution 1 Since $f(x)$ stands for the second coordinates of the points, write y in place of $f(x)$. This gives $y = -5x + 40$, which we know to be a linear function with slope -5 and y-intercept 40.

Solution 2 Use an automatic grapher (which is also called a function grapher or function plotter). Enter $y = -5x + 40$ or $f(x) = -5x + 40$. (Some graphers use function notation.) A line should appear, like that shown at the right.

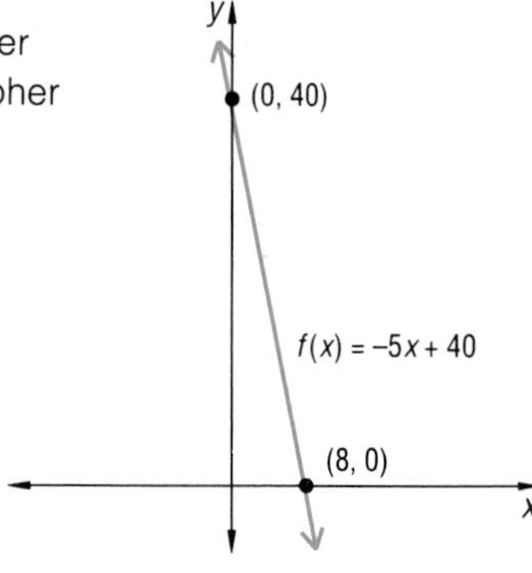

Questions

Covering the Reading

In 1–3, write out how each symbol is read.

1. P(E) **P of E**
2. $s(x)$ **s of x**
3. $f(x) = x^2$ **f of x equals x squared**

In 4–6, let $s(x) = x^2$. Give the value of:

4. $s(3)$ **9**
5. $s(-8)$ **64**
6. $s(\frac{2}{5})$ **$\frac{4}{25}$**

In 7–10, refer to Example 1.

7. *Multiple choice* The function of this example is named **(c)**
(a) A (b) n (c) $A(n)$ (d) $A(40)$

8. The average number of accidents per 50 million miles driven by a 25-year-old is _?_. **350**

9. $A(60)$ stands for _?_. **See margin.**

10. Which is larger, $A(16)$ or $A(20)$, and what does the answer mean? **A(16); see margin.**

In 11–13, consider the function f of Example 2.

11. What kind of a function is f? **linear**

12. Calculate $f(3)$ and $f(5)$. **25, 15**

13. What is the slope of f? **-5**

14. Evaluate SQR(40). **≈ 6.32**

15. Evaluate ABS(-2.5). **2.5**

Applying the Mathematics

16. **a.** According to the function in this lesson, who has more accidents on average, a 40-year-old or a 50-year old? **both have the same numbers**
b. Verify your answer by graphing the function. **See margin.**

17. At what age is there an estimated 1000 accidents per 50 million miles? **18**

18. Suppose $L(x) = 17x + 10$.
a. Calculate $L(5)$. **95**
b. Calculate $L(2)$. **44**
c. Calculate $\frac{L(5) - L(2)}{5 - 2}$. **17**
d. What have you calculated in part c? **the slope of the graph of L**

19. Let $c(n) = n^3$. **a.** Calculate $c(1)$, $c(2)$, $c(3)$, $c(4)$, and $c(5)$. **b.** What might be an appropriate name for c? **a) 1, 8, 27, 64, 125; b) cubing function**

Making Connections for Question 25: This question helps prepare students for the next lesson.

ADDITIONAL ANSWERS

9. the average number of accidents per 50 million miles driven by 60-year-olds

10. Sixteen-year-olds have more accidents per 50 million miles driven than do twenty-year-olds.

16b.

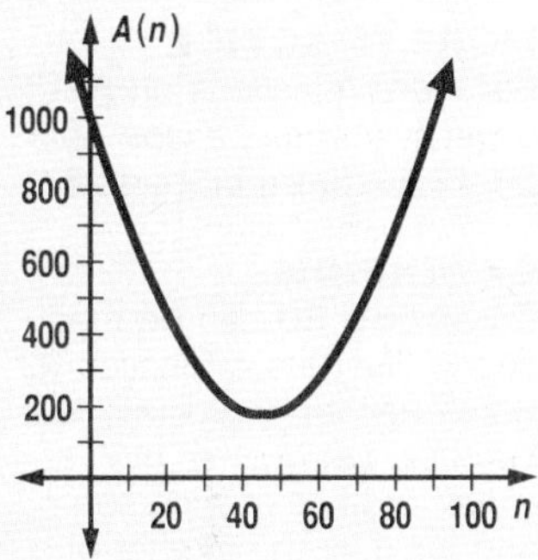

NAME ________

LESSON **MASTER 13–2**
QUESTIONS ON **SPUR** OBJECTIVES

SKILLS *Objective A (See pages 673–675 for objectives.)*
In 1–6, $f(x) = x^2 - 8x + 12$. Calculate.

1. $f(2)$ **0**
2. $f(-1)$ **21**
3. $f(0)$ **12**
4. $f(6)$ **0**
5. $f(1.5)$ **2.25**
6. $f(-\frac{9}{2})$ **68.25**
7. If $s(n) = \sqrt{n - 8}$, what is $s(12)$? **2**
8. If $g(x) = 2^x - 1$, find $g(2) + g(3)$. **10**
9. If $A(t) = -2t + 3$, calculate $\frac{A(5) - A(2)}{3}$. **-2**
10. If $A(r) = \pi r^2$, find $A(2)$. **$4\pi \approx 12.57$**

REPRESENTATIONS *Objective I*
In 11–14, graph each function.

11. $f(x) = 2(x - 1)$

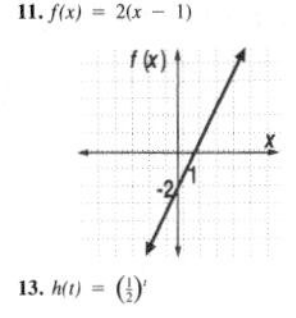

12. $g(x) = 1 - x^2$

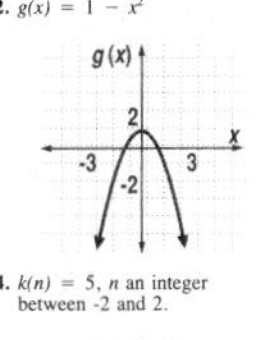

13. $h(t) = (\frac{1}{2})^t$

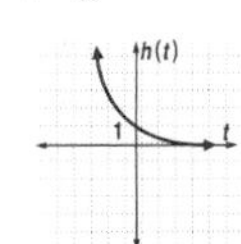

14. $k(n) = 5$, n an integer between -2 and 2.

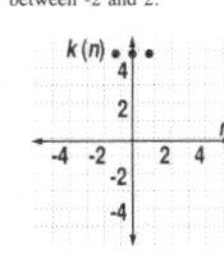

114

NOTES ON QUESTIONS
Making Connections for Question 28: You might wish to make certain that students understand there are four functions to graph. Similar questions regarding other functions are in many of the later explorations of this chapter.

FOLLOW-UP

MORE PRACTICE
For more questions on SPUR Objectives, use *Lesson Master 13-2,* shown on page 645.

EXTENSION
Question 20 can be modified to illustrate a function for which neither coordinate is a number. Let $b(p)$ = the eldest brother of a person p and $m(p)$ = the mother of a person p. Ask students to find another name for $b(m(p))$, $m(b(p))$, and $m(m(p))$. (the eldest son of the maternal grandfather of p, the mother of p, the maternal grandmother of p) Students could make up other relatives. Such functions are used in genealogy programs.

28.

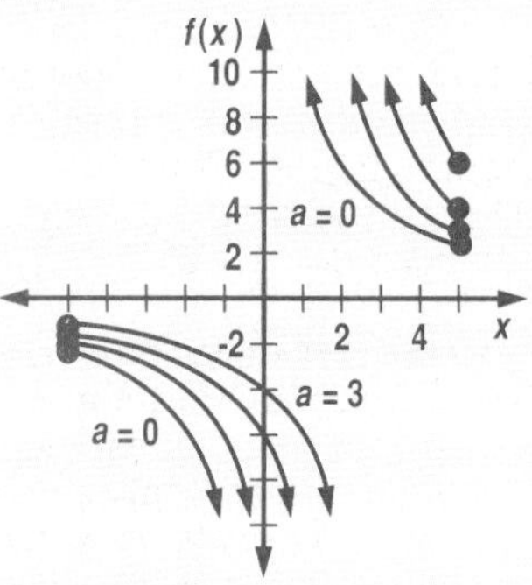

The graphs all have two branches and a value of x for which y is undefined. When a = 0, the function is undefined at x = 0. When a = 1, the function is undefined at x = 1, etc.

20. Let $s(p)$ = the number of sisters of a person p. Let $b(p)$ = the number of brothers of a person p.
a. If you are the person p, give the values of $s(p)$ and $b(p)$.
b. What does $s(p) + b(p) + 1$ stand for?
a) Answers will vary. b) total number of children in *p*'s family

21. If $SS(n)$ = the sum of the squares of the integers from 1 to n, then

$$SS(n) = \frac{n(n+1)(2n+1)}{6}.$$

a. Calculate $SS(11)$. 506
b. Evaluate $1^2 + 2^2 + 3^2 + 4^2 + 5^2 + 6^2 + 7^2 + 8^2 + 9^2 + 10^2 + 11^2 + 12^2$. 650

Review

22. *Skill sequence* Write as a single fraction. *(Lesson 2-3)*
a. $3 + \frac{2}{5}$ $\frac{17}{5}$ **b.** $3 + \frac{7}{5}$ $\frac{22}{5}$ **c.** $3 + \frac{k}{5}$ $\frac{15+k}{5}$

23. Simplify $6 \cdot 3^{-2}$. *(Lesson 9-6)* $\frac{2}{3}$

24. *Multiple choice* From a 16″ by 16″ sheet of wrapping paper, rectangles of width x'' are cut off two adjacent sides. What is the area (in square inches) of the colored region that remains? *(Lesson 10-6)* (d)

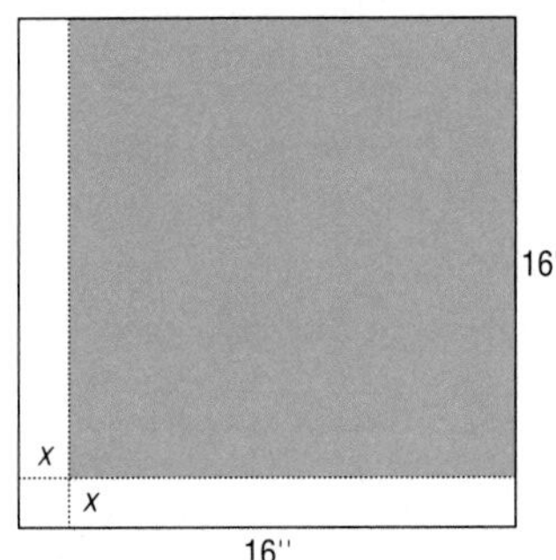

(a) $16 - x$ (b) $256 + x^2$
(c) $256 - x^2$ (d) $256 - 32x + x^2$

25. Give the value of $|x| + |-x|$ when $x = -2$. *(Lesson 7-3)* 4

26. Solve: $(t + 5)^2 = 3$. *(Lesson 7-8)* $t = -5 \pm \sqrt{3} \approx -3.3$ or -6.7

27. A case contains c cartons. Each carton contains b boxes. Each box contains 100 paper clips. How many paper clips are in the case? *(Lesson 4-2)* 100 *bc*

Exploration

28. Let $f(x) = \frac{12}{x - a}$. Using an automatic grapher, graph the function f from $x = -5$ to $x = 5$ when $a = 0$, $a = 1$, $a = 2$, and $a = 3$. What do the graphs have in common? How are they different?
See margin.

646

LESSON

13-3

Absolute Value Functions

The function with equation

$$f(x) = |x|$$

is the simplest example of an **absolute value function.** In BASIC and other computer languages, $|x|$ is written as ABS(X). By substitution, ordered pairs for this function can be found.

x	$f(x) = \|x\|$	Pair
2	$f(2) = \|2\| = 2$	(2, 2)
-8	$f(-8) = \|-8\| = 8$	(-8, 8)
0	$f(0) = \|0\| = 0$	(0, 0)

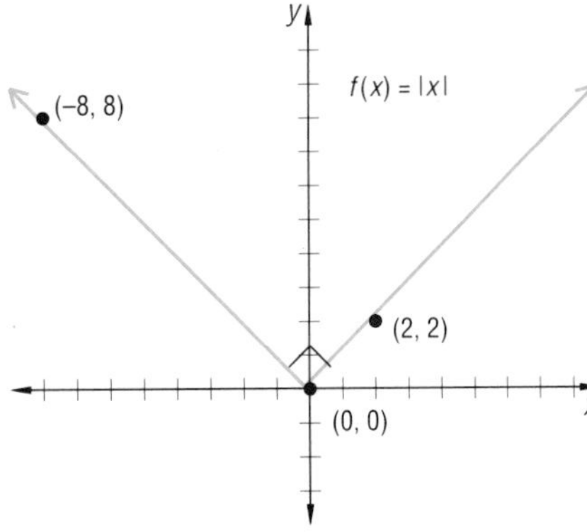

In general, when x is positive, $f(x) = x$, so the graph is part of the line $y = x$. When x is negative, then $f(x) = -x$, and the graph is part of the line $y = -x$.

The result is that the graph of the function is an angle. The angle has vertex at the origin (0, 0) and has measure 90°. It is a right angle.

You may wonder why absolute value functions are needed. (They must be needed, or computer languages would not have a special name for them and we would not have the special symbol | |.) One reason is that they occur in the study of error.

LESSON 13-3

RESOURCES
- Lesson Master 13-3
- Visual for Teaching Aid 76: Diagram for **Question 16**
- Computer Master 28

OBJECTIVES

A Find values of absolute value functions from their formulas.
D Classify functions.
I Graph absolute value functions.

TEACHING NOTES

Students often draw parabolas that look like graphs of absolute value functions. This would be a good time to discuss the difference between the two. You can illustrate with a tennis ball. A parabolic path comes from tossing the ball to someone. The ball gradually slows its climb and starts to fall. A V-shape can be shown by rolling the ball on the floor so that it bounces off a wall horizontally; it follows a straight line, then suddenly changes directions.

The two-part definition of absolute value ($|a| = a$ if $a \geq 0$, $|a| = -a$ if $a < 0$) can be related to the application and graph in **Example 1.** In **Example 1,** the error is $60 - x$ if the guess is too low; it is $x - 60$ if the guess is too high. The graph is part of the line $y = 60 - x$ for points to the left of $x = 60$. To the right, the graph is part of $y = x - 60$.

Students are not expected to write an equation to describe a situation like that given in **Example 2.** Rather, they should be able to verify that a given equation fits the information.

ADDITIONAL EXAMPLES

1. A bus driver is supposed to drive his scheduled route in 35 minutes. If x represents the number of minutes it takes him, then $|35 - x|$ is the number of minutes off-schedule he is. Graph $f(x) = |35 - x|$.

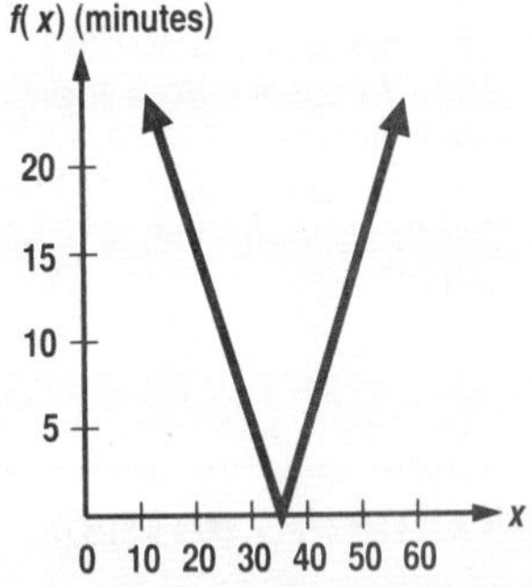

2. A train is traveling down a straight track at 80 miles per hour. Three hours after leaving the station it crosses a river and continues down the track. The distance between the train and the river t hours after leaving the station is given by $d(t) = 80|3 - t|$. Graph this function.

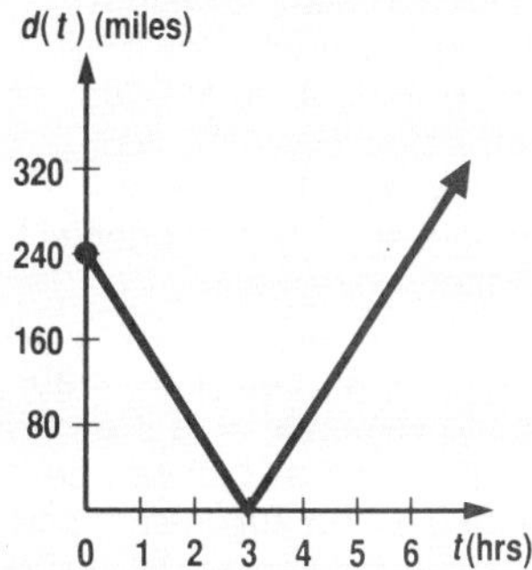

Example 1 A psychologist asked some teenagers to estimate the length of a minute. The psychologist rang a bell on a desk in front of each teenager. The teenager was to wait until he or she thought a minute was up, and then ring the bell again. The estimate x (in seconds) determines the error $|60 - x|$. Graph the function with equation

$$f(x) = |60 - x|.$$

Solution Draw axes with units of 10, so 60, clearly a key number, can fit. Make a table.

x	error: $f(x) = |60 - x|$
60	0
50	10
40	20
70	10
0	60
100	40

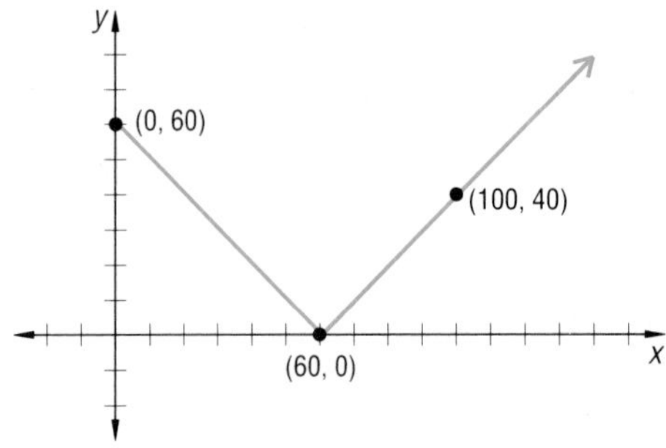

These and other points are plotted above. You can see that the graph again is a right angle, but its vertex is at (60, 0).

Another reason for absolute value functions is that they help to explain some complicated situations.

Example 2 A plane crosses a check point going due east. It then flies at 600 $\frac{\text{km}}{\text{hr}}$ for 2 hours, then returns flying due west. Is there any formula describing its distance from the check point?

Solution Let $d(t)$ = the plane's distance from the check point t hours after crossing it. The given information tells you some points on this function.

When $t = 0$, the plane is at the check point.	So $d(0) = 0$.
When $t = 1$, the plane is 600 km east.	So $d(1) = 600$.
When $t = 2$, the plane is 1200 km east.	So $d(2) = 1200$.

648

All this time the plane has been going at a constant rate. Now it turns back.

When $t = 3$, the plane is again 600 km east. So $d(3) = 600$.

When $t = 4$, the plane crosses the check point again. So $d(4) = 0$.

The graph below results from graphing these and other ordered pairs. Notice how the graph describes the situation.

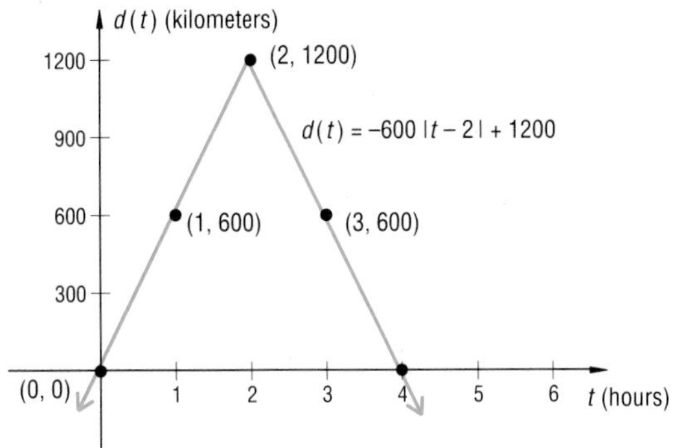

Because the graph is an angle, you should expect a formula for $d(t)$ to involve the absolute value function. And it does.

$$d(t) = -600\,|t - 2| + 1200.$$

You should check that the formula does work for the values we found and for other values.

Without knowing the graph of the absolute value function $f(x) = |x|$, you probably would never think the situation in Example 2 could involve absolute value. The formula

$$d(t) = -600\,|t - 2| + 1200$$

is a special case of the general absolute value function

$$f(x) = a\,|x - h| + k,$$

where $a = -600$, $h = 2$, and $k = 1200$. You are asked to explore what the graph of this function looks like for various values of a, h, and k. In your later study of mathematics, you will learn how to determine such formulas.

NOTES ON QUESTIONS

Question 5: You might ask if absolute value graphs always form right angles. The graph of the function of **Example 2** shows that the answer is no.

Making Connections for Question 15: Much worthwhile discussion can arise from the question of which points to mark on the x-axis. (none since $y \geq 7$). You might talk about how to find the vertex and how the vertex relates to the range of the function. (This meaning of *range* is introduced in the next lesson.) [vertex: (10, 7); range $y \geq 7$. In general, for $y = a|x-h| + k$, the vertex is (h, k). If $a > 0$, then (h, k) is a minimum point, and the range is $y \geq k$. If $a < 0$, then (h, k) is a maximum point, and the range is $y \leq k$.]

Question 16: *Teaching Aid 76* may be used.

ADDITIONAL ANSWERS

6. They occur in the study of error. They help to explain some complicated situations.

14.

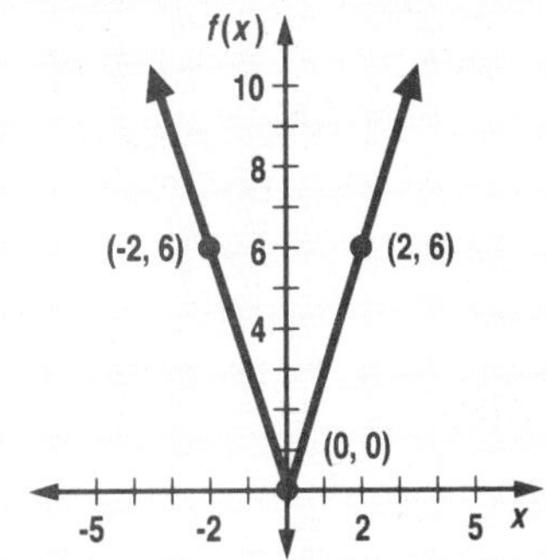

6, 14. See margin, page 649.

15.

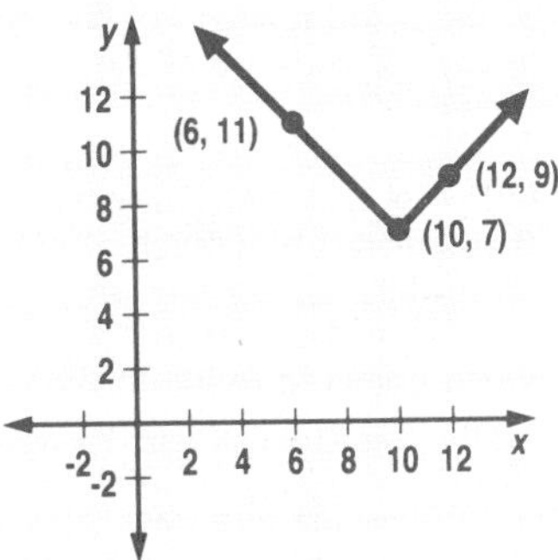

17.

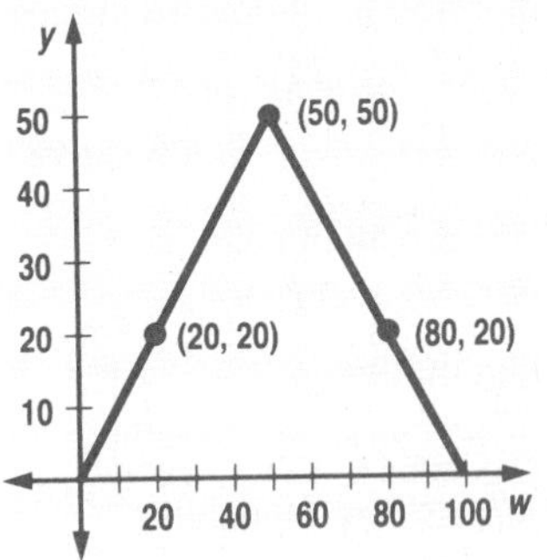

22a. sample:

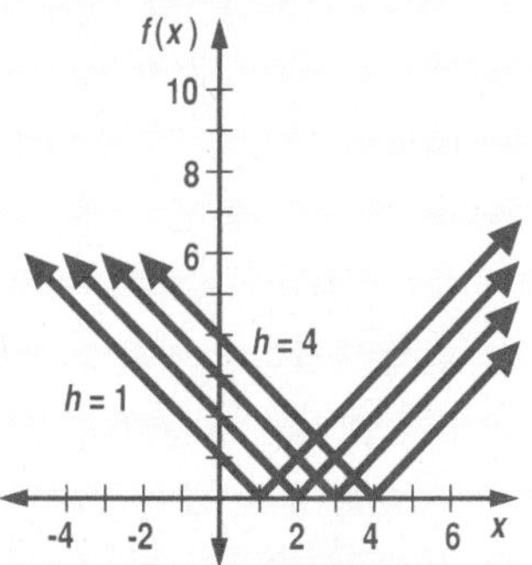

22b. The graph shifts 1 unit to the right for each increase in *h* of 1 unit.

23a. sample:

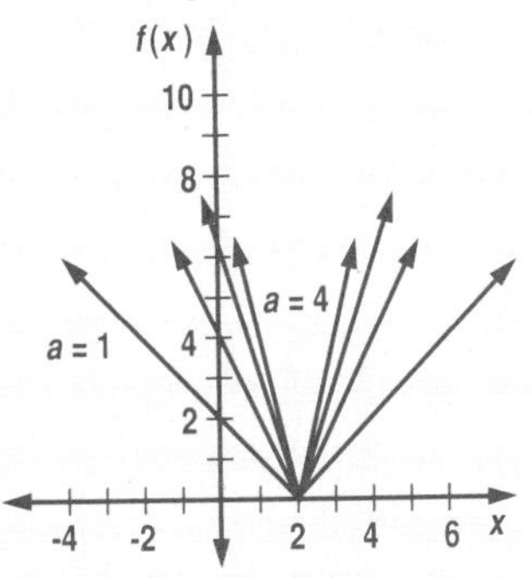

23b. The angle becomes smaller as a increases.

Earlier in this book, you would have seen the formula $d = -600|t - 2| + 1200$ without function notation. Using the $d(t)$ function notation makes it clear that the value of d depends on t. There may be other quantities that depend on the time. We could write

$a(t)$ = altitude of the plane t hours after crossing
$f(t)$ = amount of fuel used t hours after crossing
and so on.

By using $a(t)$ and $f(t)$, it is clear that the altitude and fuel used by the plane depend on time.

Questions

Covering the Reading

In 1–4, let $f(x) = |x|$. Calculate.

1. $f(-3)$ 3 **2.** $f(2)$ 2 **3.** $f(-\frac{3}{4})$ $\frac{3}{4}$ **4.** $f(0)$ 0

5. The shape of the graph of an absolute value function is __?__. an angle

6. Name two reasons for studying absolute value functions. See margin.

In 7–9, let f be the function of Example 1.

7. If $x = 90$, $f(x) =$ __?__. 30

8. The graph of f has vertex __?__. (60, 0)

9. $f(x)$ stands for the absolute difference between the actual and estimated values of __?__. the length of a minute

In 10–13, let $d(t) = -600|t - 2| + 1200$.

10. Calculate $d(0)$, $d(1)$, $d(2)$, and $d(3)$. 0, 600, 1200, 600

11. Describe a situation that can lead to the function d. sample: distance of a plane from a checkpoint

12. The function d contains (1.5, 900). What does this point represent? t = 1.5 hr; plane is 900 km east of checkpoint

13. The function d contains (5, -600). What could this point represent? t = 5 hr; plane is 600 km west of checkpoint

Applying the Mathematics

In 14 and 15, graph the function with the given equation. See margin.

14. $f(x) = |3x|$ **15.** $y = |x - 10| + 7$

650

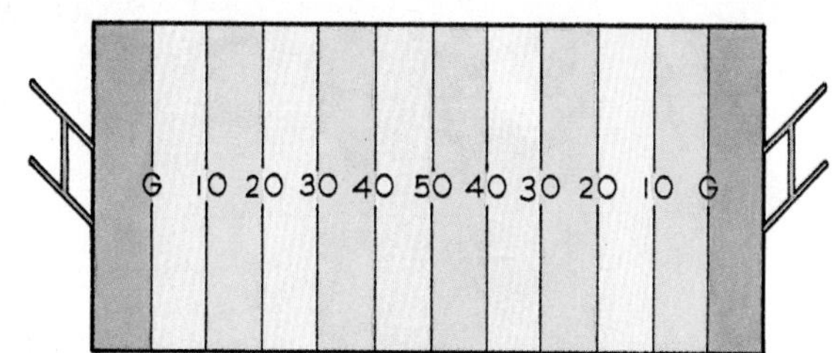

In 16 and 17, suppose you start at the goal line of a football field and walk to the other goal line. After you have walked w yards, you will be on the y yard line.

16. *Multiple choice* Which equation relates w and y? (d)
(a) $y = w$
(b) $y = |w|$
(c) $y = |50 - w| + w$
(d) $y = -|50 - w| + 50$

17. Let f be the function relating w and y. Graph f. See margin.

Review

18. *Skill sequence* Simplify. *(Lesson 2-3)*
a. $x + \frac{x}{2}$ $\frac{3x}{2}$ **b.** $\frac{x}{3} + \frac{x}{2}$ $\frac{5x}{6}$ **c.** $\frac{x}{3} + \frac{y}{2}$ $\frac{2x + 3y}{6}$

19. Let $A(x)$ = the April mean high temperature for city x, as shown in Lesson 13-1. What is A(Moscow)? *(Lesson 13-1)* about 47°F

20. Let $f(x) = \frac{2}{3}x + 5$.
a. Calculate $f(120)$. 85
b. Calculate $f(-120)$. -75
c. Describe the graph of f. *(Lesson 13-1)* a straight line

21. If 10 pencils and 7 erasers cost \$4.23 and 3 pencils and 1 eraser cost \$0.95, what is the cost of two erasers? *(Lesson 11-5)* \$0.58

Exploration

In 22 and 23, consider absolute value functions of the form $f(x) = a|x - h|$. See margin.

22. Fix $a = 1$. Then vary the value of h, choosing any numbers you wish. For instance, if you let $h = 3$, then $f(x) = |x - 3|$.
a. Graph the function f for four different values of h.
b. What effect does h have on the graphs?

23. Fix $h = 2$. Now vary the value of a, choosing any numbers you wish. For instance, if you let $a = 4$, then $f(x) = 4|x - 2|$. See margin.
a. Graph the function f for four different values of a.
b. What effect does a have on the graphs?

NOTES ON QUESTIONS

Computer for Questions 22 and 23: The graphs can be done with a function plotter (and should be done that way, if one is available). Some students may find it easier to compare four separate graphs than one diagram with four graphs.

FOLLOW-UP

MORE PRACTICE

For more questions on SPUR Objectives, use *Lesson Master 13-3,* shown below.

EXTENSION

Small Group Work Your class might enjoy carrying out the experiment in **Example 1.** Your science or physical education department may have stopwatches that you can use. In addition to calculating each student's error, the class could plot the function $n(e)$ = number of results with error e. (For a more compact graph, values of $n(e)$ can be rounded to the nearest 5 seconds.)

NAME ______

LESSON **MASTER 13–3**
QUESTIONS ON **SPUR** OBJECTIVES

SKILLS *Objective A (See pages 673–675 for objectives.)*
In 1–6, $f(x) = |24 - x|$. Calculate.

1. $f(36)$ 12 2. $f(0)$ 24
3. $f(-6)$ 30 4. $10 - f(28)$ 6
5. $f(20.5) + f(22.5)$ 5 6. $f(-3.5) - f(-1.5)$ 2

In 7 and 8, $g(t) = -150|t - 4| + 800$. Calculate.

7. $g(8)$ 200 8. $g(5.5) - g(4.5)$ -150

PROPERTIES *Objective D*
In 9–12, classify the function as (a) linear, (b) quadratic, or (c) absolute value.

9. $f(x) = 3x^2 + 2x$ b 10. $y = |\frac{1}{2}x + 5|$ c
11. $g(x) = -\frac{2}{3}x + |-7|$ a 12. $y = |-\frac{2}{3}x| - 7$ c

REPRESENTATIONS *Objective I*
In 13–16, graph each function.

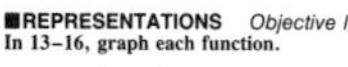

13. $g(x) = |6 - x|$ 14. $h(t) = |t| + 4$

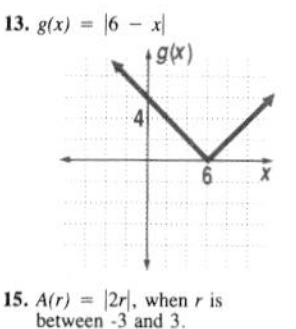

15. $A(r) = |2r|$, when r is between -3 and 3.
16. $V(t) = -|t|$, when t is an integer between -3 and 3.

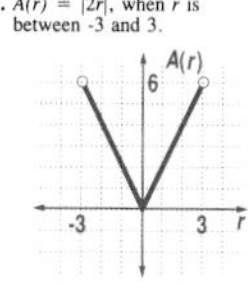

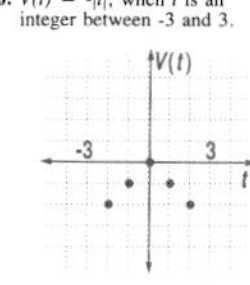

LESSON 13-4

RESOURCES
- Lesson Master 13-4
- Quiz on Lessons 13-1 Through 13-4
- Visual for Teaching Aid 77: Domain and Range of a Function

OBJECTIVE

E Find the domain and range of a function from its formula, graph, or rule.

TEACHING NOTES

Reading Your students may need some help in sorting out the different situations here. *Teaching Aid 77* may be used. The domain and range are most easily found for a small set in which you can see the ordered pairs. Questions about real world situations often can be answered by thinking about what is reasonable. In an abstract problem, finding the domain involves looking for special numbers (like zero or negative numbers) that must be restricted. Usually the range is determined by finding minimum or maximum values.

In the graphs following **Example 1** the range of $y = -x^2 + 6x - 4$ is given. Although we have not covered completing the square, your students can see this equation is equivalent to $y = -(x - 3)^2 + 5$, so y must be less than or equal to 5.

Alternate Approach Some students may appreciate a numerical explanation to **Example 2.** Since $\sqrt{x} \geq 0$, adding 4 to both sides shows $\sqrt{x} + 4 \geq 4$.

LESSON

13-4 Function Language

Every function can be thought of as a set of ordered pairs. The set of first coordinates of these pairs is called the **domain of the function.** Here are two functions with the same formula but the domains are different.

Let $f(x)$ be the price of two basketballs if one costs x dollars. Then $f(x) = 2x$.

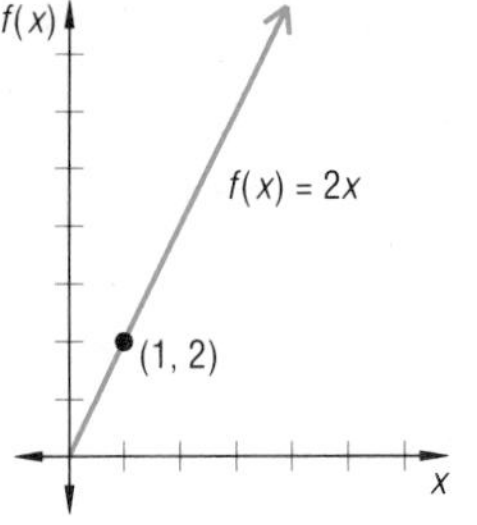

Let $g(x)$ be the number of childre in x set of twins. Then $g(x) = 2x$.

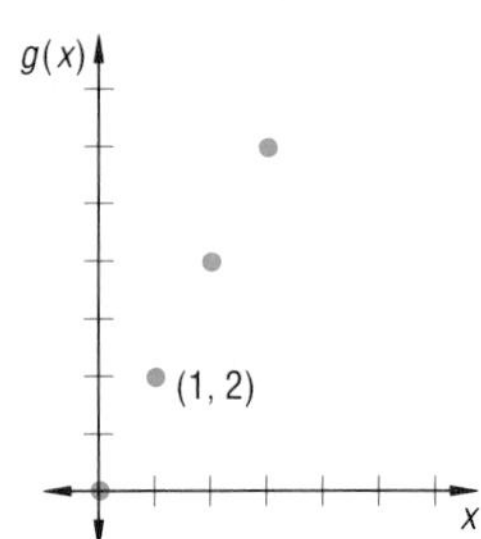

If you were to describe the above graphs by $y = 2x$, you would not be able to distinguish the functions. In this way, function language is sometimes clearer.

The domain of a function is the replacement set for the first variable. When no domain is given, the domain is assumed to be the largest set possible. For instance, if $A(t)$ stands for the area of a triangle t, then the domain is the set of all triangles. If a function is defined by the equation $f(x) = 4x + 3$ and no other information is given, we assume the domain is the set of real numbers. However, the domain of a function sometimes cannot contain particular values.

Example 1 What is the domain of the function f with rule $f(x) = \frac{x + 1}{x - 2}$?

Solution The domain is the set of allowable values for x. The numerator can be any number, so it can be ignored. Since the denominator cannot be 0, the domain is the set of all real numbers but 2.

Whereas the *domain* of a function f is the set of possible replacements for x, the **range of a function** is the set of possible values of $f(x)$. For instance, in the absolute value function with equation $f(x) = |x|$, $f(x)$ can be any positive number or zero. Thus the range of this function is the set of nonnegative real numbers.

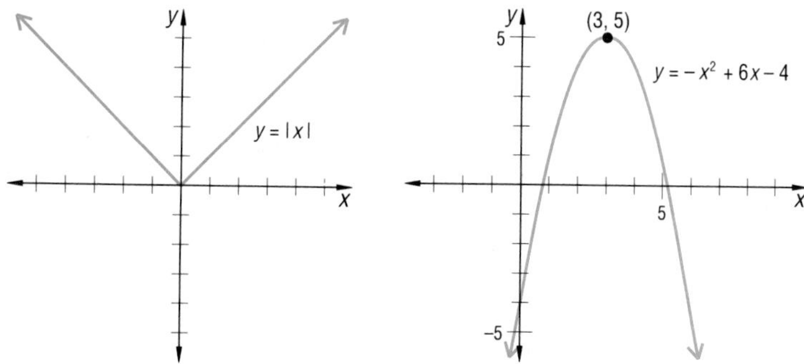

range = set of nonnegative numbers range = set of numbers less than or equal to 5

You can often determine the range of a function by examining its graph. In the graph of the quadratic function above at right, y could be any number less than or equal to 5. So the range of that function is the set of real numbers less than or equal to 5.

If you do not have a graph of a function, then calculating the range can be more difficult.

Example 2 Determine the range of the function f with equation $f(x) = \sqrt{x} + 4$.

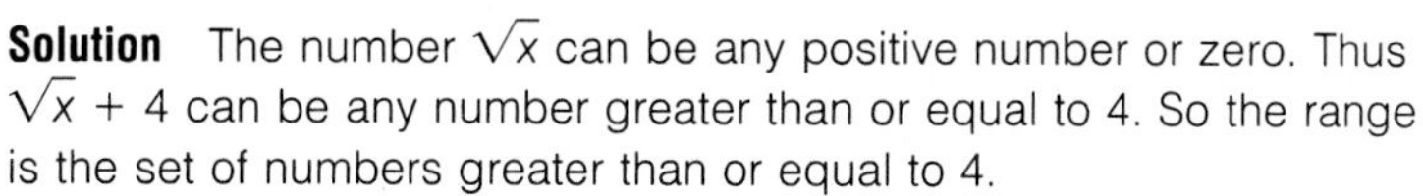

Solution The number $\sqrt{x}$ can be any positive number or zero. Thus $\sqrt{x} + 4$ can be any number greater than or equal to 4. So the range is the set of numbers greater than or equal to 4.

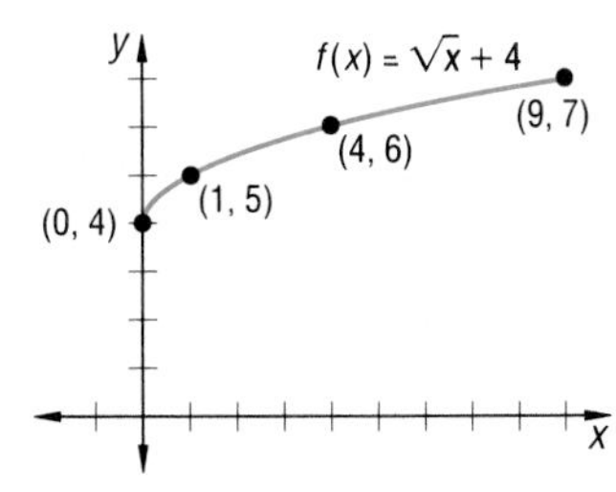

Check A graph of $f(x) = \sqrt{x} + 4$ with an automatic grapher is shown at left. The graph verifies the solution.

ADDITIONAL EXAMPLES

1. What is the domain of f if $f(x) = \frac{x}{2x + 5}$?
All real numbers except $-\frac{5}{2}$.

2. What is the range of f with rule $f(x) = |x| - 5$?
The set of real numbers greater than or equal to -5.

3. Give the domain and range of the function {(Pacific, 64.0), (Atlantic, 31.8), (Indian, 25.3), (Arctic, 5.4)}. This function relates oceans and their area in millions of square miles.
Domain = {Pacific, Atlantic, Indian, Arctic}
Range = {64.0, 31.8, 25.3, 5.4}

NOTES ON QUESTIONS

Computer for Question 8: You can use an automatic grapher to show your students the graph of the function. It has the shape of a hyperbola with a vertical asymptote at $x = 3$ and a horizontal asymptote at $y = 1$.

Question 11b: This question can be answered by using permutations. Consider the first coordinates to be set. Since there are 3! ways to arrange the second coordinates, there are 6 possible functions. This is a small enough number to list.

If the function is a finite set of ordered pairs, then you can often list the elements of the domain and range.

Example 3 Give the domain and range of the function {(1945, 51), (1965, 117), (1985, 159)} that associates a year with the number of members of the United Nations in that year. (The United Nations was formed in 1945.)

Solution Only three points are given for this function.
The domain is the set of first coordinates {1945, 1965, 1985}.
The range is the set of second coordinates {51, 117, 159}.

Questions

Covering the Reading

1. Define: domain of a function. **the replacement set for the first variable**
2. Define: range of a function. **the set of possible values of $f(x)$**

In 3–5, give the domain and range of the function.

3. {(1, 2), (3, 4), (5, 7)} **{1, 3, 5}; {2, 4, 7}**
4. The function graphed at left **$0 \le x \le 6$; $0 \le y \le 20$**

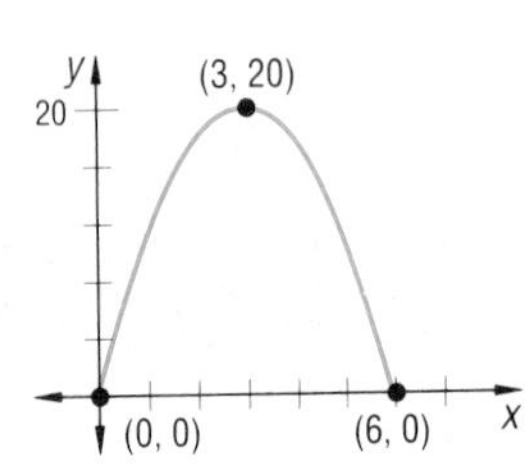

5. The function with equation $f(x) = \sqrt{x} + 4$ **$x \ge 0$; $f(x) \ge 4$**
6. When no domain is given for a function, what can you assume about the domain? **The domain is assumed to be the largest set possible.**
7. Give the domain and range of the function with equation $y = |x|$. **all real numbers; $y \ge 0$**
8. What number is not in the domain of the function g with rule $g(x) = \frac{x - 2}{x - 3}$? **$x = 3$**
9. Let $f(x)$ = the price of four tires if one costs x dollars. Let $g(x)$ = the number of people in x foursomes for bridge.
   a. Give a formula for f. **$f(x) = 4x$**
   b. Give a formula for g. **$g(x) = 4x$**
   c. How do f and g differ? **See margin.**
10. How many more members did the United Nations have in 1985 than when it was founded? **108 more members**

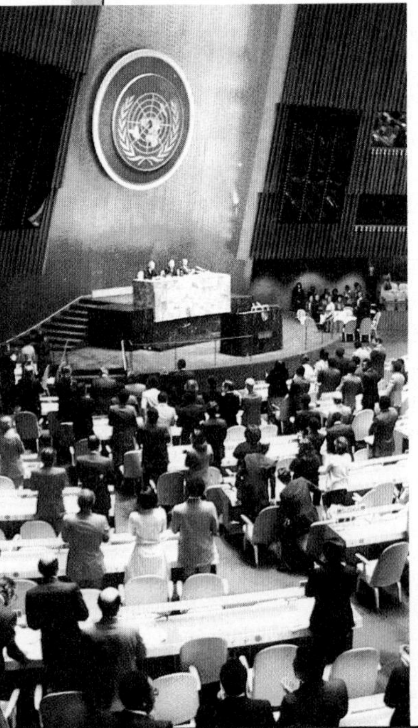

NOTES ON QUESTIONS
Alternate Approach for Question 13: Some students may solve this algebraically. Others may use a graph. Use either method to check the other.

FOLLOW-UP

MORE PRACTICE
For more questions on SPUR Objectives, use *Lesson Master 13-4,* shown on page 655.

EXTENSION
Another idea that can be discussed with functions is minimum and maximum values. These points can often be determined from an equation or graph. You can examine equations like $y = 2x^4 - 11$ or $y = (|x| + 7)^2$, or graphs like the following:

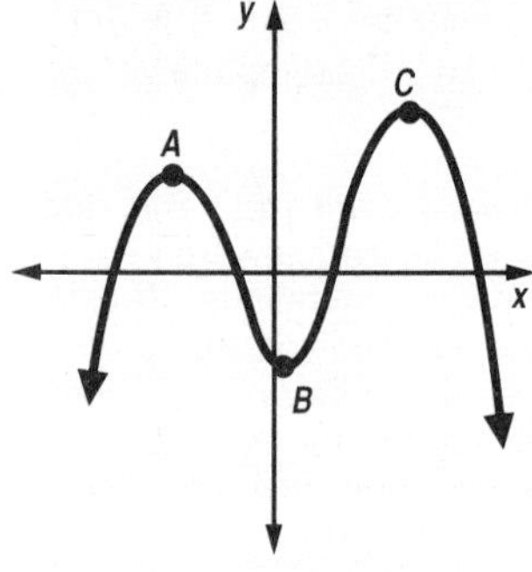

[$y = 2x^4 - 11$ has a minimum point at (0, -11); $y = (|x| + 7)^2$ has a minimum point at (0, 49); the graph has maximums at *A* and *C* and a minimum at *B*.]

EVALUATION
A quiz covering Lessons 13-1 through 13-4 is provided in the Teacher's Resource File.

Alternative Assessment
Have **small groups** of students devise descriptions of functions which have varied domains and ranges. They can use *Teaching Aid 77* as a guide.

Applying the Mathematics

11. a. Graph a function whose domain is {-1, 2, 3} and whose range is {5, 8, 0}. **See margin.**
    b. How many possible functions are there? **6**

In 12–16, give the domain and range of the function.

12. $y = 3x + 1$ **all real numbers; all real numbers**

13. $y = 2x^2 - 3$ **all real numbers; $y \geq -3$**

14. The exponential function with equation $y = 2^x$ graphed below at the left **all real numbers; all real numbers greater than 0**

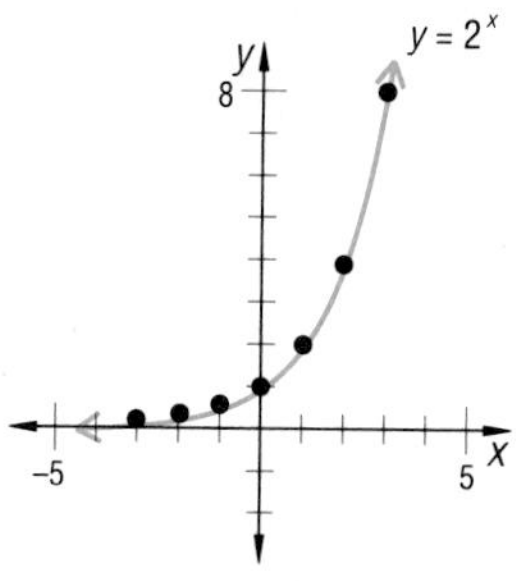

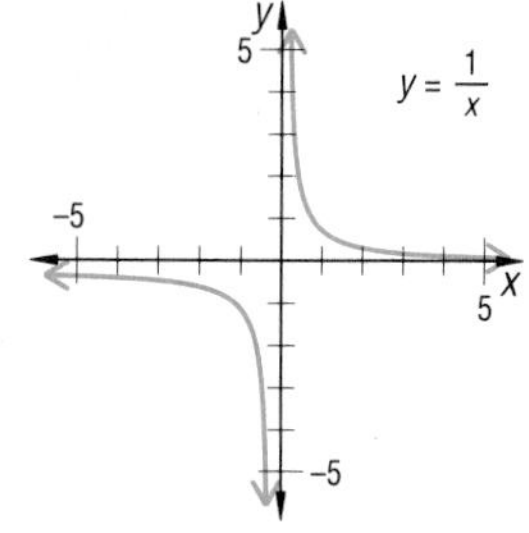

15. The function with equation $y = \frac{1}{x}$ graphed above at the right
    all nonzero real numbers; all nonzero real numbers

16. The football field walking function of Questions 16 and 17 of Lesson 13-3 **See margin.**

Review

17. The graph of $y = |x| + 3$ is _?_ with vertex _?_. *(Lesson 13-3)*
    an angle; (0, 3)

18. A poll in an election for senator predicts that candidate A will get 46% of the vote. If instead A gets x% of the vote, by how far off was the poll? *(Lesson 13-3)* **$|46 - x|$**

19. If $f(x) = (x - 1)(x + 2)$, find $f(1)$, $f(2)$, and $f(\frac{7}{3})$. *(Lesson 13-2)* **0; 4; $\frac{52}{9}$**

20. In 1986, Cuba had a population of about 10.2 million living on about 44,218 square miles of land. Mexico had a population of 81.7 million living on 761,604 square miles. Which country was more densely populated? *(Lesson 5-2)* **Cuba**

21. Solve for x: $y = 2x + 6$. *(Lesson 6-1)* **$x = \frac{1}{2}y - 3$**

22. The price of an item was increased by $\frac{1}{3}$ its former price. The new price is \$10.00.
    a. What equation can be solved to find the former price? **$(1 + \frac{1}{3})x = 10.00$**
    b. What was that price? *(Lesson 5-6)* **\$7.50**

Exploration

23. Consider the absolute value functions of the form $f(x) = |x| + k$.
    a. What is the effect of k on the graph of f? (You may need to graph f for different values of k.) **See margin.**
    b. What is the range of f in terms of k? **$f(x) \geq k$**

ADDITIONAL ANSWERS

9c. The domain for $f(x)$ can be any real number ≥ 0. The domain for $g(x)$ can only be whole numbers.

11a.

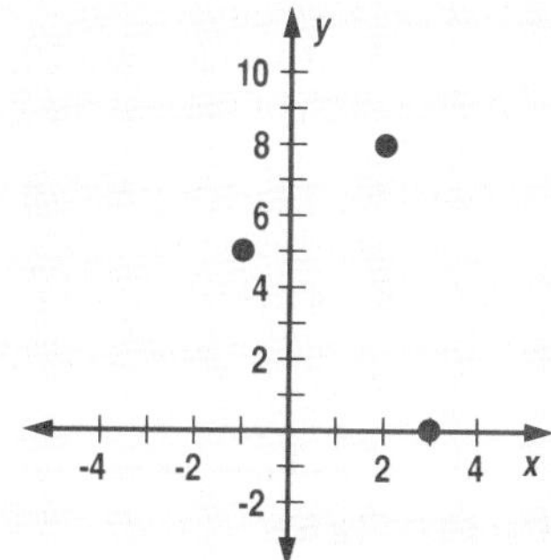

There are 5 other possibilities:
(1) (-1, 5), (2, 0), (3, 8);
(2) (-1, 8), (2, 5), (3, 0);
(3) (-1, 8), (2, 0), (3, 5);
(4) (-1, 0), (2, 5), (3, 8);
(5) (-1, 0), (2, 8), (3, 5)

16. real numbers greater than or equal to 0 and less than or equal to 100; real numbers greater than or equal to 0 and less than or equal to 50

23a. $f(x) = |x|$ has vertex (0, 0). k will move the entire graph up or down k units.

NAME __________

LESSON **MASTER 13–4**
QUESTIONS ON **SPUR** OBJECTIVES

■PROPERTIES *Objective E (See pages 673–675 for objectives.)*

1. What number cannot be in the domain of $f(x) = \frac{2}{x - 1}$? **$x = 1$**

In 2–5, give the domain for each function.

2. $f(x) = -7x + 9$ **all reals**
3. $A(t) = t^2 - 4$ **all reals**
4. $g(x) = \sqrt{x}$ **nonneg. reals**
5. $C(n) = 4.5n$, where n is the number of books bought. **nonneg. integers**

In 6–9, give the domain and range.

	Domain	Range
6. $f(x) = 2x + 5$	all reals	all reals
7. $g(x) = \|3x + 10\|$	all reals	$g(x) \geq 0$
8. $h(t) = \sqrt{t} + 5$	$t \geq 0$	$h(t) \geq 5$
9. {(1, 5), (2, 8), (3, 5)}	{1, 2, 3}	{5, 8}

10. *Multiple choice* The domain of a function is {1, 2, 3}. The range is {2, 4, 6}. Which of these could be the rule for the function?
    (a) $y = x + 2$ (b) $y = 2x$ (c) $y = .5x$ (d) $y = 2|x|$ **b, d**

In 11 and 12, give a. the domain and b. the range of each function graphed below.

11. a. domain **{-3, -2, -1, 0, 1}**
    b. range **{0, 1, 2}**

12. a. domain **$x \geq 0$**
    b. range **$y \geq 0$**

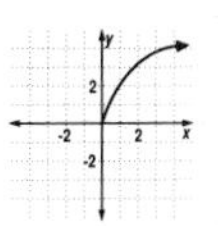

LESSON 13-5

RESOURCES

- Lesson Master 13-5
- Visual for Teaching Aid 78: A Probability Function for 2 Fair Dice
- Visual for Teaching Aid 79: Table and Graph for Additional Example

OBJECTIVES

F Determine values of probability functions.
I Graph probability functions.

TEACHING NOTES

Stress that there are many types of probability functions and that the functions have been chosen here for their relationship to content studied in earlier chapters.

Alternate Approach
Your students may enjoy making graphs of other probability functions. You might ask them to find the probabilities of different sums when rolling two eight-sided (octahedral) dice. Students can be asked to predict what the graph will look like by examining the graph of probabilities for six-sided dice. They then can make a table of values to check their predictions. Another interesting problem is to find probabilities when rolling one eight-sided die and one six-sided die.

LESSON

13-5

Probability Functions

In Monopoly™ and many other board games, two dice are thrown and the sum of the numbers that appear is used to make a move. Since the outcome of the game depends on landing or not landing on particular spaces, it is helpful to know the probability of obtaining each sum. The following picture, which first appeared in Lesson 1-7, is helpful. It shows the 36 possibilities for two fair dice. (A fair die is one on which each side is equally likely to appear up.)

If the dice are fair, then each of the 36 outcomes has a probability of $\frac{1}{36}$. Let $P(n)$ = the probability of getting a sum of n. The domain of P is the set of possible values for n, namely {2, 3, 4, 5, 6, 7, 8, 9, 10, 11, 12}. By counting, $P(n)$ has the values given on page 657. The range of the function P is thus $\{\frac{1}{36}, \frac{2}{36}, \frac{3}{36}, \frac{4}{36}, \frac{5}{36}, \frac{6}{36}\}$. This *probability function* is graphed on page 657.

n	2	3	4	5	6	7	8	9	10	11	12
$P(n)$	$\frac{1}{36}$	$\frac{2}{36}$	$\frac{3}{36}$	$\frac{4}{36}$	$\frac{5}{36}$	$\frac{6}{36}$	$\frac{5}{36}$	$\frac{4}{36}$	$\frac{3}{36}$	$\frac{2}{36}$	$\frac{1}{36}$

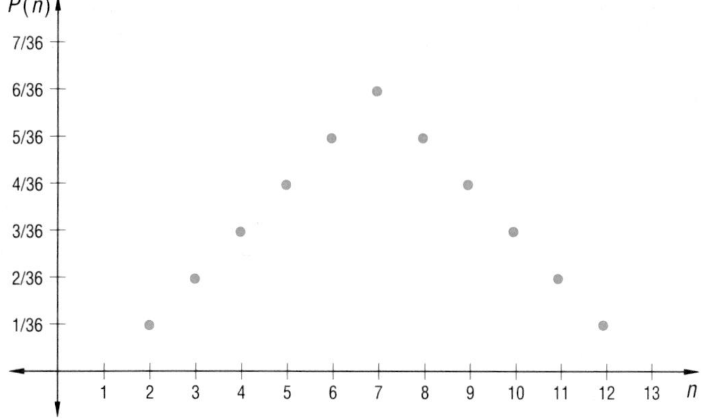

The graph is part of an angle. This suggests that there is a formula for $P(n)$ involving absolute value. In fact, there is.

$$P(n) = \frac{-1}{36}|n - 7| + \frac{1}{6}.$$

For instance, using the formula, the probability of a sum of 3, $P(3) = \frac{-1}{36}|3 - 7| + \frac{1}{6} = \frac{-1}{36}|-4| + \frac{1}{6} = \frac{-4}{36} + \frac{1}{6} = \frac{2}{36}$. Although you could substitute any real number for n, in this situation the formula has meaning only when n is in the domain of the function P.

In general, a **probability function** is a function whose domain is a set of outcomes in a situation and in which each ordered pair contains an outcome and its probability. Many probability functions have simpler formulas than that of the dice example.

Example 1 Consider the spinner at left. Assume all regions have the same probability of the spinner landing in them. Let P(n) = the probability of landing in region n. Graph the function P.

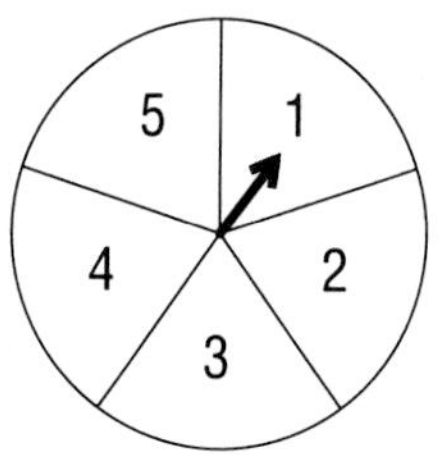

Solution Since there are five regions, each with the same probability, each has probability $\frac{1}{5}$. So $P(1) = \frac{1}{5}$, $P(2) = \frac{1}{5}$, and so on. The graph is shown at right. An equation for the function is $P(n) = \frac{1}{5}$.

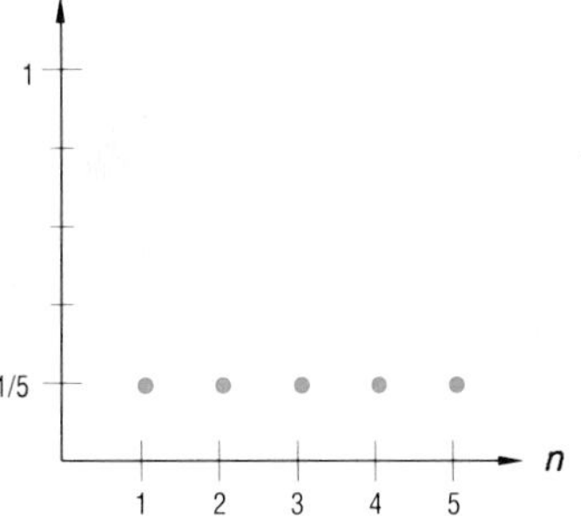

ADDITIONAL EXAMPLE
Teaching Aid 79 may be used here. The chart below shows the probability P(x) that at least two people have the same birthday out of a group of x people. Graph the function P.

x	P(x)
10	.129
15	.253
20	.411
25	.569
30	.706
40	.891
50	.970

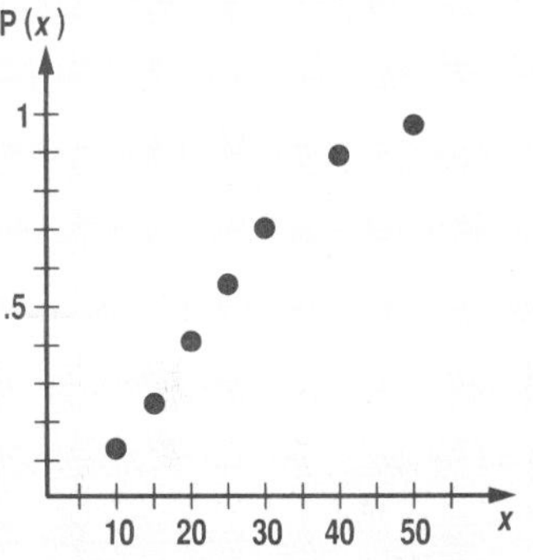

NOTES ON QUESTIONS
Questions 2-5: These questions relate to the probability function graphed on page 657. *Teaching Aid 78* may be used.

Reading for Question 16c: Your students may need some guidance. Point out that *compare* means "describe the similarities," while *contrast* means "describe the differences."

Question 17: Trial and error may be the easiest way for students to answer this question. The hint directs them to factor $2x^2 + 3x - 20$ into $(2x - 5)(x + 4)$. The product will be prime only if one of the factors is 1.

ADDITIONAL ANSWERS
1. A probability function is a function whose domain is a set of outcomes in a situation, and in which each ordered pair contains an outcome and its probability.

1. See margin, page 657.

7.

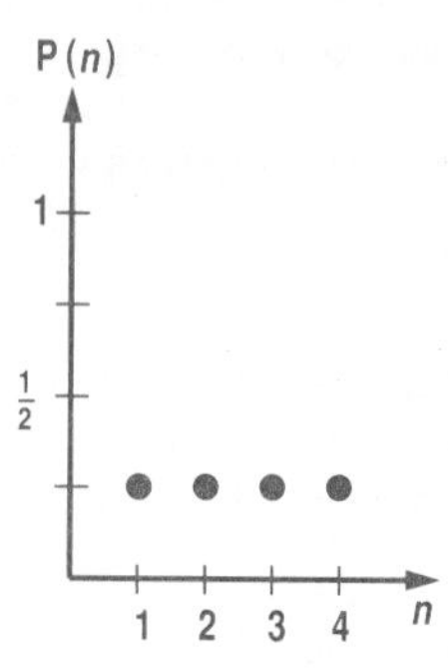

12.

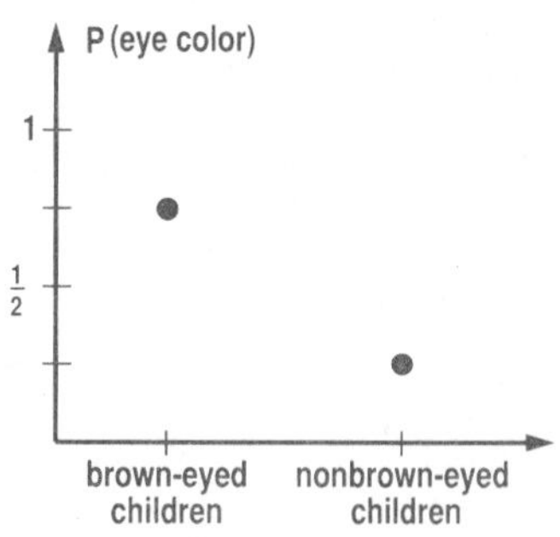

13.

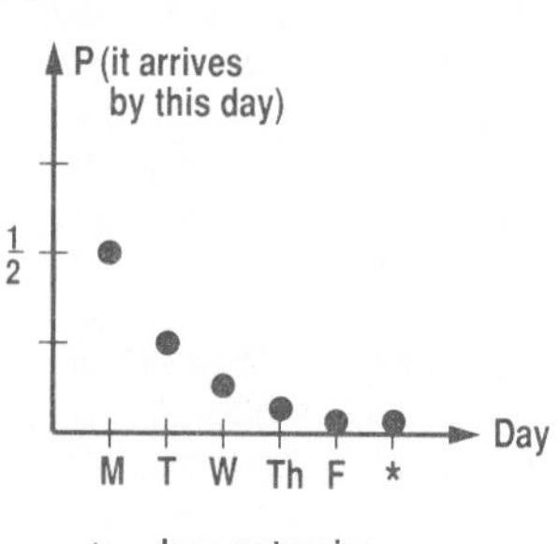

16a; b.

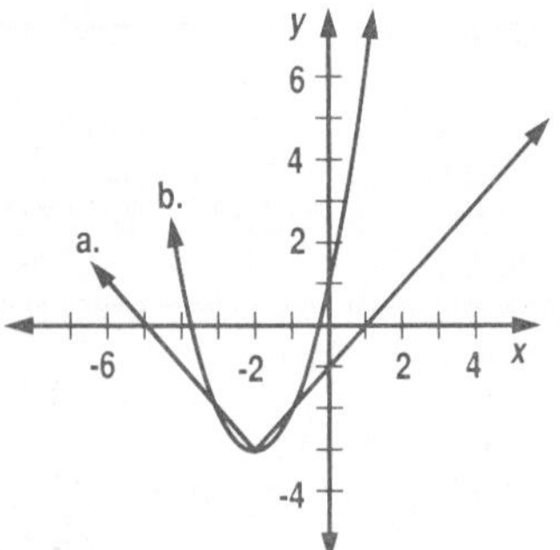

16c. Both open upward. Both have vertex (-2, -3). One is an angle, one is curved.

21a. sums of 3, 4, 5, 6, 7, 8, 9, 10, 11, 12, 13, 14, 15, 16, 17, 18

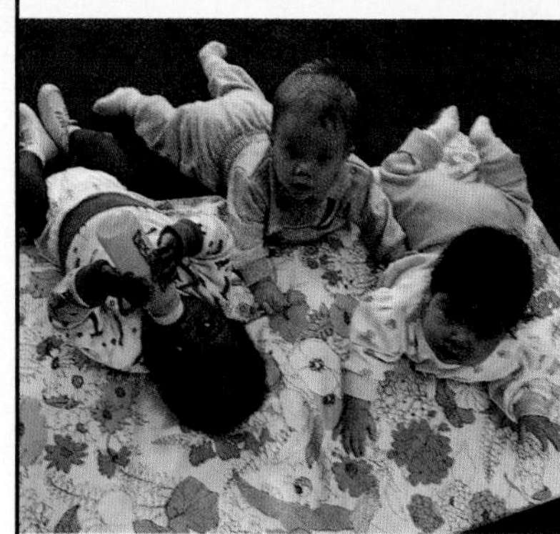

Events do not have to be numerical. Below are graphs for two functions related to the birth of boys and girls. There were about 1,928,000 boys and 1,833,000 girls born in the U.S. in 1985. The function at left assumes the two are equally likely. The function at right gives probabilities calculated from the relative frequencies of boy and girl births in 1985. A basic question for statisticians is "Could you expect relative frequencies like those at right if the probabilities at left are true?"

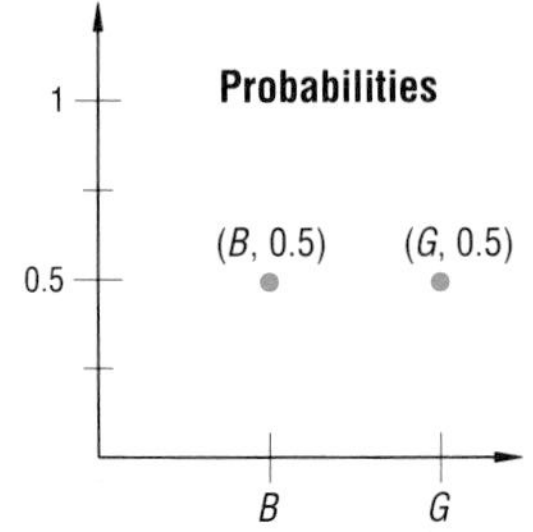

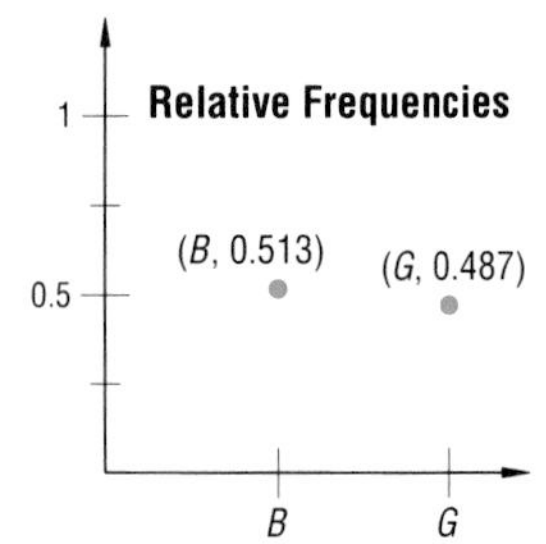

The answer in this case is "No." It is so unlikely to have such relative frequencies (with so many births) that it is possible to conclude that a baby is more likely to be a boy than a girl. In fact, in the U.S. about 105 boys are born for every 100 girls born. But women live longer, so the population contains more women than men.

Questions

Covering the Reading

1. Define: probability function. **See margin.**

In 2–5, let P(n) = the probability of getting a sum of n when two fair dice are thrown.

2. Give an algebraic formula for P(n). $P(n) = -\frac{1}{36}|n - 7| + \frac{1}{6}$

3. Verify that $P(12) = \frac{1}{36}$ using the algebraic formula. **See below.**

4. The graph of P is part of what geometric figure? **an angle**

5. If $P(n) = \frac{5}{36}$, then n = __?__ or __?__. **6; 8**

6. Why can't 2 be in the range of a probability function?
Probabilities are in the range $0 \le x < 1$.

7. Consider the spinner at left. Assume the spinner can land in each region with the same probability. Let P(n) = the probability of landing in region n. Graph the function P. **See margin.**

3. $P(12) = \frac{-1}{36}|12 - 7| + \frac{1}{6}$
$= \frac{-1}{36}|5| + \frac{1}{6}$
$= \frac{-5}{36} + \frac{6}{36} = \frac{1}{36}$

658

In 8–10, *true or false.*

8. In 1985, more boys than girls were born in the U.S. **True**

9. In 1985, more men than women were living in the U.S. **False**

10. In a single birth, the probability that a baby is a boy is $\frac{1}{2}$. **True**

Applying the Mathematics

11. At the right is a graph of a probability function for a weighted (unfair) 6-sided die.

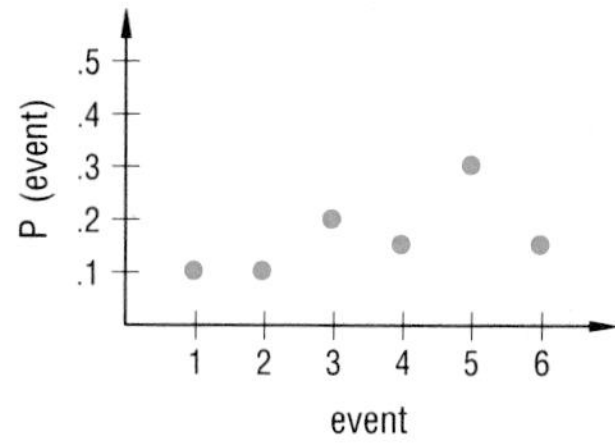

a. $P(3) =$ ___?___ **.2**

b. $P(\text{a number} > 3 \text{ appears}) =$ ___?___ **.6**

c. What would the graph look like if the die were fair?
Each point would be graphed at P = $.1\overline{6}$.

12. Graph the probability function suggested by this situation. If two brown-eyed people marry, then P(a particular child will be brown-eyed) $= \frac{3}{4}$. **See margin.**

13. A letter is mailed Saturday. P(it arrives Monday) $= \frac{1}{2}$. P(it arrives Tuesday) $= (\frac{1}{2})^2$. P(it arrives Wednesday) $= (\frac{1}{2})^3$. P(it arrives Thursday) $= (\frac{1}{2})^4$. P(it arrives Friday) $= (\frac{1}{2})^5$. Calculate P(it does not arrive by Friday) and graph the appropriate probability function.
$\frac{1}{32}$; see margin.

Review

14. If the probability that a boy is born is about 0.513, what is the probability that a family with two children has two boys? *(Lesson 4-8)*
0.263169

15. Give the domain and range of the function of Example 1 in this lesson. *(Lesson 13-4)* **{1, 2, 3, 4, 5}; $\{\frac{1}{5}\}$**

16. a. Graph $y = |x + 2| - 3$. **See margin.**
b. Graph $y = (x + 2)^2 - 3$.
c. Compare and contrast these graphs. *(Lessons 12-2, 13-3)*

17. Find a value of x for which $2x^2 + 3x - 20$ is a prime number. (Hint: Factor the trinomial.) *(Lesson 12-8)* **$x = 3$**

18. Do this problem in your head. Since one thousand times one thousand equals one million, $1005 \cdot 995 =$ ___?___. *(Lesson 10-9)* **999,975**

19. Simplify $\sqrt{12} + \sqrt{3}$. *(Lesson 7-6)* **$3\sqrt{3}$**

Exploration

Answers will vary.

20. a. Toss two dice a large number of times (at least 60).
b. Do you think your dice are fair?

21. Imagine tossing *three* fair dice. **See margin.**
a. What are the possible outcomes?
b. What is the probability of each possible sum?
c. Is the graph part of an absolute value function?

FOLLOW-UP

MORE PRACTICE

For more questions on SPUR Objectives, use *Lesson Master 13-5,* shown below.

EXTENSION

You might ask your class to calculate the probabilities of rolling different sums with two dice that are weighted like the one described in **Question 11.** Counting the outcomes (as for two fair dice) will not work because all the outcomes are not equally likely. However, the probability of each of the outcomes can be found by multiplying. For instance, the probability of rolling a 5 on the first die and a 6 on the second is P(5) • P(6) = .3(.1) = .03.

21b. 3: $\frac{1}{216}$; 4: $\frac{3}{216}$; 5: $\frac{6}{216}$; 6: $\frac{10}{216}$; 7: $\frac{15}{216}$; 8: $\frac{21}{216}$; 9: $\frac{25}{216}$; 10: $\frac{27}{216}$; 11: $\frac{27}{216}$; 12: $\frac{25}{216}$; 13: $\frac{21}{216}$; 14: $\frac{15}{216}$; 15: $\frac{10}{216}$; 16: $\frac{6}{216}$; 17: $\frac{3}{216}$; 18: $\frac{1}{216}$;

21c. No

NAME ______

LESSON **MASTER 13–5**
QUESTIONS ON **SPUR** OBJECTIVES

■**USES** *Objective F (See pages 673–675 for objectives.)*
In 1–4, use the spinner to determine the probabilities.

1. P(A) $\frac{1}{3}$
2. P(B) $\frac{1}{6}$
3. P(C) $\frac{1}{6}$
4. P(D) $\frac{1}{3}$

In 5–9, two dice in the shape of a triangular base pyramid are tossed. The faces are numbered 1 to 4, and are equally likely to appear.

5. P(sum is 2) $\frac{1}{16}$
6. P(sum is 4) $\frac{3}{16}$
7. P(sum is 7) $\frac{1}{8}$
8. P(sum is even) $\frac{1}{2}$

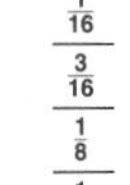

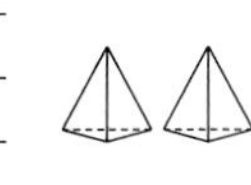

9. The batting average of a baseball player is an indication of the probability that the player will get a hit in a time at bat. In 1987, Tony Gwynn of San Diego had a batting average of .369. What was the probability that he would not get a hit in a time at bat?
.631

■**REPRESENTATIONS** *Objective I*

10. Graph the probability function for the numbers on the spinner.

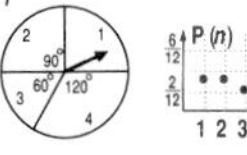

11. Three table tennis balls are numbered 1, 2, or 3. A ball is chosen from a box, replaced, and then another is chosen. Graph the probability function for all possible sums.

LESSON 13-6

RESOURCES
■ Lesson Master 13-6

OBJECTIVES

B Find and analyze values of tangent functions.
G Find lengths and angle measures in triangles using the tangent function.

TEACHING NOTES

Reading Your students may need help identifying the opposite and adjacent legs when relating the definition of tan *A* to the figure.

To convince your students that tan *A* depends on the size of $\angle A$, not on the size of the triangle, calculate the tangent of corresponding angles in similar triangles. Relate the example that opens the lesson to triangles with sides 6, 8, and 10 or other multiples of 3, 4, and 5.

On most calculators, two keys must be pressed to find *A* given tan $A = k$. The text mentions the key sequence

k [INV] [tan].

On some calculators the key sequence is

k [2nd] [tan].

You might mention that these keys undo the tangent function in much the same way that the square root key undoes squaring. The symbol for the undoing function is $\tan^{-1}$ and may appear on some calculators. Emphasize that calculators must be set to degrees, not radians.

LESSON

The Tangent of an Angle

Consider right triangle *ABC* below. Its *legs* (the sides forming the right angle) have lengths 3 and 4. $\angle C$ is a right angle and is thus a 90° angle. Since the measures of the three angles of a triangle add up to 180°, $m\angle A + m\angle B = 90$.

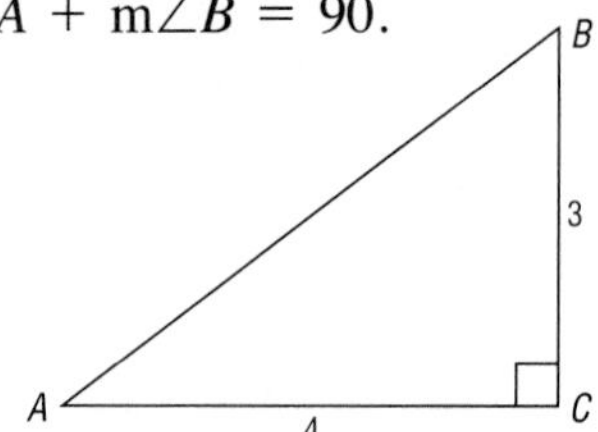

It is possible to determine the measures of the angles of this triangle using a function called the **tangent function.** The **tangent of angle *A*** in a right triangle, abbreviated **tan A,** is defined as a ratio of legs in the triangle.

Definition:

In a right triangle with acute angle *A*,

$$\tan A = \frac{\text{length of the leg opposite angle } A}{\text{length of the leg adjacent to angle } A}.$$

Above, *BC* is the leg opposite $\angle A$, and *AC* is the leg adjacent to $\angle A$. So $\tan A = \frac{BC}{AC}$. In BASIC, TAN(*A*) stands for tan *A*. Most scientific calculators have a [tan] key. In this lesson, the domain of the tangent function is the set of acute angles in right triangles. In later courses you will study this function with a larger domain.

Example 1 In $\triangle ABC$ above, (a) find tan *A*; (b) find $m\angle A$.

Solution

(a) Substitute the lengths for $\triangle ABC$ in the definition.

$$\tan A = \frac{\text{length of the leg opposite angle } A}{\text{length of the leg adjacent to angle } A} = \frac{BC}{AC} = \frac{3}{4}$$

(b) Use your calculator. Be sure it is set to degrees. When $\tan A = \frac{3}{4} = .75$, the key sequence

0.75 [INV] [tan]

undoes the tangent and gives the result. $m\angle A \approx 37°$.

One of the wondrous sights in Seattle is the peak of Mt. Rainier.

Example 2 From Seattle, which is at sea level, it is 58 miles to Mount Rainier. Mount Rainier towers 14,410 ft above sea level. When viewed from Seattle, how far is the peak of Mount Rainier above the horizon?

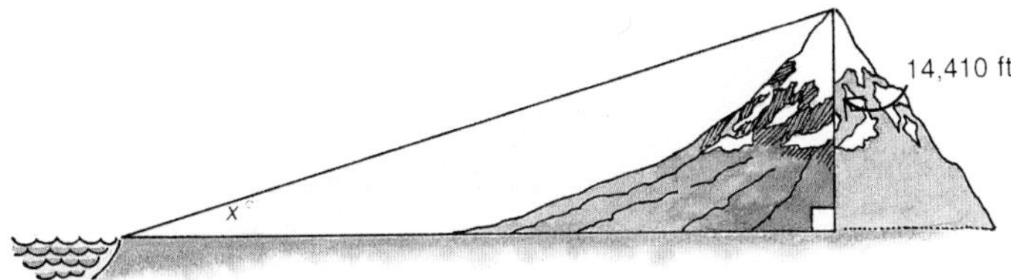

Solution The picture above, though not drawn to scale, represents the situation. Since the tangent is a ratio, the sides must be measured in the same units. Change miles to feet.

$$58 \text{ miles} \cdot \frac{5280 \text{ ft}}{1 \text{ mile}} = 306{,}240 \text{ feet}$$

Thus,

$$\tan x = \frac{14{,}410 \text{ ft}}{306{,}240 \text{ ft}} \approx 0.047$$

The key sequence .047 INV tan reveals that $x \approx 2.7°$.

The solution in Example 2 ignores the curvature of the earth, which lowers the perceived height by about 2240 feet. Even with this correction, the peak of Mount Rainier is 2.3° above the horizon. The diameter of the moon is about 0.5°. Since $2.3° > 4 \cdot 0.5°$, Mount Rainier is over 4 moon diameters above the horizon.

In **Example 1** you can ask your students to find $m\angle B$ using the tangent ratio. They can then check their result by using $m\angle A + m\angle B + m\angle C = 180$.

Error Analysis It may be difficult for students to differentiate the two types of questions in this lesson, those that use the tangent to find a length and those that use the inverse tangent to find an angle. You can illustrate the inverse relationship between the two by having students enter a value into their calculator, then alternately press tan and INV tan.

ADDITIONAL EXAMPLES

1. In $\triangle PQR$ find **a.** tan P and **b.** m$\angle P$.

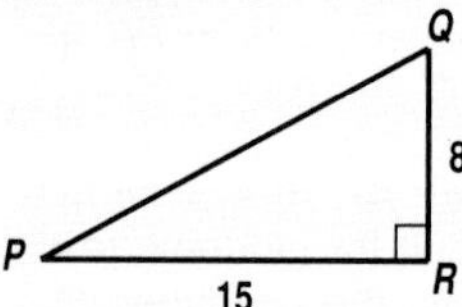

a. 0.533; b. 28°

2. Bob is 75 inches tall and his little sister Betsy is only 40 inches tall. If they are standing 4 feet apart, what is the approximate size of the angle at which Betsy must look up to see Bob's face?
36°

3. Suppose an airplane takes off at a 15° angle. After it has traveled 600 feet horizontally, how far above the ground is it?
161 feet

In Examples 1 and 2, the calculator sequence [INV] [tan] gives you an angle when given the tangent. When you know an angle with measure x, the sequence X [tan] gives you the tangent. This sequence is used in Example 3.

Example 3 Nancy had to look up 50° to see the top of a tree 5 meters away. If her eyes are 1.5 meters above the ground, how tall is the tree?

Solution If h is the height of the tree *above eye level,* then the height of the tree is $h + 1.5$. First use the triangle to find h, then add 1.5. To find h, note that

$$\tan 50° = \frac{h}{5}.$$

To compute tan 50° use the key sequence 50 [tan].

$$\tan 50° \approx 1.19.$$

Substituting,

$$\frac{h}{5} \approx 1.19.$$
$$h \approx 5 \cdot 1.19$$
$$h \approx 6.0.$$

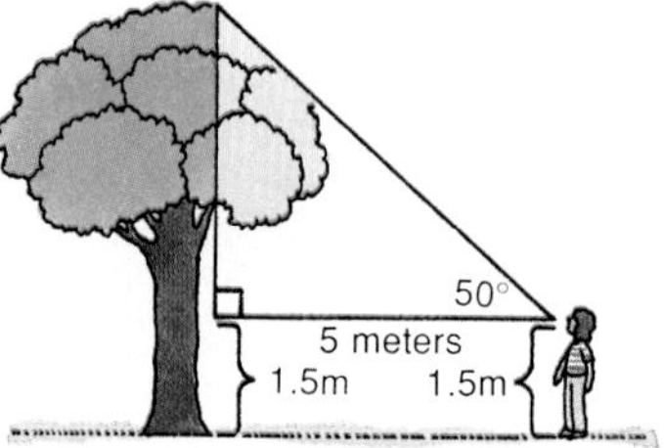

So the full height of the tree is about $h + 1.5 \approx 6.0 + 1.5 = 7.5$ m.

You may not realize it, but you have already calculated tangents on the coordinate plane. Consider the line $y = \frac{2}{3}x - 4$. This is a line with a slope of $\frac{2}{3}$. It crosses the x-axis at (6, 0) and also goes through $(7, \frac{2}{3})$.

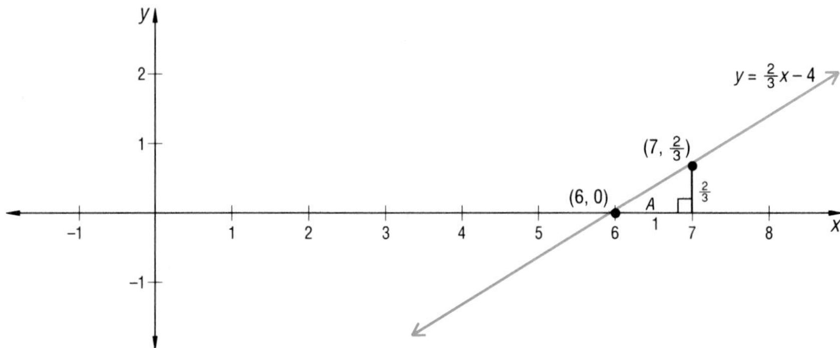

662

Let A be the angle of the upper half of the line with the positive ray of the x-axis. From the graph on page 662 you can see that

$$\tan A = \frac{\frac{2}{3}}{1} = \frac{2}{3}.$$

This is the slope of the line!

If A is the angle formed by the upper half of the oblique line $y = mx + b$ and the positive ray of the x-axis, then

$$\tan A = m.$$

The tangent function is quite a function; it combines the concepts of slope, graphing, angles, ratios, and triangles.

Questions

Covering the Reading

In 1 and 2, use right triangle DEF below.

1. **a.** $m\angle D + m\angle E =$ _?_. 90
   b. The relationship in part a means that $\angle D$ and $\angle E$ are _?_ angles. complementary

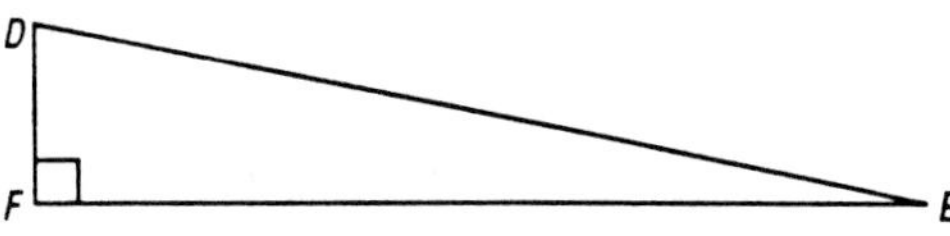

2. **a.** Name the side opposite $\angle E$. $\overline{DF}$
   b. Name the side adjacent to $\angle E$. $\overline{EF}$
   c. What is tan E? $\frac{DE}{EF}$

3. What is the domain of the tangent function in this lesson?
   the set of acute angles in right triangles

In 4 and 5, estimate $m\angle A$ to the nearest degree for the given value of tan A.

4. $\tan A = 1.963$ 63°
5. $\tan A = 0.5$ 27°

6. Refer to $\triangle GHI$ below.
   a. Find tan I. $0.5\overline{3}$
   b. Find $m\angle I$. ≈ 28°

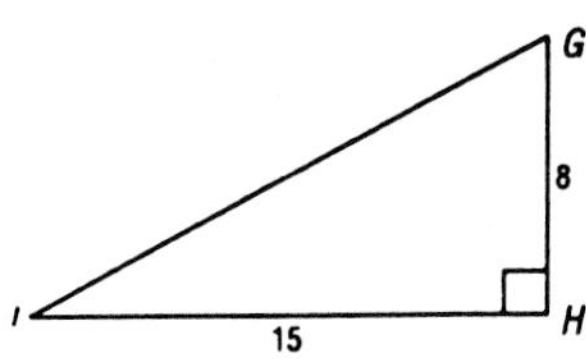

NOTES ON QUESTIONS
Questions 9 and 10: Encourage students to make drawings as their first step.

Question 12: Students must use the Pythagorean Theorem to find *AC*.

ADDITIONAL ANSWERS
19c.

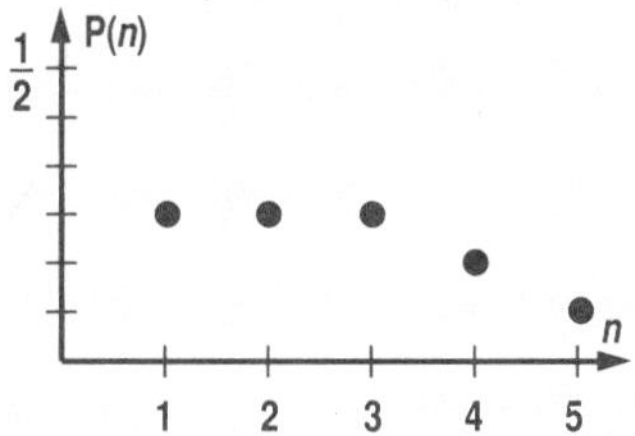

20.

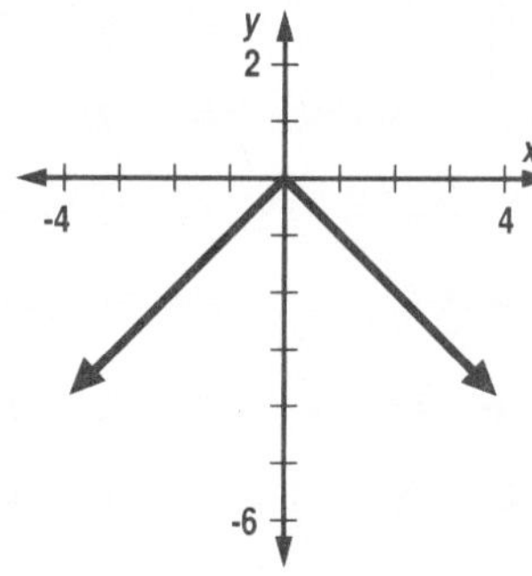

In 7 and 8, use your calculator. Give a three-place decimal approximation.

7. tan 57°; **1.540** **8.** tan 3°. **0.052**

9. Lester had to look up 65° to see the top of a tree 6 meters away. If his eyes are 1.7 meters above the ground, how tall is the tree? **14.57 m**

10. From sea level in Tacoma, Washington it is 42 miles to Mount Rainier. Find the measure of the angle needed to see the peak of Mount Rainier from Tacoma. **≈ 3.7°**

11. What is the relationship between the tangent function and the slope of a line $y = mx + b$? **tan *A* = *m***

Applying the Mathematics

12. Refer to △*ABC* at right.
a. Find *AC*. **24**
b. Find m∠*A*. **≈ 16°**
c. Find m∠*B*. **74°**

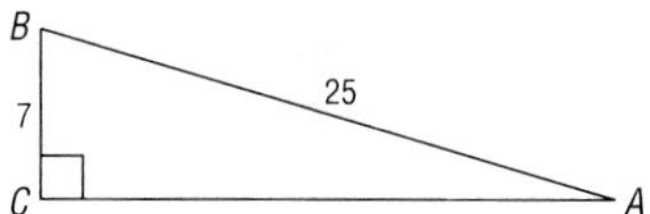

13. To the nearest degree, find the measure of the angle formed by the upper half of the line $y = 4x - 3$ and the positive ray of the *x*-axis. **76°**

14. Line *P* goes through the origin and the upper half makes an angle of 140° with the positive ray of the *x*-axis.
a. Find the slope of line *P*. **≈-0.84**
b. Find an equation for line *P*. **y = -0.84x**

15. A meter stick casts a shadow 0.6 meters long. Find the measure of the angle needed to see the sun. (This is called the *angle of elevation* of the sun.) **≈ 59°**

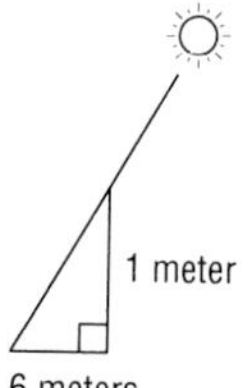

16. Joan had to look up 40° to see the top of a flagpole 20 feet away. The situation is pictured below. If her eyes are 5 feet above the ground, how high is the flagpole? **21.8 ft**

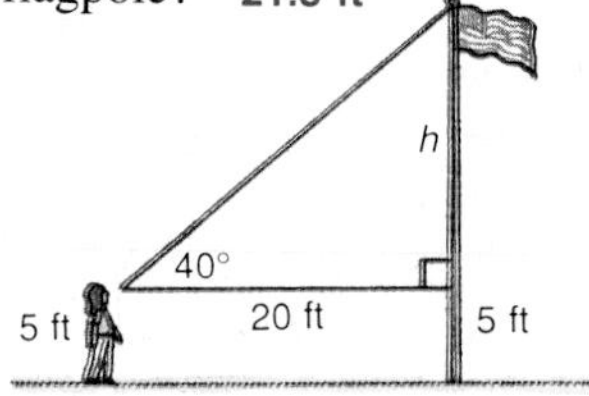

17. The Sears Tower in Chicago is about 443 meters tall. If a person two meters tall is 100 meters from the front door, about what is the measure of the angle needed to see the top? **≈ 77°**

Review

18. In right triangle DEF, $\angle D$ is a right angle. If $m\angle E$ is four times $m\angle F$, find $m\angle E$. *(Lesson 3-8)* **72**

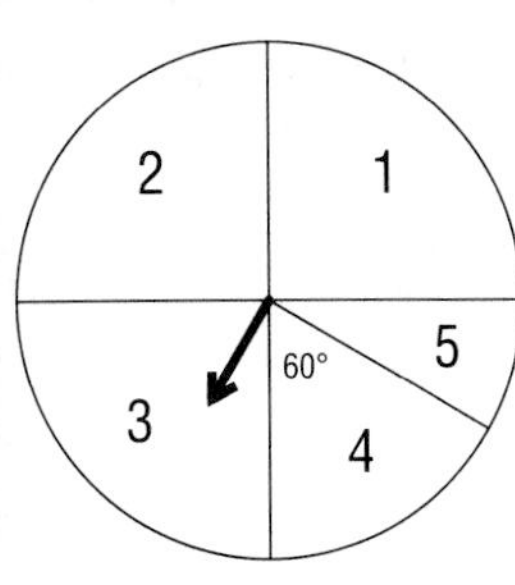

19. In the spinner at left, you receive the number of points indicated when the spinner lands in the region. The two diameters are perpendicular and the angle of region 4 has a measure of 60°.

a. What is the measure of the angle in region 5? **30°**

b. Give P(landing in region n) for $n = 1, 2, 3, 4$, and 5. $\frac{1}{4}, \frac{1}{4}, \frac{1}{4}, \frac{1}{6}, \frac{1}{12}$

c. Graph the probability function P. *(Lesson 13-5)* **See margin.**

20. Graph $y = -|x|$. *(Lesson 13-3)* **See margin.**

21. What number is not in the domain of the function f if $f(x) = \frac{x - 1}{2x + 4}$? *(Lesson 13-4)* $x = -2$

22. a. If $y = 3(x + 1)^2 - 4$, what is the smallest possible value of y? **-4**

b. If $y = 3|x + 1| - 4$, what is the smallest possible value of y? **-4**

c. If $y = 3\sqrt{x + 1} - 4$, what is the smallest possible value of y? *(Lessons 12-2, 13-2, 13-4)* **-4**

23. Solve for x: $ax^2 + bx + c = 0$. *(Lesson 12-4)* $x = \frac{-b \pm \sqrt{b^2 - 4ac}}{2a}$

24. If $\frac{(a^{11})^{12} \cdot a^{13}}{a^{14}} = a^t$, what is the value of t? *(Lessons 9-5, 9-7)* **131**

Exploration

25. When $x = \frac{\pi A}{180°}$, $\tan A \approx \frac{2x^5 + 5x^3 + 15x}{15}$.

a. Let $A = 10°$. How close is the polynomial approximation to the calculator value of tan A? **tan 10 ≈ calculator value 0.1763270, approximation 0.1763267, .0000003 off**

b. Repeat part a when $A = 70°$. **calculator value 2.7474774, approximation 2.192516, off by 0.554961**

26. What became of the man who sat on a beach along the Gulf of Mexico? **He became a tangent.**

FOLLOW-UP

MORE PRACTICE

For more questions on SPUR Objectives, use *Lesson Master 13-6,* shown below.

NAME ____________

LESSON **MASTER 13–6**

QUESTIONS ON **SPUR** OBJECTIVES

■**SKILLS** *Objective B (See pages 673–675 for objectives.)*

In 1–6, use a calculator to find each of the values to the nearest thousandth.

1. tan 22.5° **0.414** 2. tan 72.6° **3.191** 3. tan 62.7° **1.937**

4. tan 7.1° **0.125** 5. $(\tan 60°)^2$ **3.000** 6. $\frac{1}{\tan 45°}$ **1.000**

In 7–10, find the measure of each angle to the nearest tenth of a degree.

7. $m\angle A$ if $\tan A = 1.036$ **46.0°** 8. $m\angle B$ if $\tan A = .556$ **29.1°**

9. $m\angle C$ if $\tan A = .048$ **2.7°** 10. $m\angle D$ if $\tan A = 3.549$ **74.3°**

In 11–14, use the picture.

11. $\tan A =$ $\frac{5}{12}$ 12. $m\angle A =$ **22.6°**

13. $\tan B =$ $\frac{12}{5}$ 14. $m\angle B =$ **67.4°**

B, C, A; 5, 13, 12

■**USES** *Objective G*

15. Sara looks up at an angle of 35° to the top of the Gateway Arch in St. Louis from a viewing point 900 feet from the base of the Arch. Approximately how tall is the Arch if Sara's eyes are 5 feet above the ground? **about 635 feet**

16. Ben's eyes are 170 cm above the ground. When he stands 20 m from the base of a fire tower, he has to look up at an angle of 40° to see the top. How high is the tower? **about 18.5 m**

17. What angle does the upper half of the line $y = -0.6x + 2$ make with the positive ray of the x-axis? **31°**

18. What is the slope of a line which makes an angle of 68° with the positive ray of the x-axis? **about 2.48**

118

LESSON 13-7

RESOURCES
- Lesson Master 13-7
- Visual for Teaching Aid 80: Graphs of $y = \tan(x)$, $y = \sin(x)$, and $y = \log(x)$
- Computer Master 29

OBJECTIVE

B Find and analyze values of functions.

TEACHING NOTES

We suggest that you teach this lesson with the following goals in mind: (1) Give an extremely brief look at other functions that appear on a calculator; (2) Do not expect students to do more than evaluate the functions presented here using a calculator or a graph.

The opening paragraph mentions error messages. Remind students that error messages do not always arise from attempting to do a function calculation with a number not in the domain. Sometimes an error message signals that a number is too large or too small for the calculator to handle.

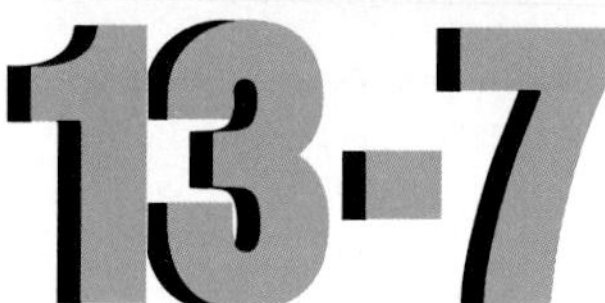

LESSON

13-7 Functions on Calculators

Calculators use the idea of functions. Rules programmed into calculators are designed to give you single answers when you enter a value of the domain. A calculator will indicate an error message when you enter a value not in the domain. Here are some familiar keys and their domains.

Key	Function	Domain	Errors
the square root key $\sqrt{\ }$	$SQR(x) = \sqrt{x}$	set of nonnegative reals	$x < 0$
the factorial function key !	$FACT(n) = n!$	set of nonnegative integers	nonintegers
reciprocal function key $\frac{1}{x}$	$f(x) = \frac{1}{x}$	set of nonzero reals	$x = 0$
the squaring key x^2	$s(x) = x^2$	set of all reals	none

In Lesson 13-6, you used the tan key. This key defines the tangent function. Its equation is $y = \tan x$. Below is a graph of this function for values of x between 0° and 90°

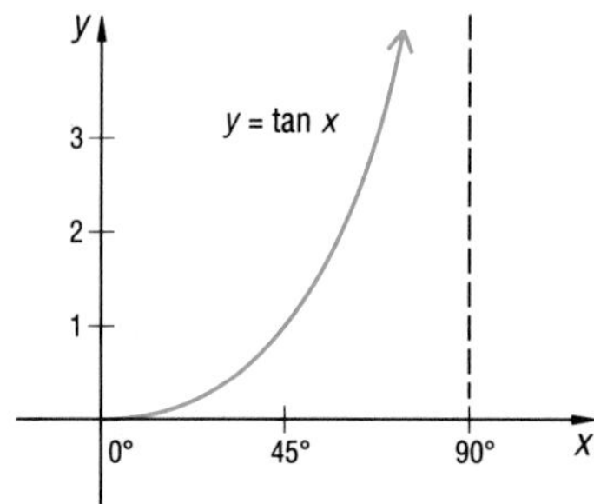

You have learned some applications for the tangent function. In this lesson, we introduce you to some of the other keys on your scientific calculator.

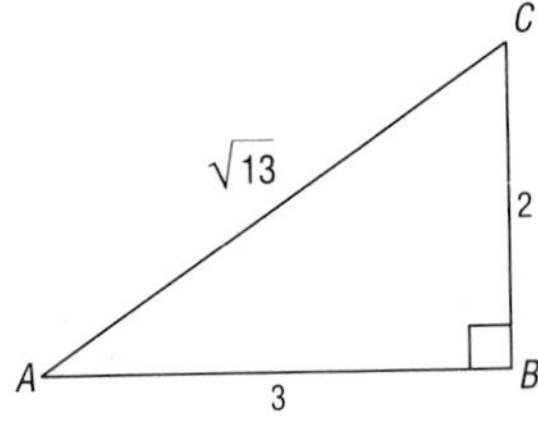

Two keys related to the tangent key are the sine key sin and the cosine key cos. These keys also give values of ratios of sides in right triangles. Again consider a right triangle ABC.

$$\textbf{sin } A = \frac{\text{length of the leg opposite angle } A}{\text{hypotenuse}}$$

$$\textbf{cos } A = \frac{\text{length of leg adjacent to angle } A}{\text{hypotenuse}}$$

So in this case, $\sin A = \frac{2}{\sqrt{13}}$ and $\cos A = \frac{3}{\sqrt{13}}$.

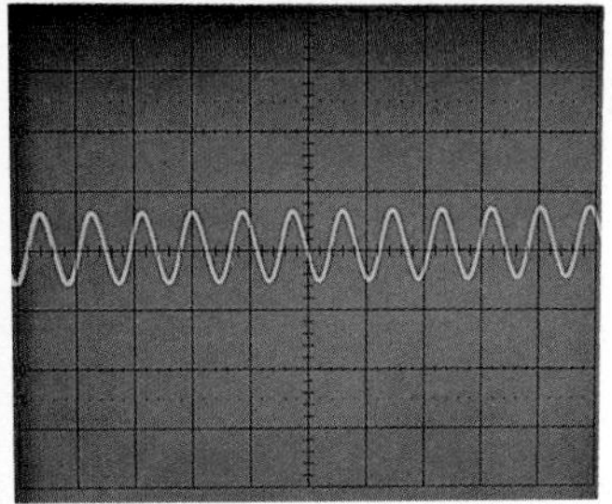

It is possible to define these functions and the tangent function for any degrees. A surprise comes when the sine or cosine function is graphed. Below is the graph of $y = \sin x$.

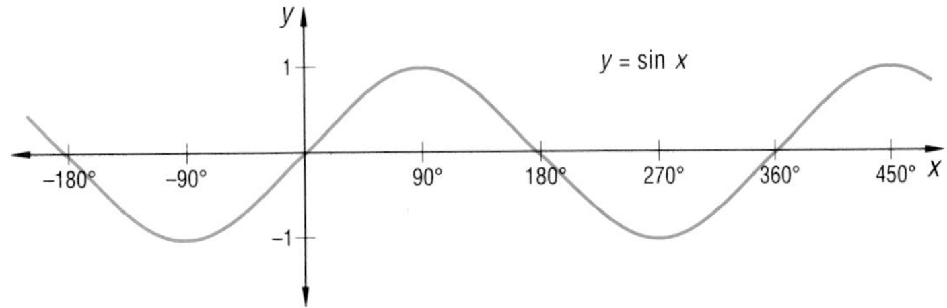

The curve is called a *sinusoidal curve*, and it has the same shape as sound waves and radio waves. The sine, cosine, and tangent functions are part of the area of mathematics called trigonometry. These functions are so important that most high schools offer a full course in trigonometry devoted to studying them and their applications.

Another function key on almost all scientific calculators is the **common logarithm key** [log]. This key defines a function $y = \log x$, read "y equals the common logarithm of x." The common logarithm of a number is the power to which 10 must be raised to equal that number. So, since 1 million = 10^6, log (1 million) = 6. Logarithms provide a way to deal easily with very large or very small numbers. A graph of the common logarithm function is given below.

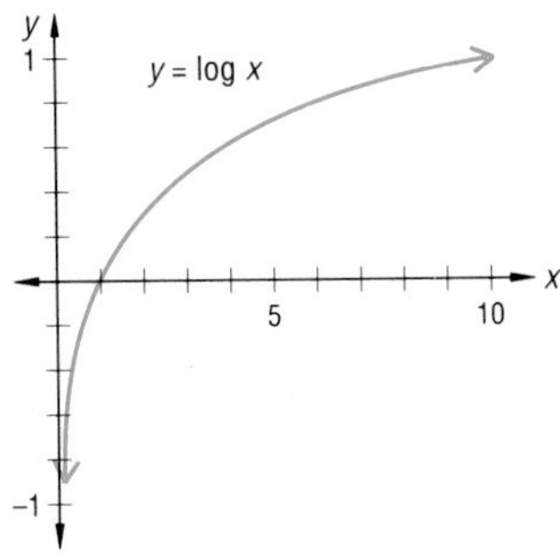

This graph pictures the kind of growth often found in learning. At first, one learns an idea quickly, so the curve increases quickly. But after a while it is more difficult to improve, so the curve increases more slowly.

NOTES ON QUESTIONS

Question 9: Students may be surprised that they do not get an error message when evaluating 0! Explain that 0! is defined to be 1 so that patterns which arise in working with factorials are consistent. One such pattern is

$$(n+1)! = (n+1) \cdot n!$$

and if $n = 0$, then

$$(0+1)! = (0+1) \cdot 0!$$

So, $1! = 1 \cdot 0!$,

from which $0! = 1$.

They will study these patterns (in connection with combinations and permutations) in later courses.

Making Connections for Question 21: Students should refer back to the graph at the beginning of Lesson 13-5.

Alternate Approach for Question 24: The reference to Lesson 8-6 suggests that this question be solved by writing the equation of a line. Another method is to calculate the speed traveled, then find the time to travel 13 km.

ADDITIONAL ANSWERS

16a.

x	cos x	x	cos x
-90	0	140	-0.77
-80	0.17	150	-0.87
-70	0.34	160	-0.94
-60	0.50	170	-0.98
-50	0.64	180	-1
-40	0.77	190	-0.98
-30	0.87	200	-0.94
-20	0.94	210	-0.87
-10	0.98	220	-0.77
0	1	230	-0.64
10	0.98	240	-0.50
20	0.94	250	-0.34
30	0.87	260	-0.17
40	0.77	270	0
50	0.64	280	0.17
60	0.50	290	0.34
70	0.34	300	0.50
80	0.17	310	0.64
90	0	320	0.77
100	-0.17	330	0.87
110	-0.34	340	0.94
120	-0.50	350	0.98
130	-0.64	360	1

16a. See margin, page 667.
16b.

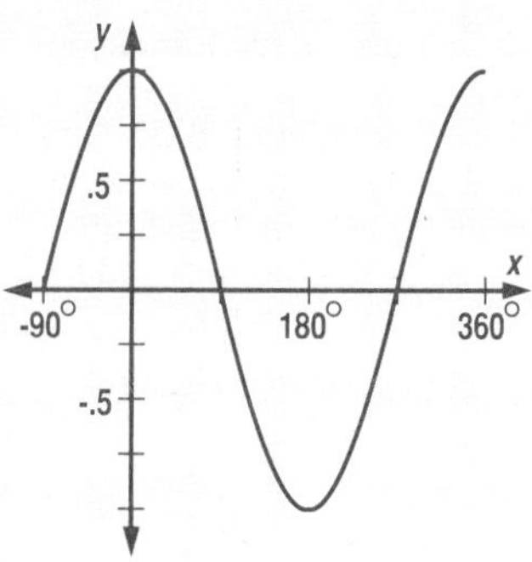

17a. It depends on how your BASIC defines LOG X.

X	LOG X (base 10)	or	LOG X (base e)
1	0		0
2	0.30103		.69315
3	0.47712		1.0986
4	0.60206		1.3863
5	0.69897		1.6094
6	0.77815		1.7918
7	0.84510		1.9459
8	0.90309		2.0794
9	0.95424		2.1972
10	1		2.3026

17b.

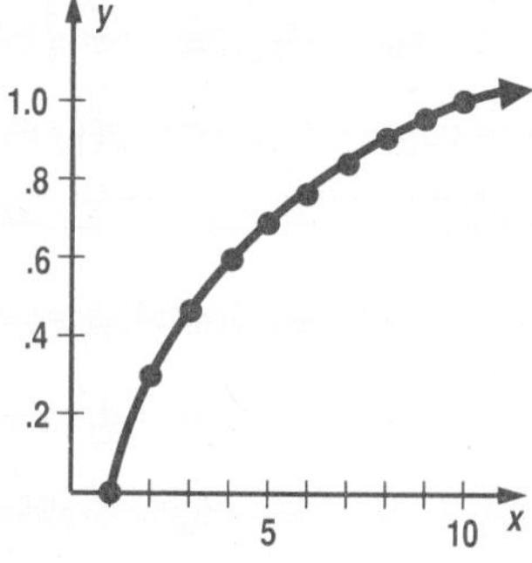

17c. It passes through the point (1, 0), but then goes up faster.

18a.

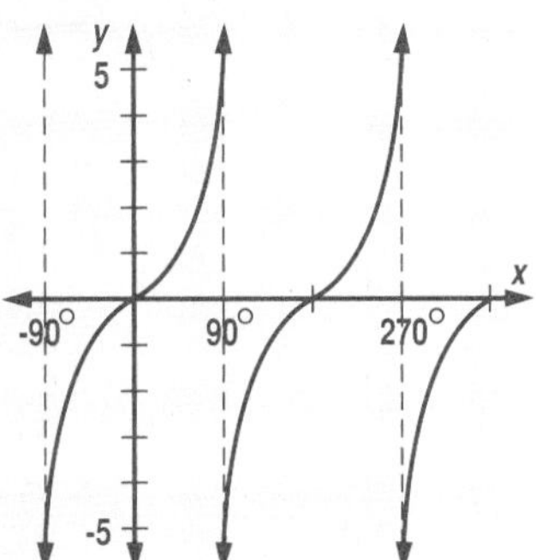

approximately -0.2

Most scientific calculators have other function keys. These keys would not be there unless many people needed to get values of that function. Calculators have made it possible for people to obtain values of these functions more easily than most people ever imagined. The algebra that you have studied this year gives you the background to understand these functions and to deal with them.

Questions

Covering the Reading

In 1–6, approximate each value to the nearest thousandth using a calculator.

1. tan 11° 0.194 **2.** sin 45° 0.707 **3.** cos 47° 0.682

4. log (10^6) 6 **5.** $(-3.489)^2$ 12.173 **6.** $\sqrt{0.5}$ 0.707

In 7–9, consider the [√], [!], [1/x], and [x²] function keys on your calculator. Which produce error messages when the given is entered?

7. 3.5 ! **8.** -4 √, ! **9.** 0 1/x

10. Which function has a graph that is the shape of a sound wave?
sine and cosine

11. Which function has a graph that is sometimes used to model learning?
common logarithm

12. Use $\triangle ABC$ at right. Give the value of:
  a. AC 29
  b. $\sin A$ ≈0.690
  c. $\cos A$ ≈0.724

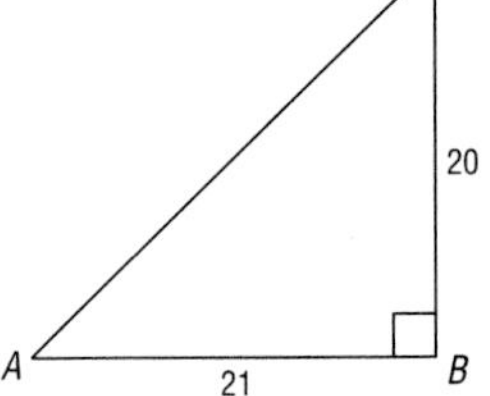

In 13–15, refer to the graph of $y = \sin x$ in this lesson.
a. Estimate the value from the graph.
b. Use a calculator to check your estimate.

13. sin 90° a) 1; b) 1 **14.** sin 360° a) 0; b) 0 **15.** sin(-70°) a) -0.9; b) -0.940

Applying the Mathematics

16. **a.** Make a table of values for $y = \cos x$ for values of x from -90° to 360° in increments of 10°. See margin.
  b. Carefully graph this function.
  c. What graph in this lesson does the graph of $y = \cos x$ most resemble? sin x

668

17. Many computers use the name LOG to refer to a different logarithm function than the one in the lesson. **See margin.**

a. Run this program or use your calculator to determine what is printed.

```
10 PRINT "X", "LOG X"
20 FOR X = 1 TO 10
30    Y = LOG(X)
40    PRINT X, Y
50 NEXT X
60 END
```

b. Graph the ordered pairs that are printed.

c. Is your graph like that in the lesson, or is it different? If it is different, how does it differ?

18. a. Graph $y = \tan x$ on an automatic plotter with x set for degrees. Use the graph to estimate tan (-10°). **See margin.**

b. Verify the value of tan (-10°) on your calculator. **-0.18**

19. Graph the reciprocal function $f(x) = \frac{1}{x}$. **See margin.**

20. The graph of the squaring function $s(x) = x^2$ is what curve? **a parabola**

Review

21. a. In tossing two fair dice, what number is the most likely sum to appear? **7**

b. What is its probability of occurring? *(Lesson 13-5)* $\frac{1}{6}$

22. In $\triangle ABC$ at the left, find the measure of $\angle A$ to the nearest degree. *(Lesson 13-6)* **37°**

23. Graph $f(x) = 2|x - 3| + 4$. *(Lesson 13-3)* **See margin.**

24. The explorers were 13 km from home base at 2 P.M. and 10 km from home base at 3:30 P.M. At this rate, when will they reach home? *(Lesson 8-6)* **6.5 hours; 8:30 P.M.**

19.

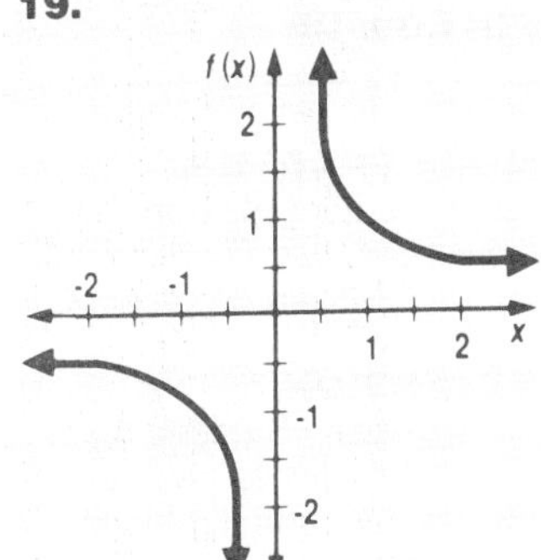

23.

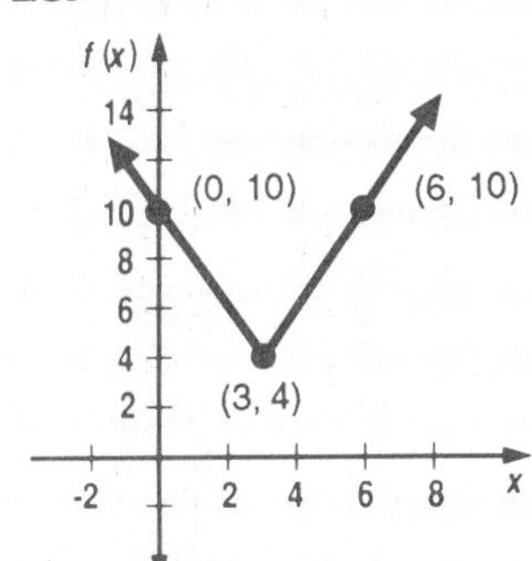

NAME ______

LESSON **MASTER 13–7**
QUESTIONS ON **SPUR** OBJECTIVES

SKILLS *Objective B (See pages 673–675 for objectives.)*
In 1–14, approximate to the nearest thousandth.

1. $\sqrt{21,443}$	146.434	2. 11!	39,916,800
3. $\frac{1}{13}$	0.077	4. SQR(11.4)	3.376
5. tan 48°	1.111	6. sin 26.5°	0.446
7. log 1000	3	8. cos 143°	-0.799
9. $(2.63)^{-2}$	0.145	10. tan (-25°)	-0.466
11. 3! · 4!	144	12. sin 1285°	-0.423
13. $\sqrt{0.0256}$	0.160	14. log 0.789	-0.103

Multiple choice **In 15–19, tell which number is not in the domain of the given function.**

15. SQR	(a) 0.5	(b) -4	(c) $(3)^{-2}$	(d) 0	b
16. LOG	(a) 0.5	(b) -4	(c) $\frac{1}{3}$	(d) 1600	b
17. tan	(a) 0.5°	(b) -4°	(c) 1000°	(d) 90°	d
18. FACT	(a) 0.5	(b) 2140	(c) 3^2	(d) 0	a
19. $\frac{1}{x}$	(a) 0.5	(b) -4	(c) $(3)^2$	(d) 0	d

 119

FOLLOW-UP

MORE PRACTICE
For more questions on SPUR Objectives, use *Lesson Master 13-7,* shown on page 669.

EXTENSION
Computer Students can use computers to investigate the sin, tan, and log functions. Since these are preprogrammed functions in BASIC, it is easy to write a short program that will print a table of values for these functions. Example:

```
10 PRINT "X (IN DEG.)",
   "TAN(X)"
20 FOR X=0 TO 89
30 PRINT
   X, TAN (X*3.1416/180)
40 NEXT X
50 END
```

Notice that in line 30, we multiply X by π/180 when finding the tangent. This is done to convert X from degrees to radians (used in BASIC). You might at this time also introduce students to radian measure and investigate radian-degree equivalents.

EVALUATION
Alternative Assessment
You may wish to once again use an informal questionnaire of the kind suggested with Lesson 1-1. (See page 8.) You and your students might find it interesting to compare their earlier responses, at the beginning of the course, with their responses now, at the conclusion of the course.

31a.

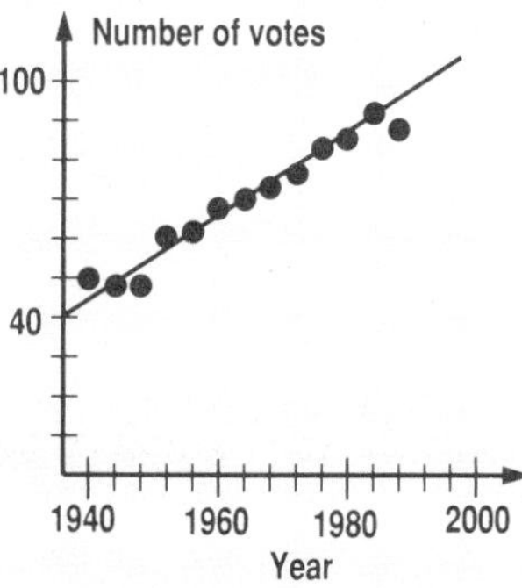

In 25 and 26, $S(x) = x + \frac{x^2}{20}$ gives the number of feet a car traveling at x miles per hour will take to stop. $B(x) = \frac{x^2}{20}$ gives the number of feet after brakes are applied.

25. About how many feet does it take to stop at 40 mph? *(Lesson 13-2)* **120 ft**

26. If skid marks in an accident are 100 feet long, at least how fast was the car going? *(Lesson 13-2)* **at least 44.7 miles per hour**

27. If you read 17 pages of a 300-page novel in 45 minutes, about how long will it take you to read the entire novel? *(Lesson 5-7)* **794.12 min, or 13 hr 14.12 min**

In 28–30, solve.

28. $\sqrt{v - 6} = 4$ *(Lesson 7-4)* **$v = 22$**

29. $\frac{m}{2} = \frac{m + 36}{11}$ *(Lesson 5-7)* **$m = 8$**

30. $3x + 9 > x$ *(Lesson 6-7)* **$x > -\frac{9}{2}$**

31. Here are the total numbers of votes (to the nearest million) cast for major candidates in the presidential elections since 1940.

Year	Number of Votes (millions)	Winner
1940	50	Franklin D. Roosevelt
1944	48	Franklin D. Roosevelt
1948	48	Harry S Truman
1952	61	Dwight D. Eisenhower
1956	62	Dwight D. Eisenhower
1960	68	John F. Kennedy
1964	70	Lyndon B. Johnson
1968	73	Richard M. Nixon
1972	76	Richard M. Nixon
1976	83	Jimmy Carter
1980	85	Ronald Reagan
1984	92	Ronald Reagan
1988	88	George Bush

a. Graph the ordered pairs. **See margin.**

b. Use the graph to predict how many votes will be cast for major candidates in the presidential election of 2000. *(Lesson 8-7)* **sample: 120 million**

Exploration

32. List all the function keys of a scientific calculator to which you have access. Separate those you have studied from those you have not. Identify at least one situation in which each function you have studied might be used. **Answers will vary.**

Summary

A function is a set of ordered pairs in which each first coordinate appears with exactly one second coordinate. A function may be described by a graph, by a written rule, by listing the pairs, or by an equation. The key idea in functions is that knowing the first coordinate of a pair is enough to determine the second coordinate of the pair. For this reason, functions exist whenever one variable determines another.

If a function f contains the ordered pair (a, b), then we write $f(a) = b$. We say that b is the value of the function at a. The set of possible values of a is the domain of the function. The set of possible values of b is the range of the function. If a and b are numbers, then the function can be graphed on the coordinate plane and values of the function can be found or approximated by reading the graph. The purpose of automatic graphers is to graph functions. Though convenient, it is not necessary to use $f(x)$ notation for functions; y is often used to stand for the second coordinate. Many of the graphs you studied in earlier chapters describe functions.

Equation	Graph	Type of function
$f(x) = mx + b$	line	linear
$f(x) = ax^2 + bx + c$	parabola	quadratic
$f(x) = b^x$	exponential curve	exponential
$f(x) = a\lvert x - h\rvert + k$	angle	absolute value

When the domain of a function is a set of outcomes in a situation and the range of the function the probabilities of these outcomes, then the function is a probability function. Graphs of probability functions take on various shapes.

Calculator keys determine values of functions. The tan key evaluates the tangent function, which can be used to determine lengths of sides and measures of angles in right triangles. You will encounter this function and many others in your future work in mathematics.

Vocabulary

Below are the most important terms and phrases for this chapter. You should be able to give a general description and a specific example of each.

Lesson 13-1
function
relation
value of a function
linear function
quadratic function

Lesson 13-2
$f(x)$ notation

Lesson 13-3
absolute value function

Lesson 13-4
domain of a function
range of a function

Lesson 13-5
probability function

Lesson 13-6
tangent function
tangent of an angle in a right triangle, tan A
tan, INV tan

Lesson 13-7
function key on a calculator
sine of an angle in a right triangle, sin A
cosine of an angle in a right triangle, cos A
sin, cos
logarithm key log

SUMMARY

The Summary gives an overview of the entire chapter and provides an opportunity for students to consider the material as a whole. Thus, the Summary can be used to help students relate the concepts presented in the chapter.

VOCABULARY

Terms, symbols, and properties are listed by lesson to provide a checklist of things a student must know. Emphasize to students that they should read the vocabulary list carefully before starting the Progress Self-Test. If students do not understand the meaning of a term, they should refer back to the indicated lesson.

Definitions or descriptions of all terms in the vocabulary list may be found in the Glossary.

ADDITIONAL ANSWERS

14.

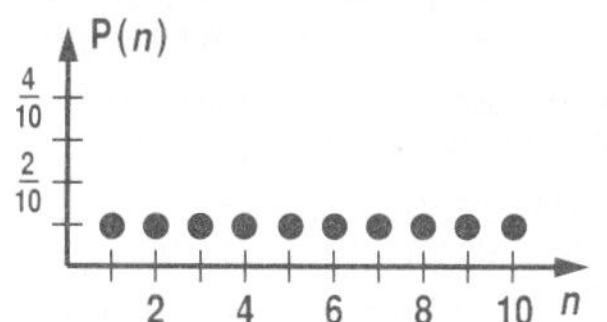

16.

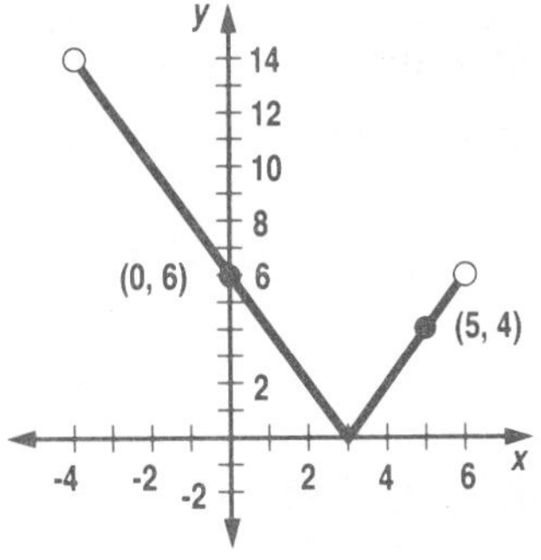

PROGRESS SELF-TEST

We cannot overemphasize the importance of these end-of-chapter materials. It is at this point that the material "gels" for many students, allowing them to solidify skills and understanding. In general, student performance should be markedly improved after these pages.

USING THE PROGRESS SELF-TEST

Assign the Progress Self-Test as a one-night assignment. Worked-out *solutions* for all questions are in the Selected Answers section at the back of the student book. Encourage students to take the Progress Self-Test honestly, grade themselves, and then be prepared to discuss the test in class.

Advise students to pay special attention to those Chapter Review questions (pages 673–675) which correspond to questions missed on the Progress Self-Test. A chart provided in the Selected Answers section in the student text keys the Progress Self-Test questions to the lettered SPUR Objectives in the Chapter Review or to the Vocabulary. It also keys the questions to the corresponding lessons where the material is covered.

14, 16. See margin, page 671.

17.

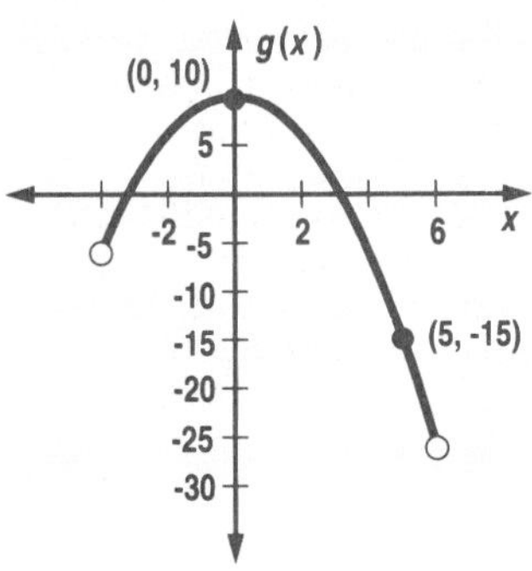

Progress Self-Test

Take this test as you would take a test in class. You will need graph paper and a calculator. Then check your work with the solutions in the Selected Answers section in the back of the book.

1. If $f(x) = 3x + 5$, then $f(2) =$ _?_. 11
2. If $g(t) = t^2 + 4t$, solve for t: $g(t) = 5$. $t = -5$ or $t = 1$
3. Estimate tan 82° to the nearest thousandth. 7.115
4. Give the value of sin 30°. 0.50
5. Define: function. See below.
6. **a.** Give an example of a quadratic function.
   b. The graph of the quadratic function in part (a) is a _?_. parabola; 6a) Answers will vary.
7. Explain why the equation $x = |y|$ does not describe a function. See below.
8. If the set {(10, 4), (x, 5), (30, 6)} is a function, what values can x not have? 10 or 30

In 9 and 10, tell whether the graph represents a function. If so, give its domain and range. If not, tell why not.

9. Yes; {0, 1, 2, 3, 4}; {1, 2}

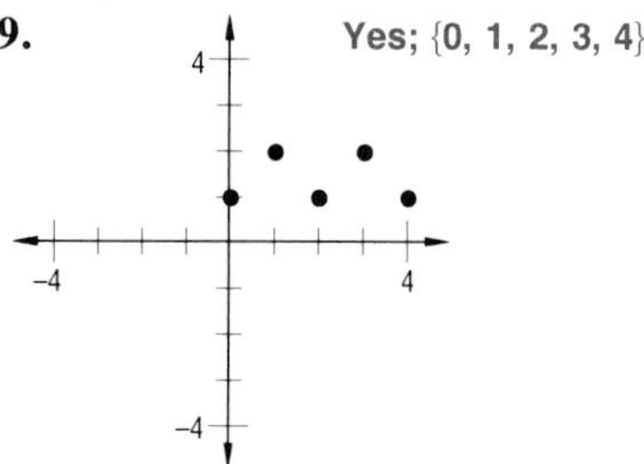

10. No; $x = 0$ is paired with 1 and -1 for y.

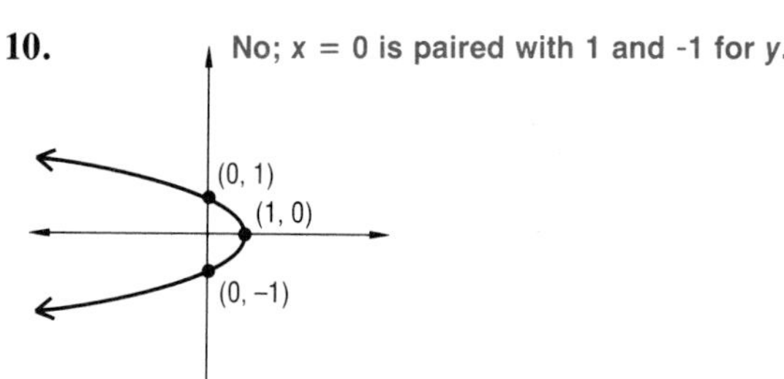

5. A function is a set of ordered pairs in which each first coordinate appears with exactly one second coordinate.

7) One positive value of x yields two values of y.

11. In the tossing of two fair dice, what is the probability of obtaining a sum of 10? $\frac{3}{36}$
12. In the plane crossing a check point example of Lesson 13-3, $d(t) = -600|t - 2| + 1200$. Calculate $d(2.5)$ and tell what that means. 900; When $t = 2.5$, the plane is 900 km east.

In 13 and 14, assume each of ten regions in the circle below has the same probability that the spinner will land on it. Let P(n) = the probability of landing in region n.

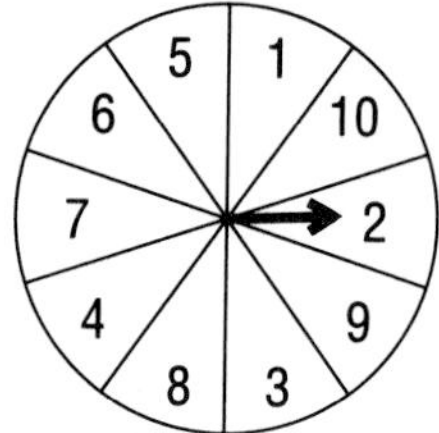

13. Calculate P(2). $\frac{1}{10}$
14. Graph the function P. See margin.
15. In $\triangle PQR$ below, determine the measure of $\angle P$ to the nearest degree. 46°

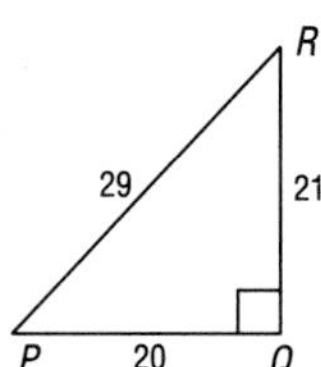

In 16 and 17, graph the function for values of x between -4 and 6. See margin.

16. $f(x) = 2|x - 3|$
17. $g(x) = 10 - x^2$

672

Chapter Review

Questions on SPUR Objectives

SPUR stands for **S**kills, **P**roperties, **U**ses, and **R**epresentations. The Chapter Review questions are grouped according to the SPUR Objectives for this chapter.

SKILLS deal with the procedures used to get answers.

■ **Objective A.** *Find values of functions from their formulas. (Lessons 13-2, 13-3)*

In 1–4, $f(x) = x^2 - 3x + 8$. Calculate:

1. $f(2)$ 6 **2.** $f(3)$ 8

3. $f(-7)$ 78 **4.** $f(0)$ 8

5. If $A(t) = 2|t - 5|$, calculate $A(1)$. 8

6. If $g(n) = 2^n$, calculate $g(3) + g(4)$. 24

7. If $f(x) = -x$, what is $f(-1.5)$? 1.5

8. If $h(t) = 64t - 16t^2$, find $h(4)$. 0

■ **Objective B.** *Find and analyze values of functions. (Lessons 13-6, 13-7)*

9. If $f(x) = |x + 3|$, solve $f(x) = 5$. 2 or -8

10. Let N(t) = the number of chirps of a cricket in a minute at a temperature t° Fahrenheit. If $N(t) = \frac{1}{4}t + 37$, for what value of t is $N(t) = 60$? $t = 92$

11. What is the largest possible value of the function f, where $f(x) = -x^2 + 10$? 11) $f(x) = 10$

12. What is the smallest possible value of the function A with equation $A(n) = 5|n - 3| - 9$? $A(n) = -9$

In 13–20, approximate to the nearest thousandth.

13. $\frac{1}{17}$ 0.059 **14.** 10! 3,628,800

15. $\sqrt{11469}$ 107.093 **16.** 0.8^{-3} 1.953

17. tan 30° 0.577 **18.** SQR(6.5) 2.550

19. sin 82.4° 0.991 **20.** log 5 0.699

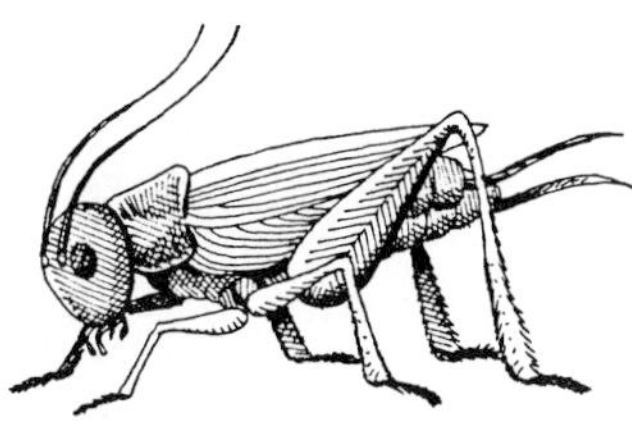

PROPERTIES deal with the principles behind the mathematics.

■ **Objective C.** *Determine whether a set of ordered pairs is a function. (Lesson 13-1)*

In 21–24, tell whether or not the equation determines a function.

21. $x = |y + 1|$ No

22. $x^2 = \sqrt{y}$ Yes

23. $3x - 5y = 7$ Yes

24. $y = \tan x$ Yes

In 25–27, tell whether or not the set of ordered pairs is a function.

25. {(0, 1), (1, 2), (2, 3), (3, 4)} Yes

26. {(1, 8), (1, 9), (1, 10), (1, 11)} No

27. the set of pairs (students, age) for students in your class. Yes

RESOURCES
- ■ Chapter 13 Test, Form A
- ■ Chapter 13 Test, Form B
- ■ Chapter 13 Test, Cumulative Form
- ■ Comprehensive Test, Chapters 1-13

CHAPTER REVIEW

The main objectives for the chapter are organized here into sections corresponding to the four main types of understanding this book promotes: Skills, Properties, Uses, and Representations.

USING THE CHAPTER REVIEW

Whereas end-of-chapter material may be considered optional in some texts, in *Algebra* we have selected these objectives and questions with the expectation that they will be covered. Students should be able to answer these questions with about 85% accuracy after studying the chapter.

You may assign these questions over a single night to help students prepare for a test the next day, or you may assign the questions over a two-day period.

If you work the questions over two days, then we recommend assigning the *evens* for homework the first night so that students get feedback in class the next day, then assigning the *odds* the night before the test so the students can use the answers provided in the book.

ADDITIONAL ANSWERS

35. domain {1850, 1900, 1950, 1960, 1970, 1980} range {1610, 102,479, 1,970,358, 2,479,015, 2,811,801, 2,966,850}

52.

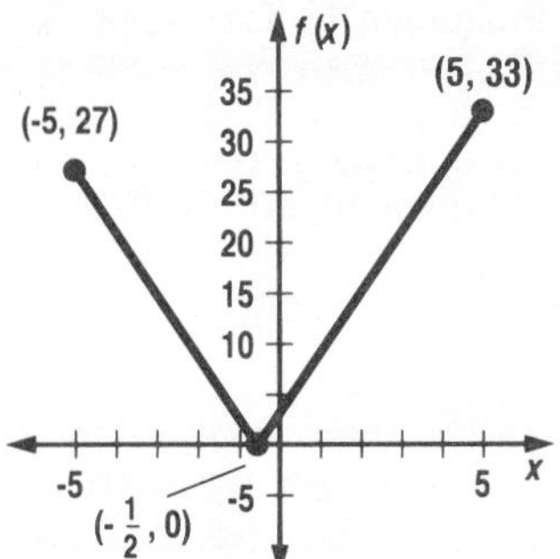

53.

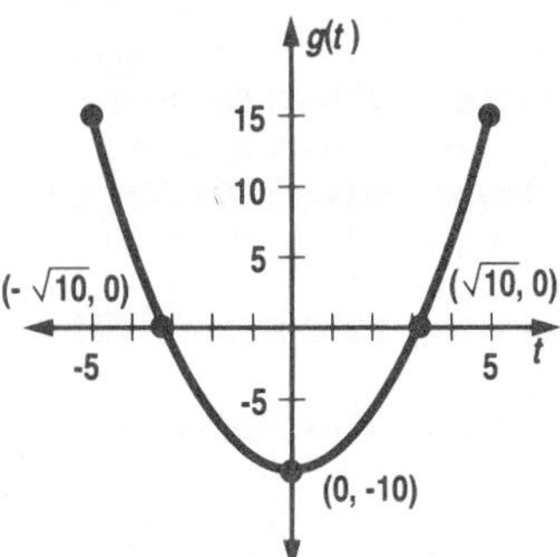

54.

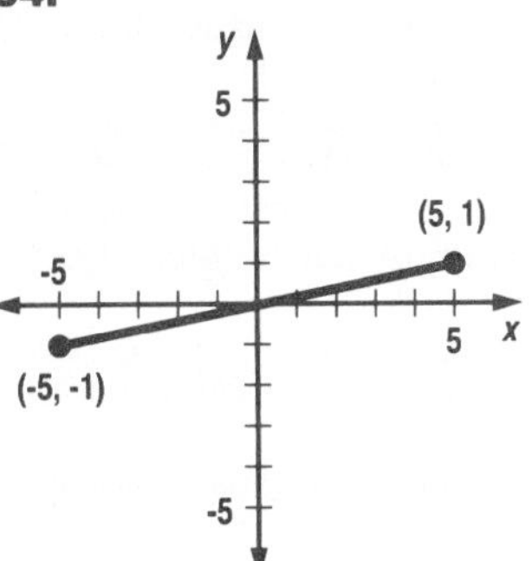

55.

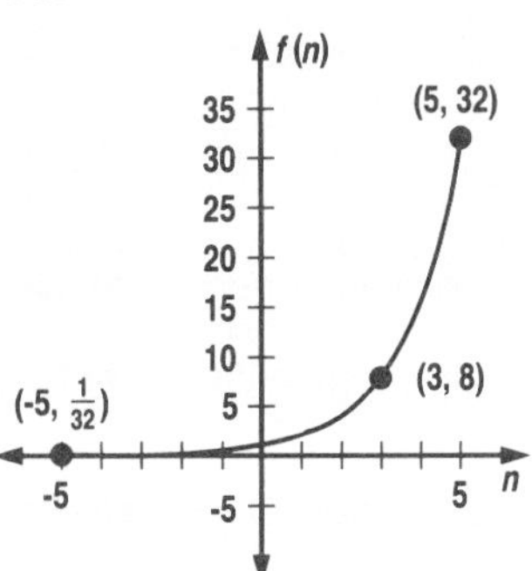

■ **Objective D.** *Classify functions. (Lessons 13-1, 13-3)*

In 28–33, classify the function as linear, quadratic, exponential, absolute value, or other.

28. $f(x) = 4^x$ **exponential**

29. $g(x) = \frac{x^2}{5} + \frac{x}{3}$ **quadratic**

30. $x + y = 1$ **linear**

31. $y = |3x + 4| - 2$ **absolute value**

32. $y = mx + b$ **linear**

33. $f(t) = t^{10} - t^9 + t^8 - t^7$ **other**

■ **Objective E.** *Find the domain and range of a function from its formula, graph, or rule. (Lesson 13-4)* **the largest replacement set possible**

34. If the domain of a function is not given, what should you assume?

35. Give the domain and range of this population function for Los Angeles, California. {(1850, 1610), (1900, 102479), (1950, 1970358), (1960, 2479015), (1970, 2811801), (1980, 2966850)}.
See margin, page 673.

36. *Multiple choice* The domain of a function is {1, 2, 3}. The range is {4, 5, 6}. Which of these could not be a rule for the function? **(c)**

(a) $y = x + 3$ (b) $y = 7 - x$

(c) $y = x - 3$ (d) $y = |x| + 3$

37. What is the range of the function $A(x) = |x - 2|$? **set of nonnegative real numbers**

In 38 and 39, determine the domain and range of the function from its graph.

38. {**all real numbers**}; {$y \leq 1$}

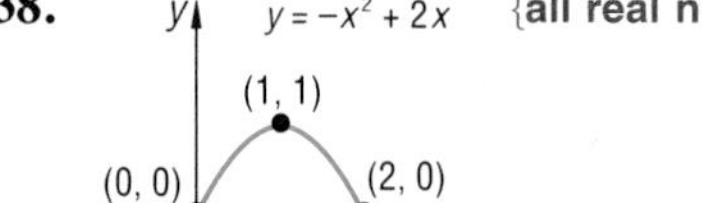

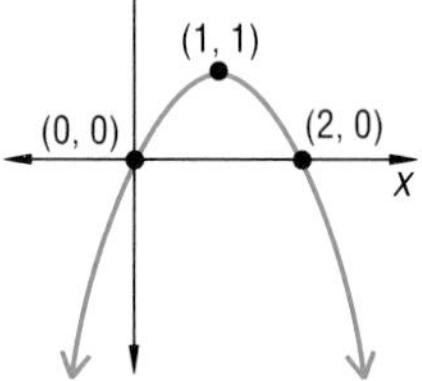

39. {$0 \leq x \leq 18$}; {$0 \leq y \leq 6$}

y
(0, 6)
3y + x = 18
(18, 0) x

USES deal with applications of mathematics in real situations.

■ **Objective F.** *Determine values of probability functions. (Lesson 13-5)*

40. If the spinner below has the same probability of landing in any direction, find each of the following:

a. $P(1)$ $\frac{1}{2}$

b. $P(2)$ $\frac{1}{3}$

c. $P(3)$ $\frac{1}{6}$

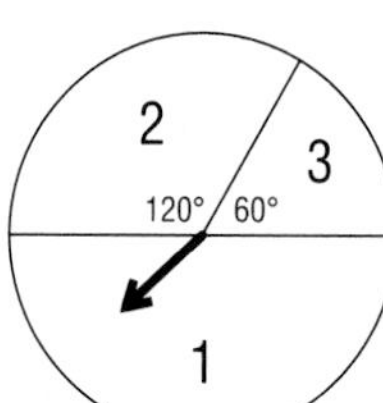

41. What is the probability of tossing a sum of 12 with two fair dice? $\frac{1}{36}$

42. If you guess on three multiple-choice questions with four choices each, the probability you will get exactly n correct is $\frac{3!}{n!(3-n)!} \cdot (\frac{1}{4})^n \cdot (\frac{3}{4})^{3-n}$. Calculate the probability you will get exactly 2 correct. $\frac{9}{64}$

43. A letter is mailed. Suppose P (the letter arrives the next day) = 0.75. What is P(the letter does not arrive the next day)? **0.25**

674

■ **Objective G.** *Find lengths and angle measures in triangles using the tangent function.* (*Lesson 13-6*)

44. Find m∠A to the nearest degree in the triangle below. **41°**

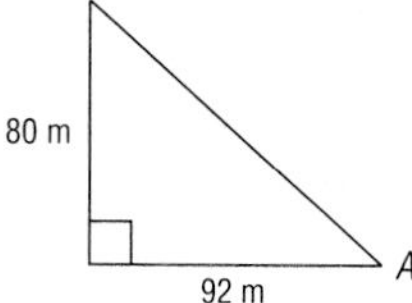

45. Two friends are 200 feet apart. At the same time one of the friends looks straight up at a kite, the other has to look up 20°. How high is the kite? **≈73 ft**

46. On a field trip, a girl whose eyes are 150 cm above the ground sights a nest high on a pole 25 meters away. If she has to raise her eyes 50° to see the nest, how high is the nest? **31.3 m**

47. What is the slope of line ℓ graphed below? **tan 18° ≈ 0.325**

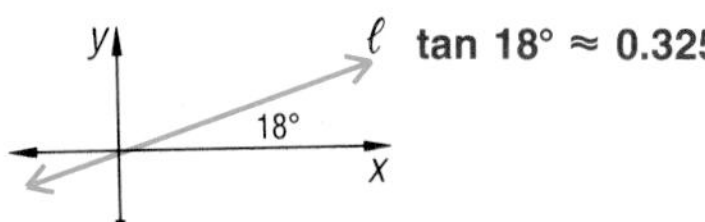

REPRESENTATIONS deal with pictures, graphs, or objects that illustrate concepts.

■ **Objective H.** *Determine whether or not a graph represents a function.* (*Lesson 13-1*)

In 48–51, tell whether or not the set of ordered pairs graphed is a function.

48. **Yes**

49. **No**

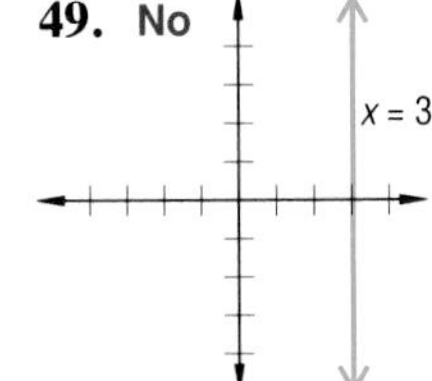

50. **Yes**

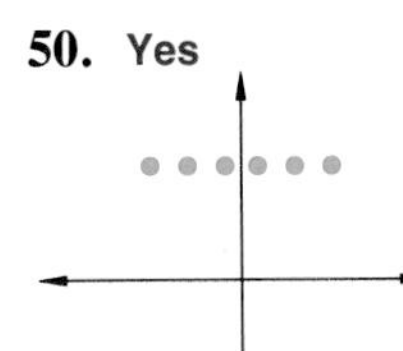

51. **Yes**

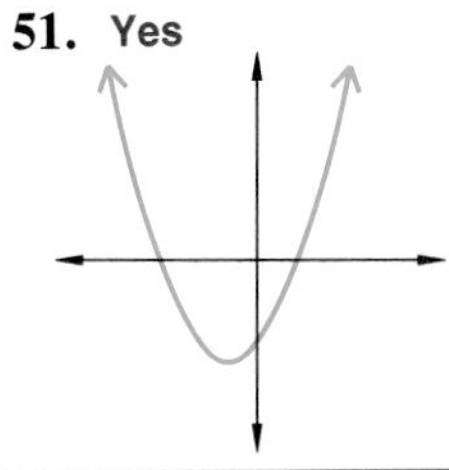

■ **Objective I.** *Graph functions.* (*Lessons 13-2, 13-3, 13-5*)

In 52–55, graph each function over the domain $\{x: -5 \le x \le 5\}$. **See margin.**

52. $f(x) = 3|2x + 1|$

53. $g(t) = t^2 - 10$

54. $y = \frac{1}{5}x$

55. $f(n) = 2^n$, n an integer

56. A weighted die has the following possibilities of landing on its sides. P(1) = 0.12; P(2) = 0.19; P(3) = 0.09; P(4) = 0.21; P(5) = 0.15. Find P(6) and graph the probability function. **0.24; see margin.**

57. Graph the probability function for a fair die. **See margin.**

EVALUATION

Three tests are provided for this chapter in the Teacher's Resource File. Chapter 13 Test, Forms A and B, cover just Chapter 13. The third test is Chapter 13 Test, Cumulative Form. About 50% of this test covers Chapter 13; 25% covers Chapter 12, and 25% covers earlier chapters. A Comprehensive Test covering Chapters 1–13 is also included with this chapter. This test can be used as the Final Examination for the course. For more information on grading, see *General Teaching Suggestions: Grading* on page T44 in the Teacher's Edition.

56.

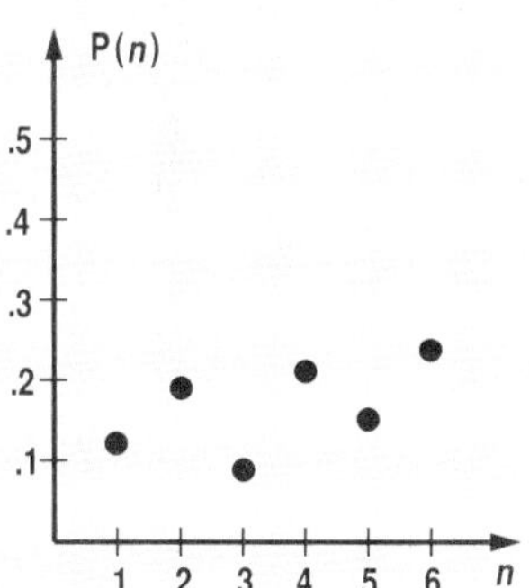

57.

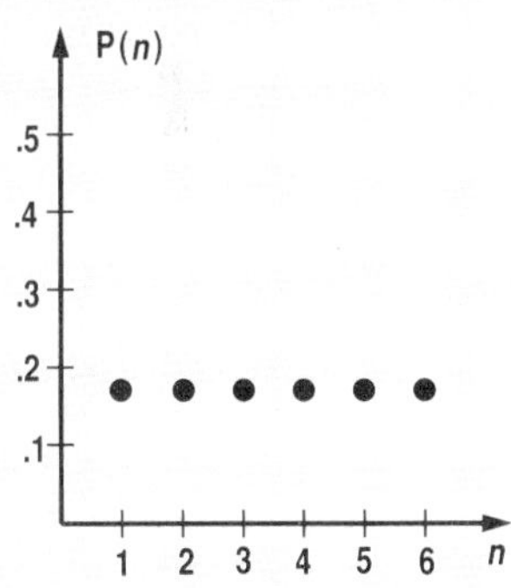

APPENDIX A

Scientific Calculators

You will be using a scientific calculator for many lessons in this book so it is important for you to know how your calculator works. Use your calculator to do all the calculations described in this appendix. Some of the problems are very easy. They were selected so that you can check whether your calculator does the computations in the proper order.

Suppose you want to use your calculator to find 3 + 4. Here is how to do it:

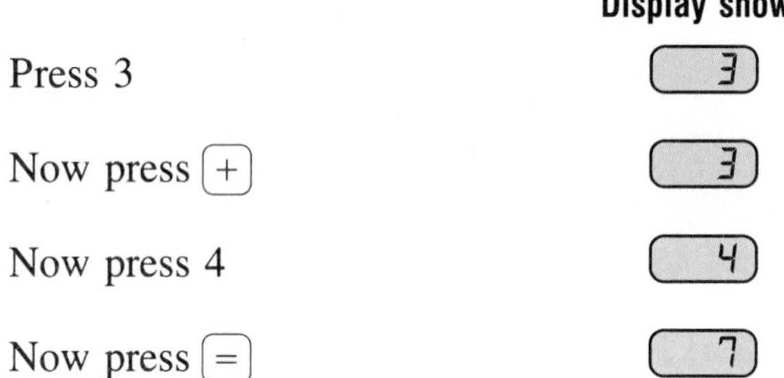

Pressing calculator keys is called **entering** or **keying in.** The set of instructions in the left column is called the **key sequence** for this problem. We write the key sequence for this problem using boxes for everything pressed except the numbers.

3 [+] 4 [=]

Sometimes we put what you would see in the calculator display underneath the key presses.

Key sequence	3	[+]	4	[=]
Display	3	3	4	7

Next consider 12 + 3 · 5. In Lesson 1-4, you learned that multiplication should be performed before addition. Perform the key sequence below on your calculator. See what your calculator does.

Key sequence	12	[+]	3	[×]	5	[=]
Display	12	12	3	3	5	27

Different calculators may give different answers even when the same buttons are pushed. If you have a calculator appropriate for algebra, the calculator displays 27. **Scientific calculators** which follow the order of operations used in algebra should be used with this book. If your calculator gave you the answer 75, then it has done the addition first and does not follow the algebraic order of operations. Using such a calculator with this book may be confusing.

Example 1 Evaluate $ay + bz$ when $a = 0.05$, $y = 2000$, $b = 0.06$ and $z = 9000$. (This is the total interest in a year if $2000 is earning 5% and $9000 is earning 6%.)

Solution

Key sequence: a [×] y [+] b [×] z [=]

Substitute in the key sequence:

0.05 [×] 2000 [+] 0.06 [×] 9000 [=]

Display:

[0.05] [0.05] [2000] [100] [0.06] [0.06] [9000] [640]

(The total interest is $640.)

Most scientific calculators have parentheses keys, [(] and [)]. To use them just enter the parentheses when they appear in the problem. Remember to use the [×] key every time you do a multiplication, even if × is not in the expression.

Example 2 Use the formula $A = 0.5h(b_1 + b_2)$ to calculate the area of the trapezoid at the right.

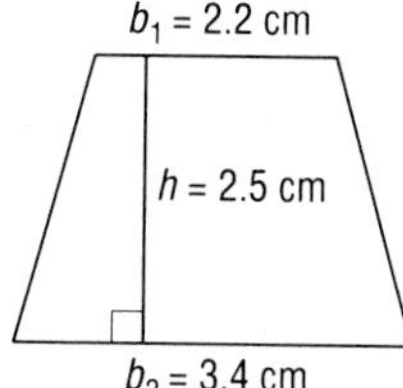

Solution

Remember that $0.5h(b_1 + b_2)$ means $0.5 \cdot h \cdot (b_1 + b_2)$.

Key sequence: 0.5 [×] h [×] [(] b_1 [+] b_2 [)] [=]

Substitute: 0.5 [×] 2.5 [×] [(] 2.2 [+] 3.4 [)] [=]

Display:

[0.5] [0.5] [2.5] [1.25] [1.25] [2.2] [2.2] [3.4] [5.6] [7.]

The area of the trapezoid is 7 square centimeters.

Some numbers are used so frequently that they have special keys on the calculator.

Example 3 Find the circumference of the circle at the right.

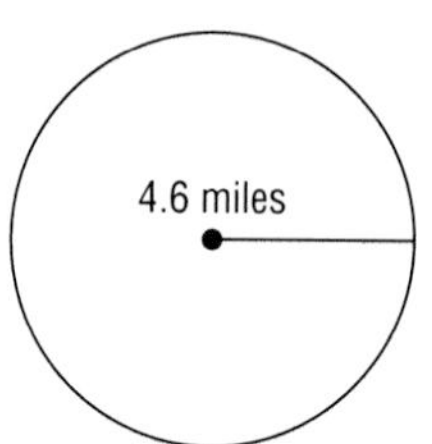

Solution
The circumference is the distance around the circle, and is calculated using the formula $C = 2\pi r$, where $C =$ circumference, and $r =$ radius. Use the π key.

Key sequence: 2 [×] [π] [×] r [=]

Substitute: 2 [×] [π] [×] 4.6 [=]

[2] [2] [3.1415927] [6.2831853] [4.6] [28.902652]

Rounding to the nearest tenth, the circumference is 28.9 miles.

As a decimal, $\pi = 3.141592653\ldots$ and the decimal is unending. Since it is impossible to list all the digits, the calculator rounds the decimal. Some calculators, like the one in Example 3, round to the nearest value that can be displayed. Some calculators truncate or round down. If the calculator in the example had truncated, it would have displayed 3.1415926 instead of 3.1415927 for π.

On some calculators you must press two keys to display π. If there is a small π written next to a key, two keys are probably needed. Then you should press [INV], [2nd], or [F] before pressing the key next to π.

Negative numbers can be entered in your calculator using the plus-minus key [±] or [+/-]. For example, to enter -19, use the following key sequence:

Key sequence: 19 [±]

Display: [19] [-19]

You will use powers of numbers throughout this book. The scientific calculator has a key [y^x] (or [x^y]) which can be used to raise numbers to powers. The key sequence for

3^4 is 3 [y^x] 4 [=]

You should see displayed [3] [3] [4] [81].

$3^4 = 81$.

Example 4 A formula for the volume of a sphere is $V = \frac{4\pi r^3}{3}$, where r is the radius. The radius of the moon is about 1080 miles. Find its volume.

Solution

Key sequence: 4 [×] [π] [×] r [y^x] 3 [÷] 3 [=]

Substitute: 4 [×] [π] [×] 1080 [y^x] 3 [÷] 3 [=]

You see

The display shows the answer in scientific notation. If you do not understand scientific notation, read Appendix B.

The volume of the moon is about $5.28 \cdot 10^9$ cubic miles.

Note: You may be unable to use a negative number as a base on your calculator. Try the key sequence 2 [±] [y^x] 5 to evaluate $(-2)^5$. The answer should be -32. However, some calculators will give you an error message. You can, however, use negative *exponents* on scientific calculators.

Questions

Covering the Reading

1. What is meant by the phrase "keying in"? **pressing calculator keys**

2. To calculate 28.5 · 32.7 + 14.8, what key sequence should you use?
28.5 [×] 32.7 [+] 14.8 [=]

3. Consider the key sequence 13.4 [−] 15 [÷] 3 [=]. What arithmetic problem does this represent? **13.4 − 15 ÷ 3**

4. a. To evaluate $ab - c$ on a calculator, what key sequence should you use? **a [×] b [−] c [=]**
   b. Evaluate 297 · 493 − 74,212. **72,209**

5. Estimate 26π to the nearest thousandth. **81.681**

6. What number does the key sequence 104 [+/−] yield? **-104**

7. a. Write a key sequence for -104 divided by 8. **104 [+/−] [÷] 8 [=]**
   b. Calculate -104 divided by 8 on your calculator. **-13**

8. Calculate the area of the trapezoid below. **36.08**

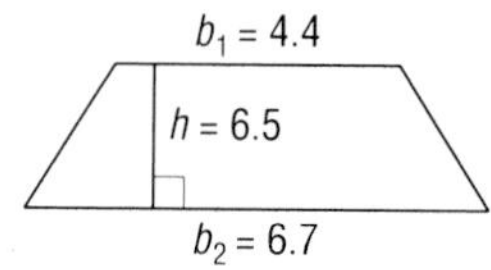

9. Find the circumference of a circle with radius 6.7 inches. **42.10**

10. Which is greater, $\pi \cdot \pi$ or 10? **10**

11. What expression is evaluated by 5 [y^x] 2 [=]? **5^2**

12. A softball has a radius of about 1.92 in. What is its volume?
29.65 in.^{3}

13. What kinds of numbers may not be allowed as bases when you use the [y^x] key on some calculators? **negative numbers**

Applying the Mathematics

14. Use your calculator to help find the surface area $2LH + 2HW + 2LW$ of the box at right. **455.3 sq in.**

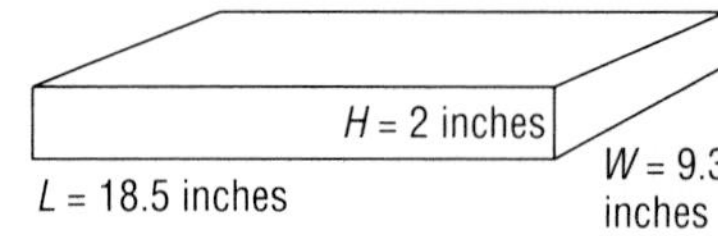

15. Remember that $\frac{2}{3} = 2 \div 3$. **Answers will vary.**
   a. What decimal for $\frac{2}{3}$ is given by your calculator?
   b. Does your calculator *truncate* or *round to the nearest?*

16. Order $\frac{3}{5}$, $\frac{4}{7}$, and $\frac{5}{9}$ from smallest to largest. **$\frac{5}{9}$, $\frac{4}{7}$, $\frac{3}{5}$**

17. Use the clues to find the mystery number y.
   Clue 1: y will be on the display if you alternately press 2 and [×] again and again ...
   Clue 2: $y > 20$.
   Clue 3: $y < 40$. **32**

18. $A = \pi r^2$ is a formula for the area A of a circle with radius r. Find the area of the circle in Example 3. **66.5**

19. What is the total interest in a year if \$350 is earning 5% and \$2000 is earning 8%? (Hint: Use Example 1.) **\$177.50**

20. To multiply the sum of 2.08 and 5.76 by 2.24, what key sequence can you use? **[( ] 2.08 [+] 5.76 [ )] [×] 2.24 [=]**

APPENDIX B

Scientific Notation

The first three columns in the chart on page 683 show three ways to represent integer powers of ten: in exponential notation, with word names, and as decimals. The fourth column describes a distance or length in meters. For example, the top row tells that Mercury is about ten billion meters from the sun.

You probably know the quick way to multiply by 10, 100, 1000, and so on. Just move the decimal point as many places to the right as there are zeros.

$$84.3 \cdot 100 = 8430 \qquad 84.3 \cdot 10{,}000 = 843{,}000$$

It is just as quick to multiply by these numbers when they are written as powers.

$$489.76 \cdot 10^2 = 48{,}976 \qquad 489.76 \cdot 10^4 = 4{,}897{,}600$$

The general pattern is as follows.

To multiply by a positive power of 10, move the decimal point to the *right* as many places as indicated by the exponent.

The patterns in the chart on the following page help to explain powers of 10 where the exponent is negative. Each row describes a number that is $\frac{1}{10}$ of the number in the row above it. So 10^0 is $\frac{1}{10}$ of 10^1.

$$10^0 = \tfrac{1}{10} \cdot 10 = 1$$

To see the meaning of 10^{-1}, think: 10^{-1} is $\frac{1}{10}$ of 10^0 (which equals 1).

$$10^{-1} = \tfrac{1}{10} \cdot 1 = \tfrac{1}{10} = 0.1$$

Remember that to multiply a decimal by 0.1, just move the decimal point one unit to the left. Since $10^{-1} = 0.1$, to multiply by 10^{-1}, just move the decimal point one unit to the left.

$$435.86 \cdot 10^{-1} = 43.586$$

To multiply a decimal by 0.01, or $\frac{1}{100}$, you move the decimal point two units to the left. since $10^{-2} = 0.01$, the same is true for multiplying by 10^{-2}.

$$435.86 \cdot 10^{-2} = 4.3586$$

The following pattern emerges.

To multiply by a negative power of 10, move the decimal point to the *left* as many places as indicated by the exponent.

Integer Powers of Ten

Exponential Notation	Word Name	Decimal	Something about this length in meters
10^{10}	ten billion	10,000,000,000	distance of Mercury from Sun
10^{9}	billion	1,000,000,000	radius of Sun
10^{8}	hundred million	100,000,000	diameter of Jupiter
10^{7}	ten million	10,000,000	radius of Earth
10^{6}	million	1,000,000	radius of Moon
10^{5}	hundred thousand	100,000	length of Lake Erie
10^{4}	ten thousand	10,000	average width of Grand Canyon
10^{3}	thousand	1,000	5 long city blocks
10^{2}	hundred	100	length of football field
10^{1}	ten	10	height of shade tree
10^{0}	one	1	height of waist
10^{-1}	tenth	0.1	width of hand
10^{-2}	hundredth	0.01	diameter of pencil
10^{-3}	thousandth	0.001	thickness of window pane
10^{-4}	ten thousandth	0.000 1	thickness of paper
10^{-5}	hundred thousandth	0.000 01	diameter of red blood corpuscle
10^{-6}	millionth	0.000 001	mean distance between successive collisions of molecules in air
10^{-7}	ten millionth	0.000 000 1	thickness of thinnest soap bubble with colors
10^{-8}	hundred millionth	0.000 000 01	mean distance between molecules
10^{-9}	billionth	0.000 000 001	size of air molecule
10^{-10}	ten billionth	0.000 000 000 1	mean distance between molecules in a crystal

Example 1 Write $68.5 \cdot 10^{-6}$ as a decimal.

Solution
To multiply by 10^{-6}, move the decimal point six places to the left. So $68.5 \cdot 10^{-6} = .0000685$.

The names of the negative powers are very similar to those for the positive powers. For instance, 1 billion = 10^9 and 1 billionth = 10^{-9}.

Example 2 Write 8 billionths as a decimal.

Solution
8 billionths = $8 \cdot 10^{-9} = .000000008$.

Most calculators can display only the first 8, 9, or 10 digits of a number. This is a problem if you need to key in a large number like 455,000,000,000 or a small number like .00000000271. However, powers of 10 can be used to rewrite these number in **scientific notation.**

$$455{,}000{,}000{,}000 = 4.55 \cdot 10^{11}$$
$$.00000000271 = 2.71 \cdot 10^{-9}$$

Definition:

In scientific notation, a number is represented as $x \cdot 10^n$, where $1 \leq x \leq 10$ and n is an integer.

Scientific calculators can display numbers in scientific notation. The display for $4.55 \cdot 10^{11}$ will usually look like one of these shown here.

4.55 E 11 | 4.55 11 | 4.55 x10 11

The display for $2.71 \cdot 10^{-9}$ is usually one of these

2.71 E -0.9 | 2.71 -09 | 2.71 x10 -09

Numbers written in scientific notation are entered into a calculator using the EXP or EE key. For instance, to enter $6.0247 \cdot 10^{23}$ (known as Avogadro's number), key in

6.0247 EE 23.

You should see this display.

6.0247   23

In general, to enter $x \cdot 10^n$, key in x [EE] n.

Example 3 The total number of hands possible in the card game bridge is about 635,000,000,000. Write this number in scientific notation.

Solution

First, move the decimal point to get a number between 1 and 10. In this case the number is 6.35. This tells you the answer will be:

$$6.35 \cdot 10^{\text{exponent}}$$

The exponent of 10 is the number of places you must move the decimal point in 6.35 to get 635,000,000,000. You must move it 11 places to the right, so the answer is $6.35 \cdot 10^{11}$

Example 4 The charge of an electron is .00000000048 electrostatic units. Put this number in scientific notation.

Solution

First move the decimal point to get a number between 1 and 10. The result is 4.8. To find the power of 10, count the number of places you must move the decimal to change 4.8 to .00000000048. The move is 10 places to the left, so the charge of the electron is $4.8 \cdot 10^{-10}$ electrostatic units.

Example 5 Enter 0.00000000123 into a calculator.

Solution

Rewrite the number in scientific notation.
$0.00000000123 = 1.23 \cdot 10^{-9}$.

Key in 1.23 [EE] 9 [+/−].

Questions

Covering the Reading

1. Write one million as a power of ten. 10^6

2. Write 1 billionth as a power of 10. 10^{-9}

In 3–5, write as a decimal.

3. 10^{-4}
0.0001

4. $28.5 \cdot 10^7$
285,000,000

5. 10^0
1

6. To multiply by a negative power of 10, move the decimal point to the _?_ as many places as indicated by the _?_. left, exponent

7. Write $2.46 \cdot 10^{-8}$ as a decimal. .0000000246

8. Why is $38.25 \cdot 10^{-2}$ not in scientific notation?
38.25 is not between 1 and 10

9. Suppose $x \cdot 10^y$ is in scientific notation.
a. What is the domain of x? set of real numbers greater than or equal to 1 and less than 10
b. What is the domain of y? set of integers

In 10–14, rewrite the number in scientific notation.

10. 5,020,000,000,000,000,000,000,000,000 tons, the mass of Sirius, the brightest star 5.02×10^{27}

11. 0.0009 meters, the approximate width of a human hair 9×10^{-4}

12. 763,000
7.63×10^5

13. 0.00000328
3.28×10^{-6}

14. 754.9876
7.549876×10^2

15. One computer can do an arithmetic problem in 2.4×10^{-9} seconds. What key sequence can you use to display this number on your calculator. 2.4 [EE] 9 [+/−]

Applying the Mathematics

In 16 and 17, write in scientific notation.

16. 645 billion
6.45×10^{11}

17. 27.2 million
2.72×10^7

In 18–22, use the graph below.
Write the world population in the given year: **a.** as a decimal; **b.** in scientific notation.

18. 10,000 B.C. a) 10,000,000 b) 10^6 **19.** A.D. 1 a) 300,000,000 b) 3×10^8

20. 1700 a) 625,000,000 b) 6.25×10^8 **21.** 1970 a) 3,575,000,000 b) 3.575×10^9

World Population Growth 10,000 B.C. to 1987

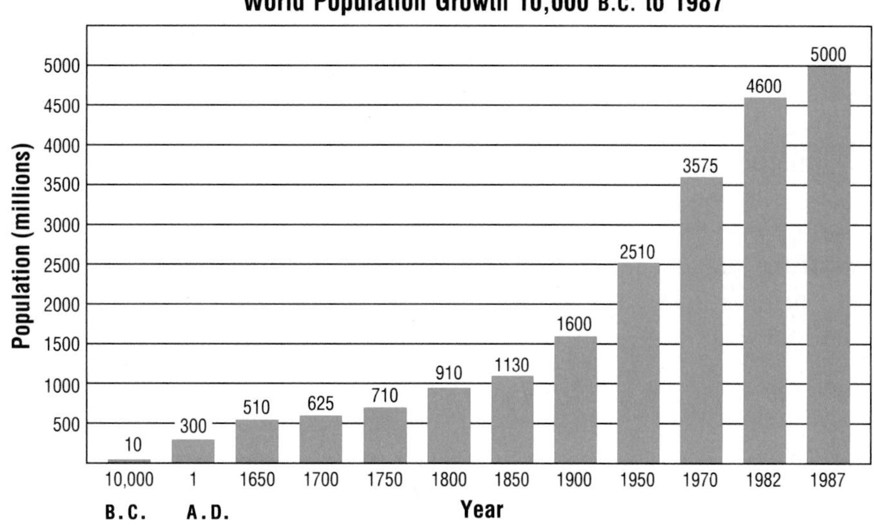

22. How can you enter the world population in 1987 into your calculator? 5 [EE] 9

23. How many digits are in 1.7×10^{100}? 101

In 24–26, write the number in scientific notation.

24. 0.00002 2×10^{-5} **25.** 0.0000000569 5.69×10^{-8}

26. 400.007 4.00007×10^2

In 28–30, write as a decimal.

28. $3.921 \cdot 10^5$ 392,100 **29.** $3.921 \cdot 10^{-5}$ .00003921

30. $8.6 \cdot 10^{-2}$ .086

Exploration

31. a. What is the largest number you can display on your calculator? Answers may vary.
b. What is the smallest number you can display? (Use scientific notation and consider negative numbers.) Answers may vary.
c. Find out what key sequence you could use to enter -5×10^{-7} in your calculator. sample: 5 [+/–] [EE] 7 [+/–]

APPENDIX C

BASIC

In BASIC (Beginner's All-Purpose Symbolic Instruction Code), the arithmetic symbols are: + (for addition), − (for subtraction), * (for multiplication), / (for division), and ^ (for powering). In some versions of BASIC, ↑ is used for powering. The computer evaluates expressions according to the usual order of operations. Parentheses ( ) may be used. The comparison symbols =, >, < are also used in the standard way, but BASIC uses <= instead of ≤, >= instead of ≥, and <> instead of ≠.

Variables are represented by letters or letters in combination with digits. Consult the manual for your version of BASIC for restrictions on the length or other aspects of variable names. Examples of variable names allowed in most versions are N, X1, and AREA.

Commands

The BASIC commands used in this course and examples of their uses are given below.

LET ... A value is assigned to a given variable. Some versions of BASIC allow you to omit the word LET in the assignment statement.

LET X = 5	The number 5 is stored in a memory location called X.
LET N = N + 2	The value in the memory location called N is increased by 2 and then restored in the location called N.

PRINT ... The computer prints on the screen what follows the PRINT command. If what follows is a constant or variable, the computer prints the value of that constant or variable. If what follows is in quotes, the computer prints exactly what is in quotes.

PRINT X	The computer prints the number stored in memory location X.
PRINT "X-VALUES"	The computer prints the phrase X-VALUES.

INPUT ... The computer asks the user to give a value to the variable named, and stores that value.

INPUT X	When the program is run, the computer will prompt you to give it a value by printing a question mark, and then store the value you type in memory location X.
INPUT "HOW OLD?"; AGE	The computer prints HOW OLD? and stores your response in memory location AGE.

REM ... This command allows remarks to be inserted in a program. These may describe what the variables represent, what the program does or how it works. REM statements are often used in long complex programs or programs others will use.

REM PYTHAGOREAN THEOREM	The statement appears when the LIST command is given, but it has no effect when the program is run.

FOR ...
NEXT ...
STEP ... The FOR command assigns a beginning and ending value to a variable. The first time through the loop, the variable has the beginning value in the FOR command. When the computer hits the line reading NEXT, the value of the variable is increased by the amount indicated by STEP. The commands between FOR and NEXT are then repeated. When the incremented value of the variable is larger than the ending value in the FOR command, the computer leaves the loop and executes the rest of the program. If STEP is not written the computer increases the variable by 1 each time through the loop.

```
10 FOR N = 3 TO 6 STEP 2
20   PRINT N
30 NEXT N
40 END
```

The computer assigns 3 to N and then prints the value of N. On reaching NEXT, the computer increases N by 2 (the STEP amount), and prints 5. The next N would be 7 which is too large. The computer executes the command after NEXT, ending the program.

IF ... THEN ... The computer performs the consequent (the THEN part) only if the antecedent (the IF part) is true. When the antecedent is false, the computer *ignores* the consequent and goes directly to the next line of the program.

```
IF X > 100 THEN END
PRINT X
```

If the X-value is less than or equal to 100, the computer ignores "END," goes to the next line, and prints the value stored in X. If the X-value is greater than 100, the computer stops and the value stored in X is not printed.

GO TO ... The computer goes to whatever line of the program is indicated. GOTO statements are generally avoided because they interrupt program flow and make programs hard to interpret.

GOTO 70	The computer goes to line 70 and executes that command.

END ... The computer stops running the program. No program should have more than one end statement.

Functions

The following built-in functions are available in most versions of BASIC. Each function name must be followed by a variable or constant enclosed in parentheses.

ABS The absolute value of the number that follows is calculated.

LET X = ABS (-10)	The computer calculates $\|-10\| = 10$ and assigns the value 10 to memory location X.

SQR The square root of the number that follows is calculated.

C = SQR (A * A + B * B)	The computer calculates $\sqrt{A^2 + B^2}$ using the values stored in A and B and stores the result in C.

Programs

A program is a set of instructions to the computer. In most versions of BASIC every step in the program must begin with a line number. We usually start numbering at 10 and count by tens, so intermediate steps can be added later. The computer reads and executes a BASIC program in order of the line numbers. It will not go back to a previous line unless told to do so.

To enter a new program type NEW, and then the lines of the program. At the end of each line press the key named RETURN or ENTER. You may enter the lines in any order. The computer will keep track of them in numerical order. If you type LIST the program currently in the computer's memory will be printed on the screen. To change a line re-type the line number and the complete line as you now want it.

To run a new program after it has been entered, type RUN, and press the RETURN or ENTER key.

Programs can be saved on disk. Consult your manual on how to do this for your version of BASIC. To run a program already saved on disk you must know the exact name of the program including any spaces or punctuation. To run a program called TABLE SOLVE, type RUN TABLE SOLVE, and press the RETURN or ENTER key.

The following program illustrates many of the commands used in this course.

10 PRINT "A DIVIDING SEQUENCE"	The computer prints A DIVIDING SEQUENCE.
20 INPUT "NUMBER PLEASE" X	The computer prints NUMBER PLEASE? and waits for you to enter a number. You must give a value to store in the location X. Suppose you use 20. X now contains 20.
30 LET Y = 2	2 is stored in location Y.
40 FOR Z = -5 TO 4	Z is given the value -5. Each time through the loop, the value of Z will be increased by 1.

50 IF Z = 0 THEN GOTO 70	When Z $=$ 0 the computer goes directly to line 70. When Z $\neq$ 0 the computer executes line 60.
60 PRINT (X * Y) / Z	On the first pass through the loop, the computer prints -8 because $(20 \cdot 2)/(-5) = -8$.
70 NEXT Z	The value in Z is increased by 1 to -4 and the computer goes back to line 50.
80 END	After going through the FOR ... NEXT ... loop with Z $= 4$, the computer stops.

The output of this program is

```
A DIVIDING SEQUENCE
NUMBER PLEASE? 20
- 8
-10
-13.3333
-20
-40
 40
 20
 13.3333
 10
```

SELECTED ANSWERS

LESSON 1-1 (pp. 4-8)
1. 1.6 miles **3.** Yes **5.** Yes **7.** 5 and 9 **9. a.** $m > 3$ **b. See below.** **11.** b **13.** $\frac{5}{6} < \frac{17}{20}$ or $\frac{17}{20} > \frac{5}{6}$ **15.** $q < 15$ **17.** c **19.** 3.375 **21.** $112.9\overline{3}$ **23. a.** sample: 4 (any number greater than 3) **b.** sample: 1 (any number less than 3) **c.** 3 **25.** -3, -2 and 7 **27.** $\frac{2}{3}$, $\frac{7}{10}$, $\frac{3}{4}$

9. b.

LESSON 1-2 (pp. 9-13)
1. a. 1 student **b.** 12 **c.** 79.875, or about 80 **3.** median **5. a.** 66.25 **b.** 66.5 **c.** 80 **d.** mode **7. a.** 8 days **b.** 24 days **c.** 9° and 13° **d.** 6° **11. a.** $C > 100$ **b. See below.** **13.** -15, -10, -4, -2, 0, 5, 6.8 **15.** -4 **17.** $350 **19.** 40 **21.** $\frac{6}{35}$ **23.** 4

11. b.

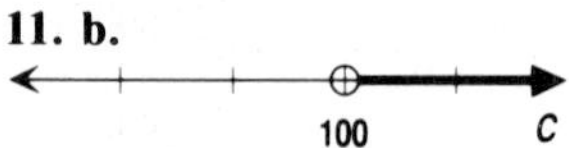

LESSON 1-3 (pp. 14-19)
3. a. 47% ± 5% **b.** 42% and 52% **5. a.** $5 \le a \le 12$ **b.** closed **c.** 7 **7. a.** $5 \le n \le 35$ **b. See below.** **c.** from 5 to 35 hours **9. a.** $20 \le g \le 20.5$ **b.** 20.25 **11. See below.** **13.** $\frac{3}{8} \le x \le \frac{5}{8}$ **15. a.** $d > 1800$ **b. See below.** **17. a. See below.** **b.** 0 **c.** 1 **19. a.** 3.6 **b.** 25.2 **c.** 54.75 or, in leap years, 54.9 **21. a.** $\frac{13}{5}$ **b.** $\frac{17}{10}$ **c.** $\frac{89}{55}$ **23. a.** -56 **b.** -56 **c.** 56

7. b. **11.**

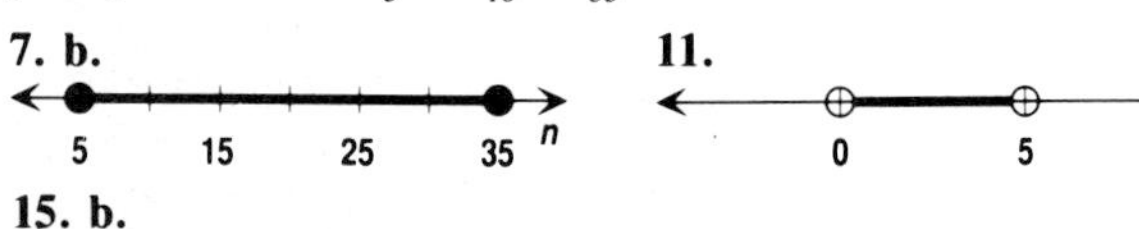

15. b.

1799 1800 1801 d

17. a.

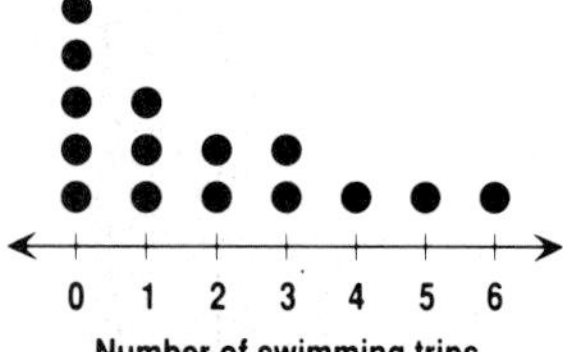

LESSON 1-4 (pp. 20-24)
1. numerical **3.** algebraic **5.** 4 **7.** 6 **9.** 8
11.

```
10 PRINT "ANSWER TO QUESTION 11"
20 LET M = 2.4
30 LET N = .2
40 PRINT ((M + 12.5)/(N + 3))^10
50 END
```

13. 5 * X + 3 * Y ^10 **15.** 110 mm **17.** $(1.4x - 2.3y)$, $4xy$ **19. See below.** **21. a.** $0 < P < 7.98$ **b. See below.** **23. a. See below.** **b.** 80 **c.** 80 **d.** 72 **e.** 70 **25. a.** -85.7 **b.** -85.7 **c.** 85.7 **27.** a and c **29.** $\frac{11}{16}$

19. **21. b.**

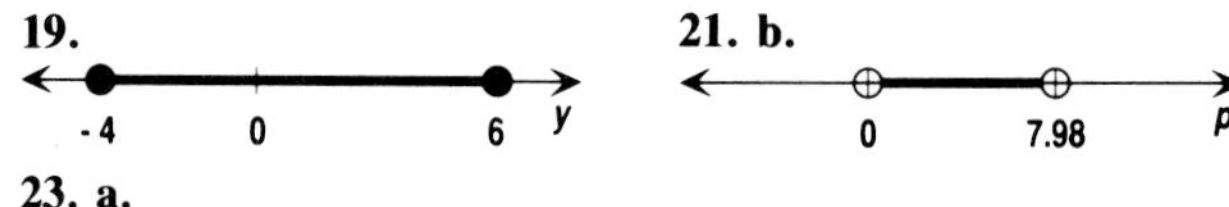

23. a.

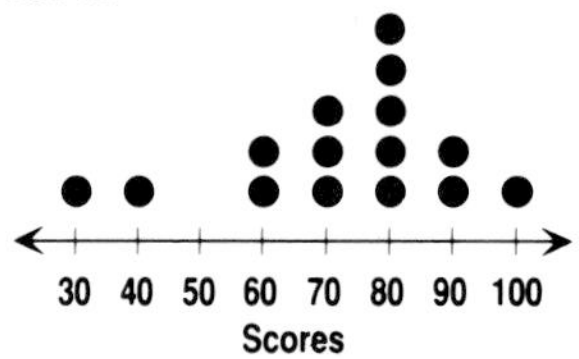

LESSON 1-5 (pp. 25-29)
1. L, d and s **3.** 634 **5.** $H = .8(200 - A)$ **7.** d **9.** pause and wait for a value to be typed in **11.** ≈ 22.9 in. **13. a.** 18.75 lb **b.** It increases **c.** a heavy person **15. a.** 0 lb **b.** 40 in. is outside the domain of most adult heights, and the answer has no meaning. (No one has an ideal weight of 0.) **17.** 82°F **19.** 3125 **21.** ANSWER TO QUESTION 21
15.24
23.

```
10 PRINT "ANSWER TO QUESTION 23"
20 LET X = 5.7
30 LET Y = 2.006
40 LET Z = 51.46
50 PRINT X + Y + 3 * Z
60 END
```

25. a. 1 **b.** $\frac{5}{8}$ **c.** $\frac{11}{20}$ **27.** 29,360,000

LESSON 1-6 (pp. 30-35)
3. a. discrete **b.** sample: sister **5. a.** continuous **b.** sample: any real number except 2 **7.** I or R **9.** R **11. a.** {0, 1, 2} **b.** 3 **15.** sample: $\frac{a + b}{2}$ **17. a.** the set of real numbers **b.** $0 \le E \le 6194$ **c.** the set of real numbers between 0 and 6194 (closed interval) **c. See below.** **21.** discrete **23.** {2, 4} **25. See below.** **27. See below.** **29.** {5, 7, 9} **31.** $7\frac{1}{2}$ **33.** 35 − (20 − 7) = 22 **35. a.** -6 **b.** 9 **c.** 8 **d.** -9

17. c. **25.** **27.**

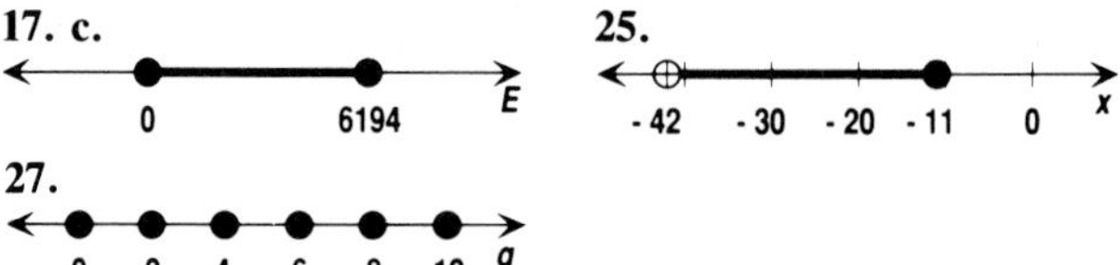

LESSON 1-7 (pp. 36-41)
1. $\frac{1}{400}$ **5.** $\frac{2}{6} = \frac{1}{3}$ **7.** $\frac{1}{52}$ **9. a.** $\frac{2}{5}$ **b.** $\frac{3}{5}$ **c.** 1 **11. a.** (4, 6), (6, 4), (5, 5), (5, 6), (6, 5), (6, 6) **b.** $\frac{6}{36} = \frac{1}{6}$ **13.** 8 prizes

15. a. $\frac{1}{4}$ **b.** $\frac{2}{4} = \frac{1}{2}$ **17. a.** You cannot have more successes than possible outcomes. **b.** You cannot have a negative number of outcomes. **c.** The largest probability possible is 1, when all possible outcomes are successes. **19.** $\frac{11}{26}$
21. $10 \cdot (-3)^2 = 90$; $10 \cdot 0^2 = 0$; $10 \cdot 5^2 = 250$
23. sample: $\frac{x + y}{2}$ **25.** b **27. a.** 221.34 **b.** 22.134
c. 2.2134 **29.** 15%

LESSON 1-8 (pp. 42–47)
1. a. about .505 **b.** 50.5% **c.** It's smaller **d.** 49.5%
3. ≈ .052 or 5.2% **7. a.** $\frac{5}{17}$ **b.** $\frac{1}{10}$ **c.** $\frac{4}{y}$ **9. a.** 60 people
b. 300 people **c.** 3 people **11.** No, the event did not occur.
13. c **15. a.** X **b.** No, but it probably would. **17.** 1 **19.** a
21. 3 **23.** 40% **25. a.** $\frac{1}{52}$ **b.** $\frac{13}{52} = \frac{1}{4}$ **c.** $\frac{4}{52} = \frac{1}{13}$
27. a. 8.85 **b.** .885 **c.** $38.43 **29.** 1 **31.** $\frac{7}{2}$

CHAPTER 1 PROGRESS SELF-TEST (p. 49)

1. $2(a + 3b)$ when $a = 3$ and $b = 5$; $2(3 + 3 \cdot 5) = 2(18) = 36$ **2.** $5 \cdot 6^n = 5 \cdot 6^4 = 5 \cdot 1296 = 6480$
3. $\frac{p + t^2}{p + t}$ when $p = 5, t = 2$ $\frac{5 + 2^2}{5 + 2} = \frac{9}{7}$ **4.** $\frac{3}{5}$
5. $\frac{7 \cdot 9abc}{7 \cdot 4b} = \frac{9ac}{4}$ **6.** $\frac{50.7}{4} \approx 12.7$ **7.** $10, $6, $6, $5, $5, $4.50; $\frac{\$6 + \$5}{2} = \$5.50$
8. ANSWER TO QUESTION 8
8.82

9. See below.
10. $S > 25$ **11.** positive real numbers **12.** integers, real numbers **13.** 67% + 3% = 70%; 67% − 3% = 64% **14.** 8
15. sample: 0, 2, 4 **16.** $c = 20(4 - 1) + 25$; $c = 60 + 25$; $c = 85¢$ **17.** $A = \pi r^2 = 3.14159(3)^2 \approx 28$ m²
18. a. 3 bars **b.** 8 bars **19.** $8 \le c \le 31$ **20.** $\frac{2284}{100{,}000}$ or ≈ .02 **21.** $\frac{8}{300}$ or $\frac{2}{75}$ **22.** $\frac{4}{26}$ or $\frac{2}{13}$ **23.** Donna **24.** See below. **25.** 11

9.
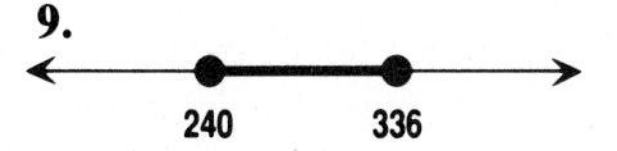

24.
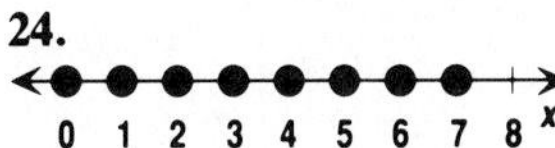

The chart below keys the **Progress Self-Test** questions to the objectives in the **Chapter Review** on pages 50–53 or to the **Vocabulary** (Voc.) on page 48. This will enable you to locate those **Chapter Review** questions that correspond to questions you missed on the **Progress Self-Test.** The lesson where the material is covered is also indicated in the chart.

Question	**1-3**	**4**	**5**	**6-7**	**8**	**9**	**10**	**11**	**12**
Objective	C	A	A	H	D	K	K	G	Voc.
Lesson	1-4	1-1	1-8	1-2	1-4	1-3	1-1	1-6	1-6
Question	**13**	**14-15**	**16-17**	**18-19**	**20**	**21-22**	**24**	**25**	
Objective	K	B	I	L	J	F	K	E	
Lesson	1-3	1-1	1-5	1-2	1-8	1-7	1-6	1-6	

CHAPTER 1 REVIEW (pp. 50–53)

1. $\frac{1}{6} > \frac{3}{20}$ or $\frac{3}{20} < \frac{1}{6}$ **3.** $\frac{3}{4}$ **5.** $\frac{11q}{12m}$ **7.** $\frac{7}{60}$ **9.** 4 **11.** sample: 75, 10^2, 387.2 **13.** -7 **15.** 45 **17.** 33.6 **19.** 250 **21.** 10
23. ANSWER TO QUESTION 23
ENTER A NUMBER
?2
6
25. a. -1, 0, 1, 2, 3 **b.** 5 **27.** True **29.** 50 **31.** 5 **33.** $\frac{4}{52} = \frac{1}{13}$ **35. a.** B **b.** A **37.** whole numbers, discrete **39.** positive real numbers, continuous **41.** True **43.** True **45.** ≈ 1357 cm³
47. $159.73 **49.** 240 women **51.** ≈ 82% **53.** a
55. a. $45 \le s \le 65$ **55. b.** See below. **57. a.** See below.
57. b. See below. **59.** b **61. a.** 3 states **b.** 16 states **c.** 118°

55. b.
45 65 s

57. a.
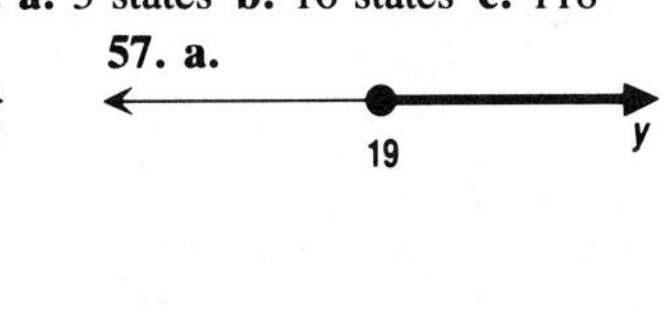

57. b.
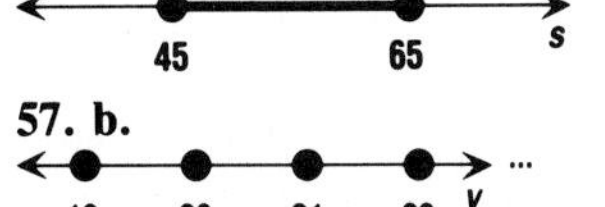

CHAPTER 2 REFRESHER (p. 53)
1. 7.8 **2.** 133.56 **3.** 11.0239 **4.** $3\frac{3}{4}$ **5.** 9 **6.** $\frac{209}{210}$ **7.** 18%
8. 31.2% **9.** 11.03 cm **10.** 2.3 km **11.** 3′ **12.** 7′3″
13. 9 lb 14 oz **14.** 7 lb 9 oz **15.** 24 **16.** -15 **17.** 1 **18.** 13
19. -4 **20.** -16 **21.–29.** See below. **30.** $x = 8$ **31.** $z = 31$
32. $w = 407$ **33.** $m = 5$ **34.** $n = 539$ **35.** $s = 299$

21.–29.
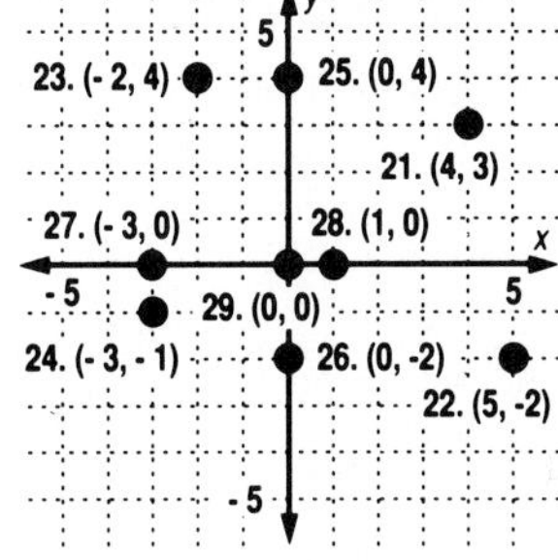

LESSON 2-1 (pp. 56–61)

3. 1988 **5.** Let E be the amount available for other expenses. Then $52.50 + 23.75 + 20 + E = 115$. **7. a.** 17 cm **b.** 15 cm **11.** a **13.** b **15.** $50 + x = 54$ **17.** There is overlap; zero is in both sets. **19.** $p + q + 26$ **21.** $49.95 + .05 + 59.28 + .72 = (49.95 + .05) + (59.28 + .72) = 50 + 60 = 110$ **23. a.** No **b.** Yes **c.** No **d.** Sample: brushing your teeth followed by combing your hair; yes **25.** $\frac{35}{68}$ or $\approx .515$ **27. a.** $\frac{2}{3}$ **b.** $\frac{2y}{3z}$ **c.** $\frac{2a}{3n}$ **29. a.** $\frac{26}{3}$ **b.** $-\frac{26}{3}$ **c.** $\frac{53}{10}$

LESSON 2-2 (pp. 62–67)

1. a. **See below.** **b.** gain of 4 yards **3. a.** -23 **b.** $-2x$ **c.** -143 **5.** $y + -11$ **9.** any negative value, such as -6 **11.** Property of Opposites **13.** Adding Like Terms Property **15.** $3 + 8 \cdot 4 \neq 44$ **17.** $x + -3 + 5$ **19.** $40 - n + 2n$ or $40 + n$ **21.** 18 **23.** $-c$ **25.** 0 **27.** $14a - 4$ **29.** $(87 + k)$ sq cm **31. a.** F = W * A/G **b.** 12.6 pounds **33.** 9

1. a.

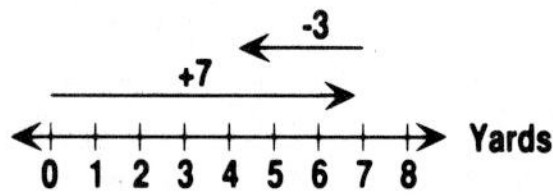

LESSON 2-3 (pp. 68–73)

3. **See below.** **5.** -.625, -.625 **7.** $4\frac{1}{2}$ **9.** 3 **11. a.** $\frac{8x}{15}$ **b.** $\frac{8}{x}$ **c.** $\frac{5f + 3g}{5g}$ **d.** $\frac{bx + 3c}{cx}$ **13.** $\frac{17k}{12}$ **15.** $f + \frac{1}{3}$ or $\frac{3f + 1}{3}$ **17.** c **19.** $60\% = .60 = \frac{3}{5}$; $5\% = .05 = \frac{1}{20}$; $10\% = .10 = \frac{1}{10}$ **21.** sample: The temperature ranged from -3 to 4 degrees. **23.** 11 **25.** About 11.1 **27.** perpendicular lines

3.

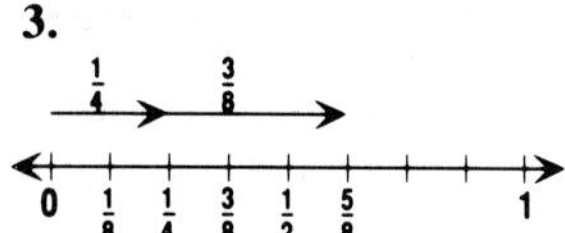

LESSON 2-4 (pp. 74–79)

3. a. 2 **b.** Beth, 60 minutes; Gary, 90 minutes **5.** to make the graph easier to use and to read. **7.** \$126 billion less **9.** 30 mph **13.** 31 minutes **15.** c **17. a.** 4 **b.** $4m$ **19.** $\frac{1}{8}$ **21.** $\frac{17}{5a}$ **23. a.** -17.3 **b.** Property of Opposites **25.** $x + 7 + y = 140$ **27.** 1460 **29.** 8.232

LESSON 2-5 (pp. 80–84)

3. (-3.5, 5) **5.** **See below.** **7. a.** $(x + 3, y + -7)$ **b.** sample: $x = 2$, $y = 0$; $(2 + 3, 0 + -7) = (5, -7)$ **See below.** **9.** (4, -10) **11.** samples: 2N, 4E, 2N; 4E, 4N; 4N, 4E **13.** **See below.** **15.** $\frac{6 + 7x}{21}$ **17.** -\$1.8 million **19.** $1\frac{1}{3}$ **21.** 40 **23. a.** Commutative Property of Addition **b.** $x + y$ **25.** **See below.**

5.

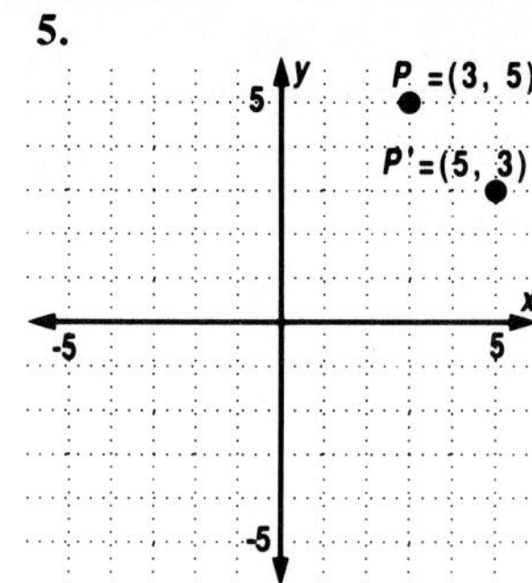

7. b.

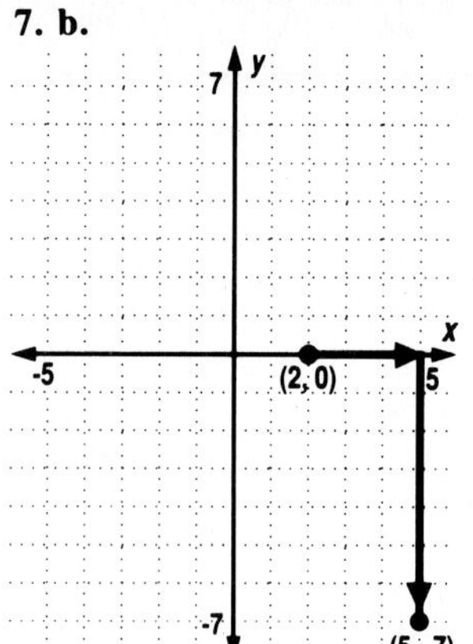

13.

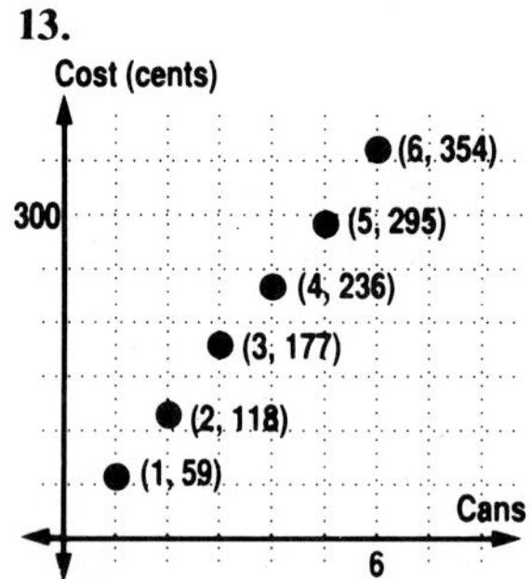

25.

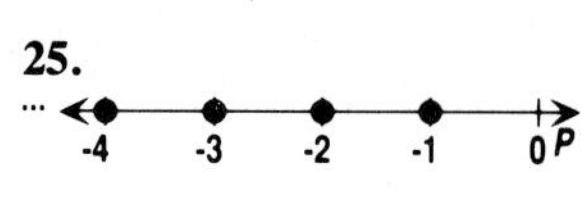

LESSON 2-6 (pp. 85–90)

1. My friend and I are the same age. **3.** Six years ago we were also the same age. **7.** Additive Identity Property **9. a.** 12 **b.** $y = -229$ **c.** Does $-12 + -229 = -241$? Yes. **11. a.** $a + b + c = p$ **b.** $b = p + -a + -c$ **c.** $b = 33$ **13.** b **15. a.** $C + 43 = 120$ **b.** $C = 77$. Does $77 + 43 = 120$? Yes. **17. a.** $7\frac{1}{4}$ **b.** Does $3\frac{1}{4} + 7\frac{1}{4} = 10\frac{1}{2}$? $3 + 7 + \frac{1}{4} + \frac{1}{4} = 10\frac{1}{2}$? Yes. **19.** $d = c + -a$ **21.** $25 + c = -12$, $c = -37$, fallen 37°, $25 + -37 = -12$ **23. a.** 2 right, 4 down; **b.** $D' = (2, -4)$; $E' = (3, 0)$ **25.** B **27.** Merry Berry **29.** 18.5¢

LESSON 2-7 (pp. 91–95)

1. $x < y$ **3.** $x + -6 < y + -6$ **5.** $y \geq 0.19$ **7.** d **9. a.** $z + 2 \geq 18$ **b.** $z \geq 16$ **11.** True **13. a.** $129 + p \leq 162$; $p \leq 33$ **b.** **See below.** **15.** $x \geq 1\frac{3}{4}$. Step 1: Does $\frac{1}{2} + 1\frac{3}{4} + \frac{3}{4} = 3$? Yes. Step 2: Try 3. Is $\frac{1}{2} + 3 + \frac{3}{4} \geq 3$? Yes, $4\frac{1}{4} \geq 3$. **17.** 0 **19.** $-5\frac{1}{2}$ **21.** $B = -20.6$ **23.** 60° **25.** (7, 12) **27. a.** (0, -2), (1, -1), (2, 0), (3, 1), (4, 2), (5, 3) **b.** **See below.** **29.** $\frac{3}{16}$

13. b.

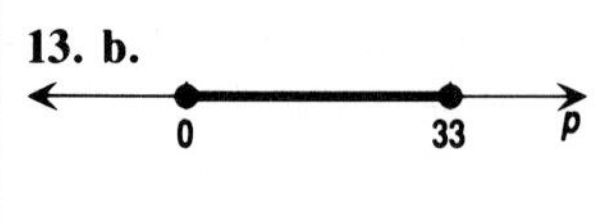

27. b.

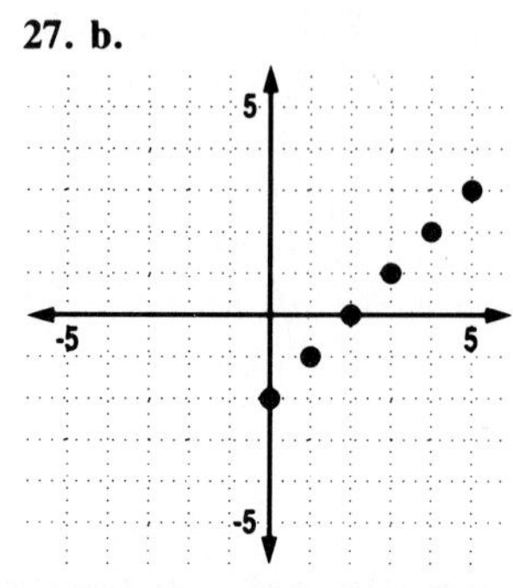

LESSON 2-8 (pp. 96–99)
1. $10 + d$ **5. a.** $4 + 5 > x, x + 4 > 5, x + 5 > 4$ **b.** $x < 9, x > 1, x > -1$ **c.** 9 **d.** 1 **e.** 1, 9 **7.** 0.5 km, 2.1 km **9.** because $1 + 2 < 4$ **11.** $2.6 < m < 20$ light-years **13.** $\frac{7}{6}$ or $1\frac{1}{6}$ **15.** 8 **17.** 0 **19. a.** 15 **b.** 9 **c.** 15 **21.** They are equal. **23.** $-50 + c + -20 = 210$; $c = 280$

CHAPTER 2 PROGRESS SELF-TEST (p. 101)

1. Associative Property of Addition **2.** $x + y + 35 = 6 \cdot 12$ **3.** $-10 + d = t$ **4.** 27 **5.** $x + -3$ **6.** $\frac{2 + m}{n}$ **7.** $\frac{3}{4} + \frac{3}{5} + \left(\frac{-3}{10}\right) = \frac{3}{4} + \frac{3}{10} = \frac{15 + 6}{20} = \frac{21}{20}$ or $1\frac{1}{20}$ **8.** $-11\frac{5}{6}$ **9.** $-p$ **10.** $-2x + 4y$ **11.** d **12. a.** $-4 + 1\frac{1}{2} + -3 + L = -10$ **b.** $-5\frac{1}{2} + L = -10$; $L = -4\frac{1}{2}$; she must lose $4\frac{1}{2}$ lb. **13.** Addition Property of Equality **14.** 16 **15.** $a > 13.7$ **16.** $\frac{7}{4}$ **17.** $1 > z + -10$, $11 > z$, $z < 11$ **18.** $b = 100 + -a$ **19.** Is $15 \le -100 + 87$? Is $15 \le -13$? No **20.** $-13 \ge x$; **See below.** **21.** $m + 47.50 \ge 150$ **22.** $9 + b + 21 = 43$; $b + 30 = 43$; $b = 13$ **23.** $C + -7$ **24.** $(5 + -4, -2 + 5) = P' = (1, 3)$ **25.** $-4 + a = 6$, $a = 10$; $7 + b = 5$, $b = -2$; $(-5 + 10, -2 + -2) = B' = (5, -4)$ **26.** $x \le 30 + 12$, $x + 12 \ge 30$, and $x + 30 \ge 12$ gives $x \le 42$ and $x \ge 18$ $(18 \le x \le 42)$ **27.** 18 km **28.** $b + g = 45$ **29.** (10, 35), (20, 25), (23, 22), (44, 1) **30. See below.**

20.

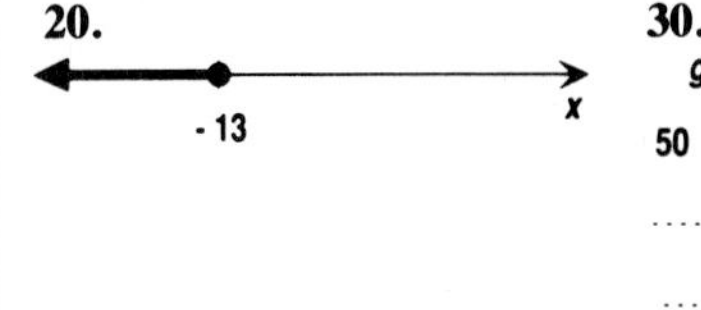

30.

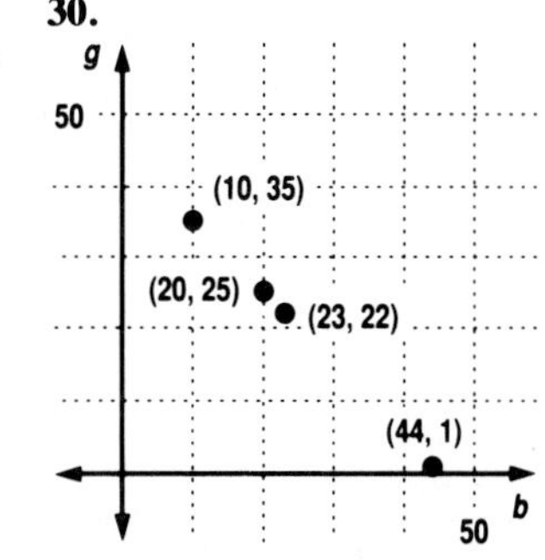

The chart below keys the **Progress Self-Test** questions to the objectives in the **Chapter Review** on pages 102–105 or to the **Vocabulary** (Voc.) on page 100. This will enable you to locate those **Chapter Review** questions that correspond to questions you missed on the **Progress Self-Test.** The lesson where the material is covered is also indicated in the chart.

Question	**1**	**2**	**3**	**4, 5**	**6–8**	**9**	**10**	**11**	**12**	**13**	**14**	**15**
Objective	E	H	H	B	A	E	B	A	H	F	C	D
Lesson	2-1	2-1	2-2	2-2	2-3	2-2	2-2	2-2	2-6	2-6	2-6	2-7
Question	**16**	**17**	**18**	**19**	**20**	**21**	**22, 23**	**24, 25**	**26, 27**	**28**	**29, 30**	
Objective	C	D	C	D	J	H	H	L	G, I	H	K	
Lesson	2-6	2-7	2-6	2-7	2-7	2-7	2-6	2-5	2-8	2-6	2-4	

CHAPTER 2 REVIEW (pp. 102–105)

1. $\frac{13}{12}$ **3.** $-\frac{21}{20}$ **5.** $\frac{x + y}{3}$ **7.** $\frac{mq + np}{nq}$ **9.** 5 **11.** $12a + 2b + -5$ **13.** $3t + 3$ **15.** $6b$ **17.** $m = 10$; does $2 + 10 = 12$? Yes **19.** $t = -0.6$; does $2.5 = -0.6 + 3.1$? Yes **21.** $m = 7487$; does $21{,}625 + 7487 = 29{,}112$? Yes **23.** $y = -1$; does $-2 + -1 = -3$? Yes **25.** $r = 5p$ **27.** $x > 5$ **29.** $x > 1$ **31.** $15 + 35 = 50$; not correct **33.** Additive Identity Property **35.** Op-op Property **37.** Adding Like Terms Property **39.** Addition Property of Equality **41.** c **43.** $a + b > c$, $b + c > a$, $c + a > b$ **45.** $0.2 < y < 4.6$ **47.** 24° **49.** $5.4 + d + 7.50 < 26$ **51.** $T_1 + C > T_2$ **53.** $+\frac{5}{8}$ **55.** It would take more than 10 minutes and less than 50 minutes. **57. See below.** **59. See below.** **61.** halfway up **63.** Ohio **65.** 1950 to 1960 **67.** $(x + 4, y + -10)$ **69. See below.**

57.

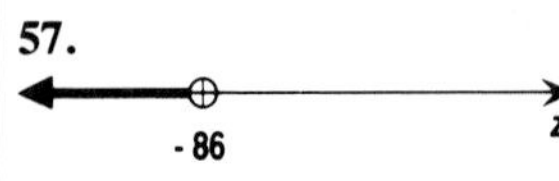

59.

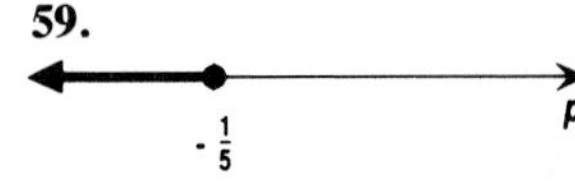

69.

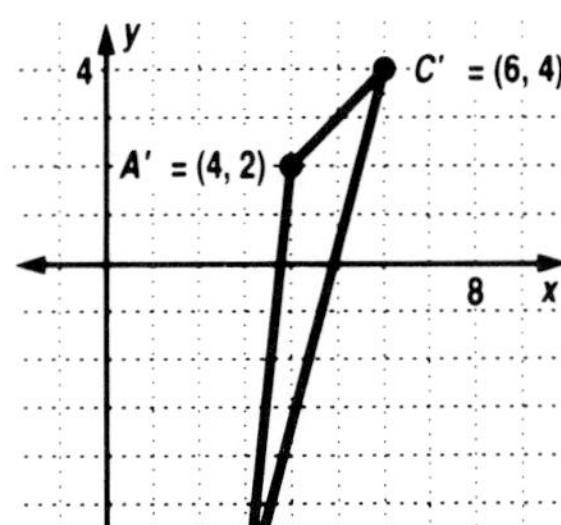

CHAPTER 3 REFRESHER (p. 105)
1. -160 **2.** -3 **3.** -8 **4.** -1 **5.** 199 **6.** 1 **7.** b **8.** c **9.** 75° **10.** 120° **11. See below.** **12.** $x = 51$ **13.** $909 = y$ **14.** $w = 113$ **15.** $502 = z$

11.

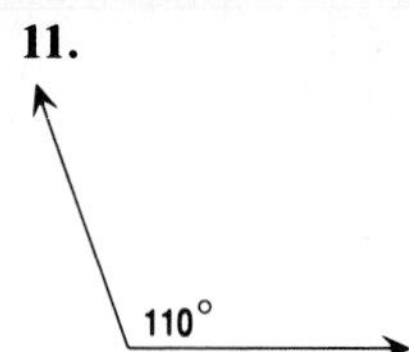

CHAPTER 3 OPENER (p. 107)
1.–6. See below.

1. IX + VI = XV
2. VII + I = VIII
3. V − III = II
4. VII − IV = III
5. XI − V = VI
6. VII − VI = I

LESSON 3-1 (pp. 108–112)
1. a. 12 + -15 **b.** 12 − 15 **3.** -2 + -7 **5.** $x + d$ **7. a.** $\frac{3}{5} + \frac{7}{10}$ **b.** $\frac{13}{10}$ **9. a.** False **b.** Associative Property of Subtraction **11.** -57 **13.** $10p + 6q + 4$ **15.** -22 **17.** 0 **19. a.** -4 + -3 + -3 + 5 **b.** -4 − 3 − 3 + 5 **c.** -5 lb **21.** -1, 1 **23. a.** $-15x$ **b.** $-14y$ **c.** $2x + 32$ **d.** $4x$ **25. a.** $x = 4$ **b.** $y = 0.7$ **c.** $z = \frac{1}{2}$ **27. a.** 17 **b.** 10 **c.** 800 **29.** $y = 21x + 3$

LESSON 3-2 (pp. 113–117)
5. $18 - A$ **7.** $1600 - b^2$ **9. a.** Bernie **b.** 7 years **11. a.** 0.5° **b.** -1.5° **13.** 47° **15.** $(x - 3)$ feet **17.** $4x$ **19.** -24.73 **21.** $-13ab - 2a - 4b$ **23. a.** -10 **b.** $-6 + n$ **25.** 37 **27.** $x = 3$, $y = 1$ **29.** $\frac{E}{G}$ **31. a.** $\frac{1}{2}b^2$ **b.** $6h^2$ **c.** $\frac{1}{16}$

LESSON 3-3 (pp. 118–122)
3. a. $s + -1240 = 20{,}300$ **b.** $s = 21{,}540$ **5. a.** $x + 60 < 140$ **b.** $x < 80$ **7. a.** Definition of subtraction **b.** Addition Property of Inequality **c.** Property of Opposites **d.** Additive Identity Property **9.** $A - 2768 \geq 1000$ **11.** $x \leq y + 35$ **13. a.** Definition of subtraction **b.** Addition Property of Equality **c.** Associative Property of Addition **d.** Property of Opposites **e.** Additive Identity Property **15.** 3 **17.** $100\frac{1}{2}$ **19.** $q > 31$ **See below.** **21.** $2a + a = 3a$ **23.** $2000 - n$ **25.** \$5500 − 4500 = \$1000 **27.** -14 **29. a.** 200,000 **b.** 10 **c.** 5

19.

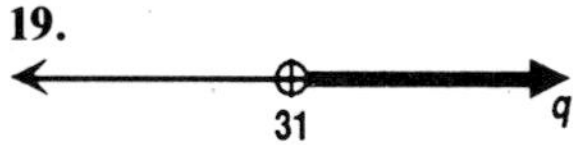

LESSON 3-4 (pp. 123–127)
3. {6, 12} **5. See below.** **7.** $\frac{1}{3}$ **11. a. See below. b. See below.** **13.** $\frac{4}{26}$ **15.** $\frac{15}{30}$ or $\frac{1}{2}$ **17. a.** {1, 7} **b.** {1} **19. a.** $T + S - B$ **21.** $t = 141$ **23.** $b = 4$ **25.** -4 **27. a.** -3 **b.** $-\frac{3}{5}$ **c.** $\frac{-3}{x}$

5.

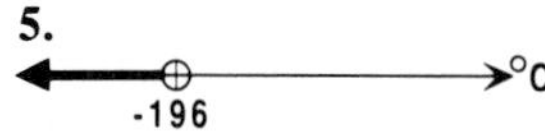

11. a.

11. b.

LESSON 3-5 (pp. 128–132)
1. The Greens beat the Reds and the Blues beat the Purples. **3.** {2, 3, 4, 6, 8, 9, 10, 12, 15} **5. a.** I **b.** III **c.** II **7. a.** ≈ 6% **b.** ≈ 56% **9. a.** {3} **b.** {1, 2, 3, 5, 6, 7, 9} **11. See below.** **13. See below.** **15. See below.** **17. a.** $x = 7.4$ **b.** $y = 2\frac{1}{2}$ **c.** $z = -1.5$ **19.** $\frac{7}{5}x = -5$ **21. a.** $\frac{1}{2} - \frac{2}{3} = \frac{-1}{6}$ **b.** $\frac{x}{2} + \frac{-2x}{3} = \frac{-x}{6}$ **c.** $\frac{x}{2a} + \frac{2x}{3a} = \frac{7x}{6a}$ **23.** $0 < s < 24$ where s is length of third side **25.** a **27.** a

11.

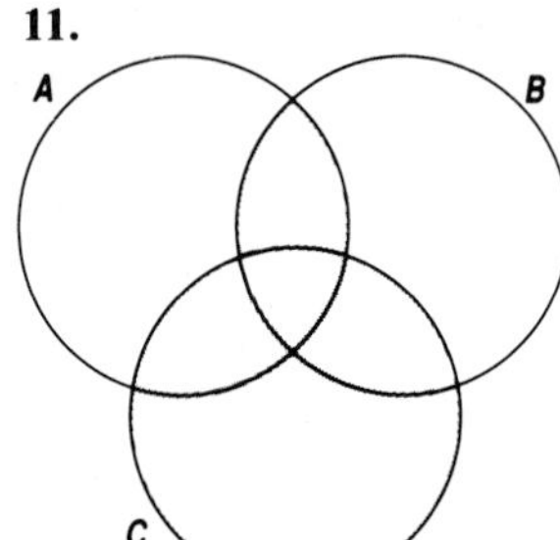

13. / **15.**

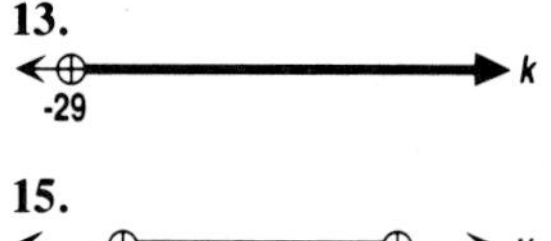

LESSON 3-6 (pp. 133–137)
5. 25 **9.** .87 **11.** 6 **13. a.** 6 **b. See below.** **15.** $\frac{7}{12}$ **17. a.** $x = 9$ **b.** $y = 6$ **c.** $z = 2$ **19. a.** $y - 12$ **b.** $y + 38$ **21.** ≈ .5 **23.** $\frac{4}{9}$; slightly above par

13.

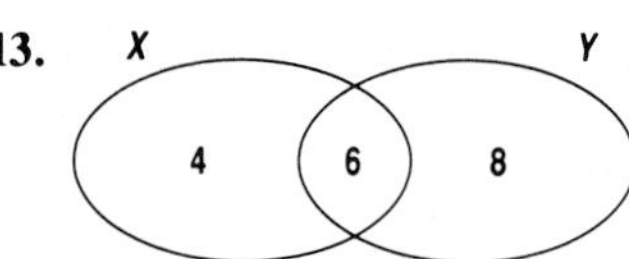

LESSON 3-7 (pp. 138–142)
5. a. See below. **5. b. See below.** **7. a.** (1, 7), (2, 6), (3, 5), (4, 4), (5, 3), (6, 2), (7, 1) **b.** 3 **9.** (0, 3), (1, 2), (2, 1), (3, 0); c **11.** $y = x + 5$ **13.** 22.6 **15.** 2326 **17. a.** 95% **b.** 430 **19.** samples: violin, piano, kettle drum **21.** a **23.** \$9.50 **25. a.** 1000 **b.** 2000 **c.** 125

5. a.

x Xandra	y Yvonne	(x, y) Ordered Pairs
1	6	(1, 6)
2	7	(2, 7)
3	8	(3, 8)
4	9	(4, 9)
5	10	(5, 10)
6	11	(6, 11)

5. b.

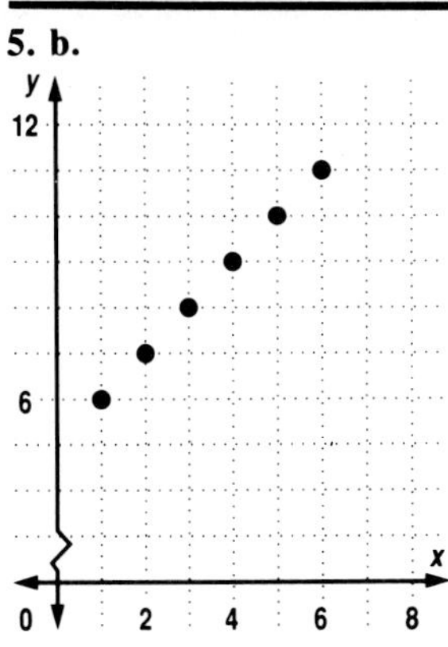

LESSON 3-8 (pp. 143–147)
1. 138° **5.** 65° **7.** $m = 48$ **9.** True **11. a.** sample: 10° and 80°; 30° and 60°; 45° and 45°, 70° and 20°; 85° and 5° (10, 80); (30, 60); (45, 45); (70, 20); (85, 5) **b. See below. c. See below. 13.** $m\angle C = 25°$, $m\angle T = 65°$ **15.** 50° **17.** $m\angle C = 180 - (m\angle A + m\angle B)$ **19.** $z < 108$ **21.** $x = 10$ **23.** 3279 **25.** 961 **27.** EVALUATE A * B
GIVE A AND B
?13.94, 6.06
84.4764
29. b **31.** $-\frac{7}{12}x$

11. b. 11. c.

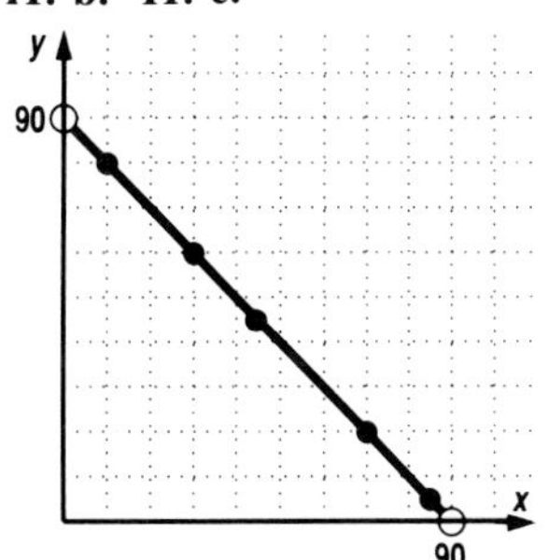

CHAPTER 3 PROGRESS SELF-TEST (p. 149)

1. subtracting 7 **2.** $1n + -16 + -2n + 12 = -1n + -4 = -n - 4$ **3.** $-8x + -2x + x = -10x + 1x = -9x$ **4.** $\frac{3}{4} + -\frac{7}{8} = \frac{6}{8} + -\frac{7}{8} = -\frac{1}{8}$ **5.** $\frac{2m}{4a} + -\frac{3m}{4a} = \frac{-1m}{4a} = -\frac{m}{4a}$ **6.** $y + -13 = -7$; $y + -13 + 13 = -7 + 13$; $y + 0 = 6$; $y = 6$ **7.** $m + -2 < 6$; $m + -2 + 2 < 6 + 2$; $m + 0 < 8$; $m < 8$ **8.** $b + -a = 100$; $b + -a + a = 100 + a$; $b + 0 = 100 + a$; $b = 100 + a$ **9.** $m + -7n = -22n$; $m + -7n + 7n = -22n + 7n$; $m + 0 = -15n$; $m = -15n$ **10.** {-3, 3} **11.** { -6, -3, -1, 0, 1, 3, 5, 6, 7, 9} **12. See below. 13. See below. 14.** $(321 + 215) - 480 = 56$ **15.** $V - H$ **16.** $B - S - 3 + N$ **17.** $15 + 11 - 20 = 6$, $\frac{6}{30} = \frac{1}{5}$ **18.** c **19. See below. 20. See below. 21.** c

12.

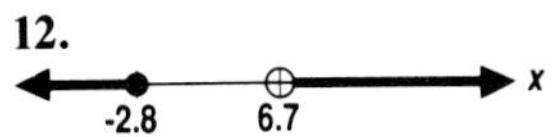

13.

19.

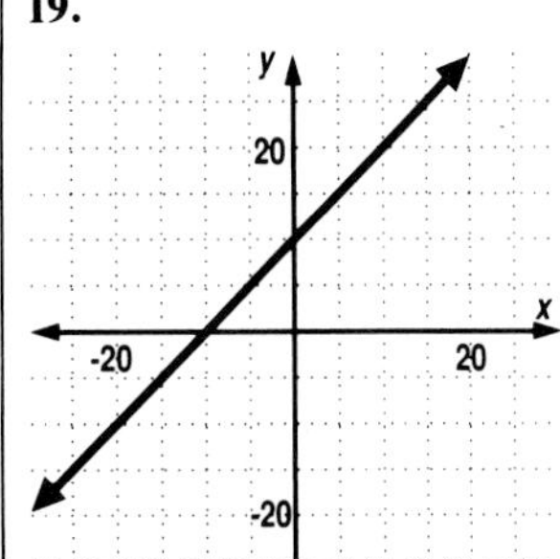

20.

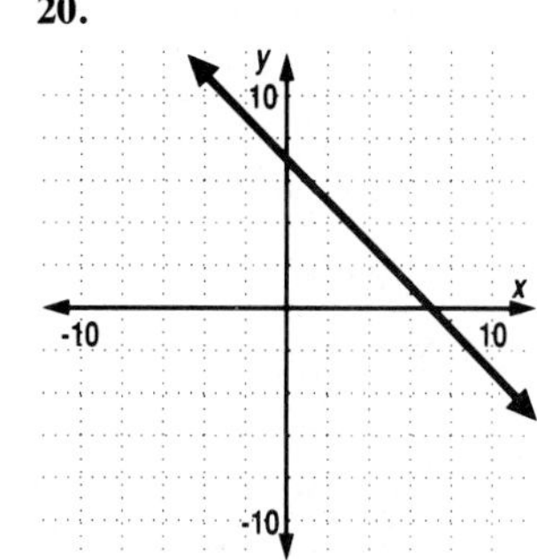

The chart below keys the **Progress Self-Test** questions to the objectives in the **Chapter Review** on pages 150–152 or to the **Vocabulary** (Voc.) on page 148. This will enable you to locate those **Chapter Review** questions that correspond to questions you missed on the **Progress Self-Test.** The lesson where the material is covered is also indicated in the chart.

Question	**1**	**2–5**	**6, 7**	**8, 9**	**10**	**11**	**12**	**13**	**14**	**15, 16**	**17**
Objective	E	D	B	B	A	A	H	H	G	F	G
Lesson	3-1	3-1	3-3	3-3	3-4	3-5	3-5	3-4	3-6	3-2	3-6
Question	**18**	**19, 20**	**21**								
Objective	C	J	I								
Lesson	3-8	3-7	3-5								

CHAPTER 3 REVIEW (pp. 150–152)

1. {15, 25} **3.** {8, 9} **5.** $x = 45$; Does $45 - 47 = -2$? Yes **7.** $y = -\frac{1}{2}$ Does $\frac{3}{2} + -\frac{1}{2} - \frac{1}{4} = \frac{3}{4}$? Yes **9.** $z < 23$ Does $23 - 12 = 11$? Yes; try 3: Is $3 - 12 < 11$? Yes **11.** Does $10 - 30 = 40$? No. He is wrong. **13.** $-z = y$ **15.** 27.5° **17.** $x + z = 90$ **19.** $-1\frac{7}{15}$ **21.** $-25\frac{1}{3}$ **23.** 0 **25.** $1 + -3z^3$ **27.** $-8 + -v = 42$ **29.** d **31.** $p + 80 > L$ where

p = weight of other passengers; $p > L - 80$ **33.** $S - 40 < 3$; $S < 43$ **35.** 31,500 feet **37.** $5000 - H$ **39.** $\frac{22}{25}$ **41.** 91 **43.** **See below.** **45.** **See below.** **47.** {-11, -1, 2} **49.** **See below.** **51.** **See below.** **53.** **See below.**

43.

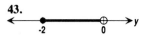

45.

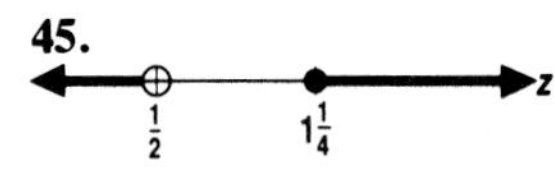

49.

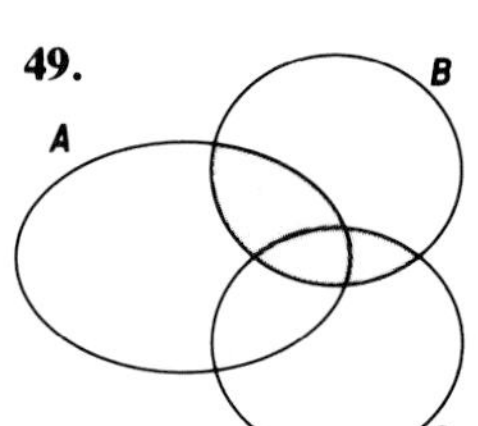

51.

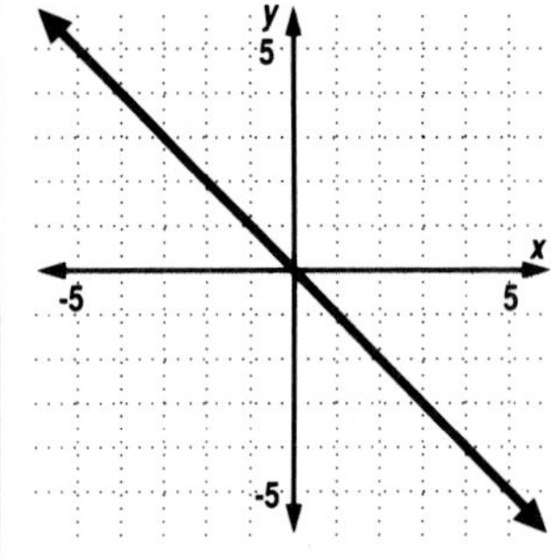

53.

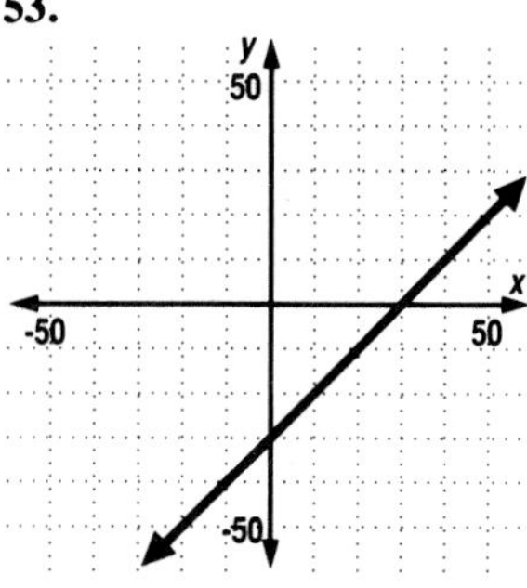

CHAPTER 4 REFRESHER (p. 153)

1. 15.087 **2.** 12.48 **3.** 0.00666 **4.** 0.0034 **5.** 20 **6.** $27\frac{1}{2}$ **7.** $\frac{1}{6}$ **8.** $\frac{1}{24}$ **9.** $2\frac{21}{32}$ **10.** $33\frac{1}{3}$ **11.** $39.27 **12.** $93.75 **13.** $5\frac{1}{4}$ inches **14.** 36 **15.** $180 **16.** 78.75 **17.** -6 **18.** -121 **19.** -24 **20.** 25 **21.** 0 **22.** -1820 **23.** 3540 **24.** 6 **25.** $x = 4$ **26.** $y = 22$ **27.** $z = \frac{1}{2}$ **28.** $\frac{1}{9} = w$ **29.** $\frac{3}{25} = a$ **30.** $b = \frac{2}{3}$ **31.** $c = \frac{1}{2}$ **32.** $3\frac{1}{2} = d$ **33.** 180 in.^{2} **34.** 14.4 cm^2 **35.** 8 m^2 **36.** 8200 ft^2 **37.** 96 cm^3 **38.** 162 in.^{3} **39.** $\frac{1}{8}$ ft^3 **40.** 30,000 m^3

LESSON 4-1 (pp. 156–161)

3. square inches **5.** $8y$ in.^{2} **7.** 3984 **9.** $21xy$ cubic units **11.** $45ab$ **13.** **a.** kn **b.** $2k + 2n$ **15.** $12x^3$ cm^3 **17.** **a.** $\frac{1}{2}$ in. • $\frac{3}{4}$ in. **b.** $\frac{3}{8}$ **c.** $\frac{3}{8}$ **19.** 576 m^2 **21.** samples: 3 by 4 by 7, 2 by 6 by 7, 14 by 2 by 3, 28 by 1 by 3, $\frac{1}{2}$ by $\frac{1}{2}$ by 336 **23.** $240x^2$ **25.** 17 **27.** 175 **29.** **a.** If p pounds of meat are eaten, then $17 \leq p \leq 23$ **29. b. See below.**

29. b.

LESSON 4-2 (pp. 162–167)

1. $\frac{10}{33}$ **3.** $\frac{7m^2}{3n}$ **5.** $6k$ **7.** **a.** A typist types 70 words per minute **b.** 70 words/minute **c.** $70\frac{\text{words}}{\text{minute}}$ **9.** 17.55 miles **11.** **a.** -1.5 inches **b.** -1 5 **13.** (b) **15.** **a.** 30 **b.** A printer is printing 15-page documents at the rate of $\frac{1}{2}$ page per minute. How many minutes will it take to print each document? **17.** $\frac{60ab}{x}$ **19.** **a.** 1536 oz **b.** $128c$ oz **21.** 3,503,000 babies **23.** Ds dollars **25.** ≈ 11.4 sec **27.** $\frac{1}{2}$ in.^{2} **29.** 5 12 534.072 **31.** **a.** True **b.** True **c.** False

LESSON 4-3 (pp. 168–172)

5. **a.** opposites or additive inverses, zero **b.** reciprocals, one **7.** $\frac{1}{10}$; $10 \cdot \frac{1}{10} = 1$ **9.** $\frac{5}{23}$; $\frac{23}{5} \cdot \frac{5}{23} = 1$ **11.** $-\frac{7}{6}$; $-\frac{6}{7} \cdot -\frac{7}{6} = 1$ **13.** **a.** 10 in. • $2.54\frac{\text{cm}}{\text{in.}}$ = 25.4 cm **b.** x in. • $2.54\frac{\text{cm}}{\text{in.}}$ = $2.54x$ cm **15.** $abcde$ **17.** a and d **19.** Yes **21.** $a = 1$, $b = 0$ **23.** $10x$ **25.** **a.** $32p$ **b.** -125 **c.** x^2 **27.** 33 math problems/night **29.** **a.** 3080 ft^2 **b.** 513 people **31.** $T - \frac{3}{2}$ hours

LESSON 4-4 (pp. 173–177)

3. **a.** -32 **b.** $-\frac{1}{32}$ **c.** -13 **5.** **a.** $\frac{3}{32}$ **b.** $\frac{32}{3}$ **c.** 8 **7.** -.05 **11.** No **13.** 200 cm from the turning point **15.** 12.41 cm **17.** **a.** $DV = M$ **b.** 648.96 pounds **19.** (a) **21.** 16.2 minutes **23.** ≈ 171 cm^2 **25.** **a.** $a = -7$ **b.** $a \leq 48$ **c.** $a > 166 - c$ **27.** **a.** 24% **b.** 30% **c.** 140%

LESSON 4-5 (pp. 178–181)

1. 0 has no reciprocal. **3.** **a.** There is no solution. **b.** { } or ∅ **7.** $x = -40$ **9.** $z = 0$ **11.** $v = 3.74$ **13.** $x = 89$ seconds **15.** **a.** $y = m - 25$ **b.** $2 = 27 - 25$ **17.** $N = 0$ **19.** $p = -3$ **21.** $r = 30$ **23.** -238 **25.** **a.** 1 **b.** -1 **c.** When the number of factors is even, the value is 1. When the number of factors is odd, the value is -1. **27.** 4 + -3 **29.** -432 • -175

LESSON 4-6 (pp. 182–185)

1. 120 < 180 **3.** -80 > -120 **7.** **a.** No **b.** No **c.** Yes **d.** No **e.** No **f.** No **9.** $y > -100$ **11.** $\frac{13}{2} > z$ **13.** $-0.01 < c$ **15.** $m > -8$ **17.** $t > 0$ **19.** 30 rows **21.** $n < 272$ **23.** $x = 4$ **25.** $b = 10$ **27.** $d = 7$ **29.** $30 = d$ **31.** 57 cubic units **33.** **a.** $\frac{1}{2}$ **b.** $\frac{1}{2}$ **c.** $\frac{1}{3}$ **d.** $\frac{2}{3}$ **35.** $A = \frac{1}{2}s^2$ **37.** **a.** $1\frac{1}{5}$ **b.** 6 **c.** 7.5 **d.** $\frac{1}{6}$

LESSON 4-7 (pp. 186–190)

5. See below. **7.** $5m^2n^4$ **9.** **a.** $2^{20} = 1{,}048{,}576$ **b.** $\frac{1}{1{,}048{,}576}$ **11.** Takeshi and Reiko, Takeshi and Akiko, Takeshi and Kimiko, Satoshi and Reiko, Satoshi and Akiko, Satoshi and Kimiko, Izumi and Reiko, Izumi and Akiko, Izumi and Kimiko, Mitsuo and Reiko, Mitsuo and Akiko, Mitsuo and Kimiko **13.** 144 **15.** 72 **17.** 2^{ℓ} **19.** $k = -\frac{1}{50}$ **21.** $m < \frac{1}{40}$ **23.** $d < 13$ **25.** 5.9 **27.** $(2w + 5)w$ **29.** Commutative Property of Multiplication **31.** Property of Opposites **33.** ≈ 38.8 **35.** **a.** $\frac{1}{4}$ **b.** $\frac{11}{2}$ **c.** -1 **37.** 70%

5.

		South Gate I	South Gate F	South Gate E
North Gate	A	(A, I)	(A, F)	(A, E)
	B	(B, I)	(B, F)	(B, E)
	C	(C, I)	(C, F)	(C, E)

LESSON 4-8 (pp. 191–196)

1. b. $\frac{2}{30}$ or $\frac{1}{15}$ **5.** $\frac{3}{70} \approx .043$ or 4.3% **7.** $\frac{19}{34}$ **9.** $\approx$ 18% **11.** (b) **13.** 30% **15. a.** $\frac{1}{2}$ **b.** $\frac{7}{19}$ **c.** $\frac{7}{38}$ **17.** $\frac{5m^2}{9n^2}$ **19. a.** $\frac{1}{4}$ **b.** $\frac{1}{8}$ **21.** 17,576,000 **23.** $cr = d$ **25.** $\frac{6}{5}$ **27.** $\frac{1}{a}$ **29.** $x = -\frac{12}{m}$ **31. a.** (1, -3) **b.** $(-7, r + 2)$ **c.** $(-7 + m, 2 - n)$

LESSON 4-9 (pp. 197–201)

1. Bird, Jordan, Johnson; Bird, Johnson, Jordan; Jordan, Johnson, Bird; Jordan, Bird, Johnson; Johnson, Bird, Jordan; Johnson, Jordan, Bird **5. a.** 1 **b.** 2 **c.** 6 **d.** 24 **e.** 120 **f.** 720 **g.** 5040 **h.** 40,320 **7.** 2.6525×10^{32} **9.** 100 **13.** 720 **15. a.** $8 \cdot 7 = 56$ **b.** $8! = 40{,}320$ **17. a.** 10 **b.** $\frac{n!}{(n-1)!} = n$ **19. a.** $\frac{12}{25}$ **b.** $\frac{2}{6}$ or $\frac{1}{3}$ **c.** $\frac{6}{25} \cdot \frac{2}{6} = \frac{2}{25}$ **21.** 72.3 **23.** $y < \frac{10}{3}$ **25.** $t \geq -8$ **27.** 0 **29.** $\approx$ 691,200,000 grains **31.** $6.6a$ **33.** $64c^2$

CHAPTER 4 PROGRESS SELF-TEST (p. 203)

1. $\frac{5 \cdot 4 \cdot 3 \cdot 2 \cdot 1}{3 \cdot 2 \cdot 1 \cdot 2 \cdot 1} = \frac{5 \cdot 4}{2} = \frac{20}{2} = 10$ **2.** $7(2.4 + 2.9)(2 \cdot 2.4 + 3.1)(0) = 0$ **3.** $\frac{5}{3} \cdot \frac{x}{5} = \frac{x}{3}$ **4. a.** sample: $(2 \cdot 5) \cdot 8 = 2 \cdot (5 \cdot 8)$ **b.** sample: $6 \cdot \frac{1}{6} = \frac{1}{6} \cdot 6 = 1$ **5. See below.** **6.** $\frac{1}{30} \cdot 30x = \frac{1}{30} \cdot 10$; $x = \frac{10}{30}$; $x = \frac{1}{3}$ **7.** $4 \cdot \frac{1}{4}k = 4 \cdot -24$; $k = -96$ **8.** $\frac{1}{3} \cdot 15 \leq \frac{1}{3} \cdot 3m$; $\frac{15}{3} \leq m$; $5 \leq m$ **9.** $-y \leq -2$; $y \geq 2$ **10.** $1.46 = 2.7 + -t$; $2.7 + 1.46 = -2.7 + 2.7 + -t$; $-1.24 = 0 + -t$; $1.24 = t$ **11.** $\frac{1}{3m}$ **12.** $n \cdot 1 = n$ **13.** $11 \cdot (14 + 6 + 4) - (5 \cdot 6) = (11 \cdot 24) - 30 = 264 - 30 = 234$ **14.** $4 \cdot 5 = 20$ **15.** $5! = 120$ **16.** \$15.50s **17.** 300 mi. $\cdot \frac{1}{55} \frac{\text{hour}}{\text{mile}} = 5.\overline{45}$ hours, or about $5\frac{1}{2}$ hours **18.** 8 inches $\cdot\ 2.54 \frac{\text{cm}}{\text{in.}} = 20.32$ cm **19.** $\frac{3}{7} \cdot \frac{2}{6} = \frac{6}{42} = \frac{1}{7}$ **20. a.** 16 cm $\cdot\ w \cdot$ 5 cm = 1000 cm^3 **b.** $80w$ = 1000 cm; $\frac{1}{80} \cdot 80w = \frac{1}{80} \cdot$ (1000 cm); w = 12.5 cm **21.** $\frac{14}{40} \cdot \frac{1}{2} = \frac{7}{40}$

5.

$\frac{1}{5}$ $\frac{1}{5}$ $\frac{1}{5}$ $\frac{1}{5}$ $\frac{1}{5}$

$\frac{1}{2}$

$\frac{1}{2}$

The chart below keys the **Progress Self-Test** questions to the objectives in the **Chapter Review** on pages 204–207 or to the **Vocabulary** (Voc.) on page 202. This will enable you to locate those **Chapter Review** questions that correspond to questions you missed on the **Progress Self-Test.** The lesson where the material is covered is also indicated in the chart.

Question	**1**	**2**	**3**	**4**	**5**	**6**	**7**	**8, 9**	**10**	**11, 12**
Objective	E	F	A	F	L	B	B	D	C	F
Lesson	4-9	4-3	4-2	4-3	4-1	4-4	4-5	4-6	4-5	4-3
Question	**13**	**14**	**15**	**16, 17, 18**	**19**	**20**	**21**			
Objective	G	H	J	G	I	K	I			
Lesson	4-2	4-7	4-2	4-9	4-8	4-4	4-8			

CHAPTER 4 REVIEW (pp. 204–207)

1. $\frac{27}{40}$ **3.** $\frac{c}{d}$ **5.** $m = 150$; Does $2.4m = 2.4 \cdot 150 = 360$? Yes **7.** $f = -2.3$; Does $-10f = -10 \cdot -2.3 = 23$? Yes **9.** $A = \frac{15}{2}$; Does $\frac{4}{25}A = \frac{4}{25} \cdot \frac{15}{2} = \frac{30}{25} = \frac{6}{5}$? Yes **11.** $x = -12$; Does $31 - -12 = 31 + 12 = 43$? Yes **13.** $z = -\frac{1}{5}$; Does $\frac{1}{5} - -\frac{1}{5} = \frac{1}{5} + \frac{1}{5} = \frac{2}{5}$? Yes **15.** $m \leq 2$; Step 1: Does $8 \cdot 2 = 16$? Yes; Step 2: Try 0. Is $8 \cdot 0 \leq 16$? Yes **17.** $u > -2$; Step 1: Does $6 \cdot -2 = -12$? Yes; Step 2: Try 0. Is $6 \cdot 0 > -12$? Yes **19.** $g \leq 10$; Step 1: Does $\frac{1}{2} \cdot 10 = 5$? Yes; Step 2: Try 4. Is $\frac{1}{2} \cdot 4 \leq 5$? Yes **21.** 30 **23.** 240 **25.** 20 [x!] [÷] 15 [x!] [=] [÷] 5 [x!] [=] 15,504 **27. a.** $2200x$ **b.** Associative and Commutative Properties of Multiplication **29.** $n \cdot \frac{1}{n} = 1$ **31.** $\frac{1}{0.6}$ or $\frac{5}{3}$ **33. a.** $(-6.2 + 3.8)(4.3 - -6.2)(0) = 0$ **b.** Multiplication Property of Zero **35.** opposite **37.** sample: $0x = 5$ **39.** 48 ft^2 **41.** \$350k **43.** 1,045,440 sq ft **45.** C bookcases $\cdot\ 24 \frac{\text{ft}}{\text{bookcase}} \cdot B \frac{\text{books}}{\text{ft}} = 24 \cdot B \cdot C$ books **47.** 9,765,625 **49.** $\frac{1}{3} \cdot \frac{2}{8} = \frac{1}{12}$ **51. a.** $\frac{2}{10}$ or $\frac{1}{5}$ **b.** $\frac{10}{30} \cdot \frac{2}{10} = \frac{2}{30}$ or $\frac{1}{15}$ **53. a.** $\frac{13}{52} \cdot \frac{12}{51} = \frac{3}{51}$ **b.** $\frac{4}{52} \cdot \frac{3}{51} = \frac{1}{221}$ **55. a.** $9! = 362{,}880$ **b.** $\underline{3}.6288 \times 10^5$ **57.** 8.22 hr or $\approx$ 8 hr 15 min

59. $d \le 12.2$; at most 12 days **61.** Commutative Property of Multiplication **63.** See below. **65.** $\frac{3}{4} \cdot \frac{2}{5} = \frac{6}{20}$ or $\frac{3}{10}$ **67.** $20q$ tiles **69.** $24k^3$

63.

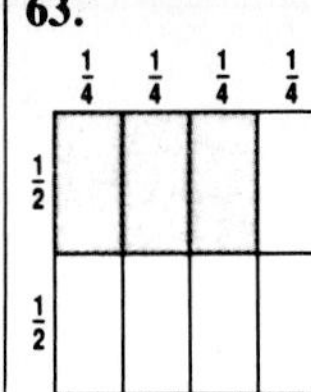

CHAPTER 5 REFRESHER (p. 207)

1. 0.40 **2.** 2.5 **3.** 2.4 **4.** 1,600 **5.** .2 **6.** .2 **7.** .0016 **8.** $\approx$ 4.8 **9.** 6 **10.** $\frac{4}{5}$ **11.** $\frac{2}{3}$ **12.** $1\frac{7}{8}$ **13.** 3 ft **14.** $2.5m$ **15.** $14\frac{2}{7}$ kg **16.** .24 lb **17.** .5; 50% **18.** .75; 75% **19.** .025; 2.5% **20.** .73; 73% **21.** .14 **22.** 6.67 **23.** 6.47 **24.** 3.14 **25.** 220% **26.** 27% **27.** 89% **28.** 18% **29.** .3; $\frac{3}{10}$ **30.** .01; $\frac{1}{100}$ **31.** 3.0; $\frac{3}{1}$ **32.** .0246; $\frac{123}{5000}$ **33.** .0003; $\frac{3}{10{,}000}$ **34.** .0025; $\frac{1}{400}$ **35.** \$240 **36.** 68 questions **37.** 2942 voters **38.** 12,000 square miles **39.** 0 **40.** 2 **41.** -8 **42.** -.5 **43.** -.025 **44.** $\frac{1}{2}$ **45.** -100 **46.** divisor 3; dividend 21; quotient 7 **47.** divisor 100; dividend 20; quotient 0.2 **48.** divisor 7; dividend 56; quotient 8

LESSON 5-1 (pp. 210–214)

1. $32 \div 6 = 5.\overline{33}$; $32 \cdot \frac{1}{6} = 5.\overline{33}$ **3. a.** n **b.** $\frac{1}{n}$ **5. a.** 2 **b.** 2 **c.** $\frac{1}{2}$ **d.** 100 **7.** $\frac{25}{2n}$ **9. a.** $\frac{6}{25} \div \frac{10}{7}$ **b.** $\frac{6}{25} \cdot \frac{7}{10}$ **c.** $\frac{42}{250} = \frac{21}{125}$ **11. a.** $-\frac{1}{3}$ **b.** -3 **13.** 50 **15.** $\frac{1}{2}$ **17.** $\frac{1}{6}$ **19. a.** -3.5, -3.5, and -3.5 **b.** $-.\overline{27}$, $-.\overline{27}$, and $-.\overline{27}$ **c.** $\frac{-x}{y} = \frac{x}{-y} = -\frac{x}{y}$ **21.** A positive number divided by a positive number is positive; a negative number divided by a negative number is positive; a negative number divided by a positive number is negative; a positive number divided a negative number is negative. **23.** $t + b = 5$; $t \ge 0$; $b \ge 0$; **See below.** **25.** 120 **27. a.** 3 **b.** 10 **29.** 4.5 m²

23.

x (turkey)	y (beef)
0	5
1	4
2	3
3	2
4	1
5	0

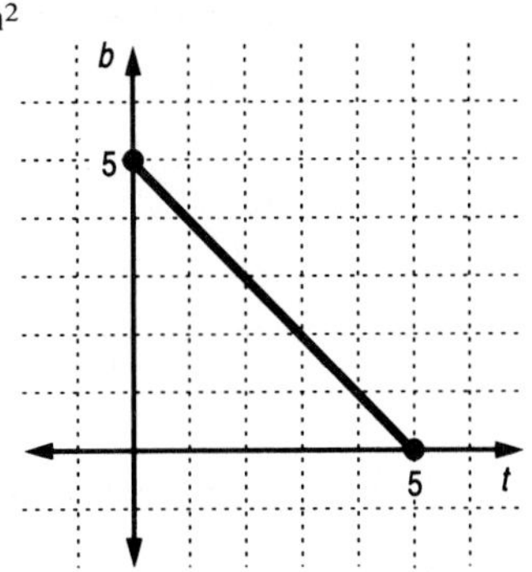

LESSON 5-2 (pp. 215–220)

1. a. 37.5 mph **b.** $\frac{2}{75}$ or $\approx$ .027 hour **3. a.** degrees, hours **b.** -2.2 degrees per hour **5.** \$55 per day **7.** $\approx$ 34.6 miles per gallon **9.** -1 **11.** so that the program will divide by the result of $K - 5$ **13. a.** 1544.1 people per sq mi **b.** .06 person per sq mi **15.** (b) **17.** An error message (E) appears. **19.** $\frac{x}{3} \cdot \frac{1}{5}$ **21.** $\frac{1}{2}$ **23.** 12 **25.** $x = -300$ **27.** $-\frac{10}{t}$ **29.** $\approx$ 738 francs **31.** 13; Does 8 = 13 − 5? Yes **33.** $\frac{15}{4}$; Does $13 - 15 + \frac{15}{4} = 2\frac{1}{2} + \frac{-3}{4}$? Yes

LESSON 5-3 (pp. 221–225)

1. Yes **5.** $\approx$ 7% **9.** b **11.** $\frac{w}{h} > 1$ **13.** $\approx$ 148 **15. a.** $\frac{.64}{16} = \frac{1}{25}$ **b.** 4% **17.** $\frac{6}{4} = \frac{3}{2}$ **19.** $\frac{y}{x}$ **21.** $-\frac{16}{21}$ **23.** .12 **25. a.** 13.5 ft² **b.** $\frac{1}{3}$ m² **c.** $6x^2$ **27. a.** \$65,000 **b.** \$67,500 **29.** 11

LESSON 5-4 (pp. 226–230)

5. 1100 **7.** $\approx$ 17% **9. a.** $.124x = 70{,}000$ **b.** $x = 564{,}516$ **11.** 33% **13.** 33% **15.** 25% **17.** \$88,000 **19.** $\approx$ 166% **21.** $66\frac{2}{3}$% **23.** \$8.50 **25.** -6 **27.** 130.5 **29.** $y = \frac{14x}{3}$ **31.** $c > \frac{2}{5}$

LESSON 5-5 (pp. 231–235)

1. a. $\approx$ .08 **b.** $\approx$ 8% **3.** .5 **5.** $\frac{13}{36}$ **7. a.** 100 **b.** $100 - 25\pi \approx 21.5$ **c.** $\frac{\pi}{4} \approx 78.5\%$ **d.** 100%; $p + q$ is the area of the whole region **9. a.** $\approx$ .28 **b.** $\approx$ .21 **11.** $\frac{ab}{pq}$ **13.** $\approx$ 26.3% **15.** $\frac{98}{135}$ **17.** ad **19.** more than $\frac{85}{6}$ ($\approx$ 14.2) cm **21. a.** 3,628,800 **b.** 132 **c.** 56 **23.** See below.

23.

LESSON 5-6 (pp. 236–241)

5. 6.4 in. by 9.6 in. **9.** $(8x, 8y)$ **11. a.** $J' = (-3, 0)$; $K' = (-3, 6)$, $L' = (0, 10.5)$; $M' = (9, 6)$, $N' = (9, 0)$ **b.** See below. **13.** \$7.80/hr **15.** 150 **17. a.** The image is the same as the original figure. **b.** Multiplicative Identity Property of 1 **19.** $\approx$ 14% **21. a.** 70% **b.** $c = .7(23.95)$ **c.** \$16.77 **23.** $18 \le x$ **25.** $y = \frac{53}{x}$ **27. a.** $\frac{5}{8} + x = 80$ **b.** $79\frac{3}{8}$ **29.** $\approx$ 100 **31.** $\approx$ 8 **33. a.** positive **b.** negative **35.** 144

11. b.

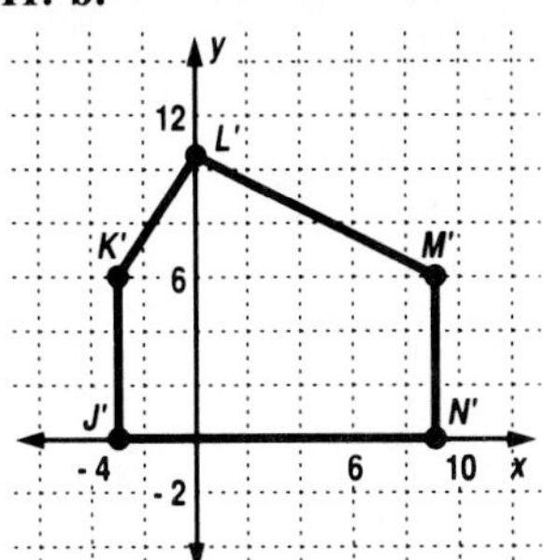

LESSON 5-7 (pp. 242–246)

1. True **3.** Yes **5.** No **7.** ≈328.7 miles **9. a.** $21 = 5n$ **b.** $15 = 7n$ **c.** $21 = 5n$ **d.** b **11. a.** $11x = 21$ **b.** $x = \frac{21}{11}$ **13.** $\frac{13}{40}$ or .325 of a picture **15.** 2.25 inches **17.** $b = \frac{2}{7}$ **19.** equal **21. a.** (5, -10) **b.** expansion **23.** $\frac{4x - 3y}{4x}$ or $1 - \frac{3y}{4x}$ **25. a.** $\frac{3,120,348}{5,232,113}$ **b.** ≈ 59% **27.** -3

LESSON 5-8 (pp. 247–252)

3. a. $\overline{BG}$ **b.** $\overline{IG}$ **5. a.** $\frac{2}{0.8} = \frac{3}{x}$ or (equivalent) **b.** $x = 1.2$ **c.** .4 or 2.5 **7.** sample: $\frac{p}{t} = \frac{a}{s} = \frac{r}{e} = \frac{k}{w}$ **9. a. See below. b.** $\frac{t}{6} = \frac{25}{10}$ **c.** 15 ft **11. a.** $\frac{1.5 \text{ in.}}{30 \text{ ft.}}$ **b.** $\frac{1.5}{30} = \frac{1}{x}$ **c.** 20 ft **13.** $A = \frac{1}{4}$ **15.** $C = \frac{15}{2}$ **17.** 90 students per year **19.** $\frac{1}{38}$ **21.** ≈ 19% **23.** $\frac{15}{y^2}$ **25.** 42 **27.** $a \leq 15$ **29.** $b \leq 75$

9. a.

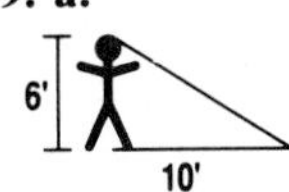

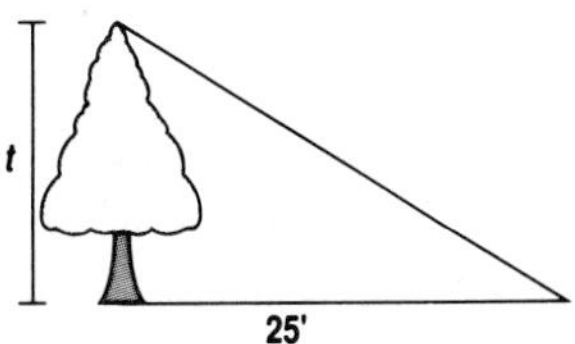

CHAPTER 5 PROGRESS SELF-TEST (pp. 254–255)

1. $15 \cdot -\frac{2}{3} = -10$ **2.** $\frac{x}{9} \cdot \frac{3}{2} = \frac{x}{6}$ **3.** $\frac{2b}{3} \cdot \frac{3}{b} = 2$ **4.** $\frac{4}{7} \cdot \frac{m}{3} = \frac{4m}{21}$ **5.** $23y = 22$; $y = \frac{22}{23}$ **6.** $60 = 15y$, $y = 4$ **7.** $.14 \cdot b = 60$, $b \approx 428.6$ **8.** $.25n = 4.5$, $n = 18$ **9.** $\frac{1}{2} = x \cdot \frac{4}{5}$; $x = 62.5\%$ **10.** $\frac{1}{8}$ **11.** 3 and x **12.** $v + 1 = 0$; $v = -1$; v cannot be -1. **13.** False **14. a.** $\frac{36}{30} = 1.2 = 120\%$ **b.** 20% **15.** $n \cdot c = d$, $n = \frac{d}{c}$ **16.** p pages in $7y$ minutes **17.** $40p = 16$, $p = .4 = 40\%$ **18.** $\frac{1}{12}$ **19.** $\frac{35 \text{ days}}{3 \text{ chapters}} \cdot 13 \text{ chapters} \approx 152$ days **20.** $\frac{250 \text{ miles}}{12 \text{ gallons}} \cdot 14 \text{ gallons} \approx 292$ miles **21.** $B = 5$ **22. a. See below. b. See below. 23.** $\frac{9}{12} = \frac{4}{z}$, $9z = 48$, $z = \frac{48}{9} = 5\frac{1}{3}$ **24.** $\frac{2x}{7} = \frac{5}{10}$, $20x = 35$, $x = \frac{35}{20} = \frac{7}{4} = 1\frac{3}{4}$ **25.** $25 \cdot \frac{20}{27} \cdot 39 = \frac{500}{1053} \approx .47$

22. a.

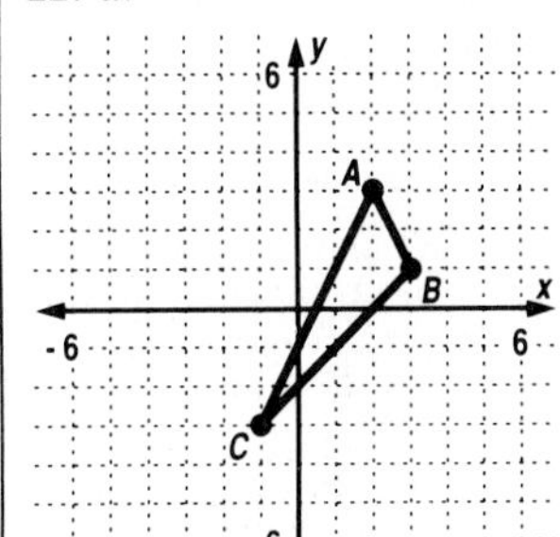

22. b.

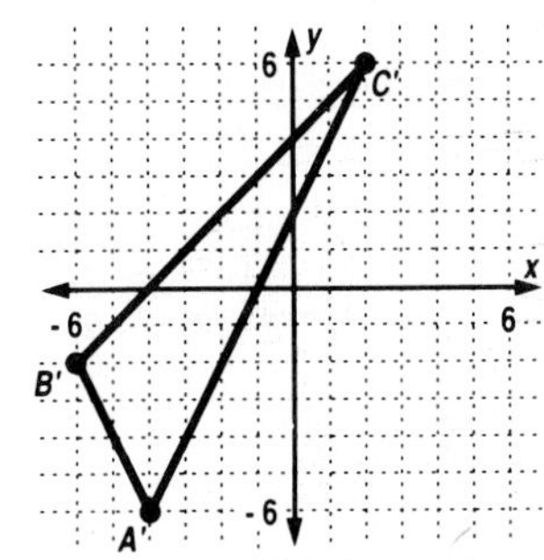

The chart below keys the **Progress Self-Test** questions to the objectives in the **Chapter Review** on pages 256–259 or to the **Vocabulary** (Voc.) on page 253. This will enable you to locate those **Chapter Review** questions that correspond to questions you missed on the **Progress Self-Test.** The lesson where the material is covered is also indicated in the chart.

Question	**1–4**	**5, 6**	**7–9**	**10**	**11**	**12**	**13**	**14**	**15**
Objective	A	C	B	A	E	D	E	G	F
Lesson	5-1	5-7	5-4	5-1	5-7	5-2	5-7	5-3	5-2

Question	**16**	**17**	**18**	**19, 20**	**21**	**22**	**23, 24**	**25**
Objective	H	I	J	F	L	M	K	J
Lesson	5-4	5-7	5-5	5-2	5-2	5-6	5-8	5-5

CHAPTER 5 REVIEW (pp. 256–259)

1. 125 **3.** $\frac{6}{7}$ **5.** $\frac{4}{3}$ **7.** $\frac{ad}{cb}$ **9.** 2 **11.** 24 **13.** 3.6 **15.** 33.33% **17.** $\frac{5}{2}$ **19.** 156 **21.** $-\frac{15}{2}$ **23.** $-\frac{0.44}{2.3} \approx -0.19$ **25.** 0 **27.** .2 **29. a.** 8 and 15 **b.** 5 and 24 **31.** $\frac{3}{2}$ **33.** Sample: What was the Johnson's average speed? 40 miles per hour **35.** Sample:

What was the puppy's average weight loss? $-\frac{3}{4}$ kg per week **37.** $\frac{1}{11}$ hours per mile **39.** $\frac{1}{4}$ hr (15 min) **41.** $6w$ words in $2m$ min **43.** $\frac{17}{10}$ **45.** 40% **47. a.** $133\frac{1}{3}$% **b.** $33\frac{1}{3}$% **c.** 25% **49.** 44,590 **51.** 25% **53.** 2610 cm **55.** 48 **57.** $\approx$ \$59.11 **59.** $\frac{150}{360} = \frac{5}{12}$ **61.** $\frac{1}{2}$ **63.** 12.5 **65. a.** 5.5 **b.** 30 **67.** $\frac{27}{n}$ **69. See below. 71.** (2, 3) **73. See below.**

69.

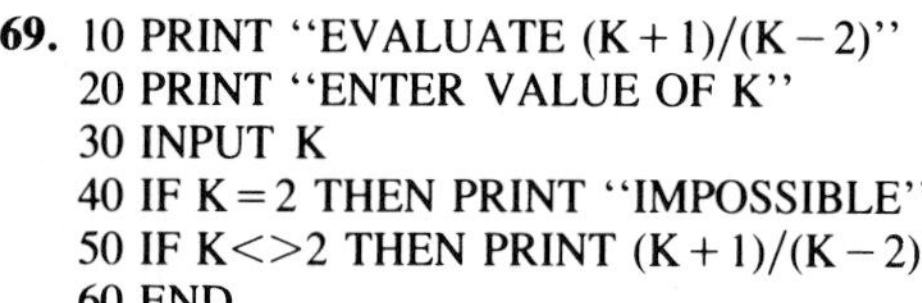

```
10 PRINT "EVALUATE (K+1)/(K-2)"
20 PRINT "ENTER VALUE OF K"
30 INPUT K
40 IF K=2 THEN PRINT "IMPOSSIBLE"
50 IF K<>2 THEN PRINT (K+1)/(K-2)
60 END
```

73.

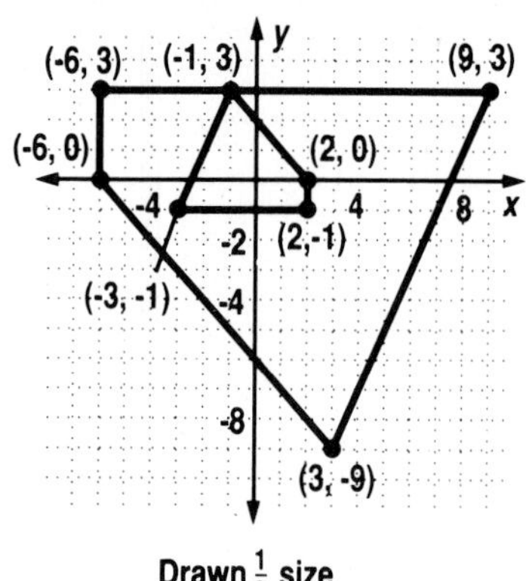

Drawn $\frac{1}{2}$ size

LESSON 6-1 (pp. 262–266)

1. a. If B equals the weight of each box, then $2B + 4 = 12$. **b.** One: remove 4 kg from each side of the balance. Two: remove half the contents of each side of the balance. **3. a.** Add 61 to each side. **b.** Divide each side by 55. **5.** $y = 9$; Does $7 \cdot 9 - 11 = 52$? Does $63 - 11 = 52$? Yes **7.** $z = 128$; Does $2 \cdot 128 + 32 = 288$? Does $256 + 32 = 288$? Yes **9.** $w = 7$; Does $312 = 36 \cdot 7 + 60$? Does $312 = 252 + 60$? Yes **11.** $t = 25$; Does $7 + 8 \cdot 25 = 207$? Does $7 + 200 = 207$? Yes **13.** b **15.** $x = \frac{-15}{7}$; Does $7 \cdot \frac{-15}{7} + 11 = -4$? Does $-15 + 11 = -4$? Yes **17.** $266\frac{2}{3}$ days **19.** $11\frac{2}{3}$ in. **21. a.** $3x + 16$ **b.** $x = 10$ **23.** -312 **25.** -85 **27. a.** $x = -15$ **b.** $y = 15$ **c.** $z = 45$ **29.** 11.25 feet

LESSON 6-2 (pp. 267–270)

3. $x = 18$; Does $\frac{2}{3} \cdot 18 + 15 = 27$? Does $12 + 15 = 27$? Yes **5.** C = 20° **7. a.** Add 3.5 and 5.6. **b.** $x = .45$; Does $3.5 + 2 \cdot .45 + 5.6 = 10$? Does $3.5 + .9 + 5.6 = 10$? Yes **9.** $n = -2.7$; Does $6 - 30 \cdot -2.7 - 18 = 69$? Does $6 + 81 - 18 = 69$? Yes **11.** $x = 28$; Does $-4 \cdot 28 + 12 = -100$? Does $-112 + 12 = -100$? Yes **13.** $f \approx 42.5$ cm **15.** $x = \frac{c - b}{a}$ **17.** $x = 0$ **19.** $y = -37$ **21. a.** \$35,000 **b.** $x \approx 51.6$ or 52 concerts **23.** 2.0625 in.^{2}

LESSON 6-3 (pp. 271–275)

1. $h = 20.5$ **3.** $g = 8400$ **5.** $h + h + \frac{1}{4}h = 90{,}000$ Two heirs receive \$40,000 each; third receives \$10,000. **7.** \$411.76 **9.** \$11.00 **11.** $.7F$ **13. a.** $s + .06s = 2650$ **b.** \$2500 **15.** $\approx$ 52% **17.** $x = \frac{17}{5}$ **19.** $y = 4.5$ **21.** $c = -2.81$ **23.** $C = 0$ **25.** 4.98×10^{-23} **27.** $(x + 2, y - 4)$

LESSON 6-4 (pp. 276–281)

1. a. t is the number of hours the car is parked. **b.** The \$0.80 is the charge for each additional hour beyond the first. **c.** \$40.70 **3.** 43 hr **5.** 82nd **7.** 9th **9.** 517 **11. a.** $1000 - 3(n - 1)$ **b.** 835 **c.** 201st **13. a.** i **b.** ii **c.** iii **d.** They are discrete points which lie on a line. **15.** $\frac{1}{5} + \frac{1}{6}p$ **17.** $x = 2$ **19.** $m\angle A = 30$, $m\angle B = 60$, $m\angle C = 90$ **21.** $x = \frac{3}{5}$ **23.** $z < 77$ **25. a.** January, February, March, April, May, June, October, November **b.** July and August **c.** zero inches **d.** June and July **27. a.** 3 **b.** 9 **c.** 21 **d.** 16

LESSON 6-5 (pp. 282–283)

1. $a = -1$ **3.** $c = \frac{2}{3}$ **5.** $e = -\frac{3}{7}$ **7.** $g = 3$ **9.** $i = 11$ **11.** $k = -2$ **13.** $m = \frac{1}{36}$ **15.** $p = 100$ **17.** $r = 1200$ **19.** \$680.00 **21.** 56 persons **23.** \$1.75 **25.** 28 cards **27.** $3 + 8(n - 1) = 331$; 42nd term **29.** $1000 - 6n = 100$; 150 days

LESSON 6-6 (pp. 284–289)

1. a. Let B = weight of 1 box, then $5B + 6 = 3B + 10$. **b.** Remove 3 boxes from both sides, remove 6 kg from both sides, and divide the contents of both sides in half. **3.** $y = 10$ **5.** $w = 2$ **7.** $z = \frac{1}{3}$ **9.** $a = 6$ **11.** -70 **13. a.** 13 **b.** 91 **15. a.** $54.73 - .33x$ **b.** $49.36 - .18x$ **c.** $\approx$ 36 yr **17. a.** 16 **b.** 20 **c.** -160 **19.** samples: *yxz, xzy, zyx, zxy, yzx* **21.** $1.05c = 10$ **23. a.** $\frac{2}{3}A = 9 \cdot 12$ **b.** $A = 162$ square feet **25.** $z = \frac{6}{7}$

LESSON 6-7 (pp. 290–295)

1. $ax + b = cx + d$ **3.** $x < 5$; **See below. 5.** $-1 \le b$; **See below. 7.** 59 **9.** 8 **11.** packages weighing more than 31.25 ounces **13.** $x = -3$ **15.** $m = 6$ **17.** $-(a - b) = b - a$ **19.** 7800 **21.** 9 **23.** 25% **25.** 9 **27.** $\frac{1}{3}$ **29.** 7.25×10^{11} **31.** $\frac{mn}{48}$

3. **5.**

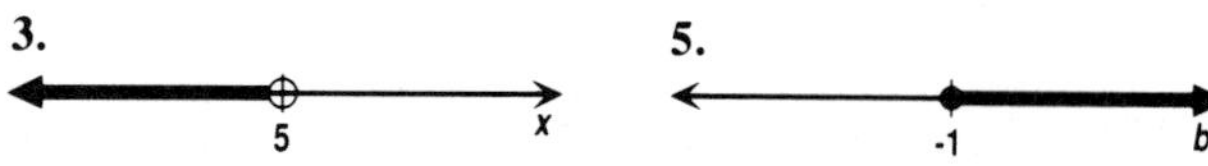

LESSON 6-8 (pp. 296–300)

3. $12k + 60$ **5.** $21a - 35ab$ **7.** $2xy + 3x$ **9.** $5(7.96) = 5(8.00) - 5(.04) = 40.00 - .20 = \$39.80$ **11.** \$21.00 **13.** $m = 73$; Does $4(73 + 7) = 320$? Does $4(80) = 320$? Yes **15.** $x = 1.8$; Does $2(1.8 + 3.1) = 9.8$? Does $2 \cdot 4.9 = 9.8$? Yes **17.** 5,999,994 **19. a.** $\frac{1}{2}x = \frac{11}{15} + -\frac{2}{3}$; $\frac{1}{2}x = \frac{1}{15}$; $x = \frac{2}{15}$ **b.** $15x + 20 = 22$; $x = \frac{2}{15}$ **21.** $b_2 = 15$ cm **23.** $n \le -\frac{1}{8}$ **25.** $\frac{9}{4}$ **27.** $x < -\frac{1}{2}$ **29.** $4b$ **31.** $\frac{1}{3}$ lb **33.** 2,657,638

LESSON 6-9 (pp. 301–305)
3. a **5.** $-4n + 3m$ **7.** $-2y - 5$ **9.** -23 **11.** $D - (L + 10)$, $D - L - 10$ **13. a.** $16 - 2y$ **b.** $y = -1$ **15.** $x = -\frac{13}{3}$ **17.** $x = \frac{15}{2}$ **19.** $96 - (R + S)$ or $96 - R - S$ **21.** No **23.** c **25.** $x = -1$ **27.** $z = 10.4$ **29.** $\$100$ **31. a.** 720 **b.** 120 **c.** 857,280 **33. a.** $\$80$ **b.** $\$6$

PROGRESS SELF-TEST (p. 307)

1. $.77m$ **2.** $4k + 9$ **3.** $10v + 250 - \frac{5}{2}w$ **4.** $14t - 18$ **5.** $r = 7.5$ **6.** $q = -3$ **7.** $w = -36$ **8.** $x = 2$ **9.** $m = 2$ **10.** $x \le -6$ **11.** $v < -1$ **12.** $h = 0$ **13.** $5x + 3 = 12$ **14.** $6(3 - .01) = 18 - .06 = 17.94$ **15.** $\$550$ **16.** $\$18.90$ **17.** term $= -10 + 12n$; $470 = -10 + 12n$; $n = 40$; 40th term; **See below.** **18.** term $= 1100 - 6n$; $350 = 1100 - 6n$; $n = 125$ min; **See below.** **19.** $C = 10°$ **20.** $137.25 + 2.50w$ **21.** Let x = amount Jill will receive; $x + 2x = 19.50$; $x = \$6.50$ **22.** Let n = number of years; $25{,}000 + 1200n = 37{,}000 - 200n$; $n = 12$ years **23.** The picture shows that the area can be calculated in two ways: $c(a + b)$ or $ca + cb$ **24.** 62.6 years **25.** $y - (c + 15)$; $y - c - 15$

17.

term no.	term
0	-10
1	$2 = -10 + 12 \cdot 1$
2	$14 = -10 + 12 \cdot 2$
3	$26 = -10 + 12 \cdot 3$
4	$38 = -10 + 12 \cdot 4$

18.

term no.	term
0	1100
1	$1100 - 6 \cdot 1$
2	$1100 - 6 \cdot 2$

The chart below keys the **Progress Self-Test** questions to the objectives in the **Chapter Review** on pages 308–311 or to the **Vocabulary** (Voc.) on page 306. This will enable you to locate those **Chapter Review** questions that correspond to questions you missed on the **Progress Self-Test.** The lesson where the material is covered is also indicated in the chart.

Question	**1**	**2, 3**	**4**	**5**	**6**	**7**	**8**	**9**	**10, 11**
Objective	A	A	A	B	B	B	B	B	C
Lesson	6-3	6-8	6-9	6-5	6-1	6-6	6-8	6-9	6-7
Question	**12**	**13**	**14**	**15, 16**	**17**	**18**	**19**	**20**	**21, 22**
Objective	B	D	E	F	G	G	H	I	I
Lesson	6-2	6-1	6-3	6-3	6-4	6-6	6-2	6-3	6-6
Question	**23**	**24**	**25**						
Objective	J	H	J						
Lesson	6-8	6-2	6-8						

CHAPTER 6 REVIEW (pp. 308–311)

1. $\frac{3}{2}c$ **3.** $.92m$ **5.** $3a + 6b$ **7.** $17x + 10$ **9.** $2 - z$ **11.** $n = 3$ **13.** $x = 68$ **15.** $m = -5$ **17.** $A = 2$ **19.** $w = 142$ **21.** $a = \frac{3}{2}$ **23.** $g = 4$ **25.** $x < 95$ **27.** $-\frac{1}{9} < g$ **29.** $y > -13$ **31.** $y \ge -1$ **33.** Distributive Property **35.** Addition Property of Inequality **37.** $2 < a + 4$ **39.** $B - 6B + 4B + 8 \ge B - 5$ **41.** $7(3 + 0.4) = \$21.28$ **43.** $9(20.00 - 0.01) = \$179.91$ **45.** $\$55.50$ **47.** $\$9.00$ **49.** 50 weeks **51.** 20 months **53. a.** 5507 **b.** 35th term **55.** $12\frac{1}{3}$ in. **57.** ≈ 38.2 cm **59.** up to 5 ounces **61.** more than 41.3 hr **63. a.** $3B + 2 = 8$ **b.** 2 kg **65.** $1.5(.5 + 2.5)$; $1.5(.5) + 1.5(2.5)$

LESSON 7-1 (pp. 314–318)

5. 2 in. **7. a.** 0 **b.** Yes **9.** 40 LET Y = 8 * X − 3 **11.** $\frac{2}{3}$ **13.** b **15. a.–b. See below.** **c.** (0, 0) **17.** $3.35h - .14y$ **19.** $x = 62$ **21.** $-\frac{9}{2}$ **23.** 60 **25.** $3.326 \cdot 10^6$ **27. a.** .25 **b.** 2.5 **c.** 25 **d.** 250,000

15. a.–b.

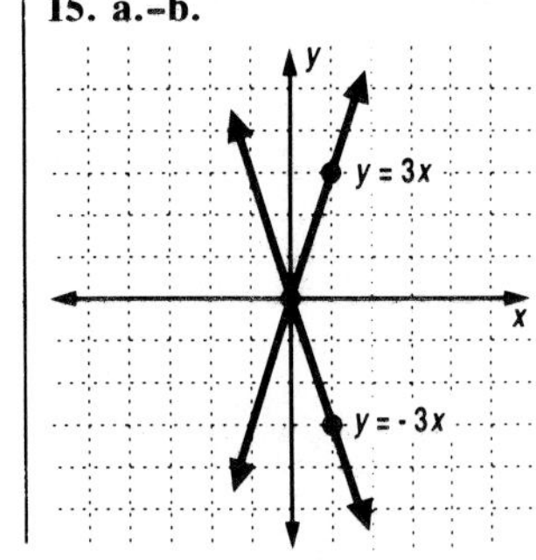

LESSON 7-2 (pp. 319–323)

3. True **5. a.–b. See below. 7. a.–b. See below.** **9.** $x = 1$ **11.** $x \geq -3$ **13. a. See below. b. See below. 15.** $x = -6$ **17. See below. 19. a.** $y = 0$ **b.** $x = 0$ **21. See below. 23.** $t = 25 + 2w$ **25.** $16x^2 + 45x - 33$ **27.** $25 \cdot 9.8 + 25 \cdot 14.2$; $25(9.8 + 14.2)$ **29.** $w \approx 13.48$ **31.** $x = .75$

5. a.

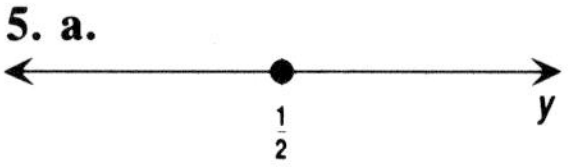

7. a.

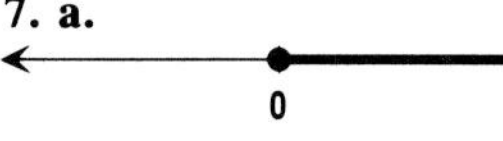

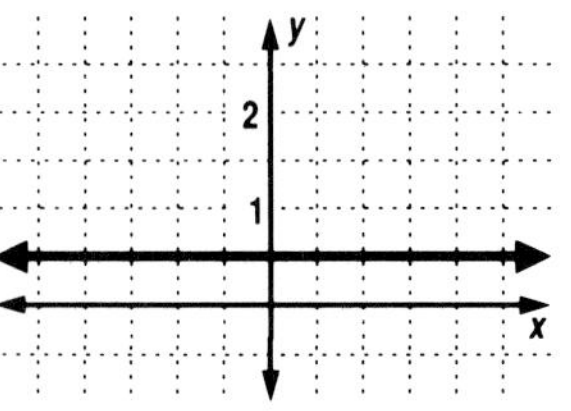

7. b.

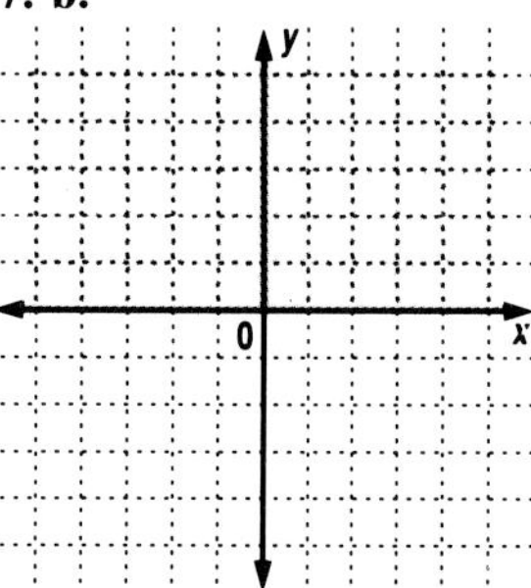

13. a.

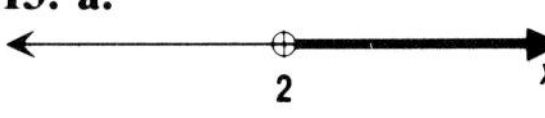

13. b.

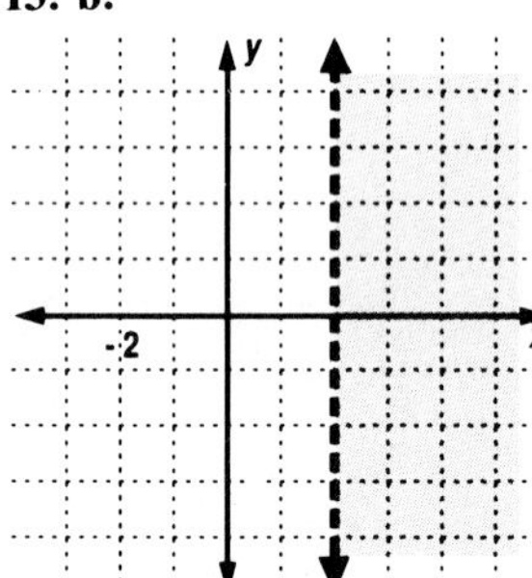

17.

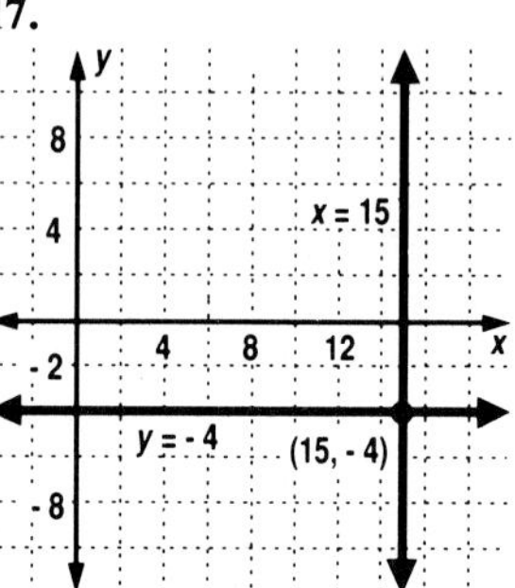

21.
```
10 PRINT "TABLE OF (X, Y) VALUES"
20 PRINT "X VALUES", "Y VALUES"
30 FOR X = 0 TO 5
40 LET Y = -0.63 + 19 * X
50 PRINT X, Y
60 NEXT X
70 END
```

LESSON 7-3 (pp. 324–330)

1. a. 49 **b.** 25 **c.** $|487 - G|$ **3.** 72 **5.** 0 **7.** 1 **9.** 39 **11.** $|17.5 - x|$ **13.** THE DISTANCE IS 38 **15.** 8 **17.** $x = 290$ or $x = 310$; **See below. 19. a.** 4 **b.** -6 **21. a.** a **23.** 36 **25. a.** $m + 4$ **b.** $m - 4$ **c.** 4 **d.** 8 **27. See below. 29. See below. 31.** $108x^2$ sq cm

17.

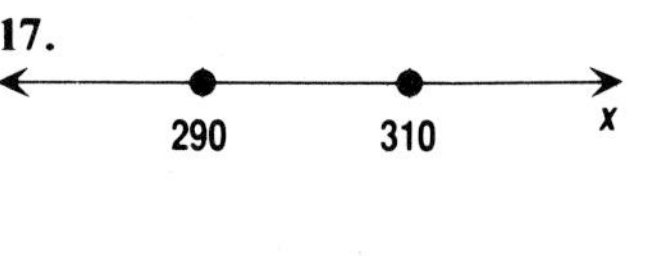

27.

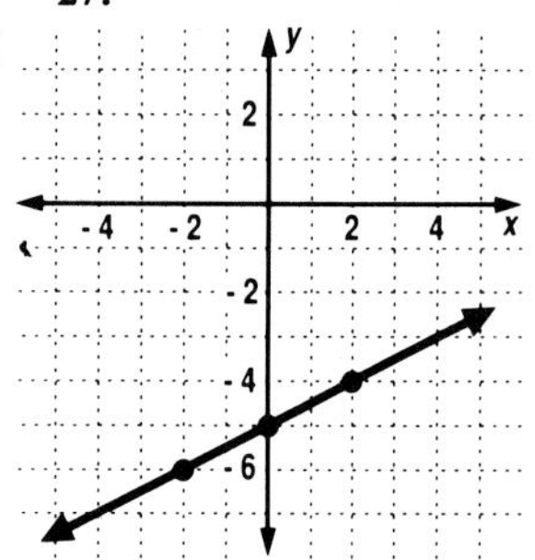

29.

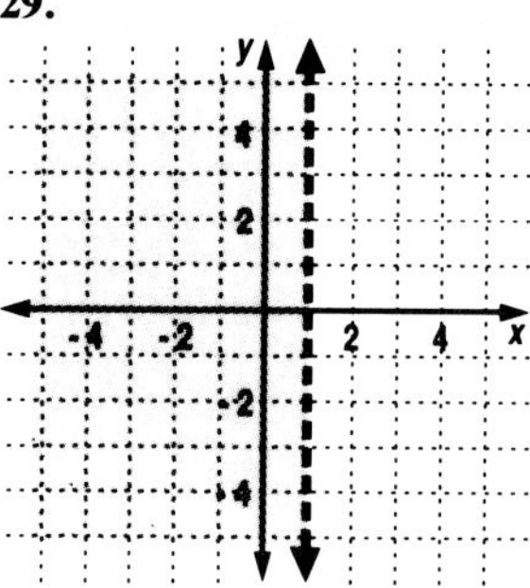

LESSON 7-4 (pp. 331–336)

1. square root **3.** square **5. a.** 10 **b.** -9 **c.** 144 **7.** 3 and 4 **11.** $\sqrt{301}$ or $-\sqrt{301}$, ≈ 17.35, or ≈ -17.35 **13.** 400 **15.** no real solutions

17. TYPE IN A NUMBER
CALCULATE SQUARE ROOTS
NO REAL SQUARE ROOTS

19.

1.732	3.464
2	3.606
2.236	3.742
2.449	3.873
2.646	4
2.828	4.123
3	4.243
3.162	4.359
3.317	4.472

21. 0.6561 **23.** 90 **25.** $x = 7$ or $x = -1$ **27. a.** $x = 0$ **b.** y-axis **29.** -7 **31.** -16 **33.** $\approx .215$

LESSON 7-5 (pp. 337–341)

5. a. 29 **b.** 41 **7.** 25 **9.** $\sqrt{119}$ ft ≈ 10.9 ft **11.** 7 **13. a.** 9 cm **b.** $\sqrt{162} \approx 12.73$ cm **15.** $2\frac{1}{2}$ seconds **17.** > **19.** 177 **21. a.** 11 or -11 **b.** 14,641 **c.** 121 or -121 **23. a.** $y = -\frac{7}{2}x + 7$ **b. See below. 25.** w words in m minutes **27.** b **29.** 300

23. b.

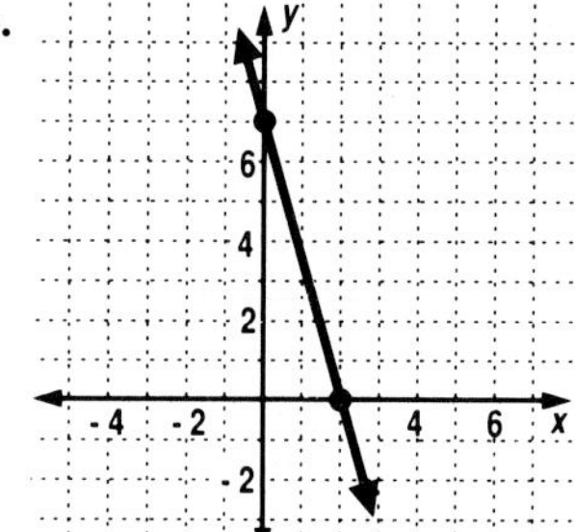

LESSON 7-6 (pp. 342–346)

3. a. 2.65 **b.** 2.24 **c.** 5.92 **d.** 5.92 **5. a.** $\sqrt{25} \cdot \sqrt{2}$ **b.** $5\sqrt{2}$ **7.** $\sqrt{128} \approx 11.314$, $8\sqrt{2} = 11.314$ **9.** $10\sqrt{2}$ **11.** $3\sqrt{3}$ **13.** $a = \sqrt{6}$ or $-\sqrt{6}$ Does $(2 \cdot \pm\sqrt{6})^2 = 24$? Does $4 \cdot 6 = 24$? Yes **15. a.** $5\sqrt{3}$ **b.** $2\sqrt{3}$

c. $7\sqrt{3}$ **17.** $2w\sqrt{5}$ **19.** $\frac{10\sqrt{3}}{5} = 2\sqrt{3}$ **21.** 540 **23. a. See below. b. See below. 25. a.** {1, 2, 3, 4, 5, 6, 7, 8, 10, 12} **b.** ∅ **c.** {1, 2, 3, 4, 5, 6, 7, 8} **27. a.** 12.25 **b.** 12.25 **c.** 12.25 **29.** $.25q + .10d \geq 5.20$ **31.** 3

23. a.

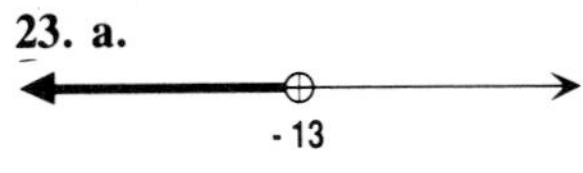

23. b.

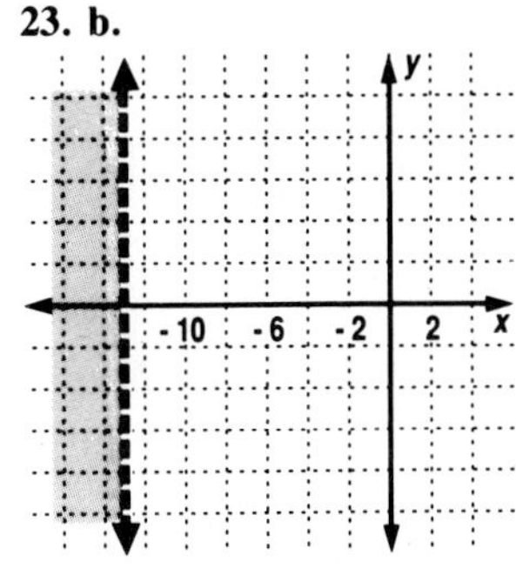

LESSON 7-7 (pp. 347–352)

1. a. 11 **b.** $\sqrt{73} \approx 8.5$ **3. a.** 8 **5.** 5 **c.** ≈ 9.4 **5.** $\sqrt{173} \approx 13.15$ **7.** 7 miles **9.** $\sqrt{5} \approx 2.2$ miles **11.** 1000 m **13.** 29.732137 **15. a.** 20 **b.** 100 **c.** 195 **d.** 10 **17.** $\sqrt{180}$ or $6\sqrt{5}$ **19.** $2(2x + 1 - x) = (4x + 6) - 20$; 8 **21.** $\frac{164}{15}$ or $10\frac{14}{15}$ **23.** $a = 3$ **25.** $m = 0$ **27. a.** $m = wa$ **b.** $t = \frac{s}{z}$ **c.** $k = b(x + 1)$

LESSON 7-8 (pp. 353–357)

3. 46 **5.** 12 or -18 **7.** 7, -8 **9.** $\frac{x - 8}{x + 8}$ **11.** $12\frac{1}{2}$ **13.** 2, -2 **15.** -3.45, -18.55 **17.** $7\sqrt{5}$ **19. a.** 36 **b.** 18 **c.** 90 **21.** $\frac{12}{5}$ **23. a.** 10 **b.** 15 **25.** 3.8 **27. See below. 29.** $T = sd$ **31. a. See below. b.** preimage: $4x + 7y + 10$, image: $32x + 56y + 80$

27.

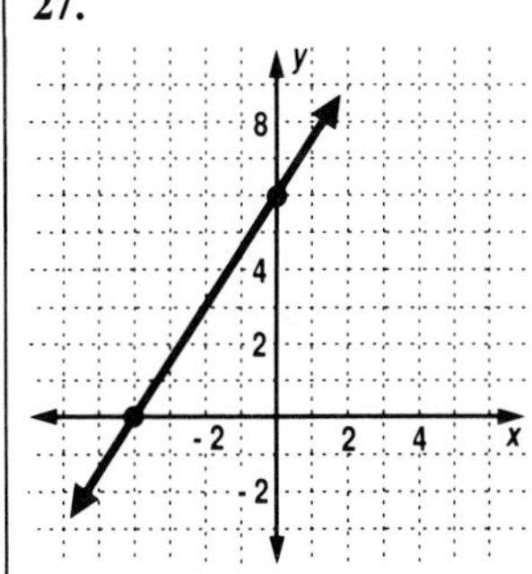

31. a.

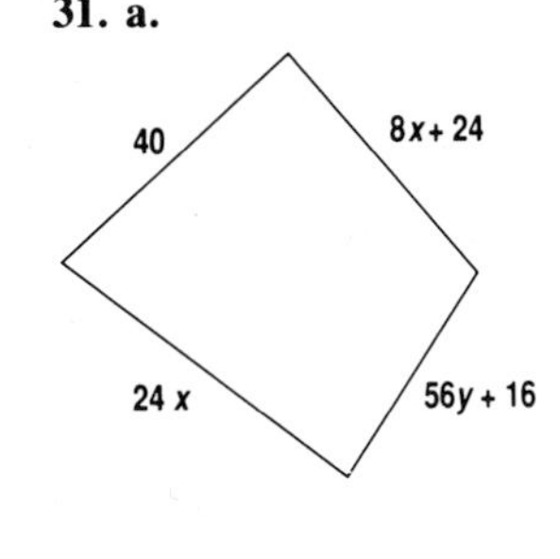

CHAPTER 7 PROGRESS SELF-TEST (p. 359)

1. 30 **2.** 72 **3.** 27 **4.** $|13x|$ or $13|x|$ **5.** 14.49 **6.** $\sqrt{29}$ cm **7.** 9 **8.** $8ab$ **9.** $3\sqrt{5}$ **10.** $2\sqrt{11}$ **11.** 14.5 **12.** $n = 24$ or -24 **13.** no solutions **14.** $y = 16$ **15.** $y = 4$ or -4 **16.** $x = 7\sqrt{2}$ or $-7\sqrt{2}$ **17.** 10 or -1 **18.** $x < -4$ or $x > 10$ **19.** $-2 \leq y \leq 6$ **20.** 17 ft **21.** $\sqrt{609} \approx 24.7$ **22.** $y = 6$ **23.** 800 m **24.** $200\sqrt{10}$ m ≈ 632 m **25.** $AB = \sqrt{145}$ **26.** (-2, 8), (-1, 5), (0, 2), (1, -1), (2, -4) **27. See below. 28. See below. 29. See below.**

27.

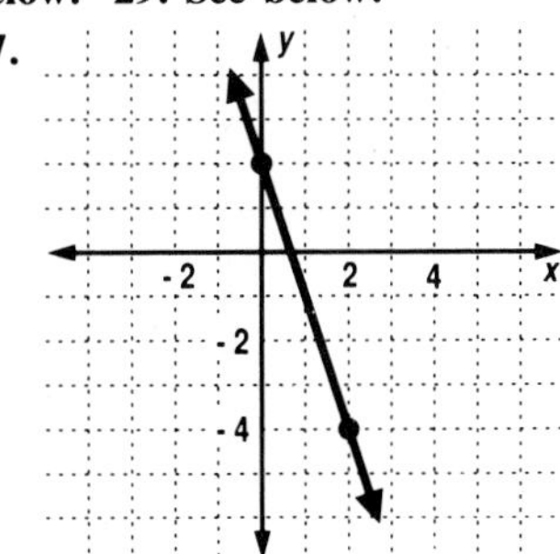

28.

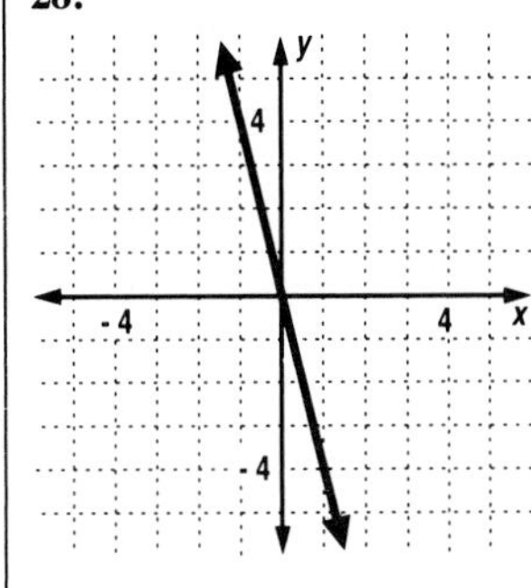

29.

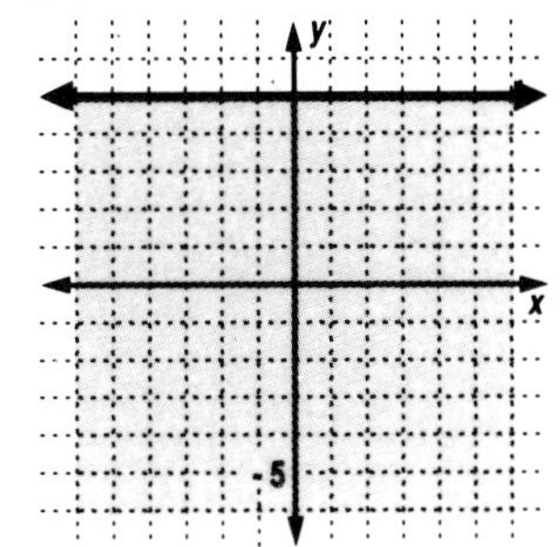

The chart below keys the **Progress Self-Test** questions to the objectives in the **Chapter Review** on pages 360–363 or to the **Vocabulary** (Voc.) on page 358. This will enable you to locate those **Chapter Review** questions that correspond to questions you missed on the **Progress Self-Test.** The lesson where the material is covered is also indicated in the chart.

Question	**1, 2**	**3, 4**	**5**	**6**	**7**	**8–10**	**11**	**12–16**	**17–19**
Objective	A	G	B	F	B	E	D	C	D
Lesson	7-3	7-3	7-4	7-4	7-4	7-6	7-8	7-4	7-8
Question	**20**	**21**	**22**	**23–25**	**26–28**	**29**			
Objective	F	J	I	K	H	L			
Lesson	7-6	7-5	7-2	7-7	7-1	7-3			

CHAPTER 7 REVIEW (pp. 360–363)

1. 43 **3.** 6 **5.** -5 **7.** 10 **9.** $d = 16$ or -16 **11.** 277 or 323 **13.** 4 and 5 **15.** -10 **17.** 33 **19.** $x = \pm 2\sqrt{10}$ **21.** $q = \pm 4\sqrt{5}$ **23.** no solution **25.** 25 **27.** 67.6 **29.** 16 or -8 **31.** $39\frac{2}{3}$ **33.** no solution **35.** $-1 < x < 7$ **37.** $10\sqrt{5}$ **39.** $\frac{5\sqrt{6}}{5} = \sqrt{6}$ **41.** -6 **43.** $x\sqrt{5}$ **45.** $7y\sqrt{3}$ if $y > 0$ **47.** ≈ 316 ft **49.** ≈ 16.6 m + Megan's height **51.** 24 **53.** $|j - d|$ or $|d - j|$ **55. a. See below. b.** -9 **57. a.** $t = 15 + 2w$ **b. See below. 59.** True **61. See below. 63.** $y \leq -2$ **65.** 37 **67.** $2\sqrt{21} \approx 9.2$ **69. a.** 8 **b.** 11 **c.** $\sqrt{185} \approx 13.6$ **71.** 6 **73.** $\sqrt{241}$ **75. a.** (-2, -7); (8, 13) **b.** $10\sqrt{5}$ **77.** 14 miles **79. See below. 81. See below 83. See below.**

55. a.

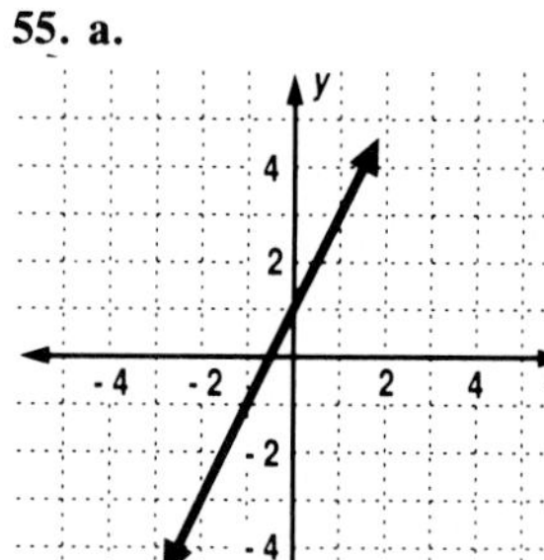

57. b.

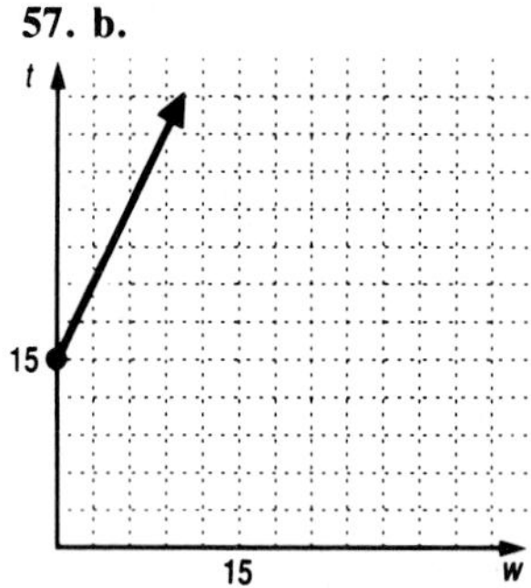

61.

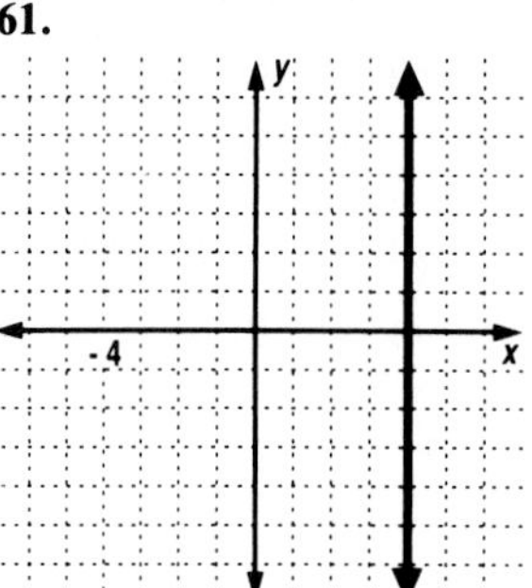

79.

81.

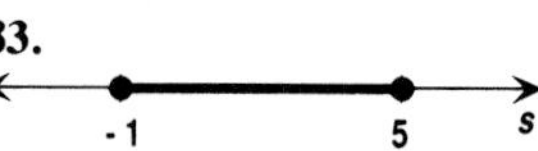

83.

LESSON 8-1 (pp. 366–370)

3. a. .75 inches per year **b.** from age 9 to 11 **5.** increase **7.** -11,094.8 people per year **11. a. See below. b.** from age 10 to 12 **c.** 4 inches per year **13.** 0 meters per second **15.** positive **17.** $\frac{4'3'' - h}{2 \text{ yrs}}$ **19. a.–b. See below. c.** (0, 2) **21.** $-\frac{1}{2}$ **23. a.** 5.25 **b.** $\frac{3}{4}x - 3$ **c.** $\frac{a}{4}x - 3$ **25. a.** $\frac{1}{a}$ **b.** $\frac{1}{3 + 4x}$ **c.** $x = -\frac{4}{5}$

11. a.

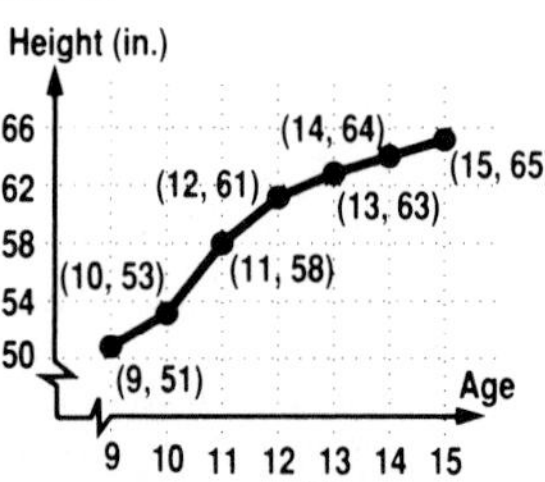

19. a.–b.

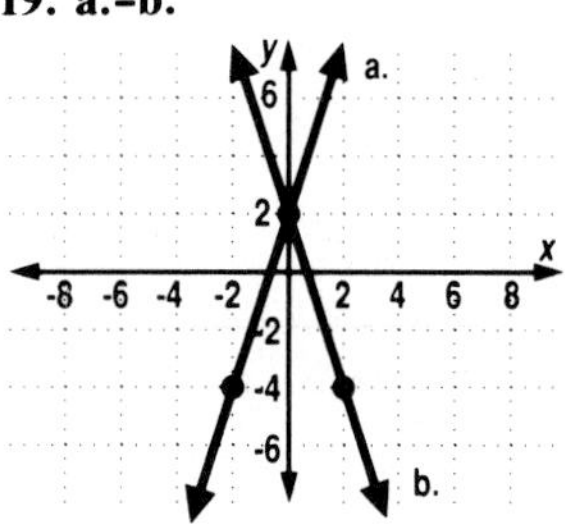

LESSON 8-2 (pp. 371–375)

3. a. See below. b. $\frac{1}{3}$ ft per minute **5.** sample: using (1, 2) and (-1, 0), $\frac{0 - 2}{-1 - 1} = 1$; using (0, 1) and (-1, 0), $\frac{0 - 1}{-1 - 0} = 1$ **7. a.** sample (9, 6) and (6, 8) **b.** $-\frac{2}{3}$ **9.** 8 **11.** $5\frac{1}{5}$ or 5.2 **13.** C; D **15. a.** 0 **b.** 0 **c.** The slope is 0. **17. a.** r **b.** q **c.** p **19. a.** 1980–85 **b.** 1960–65 and 1965–70 **c.** .5 cent per year **d.** The cost of stamps does not gradually rise over each 5-year period. For instance, the cost was never 4.3 cents.

21. See below. 23. $100 - 4x$ **25. a.** $\frac{5}{3}$ **b.** $-\frac{1}{3}$ **c.** $\sqrt{15}$, $-\sqrt{15}$ **27. a.** 60 **b.** $5b$, if $b \geq 0$ **c.** $3\sqrt{2}$

3. a.

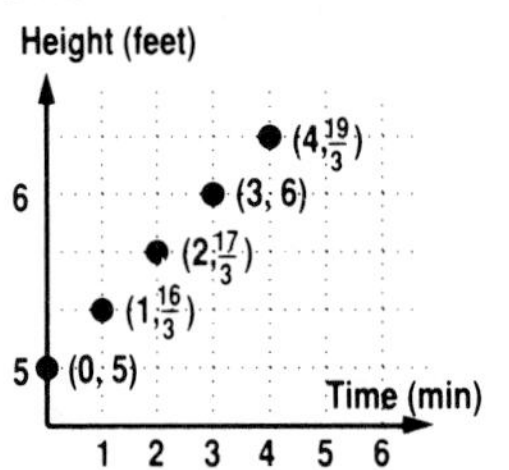

21.

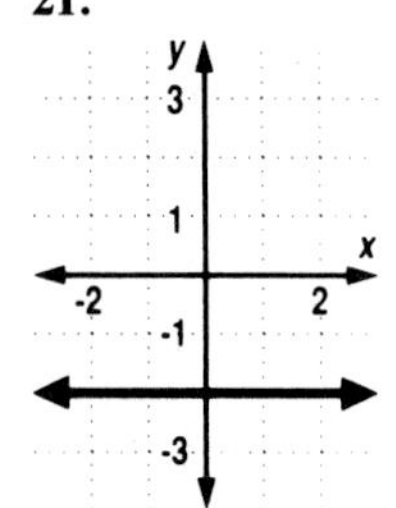

LESSON 8-3 (pp. 376–380)

1. -0.5 **5. See below. 7.** $c = .25 + .20(9 - 1)$; $c = 1.85$ **9.** 1 **11.** sample: (-4, 9) **13.** sample: $\left(1, \frac{5}{4}\right)$ or (4, 5) **15. See below. 17.** $-\frac{5}{3}$ **19.** 3 **21. a.** 1982–1983 **b.** 1983–1984 **23.** -10 **25.** 7 or -9 **27. a.** $2T - 8$ **b.** $\frac{2T - 8}{T}$ **c.** 12

5.

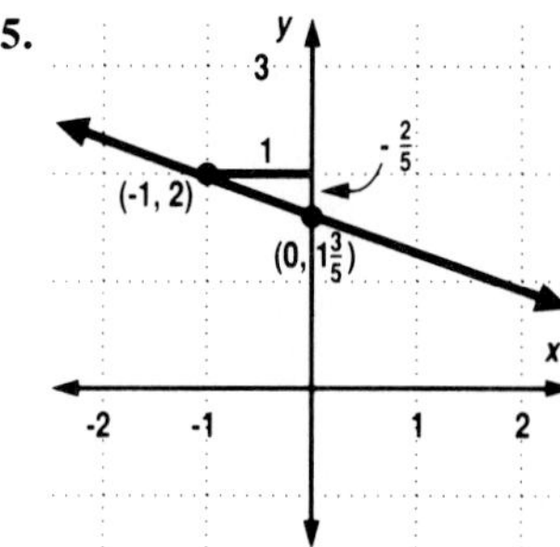

15.

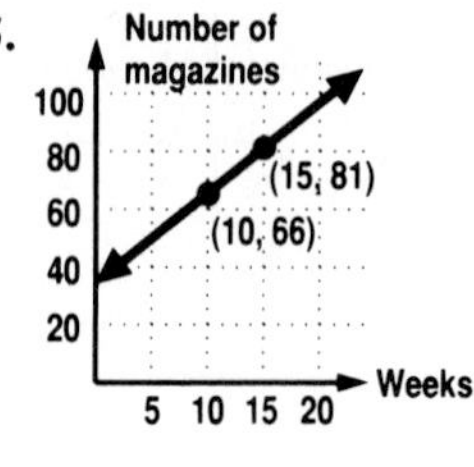

LESSON 8-4 (pp. 381–386)

3. a. 4 **b.** 2 **5. a.** ii **b.** 8 **c.** 100 **7. a.** iii **b.** 4 **c.** -350 **11.** $y = \frac{2}{3}x + -1$ or $y = \frac{2}{3}x - 1$ **13. a.** $y = -\frac{1}{6}x + \frac{7}{6}$ **b.** $-\frac{1}{6}$ **15. a.** 1 **b.** 0 **17. See below. 19. a.** u **b.** v **c.** t **d.** s **21. a.** $y = 9 - 6x$ **b. See below. 23.** $y = 3x - 7$ or $y = 3x + -7$ **25.** (b) **27.** $\sqrt{176} \approx 13.3$ feet **29.** $-\frac{11}{17}$ **31.** 2

17.

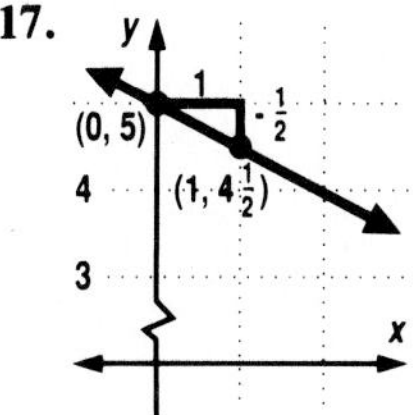

21. b.

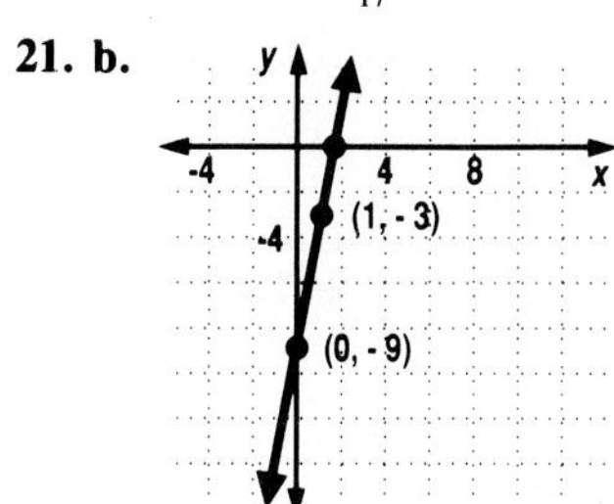

LESSON 8-5 (pp. 387–390)

3. $y = -2x - 17$ **5.** $y = -\frac{1}{2}$ **7.** $y = -3x + 110$ **9.** 10,143,00 **11. a.** $\frac{1}{2}$ **b.** $y = \frac{1}{2}x + 2$ **13. a.** q **b.** n **c.** p **d.** m **15.** No **17. a.** A **b.** C **c.** All sections show some change. **19. See below. 21. a.** $2\sqrt{6}$ or $-2\sqrt{6}$ **b.** 576 **c.** $n = 4$ **23. a.** $\frac{3}{2}$ **b.** $\frac{3}{2}$ **c.** $\frac{c}{b}$

19.

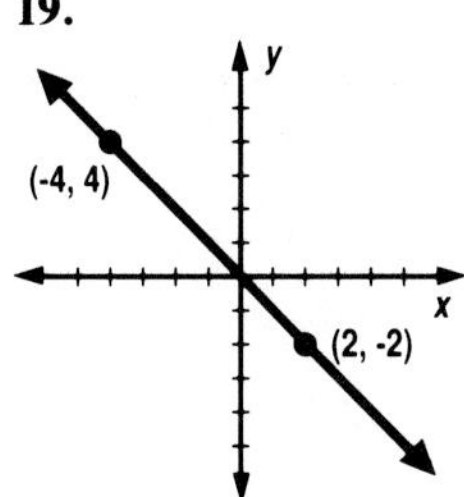

LESSON 8-6 (pp. 391–397)

1. $y = -x + 10$ **3.** $y = \frac{-11}{13}x + 11$ **5.** \$8.88 **9.** about 132 **11.** $S = 180n - 360$ **13. a.** $C = \frac{5}{9}F - \frac{160}{9}$ **b.** $\approx 65.6°C$ **c.** 302°F **15. See below. 17. a.** $\frac{15}{2}$ **b.** $\frac{2}{5}$ or $\frac{5}{2}$ **19. a.** 93 **b.** any score greater than or equal to 88 **c.** 88 **21. a.** $\frac{1}{12}$ **b.** $\frac{1}{3}$ **c.** $\frac{1}{d}$

15.

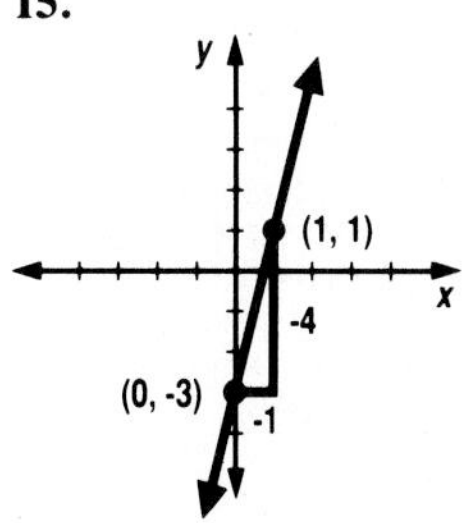

LESSON 8-7 (pp. 398–403)

9. b, c **13.** $y = \frac{3}{5}x + \frac{1}{5}$ **15. a. See below. b. See below. 17.** about 91 **19.** $\approx$ 74 miles **21. a.** 6 **b.** 6 **c.** -6

15. a.

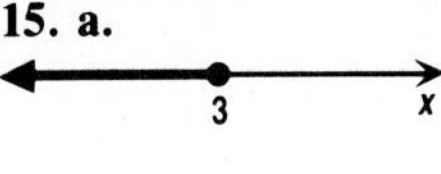

15. b.

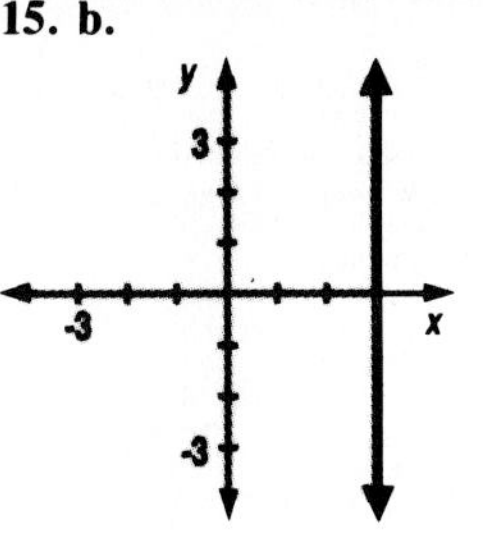

LESSON 8-8 (pp. 404–409)

7. $A = 1, B = -8, C = 2$ **9.** $-4x + y = 0; A = -4, B = 1, C = 0$ or $4x - y = 0; A = 4, B = -1, C = 0$ **11.** (0, 6) and (10, 0); **See below. 13.** sample: (4, 6), (6, 5), (8, 4) **15.** $2x + 4y = 100$ **17.** $y + 2x = 4$ **19. a. See below. b.** samples: Using (1900, 35) and (1960, 60), we get $y = .42x - 763$. **c.** $\approx$ 72 meters **d.** sample: The line is an estimate. **21. See below. 23.** Yes **25.** $\frac{1}{12}$ **27. a.** 2 **b.** 10 **c. See below.**

11.

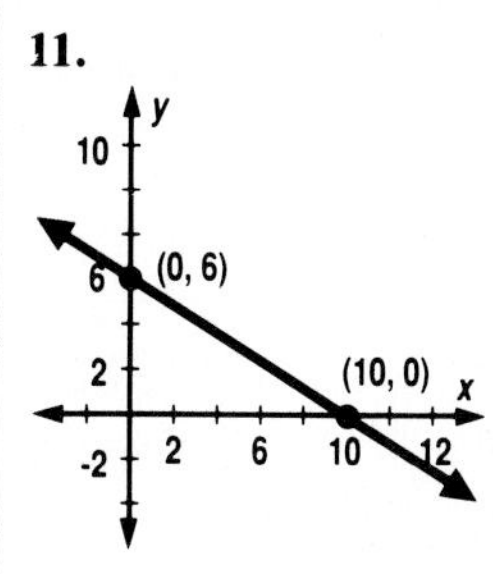

19. a.

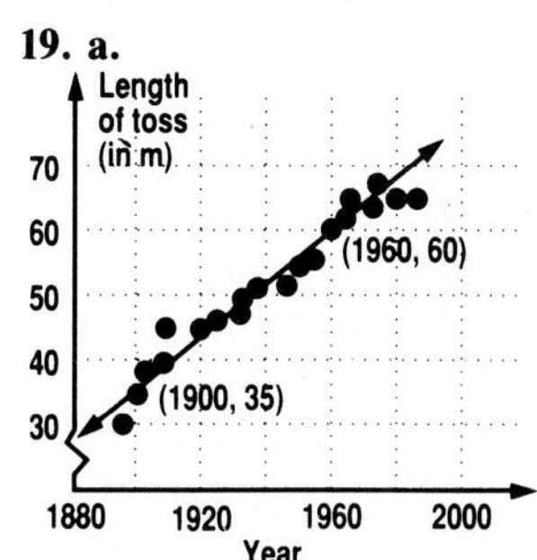

21.

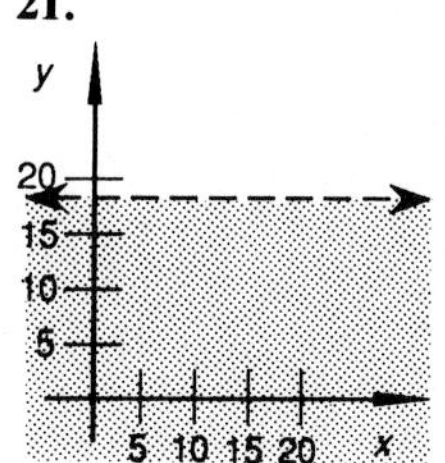

27. c.

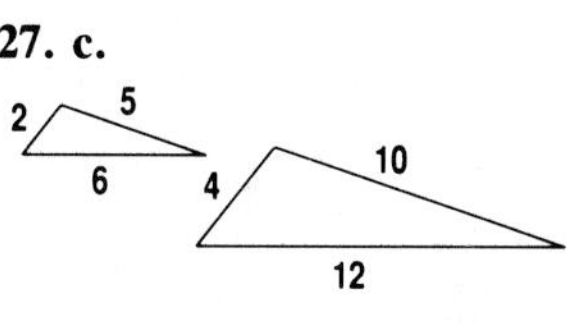

LESSON 8-9 (pp. 410–415)

7. See below. 9. See below. 11. a. $2W + T \geq 20$ **b. See below. 13. a. See below. b.** The graph is the strip of infinite length that lies between the two boundary lines. **15.** $25c + 5f = 55,000$ **17.** $\approx$ 83.8 yd **19. a.** 0.1 **b.** .03 **c.** 0.00001 **21.** 3,603,266

7.

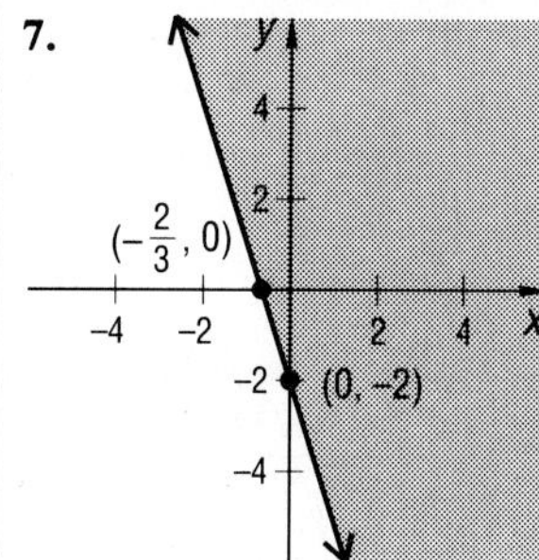

9.

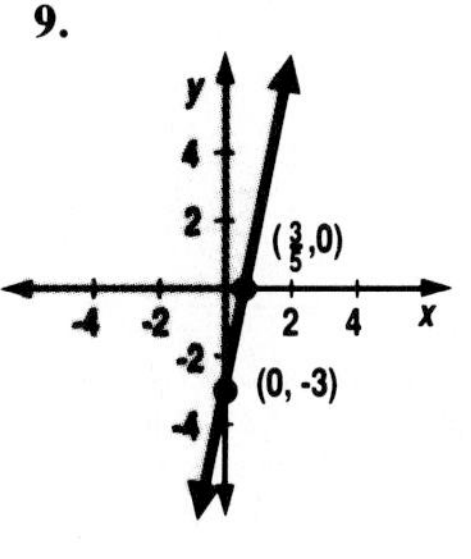

11. b.

13. a.

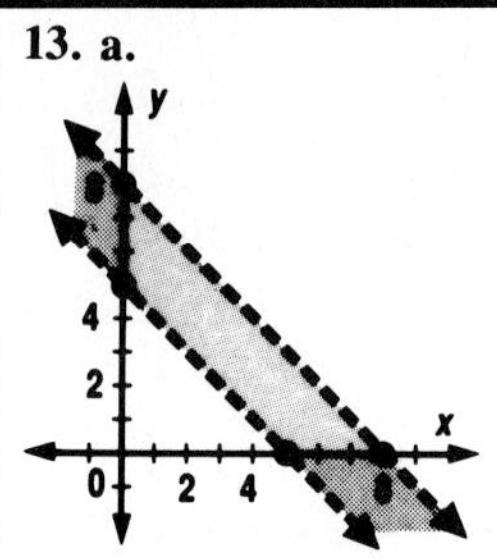

CHAPTER 8 PROGRESS SELF-TEST (p. 417)

1. $\frac{5 - 0}{0 - 2} = -\frac{5}{2}$ **2. a.** 5 **b.** 2 **3.** $\frac{1 - -5}{-2 - 4} = \frac{6}{-6} = -1$; $\frac{-20 - 1}{20 - -2} = \frac{-21}{22}$ Since $-1 \neq \frac{-21}{22}$, the points do not lie on the same line. **4.** Rewrite as $y = -4x + 8$, so the slope is -4 and the y-intercept is 8. **5.** Rewrite as $y = \frac{-5}{2}x + \frac{1}{2}$, so the slope is $\frac{-5}{2}$ and the y-intercept $\frac{1}{2}$. **6.** Substitute $m = -2$ and $(x, y) = (-5, 6)$ into $y = mx + b$ and get $y = \frac{3}{4}x + 13$. **7.** Substitute $m = -2$ and $(x, y) = (5, 6)$ into $y = mx + b$ to get $y = -2x - 4$. **8.** Add $-5x$ to both sides; $-5x + y = -2$ with $A = -5$, $B = 1$, and $C = -2$. (You could also write $5x - y = 2$ with $A = 5$, $B = -1$, and $C = 2$.) **9.** Slope is 0. **10.** up $\frac{3}{5}$ unit

11. Do a quick estimate. Between 1942 and 1944 the increase was from about 3 million to about 8 million, or 5 million personnel. From 1943 to 1945 the increase was a little over 1 million. From 1944 to 1946 was a decrease. So the greatest 2-year increase was from 1942 to 1944.

12. $\frac{1{,}889{,}690 - 3{,}074{,}184}{1946 - 1942} \approx 296{,}123$ personnel per year

13. $2x + y = 67$ **14.** slope = 5, y-intercept = 100

15. First find the rate of increase of weight; $\frac{50 - 43}{14 - 12} = \frac{7}{2}$ kg per year. Next substitute $m = \frac{7}{2}$ and $(x, y) = (14, 50)$ into $y = mx + b$ and solve for b: $50 = \frac{7}{2} \cdot 14 + 6$, $50 = 49 + b$, $b = 1$. Substitute $m = \frac{7}{2}$ and $b = 1$ into $y = mx + b$ to get $y = \frac{7}{2}x + 1$. **16. See below. 17.** First graph $y = x + 1$. It has y-intercept 1 and slope 1. Then test (0, 0) in $y < x + 1$; $0 < 0 + 1$, $0 < 1$. So (0, 0) is a solution and the region below the line is shaded. **See below. 18.** about 115 feet **19. a. See below. b.** Using (60, 70) and (120, 140) from the graph, $m \approx \frac{140 - 70}{120 - 60} = \frac{70}{60} = \frac{7}{6}$ **20.** $y = \frac{7}{6}x$

21. About 117 ft

16.

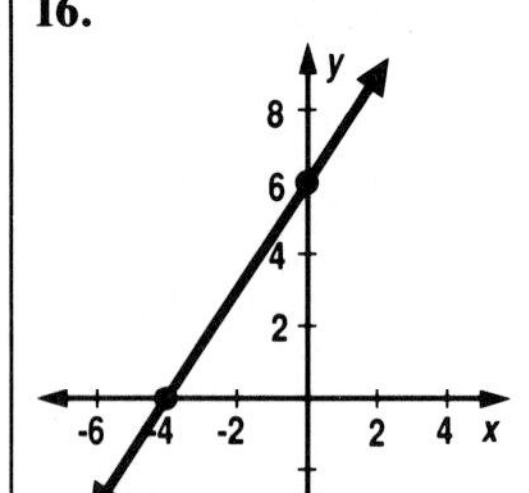

17.

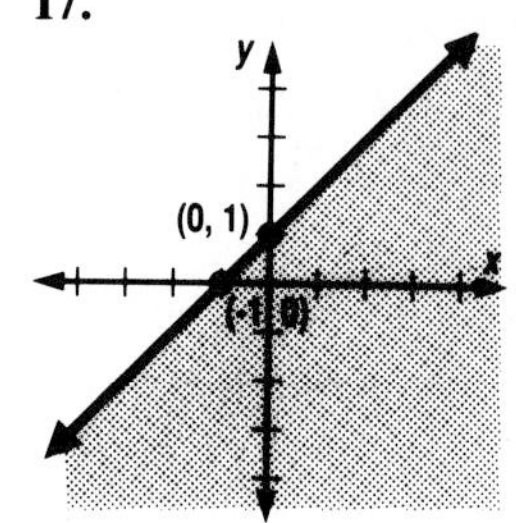

19. a.

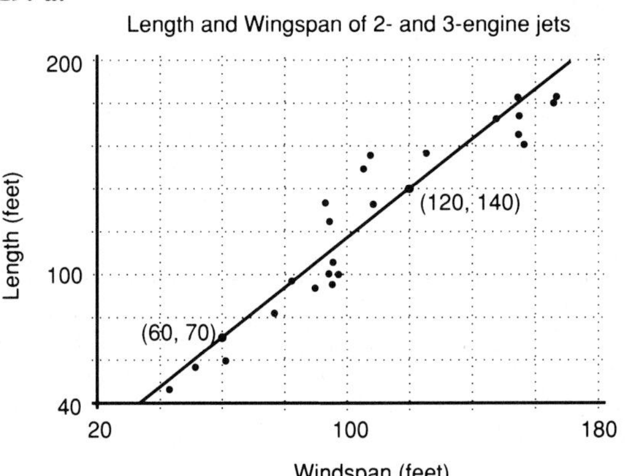

The chart below keys the **Progress Self-Test** questions to the objectives in the **Chapter Review** on pages 418–421 or to the **Vocabulary** (Voc.) on page 416. This will enable you to locate those **Chapter Review** questions that correspond to questions you missed on the **Progress Self-Test.** The lesson where the material is covered is also indicated in the chart.

Question	**1-3**	**4, 5**	**6, 7**	**8**	**9**	**10**	**11, 12**	**13-15**
Objective	A	F	B	E	D	D	G	H
Lesson	8-2	8-4	8-5	8-8	8-2	8-3	8-1	8-8
Question	**16**	**17**	**18, 19**	**20**	**21**			
Objective	I	K	J	C	H			
Lesson	8-4	8-9	8-7	8-6	8-8			

CHAPTER 8 REVIEW (pp. 418–421)

1. $-\frac{1}{2}$ **3.** $\frac{3}{5.5} = .\overline{54}$ **5.** $y = 4x + 3$ **7.** $y = -2x - 7$ **9.** $y = 30x - \frac{359}{4}$ **11.** $y = \frac{1}{2}x - \frac{9}{2}$ **13.** height; right **15. a. See below. b.** 0.46 **17.** $x - 5y = 22$; $A = 1$, $B = -5$, $C = 22$ or $-x + 5y = -22$; $A = -1$, $B = 5$, $C = -22$ **19.** $y = -2x + 4$ **21.** $m = 7$, $b = -3$ **23.** $m = -1$, $b = 0$ **25.** 4.3 kg per yr **27.** -0.5° per hour **29.** $m = 0.25$, $b = 15$ **31.** $y = 3x + 50$ **33.** $w = .2d + 37.2$ **35.** Using (21, 1976), (20, 1972), $y = 4n + 1892$ **37. See below. 39. See below. 41. See below. 43. See below. 45.** Answers will vary. **a. See below. b.** Using (1960, 4.84) and (1980, 4.15), $m \approx -.035$. **c.** $y = -.035x + 73.45$ **d.** 3.73 minutes **47.** $.05x + .25y < 2.00$; **See below. 49. See below. 51. See below.**

15. a.

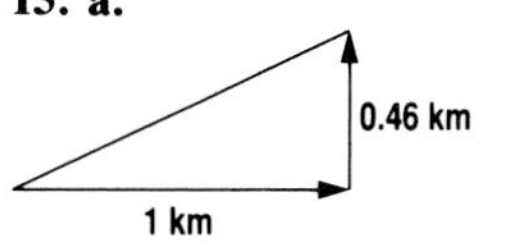

37.

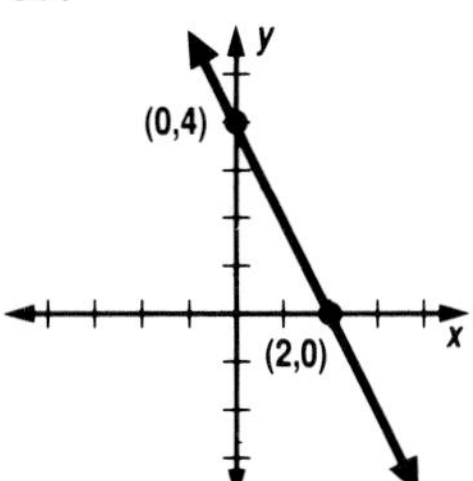

39.

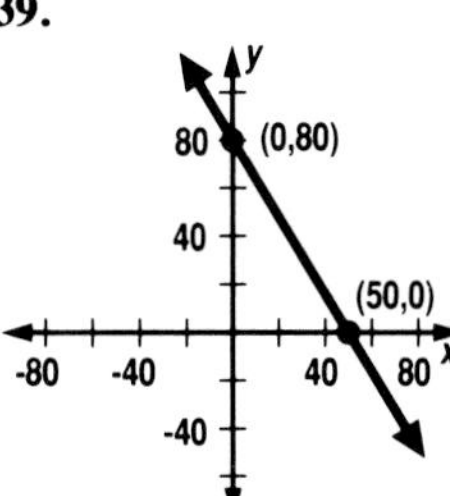

41.

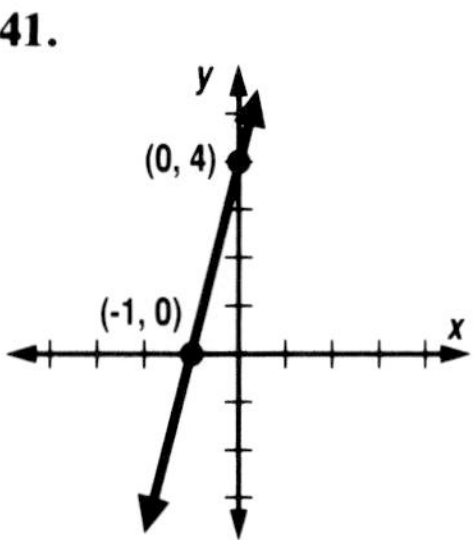

43.

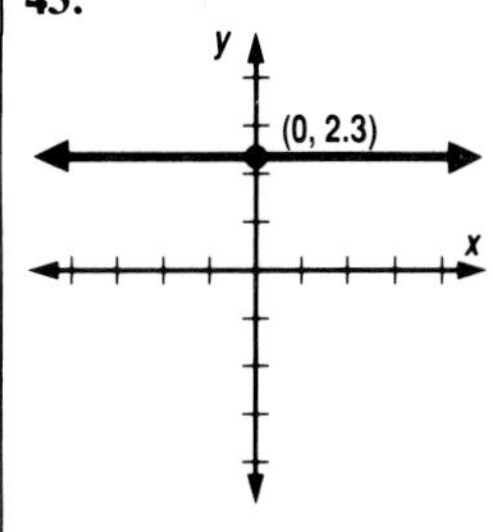

45. a.

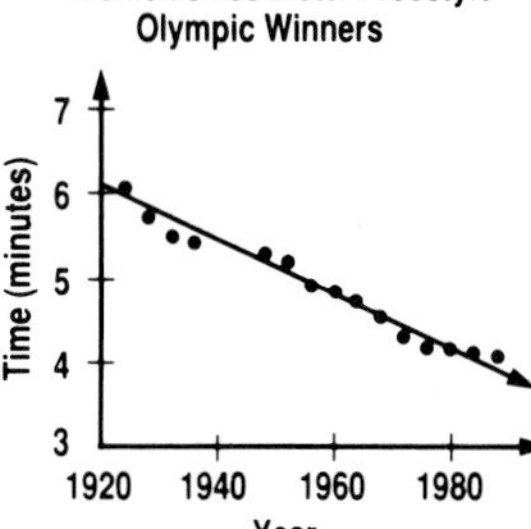

47.

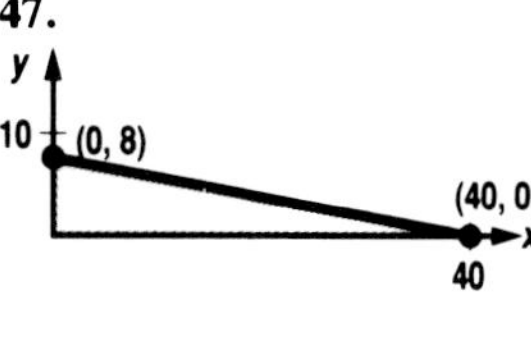

49.

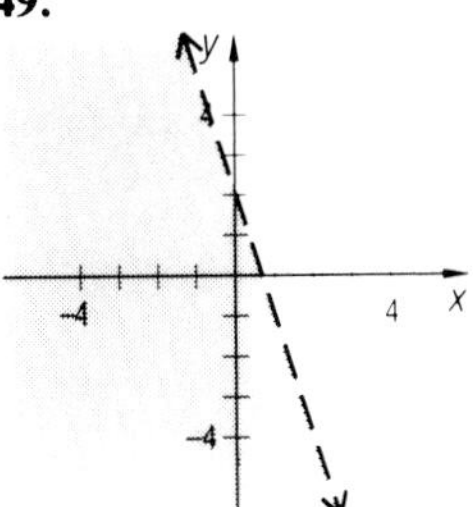

51.

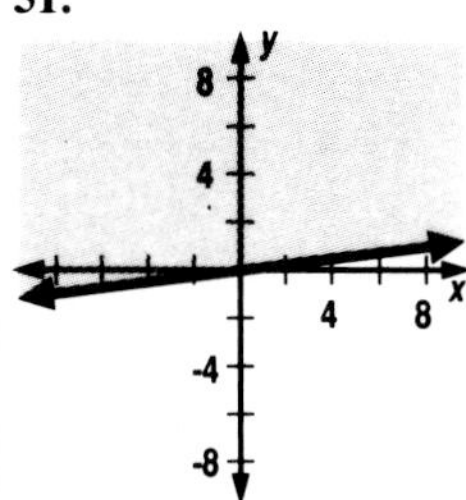

LESSON 9-1 (pp. 424–428)

3. B **5.** $P(1.06)$ **7.** 573 [×] 1.063 [y^x] 24 [=] **9. a.** \$123.88 **b.** \$23.88 **11.** \$232.18 **13. a.** Susan, \$10.25; Jake, \$21.00 **b.** No **15.** in about 9 years **17.** 79 **19. a.** $T = 7 + 2W$ **b. See below. 21.** $\approx .29$, ≈ -2.29

19. b.

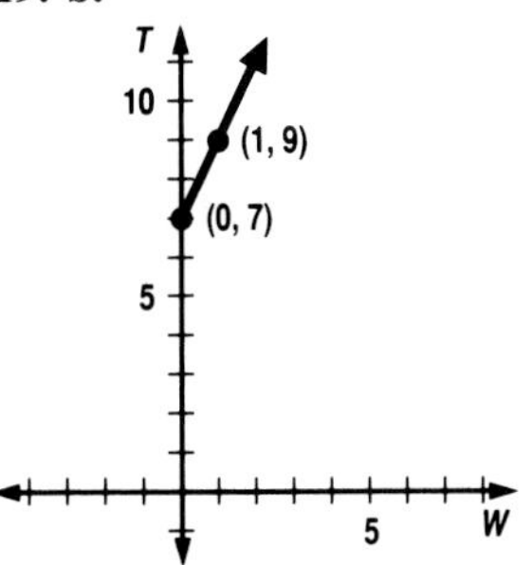

LESSON 9-2 (pp. 429–433)

1. a. 14 **b.** 409,600 **3.** 1,476,225 **5.** (1) \$1510 (2) \$1,917,510.60 **7. a.** \$2000 **b.** There is no time for the money to earn interest. **9.** 638 **11. a.** 20 minutes **b.** 6 **c.** 1,458,000 **d.** 1,062,882,000 **13.** 1605 **15.** $\approx$ \$2.92 trillion **17.** 80,000 **19.** 343 **21.** $1\frac{4}{9}$ **23. a.** $x \cdot 1.07^2 = 915.92$ **b.** \$800 **25.** $\frac{3}{26}$ **27.** $14n + 44$ **29.** $\frac{1}{128}$ **31. a.** $\frac{1}{2}$ **b.** $\frac{1}{3}$ **c.** $\frac{a}{c}$

LESSON 9-3 (pp. 434–437)

1. ≈ 48 **3.** 63,650 **5.** .937 **7.** $\approx$ 1.4 in. by 1.8 in. **9. a.** 5832 **b.** $\approx .01$ **c.** 100,000, 1.02, and 10 **11. a.** 96 **b.** 24,576 **13.** n^x **15. See below. 17.** $k(36 - k)$ **19. a.** \$5.88 **b.** \$60.20 **c.** \$6.00 **21.** 256 **23. a.** $\frac{7}{9}$ **b.** $\frac{11}{9}$ **c.** 27

15.

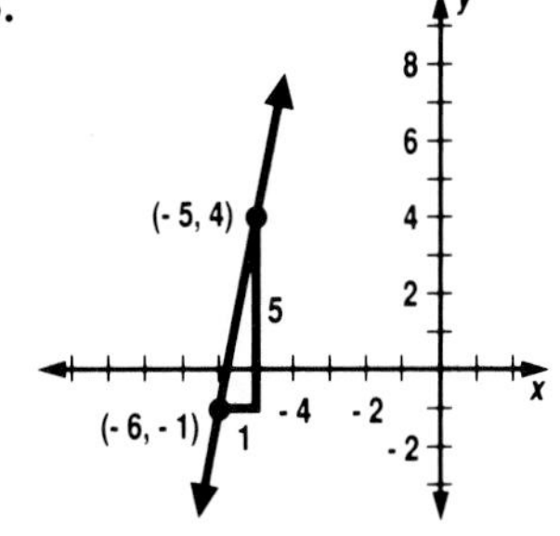

LESSON 9-4 (pp. 438–443)

3. The graph of linear decrease is a line. The graph of exponential decay is a curve. **7.** ≈ 1300 **9. a.** 27 **b.** 20 **11.** a, c, d **13.** sample: **See below.** **15.** ≈ 2156 **17.** $k = 30(1.05)^n$ **19.** -13,824 **21. a.** 100 * 1.06 ^ YEAR **b.** 20 320.71355 **c.** 30 FOR YEAR = 1 TO 100 **d.** 100 33930.208 **23.** $6a^3 + 12a^2 - 2a$ **25. a.** \$180 **b.** \$160 **c.** \$134

13.

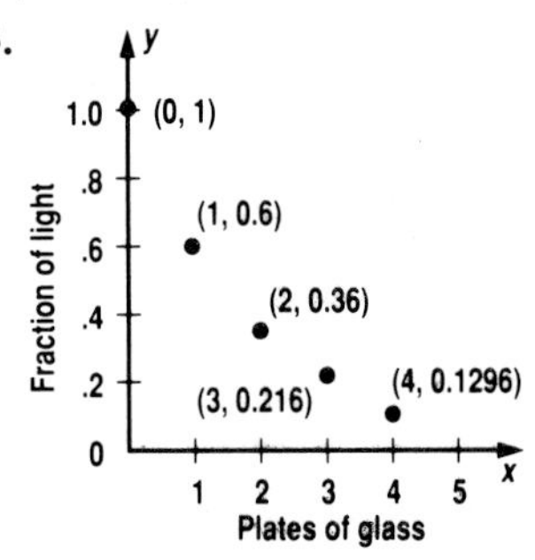

LESSON 9-5 (pp. 444–447)

1. a. $x^6 = x \cdot x \cdot x \cdot x \cdot x \cdot x$ **b.** x^6 is the growth factor after 6 years if there is growth by a factor x in each one-year interval. **3.** The expression has two different bases. **5. a.** $2000 \cdot 2^{11}$ **b.** $(2000 \cdot 2^{11}) \cdot 2^6$ or $2000 \cdot 2^{17}$ **9.** n^{12} **11.** x^{55} **13.** $(1.5)^{10}$ **15.** $2x^7$ **17.** $15m^6$ **19.** 12^{101} **21.** $a^5 + 4a^6$ **23. a.** -1; 1; -1; 1; -1; 1; -1; 1 **b.** 1 **25. See below.**

27. a. $7x + 7y = 26$ or $-7x - 7y = -26$ **b.** $y = -x + \frac{26}{7}$

29. 2.439×10^6 **31.** 8.97×10^{-1}

25.

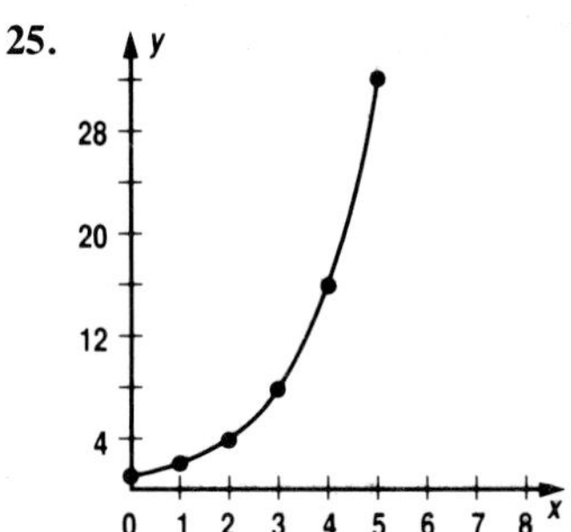

LESSON 9-6 (pp. 448–452)

1. $4^{-1} = \frac{1}{4}$, $4^{-2} = \frac{1}{16}$, $4^{-3} = \frac{1}{64}$ **3.** $\frac{1}{25}$ **5.** $\frac{1}{7}$ **7.** $\frac{x^5}{y^2}$ **9.** $\frac{1}{2^n}$

11. a. 0.000000001 **b.** $\frac{1}{1{,}000{,}000{,}000}$ **13. a.** \$3434.58 **b.** \$3209.89 **15.** -11 **17.** t^{-6} **19. a. See below. b. See below.** **21.** ≈ 4.60 **23.** a^7 **25.** $12c^7$ **27.** c **29.** $y = -5x + 9$

31. $\frac{3}{4}$ **33.** $\frac{4}{21}$

19. a.

x	y
2	9
1	3
0	1
-1	$\frac{1}{3}$
-2	$\frac{1}{9}$
-3	$\frac{1}{27}$

19. b.

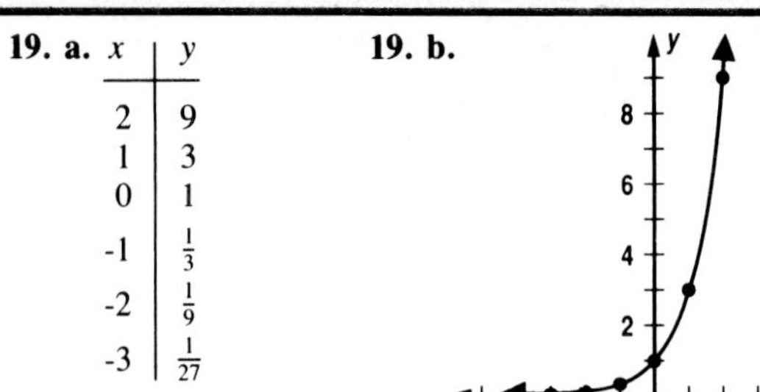

LESSON 9-7 (pp. 453–457)

1. $2^6 \cdot 2^8 = 2^{14}$ **3.** $\frac{9.29 \cdot 10^8}{2.27 \cdot 10^8} = \frac{9.29}{2.27} \approx 4 \frac{\text{five-dollar bills}}{\text{person}}$

5. $\frac{1}{3^6} = \frac{1}{729}$ **7.** $\frac{z^3}{42}$ **9.** bases are different **11.** $\approx .018 \frac{\text{pound}}{\text{person}}$

13. x^{9n} **15.** 1 **17.** $5p$ **19.** $\approx .32 \frac{\text{people}}{\text{sq km}}$ **21.** .015625

23. y^{12} **25.** x^{15}; try $x = 3$; $3^5 \cdot 3^5 \cdot 3^5 = 243 \cdot 243 \cdot 243 = 14{,}348{,}907$; $3^{15} = 14{,}348{,}907$ **27.** $\frac{4}{9}$ **29. a.** $4x + 32$ **b.** $24x + 48$ **c.** 11 **31.** $x \geq -\frac{25}{4}$ **33.** $x \leq -6$

LESSON 9-8 (pp. 458–462)

1. a. $125x^3$ **b.** $(5 \cdot 2)^3 = 10^3 = 1000$; $125(2)^3 = 125 \cdot 8 = 1000$ **3. a.** 1953.125 cu ft **b.** 15,625 cu ft **5. a.** ≈ 23,350,000,000 km³ **b.** $\approx 2.335 \cdot 10^{10}$ km³

7. $\frac{343}{1000}$ **9.** $512y^3$ **11.** $\frac{k^2}{L}$ **13.** True **15.** a; x^{13} **17.** b; k^3

19. c; v^{-6} **21.** $\frac{a^{-3}}{b^{15}}$ or $\frac{1}{a^3b^{15}}$ **23.** 1 **25.** $18k^7q^{13}$

27. a. k^3 in.³ **b.** $125k^3$ in.³ **29.** $\frac{1}{5}$ or .2 **31. a.** $2x^5$ **b.** x^9 **c.** x^{10} **33.** \$29.66 **35.** 414 sq units

LESSON 9-9 (pp. 463–468)

1. a. $\frac{8}{125}$ **b.** .064 **3.** d; sample: $\left(\frac{3}{4}\right)^2 = \frac{9}{16}$; $\frac{3^2}{4^2} = \frac{9}{16}$

5. a. Yes **b.** Yes **c.** Yes **d.** No **9.** No, plan (2) yields more. **11.** The pattern is false. Sample: let $x = 0$: $(2 \cdot 0)^3 = 0^3 = 0$, $2 \cdot 0^3 = 2 \cdot 0 = 0$, and the pattern holds. Let $x = 1$: $(2 \cdot 1)^3 = 2^3 = 8$, $2 \cdot 1^3 = 2 \cdot 1 = 2$, and the pattern does not hold. **13.** b; sample: $a = 25$; $\frac{25}{b} = b$; $b^2 = 25$; $b = 5$; Does $\sqrt{25} = 5$? Yes **15.** $\frac{36}{625x^4}$

17. 9 **19.** $2^{((14)^{92})}$ **21.** The longest segment connects opposite corners of the card. If its length is d, then $d^2 = 3^2 + 5^2$, $d^2 = 9 + 25$, $d^2 = 34$, $d = \sqrt{34} \approx 5.8$ in. **23. a.-d.:** $y = -\frac{2}{3}x + \frac{4}{3}$ **25.** 30% **27.** $\frac{193}{225} \approx .86$

CHAPTER 9 PROGRESS SELF-TEST (p. 470)

1. $b^7 \cdot b^{11} = b^{7+11} = b^{18}$ **2.** $\frac{5x^2y}{15x^{10}} = \frac{5y}{5 \cdot 3x^{10-2}} = \frac{y}{3x^8}$

3. $70 + 3 \cdot 1 + 6 \cdot 0.1 = 70 + 3 + 0.6 = 73.6$ **4.** $-\frac{1}{32{,}768}$

5. $\frac{3z^{6-4}}{3 \cdot 4} = \frac{z^2}{4} = 4^{-1}z^2 = .25z^2$ or $\frac{z^2}{4}$ **6.** $-5^4 = -5 \cdot 5 \cdot 5 \cdot 5 = -625$ **7.** $\frac{3^2}{x^2} \cdot \frac{x^4}{3^4} = \frac{x^{4-2}}{3^{4-2}} = \frac{x^2}{3^2} = \frac{x^2}{9}$ **8.** $3^4(y^2)^4 = 81y^{2 \cdot 4} = 81y^8$ **9.** $6(11)^0 = 6 \cdot 1 = 6$ **10.** $3^{-1} = \frac{1}{3} \neq -3$

11. a. Sample: Does $3^2 - 2^2 = (3 - 2)(3 + 2)$? $9 - 4 = 1 \cdot 5$? Yes; Does $(-4)^2 - (3)^2 = (-4 - 3)(-4 + 3)$? $16 - 9 = (-7)(-1)$? Yes; Does $(-10)^2 - (-9)^2 = (-10 + 9)(-10 - 9)$? $100 - 81 = (-1)(-19)$? Yes **b.** True **12.** Product of a Power Property, of $b^j \cdot b^k = b^{j+k}$ **13.** \$6500 •

$(1 + .0571)^5 = \$6500(1.0571)^5 \approx \$8580.13$ **14.** $\$1900(1 + .058)^3 = \$1900(1.058)^3 \approx \$2250.15$, $2250.15 - 1900 \approx \$350.15$ **15.** $P \cdot (1 + .03)^{15} = P(1.03)^{15} \approx 1.56P$ **16.** $T - 100{,}000(1.03) \approx 94{,}260$ people **17.** a and d **18.** **See below.** **19.** $(1.30)^3 = 2.197$ times as large **20.** $v = \frac{4}{3}(\pi)(433.10^5)^3 = \frac{4}{3}\pi(4.33)^3 \cdot (10^5)^3 = \frac{4}{3}\pi(81.183) \cdot 10^{15} \approx 340.058 \times 10^{15} \approx 3.40058 \times 10^{17}$ miles^3

18.

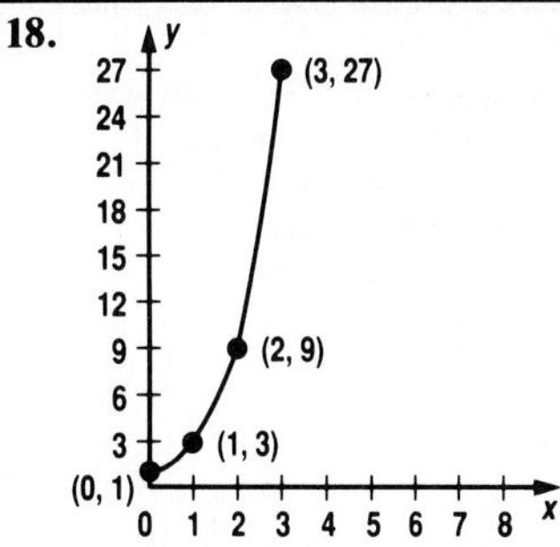

The chart below keys the **Progress Self-Test** questions to the objectives in the **Chapter Review** on pages 471–473 or to the **Vocabulary** (Voc.) on page 469. This will enable you to locate those **Chapter Review** questions that correspond to questions you missed on the **Progress Self-Test.** The lesson where the material is covered is also indicated in the chart.

Question	**1**	**2**	**3**	**4, 5**	**6**	**7, 8**	**9**	**10, 11**
Objective	B	B	A	B	A	C	E	D
Lesson	9-5	9-7	9-2	9-7	9-2	9-8	9-2	9-9
Question	**12**	**13, 14**	**15**	**16**	**17**	**18**	**19**	**20**
Objective	E	F	G	G	Voc.	I	H	H
Lesson	9-5	9-1	9-2	9-3	9-2	9-4	9-6	9-8

CHAPTER 9 REVIEW (pp. 471–473)

1. a. 81 **b.** -81 **c.** 81 **3.** 4 **5.** 703.04 **7.** $-\frac{1}{125}$ **9.** $\frac{8}{343}$ **11.** 81 **13.** x^{11} **15.** x^3y^{12} **17.** 1 **19.** $5^{-1}m^4 = .2m^4$ **21.** $\frac{x}{y^2}$ **23.** $\frac{y^3}{x^3}$ **25.** $\frac{a^5}{b^5}$ **27.** $\frac{4k^3}{27}$ **29.** a, b **31.** Does $(3 + 4)^3 = 3^3 + 4^3$? Does $7^3 = 27 + 64$? No **33.** Power of a Product Property **35.** Zero Exponent Property **37.** Power of a Quotient Property **39.** Negative Exponent Property **41.** \$3123.11 **43.** \$1348.32 **45.** \$11.41 **47. a.** 128,000 **b.** After 4 hours there will be 128,000 bacteria. **49.** 1,106,136 **51. a.** $\frac{9}{4}$ **b.** $\frac{243}{32}$ **53.** ≈ 34 **55. See below.** **57.** $y = 56 \cdot (1.04)^x$ **59. See below. b. See below. c. See below.**

55.

x	y
-4	$\frac{1}{16}$
-3	$\frac{1}{8}$
-2	$\frac{1}{4}$
-1	$\frac{1}{2}$
0	1
1	2
2	4
3	8
4	16

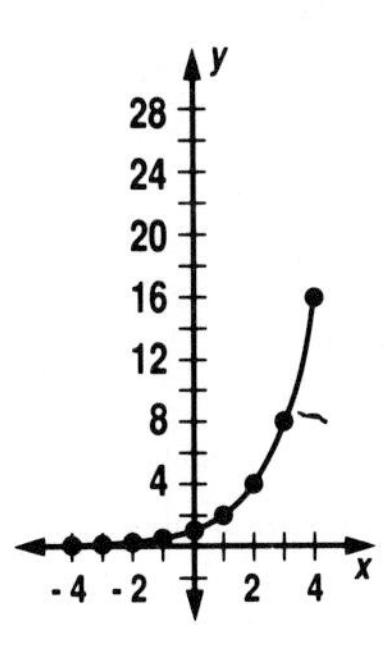

59. a.

year	0	5	10	15
amount	200	200	200	200

59. b.

year	0	5	10	15
amount	200	255.26	325.78	415.79

59. c.

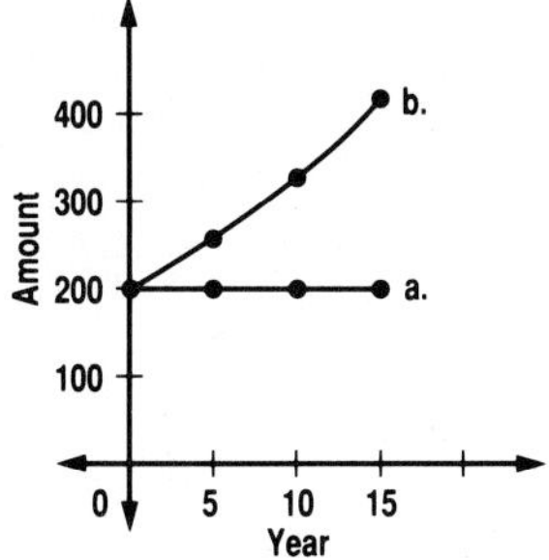

LESSON 10-1 (pp. 476–480)
1. \$1150.15 **3.** \$47.75 **5. a.** 10 dollars **b.** $10x + 20$ dollars **c.** $10x^2 + 20x + 15$ dollars **d.** $10x^3 + 20x^2 + 15x +$ 30 dollars **7. a.** $x^5 - 90x^3 + 4x^2 + 3$ **b.** 5' **9.** False **11.** $160y^3 + 220y^2 + 180y + 250$ **13. a. See below.**
b. Change line 10 to
PRINT "VALUES of POLYNOMIAL X ^ 2 − 8X + 16"
Change line 30 to
30 FOR X = -6 TO 6
and line 40 to
40 LET V = X * X − 8 * X + 16
15. a. \$110 **b.** \$99 **17. a.** $\approx .51$ **b.** $\approx .49$ **19.** $6x + 13$ **21.** $\frac{1}{2}$ **23.** 3 **25.** $\frac{1}{5}$

13. a.

X	VALUE
-3	0
-2	-3
-1	-4
0	-3
1	0
2	5
3	12

LESSON 10-2 (pp. 481–485)
3. $16y^2 + y - 17$ **5.** $7k^2 - 5k - 7$ **7. a.** $8p(4p + 2) = 32p^2 + 16p$ **b.** $3p(p + 1) = 3p^2 + 3p$ **c.** $29p^2 + 13p$ **9.** $-2x^2 - 16x - 7$ **11.** $120y^4 + 50y^3 + 160y^2 + 150y + 24$ **13. a.** $2n^2 + 20n$ **b.** $18n^2 + 120n$ **c.** $16n^2 + 100n$ **15. a.** simplified **b.** x^{m+n} **c.** x^{m-n}
17. 98 **19.** $\frac{5}{4}$ **21.** 38, 22, or 18 **23.** 20 **25.** ab^2c

LESSON 10-3 (pp. 486–489)
1. $2h(L_1 + L_2 + L_3 + L_4)$, $2hL_1 + 2hL_2 + 2hL_3 + 2hL_4$ **3.** $zq + zr - 13z$ **5.** $-12wy^2 + 6w^2y + 3wy$ **7.** $50x^8 + 70x^7 + 60x^6$ dollars **9.** $-x^2 + 6x$ **11.** $2m^4 + 2m^3 + 6m^2$ **13. a.** $9r^2$ **b.** πr^2 **c.** $9r^2 - \pi r^2$ **d.** $5(9r^2 - \pi r^2)$ or $45r^2 - 5\pi r^2$ **15.** $4n^4 + 15n^3 - 2n^2 - 9n + 25$ **17.** $10x$ **19. a.** $25x^2 + 25x + 25$ dollars **b.** $17x^2 + 24x + 31$ dollars **c.** $42x^2 + 49x + 56$ dollars **21.** $y = -2x + 5$
23. $y = 2x + 18$ **25. a.** $\dfrac{28c}{39}$ **b.** $\dfrac{c + 5cq}{13}$ **c.** $\dfrac{12c + 65cq}{156q}$

LESSON 10-4 (pp. 490–494)
3. x^2; 5 **5.** $7xy$; 3; x^2 **7. a.** a^2 **b.** $a^2(23a + 1)$ **9. a.** $6y^3$
b. $6y^3(5xy - 2 + 3x^3y^2)$ **11.** $\dfrac{3n(4n + 5)}{3n} = 4n + 5$
13. $20y^2 - 11y + 6$ **15.** True **17.** $-x + 2 - 3y$
19. \$550.19 **21.** $5x^2 + x + 9$ **23.** $4v^3 + 8v^2 + 4v$ **25.** 9
27. $\approx$ -.31 kg per day **29.** $b = \dfrac{d - c}{x}$

LESSON 10-5 (pp. 495–498)
1. a. $(w^2 + 5w + 4)(w + 6)$ **b.** $w^3 + 11w^2 + 34w + 24$ **3.** $y^3 + 13y^2 + 44y + 12$ **5.** $3m^4 + 26m^3 - 33m^2 - 32m - 6$ **7.** $(5 \cdot 2^2 + 4 \cdot 2 + 3)(2 + 7) = 31 \cdot 9 = 279$; $5 \cdot 2^3 + 39 \cdot 2^2 + 31 \cdot 2 + 21 = 40 + 156 + 62 + 21 = 279$ **9.** $x^4 + 64$ **11.** $49 - 9x^2$ **13.** $x^2 + 32$ **15. a.** Let $x = 3$; Does $(5 \cdot 3 + 3)(5 \cdot 3 - 2) = 25 \cdot 3^2 = 6$? Does $18 \cdot 13 = 225 - 6$? No **b.** 0 **17.** $2v(2v - 1)$ **19.** $3xy^3(x + 1)$
21. $-x^2 - 3x + 25$ **23.** $\sqrt{128}$ or $8\sqrt{2}$ km **25.** $\dfrac{7a^2}{3b}$

LESSON 10-6 (pp. 499–503)
1. a. $(2w + 6)(w + 7)$ **b.** $2w^2 + 20w + 42$ **3.** $ac + ad + bc + bd$ **5.** $y^2 + 11y + 30$ **7.** $9k^2 - 19k - 24$ **9.** $a^2 - b^2$ **11. a.** 892,500 **b.** $(f + p)(j + s)$ or $fj + fs + pj + ps$ **13. a.** $x^5 + 2x^3 - x^2 - 2$ **b.** $(4^2 + 2)(4^3 - 1) = 18 \cdot 63 = 1134$; $4^5 + 2 \cdot 4^3 - 4^2 - 2 = 1024 + 128 - 16 - 2 = 1134$ **15.** $n^3 + 3n^2 + 2n$ **17.** $300q - 225r$ **19.** $4w^3z^4 - 3w^2z^5 + 2wz^3$ **21.** $14x^2 + 10x - 60$
23. 150 feet **25.** $xy(3x^2 + 2y^2)$ **27.** $y = \frac{1}{2}x + \frac{17}{2}$

LESSON 10-7 (pp. 504–507)
3. a. $(3x + 7)^2$ **b.** $9x^2 + 42x + 49$ **5.** $x^2 - 2xy + y^2$ **7.** $-24p$ **9.** $(1 + .02)^2 = 1 + .04 + .0004 = 1.0404$ **11.** $(40 - 3)^2 = 1600 - 240 + 9 = 1369$ **13.** $324 + 72y + 4y^2$ **15. a.** $(2 + 7)^2 = 81$, $2^2 + 7^2 = 53$ **b.** 28 **c.** 28; It's the same. **17.** $(32t + 20)(t + 3)$ or $32t^2 + 116t + 60$ feet **19.** $z^2 - 3z - 88$ **21. a.** $52x^4 - 8x^3$ **b.** $52x^4 - 8x^3 + 78x^2 + x - 2$ **c.** $52x^3 - 12x^2 + 7x - 1$
23. $60xy(x + y + 1)$ **25.** $-\frac{1}{2}$

LESSON 10-8 (pp. 508–512)
3. No **5.** No **7. a.** $(x + 5)$ **b.** -2 or 8 **9. a.** i or iii **b.** No, $576 = 24^2$, but 776 is not a perfect square. **11.** Yes **13. a.** $4x - 2y$ **b.** THEY ARE NOT EQUAL.
15. $\frac{1}{2}m^2 + 3mn + \frac{9}{2}n^2$ **17.** $a^2 - b^2$ **19.** $6x^2 + 8x$
21. $\frac{1}{11{,}250{,}000} \approx 8.9 \cdot 10^{-8}$ **23. a.** II **b.** I **c.** III

LESSON 10-9 (pp. 513–516)
3. $25y^2 - 49$ **5.** b **7.** $(90 - 5)(90 + 5) = 90^2 - 5^2 = 8075$ **9.** $(x + 1)(x - 1)$ **11.** $(6m - 5n)(6m + 5n)$
13. $9^2 - \left(\frac{1}{2}\right)^2 = 80\frac{3}{4}$ **15.** $\frac{1}{4} - 9m^4$ **17. a.** $(x^2 - 9)(x^2 + 9)$ **b.** $(x - 3)(x + 3)(x^2 + 9)$ **19.** False **21. a.** 441 **b.** 1.21 **23.** $3x^2(-3 + 8x + 6x^2)$ **25. a.** $-28x^2 + 6x - 8$ **b.** 2 **27. See below.** **29. a.** $x = 0$ **b.** $x < 0$

27.

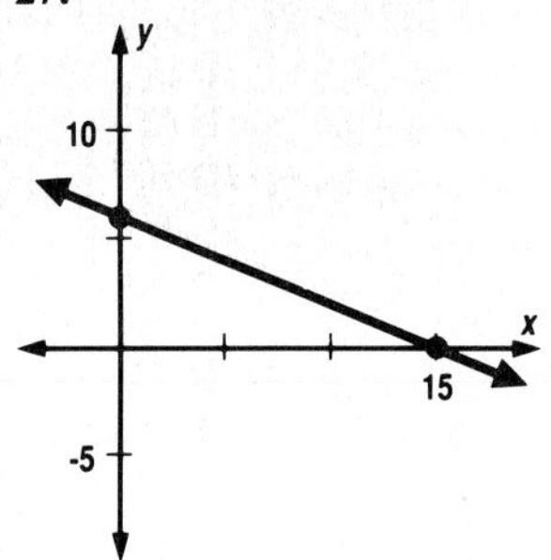

LESSON 10-10 (pp. 517–520)
3. 0, $\frac{5}{3}$ **5.** 15, $\frac{8}{9}$ **7.** 2.8125 **9.** 0, 11, $-\frac{7}{2}$ **11.** 5 **13.** c
15. a. $t^2 - 6t = 0$; $t(t - 6) = 0$; $t = 0$ or $t = 6$ **b.** $(t - 3)^2 = 9$; $t - 3 = 3$ or $t - 3 = -3$; $t = 6$ or $t = 0$ **17.** -3, -2, -1, 0 **19.** $(7p - q)(7p + q)$ **21.** $9x^2 - 49$ **23.** $(4e + 1)^2$ or $16e^2 + 8e + 1$ **25. See below.** **27.** 9 **29.** 6 or -6

25.

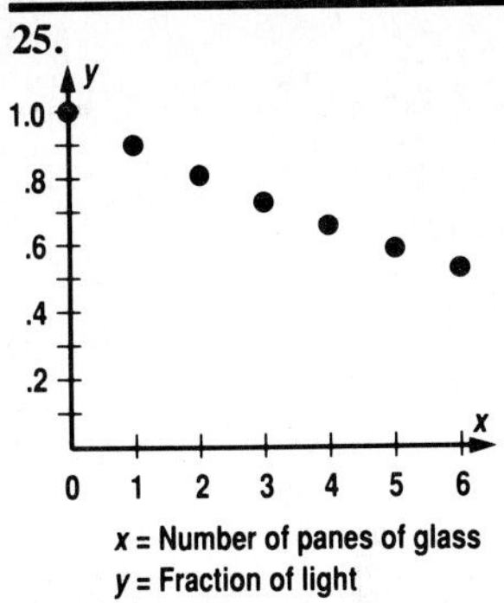

LESSON 10-11 (pp. 521–524)

3. a. $(x + 10)(x - 1) = x^2 + 9x - 10$ **b.** Sample: let $x = 3$; $(13)(2) = 26$, and $3^2 + 9 \cdot 3 - 10 = 26$. Let $x = -4$; $(6)(-5) = -30$, and $(-4)^2 + 9(-4) - 10 = -30$. **7.** c **9.** e **11.** c **13.** b **15. a.** 2 **b.** 0, 2 **c.** $\frac{-4}{3}$, 2 **d.** 5, $\frac{-4}{3}$, 2 **17.** $100(x - y + w - z)$

CHAPTER 10 PROGRESS SELF-TEST (p. 526)

1. a. $4x^2 + 9x^2 - 7x - 12 - 11 = 13x^2 - 7x - 23$ **b.** 2nd **2.** $4k^3 + 7k^3 - k^2 - 4k^2 + 6k + 8 - 2 = 11k^3 - 5k^2 + 6k + 6$ **3.** $(9v^2 + 2) - (2v^2 + 5) = 9v^2 + 2 + -2v^2 + -5 = 7v^2 - 3$ **4.** $4(3v^2 - 9 + 2v) = 12v^2 - 36 + 8v$ **5.** $18x^2 - 12x + 6 - 12x + 32 = 18x^2 - 12x - 12x + 6 + 32 = 18x^2 - 24x + 38$ **6.** $-5z(z^2) - 5z(-7z) - 5z(8) = -5z^3 + 35z^2 - 40z$ **7.** $x \cdot x + 9 \cdot x - 7 \cdot x - 7 \cdot 9 = x^2 + 2x - 63$ **8.** $4y \cdot 3y - 4y \cdot 16 - 2 \cdot 3y + 2 \cdot 16 = 12y^2 - 70y + 32$ **9.** $q^2 - 2 \cdot 1 \cdot 7 \cdot q + 7^2 = q^2 - 14q + 49$ **10.** $(3x)^2 - (8)^2 = 9x^2 - 64$ **11.** $2a \cdot a^2 + 2a \cdot 5ab + 2a \cdot 7b^2 - 3 \cdot a^2 - 3 \cdot 5ab - 3 \cdot 7b^2 = 2a^3 + 10a^2b + 14ab^2 - 3a^2 - 15ab - 21b^2$ **12.** No; $(2x - 5)^2 = 4x^2 - 20x + 25$, not $4x^2 - 10x + 25$. **13.** $6 \cdot 2m^3 - 2m^3 \cdot m^2 = 2m^3(6 - m^2)$ **14.** $50y \cdot 10x^2 + 50y \cdot 2x + 50y \cdot 1 = 50y(10x^2 + 2x + 1)$ **15.** $z^2 - 9^2 = (z + 9)(z - 9)$ **16.** $y^2 + 2 \cdot 6 \cdot y + 6^2 = (y + 6)(y + 6)$ **17.** $\frac{4c(2c + 1)}{c} = 4(2c + 1)$ **18.** $(30 - 1)(30 + 1) = 900 - 1 = 899$ **19.** a **20.** $z = 0$ or $5z - 2 = 0$, $z = 0$ or $\frac{2}{5}$ **21.** $x - 13 = 0$ or $2x + 15 = 0$, $x = 13$ or $-\frac{15}{2}$ **22.** $80x^2 + 60x + 90$ **23.** $8t^2 - 5t^2 = 0$ at ground level. So $t(8 - 5t) = 0$, $t = 0$ or $8 - 5t = 0$, $t = 0$ or $\frac{8}{5}$, after $\frac{8}{5}$ seconds. **24.** See below. **25.** $2y(5y - 3)(y + 9) = 2y(5y^2 + 42y - 27) = 10y^3 + 84y^2 - 54y$

24.

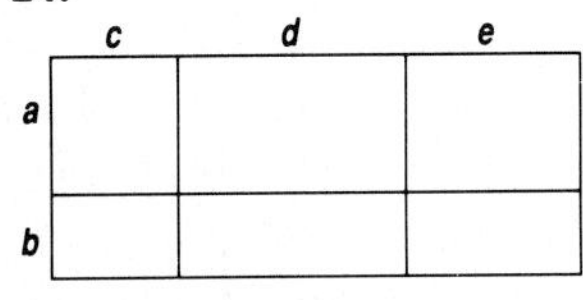

The chart below keys the **Progress Self-Test** questions to the objectives in the **Chapter Review** on pages 527–529 or to the **Vocabulary** (Voc.) on page 525. This will enable you to locate those **Chapter Review** questions that correspond to questions you missed on the **Progress Self-Test.** The lesson where the material is covered is also indicated in the chart.

Question	**1, 2, 3**	**4**	**5, 6**	**7, 8**	**9**	**10**	**11**	**12**	**13, 14**
Objective	A	B	B	B	B	F	B	C	D
Lesson	10-1, 10-2	10-3	10-3	10-6	10-7	10-9	10-5	10-8	10-4
Question	**15**	**16**	**17**	**18**	**19**	**20, 21**	**22**	**23**	**24, 25**
Objective	E	E	D	F	H	G	I	I	J
Lesson	10-9	10-8	10-4	10-7, 10-9	10-11	10-10	10-3	10-10	10-3

CHAPTER 10 REVIEW (pp. 527–529)

1. a. $7x^2 + 4x + 1$ **b.** 2nd **3.** $3.9x^2 + 1.7\overline{x} + 19$ **5.** $-k^2 + k - 5$ **7.** $8x^2 + 10x - 36$ **9.** $4x - 4x^3$ **11.** $-6m^2n + 4mn^2 - 8mn$ **13.** $x^2 + 4x - 21$ **15.** $ac - ad - bc + bd$ **17.** $d^2 - 2d + 1$ **19.** $a^2 - 225$ **21.** $a^3 - 1$ **23.** Yes **25.** No **27.** No **29.** x^3; 7 **31.** $m^2(14m^2 + 1)$ **33.** $6z^2 - 1$ **35.** $(m + 8)^2$ **37.** $(a + 2)(a - 2)$ **39.** $(2x + 1)(2x - 1)$ **41.** 1681 **43.** 3591 **45.** For any two numbers a and b, if $ab = 0$, then $a = 0$ or $b = 0$. **47.** There is no product. **49.** 3, 1 **51.** 3, $\frac{1}{2}$, $-\frac{1}{2}$ **53. a.** $x^2 + 5x - 6$ **b.** Sample: $3^2 + 5 \cdot 3 - 6 = 18$, $(3 + 6)(3 - 1) = 9 \cdot 2 = 18$. $4^2 + 5 \cdot 4 - 6 = 30$, $(4 + 6)(4 - 1) = 10 \cdot 3 = 30$ **55.** b **57.** \$811.60 **59.** $25x^6 + 50x^5 + 75x^4$ **61.** $\frac{25}{8}$ **63. a.** $xy + 3y + 2x + 6$ **b.** $(x + 3)(y + 2)$ **c.** Yes **65.** $21x^2 - \pi x^2$ or $x^2(21 - \pi)$ **67.** $x^3 - x$

LESSON 11-1 (pp. 532–535)

5. a. $\begin{cases} y = 2x + 4 \\ x + 2y = 3 \end{cases}$ **b.** (-1, 2) **7. a.** $x + y = 18$, $x - y = 8$ **b. See below. c.** 13 and 5 **9.** Any two of: $(x, y) = (-1, -9)$; $x = -1$ and $y = -9$; or $\{(-1, -9)\}$. **11. See below. 13.** $-0.185(2013) + 416.7 \approx 44.3$; $-0.313(2013) + 674.41 \approx 44.3$ **15.** $x = 2$ **17.** $12x - 3y$ **19. a.** 20 quarts **b.** $4n$ quarts **21.** 10¢ per second **23. a.** sample: $\frac{325}{1} = \frac{x}{4\frac{3}{4}}$ **b.** ≈ 1544 **25. a.** $\frac{-20}{3} = -6\frac{2}{3}$ **b.** -10 **c.** $\frac{24}{7} = 3\frac{3}{7}$

7. b.

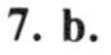
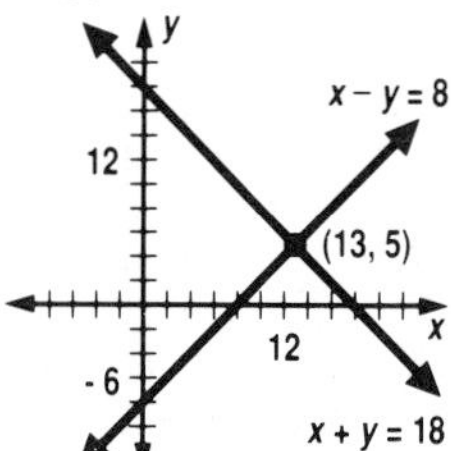

11.

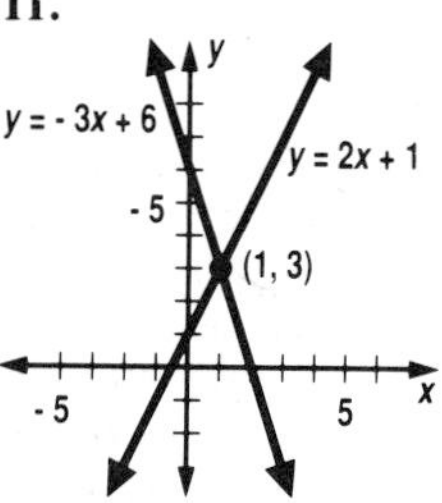

LESSON 11-2 (pp. 536–540)

1. \$135 for the boys, \$45 for the girls **3.** 15 quarts of orange juice and 5 quarts of ginger ale **5.** Does $\frac{24}{11} + \frac{86}{11} = \frac{110}{11} = 10$? Yes.; Does $\frac{32}{11} + \frac{11}{11} = \frac{43}{11}$? Yes. **7. a.** (0, -6) **b.** Does $12(0) - 5(-6) = 30$? Yes.; Does $-6 = 2(0) - 6$? Yes. **9. a.** (-12, -3) **b.** Does $2(-12) - 3(-3) = -15$? Yes.; Does $-12 = 4(-3)$? Yes. **11. a.** $\begin{cases} J = 3M \\ J + M = 11{,}000 \end{cases}$ **b.** Mary gets \$2750 and John gets \$8250. **13.** $L = \$800{,}000$ and $T = \$1{,}000{,}000$ **15. a. See below. b.** There is no answer to check. **17.** $2x^2 - 2x + 1$ **19. See below. 21.** 21

15. a.

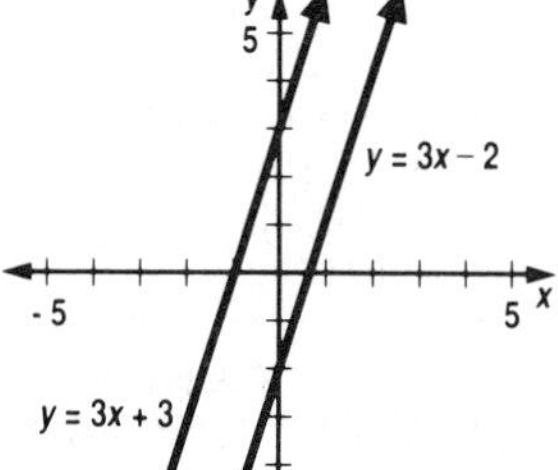

19.

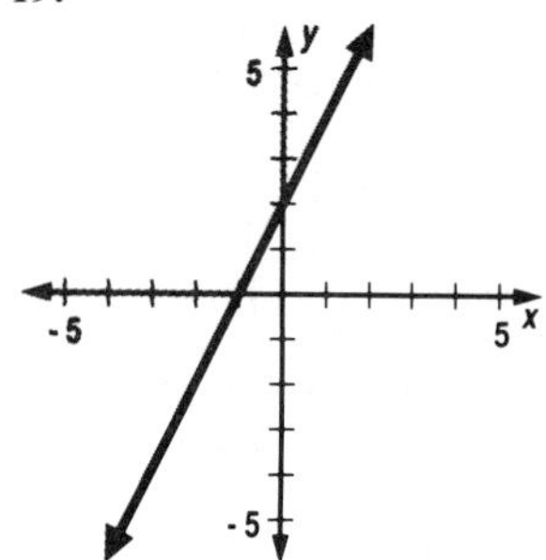

LESSON 11-3 (pp. 541–544)

1. False **3.** (-55, -610) **5.** \$4.25 **7.** distances greater than 8 tenths of a mile **9. See below. 11.** (-31, -17); Does $-31 = 2(-17) + 3$? Yes. Does $-31 = 3(-17) + 20$? Yes. **13. a.** 30 **b.** \$440 **15. a.** 12.2 years **b.** 546,000 **17.** $b = -1.9$; $a = -4.6$ **19. a.** -2 **b.** 7 **c.** -7 **21. See below. 23. a.** 9 **b.** 3 or -3 **c.** 0 or 9

9.

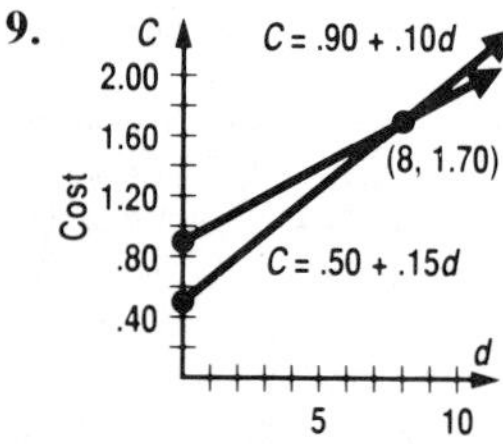

21.

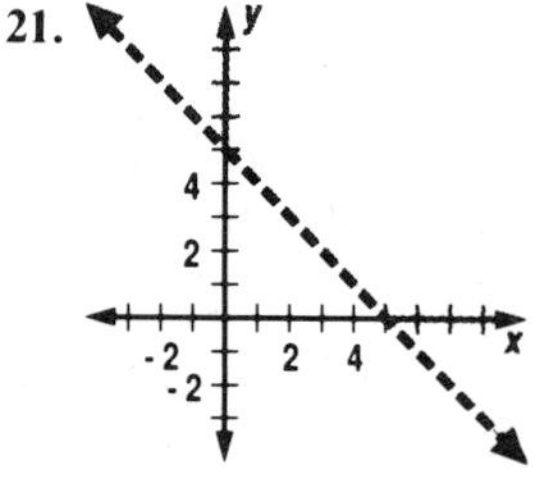

LESSON 11-4 (pp. 545–550)

1. to eliminate one variable **3.** $\left(-\frac{14}{3}, 2\right)$ **5.** plane speed is 108 mph; wind speed is 12 mph **7.** $\left(2, -\frac{1}{3}\right)$ **9.** \$49 per night and \$8 per meal **11.** $\left(6, -\frac{5}{3}\right)$ **13.** 45¢ **15.** 2 and -3 **17.** (-1, -3) **19.** sample: $P = 20, H = 0$; $P = 14, H = 5$; $P = 8, H = 10$ **21.** $2b^4$ **23. See below. 25.** $8x + y = -15$ or $-8x - y = 15$ **27.** $4x - 7y = -8$ or $-4x + 7y = 8$

23.

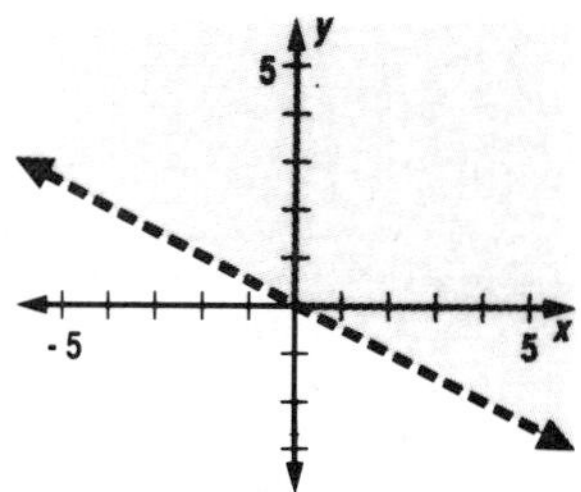

LESSON 11-5 (pp. 551–556)

1. the Multiplication Property of Equality **3. a.** -2 **b.** $(u, v) = \left(\frac{3}{4}, \frac{1}{2}\right)$ **5. a.** $10b = -20$ **b.** $15a = 80$ **c.** $\left(\frac{16}{3}, -2\right)$ **7.** $(m, n) = (57, 48)$ **9.** $(x, y) = (7, -5)$ **11.** Yes; make 7 pentagons and 8 rectangles. **13.** $m = 17$ and $t = 33$ **15.** $(x, y) = (1, -1)$ **17.** $(x, y) = (-30, -12)$ **19.** $\pm\sqrt{8} = \pm 2\sqrt{2}$ **21.** ≈ 9 days **23.** $\frac{5}{36}$

LESSON 11-6 (pp. 557–561)

1. a. $\frac{6}{8}, \frac{2}{8}$ **b.** 78.25 **5.** \$3.73 **7.** ≈ 34.4 mph **9.** ≈ 1.7 siblings **11.** ≈ 444 mph **13. a.** ≈ 7.6 hours **b.** $\left(\frac{5}{7}x + \frac{2}{7}y\right)$ hours **15.** No **17.** (4, -3) **19. a.** $\begin{cases} 2n + 3m = 22 \\ n - m = 31 \end{cases}$ **b.** 23 and -8 **21.** $\pm\sqrt{32}$ or $\pm 4\sqrt{2}$

LESSON 11-7 (pp. 562–565)

1. With a \$9 average, more than half are \$10; the balance must be less than \$9. **3.** \$9.29 **5.** $(q, z) = (20, 11)$ **7.** 0.75 hours or 45 minutes **9.** 76 **11.** 17.5 **13.** 48% **15.** No **17.** $\frac{8}{30} = \frac{4}{15}$ **19.** $0 < x < 12$

LESSON 11-8 (pp. 566–569)

1. sample: $\begin{cases} 2x + 3y = -6 \\ 4x + 6y = 24 \end{cases}$ **3.** slope **5. a.** nonintersecting **b. See below. 11.** nonintersecting **13.** intersecting **15.** Yes **17.** 2 hours **19.** $\left(\frac{7}{2}, -\frac{7}{3}\right)$ **21.** $(x - 7)^2$ **23. a.** $y = -12$ **b.** $x = 8$

5. b.

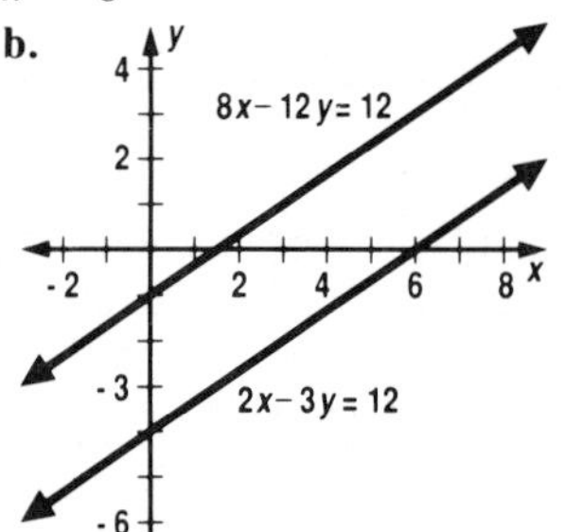

LESSON 11-9 (pp. 570–573)

1. a. always **b.** Let y = number of years employed. $6.20 + 1.00y > 6.00 + 1.00y$; $6.20 > 6.00$ **3. a.** $9 = 3 + 6$

b. y may be any real number. **5.** x may be any real number. **7.** no solution **9. a.** $375m + 500 < 315m + 400 + 60m$ **b.** $500 < 400$; Apartment A is never cheaper. **11.** B **13.** \$4.00 **15.** $\frac{1}{3}$ **17.** $525w$ **19.** ≈ 143 m

LESSON 11-10 (pp. 574–579)
1. intersection **3.** An equal sign means the boundary is included. **5.** first **7.** (0, 50), (50, 0), (25, 0) and (0, 25) **9.** sample: 20 free throws and no baskets; 10 free throws and 5 baskets; 10 baskets and no free throws. **11.** on or above the b-axis **13.** $\begin{cases} x \geq 0 \\ y \geq 0 \\ x + 2y \leq 10 \end{cases}$ **15. See below. 17. See below.**

19. no solution **b.** y may be any real number. **21.** intersecting **23.** (3, -1) **25.** 9 **27.** \$1503.66

15.

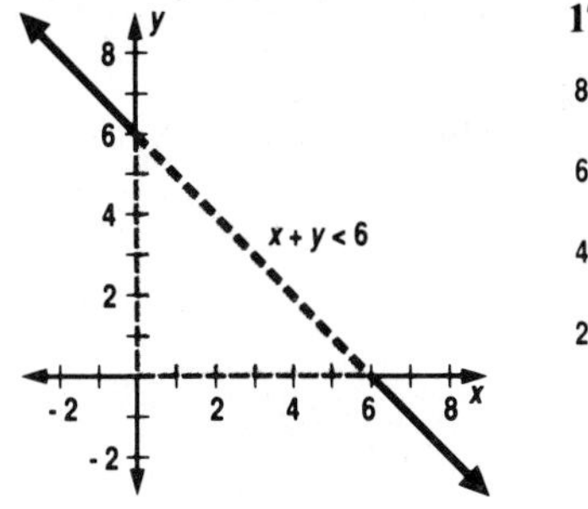

17.

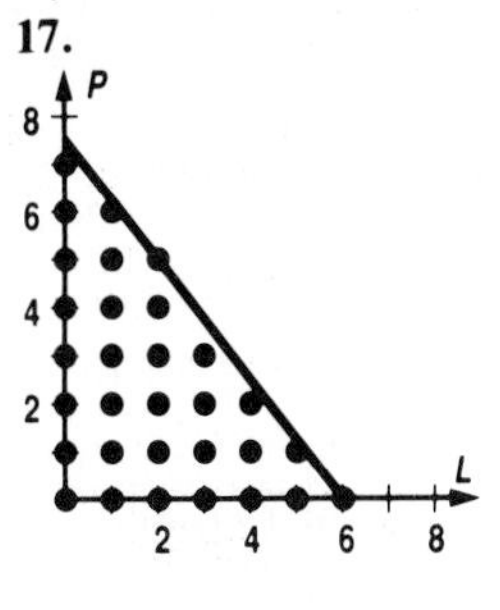

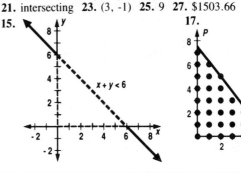

CHAPTER 11 PROGRESS SELF-TEST (p. 581)

1. $a - 3(3a) = -8$, $a - 9a = -8$, $-8a = -8$, $a = 1$; so $b = 3(1) = 3$. The solution is $(a, b) = (1, 3)$. **2.** $5r + 80 = -7r - 40$, $12r = -120$, $r = -10$; so $p = 5(-10) + 80$, $p = -50 + 80 = 30$. The solution is $(p, r) = (30, -10)$. **3.** $-5x - 15 = x - 3$, $-12 = 6x$, $x = -2$; so $y = -2 - 3 = -5$. The solution is $(x, y) = (-2, -5)$. **4.** Add the equations and get $n = 3$; so $m - 3 = -1$, $m = 2$. The solution is $(m, n) = (2, 3)$. **5.** Multiply one equation by -1 and add. We use the first equation and get $2y = 16$, $y = 8$; so $2x + 8 = -6$, $2x = -14$, $x = -7$. The solution is $(x, y) = (-7, 8)$. **6.** Multiply the second equation by 3 and add. $19x = 19$, $x = 1$; so $4(1) - y = 6$, $4 - y = 6$, $-y = 2$, $y = -2$. The solution is $(x, y) = (1, -2)$. **7.** Multiply the first equation by -2 (or the second by $-\frac{1}{2}$) and add. The result is $0 = 0$, so the lines are coincident. **8.** $2x + 7 - 2x = 3$, $7 = 3$ is not true, so the lines are parallel. **9.** Add $-12z$ to both sides to get $8 = -3$. This is not true, so there is no solution. **10.** Add $19p$ to both sides to get $0 < 22$. This is always true, so p may be any real number. **11.** Let L = Lisa's weight and B = baby's weight. Then $L = 4B$ and $L + B = 92$. So $4B + B = 92$, $5B = 92$, $B = 18.4$. Then $L = 4(18.4) = 73.6$. Lisa weighs 73.6 pounds and the baby weighs 18.4 pounds. **12.** Let h = cost of a burger and s = cost of a salad. Then $3h + 4s = 21.30$ and $5h + 2s = 22.90$. Multiply the second equation by -2 and add to get $-7h = -24.50$, $h = 3.50$. Then $3(3.50) + 4s = 21.30$, $4s = 10.80$, $s = 2.70$. A salad costs \$2.70. **13.** Let r = cost per rose and d = cost per daffodil. Then $10r + 15d = 35$ and $2r + 3d = 8$. Multiply the second equation by -5 and add to get $0 = -5$. The situation could not happen. **14.** Never. Since the populations are not equal in 1980 and the growth rates are the same, South Carolina population will never catch up to Louisiana population. **15.** $\frac{14}{20} \cdot 40\% + \frac{6}{20} \cdot 80\% = 28\% + 24\% = 52\%$ salt **16.** Let x = time traveled at 40 mph and y = total time traveled. Then $\frac{3}{y} \cdot 55 + \frac{x}{y} \cdot 40 = 45$, and $x + 3 = y$. Simplify the first equation to get $165 + 40x = 45y$, $33 + 8x = 9y$. Substitute $x + 3$ for y to get $33 + 8x = 9x + 27$, $6 = x$; it can travel 6 hours at 40 mph. **17. See below. 18. See below.**

17.

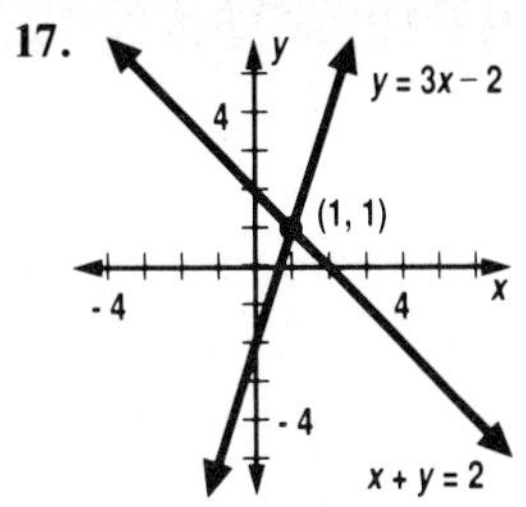

18.

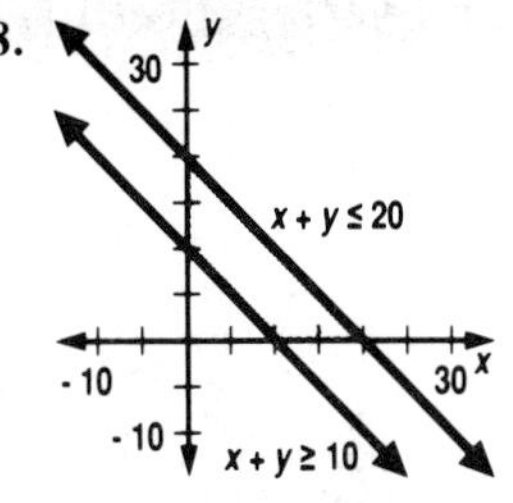

The chart below keys the **Progress Self-Test** questions to the objectives in the **Chapter Review** on pages 582–585 or to the **Vocabulary** (Voc.) on page 581. This will enable you to locate those **Chapter Review** questions that correspond to questions you missed on the **Progress Self-Test.** The lesson where the material is covered is also indicated in the chart.

Question	**1, 2**	**3**	**4**	**5, 6**	**7, 8**	**9, 10**	**11**	**12**	**13, 14**
Objective	A	A	B	C	E	D	F	F	D
Lesson	11-2	11-3	11-4	11-5	11-8	11-9	11-2	11-5	11-9
Question	**15**	**16**	**17**	**18**					
Objective	G	G	H	I					
Lesson	11-6	11-7	11-1	11-10					

CHAPTER 11 REVIEW (pp. 583–585)

1. $(a, b) = (15, 45)$ **3.** $c = 10$, $p = 20$, $q = 30$ **5.** $(x, y) = (5, 10)$ **7.** $(a, b) = (-31, -17)$ **9.** $(x, y) = (-9, -43)$ **11.** $(m, b) = (-22, 77)$ **13.** $(x, y) = (-3, -7.25)$ **15.** Different numbers could be used to multiply. This is one approach. **a.** Multiply $5x + y = 30$ by 4, $20x + 4y = 120$. **b.** $(x, y) = (7, -5)$ **17.** $(y, z) = (3, 3)$ **19.** $(a, b) = (4, -1)$ **21.** no solutions **23.** 0 (one solution) **25.** coincide **27.** coincide **29.** Marty earned \$52.50. Joe earned \$157.50.

31. \$.45 for an egg and \$.90 for a muffin **33.** Yes **35.** always **37.** ≈ 44.4 mph **39.** 55% **41.** 15 pounds **43. See below. 45. See below. 47.** c **49. See below. 51. See below. 53. See below.**

43.

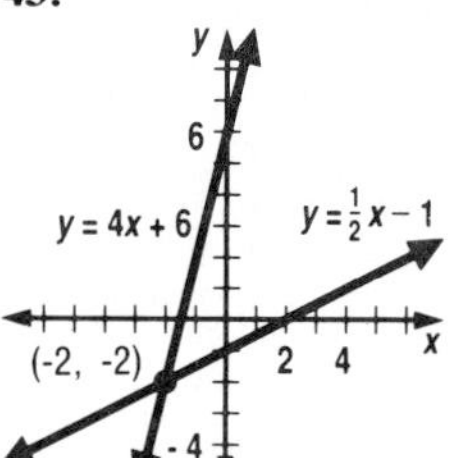

45.

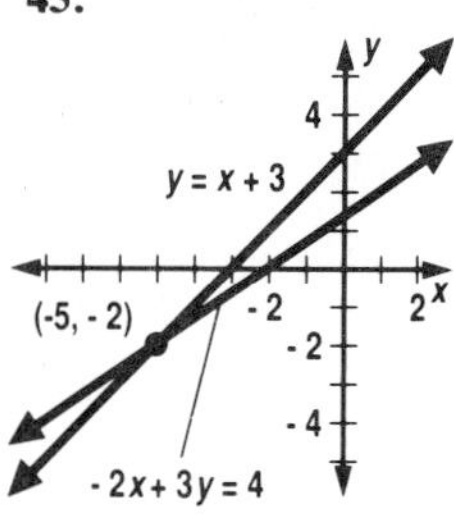

49.

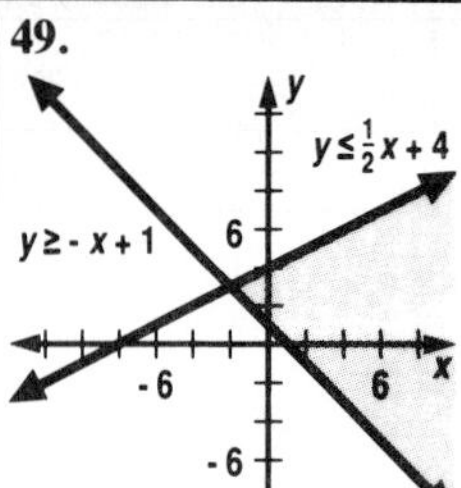

51.

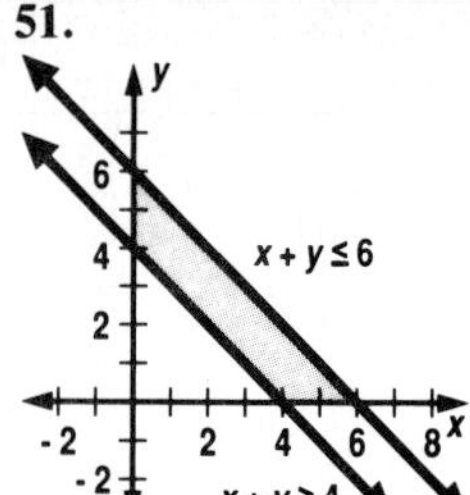

53.

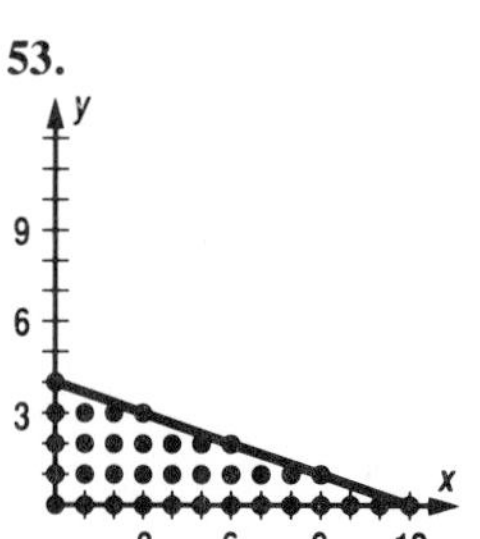

LESSON 12-1 (pp. 588–593)

3. a parabola that opens upward, vertex at (0, 0)

7. a.

x	-3	-2	-1	0	1	2	3
y	27	12	3	0	3	12	27

b. See below.

9. a.

x	-3	-2	-1	0	1	2	3
y	-32	-17	-8	-5	-8	-17	-32

b. See below. 11. a. See below. b. See below. 13. a. iii **b.** iv **c.** i **d.** ii **15.** 8 **17.** $4x^2 - 10x - 8 = 0$ or $-4x^2 + 10x + 8 = 0$ **19.** a^3 **21.** $-2 + 3x$ **23.** c **25.** $7500 - 1800 - k$ or $5700 - k$

7. b.

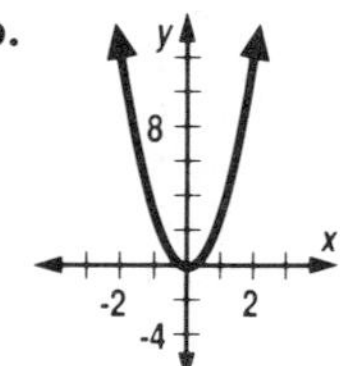

9. b.

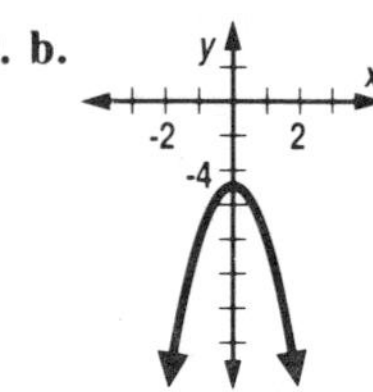

11. a.

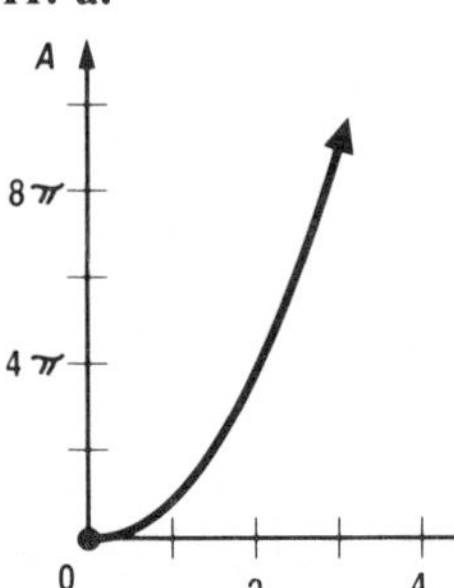

11. b.

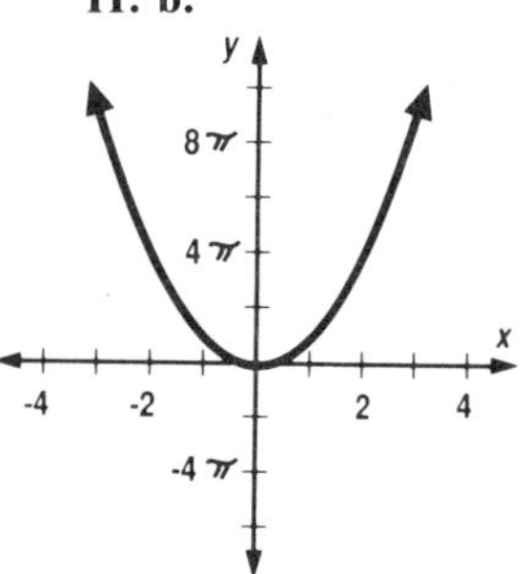

LESSON 12-2 (pp. 594–598)

3. No **5.** Yes **7.** ≈ (-.7, -3.3) **9.** $-50 \le x \le 30$; $-10 \le y \le 4$ **11.** ≈ -35 and 12 **13.** 3 **15. a. See below. b. See below. c.** The graph in part a gives you a "bigger" picture. It lets you see what is happening over more points. The graph in part b zooms into the graph in part a. You see more detail.

17. a. See below. b. As a gets smaller, the parabola appears thinner. **19. a.** $-4ac = -4(2)(4) = -32$ **b.** $b^2 - 4ac = 3^2 - 4(2)(4) = 9 - 32 = -23$ **c.** $\sqrt{b^2 - 4ac} = \sqrt{-23}$

21. ≈ 4.47 **23.** $2 - \sqrt{5}$ **25. a.** $20 \text{ ft} \cdot \frac{1 \text{ min}}{3 \text{ ft}} \approx 6.67$ min

b. $f \text{ ft} \cdot \frac{1 \text{ min}}{3 \text{ ft}} = \frac{f}{3}$ min **27. a.** $(2x + 3)(3x + 2) = 6x^2 + 4x + 9x + 6 = 6x^2 + 13x + 6$

b. $(6x - 1)(x - 6) = 6x^2 - 36x - x + 6 = 6x^2 - 37x + 6$

15. a.

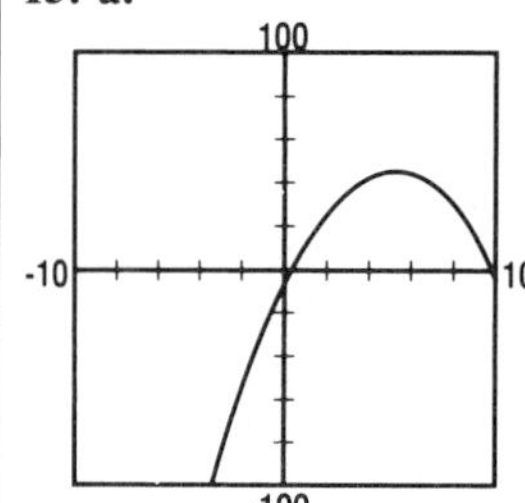

15. b.

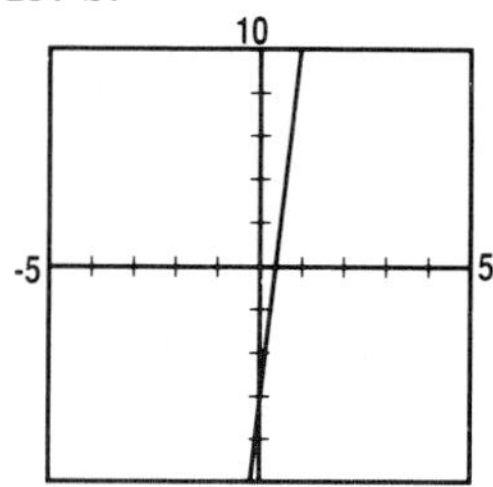

17. a. $y = -\frac{1}{2}x^2$

x	-3	-2	-1	0	1	2	3
y	-4.5	-2	$\frac{1}{2}$	0	$\frac{-1}{2}$	-2	-4.5

$y = -x^2$

x	-2	-1	0	1	2
y	-4	-1	0	1	-4

$y = -2x^2$

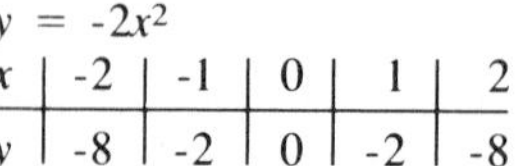

x	-2	-1	0	1	2
y	-8	-2	0	-2	-8

$y = -3x^2$

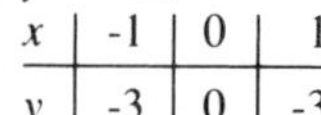

x	-1	0	1
y	-3	0	-3

17. a.

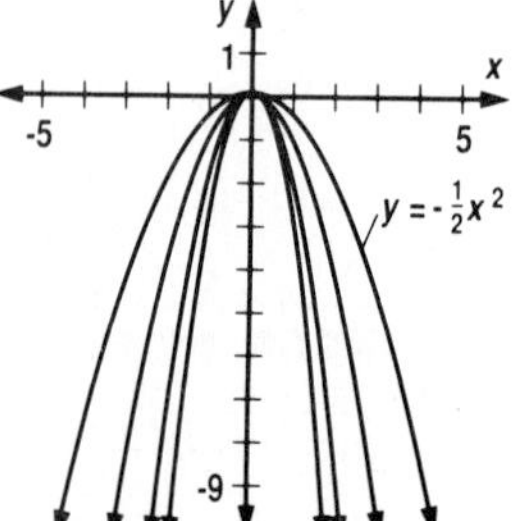

b. As a gets smaller, the parabola appears thinner

LESSON 12-3 (pp. 599–602)

3. a. 6.975 feet **b.** about 6 feet $11\frac{7}{10}$ inches **5.** $\approx$ 11.1 feet **7.** 20 yards **9.** $\approx$ 1.5 and 2.5 seconds **11.** 2 seconds **13.** 25 meters **15.** 35 meters

17. a. sample:

x	-2	-1	0	1	2
y	2	$\frac{1}{2}$	0	$\frac{1}{2}$	2

b. **See below.** **19.** 0, 4, 3 **21.** a **23.** (-3, -5)

17. b.

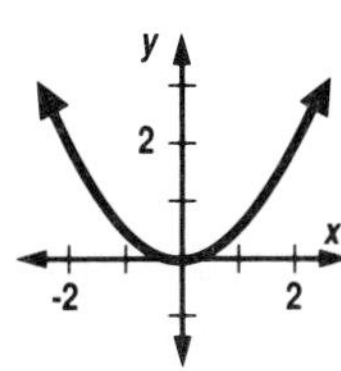

LESSON 12-4 (pp. 603–608)

3. Substitute $x = 5$; does $5^2 - 2 \cdot 5 - 15 = 0$? Yes. Substitute $x = -3$; does $(-3)^2 - 2 \cdot -3 - 15 = 0$? Yes. **5. a.** $a = 12, b = 7, c = 1$ **b.** $-\frac{1}{4}$ or $-\frac{1}{3}$ **7.** Substitute $m = 5.53$; $(5.53)^2 - 3(5.53) - 14 = -0.01$. Substitute $m = -2.53$; $(-2.53)^2 - 3(-2.53) - 14 = -0.01$. Both are close enough to zero to give the approximations. **9. a.** The simplest is $m^2 - 4m - 16 = 0$. **b.** $2 \pm 2\sqrt{5} \approx -2.47, 6.47$ **11.** $a = 3, b = -1, c = -5$; 1.47 or -1.14 **13.** $\frac{12 \pm \sqrt{96}}{24} \approx$ .908 or .092 **15. a.** 2.5, 5 **b.–c. See below.** **17. a.** 5 meters above **b.** 15 meters below **19.** d **21.** none **23.** 540 **25. a.** $x^2 + 2x + 1$ **b.** $9x^2 - 12x + 4$ **c.** $4a^2x^2 + 4abx + b^2$

15. b.–c.

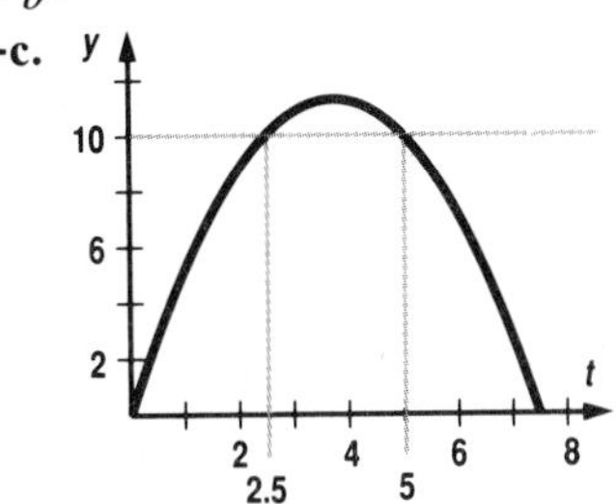

LESSON 12-5 (pp. 609–614)

3. 0 **9. a.** -119 **b.** 0 **c.** no real solution **11. a.** -11 **b.** 0 **c.** no real solution **13.** never **15. a.** $\frac{1}{2}, -\frac{5}{2}$ **b.** $\frac{-8 \pm \sqrt{48}}{8} \approx$ -.13 or -1.9 **c.** no real solution **17.** 2.25 **19. a.** $\approx$ 1.07 **b.** about 7% **21.** down **23. a.** $a < \frac{1}{3}$ **b.** $b > \frac{1}{3}$ **c.** $c < 0$ **25. a.** 48 feet **b.** $\approx$ 3.5 feet

LESSON 12-6 (pp. 615–617)

3. rational, sample: $\frac{3}{4}$ **5.** rational, sample: $\frac{-3}{2}$ **7.** rational, sample: $\frac{2}{6}$ **9.** rational, sample: $\frac{4}{1}$ **11. a.** two rational **b.** $-\frac{2}{3}$ or $-1\frac{1}{2}$ **13. a.** no rational **b.** $\approx$ 1.414 or $\approx$ -1.414 **15. a.** two rational **b.** .5 or -.2 **17. a.** no rational **b.** $\approx$ .525 or $\approx$ -9.525 **19.** samples: $3x^2 + 8x + -k = 0$ (with rational solutions); $b^2 - 4ac$ = a perfect square; $64 - 4(3)(k) = 1$; $64 - 12k = 1$; $-12k = -63$; $k = \frac{63}{12} = \frac{21}{4}$, $64 - 12k = 25$; $-12k = -39$; $k = \frac{39}{12}$ **21.** $\approx$ -9.525 or $\approx$ .525 **23.** 44.1 ft **25. a.** $d = 4.9t^2$ **b.** $1.43 \approx t$ **27. a.** $13x$ **b.** $5y^2$ **c.** $65xy^2$ **29.** 300

LESSON 12-7 (pp. 618–622)

3. Multiply the two binomials or substitute a number. **5. a.** yes; **b.** $(x + 10)(x + 11)$ **7. a.** yes; **b.** $(y + 9)(y + 1)$ **9. a.** yes; **b.** $(t + 5)(t - 6)$ **11. a.** $11^2 - 4(3)(-4) = 169$; yes; **b.** $(3x - 1)(x + 4)$ **13.** $k = 5$ **15.** No **17. a.** $\frac{5 \pm \sqrt{13}}{6}$ **b.** 1.4 or 0.2 **19.** $(2a + 2b)(a - b) = 2(a^2 - b^2)$ **21.** $m = \frac{8}{5}, b = \frac{-1}{5}$ **23.** $2x^2$ **25.** 5

LESSON 12-8 (pp. 623–626)

1. factor, Zero Product **3.** 5, -1 **5. a.** $3x(3x^2 + 4x - 4) = 0$; **b.** 0, $\frac{2}{3}$, -2 **7.** 12 **9.** -13, -2 **11.** 0, $-\frac{1}{4}$, 5 **13.** $v = -\frac{5}{2}$ or 7 **15.** sample: $20x^2 + x - 1$ **17.** True **19.** irrational **21.** irrational **23.** rational **25.** $\frac{5}{a + b}$ **27.** $\left(\frac{1}{2}y - 3\right)\left(\frac{1}{2}y + 3\right)$

LESSON 12-9 (pp. 627–630)

3. $x = \frac{-(-7) \pm \sqrt{49 - 4(10)}}{2} = 5$ or 2; $(x - 2)(x - 5)$ **5.** $k = \frac{-(-8) \pm \sqrt{64 - 4(5)(-4)}}{10} = \frac{-2}{5}$ or 2; $5k = -2$ or $k = 2$; $5k + 2 = 0$ or $k - 2 = 0$; $(5k + 2)(k - 2)$ **7.** $(x - 1)$ **9.** $(x + 8)^2$ **11.** $4m(4m^2 - 11m + 30)$ **13.** $x + 6$ **15.** $3x - 4$ **17.** 0, -5, 2 **19.** 8.96 meters high **21.** $\approx$ 53.6°F **23.** \$3650 **25.** as soon as he passes 9 weeks

CHAPTER 12 PROGRESS SELF-TEST (p. 632)

1. $x = \frac{-(-9) \pm \sqrt{(-9)^2 - 4 \cdot 1 \cdot 20}}{2 \cdot 1} = \frac{9 \pm \sqrt{81 - 80}}{2} = \frac{9 \pm \sqrt{1}}{2}$; so $x = 4$ or $x = 5$ (This could also be factored to $(x - 4)(x - 5) = 0$ and solved using the Zero Product Property.) **2.** $5y^2 - 3y - 11 = 0$; $y = \frac{-(-3) \pm \sqrt{(-3)^2 - 4 \cdot 5 \cdot -11}}{2 \cdot 5} = \frac{3 \pm \sqrt{9 + 220}}{10} = \frac{3 \pm \sqrt{229}}{10}$ **3.** Factor out 3; $6z^2 - z + 8 = 0$. **4.** $k = \frac{-(-6) \pm \sqrt{(-6)^2 - 4 \cdot 1 \cdot -3}}{2 \cdot 1} = \frac{6 \pm \sqrt{36 + 12}}{2} = \frac{6 \pm \sqrt{48}}{2}$; $k = 6.46$ or $k = -0.46$ **5.** $r = \frac{-15 \pm \sqrt{15^2 - 4 \cdot 3 \cdot 8}}{2 \cdot 3} = \frac{-15 \pm \sqrt{225 - 96}}{6} = \frac{-15 \pm \sqrt{129}}{6}$; $r = -0.61$ or $r = -4.39$ **6.** $8x^2 - 7x + 11 = 0$; the value of the discriminant is $(-7)^2 - 4 \cdot 8 \cdot 11 = -303$, so the equation has no real solutions. **7.** $z^2 - 16z + 64 = 0$; factor to $(z - 8)^2 = 0$. $z = 8$ **8.** True **9.** False **10.** $(x + 2)(x - 18)$ **11.** Solve $x^2 + 8x + 19 = 0$; the discriminant is $8^2 - 4 \cdot 1 \cdot 19 = -12$, so the equation has no solutions and the expression does not factor. **12.** $(x - 7)(x - 5)$ **13.** $(x - 7)(x + 6) = 0$; $(x - 7) = 0$ or $(x + 6) = 0$; $(x - 7) = 0$ or $(x + 6) = 0$; so $x = 7$ or $x = -6$ **14.** $h = -.07(2 - 10)^2 + 12 \approx 7.5$ ft **15.** $0 = -.07(x - 10)^2 + 12$; 23 yd

16. **a.** sample:

x	-2	-1	0	1	2
y	-8	-2	0	-2	-8

b. See below.

17. **a.** sample:

x	0	1	2	3	4
y	3	0	-1	0	3

b. See below.

18. a **19.** A number that can be written as a fraction, using whole numbers in the numerator and denominator. A number that has a repeating pattern or decimal is a rational number. **20.** c

16. b.

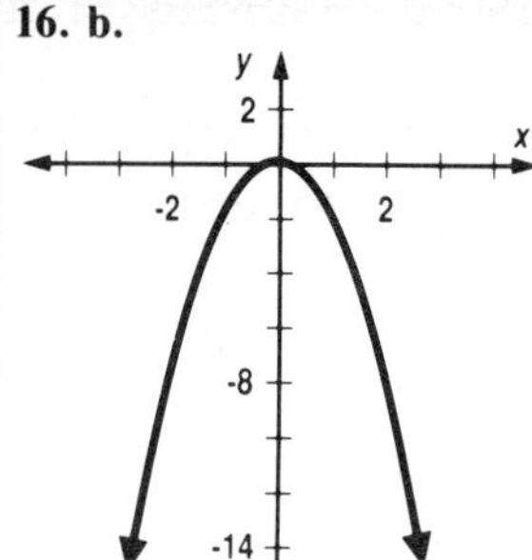

17. b.

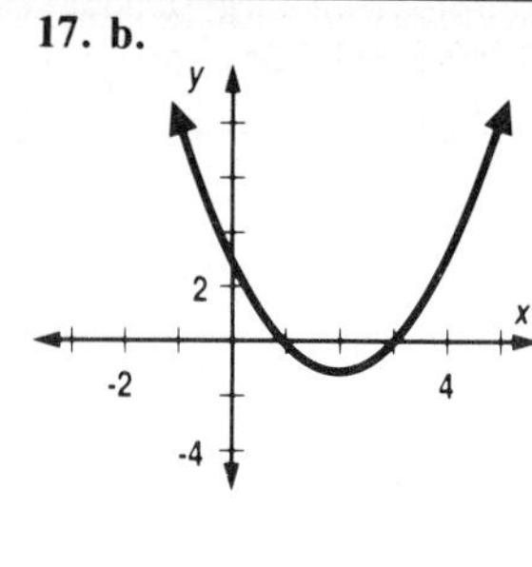

The chart below keys the **Progress Self-Test** questions to the objectives in the **Chapter Review** on pages 633–635 or to the **Vocabulary** (Voc.) on page 631. This will enable you to locate those **Chapter Review** questions that correspond to questions you missed on the **Progress Self-Test.** The lesson where the material is covered is also indicated in the chart.

Question	**1**	**2**	**3**	**4**	**5**	**6**	**7**	**8**	**9**	**10**	**11**
Objective	A	A	B	A	A	A	B	E	D	B	E
Lesson	12-4	12-4	12-7	12-4	12-4	12-5	12-7	12-5	12-1	12-7	12-5
Question	**12**	**13**	**14**	**15**	**16**	**17**	**18**	**19**	**20**		
Objective	B	C	G	G	H	H	H	F	F		
Lesson	12-7	12-8	12-3	12-3	12-1	12-1, 12-2	12-1	12-6	12-6		

CHAPTER 12 REVIEW (pp. 633–635)

1. $-\frac{5}{2}, \frac{4}{3}$ **3.** $4, -\frac{3}{4}$ **5. a.** $m^2 - 5m + 3 = 0$ **b.** $\frac{5 \pm \sqrt{13}}{2} \approx 4.3$ or 0.7 **7.** 7.27, -0.27 **9.** no real solution **11.** 0.36, -0.43 **13.** 2, 7 15. $(x + 6)(x - 1)$ **17.** $(5a - 7)(2a - 1)$ **19.** $(5x + 6)(x - 1)$ **21.** $(x + 3)(x - 17)$ **23.** $\frac{1}{2}, \frac{2}{3}$ **25.** 0, 2 **27.** a parabola **29.** $ax^2 + bx + c = 0$ **31.** $\frac{-b \pm \sqrt{b^2 - 4ac}}{2a}$ **33.** True **35.** no real solution **37.** no real solution **39.** irrational **41.** rational **43.** irrational **45. a.** 34 yards **b.** Yes **47.** 2.5 and 10 sec **49. a.** sample:

x	-2	-1	0	1	2
y	12	3	0	3	12

b. See below. **51. a.**

x	-4	-3	-2	-1	0
y	2	0	0	2	6

b. See below. **53.** b **55.** $-35 \le x \le 35$; $-20 \le y \le 10$

49. b.

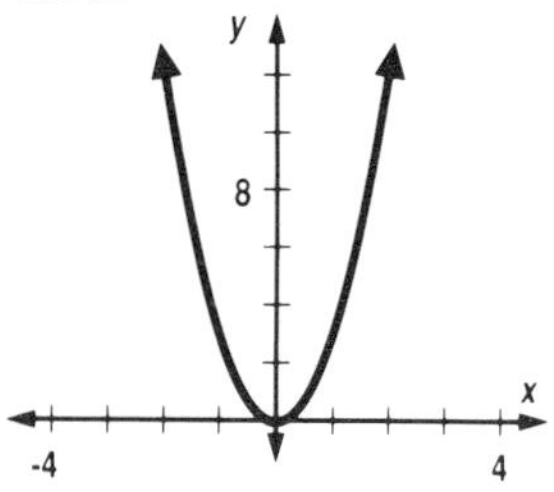

51. b.

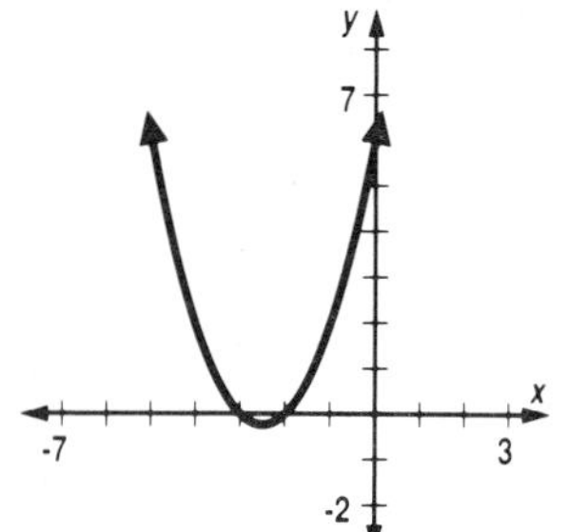

LESSON 13-1 (pp. 638–642)

3. a. $C = 0°C$, $C = 100°C$ **b.** Yes **5. a.** $y = -648$; $y = -701$ **b.** Yes **9.** $y = \frac{1}{3}x - 2$; Each value of x corresponds to one value of y, so the equation describes a function. **11.** One x value is paired with infinitely many y values. **13.** Yes **15.** typical points

x	-2	0	2
y	5	3	5

; **See below.**

17. $y = 3.00 + .50x$; **See below.** **19. a.** $\frac{5}{6}$ **b.** $\frac{x + y}{xy}$ **c.** $\frac{a + b - 1}{(a + 1)(b - 2)}$ **21.** $\frac{1}{n}$ **23.** $\frac{9}{64}$

15.

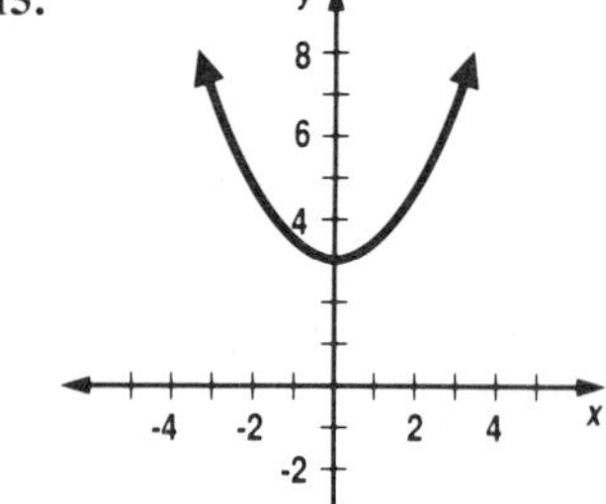

17. samples:

x	y	
0	3.00	3.00 + .50(0)
1	3.50	3.00 + .50(1)
2	4.00	3.00 + .50(2)

(0, 3.00), (1, 3.50), (2, 4.00)

LESSON 13-2 (pp. 643–646)

3. f of x equals x squared **5.** 64 **9.** the average number of accidents per 50 million miles driven by 60-year olds **13.** -5 **15.** 2.5 **17.** age 18 **19. a.** 1, 8, 27, 64, 125 **b.** cubing function **21. a.** 506 **b.** 650 **23.** $\frac{2}{3}$ **25.** 4 **27.** $100bc$

LESSON 13-3 (pp. 647–651)

1. 3 **3.** $\frac{3}{4}$ **7.** 30 **9.** the length of a minute **11.** describing the distance of a plane from a check point **13.** When $t = 5$ hours, the plane is 600 kilometers west of the checkpoint.

15.

x	12	11	10	9	8	7
y	9	8	7	8	9	10

; **See below.**

17. See below. 19. 45 **21.** $0.58

15.

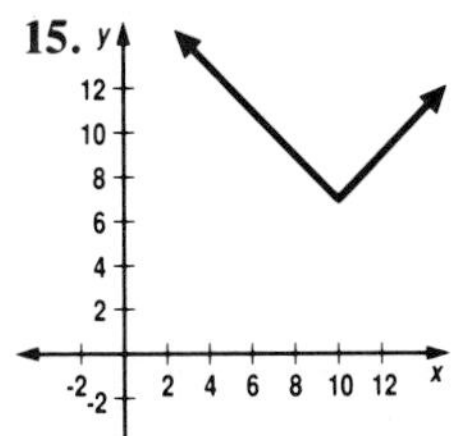

17.

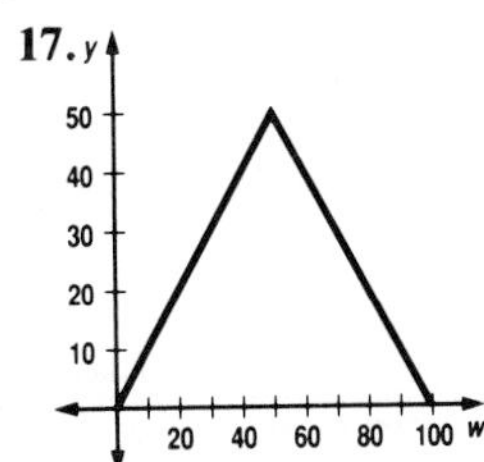

LESSON 13-4 (pp. 652–655)

1. the replacement set for the first variable **3.** {1, 3, 5}; {2, 4, 7} **5.** $x \geq 0; f(x) \geq 4$ **7.** all real numbers; $y \geq 0$ **9. a.** $f(x) = 4x$ **b.** $g(x) = 4x$ **c.** The domain for $f(x)$ can be any real number ≥ 0. The domain for $g(x)$ can only be whole numbers. **11. a. See below. b.** 6 **13.** all real numbers; $y \geq -3$ **15.** all nonzero real numbers; all nonzero real numbers **17.** an angle; (0, 3) **19.** 0; 4; $\frac{52}{9}$ **21.** $x = \frac{1}{2}y - 3$

11. a. sample:
b. 6

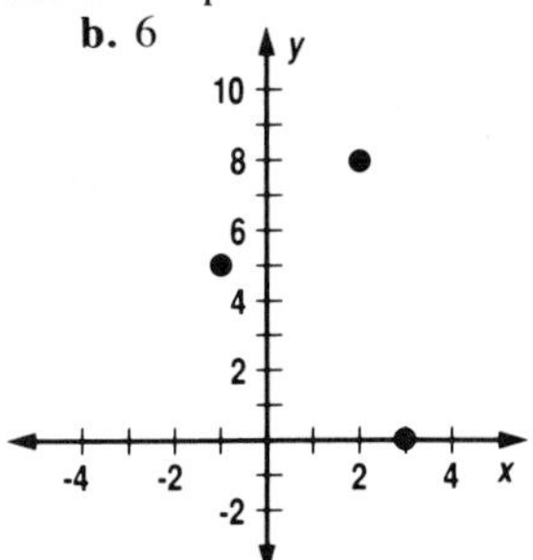

LESSON 13-5 (pp. 656–659)

3. $P(12) = -\frac{1}{36}|12 - 7| + \frac{1}{6} = -\frac{1}{36}|5| + \frac{1}{6} = -\frac{1}{36}(5) + \frac{1}{6} = -\frac{5}{36} + \frac{6}{36} = \frac{1}{36}$ **5.** 6; 8 **7. See below. 9.** False **11. a.** .2 **b.** .6 **c.** Each point would be graphed at $P = .\overline{16}$. **13.** $1 - \frac{31}{32} = \frac{1}{32}$; **See below. 15.** {1, 2, 3, 4, 5}; $\left\{\frac{1}{5}\right\}$ **17.** $x = 3$ **19.** $3\sqrt{3}$

7.

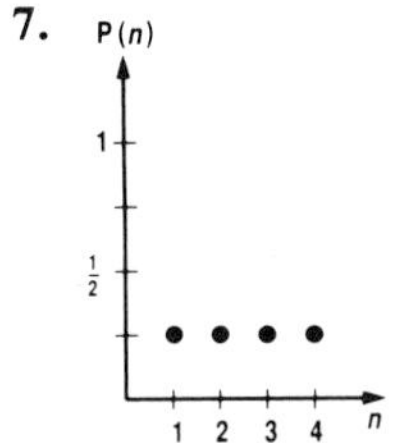

13.

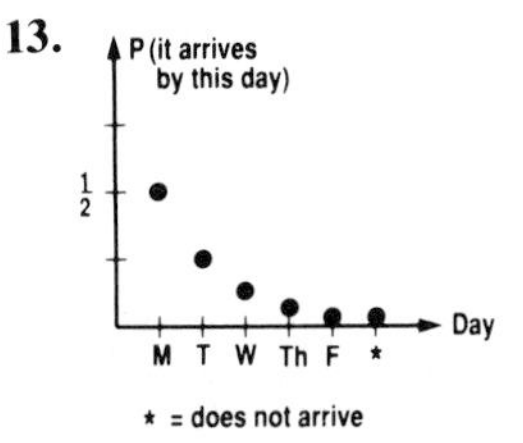

LESSON 13-6 (pp. 660–665)

1. a. 90 **b.** complementary **5.** 27° **7.** 1.540 **9.** 14.57 m **11.** tan A = m **13.** 76° **15.** ≈ 59° **17.** ≈ 77° **19. a.** 30° **b.** $\frac{1}{4}, \frac{1}{4}, \frac{1}{4}, \frac{1}{6}, \frac{1}{12}$ **c. See below. 21.** $x = -2$

23. $x = \dfrac{-b \pm \sqrt{b^2 - 4ac}}{2a}$

19. c.

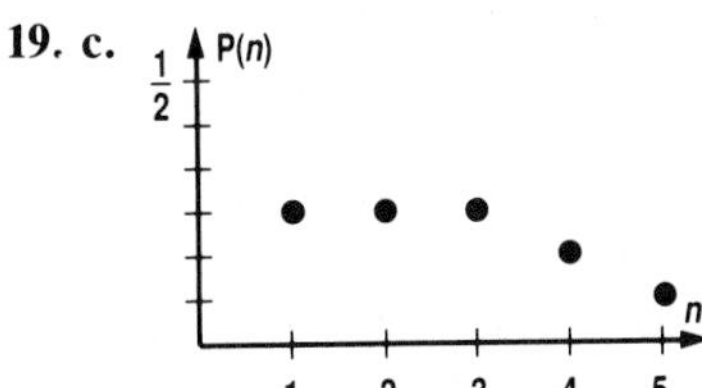

LESSON 13-7 (pp. 666–670)

1. 0.194 **3.** 0.682 **5.** 12.173 **7.** ! **9.** $\frac{1}{x}$ **11.** common logarithm **13. a.** 1 **b.** 1 **15. a.** -0.9 **b.** -0.940

17. a.

X	LOG X	or LOG X
1	0	0
2	0.301029995	.69315
3	0.477121254	1.0986
4	0.602059991	1.3863
5	0.698970004	1.6094
6	0.77815125	1.7918
7	0.84509804	1.9459
8	0.903089987	2.0794
9	0.954242509	2.1972
10	1	2.3026

b. See below. c. almost the same, none of the graph is below the x-axis **19. See below. 21. a.** 7 **b.** $\frac{1}{6}$

23.

x	0	1	2	3	4	5	6	7
$f(x)$	10	8	6	4	6	8	10	12

See below.

25. 120 ft **27.** 794.12 min, or 13 hr 14.12 min **29.** $m = 8$ **31. a. See below. b.** Sample: 120 million

17. b.

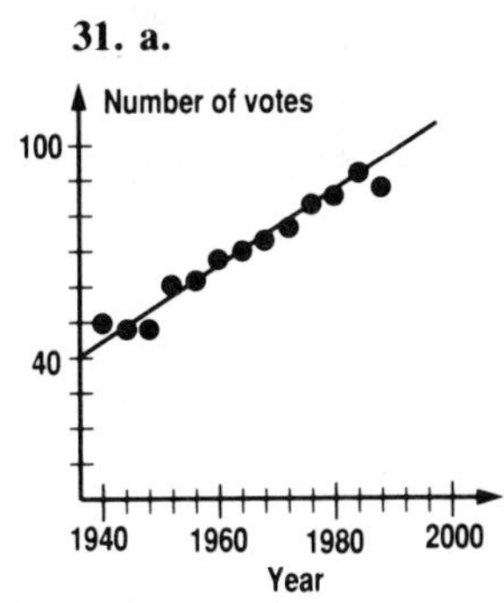

31. a.

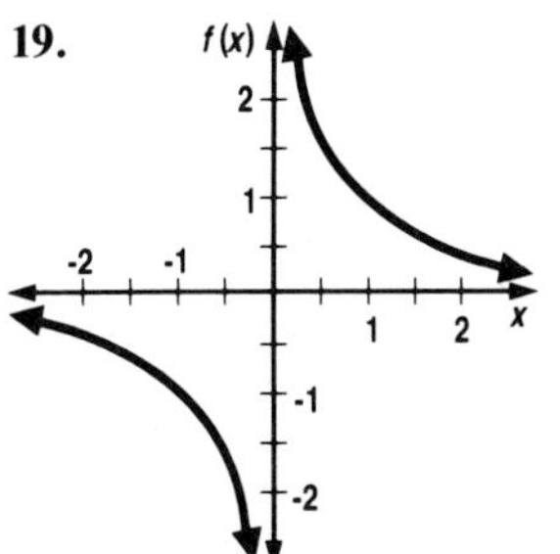

19.

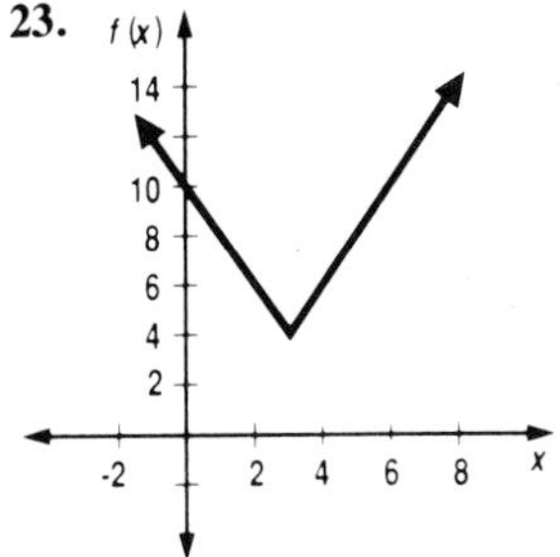

23.

CHAPTER 13 PROGRESS SELF-TEST (p. 672)

1. $3(2) + 5 = 6 + 5 = 11$ **2.** $5 = t^2 + 4t$; $t^2 + 4t - 5 = 0$; $(t + 5)(t - 1) = 0$; $t + 5 = 0$ or $t - 1 = 0$; $t = -5$ or $t = 1$ **3.** 7.115 **4.** 0.50 **5.** A function is a set of ordered pairs in which each first coordinate appears with exactly one second coordinate. **6. a.** Answers will vary. **b.** parabola **7.** One positive value of x yields two values of y. **8.** 10 or 30 **9.** Yes; domain: {0, 1, 2, 3, 4}; range: {1, 2} **10.** No; $x = 0$ is paired with 1 and -1 for y. **11.** (6, 4), (4, 6), (5, 5); $\frac{3}{36}$ **12.** $d(2.5) = -600|2.5 - 2| + 1200 = -600|0.5| + 1200 = -600(0.5) + 1200 = -300 + 1200 = 900$; When $t = 2.5$, the plane is 900 km east. **13.** $\frac{1}{10}$ **14.** See below. **15.** $\tan P = \frac{21}{20} = 1.05$, 1.05 INV TAN $\approx 46°$

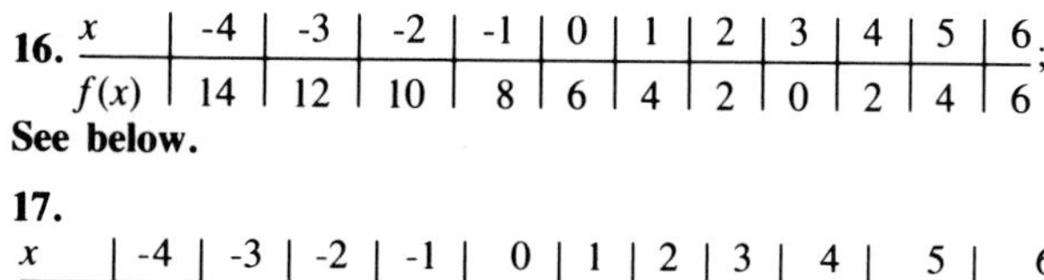

16.

x	-4	-3	-2	-1	0	1	2	3	4	5	6
$f(x)$	14	12	10	8	6	4	2	0	2	4	6

; See below.

17.

x	-4	-3	-2	-1	0	1	2	3	4	5	6
$g(x)$	-6	1	6	9	10	9	6	1	-6	-15	-26

; See below.

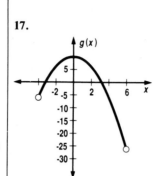

14. **16.**

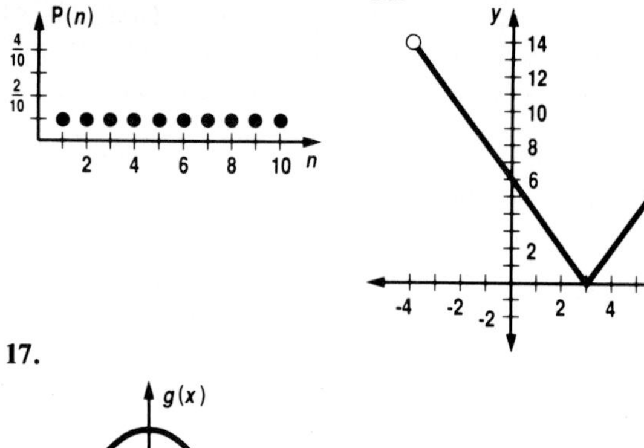

17.

The chart below keys the **Progress Self-Test** questions to the objectives in the **Chapter Review** on pages 673–675 or to the **Vocabulary** (Voc.) on page 671. This will enable you to locate those **Chapter Review** questions that correspond to questions you missed on the **Progress Self-Test.** The lesson where the material is covered is also indicated in the chart.

Question	**1–2**	**3**	**4**	**5**	**6**	**7**	**8**	**9–10**	**11**
Objective	A	G	B	C	D	I	E	H	F
Lesson	13-2	13-6	13-7	13-1	13-1	13-3	13-4	13-1	13-5
Question	**12**	**13**	**14**	**15**	**16**	**17**			
Objective	I	F	I	G	I	I			
Lesson	13-3	13-5	13-5	13-6	13-3	13-2			

CHAPTER 13 REVIEW (pp. 673–675)

1. 6 **3.** 78 **5.** 8 **7.** 1.5 **9.** 2 or -8 **11.** $f(x) = 10$ **13.** 0.059 **15.** 107.093 **17.** 0.577 **19.** 0.991 **21.** No **23.** Yes **25.** Yes **27.** Yes **29.** quadratic **31.** absolute value **33.** other **35.** domain {1850, 1900, 1950, 1960, 1970, 1980}; range {1610, 102,479, 1,970,358, 2,479,015, 2,811,801, 2,966,850} **37.** set of nonnegative real numbers **39.** domain $\{0 \le x < 18\}$; range $\{0 \le y \le 6\}$ **41.** $\frac{1}{36}$ **43.** 0.25 **45.** $\approx$ 73 ft; **See below.** **47.** $\tan 18° \approx 0.325$ **49.** No **51.** Yes

53.

t	-5	-4	-3	-2	-1	0	1	2	3	4	5
$g(t)$	15	6	-1	-6	-9	-10	-9	-6	-1	6	15

; See below.

55.

n	-5	-4	-3	-2	-1	0	1	2	3	4	5
$f(n)$	$\frac{1}{32}$	$\frac{1}{16}$	$\frac{1}{8}$	$\frac{1}{4}$	$\frac{1}{2}$	1	2	4	8	16	32

; **See below.** **57.** **See below.**

53. **55.** **57.**

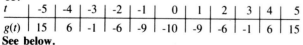

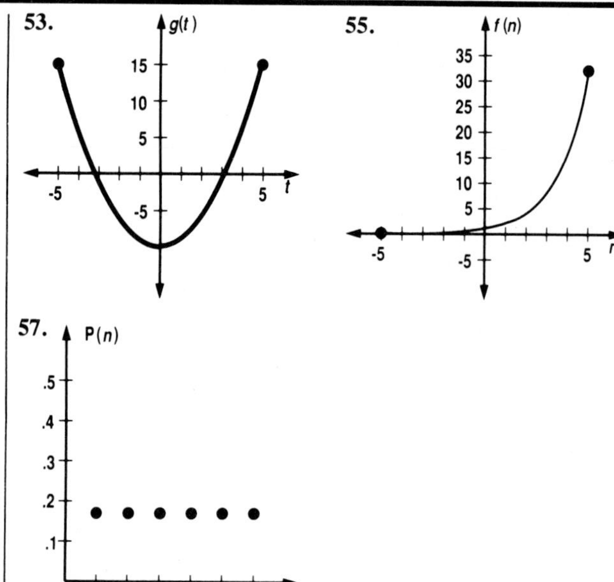

Table of Symbols

Symbol	Meaning
$=$	is equal to
$\neq$	is not equal to
$<$	is less than
$\leq$	is less than or equal to
$\approx$	is approximately equal to
$>$	is greater than
$\geq$	is greater than or equal to
$\pm$	plus or minus
$\{\ldots\}$	the symbol used for a set
$\emptyset$, $\{\ \}$	the empty or null set
$A \cap B$	the intersection of sets A and B
$A \cup B$	the union of sets A and B
W	the set of whole numbers
I	the set of integers
R	the set of real numbers
⌐	symbol for 90° angle
%	percent
$\sqrt{\ }$	square root symbol; radical sign
$\lvert x \rvert$	the absolute value of x
N(E)	the number of elements in set E
P(E)	the probability of an event E
P(A and B)	the probability that A and B occur
P(B given A)	the probability that B occurs given A
$n!$	n factorial
$f(x)$	function notation "f of x"; the second coordinates of the points of a function
tan A	tangent of $\angle A$
sin A	sine of $\angle A$
cos A	cosine of $\angle A$
[%]	calculator percent key
[1/x]	calculator reciprocal key
[y^x]	calculator key for powering
[x^2]	calculator squaring function key
[$\sqrt{\ }$]	calculator square root function key
[x!]	calculator factorial function key
[tan]	calculator tangent function key
[INV] [tan]	calculator inverse tangent keys
[sin]	calculator sine function key
[cos]	calculator cosine function key
[log]	calculator logarithm function key
ABS (X)	in BASIC, the absolute value of X
SQR (X)	in BASIC, the square root of X
X * X	in BASIC, X • X
X ^ Y	in BASIC, X^Y

absolute value If $n < 0$, then the absolute value of n equals $-n$; if $n \geq 0$, then the absolute value of n is n. The absolute value of a number is its distance from the origin.

absolute value function A function of the form $f(x) = a|x - b| + c$.

adding fractions property For all real numbers a, b, and c, with $c \neq 0$, $\frac{a}{c} + \frac{b}{c} = \frac{a + b}{c}$.

adding like terms property For any real numbers, a, b, and x, $ax + bx = (a + b)x$.

addition method for solving a system The method of adding the sides of two equations to yield a third equation that contains solutions to the system.

addition property of equality For all real numbers a, b, and c: if $a = b$, then $a + c = b + c$.

addition property of inequality For all real numbers a, b, and c: if $a < b$, then $a + c < b + c$.

additive identity The number 0, because if 0 is added to any number, that number keeps its "identity."

additive identity property For any real number a: $a + 0 = a$.

additive inverse The additive inverse of any real number x is $-x$. Also called *opposite*.

algebraic definition of division For any real numbers a and b, $b \neq 0$: $a \div b = a \cdot \frac{1}{b}$.

algebraic expression An expression that includes one or more variables.

and The word used to speak about the intersection of sets. If A and B are sets, $A \cap B$ is read "A and B."

annual yield The percent the money in an account earns per year.

area model (discrete version) The number of elements in a rectangular array with x rows and y columns is xy.

area model for multiplication The area of a rectangle with length ℓ and width w is ℓw.

associative property of addition For any real numbers a, b, and c: $(a + b) + c = a + (b + c)$.

associative property of multiplication For any real numbers a, b, and c: $(ab)c = a(bc)$.

"as the crow flies" The straight line distance between two points.

automatic grapher A graphing calculator or computer graphing program.

axes The perpendicular number lines in a coordinate graph.

axis of symmetry The line over which a graph could be folded to yield two coinciding halves.

base In the power x^n, x is the base.

BASIC A type of computer language standing for Beginner's All-Purpose Symbolic Instruction Code.

bar graph A way of displaying data using different sized rectangles or bars.

binomial A polynomial with two terms.

boundary line A line that separates two regions in a plane.

changing the sense (direction) of an inequality Changing from $<$ to $>$, or from $\leq$ to $\geq$, or vice-versa.

chunking The process of grouping some small bits of information into a single piece of information. In algebra, viewing an entire algebraic expression as one variable.

closed interval An interval that includes its endpoints.

coefficient In the term ax, a is the coefficient of x.

coincident lines The name given to two lines that have the same graph or coincide.

common denominator The same denominator for two or more fractions.

common monomial factoring Isolating the largest common factor from each individual term of a polynomial.

commutative property of addition For any real numbers a and b: $a + b = b + a$.

commutative property of multiplication For any real numbers a and b: $ab = ba$.

comparison model for subtraction The quantity $x - y$ tells how much quantity x differs from the quantity y.

complementary angles Two angles the sum of whose measures is 90°. Also called *complements*.

compound interest A form of interest payment in which the interest is placed back into the account so that it too earns interest.

compound interest formula $T = P(1 + i)^n$, where T is the total after n years if a principal P earns an annual yield of i.

conditional probability The probability that one event occurs given that another event occurs.

conditional probability formula P(A and B) = P(A) • P(B given A).

constant decrease A negative rate of change that is the same between any two points of a line.

constant term A term without a variable in a polynomial; a term in a polynomial that is a number.

continuous A situation in which numbers between any two numbers have meaning.

contraction A size change in which the size change factor k is between -1 and 1 ($k \neq 0$).

coordinate graph A graph displaying points as ordered pairs of numbers.

cosine of an angle in a right triangle (cos *A*) A ratio of sides in a right triangle given by $\cos A = \frac{\text{length of leg adjacent to angle } A}{\text{hypotenuse}}$.

counterexample A special case for which a pattern is false.

default window The window automatically picked by an automatic grapher if a particular window is not chosen.

definition of subtraction For all real numbers a and b: $a - b = a + -b$.

density property Between any two real numbers are many other real numbers.

degree of the polynomial The largest exponent in a polynomial with one variable, the largest sum of exponents in a polynomial with terms containing more than one variable.

difference of squares An expression of the form $x^2 - y^2$.

difference of two squares pattern $(a + b)(a - b) = a^2 - b^2$.

dimensions The number of rows and columns of an array. The lengths of sides of a polygon.

discount The percent by which the original price of an item is lowered.

discrete A situation in which numbers between given numbers do not have meaning.

discriminant In the quadratic equation $ax^2 + bx + c = 0$, $b^2 - 4ac$.

discriminant property Suppose $ax^2 + bx + c = 0$ and a, b, and c are real numbers. Let $D = b^2 - 4ac$. Then when $D > 0$, the equation has exactly two real solutions. When $D = 0$, the equation has exactly one real solution. When $D < 0$, the equation has no real solutions.

distance formula on a number line If two points on a line have coordinates x_1 and x_2, the distance between them is $|x_1 - x_2|$.

distributive property For any real numbers a, b, and c: $ac + bc = (a + b)c$ and $ac - bc = (a - b)c$.

domain The values that may be meaningfully substituted for a variable.

domain of a function The set of possible replacements for the first coordinate in a function.

dot frequency diagram A way of displaying data using dots above a horizontal number line.

element An object that is in a set.

eliminate parentheses To use the Distributive Property to rewrite an expression without parentheses.

empty set A set that has no elements in it.

endpoints The smallest and largest numbers in an interval. The points A and B in the segment $\overline{AB}$.

equal fractions property If $k \neq 0$ and $b \neq 0$: then $\frac{a}{b} = \frac{ak}{bk}$.

equal sets Two sets that have the same elements.

equally-likely outcomes Outcomes in a situation where each outcome is assumed to occur as often as every other outcome.

equation A sentence with an equal sign.

expanding a power of a polynomial Using the Extended Distributive Property to multiply a polynomial by itself. Example: $(5a + 1)^2 = 25a^2 + 10a + 1$ in expanded form.

expansion A size change in which the factor k is greater than 1 or less than -1.

exponent In the power x^n, n is the exponent.

exponential decay A situation in which the original amount is repeatedly multiplied by a growth factor smaller than one.

exponential growth A situation in which the original amount is repeatedly multiplied by a nonzero growth factor.

extended distributive property To multiply two sums, multiply each term in the first sum by each term in the second sum.

extremes The numbers a and d in the proportion $\frac{a}{b} = \frac{c}{d}$.

fitting a line to data Finding a line that closely describes data points which themselves may not all lie on a line.

FOIL algorithm A method for multiplying two binomials; the sum of the product of the First terms, plus the product of the Outside terms, plus the product of the Inside terms, plus the product of the Last terms.
$(a + b)(c + d) = ac + ad + bc + bd$.

formula A sentence in which one variable is given in terms of other variables and numbers.

FOR/NEXT loop A BASIC command that tells the computer the number of times to execute a loop.

function A set of ordered pairs in which each first coordinate appears with exactly one second coordinate.

function key on a calculator A key that produces the value of a function when a value of the domain is entered.

fundamental principle of counting Let A and B be finite sets. Then
$N(A \cup B) = N(A) + N(B) - N(A \cap B)$.

general form of a quadratic equation A quadratic equation in which one side is 0 and the other side is arranged in descending order of exponents: $ax^2 + bx + c = 0$, where a $\neq 0$.

general linear equation An equation of the form $ax + b = cx + d$.

generalized addition property of equality For all numbers or expressions a, b, c, and d: if $a = b$ and $c = d$, then $a + c = b + d$.

growth factor In exponential growth, the nonzero number that is repeatedly multiplied by the original amount.

growth model for powering When an amount is multiplied by g, the growth factor in each of x time periods, then after the x periods, the original amount will be multiplied by g^x.

half-plane In a plane, the region on either side of a line.

horizontal line A line with an equation of the form $y = k$, where k is a fixed real number.

hypotenuse The longest side of a right triangle.

IF . . . THEN A BASIC command that tells the computer to perform the THEN part only if the IF part is true.

image The final position of a figure resulting from a transformation.

inequality A sentence with one of the following signs: "$\neq$", "$<$", "$>$", "$\leq$", "$\geq$", or "$\approx$".

INPUT A BASIC statement that makes the computer pause and wait for you to type in a value.

integers The whole numbers and their opposites.

interest The money the bank pays on the principal in an account.

intersection of sets The set of elements in both set A and set B, written $A \cap B$.

interval The set of numbers between two numbers a and b, possibly including a and b.

irrational number A real number that is not rational. An infinite decimal that is not repeating.

leg of a right triangle One of the sides forming the right angle of a triangle.

LET A BASIC command that assigns a value to a given variable.

like terms Terms in which the variables and corresponding exponents are the same.

linear equation An equation in which the variable or variables are all to the first power and none multiply each other.

linear function A function that has an equation of the form $y = mx + b$.

linear inequality A linear sentence with an inequality symbol.

linear sentence A sentence in which the variable or variables are all to the first power and none multiply each other.

magnitude of the size change The size change factor.

markup A percent by which the original price of an item is raised.

mean The average of a set of numbers.

means The numbers b and c in the proportion $\frac{a}{b} = \frac{c}{d}$.

means-extremes property For all real numbers a, b, c, and d (b and d nonzero): if $\frac{a}{b} = \frac{c}{d}$, then $ad = bc$.

median The middle value of a set of numbers written in increasing order.

mode The most frequently occurring value in an ordered set of numbers.

monomial A polynomial with one term.

multiplication counting principle If one choice can be made in m ways and a second choice can be made in n ways, then there are mn ways of making the choices in order.

multiplication method for solving a system Multiplying both sides of an equation in a system by a number so that the addition method can be used on the result.

multiplication property of -1 For any real number a: $a \cdot -1 = -1 \cdot a = -a$.

multiplication property of equality For all real numbers a, b, and c: if $a = b$, then $ca = cb$.

multiplication property of inequality If $x < y$ and a is positive, then $ax < ay$. If $x < y$ and a is negative, then $ax > ay$.

multiplication property of zero For any real number a: $a \cdot 0 = 0 \cdot a = 0$.

multiplicative identity The number 1, because if any number is multiplied by 1, that number keeps its "identity."

multiplicative identity property of one For any real number a: $a \cdot 1 = 1 \cdot a = a$.

multiplicative inverse The multiplicative inverse of a number n is $\frac{1}{n}$, where $n \neq 0$. Also called *reciprocal*.

n factorial The product of the integers from 1 to n. In symbols, $n!$

negative exponent property For any nonzero b, $b^{-n} = \frac{1}{b^n}$, the reciprocal of b^n.

nth power The nth power of a number x is the number x^n.

null set A set that has no elements in it. Also called *empty set*.

numerical expression An expression that includes only numbers.

op-op property For any real number a: $-(-a) = a$.

open interval An interval that does not include its endpoints.

open sentence A sentence that contains at least one variable.

opposite The opposite of any real number x is $-x$. Also called *additive inverse*.

or The word used to speak about the union of sets. If A and B are sets, $A \cup B$ is read "A or B."

order of operations The correct order of evaluating numerical expressions: first do operations within parentheses or other grouping symbols; within grouping symbols or if there are no grouping symbols—do all powers from left to right, do all multiplications and divisions from left to right, do all additions and subtractions from left to right.

origin The point (0, 0) on a coordinate plane.

outcome A result of an experiment, such as the result of the toss of a die.

parabola A graph whose equation is of the form $y = ax^2 + bx + c$, where $a \neq 0$.

P(E) The probability of E, or "P of E." The letter E names an event and P(E) names the probability of that event.

percent %, times $\frac{1}{100}$, or "per 100".

percent of discount The ratio of the discount to the selling price.

perfect square A number that is the square of a whole number.

perfect square trinomial A trinomial that is the square of a binomial.

perfect square trinomial patterns $(a + b)^2 = a^2 + 2ab + b^2$ and $(a - b)^2 = a^2 - 2ab + b^2$.

permutation An arrangement of letters, names, or objects.

permutation theorem There are $n!$ possible permutations of n different objects, when each object is used exactly once.

polynomial An algebraic expression formed by adding, subtracting, or multiplying numbers and variables.

polynomial in the variable x A polynomial whose only variable is x.

power of a power property When $b \geq 0$, for all m and n: $(b^m)^n = b^{mn}$.

power of a product property For all a and b, and any integer n: $(ab)^n = a^n \cdot b^n$.

power of a quotient property For all a and nonzero b, and any integer n: $\left(\frac{a}{b}\right)^n = \frac{a^n}{b^n}$.

preimage The original position of a figure before a transformation takes place.

principal Money deposited in an account.

PRINT A BASIC command that tells the computer to print what follows the command.

probability formula for geometric regions If all points occur randomly in a region, then the probability P of an event is given by P = $\frac{\text{measure (area, length, etc.) of region for event}}{\text{measure of entire region}}$.

probability function A function whose domain is a set of outcomes in a situation and in which each ordered pair contains an outcome and its probability.

probability of success The ratio $\frac{S}{T}$, where S is the number of outcomes that are successes and T is the total number of outcomes.

probability of a union of events $P(A \cup B) = P(A) + P(B) - P(A \cap B)$.

product of powers property When b^m and b^n are defined: $b^m \cdot b^n = b^{m+n}$.

property of opposites For any real number a: $a + -a = 0$.

property of reciprocals For any nonzero real number a: $a \cdot \frac{1}{a} = \frac{1}{a} \cdot a = 1$.

proportion A statement that two fractions are equal. Any equation of the form $\frac{a}{b} = \frac{c}{d}$.

putting-together model for addition A quantity x is put together with a quantity y with the same units. If there is no overlap, then the result is the quantity $x + y$.

Pythagorean distance formula The distance AB between points $A = (x_1, y_1)$ and $B = (x_2, y_2)$ is $AB = \sqrt{(x_2 - x_1)^2 + (y_2 - y_1)^2}$.

Pythagorean theorem In a right triangle with legs a and b and hypotenuse c, $a^2 + b^2 = c^2$.

quadrant One of four parts of the coordinate plane resulting from dividing it by the x-axis and y-axis.

quadratic equation An equation that can be simplified into the form $ax^2 + bx + c = 0$.

quadratic formula If $ax^2 + bx + c = 0$ and $a \neq 0$, then $x = \frac{-b \pm \sqrt{b^2 - 4ac}}{2a}$.

quadratic function A function with an equation of the form $y = ax^2 + bx + c$ or $y = \frac{k}{x}$.

quantity (in parentheses) An expression in parentheses.

quotient of powers property If b^m and b^n are defined and $b \neq 0$: $\frac{b^m}{b^n} = b^{m-n}$.

random outcomes Outcomes in a situation where each outcome is assumed to have the same probability.

range The length of an interval. Range = maximum value − minimum value.

range of a function The set of possible values of a function.

rate factor model for multiplication When a rate is multiplied by another quantity, the unit of the product is the product of units. Units are multiplied as though they were fractions. The product has meaning when the units have meaning.

rate of change The rate of change between points (x_1, y_1) and (x_2, y_2) is $\frac{y_2 - y_1}{x_2 - x_1}$.

rate model for division If a and b are quantities with different units, then $\frac{a}{b}$ is the amount of quantity a per quantity b.

ratio A quotient of quantities with the same units.

ratio model for division Let a and b be quantities with the same units. Then the ratio $\frac{a}{b}$ compares a to b.

ratio of similitude The ratio of corresponding sides for two similar figures.

rational number A number that can be written as the ratio of two integers.

real numbers Numbers that can be represented as finite or infinite decimals.

reciprocal The reciprocal of a number n is $\frac{1}{n}$, where $n \neq 0$. Also called *multiplicative inverse*.

reciprocal rates Equal rates in which the quantities are compared in reverse order.

rectangular array A two-dimensional display of numbers or symbols arranged in rows and columns.

rectangular solid A box.

relation Any set of ordered pairs.

relative frequency The ratio of the number of times an event occurred to the total number of possible occurrences.

REM A BASIC statement for a remark or explanation that will be ignored by the computer.

replacement set The values that may be meaningfully substituted in a formula.

rule for multiplication of fractions For all real numbers a, b, c, and d, with b and d not zero: $\frac{a}{b} \cdot \frac{c}{d} = \frac{ac}{bd}$.

ruling out possibilities Arriving at the right answer by eliminating wrong ones.

scale factor The amount by which interest changes in a polynomial expression.

scattergram A two-dimensional coordinate graph that shows data.

sentence Two algebraic expressions connected by "=", "≠", "<", ">", "≤", "≥", or "≈".

set A collection of objects called elements.

similar figures Two or more figures that have the same shape.

simplifying radicals Rewriting a radical with a smaller integer under the radical sign.

sine of an angle in a right triangle (sin *A*) In a right triangle, $\sin A = \frac{\text{length of the leg opposite angle } A}{\text{hypotenuse}}$.

size change factor A number that multiplies other numbers to change their size.

size change model for multiplication If a quantity x is multiplied by a size change factor k, $k \neq 0$, then the resulting quantity is kx.

slide model for addition If a slide x is followed by a slide y, the result is the slide $x + y$.

slope The name for the constant rate of change between points on a line. The amount of change in the height of the line as you go 1 unit to the right. The slope of the line through (x_1, y_1) and (x_2, y_2) is $\frac{y_2 - y_1}{x_2 - x_1}$.

slope-intercept form An equation of a line in the form $y = mx + b$, where m is the slope and b is the y-intercept.

slope-intercept property The line with equation $y = mx + b$ has slope m and y-intercept b.

solution A replacement of the variable in a sentence that makes the statement true.

solution set The set of numbers that are solutions to a given open sentence.

solution set to a system The intersection of the solution sets for each of the conditions in the system.

square root If $A = s^2$, then s is the square root of A.

square root of a product property If $a \geq 0$ and $b \geq 0$, then $\sqrt{ab} = \sqrt{a} \cdot \sqrt{b}$.

stacked bar graph A way of displaying data using different sized rectangles or bars stacked on top of each other.

standard form for an equation of a line An equation of the form $Ax + By = C$.

standard form of a quadratic equation An equation of the form $ax^2 + bx + c = 0$, where $a \neq 0$.

statistics Numbers that represent sets of data.

substitution method for solving a system A method in which one variable is written in terms of other variables, and then this expression is used in place of the original variable in subsequent equations.

supplementary angles Two angles, the sum of whose measures is 180°. Also called *supplements.*

system A set of conditions separated by the word *and.*

system of inequalities A system in which the conditions are inequalities.

take-away model for subtraction If a quantity y is taken away from an original quantity x, the quantity left is $x - y$.

tangent function A function defined by $y = \tan x$.

tangent of an angle *A* in a right triangle (tan *A*) A ratio of sides given by $\tan A = \frac{\text{length of leg opposite angle } A}{\text{length of leg adjacent to angle } A}$.

term A single number or a product of numbers and variables.

testing a special case A strategy for finding a pattern by trying out a specific instance.

tree-diagram A tree-like way of organizing the possibilities of choices in a situation.

triangle inequality The sum of the lengths of two sides of any triangle is greater than the length of the third side.

triangle-sum In any triangle with angle measures a, b, and c: $a + b + c = 180$.

trinomial A polynomial with three terms.

two-dimensional slide A movement that can be broken into a horizontal and a vertical slide. A transformation in which the image of (x, y) is $(x + h, y + k)$.

union of sets The set of elements in either set A or set B, written $A \cup B$.

value of function A value of the second variable (often called y) in a function.

variable A letter or other symbol that can be replaced by any numbers (or other objects).

Venn diagram A diagram used to show relationships among sets.

vertex The intersection of a parabola with its axis of symmetry.

vertical line A line with an equation of the form $x = h$, where h is a fixed real number.

weighted average $W_1x_1 + W_2x_2 + \ldots + W_nx_n$, where n quantities $x_1, x_2, \ldots, x_n$ having weights $W_1, W_2, \ldots, W_n$ with $W_1 + W_2 + \ldots + W_n = 1$.

weights The parts or percents of the total accounted for by each amount.

whole numbers The set of numbers $\{0, 1, 2, 3, \ldots\}$.

window The part of the coordinate grid that is shown on an automatic grapher.

x-axis The horizontal axis in a coordinate graph.

x-coordinate The first coordinate of a point.

x-intercept The x-coordinate of a point where a graph crosses the x-axis.

y-axis The vertical axis in a coordinate graph.

y-coordinate The second coordinate of a point.

y-intercept The y-coordinate of a point where a graph crosses the y-axis.

zero exponent property If g is any nonzero real number, then $g^0 = 1$.

zero product property For any real numbers a and b, if the product of a and b is 0, then $a = 0$ or $b = 0$.

zoom feature A feature on an automatic grapher by which a window can be changed without retyping the intervals for x and y.

Professional Sourcebook For UCSMP

1 Overview of UCSMP

The Reasons for UCSMP

Recommendations for Change

The mathematics curriculum has undergone changes in every country of the world throughout this century, as a result of an increasing number of students staying in school longer, a greater number of technically competent workers and citizens being needed, and because of major advances in mathematics itself. In the last generation, these developments have been accelerated due to the widespread appearance of computers with their unprecedented abilities to handle and display information.

In the last 100 years, periodically there have been national groups examining the curriculum in light of these changes in society. (A study of these reports can be found in *A History of Mathematics Education in the United States and Canada,* the 30th Yearbook of the National Council of Teachers of Mathematics, 1970.) The most recent era of reports can be said to have begun in the years 1975–1980, with the publication of reports by various national mathematics organizations calling attention to serious problems in the education of our youth.

Beginning in 1980, these reports were joined by governmental and private reports on the state of American education with broad recommendations for school practice. Two of these are notable for their specific remarks about mathematics education.

1983: National Commission on Excellence in Education.
A Nation At Risk.

"The teaching of mathematics in high school should equip graduates to: (a) understand geometric and algebraic concepts; (b) understand elementary probability and statistics; (c) apply mathematics in everyday situations; and (d) estimate, approximate, measure, and test the accuracy of their calculations. In addition to the traditional sequence of studies available for college-bound students, new, equally demanding mathematics curricula need to be developed for those who do not plan to continue their formal education immediately." (p. 25)

1983: College Board (Project EQuality).
Academic Preparation for College: What Students Need to Know and Be Able to Do.

All students (college-bound or not) should have:
"The ability to apply mathematical techniques in the solution of real-life problems and to recognize when to apply those techniques.
Familiarity with the language, notation, and deductive nature of mathematics and the ability to express quantitative ideas with precision.
The ability to use computers and calculators.
Familiarity with the basic concepts of statistics and statistical reasoning.
Knowledge in considerable depth and detail of algebra, geometry, and functions." (p. 20)

The specific remarks about school mathematics in these documents for the most part mirror what appeared in the earlier reports. Thus, **given what seemed to be a broad consensus on the problems and desirable changes in precollege mathematics instruction, it was decided at the outset of UCSMP, that UCSMP would not attempt to form its own set of recommendations, but undertake the task of translating the existing recommendations into the reality of classrooms and schools.**

At the secondary (7–12) level, these reports respond to two generally perceived problems pursuant to mathematics education.

GENERAL PROBLEM 1: Students do not learn enough mathematics by the time they leave school.

Specifically:

(A) Many students lack the mathematics background necessary to succeed in college, on the job, or in daily affairs.

(B) Even those students who possess mathematical skills are not introduced to enough applications of the mathematics they know.

(C) Students do not get enough experience with problems and questions that require some thought before answering.

(D) Many students terminate their study of mathematics too soon, not realizing the importance mathematics has in later schooling and in the marketplace.

(E) Students do not read mathematics books and, as a result, do not learn to become independent learners capable of acquiring mathematics outside of school when the need arises.

These situations lead us to want to **upgrade students' achievement.**

GENERAL PROBLEM 2: The school mathematics curriculum has not kept up with changes in mathematics and the ways in which mathematics is used.

The UCSMP grades 7–12 can be considered to be the first mathematical sciences curriculum.

Specifically:

(A) Current mathematics curricula have not taken into account today's calculator and computer technology.

(B) Students who do succeed in secondary school mathematics are prepared for calculus, but are not equipped for the other mathematics they will encounter in college.

(C) Statistical ideas are found everywhere, from newspapers to research studies, but are not found in most secondary school mathematics curricula.

(D) The emergence of computer science has increased the importance of a background in discrete mathematics.

(E) Mathematics is now applied to areas outside the realm of the physical sciences, as much as within the field itself, but these applications are rarely taught and even more rarely tested.

(F) Estimation and approximation techniques are important in all of mathematics, from arithmetic on.

These existing situations lead us to a desire to **update the mathematics curriculum.**

Since the inception of UCSMP, reports from national groups of mathematics educators have reiterated the above problems, and research has confirmed their existence. Three reports are of special significance to UCSMP.

Universities have for many years had to recognize that mathematics encompasses far more than algebra, geometry, and analysis. The term **mathematical sciences** is an umbrella designation which includes traditional mathematics as well as a number of other disciplines. The largest of these other disciplines today are statistics, computer science, and applied mathematics. In 1983, the Conference Board of the Mathematical Sciences produced a report, *The Mathematical Sciences Curriculum: What Is Still Fundamental and What Is Not.* THE UCSMP GRADES 7–12 CAN BE CONSIDERED TO BE THE FIRST MATHEMATICAL SCIENCES CURRICULUM.

The Second International Mathematics Study (SIMS) was conducted in 1981–82 and involved 23 populations in 21 countries. At the eighth-grade level, virtually all students attend school in all those countries. At the 12th-grade level, the population tested consisted of those who are in the normal college preparatory courses, which, in the United States, include precalculus and calculus classes.

At the eighth-grade level, our students scored at or below the international average on all five subtests: arithmetic, measurement, algebra, geometry, and statistics. We are far below the top: Japan looked at the test and decided it was too easy for their 8th-graders, and so gave it at 7th grade. Still, the median Japanese 7th-grader performed at the 95th percentile of United States 8th-graders. These kinds of results have been confirmed in other studies, comparing students at lower-grade levels.

At the twelfth-grade level, about 13% of our population is enrolled in precalculus or calculus; the mean among developed countries is about 16%. Thus, the United States no longer keeps more students in mathematics than other developed countries, yet our advanced placement students do not perform well when compared to their peers in other countries. SIMS found:

1987: Second International Mathematics Study (SIMS). *The Underachieving Curriculum.*

In the U.S., the achievement of the Calculus classes, the nation's **best** mathematics students, was at or near the average achievement of the advanced secondary school mathematics students in other countries. (In most countries, **all** advanced mathematics students take calculus. In the U.S., only about one-fifth do.) The achievement of the U.S. Precalculus students (the majority of twelfth grade college-preparatory students) was substantially below the international average. In some cases the U.S. ranked with the lower one-fourth of all countries in the Study, and was the lowest of the advanced industrialized countries. (*The Underachieving Curriculum, p. vii.*)

The situation is, of course, even worse for those who do not take precalculus mathematics in high school. Such students either have performed poorly in their last mathematics course, a situation which has caused them not to go on in mathematics, or they were performing poorly in junior high school and had to take remedial mathematics as 9th-graders. If these students go to college, they invariably take remedial mathematics, which is taught at a faster pace than in high school, and the failure rates in such courses often exceed 40%. If they do not go to college but join the job market, they lack the mathematics needed to understand today's technology. IT IS NO UNDERSTATEMENT TO SAY THAT UCSMP HAS RECEIVED ITS FUNDING FROM BUSINESS AND INDUSTRY BECAUSE THOSE WHO LEAVE SCHOOLING TO JOIN THE WORK FORCE ARE WOEFULLY WEAK IN THE MATHEMATICS THEY WILL NEED.

SIMS recommended steps to renew school mathematics in the United States. **The UCSMP secondary curriculum implements the curriculum recommendations of the Second International Mathematics Study.**

In 1986, the National Council of Teachers of Mathematics began an ambitious effort to detail the curriculum it would like to see in schools. The "NCTM Standards," as they have come to be called, involve both content and methodology. The *Standards* document is divided into four sections, K–4, 5–8, 9–12, and Evaluation. Space limits our discussion here to just a few quotes from the 5–8 and 9–12 standards.

It is no understatement to say that UCSMP has received its funding from business and industry because those who leave schooling to join the work force are woefully weak in the mathematics they will need.

1989: National Council of Teachers of Mathematics. *Curriculum and Evaluation Standards for School Mathematics*

"The 5-8 curriculum should include the following features:

- Problem situations that establish the need for new ideas and motivate students should serve as the context for mathematics in grades 5-8. Although a specific idea might be forgotten, the context in which it is learned can be remembered and the idea can be re-created. In developing the problem situations, teachers should emphasize the application to real-world problems as well as to other settings relevant to middle school students.
- Communication with and about mathematics and mathematical reasoning should permeate the 5-8 curriculum.
- A broad range of topics should be taught, including number concepts, computation, estimation, functions, algebra, statistics, probability, geometry, and measurement. Although each of these areas is valid mathematics in its own right, they should be taught together as an integrated whole, not as isolated topics; the connections between them should be a prominent feature of the curriculum.
- Technology, including calculators, computers, and videos, should be used when appropriate. These devices and formats free students from tedious computations and allow them to concentrate on problem solving and other important content. They also give them new means to explore content. As paper-and-pencil computation becomes less important, the skills and understanding required to make proficient use of calculators and computers become more important." (pp. 66-67)

"The standards for grades 9-12 are based on the following assumptions:

- Students entering grade 9 will have experienced mathematics in the context of the broad, rich curriculum as outlined in the K-8 standards.
- The level of [paper-and-pencil] computational proficiency suggested in the K-8 standards will be expected of all students; however, no student will be denied access to the study of mathematics in grades 9-12 because of a lack of computational facility.
- Although arithmetic computation will not be a direct object of study in grades 9-12, conceptual and procedural understandings of number, numeration, and operations, and the ability to make estimations and approximations and to judge the reasonableness of results will be strengthened in the context of applications and problem solving, including those situations dealing with issues of scientific computation.
- Scientific calculators with graphing capabilities will be available to all students at all times.
- A computer will be available at all times in every classroom for demonstration purposes, and all students will have access to computers for individual and group work.
- At least three years of mathematical study will be required of all secondary school students.
- These three years of mathematical study will revolve around a core curriculum differentiated by the depth and breadth of the treatment of topics and by the nature of applications.
- Four years of mathematical study will be required of all college-intending students.
- These four years of mathematical study will revolve around a broadened curriculum that includes extensions of the core topics and for which calculus is no longer viewed as *the* capstone experience.
- All students will study appropriate mathematics during their senior year." (pp. 124-125)

THE UCSMP SECONDARY CURRICULUM IS THE FIRST FULL MATHEMATICS CURRICULUM THAT IS CONSISTENT WITH THE RECOMMENDATIONS OF THE NCTM STANDARDS.

The UCSMP secondary curriculum is the first full mathematics curriculum that is consistent with the recommendations of the NCTM Standards.

Accomplishing the Goals

We at UCSMP believe that the goals of the various reform groups since 1975 can be accomplished, but not without a substantial reworking of the curriculum. It is not enough simply to insert applications, a bit of statistics, and take students a few times a year to a computer. Currently the greatest amount of time in arithmetic is spent on calculation, in algebra on manipulating polynomials and rational expressions, in geometry on proof, in advanced algebra and later courses on functions. These topics—the core of the curriculum—are the most affected by technology.

It is also not enough to raise graduation requirements, although that is the simplest action to take. Increases in requirements characteristically lead to one of two situations. If the courses are kept the same, the result is typically a greater number of failures and even a greater number of dropouts. If the courses are eased, the result is lower performance for many students as they are brought through a weakened curriculum.

The fundamental problem, as SIMS noted, is the curriculum, and the fundamental problem in the curriculum is **time.** There is not enough time in the current 4-year algebra-geometry-algebra-precalculus curriculum to prepare students for calculus, and the recommendations are asking students to learn even more content.

Fortunately, there is time to be had, because the existing curriculum wastes time. It underestimates what students know when they enter the classroom and needlessly reviews what students have already learned. This needless review has been documented by Jim Flanders, a UCSMP staff member (''How Much of the Content in Mathematics Textbooks is New?'' *Arithmetic Teacher,* September, 1987). Examining textbooks of the early 1980s, Flanders reports that at grade 2 there is little new. In grades 3–5, about half the pages have something new on them. But over half the pages in grades 6–8 are totally review.

And then in the 9th grade the axe falls. Flanders found that almost 90% of the pages of first-year algebra texts have content new to the student. The student, having sat for years in mathematics classes where little was new, is overwhelmed. Some people interpret the overwhelming as the student ''not being ready'' for algebra, but we interpret it as the student being swamped by the pace. When you have been in a classroom in which at most only 1 of 3 days is devoted to anything new, you are not ready for a new idea every day.

This amount of review in grades K–8, coupled with the magnitude of review in previous years, effectively decelerates students at least 1–2 years compared to students in other countries. It explains why almost all industrialized countries of the world, except the U.S. and Canada (and some French-speaking countries who do geometry before algebra), can begin concentrated study of algebra in the 7th or 8th grade.

Thus we believe that ALGEBRA SHOULD BE TAUGHT ONE YEAR EARLIER TO MOST STUDENTS THAN IS CURRENTLY THE CASE.

However, we do not believe students should take calculus one year earlier than they do presently. It seems that most students who take four years of college preparatory mathematics successfully in high schools do not begin college with calculus. As an example, consider the data reported by Bert Waits and Frank Demana in the *Mathematics Teacher* (January, 1988). Of students entering Ohio State University with exactly four years of college preparatory high-school mathematics, only 8% placed into calculus on the Ohio State mathematics placement test. The majority placed into precalculus, with 31% requiring one semester and 42% requiring two semesters of work. The remaining 19% placed into remedial courses below precalculus.

Those students who take algebra in the 8th grade and are successful in calculus at the 12th grade are given quite a bit more than the normal four years of college preparatory mathematics in their ''honors'' or ''advanced'' courses. It is not stretching the point too much to say that they take five years of mathematics crammed into four years.

Thus, even with the current curriculum, four years are not enough to take a typical student from algebra to calculus. Given that the latest recommendations ask for students to learn more mathematics, **we believe five years of college preparatory mathematics *beginning with algebra* are necessary to provide the time for students to learn the mathematics they need for college in the 1990s.** The UCSMP secondary curriculum is designed with that in mind.

. . . algebra should be taught one year earlier to most students than is currently the case.

The UCSMP Secondary Curriculum

The UCSMP curriculum for grades 7–12 consists of these six courses:

Transition Mathematics

Algebra

Geometry

Advanced Algebra

Functions, Statistics, and Trigonometry with Computers

Precalculus and Discrete Mathematics

EACH COURSE IS MEANT TO STAND ALONE. Each course has also been tested alone. HOWEVER, TO TAKE BEST ADVANTAGE OF THESE MATERIALS, AND TO HAVE THEM APPROPRIATE FOR THE GREATEST NUMBER OF STUDENTS, IT IS PREFERABLE TO USE THEM IN SEQUENCE.

Each course is meant to stand alone. . . . However, to take best advantage of these materials, and to have them appropriate for the greatest number of students, it is preferable to use them in sequence.

Content Features

Transition Mathematics: This text weaves three themes—applied arithmetic, pre-algebra and pre-geometry—by focusing on arithmetic operations in mathematics and the real world. Variables are used as pattern generalizers, abbreviations in formulas, and unknowns in problems, and are represented on the number line and graphed in the coordinate plane. Basic arithmetic and algebraic skills are connected to corresponding geometry topics.

Algebra: This text has a scope far wider than most other algebra texts. It uses statistics and geometry as settings for work with linear expressions and sentences. Probability provides a context for algebraic fractions, functions, and set ideas. There is much work with graphing. Applications motivate all topics, and include exponential growth and compound interest.

Geometry: This text presents coordinates, transformations, measurement formulas, and three-dimensional figures in the first half of the book. Concentrated work with proof-writing is delayed until midyear and later, following a carefully sequenced development of the logical and conceptual precursors to proof.

Advanced Algebra: This course emphasizes facility with algebraic expressions and forms, especially linear and quadratic forms, powers and roots, and functions based on these concepts. Students study logarithmic, trigonometric, polynomial, and other special functions both for their abstract properties and as tools for modeling real-world situations. A geometry course or its equivalent is a prerequisite, for geometric ideas are utilized throughout.

Functions, Statistics, and Trigonometry with Computers (FST): FST integrates statistical and algebraic concepts, and previews calculus in work with functions and intuitive notions of limits. Computers are assumed available for student use in plotting functions, analyzing data, and simulating experiments. Enough trigonometry is available to constitute a standard precalculus course in trigonometry and circular functions.

Precalculus and Discrete Mathematics (PDM): PDM integrates the background students must have, to be successful in calculus, with the discrete mathematics helpful for computer study. The study of number systems, three-dimensional coordinate geometry, and some linear algebra is also included. Mathematical thinking, including specific attention to formal logic and proof, is a theme throughout.

General Features

Wider Scope: Geometry and discrete mathematics are present in all courses. Substantial amounts of statistics are integrated into the study of algebra and functions. The history of concepts and recent developments in mathematics and its applications are included as part of the lessons themselves.

Reality Orientation: Each mathematical idea is studied in detail for its applications to the understanding of real-world situations, or the solving of problems like those found in the real world. The reality orientation extends also to the approaches allowed the student in working out problems. Students are expected to use scientific calculators. Calculators are assumed throughout the series (and should be allowed on tests), because virtually all individuals who use mathematics today use calculators.

Problem Solving: Like skills, problem solving must be practiced. When practiced, problem solving becomes far less difficult. All lessons contain a variety of questions so that students do not blindly copy one question to do the next. Explorations are a feature of the first four years, and Projects are offered in the last two years. Some problem-solving techniques are so important that at times they (rather than the problems) are the focus of instruction.

Enhancing Performance: Each book's format is designed to maximize the acquisition of both skills and concepts, with lessons meant to take one day to cover. Within each lesson there is review of material from previous lessons from that chapter or from previous chapters. This gives the student more time to learn the material. The lessons themselves are sequenced into carefully constructed chapters. Progress Self-Test and Chapter Review questions, keyed to objectives in all the dimensions of understanding, are then used to solidify performance of skills and concepts from the chapter, so that they may be applied later with confidence. (See pages T35–T36 for more detail.)

Reading: Reading is emphasized throughout. Students can read; they must learn to read mathematics in order to become able to use mathematics outside of school. Every lesson has reading and contains questions covering that reading. (See page T37 for more detail.)

Understanding: Four dimensions of understanding are emphasized: skill in carrying out various algorithms; developing and using mathematical properties and relationships; applying mathematics in realistic situations; and representing or picturing mathematical concepts. We call this the SPUR approach: **S**kills, **P**roperties, **U**ses, **R**epresentations. On occasion, a fifth dimension of understanding, the historical dimension, is discussed. (See pages T38–T39 for more detail.)

Technology: Scientific calculators are recommended because they use an order of operations closer to that found in algebra and have numerous keys that are helpful in understanding concepts at this level. Work with computers is carefully sequenced within each year and between the years, with gradual gain in sophistication until FST, where computers are an essential element. In all courses, integrated computer exercises show how the computer can be used as a helpful tool in doing mathematics. Students are expected to run and modify programs, but are not taught programming. (See pages T40–T43 for more detail.)

Target Populations

We believe that all high-school graduates should take courses through *Advanced Algebra,* that all students planning to go to college should take courses through *Functions, Statistics, and Trigonometry with Computers*, and that students planning majors in technical areas should take all six UCSMP courses.

The fundamental principle in placing students into the first of these courses is that entry should not be based on age, but on mathematical knowledge. Our studies indicate that about 10% of students nationally are ready for *Transition Mathematics* at 6th grade, about another 40% at 7th grade, another 20% at 8th grade, and another 10–15% at 9th grade. We caution that these percentages are national, not local percentages, and the variability in our nation is enormous. We have tested the materials in school districts where few students are at grade level, where *Transition Mathematics* is appropriate for no more than the upper half of 8th-graders. We have tested also in school districts where as many as 90% of the students have successfully used *Transition Mathematics* in 7th grade.

However, the percentages are not automatic. Students who do not reach 7th-grade competence until the 9th-grade level often do not possess the study habits necessary for successful completion of these courses. At the 9th-grade level, *Transition Mathematics* has been substituted successfully either for a traditional pre-algebra course or for the first year of an algebra course spread out over two years. It does not work as a substitute for a general mathematics course in which there is no expectation that students will take algebra the following year.

On page T27 is a description of this curriculum and the populations for which it is intended. The percentiles are national percentiles on a 7th-grade standardized mathematics test using 7th-grade norms, and apply to students entering the program with *Transition Mathematics*. Some school districts have felt that students should also be reading at least at a 7th-grade reading level as well. See page T28 for advice when starting with a later course.

Top 10%: The top 10% nationally reach the 7th-grade level of competence a year early. They are ready for *Transition Mathematics* in 6th grade and take it then. They proceed through the entire curriculum by 11th grade and can take calculus in 12th grade. We recommend that these students be expected to do the Extensions suggested in this Teacher's Edition. Teachers may also wish to enrich courses for these students further with problems from mathematics contests.

50th–90th percentile: These students should be expected to take mathematics at least through the 11th grade, by which time they will have the mathematics needed for all college majors except those in the hard sciences and engineering. For that they need 12th-grade mathematics.

30th–70th percentile: These students begin *Transition Mathematics* one year later, in 8th grade. The college-bound student in this curriculum is more likely to take four years of mathematics because the last course is hands-on with computers and provides the kind of mathematics needed for any major.

15th–50th percentile: Students who do not reach the 7th-grade level in mathematics until 9th grade or later should not be tracked into courses that put them further behind. Rather, they should be put into this curriculum and counseled on study skills. The logic is simple: mathematics is too important to be ignored. If one is behind in one's mathematical knowledge, the need is to work more at it, not less.

Even if a student begins with *Transition Mathematics* at 9th grade, that student can finish *Advanced Algebra* by the time of graduation from high school. That would be enough mathematics to enable the student to get into most colleges.

UCSMP Target Populations in Grades 7–12

Each course is meant to stand alone. However, to take best advantage of these materials, and have them appropriate for the greatest number of students, it is preferable to use them in sequence. Although it is suggested that students begin with *Transition Mathematics,* students may enter the UCSMP curriculum at any point. Below is a brief description of the UCSMP curriculum and the populations for which it is intended.

The top 10% of students are ready for *Transition Mathematics* at 6th grade. These students can proceed through the entire curriculum by 11th grade and take calculus in the 12th grade.

Students in the 50th–90th percentile on a 7th-grade standardized mathematics test should be ready to take *Transition Mathematics* in 7th grade.

Students who do not reach the 7th-grade level in mathematics until the 8th grade **(in the 30th–70th percentile)** begin *Transition Mathematics* in 8th grade.

Students who don't reach the 7th-grade level in mathematics until the 9th grade **(in the 15th–50th percentile)** begin *Transition Mathematics* in the 9th grade.

Grade	Top 10%	50th–90th percentile	30th–70th percentile	15th–50th percentile
6	Transition Mathematics			
7	Algebra	Transition Mathematics		
8	Geometry	Algebra	Transition Mathematics	
9	Advanced Algebra	Geometry	Algebra	Transition Mathematics
10	Functions, Statistics, and Trigonometry with Computers	Advanced Algebra	Geometry	Algebra
11	Precalculus and Discrete Mathematics	Functions, Statistics, and Trigonometry with Computers	Advanced Algebra	Geometry
12	Calculus (Not part of UCSMP)	Precalculus and Discrete Mathematics	Functions, Statistics, and Trigonometry with Computers	Advanced Algebra

Starting in the Middle of the Series

From the beginning, every UCSMP course has been designed so that it could be used independently of other UCSMP courses. Accordingly, about half of the testing of UCSMP courses after *Transition Mathematics* has been with students who have not had any previous UCSMP courses. We have verified that any of the UCSMP courses can be taken successfully following the typical prerequisite courses in the standard curriculum.

ALGEBRA:
No additional prerequisites other than those needed for success in any algebra course are needed for success in UCSMP *Algebra*. Students who have studied *Transition Mathematics* tend to cover more of UCSMP *Algebra* than other students because they tend to know more algebra, because they are accustomed to the style of the book, and because they have been introduced to more of the applications of algebra.

UCSMP *Algebra* prepares students for any standard geometry course.

GEOMETRY:
No additional prerequisites other than those needed for success in any geometry course are needed for success in UCSMP *Geometry*. UCSMP *Geometry* can be used with faster, average, and slower students who have these prerequisites. Prior study of *Transition Mathematics* and UCSMP *Algebra* insures this background, but this content is also found in virtually all existing middle school or junior high school texts.

Classes of students who have studied UCSMP *Algebra* tend to cover more UCSMP *Geometry* than other classes because they know more geometry and are better at the algebra used in geometry.

Students who have studied UCSMP *Geometry* are ready for any second-year algebra text.

ADVANCED ALGEBRA:
UCSMP *Advanced Algebra* should not be taken before a geometry course but can be used following any standard geometry text. Students who have studied UCSMP *Advanced Algebra* are prepared for courses commonly found at the senior level, including trigonometry or precalculus courses.

FUNCTIONS, STATISTICS,
AND TRIGONOMETRY WITH COMPUTERS:
FST assumes that students have completed a second-year algebra course. **No additional prerequisites other than those found in any second-year algebra text are needed for success in *FST*.**

PRECALCULUS AND DISCRETE MATHEMATICS
PDM can be taken successfully by students who have had *FST*, by students who have had typical senior level courses that include study of trigonometry and functions, and by top students who have successfully completed full advanced algebra and trigonometry courses.

PDM provides the background necessary for any typical calculus course, either at the high school or college level, including advanced placement calculus courses.

Development Cycle for UCSMP Texts

The development of each text has been in four stages. First, the overall goals for each course are created by UCSMP in consultation with a national advisory board of distinguished professors, and through discussion with classroom teachers, school administrators, and district and state mathematics supervisors.

The Advisory Board for the Secondary Component at the time of this planning consisted of Arthur F. Coxford, Jr., University of Michigan; David Duncan, University of Northern Iowa; James Fey, University of Maryland; Glenda Lappan, Michigan State University; Anthony Ralston, State University of New York at Buffalo; and James Schultz, Ohio State University.

As part of this stage, UCSMP devoted an annual School Conference, whose participants were mathematics supervisors and teachers, to discuss major issues in a particular area of the curriculum. Past conferences have centered on the following issues:

1984 Changing the Curriculum in Grades 7 and 8

1985 Changing Standards in School Algebra

1986 Functions, Computers, and Statistics in Secondary Mathematics

1987 Pre-College Mathematics

1988 Mathematics Teacher Education for Grades 7–12

At the second stage, UCSMP selects authors who write first drafts of the courses. Half of all UCSMP authors currently teach mathematics in secondary schools, and all authors and editors for the first five courses have secondary school teaching experience. The textbook authors or their surrogates initially teach the first drafts of Secondary Component texts, so that revision may benefit from first-hand classroom experience.

After revision by the authors or editors, materials enter the third stage in the text development. Classes of teachers not connected with the project use the books, and independent evaluators closely study student achievement, attitudes, and issues related to implementation. For the first three years in the series, this stage involved a formative evaluation in six to ten schools, and all teachers who used the materials periodically met at the university to provide feedback to UCSMP staff for a second revision. For the last three years in the series, this stage has involved a second pilot.

The fourth stage consists of a wider comparative evaluation. For the first three books, this evaluation has involved approximately 40 classrooms and thousands of students per book in schools all over the country. For the last three books in the series, this stage has involved a careful formative evaluation. As a result of these studies, the books have been revised for commercial publication by Scott, Foresman and Company, into the edition you are now reading. (See pages T46–T50 for a summary of this research.)

2 UCSMP *Algebra*

Problems UCSMP *Algebra* Is Trying to Address

This book is different from many other algebra books. The differences are due to its attempt to respond to seven serious problems which cannot be treated by small changes in content or approach.

PROBLEM 1:
Large numbers of students do not see why they need algebra.

Some algebra courses have been motivated almost exclusively by the needs of a minority of the population, those who will take calculus four or five years later. Other algebra courses consist entirely of dozens of problems of one type, followed by dozens of another, or of one skill after another, introduced without motivation, ostensibly designed for the slower student, but actually of ultimate use to few if any students.

It is no surprise, then, that many adults—even many of those most educated—wonder why they studied algebra. We believe that this is a result of the kind of algebra courses they studied, and the lack of applications in them. Algebra has many real-world applications even though school algebra has often ignored them. Most age, digit, work, and other so-called ''word problems'' or ''story problems'' do not constitute applications; problems like those are not encountered outside of school.

The UCSMP *Algebra* response: Instead of holding off on applications until after skills have been developed, applications are used to motivate all concepts and skills. The ability to apply algebra is made a priority. Word problems that have little or no use are replaced by more meaningful types of problems. Algebra is continually connected with the arithmetic the student knows and the geometry the student will study. We have evidence that we have greatly reduced and almost eliminated the ''Why are we studying this?'' kind of question.

PROBLEM 2:
The mathematics curriculum has been lagging behind today's widely available and inexpensive technology.

The UCSMP *Algebra* response: There is unanimous sentiment in recent national reports on mathematics education in favor of the use of calculators in all mathematics courses. Scientific calculators are used starting in the first chapter. There are many reasons for using scientific calculators rather than simpler, 4-function calculators. (See pages T40–T41.) If a student is to buy a calculator, it should be one that will be useful for more than a single year of study. We strongly recommend using solar-powered scientific calculators to avoid problems with batteries.

Many connections with computers are given in this course. We give templates for programs and talk about computer notation and language. In this we are following current practice in schools. But the influence of computers ranges beyond this. Certain content has been included because of its importance in a computer age, including discrete and continuous domains, iteration, interpretation of algorithms, and a great deal of graphing.

PROBLEM 3:
Too many students fail algebra.

The UCSMP *Algebra* response: It is too much to expect students to learn all of traditional first-year algebra in a single year. *Transition Mathematics* students work not only on the transition into algebra, but also on the important concepts of algebra. Students who have not had prior experience with algebra rarely master all the concepts of first-year algebra in a single year. The evidence from our studies is that students using *Transition Mathematics* knew much more algebra at the end of their year than students in comparison classes. Thus, though we expect students to do well in this course even if they have not had *Transition Mathematics*, we expect much better performance from those who have had that kind of rich experience.

***PROBLEM* 4:**
Even students who succeed in algebra often do poorly in geometry.

The UCSMP *Algebra* response: The evidence is that the knowledge of geometry among 9th-graders and among entering geometry students is quite poor. As with algebra, it is too much to expect students to learn all of geometry in a single year in high school. The best predictor of success with proof is a student's geometry knowledge at the beginning of a course. UCSMP *Algebra* continues the strong emphasis on geometry that is found in *Transition Mathematics*, with particular attention paid to the numerical relationships involving lines, angles, and polygons.

The evidence from our studies of UCSMP *Algebra* and *Transition Mathematics* validates the UCSMP integration of geometry into these courses. In the *Transition Mathematics* summative evaluation, students in comparison classes showed no increase in geometry knowledge from September to June. However, students using *Transition Mathematics* knew almost as much at the end of the year as typical students entering a geometry class. The results of the summative evaluation study of UCSMP *Algebra* showed that UCSMP students did better than the comparison students on *every* geometry question on the final examinations.

***PROBLEM* 5:**
Students don't read.

The UCSMP *Algebra* response: We have paid careful attention to the explanations, examples, and questions in each lesson. Students using traditional texts tell us they don't read because (1) the text is uninteresting, and (2) they don't have to read; the teacher explains it for them. But students *must* learn to read for future success in mathematics. So every lesson in this book contains reading and questions covering the reading. UCSMP *Algebra* is more than a resource for questions; it is a resource for information, for examples of how to do problems, for the history of major ideas, for applications of the ideas, for connections between ideas in one place in the book and in another, and for motivation.

Teachers of UCSMP *Algebra* who had not taught *Transition Mathematics* were skeptical at first about the amount of reading in the book. As the year progressed, they joined those who had taught *Transition Mathematics* in viewing the reading as one of the strongest features of this series. Some teachers felt that UCSMP was teaching reading comprehension; they all felt that the requirement to read helped develop thinkers who were more critical and aware.

Student comments confirm this. In 1986–87 one group of 8th-grade students used UCSMP *Algebra* in their home school. They simultaneously studied algebra from a standard text at a nearby high school. Their comments comparing the two texts: ". . . the UCSMP book allows me to figure out things for myself. I feel it makes me more independent in terms of doing my homework." "UCSMP is easier to understand." "The UCSMP homework is much easier to do at home. Applying the Reading [the section of problems now called "Applying the Mathematics"] makes you think."

***PROBLEM* 6:**
High-school students know very little statistics and probability.

It is often assumed that students learn the most basic of statistics and probability before high school; such content has been in schoolbooks for some time. Our evidence is that such learning is meager at best. In the summative evaluation of UCSMP *Algebra*, students were asked to find the median of a set of nine numbers given in increasing order. Whereas

75% of UCSMP *Algebra* students correctly responded, only 36% of comparison students could do so. On an item to calculate a probability from the results of a poll, the percentages were 61% for UCSMP *Algebra* students and 37% for comparison students.

Customarily, the only time probability is discussed in high schools has been together with the study of permutations and combinations in second-year algebra. Statistics has not been discussed at all. The result is that most high-school students never encounter either of these subject areas.

The UCSMP response to this problem is to give strong attention to statistics and probability in two places: first, in *Algebra,* and second, in *Functions and Statistics with Computers.*

In *Algebra,* we assume no prior statistics knowledge except the calculation of averages (means) and no prior knowledge of probability. Since statistics starts with data, we use data throughout this book, so that students become accustomed to it. We ask students to graph, organize, and interpret data. These are easy things for students to do, but they are often ignored. Then, as algebra topics relate to statistical ideas, we do the statistics. Probability begins in the first chapter so that intuitions regarding probability are established early and then applied throughout the course.

Problem 7:
Students are not skillful enough, regardless of what they are taught.

The evidence is that students are rather skillful at routine problems, but not with problems involving complicated numbers, different wordings, or new contexts. It is obvious that in order to obtain such skill, students must see problems with all sorts of numbers, a variety of wordings, and many different contexts. We also ask that students do certain problems mentally, which expands the level of competence expected of algebra students.

The UCSMP *Algebra* response: Encountering such problems is not enough. UCSMP *Algebra* employs a four-stage approach to develop skill.

■ **Stage 1** involves a concentrated introduction to the ideas surrounding the skill: why it is done, how it is done, and the kinds of problems that can be solved with it. Most books are organized to have this stage, because teachers recognize that explanations of an idea require time. At the end of this stage, typically only the best students have the skill. But in UCSMP *Algebra* this is only the beginning.

■ **Stage 2** occupies the following lessons in the chapter and consists of questions designed to establish some competence in the skill. These are found in the review exercises. By the end of the lessons of the chapter, most students should have some competence in the skills, but some may not have enough.

■ **Stage 3** involves mastery learning. At the end of each chapter is a Progress Self-Test for students to take and judge how they are doing. Worked-out solutions are included to provide feedback and help to the student. This is followed by a list of objectives with review questions for students to acquire those skills they don't have when taking the Progress Self-Test. Teachers are expected to spend 1–3 days on these sections to give students time to reach mastery. By the end of this stage, students should have gained mastery at least at the level of typical students covering the content.

■ **Stage 4** continues the review through the daily Review sections in the subsequent chapters. Vital algebra skills, such as solving linear equations, receive consistent emphasis throughout the book. Included also are *skill sequences* consisting of 3 to 4 questions that provide practice on related problems. The evidence (see pages T48–T49) is that this four-stage process enables students to gain competence over a wider range of content than comparable students normally possess.

Goals of UCSMP *Algebra*

It would be too easy and somewhat misleading to state that the goals of UCSMP *Algebra* are to remove forever the problems detailed above. Obviously we want to make headway in solving these. Nevertheless, it is more accurate to think of this book as an attempt to convey all the dimensions of the understanding of algebra: its skills, its properties, its uses, and its representations. In each, we want to update the curriculum and upgrade students' achievement. Specifically, we want students to be better able to apply algebra, and to be more successful in future years in their study of mathematics.

We have another, more lofty goal. WE WANT STUDENTS TO VIEW THEIR STUDY OF MATHEMATICS AS WORTHWHILE, AS FULL OF INTERESTING AND ENTERTAINING INFORMATION, AS RELATED TO ALMOST EVERY ENDEAVOR. We want them to realize mathematics is still growing and is changing fast. We want them to look for and recognize mathematics in places they haven't before, to use the library, to search through newspapers or almanacs, to get excited by knowledge.

We want students to view their study of mathematics as worthwhile, as full of interesting and entertaining information, as related to almost every endeavor.

Who Should Take UCSMP *Algebra?*

Virtually all students who expect to graduate from high school should take algebra. The reasons for college-bound students to take algebra are obvious: algebra is required for admission to almost all colleges; algebra is found on all college-entrance examinations; algebra is necessary to understand even the basics of science, statistics, computers, and economics, and helps to understand the social sciences and business. Without algebra, doors are open to only a few colleges; even at those colleges a student who has no algebra has the choice of only a few college majors.

There are just as many reasons for non-college-bound students to take algebra. Technical schools, such as those for the trades, require that students be familiar with formulas and with graphs, for which algebra provides the most effective exposure. Computers abound in the workplace; algebra is the language of programs and algebraic thinking underlies the operation of spreadsheets and many other software packages. Algebra is the language of generalization; without it arithmetic is often seen merely as a collection of unrelated rules and procedures; it is no surprise that study of algebra helps competence in arithmetic.

3 General Teaching Suggestions

While it is true that most of the content in this book is found in other algebra books, both the content and the approach of UCSMP *Algebra* represent rather significant departures from standard practice. *A teacher should not expect to use this book to teach exactly the same material in exactly the same way he or she has been accustomed to teaching.*

The suggestions found on this and the following pages are given to provide ideas which have led to success and to discourage practices which do not lead to success. They should not be construed as rigid guidelines; students, teachers, classes, schools, and school systems vary greatly. But they should not be ignored. These suggestions come from users, from our extensive interviews with teachers of earlier versions of these materials, and from test results.

Optimizing Learning

Pace

Students adjust to the pace set by the teacher. It is especially important that Chapter 1 be taught at a one-day-per-lesson pace. The end of the chapter, with its Progress Self-Test and Chapter Review, is the time to take a few days to cinch the major skills. We know from our studies that this pace produces the highest performance levels. Students need to be exposed to content in order to learn it.

There is a natural tendency, when using a new book, to go more slowly, to play it safe should one forget something. Teachers using these materials for the first time have almost invariably said that they would move more quickly the next year. Do not be afraid to move quickly.

Some classes in our studies of this book went very slowly; those teaching them seemed reluctant to move to new content. Where this happens, the students get into a rut. Better students are bored because they know the material. Slower students are frustrated because they are being asked to spend more time on the stuff they don't know. They all get discouraged and perform far lower than any other comparable students at the end of the year. We emphasize:

**One day per lesson almost always,
two or three days at the end of each chapter
on the Progress Self-Test and Chapter Review,
and then a Chapter Test.**

In classes with slower students, allow a half-day for each quiz. The Teacher's Edition provides a Daily Pacing Chart before each chapter, detailing two alternate ways to pace the chapter.

There are times when it will be difficult to maintain this pace. But be advised: a slow pace can make it too easy to lose perspective and relate ideas. You need to get to later content to realize why you were asked to learn earlier content! If necessary, spend more time on end-of-chapter activities. If you spend too much time in the lessons, you may find that your slowest students may have learned more by having gone through content slowly, but all the other students will have learned less. Try to strike a balance, going quickly enough to keep things interesting but slowly enough to have time for explanations.

Review

Every lesson includes Review questions. These questions serve a variety of purposes. First, they develop competence in a topic. Because we do not expect students to master a topic on the day they are introduced to it, these questions, coming *after* the introduction of the topic, help to solidify the ideas. Second, they maintain competence from preceding chapters. This review is particularly effective with topics that have not been studied for some time.

At times we are able to give harder questions in reviews than we could expect students to be able to do on the day they were introduced to the topic. Thus the reviews sometimes serve as questions which integrate ideas from previous lessons.

Finally, we occasionally review an idea that has not been discussed for some time, just before it is to surface again in a lesson. The Notes on Questions in the Teacher's Edition usually alert you to this circumstance.

Teachers in classes that perform the best, assign all the Review questions, give students the answers each day, and discuss them when needed. Those who do not assign all Review questions tend to get poorer performance. *The Review questions must be assigned to ensure optimum performance.*

The evidence is substantial that use of the chapter end-matter materials promotes higher levels of performance.

Mastery

The mastery strategy used at the end of each chapter of UCSMP *Algebra* is one that has been validated by a great deal of research. Its components are a Progress Self-Test (literature on mastery learning may refer to this as the "formative test"), worked-out solutions to that test in the student textbook (the "feedback"), Chapter Review questions tied to the same objectives (the "correctives"), and finally a Chapter Test, again covering the same objectives.

To follow the strategy means assigning the Progress Self-Test as homework to be done *under simulated test conditions*. The next day should be devoted to answering student questions about the problems and doing some problems from the Chapter Review, if there is time. If a particular topic is causing a great deal of trouble, the corresponding Lesson Master (in the Teacher's Resource File) may be of help.

For most classes, as a second night's assignment, we suggest the *even-numbered* Chapter Review questions. Answers for the *even-numbered* Chapter Review questions are not in the student text, so students will have to work on their own. Discuss those Chapter Review questions the next day in class.

A Chapter Test (available in the Teacher's Resource File) should be given on the third day. The odd-numbered Chapter Review questions, for which answers are given in the student text, can be useful for studying for the test. In some classes, a third day before the test may be needed. If so, either the odd-numbered Chapter Review questions or selected Lesson Masters can be used as sources of problems.

We strongly recommend that, except for classes of exceptionally talented students (where less review may be needed), teachers follow this strategy. THE EVIDENCE IS SUBSTANTIAL THAT USE OF THE CHAPTER END-MATTER MATERIALS PROMOTES HIGHER LEVELS OF PERFORMANCE.

Reading

To become an independent learner of mathematics, a student must learn to learn mathematics from reading. You should expect students to read all lessons. At the beginning of the course, this may require oral reading in class. We have connected the text reading to exercises to emphasize the importance of reading in mathematics and to help the student develop better reading skills.

In general, we should note that the typical student in this course can read English rather well, but cannot read mathematics well. Students may not be able to read certain numbers, and they may have no vocabulary for symbols such as $+$, $-$, $\times$, $\div$, $=$, or $<$. Many of us have trouble reading Greek letters such as μ or δ, because we have never had to give their names out loud. For many students the same is true for common everyday mathematics symbols. Thus it is important to have students read out loud, as well as to give them assignments that involve reading.

The typical algebra student who has not used *Transition Mathematics* has never been asked to read mathematics. As a result, it is common for students to ask why they have to read.

We tell them: You must read because you must learn to read for success in all future courses that use mathematics, not just in mathematics; because you must learn to read for success in life outside of school and on any job; because the reading will help you understand the uses of mathematics; because the reading contains interesting information; because the reading tells you how the material from one lesson is related to other material in the book; because there is not enough time in class to spend doing something that you can do in a study period or at home.

Teachers of UCSMP *Algebra* have handled reading in a variety of ways. These methods differ, depending on the backgrounds of the students, the difficulty of the particular lesson, and the personality of the teacher. Prior exposure to *Transition Mathematics* is extremely helpful; many teachers report that students who have studied from *Transition Mathematics* need no special directions concerning reading.

One approach in class is to consistently assign the reading for each lesson in advance without having gone over the content. In this approach the typical assignment is all the questions on that lesson. Accustom students to that pace. Spend most classes going over the problems in order. The questions have been designed to teach the lesson. If gone through in order, all concepts will be developed and covered.

A second approach is to assign the reading and all questions as in the first approach, but the next day have students read the lesson out loud in class. Then intersperse the questions with the reading as appropriate.

A third approach is to assign for homework the reading of a new lesson, along with some questions from that lesson and from the previous one. The idea is as follows: Assign the reading and questions Covering the Reading from a new lesson. Assign the questions Applying the Mathematics, the Review, and the Exploration from the previous lesson.

We strongly encourage teachers to present their own explanations and not to rely on the book for everything. We do, however, wish to discourage the practice of always doing these explanations *before* the students have had the opportunity to learn on their own.

Specific reading comprehension tips and strategies are provided in the Teacher's Edition margin notes for appropriate lessons.

Understanding— The SPUR Approach

"Understanding" is an easy goal to have, for who can be against it? Yet understanding means different things to different people. In UCSMP texts an approach is taken that we call the SPUR approach. It involves four different aspects, or dimensions, of understanding.

SKILLS: For many people, understanding mathematics means simply knowing *how* to get an answer to a problem with no help from any outside source. But in classrooms, when we speak of understanding how to use a calculator or a computer, we mean using a computer to do something for us. In UCSMP texts, these are both aspects of the same kind of understanding, the understanding of algorithms (procedures) for getting answers. This is the S of SPUR, the Skills dimension, and it ranges from the rote memorization of basic facts to the development of new algorithms for solving problems.

PROPERTIES: During the 1960s, understanding *why* became at least as important as understanding *how*. Mathematicians often view this kind of understanding as the ultimate goal. For instance, mathematics courses for prospective elementary school teachers assume these college students can do arithmetic, and instead teach the properties and principles behind that arithmetic. This is the P of SPUR, the Properties dimension, and it ranges from the rote identification of properties to the discovery of new proofs.

. . . in UCSMP texts we have adopted the view that the understanding of mathematics is a multi-dimensional entity.

USES: To the person who applies mathematics, neither knowing how to get an answer nor knowing the mathematical reasons behind the process is as important as being able to *use* the answer. For example, a person does not possess full understanding of linear equations until that person can apply them appropriately in real situations. This is the U of SPUR, the Uses dimension. It ranges from the rote application of ideas (for instance, when you encounter a take-away situation, subtract) to the discovery of new applications or models for mathematical ideas. UCSMP *Algebra* is notable for its attention to this dimension of understanding.

REPRESENTATIONS: To some people, even having all three dimensions of understanding given above does not comprise full understanding. They require that students *represent* a concept, and deal with the concept in that representation in some way. Ability to use concrete materials and models, or graphs and other pictorial representations, demonstrates this dimension of understanding. This is the R of SPUR, the Representations dimension, and it ranges from the rote manipulation of objects to the invention of new representations of concepts.

The four types of understanding have certain common qualities. For each there are people for whom that type of understanding is preeminent, and who believe that the other types do not convey the *real* understanding of mathematics. Each has aspects that can be memorized and the potential for the highest level of creative thinking. Each can be, and often is, learned in isolation from the others. We know there are students who have S and none of the others; in the 1960s some students learned P and none of the others; there are people on the street who have U and none of the others; and some people believe that children cannot really acquire any of the others without having R. There are continual arguments among educators as to which dimension should come first and which should be emphasized.

Because of this, IN UCSMP TEXTS WE HAVE ADOPTED THE VIEW THAT THE UNDERSTANDING OF MATHEMATICS IS A MULTI-DIMENSIONAL ENTITY. We believe each dimension is important, that each dimension has its easy aspects and its difficult ones. Some skills (for example, long division) take at least as long to learn as geometry proofs; some uses are as easy as putting together beads.

For a specific example of what understanding means in these four dimensions, consider solving $100 + 5x = 50 + 10x$, and what would constitute evidence of that understanding.

Skills understanding means knowing a way to obtain a solution. (Obtain $x = 10$ by some means.)

Properties understanding means knowing properties which you can apply. (Identify or justify the steps in obtaining an answer.)

Uses understanding means knowing situations in which you could apply the solving of this equation. (Set up or interpret a solution: If one person has 100 tapes and buys 5 tapes a month, and another person has 50 tapes and buys 10 tapes a month, in how many months will they have the same number of tapes?)

Representations understanding means having a representation of the solving process, or a graphical way of interpreting the solution. (Graph $y = 100 + 5x$ and $y = 50 + 10x$ and interpret the x-coordinate of the point of intersection.)

We believe there are students who prefer one of these dimensions over the others when learning mathematics. Some students prefer applications, some would rather do manipulative skills, some most want to know the theory, and still others like the models and representations best. Thus the most effective teaching allows students opportunities in all these dimensions.

The SPUR approach is not a perfect sorter of knowledge; many ideas and many problems involve more than one dimension. For instance, the mathematics behind an algorithm may involve both S and P. And some understandings do not fit any of these dimensions. In some UCSMP texts, we add a fifth dimension H—the Historical dimension—for it provides still another way of looking at knowledge. (The ninth century Arabian mathematician Al-Khowarizmi, from whose name we get the word "algorithm," was the first to solve equations like $100 + 5x = 50 + 10x$ by performing the same operations on both sides of the equation; his work, "Hisab al-jabr w'al muqabalah," was so influential in Europe that its second word became synonymous with such problems. Hence comes our word "algebra." But not until François Vieté in the late 1500s did we have variables and use today's notation.)

In this book, you see the SPUR categorization at the end of each chapter in a set of Objectives and corresponding Chapter Review questions. The Progress Self-Test for each chapter and the Lesson Masters (in the Teacher's Resource File) are keyed to these objectives. We never ask students (or teachers) to categorize tasks into the various kinds of understanding; that is not a suitable goal. The categorization is meant only to be a convenient and efficient way to ensure that the book provides the opportunity for teachers to teach, and for students to gain a broader and deeper understanding of mathematics than is normally the case.

You may wonder why the Chapter Review and the Lesson Masters are organized using the SPUR categorization. It is because we believe that practice is essential for mastery, but that blind practice, in which a student merely copies what was done in a previous problem to do a new one, does not help ultimate performance. The practice must be accompanied by understanding. The properties, uses, and representations enhance understanding and should be covered to obtain mastery, even of the skills.

The Lesson Masters are particularly appropriate for students who wish more practice; for helping students individually with problems they have not seen; after a chapter test has been completed, if you feel that students' performance was not high enough; and for in-class work on days when a normal class cannot be conducted. However, they should be used sparingly. *The Lesson Masters should not be part of the normal routine* and should seldom be used when they would delay moving on to the next lesson.

Using Technology

We use calculators and computers in UCSMP because they make important mathematical ideas accessible to students at an early age; they relieve the drudgery of calculation and graphing, particularly with numbers and equations encountered in realistic contexts; and they facilitate exploration and open-ended problem solving by making multiple instances easy to examine. Furthermore, as indicated in the section on Research and Development (pages T46–T50), our use of technology has resulted in no loss of paper-and-pencil skill in arithmetic, and has freed up time in the curriculum to spend on other topics that lead to overall better performance by UCSMP students.

Inevitably, calculators will be considered as natural as pencils for doing mathematics.

Calculators

Hand-held calculators first appeared in 1971. Not until 1976 did the price of a four-function calculator come below $50 (equivalent to well over $100 today). Still, in 1975, a national commission recommended that hand-held calculators be used on all tests starting in eighth grade, and in 1980 the National Council of Teachers of Mathematics recommended that calculators be used in all grades of school from kindergarten on. It is reported that the Achievement section of the College Board exams will allow calculators beginning in 1990, and that the Advanced Placement exam will again allow calculators in the near future. Several standardized test batteries are being developed with calculators. And slowly but surely calculators are being expected on more and more licensing exams outside of school.

The business and mathematics education communities generally believe that paper-pencil algorithms are becoming obsolete. (The long division algorithm we use was born only in the late 1400s. Before that time, the abacus was used almost exclusively to get answers to problems. So mechanical means to do problems are really older than paper-and-pencil means.) Increasingly, businesses do not want their employees to use paper-and-pencil algorithms to get answers to arithmetic problems. Banks require that their tellers do all arithmetic using a calculator.

INEVITABLY, CALCULATORS WILL BE CONSIDERED AS NATURAL AS PENCILS FOR DOING MATHEMATICS. A century from now people will be amazed when they learn that some students as recent as the 1980s went to schools where calculators were not used.

It is wonderful to live in the age when calculators have been developed that quickly and efficiently do arithmetic. This frees us to use arithmetic more and, as teachers, to spend more time on mental arithmetic, estimation, and understanding algebra.

Section 3: General Teaching Suggestions

UCSMP *Algebra* assumes the student has a scientific calculator. There are five basic reasons why 4-function non-scientific calculators do not suffice.

(1) Applications require the ability to deal with large and small numbers. On many 4-function calculators, a number as large as the population of the U.S. cannot be entered, and on all of them the national debt or the world population could not be entered. The calculator must have the ability to display numbers in scientific notation.

(2) 4-function calculators give error messages which do not distinguish between student error and calculator insufficiency. This restricts the kinds of problems one can assign.

(3) There are keys on scientific calculators that are very useful in algebra. The π, square root, power, factorial, and parentheses keys are all utilized in this book. These keys are not found on many 4-function calculators.

(4) Order of operations on a scientific calculator is the same as in algebra, so this kind of calculator motivates and reinforces algebra skills. In contrast, order of operations on a 4-function calculator is often different from that used in algebra and could confuse students.

(5) A scientific calculator can be used for later courses a student takes; it shows the student there is much more to learn about mathematics.

Students will overuse calculators. Part of learning to use any machine is to make mistakes: using it when you shouldn't, not using it when you should. Anyone who has a word processor has used it for short memos that could much more easily have been handwritten. Anyone who has a microwave has used it for food that could have been cooked either in a conventional oven or on top of the stove.

The overuse dies down, but it takes some months. In the meantime, stress that there are three ways to get answers to arithmetic problems: by paper and pencil, mentally, or by using some automatic means (a table, a calculator, a trusty friend, and so on). Some problems require more than one of these means, but the wise applier of arithmetic knows when to use each of these ways.

Generally this means that good arithmeticians do a lot of calculations mentally, either because they are basic facts (such as 3×5) or because they can be gotten by simple rules (such as $2/3 \times 4/5$, or 100×4.72). They may not use a calculator on these because the likelihood of making an error entering or reading is greater than the likelihood of making a mental error. As a rule, we seldom say, "Do not use calculators here." We want students to learn for themselves when calculator use is appropriate and when not. However, you may feel the need to prod some students to avoid the calculator. An answer of 2.9999999 to $\sqrt{9}$ should be strongly discouraged.

Many lessons include questions to be done "in your head." These are designed to develop skill in mental arithmetic and show students situations in which mental calculation is an appropriate approach to calculation. You may wish to give quizzes on these kinds of problems and have a "no calculator" rule for these problems.

Computers and Graphing Calculators

The computer is a powerful tool for you to use in your classroom to demonstrate the relationships, patterns, properties, and algorithms of algebra. A desirable computer has the ability to deal with a good amount of data and to display graphs with accuracy and precision.

From the very first chapter of this book, computer programs appear in examples and exercises as contemporary representations of algebra. Do not ignore the computer questions even if you do not have computers available. **The goal is not to teach computer programming, but to use the computer as an application and as a concrete illustration of the role of variables.** Students are asked to analyze and write short programs. Expect a wide variety of correct solutions.

Some questions ask students to use an *automatic grapher*. By this we mean a computer with a function grapher or a graphing calculator; those graphers will display the graph of any function students encounter in this course. If students do not have access to a computer or automatic grapher, exercise caution in your assigning of such questions and, if assigned, do not have high expectations of student success. It takes time to do a good graph and many of these questions require comparing two or more graphs.

A good graphing calculator should display as many as four graphs simultaneously, be able to graph all of the functions in this book, allow the window to be changed with ease, and in general be easy to use.

The BASIC computer language was selected for use in this book because it is packaged for the microcomputers which are most popular in American schools. The programs have been kept short so that students can type them relatively quickly. It is not necessary for every student to type and run the program. Most programs can be used as classroom demonstrations.

Computer educators have recommended that students be required to provide a block structure to programs; document their programs with abundant remarks; and declare variables. Since this is an algebra course, not a programming course, you should emphasize the *computational* steps of a program. Can the students follow the steps of a program and tell what the output will be? Can the student modify a given program to solve an exercise with different values?

Programs which are printed in the text of this book follow several conventions.

1. Most programs start with a PRINT statement which serves a dual purpose: it is a title for the program LISTing and a title for the program output.

2. Extended remarks are offset from the body of the program. Brief comments appear as REM statements (remarks) in longer programs.

3. Indentation in program lines has been used to indicate blocking of lines, particularly in loops. This aid to program readability is not exploited on many computers. You will probably find that these spaces do not appear on your computer screen, and therefore need not be typed.

4. Variable names are kept short, sometimes only one character long. This reduces the amount of typing needed; is implementable on all computer forms of BASIC; and reflects the use of single letters for variables in algebra.

5. Tests for exceptional cases are frequently omitted unless the meaning of the topic is enhanced by the cases. In a program for solving $ax + b = c$, it is not really necessary for a student to write

IF $a <> 0$ THEN . . .

because he or she should recognize 0 will not work before using the computer. However, in a program to compute slope, a zero division is not as obvious to students, so the IF-THEN statement is included.

6. We do not type NEW, which students might have to type if they are not the first user of the day on the computer. We also do not type RUN, which students must do in order to execute their program. And we do not indicate that students must press the RETURN key after each line.

Here are two examples of programs like those found in UCSMP *Algebra*. If you understand these, you know enough about programs to be able to handle the programs in the book.

EXAMPLE 1

```
10 PRINT "TABLE OF DECIMAL EQUIVALENTS"
        Anything within quotes will be printed, symbol for
        symbol.
20 PRINT "GIVE THE DENOMINATOR."
30 INPUT N
        When executed, the computer will pause at line 30
        and ask for a value of N to be inputted by flashing a
        question mark.
        Lines 40 through 70 loop through
        J = 0, 1, 2, . . . , N. For each value of J
        the fraction J/N and its corresponding
        decimal value are displayed.
40 FOR J = 0 TO N
50      LET F = J/N
60      PRINT J, J; "/"; N, F
70 NEXT J
80 END
```

EXAMPLE 2

```
10 PRINT "SLOPE DETERMINED BY TWO POINTS"
        This program will compute the slope
        determined by the points
        (x1, y1) and (x2, y2).
20 PRINT "ENTER FIRST POINT COORDINATES."
30 INPUT X1, Y1
        When run, the program will ask for
        two values here, the first being x1, the second y1.
40 PRINT "ENTER SECOND COORDINATES."
50 INPUT X2, Y2
        The computer will ignore line 60 if x2 ≠ x1.
60 IF X2 - X1 = 0 THEN PRINT
   "UNDEFINED SLOPE"
        Now compute slope if (x2 - x1) ≠ 0.
70 IF X2 - X1 ≠ 0 THEN LET M = (Y2 - Y1)/
   (X2 - X1)
80 IF X2 - X1 ≠ 0 THEN PRINT "THE SLOPE IS"; M
90 END
```

Whether you are a novice or expert in BASIC, we encourage you to try the programs we provide on your own system. Appendix C of the student text contains a glossary of commands in BASIC. Each version of BASIC and each computer has slightly different characteristics, and our generic programs may need to be modified slightly for your system.

Evaluating Learning

Grading

No problem seems more difficult than the question of grading. If a teacher has students who perform so well that they all deserve A's and the teacher gives them A's as a result, the teacher will probably not be given plaudits for being successful but will be accused of being too easy. This suggests that the grading scale ought to be based on a fixed level of performance, which is what we recommend.

Never in this book are there ten similar questions in a row. To teach students to be flexible, the wording of questions is varied, and principles are applied in many contexts. Learning to solve problems in a variety of contexts or to discern relationships between properties is more difficult than learning to perform a routine skill. Thus, a natural question that arises is "How should I grade students in UCSMP courses?"

One way is to increase the number of points on the test to 110 or 120 and use your old scale. (However, do not convert the scores to percents.) A second way is to change the grading scale. One used successfully by many UCSMP pilot teachers is 85–100, A; 72–84, B; 60–71, C; 50–59, D; 0–49, F. Such a low curve may alarm some teachers, but as outlined on pages T46–T49, UCSMP students have performed well on standardized tests compared to students in other classes. STUDENTS IN UCSMP COURSES GENERALLY LEARN MORE MATHEMATICS OVERALL THAN STUDENTS IN COMPARISON CLASSES. We believe that each of the above grading policies rewards students fairly for work well done.

Students in UCSMP courses generally learn more mathematics overall than students in comparison classes.

We have also found that a word to your students about why your grading scale is "different" is helpful. They may be so accustomed to another grading scale that they feel they are doing poorly, while you think they are doing well. To encourage students, we often make a basketball analogy. In UCSMP *Algebra,* almost every question is a different shot (a problem), some close in, some from middle distance, a few from half-court. In a traditional course, most of the shots students try are done over and over again from the same court position close to the basket. ("Do the odd-numbered exercises from 1–49." Since the variability of the shots in UCSMP *Algebra* is much greater, it is unrealistic to expect percents of correct shots to be the same.

There are times, however, when you want to practice one specific shot to make it automatic. We suggest focusing in on a few topics for quizzes. The Teacher's Resource File contains at least one quiz for each chapter. If students perform well on quizzes and tests, it has a real effect on interest and motivation. We would like to see grading as a vehicle for breeding success as well as for rating students.

In the light of all this, here are some general suggestions pertaining to grading:

(1) Let students know what they need to know in order to get good grades. All research on the subject indicates that telling students what they are supposed to learn increases the amount of material covered and tends to increase performance.

(2) Have confidence in your students. Do not arbitrarily consign some of them to low grades. Let them know that it is possible for all of them to get A's if they learn the material.

(3) Some teachers have found that because of the way that the Review questions maintain and improve performance, *cumulative tests* give students an opportunity to do well. For your convenience, the Teacher's Resource File has Chapter Tests in Cumulative Form (in addition to the regular Chapter Tests) for each chapter, beginning with Chapter 2. The Cumulative Tests allow students a chance to show what they have learned about a topic in the intervening weeks.

Standardized Tests

At our first conference with school teachers and administrators early in the project, we were told in the strongest terms, "Be bold, but remember that you will be judged by old standardized tests."

In *Algebra,* we work in the four dimensions of understanding: Skills, Properties, Uses, and Representations. While it is thought that traditional algebra standardized tests are almost entirely devoted to skills, this is not the case. *School-made placement tests* are most likely to be so distorted, because Properties seem out of favor these days and items for Uses and Representations are felt to be the most difficult to find. Standardized tests are usually more balanced.

We have done an in-depth study of standarized tests. Our conclusions are as follows: Students studying UCSMP courses are likely to do better on the College Board SAT-M than other students. The SAT-M is a problem-solving test, and far more questions on the SAT-M cover content likely to be unfamiliar to other students than to UCSMP students. The ACT exams seem at least as favorable to our students as to students in other books. However, if the UCSMP idea is followed and more students take *Algebra* in the 8th grade, then there is no question that students in the UCSMP curriculum will far outscore comparable students who are a course behind.

In our large summative field study (see pages T46–T49), we used both a traditional standarized algebra test (published by American Testronics) and two other tests of first-year algebra that cover the broader range of content found in UCSMP *Algebra.* The overall results were quite positive. UCSMP students performed as well as other algebra students on the standardized test. UCSMP students significantly outperformed other students on the tests of broader algebra content.

Finally, a note about curriculum projects. Many people treat books from curriculum projects as "experimental." Few commercial textbooks, however, have been developed on the basis of large-scale testing. (See pages T46–T50 for details on the testing of this text.) Few have been produced as part of a coherent 7–12 curriculum design. This text has gone through extensive prepublication analysis and criticism. It has been revised on the basis of comments and evaluations of the pilot, formative, and summative evaluation teachers. It is the intention of UCSMP to provide materials which are successful as well as teachable. SINCE UCSMP *ALGEBRA* HAS BEEN SUCCESSFULLY TESTED AND REVISED, IT SHOULD BE VIEWED AS A *NEW* TEXT, NOT AS AN EXPERIMENTAL TEXT.

Since UCSMP *Algebra* has been successfully tested and revised, it should be viewed as a *new* text, not as an experimental text.

4 Research and Development of UCSMP *Algebra*

Writing, Pilot, and Formative Evaluation

In the spring of 1985, John McConnell, Instructional Supervisor of Mathematics at Glenbrook South High School and Coordinator of Educational Technology for the Glenbrook High Schools, was asked to lead the writing team for UCSMP *Algebra*. Dr. McConnell was chosen because of a unique combination of qualifications. He had been president of the Illinois Council of Teachers of Mathematics, which made him well-acquainted with the issues that UCSMP is trying to address. He was familiar with the use of technology, having been a member of the committee that wrote a pamphlet for that council entitled, ''Illinois Council of Teachers of Mathematics Recommendations for Secondary School Computer Science Content,'' and is an author of commercially published software. He had initiated a course in statistics at his high school and had written materials for that course. This gave him the experience to implement plans to incorporate statistics into UCSMP *Algebra*. And he had a particular interest in algebra; his doctoral dissertation at Northwestern University (1978) was entitled ''Relationships Among High Inference Measures of Teacher Behaviors and Student Achievement and Attitude in Ninth-Grade Algebra Classes.''

The other authors for UCSMP Algebra were chosen by a unique procedure. Announcements that UCSMP was looking for authors were placed in several national newsletters, including those of the National Council of Supervisors of Mathematics, the National Council of Teachers of Mathematics, and the Special Interest Group on Research in Mathematics Education of the American Educational Reseach Association. Those who responded (over 80 in number) were sent a long application in which they were asked for personal information, their opinions about various issues, asked to edit a lesson enclosed with the application, and to enclose a lesson of their own choosing. Of the 45 individuals who completed applications, 13 were invited to the University to spend a day in a mock planning-writing session. Of these 13, five (Susan Brown, Susan Eddins, Margaret Hackworth, Leroy Sachs, and Ernest Woodward) were chosen to be a member of the *Algebra* writing team.

In the summer of 1985, these individuals spent eight weeks at the University of Chicago writing the first draft of UCSMP *Algebra*. This draft was edited in Chicago by UCSMP staff (all experienced mathematics teachers) and used in six schools in the year 1985–86. The teachers during that year received loose-leaf materials a chapter at a time, often only days before they had to teach from them.

In the summer of 1986, four of the authors returned to revise the materials. The revision was guided by the comments of the pilot teachers and by the algebra needed for UCSMP *Geometry*, which was then in its planning stages. The formative evaluation in 1986–87 took place in a dozen schools. (The teachers in this and the previous year's evaluations are acknowledged on page *iii*.) Teachers periodically came to the University and commented on how things were going, what they thought were strong and weak points, how long it took to cover various lessons, which questions were most interesting, which questions might be deleted, and so on. Evaluators visited classes and interviewed students, teachers, and administrators. Comparison classes were tested, but there was no attempt at careful selection of these classes.

The results of the 1986–87 evaluations showed that students generally performed well but were not as skillful at linear sentences as we desired. (We desire very high performance on this all-important skill.) Simplification of radicals used in geometry was also not covered as much as desired. A careful examination of the questions was made and the materials were revised to correct these flaws.

Summative Evaluation and Test Results

In 1987–88, a carefully controlled study involving 40 matched pairs of classes in 9 states, half using UCSMP *Algebra* and half using algebra texts, was conducted by the Evaluation Component of UCSMP. This and all other studies of UCSMP materials are designed, conducted, and controlled independently from the writing of the materials. The design chosen by the Evaluation Component did not allow any 8th-grade UCSMP *Algebra* class to be tested against a comparison group of students not taking algebra because it was felt that an algebra final exam would be totally unfair and possibly quite disturbing to the comparison students.

No teacher in this study taught both UCSMP and comparison classes. The size of the study, approximately 2400 students, was so that evaluators could eliminate classes which did not match for any reason and still be left with enough pairs to judge overall results and enough students to conduct comparative item analyses. Information on obtaining the detailed results of this study is available by writing the UCSMP Evaluation Component, 5835 S. Kimbark Avenue, Chicago IL 60637. Herein is a summary:

Students were pretested on arithmetic, geometry, and algebra readiness. This uncovered several pairs of classes which did not match. (Since we have evidence from studies of *Transition Mathematics* that students using that book significantly outscore comparison classes on algebra and geometry readiness, this also served to remove an advantage that some UCSMP classes likely had from their previous year's study. On the other hand, this ensured that effects were due to UCSMP *Algebra* rather than to a two-year exposure to UCSMP materials.) Sometimes this mismatch occurred when one group was an honors class and the other a regular class.

If anything unusual happened to one class, both classes of the pair were removed from the detailed analysis (though kept in the study for overall analysis). Some classes were depleted at the semester. In one class, the teacher did not give all the tests, so both classes of the pair had to be dropped from the analysis.

Students were tested again in the late spring a few weeks before the end of the year. To keep the match, the fall scores of students who took the spring tests in these classes had to match. That is, those students who were left in the classes had to have been well-matched at the beginning of the year. These matching criteria eliminated 23 of the 40 pairs.

Six of the 17 remaining matched pairs of classes required some statistical equating to be matched. For the analysis, these six pairs were removed, because item analyses are not as reliable if equating is needed. The 11 remaining pairs of classes were from seven states, California, Colorado, Connecticut, Michigan, Ohio, South Carolina, and Wisconsin, representing rural, urban, and suburban areas and including both 8th- and 9th-grade students. The statistics are based on all 226 students in the 11 UCSMP *Algebra* classes and the 190 students in the 11 comparison algebra classes who took all tests in the fall and spring.

Three tests were given. First was a standarized test, the American Testronics *High School Subjects Test: Algebra* (HSST) 40-question multiple-choice test, chosen because it seems rather representative of such tests, and is new and thus less likely to be familiar to any teacher. Calculators were not permitted on this test. Students in all classes were tested for two other complete periods, during which they were given 70 additional items selected to represent either the wider range of content found in UCSMP *Algebra* or topics deemed of particular importance to all classes. These tests are called Algebra, Part I and Algebra Part II, and calculators were permitted. It was felt that the first test would be biased against UCSMP students and the remaining two tests biased in favor. The results for the sample of students follow.

Mean percentages correct for all students in the sample of well-matched pairs

Test	UCSMP (n = 226)	Comparison (n = 190)	Difference (UCSMP minus Comparison)
High School Subjects Test: Algebra (HSST)	51.5	50.3	+1.2
Algebra Part I	51.1	36.9	+14.2
Algebra Part II	57.6	43.1	+14.5

The independent evaluators wrote: "The most striking feature [of the table] is that on no subtest did the Comparison classes score higher."

Analysis of the High School Subjects Test: Algebra (HSST)

One might have expected the comparison classes to outperform the UCSMP classes on this test. The typical algebra class spends about two months on factoring and rational expressions, for example, so it was reasonable to expect that comparison classes would do better on many items which tested those topics. UCSMP students use calculators on tests throughout the course. They were not permitted to use calculators, however, on this test. Nevertheless, THE MEAN SCORE FOR THE UCSMP CLASSES ON THE HSST WAS 1.2 POINTS HIGHER THAN THE MEAN SCORE FOR THE COMPARISON CLASSES! The independent evaluators wrote:

> "The overall conclusion from the data presented [on the HSST] is that there were no significant differences between UCSMP and Comparison classes on what could be considered traditional algebra concepts and skills."

The item analyses for this test showed, in the words of the evaluators, that "UCSMP students did better [over 10% higher] on items which asked students to:

justify a property,
identify an inequality on a number line,
select the equation for a line given two points,
find the slope of a line,
determine when an expression is undefined,
find an equation to represent a graphed line,
identify a linear expression for a word problem,
and determine when an arrow shot in the air will be at a certain height.

Items Comparison students did better [scored over 10% better] on asked them to:

multiply binomials,
reduce a rational expression with powers,
factor a simple trinomial,
subtract radicals, and
divide a trinomial by a binomial."

Relative performance of well-matched pairs on all subtests

Subtest	*Pair* 1	4	5	6	9	10	12	13	14	16	17
Applied Geometry	0	0	0	+	+	+	+	+	0	+	0
Probability	+	+	+	+	+	0	+	0	0	+	0
Statistics	+	0	0	0	0	0	0	0	+	0	0
Linear Equations	+	0	0	+	+	+	0	0	0	0	0
Quadratics	0	0	0	0	0	0	+	0	0	+	0
Models for Operations	+	+	0	+	+	0	+	0	0	0	0
Calculators or Computers	+	+	+	+	+	0	+	0	+	0	+
Exponential Models	+	0	+	+	+	0	+	0	+	0	0
Applications	+	0	0	+	+	0	+	0	0	0	0
Arithmetic	0	0	0	0	0	0	0	0	0	0	0
Linear Systems	0	0	0	0	+	0	0	0	0	+	+

■ Analysis of the Algebra Test, Parts I and II

The 70 items on these tests were grouped into 11 subtests. The results are summarized here in terms of statistical significant differences at the .05 level on a t-test for a given subtest in a given pair. A "+" sign means a significant difference favoring UCSMP students; a "–" sign means a significant difference favoring Comparison students; a "0" means no significant difference.

THE INDEPENDENT EVALUATORS WROTE: "THE MOST STRIKING FEATURE [OF THE TABLE] IS THAT ON NO SUBTEST DID THE COMPARISON CLASSES SCORE HIGHER. . ."

At the item level, UCSMP students outperformed Comparison students by more than 25% correct on:

finding the third angle in a triangle,
applying a formula,
obtaining the median of a set of 9 numbers,
evaluating $\frac{102!}{100!}$
finding the area between rectangles,
calculating a probability,
applying the multiplication counting principle,
determining the output of a BASIC program,
calculating compound interest, and
finding a length in similar triangles.

On no item on these two tests did comparison students score more than 5% above UCSMP students.

Globally, the evaluators concluded: **"These student achievement data can be interpreted as a fairly strong statement in favor of UCSMP *Algebra*. . . ."**

Despite the widespread belief that conditions favor newer materials in such studies, there is at least as much evidence that comparison classes have an advantage. In this study, teachers of comparison classes knew they were being tested from the first day of the year; we have evidence that comparison classes tested at the beginning of the year score higher on our spring tests than classes not tested at the beginning of the year. It is possible that some UCSMP and comparison classes covered a wider range of content than normal because their teachers knew what is in the other book and wanted to make sure their students had been exposed to it. UCSMP teachers had the advantage of the excitement of using materials for the first time. However, for the most part the UCSMP teachers were using their texts for the first time and did not even have both parts of the text at the beginning of the school year. Some comparison teachers may have had the advantage of many years of teaching out of the books they use.

Because of the changes made, we expect results from the summative evaluation to extend to the Scott, Foresman version, further enhancing student performance.

Continuing Research and Development

The summative evaluation convinced us that the approach is not only sound but quite effective and that no major changes should be made in the materials. However, many minor changes were made, based either on careful readings given to the materials by UCSMP and Scott, Foresman editors, on the test results above, or on remarks on detailed forms returned by the teachers in the summative evaluation. In particular, teachers told us where they supplemented and where they felt there was not enough work. Lesson 6-5, unique for this book, arose in this way.

Some material was added to satisfy teachers' requests for certain content. Notable is Chapter 13, Functions, which did not exist in earlier editions. It replaces two short chapters whose content is now integrated with the rest of the book.

The present version of UCSMP *Algebra* also includes the appearance of four colors, of attractive pictures, and of many more supplements for teachers and students. Teachers, of course, will now have have the benefit of having the full text at the beginning of the year. Because of the changes made, we expect results from the summative evaluation to extend to the Scott, Foresman version, further enhancing student performance.

Since November of 1985, UCSMP has sponsored an annual ''Users' Conference'' at the University of Chicago at which users and prospective users of its materials can meet with each other and with authors. This conference now includes all components of the project. It provides a valuable opportunity for reports on UCSMP materials from those not involved in formal studies. We encourage users to attend this conference.

We desire to know of any studies school districts conduct using these materials. UCSMP will be happy to assist school districts by supplying a copy of the noncommercial tests we used in our summative evaluation and other information as needed.

Both Scott, Foresman and Company and UCSMP welcome comments on our books. Please address comments either to Mathematics Product Manager, Scott, Foresman and Company, 1900 East Lake Avenue, Glenview, IL 60025, or to Zalman Usiskin, Director, UCSMP, 5835 S. Kimbark Avenue, Chicago, IL 60637.

5 Bibliography

REFERENCES for Sections 1–4 of Professional Sourcebook

College Board. **Academic Preparation for College: *What Students Need To Know and Be Able To Do.*** New York: College Board, 1983.

Flanders, James. **"How Much of the Content in Mathematics Textbooks Is New?"** *Arithmetic Teacher,* September 1987, pp. 18–23.

Jones, Philip, and Coxford, A. ***A History of Mathematics Education in the United States and Canada.*** 30th Yearbook of the National Council of Teachers of Mathematics. Reston, VA: NCTM, 1970.

McNight, Curtis, et al. ***The Underachieving Curriculum: Assessing U.S. School Mathematics from an International Perspective.*** Champaign, IL: Stipes Publishing Company, 1987.

National Commission on Excellence in Education. ***A Nation at Risk: The Imperative for Educational Reform.*** Washington, D.C.: U.S. Department of Education, 1983.

National Council of Teachers of Mathematics. ***Curriculum and Evaluation Standards for School Mathematics.*** Reston, VA: NCTM, 1989.

Waits, Bert, and Demana, Franklin. **"Is Three Years Enough?"** *Mathematics Teacher,* January 1988, pp. 11–15.

ADDITIONAL GENERAL REFERENCES

Hirsch, Christian R., and Zweng, Marilyn J., editors. ***The Secondary School Mathematics Curriculum.*** Reston, VA: NCTM, 1985.
This forward-looking NCTM yearbook gives background for many of the ideas found in UCSMP texts.

Johnson, David R. ***Every Minute Counts.*** Palo Alto, CA: Dale Seymour Publications, 1982.
Making Minutes Count Even More. Palo Alto, CA: Dale Seymour Publications, 1986.
These booklets provide practical suggestions for using class time effectively. Comments on correcting homework, communicating in the classroom, and opening and closing activities are particularly good.

Kieran, Carolyn, and Wagner, Sigrid, editors. ***Research Issues in Learning and Teaching Algebra.*** Reston, VA: NCTM, 1989.
An overview of recent research and its implications for learning and teaching algebra. See particularly the chapters by Fey and Senk on the impact of computer technology.

The Mathematics Teacher. National Council of Teachers of Mathematics. 1906 Association Drive, Reston, VA 22091.
This journal is an excellent source of applications and other teaching suggestions. We believe that every secondary school mathematics teacher should join the NCTM and read this journal regularly.

The UMAP Journal, Consortium for Mathematics and Its Applications Project, Inc. 271 Lincoln Street, Suite Number 4, Lexington, MA 02173
This journal is a wonderful source of applications, although many of them are at the college level. COMAP also publishes a quarterly newsletter called *Consortium* that includes "The HMAP Pull-Out Section." *Consortium* provides information on COMAP modules that are appropriate for high schools.

Usiskin, Zalman. **"Why Elementary Algebra Can, Should, and Must Be an Eighth-Grade Course for Average Students."** *Mathematics Teacher*, September 1987, pp. 428–438.

Section 5: Bibliography

SOURCES for Additional Problems

Coxford, Arthur F., and Shulte, Albert P., editors. ***The Ideas of Algebra, K–12.*** Reston, VA: National Council of Teachers of Mathematics, 1988. This NCTM yearbook contains 34 articles on all aspects of the teaching of algebra.

The Diagram Group. ***Comparisons.*** New York: St. Martin's Press, 1980. This is an excellent source of visual and numerical data on such quantities as distance, area and volume, and time and speed.

Eves, Howard. ***An Introduction to the History of Mathematics.*** 5th ed. Philadelphia: Saunders College Publishing, 1983. This comprehensive history includes references to recent 20th-century mathematics, such as the proof of the four-color theorem. There is an outstanding collection of problems.

Hanson, Viggo P., and Zweng, Marilyn J, editors. ***Computers in Mathematics Education.*** Reston, VA: NCTM, 1984. This NCTM yearbook provides practical suggestions about some computer activities that can be added to mathematics classes. Chapter 15 is a particularly good overview of how programming related exercises can help teach mathematics.

Hoffman, Mark, editor. ***The World Almanac and Book of Facts, 1989.*** New York: World Almanac, 1989.

Johnson, Otto, executive ed. ***The 1989 Information Please Almanac.*** Boston: Houghton Mifflin Company, 1989. Almanacs are excellent sources of data for problems.

Joint Committee of the Mathematical Association of America and the National Council of Teachers of Mathematics. ***A Sourcebook of Applications of School Mathematics.*** Reston, VA: National Council of Teachers of Mathematics, 1980. This outstanding, comprehensive source of applied problems is organized in sections by mathematical content (advanced arithmetic through combinatorics and probability).

Sharron, Sidney, and Reys, Robert E., editors. ***Applications in School Mathematics.*** Reston, VA: NCTM, 1979. This NCTM yearbook is a collection of essays on applications, ways of including applications in the classroom, mathematical modeling, and other issues related to applications. There is an extensive bibliography on sources of applications.

U.S. Bureau of the Census. ***Statistical Abstract of the United States: 1989.*** 109th ed. Washington, D.C., 1988. This outstanding data source, published annually since 1878, summarizes statistics on the United States and provides reference to other statistical publications.

SOFTWARE

Algebra Arcade. Wadsworth Electronic Publishing. 10 Davis Drive, Belmont, CA 94002
This software is available for the Apple II family and the IBM-PC. It can be used as a game for one or two players. The object of the game is to earn points by inputting equations whose graphs pass through randomly placed Algebroids on a coordinate grid. Features allow the user to choose particular types of equations to be used (linear, quadratic, trigonometric, and so on), or to have free choice. The software may also be used as a function plotter independently of the game.

Algebra Electronic Blackboard. Wadsworth Electronic Publishing. 10 Davis Drive, Belmont, CA 94002.
This software is available for the Apple II family. It can be used in three modes: display, which introduces the content; interactive, in which the user picks parameter values for his or her own graphs; and target, in which the computer draws a graph and the user is challenged to give parameters that will match the graphs.

Functions. Developed by the North Carolina School of Science and Mathematics. Durham, NC 27705.
This is a function plotter for the IBM-PC with 512K memory. It is available for a nominal charge by writing to Helen Compton at NCSSM. NCSSM has also developed software for data analysis and geometric probability.

Green Globs and Graphing Equations. Sunburst Educational Computer Courseware, 39 Washington Ave., Pleasantville, NY 10570-9971.
This software, which has function plotting capability, is available for the Apple II family, the IBM-PC and PCjr., and Tandy 1000. It has two games which have students find equations of linear and/or quadratic relations. The game called "Green Globs" enables students to write equations of relations that pass through points on the plane.

Master Grapher. Addison-Wesley Publishing Company, 2725 Sand Hill Road, Menlo Park, CA 94025.
This flexible function plotter, developed by Bert Waits and Frank Demana at Ohio State University, is available for the Apple II family, the Macintosh, and the IBM-PC.

ACKNOWLEDGMENTS

For permission to reproduce indicated information on the following page, acknowledgment is made to:

page 35 DENNIS THE MENACE® used by permission of Hank Ketcham and © by North American Syndicate

page 415 "We're waiting to marry" by Karren Loeb, *USA Today*, September 10, 1987. Copyright © by 1987 *USA Today*. Reprinted with permission.

Illustration Acknowledgments

Phil Renaud
54–55, 91, 166, 193, 195, 215, 236, 240, 272, 281, 295, 302, 340, 369, 371, 376, 378, 389, 391, 397, 400, 408, 420, 435, 494, 603, 608, 611, 612

Jack Wallen
160, 176, 210, 218, 234, 241, 248, 249, 250, 251, 252, 256, 262, 264, 266, 284, 287, 300, 311, 339, 345, 350, 359, 361, 356, 386, 418, 436, 486, 520, 539, 563

Jill Ruter
23, 55, 56, 74, 90, 140, 143, 147, 162, 165, 178, 186, 203, 208, 209, 221, 237, 241, 246, 258, 276, 290, 296, 335, 337, 350, 356, 364, 398, 410, 415, 417, 422, 434, 448, 472, 500, 623

Unless otherwise acknowledged, all photos are the property of Scott, Foresman and Company. Page positions are as follows: (t) top, (c) center, (b) bottom, (l) left, (r) right, (ins) inset

CHAPTER 1
2-3 Milt & Joan Mann/Cameramann International, Ltd. 2-3 (INS) Translation from *The Rhind Mathematical Papyrus*, by Arnold Buffum Chase, Courtesy The National Council of Teachers of Mathematics. 4 Stuart Westmorland/Aperture Photobank 7 David Madison/Focus On Sports 12 David Black 14 Bob Daemmrich/Click/Chicago/Tony Stone 16 Mickey Pfleger 18 Norma Morrison 23 Carl Purcell 25 Brent Jones 30 Lynn M. Stone 34 Pat and Tom Lesson/Alaska Photo 36 Space Science & Engineering Center, University of Wisconsin, Madison 41 Brent Jones 46 David R. Frazier Photolibrary

CHAPTER 2
56 © Robert Perron 61 Brent Jones 62 Focus On Sports 67 Milt & Joan Mann/Cameramann International, Ltd. 70 Milt & Joan Mann/Cameramann International, Ltd. 73 Focus On Sports 76 David R. Frazier Photolibrary 79 Milt & Joan Mann/Cameramann International, Ltd. 94 Charles Krebs/Aperture Photobank 99 Jim Shives/Aperture Photobank 104 Brent Jones

CHAPTER 3
108 David Lissy/Focus On Sports 109 David R. Frazier Photolibrary 113 Milt & Joan Mann/Cameramann International, Ltd. 115 Carl Purcell 116 Bruce Forster/Aperture Photobank 121 Courtesy Patricia Dolan 122 Travelpix/FPG 123 Ellis Herwig/Stock Boston 126 Mickey Pfleger 129 Norma Morrison 135 David R. Frazier Photolibrary 137 David Black 140 Marty Snyderman 141 Milt & Joan Mann/Cameramann International, Ltd. 147 Focus On Sports 149 Carl Purcell 151 Virginia Historical Society

CHAPTER 4
154–155 California Institute of Technology & Carnegie Institute of Washington 163 David R. Frazier Photolibrary 167 Guy Sauvage Agency/Vandystadt/ALLSPORT USA 173 James R. Rowan 177 Focus On Sports 178 David R. Frazier Photolibrary 181 Randy Wells/Aperture Photobank 184 Norma Morrison 186 Rudi Von Briel 189 Viesti Associates 190 Roy Morsch/The Stock Market 197L Focus On Sports 197CL Focus On Sports 197CR Focus On Sports 197R Focus On Sports 198 David Black 200 David R. Frazier Photolibrary 203 COMSTOCK INC.

CHAPTER 5
219 Ahmed/David R. Frazier Photolibrary 222 ANIMALS ANIMALS/Ted Levin 223 Ann Purcell 227 Brent Jones 229 Christopher Morrow/Black Star 234 NASA 238 Ann Purcell 239 Rick McIntyre/Aperture Photobank 245 Susan Copen Oken/Dot Picture Agency 252 Carl Purcell 254 ANIMALS ANIMALS/H. Ausloos 257 Steve McCutcheon/Alaska Photo

CHAPTER 6
260–261 Frans Lanting 268 Carl Purcell 270 Deutsches Museum, Munchen 274 Thomas Valentin 275 Wolfgang Bayer Productions 276 Art Pahlke 278 Mitch Kezar 283 Brent Jones 286 Alan Magayne-Roshak/Third Coast 288 Thomas Valentin 291 Grant Heilman Photography 293 Robert Frerck/Odyssey Productions 297 Milt & Joan Mann/Cameramann International, Ltd. 303 John McGrail 310 Focus On Sports

CHAPTER 7
312–313 J. Taposchaner/FPG 315 Mark Reinstein/Stock Imagery 317 Art Pahlke 319 Milt & Joan Mann/Cameramann International, Ltd. 323 Milt & Joan Mann/Cameramann International, Ltd. 346 Bruce McAllister/Stock Imagery 347 © 1988 Color-Art, Inc., St. Louis, Mo. 356 Francis de Richemond/The Image Works 361 Into The Wind 362 Milt & Joan Mann/Cameramann International, Ltd.

CHAPTER 8
364–365 Chuck O'Rear/West Light 368 Brent Jones 376 Milt & Joan Mann/Cameramann International, Ltd. 381 Chet Hanchett/Photographic Resources, Inc. 385 David Brownell 387 DRS Productions/The Stock Market 390 G. Newman Haynes/The Image Works 393 Jeff Foott/Bruce Coleman Inc. 395 Steinhart Aquarium/Photo Researchers 400B Robert Frerck/Odyssey Productions 401T Robert Frerck/Odyssey Productions 404 Martha Swope 406 Martha Swope 413 Focus On Sports 419 Courtesy United Airlines 421 Bob Daemmrich/Stock Boston

CHAPTER 9
423 David Black 429 Barry L. Runk/Grant Heilman Photography 432 Michael Fredericks Jr./Earth Scenes 433 Alfred Pasieka/Bruce Coleman Inc. 437 Rudi Von Briel 439 Tom Raymond/Bruce Coleman Inc. 442 Robert Frerck/Odyssey Productions 447 Frank Siteman/Stock Boston 454 Milt & Joan

Mann/Cameramann International, Ltd. 457 Art Pahlke 461 NASA 462 NASA

CHAPTER 10
474–475 Brent Jones 476 Milton Feinberg/Stock Boston 479 Robert Frerck/Odyssey Productions 503 Mark Antman/The Image Works 512 Guido A. Rossi/Agency Vandystadt/Photo Researchers, Inc. 523 John Serrao/Photo Researchers 529 Richard Pasley/Stock Boston

CHAPTER 11
530–531 Richard Mackson/*Sports Illustrated* 544 Martin W. Grosnick/Bruce Coleman Inc. 546 Judith McClung/FPG 553 Milt & Joan Mann/Cameramann International, Ltd. 555 Mark Greenberg/Visions 558 Bruce Coleman Inc. 566 Gregg Mancuso/Stock Boston 577 Focus On Sports

CHAPTER 12
598 Bob Daemmrich/The Image Works 599 Allen Steele/ALLSPORT USA 603 Dennis Hallinan/FPG 624 John Chiasson/Gamma-Liaison 629 North Carolina Div. of Travel & Tourism

CHAPTER 13
636 William Johnson/Stock Boston 638 D. & J. Heaton/Stock Boston 639 Novosti/Gamma-Liaison 644 Disario/The Stock Market 649 Jacques Lowe/Woodfin Camp & Associates 652 Scott McKiernan/Gamma-Liaison 654 Maggie Steber/Stock Boston 658 Bob Daemmrich/The Image Works 661 Bill Ross/West Light 665 Bob Daemmrich/Stock Boston 667 E. R. Degginger/Bruce Coleman, Inc. 669 Warren Morgan/West Light 670 David Kennerly/Gamma-Liaison 675 Billy Barnes/Stock Boston